University Casebook Series

November, 1988

ACCOUNTING AND THE LAW, Fourth Edition (1978), with Problems Pamphlet (Successor to Dohr, Phillips, Thompson & Warren)

George C. Thompson, Professor, Columbia University Graduate School of Business.

Robert Whitman, Professor of Law, University of Connecticut.

Ellis L. Phillips, Jr., Member of the New York Bar.

William C. Warren, Professor of Law Emeritus, Columbia University.

ACCOUNTING FOR LAWYERS, MATERIALS ON (1980)

David R. Herwitz, Professor of Law, Harvard University.

ADMINISTRATIVE LAW, Eighth Edition (1987), with 1983 Problems Supplement (Supplement edited in association with Paul R. Verkuil, Dean and Professor of Law, Tulane University)

Walter Gellhorn, University Professor Emeritus, Columbia University.

Clark Byse, Professor of Law, Harvard University.

Peter L. Strauss, Professor of Law, Columbia University.

Todd D. Rakoff, Professor of Law, Harvard University.

Roy A. Schotland, Professor of Law, Georgetown University.

ADMIRALTY, Third Edition (1987), with Statute and Rule Supplement

Jo Desha Lucas, Professor of Law, University of Chicago.

ADVOCACY, see also Lawyering Process

AGENCY, see also Enterprise Organization

AGENCY—PARTNERSHIPS, Fourth Edition (1987)

Abridgement from Conard, Knauss & Siegel's Enterprise Organization, Fourth Edition.

AGENCY AND PARTNERSHIPS (1987)

Melvin A. Eisenberg, Professor of Law, University of California, Berkeley.

ANTITRUST: FREE ENTERPRISE AND ECONOMIC ORGANIZATION, Sixth Edition (1983), with 1983 Problems in Antitrust Supplement and 1988 Case Supplement

Louis B. Schwartz, Professor of Law, University of Pennsylvania.

John J. Flynn, Professor of Law, University of Utah.

Harry First, Professor of Law, New York University.

BANKRUPTCY (1985)

Robert L. Jordan, Professor of Law, University of California, Los Angeles.

William D. Warren, Professor of Law, University of California, Los Angeles.

BANKRUPTCY AND DEBTOR–CREDITOR LAW, Second Edition (1988)

Theodore Eisenberg, Professor of Law, Cornell University.

BUSINESS ORGANIZATION, see also Enterprise Organization

BUSINESS PLANNING, Temporary Second Edition (1984)

David R. Herwitz, Professor of Law, Harvard University.

BUSINESS TORTS (1972)

Milton Handler, Professor of Law Emeritus, Columbia University.

CHILDREN IN THE LEGAL SYSTEM (1983) with 1988 Supplement

Walter Wadlington, Professor of Law, University of Virginia.
Charles H. Whitebread, Professor of Law, University of Southern California.
Samuel Davis, Professor of Law, University of Georgia.

CIVIL PROCEDURE, see Procedure

CIVIL RIGHTS ACTIONS (1988), with 1988 Supplement

Peter W. Low, Professor of Law, University of Virginia.
John C. Jeffries, Jr., Professor of Law, University of Virginia.

CLINIC, see also Lawyering Process

COMMERCIAL AND DEBTOR–CREDITOR LAW: SELECTED STATUTES, 1988 EDITION

COMMERCIAL LAW, Second Edition (1987)

Robert L. Jordan, Professor of Law, University of California, Los Angeles.
William D. Warren, Professor of Law, University of California, Los Angeles.

COMMERCIAL LAW, Fourth Edition (1985)

E. Allan Farnsworth, Professor of Law, Columbia University.
John Honnold, Professor of Law, University of Pennsylvania.

COMMERCIAL PAPER, Third Edition (1984)

E. Allan Farnsworth, Professor of Law, Columbia University.

COMMERCIAL PAPER, Second Edition (1987) (Reprinted from COMMERCIAL LAW, Second Edition (1987))

Robert L. Jordan, Professor of Law, University of California, Los Angeles.
William D. Warren, Professor of Law, University of California, Los Angeles.

COMMERCIAL PAPER AND BANK DEPOSITS AND COLLECTIONS (1967), with Statutory Supplement

William D. Hawkland, Professor of Law, University of Illinois.

COMMERCIAL TRANSACTIONS—Principles and Policies (1982)

Alan Schwartz, Professor of Law, University of Southern California.
Robert E. Scott, Professor of Law, University of Virginia.

COMPARATIVE LAW, Fifth Edition (1988)

Rudolf B. Schlesinger, Professor of Law, Hastings College of Law.
Hans W. Baade, Professor of Law, University of Texas.
Mirjan P. Damaska, Professor of Law, Yale Law School.
Peter E. Herzog, Professor of Law, Syracuse University.

COMPETITIVE PROCESS, LEGAL REGULATION OF THE, Third Edition (1986), with 1987 Selected Statutes Supplement

Edmund W. Kitch, Professor of Law, University of Virginia.
Harvey S. Perlman, Dean of the Law School, University of Nebraska.

CONFLICT OF LAWS, Eighth Edition (1984), with 1987 Case Supplement

Willis L. M. Reese, Professor of Law, Columbia University.
Maurice Rosenberg, Professor of Law, Columbia University.

CONSTITUTIONAL LAW, Seventh Edition (1985), with 1988 Supplement

Edward L. Barrett, Jr., Professor of Law, University of California, Davis.
William Cohen, Professor of Law, Stanford University.

CONSTITUTIONAL LAW, CIVIL LIBERTY AND INDIVIDUAL RIGHTS, Second Edition (1982), with 1987 Supplement

William Cohen, Professor of Law, Stanford University.
John Kaplan, Professor of Law, Stanford University.

CONSTITUTIONAL LAW, Eleventh Edition (1985), with 1988 Supplement (Supplement edited in association with Frederick F. Schauer, Professor of Law, University of Michigan)

Gerald Gunther, Professor of Law, Stanford University.

CONSTITUTIONAL LAW, INDIVIDUAL RIGHTS IN, Fourth Edition (1986), (Reprinted from CONSTITUTIONAL LAW, Eleventh Edition), with 1988 Supplement (Supplement edited in association with Frederick F. Schauer, Professor of Law, University of Michigan)

Gerald Gunther, Professor of Law, Stanford University.

CONSUMER TRANSACTIONS (1983), with Selected Statutes and Regulations Supplement and 1987 Case Supplement

Michael M. Greenfield, Professor of Law, Washington University.

CONTRACT LAW AND ITS APPLICATION, Fourth Edition (1988)

Arthur Rosett, Professor of Law, University of California, Los Angeles.

CONTRACT LAW, STUDIES IN, Third Edition (1984)

Edward J. Murphy, Professor of Law, University of Notre Dame.
Richard E. Speidel, Professor of Law, Northwestern University.

CONTRACTS, Fifth Edition (1987)

John P. Dawson, Professor of Law Emeritus, Harvard University.
William Burnett Harvey, Professor of Law and Political Science, Boston University.
Stanley D. Henderson, Professor of Law, University of Virginia.

CONTRACTS, Fourth Edition (1988)

E. Allan Farnsworth, Professor of Law, Columbia University.
William F. Young, Professor of Law, Columbia University.

CONTRACTS, Selections on (statutory materials) (1988)

CONTRACTS, Second Edition (1978), with Statutory and Administrative Law Supplement (1978)

Ian R. Macneil, Professor of Law, Cornell University.

COPYRIGHT, PATENTS AND TRADEMARKS, see also Competitive Process; see also Selected Statutes and International Agreements

COPYRIGHT, PATENT, TRADEMARK AND RELATED STATE DOCTRINES, Second Edition (1981), with 1988 Case Supplement, 1987 Selected Statutes Supplement and 1981 Problem Supplement

Paul Goldstein, Professor of Law, Stanford University.

COPYRIGHT, Unfair Competition, and Other Topics Bearing on the Protection of Literary, Musical, and Artistic Works, Fourth Edition (1985), with 1985 Statutory Supplement

Ralph S. Brown, Jr., Professor of Law, Yale University.
Robert C. Denicola, Professor of Law, University of Nebraska.

CORPORATE ACQUISITIONS, The Law and Finance of (1986), with 1988 Supplement

Ronald J. Gilson, Professor of Law, Stanford University.

CORPORATE FINANCE, Third Edition (1987)

Victor Brudney, Professor of Law, Harvard University.
Marvin A. Chirelstein, Professor of Law, Columbia University.

CORPORATE READJUSTMENTS AND REORGANIZATIONS (1976)

Walter J. Blum, Professor of Law, University of Chicago.
Stanley A. Kaplan, Professor of Law, University of Chicago.

CORPORATION LAW, BASIC, Third Edition (1989), with Documentary Supplement

Detlev F. Vagts, Professor of Law, Harvard University.

CORPORATIONS, see also Enterprise Organization

CORPORATIONS, Sixth Edition—Concise (1988), with Statutory Supplement (1988)

William L. Cary, late Professor of Law, Columbia University.
Melvin Aron Eisenberg, Professor of Law, University of California, Berkeley.

CORPORATIONS, Sixth Edition—Unabridged (1988), with Statutory Supplement (1988)

William L. Cary, late Professor of Law, Columbia University.
Melvin Aron Eisenberg, Professor of Law, University of California, Berkeley.

CORPORATIONS AND BUSINESS ASSOCIATIONS—STATUTES, RULES AND FORMS (1988)

CORPORATIONS COURSE GAME PLAN (1975)

David R. Herwitz, Professor of Law, Harvard University.

CORRECTIONS, SEE SENTENCING

CREDITORS' RIGHTS, see also Debtor-Creditor Law

CRIMINAL JUSTICE ADMINISTRATION, Third Edition (1986), with 1988 Case Supplement

Frank W. Miller, Professor of Law, Washington University.
Robert O. Dawson, Professor of Law, University of Texas.
George E. Dix, Professor of Law, University of Texas.
Raymond I. Parnas, Professor of Law, University of California, Davis.

CRIMINAL LAW, Fourth Edition (1987)

Fred E. Inbau, Professor of Law Emeritus, Northwestern University.
Andre A. Moenssens, Professor of Law, University of Richmond.
James R. Thompson, Professor of Law Emeritus, Northwestern University.

CRIMINAL LAW AND APPROACHES TO THE STUDY OF LAW (1986)

John M. Brumbaugh, Professor of Law, University of Maryland.

CRIMINAL LAW, Second Edition (1986)

Peter W. Low, Professor of Law, University of Virginia.
John C. Jeffries, Jr., Professor of Law, University of Virginia.
Richard C. Bonnie, Professor of Law, University of Virginia.

CRIMINAL LAW, Fourth Edition (1986)

Lloyd L. Weinreb, Professor of Law, Harvard University.

CRIMINAL LAW AND PROCEDURE, Sixth Edition (1984)

Rollin M. Perkins, Professor of Law Emeritus, University of California, Hastings College of the Law.
Ronald N. Boyce, Professor of Law, University of Utah.

CRIMINAL PROCEDURE, Third Edition (1987), with 1988 Supplement

James B. Haddad, Professor of Law, Northwestern University.
James B. Zagel, Chief, Criminal Justice Division, Office of Attorney General of Illinois.
Gary L. Starkman, Assistant U. S. Attorney, Northern District of Illinois.
William J. Bauer, Chief Judge of the U.S. Court of Appeals, Seventh Circuit.

CRIMINAL PROCESS, Fourth Edition (1987), with 1988 Supplement

Lloyd L. Weinreb, Professor of Law, Harvard University.

DAMAGES, Second Edition (1952)

Charles T. McCormick, late Professor of Law, University of Texas.
William F. Fritz, late Professor of Law, University of Texas.

DECEDENTS' ESTATES AND TRUSTS, Seventh Edition (1988)

John Ritchie, Late Professor of Law, University of Virginia.
Neill H. Alford, Jr., Professor of Law, University of Virginia.
Richard W. Effland, Professor of Law, Arizona State University.

DISPUTE RESOLUTION, Processes of (1989)

John S. Murray, President and Executive Director of The Conflict Clinic, Inc., George Mason University.
Alan Scott Rau, Professor of Law, University of Texas.
Edward F. Sherman, Professor of Law, University of Texas.

DOMESTIC RELATIONS, see also Family Law

DOMESTIC RELATIONS, Successor Edition (1984) with 1988 Supplement

Walter Wadlington, Professor of Law, University of Virginia.

EMPLOYMENT DISCRIMINATION, Second Edition (1987), with 1988 Supplement

Joel W. Friedman, Professor of Law, Tulane University.
George M. Strickler, Professor of Law, Tulane University.

EMPLOYMENT LAW (1987), with 1987 Statutory Supplement and 1988 Case Supplement

Mark A. Rothstein, Professor of Law, University of Houston.
Andria S. Knapp, Adjunct Professor of Law, University of California, Hastings College of Law.
Lance Liebman, Professor of Law, Harvard University.

ENERGY LAW (1983) with 1986 Case Supplement

Donald N. Zillman, Professor of Law, University of Utah.
Laurence Lattman, Dean of Mines and Engineering, University of Utah.

ENTERPRISE ORGANIZATION, Fourth Edition (1987), with 1987 Corporation and Partnership Statutes, Rules and Forms Supplement

Alfred F. Conard, Professor of Law, University of Michigan.
Robert L. Knauss, Dean of the Law School, University of Houston.
Stanley Siegel, Professor of Law, University of California, Los Angeles.

ENVIRONMENTAL POLICY LAW 1985 Edition, with 1985 Problems Supplement (Supplement in association with Ronald H. Rosenberg, Professor of Law, College of William and Mary)

Thomas J. Schoenbaum, Professor of Law, University of Georgia.

EQUITY, see also Remedies

EQUITY, RESTITUTION AND DAMAGES, Second Edition (1974)

Robert Childres, late Professor of Law, Northwestern University.
William F. Johnson, Jr., Professor of Law, New York University.

ESTATE PLANNING, Second Edition (1982), with 1985 Case, Text and Documentary Supplement

David Westfall, Professor of Law, Harvard University.

ETHICS, see Legal Profession, Professional Responsibility, and Social Responsibilities

ETHICS AND PROFESSIONAL RESPONSIBILITY (1981) (Reprinted from THE LAWYERING PROCESS)

Gary Bellow, Professor of Law, Harvard University.
Bea Moulton, Legal Services Corporation.

EVIDENCE, Sixth Edition (1988 Reprint)

John Kaplan, Professor of Law, Stanford University.
Jon R. Waltz, Professor of Law, Northwestern University.

EVIDENCE, Eighth Edition (1988), with Rules, Statute and Case Supplement (1988)

Jack B. Weinstein, Chief Judge, United States District Court.
John H. Mansfield, Professor of Law, Harvard University.
Norman Abrams, Professor of Law, University of California, Los Angeles.
Margaret Berger, Professor of Law, Brooklyn Law School.

FAMILY LAW, see also Domestic Relations

FAMILY LAW Second Edition (1985), with 1988 Supplement

Judith C. Areen, Professor of Law, Georgetown University.

FAMILY LAW AND CHILDREN IN THE LEGAL SYSTEM, STATUTORY MATERIALS (1981)

Walter Wadlington, Professor of Law, University of Virginia.

FEDERAL COURTS, Eighth Edition (1988)

Charles T. McCormick, late Professor of Law, University of Texas.
James H. Chadbourn, late Professor of Law, Harvard University.
Charles Alan Wright, Professor of Law, University of Texas, Austin.

INSTITUTIONAL INVESTORS, (1978)

David L. Ratner, Professor of Law, Cornell University.

INSURANCE, Second Edition (1985)

William F. Young, Professor of Law, Columbia University.
Eric M. Holmes, Professor of Law, University of Georgia.

INTERNATIONAL LAW, see also Transnational Legal Problems, Transnational Business Problems, and United Nations Law

INTERNATIONAL LAW IN CONTEMPORARY PERSPECTIVE (1981), with Essay Supplement

Myres S. McDougal, Professor of Law, Yale University.
W. Michael Reisman, Professor of Law, Yale University.

INTERNATIONAL LEGAL SYSTEM, Third Edition (1988), with Documentary Supplement

Joseph Modeste Sweeney, Professor of Law, University of California, Hastings.
Covey T. Oliver, Professor of Law, University of Pennsylvania.
Noyes E. Leech, Professor of Law Emeritus, University of Pennsylvania.

INTRODUCTION TO LAW, see also Legal Method, On Law in Courts, and Dynamics of American Law

INTRODUCTION TO THE STUDY OF LAW (1970)

E. Wayne Thode, late Professor of Law, University of Utah.
Leon Lebowitz, Professor of Law, University of Texas.
Lester J. Mazor, Professor of Law, University of Utah.

JUDICIAL CODE and Rules of Procedure in the Federal Courts, Students' Edition, 1988 Revision

Daniel J. Meltzer, Professor of Law, Harvard University.
David L. Shapiro, Professor of Law, Harvard University.

JURISPRUDENCE (Temporary Edition Hardbound) (1949)

Lon L. Fuller, late Professor of Law, Harvard University.

JUVENILE, see also Children

JUVENILE JUSTICE PROCESS, Third Edition (1985)

Frank W. Miller, Professor of Law, Washington University.
Robert O. Dawson, Professor of Law, University of Texas.
George E. Dix, Professor of Law, University of Texas.
Raymond I. Parnas, Professor of Law, University of California, Davis.

LABOR LAW, Tenth Edition (1986), with 1986 Statutory Supplement

Archibald Cox, Professor of Law, Harvard University.
Derek C. Bok, President, Harvard University.
Robert A. Gorman, Professor of Law, University of Pennsylvania.

LABOR LAW, Second Edition (1982), with Statutory Supplement

Clyde W. Summers, Professor of Law, University of Pennsylvania.
Harry H. Wellington, Dean of the Law School, Yale University.
Alan Hyde, Professor of Law, Rutgers University.

LAND FINANCING, Third Edition (1985)

The late Norman Penney, Professor of Law, Cornell University.
Richard F. Broude, Member of the California Bar.
Roger Cunningham, Professor of Law, University of Michigan.

LAW AND MEDICINE (1980)

Walter Wadlington, Professor of Law and Professor of Legal Medicine, University of Virginia.

Jon R. Waltz, Professor of Law, Northwestern University.

Roger B. Dworkin, Professor of Law, Indiana University, and Professor of Biomedical History, University of Washington.

LAW, LANGUAGE AND ETHICS (1972)

William R. Bishin, Professor of Law, University of Southern California.

Christopher D. Stone, Professor of Law, University of Southern California.

LAW, SCIENCE AND MEDICINE (1984), with 1989 Supplement

Judith C. Areen, Professor of Law, Georgetown University.

Patricia A. King, Professor of Law, Georgetown University.

Steven P. Goldberg, Professor of Law, Georgetown University.

Alexander M. Capron, Professor of Law, University of Southern California.

LAWYERING PROCESS (1978), with Civil Problem Supplement and Criminal Problem Supplement

Gary Bellow, Professor of Law, Harvard University.

Bea Moulton, Professor of Law, Arizona State University.

LEGAL METHOD (1980)

Harry W. Jones, Professor of Law Emeritus, Columbia University.

John M. Kernochan, Professor of Law, Columbia University.

Arthur W. Murphy, Professor of Law, Columbia University.

LEGAL METHODS (1969)

Robert N. Covington, Professor of Law, Vanderbilt University.

E. Blythe Stason, late Professor of Law, Vanderbilt University.

John W. Wade, Professor of Law, Vanderbilt University.

Elliott E. Cheatham, late Professor of Law, Vanderbilt University.

Theodore A. Smedley, Professor of Law, Vanderbilt University.

LEGAL PROFESSION, THE, Responsibility and Regulation, Second Edition (1988)

Geoffrey C. Hazard, Jr., Professor of Law, Yale University.

Deborah L. Rhode, Professor of Law, Stanford University.

LEGISLATION, Fourth Edition (1982) (by Fordham)

Horace E. Read, late Vice President, Dalhousie University.

John W. MacDonald, Professor of Law Emeritus, Cornell Law School.

Jefferson B. Fordham, Professor of Law, University of Utah.

William J. Pierce, Professor of Law, University of Michigan.

LEGISLATIVE AND ADMINISTRATIVE PROCESSES, Second Edition (1981)

Hans A. Linde, Judge, Supreme Court of Oregon.

George Bunn, Professor of Law, University of Wisconsin.

Fredericka Paff, Professor of Law, University of Wisconsin.

W. Lawrence Church, Professor of Law, University of Wisconsin.

LOCAL GOVERNMENT LAW, Second Revised Edition (1986)

Jefferson B. Fordham, Professor of Law, University of Utah.

MASS MEDIA LAW, Third Edition (1987)

Marc A. Franklin, Professor of Law, Stanford University.

MENTAL HEALTH PROCESS, Second Edition (1976), with 1981 Supplement

Frank W. Miller, Professor of Law, Washington University.
Robert O. Dawson, Professor of Law, University of Texas.
George E. Dix, Professor of Law, University of Texas.
Raymond I. Parnas, Professor of Law, University of California, Davis.

MUNICIPAL CORPORATIONS, see Local Government Law

NEGOTIABLE INSTRUMENTS, see Commercial Paper

NEGOTIATION (1981) (Reprinted from THE LAWYERING PROCESS)

Gary Bellow, Professor of Law, Harvard Law School.
Bea Moulton, Legal Services Corporation.

NEW YORK PRACTICE, Fourth Edition (1978)

Herbert Peterfreund, Professor of Law, New York University.
Joseph M. McLaughlin, Dean of the Law School, Fordham University.

OIL AND GAS, Fifth Edition (1987)

Howard R. Williams, Professor of Law, Stanford University.
Richard C. Maxwell, Professor of Law, University of California, Los Angeles.
Charles J. Meyers, Dean of the Law School, Stanford University.
Stephen F. Williams, Judge of the United States Court of Appeals.

ON LAW IN COURTS (1965)

Paul J. Mishkin, Professor of Law, University of California, Berkeley.
Clarence Morris, Professor of Law Emeritus, University of Pennsylvania.

PATENTS AND ANTITRUST (Pamphlet) (1983)

Milton Handler, Professor of Law Emeritus, Columbia University.
Harlan M. Blake, Professor of Law, Columbia University.
Robert Pitofsky, Professor of Law, Georgetown University.
Harvey J. Goldschmid, Professor of Law, Columbia University.

PLEADING AND PROCEDURE, see Procedure, Civil

POLICE FUNCTION, Fourth Edition (1986), with 1988 Case Supplement

Reprint of Chapters 1–10 of Miller, Dawson, Dix and Parnas's CRIMINAL JUSTICE ADMINISTRATION, Third Edition.

PREPARING AND PRESENTING THE CASE (1981) (Reprinted from THE LAWYERING PROCESS)

Gary Bellow, Professor of Law, Harvard Law School.
Bea Moulton, Legal Services Corporation.

PROCEDURE (1988), with Procedure Supplement (1988)

Robert M. Cover, late Professor of Law, Yale Law School.
Owen M. Fiss, Professor of Law, Yale Law School.
Judith Resnik, Professor of Law, University of Southern California Law Center.

PROCEDURE—CIVIL PROCEDURE, Second Edition (1974), with 1979 Supplement

The late James H. Chadbourn, Professor of Law, Harvard University.
A. Leo Levin, Professor of Law, University of Pennsylvania.
Philip Shuchman, Professor of Law, Cornell University.

PROCEDURE—CIVIL PROCEDURE, Fifth Edition (1984), with 1988 Supplement

Richard H. Field, late Professor of Law, Harvard University.
Benjamin Kaplan, Professor of Law Emeritus, Harvard University.
Kevin M. Clermont, Professor of Law, Cornell University.

PROCEDURE—CIVIL PROCEDURE, Fourth Edition (1985), with 1988 Supplement

Maurice Rosenberg, Professor of Law, Columbia University.
Hans Smit, Professor of Law, Columbia University.
Harold L. Korn, Professor of Law, Columbia University.

PROCEDURE—PLEADING AND PROCEDURE: State and Federal, Fifth Edition (1983), with 1988 Supplement

David W. Louisell, late Professor of Law, University of California, Berkeley.
Geoffrey C. Hazard, Jr., Professor of Law, Yale University.
Colin C. Tait, Professor of Law, University of Connecticut.

PROCEDURE—FEDERAL RULES OF CIVIL PROCEDURE, 1988 Edition

PRODUCTS LIABILITY (1980)

Marshall S. Shapo, Professor of Law, Northwestern University.

PRODUCTS LIABILITY AND SAFETY (1980), with 1985 Case and Documentary Supplement

W. Page Keeton, Professor of Law, University of Texas.
David G. Owen, Professor of Law, University of South Carolina.
John E. Montgomery, Professor of Law, University of South Carolina.

PROFESSIONAL RESPONSIBILITY, Fourth Edition (1987), with 1988 Selected National Standards Supplement

Thomas D. Morgan, Dean of the Law School, Emory University.
Ronald D. Rotunda, Professor of Law, University of Illinois.

PROPERTY, Fifth Edition (1984)

John E. Cribbet, Professor of Law, University of Illinois.
Corwin W. Johnson, Professor of Law, University of Texas.

PROPERTY—PERSONAL (1953)

S. Kenneth Skolfield, late Professor of Law Emeritus, Boston University.

PROPERTY—PERSONAL, Third Edition (1954)

Everett Fraser, late Dean of the Law School Emeritus, University of Minnesota.
Third Edition by Charles W. Taintor, late Professor of Law, University of Pittsburgh.

PROPERTY—INTRODUCTION, TO REAL PROPERTY, Third Edition (1954)

Everett Fraser, late Dean of the Law School Emeritus, University of Minnesota.

PROPERTY—REAL AND PERSONAL, Combined Edition (1954)

Everett Fraser, late Dean of the Law School Emeritus, University of Minnesota.
Third Edition of Personal Property by Charles W. Taintor, late Professor of Law, University of Pittsburgh.

PROPERTY—FUNDAMENTALS OF MODERN REAL PROPERTY, Second Edition (1982), with 1985 Supplement

Edward H. Rabin, Professor of Law, University of California, Davis.

PROPERTY—PROBLEMS IN REAL PROPERTY (Pamphlet) (1969)

Edward H. Rabin, Professor of Law, University of California, Davis.

PROPERTY, REAL (1984), with 1988 Supplement

Paul Goldstein, Professor of Law, Stanford University.

PROSECUTION AND ADJUDICATION, Third Edition (1986), with 1988 Case Supplement

Reprint of Chapters 11–26 of Miller, Dawson, Dix and Parnas's CRIMINAL JUSTICE ADMINISTRATION, Third Edition.

PSYCHIATRY AND LAW, see Mental Health, see also Hinckley, Trial of

PUBLIC REGULATION OF DANGEROUS PRODUCTS (paperback) (1980)

Marshall S. Shapo, Professor of Law, Northwestern University.

PUBLIC UTILITY LAW, see Free Enterprise, also Regulated Industries

REAL ESTATE PLANNING, Second Edition (1980), with 1980 Problems, Statutes and New Materials Supplement

Norton L. Steuben, Professor of Law, University of Colorado.

REAL ESTATE TRANSACTIONS, Revised Second Edition (1988), with Statute, Form and Problem Supplement (1988)

Paul Goldstein, Professor of Law, Stanford University.

RECEIVERSHIP AND CORPORATE REORGANIZATION, see Creditors' Rights

REGULATED INDUSTRIES, Second Edition, (1976)

William K. Jones, Professor of Law, Columbia University.

REMEDIES, Second Edition (1987)

Edward D. Re, Chief Judge, U. S. Court of International Trade.

RESTITUTION, Second Edition (1966)

John W. Wade, Professor of Law, Vanderbilt University.

SALES, Second Edition (1986)

Marion W. Benfield, Jr., Professor of Law, University of Illinois.
William D. Hawkland, Chancellor, Louisiana State Law Center.

SALES AND SALES FINANCING, Fifth Edition (1984)

John Honnold, Professor of Law, University of Pennsylvania.

SALES LAW AND THE CONTRACTING PROCESS (1982)

Reprint of Chapters 1–10 of Schwartz and Scott's Commercial Transactions.

SECURED TRANSACTIONS IN PERSONAL PROPERTY, Second Edition (1987) (Reprinted from COMMERCIAL LAW, Second Edition (1987))

Robert L. Jordan, Professor of Law, University of California, Los Angeles.
William D. Warren, Professor of Law, University of California, Los Angeles.

SECURITIES REGULATION, Sixth Edition (1987), with 1988 Selected Statutes, Rules and Forms Supplement and 1988 Cases and Releases Supplement

Richard W. Jennings, Professor of Law, University of California, Berkeley.
Harold Marsh, Jr., Member of California Bar.

SECURITIES REGULATION, Second Edition (1988), with Statute, Rule and Form Supplement (1988)

Larry D. Soderquist, Professor of Law, Vanderbilt University.

SECURITY INTERESTS IN PERSONAL PROPERTY, Second Edition (1987)

Douglas G. Baird, Professor of Law, University of Chicago.
Thomas H. Jackson, Professor of Law, Stanford University.

SECURITY INTERESTS IN PERSONAL PROPERTY (1985) (Reprinted from Sales and Sales Financing, Fifth Edition)

John Honnold, Professor of Law, University of Pennsylvania.

SENTENCING AND THE CORRECTIONAL PROCESS, Second Edition (1976)

Frank W. Miller, Professor of Law, Washington University.
Robert O. Dawson, Professor of Law, University of Texas.
George E. Dix, Professor of Law, University of Texas.
Raymond I. Parnas, Professor of Law, University of California, Davis.

SOCIAL RESPONSIBILITIES OF LAWYERS, Case Studies (1988)

Philip B. Heymann, Professor of Law, Harvard University.
Lance Liebman, Professor of Law, Harvard University.

SOCIAL SCIENCE IN LAW, Cases and Materials (1985)

John Monahan, Professor of Law, University of Virginia.
Laurens Walker, Professor of Law, University of Virginia.

TAX, POLICY ANALYSIS OF THE FEDERAL INCOME (1976)

William A. Klein, Professor of Law, University of California, Los Angeles.

TAXATION, FEDERAL INCOME, Second Edition (1988)

Michael J. Graetz, Professor of Law, Yale University.

TAXATION, FEDERAL INCOME, Sixth Edition (1987)

James J. Freeland, Professor of Law, University of Florida.
Stephen A. Lind, Professor of Law, University of Florida and University of California, Hastings.
Richard B. Stephens, Professor of Law Emeritus, University of Florida.

TAXATION, FEDERAL INCOME, Successor Edition (1986), with 1988 Legislative Supplement

Stanley S. Surrey, late Professor of Law, Harvard University.
Paul R. McDaniel, Professor of Law, Boston College.
Hugh J. Ault, Professor of Law, Boston College.
Stanley A. Koppelman, Professor of Law, Boston University.

TAXATION, FEDERAL INCOME, VOLUME II, Taxation of Partnerships and Corporations, Second Edition (1980), with 1988 Legislative Supplement

Stanley S. Surrey, late Professor of Law, Harvard University.
William C. Warren, Professor of Law Emeritus, Columbia University.
Paul R. McDaniel, Professor of Law, Boston College.
Hugh J. Ault, Professor of Law, Boston College.

TAXATION, FEDERAL WEALTH TRANSFER, Successor Edition (1987)

Stanley S. Surrey, late Professor of Law, Harvard University.
Paul R. McDaniel, Professor of Law, Boston College.
Harry L. Gutman, Professor of Law, University of Pennsylvania.

TAXATION, FUNDAMENTALS OF CORPORATE, Second Edition (1987)

Stephen A. Lind, Professor of Law, University of Florida and University of California, Hastings.
Stephen Schwarz, Professor of Law, University of California, Hastings.
Daniel J. Lathrope, Professor of Law, University of California, Hastings.
Joshua Rosenberg, Professor of Law, University of San Francisco.

TAXATION, FUNDAMENTALS OF PARTNERSHIP, Second Edition (1988)

Stephen A. Lind, Professor of Law, University of Florida and University of California, Hastings.
Stephen Schwarz, Professor of Law, University of California, Hastings.
Daniel J. Lathrope, Professor of Law, University of California, Hastings.
Joshua Rosenberg, Professor of Law, University of San Francisco.

TAXATION, PROBLEMS IN THE FEDERAL INCOME TAXATION OF PARTNER-SHIPS AND CORPORATIONS, Second Edition (1986)

Norton L. Steuben, Professor of Law, University of Colorado.
William J. Turnier, Professor of Law, University of North Carolina.

TAXATION, PROBLEMS IN THE FUNDAMENTALS OF FEDERAL INCOME, Second Edition (1985)

Norton L. Steuben, Professor of Law, University of Colorado.
William J. Turnier, Professor of Law, University of North Carolina.

TAXES AND FINANCE—STATE AND LOCAL (1974)

Oliver Oldman, Professor of Law, Harvard University.
Ferdinand P. Schoettle, Professor of Law, University of Minnesota.

TORT LAW AND ALTERNATIVES, Fourth Edition (1987)

Marc A. Franklin, Professor of Law, Stanford University.
Robert L. Rabin, Professor of Law, Stanford University.

TORTS, Eighth Edition (1988)

William L. Prosser, late Professor of Law, University of California, Hastings.
John W. Wade, Professor of Law, Vanderbilt University.
Victor E. Schwartz, Adjunct Professor of Law, Georgetown University.

TORTS, Third Edition (1976)

Harry Shulman, late Dean of the Law School, Yale University.
Fleming James, Jr., Professor of Law Emeritus, Yale University.
Oscar S. Gray, Professor of Law, University of Maryland.

TRADE REGULATION, Second Edition (1983), with 1987 Supplement

Milton Handler, Professor of Law Emeritus, Columbia University.
Harlan M. Blake, Professor of Law, Columbia University.
Robert Pitofsky, Professor of Law, Georgetown University.
Harvey J. Goldschmid, Professor of Law, Columbia University.

TRADE REGULATION, see Antitrust

TRANSNATIONAL BUSINESS PROBLEMS (1986)

Detlev F. Vagts, Professor of Law, Harvard University.

TRANSNATIONAL LEGAL PROBLEMS, Third Edition (1986) with Documentary Supplement

Henry J. Steiner, Professor of Law, Harvard University.
Detlev F. Vagts, Professor of Law, Harvard University.

TRIAL, see also Evidence, Making the Record, Lawyering Process and Preparing and Presenting the Case

TRIAL ADVOCACY (1968)

A. Leo Levin, Professor of Law, University of Pennsylvania.
Harold Cramer, of the Pennsylvania Bar.
Maurice Rosenberg, Professor of Law, Columbia University, Consultant.

TRUSTS, Fifth Edition (1978)

George G. Bogert, late Professor of Law Emeritus, University of Chicago.
Dallin H. Oaks, President, Brigham Young University.

TRUSTS AND SUCCESSION (Palmer's), Fourth Edition (1983)

Richard V. Wellman, Professor of Law, University of Georgia.
Lawrence W. Waggoner, Professor of Law, University of Michigan.
Olin L. Browder, Jr., Professor of Law, University of Michigan.

UNFAIR COMPETITION, see Competitive Process and Business Torts

UNITED NATIONS LAW, Second Edition (1967), with Documentary Supplement (1968)

Louis B. Sohn, Professor of Law, Harvard University.

WATER RESOURCE MANAGEMENT, Third Edition (1988)

Charles J. Meyers, Esq., Denver, Colorado, formerly Dean, Stanford University Law School.
A. Dan Tarlock, Professor of Law, II Chicago-Kent College of Law.
James N. Corbridge, Jr., Chancellor, University of Colorado at Boulder, and Professor of Law, University of Colorado School of Law.
David H. Getches, Professor of Law, University of Colorado School of Law.

WILLS AND ADMINISTRATION, Fifth Edition (1961)

Philip Mechem, late Professor of Law, University of Pennsylvania.
Thomas E. Atkinson, late Professor of Law, New York University.

WORLD LAW, see United Nations Law

University Casebook Series

V7204—16g

ADMINISTRATIVE LAW

CASES AND COMMENTS

By

WALTER GELLHORN
University Professor Emeritus, Columbia University

CLARK BYSE
Byrne Professor of Administrative Law Emeritus,
Harvard University

PETER L. STRAUSS
Betts Professor of Law, Columbia University

TODD RAKOFF
Professor of Law, Harvard University

and

ROY A. SCHOTLAND
Professor of Law, Georgetown University Law Center

EIGHTH EDITION

Mineola, New York
THE FOUNDATION PRESS, INC.
1987

Library of Congress Cataloging in Publication Data

Administrative law.

  (University casebook series)
  Includes bibliographical references and index.
   1. Administrative law—United States—Cases.
1. Gellhorn, Walter, 1906– . II. Series.
KF5402.A4A35 1986   342.73'06   86–25730
ISBN 0–88277–523–5   23–5347.3026

G., B., S., R. & S.–Cs.Admin.Law 8th Ed. UCB
4th Reprint—1989

PREFACE

The act of writing a preface for materials such as these, published in varying editions over almost half a century, invites reflection on the continuing concerns and fluidity of Administrative Law. Some of the most recent cases in this edition appear to reinvigorate a problem, separation of powers, that dominated the very first of the modern case books—that of Frankfurter and Davidson in 1932. Other materials added here also reflect changing attitudes towards matters that have long marked preceding editions of this book—political involvement in administrative action, claims to participation and procedure before the agency itself, judicial review of administrative action, and openness in government. And the text reflects as well concerns that have emerged more recently, such as continuing uncertainties about the resolution of disputes over technological issues, the move in some contexts to larger reliance on market forces in lieu of regulation, and the increasing relevance to "administrative law" of the contributions of other disciplines. In the intensely human and ultimately political business of striving for sound government, your editors do not suppose that such movement will ever cease.

One should start the enterprise of learning about American administrative process by acknowledging that it is a figment of the imagination. No political theory has proposed it. No person has created it. It cannot be described, because it does not exist. To be sure, public administration exists in abundance. What does not exist is any integrated, coherent, unwavering element of government that can be identified as the administrative process. There are innumerable processes rather than one.

Yet your editors also believe that common elements may be recognized in the affairs of administrative agencies. We entirely repudiate the notion that a single set of rules can effectively govern agencies having such diverse tasks as superintending imports and immigration, licensing airlines and attorneys, regulating farm prices and food additives, administering aid to the aged and nuclear energy, directing rent control and radio broadcasting, and controlling liquor distribution and labor relations. Even so, each of the many duties performed by administrators does have certain resemblances to other governmental activities. Our effort in this volume is to facilitate identification of resemblances as well as of differences, in the hope that capacity to make critical and predictive judgments about administrative and judicial behavior will thus be enhanced.

Of particular importance to your editors in making this effort is inviting your attention to the other-than-judicial worlds in which agencies act and to which they respond; and also stressing that no single set of values can be identified against which to measure their success or failure. Concerning the first of these, the following pages will refer again and again to the difficult problems that arise when the world of politics comes within judicial view. Each of our past two Presidents, first a Democrat then a Republican, was elected to office after a campaign in which he ran, in effect, against the federal government and promised to bring it under control. Each of them took a series of actions intended to carry out those campaign promises and assert political leadership over the "faceless federal bureaucracy." Congress, too, has been active both formally and informally. At what points and in what respects must the worlds of politics and law answer to each other?

As for the problem of competing values (of which reconciling "politics" and "law" might be regarded as merely an example), consider the trio of not readily accommodated values that have been articulated in the Supreme Court's recent decisions about "due process" in administrative adjudication, the subject of Chapter 4. Fairness to interested persons, accuracy in decision-making, and reasonable social costs are all desirable—and none of them is achievable without cost to the others. It is fair that the interested or aggrieved person participate in the process. It is fair that she be given appropriate procedural weapons (including access to judicial review) with which to confront an often impersonal, sometimes blundering bureaucracy. Yet the longer and more complex proceedings thus brought about may result in others being denied needed public services, significant additions to the cost of building a planned facility, or loss of the business required to keep a private concern economically viable. "Stopping the government in its tracks" would be a furtherance of fairness if the governmental tracks always went in the wrong direction; but few believe so unreservedly that that government is best which governs least. For the rest of us, fairness is not a likely product of governmental immobilization. Nor is it sound to view competition in values as occurring mostly between a public interest and a special interest. Identifiable Good Guys and Bad Guys may appear in tales of the West-that-never-was, but not (or certainly not clearly) in most modern affairs. In any interesting dispute, many public interests compete for consideration; rarely can an individual truly speak for *the* public interest rather than, far more modestly, for *a* public interest.

Difficult choices are inescapable—not soft choices between Definitely Good and Plainly Bad, but hard choices between one Good and another Good (or, more commonly, among a number of Goods that cannot be simultaneously achieved, so that some must be preferred over others). The desire to design procedures giving maximum assurance of fairness rubs against the desire to expedite governmental processes. The desire to give everybody a full chance to be heard rubs against a grudging suspicion that adversary proceedings may not invariably be the best solvent of disagreements. The desire to bring administration into public view rubs against awareness that sometimes confidentiality facilitates resolution of difficult problems and may be as eagerly sought by members of the public as by members of the bureaucracy. The desire to encourage administrators to become fully informed before promulgating regulations having the force of law rubs against the fear of back door approaches to and surreptitious pressure upon the rulemakers.

Frictions like these generate considerable heat. Sometimes the heat produces litigation (which regardless of outcome can create further heat).

Sometimes efforts to resolve matters in the legislature succumb to realities that produce gaps in statutory directions or cloudy language that thrusts upon administrators the responsibility—and the attendant heat—for value choices the lawmakers themselves could not agree upon. Criticizing what officials do may be far easier and more congenial than doing the job oneself. The techniques of law are unlikely to point to a single outcome or provide a settled resolution.

With all that said, it is still true that this is a law book about the administrative process, not a political-science text. The forms and trappings of law are ever-present in American government. Partly this is so, because many administrators have been legally trained; partly, because bureaucratic organizations need the formal structures we associate with law; partly, because many agency actions are subject to judicial review, and therefore come directly into the hands of the law in its most formal aspect. But the matter does not rest on institutional realities alone. Deep in the American spirit is the proposition that we ought to be governed by laws, not men; that the quest for law is part of the quest for freedom. From this point of view, administrative law is a normative enterprise that attempts to make the vast apparatus of the modern state conform to the standards which make the existence of that public power tolerable. Or, at least, the student of administrative law must always ask, to what extent does this subject rest on legal traditions rather than growing from the functional requisites of government alone.

In what follows, we have avoided presenting as "settled doctrines" what are in fact still evolving patterns of interaction. We have sought instead to offer material that reveals the present state of evolution and that provides bases for realistic speculation concerning future growth of the law. As in earlier editions, we have omitted many citations and footnotes when we have reproduced opinions and other writings, renumbering the footnotes that we have retained.

CLARK BYSE
PETER L. STRAUSS
TODD RAKOFF
ROY A. SCHOTLAND

August 1986

*

SUMMARY OF CONTENTS

APPENDICES

TABLE OF CONTENTS

TABLE OF CONTENTS

TABLE OF CONTENTS

APPENDICES

TABLE OF CASES

The principal cases are in italic type. The cases appearing in the notes and the cases cited are roman type.

Cases are listed by both the name of the plaintiff and of the defendant. The references are to Pages.

lv

TABLE OF TEXT AND PERIODICAL CITATIONS

S

Reports of Commissions and Committees

TABLE OF STATUTES

TABLE OF STATUTES

ADMINISTRATIVE LAW

CASES AND COMMENTS

Chapter I

INTRODUCTION

"Administrative Law" means different things to different people. In the setting of the law school course for which this book has been designed, the term refers to the body of largely procedural requirements resting upon administrative agencies which affect private interests through making rules, adjudicating cases, investigating, threatening, prosecuting, publicizing, disbursing benefits, and advising. The stress is chiefly on requirements that are judicially enforceable, and that therefore are the special domain of lawyers. Attention is also directed, however, to aspects of control over administrators exercised by the legislative and executive branches of the government. The most pervasive control of all—that is, self-control, reinforced by professional attitudes within the public service—is difficult to depict; but assuredly it must not be overlooked, for without it the external controls would be of small moment. And, since most agencies have attorneys, this self-control is also often of special concern to lawyers.

Shortness of time prevents describing or fully evaluating the law which the agencies themselves produce—labor law, utility law, corporation finance, land use (e.g., zoning and planning), trade regulation, health and safety, and so on. That substantive law must be considered in other appropriate courses, where it can be integrated with the judicial and legislative contributions to those respective subject matters. Yet the student of Administrative Law must constantly be mindful of substantive matters. Plainly, the nature of an administrative agency's program affects its mode of operation. An agency's procedures are shaped by an agency's duties as well as by generalized propositions or traditions—just as the architecture of an office building differs from the architecture of an airport because the two structures have different functions, though in both instances the architects have no doubt utilized common principles in some phases of their plans. The converse is true, too: the legal effect of an agency's substantive decisions often turns on the process which has been used.

One may note an increasing tendency on the part of courts, especially the Supreme Court, to give elaborate statements of the procedural context of agency action in their opinions. However unconscious this opinion-writing behavior may be, it serves to promote understanding of the particular agency and its circumstances and so to suggest natural limits for what may appear a more general statement of law. There are, indeed, those who believe that administrative procedure cannot be studied with profit apart from the particular substantive functions that procedure serves in a given instance.[1]

1. E. Gellhorn and G. Robinson, Perspectives on Administrative Law, 75 Colum.L.Rev. 771 (1975); R. Rabin, Administrative Law in Transition: A Discipline in Search of an Organizing Principle, 72 Nw.U.L.Rev. 120 (1977).

That view, to the extent it is a characterization of the forms of law, is one the authors of this text reject—and, we might add, that we doubt is the view of the courts themselves. If general rules applicable to the behavior of the thousands of diverse instruments of government did not exist, surely judges and lawyers would be obliged to invent them, to assure the possibility of control and avoid unsustainable specialization. Nonetheless, the interactions between procedural choices and substantive responsibilities cannot be denied; procedures appropriate for allocation of a valuable radio license may poorly suit decisions on truck routing or welfare benefits. As important, the institutions which must apply or follow given prescriptions are not abstractions. They have structure, finite resources, a "point of view." One need not be familiar with the detail of an agency's substantive program to acquire a sense of this concrete setting for procedural options.

The skeptical view of our enterprise set out above could also be stated as a proposition about administrative law *practice.* One of your editors once heard Peter Hutt, a distinguished Washington lawyer, tell a convention of administrative law professors that their courses overemphasized courts and litigation. ". . . Over 90 percent of his practice . . . is entirely informal, occurring outside hearings of any character. Litigation is avoided where it can be, and what the administrative law teacher must do is bring students to understand the variety of ways in which this can be done. The ideal course, working from the bottom up rather than from the top down, would begin with a sense of the history and mission of the agency with which one is concerned, a history which often predetermines both procedure and substance. A look at the statute will provide a sense of how to use it, of what procedures and what choices it opens. Much the larger proportion of the impact of any given statute can be inferred from the regulatory mechanism it establishes. Then one may consider what the style of given regulation is (hard-line enforcement or softer); what the agency's budget is and how the agency is treated by its appropriation committee; what the political atmosphere is and the attitude of important congressmen; what relationships exist between the agency and other federal agencies; what procedures it employs; who its personnel are and what their attitudes are; how competitors use or manipulate the statute for their own purposes; what the role of chance is in shaping the agency's agenda; what the general competence is of the staff being dealt with. One must know not only how to get meetings with agency officials but also what the publicity consequences are going to be of meeting with officials at varying levels; one must know what policy is likely to be driving the agency, for that will drive the procedures the agency chooses. And then there is the need to become thoroughly familiar with the mass of detail that bears on the particular issues to be presented for decision. Only then does one come to the point of exposure to public materials or public processes." [2]

2. P. Strauss, Teaching Administrative Law: The Wonder of the Unknown, 33 J.Leg.Ed. 1, 8 (1983).

Mr. Hutt speaks the truth about administrative law practice, and the pages that follow attempt to be suggestive about the worlds of politics and bureaucratic function he suggests. Yet your editors are not persuaded by Mr. Hutt's suggestions as ones for administrative law *instruction.* "[T]he perception was possible, if not demanded, that our plate was being piled higher with necessary comestibles than any professor—much less student—could possibly digest. Here . . . one might have discerned the question, what is the role of theory in law teaching, particularly in teaching administrative law? . . . A workable theory, like the assertion that there exists a general administrative law, permits a sense of mastery, an order, a structure from which ventures into the chaos of the real world can perhaps more safely be made. One might believe that only if one has a perspective from which to understand the world, simplified though it might be, can the effort at digestion of the world's rich body of data even begin." [3]

SECTION 1. REASONS FOR ESTABLISHMENT OF ADMINISTRATIVE AGENCIES

JAMES M. LANDIS,* THE ADMINISTRATIVE PROCESS †
(Yale University Press, 1938) pp. 7–12, 23–26, 30–38, 46.

Two tendencies in the expanding civilization of the late nineteenth century seem to me to foreshadow the need for methods of government different in kind from those that had prevailed in the past. These are the rise of industrialism and the rise of democracy. Naturally, these two tendencies combined and interacted each upon the other, so that it becomes difficult to isolate cause and effect. For as a dynamic society does not move *in vacuo,* so an abstract classification of tendencies can have only a relative value. The rise of industrialism and the rise of democracy, however, brought new and difficult problems to government. A world that scarcely a hundred years ago could listen to Wordsworth's denunciation of railroads because their building despoiled the beauty of his northern landscapes is different, very different, from one that in 1938 has to determine lanes and flight levels for air traffic. While it was true that advances in transportation, communication, and mass production were in themselves disturbing elements, the profound problems were the social and economic questions that flowed from the era of mechanical invention. To their solution some contribution derived from the rise of humanitarianism. But the driving force was the recognition by the governing classes of our civilization of their growing dependence upon the promotion of the welfare of the governed. Concessions to rectify social maladjustments thus had to be made, however grudgingly. And as the demands for positive solutions increased and, in the form of legislative measures, were precipitated

---

3. Ibid.

* The late James Landis was Dean of Harvard Law School at the time he delivered these remarks as part of his Storrs Lectures at Yale Law School. He had earlier been Federal Trade Commissioner and Securities and Exchange Commission Chairman, "an active, dedicated missionary of the New Deal." A. Sutherland, The Law at Harvard 305 (1967).

upon the cathodes of governmental activity, *laissez faire*—the simple belief that only good could come by giving economic forces free play— came to an end.

. . .

These [developments] can be traced by their concrete manifestations in the growth and forms of the administrative process. The high level of transportation charges and the existence of tariffs that discriminated between communities, commodities, and individuals had made the railroads a political issue. The first attempts at a direct legislative control of rates and charges proved crude and useless. Such remedies as the common law and the courts afforded depended upon the initiative of aggrieved shippers. . . . The need for nondiscriminatory and reasonable rates, uniformly applicable, could not be achieved through the intermittent intervention of the judicial process. . . . Some federal mechanism of necessity had to be invented if the rudiments of a national railroad policy were to be developed.

More important than the immediate powers that in 1887 were vested in the Interstate Commerce Commission was the creation of the Commission itself. A government had to be provided to direct and control an industry, and governance as a practical matter implied not merely legislative power or simply executive power, but whatever power might be required to achieve the desired results. It is not too important to our purposes that in 1887 the powers granted to the Interstate Commerce Commission were meager and that the objectives for which they had been created were of themselves limited. . . . What was important was the deliberate organization of a governmental unit whose single concern was the well-being, in a broad public sense, of a vital and national industry.

If in private life we were to organize a unit for the operation of an industry, it would scarcely follow Montesquieu's lines. As yet no organization in private industry either has been conceived along those triadic contours, nor would its normal development, if so conceived, have tended to conform to them. Yet the problems of operating a private industry resemble to a great degree those entailed by its regulation. The direction of any large corporation presents difficulties comparable in character to those faced by an administrative commission. . . . The significance of this comparison is not that it may point to a need for an expanding concept of the province of governmental regulation, but rather that it points to the form which governmental action tends to take. As the governance of industry, bent upon the shaping of adequate policies and the development of means for their execution, vests powers to this end without regard to the creation of agencies theoretically independent of each other, so when government concerns itself with the stability of an industry it is only intelligent realism for it to follow the industrial rather than the political analogue. It vests the necessary powers with the administrative authority it creates, not too greatly concerned with the extent to which such action does violence to the traditional tripartite theory of governmental organization. . . .

The advantages of specialization in the field of regulatory activity seem obvious enough. But our governmental organization of the nineteenth century proceeded upon a different theory. Indeed, theorists have lifted the inexpertness that characterized our nineteenth-century governmental mechanisms to the level of a political principle. Such a practical politician as Andrew Jackson took occasion to urge the Congress to take measures against permitting the civil servants of the government a "long continuance" in office. But expertness cannot derive otherwise. It springs only from that continuity of interest, that ability and desire to devote fifty-two weeks a year, year after year, to a particular problem. With the rise of regulation, the need for expertness became dominant; for the art of regulating an industry requires knowledge of the details of its operation, ability to shift requirements as the condition of the industry may dictate, the pursuit of energetic measures upon the appearance of an emergency, and the power through enforcement to realize conclusions as to policy.

. . .

I have mentioned a broad distinction which underlies types of administrative agencies now in existence. That distinction relates to the difference between those administrative bodies whose essential concern is the economic functioning of the particular industry and those which have an extended police function of a particular nature. Although it is dangerous to deal in motives, yet the reasons which prompted a resort to the administrative process in the latter area would seem to be reasonably clear. In large measure these reasons sprang from a distrust of the ability of the judicial process to make the necessary adjustments in the development of both law and regulatory methods as they related to particular industrial problems.

Admittedly, the judicial process suffers from several basic and more or less unchangeable characteristics. One of these is its inability to maintain a longtime, uninterrupted interest in a relatively narrow and carefully defined area of economic and social activity. As Ulpian remarked, the science of law embraces the knowledge of things human and divine. A general jurisdiction leaves the resolution of an infinite variety of matters within the hands of courts. In the disposition of these claims judges are uninhibited in their discretion except for legislative rules of guidance or such other rules as they themselves may distill out of that vast reserve of materials that we call the common law. This breadth of jurisdiction and freedom of disposition tends somewhat to make judges jacks-of-all-trades and masters of none. . . . If the problem is a business problem, the answer must be derived from that source. But incredible areas of fact may be involved in the disposition of a business problem that calls not only for legal intelligence but also for wisdom in the ways of industrial operation. This difficulty is intrinsic to the judicial process. . . .

To these considerations must be added two others. The first is the recognition that there are certain fields where the making of law springs less from generalizations and principles drawn from the majestic authority of textbooks and cases, than from a "practical" judgment which is based upon all the available considerations and which has in mind the most desirable and pragmatic method of solving that particular problem. In the period preceding the World War commentators upon decisions relating to these problems frequently pointed to the fact that such judgments were determined much less by accepted "legal principles" than by given political, economic, and social considerations—a pedantic way of expressing the term "practical." . . .

The second consideration is, perhaps, even more important. It is the fact that the common-law system left too much in the way of the enforcement of claims and interests to private initiative. Jhering's analysis of the "struggle for law"—the famous essay in which he indicated that the process of carving out new rights had resulted from the willingness of individuals as litigants or as criminal defendants to become martyrs to their convictions—pointed only to a slow and costly method of making law. . . .

True, the criminal law offered a partial solution of the difficulty, but an insufficient one. A criminal action changes the entire atmosphere of litigation. The traditions of the common law in criminal cases erect new and imposing barriers to prosecution. Juries are always an uncertain factor, while a judge, in his charge, may exhibit such disrespect for the policy of the law as to make acquittal almost certain. Moreover, prosecuting agencies, like courts, have difficulty in developing that single-mindedness of devotion to a specific problem. Without such devotion their power and efficiency may be effective in particular cases but it would fall substantially short of promoting an enlightened long-term development of law and administration in a particular field. . . .

The power to initiate action exists because it fulfils a long-felt need in our law. To restrict governmental intervention, in the determination of claims, to the position of an umpire deciding the merits upon the basis of the record as established by the parties, presumes the existence of an equality in the way of the respective power of the litigants to get at the facts. Some recognition of the absence of such equality is to be found in rules shifting the burden of proof and establishing *prima facie* and even conclusive presumptions of fact or of law. In some spheres the absence of equal economic power generally is so prevalent that the umpire theory of administering law is almost certain to fail. Here government tends to offer its aid to a claimant, not so much because of the grave social import of the particular injury, but because the atmosphere and conditions created by an accumulation of such unredressed claims is of itself a serious social threat. . . .

One other significant distinction between the administrative and the judicial processes is the power of "independent" investigation possessed by the former. The test of the judicial process, traditionally, is not the fair disposition of the controversy; it is the fair disposition of the controversy *upon the record as made by the parties*. . . . The administrative process is, in essence, our generation's answer to the inadequacy of the judicial and the legislative processes. It represents our effort to find an answer to those inadequacies by some other method than merely increasing executive power. If the doctrine of the separation of power implies division, it also implies balance, and balance calls for equality. The creation of administrative power may be the means for the preservation of that balance, so that paradoxically enough, though it may seem in theoretic violation of the doctrine of the separation of power, it may in matter of fact be the means for the preservation of the content of that doctrine.

NOTE

A. SUTHERLAND, THE LAW AT HARVARD 305–306 (1967):

The Administrative Process is an eloquent declaration of faith in discretionary government carried on by an assumed enlightened and apolitical elite. The only serious shortcoming of the book is its author's neglect of the possibility that a governing elite might be neither enlightened, nor apolitical, nor wisely selected. Time was to disconcert many men, including Landis, by demonstrating this possibility.

CHARLES SCHULTZE,* THE PUBLIC USE OF PRIVATE INTEREST [†]
(Brookings Institution, 1977) pp. 7–12.

In 1929, one hundred and forty years after the birth of the Republic, some 9 percent of the gross national income was spent by federal, state, and local governments for purposes other than national defense and foreign affairs. Between 1929 and 1960, however, the proportion of gross national income spent for domestic programs rose to 17½ percent. Today, only sixteen years later, that figure is 28 percent. . . . .

The growth of federal regulatory activities has been even more striking. There is no good way to quantify regulatory growth, but a few figures will illustrate its speed. Even as late as the middle 1950s the federal government had a major regulatory responsibility in only four areas: antitrust, financial institutions, transportation, and communications.[1] In 1976, eighty-three federal agencies were engaged in regulating some aspect of private activity. Thirty-four of those had been created since 1960 and all but eighteen since 1930. By one count about 100,000 federal employees are engaged in regulatory activity. The number of laws establishing or expanding regulatory activities has grown faster than the number of agencies. In the highly publicized case of the discharge of the toxic chemical Kepone into the public sewage system of Hopewell, Virginia, for example, four different federal

* Mr. Schultze is a distinguished academic economist who served as Director of the Bureau of the Budget in the Johnson Administration and as Chairman of the President's Council of Economic Advisers in the Carter Administration.

1. There were other regulatory activities—for example, meat inspection and food and drug regulation—but at the time their impact on the economy was small.

regulatory laws were potentially applicable to the situation, all written in 1970 or later: the Clean Air Amendments of 1970; the Federal Water Pollution Control Act Amendments of 1972; the Federal Environmental Pesticide Control Act of 1972; and the Occupational Safety and Health Act of 1970.

. . . Until recently, federal intervention not only was limited in extent, but was carried out in a relatively uncomplicated way. The decision in the 1930s to launch a compulsory social security program represented a major political watershed. To reach it, important value conflicts had to be compromised or overridden. But once the decision was made, carrying it out efficiently—getting checks in the mail for the right amounts to the right people—was essentially simple. . . .

Addressed to much more intricate and difficult objectives, the newer programs are different; and the older ones have taken on more ambitious goals.

In the field of energy and the environment the generally accepted objectives of national policy imply a staggeringly complex and interlocking set of actions, directly affecting the production and consumption decisions of every citizen and every business firm. Consider for a moment the chain of collective decisions and their effects just in the case of electric utilities. Petroleum imports can be conserved by switching from oil-fired to coal-fired generation. But barring other measures, burning high-sulfur Eastern coal substantially increases pollution. Sulfur can be "scrubbed" from coal smoke in the stack, but at a heavy cost, with devices that turn out huge volumes of sulfur wastes that must be disposed of and about whose reliability there is some question. Intermittent control techniques (installing high smokestacks and switching off burners when meteorological conditions are adverse) can, at lower cost, reduce local concentrations of sulfur oxides in the air, but cannot cope with the growing problem of sulfates and widespread acid rainfall. Use of low-sulfur Western coal would avoid many of these problems, but this coal is obtained by strip mining. Strip-mine reclamation is possible, but substantially hindered in large areas of the West by lack of rainfall. Moreover, in some coal-rich areas the coal beds form the underground aquifer and their removal could wreck adjacent farming or ranching economies. Large coal-burning plants might be located in remote areas far from highly populated urban centers in order to minimize the human effects of pollution. But such areas are among the few left that are unspoiled by pollution, and both environmentalists and the residents (relatively few in number compared with those in metropolitan localities but large among the voting population in the particular states) strongly object to this policy. Fears, realistic or imaginary, about safety and about accumulation of radioactive waste have increasingly hampered the nuclear option. Court actions have delayed site selections, and increasingly stringent safety requirements and certification procedures have slowed construction and increased costs.

Complex as is this bare-boned outline, it deals with the case of public utilities, which has a much simpler environmental problem than that in many other fields. There are only about 1,000 electric utility plants, whose major environmental problems, nuclear aside, are confined to sulfur, particulates, and in some cases thermal pollution. But there are 62,000 point sources of water pollution, discharging a much larger variety of known, and probably some as yet unknown, pollutants. There are 100 million pollution-emitting vehicles on the road, whose contribution to the environmental problem depends not only on the particular pollution controls built into the vehicle but on the density of traffic, the time of day, local atmospheric conditions, the tuning of older engines, and the speed of travel.

The federal government has recently entered in a big way the field of regulating health and safety in workplaces throughout the country. The complexities of controlling industrial accidents, and over the longer run the even greater problem of identifying and dealing with industrial health problems in a chemically inventive society, are as great as those of energy and the environment.

On a quite different plane, over the last twenty years the federal government has become deeply involved for the first time in what might loosely be called social investments and social services. It not only provides heavy financial support for health care through Medicare and Medicaid, but actively seeks to influence the structure of the private health care system—through those programs, through manipulating its support of medical schools, and through various grant-in-aid programs. . . .

Even the goals of older programs have become more ambitious and correspondingly more complex. The purpose of federal highway grants in the late 1950s and early 1960s was simple: to help finance a highway network that would transport people and goods safely and conveniently from one place to another. Now the federal government, by making comprehensive transportation and urban development plans a condition of highway and mass-transit grants, at least attempts to deal with the broader problems of transportation and even beyond that to influence urban structure and growth. . . .

The single most important characteristic of the newer forms of social intervention is that their success depends on affecting the skills, attitudes, consumption habits, or production patterns of hundreds of millions of individuals, millions of business firms, and thousands of local units of government. The tasks are difficult, not so much because they deal with technologically complicated matters as because they aim ultimately at modifying the behavior of private producers and consumers. The boundaries of the "public administration" problem have leapt far beyond the question of how to effectively organize and run a public institution [2] and now encompass the far more vexing question of how to change some aspect of the behavior of a whole society.

2. The principal exception to this description [of the relatively straightforward tasks which, until very recently, were characteristic of federal interventions] was federal regulation of transportation. Here the ultimate actors were not government employees but private railroads, airlines, trucking firms, and barge lines. And it is precisely here that the most abysmal failure of government intervention has occurred. The federal government's powers, originally granted to prevent monopolistic

THOMAS K. McCRAW,* PROPHETS OF REGULATION†
(Belknap Press, 1984), pp. 300–309.

Over time, regulation has performed not only economic tasks, but political, legal, and cultural ones as well. Among the many particular functions that regulation has been used to serve are the functions of:

(a) disclosure and publicity (SEC, . . .);

(b) protection and cartelization of industries (ICC, FCC, CAB . . .);

(c) containment of monopoly and oligopoly (FPC, FTC, Antitrust Division, state utility commissions);

(d) promotion of safety for consumers and workers (Consumer Product Safety Commission, Occupational Safety and Health Administration);

(e) legitimization of the capitalist order (SEC, Environmental Protection Agency).

Obviously such a list could be longer or differently stated. The general point is that regulation has served a variety of purposes, some of which (such as items b and c above) have been mutually inconsistent.

In view of these diverse and sometimes contradictory functions, all overarching theories and heroic generalizations about "Regulation" (with a capital R) run an extremely high risk of being in error. No single theory from any academic discipline can predict precisely which industries will be regulated and which will not. . . . Like the application of regulation to industries, the behavior of regulatory commissions, once they have been created, shows no clear single pattern. All agencies do not follow a standard "life cycle," for example, going from youthful exuberance to middle age, then finally to geriatric decrepitude. Instead, young agencies sometimes behave sluggishly (as did the early FTC) and old ones vigorously (the CAB under Alfred Kahn). . . .

The single constant in the American experience with regulation has been controversy. Here the reason why is not hard to find. . . . As in so many other aspects of American politics, the fundamental controversy underlying the history of regulation has been an ongoing need to work out the inevitable tradeoffs between the good of the whole society, on the one hand, and the rights of the individual, on the other. In regulation, these tradeoffs have appeared most clearly as ways of relieving the persistent tension between the forces seeking to implement economic efficiency for the broad benefit of American society, and those dedicated to guaranteeing the observance of legal due process for every individual member of that society. At different times in our

practices, not only have failed in that purpose but in fact have been used to protect—indeed, to create—such practices. To a much lesser degree the same thing can be said of at least some aspects of federal regulation of financial institutions.

* Professor, Graduate School of Business Administration, Harvard University.

history, each party to these fundamental tensions has established a clear advantage over the other. On balance, however, it seems clear that the concern about legal process has controlled the outcome of regulation more often than has the concern about the substance of economic efficiency. In economists' language, this means that the concern for equity has generally triumphed over the quest for efficiency. In lawyers' terms, it means that in regulation the judicial model has usually triumphed over the legislative and administrative model. In cultural terms, it means that the concern for fairness and for the protection of the diverse interests of all affected individuals has most often won out over the concern for overall growth in the national economy. More generally in political terms, it means that regulation is best understood as a political settlement, undertaken in an effort to keep peace within the polity.

Overall, the conclusion appears inescapable that regulation in America has more often functioned as a protective device rather than as a promotional or developmental one. Of course, protection was not always inappropriate. By holding in check socially destructive forms of behavior, protective regulation often cushioned the impact of rapid industrial change. In America, in contrast to older societies, so many other forces consistently acted to promote pell-mell economic growth that regulation can hardly be condemned for not always doing so. . . .

Ideas about regulation . . . , vary with time. During the 1930s, national policymakers generally held the powerful conviction that market mechanisms left to themselves would produce widespread injustice and even inefficiency. Hence they believed that an active federal government was essential for the protection of the public interest. So these political activists created a broad portfolio of new, independent agencies: the SEC, the FCC, the CAB, and so on. A few decades later, during the 1960s and 1970s, a new generation of policymakers embraced a very different idea. Rather than applauding the old activism, they became convinced that many of the independent commissions created during the 1930s had since been captured by the very interests that these agencies had been set up to regulate.

Partly as a result of the capture idea, there arose during the 1960s a curious two-pronged reform movement: pointing, on the one hand, toward deregulation and, on the other, toward a new wave of large-scale social and environmental regulation. These new rules were to be enforced not by independent commissions of the 1930s variety, which usually administered brief general statutes designed to give broad discretion to a group of commissioners acting collegially; but rather by an entirely different type of agency, with a single executive at its head (who could be held individually responsible for success or failure) and an agenda set in advance by the explicit provisions of extremely detailed legislation. New laws such as the Clean Air Act and the Occupational Safety and Health Act, often running to scores of pages in length, were calculated to minimize administrative discretion and to close all possible loopholes. Meanwhile, on the other prong, the deregulation movement—whose basic intellectual premise was that economic markets *do* work well—also advanced, simultaneously but contradictorily, gaining momentum alongside the companion movement toward growth of regulation in the areas of social and environmental policy.

The result, by the 1980s, presented a most peculiar spectacle. In an ironic historical example of the ways in which ideas can move policymakers in opposite directions, significant deregulation had been instituted for such industries as airlines, trucking, railroads, financial markets, and telecommunications. At the same time, additional social and environmental regulation had become firmly embedded in the structure of state and federal government in such a form as to make any capture by regulated interests very difficult, if not impossible.

The movement of ideas alone, of course, had not produced this ironic result. . . . The disparate sets of ideas underlying the initial imposition of regulation in airlines and trucking during the 1930s, and the later deregulation of these same industries in the 1970s and 1980s, could not both have been correct, in the absolute sense. Yet both sets of ideas became institutionalized. What had changed was the historical context in which opposing ideas about the legitimacy and actual performance of economic markets were defined.

During the 1930s, a period not only of depression but also of economic *de*flation, policymakers searched for some way to stabilize prices, as a means of preventing further economic decline. By the 1970s, however, deflation no longer provided the historical filter; indeed, it had become almost inconceivable as a problem for policy to solve. Instead, *in*flation was now the pressing issue, and thus the same protectionist regulations that had been applied in the 1930s to combat deflation now seemed inappropriate to the new economic context. Both ideas remained alive, but a different time meant a different choice for public policy. To state the same point in a more general sense, it is clear that in American history both the producer-oriented protectionist tradition, on the one hand, and the consumer-oriented anticartelist tradition on the other have remained hostage to immediate economic conditions. The strengths of each tradition have ebbed and flowed in response to several external forces: the business cycle, the different degrees of maturity reached by different product markets, and the conditions of international war and peace.

In speculating about the future, it is difficult to foresee with much additional precision what new historical contexts for regulation might develop. . . . [T]he "economist's hour" of the 1970s and 1980s, for example, represents a phenomenon of unpredictable duration. . . . Economic analysis, however, will always remain directly relevant to regulatory policy. This is true because every industry, whether regulated or not, does possess a certain underlying economic structure: characteristics that make it different from other industries and that help to shape the internal conditions for regulatory opportunities and constraints. *More than any other single factor, this underlying structure of the particular industry being regulated has defined the context in which regulatory agencies have operated.* Sometimes the differences between industry structures can be radical: the railroad industry, with its huge fixed costs and enormous scale economies, could hardly differ more fundamentally from the securities industry, with its paper assets and labor-intensive structure.   In other cases the differences can be more subtle, as in the contrast between center and peripheral firms, and the related distinction between tight and loose forms of horizontal combination.

Because the underlying characteristics of the industry so often shape the limits of governmental action, the industry may be regarded as the dog, the regulatory agency only as the tail.   Yet many students of regulation have assumed that tails wag dogs and, further, that one standard type of tail can wag whatever breed of dog may be attached. Such observers, by focusing primarily on the similarities of regulatory commissions (most of which were bipartisan, appointed by the executive, expert in their fields, and so on), have missed a larger truth: the industries that these similarly-structured commissions regulated were extremely diverse.   Thus these observers have duplicated the errors made historically by many regulators themselves, who often paid more attention to legal processes and administrative procedures than to the greater task of framing strategies appropriate to the particular industries they were regulating.   For all parties who seek to understand regulation, the most important single consideration is the appropriateness of the regulatory strategy to the industry involved.

The process of fitting regulatory strategies to particular industries is a difficult task, partly because industrial structures, like regulatory ideas, can change over time.   The railroad industry represented a true natural monopoly when the Interstate Commerce Commission first emerged to regulate it during the 1880s.   But several decades later, this natural monopoly status of railroads had disappeared before the rise of alternative modes of transportation—the automobile, truck, and airplane.   Clearly, by the 1930s, some central assumptions behind the whole scheme of national railroad regulation needed to be revised, and regulatory policy adjusted accordingly.   Yet until the 1970s little was done, as assumptions remained those of the 1880s.   In the meantime, the Interstate Commerce Commission kept rates inflexible, prevented industry rationalization by blocking truck-rail mergers, and delayed for years the widespread application of unit-train technology.   The ICC took so much time to recognize the revolutionary changes in the transportation industries that regulatory policy lagged badly behind market reality, causing unintended injury to the very railroad industry the commission was trying to protect.

To cite still another example, a situation of natural monopoly prevailed for many years in long-distance telephoning, based on the once-valid principle that a single set of transcontinental wires could most economically serve consumers' needs.   But in the 1960s and 1970s, a technological revolution in microwave communication destroyed that premise and ended the natural monopoly in long-distance telephoning. As the significance of this technological shift became clear, new companies emerged to compete for long-distance telephone business, and just

as quickly a movement to deregulate the telephone industry began. By 1984, the giant Bell System, once the most conspicuous natural monopoly in America, had divided itself into a number of much smaller companies. What had been a thoroughgoing center industry (telephoning) now became part center (local telephone service, heavy equipment manufacturing) and part peripheral (long-distance service, high-technology research and development, and light manufacturing). As a result of these seismic changes in industry structure, the regulation of telecommunications became during the 1980s one of the most publicized and controversial problems of state and federal government.
. . .

In thinking about the future of regulation, whether in broadcasting, telephones, or any other industry, it is important to keep in mind the ambiguous record of the past. Even though much of regulatory history is tinged with apparent failure, regulation cannot properly be said either to have "failed" or "succeeded" in an overall historical sense. Instead, individual regulatory experiments and episodes must be judged against a standard true to the particular historical moment. Many observers hold a contrary view and insist on a single overriding verdict of failure. Because of this prevailing opinion in our time, it becomes useful to speculate about ways in which the same judgment might be applied to other parts of government. Can it be said with equal justice, for example, that legislation in general has failed historically, or that the court system has failed, or that the office of the presidency has failed—without specifying exactly which legislation, which court on what case, and which president on what issue? Although the answer might seem self-evident, the fact remains that in popular perceptions over the last three decades regulation has been regarded as a synonym for failure. . . .

To weigh against these multiple theories premised on failure, we have only one premised on success. But it is a very useful one: the theory of "public use of private interest." According to this idea, regulators should always exploit the natural incentives of regulated interests to serve particular goals that the regulators themselves have carefully defined in advance. And, in fact, the historical record suggests that regulation in America has succeeded best when it has respected these incentives instead of ignoring them; when it has based its strategies less on some idealized vision of what the economy should do and more on a clear understanding of what the economy actually is doing. Regulatory strategies framed in ignorance or disregard of real economic conditions and market incentives—and the number of such attempts has been legion—have usually led only to unfortunate results. By contrast, strategies framed with these conditions and incentives in mind have often produced strikingly successful outcomes . . . . .

NOTES

(1) As the last excerpt suggests, recent years have witnessed sharp debate over the utility of economic regulation, and a retreat from much of it. The CAB is no more, eliminated when Congress became persuad-

ed that rate and entry regulation made air transport more costly for the American public, that air transport works well as a competitive industry.[1] ICC regulation of other modes of transportation has been sharply curbed, and it too may be headed for extinction; the Federal Power Commission is now the Federal Energy Regulatory Commission, merged into a cabinet department (the Department of Energy) and enjoying much less authority over energy rates than it formerly had. The well-regarded report of the American Bar Association's Commission on Law and the Economy, Federal Regulation: Roads to Reform (1979) typified the critical thinking that produced these changes in its four "rules of thumb" for use in avoiding

"mismatches between a particular need for government intervention and the regulatory method used to meet that need . . .

"(a) In structurally competitive industries, consideration should be given to greater reliance on market forces in lieu of classical price and entry regulation.

"(b) Classical price and entry regulation does not deal effectively with the need to control 'windfall' profits over a substantial period. Although it is recognized that in emergencies this type of regulation may be politically necessary, consideration should be given to substituting a tax system.

"(c) Cost-of-service ratemaking appears to be reasonably suited to the 'natural monopoly' problem but when applied to complex industries, it may create substantial difficulties.

"(d) Classical standard-setting is needed to protect the public by controlling dangerous conditions and substances. Where possible, however, in dealing with problems of 'spillovers' (such as environmental pollution or safety), less restrictive tools (such as taxes, disclosure, or bargaining) should be considered as supplements to, or as partial substitutes for, classical standard-setting." [2]

The idea of "mismatch" implies that proper matches are still to be desired. While much regulation of entry and rates may reflect industrial more than public interest,[3] the proposition that restoration of the

---

1. The Airline Deregulation Act of 1978, P.L. 95–504, 92 Stat. 1705, drew substantial support from the success of Southwest Airlines of Texas and Pacific Southwest Airlines of California in promoting and maintaining scheduled air services at rates much below those charged by the national airlines under CAB regulation. See A. Kahn, Applying Economics to an Imperfect World, Regulation, Vol. 2, No. 6 p. 17 (Nov./Dec.1978).

2. At I. These "rules of thumb" are discussed in some detail in Chapters 3 and 4 of the report, and elaborated upon in Professor (now U.S. Circuit Court Judge) Steven Breyer's influential book, Regulation and Its Reform (1982).

3. "No industry offered the opportunity to be regulated should decline it. Few industries have done so. . . . Regulation protects industries against competition from outsiders and from within the industry. It provides protection from antitrust attack. It provides a degree of protection from Congressional investigation. Regulation greatly reduces the risk of bankruptcy from causes other than competition. And, while regulation may make very high rates of return difficult to achieve, it does virtually guarantee a steady stream of adequate profits." B. Owen and R. Braentigam, The Regulation Game, Strategic Use of the Administrative Process 2 (1978).

free market will maximize public benefits is also open to doubt.[4] As one thoughtful scholar recently wrote, "[A] half-century after the New Deal—a century after the birth of the federal regulatory system—. . . the system has grown by leaps and bounds, yet it remains devoid of any coherent ideological framework." R. Rabin, Federal Regulation in Historical Perspective, 38 Stan.L.Rev. 1189, 1325 (1986).

(2) As the last of the ABA's "rules of thumb" suggests, questions about whether, to what extent, and in what form regulation is required characterize social (e.g., health and safety) as well as economic regulation. While most agree that industrialists should be inhibited by law from polluting water supplies, for example, debate rages fiercely over how that inhibition should best be accomplished.[5] Presumably even if there were no formal "regulatory" regime, the common law of tort and nuisance would establish some legal controls. But agency rule-making and norm-enforcement are not the only alternatives to judicial implementation of "background" rules. Thus, later in his Godkin Lectures on "The Public Use of Private Interest," Mr. Schultze addressed himself to the possible advantages of "effluent charges" over pollution discharge permits as a means for assuring clean water in our nation's rivers, lakes, and aquifers:

"In effect, the current law sets up a central agency to determine a detailed control strategy for every polluting source, balancing environmental gains against economic costs. Difficult as this task is in a static context, it is dwarfed by the continuing problem of pacing the guidelines to economic growth and technological change. And the very nature of the controls discourages pollution-reducing technological change. The 1983 criteria base effluent limits on 'best available technology.' But will firms in polluting industries sponsor research or undertake experimentation to develop a new means of reducing pollution still further if its very availability will generate new and more stringent regulations?

"The entire approach provides strong and positive incentives for polluters to use the legal system to delay progress toward effective

---

4. "The free-market model depends ultimately on the assumption that the free market will best satisfy public values through the instrumentality of the invisible hand. Yet the evidence is overwhelming that public values and the goals of firms diverge sharply. Cigarette firms, for example, felt no need to warn consumers of their product's dangers, nor did automobile manufacturers voluntarily make cars safer. Indeed, the enormous volume of fraud that the F.T.C. and various federal, state, and local bodies have uncovered points to the inescapable conclusion that when profit and sales goals conflict with public values, the latter must yield in business calculations. . . . [P]rofits and growth are the supreme values for corporations. If firms' discretion were further enlarged through the operation of the free-market principle, we might expect that in some

areas their derelictions would expand correspondingly, even if some market distortions attributable to regulation disappeared. Natural gas would flow again, and new drugs would be produced again. But the costs of the free-market approach might very well outweigh the benefits; if nineteenth-century experience is any guide, snake oil and placebos would join new drugs in the marketplace." A. Stone, Economic Regulation and the Public Interest 267–68 (1977).

5. See, e.g., H. Latin, Ideal versus Real Regulatory Efficiency: Implementation of Uniform Standards and "Fine-Tuning Regulatory Reforms, 37 Stan.L.Rev. 1267 (1985) and B. Ackerman & R. Stewart, Reforming Environmental Law, 37 Stan.L. Rev. 1333 (1985).

cleanup. It forces a central control agency to make thousands of decisions resting on detailed knowledge it cannot possibly have and, even less, keep up with over time. And most important, it provides absolutely no incentives to firms and municipalities to channel technological innovation toward the efficient reduction of pollution.

"It is possible, on the other hand, to put a common price—via an effluent charge—on each of the major forms of water pollutants. If the polluting side effects of industrial activity were priced, several consequences would follow. Depending on the size of the effluent charge, firms would have incentives to reduce pollution in order to increase their own profits, or to avoid losses. The higher ι̇ e charge, the greater the reduction; hence the fee could be adjusted to achieve any desired set of water-quality standards. Firms with low costs of reducing pollution would reduce their waste discharges by more than firms with high costs of reduction, which is precisely what is needed to achieve any given environmental standard at the lowest national cost. Even when the standards were met, firms would still have incentives to look for ways of reducing pollution still further because they would be paying a fee on residual pollutants. And again, most important, there would be strong incentives throughout industry for the continuing development of new technology for reducing pollution.

"Enough studies have been carried out on river basins to provide guidance on the magnitude of effluent charges needed to achieve particular water-quality standards. But effluent charges are by no means the sole answer. Since we have had no experience with them they would have to be introduced gradually—you cannot create a large new market overnight. Regulations are already in force and they cannot simply be junked; effluent charges would have to supplement the regulations at first, not replace them. Moreover, as I stressed earlier, some exotic and highly dangerous chemical discharges will always have to be controlled by regulation rather than incentive. After all the qualifications, however, an incentive-oriented approach has a very large potential role, and its absence is very costly." At 53–54.

Your editors have no wish to take a position on the particular merits or demerits of effluent charges as a means for protecting the nation's water resources. They are enthusiastically in favor of reducing waste and cost, and of adopting measures which maximize individual initiative while achieving needed public ends; they fully agree that careful and continuing social consideration is called for regarding what ends can effectively be served by regulation, and what means will most efficiently, accurately, and fairly tend to promote those ends. They are also impressed with the observations of Herbert Kaufman, Mr. Schultze's Brookings Institution colleague at the time of his Godkin lectures, in a slim contemporary volume entitled Red Tape, Its Origins, Uses and Abuses (1977). "Big government" and its associated red tape, Mr. Kaufman concluded, are basically the product of public demand. Giving up government will require us to resubmit to the evils we had decided to prevent; we can eliminate only that which present analysis reveals to be ineffective or superfluous.[6] Changing the balance of authority as between Washington and the States—another frequently mentioned nostrum for excessive government—only redistributes power, and may add complexity and delay. And while pollution taxes may indeed offer hope for improvement in some settings, tax collection, too, involves the administrative process in all its manifestations.

To sum up, you will wish as a professional to be vigilant always to detect the opportunities for incremental improvement that are the very stuff of reform. In analyzing the failures and disappointments of administrative action, well enough represented in these pages, you will want carefully to distinguish those failures which are the product of a misguided task, from those which stem from inappropriate procedure or from a "mismatch" between regulatory goal and regulatory process and those which are the product of error or maladministration. But the emphasis on these pages will be on the basic and evolving forms of procedure within agencies, and external controls over agency action, which seem likely to persist in general law—however much specific regulatory mandates may change. Whether government can profitably act at all is a question not to be confused with what procedures it should best, or in the interests of fairness must, employ.

(3) Implicit in the preceding is a characteristic of agencies that distinguishes them from general-purpose bodies such as courts: an administrative agency has a focused responsibility for achieving particular results—Congress has charged it with accomplishing or attempting to accomplish some end specified by a statute. "Taken together, the various Federal administrative agencies have the responsibility for making good to the people of the country a major part of the gains of a hundred and fifty years of democratic government. This means that the agencies cannot take a wholly passive attitude toward the issues which come before them. Out of this fact flow perhaps the most difficult of the problems relating to the administrative process. Administrative agencies constitute a large measure of the motive power of Government; a problem of motive power is a problem also of brakes; but the necessity of both must be faced frankly when either is in question." [7]

The character of the results being sought has changed in recent years, in ways having striking implications for the purpose, scope and structure of the regulatory enterprise.

"While traditional economic regulation focuses above all on the problem of monopoly and its effect on prices, the new regulation focuses

---

6. "[R]egulation is the connective tissue of a civilized society. As technological and scientific advances lead us into unknown worlds with unimaginable dangers, society needs more protection, not less. This means more government regulation, intelligently crafted, skillfully managed, and sensitively enforced. It means a new appreciation of government's role, born of a new sophistication in public attitudes. Finally, it means a shift in our national values to assure the public's protection in an increasingly hazardous world, and a realization that the power and resources to achieve that goal can be provided only by government." S. and M. Tolchin, Dismantling America—The Rush to Deregulate, 276 (1983).

7. Final Report of the Attorney General's Committee on Administrative Procedure, Sen.Doc. No. 8, 77th Cong., 1st Sess. 20 (1941).

primarily on the quality of the products of the industrial system, namely consumer goods and externalities. The purpose of most traditional regulation is to prevent firms from using their monopoly position to charge excessive prices or to curtail service. To do this, regulators can break up existing monopolies ('trust-busting'), prevent new ones from forming (stopping mergers and outlawing unfair trade practices), or set maximum rates and minimum service levels. The purpose of most recent regulation, in contrast, is to reduce the health and safety risk created by consumer goods (such as automobiles, drugs, and toys) and by externalities (such as air pollution, water pollution, and hazards in the workplace).

"The goal of protecting the well-being of citizens brings with it more political controversy than does the goal of ensuring fair and efficient pricing. It is relatively easy to delegate the task of achieving the latter to economists and other experts. But experts cannot so readily claim to know whether a consumer product is sufficiently safe and effective or whether the environment is sufficiently healthy, enjoyable, or even aesthetically pleasing. It is, moreover, somewhat easier to become angry about cancer-causing pollution than about windfall profits.

"This change in the purpose of the regulation in turn expands its scope. Traditional regulation selected a few natural monopolies, near monopolies, or supposed monopolies for special treatment. The Interstate Commerce Commission first regulated only railroads and later added trucking and inland water transport . . . ; the Federal Communications Commission [regulates] broadcasters and interstate telephone service; state public utilities commissions, intrastate electric power and telephone service. The new regulatory agencies exercise control over hundreds of industries and thousands of companies. The EPA's actions directly affect every facility that produces air pollution, water pollution, noise, solid waste, radiation, or pesticides—which means virtually every firm and government unit in the country. Similarly the Occupational Safety and Health Administration regulates working conditions in nearly every factory, store, and construction site in the nation. The Consumer Product Safety Commission has authority to set standards for almost any consumer good sold by American industry.

"Not only does the new regulation directly touch more lives than does the old, but officials administering these new laws are less likely to see their job as promoting the effective management of one sector of the economy. This helps explain the continuing hostility between these agencies and the business community.

"The authors of the regulatory statutes passed in the late 1960s and 1970s attempted to meet criticisms aimed at traditional regulation and to instill in regulators an enduring sense of mission. Lectured incessantly about its failure to provide regulators with specific standards, Congress wrote lengthy statutes that did far more than tell administrators to grant licenses 'in the public interest' or to guarantee 'fair and reasonable rates.' Many of the laws passed during this period included relatively specific standards, deadlines, and procedures. For example, the Clean Air Act, which by 1977 had expanded to cover almost 200 pages, specifies which industries must comply with emission limitations by 1977, which by 1979, and which by 1981; that the levels of sulfur dioxide in the air over national parks can increase by only two micrograms per cubic meter over 1977 levels; and that cars produced in 1981 can emit no more than one gram of nitrogen oxides per mile." R.S. Melnick, Regulation and the Courts: The Case of the Clean Air Act 6–8 (1983).

(4) A *choice* between governmental action and non-action is always available. Nothing *compels* the assignment of a traffic policeman to a busy corner, or the imposition of price control, or licensing barbers and cosmetologists, or seeking to eliminate business monopolies. Whichever way the choice may be made, almost inevitably someone gains and someone loses from the decision.

Those who are devoted to "rugged individualism" argue in effect that that government is best which governs least. One must ask, "Best for *whom?*" Unwise action by governmental agencies and unwise policy choices by legislators may produce great harm, to be sure. Does this fact support the argument that governmental action should be reduced to a minimum? Emmette S. Redford, a well known political scientist, expects continued expansion of the administrative state because three propositions limit acceptability of a laissez-faire concept: [8]

"First, escape from the administrative state would not mean escape from the administered society. The latter is ubiquitous and exists in both public and private sectors: for the business of society, the whole of society, is conducted by organizations with specialized functions. On the private side, organizations—corporations, unions, associations—are now the dominant factor in the economy. Man must live within them if he is to be sustained by his own employment, and he must buy from them and borrow from them if he is to enjoy even the minimum essentials of life. Their policies and managerial decisions—on production, wages, prices, advertising, etc.—allocate advantages and disadvantages to men. Man is, in other words, inescapably a subject of private administration.

"Second, the ballot of the market place does not provide to man an adequate means of protecting and promoting his interests. Man casts his ballot much more frequently in the market place than he does in the political system. He votes when he chooses a product, or elects to buy or not to buy, to sell or not to sell, to borrow or not to borrow, to patronize one dealer rather than another. Yet in spite of the multitude of individual ballots, continuously cast, there are grave limitations on the capacity of the economic vote:

    1. It cannot provide many common services desired by all or by significant groups.

    2. It cannot correct abuses and injustices in the operation of the economic system.

8. E.S. Redford, Democracy in the Administrative State (1969), at pp. 180–182.

3. It cannot deal successfully with the interrelationships and the interdependencies within the economy.

4. Money is the usual means of economic balloting and the lack of it deprives many of the ability to vote.

". . . Man has turned to politics and to creation of the administrative state because his ballot in the market place did not satisfy all of his interests.

"Third, the public and the private sectors of the administered society are interlocked. The private sector is dependent upon the public, just as the public sector is dependent upon the private. The private sector is propped and serviced in innumerable ways by the administrative state."

(5) Direct government ownership of business is one possible means of achieving control over private interests in whose hands economic power has been concentrated.[9] "Government ownership" has another aspect, however. It can be considered as a method of accomplishing what might otherwise remain undone because private interests may wield too little rather than too much power.

The Tennessee Valley Authority may serve as a grandiose example. The T.V.A. is a corporation created by statute. The United States became at the outset its sole stockholder. Its directors are appointed by the President. Its stated purposes are to act "in the interest of national

---

9. The late James M. Landis spelled out this thought as follows: "I have always contended that the function of the administrative process is to try to make administrative regulation sufficiently effective so as to enable capitalism to live up to its own pretensions and that if administrative regulation were to fail, collectivism would be the only answer. Wall Street and big business seem to me singularly unaware of this possibility. They build as the German industrialists did—perilously close to collectivism—not only because they build instruments of power which can be so easily seized by the government but also because these instruments of power if inefficiently regulated may be required to be taken over by the government." Report of the Committee on Cartels and Monopoly, ch. 16 of G.W. Stocking and N.W. Watkins, Monopoly and Free Enterprise 550 (1951).

Alan Stone, Economic Regulation and the Public Interest 269–270 (1977), suggests a greater willingness to take the next step:

"The great [advantage of public ownership] is that conflict between public goals and corporate profits can disappear since theoretically the latter have no further role. This is not by any means to say that accounting disappears, but rather that turning a profit becomes only one of several goals for an enterprise. But the public enterprise model raises the question of whether an alternative system of

effective incentives can replace the pecuniary system of incentives under capitalism. For public ownership is not necessarily a panacea, as the U.S. Postal Service and the French matchbook industry attest. And public ownership has been associated with so many repressive regimes that one must wonder whether public ownership and totalitarianism are inexorably linked, as F.A. Hayek and others argue. The dangers associated with a concentration of economic and political power in a few hands need not be belabored; several nations provide dramatic illustrations.

". . . Why did the Soviet Union and China become totalitarian? Can it not plausibly be argued that their political excesses sprang from their underdeveloped status rather than from their economic system? Could not widespread public ownership operate in the United States, or in any other developed society, within a democratic framework? These questions require exploration and deserve not to be ignored. All of the models that operate within a capitalist framework have glaring deficiencies. To expect any of them to play a major role in upholding public values is like asking a cat to bark; we can be assured, though, that public and private decision makers will roar like lions in proclaiming their devotion to the public interest."

defense and for agricultural and industrial development" by seeking "to improve navigation in the Tennessee River and to control the destructive flood waters . . . ".

Might these same goals have been achieved through private development under the control of an administrative agency such as the Federal Power Commission? In this instance probably not, because of the vast initial investment and the long developmental effort needed to transform an entire region.

These same considerations have not appeared with equal force in all the instances of public use of the corporate device, as in the various turnpike authorities, port authorities, recreational area authorities, and lending or insuring bodies that have become commonplace in America.[10] What, then, are the advantages of the corporate form? Why do American legislatures turn to a business instrumentality instead of relying on more plainly governmental mechanisms to reach the ends sought? [11]

Among the answers that have been given is the supposedly greater freedom of a corporate organization concerning (1) choosing and disciplining its staff, (2) budgetary and accounting controls over purchases and expenditures, (3) financing the enterprise through earnings or borrowings without having to go through legislative appropriations committees. Moreover, promotional activities—especially if they involve the coordinated development and the integrated operation of multipurpose projects—are not the kind in which administrative organizations have acquired a reputation for expertness or adeptness. Perhaps, as one scholar has suggested, recourse to the corporate form simply improves "the semantic position of the operation for people who are accustomed to corporate, but not government, business activities".[12]

(6) Still another mechanism of government control, involving neither ownership nor regulatory agencies nor litigation, uses contract as a means of achieving public objectives. Government simply sets the terms on which it is willing to do business. Since the United States has itself become the nation's largest consumer of goods and services, its purchasing power is enormous; when to this is added the purchasing power of the fifty states and their subdivisions, one must recognize that governmental pressure can indeed be brought to bear heavily on those who seek to do business with public agencies.

Some provisions of federal procurement contracts have become "boilerplate" paragraphs, unchangeable in form or content, aimed at enforcing policies only tangentially related (if related at all) to what is then being procured. A supplier of goods or services must promise, for example, to be non-discriminatory in hiring and promoting employees; to observe various standards of wages, hours of labor, and working

---

10. See R. Gerwig, Public Authorities in the United States, 26 L. & Contemp. Probs. 591 (1961); Council of State Governments, Public Authorities in the States (1953).

11. The point should perhaps be stressed here that recourse to government

corporations is not a peculiarly American development. The contrary is the case. See W. Friedmann and J.F. Garner, Government Enterprise: A Comparative Study (1970).

12. L. Schwartz, Free Enterprise and Economic Organization (1952).

conditions; to maintain personnel security practices calculated to preserve secrecy; to utilize only "humane slaughter" methods when meat products are involved; to make certain dispositions of patent rights that incidentally emerge from performing the contract; and to "renegotiate" the contract if, as matters develop, excessive profits flow from the original agreement.

An especially telling article by Arthur S. Miller, Administration by Contract: A New Concern for the Administrative Lawyer, 36 N.Y.U.L. Rev. 957 (1961), suggests that even more important than regulation by contract is the mounting practice of governmental contracting with private institutions for the direct accomplishment of functions previously performed (or, at least, performable) by the government itself. Contracts with corporations, institutes, and universities to conduct research that would in times past have been done in official laboratories are now common. Planning future operations—sheer thinking, in short—is often done by outside contractors rather than by inside officials. Designing entire "weapons systems" and then executing the designs have been shifted from Defense Department and military officers into the hands of large corporations. Even the active operation of publicly owned property has been "contracted out," as has been done notably in the nuclear energy field.

"Contract" has thus become, in the course of the years, an additional mechanism of government control, for the gains derived from doing business with (or on behalf of) the government make contractors ready to accept constraints upon managerial choices.[13] The other side of the coin, however, must be examined, too. Governmental reliance on private contractors creates a condition of public dependency as well as a public pressure. Something of this kind must have been in President Eisenhower's mind when, in his farewell message on January 17, 1961, he warned: "In the councils of government, we must guard against the acquisition of unwarranted influence, whether sought or unsought, by the military-industrial complex. The potential for the disastrous rise of misplaced power exists and will persist. We must never let the weight of this combination endanger our liberties or democratic processes. . . . ."[14]

And as Professor Miller has remarked in the paper cited above (at 982): "By placing the influence over, and sometimes even control of, important decisions one step further away from the public and their elected representatives, the [contractual] system further exacerbates the problem of discretion. In brief, subdelegation of power which is itself almost unrestricted has significant implications for a democratic society."[15]

13. For illustration of "the erosion of independence," see C.A. Reich, The New Property, 73 Yale L.J. 733, 756–757, 766 (1964).

14. Public Papers of the Presidents, 1960–61, at 1038.

15. [Ed.] See also H. Leventhal, Public Contracts and Administrative Law, 52 A.B. A.J. 35 (1966). In this article, Judge Leventhal suggests that the principles of administrative law which have been developed for regulatory programs are of increasing relevance for the federal government's procurement activities. Although not advocating any wholesale transference of regulatory administrative law doctrines to the procurement process, he predicts extensions of the concept of public account-

(7) Apart from control by contract, the federal government has vastly extended its direction of state and local administrators by making financial grants which are conditioned upon acceptance of national policies and administrative prescriptions. This occurs chiefly in matters which are not thought of as regulatory; but in fact regulatory activity by non-federal officials may be generated by federal grants. Money for highway building, for example, may be given on condition that outdoor advertising displays be brought under control. Similarly, hospital construction may be subsidized if suitable measures are taken to prevent improprieties in professional staffing and in the admission of patients.

The great enlargement of the federal government's recognition of social welfare responsibilities has not, however, caused a corresponding displacement of administration at other levels of government. The federal Department of Health, Education, and Welfare, for example, "operates directly only the retirement, survivors, disability, and hospital-medical programmes set up under federal law. Other programmes affecting health, education, and welfare are provided for and administered by the states and their subdivisions—though with substantial federal assistance. This is eminently true in the fields of education and welfare assistance, where it is the states which still have the primary administrative responsibility. It is also true in fields like public housing, urban development, town planning, zoning, and the like. . . .

"What the federal government has done recently has been greatly to increase its financial participation in those fields of social welfare in which the law does not provide for direct federal administration. A major portion of the state and local budgets for education and welfare is underwritten by congressional appropriations. This has enabled the federal government, by paying the piper, to call the tune. Federal aid is extended only on terms dictated from Washington. Federal statutes may in this way require state welfare agencies to hold judicialized hearings; federal statutes and regulations may similarly require state laws to be administered without racial discrimination. The power to cut off federal funds is a simple and effective sanction.

"The result has been to modify considerably the established division between national and state authority. Some may consider that the federal government's encroachments are inconsistent with constitutional fundamentals. But in such ways must progress be made." B. Schwartz and H.W.R. Wade, Legal Control of Government (1972), at 10.

SECTION 2. AGENCY STRUCTURE AND AGENCY FUNCTION

Discussion to this point has revealed the variety of tasks that agencies perform, and has suggested the likely durability of public administration as an enterprise—however much the specific tasks assigned it may change with time. It may now be useful to provide some

ability of public officials and discusses specific areas where the process might be improved.

models, both of agencies and of their decisional processes, against which the legal constraints on public administration which are the focus of this course may be considered. Just as the study of Corporations is aided by a passing acquaintance with the characteristics of corporate form and corporation decision, administrative law is difficult to consider without having some initial impressions of the organization of an agency and how it may act.

The student would be ill-advised to regard the sketches that follow as definitive. They are intended merely to suggest models which may be helpful in understanding the materials of this book. Thus the two federal agencies shortly to be compared are both large, well-staffed, and rigidly bureaucratic organizations when compared to the Virginia State Corporation Commission or the Hempstead Town Zoning Board. The enormous variation in fact of decision processes among and within federal agencies is suggested by the twenty-seven monographs published by the Attorney General's Committee on Administrative Procedure in 1940, each describing in detail the procedures and decisional processes employed by one agency.[1] A survey of state and local agency practice would doubtless show even greater variation. In 1978, in response to an Executive Order, over thirty federal agencies described in the pages of the Federal Register the manner in which they decide issues of rulemaking.[2] These pages quickly show that, as with the biological description "bird", the term "rulemaking" encompasses enormous variety as well as some prominently shared characteristics. The materials of this book speak, as judges and lawyers do, at the level of "mammal," "bird," and "reptile." But the sketches, like the circumstances of any concrete case, may more immediately suggest squirrel, thrush, or lizard. The student—like the judge—must take pains to avoid letting his view of the mammalian class as a whole be distorted by his having encountered a squirrel—or, perhaps, a skunk.

The organizational charts of two federal agencies are set out on the immediately following pages. The Nuclear Regulatory Commission is an independent agency with a relatively simple structure. In Fiscal Year 1985, it had 3,498 employees and a budget of $448 million. The much larger and more complex Department of Agriculture is a part of the Executive Branch. In Fiscal Year 1985, it had more than 106,000 employees and spent more than $55 billion. Strikingly, however, the tables of organization of these two agencies reveal substantial commonalities. The head of the agency—five Commissioners in case of the NRC, the Secretary in case of the Department—has a small cadre of advisers immediately responsible to it; but the great bulk of the agency's personnel serves in "administrations," "services," "offices," or like subordinate units with particular substantive or administrative support responsibilities (and each with its own similarly hierarchical infrastructure). Detailed knowledge about control devices for nuclear

1. S.Doc. 186, 76th Cong. 3d Sess. (1940); S.Doc. 8, 77th Cong. 1st Sess. (1941).

2. Executive Order 12044, 43 Fed.Reg. 12661 (March 24, 1978). Initial responses to the order appear almost daily in Federal Register issues between late May and July, 1978.

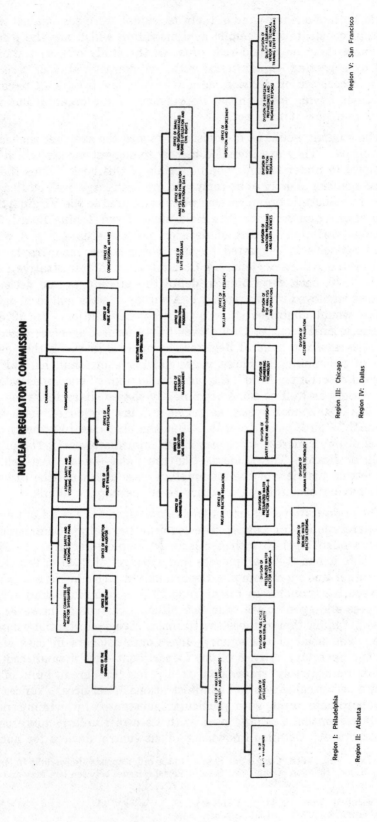

NUCLEAR REGULATORY COMMISSION

Region I: Philadelphia

Region II: Atlanta

Region III: Chicago

Region IV: Dallas

Region V: San Francisco

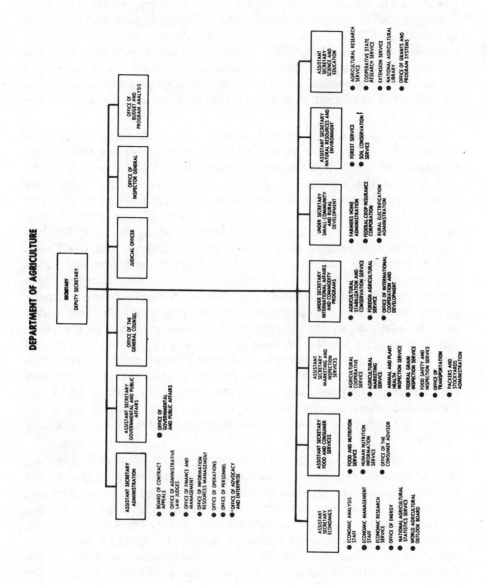

power plants resides in the twenty or so members of the Electrical Instrumentation Branch of the Division of Safety Review and Oversight of the NRC's Office of Nuclear Reactor Regulation; the extent of gypsy moth infestation and knowledge of measures useful to control it is the immediate concern of a group of specialists within the Animal and Plant Health Inspection Service, which in turn is supervised by the Department's Assistant Secretary for Marketing and Inspection Services.

Other organizational units, of course, may be concerned with these issues, or have particular support skills to offer respecting them. The inspectors of the NRC's Office of Inspection and Enforcement or the engineers of the Division of Human Factors Technology may have practical experience with the functioning of control systems; its Office of Nuclear Regulatory Research may be supervising, or know of, relevant experimentation in innovative design. The Agricultural Marketing Service, the Federal Crop Insurance Corporation, and the Forest Service may each need to know about the gypsy moth problem for its own purposes, or be able to contribute to its control. Lawyers, data service operators, comptrollers, and policy planners—isolated in each agency into discrete "staff support" offices—may also be, or feel, called upon to take part in any consideration of these problems as they may arise. Note that lawyers in both agencies are segregated into special law offices; often the internal structure of these offices mirrors the structure of the agency as a whole, so that a small group of attorneys may be particularly cognizant of the problems of the Animal and Plant Health Inspection Service, without, however, coming under the direct control of the Service Chief or of the Assistant Secretary for Marketing Services.

One organizational choice common to the two agencies (and all federal agencies engaged in substantial adjudication) is central to the following discussion: the administrative law judges and the appellate tribunal of the agency are wholly separated from both "staff" and "counsel" in the agency. The Assistant Secretary for Administration, to whom the Department's Office of Administrative Law Judges reports, is an officer divorced from the substantive concerns of the Department; the Judicial Officer, who holds its final adjudicatory authority, is responsible only to the Secretary. The Commission's Atomic Safety and Licensing Board Panel and Atomic Safety and Licensing Appeal Panel are equally free of ties to the NRC's operating staff. Counsel in both agencies serve under other officers, officers lacking any authority over the adjudicatory function. Indeed, the Commission has created two groups of lawyers, one to serve it directly and the other to satisfy the legal needs of its staff; other agencies commonly create the same type of distinction within their General Counsel's Office, to permit legal advice to be given staff taking a possibly adversary role in agency proceedings without compromising the access of the agency head to legal advice at later stages in the proceedings.

To assume that organizations so complex are as integrated as a single individual, or that the decisions attributed to such organizations are generally taken at the very top of their organizational structure, would be naive. The realities of bureaucratic behavior and the pressures of time serve to defeat these assumptions. While the employees of the Department of Agriculture doubtless share a certain esprit de corps, those who have themselves served in a complex administrative agency may smile wryly at the notion that the Inspection Service, the Marketing Service, the Crop Insurance Corporation, the Forest Service, the General Counsel's Office and all others who may be concerned with the gypsy moth problem will act as one in dealing with it—politely acquiescing in each other's views or excusing, even covering up, mistakes and injustices of other parts of the Department. In governmental organizations, bitter infighting and tense inter-divisional rivalries are much more commonplace than is the Spirit of the Three Musketeers. Of course at any given moment common goals and policies may be shared from top to bottom within an agency; in fact, unless such a sharing does substantially occur, the operations of the organization become chaotic and unpredictable, usually to the dismay of all who are affected. But in any particular instance this concurrence as to end objectives rarely guarantees frictionless or mutually uncritical interactions of the agency's several parts. Even when superior officials think they have given explicit instructions (let alone when they rely on anything so amorphous as esprit de corps), they cannot be at all sure that their subordinates will behave exactly as desired. An astute commentator on public administration, summing up a year's observation of the work of six federal bureau chiefs, remarked:

> [B]eing a Chief is gratifying only for those who derive pleasure from accomplishments on a small scale and from the chance that some . . . may lead to larger benefits in the future. The chiefs . . . certainly do calculate and negotiate to accomplish all they can. But they make their marks in inches, not miles, and only as others allow.[3]

H. Kaufman, The Administrative Behavior of Federal Bureau Chiefs 174 (Brookings 1981).

3. The chiefs studied headed The Animal and Plant Health Inspection Service, the Forest Service, the Food and Drug Administration, the Social Security Administration, the Customs Service and the Internal Revenue Service. An earlier work of Kaufman's, The Forest Ranger (1960), also provides a subtle and probing study of hierarchical functioning and control in administration. Compare H.A. Simon, Administrative Behavior (1957), at 13–14.

WARNER W. GARDNER,* THE ADMINISTRATIVE
PROCESS†

Legal Institutions Today and Tomorrow (M.G. Paulsen ed. 1959) pp. 116–118,
120, 124–129, 133, 142, 147, 148.

. . . [I]n most agencies the commissioner or the head is in no sense an expert. In more cases than not he will to one degree or another have a political background, and in more cases than not his qualifications would point to government service in general rather than to the particular agency to which he is appointed. This is not a bad thing. I for one believe we get better government from nonspecialists, indeed from politicians, than we get from experts. And with the passage of enough time in office, the nonexpert is likely to become at least experienced, if not expert. But even though it be a good thing to have nonexpert agency heads, it is not also a good thing to build up our law and our thinking on the fiction of their invariable expertise.

The agency staff, in contrast, can more often than not be described as expert. It is an expertness based usually upon a good many years of familiarity with the regulation of the industry, and only rarely upon any substantial experience in the operation of the industry. It is, therefore, ordinarily true, as John Dickinson has said, that they "are experts as students or analysts, observing, but always from the outside and with a touch of unfamiliarity." But, as expertise goes in the world of government, we must grant it to the usual agency staff.

The staff expertise will not always be transferred to the agency when it makes its decisions. Sometimes this may be because of the technical complexity of the problem. Agency heads as well as reviewing courts will often or even ordinarily take on compulsory faith the more technical and complex proposals of the staff. At other times it may be because our search for disinterested justice has, by a vigorous separation of functions, insured only that we have an uninformed dispensation of justice. But let us assume that the expertise has been transferred, and that the agency decision reflects the accumulated information and insight of the staff. There is no reason, even in that event, to pay the same deference to the expertise of the agency when it determines whether a book is "obscene, lewd or lascivious" as when it decides an issue of oil proration, touching "matters of geography and geology and physics and engineering." . . .

. . . I believe . . . [the administrative agency's] chief sources of guidance are three, and that since they are more often opposed than united the result is tolerably good government.

The main source of guidance is the agency's permanent staff. In the course of a quarter of a century in Washington I have encountered only one clear instance where the head of an already established agency or department succeeded in subjugating his employees to the

* Mr. Gardner is a member of the Washington, D.C., law firm of Shea & Gardner. He was formerly Solicitor of the Departments of Labor and Interior, and was Assistant Secretary of the Interior in 1946– 1947. He has been active in the Administrative Conference of the United States.

† Copyright 1959 Columbia University Press. Reprinted by permission.

point that the clear preponderance of the departmental actions, where there was room for choice, reflected his views rather than those held by his staff when he took office. . . .[4]

This is no reflection either on the agency heads or the staffs. It is instead inevitable. The permanent staff knows the technical subject, it knows the statute and the regulations, and it knows the precedents—in each case far better than its superior officer. . . .

The countervailing influence upon the agency which regulates a particular industry is the industry itself. It operates to a lesser degree in the agencies which cut across many industries. But it is not, I would be bold enough to guess, negligible even there. The "industry-mindedness" of the established administrative agency has been deplored. But, as Professor Jaffe reminds us, this may be just what the Congress wanted when it gave the agency the job not only of regulating but of supporting and developing the industry. And certainly . . . we expect the Department of Agriculture to be guardian of the farmers' interests, and we hope, if we do not always expect, that the Office of Indian Affairs will do the same for its wards. I believe it in any case to be inevitable. One cannot spend his time immersed in the problems of a single industry without becoming both aware of these problems and sympathetic toward their solution. . . .

The third major influence upon the administrative agency is, I believe, and certainly hope, the bar which practices before it. The agency's work must inevitably be better done if it has the benefit of careful research, thoughtful consideration, and effective advocacy on behalf of the interested parties. Its work must inevitably be more quickly dispatched if its practitioners can move with speed, can understand what is both relevant and important, and can discharge their responsibilities without the wrangling which no court would permit. . . .

a. Executive Decision

Far the most common sort of decision taken within administrative agencies is that of day-to-day administration, which rarely comes to the attention of outside lawyers or courts. How shall the Department respond to Congressman Jones' irate letter of September 3, complaining of uncontrolled spread of gypsy moths in Herkimer County, and Congressman Smith's letter of August 21, forwarding a constituent's complaint that she was obliged to bake for four hours in the August sun on the way home from her vacation while awaiting departmental inspection and decontamination of a recreational vehicle which she had driven into an area contaminated by the moths? What budget shall be sought for the control program for the coming year? What priority shall the current year's effort be given as against the emerging problem of corn rust in the midwest? What parts of the country appear most

---

4. [Ed.] For elaboration on the difficulties Presidential appointees experience in subduing their civil service staffs, consult H. Heclo, A Government of Strangers (1977); see also R.O. Berner, Constraints on the Regulatory Process: A Case Study of Regulation of Cable Television (1976).

threatened? To what ends (commercial forest protection, recreational area protection, containment of existing infestation, eradication efforts) should existing resources be committed? These are not legal questions, to be sure (although laws, including appropriations acts, may influence the range of possible answers), nor are they necessarily contentious or complex. But understanding the common mode of agency decision may assist in acquiring perspective on the more formal modes of rulemaking and adjudication that mark this book's principal concern.

It would be reasonable to expect each of these matters to be referred initially to the Animal and Plant Health Inspection Service; and within that Service they would find their way to gypsy moth (and corn rust) specialists. But plainly they cannot be resolved at one desk. Information may be needed from the Statistical Reporting Service; the Office of Governmental and Public Affairs may contribute insight into the delicate issues of corresponding with the Congress; the Forest Service, the Federal Crop Insurance Corporation, and others will have views on the allocation of current effort; next year's budget may require judgments about relative importance respecting the whole of the Department's operations. The individual to whom the assignment is made, then, will be given the responsibility of consulting with counterparts in other organizational divisions to see that they are "on board", or, if not, what might bring them around. He may also be responsible for checking with concerned private organizations or individuals. The written response he makes to his assignment will carry an indication of the consultations he has made and their result, and will embody a proposed response or course of action. It will move to his supervisor, and his supervisor's supervisor, each of whom may in turn consult with her own counterparts elsewhere in the Department. Someone in the General Counsel's Office will review the document for legal problems; there or elsewhere it will be reviewed for consistency with Departmental policy and for what it may reveal respecting future needs for policy development.

If the matter turns out not to be controversial, or any initial controversy can be mediated at the working level, it is unlikely ever to come to the attention of the Secretary, the Undersecretary, the Assistant Secretaries, or even individual office heads.[1] Controversy between

---

1. "[T]he priority of presidential demands and national policy issues over departmental administration has been offered as an explanation for the weakness of secretarial direction of bureaus. For example, [Michael Blumenthal,] a recent secretary of the treasury observed:

'I remember asking a former secretary of the Treasury years ago, when I never dreamed that I would be in his job: Why don't you do something about the U.S. Customs Service? Why don't you do something about what I saw as the excessive number of customs agents going through bags, on the grounds that they're unlikely to catch much that way? If you want to catch people who smuggle in drugs or dangerous weapons, you have to do it a different way, perhaps with spot checks and not by going through people's individual bags. And he shrugged his shoulders and said, I have not time for that. And I thought to myself, if I were ever in a position of authority, I really would want to do something about that, because as a citizen coming through the U.S. Customs, I always resented that kind of thing, comparing it to Europe.

'Now that I'm the Secretary, I realize what he meant, and I haven't done anything about it, because I've spent my time working with the President and my Cabinet colleagues on things that are more important, like economic policy.' "

the corn rust and gypsy moth specialists might be resolved within the Service by its Administrator or his delegate—this after memoranda had been written, or perhaps an informal meeting had been held to present the contending views. If, on the other hand, services responding to differing Assistant Secretaries are in controversy, and the Assistant Secretaries cannot themselves resolve the differences, the Secretary's office may have to be involved.[2] If broad and contentious public debate is anticipated, however low the level of controversy within the Department, it may insist on being involved. His consideration is likely to take the same form: he may receive a decision memorandum setting forth, in a set format, the varying views with supporting information; or he may preside at a meeting with the affected offices, at which each can briefly present its views in discussion with him. The common elements here are notable: only controversy rises through the hierarchy for decision; the hierarchy is structured to permit the identification, but encourage the mediation, of such controversies; in general, issues are left for decision to the specialists presumed to know the most about them; and when controversy does arise, it is resolved with their direct participation and on the facts which they choose to state. The Secretary does not have a separate bank of gypsy moth and corn rust specialists to which he can turn for advice in resolving any dispute among those in his Animal and Plant Health Inspection Service; to acquire the understanding he needs, he necessarily depends on interchanges with and the advice of the disputants themselves.[3]

H. Kaufman, The Administrative Behavior of Federal Bureau Chiefs 187 (Brookings, 1983).

2. "The Secretary" may not always be personally involved when his office is, just as "the White House" does not mean the President. A Secretary's personal aides regularly can and do indicate to the staff how "the Secretary" wants something to be handled without having explicit instructions on the point. While such behavior is sometimes regarded as involving a bluff deserving to be called, it is generally known within the Department who has the Secretary's ear, and understood that few department heads could possibly have the time and energy to deal personally with all departmental affairs laid on their desks.

3. One should not underestimate the force of precedent in large organizations. If in fact responding to Congressman Jones and Congressman Smith often necessitated extensive consultations and debates, governmental processes would be even slower than in fact they are. So of course staff members rely on "policy" (formally recorded or reflected in past incidents), reason by analogy, and so on. Indeed, the burdensomeness of reexamining an issue through the steps described is one of the main explanations of "bureaucratic rigidity" and similar asserted ills of the body politic.

The Secretary's dependence on his specialists also creates in that staff a substantial reservoir of power. As Richard O. Berner has noted in his case study of regulation of cable television by the FCC, "Constraints on the Regulatory Process" 66–67, 69, 71 (1976), "a Staff has initial control over the flow of information to the Commission within its specialized area, . . . routinely decides on the cases to which the Commission will address itself . . . [and] must use its judgment in deciding which previous Commission decisions . . . have a bearing on [those cases] . . . The procedure whereby the bureau writes up a proposed Commission decision in advance [of the meeting at which that decision will be considered, often summarily,] creates the expectation that the Commission will adopt the recommended action of the bureau." This influence is only enhanced by the staff's presumed expertise; it is the more striking when it is found to operate (as it does) even when the Commissioners themselves do not share the bureau's attitude.

In general, see Herbert Kaufman's excellent study, The Administrative Behavior of Federal Bureau Chiefs (1983).

b. Rulemaking

The statutory procedures for federal notice and comment rulemaking, set out in Section 553 of the Administrative Procedure Act, are neither elaborate nor demanding. An agency must publish a notice of its proposal in the Federal Register, a daily governmental publication of wide circulation. The notice must indicate the public procedures to be followed in adopting the rule and the authority claimed for its adoption, but the statute says it need only indicate the terms or substance of the proposal or describe the subjects and issues involved. An opportunity of unspecified duration is to be provided for written comment; the agency's only stated obligation of response is to "incorporate in the rules adopted a concise general statement of their basis and purpose." In fact, as we shall see, a good deal of law has been generated out of these sparse provisions; as important at this point, however, is grasping the internal agency behavior of rulemaking. The following description, while a decade old, effectively captures that perspective:

WILLIAM F. PEDERSEN, JR.,* FORMAL RECORDS AND INFORMAL RULEMAKING
85 Yale Law Journal 38, 51–59[†] (1975).

. . .

The Administrative Procedure Act is only a statute; it is not the source of all agency procedures. Commentators who focus too narrowly on the APA may forget what lies behind it, and the long paths an agency rule may have to trace before even being proposed for comment. Those who hope to improve agency rulemaking should first understand how agencies work internally. . . .

A. *Internal procedures: lead offices, working groups, steering committees and OMB*

. . .

Under internal EPA directives, the first formal step in drafting a regulation is to assemble an ad hoc "working group" composed of EPA staff members who have a particular interest or competence in a field. Needless to say, not all members of the working group participate actively; often most of the work is done by a few members. The most active are usually those representing the "lead office" or "office of primary interest"—the office which first had the idea for the rule or has been assigned responsibility for it. This office typically will far outdistance others in familiarity with the technical issues involved. Indeed, the evidence of that familiarity, when written down at all, may be very difficult for those outside the lead office to examine since it is often scattered through various studies, correspondence, and contrac-

---

* Mr. Pedersen was Deputy General Counsel, Environmental Protection Agency; he also served as a member of the staff of the Senate Committee on Government Operations during its Study of Federal Regulation pursuant to S.Res. 71, 95th Cong.

† Reprinted by permission of the author, The Yale Law Journal Company and Fred B. Rothman & Co.

tors' reports in the possession of the lead office. More data, of course, may be similarly scattered through other offices. There is no formal mechanism to specify what the working groups should consider, or even to make sure that all members have a chance to consider the same information. Disputes are raised and resolved in a catch-as-catch-can way until all the apparent issues have been thrashed out.

The working group then prepares a set of documents for review within EPA. Typically these consist of (1) the draft regulation, complete with explanatory preamble; (2) a technical support document cited in the preamble which contains background information too voluminous to be reprinted in the Federal Register; and (3) an "action memorandum" addressed to the EPA Administrator to highlight the major uncertainties, policy issues and probable objections to the regulations. Where required, an environmental impact statement and an inflation impact statement also will be included. After these materials are assembled, the regulation is ready to move on to the next stage.

This second stage consists of review by the "steering committee." The steering committee is composed of permanent representatives from each of the major sections of EPA plus a few permanent committee staff members. Others may also attend,[1] and in practice the steering committee's weekly meetings generally have a minimum of 15 people in attendance. Steering committee review of draft regulations is limited to consideration of the documents assembled by the working group. Passage through the steering committee is meant to ensure that no significant part of EPA is denied the opportunity to comment from its own perspective when new regulations are developed, and that all new regulations become the subject of disinterested analysis by the permanent staff of the steering committee.

After the steering committee has approved a proposed regulation, but before it is sent to the Administrator for signature, copies of the regulation and the various supporting documents are supplied to the Office of Management and Budget and to other interested agencies and departments for analysis and comment.[2] Some of these recipients release their copies to industries that would be affected by the proposed regulation and thereafter serve as conduits for industry views. Problems that arise during this review are bargained out between the agencies concerned, with OMB playing a role halfway between that of a judge and that of a moderator. EPA has occasionally been able to get its way even on highly controversial points in this forum. Only after the regulations have cleared OMB are they signed by the Administrator and put out for the public comment contemplated by the APA. After

1. EPA has 19 Deputy Assistant Administrators who rank just below and (with one exception) report to the heads of the five major divisions of the agency. These officials, to oversimplify, serve as the link between the top of the agency, which is basically concerned with policy and with representing EPA to the world outside, and the lower levels at which the more detailed technical work is done. Originally it was expected that they would attend the steering committee meetings; in practice they generally stay away and send one or more representatives. Members of working groups which have items on the agenda often also attend.

2. [Ed. The current structure of OMB review is considered in Chapter 2, below.]

comments have been received, the working group analyzes them and, when necessary, revises the regulations, technical support document, or action memorandum. The revised regulations are then reviewed once again by the steering committee and OMB before promulgation in final form.

B. *The process as it actually works*

Simply to outline the formal procedures established for developing and reviewing rules inside the executive branch may give an exaggerated idea of their importance. They do indeed provide a structure through which most [3] agency actions must pass, but other factors tend to diminish their influence.

In most cases the office of primary interest will care far more about a given rule than any other group. . . . [T]he dominance of the lead office makes the role of the working group far less significant than a description of the system of review might suggest. . . . Working groups are supposed to be forums for resolving differences of opinion within the agency before the agency position is fixed in a proposed rule. But to the extent that serious disagreement actually arises, . . . [issues are escalated at least to the Deputy Assistant-Administrator] level and maybe higher for resolution. . . . The steering committee typically makes even less of a contribution to proposed rules than do the working groups.

. . . A main job of higher EPA officials, above the steering committee level, is to remain in contact with outside groups such as industry, environmentalists, Congress and state and local officials and, of course, with their own staffs. When a vital issue arises, in the nature of things it will be swiftly brought to the attention of these officials. A round of informal discussions is likely to ensue, which often takes the main burden of resolving complex or controversial issues.

Another set of problems arises because the controversial issues at EPA also tend to be very technical and complex. . . . To take one example, the question whether power plants should be required to install scrubbers to remove sulfur compounds from their stack gasses turns in the first instance on whether the scrubbers will work. But if a

---

3. Some of the most important agency actions escape both internal EPA review and OMB review. These have included the various suspensions of auto emission standards, the decision to start proceedings to summarily prohibit the use of the pesticide aldrin/dieldrin, and the promulgation of transportation control plans to reduce traffic in urban areas. Here a combination of time pressure and the complexity of the subject matter has swamped the usual intra-agency procedures. OMB review has been cut out both for this reason and, in the first two cases, because the statute was very clear that the Administrator of EPA was to make the decision and specified at least a fairly formal procedure for him to use.

In such cases, the Administrator or his top aides have typically worked directly with the staff members most directly concerned. On balance, I believe the decisions made in this manner have been at least as good as those that have gotten the full steering committee/OMB treatment, though of course the Administrator can only become involved in a handful of decisions.

given scrubber doesn't work, that may well stem from a lack of proper maintenance, from the omission of some easy adjustment, or from routine development problems that will quite predictably be cleared up as the technology advances. The fact that a scrubber has worked may be due to the nature of the particular fuel or facility, so that no lesson has been learned about the efficacy of the technology generally. When such uncertainties arise, as they do early in the discussion of any even moderately controversial issue, there is really no way to answer them short of a thoroughgoing immersion in the data. Yet high government officials, at EPA and certainly still more at OMB (and, I am sure, in other agencies), do not want to be bothered with the details of technical matters if they can possibly avoid it.

What is more, the briefing package to which the discussion of a proposed rule is reduced at the steering committee stage is often unable to convey an adequate notion of the complex, uncertain and ambiguous nature of the information and the choices involved. Even when officials realize this and the matter is important, they are often far too busy to master the data. The attitude of these officials toward the regulation in question is thus significantly influenced by which staff members are trusted, which present their case more plausibly, who won last time, and other considerations extraneous to the technical complexities of the regulation itself.

The bureaucratic weight and inertia and the relatively coarse mesh of the review process have two adverse (and seemingly contrary) effects on those who develop regulations. First, stiff or problematical regulations may simply not be pushed because too much bureaucratic counterpressure will be generated. . . . Second, regulations that do get pushed may still be arbitrary to some degree, particularly in the direction from which opposition is unlikely. The upper levels of review cannot be thorough enough to catch the technical errors or errors of detail on which the legality and, indeed, the wisdom of the regulations may depend.[4]

4. [Ed.] See also J. Quarles, Cleaning Up America (1976) for accounts of particular EPA rulemakings. The "rulemaking" Mr. Pedersen describes is that looking toward formulation of a so-called "legislative rule," the most formal product of rulemaking behaviors. Codified in the Code of Federal Regulations, a collection now filling several library shelves, such rules assume the form and have the impact of statutes. If valid, they have the force of law, binding agency, court and citizen alike. Other behaviors which would be regarded as "rulemaking" include setting rates, announcing policies, issuing guidelines, stating interpretations, and promulgating staff procedures; each involves the formulation of more or less abstract policy for possible but not always mandatory application to future events.

c. Adjudication

ARCHIBALD COX, DEREK BOK AND ROBERT GORMAN,*
CASES AND MATERIALS ON LABOR LAW †

(Foundation Press, Tenth Ed., 1986) pp. 104–107.

NLRB ORGANIZATION AND PROCEDURE

Although it is customary to speak of "the Board" as if the National Labor Relations Board and its large staff of employees thought and acted as a single person, this usage is highly misleading. In reality, the NLRB is composed of various categories of persons exercising quite different responsibilities. The adjudicative responsibilities of the agency are ultimately entrusted to the five members of the Board, appointed by the President of the United States for five-year terms by and with the consent of the Senate. In the course of the Taft-Hartley amendments of 1947, the Congress also established the office of General Counsel, appointed to a four-year term by the President by and with the consent of the Senate. The General Counsel has authority to investigate charges of unfair labor practices, to decide whether complaints should be issued on the basis of these charges and to direct the prosecution of such complaints. The General Counsel also represents the Board in court proceedings to enforce or review Board decisions.

To assist the Board members and the General Counsel in discharging their responsibilities, a large staff has been created. Organizationally, the staff is divided between the Washington office and over thirty Regional Offices. The Regional Offices are under the general supervision of the General Counsel. Each Regional Office is under the direction of a Regional Director aided by a Regional Attorney. Their staff consists principally of Field Examiners and Field Attorneys, who investigate charges, conduct elections, and prosecute complaints at hearings before Administrative Law Judges (called Trial Examiners prior to August 1972).

The General Counsel may issue a complaint only upon a formal charge that the employer or the union has engaged in an unfair labor practice. Such a charge may be filed by "any person" in the office for the region in which the alleged unfair labor practice occurred. . . . When a charge is filed, the Regional Director normally requires the person making the charge to submit the supporting evidence in the form of affidavits, lists of witnesses, etc. The charged party (respondent) will then be asked to submit a reply and a Field Examiner or Attorney will make a thorough investigation of the facts and surrounding circumstances. . . .

---

* The authors are, respectively, Professor of Law Emeritus at Harvard University. President of Harvard University, and Professor of Law at the University of Pennsylvania.

† Reprinted by permission of the authors and publisher.

If this preliminary investigation discloses that the charge is without foundation, the case is likely to be dropped forthwith. Otherwise, further investigation may ensue and there will commonly be an informal conference at the local office of the Board, attended by both the respondent and the charging party, at which the alleged unfair practices are thoroughly discussed and possible settlements considered. It is important to emphasize the informality of these investigations, conferences and settlements. Except for such steps as are required by sound administration, including the reduction to writing of any settlement agreement, the entire procedure up to this point is conducted with all possible informality and an eye to amicable adjustments.

The overwhelming preponderance of unfair labor practice cases have traditionally been disposed of in one way or another in the Regional Offices by these informal personal negotiations. In the fiscal year ending June 30, 1982 . . ., for example, of the 36,400 unfair labor practice charges that were "closed," 94 percent were closed by the NLRB Regional Offices prior to a formal hearing. (Within those cases, approximately 35 percent were disposed of by dismissing the charge involved, 40 percent by voluntary withdrawal of the charge, and 25 percent by settlement.)

If it is impossible to dispose of an unfair labor practice case in the Regional Office, formal proceedings are commenced by the filing of a complaint. The General Counsel has delegated to the Regional Directors authority to issue complaints except in cases "involving novel and complex issues." Should the Regional Director refuse to issue a complaint, the matter may be appealed to the General Counsel. . . .

. . .

The complaint, which is drafted by the Regional Attorney or a member of his or her staff, specifies the violations of the Act which the company is alleged to have committed and contains a notice of the time and place of hearing. The Act and the Board's rules give the respondent the right to answer a complaint. The answer is filed with the Regional Director, as are all motions made prior to the hearing.

The hearing is usually held in the city or town where the alleged violation occurred before an Administrative Law Judge appointed from the Division of Administrative Law Judges in Washington (or from one of the geographically decentralized divisions which the Board has recently established). The case is prosecuted for the Board by an attorney from the Regional Office. The charging party is permitted to intervene, and its attorneys may take part in the proceedings. The respondent, of course, may and usually does appear by an attorney. Section 10(b) of the Act provides that unfair labor practice proceedings "shall, so far as practicable, be conducted in accordance with the rules of evidence applicable in the district courts" under the rules of civil procedure adopted by the Supreme Court. Evidence is introduced through witnesses and documents, just as in an ordinary civil trial. At the conclusion of the hearing both parties are entitled as a matter of right to argue orally before the Administrative Law Judge and file a written brief. In practice, however, it has not been customary for either party to make an oral argument.

After the hearing is completed, the Administrative Law Judge prepares a decision containing proposed findings of fact and recommendations for the disposition of the case. The Administrative Law Judge's decision is then filed with the Board, and a copy is served on the respondent and any other parties. Exceptions to the Administrative Law Judge's decision may then promptly be filed by counsel for any party, including the General Counsel. . . . If no exceptions are filed, the Board normally adopts the decision of the Administrative Law Judge.

In cases in which exceptions have been filed and briefs submitted, the Executive Secretary forwards the complete record to one of the five Board members, determined by rotation. Board members, through their legal staff of some twenty attorneys for each member, prepare a draft decision. In routine cases, a panel of three members will consider the case. When a draft opinion is sent to the other panel members, copies are also sent to members who are not on the panel so that they may consider whether the case is sufficiently important to warrant decision by the full Board; any member may ask to have a case referred to the full Board. Panel opinions may be approved by the participating members without any formal conference, but where there is a difference of opinion or an important issue is at stake a conference is held. In cases sufficiently important for decision by the full Board there is always a conference. Afterward, the opinion is prepared, approved by the members and issued by the Board.

The five members of the Board decide in this fashion more than one hundred unfair labor practice cases a month. It is obvious that in most of them the basic responsibility rested on the administrative law judge and the legal assistants who prepared draft decisions for the Board. Only a relatively small number of really important cases could receive full consideration from the members themselves, however conscientiously they attended to their duties.

ROBERT A. KAGAN,* REGULATORY JUSTICE: IMPLEMENTING A WAGE–PRICE FREEZE
(Russell Sage Foundation, 1978), pp. 28–32, 100–107.[†]

Within hours after the public announcement of [President Nixon's executive order establishing a wage-price freeze in an effort to control post-Vietnam-War inflation, and assigning administration of the order to the Cost of Living Council (CLC) and Office of Emergency Preparedness (OEP),] officials were besieged by telephone calls, telegrams, and letters. They came from trade associations, labor unions, and business corporations, from state and local government officials and congressional staff members, from individual wage earners, tenants, and consum-

* Professor Kagan is an associate professor in the Department of Political Science, University of California, Berkeley.

† Copyright © 1978 by the Russell Sage Foundation, and reprinted by permission of the author, the Foundation, and Basic Books, the publishers.

ers. These demands for action became the routine case load of the agencies. There were three kinds.

First were *complaints of violations,* primarily by ultimate consumers. They alleged, for example, that a retailer or gas station or insurance company had violated the freeze by increasing prices or that a landlord had illegally increased the rent. They demanded that the agency see to it that the increases were rolled back or the complainant's money refunded. Second, there were *inquiries,* requests for an official opinion or ruling concerning the requirements of the freeze as applied to a specific situation or transaction. . . . Most inquiries sought agency permission for a planned price or wage increase, a letter from the agency that would serve as a declaratory judgment which could be used to justify the planned increases to any challengers. Some inquirers, however, were in the posture of complainant: they sought an official ruling that they could use to block increases threatened or demanded by their suppliers or landlords or employees. Third, there were *requests for exceptions.* Whereas an inquiry asked or argued for an interpretation of the order as it applied to a specific case, an exception request acknowledged that the desired wage, price, or rent increase was prohibited as a matter of freeze law as previously articulated, but asked for an exception on grounds of hardship as a matter of administrative compassion.

The volume of inquiries far overshadowed the other types of cases. According to official OEP records, some 50,000 complaints of violations and 6,000 requests for exceptions were processed in the ninety days of the freeze. But even these enormous figures shrink to insignificance beside the 750,000 inquiries which were received and answered by the agencies. The average weekly volume of inquiries remained close to 85,000 for almost the entire freeze period. Responding to inquiries became the preeminent work of the agencies. Creation and maintenance of an efficient inquiry-response system became the principal organizational task.

This was in part a deliberate choice. . . . Prompt response to all inquiries, it was assumed, was necessary to retain public support; an inquirer whose questions were not answered quickly might be alienated and more likely to evade the freeze. In addition, to be open to inquiries would help officials identify problem areas that could be made the basis of broader public education campaigns.

. . .

DECISION IN ROUTINE CASES: EX PARTE PRESENTATIONS AND THE REGIME OF RULES

. . . In the freeze agencies, *complaints of violations* triggered an investigation by an IRS agent. Usually he simply telephoned the alleged violator and questioned him; if he felt it necessary, he visited the respondent's place of business and examined his records.[1] A series

1. The executive order required every business to "maintain available for public inspection a record of the highest prices or rents charged . . . during the thirty-day period ending August 14, 1971."

of formal procedures, however, stood between the investigation and the imposition of legal penalties. The alleged violator was first asked to give his version of the facts. If the IRS agent found a violation, the case was referred to OEP for review, and then to the Department of Justice for prosecution in a United States District Court. This route to prosecution and formal adjudication was rarely utilized, however. In 62 percent of the thousands of investigations, the IRS determined that there had been no violation. In most of the remainder, there was no dispute: the seller or landlord freely admitted violation and agreed to roll back his price or rent immediately. Only 214 cases developed into serious enough disputes to be forwarded to OEP for review. Ultimately only eight lawsuits were filed against recalcitrant violators. . . .

The agencies' approach to fact-finding for *inquiries* . . . sought to avoid all formal procedures and their usual corollaries—expense and delay. Persons or firms seeking a ruling from the OEP, for example, needed only to send a letter describing their situation and asking what the freeze order required. . . . This meant, of course, that there was no opportunity for adversarial confrontation between a landlord seeking permission for a rent increase and his tenants or between sellers and their customers. There was no opportunity for the agency officials to cross-examine the inquirer face-to-face. Almost all inquiries were decided on the basis of unverified ex parte presentations.[2] In agencies that stress enforcement, investigation, or adversarial confrontation, the greater part of official energy is devoted to resolution of factual issues. In the freeze agencies' inquiry-response system, as in appellate courts, the focus was almost exclusively on questions of policy or law, because the facts in each case were taken as given.

With respect to questions of policy, too, the agencies sought to avoid procedures that increased the risk of delay. Their goal was to have officials in the field offices issue rulings immediately. Concern for voluntary compliance, however, suggested that inquiry-responses should be not only prompt but consistent. Ad hoc policy decisions by the numerous, hastily recruited officials in the field, resulting in different decisions for similar cases, would invite mistrust of the fairness of the program, it was feared, and loss of public support. . . .

In response, CLC and [its Executive Committee] met each day to formulate detailed written rules, articulating freeze policy with respect to a growing list of specific situations. Copies of the freeze order and CLC rules were disseminated to lower-level officials, who inserted them in loose-leaf manuals called Stabilization Program Guidelines and referred to them for answers to the inquiries they received. The inquiry-response system thus became a regime of rules in which policy questions were routinely transformed into questions of "correct" rule appli-

---

2. . . . It is important to recognize that decision on the basis of facts as asserted is not at all an unusual procedure. Such "advisory opinions" are regularly given by the IRS, see Annual Report of the Commissioner; and by the Securities and Exchange Commission, and other agencies. See Lewis Lowenfels, "SEC No-Action Letters," 59 Virginia Law Review 303 (1973).

cation. Formally, there was little scope for discretion or policy judgment on the part of the inquiry-response officials.

. . .

THE SCHOOL BUS CONTRACTORS' CASE

On September 8, 1971, Mr. Reynolds, an officer of the School Bus Contractors Association of America, was ushered into GC [the general counsel's office] by Doug Johnston, the head of OEP's Correspondence Section. Johnston urged that Reynolds be given a quick answer to his inquiry, which appeared to raise a question of rule interpretation. I was asked to deal with the matter. Reynolds explained that in the spring and early summer of 1971, well before the August 15 freeze, many private school bus companies had contracted with school boards to provide service for the 1971–72 school year at rates higher than those charged during the 1970–71 year. I told Reynolds that they would appear to be frozen at last year's rates: the basic CLC rule was that the price of pre-freeze "transactions" established the ceiling price for any commodity or service. Another important rule (in Circular 7) stated that in contracts for services, "the transaction takes place when the service is performed," as opposed to the time of payment or the time of the making of the contract.

Mr. Reynolds acknowledged that, but pointed out that many bus contractors, before the freeze, had undertaken various actions to prepare for the new school year, such as scheduling routes and determining loading zones, making test drives, hiring and training drivers, and buying and repairing equipment. Those actions, he argued, were the necessary first step in performance of the new contract, and they had been completed before the freeze. Since these contractual services had been performed before the freeze, couldn't the contracted-for rate increases be charged? Besides, Reynolds said, the bus companies had relied upon getting those rate increases when they had given raises to drivers and purchased new buses. If they couldn't get those rates, many could not break even and could not provide the bus service. Reynolds also urged OEP to provide them an immediate answer, because the new school term was already beginning in thousands of districts across the country. I told him we'd have an answer for him by the next day.

Jim McAleer, an OEP lawyer who shared an office with me, overheard my conversation with Mr. Reynolds. After Reynolds left, McAleer suggested that the higher rate was not allowable. The preparatory services, he argued, were not "performance" within the meaning of the Circular 7 rule; only actual busing of students was the service contracted for, and only that would qualify under the rule. Jerry Tankel, another attorney, listened to McAleer's discussion with me and entered his disagreement; he thought the preliminary actions *did* constitute performance of a service. If a school district canceled the contract at this point, he argued, the bus company would be entitled to some compensation under ordinary contract law for what it had done. Tankel also pointed out that under one CLC rule, a teacher was entitled to receive a planned September raise if, before the freeze, he or she had come into school and begun work under the new contract, even if it was only preparatory administrative work.

Left alone for a moment, I reread Circular 7 and other CLC rules. I decided that they were certainly not clear about what "performance" meant, or whether the preparatory actions were "performance" as used in Circular 7. I also thought it was not an issue worth sending to CLC for further definition; I felt that CLC would not approve a price increase but would define performance more narrowly to mean actual transportation of school children. They would reject a broad definition of performance, I thought, because it would open the door to price increases under a lot of contracts in other areas and because it was not clear that the resulting disruption and hardship would be as unavoidable or as great as Reynolds claimed.

I consulted with Elmer Bennett (OEP's general counsel) and John Simpson, his assistant. They agreed. I drafted a letter to Reynolds for Bennett's signature, declaring that no increased contractual rate could be charged unless actual transportation of school children had been performed before August 15 at the higher rate. The letter cited Circular 7 and stated, "Preliminary and preparatory work under the contract . . . does not . . . constitute delivery or furnishing of service within the meaning of the above provisions."

THE NORMS OF RULE INTERPRETATION

Implicit in this account are several basic norms of decision making. Most fundamental are those that might easily be taken for granted or noticed only when breached—the familiar bureaucratic norms of *impersonality* (no attorney talked about Mr. Reynolds as an individual, his politics or character or motives) and *fidelity to legally constituted authority* (the discussion was about what response would be justified by CLC's rules, not about the OEP lawyers' own views of desirable school bus rates).

. . .

Conceptual analysis

. . . Matching the facts of individual cases with legal concepts or categories is always a crucial decision in rule-based systems. Lawyers, for example, often argue about whether a transaction is a "rental" or a "bailment," an "operating expense" or a "capital improvement." They do so because those concepts are embedded in prescriptive rules; specific legal outcomes flow automatically from the act of classification. Similarly, OEP officials applying CLC rules would argue whether a municipal license fee was "really" a price (and hence frozen) or a tax (and hence exempt).

In OEP, if the facts of a situation seemed to fit clearly within an existing rule, the matter would usually end there, regardless of the decision maker's personal sympathies. For example, had the bus companies *not* undertaken any preparatory action—that is, had they done nothing that was arguably "performance"—the case would have been an easy one for OEP officials, even though the result might have been financial hardship for some bus companies.

. . . [M]aintaining *consistency of treatment* was a highly salient canon of rule interpretation in OEP, but the problem, of course, was to decide what features rendered the two situations truly analogous. . . .

Analysis of consequences

A second (or simultaneous) approach to determining CLC's preference in the hard case was to inquire into the purposes that presumably lay behind the ambiguous rule and adopt the interpretation that best furthered that purpose. CLC did not make this task an easy one: it wrote no opinions explaining its rules and left no recorded legislative history. Nevertheless, by reexamining CLC's transaction rules concerning executory contracts, I concluded that overall they seemed to reflect a stringent, anti-inflationary purpose. These rules almost invariably prevented price increases during the freeze even if contracted for earlier, even if it meant contravening the ordinary law of contract and the parties' reasonable expectations. . . .

The presumption in favor of stringency was not articulated in official OEP documents. As a newcomer to the agency, I only gradually sensed its existence, inferring it from the general tenor of case discussion in various offices. New recruits sometimes asked impatiently, "What's the philosophy here, to be lenient or strict?" Older hands said, "It's not that simple. It's a matter of judgment." There was such a thing as *good* judgment, however. It meant that in doubtful cases, one should "lean" toward stringency unless the case for the accommodative ruling was clear—that is, unless a specific, accommodative CLC rule was unambiguously analogous or it appeared that a stringent interpretation almost certainly would create unavoidable disruption or hardship. . . .

In the School Bus Contractors' Case, . . . I thought that an accommodative decision would, in principle, open up a rather wide door to price increases in many other situations involving preliminary actions under executory contracts and might well stimulate protests from school districts and teachers' associations. Nor did Reynolds' arguments offset these considerations, at least in my eyes. His claims of hardship to the bus companies were neither documented nor otherwise substantiated. I was not sufficiently persuaded that freezing the bus companies for three months would seriously and inevitably disrupt the school systems of the nation. . . .

Consultation

The capstone of the process of rule interpretation in the School Bus Contractors' Case was a search for consensus. If an individual OEP official had doubts about the correct decision on a case, he or she was expected to consult with colleagues in the same office. . . . In this case, the "clincher" was General Counsel Elmer Bennett's agreement that a stringent interpretation was best and that CLC would probably decide it the same way.

Consultation also transformed the individual decision into a precedent, part of the collective memory of the office, indicative of the proper decision in similar cases that might arise in the future. The awareness—or assumption—that the decision would set a precedent affected the style of the consultation and thereby of the whole decision-making process. Consultation was oriented toward finding *general* reasons for the decision, so that it would be one the decision makers could "live with" in the future. . . .

Chapter II

LEGISLATIVE AND EXECUTIVE CONTROL OF ADMINISTRATIVE ACTION

The Constitution of the United States:

Article 1, Section 1:

All legislative Powers herein granted shall be vested in a Congress of the United States, which shall consist of a Senate and House of Representatives . . .

Article 1, Section 8:

The Congress shall have Power . . .

To make all Laws which shall be necessary and proper for carrying into Execution the foregoing Powers, and all other Powers vested by this Constitution in the Government of the United States, or in any Department or Officer thereof.

Article 2, Section 1:

The executive Power shall be vested in a President of the United States of America . . .

Article 3, Section 1:

The judicial Power of the United States, shall be vested in one supreme Court, and in such inferior Courts as the Congress may from time to time ordain and establish . . .

These familiar words accomplish two ends, one evident on the surface and the other somewhat more subtle. Civics-class simple is that they establish a "separation of powers"—legislative authority here, executive authority there, judicial power in a third place. But they also leave the shaping of government in Congress' hands. If you were to search the whole of the Constitution, you would find little about the place or function of the inferior parts of government—only Congress' sweeping authority to legislate what is necessary and proper to carry out the governmental scheme, in Article I, and a few scattered references to "departments" that are nowhere empowered or defined. Even the oldest of cabinet departments is not a constitutional given; it is for Congress to decide whether to have a Department of Justice or a Department of State, an Environmental Protection Agency or a Securities and Exchange Commission. More: we know from the preceding Chapter that, in the colloquial sense, any given agency may on the same day legislate by adopting a rule, adjudicate by resolving a dispute in an on-the-record proceeding, and execute the laws by gathering information or initiating enforcement measures. "The existence of a sprawling administrative bureaucracy with broad powers to make law . . . is constitutional fact. It must become one of the fundamental premises from which our reasoning about constitutional structure and relationships begins. . . . The changes in structure and working

47

relationships which are hinted at by the term 'the administrative state' are at least as fundamental as any of the changes in governmental institutions that have been embodied in constitutional amendments during the twentieth century." D. Elliott, INS v. Chadha: The Administrative Constitution, the Constitution, and the Legislative Veto, 1983 Sup.Ct.Rev. 125, 174. How is this "constitutional fact," this product of Congress' power to shape, to be squared with that most evident of judgments in the constitutional structure: that Congress is to legislate, the courts to adjudicate, and the President to execute, respectively; and, that these three authorities and their powers are to be kept reasonably distinct? [1]

What is the purpose of separation of powers? Here, in language few civics teachers could match, is Madison's explanation of the matter:

. . . The great security against a gradual concentration of the several powers in the same department, consists in giving to those who administer each department the necessary constitutional means and personal motives to resist encroachments of the others. The provision for defense must in this, as in all other cases, be made commensurate to the danger of attack. Ambition must be made to counteract ambition. The interest of the man must be connected with the constitutional rights of the place. It may be a reflection on human nature, that such devices should be necessary to control the abuses of government. But what is government itself, but the greatest of all reflections on human nature? If men were angels, no government would be necessary. If angels were to govern men, neither external nor internal controls on government would be necessary. In framing a government which is to be administered by men over men, the great difficulty lies in this: you must first enable the government to control the governed; and in the next place oblige it to control itself. A dependence on the people, is, no doubt, the primary control on the government; but experience has taught mankind the necessity of auxiliary precautions. [2]

Language like this, it is fair to say, is most often invoked when the behavior of Congress or the President itself is at issue—cases a law student is most likely to encounter in a course in Constitutional Law. Perhaps the most dramatic expressions in this century occurred in the "Steel Seizure" cases, which declared that President Truman could not take control of steel mills to avert a strike he feared would imperil the

1. "If we look into the constitution of the several States we find that, notwithstanding the emphatical and, in some instances, the unqualified terms in which the axiom has been laid down, there is not a single instance in which the several departments of power have been kept absolutely separate and distinct. New Hampshire, whose constitution was the last formed, seems to have been fully aware of the impossibility and inexpediency of avoiding any mixture whatever of these departments, and has qualified the doctrine by declaring 'that the legislative, executive, and judiciary powers ought to be kept as separate from, and independent of, each other as the nature of a free government will admit: or as is consistent with that chain of connection that binds the whole fabric of the constitution in one indissoluble bond of unity and amity.'" The Federalist, # 47 (Madison).

2. The Federalist, # 51.

national defense; Congress had not authorized the action, nor did it lie within the President's constitutional authority as chief executive or as commander in chief.[3]   "[T]he President's power to see that the laws are faithfully executed refutes the idea that he is to be a lawmaker," Justice Black wrote for the majority; Justice Douglas, quoting an earlier Brandeis dissent,[4] added, "The doctrine of the separation of powers was adopted by the Convention of 1787, not to promote efficiency but to preclude the exercise of arbitrary power.   The purpose was not to avoid friction, but, by means of the inevitable friction incident to the distribution of the governmental powers among three departments, to save the people from autocracy." [5]

When they have encountered the subordinate organs of law-administration, creatures of statute, the Justices have often sounded less sure, more puzzled.   Justice Robert Jackson remarked in an often-quoted passage that:

> [Administrative bodies such as the FTC] have become a veritable fourth branch of Government, which has deranged our three-branch legal theories.   .   .   .   Administrative agencies have been called quasi-legislative, quasi-executive or quasi-judicial, as the occasion required in order to validate their functions within the separation-of-powers scheme of the Constitution.   The mere retreat to the qualifying "quasi" is implicit with confession that all recognized classifications have broken down, and "quasi" is a smooth cover which we draw over our confusion as we might use a counterpane to cover a disordered bed.

FTC v. Ruberoid Co., 343 U.S. 470, 487 (1952) (dissent).   It is sometimes assumed this remark is addressed to the so-called independent regulatory commissions.   But is it any less apt for the Department of Agriculture?   That body, too, adjudicates cases on the record before its administrative law judges and judicial officer, and adopts legislative rules having the force and effect of statutes under delegation from Congress.[6]   Perhaps, as one of your editors has written,

> the important fact is that an agency is neither Congress nor President nor Court, but an inferior part of government.   Each agency is subject to control relationships with some or all of the three constitutionally named branches, and those relationships give an assurance—functionally similar to that provided

3. Youngstown Sheet and Tube Co. v. Sawyer, 343 U.S. 579, 593 (1952).

4. Myers v. United States, 272 U.S. 52, 293 (1926).

5. The theory has had important critics—for example, Woodrow Wilson, who wrote:

"The trouble with the theory is that government is not a machine, but a living thing.   .   .   .   No living thing can have its organs offset against each other as checks, and live.   On the contrary, its life is dependent upon their quick cooperation, their ready response to the commands of instinct or intelligence, their amicable community of purpose.   Government is not a body of blind forces; it is a body of men, with highly differentiated function, no doubt, in our modern day of specialization, but with a common task and purpose.   Their cooperation is indispensible, their warfare fatal.   There can be no successful government without leadership or without the intimate, almost instinctive, coordination of the organs of life and action.   This is not theory, but fact, and displays its force as fact, whatever theories may be thrown across its track," Wilson, Constitutional Government in the United States 56–57 (1908).

6. See, e.g., United States v. Grimaud, p. 69 within.

by the separation-of-powers notion for the constitutionally named bodies—that they will not pass out of control. Powerful and potentially arbitrary as they may be, the Secretary of Agriculture and the Chairman of the SEC for this reason do not present the threat that led the framers to insist on a splitting of the authority of government at its very top. What we have, then, are three named repositories of authorizing power and control, and an infinity of institutions to which parts of the authority of each may be lent. The three must share the reins of control; means must be found of assuring that no one of them becomes dominant. But it is not terribly important to number or allocate the horses that pull the carriage of government.[7]

SECTION 1: THE PROBLEM OF DELEGATION

a. Federal Law

INDUSTRIAL UNION DEPARTMENT, AFL–CIO v. AMERICAN PETROLEUM INSTITUTE

Supreme Court of the United States, 1980.
448 U.S. 607.

MR. JUSTICE STEVENS announced the judgment of the Court and delivered an opinion in which THE CHIEF JUSTICE and MR. JUSTICE STEWART joined and in Parts I, II, III–A, III–B, III–C, and III–E of which MR. JUSTICE POWELL joined.

The Occupational Safety and Health Act of 1970 (Act), 29 U.S.C. § 651 et seq., was enacted for the purpose of ensuring safe and healthful working conditions for every working man and woman in the Nation. This litigation concerns a standard promulgated by the Secretary of Labor to regulate occupational exposure to benzene, a substance which has been shown to cause cancer at high exposure levels. . . .

The Act delegates broad authority to the Secretary to promulgate different kinds of standards. The basic definition of an "occupational safety and health standard" is found in § 3(8), which provides:

The term "occupational safety and health standard" means a standard which requires conditions, or the adoption or use of one or more practices, means, methods, operations, or processes, reasonably necessary or appropriate to provide safe or healthful employment and places of employment.

Where toxic materials or harmful physical agents are concerned, a standard must also comply with § 6(b)(5), which provides:

The Secretary, in promulgating standards dealing with toxic materials or harmful physical agents under this subsection, shall set the standard which most adequately assures, to the extent feasible, on the basis of the best available evidence, that no employee will suffer material impairment of health or functional capacity even if such employee has regular exposure

---

7. P. Strauss, The Place of Agencies in Government: Separation of Powers and the Fourth Branch, 84 Colum.L.Rev. 573, 579–80 (1984).

to the hazard dealt with by such standard for the period of his working life. Development of standards under this subsection shall be based upon research, demonstrations, experiments, and such other information as may be appropriate. In addition to the attainment of the highest degree of health and safety protection for the employee, other considerations shall be the latest available scientific data in the field, the feasibility of the standards, and experience gained under this and other health and safety laws.

. . .

I

Benzene is a familiar and important commodity. It is a colorless, aromatic liquid that evaporates rapidly under ordinary atmospheric conditions. Approximately 11 billion pounds of benzene were produced in the United States in 1976. Ninety-four percent of that total was produced by the petroleum and petrochemical industries, with the remainder produced by the steel industry as a byproduct of coking operations. Benzene is used in manufacturing a variety of products including motor fuels (which may contain as much as 2% benzene), solvents, detergents, pesticides, and other organic chemicals.

The entire population of the United States is exposed to small quantities of benzene, ranging from a few parts per billion to 0.5 ppm, in the ambient air. Over one million workers are subject to additional low-level exposures as a consequence of their employment. The majority of these employees work in gasoline service stations, benzene production (petroleum refineries and coking operations), chemical processing, benzene transportation, rubber manfuacturing, and laboratory operations.

. . .

Industrial health experts have long been aware that exposure to benzene may lead to various types of nonmalignant diseases. . . . In 1969 the American National Standards Institute (ANSI) adopted a national consensus standard of 10 ppm averaged over an 8-hour period with a ceiling concentration of 25 ppm for 10-minute periods or a maximum peak concentration of 50 ppm. In 1971, after the Occupational Safety and Health Act was passed, the Secretary adopted this consensus standard as the federal standard.

As early as 1928, some health experts theorized that there might also be a connection between benzene in the workplace and leukemia. . . . In a 1974 report recommending a permanent standard for benzene, the National Institute for Occupational Safety and Health (NIOSH), OSHA's research arm, noted that these studies raised the "distinct possibility" that benzene caused leukemia. . . . Between 1974 and 1976 additional studies were published. . . . In an August 1976 revision of its earlier recommendation, NIOSH stated that these studies provided "conclusive" proof of a causal connection between benzene and leukemia. . . .

In October 1976, NIOSH sent another memorandum to OSHA, seeking acceleration of the rulemaking process and "strongly" recommending the issuance of an emergency temporary standard pursuant to § 6(c) of the Act. . . . NIOSH recommended that a 1 ppm exposure limit be imposed for benzene. . . . OSHA did issue an emergency standard, effective May 21, 1977, reducing the benzene exposure limit from 10 ppm to 1 ppm, the ceiling for exposures of up to 10 minutes from 25 ppm to 5 ppm, and eliminating the authority for peak concentrations of 50 ppm. . . .

On May 19, 1977, the Court of Appeals for the Fifth Circuit entered a temporary restraining order preventing the emergency standard from taking effect. Thereafter, OSHA abandoned its efforts to make the emergency standard effective and instead issued a proposal for a permanent standard patterned almost entirely after the aborted emergency standard.

In its published statement giving notice of the proposed permanent standard, OSHA did not ask for comments as to whether or not benzene presented a significant health risk at exposures of 10 ppm or less. Rather, it asked for comments as to whether 1 ppm was the minimum feasible exposure limit. As OSHA's Deputy Director of Health Standards, Grover Wrenn, testified at the hearing, this formulation of the issue to be considered by the Agency was consistent with OSHA's general policy with respect to carcinogens. Whenever a carcinogen is involved, OSHA will presume that no safe level of exposure exists in the absence of clear proof establishing such a level and will accordingly set the exposure limit at the lowest level feasible. The proposed 1 ppm exposure limit in this case thus was established not on the basis of a proven hazard at 10 ppm, but rather on the basis of "OSHA's best judgment at the time of the proposal of the feasibility of compliance with the proposed standard by the [a]ffected industries." . . .

Public hearings were held on the proposed standard, commencing on July 19, 1977. The final standard was issued on February 10, 1978. In its final form, the benzene standard is designed to protect workers from whatever hazards are associated with low-level benzene exposures by requiring employers to monitor workplaces to determine the level of exposure, to provide medical examinations when the level rises above 0.5 ppm, and to institute whatever engineering or other controls are necessary to keep exposures at or below 1 ppm. . . . Consistent with OSHA's general policy, the regulation does not allow respirators to be used if engineering modifications are technologically feasible.[1]

. . .

The permanent standard is expressly inapplicable to the storage, transportation, distribution, sale, or use of gasoline or other fuels subsequent to discharge from bulk terminals. This exception is particularly significant in light of the fact that over 795,000 gas station

---

1. . . . OSHA's preference for engineering modifications is based on its opinion that respirators are rarely used properly (because they are uncomfortable, are often not properly fitted, etc.) and therefore cannot be considered adequate protective measures.

employees, who are exposed to an average of 102,700 gallons of gasoline (containing up to 2% benzene) annually, are thus excluded from the protection of the standard.

As presently formulated, the benzene standard is an expensive way of providing some additional protection for a relatively small number of employees. According to OSHA's figures, the standard will require capital investments in engineering controls of approximately $266 million, first-year operating costs (for monitoring, medical testing, employee training, and respirators) of $187 million to $205 million and recurring annual costs of approximately $34 million. The figures outlined in OSHA's explanation of the costs of compliance to various industries indicate that only 35,000 employees would gain any benefit from the regulation in terms of a reduction in their exposure to benzene. Over two-thirds of these workers (24,450) are employed in the rubber-manufacturing industry. Compliance costs in that industry are estimated to be rather low with no capital costs and initial operating expenses estimated at only $34 million ($1,390 per employee); recurring annual costs would also be rather low, totaling less than $1 million. By contrast, the segment of the petroleum refining industry that produces benzene would be required to incur $24 million in capital costs and $600,000 in first-year operating expenses to provide additional protection for 300 workers ($82,000 per employee), while the petrochemical industry would be required to incur $20.9 million in capital costs and $1 million in initial operating expenses for the benefit of 552 employees ($39,675 per employee).

Although OSHA did not quantify the benefits to each category of worker in terms of decreased exposure to benzene, it appears from the economic impact study done at OSHA's direction that those benefits may be relatively small. Thus, although the current exposure limit is 10 ppm, the actual exposures outlined in that study are often considerably lower. For example, for the period 1970–1975 the petrochemical industry reported that, out of a total of 496 employees exposed to benzene, only 53 were exposed to levels between 1 and 5 ppm and only 7 (all at the same plant) were exposed to between 5 and 10 ppm.

II

The critical issue at this point in the litigation is whether the Court of Appeals was correct in refusing to enforce the 1 ppm exposure limit on the ground that it was not supported by appropriate findings.

. . .

The evidence in the administrative record of adverse effects of benzene exposure at 10 ppm is sketchy at best. . . . In the end OSHA's rationale for lowering the permissible exposure limit to 1 ppm was based, not on any finding that leukemia has ever been caused by exposure to 10 ppm of benzene and that it will *not* be caused by exposure to 1 ppm, but rather on a series of assumptions indicating that some leukemias might result from exposure to 10 ppm and that the number of cases might be reduced by reducing the exposure level to 1 ppm. In reaching that result, the Agency first unequivocally concluded that benzene is a human carcinogen. Second, it concluded that industry had failed to prove that there is a safe threshold level of exposure to benzene below which no excess leukemia cases would occur. . . . Third, the Agency applied its standard policy with respect to carcinogens, concluding that, in the absence of definitive proof of a safe level, it must be assumed that *any* level above zero presents *some* increased risk of cancer. . . .

Fourth, the Agency reiterated its view of the Act, stating that it was required by § 6(b)(5) to set the standard either at the level that has been demonstrated to be safe or at the lowest level feasible, whichever is higher. If no safe level is established, as in this case, the Secretary's interpretation of the statute automatically leads to the selection of an exposure limit that is the lowest feasible. Because of benzene's importance to the economy, no one has ever suggested that it would be feasible to eliminate its use entirely, or to try to limit exposures to the small amounts that are omnipresent. Rather, the Agency selected 1 ppm as a workable exposure level, and then determined that compliance with that level was technologically feasible and that "the economic impact of . . . [compliance] will not be such as to threaten the financial welfare of the affected firms or the general economy." It therefore held that 1 ppm was the minimum feasible exposure level within the meaning of § 6(b)(5) of the Act.

Finally, although the Agency did not refer in its discussion of the pertinent legal authority to any duty to identify the anticipated benefits of the new standard, it did conclude that some benefits were likely to result from reducing the exposure limit from 10 ppm to 1 ppm. . . . In light of the Agency's disavowal of any ability to determine the numbers of employees likely to be adversely affected by exposures of 10 ppm, the Court of Appeals held this finding to be unsupported by the record. 581 F.2d, at 503.

It is noteworthy that at no point in its lengthy explanation did the Agency quote or even cite § 3(8) of the Act. It made no finding that any of the provisions of the new standard were "reasonably necessary or appropriate to provide safe or healthful employment and places of employment." Nor did it allude to the possibility that any such finding might have been appropriate.

III

Our resolution of the issues in these cases turns, to a large extent, on the meaning of and the relationship between § 3(8), which defines a health and safety standard that is "reasonably necessary and appropriate to provide safe or healthful employment," and § 6(b)(5), which directs the Secretary in promulgating a health and safety standard for toxic materials to "set the standard which most adequately assures, to the extent feasible, on the basis of the best available evidence, that no employee will suffer material impairment of health or functional capacity. . . . "

In the Government's view, § 3(8)'s definition of the term "standard" has no legal significance or at best merely requires that a standard not be totally irrational. It takes the position that § 6(b)(5) is controlling and that it requires OSHA to promulgate a standard that either gives an absolute assurance of safety for each and every worker or reduces exposures to the lowest level feasible. The Government interprets "feasible" as meaning technologically achievable at a cost that would not impair the viability of the industries subject to the regulation. The respondent industry representatives, on the other hand, argue that the Court of Appeals was correct in holding that the "reasonably necessary and appropriate" language of § 3(8), along with the feasibility requirement of § 6(b)(5), requires the Agency to quantify both the costs and the benefits of a proposed rule and to conclude that they are roughly commensurate.

In our view, it is not necessary to decide whether either the Government or industry is entirely correct. For we think it is clear that § 3(8) does apply to all permanent standards promulgated under the Act and that it requires the Secretary, before issuing any standard, to determine that it is reasonably necessary and appropriate to remedy a significant risk of material health impairment. Only after the Secretary has made the threshold determination that such a risk exists with respect to a toxic substance, would it be necessary to decide whether § 6(b)(5) requires him to select the most protective standard he can consistent with economic and technological feasibility, or whether, as respondents argue, the benefits of the regulation must be commensurate with the costs of its implementation. Because the Secretary did not make the required threshold finding in these cases, we have no occasion to determine whether costs must be weighed against benefits in an appropriate case.

A

. . . [W]e think it is clear that the statute was not designed to require employers to provide absolutely risk-free workplaces whenever it is technologically feasible to do so, so long as the cost is not great enough to destroy an entire industry. Rather, both the language and structure of the Act, as well as its legislative history, indicate that it was intended to require the elimination, as far as feasible, of significant risks of harm.

B

By empowering the Secretary to promulgate standards that are "reasonably necessary or appropriate to provide safe or healthful employment and places of employment," the Act implies that, before promulgating any standard, the Secretary must make a finding that the workplaces in question are not safe. But "safe" is not the equivalent of "risk-free." There are many activities that we engage in every day—such as driving a car or even breathing city air—that entail some risk of accident or material health impairment; nevertheless, few people would consider these activities "unsafe." Similarly, a workplace can hardly be considered "unsafe" unless it threatens the workers with a significant risk of harm.

Therefore, before he can promulgate *any* permanent health or safety standard, the Secretary is required to make a threshold finding that a place of employment is unsafe—in the sense that significant risks are present and can be eliminated or lessened by a change in practices. This requirement applies to permanent standards promulgated pursuant to § 6(b)(5), as well as to other types of permanent standards. For there is no reason why § 3(8)'s definition of a standard should not be deemed incorporated by reference into § 6(b)(5). . . . This interpretation of §§ 3(8) and 6(b)(5) is supported by the other provisions of the Act. . . .

In the absence of a clear mandate in the Act, it is unreasonable to assume that Congress intended to give the Secretary the unprecedented power over American industry that would result from the Government's view of §§ 3(8) and 6(b)(5), coupled with OSHA's cancer policy. Expert testimony that a substance is probably a human carcinogen—either because it has caused cancer in animals or because individuals have contracted cancer following extremely high exposures—would justify the conclusion that the substance poses some risk of serious harm no matter how minute the exposure and no matter how many experts testified that they regarded the risk as insignificant. That conclusion would in turn justify pervasive regulation limited only by the constraint of feasibility. In light of the fact that there are literally thousands of substances used in the workplace that have been identified as carcinogens or suspect carcinogens, the Government's theory would give OSHA power to impose enormous costs that might produce little, if any, discernible benefit.

If the Government were correct in arguing that neither § 3(8) nor § 6(b)(5) requires that the risk from a toxic substance be quantified sufficiently to enable the Secretary to characterize it as significant in an understandable way, the statute would make such a "sweeping delegation of legislative power" that it might be unconstitutional under the Court's reasoning in A.L.A. Schechter Poultry Corp. v. United States, 295 U.S. 495, 539, and Panama Refining Co. v. Ryan, 293 U.S. 388. A construction of the statute that avoids this kind of open-ended grant should certainly be favored.

C

The legislative history also supports the conclusion that Congress was concerned, not with absolute safety, but with the elimination of significant harm. The examples of industrial hazards referred to in the Committee hearings and debates all involved situations in which the risk was unquestionably significant. For example, the Senate Committee on Labor and Public Welfare noted that byssinosis, a disabling lung disease caused by breathing cotton dust, affected as many as 30% of the workers in carding or spinning rooms in some American cotton mills and that as many as 100,000 active or retired workers were then suffering from the disease. . . . Moreover, Congress specifically amended § 6(b)(5) to make it perfectly clear that it does not require the

Secretary to promulgate standards that would assure an absolutely risk-free workplace. . . .

OSHA's concessions to practicality in beginning with a 1 ppm exposure limit and using an action level concept implicitly adopt an interpretation of the statute as not requiring regulation of insignificant risks. It is entirely consistent with this interpretation to hold that the Act also requires the Agency to limit its endeavors in the standard-setting area to eliminating significant risks of harm.

Finally, with respect to the legislative history, it is important to note that Congress repeatedly expressed its concern about allowing the Secretary to have too much power over American industry. . . . This effort by Congress to limit the Secretary's power is not consistent with a view that the mere possibility that some employee somewhere in the country may confront some risk of cancer is a sufficient basis for the exercise of the Secretary's power to require the expenditure of hundreds of millions of dollars to minimize that risk.

D

Given the conclusion that the Act empowers the Secretary to promulgate health and safety standards only where a significant risk of harm exists, the critical issue becomes how to define and allocate the burden of proving the significance of the risk in a case such as this, where scientific knowledge is imperfect and the precise quantification of risks is therefore impossible. The Agency's position is that there is substantial evidence in the record to support its conclusion that there is no absolutely safe level for a carcinogen and that, therefore, the burden is properly on industry to prove, apparently beyond a shadow of a doubt, that there *is* a safe level for benzene exposure. The Agency argues that, because of the uncertainties in this area, any other approach would render it helpless, forcing it to wait for the leukemia deaths that it believes are likely to occur before taking any regulatory action.

We disagree. As we read the statute, the burden was on the Agency to show, on the basis of substantial evidence, that it is at least more likely than not that long-term exposure to 10 ppm of benzene presents a significant risk of material health impairment. . . .

E

. . .

In this case the record makes it perfectly clear that the Secretary relied squarely on a special policy for carcinogens that imposed the burden on industry of proving the existence of a safe level of exposure, thereby avoiding the Secretary's threshold responsibility of establishing the need for more stringent standards. In so interpreting his statutory authority, the Secretary exceeded his power.

. . .

The judgment of the Court of Appeals remanding the petition for review to the Secretary for further proceedings is affirmed.

MR. CHIEF JUSTICE BURGER, concurring.

[Chief Justice Burger's brief concurrence, while stressing the dominant roles of legislature and agency in policy formulation and application, ended with the following remarks:] When the administrative record reveals only scant or minimal risk of material health impairment, responsible administration calls for avoidance of extravagant, comprehensive regulation. Perfect safety is a chimera; regulation must not strangle human activity in the search for the impossible.

MR. JUSTICE POWELL, concurring in part and concurring in the judgment.

For the reasons stated by the plurality, I agree that §§ 6(b)(5) and 3(8) of the Occupational Safety and Health Act of 1970, 29 U.S.C. §§ 655(b)(5) and 652(8), must be read together.[2] They require OSHA to make a threshold finding that proposed occupational health standards are reasonably necessary to provide safe workplaces. . . .

Although I regard the question as close, I do not disagree with the plurality's view that OSHA has failed, on this record, to carry its burden of proof on the threshold issues summarized above. But even if one assumes that OSHA properly met this burden, I conclude that the statute also requires the agency to determine that the economic effects of its standard bear a reasonable relationship to the expected benefits. An occupational health standard is neither "reasonably necessary" nor "feasible," as required by statute, if it calls for expenditures wholly disproportionate to the expected health and safety benefits. . . . I therefore would not lightly assume that Congress intended OSHA to require reduction of health risks found to be significant *whenever* it also finds that the affected industry can bear the costs. Perhaps more significantly, however, OSHA's interpretation of § 6(b)(5) would force it to regulate in a manner inconsistent with the important health and safety purposes of the legislation we construe today. Thousands of toxic substances present risks that fairly could be characterized as "significant." Even if OSHA succeeded in selecting the gravest risks for earliest regulation, a standard-setting process that ignored economic considerations would result in a serious misallocation of resources and a lower effective level of safety than could be achieved under standards set with reference to the comparative benefits available at a lower cost.[3] I would not attribute such an irrational intention to Congress. . . .

MR. JUSTICE REHNQUIST, concurring in the judgment.

. . . According to the Secretary, who is one of the petitioners herein, § 6(b)(5) imposes upon him an absolute duty, in regulating

---

2. [The] portions of the plurality opinion [I join] primarily address OSHA's special carcinogen policy, rather than OSHA's argument that it also made evidentiary findings. I do not necessarily agree with every observation in the plurality opinion concerning the presence or absence of such findings. I also express no view on the question whether a different interpretation of the statute would violate the nondelegation doctrine of A.L.A. Schechter Poultry Corp. v. United States, 295 U.S. 495 (1935), and Panama Refining Co. v. Ryan, 293 U.S. 388 (1935).

3. For example, OSHA's reading of § 6(b)(5) could force the depletion of an industry's resources in an effort to reduce a single risk by some speculative amount, even though other significant risks remain unregulated.

harmful substances like benzene for which no safe level is known, to set the standard for permissible exposure at the lowest level that "can be achieved at bearable cost with available technology." . . . According to respondents, § 6(b)(5), as tempered by § 3(8), requires the Secretary to demonstrate that any particular health standard is justifiable on the basis of a rough balancing of costs and benefits.

In considering these alternative interpretations, my colleagues manifest a good deal of uncertainty, and ultimately divide over whether the Secretary produced sufficient evidence that the proposed standard for benzene will result in any appreciable benefits at all. This uncertainty, I would suggest, is eminently justified, since I believe that this litigation presents the Court with what has to be one of the most difficult issues that could confront a decisionmaker: whether the statistical possibility of future deaths should ever be disregarded in light of the economic costs of preventing those deaths. I would also suggest that the widely varying positions advanced in the briefs of the parties and in the opinions of Mr. Justice Stevens, the Chief Justice, Mr. Justice Powell, and Mr. Justice Marshall demonstrate, perhaps better than any other fact, that Congress, the governmental body best suited and most obligated to make the choice confronting us in this litigation, has improperly delegated that choice to the Secretary of Labor and, derivatively, to this Court.

I

In his Second Treatise of Civil Government, published in 1690, John Locke wrote that "[t]he power of the legislative, being derived from the people by a positive voluntary grant and institution, can be no other than what that positive grant conveyed, which being only to make laws, and not to make legislators, the legislative can have no power to transfer their authority of making laws and place it in other hands." Two hundred years later, this Court expressly recognized the existence of and the necessity for limits on Congress' ability to delegate its authority to representatives of the Executive Branch: "That Congress cannot delegate legislative power to the President is a principle universally recognized as vital to the integrity and maintenance of the system of government ordained by the Constitution." Field v. Clark, 143 U.S. 649, 692 (1892).

The rule against delegation of legislative power is not, however, so cardinal a principle as to allow for no exception. The Framers of the Constitution were practical statesmen, who saw that the doctrine of separation of powers was a two-sided coin. James Madison, in Federalist Paper No. 48, for example, recognized that while the division of authority among the various branches of government was a useful principle, "the degree of separation which the maxim requires, as essential to a free government, can never in practice be duly maintained."

This Court also has recognized that a hermetic sealing-off of the three branches of government from one another could easily frustrate the establishment of a National Government capable of effectively exercising the substantive powers granted to the various branches by the Constitution. Mr. Chief Justice Taft, writing for the Court in J.W. Hampton & Co. v. United States, 276 U.S. 394 (1928), noted the practicalities of the balance that has to be struck:

> "[T]he rule is that in the actual administration of the government Congress or the Legislature should exercise the legislative power, the President or the State executive, the Governor, the executive. power, and the Courts or the judiciary the judicial power, and in carrying out that constitutional division into three branches it is a breach of the National fundamental law if Congress gives up its legislative power and transfers it to the President, or to the Judicial branch, or if by law it attempts to invest itself or its members with either executive power or judicial power. This is not to say that the three branches are not co-ordinate parts of one government and that each in the field of its duties may not invoke the action of the two other branches in so far as the action invoked shall not be an assumption of the constitutional field of action of another branch. In determining what it may do in seeking assistance from another branch, the extent and character of that assistance must be fixed according to common sense and the inherent necessities of the governmental co-ordination." Id., at 406.

During the third and fourth decades of this century, this Court within a relatively short period of time struck down several Acts of Congress on the grounds that they exceeded the authority of Congress under the Commerce Clause or under the nondelegation principle of separation of powers, and at the same time struck down state statutes because they violated "substantive" due process or interfered with interstate commerce. When many of these decisions were later overruled, the principle that Congress could not simply transfer its legislative authority to the Executive fell under a cloud. Yet in my opinion decisions such as Panama Refining Co. v. Ryan, 293 U.S. 388 (1935), suffer from none of the excesses of judicial policymaking that plagued some of the other decisions of that era. The many later decisions that have upheld congressional delegations of authority to the Executive Branch have done so largely on the theory that Congress may wish to exercise its authority in a particular field, but because the field is sufficiently technical, the ground to be covered sufficiently large, and the Members of Congress themselves not necessarily expert in the area in which they choose to legislate, the most that may be asked under the separation-of-powers doctrine is that Congress lay down the general policy and standards that animate the law, leaving the agency to refine those standards, "fill in the blanks," or apply the standards to particular cases. These decisions, to my mind, simply illustrate the above-quoted principle stated more than 50 years ago by Mr. Chief Justice Taft that delegations of legislative authority must be judged "according to common sense and the inherent necessities of the governmental co-ordination."

Viewing the legislation at issue here in light of these principles, I believe that it fails to pass muster. Read literally, the relevant portion of § 6(b)(5) is completely precatory, admonishing the Secretary to adopt the most protective standard if he can, but excusing him from that duty if he cannot. In the case of a hazardous substance for which a "safe" level is either unknown or impractical, the language of § 6(b)(5) gives the Secretary absolutely no indication where on the continuum of relative safety he should draw his line. Especially in light of the importance of the interests at stake, I have no doubt that the provision at issue, standing alone, would violate the doctrine against uncanalized delegations of legislative power. For me the remaining question, then, is whether additional standards are ascertainable from the legislative history or statutory context of § 6(b)(5) or, if not, whether such a standardless delegation was justifiable in light of the "inherent necessities" of the situation.

II

One of the primary sources looked to by this Court in adding gloss to an otherwise broad grant of legislative authority is the legislative history of the statute in question. . . .

There can be little doubt that, [in a version being considered in the House], § 6(b)(5) would have required the Secretary, in regulating toxic substances, to set the permissible level of exposure at a safe level or, if no safe level was known, at zero. When the Senate Committee on Labor and Public Welfare considered a provision identical in almost all respects to the House version, however, Senator Javits objected that the provision in question "might be interpreted to require absolute health and safety in all cases, regardless of feasibility. . . . " The Committee therefore amended the bill to provide that the Secretary "shall set the standard which most adequately *and feasibly*" assured that no employee would suffer any impairment of health. . . . Despite Senator Javits' inclusion of the words "and feasibly" in the provision, participants in the floor debate immediately characterized § 6(b)(5) as requiring the Secretary "to establish a utopia free from any hazards" and to "assure that there will not be any risk at all." 116 Cong.Rec. 37614 (1970). (remarks of Senator Dominick). . . .

Eventually, Senator Dominick and his supporters settled for the present language of § 6(b)(5). This agreement resulted in three changes from the original version of the provision as amended by Senator Javits. First, the provision was altered to state explicitly that it applied only to standards for "toxic materials or harmful physical agents," in apparent contrast with safety standards. Second, the Secretary was no longer admonished to protect employees from "any" impairment of their health, but rather only from "material" impairments. Third, and most importantly for our purposes, the phrase "most adequately and feasibly assures" was revamped to read "most adequately assures, to the extent feasible."

We have been presented with a number of different interpretations of this shift. According to the Secretary, Senator Dominick recognized that he could not delete the seemingly absolute requirements of § 6(b)(5) entirely, and instead agreed to limit its application to toxic materials or harmful physical agents and to specify that the Secretary was

only to protect employees from material impairment of their health.
. . . Mr. Justice Marshall reads this history quite differently. . . .
Respondents cast yet a third light on these events . . . .

To my mind, there are several lessons to be gleaned from this
somewhat cryptic legislative history. First, . . . to the extent that
Senator Javits, Senator Dominick, and other Members were worried
about imposing upon the Secretary the impossible burden of assuring
absolute safety, they did not view § 3(8) of the Act as a limitation on
that duty. . . . Second, and more importantly, I believe that the
legislative history demonstrates that the feasibility requirement, as
employed in § 6(b)(5), is a legislative mirage, appearing to some Members but not to others, and assuming any form desired by the beholder.
. . . Perhaps Senator Dominick himself offered the aptest description
of the feasibility requirement as "no more than an admonition to the
Secretary to do his duty . . . ." 116 Cong.Rec. 36530 (1970); Leg.
Hist. 367.

In sum, the legislative history contains nothing to indicate that the
language "to the extent feasible" does anything other than render what
had been a clear, if somewhat unrealistic, standard largely, if not
entirely, precatory. There is certainly nothing to indicate that these
words, as used in § 6(b)(5), are limited to technological and economic
feasibility. . . . I also question whether the Secretary wants to
assume the duties such an interpretation would impose upon him. In
these cases, for example, the Secretary actually declined to adopt a
standard lower than 1 ppm for some industries, not because it was
economically or technologically infeasible, but rather because "different
levels for different industries would result in serious administrative
difficulties." If § 6(b)(5) authorizes the Secretary to reject a more
protective standard in the interest of administrative feasibility, I have
little doubt that he could reject such standards for any reason whatsoever, including even political feasibility.

III

In prior cases this Court has looked to sources other than the
legislative history to breathe life into otherwise vague delegations of
legislative power. In American Power & Light Co. v. SEC, 329 U.S. 90,
104 (1946), for example, this Court concluded that certain seemingly
vague delegations "derive[d] much meaningful content from the purpose of the Act, its factual background and the statutory context in
which they appear." Here, however, there is little or nothing in the
remaining provisions of the Occupational Safety and Health Act to
provide specificity to the feasibility criterion in § 6(b)(5). It may be
true, as suggested by Mr. Justice Marshall, that the Act as a whole
expresses a distinct preference for safety over dollars. But that expression of preference, as I read it, falls far short of the proposition that the
Secretary must eliminate marginal or insignificant risks of material
harm right down to an industry's breaking point.

Nor are these cases like Lichter v. United States, 334 U.S. 742, 783
(1948), where this Court upheld delegation of authority to recapture

"excessive profits" in light of a pre-existing administrative practice. Here, the Secretary's approach to toxic substances like benzene could not have predated the enactment of § 6(b)(5) itself. Moreover, there are indications that the postenactment administrative practice has been less than uniform. . . .

In some cases where broad delegations of power have been examined, this Court has upheld those delegations because of the delegatee's residual authority over particular subjects of regulation. In United States v. Curtiss-Wright Export Corp., 299 U.S. 304, 307 (1936), this Court upheld a statute authorizing the President to prohibit the sale of arms to certain countries if he found that such a prohibition would "contribute to the reestablishment of peace." This Court reasoned that, in the area of foreign affairs, Congress "must often accord to the President a degree of discretion and freedom from statutory restriction which would not be admissible were domestic affairs alone involved." Id., at 320. . . . In the present cases, however, neither the Executive Branch in general nor the Secretary in particular enjoys any independent authority over the subject matter at issue.

Finally, as indicated earlier, in some cases this Court has abided by a rule of necessity, upholding broad delegations of authority where it would be "unreasonable and impracticable to compel Congress to prescribe detailed rules" regarding a particular policy or situation. American Power & Light Co. v. SEC, 329 U.S., at 105. See also Buttfield v. Stranahan. But no need for such an evasive standard as "feasibility" is apparent in the present cases. In drafting § 6(b)(5), Congress was faced with a clear, if difficult, choice between balancing statistical lives and industrial resources or authorizing the Secretary to elevate human life above all concerns save massive dislocation in an affected industry. That Congress recognized the difficulty of this choice is clear from the . . . remark of Senator Saxbe, who stated that "[w]hen we come to saying that an employer must guarantee that such an employee is protected from any possible harm, I think it will be one of the most difficult areas we are going to have to ascertain." 116 Cong.Rec. 36522 (1970), Leg.Hist. 345. That Congress chose, intentionally or unintentionally, to pass this difficult choice on to the Secretary is evident from the spectral quality of the standard it selected . . . ." Ibid.

IV

As formulated and enforced by this Court, the nondelegation doctrine serves three important functions. First, and most abstractly, it ensures to the extent consistent with orderly governmental administration that important choices of social policy are made by Congress, the branch of our Government most responsive to the popular will. See Arizona v. California, 373 U.S. 546, 626 (1963) (Harlan, J., dissenting in part); United States v. Robel, 389 U.S. 258, 276 (1967) (Brennan, J., concurring in result). Second, the doctrine guarantees that, to the extent Congress finds it necessary to delegate authority, it provides the recipient of that authority with an "intelligible principle" to guide the exercise of the delegated discretion. See J.W. Hampton & Co. v. United

States, 276 U.S. at 409; Panama Refining Co. v. Ryan, 293 U.S., at 430. Third, and derivative of the second, the doctrine ensures that courts charged with reviewing the exercise of delegated legislative discretion will be able to test that exercise against ascertainable standards. See Arizona v. California, supra, at 626 (Harlan, J., dissenting in part); American Power & Light Co. v. SEC, supra, at 106.

I believe the legislation at issue here fails on all three counts. The decision whether the law of diminishing returns should have any place in the regulation of toxic substances is quintessentially one of legislative policy. For Congress to pass that decision on to the Secretary in the manner it did violates, in my mind, John Locke's caveat—reflected in the cases cited earlier in this opinion—that legislatures are to make laws, not legislators. Nor, as I think the prior discussion amply demonstrates, do the provisions at issue or their legislative history provide the Secretary with any guidance that might lead him to his somewhat tentative conclusion that he must eliminate exposure to benzene as far as technologically and economically possible. Finally, I would suggest that the standard of "feasibility" renders meaningful judicial review impossible.

We ought not to shy away from our judicial duty to invalidate unconstitutional delegations of legislative authority solely out of concern that we should thereby reinvigorate discredited constitutional doctrines of the pre-New Deal era. If the non-delegation doctrine has fallen into the same desuetude as have substantive due process and restrictive interpretations of the Commerce Clause, it is, as one writer has phrased it, "a case of death by association." J. Ely, Democracy and Distrust, A Theory of Judicial Review 133 (1980). Indeed, a number of observers have suggested that this Court should once more take up its burden of ensuring that Congress does not unnecessarily delegate important choices of social policy to politically unresponsive administrators.[4] Other observers, as might be imagined, have disagreed.[5]

If we are ever to reshoulder the burden of ensuring that Congress itself make the critical policy decisions, these are surely the cases in which to do it. It is difficult to imagine a more obvious example of Congress simply avoiding a choice which was both fundamental for purposes of the statute and yet politically so divisive that the necessary decision or compromise was difficult, if not impossible, to hammer out in the legislative forge. . . .

I would invalidate the first sentence of § 6(b)(5) of the Occupational Safety and Health Act of 1970 as it applies to any toxic substance or harmful physical agent for which a safe level, that is, a level at which

---

4. See J. Ely, Democracy and Distrust, A Theory of Judicial Review 131–134 (1980); J. Freedman, Crisis and Legitimacy, The Administrative Process and American Government 78–94 (1978); T. Lowi, The End of Liberalism: Ideology, Policy, and the Crisis of Public Authority 129–146, 297–299 (1969); Wright, Beyond Discretionary Justice, 81 Yale L.J. 575, 582–587 (1972).

5. See K. Davis, Discretionary Justice: A Preliminary Inquiry 49–51 (1969); Stewart, The Reformation of American Administrative Law, 88 Harv.L.Rev. 1669, 1693–1697 (1975). Cf. Jaffe, The Illusion of the Ideal Administration, 86 Harv.L.Rev. 1183, 1190, n. 37 (1973).

"no employee will suffer material impairment of health or functional capacity even if such employee has regular exposure to [that hazard] for the period of his working life," is, according to the Secretary, unknown or otherwise "infeasible." Absent further congressional action, the Secretary would then have to choose, when acting pursuant to § 6(b)(5), between setting a safe standard or setting no standard at all. Accordingly, for the reasons stated above, I concur in the judgment of the Court affirming the judgment of the Court of Appeals.[6]

MR. JUSTICE MARSHALL, with whom MR. JUSTICE BRENNAN, MR. JUSTICE WHITE, and MR. JUSTICE BLACKMUN join, dissenting.

[The tone of Justice Marshall's 36-page dissent is evident in its opening passage: "In cases of statutory construction, this Court's authority is limited. If the statutory language and legislative intent are plain, the judicial inquiry is at an end." On the whole, the dissent was given over to a demonstration that the Secretary's action was sustainable on the record he had made, and an accusation that the plurality had mischaracterized that record, substituting its judgment of scientific and technical matters for the Secretary's. Concerning Section 3(8), the thrust of his opinion is shown in his observations that " 'reasonably necessary or appropriate' clauses are routinely inserted in regulatory legislation, and in the past such clauses have uniformly been interpreted as general provisions that regulatory authors must bear a reasonable relation to those statutory purposes set forth in the statute's substantive provinces." As to Section 6(b)(5) and the word "feasible," he thought that Congress' sole concern was that standards be economically and technologically achievable. The legislative intent was to prevent the Secretary from materially harming the financial condition of regulated industries in order to eliminate risks of impairment. Congress did not intend to preclude the Secretary from taking regulatory action where, as here, no such threat to industry is posed.]

However, even if some balancing of costs and benefits were implicit in the term, taking into account the uncertainties in existing knowledge, the Secretary made an express finding that the hazards of benzene exposure were sufficient to justify the regulation's costs. Any requirement to balance costs and benefits cannot be read to invalidate this wholly rational conclusion.

[Regarding the problem of delegation, the dissent had this to say:]

Finding obscurity in the word "feasible," my Brother Rehnquist invokes the nondelegation doctrine, which was last used to invalidate an Act of Congress in 1935. Schechter Poultry Corp. v. United States, 295 U.S. 495 (1935). While my Brother Rehnquist eloquently argues that there remains a place for such a doctrine in our jurisprudence, I am frankly puzzled as to why the issue is thought to be of any relevance here. The nondelegation doctrine is designed to assure that the most

6. [Ed.] Justice Rehnquist reiterated his view that § 6(b)(5) of the Occupational Safety and Health Act represented an unconstitutional delegation of legislative power in 1981, in American Textile Manuf. Institute v. Donovan, 452 U.S. 490, 543. This time he emphasized that Congress failed to specify whether the agency "should be either mandated, permitted, or prohibited from undertaking a cost-benefit analysis." 452 U.S. at 548. And this time Chief Justice Burger joined his opinion.

fundamental decisions will be made by Congress, the elected representatives of the people, rather than by administrators. Some minimal
definiteness is therefore required in order for Congress to delegate its
authority to administrative agencies.

Congress has been sufficiently definite here. The word "feasible"
has a reasonably plain meaning, and its interpretation can be informed
by other contexts in which Congress has used it. Since the term is
placed in the same sentence with the "no employee will suffer" language, it is clear that 'feasible' means technologically and economically
achievable. Under the Act, the Secretary is afforded considerably more
guidance than are other administrators acting under different regulatory statutes. In short, Congress has made "the critical policy decisions"
in these cases, see ante (Rehnquist, J., concurring in judgment).

The plurality's apparent suggestion that the nondelegation doctrine might be violated if the Secretary were permitted to regulate
definite but nonquantifiable risks is plainly wrong. Such a statute
would be quite definite and would thus raise no constitutional question
under Schechter Poultry. Moreover, Congress could rationally decide
that it would be better to require industry to bear 'feasible' costs than
to subject American workers to an indeterminate risk of cancer and
other fatal diseases.

NOTES

(1) To understand the range of issues at stake in "the Benzene
Case," one must distinguish two possible legal doctrines, each of which
could be used to invalidate administrative action: a prohibition of
administrative acts beyond conferred authority ("ultra vires"), and a
prohibition of legislative acts which delegate legislative power.

Except for instances in which state constitutions provide for administrative agencies or to the extent that constitutional officers—President, governor and the like—possess power by virtue of their offices, all
administrative authority is conferred (directly or by implication) by a
statute. Of necessity, because the Constitution does not itself define
the inferior parts of government, Congress has delegated governmental
power to the President and other federal officials and agencies from the
very beginnings of the federal government. Thus, at the outset, the
legislature perforce exercises some degree of control, because in enacting the statute the legislature, in broad outline at least, defines the
objective sought to be accomplished. Administrative action clearly
outside the delegated field or not designed to achieve the legislative
objective would, in an appropriate judicial proceeding, be held invalid
as being outside the power delegated.[1] Legislature and judiciary here
combine to prevent the administrative agency from acting ultra vires,
and the judiciary bases its ruling on an interpretation of a statute.
Justice Stevens' opinion, by and large, illustrates this method.

1. On the difficulty of determining
these issues, see Chapter 3, Section 4 within. Note that the courts do not invariably
insist that legislative authority be explicit.
See, e.g., Interstate Commerce Comm'n v.
American Trucking Assn, 467 U.S. 354
(1984); J. Mallamud, Courts, Statutes and
Administrative Agency Jurisdiction, A
Consideration of Limits on Judicial Creativity, 35 S.Car.L.Rev. 191 (1984).

A different method of limiting the area of administrative discretion is reflected in the proposition that "legislative power cannot be delegated." The delegation doctrine says the *statute* purporting to confer the power is invalid because the legislature cannot delegate its powers. When this doctrine is brought into play, the legislature and the judiciary are no longer collaborators in placing limits upon the agency. Here, rather, the legislature has expressed a desire to grant authority—and the judiciary has overruled the legislative choice. In this case, the judiciary bases its authority on an interpretation of one or more constitutional provisions. This is the approach of Justice Rehnquist.

What does, or ought to, move judges in choosing between these two approaches—in "agreeing" to interpret or, rather, repudiating the legislative work-product as inadequate for normal cooperation of this sort?

(2) In terms of its conceptual structure, the rule against delegation would be better termed a rule against subdelegation. The original delegation (on this reading of the Constitution) occurred when "We the People" conferred their own power to make laws on their selected delegate, the "Congress of the United States." In private law terms, what is being asserted is that an agent who has agreed to undertake a discretionary task involving judgment is not free to pass that responsibility on to someone else. See Restatement, Second, of Agency Section 78 (1958). In public law terms, the point was well made in the following passage from John Locke, Second Treatise of Civil Government Section 141 (1690), part of which Justice Rehnquist quotes:

"Fourthly, the legislative cannot transfer the power of making laws to any other hands; for it being but a delegated power from the people, they who have it cannot pass it over to others. The people alone can appoint the form of the commonwealth, which is by constituting the legislative and appointing in whose hands that shall be. And when the people have said, we will submit to rules and be governed by laws made by such men, and in such forms, nobody else can say other men shall make laws for them; nor can the people be bound by any laws but such as are enacted by those whom they have chosen and authorized to make laws for them. The power of the legislative, being derived from the people by a positive voluntary grant and institution, can be no other than what the positive grant conveyed, which being only to make laws, and not to make legislators, the legislative can have no power to transfer their authority of making laws and place it in other hands."

J. Locke, Second Treatise of Civil Government § 141 (1960).

(3) Justice Rehnquist discusses many of the Court's earlier cases on the delegation question, organizing them in a manner suggestive of neat doctrinal development. To understand the constitutional significance of what he is proposing, however, it is useful to have some sense of the course of history on the matter.

(a) *Prior to the New Deal*

The earliest case involving the lawfulness of a delegation of authority (in this case, directly to the President) is THE BRIG AURORA, 11 U.S.

(7 Cranch) 382 (1813). An act of Congress provided that if either Great Britain or France should cease violating the neutral commerce of the United States, "which fact the President of the United States shall declare by proclamation" then certain sections of a previous act which had expired should "be revived and have full force and effect." President Madison issued such a proclamation. When the revived statute was then brought into play, a litigant contended that Congress could not permissibly transfer its power to the President; the revival of the previous law had hinged upon the President's proclamation, which had thus been given the force of a law. The Court rejected this argument in an almost cursory fashion, stating, "[W]e can see no sufficient reason why the legislature should not exercise its discretion in reviving the act of March 1st, 1809, either expressly or conditionally, as their judgment should direct." [1]

Nearly eighty years later in FIELD V. CLARK, 143 U.S. 649 (1892), the Court relied on The Brig Aurora to uphold section 3 of the Tariff Act of 1890. That section provided a retaliatory tariff schedule which was to remain in effect for whatever time the President "shall deem just" if any country whose agricultural products came into the United States duty-free were subsequently to impose on American products "duties or other exactions . . . which . . . [the President] may deem to be reciprocally unequal and unreasonable . . . ." If the President did "deem" that American business was being treated unfairly, "he shall have the power and it shall be his duty" to proclaim a suspension of tariff provisions favorable to the country engaged in unfairness.

Did this result in a transfer of tariff-making power to the President? Justice Harlan and a majority of the Court thought it did not, saying: "That Congress cannot delegate legislative power to the President is a principle universally recognized as vital to the integrity and maintenance of the system of government ordained by the constitution. The act . . . under consideration is not inconsistent with that principle. It does not in any real sense invest the President with the power of legislation. . . . Legislative power was exercised when Congress declared that the suspension should take effect upon a named contingency. What the President was required to do was simply in execution of the act of Congress. It was not the making of law. He was the mere agent of the law-making department to ascertain and declare the event upon which its expressed will was to take effect. It was a part of the law itself as it left the hands of Congress that the provisions, full and complete in themselves, permitting the free introduction of sugars, molasses, coffee, tea and hides, from particular countries, should be suspended in a given contingency, and that in case of such suspensions certain duties should be imposed."

One need scarcely point out that the "fact" whose ascertainment had been entrusted to the President was not a single, objectively observable occurrence. It was, rather, a compound of international

---

1. The Judiciary Act of 1789, ch. 20 § 17(b), 1 Stat. 73, 83, had authorized the courts to adopt rules of procedure to govern proceedings before them. The early Court also had no difficulty sustaining this delegation. Wayman v. Southard, 23 U.S. (10 Wheat.) 1, 15–16 (1826).

economic and political issues whose significance (and, indeed, whose very existence) was more a matter of judgment than of fact.

Although the "contingency" or "ascertainment of a fact" formula of The Brig Aurora and Field v. Clark worked well enough to uphold the presidential participation in lawmaking there at issue, later delegations to other actors produced new justifying labels. UNITED STATES v. GRIMAUD, 220 U.S. 506 (1911), is a good illustration. An act of Congress authorized the Secretary of Agriculture to "make provision for the protection against destruction by fire and depredations upon the public forests and forest reservations . . . ; and he may make such rules and regulations and establish such service as will insure the objects of such reservations, namely, to regulate their occupancy and use, and to preserve the forests thereon from destruction. . . . " The Secretary had adopted a rule requiring ranchers to obtain a permit before their sheep could safely graze in national forests; Grimaud had pastured sheep on national forest land without this required permission. He was brought before a court and fined under a statute making violation of any such regulation punishable by a fine of up to $500 and/or imprisonment up to twelve months. He argued that this arrangement permitted the Secretary to enact criminal laws. Justice Lamar, speaking for a unanimous court, upheld the delegation on the theory that the Secretary was not legislating but was only exercising a "power to fill up the details." In authorizing the Secretary to issue regulations, "Congress was merely conferring administrative functions upon an agent, and not delegating to him legislative power." "[T]he authority to make administrative rules is not a delegation of legislative power, nor are such rules raised from an administrative to a legislative character because the violation thereof is punished as a public offense. . . . A violation of . . . [the rules] is made a crime, not by the Secretary, but by Congress. The statute, not the Secretary, fixes the penalty." [2] The determination of the questions committed to the Secretary was "a matter of administrative detail." [3]

J.W. HAMPTON, JR. & CO. v. UNITED STATES, 276 U.S. 394 (1928), involved a far more sweeping authority to regulate foreign trade. The Tariff Act of 1922, like its predecessor tariff laws, set the precise duties to be paid on various classes of imports. Then Section 312(a) added that, in order to carry out the legislative policy, "whenever the President, upon investigation of the differences in costs of production of articles wholly or in part the growth or product of the United States and of like or similar articles wholly or in part the growth or product of competing foreign countries, shall find . . . that the duties fixed in this Act do not equalize the said differences in costs of production in the

2. Grimaud is criticized in H. Abrahams and J. Snowden, Separation of Powers and Administrative Crimes: A Study of Irreconcilables, 1976 Southern Ill. U.L.J. 1. For additional discussion, see references cited by Professors Abrahams and Snowden, at 4 n. 3 and 5 n. 4.

3. Do you agree that it is the fixing of the penalty, rather than the definition of what acts may not be performed without incurring that penalty, that is the significant part of creating a crime? Would the analysis be the same if Congress had fixed the penalty at up to twenty years imprisonment and authorized the Secretary to make provision for avoiding offenses to public morality within the public forests? Was the Court, then, wrong?

United States and the principal competing country he shall . . . ascertain said differences and determine and proclaim the changes in classifications or increases or decreases in any rate of duty provided in this Act shown by said ascertained differences in such costs of production necessary to equalize the same." If the President, aided by the investigations of the United States Tariff Commission, did conclude that American producers needed additional protection against foreign competitors whose production costs were lower (or, theoretically, if he found that American consumers were being denied access to foreign products because tariffs were too high), then whatever new schedule of customs duties he might choose to "proclaim" would go into effect thirty days later.

It is true, however, as Justice Rehnquist writes, that the opinion in Hampton began its analysis with the general principle that "it is a breach of the National fundamental law if Congress gives up its legislative power and transfers it to the President," and that, in terms of how much help each branch can get from the other, "the extent and character of that assistance must be fixed according to common sense and the inherent necessities of the governmental co-ordination." But those statements are perhaps colored by what else Chief Justice Taft (who, it will be remembered, had had substantial experience in the executive department) had to say about "common sense":

> Again, one of the great functions conferred on Congress by the Federal Constitution is the regulation of interstate commerce and rates to be exacted by interstate carriers for the passenger and merchandise traffic. The rates to be fixed are myriad. If Congress were to be required to fix every rate, it would be impossible to exercise the power at all. Therefore, common sense requires that in the fixing of such rates, Congress may provide a Commission, as it does, called the Interstate Commerce Commission, to fix those rates, after hearing evidence and argument concerning them from interested parties, all in accord with a general rule that Congress first lays down, that rates shall be just and reasonable considering the service given, and not discriminatory.

More broadly, although Taft discussed Field v. Clark and the Grimaud case, he seemed to thrust beyond the bounds of "filling up the details" or ascertaining a "contingency" in the following passage:

> The same principle that permits Congress to exercise its rate making power in interstate commerce, by declaring the rule which shall prevail in the legislative fixing of rates, and enables it to remit to a rate-making body created in accordance with its provisions the fixing of such rates, justifies a similar provision for the fixing of customs duties on imported merchandise. If Congress shall lay down by legislative act an intelligible principle to which the person or body authorized to fix such rates is directed to conform, such legislative action is not a forbidden delegation of legislative power.

(b) *The New Deal*

If Justice Rehnquist's views are to be supported by holdings, not mere dicta, those holdings will have to be found in two cases of the mid-30's invalidating delegations contained in Title I of the National Industrial Recovery Act of 1933.[4] The background and purpose of that Act have been described as follows:

"The depression which began in the Fall of 1929 had, by 1933, produced an economic crisis probably unequalled in the history of the United States. At least thirteen million persons were unemployed; the average wages of those still employed in twenty-five selected industries had dropped to $16.13 per week in February 1933; wages received in mining, manufacturing, construction and transportation had declined from 17 to 6.8 billion dollars. Prices had fallen 37 per cent and industrial production had been cut almost in half. Insolvencies were mounting and the banks were closed. The amount of revenue freight carried by Class I railroads, a fair measure of the quantity of interstate commerce, had declined 51 per cent.

"Title I of the National Industrial Recovery Act, which became law June 16, 1933, was one of a series of statutes enacted by the Roosevelt Administration in an effort to halt the downward spiral of the depression and reinvigorate the national economy. While other measures dealt with different aspects of the problem, the Recovery Act grappled with the depression as it directly affected labor and industry. The deflated purchasing power of the masses was to be increased through the establishment of minimum wages and free collective bargaining; employment was to be increased through maximum-hour regulations.

---

4. Carter v. Carter Coal Co., 298 U.S. 238 (1936), marked the third and final time the Supreme Court found a statute unconstitutional on delegation grounds. In this instance the objection was not that legislative authority had been delegated to the executive, but that it had been placed outside government. The Bituminous Coal Conservation Act of 1935 provided that coal producers were either to pay a 15 percent tax on their coal or to become members of the Bituminous Coal Code. The Act also provided that once like contracts concerning wages and minimum hours had been negotiated between the producers of more than two thirds of the annual tonnage of coal produced and representatives of more than one-half of the mine workers employed, the hours and wages so fixed were to be accepted by all Code members. Government officials were to have no voice in shaping or approving the arrangements thus made—a safeguard which has been found to characterize subsequent such measures. See, e.g., Sunshine Anthracite Coal v. Adkins, 310 U.S. 381, 399 (1940).

Justice Sutherland wrote for the Court (after setting forth objections also on Commerce Clause grounds):

"The power conferred upon the majority is, in effect, the power to regulate the affairs of an unwilling minority. This is legislative delegation in its most obnoxious form; for it is not even delegation to an official or an official body, presumptively disinterested, but to private persons whose interests may be and often are adverse to the interests of others in the same business . . . . [I]n the very nature of things, one person may not be entrusted with the power to regulate the business of another, and especially of a competitor. And a statute which attempts to confer such power undertakes an intolerable and unconstitutional interference with personal liberty and private property."

Although this aspect of "delegation" has occasionally had bite in the states, see page 99ff. within, the problem has been treated as one of mechanical arrangement rather than substance at the federal level, and so has been easily avoided there. For a profound discussion of the problems raised in Carter Coal, see L. Jaffe, Law Making by Private Groups, 51 Harv.L.Rev. 201 (1937).

Business men, in combinations subject to Government approval, were to be allowed to eliminate wasteful competitive practices and cutthroat competition so as to enable them to halt the decline in prices, to pay the higher wage bills and to restore business to a healthy condition." R.L. Stern, The Commerce Clause and the National Economy, 1933–1936, 59 Harv.L.Rev. 645, 653 (1946).[5]

Section 9 of the Act dealt with the particular problem of the petroleum industry, "which had been subjected not merely to the ordinary effects of the depression but to the ruinous consequences of uncontrolled overproduction from newly discovered fields. The opening of the vast East Texas field brought prices in 1931 down to as low as five and two and one-half cents a barrel." Stern, supra, at 654. Section 9(c) provided:

"The President is authorized to prohibit the transportation in interstate and foreign commerce of petroleum and the products thereof produced or withdrawn from storage in excess of the amount permitted to be produced or withdrawn from storage by any state law or valid regulation or order prescribed thereunder, by any board, commission, officer, or other duly authorized agency of a State. Any violation of any order of the President issued under the provisions of this subsection shall be punishable by fine of not to exceed $1,000 or imprisonment for not to exceed six months, or both." 48 Stat. 200 (1933).

The Act became law on June 16, 1933. On July 11, 1933, the President issued an Executive Order which prohibited the transportation in interstate and foreign commerce of petroleum and petroleum products produced or withdrawn from storage in excess of the amount permitted by state authority. In October the Panama Refining Co. and others brought suit to enjoin enforcement of § 9(c). The district court issued an injunction, but the court of appeals reversed. Judge Sibley observed: "The delegation to the President of power to put the prohibition of § 9(c) into effect is not seriously attacked. Such a thing has been often done under varying forms of language, as appears by the review of statutes in Field v. Clark. . . . " 71 F.2d at 6.

When the case reached the Supreme Court, the Court held that § 9(c) unlawfully delegated legislative power. PANAMA REFINING CO. v. RYAN, 293 U.S. 388 (1935). Chief Justice Hughes thus posed the issue: "Assuming for the present purpose, without deciding, that the Congress has power to interdict that excess in interstate or foreign commerce, the question whether that transportation shall be prohibited by law is obviously one of legislative policy. Accordingly, we look to the statute to see whether the Congress has declared a policy with respect to that subject; whether the Congress has set up a standard for the President's action; whether the Congress has required any finding by the President in the exercise of the authority to enact the prohibition."

The opinion first considered § 9(c) and concluded that no standard could be discovered there. "So far as this section is concerned, it gives to the President an unlimited authority to determine the policy and to

5. P. Irons, The New Deal Lawyers (1982) contains a revealing account of the Act and of the litigation leading to the cases discussed in the text.

lay down the prohibition, or not to lay it down, as he may see fit. And disobedience to his order is made a crime punishable by fine and imprisonment." Nor did the other portions of § 9—which had to do with pipe line rates and operations—provide any guidance to the President when deciding whether or not to place an embargo on the interstate shipment of "hot oil."

The Chief Justice then turned to the other provisions of the Act, particularly to its "declaration of policy," to see whether they constituted an adequate legislative command to the recipient of delegated power. Congress had found in § 1 of the statute that a "national emergency" had produced "widespread unemployment and disorganization of industry, which burdens interstate and foreign commerce, affects the public welfare, and undermines the standards of living of the American people." The present enactment was a reflection (so § 1 said) of congressional policy (a) to eliminate obstructions to commerce, (b) to promote general welfare by aiding cooperative action among industrial groups, (c) to facilitate management-labor unity, (d) to erase unfair competitive practices, (e) to seek full utilization of existing productive capacity by preventing undue restrictions on production "(except as may be temporarily required)" and by stimulating consumption, (f) to reduce unemployment, (g) to improve labor standards, and (h) "otherwise to rehabilitate industry and to conserve natural resources." The Chief Justice concluded that this recital of aspirations did not improve the case at all, because "Among the numerous and diverse objectives broadly stated, the President was not required to choose. The President was not required to ascertain and proclaim the conditions prevailing in the industry which made the prohibition necessary. The Congress left the matter to the President without standard or rule, to be dealt with as he pleased."

The opinion also reviewed the precedents in which the Court had without exception upheld the congressional delegation, and concluded:

"Thus, in every case in which the question has been raised, the Court has recognized that there are limits of delegation which there is no constitutional authority to transcend. We think that § 9(c) goes beyond those limits. As to the transportation of oil production in excess of state permission, the Congress has declared no policy, has established no standard, has laid down no rule. There is no requirement, no definition of circumstances and conditions in which the transportation is to be allowed or prohibited.

"If § 9(c) were held valid, it would be idle to pretend that anything would be left of limitations upon the power of the Congress to delegate its law-making function. The reasoning of the many decisions we have reviewed would be made vacuous and their distinctions nugatory. Instead of performing its law-making function, the Congress could at will and as to such subjects as it chose transfer that function to the President or other officer or to an administrative body. The question is not of the intrinsic importance of the particular statute before us but of the constitutional processes of legislation which are an essential part of our system of government."

Only Justice Cardozo dissented. His fifteen-page opinion—about half the length of that of the Chief Justice . . . emphasized at the outset that the "nature of the *act* which the President is authorized to perform . . . is definite beyond the possibility of challenge . . . He is not left to roam at will among all the possible subjects of interstate transportation, picking and choosing as he pleases." He can only prohibit transportation of stated products produced or withdrawn in excess of state authority.

". . . Congress was aware that for the recovery of national well-being there might be need of temporary restriction upon production in one industry or another. It said so in § 1. When it clothed the President with power to impose such a restriction—to prohibit the flow of oil illegally produced—it laid upon him a mandate to inquire and determine whether the conditions in that particular industry were such at any given time as to make restriction helpful to the declared objectives of the act and to the ultimate attainment of industrial recovery. If such a situation does not present an instance of lawful delegation in a typical and classic form (Field v. Clark, 143 U.S. 649; United States v. Grimaud, 220 U.S. 506; Hampton & Co. v. United States, 276 U.S. 394), categories long established will have to be formulated anew.

"In what has been written, I have stated, but without developing the argument, that by reasonable implication the power conferred upon the President by § 9(c) is to be read as if coupled with the words that he shall exercise the power whenever satisfied that by doing so he will effectuate the policy of the statute as theretofore declared. . . . What, indeed, is the alternative? Either the statute means that the President is to adhere to the declared policy of Congress, or it means that he is to exercise a merely arbitrary will. The one construction invigorates the act; the other saps its life. A choice between them is not hard.

"I am persuaded that a reference, express or implied, to the policy of Congress as declared in § 1 is a sufficient definition of a standard to make the statute valid. Discretion is not unconfined and vagrant. It is canalized within banks that keep it from overflowing. Field v. Clark, 143 U.S. 649; United States v. Grimaud, 220 U.S. 506, and Hampton & Co. v. United States, 276 U.S. 394, state the applicable principle. Under these decisions the separation of powers between the Executive and Congress is not a doctrinaire concept to be made use of with pedantic rigor. There must be sensible approximation, there must be elasticity of adjustment in response to the practical necessities of government, which cannot foresee today the developments of tomorrow in their nearly infinite variety."

SCHECHTER POULTRY CORP. v. UNITED STATES, 295 U.S. 495 (1935), the only other case in which the Supreme Court has invalidated an attempted congressional transference of law-making power to another arm of the government, was decided five months later. It involved § 3 of the Act, which read in part as follows:

"(a) Upon the application to the President by one or more trade or industrial associations or groups, the President may approve a code or codes of fair competition for the trade or industry or subdivision thereof, represented by the applicant or applicants, if the President finds (1) that such associations or groups impose no inequitable restrictions on admission to membership therein and are truly representative of such trades or industries or subdivisions thereof, and (2) that such code or codes are not designed to promote monopolies or to eliminate or oppress small enterprises and will not operate to discriminate against them, and will tend to effectuate the policy of this title. . . .

"(b) After the President shall have approved any such code, the provisions of such code shall be the standards of fair competition for such trade or industry or subdivision thereof. Any violation of such standards in any transaction in or affecting interstate or foreign commerce shall be deemed an unfair method of competition in commerce within the meaning of the Federal Trade Commission Act. . . .

"(f) When a code of fair competition has been approved or prescribed by the President under this title, any violation of any provision thereof in any transaction in or affecting interstate or foreign commerce shall be a misdemeanor and upon conviction thereof an offender shall be fined not more than $500 for each offense, and each day such violation continues shall be deemed a separate offense." 48 Stat. 196–197 (1933).

The Schechter Poultry Corp. had been prosecuted under subsection (f) for violation of a "Live Poultry Code" adopted under the procedures of subsection (a) to govern the poultry trade in New York City. This was the major test of the NIRA, and the Court's reaction was sweeping. Chief Justice Hughes again delivered the opinion of the Court, which held the code-making authority conferred by § 3 to be an unconstitutional delegation. As in Panama Refining, the Chief Justice considered the various provisions of Title I of the Act; he concluded that none of them adequately cabined the President's authority to approve or prescribe codes of fair competition.

To reach this result, the Chief Justice had to distinguish a number of previous decisions upholding delegations with arguably vacuous standards to other authorities. Those precedents had upheld delegations of power to the Federal Trade Commission to prevent "unfair methods of competition," to the Interstate Commerce Commission to permit the acquisition by one carrier of the control of another if the acquisition were found to be "in the public interest," and to the Federal Radio Commission to issue licenses "as the public convenience, interest or necessity requires." In distinguishing each of these prior delegations, the Court emphasized the difference in procedure. In the case of the Federal Trade Commission, for example, "Congress set up a special procedure. A Commission, a quasi-judicial body, was created. Provision was made for formal complaint, for notice and hearing, for appropriate findings of fact supported by adequate evidence, and for judicial review to give assurance that the action of the Commission is taken within its statutory authority." The Interstate Commerce Commission and the Federal Radio Commission were similarly constrained. But "the National Industrial Recovery Act dispenses with this administrative procedure and with any administrative procedure of an analogous character."

Justice Cardozo wrote a concurring opinion, a portion of which is reproduced here:

"The delegated power of legislation which has found expression in this code is not canalized within banks that keep it from overflowing. It is unconfined and vagrant, if I may borrow my own words in an earlier opinion. Panama Refining Co. v. Ryan, 293 U.S. 388, 440. . . . Here, in the case before us, is an attempted delegation not confined to any single act nor to any class or group of acts identified or described by reference to a standard. Here in effect is a roving commission to inquire into evils and upon discovery correct them.

"I have said that there is no standard, definite or even approximate, to which legislation must conform. Let me make my meaning more precise. If codes of fair competition are codes eliminating 'unfair' methods of competition ascertained upon inquiry to prevail in one industry or another, there is no unlawful delegation of legislative functions when the President is directed to inquire into such practices and denounce them when discovered. For many years a like power has been committed to the Federal Trade Commission with the approval of this court in a long series of decisions. Cf. Federal Trade Comm'n v. Keppel & Bro., 291 U.S. 304, 312; Federal Trade Comm'n v. Raladam Co., 283 U.S. 643, 648; Federal Trade Comm'n v. Gratz, 253 U.S. 421. Delegation in such circumstances is born of the necessities of the occasion. The industries of the country are too many and diverse to make it possible for Congress, in respect of matters such as these, to legislate directly with adequate appreciation of varying conditions. Nor is the substance of the power changed because the President may act at the instance of trade or industrial associations having special knowledge of the facts. Their function is strictly advisory; it is the imprimatur of the President that begets the quality of law. Doty v. Love, 295 U.S. at 64. When the task that is set before one is that of cleaning house, it is prudent as well as usual to take counsel of the dwellers.

"But there is another conception of codes of fair competition, their significance and function, which leads to very different consequences, though it is one that is struggling now for recognition and acceptance. By this other conception a code is not to be restricted to the elimination of business practices that would be characterized by general acceptance as oppressive or unfair. It is to include whatever ordinances may be desirable or helpful for the well-being or prosperity of the industry affected. In that view, the function of its adoption is not merely negative, but positive; the planning of improvements as well as the extirpation of abuses. What is fair, as thus conceived, is not something to be contrasted with what is unfair or fraudulent or tricky. The extension becomes as wide as the field of industrial regulation. If that conception shall prevail, anything that Congress may do within the limits of the commerce clause for the betterment of business may be done by the President upon the recommendation of a trade association by calling it a code. This is delegation running riot. No such plenitude of power is susceptible of transfer. The statute, however, aims at nothing less, as one can learn both from its terms and from the administrative practice under it. Nothing less is aimed at by the code now submitted to our scrutiny."

(c) *From The New Deal To 1980*

As Justice Rehnquist's dissent itself reflects, Panama and Schechter did not stop the steady transfer by Congress of law-making power to administrators. Up to 1980 (and since, despite Justice Rehnquist's efforts) the Supreme Court has continued to sustain such delegations and, indeed, the delegation argument has continued to be regarded as weak. Two cases deserve particular mention:

(1) YAKUS v. UNITED STATES, 321 U.S. 414 (1944). The Emergency Price Control Act of 1942 directed the Price Administrator to adopt and issue regulations or orders fixing maximum prices of commodities and rents. Section 2(a) authorized the Administrator to promulgate regulations fixing prices of commodities which "in his judgment will be generally fair and equitable and will effectuate the purposes of this Act," namely to "stabilize prices and to prevent speculative, unwarranted, and abnormal increases in prices and rents; to eliminate and prevent profiteering, hoarding, manipulation, speculation and other disruptive practices resulting from abnormal market conditions or scarcities caused by or contributing to the national emergency; to assure that defense appropriations are not dissipated by excessive prices; to protect persons with relatively fixed and limited incomes, consumers, wage earners, investors, and persons dependent on life insurance, annuities, and pensions, from undue impairment of their standard of living; to prevent hardships to persons engaged in business, . . . and to the Federal, State, and local governments, which would result from abnormal increases in prices; to assist in securing adequate production of commodities and facilities; to prevent post emergency collapse of values; . . . " The Act also provided that "So far as practicable . . . the Administrator shall ascertain and give due consideration to the prices prevailing between October 1 and October 15, 1941. . . . " The Administrator was also to set forth a "statement of the considerations involved" in prescribing prices.

Petitioners were convicted of selling beef at prices above the maximum prescribed by the Administrator. Their convictions were affirmed by the Supreme Court, which held, per Stone, C.J., that the Act did not unconstitutionally delegate legislative power. Congress need not itself make detailed determinations, even though they be of a legislative nature—for, as the Chief Justice put it, "The Constitution as a continuously operative charter of government does not demand the impossible or the impracticable. . . . [T]he only concern of courts is to ascertain whether the will of Congress has been obeyed. This depends not upon the breadth of the definition of the facts or conditions which the administrative officer is to find but upon the determination whether the definition sufficiently marks the field within which the Administrator is to act so that it may be known whether he has kept within it in compliance with the legislative will. . . .

"Congress is not confined to that method of executing its policy which involves the least possible delegation of discretion to administrative officers. . . . It is free to avoid the rigidity of such a system, which might well result in serious hardship, and to choose instead the flexibility attainable by the use of less restrictive standards. . . . Only if we could say that there is an absence of standards for the guidance of the Administrator's action, so that it would be impossible in a proper proceeding to ascertain whether the will of Congress has been obeyed, would we be justified in overriding its choice of means for effecting its declared purpose of preventing inflation.

"The standards prescribed by the present Act, with the aid of the 'statement of considerations' required to be made by the Administrator, are sufficiently definite and precise to enable Congress, the courts and the public to ascertain whether the Administrator, in fixing the designated prices, has conformed to those standards. . . . Hence we are unable to find in them an unauthorized delegation of legislative power." Roberts, J., dissented.

(2) ARIZONA v. CALIFORNIA, 373 U.S. 546 (1963). The Boulder Canyon Project Act of 1928, which began the process of major dam and canal building that has made possible impounding waters for use in the arid southwest, gave the Secretary of the Interior vast power to choose among water users and to settle the terms of contracts when apportioning impounded waters. He was instructed to be mindful of an order of priorities—first, river regulation and flood control; second, irrigation and domestic uses and satisfaction of "present perfected rights" to use the Colorado's flow; and, third, power production. The importance of the rights thus to be allocated produced protracted legislative and litigative battles among Arizona, California, and other states over dividing the waters of the Colorado River and its tributaries. The Court did not even debate whether so gigantic a range of choice could validly be given. Referring to the network of river projects initiated by the United States, the Court said: "All this vast, interlocking machinery—a dozen major works delivering water according to congressionally fixed priorities for home, agricultural, and industrial uses to people spread over thousands of square miles—could function efficiently only under unitary management, able to formulate and supervise a coordinated plan that could take account of the diverse, often conflicting interests of the people and community of the Lower Basin States. Recognizing this, Congress put the Secretary of the Interior in charge of these works and entrusted him with sufficient power, principally the § 5 contract power, to direct, manage, and coordinate their operation."

Later in its opinion, commenting on parties' expressed fear that the Secretary might abuse some of the conflicting states' interests in times of water shortage, the Court remarked that no problem of this kind existed at the moment—and, anyway, "Congress still has broad powers over this navigable international stream. Congress can undoubtedly reduce or enlarge the Secretary's power if it wishes. Unless and until it does so, we leave in the hands of the Secretary, where Congress has placed it, full power to control, manage, and operate the Government's Colorado River works and to make contracts for the sale and delivery of water on such terms as are not prohibited by the Project Act."

Justice Harlan's partial dissent, more than once cited by Justice Rehnquist, was joined by Justices Douglas and Stewart. He protested (at 625–627) that the Secretary's authority was wholly undefined by standards. "Under the Court's construction of the Act, in other words, Congress has made a gift to the Secretary of almost 1,500,000 acre-feet of water a year, to allocate virtually as he pleases in the event of any shortage. . . .

"The delegation of such unrestrained authority to an executive official raises, to say the least, the gravest constitutional doubts. See Schechter Poultry Corp. v. United States, 295 U.S. 495; Panama Refining Co. v. Ryan, 293 U.S. 388; cf. Youngstown Sheet & Tube Co. v. Sawyer, 343 U.S. 579, 587–589. The principle that authority granted by the legislature must be limited by adequate standards serves two primary functions vital to preserving the separation of powers required by the Constitution. First, it insures that the fundamental policy decisions in our society will be made not by an appointed official but by the body immediately responsible to the people. Second, it prevents judicial review from becoming merely an exercise at large by providing the courts with some measure against which to judge the official action that has been challenged. . . .

". . . The unrestrained power to determine the burden of shortages is the power to make a political decision of the highest order. Indeed, the political pressures that will doubtless be brought to bear on the Secretary as a result of this decision are disturbing to contemplate. Furthermore, whatever the Secretary decides to do, this Court will surely be unable effectively to review his actions, since it will not know what guides were intended by Congress to govern those actions.

"These substantial constitutional doubts do not, of course, lead to the conclusion that the Project Act must be held invalid. Rather, they buttress the conviction, already firmly grounded in the Act and its history, that no such authority was vested in the Secretary by Congress. Its purpose instead was to leave these matters to state law, and developed principles of equitable apportionment, subject only to the explicit exceptions provided in the Act." [6]

(4) The scholarly literature concerning the delegation doctrine is, as one would imagine, enormous. Here is a small sampling:

(a) THEODORE LOWI, THE END OF LIBERALISM 298–299 (1969): There is . . . no reason to fear reduction of government power as a result of

---

6. See also the concurrence filed by Justice Brennan in United States v. Robel, 389 U.S. 258 (1967), an opinion on which Justice Rehnquist also relies: "Formulation of policy is a legislature's primary responsibility, entrusted to it by the electorate, and to the extent Congress delegates authority under indefinite standards, this policy-making function is passed on to other agencies, often not answerable or responsive in the same degree to the people."

serious application of the Schechter rule. . . . Interest-group liberals have less to fear from the rule-of-law requirement than they might have thought. . . . [T]he laissez-faire hope that such a requirement would help keep government small is based on a misunderstanding of the principle . . . Historically, rule of law, especially statute law, is the essence of positive government. A bureaucracy in the service of a strong and clear statute is more effective than ever. Granted, the rule-of-law requirement is likely to make more difficult the framing and passage of some policies. But why should any program be acceptable if the partisans cannot fairly clearly state purpose and means? We ask such justification even of children. It may also be true that requirement of rule of law will make government response to demands a bit slower and government implementation of goals less efficient. Good statistical analysis of the record would probably not support such a hypothesis; but even if the hypothesis were fully confirmed, one must still ask, What good is all our prosperity if we cannot buy a little more law with it?

(b) JOHN HART ELY, DEMOCRACY AND DISTRUST, A THEORY OF JUDICIAL REVIEW, 131–33 (1980): [T]he fact seems to be that on most hard issues our representatives quite shrewdly prefer not to have to stand up and be counted but rather to let some executive-branch bureaucrat, or perhaps some independent regulatory commission, "take the inevitable political heat." As Congressman Levitas put it, "When hard decisions have to be made, we pass the buck to the agencies with vaguely worded statutes." . . .

Now this is wrong, not because it isn't "the way it was meant to be" . . . but rather because it is undemocratic, in the quite obvious sense that by refusing to legislate, our legislators are escaping the sort of accountability that is crucial to the intelligible functioning of a democratic republic. . . . Coming along when it did, [in 1935,] the nondelegation doctrine became identified with others that were used in the early thirties to invalidate reform legislation, such as substantive due process and a restrictive interpretation of the commerce power—in fact Schechter itself featured the latter as an alternative holding—and when those doctrines died the nondelegation doctrine died along with them. (It was, of course, part of the New Deal religion that policy should be made by "experts.") Since that time Congress has quite commonly by statute said to administrative officials, in essence, "Find the problems in this area and solve them," and the Court, when the question has even been raised, has upheld the delegation. Writing in 1974, Justice Marshall accurately summarized the doctrine's contemporary standing: "The notion that the Constitution narrowly confines the power of Congress to delegate authority to administrative agencies, which was briefly in vogue in the 1930's, has been virtually abandoned by the Court for all practical purposes . . . This doctrine is surely as moribund as the substantive due process approach of the same era—for which the Court is fond of writing an obituary . . . if not more so. . . . "

It's a case of death by association, though. There can be little point in worrying about the distribution of the franchise and other personal political rights unless the important policy choices are being made by elected officials. Courts thus should ensure not only that administrators follow those legislative policy directions that do exist . . . but also that such directions are given.

(c) KENNETH C. DAVIS, DISCRETIONARY JUSTICE 47–50 (1969): Judge Henry Friendly, in an especially perceptive little book, The Federal Administrative Agencies, has written: "We still live under a Constitution which provides that 'all legislative Powers herein granted shall be vested in a Congress of the United States, which shall consist of a Senate and House of Representatives'; even if a statute telling an agency 'Here is the problem: deal with it' be deemed to comply with the letter of that command, it hardly does with the spirit." Although I agree with the main thrust of Judge Friendly's excellent book, this particular thought seems to me unsound and harmful. The remark is opposed to dozens of Supreme Court decisions upholding such delegations, it wrongly assumes that the words "all legislative Powers" do not include the power to determine how much delegation is desirable, it does not mention the power "to make all Laws which shall be necessary and proper for carrying into Execution the foregoing Powers," and it ignores the realities that impel legislative bodies to delegate as they do.

The first Congress, made up largely of the same men who wrote the Constitution, did not bother with standards when it delegated to the courts the power "to make and establish all necessary rules for the orderly conducting of business in the said courts, provided such rules are not repugnant to the laws of the United States";[7] . . . when it provided for military pensions "under such regulations as the President of the United States may direct";[8] . . . when it conferred discretionary power upon the Secretary of the Treasury to mitigate or remit fines and forfeitures in designated circumstances, without requiring him to mitigate or remit.[9] Nor did the first Congress define the word "proper" in authorizing superintendents to license "any proper person" to engage in trade or intercourse with the Indian tribes; it provided no standard to guide the President in providing that such superintendents "shall be governed in all things touching the said trade and intercourse, by such rules and regulations as the President shall prescribe."[10] I think it fair to say that Judge Friendly finds a "spirit" in the Constitution that members of the first Congress did not find there, even though many of them had participated in drafting the Constitution.

(d) J. SKELLY WRIGHT, REVIEW: BEYOND DISCRETIONARY JUSTICE, 81 Yale L.J. 575, 584–86 (1972): Ultimately, the arguments for broad delegation rest on the illusion that problems are solved by conflict avoidance. Congress, for one reason or another, cannot deal with a problem, so it passes some "soft" statutes which throw the mess into the lap of an administrative agency. Such a broad delegation can yield only two possible results, both of which are unfortunate. On the one hand, if the problem is really intractable, it is unlikely that the agency, with all its expertise, will do any better with it than Congress. Indeed, if there is political opposition to any contemplated action, the agency

7. 1 Stat. 83.

8. 1 Stat. 95.

9. 1 Stat. 123.

10. 1 Stat. 137.

may actually be more vulnerable than Congress. . . . Alternatively, it is possible that the agency will be able to deal with the problem forcefully. It may be that the agency is sufficiently insulated from political pressure so that it can take action which would have been unavailable to Congress, or that Congress is badly split while the agency is united. In this situation, a strong agency will be able to formulate prospective rules, develop a clear sense of purpose, and minimize unnecessary discretion. But these goals will have been accomplished at the expense of democratic decisionmaking. The putatively substantial portion of the electorate which opposes the agency action, or which is merely uncertain as to its wisdom, is likely to believe—and with some justification—that Congress has done through the back door what it could not accomplish in direct, democratic fashion.

(e) RICHARD B. STEWART, THE REFORMATION OF AMERICAN ADMINISTRATIVE LAW, 89 Harv.L.Rev. 1667, 1696–97 (1975): How does the judge differentiate [cases in which the legislature has been as specific as circumstances permit] from those where the legislature is avoiding its "proper" responsibilities? Such judgments are necessarily quite subjective, and a doctrine that made them determinative of an administrative program's legitimacy could cripple the program by exposing it to continuing threats of invalidation and encouraging the utmost recalcitrance by those opposed to its effectuation. Given such subjective standards, and the controversial character of decisions on whether to invalidate legislative delegations, such decisions will almost inevitably appear partisan, and might often be so.

This is not to deny the possibility of a more modestly conceived judicial role in policing legislative delegation of discretionary choices to agencies. Courts have applied policies of clear statement to construe narrowly statutory delegations that infringe important individual interests. Were policies of clear statement applied in the context of economic and social administration, Congress would at least have to take a fresh look at the agency's mandate before its powers were extended. Accordingly, a policy of narrow construction of statutory delegations might usefully be followed, but adoption of such a policy would hardly represent the large-scale revival of the nondelegation doctrine envisaged by Professor Lowi and Judge Wright. Obtaining greater specificity in regulatory statutes is essentially a political problem, and even if judges were to hazard a more venturesome approach, any remotely tolerable application of the nondelegation doctrine would be limited to gross instances of legislative irresponsibility.

(f) ALEXANDER M. BICKEL, THE LEAST DANGEROUS BRANCH, 160–61 (1962): To say that the doctrine of delegation is concerned with the separation of powers is merely to invoke a symbol. No doubt, as one of its side effects, it tends to support the checks and balances of the system, but the important checks and counter-checks are, after all, built into the governmental scheme in more binding ways. To say that the doctrine facilitates control by the Court of official action that might otherwise be erratic or capricious is, again, to notice a byproduct and to beg the question somewhat by assuming that judicial control (the irresponsible leading the unrepresentative) is necessary or desirable and can be effective. Other controls are possible and have been tried— through the President alone exercising power to appoint, remove, and guide; through either House or through Congress as a whole, acting by simple or concurrent resolution without approval of the President; and through committees of Congress. These mechanisms share with judicial control and administrative policy-making the fault of electoral irresponsibility or, at best, fragmented responsibility. The doctrine of delegation is concerned with the sources of policy, with the crucial joinder between power and broadly based democratic responsibility, bestowed and discharged after the fashion of representative government. . . .

"Delegation of power to administration is," however, "the dynamo of the modern social service state." It has made possible the vast, pervasive growth of the administrative process, which few now would, and no one could, abolish. When should the Court recall the legislature to its own policy-making function? Obviously, the answer must lie in the importance of the decision left to the administrator or other official. And this is a judgment that will naturally be affected by the proximity of the area of delegated discretion to a constitutional issue. The more fundamental the issue, the nearer it is to principle, the more important it is that it be decided in the first instance by the legislature.

(g) GERALD FRUG, THE IDEOLOGY OF BUREAUCRACY IN AMERICAN LAW, 97 HARV.L.REV. 1276, 1302–03 (1984): . . . The nondelegation doctrine is thus crucially dependent on the lines it seeks to draw between the appropriate functions of the legislature and those of the bureaucracy, between legitimate and illegitimate legislative decisions to delegate power, and between the proper kind of bureaucratic subjectivity and its needed objectivity.

In an attempt to draw these lines, the courts have articulated a series of "tests" that a delegation of power must meet in order to be constitutional: the legislature must lay down an "intelligible principle," decide the "fundamental policy questions," exercise the "essentials" of the legislative function. These tests appear harmoniously to combine subjectivity and objectivity—they comfort us by suggesting that, if they are met, there will be adequate legislative decisionmaking to ensure meaningful bureaucratic objectivity, yet not so much legislative decisionmaking as to prevent needed bureaucratic discretion. . . . But while their strength lies in their ability to suggest that, if they are properly applied, everything will be all right, their weakness lies in their inability to generate any consistent application. Legal argument about nondelegation consists of applying these tests to specific delegations of power, applications that generate contradictory conclusions: any delegation both does and does not satisfy the relevant tests.

(5) A number of the preceding excerpts, perhaps especially Professor Frug's, suggest the utility of viewing the "delegation" doctrine not in isolation, but as only one of a number of tools available for promoting the effective subservience of administrators to the controls of law. What does it mean, for example, to say that a legislature had delegated

some of its authority when, having acted, it continued to sit with authority to recall what it had done? To what extent should courts consider to whom a power has been delegated, and how susceptible that delegate is to continuing control by other parts of government (or, more broadly, the people as a whole)? Consider, too, whether the record of judicial use of "delegation" is the only measure by which the doctrine's success should be judged. If, for example, successful invocation of "delegation" is likely to occur only if a court can be persuaded that some agency has been placed beyond the possibility of effective control, wouldn't that lead you, as a government lawyer, to argue at all times that effective legal controls *were* available and to advise your client to structure its actions in ways that tended to support that argument? The casebook editors do not know of many instances in which government officials have claimed in court that standards were lacking on the basis of which the lawfulness of their regulatory actions could be assessed.[1] Insofar as "delegation" concerns issues of effective control of government actors, inducing respect for the obligation to act in ways demonstrably in accordance with law may itself be the measure of the doctrine's success. We need not expect to find unconstitutional delegations among statutes any more frequently than we find murderers among the populace. Insofar as "delegation" concerns John Locke's proposition, on the other hand, it must be regarded as a failure; recognition of the extent to which administrative agencies do make law—of the extent to which the legislature has created other legislators who are not directly responsible to the people—is precisely that characteristic of the administrative state most animating today's discussions of the intensity of judicial review, the appropriate breadth of intervention in administrative proceedings, and the like.

The cases cited by Justice Rehnquist in Part III of his dissent, American Power & Light Co. v. SEC and Lichter v. United States, are readily understood as resting on assurances of effective control arising outside the statute itself. Other frequently-cited cases of this character are FAHEY v. MALLONEE, 332 U.S. 245 (1947) and AMALGAMATED MEAT CUTTERS & BUTCHER WORKMEN v. CONNALLY, 337 F.Supp. 737 (D.D.C.1971). Fahey concerned a statute granting sweeping authority to bank regulator;[2] the Court sustained this seemingly standardless delegation without difficulty:

> Banking is one of the longest regulated and most closely supervised of public callings. It is one in which accumulated experience of supervisors, acting for many states under various statutes, has established well-defined practices for the appointment of conservators, receivers and liquidators. Corporate

1. Cf. The discussion within, in Chapter 9, Section 2, of the problem when judicial review of agency discretion is precluded by law.

2. Section 5(d) of the Home Owners' Loan Act gave the Federal Home Loan Bank Board "full power to provide in the rules and regulations herein authorized for the reorganization, consolidation, merger, or liquidation of such associations, including the power to appoint a conservator or a receiver to take charge of the affairs of any such association, and to require an equitable readjustment of the capital structure of the same; and to release any such association from such control and permit its further operation."

management is a field, too, in which courts have experience and many precedents have crystallized into well-known and generally acceptable standards. A discretion to make regulations to guide supervisory action in such matters may be constitutionally permissible while it might not be allowable to authorize creation of new crimes in uncharted fields.

Amalgamated Meat Cutters concerned § 202 of the Economic Stabilization Act of 1970, which authorized the President "to issue such orders and regulations as he may deem appropriate to stabilize prices, rents, wages, and salaries at levels not less than those prevailing on May 25, 1970. Such orders and regulations may provide for the making of such adjustments as may be necessary to prevent gross inequities." In sustaining the statute, the court accepted the government's concession that its authority was constrained by the patterns "of wage and price controls in two wars. The administrative practice under both of those Acts was the subject of extensive judicial interpretation and review. This substantial background of prior law and practice provides a further framework for assessing whether the Executive has stayed within the bounds authorized by Congress and provides more than adequate standards for the exercise of the authority granted by the Act."

From this perspective, the issue *is* the possibility of effective control, rather than delegation as such. Consider whether Panama Refining and Schechter Poultry may be understood just this way and, in this light, the following further views of Professor Kenneth C. Davis:

"Five principal steps should be taken to alter the non-delegation doctrine and to move toward a system of judicial protection against unnecessary and uncontrolled discretionary power: (a) the purpose of the non-delegation doctrine should no longer be either to prevent delegation or to require meaningful statutory standards; the purpose should be the much deeper one of protecting against unnecessary and uncontrolled discretionary power; (b) the exclusive focus on standards should be shifted to an emphasis more on safeguards than on standards; (c) when legislative bodies have failed to provide standards, the courts should not hold the delegation unlawful but should require that the administrators must as rapidly as feasible supply the standards; (d) the non-delegation doctrine should gradually grow into a broad requirement extending beyond the subject of delegation—that officers with discretionary power must do about as much as feasible to structure their discretion through appropriate safeguards and to confine and guide their discretion through standards, principles, and rules; (e) the protection should reach not merely delegated power but also such undelegated power as that of selective enforcement." 1 K. Davis, Admin.L.Treatise 207–208 (2d ed. 1978).

(6) While Justice Rehnquist's opinion takes the more radical stance, one ought not forget that Justice Stevens' opinion in the Benzene case, speaking as well for Chief Justice Burger and Justice Stewart, also cites Schechter Poultry and Panama Refining. The Chief Justice would join Justice Rehnquist's view in a subsequent OSHA

dispute over the validity of rules regulating cotton dust, American Textile Mfrs. Inst., Inc. v. Donovan, 452 U.S. 490 (1981). Justice Stevens' proposition is that the statute should be construed to avoid giving the agency an "open-ended grant," in order to avoid raising the constitutional issue of delegation. There is a long tradition of construing statutes to avoid raising constitutional issues of all sorts, and Justice Stevens' opinion is not the first to use this technique to narrow an administrative delegation.

KENT v. DULLES, 357 U.S. 116 (1958), is a well-known exemplar of this approach. The Passport Act of 1926 codified the authority of the Secretary of State to "grant and issue passports . . . under such rules as the President shall designate and prescribe." Executive Order No. 7856 authorized the Secretary of State "in his discretion to refuse to issue a passport." In 1952 the Secretary promulgated a regulation prohibiting issuance of passports to members or supporters of the Communist Party, or persons believed to be going abroad in order to advance the Communist movement. Another regulation required passport applicants to execute an affidavit concerning past or present membership in the Communist Party. Kent's application for a passport was denied because he refused to execute the affidavit and also because he was thought to be a Communist who had "a consistent and prolonged adherence to the Communist Party line." On review of lower court decisions denying Kent's petition for declaratory relief, the Supreme Court reversed.

Writing for the Court, Justice Douglas began by finding a threat to Kent's civil liberties. The "right to travel is a part of the 'liberty' of which the citizen cannot be deprived without due process of law. . . . If that 'liberty' is to be regulated, it must be pursuant to the lawmaking functions of the Congress. And if that power is delegated, the standards must be adequate to pass scrutiny by the accepted tests. See Panama Refining Co. v. Ryan, 293 U.S. 388, 420–430. Where such activities . . . are involved, we will construe narrowly all delegated powers that curtail or dilute them. . . . We hesitate to find in this broad generalized power an authority to trench so heavily on the rights of the citizen.

"We would be faced with important constitutional questions were we to hold that Congress . . . had given the Secretary authority to withhold passports to citizens because of their beliefs or associations. Congress has made no such provision in explicit terms; and absent one, the Secretary may not employ that standard to restrict the citizens' right of free movement."

The Court's construction that the statute did not delegate power to refuse a passport because of beliefs or associations was not based wholly on air or a judicial wish to avoid difficult issues. Prior to the Passport Act of 1926 the seemingly broad power of the Secretary of State to refuse passports had in practice been exercised only in two categories of cases: (1) lack of citizenship or allegiance and (2) illegal conduct. The Court drew on this administrative practice in refusing to impute to Congress an intention to give the Secretary an "unbridled discretion to grant or withhold a passport from a citizen for any substantive reason he may choose."

Nonetheless, four Justices (Clark, Burton, Harlan and Whittaker) sharply disagreed with the majority's interpretation of the statute, drawing on legislative history suggesting that when Congress acted to restrict travel abroad it seems to have acted on the assumption that the executive had power to deny a passport to any person whose activities abroad were thought to be detrimental to the United States. See Note, The Supreme Court, 1957 Term, 72 Harv.L.Rev. 96, 175 (1958).[3]

Is Justice Stevens' construction of a statute to avoid giving an agency "unprecedented power over American industry" similar to the analyses in Kent v. Dulles? Would a general requirement of "clear statement" by the legislature present the same problems for the relationship between court and legislature as does the "unconstitutionality" approach of the delegation doctrine?

(7) CHEVRON, U.S.A. INC. v. NATURAL RESOURCES DEFENSE COUNCIL, 467 U.S. 837 (1984)[4] is a more recent opinion by Justice Stevens, and strongly suggests that neither he nor the Court as a whole perceives any general difficulty in legislation leaving important legal questions for agency decision when Congress has been unable to agree. Before the Court was the question whether the Administrator of the Environmental Protection Agency was authorized to adopt a regulation permitting an industrial complex to be treated as if all its pollution-emitting sources were within a single "bubble," rather than independent sources each subject to regulation. The Court concluded, on a preliminary inquiry, that Congress "has not directly addressed the precise question at issue." Once this conclusion is reached, observed the Court, the question before a reviewing court is "not whether in its view the [bubble] concept is 'inappropriate' in the general context of a program designed to improve air quality, but whether the Administrator's view that it is appropriate in the context of this particular program is a reasonable one." The authority thus recognized in the agency was underscored by the Court's recognition that the question presented was one of statutory interpretation rather than application, and that it was a question that might have no determinate answer. "Perhaps [Congress] consciously desired the Administrator to strike the balance [between conflicting policies as she had done], thinking that those with great expertise and charged with responsibility for administering the provision would be in a better position to do so. Perhaps it simply did

3. Compare Haig v. Agee, 453 U.S. 280 (1981). Here the Court upheld the denial of a passport under the Passport Act; the government had asserted that Mr. Agee's travel would present a threat to national security and foreign policy, because he was engaged in a campaign to expose CIA operatives. In support of its action the government relied upon an executive practice of denying passports to security risks—a practice concededly infrequent but, the majority asserted, consistent; "the continued validity of the power is not diluted simply because there is no need to use it." The majority explained that the failure to give effect to the asserted executive policy or construction in Kent had been based on the absence of any consistent pattern in government action, and a threat to First Amendment concerns unbalanced by issues of national security. Justices Brennan and Marshall dissented.

4. The case is considered more fully within at p. 405.

not consider the question at this level; *and perhaps Congress was unable to forge a coalition on either side of the question, and those on each side decided to take their chances with the scheme devised by the agency.* [Emphasis added] For judicial purposes, it matters not which of these things occurred.

"Judges are not experts in the field, and are not part of either political branch of the Government. Courts must, in some cases, reconcile competing political interests, but not on the basis of the judges' personal policy preferences. In contrast, an agency to which Congress has delegated policymaking responsibilities may, within the limits of that delegation, properly rely upon the incumbent administration's views of wise policy to inform its judgments. While agencies are not directly accountable to the people, the Chief Executive is, and it is entirely appropriate for this political branch of the Government to make such policy choices—resolving the competing interests which Congress itself either inadvertently did not resolve, or intentionally left to be resolved by the agency charged with the administration of the statute in light of everyday realities.

"When a challenge to an agency construction of a statutory provision, fairly conceptualized, really centers on the wisdom of the agency's policy, rather than whether it is a reasonable choice within a gap left open by Congress, the challenge must fail. In such a case, federal judges—who have no constituency—have a duty to respect legitimate policy choices made by those who do. The responsibilities for assessing the wisdom of such policy choices and resolving the struggle between competing views of the public interest are not judicial ones. . . . 'Our Constitution vests such responsibilities in the political branches.' TVA v. Hill, 437 U.S. 153, 195 (1978)." [5]

(8) JERRY L. MASHAW, PRODELEGATION: WHY ADMINISTRATORS SHOULD MAKE POLITICAL DECISIONS, 1 J.Law, Ec. & Org. 81, 95–99 (1985),* draws on ideas like those expressed in the paragraphs just quoted to make an affirmative case for broad delegations. Critically reviewing the critical literature, he finds "no strong reason to believe that broad delegations of authority either delegitimize governance or produce systematically negative welfare effects." Agency action is subject to controls of a different order than legislative action.

"Does judicial review or OMB oversight ensure that agency choices will always have positive welfare effects? Hardly. Yet it is also clear that executive branch requirements that cost-benefit analyses of agency regulations be prepared, and court demands that agency explanations for rules demonstrate a reasoned assessment of competing values, surely press agencies in the direction of cost-minimizing or welfare-enhancing action. No such constraints would operate on specific legis-

---

5. The opinion was unanimous, Justices Marshall, Rehnquist and O'Connor not participating. Of course, determining whether Congress had an ascertainable intent with respect to some controverted issue will often prove difficult. See Chemical Mfrs. Assn. v. Natural Resources Defense Council, 470 U.S. 116 (1985) and more generally, Chapter 3, Section 4 within.

* Reprinted with the permission of the author and publisher.

lative choices (see, e.g., National Tire Dealers and Retreaders Association v. Brinegar, 491 F.2d 31 (D.C.Cir.1974)). . . .

"Strangely enough it may [also] make sense to imagine the delegation of political authority to administrators as a device for improving the responsiveness of government to the desires of the electorate. This argument can be made even if we accept many of the insights of the political and economic literature that premises its predictions of congressional and voter behavior on a direct linkage between benefits transferred to constituents and the election or reelection of representatives. All we need do is not forget there are also presidential elections and that, as the Supreme Court reminds us in Chevron, presidents are heads of administrations.

"Assume then that voters view the election of representatives to Congress through the lens of the most cynical interpretation of the modern political science literature on congressional behavior. . . . The voter's vision of presidential electoral politics is arguably quite different. The president has no particular constituency to which he or she has special responsibility to deliver benefits. Presidents are hardly cut off from pork-barrel politics. Yet issues of national scope and the candidates' positions on those issues are the essence of presidential politics. Citizens vote for a president based almost wholly on a perception of the difference that one or another candidate might make to general governmental policies.

"If this description of voting in national elections is reasonably plausible, then the utilization of vague delegations to administrative agencies takes on significance as a device for facilitating responsiveness to voter preferences expressed in presidential elections. The high transactions costs of legislating specifically suggests that legislative activity directed to the modification of administration mandates will be infrequent. Agencies will thus persist with their statutory empowering provisions relatively intact over substantial periods of time. Voter preferences on the direction and intensity of governmental activities however, are not likely to be so stable. Indeed, one can reasonably expect that a president will be able to affect policy in a four-year term only because being elected president entails acquiring the power to exercise, direct, or influence policy discretion. The group of executive officers we commonly call 'the Administration' matters only because of the relative malleability of the directives that administrators have in their charge. . . . Even if Congress had adopted as legislation every specific and detailed rule that subsequently has been adopted by the Occupational Safety and Health Administration, the influence of the OSHA statute might still be vastly different (indeed has been vastly different) in the Carter and Reagan administrations. In the broadest term, the statute has had a different meaning in the years 1976 to 1980 than in the years 1980 to 1984.

. . .

"Responsiveness to diversity in voter preferences is not limited to changes through time. It is surely plausible to imagine that, with a large land area and a heterogeneous citizenry, governmental responsiveness also entails situational variance at any one time. If our laws were truly specific, this would also be impossible. We could not, for example, have local draft boards exercising their discretion in accordance with their perceptions of the tolerance of the local population for particular attempts at mobilization, or granting exceptions based upon their understanding of the legitimacy of particular excuses from the local point of view. We could not have a Social Security Disability program which harnesses the national government's advantage in the collection of taxes for redistributional purposes and employs a national general criterion of disability, while permitting flexible application that takes account of local attachment to the work ethic, local employment opportunities, and other variations that are likely to be peculiar to particular regions of the country. In short, we could not have laws that say, 'Do something, but be reasonable and take account of local differences.' Or at least we could not have them if our idea of democratic responsiveness is that the Congress as a body should make all the decisions necessary to give determinant meaning to the statutes that it passes.

. . .

"There is one additional reason to believe that broad delegations to administrators might improve responsiveness. . . . Administrators at least operate within a set of legal rules (administrative law) that keep them within their jurisdiction, require them to operate with a modicum of explanation and participation of the affected interests, police them for consistency, and protect them from the importuning of congressmen and others who would like to carry logrolling into the administrative process. In short, if we are uncertain about the responsiveness of majority rule voting procedures to citizens' or even legislators' desires, perhaps vague delegations to administrators can be a technique for avoiding the more disheartening aspects of the alternatives." [6]

b. Delegation in the States

In the states, the delegation doctrine retains a certain vitality.[1] This divergence in federal and state handling of the delegation problem cannot be explained in a single phrase.

6. [Ed.] Professor Mashaw's analysis speaks to a body of economic and social choice literature employing analytic concepts not generally developed in these materials. Correspondingly, much of that analysis has been edited out; hopefully without undue distortion. However, readers familiar with that literature will want to consult the original.

1. 1 Cooper, State Administrative Law 73–91 (1965), discusses the following "eleven factors that are believed to play a predominant part in the actual course of judicial decision" in state delegation cases: (1) delegation sustained, where reference to established legal concepts has effect of limiting discretion; (2) the tradition in a particular field may control decision; (3) discretion must be more strictly limited where substantial property interests are involved; (4) broad discretionary powers may be delegated, where judicial review is available to correct abuses; (5) broad delegations sustained where statute requires notice and hearing and fair administrative procedure; (6) broad delegations are upheld where there is an obvious need for expertise; (7) delegation of power to private groups is frowned upon; (8) broad discretionary powers may be delegated where public health, safety, or morals are significantly involved; (9) delegations of power to fix penalties are not favored; (10) courts insist on preserving essential inde-

To some extent the state holdings invalidating delegations may reflect judicial lack of sympathy with the substantive regulation at issue. But as Professor Louis L. Jaffe has noted, "Judicial antipathy to social legislation has not been the only factor contributing to . . . [uncertainty and subjectivism in state courts' interpretation of the delegation doctrine]. The state courts are troubled by the spectre of discriminatory administration. In the field of general business regulation state decisions are not notably different from the federal decisions. . . . It is when delegated power affects the use of real property or the practice of a profession that the judicial nerve tingles. The doctrine of delegation is then likely to be invoked against delegations which because of an uncertainty of standards (in phrase or in fact) encourage undetectable discrimination or subjective notions of policy." Judicial Control of Administrative Action 76–77 (1965).

Justice Hans A. Linde of the Supreme Court of Oregon (formerly of the University of Oregon law faculty) and Professors George Bunn, Fredericka Paff and W. Lawrence Church point out that although in theory the techniques used by the federal courts in coping with broad delegations are available to state courts, they tend not to utilize them. "They are more likely to hold a delegation invalid because too broad. And whether striking it down or upholding it, they are more likely to interpret it by reading its text without writing standards into it based on its history and probable purpose. The resulting case law is quite inconsistent."

The authors "speculate" as follows "on the reasons for this difference: (i) The typical paucity of legislative history of state laws makes resort to it less promising, and more haphazard and unreliable when attempted. (ii) While federal law is recognized to be almost wholly statutory, counsel and judges in state courts tend to approach a public law case from a common law background of practice and with common law rather than statute law methods of briefing and argument. (iii) There may be a different degree of institutional respect and deference toward the legislative branch and its products; in any event, state courts are far less reluctant to hold that a legislature has misconstrued and exceeded its powers than federal courts are to hold that Congress has done so. (iv) Similarly state courts may have a different, and realistic, view of the professional capacity and impartiality of many agencies to whom power is delegated in the states as compared with federal agencies. Often 'excessive delegation' seems to be employed by courts to strike down action that they deem unreasonable impositions on private parties.

"A special class of problems more common in state law is the delegation of public decision-making authority to private groups, or to representatives of private groups appointed to part-time public positions. Whether because of these institutional differences in the settings of state and federal judicial review or because of a more theoretical disagreement over the principle that legislatures can and should

pendence of the departments of government; (11) broad discretionary powers may   be delegated where proprietary functions are involved.

come to grips with the substance of the policies they delegate, state courts do differ among themselves and with federal courts on the constitutional significance of standards in delegation." [2]

Various aspects of the delegation doctrine in the states are developed in the materials which follow. Typically the materials deal with judicial reaction to a particular delegation in a concrete litigation context. This particularistic, case-law approach has obvious advantages. But emphasis on judicial action may tend to obscure the fact that the delegation problem has a large legislative and drafting component.

In considering these materials, in addition to appraising the judicial reaction to the delegation in question, the student should ask, "Had I participated in drafting the statute, what would I have proposed with respect to: (1) the kind of substantive power to be delegated—to manage government property, employ civil servants, enter into contracts, grant subsidies, award welfare benefits, require disclosure, publicize misdeeds, allocate scarce resources, issue licenses, fix rates, prices or wages, establish standards, impose fines, levy taxes, incarcerate offenders; (2) the statutory language to be used in directing the agency concerning its exercise of the delegated substantive power—general versus more specific directions; (3) the identity, character, selection process and tenure of the delegate—governor, cabinet officer, independent board or commission, local elected official, members or representatives of the regulated group, appointed by whom, with or without legislative approval, for what terms, subject to removal by whom and for what reasons; (4) the nature of the processes to be utilized in exercising the delegated substantive power—rulemaking, investigating, inspecting, testing, examining, requiring reports, jaw-boning, prosecuting, adjudicating; (5) procedural safeguards to be required—publication of, and conformance to, administrative standards, notice, hearing, statement of reasons; (6) ongoing legislative controls such as legislative veto, oversight committee, annual appropriations; (7) gubernatorial authority to direct or coordinate the exercise of the delegated power; (8) participation by interested members of the public—concerning what issues in what proceedings with or without public funding; (9) the availability and scope of judicial review; and (10) the proper balance between procedural-regulatory costs and substantive benefits?"

Publication of Administrative Rules

Absence of provision for adequate publication has sometimes induced judicial hostility toward delegated legislation. In Goodlove v. Logan, 217 Iowa 98, 251 N.W. 39 (1933), which involved the power of the state highway commission to adopt rules and regulations "for the protection of the highways and the safety of the traffic thereon," the court—in striking down the delegation—emphasized its concern about failure to publicize, as follows: "[H]ow is the individual using the

2. Linde, Bunn, Paff, and Church, Legislative and Administrative Processes 477–78 (2d ed. 1981).

highways to know what rules and regulations the highway commission passes? The highway commission meets at various and different times. It might pass some rule or regulation today and revoke it next week. There is no way that the people throughout this state could know just what were the rules and regulations that the highway commission adopted." Compare People v. Soule, 238 Mich. 130, 213 N.W. 195 (1927): A statute delegating the power to regulate fishing and hunting was upheld; the rules promulgated under the statute were required to be published three weeks before their effective date and periodically thereafter; the court felt that the statute deserved its enthusiastic applause, for it made possible an orderly and readily accessible body of regulations in place of the then "overwhelming volume of chaotic and more or less conflicting game and fish laws" scattered through the statute books.[3]

Organized publication has been surprisingly late in developing, but is now well established. At the federal level, the situation was chaotic until 1935, when the Panama Refining Co. case made clear the need for action.[4] Then the statutory creation of the Federal Register, an official gazette published every working day, provided a stable means of recordation and communication.[5] The new statute also provided for codification of documents of "general applicability and legal effect." The resulting Code of Federal Regulations is issued annually in fifty titles which roughly approximate the subject areas of the United States Code.[6]

As of 1965, fourteen states published administrative regulations in a general compilation.[7] A 1982 survey indicated that thirty-five states now do so; six others publish periodic registers of state regulations;

3. And see United States v. Howard, 352 U.S. 212 (1957), in which the Court upholding a conviction for disregard of a Florida agency's regulation, spoke with obviously warm approval of a requirement that amended regulations had to be filed in county courts and published in a newspaper in each county; moreover, the agency "compiles its rules in a code book which is circulated without cost" to anyone who wants it, and the agency conducts "public hearings to give everyone an opportunity to air his own views on proposed changes in the rules."

4. See E. Griswold, Government in Ignorance of the Law—A Plea for Better Publication of Executive Legislation, 48 Harv.L.Rev. 198 (1934).

5. The Federal Register Act, 49 Stat. 500 (1935), as amended 44 U.S.C. §§ 301–314 (1958). Compare F. Newman, Government and Ignorance—A Progress Report on Publication of Federal Regulations, 63 Harv.L.Rev. 929 (1950).

6. For more detailed explanation, see J. Jacobstein and R. Mersky, Legal Research Illustrated, Chapter 12 ("Administrative Law") (2d ed. 1981).

The Division of the Federal Register also publishes annually the United States Government Manual, which contains brief descriptions of agency organizations, delegations of authority, and other general information concerning the personnel and structure of the Federal Government. As to specifications concerning matters that must be published in the Federal Register, going far beyond the topic now under discussion, consult the Administrative Procedure Act, reproduced in Appendix I.

See also Note, The Federal Register and the Code of Federal Regulations—A Reappraisal, 80 Harv.L.Rev. 439, 451 (1966). For added information about administrative regulations and departmental rulings, consult L. Schmeckebier and R. Eastin, Government Publications and Their Use 300–329 (2d rev. ed. 1969).

7. Another eight required named agencies to publish their rules separately and forty-two states required administrative agencies to deposit their regulations in a central state office such as that of the Secretary of State. M. Cohen, Publication of State Administrative Regulations—Reform in Slow Motion, 14 Buff.L.Rev. 410, 421 (1965).

and most of the remaining nine jurisdictions have "administrative codes" on the drawing board.[8] Individual agencies in most states freely distribute their own regulations to persons who are occupationally or otherwise interested in them. Compliance with filing or publication requirements has been regarded by some state courts and legislators as an absolute precondition of a regulation's having legal effect.[9]

PEOPLE v. TIBBITTS

Supreme Court of Illinois, 1973.
56 Ill.2d 56, 305 N.E.2d 152.

[Section 4.1 of an Illinois statute creating a Commission on Human Relations provided that owners of residential property who did not wish to sell or be solicited to sell their property could so notify the Commission. The Commission was directed to "compile suitable lists by *area* of the names and addresses of owners of residential property who submit such forms . . . . The Commission shall cause copies of such lists to be mailed by certified mail to those real estate agents and brokers and other persons who are *known or believed by the Commission* to be soliciting owners of residential property for the sale or listing of such property *in the area* covered by such list." (Emphasis added.)

Section 70–51(d) of the Illinois Criminal Code provided as follows: "It shall be unlawful for any person or corporation knowingly: . . . [to] solicit any owner of residential property to sell or list such residential property at any time after such person or corporation has notice that such owner does not desire to sell such residential property or does not desire to be solicited to sell or list for sale such residential property. For the purpose of this paragraph a person has such notice (1) when the Human Relations Commission has mailed to him pursuant to Section 4.1 of 'An Act to create a Commission on Human Relations and to define its powers and duties', approved August 8, 1947, as now or hereafter amended, a list containing the name and address of such owner, or (2) when he has been notified in writing that the owner does not desire to sell or list for sale such residential property."

Those who violate this section of the criminal code are guilty of a Class A misdemeanor for the first offense and of a Class 4 felony for any subsequent offense.

8. E. Fox, Status of State Administrative Codes and Registers, 2 Leg.Ref.Serv.Q. 77 (Winter 1982); see also H. Tseng and D. Podersen: Acquisition of State Administrative Rules and Regulations—Update 1979, 31 Ad.L.Rev. 405 (1979); § 2–101 of the Model State Administrative Procedure Act (1981), p. 1248 infra.

9. See, e.g., N.Y.—McKinney's Administrative Proc. Act § 202(1)(a); and People v. Cull, 10 N.Y.2d 123, 218 N.Y.S.2d 38, 176 N.E.2d 495 (1961), discussed in R. Herman, The New York Rulemaking Process 47 Alb. L.Rev. 1051, 1069–1075 (1983): The state constitution requires that administrative rules and regulations be filed in a central state office. The court refused to sustain a motorist's conviction for driving at a speed exceeding that fixed in a particular zone by the State Traffic Commission. Highway signs had given the motorist actual notice of the speed limit. But the zone speed limit had not been filed in Albany. "The spirit and design of the constitutional provision," the court said, "are best effectuated by requiring the administrator, if he wishes the rules and regulations of his agency or department to be effective, to file them no matter what label is assigned to them."

Tibbitts was charged with violating section 70–51(d). The lower court held that section 70–51(d) was unconstitutional and the State of Illinois appealed. The Supreme Court of Illinois affirmed because "the statute which provides for the giving of the notice upon which the prosecution is based constitutes an unlawful delegation of legislative authority to the Human Relations Commission and is thus invalid."]

RYAN, JUSTICE. . . .

The statute does not define what constitutes an "area" and does not specifically state who has the authority to create them. We must assume that the statute vests in the Commission the absolute and arbitrary power to divide the State of Illinois or portions thereof into "areas." The statute establishes no guidelines or standards for the Commission to follow in designating an "area," leaving it entirely to the whim of the Commission what part of the State shall be encompassed within an "area" and to a great extent who shall be prohibited from soliciting those who have executed the forms. For example, it is conceivable that a large number of such forms will be executed by people who reside in a particular neighborhood composed of a few square blocks in the city of Chicago. However, by defining the "area" as the entire city of Chicago a real estate broker who has never solicited the owners of residential property in that neighborhood but who has so solicited in other parts of the city would be barred from soliciting for the sale or listing of real estate in the neighborhood from which executed forms were received. Conversely, by defining a small geographic "area" a person who may have been soliciting owners of real estate up to the very boundaries of that neighborhood but not within it would not receive a notice from the Commission and would thus be free to solicit the owners who had executed the forms.

It is contended that section 70–51(d) of the Criminal Code is a part of "An Act to prohibit the solicitation or inducement of sale or purchase of real estate on the basis of race, color, religion, or national origin or ancestry." . . . However, nothing in section 70–51(d) of the Criminal Code or in section 4.1 of the act creating the Commission on Human Relations establishes any guidelines or standards for the Commission to follow to effectuate this purpose. The Commission has the authority to arbitrarily establish "areas" for the purpose of prohibiting the solicitation of the sale of real estate for any purpose, whether or not it is related to the purpose of the Act. In fact, by treating the State of Illinois as one "area" the Commission could effectively prohibit solicitation of those who had executed the forms by all real estate brokers or salesmen by the simple practice of sending copies of the lists to all those who are licensed by the State of Illinois to engage in those occupations. The same could be true as to any city or county. Such a legislative intent is not discernible from the statute. We express no opinion as to whether or not the legislature itself could prohibit solicitation or whether such a prohibition would be violative of a person's right of freedom of speech. However, under the arbitrary power conferred by this statute the Commission may accomplish this result and thus is vested with the authority to determine what the law shall be and to whom it shall apply, contrary to the previous decisions of this court cited above.

We also consider as vague and indefinite the requirement that the Commission shall cause copies of the lists to be mailed to those who are *known* or *believed by the Commission* to be soliciting in the area covered by such lists. It is possible that each member of the Commission or succeeding members of the Commission may differently interpret the meaning of the words "known or believed." No guidelines are established for establishing the basis upon which such a "belief" may be formed. It is a common practice for real estate brokers and salesmen to solicit the listing of property for sale either directly or through advertisement in the media. Would this practice constitute sufficient "belief" to justify the Commission in sending copies of the lists to all real estate brokers or salesmen? The Commission as it is now composed may interpret these words in a manner that will preclude certain persons from soliciting in certain "areas" whereas a later Commission may interpret the same words in such a manner as to permit the same persons to solicit in these "areas." Therefore, this vague and indefinite language likewise confers upon the Commission an arbitrary and unrestricted power to determine to whom the law will apply. . . . This court stated in Krol v. County of Will, 38 Ill.2d 587, at 593, 233 N.E.2d 417, 420: "[A] law vesting discretionary power in an administrative officer without properly defining the terms under which his discretion is to be exercised is void as an unlawful delegation of legislative power . . . ."

We thus hold that section 4.1 of "An Act to create a Commission on Human Relations" and section 70–51(d)(1) of the Criminal Code are unconstitutional. . . .

[Justice Schaefer, with whom Chief Justice Underwood and Justice Ward joined, entered a dissenting opinion.][1]

NOTE

Four years after its decision in Tibbitts, in STOFER v. MOTOR VEHICLE CAS. CO., 68 Ill.2d 361, 369 N.E.2d 875 (1977), the Supreme Court of Illinois expressed a different view in a case involving the validity of a statute which instructed the Director of Insurance to "promulgate such rules and regulations as may be necessary to effect uniformity in all basic policies of fire and lightning insurance issued in this State, to the end that there be concurrency of contract where two or more companies insure the same risk." The Director ruled that all fire and lightning policies should contain a clause requiring actions on the policies to be "commenced within twelve months next after inception of the loss." The court stated in part:

"Many of our early cases adhere to the notion that administrative rule making basically is interstitial, interpolating among the standards set by the legislature to fill in details and create a comprehensive

---

1. 1 K. Davis, Admin.L. Treatise 192 (2d ed. 1978): "[T]he Illinois court has been one of the most backward in that it has often struck down delegations that would be permitted elsewhere, as in People v. Tibbitts . . . ."

regulatory scheme. Subsequent experience, however, with the administrative regulation of highly complex and technical subjects leads us to conclude that the administrative task necessarily differs substantially from the traditional model. In determining to regulate a particularly complex subject, the legislature frequently intends only to eliminate a particular class of abuse from an otherwise lawful and valuable activity. In many cases, it simply is impractical for legislators to become and remain thoroughly apprised of the facts necessary to determine which aspects of that activity are harmful and how they might be modified. In most cases, therefore, the administrator's task is not merely to interpolate among broadly stated legislative prohibitions, but, rather, to extrapolate from the broad language of his enabling statute, and, using the regulatory tools given him by the legislature, to deal with the problems which the legislature sought to address.

"To require the legislature continually to determine the specific actions which ought to be prohibited and those which ought to be required would be to render the regulation of many matters hopelessly inefficient. Yet the demands of administrative efficiency are not dispositive of the mandate of our constitution. A structure which enables government to serve its citizens more efficiently also may enable it to oppress them more efficiently. The separation of powers and branches of government mandates a distribution of authority which may, on occasion, impede one of the branches in attempting to address a particular problem. This impediment is necessary, however, to impede the abuse of power by any one particular branch acting alone.

"At least one commentator thus views the question of separation of powers as being limited to preventing the oppression of one branch of government by another. (See 1 F. Cooper, State Administrative Law 16 (1965).) We find that analysis inadequate. It is not enough that the other branches of government remain unimpeded in their ability to remedy an abuse of power by the offending branch. Rather, the requirement of affirmative authority from more than one branch of government is itself an important protection against the misguided acts of a particular bureaucracy. It is for this reason that our earlier cases emphasized the need for intelligible legislative standards to guide administrative rule making.

"Without sufficient statutory directions against which to compare administrative regulations, the mere existence of judicial review is not a meaningful safeguard against administrative abuses. . . . [U]nless found in the statute, the restraints which the judiciary is to apply to safeguard against the abuse of discretion in administrative rule making simply do not exist.

"Accordingly, we find that the view which has developed through the decisions of this court in recent years requires that the legislature, in delegating its authority provide sufficient identification of the following:

(1) The *persons* and *activities* potentially subject to regulation;

(2) the *harm* sought to be prevented; and

(3) the general *means* intended to be available to the administrator to prevent the identified harm."

The court then applied these criteria and held that the statute constituted a valid delegation of legislative power.

Further statements were made in Thygesen v. Callahan, 74 Ill.2d 404, 24 Ill.Dec. 558, 385 N.E.2d 699 (1979), and Rockford Drop Forge v. Pollution Control Board, 79 Ill.2d 271, 37 Ill.Dec. 600, 402 N.E.2d 602 (1980). Viewing Stofer as an "attempt to endow the requisite of intelligible standards with a conceptual foundation," the court in Thygesen found the second and third criteria not satisfied by a statute authorizing relevant state officials, in so many words, to set "maximum rates [to be] charged for check cashing and writing of money orders" by local currency exchanges "according to such circumstances and conditions as [are] determine[d] to be appropriate." Although the exchanges would be subject to the impact of competition as well as regulation in deciding what to charge for their services, the court found fatal the legislature's failure "to convey, *within the Act,* the harm which it sought to remedy . . . [and] to set forth any meaningful standards to guide defendant in setting the maximum rates." (Emphasis added.) In Rockford Drop Forge, the challenged statute made it a criminal offense for anyone to "emit beyond the boundaries of his property any noise that unreasonably interferes with the enjoyment of life or with any lawful business or activity, so as to violate any regulation or standard adopted by the Board under this Act." The Stofer criteria, the court stated, "adopted as the criteria of validity that the statute sufficiently identify the persons and activities subject to regulation, the harm sought to be prevented, and the general means intended to be made available to prevent the harm. It is plain without further discussion that the provisions of title VI, including the legislative declaration, the definition of the acts prohibited, and the specification of permissible regulations, together with the provisions of section 27 of the Act, amply satisfy constitutional requirements."

Does Illinois courts' evident attention to the delegation issue have an impact on legislative behavior in that state? In 1983, Professor George Bunn of the University of Wisconsin Law School published with Kathleen Irwin and F. Kyra Sido the results of a comparative study they had made of the operation of the delegation doctrine in Wisconsin and Illinois.[1] Wisconsin courts had invalidated only two statutes on delegation grounds during the period 1928–1977, both during the 1930's and on what the authors regarded as special grounds; that state, they thought, was as liberal as any in the nation. In the shorter period 1945–1977 Illinois courts had struck down "approximately fifteen" statutes on delegation grounds; they found no state with a stricter delegation doctrine. The results suggest little support for those believing that stricter judicial enforcement of delegation standards will result in more legislative attention to statute drafting: While the particular Illinois statutes challenged tended to be reenacted in terms that "gave

---

1. No Regulation Without Representation: Would Judicial Enforcement of a Stricter Nondelegation Doctrine Limit Administrative Lawmaking?, 1983 Wisc.L. Rev. 341.

significantly less discretion to the agency than its Wisconsin counterpart," in general a "[c]omparison of statutes in Illinois and Wisconsin shows no significant pattern of difference in the amount of discretion given to agencies for resolving policy questions." Other differences between the states, of course, existed that might have explained their political and legal variations; yet the authors thought that "a doctrine that does no more than narrow [particular delegations] every other year on the average seems to have little impact. To have a significant influence, the doctrine must deter legislators in their everyday lawmaking, rather than result merely in repairs to invalidated statutes. . . . [I]t is doubtful that the doctrine's revival by state or federal courts would be worth the resulting added uncertainty of statutory validity."

ALLEN v. CALIFORNIA BD. OF BARBER EXAMINERS

Court of Appeals of California, Fourth District, Division Two, 1972.
25 Cal.App.3d 1014, 102 Cal.Rptr. 368.

KAUFMAN, J.

Respondents are an apprentice barber, a journeyman barber and two owners of a barbershop, all duly certificated. Their certificates were revoked by appellant Board of Barber Examiners (hereinafter Board) for furnishing barbering services at prices below those prescribed in the minimum price schedule established by the Board for San Diego County. In the trial court, respondents sought a writ of mandate directed to the Board commanding it to vacate and set aside its orders revoking respondents' certificates. The court found the minimum price schedules invalid and issued a peremptory writ of mandate. The Board appeals.

. . .

In 1941 the Legislature added to the statutes regulating the barbering industry (hereinafter the Barbers' Act) Business and Professions Code, sections 6551 through 6557 authorizing the Board of Barber Examiners to establish minimum price schedules for barbering services for any city or county. . . . [These sections directed that in] "establishing a minimum price schedule, the board shall consider all conditions affecting the practice of barbering in that city and county, . . . , the relation of those conditions to the public health and safety [and the] necessary costs incurred in that city or county in maintaining a barber shop in a clean, healthful and sanitary condition. [The Board may] modify a previously established minimum price schedule if, after investigation, the Board "determines that the minimum prices so established . . . are insufficient properly to provide healthful services to the public and to maintain a sanitary barber shop, or that any minimum price set creates an undue hardship on barber shop owners and operators . . . ." "At the conclusion of an investigation therefor, the board may establish a reasonable and just minimum price schedule conforming to the requirements of this article." . . .

[These provisions, the court stated] are substantially identical to the minimum price provisions of the Dry Cleaners' Act enacted by the Legislature in 1945. . . . In State Board v. Thrift-D-Lux Cleaners, 40

Cal.2d 436, 440–446 [254 P.2d 29], over the vigorous dissent of three justices, the majority of the California Supreme Court held . . . that the minimum price provisions of the Dry Cleaners' Act constituted an unlawful delegation of legislative power to the State Board of Dry Cleaners; the Thrift-D-Lux court reviewed the standards set forth in the legislation and found them insufficient, particularly in view of the fact that the price-fixing power was delegated to a seven-man board, six of whom were active members of the dry cleaning industry. The Thrift-D-Lux case was distinguished on this point in Wilke & Holzheiser, Inc. v. Dept. of Alcoholic Bev. Control, 65 Cal.2d at pages 366–367, but in distinguishing the case the court expressed no disapproval of its rationale or conclusion. On the contrary, the Wilke & Holzheiser opinion indicates approval of the Thrift-D-Lux decision on this point and serves to reinforce it. "When the power which the Legislature purports to confer is the power to regulate the business of one's competitors, as in Thrift-D-Lux, . . . a real danger of abuse arises, and the courts accordingly insist upon stringent standards to contain and guide the exercise of the delegated power. [Fn. omitted.]"

Appellant first seeks to distinguish the Barbers' Act from the Dry Cleaners' Act on a difference in the makeup of the governing board. The seven members of the State Board of Dry Cleaners consists of "one public member and the owners of two retail plants, two wholesale plants, and two shops." (Bus. & Prof. Code, § 9530.) Thus, the six industry members are all "owners." The State Board of Barber Examiners consists of five members including one public member and four barbers who have engaged in the practice of barbering in California for at least five years immediately prior to their appointments. Of the four, one member "shall be a journeyman barber and one member shall be a barber employing one or more journeyman barbers." (Bus. & Prof. Code, § 6501.) Thus, only one member of the State Board of Barber Examiners need be an "owner." We do not find this distinction meaningful in terms of the rationale of the Thrift-D-Lux and Wilke & Holzheiser cases. The legislation "attempts to delegate . . . powers to an administrative board made up of interested members of the industry, the majority of which can initiate regulatory action by the board in that industry. . . . " (State Board v. Thrift-D-Lux Cleaners, supra, 40 Cal.2d at p. 449.) The power which the legislation "purports to confer is the power to regulate the business of one's competitors. . . . " (Wilke & Holzheiser, Inc. v. Dept. of Alcoholic Bev. Control, supra, 65 Cal.2d at p. 367.) A journeyman barber whose compensation is undoubtedly affected by the price of barbering services is as personally interested in the price of such services as an "owner."

Next, it is asserted that additional standards are contained in the Barbers' Act not found in the Dry Cleaners' Act. In this, appellant is incorrect. The minimum price provisions of the two acts are substantially identical.

[A]ppellant cites a number of cases in which it asserts that delegations of legislative power to administrative agencies were upheld where the standards set forth were no more definite than those in the Barbers'

Act. . . . None of the cited cases, however, involve the delegation of a power to fix prices to an administrative agency made up of interested members of the industry. As heretofore noted, under such circumstances "the courts . . . insist upon stringent standards to contain and guide the exercise of the delegated power." . . . State Board v. Thrift-D-Lux Cleaners, supra, 40 Cal.2d at pp. 448–449; Bayside Timber Co. v. Board of Supervisors, 20 Cal.App.3d 1, 12–13 [97 Cal.Rptr. 431].)

The judgment is affirmed.

TAMURA, Acting P.J., and GABBERT, J., concurred.

A petition for a rehearing was denied June 15, 1972, and appellant's petition for a hearing by the Supreme Court was denied July 26, 1972.[2]

NOTE

Is the objection to the delegation of power to private groups one of fairness to particular persons who may be affected by its exercise, or the expression of broader structural concerns? The fairness rationale was rejected by the United States Supreme Court in Friedman v. Rogers, 440 U.S. 1 (1979). Texas had placed control of the profession of optometry in control of a board dominated by independent optometrists, one of two contending professional groups. The Supreme Court found no problem of federal due process raised by this arrangement, which was challenged by a salaried, or commercial, optometrist—a member of the disfavored group. In any disciplinary hearing, the plaintiff could protect his "constitutional right to a fair and impartial hearing" by seeking disqualification of board members on conflict of interest grounds. See Gibson v. Berryhill, 411 U.S. 564 (1973), discussed at p. 956 infra. Plaintiff had "no constitutional right to be regulated by a Board . . . sympathetic to the commercial practice of optometry."

Perhaps federal courts reach these results—and should do so—because of a disinclination to upset state legislative choices. With the discrediting of "substantive due process," judgments about the political suitability of state law choices are emphatically to be left to state officials; [1] to say, however, that *federal* standards may not prohibit state legislatures from delegating their power to private groups leaves open the question whether a particular state's standards do. And occupational licensure rules, in particular, may frequently seem to raise such questions.[2]

2. [Ed.] Calif.Stats. 1973, c. 319, § 27 repealed sections 6551–6558. West's Ann. Cal. Bus. and Prof.Code § 723 (1974).

1. Of course it does not follow from the unwillingness of federal courts to interfere with state economic judgments that economic analysis of regulatory impact has nothing to tell us. See, e.g., P. Aranow, E. Gellhorn and G. Robinson, A Theory of Legislative Delegation, 68 Corn.L.Rev. 1, 64–65 (1983); R. Posner, Theories of Economic Regulation, 5 Bell J.Econ. 335 (1974); G. Steigler, The Theory of Economic Regulation, 2 Bell J.Eco. & Man.Sci. 3 (1971).

2. For discussion of the various facets of delegation of governmental power to private parties, see W. Gellhorn, The Abuse of Occupational Licensing, 44 U.Chi.L.Rev. 6 (1976); G. Liebmann, Delegation to Private Parties in American Constitutional Law, 50 Ind.L.J. 650 (1975); J. Barron, Business and Professional Licensing—California, A Representative Example, 18 Stan.L.Rev. 640 (1966); L. Jaffe, Law Making by Private Groups, 51 Harv.L.Rev. 201 (1937); J.

LINCOLN DAIRY CO. v. FINIGAN
Supreme Court of Nebraska, 1960.
170 Neb. 777, 104 N.W.2d 227.

[The Nebraska Grade A Milk Control Act provided in part, "The director is hereby authorized to adopt by regulation minimum standards for the sanitary quality, production, processing, distribution, and sale of Grade A milk and Grade A milk products, and for labeling of the same. Such regulations shall comply generally with the Milk Ordinance and Code—1953 recommendations of the Public Health Service of the Department of Health, Education and Welfare of the United States. . . . Any person or persons violating the provisions of [the Act] or the rules and regulations issued thereunder . . . shall be guilty of a misdemeanor and shall, upon conviction thereof, be fined not less than twenty-five dollars nor more than one hundred dollars. . . . " Plaintiffs sought a declaratory judgment that the statute was unconstitutional.]

CARTER, JUSTICE. . . .

The act authorizes the director to adopt, by regulation, minimum standards for the sanitary quality, production, processing, distribution, and sale of Grade A milk and Grade A milk products, and for the labeling of the same. No limitation is placed upon the power of the director or the standards by which such granted power is to be exercised except that they are to comply generally with the Milk Ordinance and Code—1953 recommendations of the Public Health Service of the Department of Health, Education and Welfare of the United States. It will be observed that the ordinance and code referred to are recommendations only. They constitute a suggested model to be used in making regulations for the production and sale of Grade A milk and other grades as well. They have not been promulgated or published as regulations by any department of the United States government. They are not required to be filed in any public office or registry and their content can be established only by extrinsic evidence since this court cannot take judicial notice of their existence or what they may contain.

It will be noted also that [the statute] provides criminal penalties for violation of the Grade A Milk Act and the regulations promulgated by the director. The validity of the regulations is dependent upon proof by extrinsic evidence, which is uncertain as to status and not readily available. Their validity cannot be ascertained from the authorizing statute. Criminal prosecution cannot be grounded on such nebulous definitions of crime. All crimes are statutory in this state. The validity of a statute purporting to define a crime cannot be based on such an indefinite, uncertain, and obscure basis of validity as is presented by the statute before us. . . .

The Legislature purported to grant authority to the director to make regulations which comply generally with the described milk ordinance and code, and provided that a violation of such regulations constituted a criminal offense with a fixed penalty. The director was

Freedman, Delegation of Power and Institutional Competence, 43 U.Chi.L.Rev. 307, 331–335 (1976). Additional references are cited by Professor Freedman at 331 n. 124.

thereby empowered to arbitrarily promulgate any regulations he saw fit if they complied generally with the milk ordinance and code. The effect is that the director was authorized to select any regulations he chose which were within the scope of the described model milk ordinance and code, the violation of which was to be a criminal offense. The attempt of the Legislature to thus grant to the director the power to create criminal offenses violates all fundamental concepts relating to the delegation of legislative authority. By this statute the director and not the Legislature defines what shall be criminal offenses. It is axiomatic that the power to define crimes and criminal offenses is in the Legislature and it may not delegate such power to an administrative agency. . . .

To uphold such a delegation of legislative power to an administrative officer or agency, as was attempted in the present case, would lead to far-reaching and dangerous consequences. Since regulations can be changed at any time by the director, it is within his power to change or add to regulations previously promulgated, file them with the Secretary of State, and immediately they have the effect of law for a violation of which one may be punished criminally.

The public has a right to know what acts constitute crimes in this state and the punishments provided therefor. They may properly assume that crimes and punishment are purely a legislative function and that the definition of all crimes and the punishment therefor will be found in the duly enacted statutes of this state. The public may properly rely on the fact that the Legislature meets only at stated intervals and that criminal laws may be enacted, amended, and repealed only during such legislative sessions. For this court to hold that administrative or executive officers, or departments, could make rules and regulations from time to time according to judgment or whim, which would have the effect of law and the violation of which would be punishable as crimes, would be to deprive the people of the protection of the personal rights for which constitutions were devised to protect. The Grade A Milk Act is clearly unconstitutional in that it unlawfully delegates legislative powers to the Director of the Department of Agriculture and Inspection. The Legislature may not avoid by delegation the performance of its exclusive function to define crimes and provide the punishment therefor.

We do not hold that the Legislature may not adopt a law or regulation of another jurisdiction by reference. It may even adopt such except insofar as it is not in conflict with existing laws of this state. But it may not adopt by reference only to the extent that an administrative agency or officer shall see fit to adopt it. To so do is to delegate to the administrative agency or officer the determination of matters which are legislative and, consequently, for the determination of the Legislature.

NOTES

(1) The Lincoln Dairy Co. case was distinguished in STATE v. CUTRIGHT, 193 Neb. 303, 226 N.W.2d 771 (1975), in which defendant—a self styled "inveterate swimmer" who "as a general practice [swam] in

complete disregard" of the rules—was convicted of violating a statute which provided that "any person who shall swim . . . on any area under the ownership or control of the [Game and Park Commission] unless the Commission shall have given permission for such activity . . . . shall be guilty of a misdemeanor. . . . " The court first summarized the holding in Lincoln Dairy Co. as follows: "The court held that the Legislature could not delegate its power to create criminal offenses and prescribe penalties to an administrative or executive authority; that such powers are exclusively legislative and may not be delegated to the executive branch of the government under the doctrine of division of powers contained in the state Constitution; and, further, that the grant of power by the Legislature to the Director of the Department of Agriculture and Inspection to promulgate rules and regulations in general compliance with a model code, in accordance with his judgment or whim, the violation of which are made crimes subject to punishment, is an unconstitutional delegation of legislative power to an administrative authority. This court found that under that statute, the Director, and not the Legislature, defined what should be criminal offenses."

But in this case, said the Court: "The Legislature itself actually established the crime and the penalty for violation of the statute. To paraphrase the language of the Legislature, it is provided that any person who shall swim in any area under the ownership or control of the commission, without permission from the commission, shall be guilty of a misdemeanor, and punished accordingly. The only thing that is left to the decision or discretion of the commission is the designation of the appropriate areas where swimming may be permitted, and the posting of the proper notices for such areas. Obviously the filling in of the minor details relative to the implementation of the statute would have to be delegated by the Legislature, as it is not to be expected and, in fact, would be a physical impossibility for the Legislature to visit all the state lakes personally, and make its own determination of where swimming should be permitted.

"On the other hand, the act involved in Lincoln Dairy Co. v. Finigan, supra, did not contain a legislative definition of the crime itself, as did the statute in this case. It merely provided that the Director should have the power to make rules and regulations, and if he did so the Legislature provided that a violation of such regulations would be a misdemeanor, and punishable as such. In other words, the Director, under that act, was given the absolute power to determine what conduct would be punishable under the regulations that he drew. This clearly would be an unconstitutional delegation of its power by the Legislature to an administrative agency or an executive of the government; and this court so held. The statute involved in this case is totally unlike the act involved in the Lincoln Dairy Co. case for the reasons previously stated; and we conclude that there is no unconstitutional delegation of legislative power involved in the statute in this case."

(2) Compare UNITED STATES v. GRIMAUD, 220 U.S. 506 (1911), . . . p. 69 supra.

SECTION 2: LEGISLATIVE REASSIGNMENT OF "JUDICIAL" AUTHORITY

The cases thus far considered involve the validity of legislative attempts to authorize administrators to prescribe the standards for governmental action or the rules by which private conduct will be judged—the problem of delegation of legislative power. We have seen little indication that delegation of the authority to decide individual cases—that is to adjudicate—is problematic. Although it might be thought that attempts to vest adjudicatory powers in non-judicial hands necessarily violate the separation of powers principle, courts have not often invalidated statutes on this basis.

At the federal level, the general validity of such delegations has long been regarded as settled by CROWELL v. BENSON, 285 U.S. 22 (1932). The case involved a proceeding under the Longshoremen's and Harbor Workers' Act, a federal workmen's compensation law covering certain maritime employments. An award of compensation had been made by Crowell, deputy commissioner of the United States Employees' Compensation Commission; it ran in favor of Knudsen and rested on the finding that he had been injured while in Benson's employ and while performing services on the navigable waters of the United States. Benson denied that Knudsen was his employee. Under the Act, the Deputy Commissioner's decision was reviewable in U.S. District Court, which was to have plenary authority in deciding any questions of law, but only limited authority to review the Deputy Commissioner's conclusions about the facts. In the court review proceedings, Benson claimed, inter alia, that Congress could not constitutionally vest fact-finding authority in the deputy commissioner rather than an Article III court, given the Constitution's placement of "all cases of admiralty and maritime jurisdiction" in the judicial power of the United States. The Court agreed with that argument for only a limited set of issues (which it called "jurisdictional") discussed at some length at pp. 530–538 within. Of interest here are its preliminary observations, generally taken to validate the use of administrative agencies for adjudication, at least so long as they remain subject to the controls of judicial review:[1]

"The question in the instant case, in this aspect, can be deemed to relate only to determinations of fact. The reservation of legal questions is to the same court that has jurisdiction in admiralty, and the mere fact that the court is not described as such is unimportant. . . . The Congress did not attempt to define questions of law, and the generality of the description leaves no doubt of the intention to reserve to the Federal court full authority to pass upon all matters which this Court had held to fall within that category. There is thus no attempt to interfere with, but rather provision is made to facilitate, the exercise by the court of its jurisdiction to deny effect to any administrative finding which is without evidence or 'contrary to the indisputable character of

---

1. See also H.M. Hart, Jr., The Power of Congress to Limit the Jurisdiction of the   Federal Courts: An Exercise in Dialectic, 66 Harv.L.Rev. 1362 (1953).

the evidence,' or where the hearing is 'inadequate,' or 'unfair,' or arbitrary in any respect.

"As to determinations of fact, the distinction is at once apparent between cases of private right and those which arise between the Government and persons subject to its authority in connection with the performance of the constitutional functions of the executive or legislative departments. The Court referred to this distinction in Murray's Lessee v. Hoboken Land and Improvement Company [18 How. 272,] pointing out that 'there are matters, involving public rights, which may be presented in such form that the judicial power is capable of acting on them, and which are susceptible to judicial determination, but which Congress may or may not bring within the cognizance of the courts of the United States, as it may deem proper.' Thus the Congress, in exercising the powers confided to it, may establish 'legislative' courts (as distinguished from 'constitutional courts in which the judicial power conferred by the Constitution can be deposited') which are . . . to serve as special tribunals 'to examine and determine various matters, arising between the government and others, which from their nature do not require judicial determination and yet are susceptible of it.' But 'the mode of determining matters of this class is completely within congressional control. Congress may reserve to itself the power to decide, may delegate that power to executive officers, or may commit it to judicial tribunals.' Ex parte Bakelite Corporation, 279 U.S. 438, 451. Familiar illustrations of administrative agencies created for the determination of such matters are found in connection with the exercise of the congressional power as to interstate and foreign commerce taxation, immigration, the public lands, public health, the facilities of the post office, pensions and payments to veterans.

"The present case does not fall within the categories just described but is one of private right, that is, of the liability of one individual to another under the law as defined. But in cases of that sort, there is no requirement that, in order to maintain the essential attributes of the judicial power, all determinations of fact in constitutional courts shall be made by judges. On the common law side of the Federal courts, the aid of juries is not only deemed appropriate but is required by the Constitution itself. In cases of equity and admiralty, it is historic practice to call to the assistance of the courts, without the consent of the parties, masters and commissioners or assessors, to pass upon certain classes of questions, as, for example, to take and state an account or to find the amount of damages. While the reports of masters and commissioners in such cases are essentially of an advisory nature, it has not been the practice to disturb their findings when they are properly based upon evidence, in the absence of errors of law, and the parties have no right to demand that the court shall redetermine the facts thus found.

. . .

"The statute has a limited application, being confined to the relation of master and servant, and the method of determining the questions of fact, which arise in the routine of making compensation awards to employees under the Act, is necessary to its effective enforcement. . . . For the purposes stated, we are unable to find any constitutional obstacle to the action of the Congress in availing itself of a method shown by experience to be essential in order to apply its standards to the thousands of cases involved, thus relieving the courts of a most serious burden while preserving their complete authority to insure the proper application of the law."

Note that two differing theories are presented. For disputes between the government and its citizens of a character Congress could freely choose to withhold from the courts entirely, cases involving "public rights," Congress may use its authority under the necessary and proper clause of the Constitution to involve the courts on aspects "susceptible of judicial determination" to whatever extent it chooses. Separation of powers appears to present no issue; although the agency's function may be judicial in character it is not regarded as an exercise of Article III judicial power, and so it is not problematic that the function is not placed in a court. For cases "of private right, that is, of the liability of one individual to another under the law as defined," the judicial power *is* involved; hence a court *must* be used; but the Court saves the day (for most purposes) by characterizing the administrative agency as if it were a special master, commissioner, or assessor—an adjunct to the court, and hence within the Article III structure. This characterization, however, limits Congress's freedom of choice; certain functions (e.g., "full authority . . . to deal with matters of law") must be reserved to the Article III judge.

During the early 1980's, this rather formal and theoretical analysis was tested in a series of three Supreme Court decisions, Northern Pipeline Construction Co. v. Marathon Pipe Line Co., 458 U.S. 50 (1982); Thomas v. Union Carbide Agricultural Products Co., 105 S.Ct. 3325 (1985); and Commodity Futures Trading Commission v. Schor, 106 S.Ct. 3245 (1986). The last of these—the most recent, the least disputatious, and the most clearly administrative—is set out below as a principal case; Northern Pipeline and Thomas are noted in the following pages. What, now, are the constraints on Congress' power to assign dispute resolution to tribunals other than Article III courts?

COMMODITY FUTURES TRADING COMMISSION v. SCHOR

Supreme Court of the United States, 1986.
106 S.Ct. 3245.

JUSTICE O'CONNOR delivered the opinion of the Court.

The question presented is whether the Commodity Exchange Act (CEA or Act), 7 U.S.C. § 1 et seq., empowers the Commodity Futures Trading Commission (CFTC or Commission) to entertain state law counterclaims in reparation proceedings and, if so, whether that grant of authority violates Article III of the Constitution.

I

The CEA broadly prohibits fraudulent and manipulative conduct in connection with commodity futures transactions. In 1974, Congress "overhaul[ed]" the Act in order to institute a more "comprehensive regulatory structure to oversee the volatile and esoteric futures trading complex." Congress also determined that the broad regulatory powers of the CEA were most appropriately vested in an agency which would be relatively immune from the "political winds that sweep Washington." H.R.Rep. No. 93–975, pp. 44, 70. It therefore created an independent agency, the CFTC, and entrusted to it sweeping authority to implement the CEA.

Among the duties assigned to the CFTC was the administration of a reparations procedure through which disgruntled customers of professional commodity brokers could seek redress for the brokers' violations of the Act or CFTC regulations. Thus, § 14 of the CEA, provides that any person injured by such violations may apply to the Commission for an order directing the offender to pay reparations to the complainant and may enforce that order in federal district court. Congress intended this administrative procedure to be an "inexpensive and expeditious" alternative to existing fora available to aggrieved customers, namely, the courts and arbitration. S.Rep. No. 95–850, p. 11 (1978).

In conformance with the congressional goal of promoting efficient dispute resolution, the CFTC promulgated a regulation in 1976 which allows it to adjudicate counterclaims "aris[ing] out of the . . . transactions or occurrences set forth in the complaint." 17 CFR § 12.23(b)(2) (1983)). This permissive counterclaim rule leaves the respondent in a reparations proceeding free to seek relief against the reparations complainant in other fora.

. . . [I]n February 1980, . . . respondents Schor and Mortgage Services of America invoked the CFTC's reparations jurisdiction by filing complaints against petitioner ContiCommodity Services, Inc. (Conti), a commodity futures broker, and Richard L. Sandor, a Conti employee. Schor had an account with Conti which contained a debit balance because Schor's net futures trading losses and expenses, such as commissions, exceeded the funds deposited in the account. Schor alleged that this debit balance was the result of Conti's numerous violations of the CEA.

Before receiving notice that Schor had commenced the reparations proceeding, Conti had filed a diversity action in Federal District Court to recover the debit balance. Schor counterclaimed in this action, reiterating his charges that the debit balance was due to Conti's violations of the CEA. Schor also moved on two separate occasions to dismiss or stay the district court action, arguing that the continuation of the federal action would be a waste of judicial resources and an undue burden on the litigants in view of the fact that "[t]he reparations proceedings . . . will fully . . . resolve and adjudicate all the rights of the parties to this action with respect to the transactions which are the subject matter of this action."

Although the District Court declined to stay or dismiss the suit, Conti voluntarily dismissed the federal court action and presented its debit balance claim by way of a counterclaim in the CFTC reparations proceeding. Conti denied violating the CEA and instead insisted that the debit balance resulted from Schor's trading, and was therefore a simple debt owed by Schor.

After discovery, briefing and a hearing, the Administrative Law Judge (ALJ) in Schor's reparations proceeding ruled in Conti's favor on both Schor's claims and Conti's counterclaims. After this ruling, Schor for the first time challenged the CFTC's statutory authority to adjudicate Conti's counterclaim. The ALJ rejected Schor's challenge, stating himself "bound by agency regulations and published agency policies." The Commission declined to review the decision and allowed it to become final, at which point Schor filed a petition for review with the Court of Appeals for the District of Columbia Circuit. Prior to oral argument, the Court of Appeals, sua sponte, raised the question of whether CFTC could constitutionally adjudicate Conti's counterclaims in light of Northern Pipeline Construction Co. v. Marathon Pipe Line Co., 458 U.S. 50 (1982) (Northern Pipeline). . . .

After briefing and argument, the Court of Appeals upheld the CFTC's decision on Schor's claim in most respects, but ordered the dismissal of Conti's counterclaims on the ground that "the CFTC lacks authority (subject matter competence) to adjudicate" common law counterclaims. In support of this latter ruling, the Court of Appeals reasoned that the CFTC's exercise of jurisdiction over Conti's common law counterclaim gave rise to "[s]erious constitutional problems" under Northern Pipeline, [and construed the statute as not conferring the counterclaim jurisdiction, to avoid these problems.] . . . This Court granted the CFTC's petition for certiorari, vacated the court of appeals' judgment, and remanded the case for further consideration in light of Thomas v. Union Carbide Agricultural Products Co., 105 S.Ct. 3325 (1985).

On remand, the Court of Appeals reinstated its prior judgment. It reaffirmed its earlier view that Northern Pipeline drew into serious question the Commission's authority to decide debit-balance counterclaims in reparations proceedings; concluded that nothing in Thomas altered that view; and again held that, in light of the constitutional problems posed by the CFTC's adjudication of common law counterclaims, the CEA should be construed to authorize the CFTC to adjudicate only counterclaims arising from violations of the Act or CFTC regulations.

II

[The Supreme Court agreed that statutes might be construed to avoid serious constitutional problems, but reminded that they are not to be rewritten or perverted. As the Court read the statute, explicit congressional purpose to confer the jurisdiction being exercised was inescapable.] . . . We therefore are squarely faced with the question of whether the CFTC's assumption of jurisdiction over common law counterclaims violates Article III of the Constitution.

III

Article III, § 1 directs that the "judicial Power of the United States shall be vested in one supreme Court and in such inferior Courts as the Congress may from time to time ordain and establish," and provides that these federal courts shall be staffed by judges who hold office during good behavior, and whose compensation shall not be diminished during tenure in office. Schor claims that these provisions prohibit Congress from authorizing the initial adjudication of common law counterclaims by the CFTC, an administrative agency whose adjudicatory officers do not enjoy the tenure and salary protections embodied in Article III.

Although our precedents in this area do not admit of easy synthesis, they do establish that the resolution of claims such as Schor's cannot turn on conclusory reference to the language of Article III. Rather, the constitutionality of a given congressional delegation of adjudicative functions to a non-Article III body must be assessed by reference to the purposes underlying the requirements of Article III. This inquiry, in turn, is guided by the principle that "practical attention to substance rather than doctrinaire reliance on formal categories should inform application of Article III." Thomas, supra, at 3336. See also Crowell v. Benson, 285 U.S., at 53.

A

Article III, § 1 serves both to protect "the role of the independent judiciary within the constitutional scheme of tripartite government," Thomas, supra, at 3336, and to safeguard litigants' "right to have claims decided before judges who are free from potential domination by other branches of government." United States v. Will, 449 U.S. 200, 218 (1980). Although our cases have provided us with little occasion to discuss the nature or significance of this latter safeguard, our prior discussions of Article III, § 1's guarantee of an independent and impartial adjudication by the federal judiciary of matters within the judicial power of the United States intimated that this guarantee serves to protect primarily personal, rather than structural, interests. . . .
[A]s a personal right, Article III's guarantee of an impartial and independent federal adjudication is subject to waiver, just as are other personal constitutional rights that dictate the procedures by which civil and criminal matters must be tried. . . . In the instant case, Schor indisputably waived any right he may have possessed to the full trial of Conti's counterclaim before an Article III court. Schor expressly demanded that Conti proceed on its counterclaim in the reparations proceeding rather than before the District Court, and was content to have the entire dispute settled in the forum he had selected until the ALJ ruled against him on all counts; it was only after the ALJ rendered a decision to which he objected that Schor raised any challenge to the CFTC's consideration of Conti's counterclaim.

Even were there no evidence of an express waiver here, Schor's election to forgo his right to proceed in state or federal court on his claim and his decision to seek relief instead in a CFTC reparations proceeding constituted an effective waiver. Three years before Schor instituted his reparations action, a private right of action under the CEA was explicitly recognized in the circuit in which Schor and Conti filed suit in District Court. See Hirk v. Agri-Research Council, Inc., 561 F.2d 96, 103, n. 8 (CA7 1977). Moreover, at the time Schor decided to seek relief before the CFTC rather than in the federal courts, the CFTC's regulations made clear that it was empowered to adjudicate all counterclaims "aris[ing] out of the same transaction or occurrence or series of transactions or occurrences set forth in the complaint." Thus, Schor had the option of having the common law counterclaim against him adjudicated in a federal Article III court, but, with full knowledge that the CFTC would exercise jurisdiction over that claim, chose to avail himself of the quicker and less expensive procedure Congress had provided him. In such circumstances, it is clear that Schor effectively agreed to an adjudication by the CFTC of the entire controversy by seeking relief in this alternative forum. Cf. McElrath v. United States, 12 Otto 426, 440, 102 U.S. 426, 440 (1880).

B

As noted above, our precedents establish that Article III, § 1 not only preserves to litigants their interest in an impartial and independent federal adjudication of claims within the judicial power of the United States, but also serves as "an inseparable element of the constitutional system of checks and balances." Northern Pipeline, 458 U.S., at 58. Article III, § 1 safeguards the role of the Judicial Branch in our tripartite system by barring congressional attempts "to transfer jurisdiction [to non-Article III tribunals] for the purpose of emasculating" constitutional courts, National Insurance Co. v. Tidewater Co., 337 U.S. 582, 644 (1949) (Vinson, C.J., dissenting), and thereby preventing "the encroachment or aggrandizement of one branch at the expense of the other." Buckley v. Valeo, 424 U.S. 1, 122 (1976) (per curiam). To the extent that this structural principle is implicated in a given case, the parties cannot by consent cure the constitutional difficulty for the same reason that the parties by consent cannot confer on federal courts subject matter jurisdiction beyond the limitations imposed by Article III, § 2. . . . [T]he limitations serve institutional interests that the parties cannot be expected to protect.

In determining the extent to which a given congressional decision to authorize the adjudication of Article III business in a non-Article III tribunal impermissibly threatens the institutional integrity of the Judicial Branch, the Court has declined to adopt formalistic and unbending rules. Thomas, supra. Although such rules might lend a greater degree of coherence to this area of the law, they might also unduly constrict Congress' ability to take needed and innovative action pursuant to its Article I powers. Thus, in reviewing Article III challenges, we have weighed a number of factors, none of which has been deemed determinative, with an eye to the practical effect that the congressional action will have on the constitutionally assigned role of the federal judiciary. Id. Among the factors upon which we have focused are the extent to which the "essential attributes of judicial power" are reserved to Article III courts, and, conversely, the extent to which the non-Article III forum exercises the range of jurisdiction and powers normally vested only in Article III courts, the origins and importance of the right to be adjudicated, and the concerns that drove Congress to depart from the requirements of Article III.

An examination of the relative allocation of powers between the CFTC and Article III courts in light of the considerations given prominence in our precedents demonstrates that the congressional scheme does not impermissibly intrude on the province of the judiciary. The CFTC's adjudicatory powers depart from the traditional agency model in just one respect: the CFTC's jurisdiction over common law counterclaims. While wholesale importation of concepts of pendent or ancillary jurisdiction into the agency context may create greater constitutional difficulties, we decline to endorse an absolute prohibition on such jurisdiction out of fear of where some hypothetical "slippery slope" may deposit us. Indeed, the CFTC's exercise of this type of jurisdiction is not without precedent. Thus, in Reconstruction Finance Corp. v. Bankers Trust Co., 318 U.S. 163, 168–171 (1943), we saw no constitutional difficulty in the initial adjudication of a state law claim by a federal agency, subject to judicial review, when that claim was ancillary to a federal law dispute. Similarly, in Katchen v. Landy, 382 U.S. 323 (1966), this Court upheld a bankruptcy referee's power to hear and decide state law counterclaims against a creditor who filed a claim in bankruptcy when those counterclaims arose out of the same transaction. We reasoned that, as a practical matter, requiring the trustee to commence a plenary action to recover on its counterclaim would be a "meaningless gesture."

In the instant case, we are likewise persuaded that there is little practical reason to find that this single deviation from the agency model is fatal to the congressional scheme. . . . The CFTC, like the agency in Crowell v. Benson deals only with a "particularized area of law," whereas the jurisdiction of the bankruptcy courts found unconstitutional in Northern Pipeline extended to broadly "all civil proceedings arising under title 11 or arising in or *related to* cases under title 11." CFTC orders, like those of the agency in Crowell, but unlike those of the bankruptcy courts are enforceable only by order of the District Court. CFTC orders are also reviewed under the same "weight of the evidence" standard sustained in Crowell, rather than the more deferential ["clearly erroneous"] standard found lacking in Northern Pipeline. The legal rulings of the CFTC, like the legal determinations of the agency in Crowell, are subject to de novo review. Finally, the CFTC, unlike the bankruptcy courts under the 1978 Act, does not exercise "all ordinary powers of district courts," and thus may not, for instance, preside over jury trials or issue writs of habeas corpus.

Of course, the nature of the claim has significance in our Article III analysis quite apart from the method prescribed for its adjudication. The counterclaim asserted in this case is a "private" right for which state law provides the rule of decision. It is therefore a claim of the kind assumed to be at the "core" of matters normally reserved to Article III courts. Yet this conclusion does not end our inquiry; just as this Court has rejected any attempt to make determinative for Article III purposes the distinction between public rights and private rights, Thomas, supra, there is no reason inherent in separation of powers principles to accord the state law character of a claim talismanic power in Article III inquiries.

We have explained that "the public rights doctrine reflects simply a pragmatic understanding that when Congress selects a quasi-judicial method of resolving matters that 'could be conclusively determined by the Executive and Legislative Branches,' the danger of encroaching on the judicial powers" is less than when private rights, which are normally within the purview of the judiciary, are relegated as an initial matter to administrative adjudication. Thomas, supra, at 3337 (quoting Northern Pipeline, supra, 458 U.S., at 68). Similarly, the state law character of a claim is significant for purposes of determining the effect that an initial adjudication of those claims by a non-Article III tribunal will have on the separation of powers for the simple reason that private, common law rights were historically the types of matters subject to resolution by Article III courts. The risk that Congress may improperly have encroached on the federal judiciary is obviously magnified when Congress "withdraw[s] from judicial cognizance any matter which, from its nature, is the subject of a suit at the common law, or in equity, or admiralty" and which therefore has traditionally been tried in Article III courts, and allocates the decision of those matters to a non-Article III forum of its own creation. Murray's Lessee v. The Hoboken Land and Improvement Co., 18 How. 272, 284 (1856). Accordingly, where private, common law rights are at stake, our examination of the congressional attempt to control the manner in which those rights are adjudicated has been searching. In this case, however, "[l]ooking beyond form to the substance of what" Congress has done, we are persuaded that the congressional authorization of limited CFTC jurisdiction over a narrow class of common law claims as an incident to the CFTC's primary, and unchallenged, adjudicative function does not create a substantial threat to the separation of powers.

It is clear that Congress has not attempted to "withdraw from judicial cognizance" the determination of Conti's right to the sum represented by the debit balance in Schor's account. Congress gave the CRTC the authority to adjudicate such matters, but the decision to invoke this forum is left entirely to the parties and the power of the federal judiciary to take jurisdiction of these matters is unaffected. In such circumstances, separation of powers concerns are diminished, for it seems self-evident that just as Congress may encourage parties to settle a dispute out of court or resort to arbitration without impermissible incursions on the separation of powers, Congress may make available a quasi-judicial mechanism through which willing parties may, at their option, elect to resolve their differences. This is not to say, of course, that if Congress created a phalanx of non-Article III tribunals equipped to handle the entire business of the Article III courts without any Article III supervision or control and without evidence of valid and specific legislative necessities, the fact that the parties had the election to proceed in their forum of choice would necessarily save the scheme from constitutional attack. But this case obviously bears no resemblance to such a scenario, given the degree of judicial control saved to the federal courts, as well as the congressional purpose behind the jurisdictional delegation, the demonstrated need for the delegation, and the limited nature of the delegation.

When Congress authorized the CFTC to adjudicate counterclaims, its primary focus was on making effective a specific and limited federal regulatory scheme, not on allocating jurisdiction among federal tribunals. Congress intended to create an inexpensive and expeditious alternative forum through which customers could enforce the provisions of the CEA against professional brokers. Its decision to endow the CFTC with jurisdiction over such reparations claims is readily understandable given the perception that the CFTC was relatively immune from political pressures, see H.R.Rep. No. 93–975, pp. 44, 70, and the obvious expertise that the Commission possesses in applying the CEA and its own regulations. This reparations scheme itself is of unquestioned constitutional validity. It was only to ensure the effectiveness of this scheme that Congress authorized the CFTC to assert jurisdiction over common law counterclaims. Indeed, as was explained above, absent the CFTC's exercise of that authority, the purposes of the reparations procedure would have been confounded.

It also bears emphasis that the CFTC's assertion of counterclaim jurisdiction is limited to that which is necessary to make the reparations procedure workable. See 7 U.S.C. § 12a(5). The CFTC adjudication of common law counterclaims is incidental to, and completely dependent upon, adjudication of reparations claims created by federal law, and in actual fact is limited to claims arising out of the same transaction or occurrence as the reparations claim.

In such circumstances, the magnitude of any intrusion on the Judicial Branch can only be termed de minimus. Conversely, were we to hold that the Legislative Branch may not permit such limited cognizance of common law counterclaims at the election of the parties, it is clear that we would "defeat the obvious purpose of the legislation to furnish a prompt, continuous, expert and inexpensive method for dealing with a class of questions of fact which are peculiarly suited to examination and determination by an administrative agency specially assigned to that task." Crowell v. Benson, 285 U.S., at 46. We do not think Article III compels this degree of prophylaxis.

Nor does our decision in Bowsher v. Synar [decided the same day and set out at p. 183 within—Ed.] require a contrary result. Unlike Bowsher, this case raises no question of the aggrandizement of congressional power at the expense of a coordinate branch. Instead, the separation of powers question presented in this case is whether Congress impermissibly undermined, without appreciable expansion of its own power, the role of the Judicial Branch. In any case, we have, consistent with Bowsher, looked to a number of factors in evaluating the extent to which the congressional scheme endangers separation of powers principles under the circumstances presented, but have found no genuine threat to those principles to be present in this case.

In so doing, we have also been faithful to our Article III precedents, which counsel that bright line rules cannot effectively be employed to yield broad principles applicable in all Article III inquiries. Rather, due regard must be given in each case to the unique aspects of the congressional plan at issue and its practical consequences in light of the larger concerns that underlie Article III. We conclude that the limited jurisdiction that the CFTC asserts over state law claims as a necessary incident to the adjudication of federal claims willingly submitted by the parties for initial agency adjudication does not contravene separation of powers principles or Article III.

.   .   .

The judgment of the Court of Appeals for the District of Columbia Circuit is reversed and the case remanded for further proceedings consistent with this opinion.

It is so ordered.

JUSTICE BRENNAN, with whom JUSTICE MARSHALL joins, dissenting.

[In his lengthy dissent, Justice Brennan took the position, earlier developed in his plurality opinion in Northern Pipeline Co. v. Marathon Pipe Line Co., p. 117 below, that Article III, § 1 generally "prohibit[s] the vesting of *any* judicial functions" outside the judiciary, subject to "three narrow exceptions" that had been recognized over time: for territorial courts, for military courts martial, and for "courts that adjudicate certain disputes concerning public rights." Only the latter was important here, and the Justice saw no way to fit the CFTC's counterclaim authority within it.

The opinion stresses both the formal theory of separation of powers already encountered and the particular function of the judiciary:] The Framers understood that a principal benefit of the separation of judicial power from the legislative and executive powers would be the protection of individual litigants from decisionmakers susceptible to majoritarian pressures. Article III's salary and tenure provisions promote impartial adjudication by placing the judicial power of the United States "in a body of judges insulated from majoritarian pressures and thus able to enforce [federal law] without fear of reprisal or public rebuke." United States v. Raddatz, 447 U.S. 667, 704 (1980) (Marshall, J., dissenting). As Alexander Hamilton observed, "[t]hat inflexible and uniform adherence to the rights of the constitution and of individuals, which we perceive to be indispensable in the courts of justice can certainly not be expected from judges who hold their offices by a temporary commission." The Federalist No. 78, p. 546. This is so because:

> "If the power of making [periodic appointments] was committed either to the Executive or Legislature, there would be danger of an improper complaisance to the branch which possessed it; if to both, there would be an unwillingness to hazard the displeasure of either; if to the People, or to persons

chosen by them for the special purpose, there would be too great a disposition to consult popularity, to justify a reliance that nothing would be consulted but the Constitution and the laws." Ibid.

"Next to permanency in office," Hamilton added, "nothing can contribute more to the independence of the Judges than a fixed provision for their support" because "*a power over a man's subsistence amounts to a power over his will.*" Id. at 548 (emphasis in original). . . .

These important functions of Article III are too central to our constitutional scheme to risk their incremental erosion. . . . More than a century ago, we recognized that Congress may not "withdraw from [Article III] judicial cognizance any matter *which, from its nature, is the subject of a suit at the common law*, or in equity, or admiralty." Murray's Lessee v. Hoboken Land and Improvement Co., 18 How. 272, 284 (1856). . . . The Court attempts to support the substantial alteration it works today in our Article III jurisprudence by pointing, inter alia, to legislative convenience; to the fact that Congress does not altogether eliminate federal court jurisdiction over ancillary state-law counterclaims; and to Schor's "consent" to CFTC adjudication of ContiCommodity's counterclaims.[1]

. . . Article III's prophylactic protections were intended to prevent . . . abdication to claims of legislative convenience. The Court requires that the legislative interest in convenience and efficiency be weighed against the competing interest in judicial independence. In doing so, the Court pits an interest the benefits of which are immediate, concrete, and easily understood against one, the benefits of which are almost entirely prophylactic, and thus often seem remote and not worth the cost in any single case. Thus, while this balancing creates the illusion of objectivity and ineluctability, in fact the result was foreordained, because the balance is weighted against judicial independence. The danger of the Court's balancing approach is, of course, that as individual cases accumulate in which the Court finds that the short-term benefits of efficiency outweigh the long-term benefits of judicial independence, the protections of Article III will be eviscerated. . . .

Moreover, in Bowsher v. Synar, we rejected the appellant's argument that legislative convenience saved the constitutionality of the assignment by Congress to the Comptroller General of essentially executive functions, stating that " 'the fact that a given law or procedure is efficient, convenient, and useful in facilitating functions of government, standing alone, will not save it if it is contrary to the Constitution. Convenience and efficiency are not the primary objectives—or the hallmarks—of democratic government. . . .' " We recognized that " '[t]he hydraulic pressure inherent within each of the

---

1. The Court also rests its holding on the fact that Congress has not assigned the same sweeping judicial powers to the CFTC that it had assigned to the bankruptcy courts under the Bankruptcy Act of 1978 and that we held violated Article III in Northern Pipeline Co. v. Marathon Pipe Line Co., 458 U.S. 50 (1982). While I agree with the Court that the grant of judicial authority to the CFTC is significantly narrower in scope than the grant to the bankruptcy courts under the 1978 Act, in my view, that difference does not suffice to cure the constitutional defects raised by the grant of authority over state-law counterclaims to the CFTC.

separate Branches to exceed the outer limits of its power, even to accomplish desirable objectives, must be resisted.' " Despite the "conflicts, confusion, and discordance" that separation of powers may at times generate, we held that it is necessary to endure the inconvenience of separated powers in order " 'to secure liberty.' " (quoting Youngstown Sheet & Tube Co. v. Sawyer, 343 U.S. 579, 635 (1952) (Jackson, J., concurring).

It is impossible to reconcile the radically different approaches the Court takes to separation of powers in this case and in Bowsher. The Framers established *three* coequal branches of government and intended to preserve *each* from encroachment by either of the others. The Constitution did not grant Congress the general authority to bypass the judiciary whenever Congress deems it advisable, any more than it granted Congress the authority to arrogate to itself executive functions.

[The consideration that the CFTC merely shares authority over the counterclaims with the federal judiciary was unpersuasive, Justice Brennan argued, because the principle established is without limit—it leaves Congress free to create alternative tribunals, competing with the Article III judiciary across an enormous range of subject matter.] [C]ontrary to the Court's intimations, dilution of judicial power operates to impair the protections of Article III regardless of whether Congress acted with the "good intention" of providing a more efficient dispute resolution system or with the "bad intention" of strengthening the Legislative Branch at the expense of the judiciary.

[Finally, Justice Brennan rejected any notion that Schor's "consent" supported the CFTC's authority.] The Court erroneously suggests that there is a clear division between the separation of powers and the impartial adjudication functions of Article III. . . . . In my view, the structural and individual interests served by Article III are inseparable. The potential exists for individual litigants to be deprived of impartial decisionmakers only where federal officials who exercise judicial power are susceptible to congressional and executive pressure. That is, individual litigants may be harmed by the assignment of judicial power to non-Article III federal tribunals only where the Legislative or Executive Branches have encroached upon judicial authority and have thus threatened the separation of powers. . . .

NOTES

(1) Justice Brennan had been the author of the plurality opinion in NORTHERN PIPELINE CONSTRUCTION CO. v. MARATHON PIPE LINE CO., 458 U.S. 50 (1982), in which Justices Marshall, Blackmun and Stevens had joined. (Note that Justices Blackmun and Stevens joined the Court's opinion in the principal case). In that case, Northern Pipeline Construction Co. had initiated a reorganization proceeding in United States Bankruptcy Court, and then attempted to sue Marathon Pipe Line Co. in that court on contract claims arising out of state law. Marathon sought to have the action dismissed on the ground that the amended Bankruptcy Act, under which the suit was brought, P.L. 95–598, 92 Stat. 2549 (1978), unconstitutionally conferred Article III Judicial

power upon bankruptcy judges, who did not qualify as Article III judges because they lacked lifetime tenure and salary protection.   These judges were given substantially all the powers of Article III judges in civil cases except the power to enjoin another court or to punish criminal contempt not committed in their presence; they might, for example, preside over a jury trial or issue declaratory judgments or writs of habeas corpus.   They were authorized to decide all matters in the bankruptcy proceedings—including issues in litigation between private parties that would ordinarily be resolved in state courts (for example, the existence of a contractual obligation), but that might be swept into the bankruptcy proceedings.   Their judgments would become final if unchallenged, but were subject to review, ultimately by Article III courts.

As appears from his dissent in Schor, Justice Brennan's opinion began with the historical background of Article III and the two "theories" of Crowell v. Benson, and stressed separation of powers principles in rather formal terms.   The bankruptcy courts did not fit the "group of cases in which this Court has upheld the constitutionality of legislative courts and administrative agencies created by Congress to adjudicate cases involving 'public rights,' [1]" he concluded, because in those cases "the Framers expected that Congress would be free to commit such matters completely to nonjudicial executive determination, and that as a result there can be no constitutional objection to Congress' employing the less drastic expedient of committing their determination to a legislative court or an administrative agency."   Bankruptcy proceedings could not be so characterized since they involved private claims, and "a matter of public rights must at a minimum arise 'between the government and others.' [2]"   Nor could bankruptcy courts be characterized as merely "adjunct" to the district court; so much authority had been vested in bankruptcy judges that it could not be said the district courts "retained 'the essential attributes of the judicial power' Crowell v. Benson, supra" or that those courts "were subject to sufficient control by the Art. III district courts."   And, "when [a] right being adjudicated is not of congressional creation . . ., substantial inroads into functions that have traditionally been performed by the Judiciary cannot be characterized merely as incidental extensions of Congress' power to define rights that it has created."

Justice Rehnquist concurred in Northern Pipeline, joined by Justice O'Connor—the author of the Court's opinion in the principal case. He stressed that Marathon was being forced to submit to bankruptcy court resolution of a claim it could ordinarily prosecute in state courts.

1.   Congress' power to create legislative courts to adjudicate public rights carries with it the lesser power to create administrative agencies for the same purpose, and to provide for review of those agency decisions in Art. III courts.   See, e.g., Atlas Roofing Co. v. Occupational Safety and Health Review Comm'n, 430 U.S. 442, 450 (1977).

2.   Congress cannot "withdraw from [Art. III] judicial cognizance *any* matter which, *from its nature,* is the subject of a suit at the common law, or in equity, or admiralty."   Murray's Lessee v. Hoboken Land & Improvement Co., 18 How. 272, 284 (1856) [emphasis added].   It is thus clear that the presence of the United States as a proper party to the proceeding is a necessary but not sufficient means of distinguishing "private rights" from "public rights."   .   .   .

"I need not decide whether these cases in fact support a general proposition with tidy exceptions, as the plurality believes, or whether instead they are but landmarks on a judicial 'darkling plain' where ignorant armies have clashed by night, as Justice White apparently believes them to be. None of the cases has gone so far as to sanction the type of adjudication to which Marathon will be subjected against its will under the provisions of the 1978 Act. To whatever extent different powers granted under that Act might be sustained under the 'public rights' doctrine of Murray's Lessee v. Hoboken Land & Improvement Co., 18 How. 272 (1856), and succeeding cases, I am satisfied that the adjudication of Northern's lawsuit cannot be so sustained."

Justice White wrote the principal dissent for himself, the Chief Justice, and Justice Powell. Conceding the plurality's approach as a historical proposition,[3] he found it untenable as a contemporary answer to the question "what limits Art. III places on Congress' ability to create adjudicative institutions designed to carry out federal policy established pursuant to the substantive authority given Congress elsewhere in the Constitution. Whether fortunate or unfortunate, at this point in the history of constitutional law that question can no longer be answered by looking only to the constitutional text." Reviewing the caselaw in "what has been characterized as one of the most confusing and controversial areas of constitutional law," Justice White concluded: "There is no difference in principle between the work that Congress may assign to an Art. I court and that which the Constitution assigns to Art. III courts. Unless we want to overrule a large number of our precedents upholding a variety of Art. I courts—not to speak of those Art. I courts that go by the contemporary name of 'administrative agencies'—this conclusion is inevitable. It is too late to go back that far; too late to return to the simplicity of the principle pronounced in Art. III and defended so vigorously and persuasively by Hamilton in The Federalist Nos. 78–82.

"To say that the Court has failed to articulate a principle by which we can test the constitutionality of a putative Art. I court, or that there is no such abstract principle, is not to say that this Court must always defer to the legislative decision to create Art. I, rather than Art. III, courts. Article III is not to be read out of the Constitution; rather, it should be read as expressing one value that must be balanced against competing constitutional values and legislative responsibilities. This Court retains the final word on how that balance is to be struck." The existence of provisions for judicial review, and the absence of issues of high political interest or moment were important among the factors persuading Justice White that the Bankruptcy Act provisions did not unacceptably

---

3. "Any reader could easily take Article III to mean that although Congress was free to establish such lower courts as it saw fit, any court that it did establish would be an 'inferior' court exercising 'judicial Power of the United States' and so must be manned by judges possessing both life-ten-ure and a guaranteed minimal income. This would be an eminently sensible reading and one that, as the plurality shows, is well founded in both the documentary sources and the political doctrine of separation of powers that stands behind much of our constitutional structure."

weaken the courts or contribute to "a dangerous accumulation of power in one of the political branches of government."

(2) Northern Pipeline engendered a sharply critical response, raising questions about implications for administrative adjudication rather similar to Justice White's dissent. See, e.g., H. Monaghan, Marbury and the Administrative State, 83 Colum.L.Rev. 1, 18–20 (1983); M. Redish, Legislative Courts, Administrative Agencies, and the Northern Pipeline Decision, 1983 Duke L.J. 197; P. Strauss, the Place of Agencies in Government: Separation of Powers and the Fourth Branch, 84 Colum.L.Rev. 573, 631–33 (1984). The Court first confronted these questions in THOMAS v. UNION CARBIDE AGRICULTURAL PRODUCTS CO., 105 S.Ct. 3325 (1985). Thomas was an action by pesticide chemical manufacturers challenging the constitutionality of 1978 amendments to the Federal Insecticide, Fungicide and Rodenticide Act (FIFRA). These amendments permitted the EPA to use one manufacturer's research data about the health, safety and environmental effects of its product in considering another manufacturer's later application to register a similar product, if the follow-on registrant had offered to compensate the first for use of the data and agreed to binding arbitration should they not agree as to amount. The arbitrator's decision is made subject to judicial review only for "fraud, misrepresentation or other misconduct." The question for the Court was whether this virtually final arbitral decision between two private litigants, about the value of the assistance provided by one to the other, took from Article III courts functions required to be theirs.

Justice O'Connor wrote for five members of the Court that Article III constraints were not offended. State law was not involved because a registrant, having disclosed their research to the EPA, pro tanto extinguished any claim it might have had to a common law trade secret; if its data was to be protected from uncompensated disclosure to its competitors, that protection would have to come from federal law. The Northern Pipeline plurality's distinction between "public" and "private" rights was then repudiated as one that "did not command a majority of the Court."

"If the identity of the parties alone determined the requirements of Article III, under appellees' theory the constitutionality of many quasi-adjudicative agencies involving claims between individuals would be thrown into doubt. . . . The Court has treated as a matter of 'public right' an essentially adversary proceeding to invoke tariff protections against a competitor, as well as an administrative proceeding to determine the rights of landlords and tenants. . . . In essence, the public rights doctrine reflects simply a pragmatic understanding that when Congress selects a quasi-judicial method of resolving matters that 'could be conclusively determined by the Executive and Legislative Branches,' the danger of encroaching on the judicial powers is reduced."

C

"Looking beyond form to the substance of what FIFRA accomplishes, we note several aspects of FIFRA that persuade us the arbitration scheme adopted by Congress does not contravene Article III. First, the right created by FIFRA is not a purely 'private' right, but bears many of the characteristics of a 'public' right. Use of a registrant's data to support a follow-on registration serves a public purpose as an integral part of a program safeguarding the public health. Congress has the power, under Article I, to authorize an agency administering a complex regulatory scheme to allocate costs and benefits among voluntary participants in the program without providing an Article III adjudication. It also has the power to condition issuance of registrations or licenses on compliance with agency procedures. . . .

"Given the nature of the right at issue and the concerns motivating the legislature, we do not think this system threatens the independent role of the judiciary in our constitutional scheme. 'To hold otherwise would be to defeat the obvious purpose of the legislation to furnish a prompt, continuous, expert and inexpensive method for dealing with a class of questions of fact which are peculiarly suited to examination and determination by an administrative agency specially assigned to that task.' Crowell v. Benson, supra, at 46.

"We note as well that the FIFRA arbitration scheme incorporates its own system of internal sanctions and relies only tangentially, if at all, on the Judicial Branch for enforcement. See supra, at 3329–3330. The danger of Congress or the Executive encroaching on the Article III judicial powers is at a minimum when no unwilling defendant is subjected to judicial enforcement power as a result of the agency 'adjudication.' See, e.g., Hart, The Power of Congress to Limit the Jurisdiction of Federal Courts: An Exercise in Dialectic, 66 Harv.L.Rev. 1362 (1953). . . . [U]nder FIFRA, the only potential object of judicial enforcement power is the follow-on registrant who explicitly consents to have his rights determined by arbitration.

"Finally, . . . FIFRA at a minimum allows private parties to secure Article III review of the arbitrator's 'findings and determination' for fraud, misconduct, or misrepresentation. § 3(c)(1)(D)(ii). This provision protects against arbitrators who abuse or exceed their powers or willfully misconstrue their mandate under the governing law. Moreover, review of constitutional error is preserved, and FIFRA, therefore, does not obstruct whatever judicial review might be required by due process. We need not identify the extent to which due process may require review of determinations by the arbitrator because the parties stipulated below to abandon any due process claims. For purposes of our analysis, it is sufficient to note that FIFRA does provide for limited Article III review, including whatever review is independently required by due process considerations. . . .

"Our holding is limited to the proposition that Congress, acting for a valid legislative purpose pursuant to its constitutional powers under Article I, may create a seemingly 'private' right that is so closely integrated into a public regulatory scheme as to be a matter appropriate for agency resolution with limited involvement by the Article III judiciary." [1]

1. The Court remanded, rather than decide, a claim that vesting authority in the arbitrator was an unlawful delegation.

The four Justices of the Northern Pipeline plurality wrote separately. Justice Stevens found standing objections to reaching the merits. Justices Brennan, Marshall and Blackmun, in an opinion by Justice Brennan, concurred in an opinion that reasserted their analysis and found the arbitration provision consistent with the "public rights" idea.

(3) ATLAS ROOFING CO., INC. v. OCCUPATIONAL SAFETY AND HEALTH REVIEW COMM., 430 U.S. 442 (1977). The Occupational Safety and Health Act of 1970 imposed a new statutory duty on employers to avoid maintaining unsafe or unhealthy working conditions, administered by the Department of Labor. On finding a violation of the Act, an inspector issues a citation to the employer fixing a reasonable time for abatement of the violation and, in his discretion, proposing a "civil penalty" ranging from very small amounts for non-serious violations, to not more than $1,000 for serious violations, to a maximum of $10,000 for willful or repeated violations. An employer may contest an abatement or penalty order at an evidentiary hearing held by an administrative law judge of the Department's Occupational Safety and Health Review Commission; her decision becomes the Commission's final and appealable order unless reviewed by the full Commission. Either the Secretary or the employer may secure review of the Commission's decision in an appropriate circuit court of appeals, where the "findings of the Commission with respect to questions of fact, if supported by substantial evidence on the record considered as a whole, shall be conclusive." If the employer does not pay the assessed penalty, the Secretary may institute a collection action in a federal district court in which neither the fact of the violation nor the propriety of the penalty assessed may be retried.

Penalties were imposed on employers who, after unsuccessfully contesting the assessments before the Commission, sought judicial review contending that the statutory assessment scheme violated the Sixth Amendment provision that in "all criminal prosecutions the accused shall enjoy the right to a speedy and public trial, by an impartial jury . . . " and if the proceeding were held not to be criminal, the requirement of the Seventh Amendment that in "Suits at common law, where the value in controversy shall exceed twenty dollars, the right of trial by jury shall be preserved. . . . " The Supreme Court considered only the Seventh Amendment issue, in an opinion written by Mr. Justice White:

. . . Petitioners claim that a suit in a federal court by the Government for civil penalties for violation of a statute is a suit for a money judgment which is classically a suit at common law, and that the defendant therefore has a Seventh Amendment right to a jury determination of all issues of fact in such a case. . . . We disagree. At least in cases in which "public rights" are being litigated—e.g., cases in which the Government sues in its sovereign capacity to enforce public rights created by statutes within the power of Congress to enact—the Seventh Amendment does not prohibit Congress from assigning the factfinding function and initial adjudication to an administrative forum with which the jury would be incompatible.[4]

Congress has often created new statutory obligations, provided for civil penalties for their violation, and committed exclusively to an administrative agency the function of deciding whether a violation has in fact occurred. . . . In sum, [our cases] stand clearly for the proposition that when Congress creates new statutory "public rights," it may assign their adjudication to an administrative agency with which a jury trial would be incompatible, without violating the Seventh Amendment's injunction that jury trial is to be "preserved" in "suits at common law." [5] Congress is not required by the Seventh Amendment to choke the already crowded federal courts with new types of litigation or prevented from committing some new types of litigation to administrative agencies with special competence in the relevant field. This is the case even if the Seventh Amendment would have required a jury where the adjudication of those rights is assigned to a federal court of law instead of an administrative agency. . . .

. . . Our prior cases support administrative factfinding in only those situations involving "public rights," e.g., where the Government is involved in its sovereign capacity under an otherwise valid statute creating enforceable public rights. Wholly private tort, contract, and property cases, as well as a vast range of other cases, are not at all implicated. . . .[6]

4. These cases do not involve purely "private rights." In cases which do involve only "private rights," this Court has accepted factfinding by an administrative agency, without intervention by a jury, only as an adjunct to an Art. III court, analogizing the agency to a jury or a special master and permitting it in admiralty cases to perform the function of the special master. Crowell v. Benson, 285 U.S. 22, 51–65 (1932). The Court there said: "On the common law side of the federal courts, the aid of juries is not only deemed appropriate but is required by the Constitution itself." Id., at 51.

5. We note that the decision of the administrative tribunal in these cases on the law is subject to review in the federal Courts of Appeals, and on the facts is subject to review by such Courts of Appeals under a substantial-evidence test. Thus, these cases do not present the question whether Congress may commit the adjudication of public rights and the imposition of fines for their violation to an administrative agency without any sort of intervention by a court at any stage of the proceedings.

6. [Ed.] The Court also demonstrated that even in matters unquestionably to be heard in court, factfinding "was never the

exclusive province of the jury under either the English or American legal systems at the time of the adoption of the Seventh Amendment; and the question whether a fact would be found by a jury turned to a considerable degree on the nature of the forum in which a litigant found himself. Critical factfinding was performed without juries in suits in equity, and there were no juries in admiralty; neither was there in the military justice system. The jury was the factfinding mode in most suits in the common-law courts, but it was not exclusively so: condemnation was a suit at common law but constitutionally could be tried without a jury. . . . The point is that the Seventh Amendment was never intended to establish the jury as the exclusive mechanism for factfinding in civil cases. It took the existing legal order as it found it, and there is little or no basis for concluding that the Amendment should now be interpreted to provide an impenetrable barrier to administrative factfinding under otherwise valid federal regulatory statutes."

The case is critically discussed in R. Kirst, Administrative Penalties and the Civil Jury: The Supreme Court's Assault on the Seventh Amendment, 126 U.Pa. L.Rev. 1281 (1978).

SECTION 3: THE POLITICAL BRANCHES' CONTROLS OVER AGENCY ACTION

Administrative law courses understandably focus attention on the structured world of laws and courts when considering controls over administrative agencies and their actions. As noted at the beginning of the previous chapter,[1] lawyers engaged in administrative practice quickly find this focus insufficient. To be sure, the final outcome of any particular proceeding may ultimately be testable by those standards and in that forum. Yet many if not most concerns a lawyer and his public or private client might have will not be efficiently addressed in this way. Judicial proceedings take time, often measured in years rather than months;[2] and for regulated as well as regulator and regulatory beneficiary the central issue will most often be to influence outcomes in real time—today. Statutes confer and (as we shall see) courts generally recognize broad ranges of discretion within which all agency choices will be sustainable, and so the central issue will most often be shaping the exercise of that discretion in choosing among outcomes any of which would be permissible in legal perspective. Judicial appraisals tend to be particularistic, focussing on *this* controversy and its outcome-in-fact rather than on the broad fabric of agency policy or questions that might have been (but were not) asked along the way; for most persons affected by administrative actions, what kinds of inquiries the agency undertakes in formulating policy and what is the general shape of its approach has great significance.

These issues can be raised within the agency itself, of course. The formal procedures for doing so are the primary focus of this course (albeit often as seen from judicial perspective). Outside instruments of control other than courts also exist, however, by which an agency's work may be shaped—and shaped in many respects for which judicial oversight is poorly adapted.

Agencies are organs of government. That should suggest that they are subject in their work to the pressures and controls that characterize government functioning generally. Agency personnel meet with citizens and those they regulate, on and off agency premises, to exchange information and views on topics that may be outside particular proceedings yet may influence the views brought to those proceedings. They deal with reporters and read widely—both the general press reporting the run of government business (usually the controversial, if anything at all about agency work is to be printed) and the trade press that exists to report normal as well as abnormal developments to those whose future course and profitability depend on what the agency chooses to do. And, of particular importance for consideration here, agencies are

---

1. P. 2 above.

2. Consider, for example, the chronology in the Vermont Yankee litigation set out at pages 248–258 infra. During 1972–1974 the Atomic Energy Commission, predecessor to the Nuclear Regulatory Commission, developed a policy for application in hearings that would themselves be the culmination of long periods of planning and development. Judicial review of what proved highly limited aspects of that development was completed only in 1983. The world had not stood still in the interim.

subject to the controls that derive from their place in government and their relationships with other parts of government—notably, the elected officials of the legislature and executive branch, and their respective staffs.[3]

Indeed, Congress and the President provide the primary direct check on the daily conduct of federal administrative agencies. On a day-to-day basis, administrators may not worry about the courts unless their general counsels bring them up short (which they learn not to do too often if they wish to remain in office); administrators *are* deeply concerned with what Senator Jones or Presidential Assistant Smith is likely to think when he encounters one or another policy direction. Presidents and legislators are able to react in real time; courts rarely can. Presidents and legislators can give forward shape; courts rarely can. And Presidents and legislators can administer systematic rewards and penalties; courts rarely can.

The remainder of this chapter is addressed to these legislative and executive controls from the general perspective of "separation of powers." That is, after identifying (in rather summary fashion) the controls that exist, the legal question here will be whether any are objectionable in general because of their possible implications for constitutional structure. We return to several of these controls later, notably in Chapter 8, to ask whether and in what circumstances particular individuals whose interests may have been frustrated by the exercise of these controls can object on the grounds that their exercise rendered a particular proceeding "unfair" or otherwise objectionable in standard administrative law terms.

a. Policy Direction

(i) Informal political controls

LOUIS L. JAFFE,* THE ILLUSION OF THE IDEAL ADMINISTRATION **

86 Harv.L.Rev. 1183, 1188-91, 1194-8 (1973).

I would propose a view of administration which recognizes the peculiar political process which provides the milieu and defines the operation of each agency. The elements of this political process are common to all potential lawmaking activity—the intensity of a given problem, the degree to which it is felt throughout an organized and stable constituency, and the representation (or lack thereof) of varying interests within and without the lawmaking body. The significance of each of these elements and the manner of their interaction are unpredictable, and likely to vary with each successive problem. Often the

---

3. See p. 32 n. 1 supra. The following pages are written largely from the perspective of federal government. For treatment of similar issues at the state level, see W. Gormley, Jr., The Politics of Public Utility Regulation (1983).

* Byrne Professor of Administrative Law Emeritus, Harvard University Law School.

outcome will be determined not by the abstracted merits of a situation, but by the character of certain interests which are cohesive and vociferous. The more important point for our purposes, however, is that the extent to which an agency is open—influenced by and responsive to a political process—is determined by the definiteness and specificity of the congressional expression of the agency's methods and objectives.

Taking the highly articulated scheme for tax administration as polar, one can proceed through a spectrum of agencies whose ends and means are less well defined and which, as a consequence, are to a greater or lesser extent centrally positioned in the uncertainties and structural deficiencies of the political process. Where the ends and means of an agency's role are highly defined, elaborately rationalized— as is the case with tax or social security—the effects of the political process on the agency are marginal, though rationalization could never go so far as totally to exclude political choice. In such agencies, the bureaucratic virtues and vices are predominant; highly rationalized administrations embody the advantages of stability, equality of treatment, order, comprehensibility and predictability, and the defects of rigidity and displacement of objectives by bureaucratic routine. . . . The monumental detail of the tax code suggests that Congress can, and does, legislate with great specificity when it regards a matter as sufficiently important. Nor can a political conflict be avoided by relegating a problem to the care of an agency and invoking the talisman of "expertise." The effect of such a transfer of function is simply to shift the legislative process to a different level, and there is no reason to believe that the agency will be able to rise above power conflicts to achieve solutions that the legislature itself cannot or does not choose to provide. The examples of the Federal Communications Commission, Civil Aeronautics Board, and Interstate Commerce Commission do not attest to any intrinsic virtue in general delegations, particularly when they express little more than a disposition to pass the buck.

. . . [I]t makes little sense to criticize an administration for failure to meet a critic's judgment of what the "public interest" requires. The action or inaction of an agency acting under a broad delegation is often the result of the political process operating on the agency, and is, after all, all that can be expected. Indeed, the criticisms of administration must be recognized as themselves a component of the political process, and critics' invocation of the "public interest" as a standard with readily discoverable content should be viewed as but a useful tactic in the political debate.

. . . In a recent faculty seminar which I attended, a speaker characterized the FCC as an agency which has broad powers to regulate the broadcast industry, but which has never been given enough money to hire a staff adequate for the exercise of those powers. This is perhaps another version of the notion that the Commission has been "captured" by the industry, by the means of industry lobbying in the congressional appropriations process. I would contend that, on the contrary, the FCC has an adequate staff *to do what Congress intended and still intends it to do* and a little left over occasionally to be pushed into ventures somewhat beyond congressional expectations.

The notion that the FCC "has" broad powers is derived from the generous verbiage of the Communications Act which empowers the Commission to license—including original licensing, sale of licenses, renewal of license and revocation—in "the public convenience, interest, or necessity." These words are thought by critics of the FCC to give it power generally "to regulate the industry," that is, to make it over pursuant to an image of "the public interest" entertained by one or another group of critics. But there is little, I think, to support this view. The meaning of a statute should be derived initially from the occasion for its enactment, and after that from its development over time, rather than from the abstract terms in which it may be phrased.

. . . [E]ven when the FCC does act within the limited margin available for reform, it has as often as not been stopped in its tracks by a Congress which is committed to the broadcasting status quo. In 1945, the Commission attempted to limit the free transfer of broadcasting licenses by requiring that a proposed buyer enter into a comparison of merit with whoever chose to offer the seller similar terms. The Commission, as it happens, found the scheme unworkable; but Congress, lest the experiment be repeated, forbade it. In another case, the Commission abandoned an attempt to limit advertising to the 16 minutes per hour which was established by a voluntary industry code, after being met with a sharp rebuke from a congressional committee.

Finally, in the political complex which defines the effective power of any particular agency, the potential of an activist court, conservative or liberal, to block, encourage, or command policy initiatives must not be overlooked. The FCC is again an excellent example. Most of its actions are exclusively reviewable by the Court of Appeals of the District of Columbia, where Judges Wright and Bazelon—a powerful activist and liberal faction—are often able to enlist the support of their brethren Robinson, Leventhal, and McGowan. Similarly, conservative judges can severely clip the wings of an agency, as they did to the Federal Trade Commission in the 1920's. The FTC's uncertain, sometimes conflicting, and heterogeneous jurisdiction made it an easy target for judicial sabotage.

. . . Progressives denigrate the administrative agency, often in terms which air their belief that agencies are inherently ineffective, as well as rather quickly captured. Yet however many attempts at reform by government regulation have failed or produced side effects as bad as the original disease, reformers almost invariably fall back on regulation to implement their programs for auto safety, products safety, clean air, unpolluted water, and safe chemicals. This persistence may indicate chronic unawareness or indefatigable optimism, but it may also reflect the truth that an administrative agency, properly mandated and organized, has a very fair chance of success. If the scheme of the reformer is to function along the lines which he assumes to be beneficial, he is most likely to succeed if he secures a specific and firm political judgment from Congress which will resolve, to the degree appropriate formulae permit, the sharp conflicts of interest which are likely to be incapable of resolution by an agency. . . . The key to success is the strong and persistent public opinion which demands a response to a given problem, which is sufficiently organized to press for the detailed legislative solution required, and which will ultimately, keep the administration on the job of implementing it.

NOTES

(1) The view that the political impulse for regulation stems from public rather than private interests has often been controverted. In his Perspectives on the Administrative Process (1979), Professor Robert L. Rabin sets out excerpts from G. Kolko, The Triumph of Conservatism (1963) and G. Stigler, The Theory of Economic Regulation, 2 Bell J. Econ. & Mgmt. Sci 1 (1971). Kolko's essay presents evidence that federal meat inspection laws owe far more to the self-interest of the Beef Trust in protecting their position in European markets from suspicion that American meat was diseased, than to the muckraking exposes of Upton Sinclair, the young journalist widely credited with the development; "it [was] business control over politics . . . rather than political regulation of the economy that [was] the significant phenomenon of the Progressive Era." Professor Stigler celebrates from the perspective of economic analysis "the general hypothesis: every industry or occupation that has enough political power to utilize the state will seek to control entry" and promote other means (such as price-fixing) by which its interests will be served.[1]

(2) Significant controls arise from the process of creating legislation. Jaffe writes of the possibility "that Congress can, and does, legislate with great specificity when it regards a matter as sufficiently important." Notwithstanding the complaints of Justice Rehnquist in the benzene case, pp. 58–65 above, it is observable that contemporary delegations to agencies are often far more specific than characterized the legislation of the New Deal.[2] As important as the public constraints thus created, however, are those that arise in the process of creating legislation. It may be, as has been observed, that for legislation as for sausages one should savor the result, but no one should observe the making. Yet agencies and those they deal with do observe the making, and that can have significant impacts for policy direction.

---

1. Prof. Stigler adds:

"The idealistic view of public regulation is deeply imbedded in professional economic thought. So many economists, for example, have denounced the ICC for its pro-railroad policies that this has become a cliche of the literature. This criticism seems to me exactly as appropriate as a criticism of the Great Atlantic and Pacific Tea Company for selling groceries, or as a criticism of a politician for currying popular support. The fundamental vice of such criticism is that it misdirects attention: it suggests that the way to get an ICC which is not subservient to the carriers is to preach to the commissioners or to the people who appoint the commissioners. The only way to get a different commission would be to change the political support for the Commission, and reward commissioners on a basis unrelated to their services to the carriers."

2 Bell J. Econ. and Mgmt. Sci. at 17–18.

2. See, e.g., R.S. Melnick, p. 19 above.

For a federal agency, the apparatus for statute-making is significantly controlled by legislative coordination and clearance procedures administered for the President by the Office of Management and Budget, an agency that is a major actor in the Executive Office of the President. Pursuant to a long-standing and detailed internal regulation, Circular A–19, no agency may submit draft legislation or even commentary on proposed legislation to Congress unless it has first been cleared with OMB. That clearance will come as a result both of a sensible coordinating process (that is, after the views of all interested agencies have been considered and conflicts resolved) and of an openly political one; conformity of the proposal to the President's program is a central issue. The circular reaches all agencies—the so-called independent regulatory commissions as well as agencies generally regarded as within the executive branch—except for a few explicitly "required by law to transmit their legislative proposals, reports, or testimony to the Congress without prior clearance." [3] Authority for the requirement seems straightforward; among the Constitution's few explicit statements about the President's domestic powers and role are the authority to "require the Opinion, in writing, of the Principal Officer of each of the executive Departments, upon any Subject relating to the Duties of their respective offices" and the responsibility to "recommend to [the Congress'] Consideration such Measures as he shall judge necessary and expedient." [4] If an agency disregards or circumvents these procedures, the result is neither invalidity for an ensuing statute nor inevitable dismissal for the offender. Yet doing so can make it more difficult to secure passage of other desired legislation, and will spend if not exhaust the agency's political capital with OMB, an agency whose responsibilities for the President's budget make its friendship important.[5] The OMB process, then, can generate compromises and understandings with a significant forward impact.

Within Congress itself, the legislative process produces not only the words of a statute, but also what is often a large and unruly body of legislative history and techniques for its enforcement. Professor Bruce A. Ackerman and William T. Hassler, in their short, informative, highly critical, and eminently readable study, "Clean Coal, Dirty Air" (1981), show both how this process worked for one important statute

3. The "independent regulatory commissions" are generally regarded to be those headed by a panel of commissioners serving staggered terms of fixed length and required in some degree to be bipartisan in their political orientation. It is often assumed that they are a wholly different breed from executive agencies, typically headed by a single administrator of the President's party whose term is indefinite—that is, who serves at the President's will. Students should be open to the question just how much difference there really is, given that both types of agencies may perform the identical sorts of regulation employing identical procedures, subject to undifferentiated judicial controls. Indeed, it can be argued that except for the differ-ences implicit in the first two sentences of this footnote, both types of agencies are also subject to undifferentiated political controls. For a fuller treatment, see P. Strauss, The Place of Agencies in Government, Separation of Powers and the Fourth Branch, 84 Colum.L.Rev. 573, 574–596 (1984).

4. U.S.Const. Art. II secs. 2 and 3.

5. See H. Linde, G. Bunn, F. Paff & W. Church, Legislative and Administrative Process 272–280 (2d ed. 1981); R. Gilmour, "Policy Formulation in the Executive Branch: Central Legislative Clearance," in J. Anderson, ed., Cases in Public Policy-Making 80 (1976).

(the reconsideration of Section 111 of the Clean Air Act, 42 U.S.C. § 7411, in 1977) and how the resulting legislative history controlled subsequent events. The legislative process they describe was unruly, covert, and directed at securing political compromise rather than "the recommendation of basic policy premises and the reflection of changes in predominant political opinion;" they found the result "easier to understand as an exercise in small group dynamics than as a serious effort to guide the bureaucratic management of a multi-billion dollar program." The greatest influence was wielded by the legislative subcommittees responsible for the legislation.

"Each subcommittee recognizes that the capacity of the full Congress to process issues is such a scarce resource that only the most salient questions will receive serious attention from the great majority of representatives. Therefore each subcommittee is in a position to manipulate the legislative process to achieve aims that would not survive if they were given clearly focused legislative attention.

"The problem is heightened by the massive increase in congressional staff over the past twenty years.[6] Although these staffers do try to alert their congressmen to important issues, their presence also makes it possible for strategically placed interest groups to generate many more legislative initiatives. The demand for low-visibility legislation may be outstripping the fixed supply of congressional attention." At 56–57.

The same subcommittees, of course, would be responsible for subsequent oversight of the agency's performance of function. That produces one strong incentive for the agency to follow the legislative history in making choices about implementation. "Government by investigation" has emerged as a major form of twentieth century congressional activity. Legislative inquiry into administrative goals and shortcomings dates from the earliest days of the Republic.[7] But investigation as a virtually daily normality has been a development of more recent years. Such hearings can consume enormous amounts of agency time and (by the preparation efforts they require) effectively shape an agency's agenda if not its substantive position.

Another incentive for agency attention to legislative history can be found in the agency's internal needs for self-justification; to a degree outsiders would find difficult to credit, legislative history is regarded as text by agency lawyers in their unending effort to assure the existence of legal authority for whatever it may be the agency proposes to do. And beyond this is a point well expressed by R. Shep Melnick in a Review Essay discussing the Ackerman-Hassler book, 1983 A.B.F. Res.J. 740, 747–48:

6. Between 1957 and 1976, staffing on congressional committees tripled, and congressmen's personal staffs grew by 180%. H. Fox & S. Hammond, Congressional Staffs: The Invisible Force in American Lawmaking 171 (1977). Committee staffing grew by 81% between 1972 and 1976 alone. Id.

7. See T. Taylor, Grand Inquest Ch. 2 (1955).

[A]dministrators have been extremely attentive to the legislative histories manufactured by congressional insiders because they know that the courts—especially the D.C. Circuit—will overrule them when they are not. Thus one cannot fully understand the boldness of well-placed members of Congress and their staff or the timidity of agency officials without seeing how the "new administrative law" has changed the political relations between these two institutions.

BARRY R. WEINGAST * AND MARK J. MORAN,** BUREAUCRATIC DISCRETION OR CONGRESSIONAL CONTROL? REGULATORY POLICYMAKING BY THE FEDERAL TRADE COMMISSION †

91 J.Polit.Econ. 765, 766–770, 775–779, 793 (1983).

I. Two Views of Agency Decision Making

The literature on agency policymaking divides into two distinct approaches. The bureaucratic, or traditional, approach argues that agencies are independent of the legislature. The second, or congressional dominance, approach argues that agencies are directly tied to (or operate in alliance with) the legislature or specific committees within the legislature. In what follows, we . . . note, on the basis of the usual sort of evidence amassed through case studies, that they . . . lead to the same observations about the relationship between agencies and Congress during periods of stable policy: (1) the lack of oversight hearings; (2) the infrequency of congressional investigations and policy resolutions; (3) the perfunctory nature of confirmation hearings of agency heads; (4) the lack of ostensible congressional attention to or knowledge about the ongoing operation and policy consequences of agency choice; and (5) the superficiality of annual appropriations hearings.

According to the traditional approach, these observations represent a failure of Congress to oversee and control the bureaucracy. Several factors contribute to the inability of Congress to control agencies. First, agencies control information from their policy area. Second, access to clientele fosters agency-clientele alliances to protect agencies from their nominal overseers in Congress. And third, the high cost of passing new legislation to redirect agency policy limits congressional action in all but the most important cases. The resulting bureaucratic insulation affords bureaucrats a degree of discretion which, in turn, is used to pursue their own private goals rather than the public purposes for which they were originally created. According to Dodd and Schott, for example, the federal bureaucracy is "in many respects a prodigal child. Although born of congressional intent, it has taken on a life of

* Professor, Center for the Study of American Business, Washington University.

** Professor of Banking and Finance, Case Western Reserve University.

† © The University of Chicago, and reprinted with its permission.

its own and has matured to a point where its muscle and brawn can be turned against its creator." [1] Similarly, J.Q. Wilson concludes that "by and large, the policies of regulatory commissions are not under close scrutiny or careful control of either the White House or of Congress. [Moreover,] . . . whoever first wished to see regulation carried on by quasi-independent agencies and commissions has had his boldest dreams come true. The organizations studied for this book operate with substantial autonomy, at least with respect to congressional or executive direction." [2] While significant differences exist among adherents of this view, these examples illustrate how each hinges on the assumption of agency independence of the legislature. Furthermore, nearly all adherents rely on observations like 1–5 above as evidence in support of their approach. Because Congress plays no easily recognizable role in agency relations, traditional analysis conclude that Congress has little influence over agency policy.

The congressional dominance approach begins with the opposite assumption about agencies and Congress. Though in the textbook version of agency control by Congress congressmen publicly debate policy alternatives and then issue directives to agencies, in practice Congress works quite differently. A less visible but nevertheless effective means for congressional control of agencies is through a system of incentives. Observations 1–5, as we shall see, are consistent with this latter view, though not with the textbook version.

The congressional dominance approach assumes that congressmen—or, more specifically, particular congressmen on the relevant committees—possess sufficient rewards and sanctions to create an incentive system for agencies. Agency mandate notwithstanding, rewards go to those agencies that pursue policies of interest to the current committee members; those agencies that fail to do so are confronted with sanctions. It follows that if the incentive system worked effectively, then agencies would pursue congressional goals even though they received little direct public guidance from their overseers. Congressmen on the relevant committees may appear ignorant of agency proceedings because they gauge the success of programs through their constituents' reactions rather than through detailed study. Public hearings and investigations are resource-intensive activities, so they will hardly be used by congressmen for those policy areas that are operating smoothly (i.e., benefiting congressional clientele). Their real purpose is to police those areas functioning poorly. The threat of ex post sanctions creates ex ante incentives for the bureau to serve a congressional clientele. This view has a striking implication; the more effective the incentive system, the less often we should observe sanctions in the form of congressional attention through hearings and investigations. Put another way, direct and continuous monitoring of inputs rather than of results is an inefficient mechanism by which a principal constrains the action of his agent.

1. L. Dodd and R. Schott, Congress and the Administrative State 2 (1979).   2. The Politics of Regulation 388, 391 (1980).

Several factors make up the congressional incentive system. First, in the budgetary process each agency competes with a host of others for budgetary favors. Congressmen pursuing their own electoral goals favor those agencies that provide the best clientele service. Case studies of particular agencies typically focus on an agency in isolation and miss the important effects of this competition that mitigate, in part, the monopoly aspects of agency service. Second, oversight plays an important role in sanctioning errant agencies. This includes new legislation, specific prohibitions on activities, and other means that serve to embarrass agency heads, hurt future career opportunities, and foil pet projects. Finally, and perhaps the most effective means of influence, Congress controls who gets appointed and reappointed. Confirmation hearings may appear perfunctory to traditional analysis because the difficult policy issues are faced at an earlier, less public stage. For instance, while the official confirmation hearings of ICC commissioners lasted an average of 17 minutes (during the period 1949–74), a closer investigation revealed that Congress played a crucial role in selecting the nominee in most cases. In sum, observations 1–5 are consistent with the smooth and effective functioning of a congressional incentive system to control agency decisions.

. . .

III. Two Alternative Explanations of Recent FTC History

In the early fall of 1979, Congress publicly lambasted the FTC for a series of its investigations and programs, branding them as examples of regulatory abuse. Policy initiatives begun during the previous decade were publicly criticized. Several FTC investigations were halted outright, and the threat of more stringent sanctions suggested new directions for the FTC. Emphasizing this, the following spring the commission was officially allowed to go "out of business" as funds for its operations were not renewed. . . . Although funds were ultimately renewed to continue the FTC's existence, the message was clear: more serious sanctions would follow if the direction and impact of policies were not changed. Responding over the next year and a half, the FTC closed nearly all of its controversial rulemaking investigations and antitrust suits. Congress had demonstrated to the agency that it held the upper hand.

Here is a clear case in which Congress actively intervened using public oversight and legislation to publicly question the direction of policy and attempted to steer the agency along a different course. The issue is, Why? How can we account for this unusual congressional action? The two approaches described [above] provide alternative answers.

The Traditional Interpretation

Remarkably, nearly all public and academic explanations fit into the traditional bureaucratic view of agency policymaking. According to the traditional approach, the congressional action in the form of a rare burst of official oversight confirmed, once again, the view of agency discretion. Congress finally caught a runaway, out-of-control bureaucracy. This demonstrated the discretion afforded by the lack of congressional attention: the FTC had operated independently for nearly a decade and, if not stopped by Congress, would have continued along these lines. Nearly the entire collection of ongoing investigations at the FTC received criticism. Examples of the wide range of targets of FTC investigations included advertising aimed at children (the so-called Kid-Vid controversy), the used car market, the insurance industry, the self-regulating professional organizations such as undertakers, and several of the major antitrust suits such as Exxon et al. (against the nation's largest oil companies) and Kellogg et al. (against the largest manufacturers of breakfast cereals).

Evidently it appeared to Congress and the press that the FTC claimed a mandate spanning the entire economy and was prepared to impose its regulatory control without hesitation. Had Congress played a more continuous role in agency decisions, so the argument goes, agency policy initiatives would have taken a different course. . . . The congressmen participating in this attack on the FTC shared this view. Senator Durkin, for example, described these hearings and sanctions as "shock therapy for bureaucrats." Congressman Levitas (D–Ga.) announced, "We are seeing the end to government by bureaucratic fiat."

These statements give the flavor of the investigation hearings in 1979 as well as of the appropriation hearings early the next year. The perception that the FTC was inattentive to congressional interests, exercised discretion, and overstepped its mandate all seems to support the traditional view of congressional-agency relations. What occurred over the course of late 1979 and early 1980 was simply a case of Congress stepping in to direct policy in an ad hoc manner, "proving" that when congressional action does occur, it has positive effects on policy.

We also note that the two most recent academic studies of the FTC are within this tradition.[3] These scholars analyze FTC behavior throughout the 1970's and conclude that Congress had little to do with FTC decision making. Clarkson, reviewing the legislative constraints on the FTC, articulates many of the important premises of the bureaucratic approach: "The ability of Congress to monitor individual FTC activities effectively is limited. Yet . . . even with its most effective tools, Congress can redirect resources into or away from specific programs only after detailed analysis at the level beyond the institutional competence of Congress except on an, at most occasional project. . . . Oversight and ad hoc monitoring seldom influence Commission activities." Similarly, Katzmann regularly details the opportunities for congressional evaluation or influence but finds little of either. Rather, congressional attention to policy details is superficial and perfunctory.

3. R. Katzmann, Regulatory Bureaucracy: The Federal Trade Commission and Antitrust Policy (1980); K. Clarkson & T. Muris, The Federal Trade Commission Since 1970: Economic Regulation and Bureaucratic Behavior (1981).

An Alternative Explanation: Congressional Choice

According to the second view, the descriptions in the popular press and the political forums had little to do with FTC policymaking during the 1970's, including the imposition of sanctions in 1979–80. Rather, all throughout this decade, the commission pursued the interests of the congressional oversight committee.

Many of the commission's major policy initiatives, important cases, and investigations had their inception and design in congressional hearings held prior to FTC action. . . . As late as 1977 Congress consistently criticized the FTC for lack of progress on their many investigations—the very investigations that drew so much criticism 2 years later.

What occurred in the late 1970's was that congressional support for an activist FTC disappeared. Between 1976 and 1979, the dominant coalition on the relevant congressional committees changed from favoring to opposing an activist FTC. This resulted from the nearly complete turnover of those on and in control of the relevant Senate oversight subcommittee. None of the senior members of the subcommittee responsible for major FTC legislation and direction for the previous decade returned after 1976. Those previously in the minority took control of the subcommittee and began reversing the policies initiated by their predecessors. The 1979 and 1980 hearings were simply the most visible culmination of this process.

The congressional choice explanation suggests that the FTC initiated controversial policies because it got strong signals to do so from Congress. Far from roaming beyond its congressional mandate as an exercise in bureaucratic discretion, the FTC aggressively implemented its new authority in concert with its congressional sponsors. With the turnover in 1977, however, the FTC lost its congressional support and thus was vulnerable to the subsequent reversals.

As evidence in favor of this view, we note that prior to the committee turnover, a small group of dedicated congressmen and senators on the FTC oversight subcommittee spent over a decade developing legislation, holding hearings, and earning a reputation in the area of consumer protection. . . . Warren Magnuson and other major senators involved in FTC activities (e.g., Frank Moss and Philip Hart) were well known for their support of the consumerist issues from the mid-1960s through the 1970s. Magnuson and Moss in the Senate and John Moss in the House worked for 5 years to pass the Magnuson-Moss Warranties and FTC Improvements Act. The latter gave the commission its official rulemaking powers, allowing it to promulgate regulations for an entire industry or industrial practice. Could they have been unaware of the consequences of this delegation? This seems unlikely, since many of the FTC's rulemaking investigations had already begun . . . Magnuson, Moss, Hart, et al. were trying to foster this process, not hinder it.

Similarly, the major antitrust suit against the petroleum industry began with congressional hearings prior to the "oil crisis" of 1973; the oil crisis markedly increased the political popularity of the case independent of its economic merits, leading to increased congressional support in 1973–74. Though the case drew substantial criticism in 1979 from the new subcommittee members, this does not contradict the large role played by the previous subcommittee in launching the case.

Finally, Michael Pertschuk, the outspoken chairman of the commission during the sanctions, played a major role in the development and passage of nearly all the new legislation entrusted to the FTC in his capacity as Senate Commerce Committee Chief of Staff and General Counsel throughout the 1970s. The appointment of Pertschuk to the head of the commission in 1977 seemed a natural culmination of this phase, not a coincidence. The irony is that, just as he left the congressional domain to manage the FTC, the congressional support for FTC activism vanished.[4] . . .

[The authors then test their hypotheses by a series of empirical measures, concluding] that FTC activity is remarkably sensitive to changes in the subcommittee composition. In addition, the evidence reveals the greater influence of the relevant oversight subcommittees compared to the rest of the body. Despite the political rhetoric about a runaway, uncontrollable bureaucracy bringing on the 1979–80 sanctions, the evidence supports our interpretation that these sanctions reflected the new subcommittee's efforts to reverse the policies of their predecessors.

Several tentative generalizations follow from this study. First, the results suggest that the same may also be true for other agencies: on the surface, little ostensible activity by Congress may mask more subtle but nonetheless strong congressional influence. Lack of regular congressional monitoring may reflect the smoothly working congressional system in which intensive monitoring is unnecessary. Second, the evidence also suggests that congressional institutions play important roles in agency decisions. It is not the entire Congress that seems of most interest but rather the specific committees. No doubt more refined models will yield more specific predictions about policymaking.

NOTES

(1) R. KATZMANN, LETTER TO THE EDITOR, Regulation Magazine, Sept./Oct. 1982, pp. 4 and 56:[1] Barry Weingast and Mark Moran presume that there are essentially two distinct and mutually exclusive approaches to agency decision making, the "bureaucratic" and the "congressional dominance" theories. . . . [T]he authors' description

4. [Ed.] Chairman Pertschuk's account may be found in Revolt Against Regulation: The Rise and Pause of the Consumer Movement (University of California 1982) and summarized in his step-son's breakfast question: "If the FTC is an arm of Congress, how come Congress wants to break its arm for making a fist?"

1. Weingast and Moran had published an abbreviated report of their findings in the May/June 1982 issue of Regulation Magazine. This excerpt from Mr. Katzmann's response is reprinted with permission of The American Enterprise Institute.

of the bureaucratic approach oversimplifies the literature, largely in political science, to which it refers. . . . [B]ureaucratic theorists do not claim that Congress fails to oversee the bureaucracy. To be sure, Congress did not rigorously use the various oversight devices at its disposal during most of the 1970s. The reason, in my view, is that it did not think it necessary to do so: congressional committees believed that the FTC was performing well. Congress did try to affect some FTC decisions in the early and mid-seventies: The Exxon case (the most expensive FTC antitrust action in history) and the food investigation, among others, both were in part prompted by vigorous congressional prodding. For the most part, the FTC used its discretion within the bounds of what it saw as the congressional will. What the bureaucratic view does hold is that agency outcomes are very much influenced by internal organizational factors—which is not to deny due weight to external variables such as the will of Congress.

. . . I do not think Weingast and Moran's congressional dominance theory offers an adequate explanation of agency decision making. To suppose that the commission's caseload is simply determined by congressional preferences is to ignore a whole list of organizational factors that affect any agency's decisions; how power is distributed among decision makers, what their professional norms and personal objectives are, and what information is gathered and how. It is also to ignore a whole list of factors specific to the FTC, such as the interaction between lawyers and economists, the value of precedents, and the role of the commissioners.

Weingast and Moran do not even provide much of a test for the argument that Congress has dominated FTC decisions, since they disregard the House of Representatives and look only at the Senate—and mostly at a single subcommittee (the Senate Commerce Committee's Subcommittee on Consumer Affairs). The turnover of membership on this subcommittee coincided with other important trends: the growing sophistication of business lobbyists, disaffection with the FTC across the political spectrum, and changing public attitudes about the efficacy of government intervention in the market. These developments all defy labeling, and their dynamics are not captured by studying almost exclusively, changes in the composition of a Senate subcommittee.

(2) The last paragraph of Katzmann's response warrants some expansion. Agencies typically deal, not with one subcommittee in one house of Congress but with several in each that may be responsible for varying aspects of their programs. Both branches of the Congress maintain standing committees, with jurisdiction over the various subject matters entrusted to the administrative agencies. The committees and active subcommittees number more than 200. In addition to "subject matter" committees and appropriations committees, both the House and the Senate have a Committee on Government Operations, charged with the duty of examining administrative activities in order to determine whether they are marked by "economy and efficiency." [2]

2. M. Ogul, Congress Oversees the Bureaucracy (1976), is a useful, realistic examination of legislative supervision; and see also T. Henderson, Congressional Over-

Every federal agency therefore finds itself answerable to at least six legislative committees, three in each branch of the Congress. As the preceding materials have suggested, these committees and their particular membership will likely have more influence than the Congress as a whole, and that influence will often be directed to seemingly small particulars—neglecting the perception that legislative action concerning those particulars may sacrifice other broader administrative considerations. The mere distraction of satisfying so many overseers may detract from the achievement of primary function; benign or censorious in intention, legislative oversight hearings can consume enormous amounts of agency time and (by the preparation efforts they require) effectively shape an agency's agenda if not its substantive position. Beyond this, as Arthur Macmahon once wrote, "The hazard is that a body like Congress, when it gets to detail, ceases to be itself; it acts through a fraction which may be a faction." [3] Another analyst, sympathetic with the need to maintain effective legislative oversight, wrote that "The splintering of responsibility for inquiries into administration among numerous congressional committees and subcommittees weakens the control that Congress might otherwise exercise, and provides the departments with many legislative controllers. In theory each of the committees is expected to exercise a somewhat different type of control, but in practice questions of program, policy, finance, and efficiency cannot be neatly divided, and when inquiries are undertaken by any one of the various committees they are likely to touch upon all aspects of the work of the department".[4]

Less formal supervision of an ongoing character is carried on by a variety of means, of which two warrant special mention. The 4000 + professional employees of the General Accounting Office, a body organized within Congress, engage in continuous hands-on oversight of agency functioning. GAO evaluators will often be assigned to agencies on a long-term basis, with offices at the site; responding to the requests of committees and of individual members of Congress, and on their own initiative, they may have dozens of investigations into the efficiency of various, often detailed aspects of agency functioning under way at any given time. Draft reports are shown to agency management for response, which often leads to correction; the final reports then made— 935 in fiscal 1980—inform congressional oversight and recommend legislative change.[5] While assuring fiscal responsibility in government

sight of Executive Agencies: A Study of the House Committee on Government Operations (1970). The chairman of the Senate Committee on Government Operations wrote in 1976 that "fragmentation" of legislative responsibility and "chronic absence of coordination and cooperation between committees" had caused inefficiency. The standing committees concerned with subject matter "do not coordinate their oversight with either the Government Operations Committees or the Appropriations Committees on a systematic basis." A. Ribicoff, Congressional Oversight and Regulatory Reform, 28 Ad.L.Rev. 415, 420 (1976). See also W. Cary, Politics and the Regulatory Agencies 55–56 (1967); S. Scher, Congressional Committee Members as Independent Agency Overseers, 54 Am. Pol.Sci.Rev. 911 (1960).

3. A. Macmahon, Congressional Oversight of Administration: The Power of the Purse II, 58 Pol.Sci.Q. 380, 414 (1943).

4. J. Harris, Congressional Control of Administration 275 (1964).

5. See generally Annual Report, United States General Accounting Office for a contemporary view of GAO's activities; F. Mosher, The GAO, The Quest for Accountabil-

affairs is the central GAO function, its evaluators have taken a broad view of their charge to promote efficiency in government, and often report on operating issues as well.[6]

Beyond this professional staff is the burgeoning staff of the Congress itself—staff both on committees and in the offices of individual members of Congress—which can be pressed into the service of overseeing any matter of concern.[7] Inquiring into the impact of "the staff explosion of the past three decades," one analyst has concluded:

"The system of individualized staff control seems also to be responsible for much of the oversight that gets accomplished outside of the General Accounting Office. Having a substantial number of staff people with appropriate investigative authority seems a necessary condition for congressional oversight of the executive branch and the independent regulatory commissions. But it is not a sufficient condition. Oversight also depends on chairmen and staffs who consider the effort worthwhile. For some reason, collegial nonpartisan committee staffs have not provided much oversight. Perhaps it is because their accessibility to all members of a committee leaves them with little time for anything else; perhaps because committees that are willing to retain nonpartisan staffs try to restrain their partisanship and maintain close relationships with their counterparts in the executive branch. Thus, the movement away from a system of collegial nonpartisan committee staffing to a more personalized one has been associated with an increase in congressional oversight activity, largely because a personalized system lets chairmen have activist staff entrepreneurs, and chairmen who use entrepreneurial staffs tend to be more interested in maintaining their independence from the executive branch.

"Yet, while the growth and use of staff has produced these beneficial results, there is a gloomier side: the effect of staffs on Congress' ability to act as a deliberative body. . . . Debate and discussion have lost their central place in the legislative process and that loss has produced serious consequences. The growing importance of staff is but one reflection of the new situation. [T]he growing dominance of large 'chairmen's staffs' has produced management problems that result in uncertainties in the flow of information from staffs to chairmen and from chairmen to others in the Senate or House. Most of the information reaching members may well be reliable, but it would take an expert to sort out the reliable from the unreliable, and even an expert cannot possibly know about material that has been stifled to serve a staff's or chairman's own interests. . . .

"The second problem with the use of staff . . . is that it has not left the members with more time to concentrate on their legislative work. . . . [W]hile representatives as recently as 1965 spent almost

ity in American Government (1979) and E. Kloman, Cases in Accountability: The Work of the GAO (1979) provide external views.

6. The perception that the Comptroller General, who heads the GAO, was performing "executive" functions was central to the dispute over the measure Congress enacted in 1985 to control mounting federal budget deficits. See p. 183 within.

7. H. Fox, Jr., and S. Hammond, The Growth of Congressional Staffs, in H. Mansfield, ed., Congress Against the President 112 (1975).

one full day every week on 'legislative research and reading,' by 1977 the time spent on reading was down to an average of eleven minutes per day.   In other words, instead of freeing the members to concentrate, the staffs contribute to the frenetic pace of congressional life that pulls members in different directions, reduces the time available for joint deliberation, and makes concentration all but impossible.   With the pressure of business thus created, it should be no surprise that members are beguiled into looking at issues as technical problems instead of political ones.   Overburdened and somewhat intimidated by the material the 'experts' throw at them, they are delighted when issues can be resolved in apparently noncontroversial, technocratic terms.   The situation feeds on itself.   The members need staff because they have so little time to concentrate, but the new work created by the staff takes even more of the members' time, indirectly elevating the power of the Washington issue networks in which the staffs play so prominent a role." [8]

The fragmentation of congressional effort is seen, finally, in the "casework" for constituents that scholars of the congressional process often see as central to each member of Congress' effort.[9]   Of course, congressional intercession in pending matters is no new phenomenon. "When I was in the Executive Branch administering the large affairs of one agency," the late Justice Douglas recalled, "there were those in Congress who did not hesitate to pound my desk demanding that a decision be made in a particular way for a constituent." [10]

The late Senator Paul H. Douglas (Dem.Ill.), a man by no means insensitive to ethical issues, insisted from the other side that such interventions were proper.   Administrative officials may readily err, or may "suffer from an undue power complex," or may be lazy or insensitive, or may allow red tape to prevail over individual needs.   Being human, "they do not like to admit mistakes and they naturally protect their own class."   For all these reasons, Senator Douglas said, "the intervention of legislators corrects injustices in a large number of cases and also helps to check tendencies of administrators towards personal and class aggrandizement."   To this ethical justification Senator Douglas added the following bit of political pragmatism: "Out of a deep instinctive wisdom, the American people have never been willing to confide their individual or collective destinies to civil servants over whom they have little control.   They distrust and dislike a self-perpetuating bureaucracy, because they believe that ultimately it will not reflect the best interest of the people.   They therefore turn to their elected representatives to protect their legitimate interests in their relationship with the public administrators.   The people feel that this is part of a legislator's duties, as indeed it is, and if a legislator washes his hands of any such responsibility and refuses so to represent his constituents, he may expect very soon to be retired to private life.

8. M. Malkin, Unelected Representation 240, 242–244 (1979).

9. E.g., D. Arnold, Congress and the Bureaucracy 26–35 (1979); M. Fiorina and R. Noll, Voters, Legislators and Bureaucracy:

Institutional Design in the Public Sector, 68 Am.Ec.Rev. 256 (1978).

10. W. Douglas, Legal Institutions in America, in M. Paulsen ed., Legal Institutions Today and Tomorrow 275, 277 (1959).

Attention to such matters, therefore, becomes a practical necessity for political survival." [11]

One key to agreement or disagreement with views like these is one's estimate of what constitute "legitimate requests" for congressional intercession. A reasonably close analysis of constituents' casework in a number of Capitol Hill offices [12] produced a belief that "at least some congressmen are little concerned about the merits. They spring into action with uncritical zeal, determined from the outset to win for the complainant because he is a constituent, not because his cause is known to be just." The files in a number of the cases examined at that time suggested no "solid foundation for the long-continued struggles to reverse the administrative judgment." Other congressmen and Senators believe that prodding the agencies into responsiveness is ample "service" to constituents and are reluctant to extend this service to the point of advocacy. In either event, thoughtful analyses have concluded, the principal impact of congressional inquiry may be to speed action on the matter inquired of—at the expense of others of equal merit.[13]

(3) Note that the President and his program are entirely missing from both the Weingast and Moran analysis and the Katzmann response.

PETER L. STRAUSS, THE PLACE OF AGENCIES IN GOVERNMENT: SEPARATION OF POWERS AND THE FOURTH BRANCH

84 Colum.L.Rev. 573, 586–595 (1984).

As Presidents and political scientists are fond of remarking,[1] the White House does not control policymaking in the Executive Departments. The President and a few hundred political appointees are at the apex of an enormous bureaucracy whose members enjoy tenure in their jobs, are subject to the constraints of statutes whose history and provisions they know in detail, and often have strong views of the public good in the field in which they work.[2] . . . The bureaucracy constitutes an independent force—indeed, that fact is in some respects

---

11. P. Douglas, Ethics in Government 85–88 (1952).

12. W. Gellhorn, When Americans Complain 71, 72 (1966).

13. A. Sofaer, The Change-of-Status Adjudication: A Case Study of the Informal Agency Process, 1 J.Leg.Stud. 349, 383–84 (1972); J. Mashaw et al., Social Security Hearings and Appeals (1978).

1. President Truman is reported to have described his authority as the power "to bring people in and try to persuade them to do what they ought to do without persuasion. That's what I spend most of my time doing. That's what the powers of the President amount to." C. Rossiter, The American Presidency 149 (2d rev. ed.

1960); see also E. Griffith, The American Presidency, The Dilemmas of Shared Power and Divided Government 43–51 (1976). H. Heclo, A Government of Strangers: Executive Politics in Washington (1977); D. James, The Contemporary Presidency 122–29 (1969); G. McConnell, The Modern Presidency 61–79 (1976); R. Neustadt, Presidential Power—The Politics of Leadership From FDR to Carter ch. 3 (1980).

2. For remarkable and sensitive accounts of the internal strengths and functioning of the American national bureaucracy, see the works of H. Kaufman, e.g., The Forest Ranger (1960) and The Administrative Behavior of Federal Bureau Chiefs (1981).

the dominating problem of the current administrative law literature [3]—
and its cooperation must be won to achieve any desired outcome.

Viewed from any perspective other than independence in policy
formation, the legal regime within which agencies function is highly
unified under presidential direction. Many administrative functions
are centrally performed, a product of congressional recognition that all
agencies share many of the administrative needs of government, for
which central management under presidential supervision is highly
desirable. Thus, the property of independent as well as executive-
branch agencies is managed by the General Services Administration,
and their contracts are entered in accordance with its procurement
regulations. The Department of Justice, to varying degrees, represents
their interests in court; the Office of Personnel Management and the
Merit Systems Protection Board regulate their employment practices,
pay scales and allocation of super-grade management posts. The protection of national secrets, with one statutory exception, occurs under
an executive order, which establishes both the regime for classification
and the requirements for access; and the executive branch performs
the investigations that qualify persons for clearance. Government
contracts contain non-discrimination clauses, and an enforcement regime housed in an executive department has been established, again on
the basis of an executive order.

Even in the arena of policy, one readily finds major respects in
which agencies' work is centrally managed.[4] The National Security
Council and the Domestic Council coordinate interagency studies to
develop national policy at the request of the President or a possibly
affected agency, without necessary regard to the independence (or lack
of it) of the agencies that may be affected. Similarly, the Office of
Management and Budget coordinates agency comments on some proposed rules, promoting conferences and other collaborative efforts in
order to produce a result maximally acceptable among all agencies
concerned. OMB plays a coordinating role also when agencies find
themselves in the jurisdictional disputes that are the inevitable consequence of the enormous number of regulatory measures Congress
enacts and the many different agencies to which it assigns responsibility.[5] Litigation or the seeking of a formal legal opinion from the
Attorney General would be possible, for example, in the face of uncertainty whether the Nuclear Regulatory Commission or the Environ-

3. K. Meier, Politics And The Bureau-
cracy: Policy-Making in The Fourth
Branch of Government (1979); H. Merry,
Five-Branch Government 59–60 (1980); E.
Hargrove, The Power of the Modern Presi-
dency 79 (1974).

4. The policy bases for central direction
are well set out in A.B.A. Comm'n On Law
And The Economy, Federal Regulation:
Roads to Reform 68–91 (1979) [hereinafter
cited as Roads to Reform]. See also Bruff,
Presidential Power and Administrative
Rulemaking, 88 Yale L.J. 451, 474–75
(1979). However, Congress has occasional-

ly made judgments precluding balancing,
which the President as much as the agency
concerned would be obliged to respect. See
American Textile Mfrs. Inst. Inc. v. Donovan, 452 U.S. 490 (1981); Verkuil, Jawboning Administrative Agencies: Ex Parte
Contacts by the White House, 80 Colum.L.
Rev. 943, 950 n. 41 (1980).

5. Roads to Reform, supra note 4, at 70–
72, lists "sixteen federal agencies, within
and outside the executive branch, each created and governed by its own separate statutes, with responsibilities that directly affect the price and supply of energy."

mental Protection Agency had primary regulatory responsibility for radioactive discharges from NRC regulated plants into EPA regulated waters, but the more usual course is to put the matter before OMB, which will more informally attempt to bring the agencies to an understanding. . . . Overall, presidential coordination is an activity of importance, one in which the agencies generally cooperate and from which they receive benefit as well as occasional constraint.[6]

The independent agencies are often free, at least in a formal sense, of other relationships with the White House that characterize the executive branch agencies. The President's influence reaches somewhat more deeply into the top layers of bureaucracy at an executive agency than at an independent commission. . . . The requirement that commission membership be at least nominally bipartisan does not prevent the appointment of political friends but doubtless lowers the political temperature. Typically, the independents have more authority to conduct their own litigation than executive branch agencies do, although not exclusive authority. One recent statute, the Paperwork Reduction Act of 1980, specifically empowers the independents to overrule by majority the Presidential directives respecting the collection of information to which executive branch agencies are bound.[7] . . .

Yet these differences are at best matters of degree. . . . Even in executive agencies, the layer over which the President enjoys direct control of personnel is very thin and political factors may make it difficult for him to exercise even those controls to the fullest. An administrator with a public constituency and mandate cannot be discharged—and understands that he cannot be discharged—without substantial political cost. Also for political reasons, one may be certain that independent commission consultation with the White House about appointments often occurs, even if subdued—as in so many other matters—by the lack of obligation so to consult.

Presidential influence over the independent agencies is heightened by the special ties existing between the President and the chairmen of almost all of the independent regulatory commissions. Although all commissioners, including the chairmen, are appointed to fixed terms as commissioners, the chairman generally holds that special post at the President's pleasure.[8] . . . [R]egulatory commission chairmen . . .

6. See, e.g., Katzmann, Regulatory Bureaucracy: The Federal Trade Commission and Antitrust Policy 140 (1980): "[M]anagement specialists in the Commission regard the OMB as a useful ally in instituting organizational changes that are designed to centralize control and are opposed by the bureau heads. Commented one commission staff member who worked closely with the executive director: 'We know the bureau heads do not like procedures which enable the chairman and the other commissioners to get a better idea about what the troops are doing. So we tell them it is just not a question of what the chairman and the other commissioners want. The Office of Management and Budget, which could make trouble for us, will react unsympathetically to requests for more attorneys if we do not accommodate them by tightening up our management systems.' "

7. 44 U.S.C. § 3507(c). By requiring initial clearance from OMB and a public, reasoned act to overrule its guidance, even that provision suggests congressional respect for the President's central, coordinative function.

8. See D. Welborn, Governance Of Federal Regulatory Agencies 6–7, 37, 141 (1977); W. Cary, Politics And The Regula-

almost completely dominate the administrative side of commission business, selecting most staff, setting budgetary policy, and as a consequence commanding staff loyalties. These administrative responsibilities, corresponding to presidential responsibilities for the government as a whole, doubtless underlie Congress' general recognition of the President's special claim to have his own choice as chairman. . . . [Respecting] commission policymaking . . . the White House connection is often less direct and generally more subtle, but consultation and coordination on general policy issues of national interest naturally occurs. . . .

The uncertainty about what "independence" means shapes the behavior of the Congress, the President and the agencies alike. Congressmen tend to talk about the independent commissions in a proprietary way—these are "our" agencies, not so much independent as independent-of-the-President. One result of this attitude—hard to measure but suggested by local belief—may be a greater intensity of congressional political oversight of the independents. Even if congressional oversight is not itself measurably more intense, it may be the more effective if not answered by counterpressures; as a former FTC Chairman recently remarked, the independent agencies "have no lifeline to the White House. [They] are naked before Congress, without protection there," because of the President's choice not to risk the political cost that assertion of his interest would entail. In any event, Congress' techniques do not vary; no particular form of dominion is asserted over "independent" agencies that is not practiced also on the agencies associated more directly with the White House. And, as already indicated, Congress generally provides for a large measure of presidential participation in the day-to-day administration, if not the policy formation, of those agencies.

Perhaps the central fact of legislative-executive management of oversight relationships with the agencies is the extent to which behavior is determined by political factors rather than law. The White House's treatment of cost-benefit analysis by independent regulatory commissions in conjunction with major rulemakings is a notable example. Both President Carter and President Reagan were advised (correctly, in my view) that they had authority to include the independents in their executive orders promoting economic analysis of proposed rules as an element of regulatory reform.[9] Neither did include those agen-

tory Agencies 5–24 (1967). The chairmen of the Federal Reserve Board and the Consumer Product Safety Commission enjoy statutory protection of tenure. 12 U.S.C. § 241 (Federal Reserve Board); 15 U.S.C. § 2053 (Consumer Product Safety Commission). The Federal Reserve Board, at least, operates in a setting in which public confidence has long been thought paramount, and Congress seeks no oversight of its own. See also H. Bruff, supra note 4, at 496, 499; Roads To Reform, supra note 4, at 85.

9. See Executive Orders Nos. 12,044, 3 CFR 152 (Carter), and 12,291, 46 Fed.Reg.

13193 (1981), reprinted in 5 U.S.C. § 601 (Reagan). [The advice appears at . . . 43 Fed.Reg. 12,260 (1978) . . . U.S. Dept. of Justice, Memorandum re Proposed Executive Order on Federal Regulation 7–13 (Feb. 12, 1981) (addressing the question of the legality of applying proposed Executive Order No. 12,291 to the independent regulatory agencies), reprinted in Role of The Office of Management and Budget in Regulation: Hearings Before the Subcomm. on Oversight and Investigations of the House Comm. on Energy and Commerce, 97th Cong., 1st Sess. 158–64 (1981)

cies, reasoning that the political costs of arousing Congressional opposition, perhaps to the order as a whole, would be too great. In fact, the independents generally have complied with these executive orders: they have participated in the Regulatory Council, publish regular agendas of rulemaking, are attentive to White House inquiries about their progress, and otherwise behave as if they were in fact subject to the discipline from which they have been excused.

The reasons for this acceptance of presidential input are clear. The president's effective power over the independents would counsel against excluding his concerns even if political loyalties did not command attention. If the President's policies make good sense, or the importance or utility of coordination or a single policy is evident, the independents can be expected to comply.[10] . . .

It can be useful to be associated with national policy, to have a big and politically powerful "friend," when appearing before Congress. The commissions need goods the President can provide: budgetary and legislative support, assistance in dealing with other agencies, legal services, office space, and advice on national policy. They share a commitment to achieving the public interest, and are likely to respect the President's motives and appreciate his political responsibility and support. They are flattered when their own advice is sought, and respectful of office when they are advised. In the circumstances, it is not surprising that the independent commissions can be susceptible to substantial presidential oversight. . . .

The limited documentation of the process by which OMB and other executive offices participate in rulemaking accounts for the informal nature of [these] conclusions . . . as well as public fears of improper pressure. Much takes place over the telephone or in informal meetings, from which documentation is unlikely. OMB naturally fears that exposure, particularly to Congress, is likely to diminish its influence. The production of written documents takes precious time and resources from other tasks. And, much as our society values openness, . . . candor and the flexibility necessary for collaboration or compromise are more likely to flourish in the shade.[11] Yet one should not rush from

10. . . . [M]any general skills required by agencies are more efficiently exercised by a central authority. Consider, for example, the frequent provision for self-representation by the independent agencies on judicial review of their decisions. See e.g., 12 U.S.C. § 1828(c)(7)(D) (comptroller of currency, Federal Reserve Board and Federal Deposit Insurance Corporations); 15 U.S.C. § 56(a)(2) (Federal Trade Commission); 28 U.S.C. § 2323 (Interstate Commerce Commission authorized to represent itself as a party); id. § 2348 (same authority granted to Federal Communications Commission, Federal Maritime Commission, and the Nuclear Regulatory Commission). Such provisions are responsive to the concern that the President's Department of Justice might not be sufficiently understanding of their posi-

tions. Yet what self-representation in court gains for the agencies in ability to defend their particular policies, it loses in capacity to deal with the common issues that characterize much judicial review of agency action: compliance with general statutes, such as the Administrative Procedure Act or the Freedom of Information Act, 5 U.S.C. § 552, standing, ripeness, and other like issues of reviewability, general standards of review, and, at an operational level, reputation and litigating competence in the judicial forum.

11. Consider the following exchange between Representative John D. Dingell (D-Mich.), Chairman of the House Committee on Energy and Commerce and of the Subcommittee on Oversight and Investigations, and James C. Miller III, Administra-

acknowledging the paucity of information to the judgment that Congress' assignments of responsibility have been undone, that the President enjoys an iron control over the work of law-administration. Both because statutes place decisional authority in the agencies, not the President, and because the White House often lacks the personnel and knowledge to make detailed judgments about policy content, actual as well as legal placement of final decision generally remains with the agencies.

(ii) Formal political controls

The preceding materials have considered what might be described as the levers of persuasion in the political world within which agencies operate—what it is that may make agencies anxious to please the wishes of a President or of powerful congressional figures in shaping policy. We turn now to ask what powers the chief executive and legislature have to command obedience—formally to control the outcomes of administrative decisionmaking. Most obvious, and important, are the statutes that create the framework, substantive and procedural, within which the agencies—and for that matter the President—must act.[1] For the moment, however, we turn to two formal measures undertaken by the President, employing the device of an executive

tor for Information and Regulatory Affairs, Office of Management and Budget, and Executive Director, Presidential Task Force on Regulatory Relief, after Dingell requested copies of the fifty-five rules returned by OMB to an agency for review:

"D: I will not ask for the originals. I will just ask for copies and the Chair will advise I will be quite content to receive those. . . .

"M: We do not have an original.

"D: Well, who has the original?

"M: Sir, the flow of paper into our office is awesome. Under the Paperwork Reduction Act, the irony is that the paperflow in our office has increased from something like 3,000 transactions to 12,000 transactions, and so we do not even . . .

"D: I am impressed but all I am asking for is copies of papers that are supposed to be in your files.

"M: I don't know how you allege that, sir, not knowing what our filing system is. I have just said that we do not keep copies of the regulations."

Hearings, supra note 9, at 112.

1. While the bill of attainder clause prohibits Congress from using statutes to penalize determinate individuals for past behavior, United States v. Lovett, 328 U.S. 303 (1946); United States v. Brown, 381 U.S. 437 (1965), the legality of using the statutory form to force outcomes of particular administrative proceedings in other contexts is unquestioned. See, e.g., National Treasury Employees Union v. Devine, 733 F.2d 114 (D.C.Cir.1984), holding that a congressional appropriations measure directing that "no funds be spent" for implementation of a designated agency rule rendered that rule "null and void" for the period governed by the appropriations measure.

That Congress *may* command obedience by statutory change does not establish that it is invariably meet for it to do so. Even if free of the formal deficiencies of the legislative veto, see pp. 164–177 within, some have found severe problems for the general health of legislative function in the reactive particularity of the practice. See C. Hardin, K. Shepsle, and B. Weingast, "Public Policy Excesses; Government by Congressional Subcommittee" (Center for the Study of American Business Publication No. 50 1982). From the agency perspective the Administrative Conference has argued, "such intervention precludes orderly development and consideration of the complex issues involved [in the interrupted administrative proceedings] and undermines respect for the administrative process." 1979 Report of the Administrative Conference of the United States 74 (1980). Looking the other way, it may be argued, are circumstances in which a politically accountable body (Congress) becomes convinced that further agency proceedings in a matter simply will not be fruitful in bringing to light potential benefits of the proposed rule or order that might influence its current negative view.

order. The following order, adopted by President Reagan barely a month after his inauguration, elaborated on requirements for discussion of the economic consequences of regulation that had been imposed by his predecessors.[2]

EXECUTIVE ORDER NO. 12291
46 Fed.Reg. 13193 (Feb. 17, 1981).

By the authority vested in me as President by the Constitution and laws of the United States of America, and in order to reduce the burdens of existing and future regulations, increase agency accountability for regulatory actions, provide for presidential oversight of the regulatory process, minimize duplication and conflict of regulations, and insure well-reasoned regulations, it is hereby ordered as follows:

Section 1. Definitions For the purposes of this Order:

(a) "Regulation" or "rule" means an agency statement of general applicability and future effect designed to implement, interpret, or prescribe law or policy or describing the procedure or practice requirements of an agency, but does not include

1. [Rulemaking based on a formal record] . . .

2. Regulations issued with respect to a military or foreign affairs function of the United States; or

3. Regulations related to agency organization, management, or personnel.

(b) "Major rule" means any regulation that is likely to result in:

1. An annual effect on the economy of $100 million or more:

2. A major increase in costs or prices for consumers, individual industries, Federal, State, or local government agencies, or geographic regions; or

3. Significant adverse effects on competition, employment, investment, productivity, innovation, or on the ability of United States-based enterprises to compete with foreign-based enterprises in domestic or export markets.

(c) "Director" means the Director of the Office of Management and Budget.

(d) "Agency" means any authority of the United States that is an "agency" under 44 U.S.C. § 3502(1), excluding those agencies specified in 44 U.S.C. § 3502(10).[3]

(e) "Task Force" means the Presidential Task Force on Regulatory Relief.

Sec. 2. General Requirements. In promulgating new regulations, reviewing existing regulations, and developing legislative proposals concerning regulation, all agencies, to the extent permitted by law, shall adhere to the following requirements:

2. See 39 Fed.Reg. 41, 501 (1974); 42 Fed.Reg. 1,017 (1977); 43 Fed.Reg. 12,661 (1978).

3. [Ed.] 44 U.S.C. § 3502(10) lists the independent regulatory commissions

(a) Administrative decisions shall be based on adequate information concerning the need for and consequences of proposed government action:

(b) Regulatory action shall not be undertaken unless the potential benefits to society for the regulation outweigh the potential costs to society:

(c) Regulatory objectives shall be chosen to maximize the net benefits to society:

(d) Among alternative approaches to any given regulatory objective, the alternative involving the least net cost to society shall be chosen; and

(e) Agencies shall set regulatory priorities with the aim of maximizing the aggregate net benefits to society, taking into account the condition of the particular industries affected by regulations, the condition of the national economy, and other regulatory actions contemplated for the future.

Sec. 3. Regulatory Impact Analysis and Review.

(a) In order to implement Section 2 of this Order, each agency shall, in connection with every major rule, prepare, and to the extent permitted by law consider a Regulatory Impact Analysis. Such Analyses may be combined with any Regulatory Flexibility Analyses performed under 5 U.S.C. §§ 603 and 604.

(b) Each agency shall initially determine whether a rule it intends to propose or to issue is a major rule, provided that, the Director, subject to the direction of the Task Force, shall have authority, in accordance with Sections 1(b) and 2 of this Order, to prescribe criteria for making such determinations [and] to order a rule to be treated as a major rule. . . .

(c) Except as provided in Section 8 of this Order, agencies shall prepare Regulatory Impact Analyses of major rules and transmit them, along with all notices of proposed rulemaking and all final rules, to the Director as follows:

1. . . .

2. . . . . [T]he agency shall prepare a preliminary Regulatory Impact Analysis, which shall be transmitted, along with a notice of proposed rulemaking to the Director at least 60 days prior to the publication of a notice of proposed rulemaking and a final Regulatory Impact Analysis, which shall be transmitted along with the final rule at least 30 days prior to the publication of the major rule as a final rule:

3. For all rules other than major rules, agencies shall submit to the Director at least 10 days prior to publication, every notice of proposed rulemaking and final rule.

(d) To permit each proposed major rule to be analyzed in light of the requirements stated in Section 2 of this Order, each preliminary and final Regulatory Impact analysis shall contain the following information:

1.   A description of the potential benefits of the rule, including any beneficial effects that cannot be quantified in monetary terms, and the identification of those likely to receive the benefits:

2.   A description of the potential costs of the rule, including any adverse effects that cannot be quantified in monetary terms, and the identification of those likely to bear the costs:

3.   A determination of the potential net benefits of the rule, including an evaluation of effects that cannot be quantified in monetary terms:

4.   A description of alternative approaches that could substantially achieve the same regulatory goal at lower cost, together with an analysis of this potential benefit and costs and a brief explanation of the legal reasons why such alternatives, if proposed, could not be adopted: and

5.   Unless covered by the description required under paragraph (4) of this subsection, an explanation of any legal reasons why the rule cannot be based on the requirements set forth in Section 2 of this Order.

(e)(1) The Director, subject to the direction of the Task Force, which shall resolve any issues raised under this Order or ensure that they are presented to the President, is authorized to review any preliminary or final Regulatory Impact Analysis, notice of proposed rulemaking or final rule based on the requirements of this Order.

(2) The Director shall be deemed to have concluded review unless the Director advises an agency to the contrary under subsection (f) of this Section:

(A) Within 60 days of a submission . . . of a preliminary Regulatory Impact Analysis or notice of proposed rulemaking under subsection (c)(2):

(B) Within 30 days of the submission of a final Regulatory Impact Analysis and a final rule under subsection (c)(2): and

(C) Within 10 days of the submission of a notice of proposed rulemaking or final rule under subsection (c)(3).

(f)(1) Upon the request of the Director, an agency shall consult with the Director concerning the review of a preliminary Regulatory Impact Analysis or notice of proposed rulemaking under this Order, and shall, subject to Section 8(a)(2) of this Order, refrain from publishing its preliminary Regulatory Impact Analysis or notice of proposed rulemaking until such review is concluded.

(2) Upon receiving notice that the Director intends to submit views with respect to any final Regulatory Impact Analysis or final rule, the agency shall, subject to Section 8(a)(2) of this Order, refrain from publishing its final Regulatory Impact Analysis or final rule until the agency has responded to the Director's views, and incorporated those views and the agency's response in the rulemaking file.

(3) Nothing in this subsection shall be construed as displacing the agencies' responsibilities delegated by law.

. . .

Sec. 5.   Regulatory Agencies.

(a) Each agency shall publish, in October and April of each year, an agenda of proposed regulations that the agency has issued or expects to issue, and currently effective rules that are under agency review pursuant to this Order.   . . .

Sec. 6.   The Task Force and Office of Management and Budget.

(a) To the extent permitted by law, the Director shall have authority, subject to the direction of the Task Force to:

1.   Designate any proposed or existing rule as a major rule in accordance with Section 1(b) of this Order:

2.   Prepare and promulgate uniform standards for the identification of major rules and the development of Regulatory Impact Analyses:

3.   Require an agency to obtain and evaluate, in connection with a regulation, any additional relevant data from any appropriate source:

4.   Waive the requirements of Sections 3, 4, or 7 of this Order with respect to any proposed or existing major rule.

5.   Identify duplicative, overlapping and conflicting rules, existing or proposed, and existing or proposed rules that are inconsistent with the policies underlying statutes governing agencies other than the issuing agency or with the purposes of this Order, and, in each such case, require appropriate interagency consultation to minimize or eliminate such duplication, overlap, or conflict:

6.   Develop procedures for estimating the annual benefits and costs of agency regulations, on both an aggregate and economic or industrial sector basis, for purposes of compiling a regulatory budget:

7.   In consultation with interested agencies, prepare for consideration by the President recommendations for changes in the agencies' statutes: and

8.   Monitor agency compliance with the requirement of this Order and advise the President with respect to such compliance.

(b) The Director, subject to the direction of the Task Force, is authorized to establish procedures for the performance of all functions vested in the Director by this Order.   The Director shall take appropriate steps to coordinate the implementation of the analysis, transmittal, review, and clearance provisions of this Order with the authorities and requirements provided for or imposed upon the Director and agencies under the Regulatory Flexibility Act, 5 U.S.C. § 601 et seq., and the Paperwork Reduction Plan Act of 1980, 44 U.S.C. § 3501 et seq.

. . .

Sec. 8.   Exemptions.

(a) The procedures prescribed by this Order shall not apply to:

1.   Any regulation that responds to an emergency situation, provided that any such regulation shall be reported to the Director as soon as is practicable, the agency shall publish in the Federal Register a

statement of the reasons why it is impracticable for the agency to follow the procedures of this Order with respect to such a rule, and the agency shall prepare and transmit as soon as is practicable a regulatory Impact Analysis of any such major rule: and

2. Any regulation for which consideration or reconsideration under the terms of this Order would conflict with deadlines imposed by statute or by judicial order, provided that, any such regulation shall be reported to the Director together with a brief explanation of the conflict, the agency shall publish in the Federal Register a statement of the reasons why it is impracticable for the agency to follow the procedures of this Order with respect to such a rule, and the agency, in consultation with the Director, shall adhere to the requirements of this Order to the extent permitted by statutory or judicial deadlines.

(c) The Director, subject to the direction of the Task Force, may, in accordance with the purposes of this Order, exempt any class or category of regulations from any or all requirements of this Order.

Sec. 9. Judicial Review. This Order is intended only to improve the internal management of the Federal government, and is not intended to create any right or benefit, substantive or procedural, enforceable at law by a party against the United States, its agencies, its officers or any person. The determinations made by agencies under Section 4 of this Order, and any Regulatory Impact Analyses for any rule, shall be made part of the whole record of agency action in connection with the rule.

. . .

Ronald Reagan

THE WHITE HOUSE, February 17, 1981.

EXECUTIVE ORDER 12498
50 Fed.Reg. 1036 (January 4, 1985).

By the authority vested in me as President by the Constitution and laws of the United States of America, and in order to create a coordinated process for developing on an annual basis the Administration's Regulatory Program, establish Administration regulatory priorities, increase the accountability of agency heads for the regulatory actions of their agencies, provide for Presidential oversight of the regulatory process, reduce the burdens of existing and future regulations, minimize duplication and conflict of regulations, and enhance public and Congressional understanding of the Administration's regulatory objectives, it is hereby ordered as follows:

Section 1. General Requirements. (a) There is hereby established a regulatory planning process by which the Administration will develop and publish a Regulatory Program for each year. To implement this process, each Executive agency subject to Executive Order No. 12291 shall submit to the Director of the Office of Management and Budget (OMB) each year, starting in 1985, a statement of its regulatory policies, goals, and objectives for the coming year and information concerning all significant regulatory actions underway or planned; however, the Director may exempt from this Order such agencies or activities as the Director may deem appropriate in order to achieve the effective implementation of this Order.

(b) The head of each Executive agency subject to this Order shall ensure that all regulatory actions are consistent with the goals of the agency and of the Administration, and will be appropriately implemented.

. . .

Sec. 2.   Agency Submission of Draft Regulatory Program.   (a) The head of each agency shall submit to the Director an overview of the agency's regulatory policies, goals, and objectives for the program year and such information concerning all significant regulatory actions of the agency, planned or underway, including actions taken to consider whether to initiate rulemaking; requests for public comment; and the development of documents that may influence, anticipate, or could lead to the commencement of rulemaking proceedings at a later date, as the Director deems necessary to develop the Administration's Regulatory Program.   This submission shall constitute the agency's draft regulatory program.

. . .

Sec. 3.   Review, Compilation, and Publication of the Administration's Regulatory Program.   (a) In reviewing each agency's draft regulatory program, the Director shall (i) consider the consistency of the draft regulatory program with the Administration's policies and priorities and the draft regulatory programs submitted by other agencies; and (ii) identify such further regulatory or deregulatory actions as may, in his view, be necessary in order to achieve such consistency.   In the event of disagreement over the content of the agency's draft regulatory program, the agency head or the Director may raise issues for further review by the President or by such appropriate Cabinet Council or other forum as the President may designate.

(b) Following the conclusion of the review process established by subsection (a), each agency head shall submit to the Director, by a date to be specified by the Director, the agency's final regulatory plan for compilation and publication as the Administration's Regulatory Program for that year.   The Director shall circulate a draft of the Administration's Regulatory Program for agency comment, review, and interagency consideration, if necessary, before publication.

(c) After development of the Administration's Regulatory Program for the year, if the agency head proposes to take a regulatory action subject to the provisions of Section 2 and not previously submitted for review under this process, or if the agency head proposes to take a regulatory action that is materially different from the action described in the agency's final Regulatory Program, the agency head shall immediately advise the Director and submit the action to the Director for review in such format as the Director may specify.   Except in the case of emergency situations, as defined by the Director, or statutory or judicial deadlines, the agency head shall refrain from taking the proposed regulatory action until the review of this submission by the Director is completed. . . .

(d) Absent unusual circumstances, such as new statutory or judicial requirements or unanticipated emergency situations, the Director may, to the extent permitted by law, return for reconsideration any rule submitted for review under Executive Order 12291 that would be subject to Section 2 but was not included in the agency's final Regulatory Program for that year, or any other significant regulatory action that is materially different from those described in the Administration's Regulatory Program for that year.

Sec. 4. Office of Management and Budget. The Director of the Office of Management and Budget is authorized to the extent permitted by law, to take such actions as may be necessary to carry out the provisions of this Order.

Sec. 5. Judicial Review. This Order is intended only to improve the internal management of the Federal government, and is not intended to create any right or benefit, substantive or procedural, enforceable at law by a party against the United States, its agencies, its officers or any person.

Ronald Reagan

THE WHITE HOUSE
January 4, 1985.

CASS SUNSTEIN *, COST-BENEFIT ANALYSIS AND THE SEPARATION OF POWERS †
23 Ariz.L.Rev. 1267 (1981).

President Reagan's Executive Order No. 12,291 is an effort to ensure that the Presidency, through the Office of Management and Budget (OMB) and the Presidential Task Force on Regulatory Relief, will control the exercise of executive agency discretion under regulatory statutes. Although there are historical antecedents for the order,[1] no other President has gone nearly so far. In particular, no other President provided that regulatory action may not be initiated unless the benefits exceed the costs, and none has accorded to officials close to the President such wide-ranging supervisory power over the basic decision whether regulatory action should be taken. . . .

Executive Order 12,291 . . . appears to accept a particular (though not necessarily exclusive) diagnosis of regulatory failure, and to accompany that diagnosis with a particular conception of the purpose of regulatory institutions.[2] The diagnosis is that regulation has been

* Professor of Law, University of Chicago.

† Copyright © 1981 by the Arizona Board of Regents and reprinted by permission.

1. Presidents Ford and Carter both issued executive orders requiring discussion of the economic consequences of regulation. See 39 Fed.Reg. 41,501 (1974); 42 Fed.Reg. 1,017 (1977); 43 Fed.Reg. 12,661 (1978).

2. . . . This paper borrows several ideas developed originally and at much greater length in R. Stewart & C. Sunstein, Public Programs and Private Rights, [95 Harv.L.Rev. (1983)]. . . .

unduly intrusive on the private sector and has imposed substantial costs without corresponding benefits. The normative conception of institutional purpose is economic in character: the purpose of regulation—at least as a general rule—is to promote economic "efficiency," or to increase production, by compensating for free rider effects and transactions cost barriers to bargaining. Both the diagnosis and the underlying conception are far from uncontroversial. Under a different diagnosis of agency failure, or a different conception of institutional purpose, an executive order on federal regulation might have been designed to promote the openness and visibility of regulatory schemes, to guarantee public participation during regulatory decisionmaking, or to ensure protection of statutory "rights" by federal agencies rather than courts. It is not difficult to perceive some danger that such goals may be undermined rather than promoted by Executive order 12,291.

. . . .

Resolution of issues of comparative institutional competence is of course notoriously difficult, and it is hazardous to reach general conclusions as to which branch is best at performing particular tasks. Nonetheless, it appears safe to say that executive officials are better equipped than the courts to assess and weigh the costs and benefits of regulatory proposals. . . . [J]udges must respond to discrete, privately initiated controversies, and are thus unlikely either to acquire a sufficiently general overview of the regulatory system or to ensure consistency or coordination in the enforcement process. Second, measurement of social preferences for collective goods, for example, public preferences for clean air in a particular geographic region, is beyond the competence of courts, which are comparatively unaccountable and unaware of public preferences. . . .

By contrast, the executive branch . . . has a distinctive ability to assess and weigh the costs and benefits of regulatory activity. The executive power is centralized, or at least capable of centralization in the President. . . . [B]oth the particular agencies which must analyze and weigh costs and benefits under the order and the Office of Management and Budget—which is closely accountable to the President—are capable of assembling an array of policy analysis to make the kind of case-by-case assessments of technical regulatory issues that cost-benefit analysis requires. In addition, because of its comparative political accountability, the Executive is probably in a better position than the courts to make cost-benefit assessments that reflect the preferences of the public.[3] . . . I do not mean to suggest that those who are charged with administering Executive Order No. 12,291 may not be susceptible to the distorting pressures that result from the disproportionate influence of well-organized regulated entities with substantial stakes in the outcome. . . . Nonetheless, it is an accept-

3. But see, for the argument that the democratic process in the United States is so skewed that no electorally accountable body is likely to be truly representative, M. Shapiro, Freedom of Speech: The Supreme Court and Judicial Review 32 (1966); Parker, The Past of Constitutional Theory—And Its Future, 42 Ohio St.L.J. 223 (1981).

ed part of our political traditions that issues of resource allocation are best decided by the political branches of government. . . .

Although the executive branch has distinct competence in developing and applying principles of cost-benefit analysis, Executive Order 12,291 raises troubling questions of institutional authority. To what extent is it appropriate for the executive branch—which is charged with implementing regulatory programs designed at least in general terms by Congress—to declare cost-benefit analysis the decisive factor in making regulatory decisions? May the Executive properly decline to enforce a statute—and thus effectively nullify it—when the statute does not promote economic "efficiency"? Under the order, cost-benefit analysis operates as a "trump." Regulatory action is barred if it redistributes social wealth without affecting its total amount. Such regulatory action is not allowed unless it is shown that its benefits outweigh its costs, despite any other consequences the action may have, and despite the fact that those consequences may have been desired by Congress.

I do not suggest that Executive Order 12,291 is unlawful. The order expressly provides that the cost-benefit requirement is to apply only "to the extent permitted by law." . . . The critical question . . . is one of scope: How broadly may Executive Order 12,291 be applied if it is not to be inconsistent with law?

In examining this question, it is important to note that as a general rule, an approach that justifies regulation on grounds of economic "efficiency" does not conform to any realistic description of the legislative process. . . . In an electoral democracy, statutes may be a response to the claims of competing interest groups for scarce social resources, or they may reflect community values developed in the regulatory process rather than purely private desires. But no plausible theory of legislation treats congressional enactments as intended to promote efficiency, save in unusual circumstances. . . . [T]he questions faced by Congress—if those questions are to be described in terms of the allocation and transfer of resources—are predominantly distributional. . . .

For purposes of analysis, it may be useful to suggest that regulatory statutes fall into three very general categories from the standpoint of the cost-benefit requirement of the order. The first category comprises statutes that are intended or that are reasonably understood as intended to promote efficiency. Certain antitrust statutes fall into this category. Also in this category may be statutes protecting against an "unreasonable risk" to health or safety. . . . The second category consists of statutes that are not plausibly regarded as maximizing or as having been designed to maximize wealth. Various civil rights statutes and certain laws protecting the environment notwithstanding the cost probably fall within this category. . . . The third category comprises statutes that have some effects which maximize wealth, and some that do not. Many antipollution statutes fall in this category. Pollution is a classic context for government intervention because of "market failure," but there can be no doubt that anti-pollution laws often have intended effects that do not promote efficiency. With respect to statutes in this category, Executive Order 12,291 enjoins regulators to enforce the law when and only when, a cost-benefit test is satisfied—unless use of that test is prohibited by law. . . .

Thus far, I have treated Executive Order 12,291 as if it adopted the efficiency criterion. The rhetoric of costs and benefits, however, might be understood as something very different: a convenient and workable means of assuring that regulatory decisions are controlled by the President or by officials who are more likely to share his views than the career bureaucrats in the various federal agencies. The very indeterminancy of the order tends to support this view. The order defines neither benefits or costs. . . . In this respect, the order accords enormous discretion to those who are charged with interpreting it. Cost and benefits, of course, cannot be weighed without some method of determining how they should be valued. An Administration determined to impose harsh regulatory provisions, would . . . . conclude that health or life has exceptionally high value, and that an exceptionally high price is justified in order to preserve it. An Administration intending to weaken or remove regulatory protections could simply undertake different calculations. Wholly subjective judgments of value are thus unavoidable in the implementation of the order; and there is no guarantee that these judgments will conform to the views expressed in the governing statute. . . .

Even if Executive Order 12,291 is treated as a genuine effort to implement a cost-benefit approach in the economic sense, it might be argued that its scope is nearly universal. Statutes generally are not intended to promote efficiency. Nonetheless, the executive branch, in coordinating the numerous statutes Congress has entrusted to it, may have discretion to implement those statutes only when the benefits outweigh the costs. Traditions of prosecutorial discretion are themselves sufficient to reveal that Congress does not intend to require the Executive to enforce regulatory statutes fully or mechanically: the Executive has considerable discretion to determine the timing, circumstances, and even the ultimate desirability of enforcement. It might thus be argued that the Executive should not be precluded from adopting a cost-benefit approach simply because Congress did not, in enacting the statute in question, explicitly provide that enforcement is authorized only when a cost-benefit test is satisfied.

This argument is unpersuasive. To be sure, the Executive is permitted broad latitude in setting priorities for enforcement action, and there is nothing to prevent an executive agency from devoting scarce prosecutorial resources to those violations that seem most egregious. But it is a long step from this proposition to the claim that the Executive has a general power to enforce only those statutes which conform to its view of what the law should be. The President's constitutional obligation is to "take Care that the Laws be faithfully executed."[4] Nothing in the Constitution authorizes the President to decide, contrary to an instruction from Congress, that a particular statute should not be enforced. When Congress passes a statute which

4. U.S. Const. art. II, § 3, cl. 4.

does not promote "efficiency," the President has no authority to refuse to enforce it on the ground that a standard based on efficiency would be preferable. For example, the Executive may not decline to enforce laws prohibiting discrimination in education on the ground that such laws redistribute wealth instead of maximizing it. . . .

These considerations suggest that the scope of the cost-benefit requirement of the order is narrower than has generally been supposed and that the requirement cannot be applied to many regulatory statutes. While the Executive often has discretion to enforce statutes selectively, he has no power to adopt a unitary conception of regulation that accords with no plausible theory of legislation. The general conclusion is that the cost-benefit requirement of Executive Order 12,291 is applicable only to those statutes, discussed above, that are designed to remedy "market failure" in the economic sense or that otherwise have efficiency-promoting applications whose exclusive implementations would not fundamentally conflict with legislative purposes. . . . [A]pplication of the cost-benefit requirement of Executive Order 12,291 in an across-the-board fashion would raise serious questions of separation of powers, and the "to the extent permitted by law" proviso operates severely to restrict the scope of that aspect of the order. The Executive may formulate enforcement priorities, and—at least with congressional approval or acquiescence—may decide to devote scarce enforcement resources to particular statutory provisions rather than others. The difference between this authority and the power to nullify statutes is in part one of degree rather than kind, but it is nonetheless a critical one. . . . Many statutes require regulatory action even when, under an economist's approach, the "costs" exceed the "benefits," and it would be an abuse of normal conceptions of separation of powers if the Executive could nullify those statutes by deciding not to implement them. . . . [I]n a government that is both democratic and dedicated to the principle of separation of powers, cost-effectiveness—and not economic "efficiency"—is probably the most that can be expected from an executive order or federal regulation. . . .[5]

NOTES

(1) The "impact analysis" technique has had Congressional as well as Presidential use as a technique for shaping (if not controlling) administrative decisions in light of desired policy perspectives. The Environmental Impact Statements required by the National Environmental Policy Act since 1969 impelled agencies unaccustomed to considering the systemic consequences of their decisions to anticipate the adverse environmental changes their projects might bring about and consider means of reducing or avoiding them—a process often produc-

---

5. [Ed.] For assessments of experience under Executive Order 12,291 suggesting substantial displacement by OMB of discretionary authority delegated to agencies, see J. Lash, A Season of Spoils (1984); E. Olson, The Quiet Shift of Power: Office of Management and Budget Supervision of Environmental Protection Agency Rulemaking Under Executive Order 12,291; 4 Va.J.Nat.Res.L. 1 (1984); G. Eads, Relief or Reform? Reagan's Regulatory Dilemma (1982).

tive of defensive measures or altered decisions.[1] Experience under NEPA, and the inflation-forced economic debate about regulatory policy choices that statute both spurred and represented, led to the economic impact analyses of E.O. 12,291 and its predecessors and also to the Regulatory Flexibility Act [2]—a statute intended to encourage the same sorts of attention to the possible impact of regulatory initiatives on small businesses and means of avoiding them, as NEPA had sought respecting impact on small fish.

The virtues of thinking systematically about the possible forward impacts of one's acts are self-evident, as are those of balancing antici-pated costs and benefits (once this analysis is undertaken) to determine whether it is worth all the trouble to act. Yet few would suppose such analyses either a panacea or a substitute for common sense. They provide a framework for organizing thought, one subject to its own frailties. The difficulties become evident when one attempts the pro-cess: the inquiry, too, has costs in time, money, and diversion of effort, especially if it can be manipulated instrumentally for purposes of obstruction or delay; prediction is inevitably imprecise;[3] many of the matters to be accounted for are either incommensurable (the value of preserving the habitat of a species of butterfly or a stretch of wild river) or politically freighted in ways that preclude agreed valuation (the value of preserving an additional human life); and other issues—for example the elimination of racial discrimination—will be decided on bases for which economic analysis is simply irrelevant.[4] The economic premises of such inquiries and their limitations are best studied, we

1. 42 U.S.C. § 4331 et seq.; see Calvert Cliffs Coordinating Comm. Inc. v. USAEC, 449 F.2d 1109 (D.C.Cir.1971).

2. 5 U.S.C. §§ 601–612. See P. Verkuil, A Critical Guide to the Regulatory Flexi-bility Act, 1982 Duke L.J. 213.

3. W.K. Viscusi, Cotton Dust Regula-tion: An OSHA Success Story? 4 J.Pol. Anal. & Man. 325 (1985) looks retrospec-tively at the standard that was the subject of American Textile Mfrs. Inst. v. Donovan, page 86 above, finding in part that "the costs of compliance were greatly exaggerat-ed," that the standard has reduced risks of byssinosis "dramatically," and still is char-acterized by costs that are "extraordinarily high by comparison with any value that can reasonably be placed upon its achieve-ments." At 339. The last of these com-ments perhaps illustrates the difficulties of valuation; earlier Viscusi finds that for each case of moderate severity prevented by the standards (impaired lung function throughout the work week), $54,000/year must be spent. On the one hand, this is a significant multiple of a cotton worker's annual wage; yet one might also choose to ask how much a sick person would be willing to pay, annually, to avoid such symptoms. And see the observations of M. Sagoff, Must Regulatory Reform Fail, 4 J.Pol.Anal. & Man. 433 (1985).

4. A more profound observation was made by Ernest Nagel in The Structure of Science 472 (1961).

"It is a common experience of mankind that, despite carefully laid plans for realiz-ing some end, the actions adopted result in entanglements that had not been foreseen and had certainly not been intended. For planned actions rarely if ever take place in a social setting over which men have total mastery. The consequences that follow a deliberate choice of conduct are the prod-ucts not simply of that conduct; they are also determined by various attendant cir-cumstances, whose relevance to the intend-ed aim or the action may not be always understood, and whose modes of operation are in any case not within complete effec-tive control of those who have made that choice. Eli Whitney did not invent the cotton gin in order to strengthen a social system based on human slavery; Pasteur would have been horrified to learn that his researches on fermentation would become the theoretical basis for bacteriological warfare; and French support of the Ameri-can revolutionary cause against England did not aim at founding a nation that would eventually make it difficult for France to continue as a colonial power in North America."

believe, in a course stressing one or another aspect of substantive regulation [5]; here, we do little more than direct your attention to a lively, influential, and on-going controversy.[6]

(2) The Constitution vests all executive power in the President and, while contemplating delegation, clearly intends focused, personal responsibility for its exercise.[7] Yet Congress could and did create responsibilities in the departments to be exercised by departmental heads, not the President. Those regimes were creatures of law, law whose faithful execution the President had as much responsibility to assure as any other; what, then, was to be his role? Attorneys general vacillated whether an appeal lay to the President from particular decisions of the secretaries, but the practice was to leave decision where the Congress placed it.[8] The difficulties were well stated in Professor Corwin's classic study of the Presidency:

"Suppose . . . that the law casts a duty upon a subordinate executive agency *eo nomine*, does the President thereupon become entitled, by virtue of his 'executive power' or of his duty to 'take care that the laws be faithfully executed' to substitute his judgment for that of the agency regarding the discharge of such duty? An unqualified answer to this question would invite startling results. An affirmative answer would make all questions of law enforcement questions of discretion, the discretion moreover of an independent and legally uncontrollable branch of the government. By the same token, it would render it impossible for Congress, notwithstanding its broad powers under the 'necessary and proper' clause, to leave anything to the

5. See, e.g., "An Analytic Framework for Environmental Law and Policy," Ch. 3 in R.B. Stewart and J.E. Krier, Environmental Law and Policy (1978).

6. The view of the Administrative Conference of the United States has generally been favorable. See Recommendation 85–2, Agency Procedures for Performing Regulatory Analysis of Rules, 1 C.F.R. § 305.85–2, based on an impressive monograph, T. McGarity, The Role of Regulatory Analysis in Regulatory Decisionmaking (1985). See also B. Ackerman, et al. The Uncertain Search for Environmental Quality (1974); E. Stokey and R. Zeckhauser, A Primer for Policy Analysis (1978); E. Gramlich, Benefit-Cost Analysis of Government Programs (1981); C.E. Lindblom, "The Science of 'Muddling Through,'" 19 Pub.Ad.Rev. 79 (1959); S. Kelman, Cost-Benefit Analysis: An Ethical Critique, Regulation Magazine, Jan./Feb. 1981, p. 33; Replies to Kelman, id., Mar./Apr. 1981, p. 39.

7. Bear in mind that "executive power" refers to the conduct of foreign relations as well as settings productive of "agency action" in the Administrative Procedure Act sense. Thus, this book discusses behavior that, in historical perspective, is not at the core of executive function. The distinction between political and administrative government had its counterpart in early writings about administrative procedure suggesting a distinction between "executive power" and "administrative power"—the first, concerned with those issues Chief Justice Marshall had identified in Marbury v. Madison as "[q]uestions . . . in their nature political," 5 U.S. (1 Cranch) 137, 170 (1803); the second, strictly statutory, and subject to presidential participation only to whatever extent might be provided by statute. See the elegant discussion of the writings of Freund, Wyman, Willoughby and Goodnow in N. Grundstein, Presidential Power, Administration and Administrative Law, 18 Geo.Wash.L.Rev. 285 (1950). One need not accept that Congress enjoys *complete* control of "administrative power" to find force in the distinction.

8. See, e.g., 1 Op. Att'y Gen. 624 (1823) (holding that no appeal would lie); 2 Op. Att'y Gen. 480 (1831) (same); 2 Op. Att'y Gen. 507 (1832) (same); 5 Op. Att'y Gen. 630 (1852) (same); 10 Op. Att'y Gen. 527 (1863) (same); 11 Op. Att'y Gen. 14 (1864) (same); 18 Op. Att'y Gen. 31 (1884) (same); 2 Op. Att'y Gen. 463 (1831) (holding that an appeal would lie); 6 Op. Att'y Gen. 326, 343 (1854) (same); 7 Op. Att'y Gen. 453, 464 (1855) (same); 15 Op. Att'y Gen. 94, 101 (1876) (same).

specially trained judgment of a subordinate executive official with any assurance that his discretion would not be perverted to political ends for the advantage of the administration in power. At the same time, a flatly negative answer would hold out consequences equally unwelcome. It would, as Attorney General Cushing quaintly phrased it, leave it open to Congress so to divide and transfer 'the executive power' by statute as to change the government 'into a parliamentary despotism like that of Venezuela or Great Britain with a nominal executive chief or president, who, however, would remain without a shred of actual power.' " [9]

The Supreme Court had indicated in Marbury v. Madison, 5 U.S. (1 Cranch) 137 (1803), that a court could direct the performance of a nondiscretionary duty given to the executive.[10] In 1837, in Kendall v. United States, 37 U.S. (12 Pet.) 524 (1838) it seemed to go further, giving the negative answer to Professor Corwin's question—that Congress could structure government so as to preclude the President from imposing his will on a cabinet officer.

Kendall was an action in mandamus, a direction to the Postmaster General to pay a specific sum of money which Congress by special statute had ordered paid but which the President wished withheld. At the time, as Marbury illustrates, a writ of mandamus was available only if it could be shown that its subject had been given no discretion in the performance of the function at issue. Finding the Postmaster under a legal obligation to pay, the Court directed that mandamus should issue. It would be "alarming," said the Court, to assert that

> Congress cannot impose upon any executive officer any duty they may think proper, which is not repugnant to any rights secured and protected by the constitution; and in such cases, the duty and responsibility grow out of and are subject to the control of the law, and not to the discretion of the president.

While this language might be understood as broadly confirming Congress' power to confer discretion on administrators beyond the President's control, the decision carefully avoided invitations to decide so large an issue. Because the "duty" actually involved in the case left no scope for judgment, there was no need to decide what voice the President might have where the law offers a choice of possible courses of action—that is, where it confers discretion on the responsible administrator. The opinion holds only that the President and other executive officials must act within the law.

That unresolved tension finds current expression in the debates, reflected in Professor Sunstein's analysis, over the President's authority to be directory. Explicit public efforts to wield such authority in the

---

9. E. Corwin, The President: Office and Powers 1787–1957, 80–81 (4th rev. ed. 1957); for contemporary efforts, see R. Neustadt, Presidential Power—The Politics of Leadership From FDR to Carter (1980); E. Hargrove, The Power of the Modern Presidency 79 (1974); and B. Ledewitz, The Uncertain Power of the President to Execute the Laws, 46 Tenn.L.Rev. 757 (1979).

10. The case's significance for administrative law is discussed at length in H. Monaghan, Marbury and the Administrative State, 83 Colum.L.Rev. 1 (1983).

regulatory context are rare, but indirect means are available and, by reports, employed. In ENVIRONMENTAL DEFENSE FUND v. THOMAS, 627 F.Supp. 566 (D.D.C.1986), the Environmental Protection Agency's adoption of rules to regulate underground storage tanks for hazardous waste had been delayed well past a statutory deadline—in part, it transpired, because of the need to obtain OMB clearance under EO 12291. On the basis of internal documents released under seal, Judge Thomas Flannery of the District Court found this delay substantially attributable to policy disagreements between OMB and EPA over what approach should be taken to this regulatory problem. While accepting the timetable now proposed by the agency for completion of the rules, Judge Flannery addressed these words to the OMB:

"A certain degree of deference must be given to the authority of the President to control and supervise executive policymaking. Yet, the use of EO 12291 to create delays and to impose substantive changes raises some constitutional concerns. Congress enacts environmental legislation after years of study and deliberation, and then delegates to the expert judgment of the EPA Administrator the authority to issue regulations carrying out the aims of the law. Under EO 12291, if used improperly, OMB could withhold approval until the acceptance of certain content in the promulgation of any new EPA regulation, thereby encroaching upon the independence and expertise of EPA. Further, unsuccessful executive lobbying on Capitol Hill can still be pursued administratively by delaying the enactment of regulations beyond the date of a statutory deadline. This is incompatible with the will of Congress and cannot be sustained as a valid exercise of the President's Article II powers. . . .

"This court declares that OMB has no authority to use its regulatory review under EO 12291 to delay promulgation of EPA regulations arising from the 1984 Amendments of the RCRA beyond the date of a statutory deadline. Thus, if a deadline already has expired, OMB has no authority to delay regulations subject to the deadline in order to review them under the executive order. If the deadline is about to expire, OMB may review the regulations only until the time at which OMB review will result in the deadline being missed. . . . While this may be an intrusion into the degree of flexibility the executive agencies have in taking their time about promulgating these regulations, this is simply a judicial recognition of law as passed by Congress and of the method for dealing with deadlines laid down by the President himself."

And see A. Morrison, OMB Interference With Agency Rulemaking: The Wrong Way To Write A Regulation, 99 Harvard Law Review 1059 (1986); C. DeMuth and D. Ginsburg, White House Review Of Agency Rulemaking, 99 Harvard Law Review 1075 (1986).

(3) Executive Order 12,498 might be regarded not only as an instrument of presidential authority, but also as a means for enhancing an agency's political heads' control over the career bureaucrats responsible to them. In putting together a draft regulatory agenda, as in developing an annual budget, the agency head would be required to confront at an early stage competing views about priorities for her

agency and to rationalize them. Thus, the head of the OMB office responsible for administering both the Paperwork Reduction Act [11] and E.O. 12291 is reported to have written President Reagan in early 1984 that

"For the past several years agencies have published 'regulatory agendas' under various statutes and executive orders; these are now compiled each April and October in the Unified Regulatory Agenda. For the most part, however, these documents have been prepared routinely at the career level, and have been devoted to plans for new regulations. They have generally not been true policy documents expressing the priorities of Cabinet officers or the Administration, and they have reflected little inclination to reassess rules and programs. Transforming the regulatory agenda into a serious policymaking process would build upon our experience to date under E.O. 12291, our annual paperwork budgeting process, and the initial efforts of the Task Force on Regulatory Relief. The Executive Order has proven an effective mechanism for screening new regulatory initiatives promoted by the bureaucracy, and for making necessary or legally required rules as cost-effective as possible; but it is largely a reactive mechanism. . . .

"A regulatory planning process could be viewed as a usurpation of the policy prerogatives of agency heads, but the reality is more complex. Cabinet Secretaries and other senior political officials know very little of the Administration's major economic policies that are effected through regulatory programs outside their own agencies—certainly much less than they know of other major economic policies. All of our days are so consumed by immediate demands and political pressures that we spend too little time trying to make fundamental changes in the policies of our own offices. Central collegial bodies, such as the Cabinet Councils, are not only essential for keeping the President and the White House informed of broad policy developments and proposals: they also enable individual agency heads to take actions they favor, but would otherwise be too constrained to accomplish." C. DeMuth, Memorandum to the Cabinet Council on Economic Affairs, reprinted in Inside The Administration, Vol. 3, No. 3, pp. 7, 8–9 (Feb. 10, 1984).

What strengths and weaknesses do you see in the analogy between preparation of a regulatory agenda and the budget process? What proper implications for OMB's role?

(4) Provisions for executive review of agency action may be found in a number of states.[12] The drafters of the 1981 Model State Administrative Procedure Act included as an optional provision § 3–202, which would permit a governor both to "rescind or suspend all or a severable portion of a rule of an agency" following public procedures and "sum-

---

11. See Ch. 5, Sec. 1 within.

12. See H. Levinson, Legislative and Executive Veto of Rules of Administrative Agencies: Models and Alternatives, 24 Wm. & Mary L.Rev. 79 (1982). Of particu-

lar interest is the California Office of Administrative Law. See M. Cohen, Regulatory Reform: Assessing the California Plan, 1983 Duke L.J. 231.

marily [to] terminate any pending rulemaking proceeding by an executive order to that effect, stating therein the reasons for the action." This approach, the drafters thought, would "facilitate ultimate coordination of all rule making, and provide a direct and easily usable political check on the rule-making process"; it "avoids the separation of powers problems that legislative veto schemes raise; it avoids the possible subversion of the governor's authority to veto legislative acts that may be inherent in legislative veto schemes; and it keeps effective political and administrative control of all law enforcement in the official who is, by the state constitution, the *chief executive,* and who is directly politically accountable to [all of] the people for the proper performance of that function." [13]

(5) Note Sections 9 and 5 of E.O.'s 12,291 and 12,498, respectively, which seek to avoid judicial enforcement of their procedural requirements; for E.O. 12,291, however, any resulting analysis is to be part of the administrative record on the basis of which the validity of any ensuing rule will be tested. Are these procedures not to be enforced because they are not "law" binding the agencies in their performance of function? Or, if they do constitute legally binding instructions for the agency, may the President simply withhold enforcement jurisdiction from the courts by defining who has standing to enforce them [14] or on analogy to the authority explicitly given Congress to make exceptions to and regulate the appellate jurisdiction of the Supreme Court? [15]

(6) Whether or not the President can exclude judicial oversight, can he protect this process (or other executive oversight) from the gaze of Congress? We have already noted some evidence of a wish to do so, at p. 145 above. If the President were to make such a claim, it would be grounded in the doctrine of executive privilege. This issue has been litigated at times, most famously in United States v. Nixon, 418 U.S. 683 (1974). However, such issues are generally settled, through the game of political hardball rather than the courts; for example, in the winter of 1982–83, oversight hearings respecting enforcement activities at the Environmental Protection Agency produced claims of privilege, congressional citations for contempt and then, before final judicial resolution could be had, a flurry of resignations and compromises over what information would be supplied, and to whom, and under what conditions of confidentiality.[16] Of course, one cost of

13. 1981 Model State APA § 3–202 comment. See A.E. Bonfield, State Law in the Teaching of Administrative Law: A Critical Analysis of the Status Quo, 61 Texas L.Rev. 95 (1982); Note, Quis Custodiet Ipsos Custodes?: Gubernatorial and Legislative Review of Agency Rulemaking Under the 1981 Model Act, 57 Wash.L.Rev. 669 (1982).

14. On the subject of standing, see Chapter 9, section 3 within.

15. See P. Raven-Hansen, Making Agencies Follow Orders: Judicial Review of Agency Violations of Executive Order

12,291, 1983 Duke L.J. 285, 353; see also United States v. Wayte, 549 F.Supp. 1376, 1387 (C.D.Cal.1982) ("clearly, an Article III court is not prescribed from reviewing the question of the enforceability of an executive order, irrespective of an attempt by the executive branch to make review an intra-branch function").

16. Note, The Conflict Between Executive Privilege and Congressional Oversight: The Gorsuch Controversy, 1983 Duke L.J. 1333; see R. Lee, Executive Privilege, Congressional Subpoena Power and Judicial Review: Three Branches, Three Powers,

such compromises may be the further politicization of processes one would rather have occur on a more objective basis.

IMMIGRATION & NATURALIZATION SERVICE v. CHADHA
Supreme Court of the United States, 1983.
462 U.S. 919.

[Jagdish Chadha was a deportable alien found by an immigration judge of the Department of Justice's Immigration and Naturalization Service (the Department) to have established a claim to a compassionate suspension of deportation under section 244 of the Immigration and Nationality Act.[1] Under that statute, refusals so to find were subject to judicial review while favorable findings are to be transmitted to Congress, to take effect only if neither the Senate nor the House of Representatives repudiated them by resolution during the two sessions following.[2] In Mr. Chadha's case, the House adopted such a resolution at the last possible moment, without printed text, debate,[3] or significant explanation. Once a number of procedural hurdles had been passed, the issue before the Court was the validity of that resolution.]

CHIEF JUSTICE BURGER delivered the opinion of the Court. . . .

III

A

We turn now to the question whether action of one House of Congress under § 244(c)(2) violates strictures of the Constitution. We begin, of course, with the presumption that the challenged statute is valid. . . .

> Since 1932, when the first veto provision was enacted into law, 295 congressional veto-type procedures have been inserted in 196 different statutes as follows: from 1932 to 1939, five statutes were affected, from 1940–49, nineteen statutes; between 1950–59, thirty-four statutes; and from 1960–69, forty-nine. From the year 1970 through 1975, at least one hundred sixty-three such provisions were included in eighty-nine laws. Abourezk, The Congressional Veto: A Contemporary Response to Executive Encroachment on Legislative Prerogatives, 52 Ind.L.Rev. 323, 324 (1977). . . .

and Some Relationships, 1978 B.Y.U.L.Rev. 231.

1. 8 U.S.C. § 1254.

2. This mechanism—the occasion for 111 out of 230 legislative vetoes ever exercised by Congress under any statute through the summer of 1982—had been adopted to substitute for a prior practice of granting all such relief through private bills passed by the Congress, while maintaining congressional control. See Smith & Struve, Aftershocks of the Fall of the Legislative Veto, 69 A.B.A.J. 1258 (1983).

3. So far as the record before the Court showed, House action was based solely on Representative Eilberg's statement from the floor that

"[i]t was the feeling of the committee, after reviewing 340 cases, that the aliens contained in the resolution [Chadha and five others] did not meet these statutory requirements, particularly as it related to hardship; and it is the opinion of the committee that their deportation should not be suspended." 121 Cong.Reg. 40,800 (1975).

Explicit and unambiguous provisions of the Constitution prescribe and define the respective functions of the Congress and of the Executive in the legislative process. Since the precise terms of those familiar provisions are critical to the resolution of this case, we set them out verbatim. Art. I provides:

All legislative Powers herein granted shall be vested in a Congress of the United States, which shall consist of a Senate and a House of Representatives. Art. I, § 1.

Every Bill which shall have passed the House of Representatives and the Senate, shall, before it become a Law, be presented to the President of the United States; . . . Art. I, § 7, cl. 2.

Every Order, Resolution, or Vote to which the Concurrence of the Senate and House of Representatives may be necessary (except on a question of Adjournment) shall be presented to the President of the United States; and before the Same shall take Effect, shall be approved by him, or being disapproved by him, shall be repassed by two thirds of the Senate and House of Representatives, according to the Rules and Limitations prescribed in the Case of a Bill. Art. I, § 7, cl. 3.

These provisions of Art. I are integral parts of the constitutional design for the separation of powers. We have recently noted that "[t]he principle of separation of powers was not simply an abstract generalization in the minds of the Framers: it was woven into the documents that they drafted in Philadelphia in the summer of 1787." Buckley v. Valeo, 424 U.S. 1, 124. . . . The very structure of the articles delegating and separating powers under Arts. I, II, and III exemplify the concept of separation of powers and we now turn to Art. I.

B

The Presentment Clauses

. . . The decision to provide the President with a limited and qualified power to nullify proposed legislation by veto was based on the profound conviction of the Framers that the powers conferred on Congress were the powers to be most carefully circumscribed. It is beyond doubt that lawmaking was a power to be shared by both Houses and the President. In The Federalist No. 73 (H. Lodge ed. 1888), Hamilton focused on the President's role in making laws:

If even no propensity had ever discovered itself in the legislative body to invade the rights of the Executive, the rules of just reasoning and theoretic propriety would of themselves teach us that the one ought not to be left to the mercy of the other, but ought to possess a constitutional and effectual power of self-defense. Id., at 457–458.

See also The Federalist No. 51. . . .

The President's role in the lawmaking process also reflects the Framers' careful efforts to check whatever propensity a particular

Congress might have to enact oppressive, improvident, or ill-considered measures. . . .

C

Bicameralism

The bicameral requirement of Art. I, §§ 1, 7 was of scarcely less concern to The Framers than was the Presidential veto and indeed the two are interdependent. By providing that no law could take effect without the concurrence of the prescribed majority of the Members of both Houses, the Framers reemphasized their belief, already remarked upon in connection with the Presentment Clauses, that legislation should not be enacted unless it has been carefully and fully considered by the Nation's elected officials. In the Constitutional Convention debates on the need for a bicameral legislature, James Wilson, later to become a Justice of this Court, commented:

> Despotism comes on mankind in different shapes. Sometimes in an Executive, sometimes in a military, one. Is there danger of a Legislative despotism? Theory & practice both proclaim it. If the Legislative authority be not restrained, there can be neither liberty nor stability; and it can only be restrained by dividing it within itself, into distinct and independent branches. In a single house there is no check, but the inadequate one, of the virtue & good sense of those who compose it. 1 M. Farrand, supra, at 254.

. . . These observations are consistent with what many of the Framers expressed, none more cogently than Hamilton in pointing up the need to divide and disperse power in order to protect liberty:

> In republican government, the legislative authority necessarily predominates. The remedy for this inconveniency is to divide the legislature into different branches; and to render them, by different modes of election and different principles of action, as little connected with each other as the nature of their common functions and their common dependence on the society will admit. The Federalist No. 51, supra, at 324.

See also The Federalist No. 62.

. . .

IV

The Constitution sought to divide the delegated powers of the new federal government into three defined categories, legislative, executive and judicial, to assure, as nearly as possible, that each Branch of government would confine itself to its assigned responsibility. The hydraulic pressure inherent within each of the separate Branches to exceed the outer limits of its power, even to accomplish desirable objectives, must be resisted.

Although not "hermetically" sealed from one another, Buckley v. Valeo, supra, 424 U.S., at 121, the powers delegated to the three Branches are functionally identifiable. When any Branch acts, it is presumptively exercising the power the Constitution has delegated to it. See Hampton & Co. v. United States, 276 U.S. 394 (1928). When the Executive acts, it presumptively acts in an executive or administrative capacity as defined in Art. II. And when, as here, one House of Congress purports to act, it is presumptively acting within its assigned sphere.

Beginning with this presumption, we must nevertheless establish that the challenged action under § 244(c)(2) is of the kind to which the procedural requirements of Art. I, § 7 apply. Not every action taken by either House is subject to the bicameralism and presentment requirements of Art. I. Whether actions taken by either House are, in law and fact, an exercise of legislative power depends not on their form but upon "whether they contain matter which is properly to be regarded as legislative in its character and effect."

Examination of the action taken here by one House pursuant to § 244(c)(2) reveals that it was essentially legislative in purpose and effect. In purporting to exercise power defined in Art. I, § 8, cl. 4 to "establish an uniform Rule of Naturalization," the House took action that had the purpose and effect of altering the legal rights, duties and relations of persons, including the Attorney General, Executive Branch officials and Chadha, all outside the legislative branch. Section 244(c) (2) purports to authorize one House of Congress to require the Attorney General to deport an individual alien whose deportation otherwise would be cancelled under § 244. The one-House veto operated in this case to overrule the Attorney General and mandate Chadha's deportation; absent the House action, Chadha would remain in the United States. Congress has acted and its action has altered Chadha's status.

The legislative character of the one-House veto in this case is confirmed by the character of the Congressional action it supplants. Neither the House of Representatives nor the Senate contends that, absent the veto provision in § 244(c)(2), either of them, or both of them acting together, could effectively require the Attorney General to deport an alien once the Attorney General, in the exercise of legislatively delegated authority,[4] had determined the alien should remain in the United States. . . .

---

4. Congress protests that affirming the Court of Appeals in this case will sanction "lawmaking by the Attorney General. . . . Why is the Attorney General exempt from submitting his proposed changes in the law to the full bicameral process?" Brief of the United States House of Representatives 40. To be sure, some administrative agency action—rule making, for example—may resemble "lawmaking." See 5 U.S.C. § 551(4), which defines an agency's "rule" as "the whole or part of an agency statement of general or particular applicability and future effect designed to implement, interpret, or prescribe law or policy. . . ." This Court has referred to agency activity as being "quasi-legislative" in character. Humphrey's Executor v. United States, 295 U.S. 602, 628 (1935). Clearly, however, "[i]n the framework of our Constitution, the President's power to see that the laws are faithfully executed refutes the idea that he is to be a lawmaker." Youngstown Sheet & Tube Co. v. Sawyer, 343 U.S. 579, 587 (1952). See Buckley v. Valeo, 424 U.S., at 123 (1976). When the Attorney General performs his duties pursuant to § 244, he does not exercise "legislative" power. See Ernst & Ernst v. Hochfelder, 425 U.S. 185, 213–214 (1976). The bicameral process is not necessary as a check on the Executive's administration of the laws because his administrative activity cannot reach beyond the limits of the statute that created it—a statute duly enacted pursuant to Art. I, §§ 1, 7. The constitutionality of the Attorney General's execution of the authority

After long experience with the clumsy, time consuming private bill procedure, Congress made a deliberate choice to delegate to the Executive Branch, and specifically to the Attorney General, the authority to allow deportable aliens to remain in this country in certain specified circumstances. . . . [T]his choice to delegate authority is precisely the kind of decision that can be implemented only in accordance with the procedures set out in Art. I. Disagreement with the Attorney General's decision on Chadha's deportation—that is, Congress' decision to deport Chadha—no less than Congress' original choice to delegate to the Attorney General the authority to make that decision, involves determinations of policy that Congress can implement in only one way; bicameral passage followed by presentment to the President. Congress must abide by its delegation of authority until that delegation is legislatively altered or revoked.[5]

. . .

The bicameral requirement, the Presentment Clauses, the President's veto, and Congress' power to override a veto were intended to erect enduring checks on each Branch and to protect the people from the improvident exercise of power by mandating certain prescribed steps. To preserve those checks, and maintain the separation of powers, the carefully defined limits on the power of each Branch must not be eroded. To accomplish what has been attempted by one House of Congress in this case requires action in conformity with the express procedures of the Constitution's prescription for legislative action: passage by a majority of both Houses and presentment to the President.[6]

delegated to him by § 244 involves only a question of delegation doctrine. The courts, when a case or controversy arises, can always "ascertain whether the will of Congress has been obeyed," Yakus v. United States, 321 U.S. 414, 425 (1944), and can enforce adherence to statutory standards. See Youngstown Sheet & Tube Co. v. Sawyer, 343 U.S. 579, 585 (1952); Ethyl Corp. v. EPA, 541 F.2d 1, 68 (D.C.Cir.1976) (en banc) (separate statement of Leventhal, J.), cert. denied, 426 (1965). L. Jaffe, Judicial Control of Administrative Action 320 (1965). [Ed.—Compare Chevron, U.S.A., Inc. v. NRDC, p. 405 within.] It is clear, therefore, that the Attorney General acts in his presumptively Art. II capacity when he administers the Immigration and Nationality Act. Executive action under legislatively delegated authority that might resemble "legislative" action in some respects is not subject to the approval of both Houses of Congress and the President for the reason that the Constitution does not so require. That kind of Executive action is always subject to check by the terms of the legislation that authorized it; and if that authority is exceeded it is open to judicial review as well as the power of Congress to modify or revoke the authority entirely. A one-House veto is clearly legislative in both character and effect and is not so checked; the need for the check provided by Art. I, §§ 1, 7 is therefore clear. Congress' authority to delegate portions of its power to administrative agencies provides no support for the argument that Congress can constitutionally control administration of the laws by way of a Congressional veto.

5. This does not mean that Congress is required to capitulate to "the accretion of policy control by forces outside its chambers." Javits and Klein, Congressional Oversight and the Legislative Veto: A Constitutional Analysis, 52 N.Y.U.L.Rev. 455, 462 (1977). The Constitution provides Congress with abundant means to oversee and control its administrative creatures. Beyond the obvious fact that Congress ultimately controls administrative agencies in the legislation that creates them, other means of control, such as durational limits on authorizations and formal reporting requirements, lie well within Congress' constitutional power. See id., at 460–461; Kaiser, Congressional Action to Overturn Agency Rules: Alternatives to the "Legislative Veto", 32 Ad.L.Rev. 667 (1980).

6. . . . Justice White suggests that the Attorney General's action under § 244(c)(1) suspending deportation is equivalent to a proposal for legislation and that

The veto authorized by § 244(c)(2) doubtless has been in many respects a convenient shortcut; the "sharing" with the Executive by Congress of its authority over aliens in this manner is, on its face, an appealing compromise. In purely practical terms, it is obviously easier for action to be taken by one House without submission to the President; but it is crystal clear from the records of the Convention, contemporaneous writings and debates that the Framers ranked other values higher than efficiency. . . . With all the obvious flaws of delay, untidiness, and potential for abuse, we have not yet found a better way to preserve freedom than by making the exercise of power subject to the carefully crafted restraints spelled out in the Constitution.

Affirmed.

[Justice Powell concurred on the ground that the House's redetermination of Chadha's case should be regarded as a judicial act and therefore unconstitutional as beyond the authority vested in Congress by the Constitution.]

[Justice Rehnquist dissented on the non-constitutional ground that Mr. Chadha lacked standing, since the provision of the statute authorizing the Attorney General to suspend deportation was not (in his view) severable from the legislative veto; if the veto was invalid, then, Mr. Chadha must still be deported.]

JUSTICE WHITE, dissenting.

Today the Court not only invalidates § 244(c)(2) of the Immigration and Nationality Act, but also sounds the death knell for nearly 200 other statutory provisions in which Congress has reserved a "legislative veto." . . .

I

The legislative veto developed initially in response to the problems of reorganizing the sprawling government structure created in response to the Depression. The Reorganization Acts established the chief model for the legislative veto. When President Hoover requested authority to reorganize the government in 1929, he coupled his request that the "Congress be willing to delegate its authority over the problem (subject to defined principles) to the Executive" with a proposal for

---

because Congressional approval is indicated "by failure to veto, the one-House veto satisfies the requirement of bicameral approval." However, as the Court of Appeals noted, that approach "would analogize the effect of the one house disapproval to the failure of one house to vote affirmatively on a private bill." 634 F.2d at 435. Even if it were clear that Congress entertained such an arcane theory when it enacted § 244(c)(2), which Justice White does not suggest, this would amount to nothing less than an amending of Art. I. The legislative steps outlined in Art. I are not empty formalities; they were designed to assure that both Houses of Congress and the President participate in the exercise of lawmaking authority. This does not mean that legislation must always be preceded by debate; on the contrary, we have said that it is not necessary for a legislative body to "articulate its reasons for enacting a statute." United States Railroad Retirement Board v. Fritz, 449 U.S. 166, 179 (1980). But the steps required by Art. I §§ 1, 7 make certain that there is an opportunity for deliberation and debate. To allow Congress to evade the strictures of the Constitution and in effect enact Executive proposals into law by mere silence cannot be squared with Art. I.

legislative review. He proposed that the Executive "should act upon approval of a joint committee of Congress or with the reservation of power of revision by Congress within some limited period adequate for its consideration." Pub. Papers 432 (1929). Congress followed President Hoover's suggestion and authorized reorganization subject to legislative review. Act of June 30, 1932, ch. 314, § 407, 47 Stat. 382, 414. Although the reorganization authority reenacted in 1933 did not contain a legislative veto provision, the provision returned during the Roosevelt Administration and has since been renewed numerous times. Over the years, the provision was used extensively. Presidents submitted 115 reorganization plans to Congress of which 23 were disapproved by Congress pursuant to legislative veto provisions.

Shortly after adoption of the Reorganization Act of 1929, Congress and the President applied the legislative veto procedure to resolve the delegation problem for national security and foreign affairs. World War II occasioned the need to transfer greater authority to the President in these areas. The legislative veto offered the means by which Congress could confer additional authority while preserving its own constitutional rule. During World War II, Congress enacted over thirty statutes conferring powers on the Executive with legislative veto provisions. President Roosevelt accepted the veto as the necessary price for obtaining exceptional authority.

Over the quarter century following World War II, Presidents continued to accept legislative vetoes by one or both Houses as constitutional, while regularly denouncing provisions by which Congressional committees reviewed Executive activity.[1] The legislative veto balanced delegations of statutory authority in new areas of governmental involvement: the space program, international agreements on nuclear energy, tariff arrangements, and adjustment of federal pay rates.

During the 1970's the legislative veto was important in resolving a series of major constitutional disputes between the President and Congress over claims of the President to broad impoundment, war, and national emergency powers. The key provision of the War Powers Resolution, 50 U.S.C. § 1544(c), authorizes the termination by concurrent resolution of the use of armed forces in hostilities. A similar measure resolved the problem posed by Presidential claims of inherent power to impound appropriations. Congressional Budget and Impoundment Control Act of 1974, 31 U.S.C. § 1403. In conference, a compromise was achieved under which permanent impoundments, termed "rescissions," would require approval through enactment of legislation. In contrast, temporary impoundments, or "deferrals," would become effective unless disapproved by one House. This compromise provided the President with flexibility, while preserving ultimate Congressional

---

1. Presidential objections to the veto, until the veto by President Nixon of the War Powers Resolution, principally concerned bills authorizing committee vetoes. As the Senate Subcommittee on Separation of Powers found in 1969, "an accommoda- tion was reached years ago on legislative vetoes exercised by the entire Congress or by one House, [while] disputes have continued to arise over the committee form of the veto." S.Rep. No. 549, 91st Cong., 1st Sess., p. 14 (1969). . . .

control over the budget.[2] Although the War Powers Resolution was enacted over President Nixon's veto, the Impoundment Control Act was enacted with the President's approval. . . .

The history of the legislative veto also makes clear that it has not been a sword with which Congress has struck out to aggrandize itself at the expense of the other branches—the concerns of Madison and Hamilton. Rather, the veto has been a means of defense, a reservation of ultimate authority necessary if Congress is to fulfill its designated role under Article I as the nation's lawmaker. While the President has often objected to particular legislative vetoes, generally those left in the hands of congressional committees, the Executive has more often agreed to legislative review as the price for a broad delegation of authority. To be sure, the President may have preferred unrestricted power, but that could be precisely why Congress thought it essential to retain a check on the exercise of delegated authority.

II

For all these reasons, the apparent sweep of the Court's decision today is regretable. . . . The reality of the situation is that the constitutional question posed today is one of immense difficulty over which the executive and legislative branches—as well as scholars and judges—have understandably disagreed. . . . We should not find the lack of a specific constitutional authorization for the legislative veto surprising, and I would not infer disapproval of the mechanism from its absence. . . . [T]he wisdom of the Framers was to anticipate that the nation would grow and new problems of governance would require different solutions. . . .

The actual art of governing under our Constitution does not and cannot conform to judicial definitions of the power of any of its branches based on isolated clauses or even single Articles torn from context. While the Constitution diffuses power the better to secure liberty, it also contemplates that practice will integrate the dispersed powers into a workable government." Youngstown Sheet & Tube Co. v. Sawyer, 343 U.S. 579, 635 (1952).

III

. . . . There is no question that a bill does not become a law until it is approved by both the House and the Senate, and presented to the President. . . . All of this, the [subject of the] Third Part of the Court's opinion, . . . does not, however, answer the constitutional question before us. The power to exercise a legislative veto is not the power to write new law without bicameral approval or presidential consideration. . . . On its face, the legislative veto no more allows

---

2. The Impoundment Control Act's provision for legislative review has been used extensively. Presidents have submitted hundreds of proposed budget deferrals, of which 65 have been disapproved by resolutions of the House or Senate with no protest by the Executive.

one House of Congress to make law than does the presidential veto confer such power upon the President. . . .

B

The Court's holding today that all legislative-type action must be enacted through the lawmaking process ignores that legislative authority is routinely delegated to the Executive branch, to the independent regulatory agencies, and to private individuals and groups.

. . . [B]y virtue of congressional delegation, legislative power can be exercised by independent agencies and Executive departments without the passage of new legislation. For some time, the sheer amount of law—the substantive rules that regulate private conduct and direct the operation of government—made by the agencies has far outnumbered the lawmaking engaged in by Congress through the traditional process. . . . When agencies are authorized to prescribe law through substantive rulemaking, the administrator's regulation is not only due deference, but is accorded "legislative effect." See, e.g. Schweiker v. Gray Panthers, 453 U.S. 34, 43–44 (1981); Batterton v. Francis, 432 U.S. 416 (1977).[3] . . .

. . . [A] resolution of disapproval under § 244(c)(2) need not again be subject to the bicameral process. Because it serves only to check the Attorney General's exercise of the suspension authority granted by § 244, the disapproval resolution—unlike the Attorney General's action—"cannot reach beyond the limits of the statute that created it—a statute duly enacted pursuant to Article I." . . . [T]he Court concedes that certain administrative agency action, such as rulemaking, "may resemble lawmaking" and recognizes that "[t]his Court has referred to agency activity as being 'quasi-legislative' in character. Humphrey's Executor v. United States, 295 U.S. 602, 628 (1935)." Ante at n. 4. Such rules and adjudications by the agencies meet the Court's own definition of legislative action for they "alter[ ] the legal rights, duties, and relations of persons . . . outside the legislative branch," and involve "determinations of policy." . . . If the effective functioning of a complex modern government requires the delegation of vast authority which by virtue of its breadth, is legislative or "quasi-legislative" in character, I cannot accept that Article I—which is, after all, the source of the non-delegation doctrine—should forbid Congress from qualifying that grant with a legislative veto.

3. "Legislative or substantive regulations are issued by an agency pursuant to statutory authority and . . . implement the statute, as for example, the proxy rules issue by the Securities and Exchange Commission. . . . Such rules have the force and effect of law. U.S. Dept. of Justice, Attorney General's Manual on the Administrative Procedures Act 30 n. 3 (1947)." Batterton v. Francis, 432 U.S. 416, 425 n. 9 (1977). Substantive agency regulations are clearly exercises of lawmaking authority; agency interpretations of their statutes are only arguably so. But as Henry Monaghan has observed, "Judicial deference to agency interpretation of law is simply one way of recognizing a delegation of lawmaking authority to an agency." H. Monaghan, Marbury and the Administrative State, 83 Colum.L.Rev. 1, 26 (1983).

C

The Court also takes no account of perhaps the most relevant consideration: However resolutions of disapproval under § 224(c)(2) are formally characterized, in reality, a departure from the status quo occurs only upon the concurrence of opinion among the House, Senate, and President. . . .

1

As its history reveals, § 244(c)(2) . . . did not alter the division of actual authority between Congress and the Executive. At all times, whether through private bills, or through affirmative concurrent resolutions, or through the present one-House veto, a permanent change in a deportable alien's status could be accomplished only with the agreement of the Attorney General, the House, and the Senate.

2

The central concern of the presentation and bicameralism requirements of Article I is that when a departure from the legal status quo is undertaken, it is done with the approval of the President and both Houses of Congress—or, in the event of a presidential veto, a two-thirds majority in both Houses. This interest is fully satisfied by the operation of § 224(c)(2). The President's approval is found in the Attorney General's action in recommending to Congress that the deportation order for a given alien be suspended. The House and the Senate indicate their approval of the Executive's action by not passing a resolution of disapproval within the statutory period. Thus, a change in the legal status quo—the deportability of the alien—is consummated only with the approval of each of the three relevant actors. . . . "The President and the two Houses enjoy exactly the same say in what the law is to be as would have been true for each without the presence of the one-House veto, and nothing in the law is changed absent the concurrence of the President and a majority in each House." Atkins v. United States, 214 Ct.Cl. 186, 556 F.2d 1028, 1064 (1977), cert. denied, 434 U.S. 1009 (1978).

. . . .

Thus understood, § 244(c)(2) fully effectuates the purposes of the bicameralism and presentation requirements. . . . [I]t may be objected that Congress cannot indicate its approval of legislative change by inaction. In the Court of Appeals' view, inaction by Congress "could equally imply endorsement, acquiescence, passivity, indecision or indifference." This objection appears more properly directed at the wisdom of the legislative veto than its constitutionality. The Constitution does not and cannot guarantee that legislators will carefully scrutinize legislation and deliberate before acting. In a democracy, it is the electorate that holds the legislators accountable for the wisdom of their choices. It is hard to maintain that a private bill receives any greater individualized scrutiny than a resolution of disapproval under § 244(c)

(2). Certainly the legislative veto is no more susceptible to this attack than the Court's increasingly common practice of according weight to the failure of Congress to disturb an Executive or independent agency's action. Earlier this Term, the Court found it important that Congress failed to act on bills proposed to overturn the Internal Revenue Service's interpretation of the requirements for tax-exempt status under § 501(c)(3) of the tax code. Bob Jones University v. United States, 461 U.S. 574, 600–601 (1983). If Congress may be said to have ratified the Internal Revenue Service's interpretation without passing new legislation, Congress may also be said to approve a suspension of deportation by the Attorney General when it fails to exercise its veto authority. The requirements of Article I are not compromised by the Congressional scheme.

IV

The Court of Appeals struck § 244(c)(2) as violative of the constitutional principle of separation of powers. It is true that the purpose of separating the authority of government is to prevent unnecessary and dangerous concentration of power in one branch. . . .

But the history of the separation of powers doctrine is also a history of accommodation and practicality. Apprehensions of an overly powerful branch have not led to undue prophylactic measures that handicap the effective working of the national government as a whole. The Constitution does not contemplate total separation of the three branches of Government. Buckley v. Valeo, 424 U.S. 1, 121 (1976). "[A] hermetic sealing off of the three branches of Government from one another would preclude the establishment of a Nation capable of governing itself effectively." Ibid.

> [I]n determining whether the Act disrupts the proper balance between the coordinate branches, the proper inquiry focuses on the extent to which it prevents the Executive Branch from accomplishing its constitutionally assigned functions. United States v. Nixon, 418 U.S. at 711–712. Only where the potential for disruption is present must we then determine whether that impact is justified by an overriding need to promote objectives within the constitutional authority of Congress. Nixon v. Administrator of General Services, 433 U.S. 425, 443 (1977).

Section 244(c)(2) survives this test. The legislative veto provision does not "prevent the Executive Branch from accomplishing its constitutionally assigned function." . . . Here, § 244 grants the executive only a qualified suspension authority and it is only that authority which the President is constitutionally authorized to execute. . . .

Nor does § 244 infringe on the judicial power, as Justice Powell would hold. Section 244 makes clear that Congress has reserved its own judgment as part of the statutory process. Congressional action does not substitute for judicial review of the Attorney General's decisions. The Act provides for judicial review of the refusal of the Attorney General to suspend a deportation and to transmit a recom-

mendation to Congress. INS v. Wang, 450 U.S. 139 (1981) (per curiam).
But the courts have not been given the authority to review whether an
alien should be given permanent status; review is limited to whether
the Attorney General has properly applied the statutory standards for
essentially denying the alien a recommendation that his deportable
status be changed by the Congress. . . .

I do not suggest that all legislative vetoes are necessarily consistent
with separation of powers principles. A legislative check on an inherently executive function, for example that of initiating prosecutions,
poses an entirely different question. But the legislative veto device
here—and in many other settings—is far from an instance of legislative
tyranny over the Executive. It is a necessary check on the unavoidably
expanding power of the agencies, both executive and independent, as
they engage in exercising authority delegated by Congress.

V

I regret that I am in disagreement with my colleagues on the
fundamental questions that this case presents. But even more I regret
the destructive scope of the Court's holding. It reflects a profoundly
different conception of the Constitution than that held by the Courts
which sanctioned the modern administrative state. Today's decision
strikes down in one fell swoop provisions in more laws enacted by
Congress than the Court has cumulatively invalidated in its history. I
fear it will now be more difficult "to insure that the fundamental policy
decisions in our society will be made not by an appointed official but by
the body immediately responsible to the people," Arizona v. California,
373 U.S. 546, 626 (1963) (Harlan, J., dissenting). I must dissent.

NOTES

(1) D. ELLIOTT, INS v. CHADHA: THE ADMINISTRATIVE CONSTITUTION,
THE CONSTITUTION, AND THE LEGISLATIVE VETO, 1983 Sup.Ct.Review 125,
134–138:

The core of the Court's reasoning is conceptual and formalistic: the
legislative veto is "legislative" because it has the effect of "altering
legal rights." The legislative veto "alters legal rights," however, only
because the Court chooses to characterize its effect that way. . . .
There is no question that "absent House action, Chadha would remain
in the United States." But does that really prove that the House
resolution had "the effect of altering . . . legal rights"? Not at all,
any more than when a prosecutor drops charges for possession of
marijuana the defendant thereby acquires the "legal right" to smoke
the substance. . . . [T]he statute authorizing the Attorney General
to suspend deportation on grounds of hardship also provided that either
house of Congress could veto the Attorney General's action. Why was
the nature of Chadha's legal rights not defined by the statute creating
them? [1] If Chadha's only right was what the statute gave him—the
right to remain in the country unless one house exercised its legislative

1. Cf. Arnett v. Kennedy, 416 U.S. 134,
152 (1974).

veto—then the House's action did not alter Chadha's rights: the possibility of a legislative veto was built into them in the first place.

These questions imply, not that the Court's analysis is incorrect, but that it is arbitrary. The legislative veto "alters legal rights" only because the Court superimposes that conceptualization on the House resolution canceling the suspension of deportation. . . . As for the . . . proposition—that Congress must "abide" its delegation of authority to the Attorney General—one can only ask "Why?" Again, the question is whether the legislative veto is a permissible technique for controlling exercises of delegated authority. Not a word of the Court's opinion is spent explaining why it would be contrary to the framers' principles of constitutional design or otherwise legally suspect for Congress to retain supervision over exercise of power that it has delegated. . . .

There may be sound reasons of constitutional significance to prohibit Congress from making partial delegations of power to the Executive, but the Court does not reach that level of analysis. Instead, the opinion rests on two legal fictions, "altering legal rights" and "delegation." The Court treats these abstractions as if they had independent and immutable existences, rather than recognizing them as constructs that serve purposes which should define their reach and measure.[2] This approach to deciding cases by manipulating formal legal concepts is a throwback to what Llewellyn called the Formal Style of conceptualistic judicial reasoning prevalent late in the nineteenth century.[3]

(2) The week following its decision in Chadha the Court summarily affirmed two holdings of the D.C. Circuit that had found legislative veto provisions (including a two-house veto) invalid in the context of independent regulatory commission rulemaking.[4] In the Consumer Energy Council case, the D.C. Circuit had reasoned, in part:

"The contention that the separation of powers doctrine does not apply to independent agencies is manifestly groundless. . . . It is true that the President, as representative of the Executive, does not have a claim to control the decisionmaking of independent agencies. But it is an enormous and unwarranted, jump from this to the conclusion that Congress may itself interfere with an independent agency's decisions without regard to separation of powers. Although FERC is substantially independent of the Executive, it nonetheless performs executive functions. The constitutionality of agency independence has not turned on a determination that certain agency functions are properly legislative rather than executive in nature. . . . [T]he constitutionality of the one-house veto does not depend on whether it is used against an executive agency or an independent agency. There has been

---

2. Cf. Holmes, Law in Science and Science in Law, 12 Harv.L.Rev. 443 (1899) ("different rights . . . stand on different grounds of policy. . . . [I]f you simply say all rights shall be [absolute], that is only a pontifical or imperial way of forbidding discussion . . . ").

3. See Llewellyn, The Common Law Tradition: Deciding Appeals 5–6 (1960).

4. Process Gas Consumers Group v. Consumer Energy Council of America, 463 U.S. 1216 (1983), aff'g Consumer Energy Council of America v. FERC, 673 F.2d 425 (D.C.Cir.1982); United States Senate v. FTC, 463 U.S. 1216 (1983), aff'g Consumers Union v. FTC, 691 F.2d 575 (D.C.Cir.1982) (en banc).

a general breakdown in any distinction between the functions of the two types of agency, and in practice the interference by Congress is identical in either case. Indeed, it is ironic that Congressional amici attempt to place great significance on the Commission's independence and on the need for having a politically accountable check on the agency's decision. The fundamental justification for making agencies independent is that since they exercise adjudicatory powers requiring impartial expertise, political interference is undesirable. By then turning around and asserting that this independence is a justification for the one-house veto, Congress attempts simultaneously to decrease the power of the Executive and increase its own power. . . .

(3) AMERICAN FEDERATION OF GOVERNMENT EMPLOYEES v. PIERCE, 697 F.2d 303 (D.C.Cir.1982), involved an annual appropriations bill for the Department of Housing and Urban Development which had provided, in part, that none of the funds it made available "may be used prior to January 1, 1983, to plan, design, implement, or administer any reorganization of the Department without the prior approval of the Committee on Appropriations." The AFGE and others challenged action by Secretary Pierce that appeared to have disregarded this limitation. The D.C. Circuit's opinion found the proviso offensive, both as a departure from the bicameral-presentment requirements of "legislative action" and as a "means for Congress to control the executive without going through the full lawmaking process, thus unconstitutionally enhancing congressional power at the expense of executive power."

Did the panel correctly characterize these measures as involving "enhanced control" rather than "enhanced flexibility," "enhanced precision," or "enhanced executive authority"? Provisos such as these are neither uncommon, nor counted in totaling up the number of legislative veto provisions or the frequency of their exercise. Presumably the Congress enacting such a proviso is not yet prepared to appropriate funds for the stated purpose, and the measure reflects a compromise with an executive seeking added flexibility that Congress is not required to afford. Even without such provisos, it is commonplace for an agency subjected to a line-item budget, and uncertain about its authority or wishing to reallocate its funds, to call the relevant appropriations committee and explain its plan; with committee approval, or perhaps absent objection, the changed expenditures can be made within the limits established by the overall appropriation. The enforcement of budgetary limitations is almost wholly internal to the political branches of government, and a matter of intense and appropriate congressional interest. Judicial controls could be invoked only with great difficulty and the provisions rarely if ever implicate private claims of right.

"Appropriations measures originate with the President and must be signed by him; his Office of Management and Budget, with but few exceptions, controls both the initial submissions and requested alterations. Housing and Urban Development Secretary Pierce is unlikely to have taken the steps that brought about the lawsuit in American Federation of Government Employees without the initial assurance of presidential backing, as he would not have sought committee approval for the otherwise forbidden expenditures without that assurance. The limited duration of appropriations measures and the practical difficulty the President in any event faces in exercising his veto authority over such measures also suggest a presentment issue far less substantial than that involved when an agency is authorized, for an indefinite term and without presidential participation, to adopt rules as binding as statutes on the public at large, rules which are then made the subject of legislative veto procedures.

"Similarly, viewing such practices as means for enhancing congressional control over the executive without use of the full legislative process, and hence violative of separation of powers, is questionable on these facts and, in addition, apparently insufficient. The full legislative process is used at least annually; although the 'one bite at the apple' theory invoked by Justice White in general defense of the legislative veto [in Chadha] raises problems when applied to measures of indefinite duration and broad authority, it seems less problematic in the budgetary context. . . . It seems doubtful that Congress would be willing to make the questioned appropriation absent some technique for later assuring itself, or its trusted agents, that an appropriation that now seems unjustified has in fact become warranted by intervening events. If that is so, it is hard to treat these measures as if only Congress gains in power and the President necessarily loses. . . . " [5]

(4) Consider also a distinction suggested by two decisions of the New Jersey Supreme Court, GENERAL ASSEMBLY v. BYRNE, 90 N.J. 376, 448 A.2d 438 (1982) and ENOURATO v. N.J., 90 N.J. 396, 448 A.2d 449 (1982). In the first case, it struck down a provision for general legislative veto of proposed agency rules; in the second, it upheld a specific provision establishing legislative veto procedures for projects proposed by the state's building authority that would require long-term leases by state agencies. In the former setting, the court thought the legislative veto threatened both to impair the balance of power within state government and to diminish the quality of initial legislative efforts. The latter measure concerned essentially political accommodations, with no diminution of gubernatorial control; the legislature's opportunity to disapprove a proposal could be thought of as creating a form of moral obligation on its part to make the future appropriations necessary to meet the proposal's terms. In this respect, the New Jersey court evidently believed that the opportunity for a legislative veto was not merely unobjectionable, but in fact served a positive function in the arrangements of state government.[6]

---

5. P. Strauss, "Was There a Baby in the Bathwater? A Comment on the Supreme Court's Legislative Veto Decision," 1983 Duke L.J. 789, 814–15 (1983); and see S. Breyer, The Legislative Veto After Chadha, 72 Geo.L.J. 785 (1984); G. Spann, Spinning the Legislative Veto, 72 Geo.L.J. 813 (1984); Symposium, Reactions to Chadha: Separation of Powers and the Legislative Veto, 35 Syr.L.Rev. 685 (1984).

6. The 1981 Model State Administrative Procedure Act embodies a suggestion that falls somewhat short of a legislative veto. Objection by designated legislative oversight committee, if not met, will result in placing a "burden . . . upon the agency in any proceeding for judicial review or for enforcement of the rule to establish that the [matter] objected to is within [its] procedural and substantive authority. . . . " § 3–204.

(5) A reorganization act [7] incorporating a one-house legislative veto, had provided the basis on which President Carter transferred investigative and enforcement authority under the Age Discrimination in Employment Act and Equal Pay Act from the Department of Labor to the Equal Employment Opportunity Commission. That reorganization was not legislatively vetoed by either house of Congress, and so took effect. In the wake of Chadha, had the EEOC authority to investigate and enforce the acts? Or should a court conclude that Congress would not have enacted the Reorganization Act without the legislative veto—rendering the Act as a whole a nullity and thus voiding the reorganization? The Fifth Circuit was persuaded the legislative veto provision was severable and, hence, the reorganization valid. EEOC v. Hernando Bank Inc., 724 F.2d 1188 (5th Cir.1984). Not so the Second Circuit—even in the face of repeated congressional appropriation to the EEOC of enforcement funds. EEOC v. CBS, Inc., 743 F.2d 969 (2d Cir.1984). Such references, "buried in lengthy and comprehensive appropriations acts" could not be taken as independent measures of validation. While the particular problem was cured by a statute validating the reorganization,[8] the general issues of severability—and, for that matter, of devising regimes to substitute for the legislative veto [9]—remain open.[10]

(6) Rather than approve or disapprove particular actions of administrators, their political overseers may seek control over the structure of administration. For the President, this may be accomplished by exercising a statutory or inherent constitutional authority to delegate to others a share of the responsibilities assigned to him by various laws [11]

7. Commencing in 1932, a succession of statutes, each designed to have only a brief life span, conferred on the President a limited means of reorganizing administration that had become disorganized or unwieldy; The Reorganization Acts expired and were later revived in 1959, 1961, 1964, 1965, 1969, and 1971; the last expired on April 1, 1973. In 1977, President Carter persuaded Congress to give him reorganization power for three years, subsequently extended to 1981; 91 Stat. 29, 5 U.S.C. §§ 901–912; 94 Stat. 329 (1980); 96 Stat. 1086 (1982); the Reorganization Act Amendments of 1984, P.L. 98–614, reinstated the President's authority for the period Nov. 9—Dec. 31, 1984, but changed the mechanism for congressional participation in response to Chadha by requiring a joint resolution of approval within a stated period, an action requiring in turn, presidential approval. Each of the enactments empowered the President to consolidate, abolish, and transfer agencies and functions in order to achieve coordination and economy. H. Mansfield, Federal Executive Reorganization: Thirty Years of Experience, 29 Pub.Admin.Rev. 341 (1969): ". . . reorganization plans have proved a serviceable device for shifting bureaus, realigning jurisdictions, regrouping activities, and upsetting some ties of influence." But cf. H. Kaufman, Reflections on Administrative Reorganization, in J. Pechman (ed.), Setting National Priorities: The 1978 Budget (Brookings, 1977), at 401–403.

8. P.L. 95–454, 92 Stat. 1224, 5 U.S.C. § 1101 (note) and (c).

9. See, e.g., S. Breyer, The Legislative Veto After Chadha, 72 Geo.L.J. 785 (1984).

10. See, e.g. Alaska Airlines, Inc. v. Donovan, 766 F.2d 1550 (D.C.Cir.1985), cert. granted 106 S.Ct. 1259 (1986); Note, The Aftermath of Chadha: The Impact of the Severability Doctrine on the Management of Intragovernmental Relations, 71 Va.L.Rev. 1211 (1985).

11. To allay doubt about the President's power to delegate, Congress in 1950 adopted the Presidential Subdelegation Act, 64 Stat. 419 (1950), 65 Stat. 712 (1951), 3 U.S.C. § 301, authorizing him to empower some other official whose appointment was confirmed by the Senate to perform "any function which is vested in the President by law," unless subdelegation has been affirmatively prohibited or unless a statute limits subdelegation to a specifically identified officer or officers. Although this language seems to confine the President's

or, perhaps more familiarly, by reorganizing government to redirect the performance of duties directly granted others by statute. Corresponding legislative controls over agency authorization have increasingly been regularized in recent years under the rubric of "sunset legislation." Such legislation typically establishes a cycle, say of ten years, within which each agency's performance is reviewed; unless the agency's authorizing legislation is reenacted (with or without change, as the legislature finds appropriate), the agency and its rules and regulations simply cease to be. Sunset laws have been adopted in almost three quarters of the states [12] and are reported by Common Cause, which for the last decade has been their enthusiastic proponent, to be well received there.[13]

The process has obvious attractions. Compelling an agency to justify its continued existence may in fact invigorate its personnel. It may, too, give the agency a needed opportunity to air its own complaints concerning the limits others have placed on its functioning.[14] At least theoretically, moreover, the periodic life-or-death review may draw legislative attention to an obsolete agency that would otherwise remain mindlessly in existence though its reason for being had disappeared.

Potential disadvantages of the sunset review, apart from its burdensomeness, need to be noted as well. "An organization which aggressively pursues its duties invariably makes enemies," a commentator has remarked.

> The legislative process is fraught with roadblocks and an agency or program could conceivably be eliminated in the legislative maze by an influential legislator. The fear of rankling a key legislator could well have a chilling effect on an agency's activity. Another drawback of sunset review is its potential impact upon agency morale. The periodic trauma of threatened program abolition, with its resultant loss of jobs, may dishearten agency personnel. Advocates of sunset, of course, argue that a periodic review will give agency employ-

choice of a delegate to officials appointed by and with the consent of the Senate, a later portion of the statute provides that "This chapter shall not be deemed to limit or derogate from any existing or inherent right of the President to delegate the performance of functions vested in him by law. . . . " For an interesting account of the formality thus imposed on Congress, see H. Bruff, Legislative Formality, Administrative Rationality, 63 Texas L.Rev. 207 (1984).

12. See Staff Report: A Compilation of Sunset Statutes With Background Information on State Sunset Laws, House Comm. on Rules, Subcomm. on the Legislative Process, 98th Cong., 1st Sess. (Oct.1983), which sets out the text of thirty-six state statutes.

13. The Status of Sunset in the States: A Common Cause Report (1982); for a somewhat earlier, more critical view, see L.

Davis, Review Procedures and Public Accountability in Sunset Legislation: An Analysis and Proposal for Reform, 33 Ad.L. Rev. 393 (1981).

14. In 1978, for example, the Commodity Futures Trading Commission—created in 1974 but operating only since 1975 (7 U.S.C. § 4a)—was called on the Senatorial carpet to account for its seeming laxity in enforcement work. This gave the CFTC a chance to "go public" in its complaints about inadequate appropriations. The CFTC at the time had a staff of 440 to regulate all aspects of trading in commodities futures, throughout the country. Its chairman reportedly said that the Commission was allowed to employ only 26 investigators to cover activities in ten markets; a suburban police department, he added, has that many officers on duty on the night shift. Time, April 17, 1978, p. 84.

ees, lulled into complacency by heretofore unchallenged job security, a much-needed jolt. But the periodic termination threat could result in unease, uncertainty, and distraction as the sunset deadline approaches, particularly if a renewal bill becomes mired in the legislative mill.[15]

Too brief a life expectancy would have a further disadvantage for official bodies, as for human bodies, inhibiting long term planning and personnel deployment. Worrying about the immediacies of today that will be the focus of scrutiny tomorrow may or may not make for accomplishment of worthy goals. A freshly scrubbed exterior may or may not accord with inner reality.[16] Moved by these political risks, recent federal proposals for periodic review of regulatory programs have omitted the automatic termination feature of sunset. They seek other forcing mechanisms, such as a requirement of presidential analyses and recommendations that are to be given priority status as legislative business once received; "high noon," rather than "sunset," review is the appellation given this not-yet-enacted approach.[17]

b. Personnel and Resources for Administration

[The President,] by and with The Advice and Consent of the Senate, shall appoint Ambassadors, other public Ministers and Consuls, Judges of the Supreme Court, and all other officers of the United States, whose Appointments are not herein otherwise provided for, and which shall be established by Law: but Congress may by Law vest the Appointment of such inferior officers, as they think proper, in the President (alone, in the Courts of Law, or in the Heads of Departments.)

United States Constitution, Article II, Section 2

Effective presidential influence over the actions of subordinates will transparently be a function of the President's authority to select and remove those persons. Control is established both by the initial assurance that a position is held by a person who can confidently be expected to carry out one's policies, and by the subsequent power to enforce one's wishes by removing persons in whom one lacks that confidence (or, less broadly, who disobey one's valid directions). Consider, however, whether the powers to appoint and to remove are properly equated. Only appointment is mentioned in the Constitutional text, and the more natural source of the disciplinary authority suggested by removal may lie in "the executive power" and the President's corresponding responsibility to "take care that the laws be faithfully executed." See C. Thach, The Creation of the Presidency 1775–1789, pp. 88–89 (1923).

---

15. A. Licata, Zero-Base Sunset Review, 14 Harv. J.Legis. 505, 539 (1977).

16. Compare R. Neustadt, Politics and Bureaucrats, in D. Truman ed., The Congress and America's Future 106 (1965): "From the standpoint of good management as understood in private corporations or as preached by the apostles of administrative rationality, devices of this sort create a host of troubles for an agency official and for his executive superiors. Annual authorization causes turmoil every year especially in personnel administration."

17. See S. Breyer, Two Models of Regulatory Reform, 34 S.Car.L.Rev. 629 (1983).

For the great mass of federal employers, in any event, Congress long ago placed the gaining and losing of jobs outside political control by its creation of the Civil Service System (now administered by the Office of Personnel Management, an "executive" agency, and the Merit System Protective Board, an "independent" one). "We have no doubt," the Supreme Court remarked in sustaining naval engineers' claims for pay in the face of a discharge prior to the expiration of their statutory term, "that when Congress, by law, vests the appointment of inferior officers in the heads of Departments it may limit and restrict the power of removal as it deems best for the public interest. . . . The head of a Department has no constitutional prerogative of appointment to offices independently of the legislation of Congress, and by such legislation he must be governed, not only in making appointments but in all that is incident thereto." [1] More recently the Court has found constitutional limitations on the grounds that could be used to remove (and perhaps appoint) most government officials. Political affiliation—to politicians, the most popular of tests of office—may be used to support a removal only "if an employee's private political beliefs would interfere with the discharge of his public duties. . . . [T]he ultimate inquiry is whether the hiring authority can demonstrate that party affiliation is an appropriate requirement for the effective performance of the public office involved." Branti v. Finkel, 445 U.S. 507, 517–518 (1980). An assistant public defender—who from some perspectives participates in the formation of policy, and enjoys a confidential working relationship with the public defender who appointed him—is not such an employee.[2]

But what of those who serve as "Heads of Departments," for whom appointments are necessarily the President's and "advice and consent" is invariably reserved? Here, the President can change the tempo and outlook of even the supposedly "independent" regulatory agencies. Federal Reserve Board members are appointed for 14-year terms, but the members of most commissions and boards are chosen for five, six, or seven years, as the case may be, with one member's appointment expiring each year. Within a single presidential term, therefore, a President will have had opportunity to name at least a majority of the top-level people in the several agencies. In point of fact, the members of the independent agencies tend not to serve for the full period of their appointment.[3] Hence the President's choice is even more tellingly significant than the underlying statutes suggest. Despite the continuity and strength provided by an agency's career staff, newly appointed agency heads have enough power—within the range of their delegated

---

1. United States v. Perkins, 116 U.S. 483, 485 (1886).

2. The result suggests that the realm of permissible political removals is shrinking. Earlier, in a case involving employees of the Cook County, Illinois Sheriff's office complaining of their political discharge, two justices whose votes were essential to that outcome stressed that the employees in question had *no* policy responsibilities

and did *not* enjoy a confidential relationship with their boss. Elrod v. Burns, 427 U.S. 347 (1976) (Stewart and Blackmun, concurring). Justice Stewart underscored the Branti Court's softening of these lines with a vigorous dissent, 445 U.S. at 520.

3. See C. Goodsell and C. Gayo, Appointive Control of Federal Regulatory Commissions, 23 Ad.L.Rev. 291 (1971).

discretion—to shift the emphasis of the regulatory program in the general direction of "Administration policy," if one exists.[4]

Given the constitutional text—one of the very few explicit statements Article II makes about the President's authority over domestic affairs—appointments power issues have rarely arisen in the courts. Consider, however, the following:

BOWSHER v. SYNAR
Supreme Court of the United States, 1986.
106 S.Ct. 3181.

CHIEF JUSTICE BURGER delivered the opinion of the Court.

The question presented by these appeals is whether the assignment by Congress to the Comptroller General of the United States of certain functions under the Balanced Budget and Emergency Deficit Control Act of 1985 violates the doctrine of separation of powers.

I

A

On December 12, 1985, the President signed into law the Balanced Budget and Emergency Deficit Control Act of 1985, Pub.L. 99–177, 99 Stat. 1038, 2 U.S.C.A. § 901 et seq. (Supp.1986), popularly known as the "Gramm-Rudman-Hollings Act." The purpose of the Act is to eliminate the federal budget deficit. To that end, the Act sets a "maximum deficit amount" for federal spending for each of fiscal years 1986 through 1991. The size of that maximum deficit amount progressively reduces to zero in fiscal year 1991. . . . Each year, the Directors of the Office of Management and Budget (OMB) and the Congressional Budget Office (CBO) independently estimate the amount of the federal budget deficit for the upcoming fiscal year. If that deficit exceeds the maximum targeted deficit amount for that fiscal year by more than a specified amount, the Directors of OMB and CBO independently calculate, on a program-by-program basis, the budget reductions necessary to ensure that the deficit does not exceed the maximum deficit amount. The Act then requires the Directors to report jointly their deficit estimates and budget reduction calculations to the Comptroller General.

The Comptroller General, after reviewing the Directors' reports, then reports his conclusions to the President. § 251(b). The President in turn must issue a "sequestration" order mandating the spending reductions specified by the Comptroller General. § 252. There follows a period during which Congress may by legislation reduce spending to obviate, in whole or in part, the need for the sequestration order. If such reductions are not enacted, the sequestration order becomes effective and the spending reductions included in that order are made.

4. See P. Strauss, The Place of Agencies in Government: Separation of Powers and the Fourth Branch, 84 Colum.L.Rev. 573 (1984); D. Welborn, Governance of Federal Regulatory Agencies (1977); W. Cary, Poli- tics and the Regulatory Agencies 8, 37 (1967); S. Scher, Regulatory Agency Control Through Appointment, 23 J.Pol. 667 (1961).

Anticipating constitutional challenge to these procedures, the Act also contains a "fallback" deficit reduction process to take effect "[i]n the event that any of the reporting procedures described in section 251 are invalidated." § 274(f). Under these provisions, the report prepared by the Directors of OMB and the CBO is submitted directly to a specially-created Temporary Joint Committee on Deficit Reduction, which must report in five days to both Houses a joint resolution setting forth the content of the Directors' report. Congress then must vote on the resolution under special rules, which render amendments out of order. If the resolution is passed and signed by the President, it then serves as the basis for a Presidential sequestration order.

B

Within hours of the President's signing of the Act, Congressman Synar, who had voted against the Act, filed a complaint seeking declaratory relief that the Act was unconstitutional. Eleven other Members later joined Congressman Synar's suit. A virtually identical lawsuit was also filed by the National Treasury Employees Union. The Union alleged that its members had been injured as a result of the Act's automatic spending reduction provisions, which have suspended certain cost-of-living benefit increases to the Union's members.

A three-judge District Court, appointed pursuant to 2 U.S.C.A. § 922(a)(5) (Supp.1986), invalidated the reporting provisions. Synar v. United States, 626 F.Supp. 1374 (DC 1986) (Scalia, Johnson, Gasch, JJ.). . . . Although the District Court concluded that the Act survived a delegation doctrine challenge, it held that the role of the Comptroller General in the deficit reduction process violated the constitutionally imposed separation of powers. . . . Appeals were taken directly to this Court pursuant to § 274(b) of the Act. We noted probable jurisdiction and expedited consideration of the appeals. 475 U.S. ___ (1986). We affirm.

II

A threshold issue is whether the Members of Congress, members of the National Treasury Employees Union, or the Union itself have standing to challenge the constitutionality of the Act in question. It is clear that members of the Union, one of whom is an appellee here, will sustain injury by not receiving a scheduled increase in benefits. This is sufficient to confer standing under § 274(a)(2) and Article III. We therefore need not consider the standing issue as to the Union or Members of Congress. . . .

III

. . . Even a cursory examination of the Constitution reveals the influence of Montesquieu's thesis that checks and balances were the foundation of a structure of government that would protect liberty. The Framers provided a vigorous legislative branch and a separate and wholly independent executive branch, with each branch responsible ultimately to the people. The Framers also provided for a judicial branch equally independent with "[t]he judicial Power . . . extend[ing] to all Cases, in Law and Equity, arising under this Constitution, and the Laws of the United States." Art. III, § 2.

Other, more subtle, examples of separated powers are evident as well. Unlike parliamentary systems such as that of Great Britain, no person who is an officer of the United States may serve as a Member of the Congress. Art. I, § 6. Moreover, unlike parliamentary systems, the President, under Article II, is responsible not to the Congress but to the people, subject only to impeachment proceedings which are exercised by the two Houses as representatives of the people. Art. II, § 4. And even in the impeachment of a President the presiding officer of the ultimate tribunal is not a member of the legislative branch, but the Chief Justice of the United States. Art. I, § 3.

That this system of division and separation of powers produces conflicts, confusion, and discordance at times is inherent, but it was deliberately so structured to assure full, vigorous and open debate on the great issues affecting the people and to provide avenues for the operation of checks on the exercise of governmental power.

The Constitution does not contemplate an active role for Congress in the supervision of officers charged with the execution of the laws it enacts. The President appoints "Officers of the United States" with the "Advice and Consent of the Senate. . . ." Article II, § 2. Once the appointment has been made and confirmed, however, the Constitution explicitly provides for removal of Officers of the United States by Congress only upon impeachment by the House of Representatives and conviction by the Senate. An impeachment by the House and trial by the Senate can rest only on "Treason, Bribery or other high Crimes and Misdemeanors." Article II, § 4. A direct congressional role in the removal of officers charged with the execution of the laws beyond this limited one is inconsistent with separation of powers.

This was made clear in debate in the First Congress in 1789. When Congress considered an amendment to a bill establishing the Department of Foreign Affairs, the debate centered around whether the Congress "should recognize and declare the power of the President under the Constitution to remove the Secretary of Foreign Affairs without the advice and consent of the Senate." Myers v. United States, 272 U.S. 52, 114 (1926). James Madison urged rejection of a congressional role in the removal of Executive Branch officers, other than by impeachment, saying in debate:

> "Perhaps there was no argument urged with more success, or more plausibly grounded against the Constitution, under which we are now deliberating, than that founded on the mingling of the Executive and Legislative branches of the Government in one body. It has been objected, that the Senate have too much of the Executive power even, by having a control over the President in the appointment to office. Now, shall we extend this connexion between the Legislative and Executive departments, which will strengthen the objection, and diminish the responsibility we have in the head of the Executive?" 1 Annals of Cong. 380.

Madison's position ultimately prevailed, and a congressional role in the removal process was rejected. This "Decision of 1789" provides "contemporaneous and weighty evidence" of the Constitution's meaning since many of the Members of the first Congress "had taken part in framing that instrument." Marsh v. Chambers, 463 U.S. 783, 790 (1983).

This Court first directly addressed this issue in Myers v. United States, 272 U.S. 52 (1925). At issue in Myers was a statute providing that certain postmasters could be removed only "by and with the advice and consent of the Senate." The President removed one such postmaster without Senate approval, and a lawsuit ensued. Chief Justice Taft, writing for the Court, declared the statute unconstitutional on the ground that for Congress to "draw to itself, or to either branch of it, the power to remove or the right to participate in the exercise of that power . . . would be . . . to infringe the constitutional principle of the separation of governmental powers." Id., at 161.

A decade later, in Humphrey's Executor v. United States, 295 U.S. 602 (1935), relied upon heavily by appellants, a Federal Trade Commissioner who had been removed by the President sought back pay. Humphrey's Executor involved an issue not presented either in the Myers case or in this case—i.e., the power of Congress to limit the President's powers of removal of a Federal Trade Commissioner. 295 U.S., at 630.[1] The relevant statute permitted removal "by the President," but only "for inefficiency, neglect of duty, or malfeasance in office." Justice Sutherland, speaking for the Court, upheld the statute, holding that "illimitable power of removal is not possessed by the President [with respect to Federal Trade Commissioners]." 295 U.S., at 628–629. The Court distinguished Myers, reaffirming its holding that congressional participation in the removal of executive officers is unconstitutional. Justice Sutherland's opinion for the Court also underscored the crucial role of separated powers in our system:

> "The fundamental necessity of maintaining each of the three general departments of government entirely free from the control or coercive influence, direct or indirect, of either of the others, has often been stressed and is hardly open to serious question. So much is implied in the very fact of the separation of the powers of these departments by the Constitution; and in the rule which recognizes their essential co-equality." 295 U.S., at 629–630.

The court reached a similar result in Wiener v. United States, 357 U.S. 349 (1958), concluding that, under Humphrey's Executor, the President

---

1. Appellants therefore are wide of the mark in arguing that an affirmance in this case requires casting doubt on the status of "independent" agencies because no issues involving such agencies are presented here. The statutes establishing independent agencies typically specify either that the agency members are removable by the President for specified causes, see, e.g., 15 U.S.C. § 41 (members of the Federal Trade Commission may be removed by the President "for inefficiency, neglect of duty, or malfeasance in office"), or else do not specify a removal procedure, see, e.g., 2 U.S.C. § 437c (Federal Election Commission). This case involves nothing like these statutes, but rather a statute that provides for direct Congressional involvement over the decision to remove the Comptroller General. Appellants have referred us to no independent agency whose members are removable by the Congress for certain causes short of impeachable offenses, as is the Comptroller General.

did not have unrestrained removal authority over a member of the War Crimes Commission.

In light of these precedents, we conclude that Congress cannot reserve for itself the power of removal of an officer charged with the execution of the laws except by impeachment. To permit the execution of the laws to be vested in an officer answerable only to Congress would, in practical terms, reserve in Congress control over the execution of the laws. . . . The structure of the Constitution does not permit Congress to execute the laws; it follows that Congress cannot grant to an officer under its control what it does not possess.

Our decision in INS v. Chadha, 462 U.S. 919 (1983), supports this conclusion. . . . To permit an officer controlled by Congress to execute the laws would be, in essence, to permit a congressional veto. Congress could simply remove, or threaten to remove, an officer for executing the laws in any fashion found to be unsatisfactory to Congress. This kind of congressional control over the execution of the laws, Chadha makes clear, is constitutionally impermissible.

The dangers of congressional usurpation of Executive Branch functions have long been recognized. "[T]he debates of the Constitutional Convention, and the Federalist Papers, are replete with expressions of fear that the Legislative Branch of the National Government will aggrandize itself at the expense of the other two branches." Buckley v. Valeo, 424 U.S. 1, 129 (1976). Indeed, we also have observed only recently that "[t]he hydraulic pressure inherent within each of the separate Branches to exceed the outer limits of its power, even to accomplish desirable objectives, must be resisted." Chadha, 462 U.S., at 951. With these principles in mind, we turn to consideration of whether the Comptroller General is controlled by Congress.

IV

Appellants urge that the Comptroller General performs his duties independently and is not subservient to Congress. We agree with the District Court that this contention does not bear close scrutiny.

The critical factor lies in the provisions of the statute defining the Comptroller General's office relating to removability. Although the Comptroller General is nominated by the President from a list of three individuals recommended by the Speaker of the House of Representatives and the President pro tempore of the Senate, see 31 U.S.C. § 730(a)(2),[2] and confirmed by the Senate, he is removable only at the initiative of Congress. He may be removed not only by impeachment but also by Joint Resolution of Congress "at any time" resting on any one of the following bases:

2. We reject appellants' argument that consideration of the effect of a removal provision is not "ripe" until that provision is actually used. As the District Court concluded, "it is the Comptroller General's presumed desire to avoid removal by pleasing Congress, which creates the here-and-now subservience to another branch that raises separation-of-powers problems." Synar v. United States, 626 F.Supp. 1374, 1392 (DC 1986). The Impeachment Clause of the Constitution can hardly be thought to be undermined because of non-use.

(i) permanent disability;

(ii) inefficiency;

(iii) neglect of duty;

(iv) malfeasance; or

(v) a felony or conduct involving moral turpitude."

31 U.S.C. § 703(e)(1).[3]

This provision was included, as one Congressman explained in urging passage of the Act, because Congress "felt that [the Comptroller General] should be brought under the sole control of Congress, so that Congress at the moment when it found he was inefficient and was not carrying on the duties of his office as he should and as the Congress expected, could remove him without the long, tedious process of a trial by impeachment." 61 Cong.Rec. 1081 (1921). . . . The ultimate design was to "give the legislative branch of the Government control of the audit, not through the power of appointment, but through the power of removal." 58 Cong.Rec. 7211 (1919) (Rep. Taylor).

Justice White contends that "[t]he statute does not permit anyone to remove the Comptroller at will; removal is permitted only for specified cause, with the existence of cause to be determined by Congress following a hearing. Any removal under the statute would presumably be subject to post-termination judicial review to ensure that a hearing had in fact been held and the finding of cause for removal was not arbitrary." . . . [Yet] the dissent's assessment of the statute fails to recognize the breadth of the grounds for removal. The statute permits removal for "inefficiency," "neglect of duty," or "malfeasance." These terms are very broad and, as interpreted by Congress, could sustain removal of a Comptroller General for any number of actual or perceived transgressions of the legislative will. The Constitutional Convention chose to permit impeachment of executive officers only for "Treason, Bribery, or other high Crimes and Misdemeanors." It rejected language that would have permitted impeachment for "maladministration," with Madison arguing the "[s]o vague a term will be equivalent to a tenure during pleasure of the Senate." 2 Farrand 550. . . . Surely no one would seriously suggest that judicial independence would be strengthened by allowing removal of federal judges only by a joint resolution finding "inefficiency," "neglect of duty," or "malfeasance."

. . .

This much said, we must also add that the dissent is simply in error to suggest that the political realities reveal that the Comptroller General is free from influence by Congress. The Comptroller General heads the General Accounting Office, "an instrumentality of the United States Government independent of the executive departments," 31 U.S.C. § 702(a), which was created by Congress in 1921 as part of the

---

3. Although the President could veto such a joint resolution, the veto could be overridden by a two-thirds vote of both Houses of Congress. Thus, the Comptroller General could be removed in the face of Presidential opposition. Like the District Court, 626 F.Supp., at 1393 n. 21, we therefore read the removal provision as authorizing removal by Congress alone.

Budget and Accounting Act of 1921, 42 Stat. 23. . . . It is clear the Congress has consistently viewed the Comptroller General as an officer of the Legislative Branch. . . . Over the years, the Comptrollers General have also viewed themselves as part of the Legislative Branch. In one of the early Annual Reports of Comptroller General, the official seal of his office was described as reflecting:

> "the independence of judgment to be exercised by the General Accounting Office, subject to the control of the legislative branch. . . . The combination represents an agency of the Congress independent of other authority auditing and checking the expenditures of the Government as required by law and subjecting any questions arising in that connection to quasi-judicial determination." GAO Ann.Rep. 5–6 (1924).

. . . And, in one conflict during Comptroller General McCarl's tenure, he asserted his independence of the Executive Branch, stating:

> "Congress . . . is . . . the only authority to which there lies an appeal from the decision of this office. . . .
>
> ". . . I may not accept the opinion of any official, inclusive of the Attorney General, as controlling my duty under the law." 2 Comp.Gen. 784, 786–787 (1923). . . .

Against this background, we see no escape from the conclusion that, because Congress had retained removal authority over the Comptroller General, he may not be entrusted with executive powers. The remaining question is whether the Comptroller General has been assigned such powers in the Balanced Budget and Emergency Deficit Control Act of 1985.

V

[The Court concluded that the Comptroller General's functions under the statute were ones "plainly entailing execution of the law in constitutional terms."]

Congress of course initially determined the content of the Balanced Budget and Emergency Deficit Control Act; and undoubtedly the content of the Act determines the nature of the executive duty. However, as Chadha makes clear, once Congress makes its choice in enacting legislation, its participation ends. Congress can thereafter control the execution of its enactment only indirectly—by passing new legislation. By placing the responsibility for execution of the Balanced Budget and Emergency Deficit Control Act in the hands of an officer who is subject to removal only by itself, Congress in effect has retained control over the execution of the Act and has intruded into the executive function. The Constitution does not permit such intrusion.

VI

We now turn to the final issue of remedy. Appellants urge that rather than striking down § 251 and invalidating the significant power Congress vested in the Comptroller General to meet a national fiscal emergency, we should take the lesser course of nullifying the statutory provisions of the 1921 Act that authorizes Congress to remove the Comptroller General. . . . The language of the Balanced Budget and Emergency Deficit Control Act itself settles the issue. In § 274(f), Congress has explicitly provided "fallback" provisions in the Act that take effect "[i]n the event . . . *any* of the reporting procedures described in section 251 are invalidated." § 274(f)(1) (emphasis added). The fallback provisions are " 'fully operative as a law,' " Buckley v. Valeo, 424 U.S., at 108 (quoting Champlin Refining Co. v. Corporation Comm'n of Oklahoma, 286 U.S. 210, 234 (1932)). Assuming that appellants are correct in urging that this matter must be resolved on the basis of congressional intent, the intent appears to have been for § 274(f) to be given effect in this situation. . . .

VII

No one can doubt that Congress and the President are confronted with fiscal and economic problems of unprecedented magnitude, but "the fact that a given law or procedure is efficient, convenient, and useful in facilitating functions of government, standing alone, will not save it if it is contrary to the Constitution. Convenience and efficiency are not the primary objectives—or the hallmarks—of democratic government. . . ." Chadha, supra, at 944.

We conclude the District Court correctly held that the powers vested in the Comptroller General under § 251 violate the command of the Constitution that the Congress play no direct role in the execution of the laws. Accordingly, the judgment and order of the District Court are affirmed.

Our judgment is stayed for a period not to exceed 60 days to permit Congress to implement the fallback provisions.

JUSTICE STEVENS, with whom JUSTICE MARSHALL joins, concurring in the judgment.

. . . . It is not the dormant, carefully circumscribed congressional removal power that represents the primary constitutional evil. . . . Rather, I am convinced that the Comptroller General must be characterized as an agent of Congress because of his longstanding statutory responsibilities; that the powers assigned to him under the Gramm-Rudman-Hollings Act require him to make policy that will bind the Nation; and that, when Congress, or a component or an agent of Congress, seeks to make policy that will bind the Nation, it must follow the procedures mandated by Article I of the Constitution—through passage by both Houses and presentment to the President. In short, Congress may not exercise its fundamental power to formulate national policy by delegating that power to one of its two Houses, to a legislative committee, or to an individual agent of the Congress such as the Speaker of the House of Representatives, the Sergeant at Arms of the Senate, or the Director of the Congressional Budget Office. INS v. Chadha, 462 U.S. 919 (1983). That principle, I believe, is applicable to the Comptroller General.

I

. . .

The notion that the removal power at issue here automatically creates some kind of "here-and-now subservience" of the Comptroller General to Congress is belied by history. There is no evidence that Congress has ever removed, or threatened to remove, the Comptroller General for reasons of policy. Moreover, the President has long possessed a comparable power to remove members of the Federal Trade Commission, yet it is universally accepted that they are independent of, rather than subservient to, the President in performing their official duties. Thus, the statute that the Court construed in Humphrey's Executor v. United States, 295 U.S. 602 (1935), provided:

> "Any commissioner may be removed by the President for inefficiency, neglect of duty, or malfeasance in office." 38 Stat. 718.

In upholding the congressional limitations on the President's power of removal, the Court stressed the independence of the Commission from the President. There was no suggestion that the retained Presidential removal powers—similar to those at issue here—created a subservience to the President.[4] . . . [T]he Humphrey's Executor analysis at least demonstrates that it is entirely proper for Congress to specify the qualifications for an office that it has created, and that the prescription of what might be termed "dereliction-of-duty" removal standards does not itself impair the independence of the official subject to such standards.[5] . . .

4. The manner in which President Roosevelt exercised his removal power further underscores the propriety of presuming that Congress, and the President, will not use statutorily prescribed removal causes as pretexts for other removal reasons. President Roosevelt never claimed that his removal of Humphrey was for one of the statutorily prescribed reasons—inefficiency, neglect of duty, or malfeasance in office. The President's removal letter merely stated:

> " 'Effective as of this date you are hereby removed from the office of Commissioner of the Federal Trade Commission.' " See, id., at 619, 55 S.Ct., at 870.

Previously, the President had written to Commissioner Humphrey stating:

> " 'You will, I know, realize that I do not feel that your mind and my mind go along together on either the policies or the administering of the Federal Trade Commission, and, frankly, I think it is best for the people of this country that I should have a full confidence.' " Ibid.

5. Indeed, even in Myers v. United States, 272 U.S. 52 (1926), in its challenge to the provision requiring Senate approval of the removal of a postmaster, the Federal Government assumed that Congress had power to limit the terms of removal to reasons that relate to the office. Solicitor General Beck recognized "that the power of removal may be subject to such general laws as do not destroy the exercise by the President of his power of removal, and which leaves to him the exercise of the power subject to such general laws as may fairly measure the standard of public service." Substitute Brief for United States on Reargument in No. 2, O.T. 1926, p. 9. At oral argument, the Solicitor General explained his position:

> "Mr. Beck . . . Suppose the Congress creates an office and says that it shall only be filled by a man learned in the law; and suppose it further provides that, if a man ceases to be member of the bar, he shall be removed. I am not prepared to say that such a law can not be reconciled with the Constitution. What I do say is that, when the condition imposed upon the creation of the office has no reasonable relation to the office; when it is not a legislative standard to be applied by the President, and is not the declaration of qualifications, but is the creation of an appointing power other than the President, then Congress has crossed the dead line, for it has usurped

II

[Reviewing the full range of the Comptroller General's responsibilities, Justice Stevens found "little doubt that one of the identifying characteristics of the Comptroller General is his statutorily required relationship to the Legislative Branch."]

The Comptroller General's responsibilities are repeatedly framed in terms of his specific obligations to Congress. Thus, one provision specifies in some detail the obligations of the Comptroller General with respect to an individual committee's request for a program evaluation:

"On request of a committee of Congress, the Comptroller General shall help the committee to—

"(A) develop a statement of legislative goals and ways to assess and report program performance related to the goals, including recommended ways to assess performance, information to be reported, responsibility for reporting, frequency of reports, and feasibility of pilot testing; and

"(B) assess program evaluations prepared by and for an agency." 31 U.S.C. § 717(d)(1).

Similarly, another provision requires that, on "request of a member of Congress, the Comptroller General shall give the member a copy of the material the Comptroller General compiles in carrying out this subsection that has been released by the committee for which the material was compiled." § 717(d)(2).

.   .   .

This is not to say, of course, that the Comptroller General has no obligations to the Executive Branch, or that he is an agent of the Congress in quite so clear a manner as the Doorkeeper of the House. . . . The Comptroller General must "give the President information on expenditures and accounting the President requests." 31 U.S.C. § 719(f). Although the Comptroller General is required to provide Congress with an annual report, he is also required to provide the President with the report if the President so requests. § 719(a). . . . Obligations to two Branches are not, however, impermissible and the presence of such dual obligations does not prevent the characterization of the official with the dual obligations as part of one branch.[6] It is at

the prerogative of the President." 272 U.S. at 96–97.

6. See Pennsylvania Bureau of Correction v. United States Marshals Service, 474 U.S. ___, ___ (1985) (reviewing the Marshals' statutory obligations to the Judiciary and the Executive Branch, but noting that the "Marshals are within the Executive Branch of the Federal Government"). Cf. Report by the Comptroller General, U.S. Marshals' Dilemma: Serving Two Branches of Government 14 (1982) ("It is extremely difficult for one person to effec-

tively serve two masters"). Surely no one would suggest that the fact that the Chief Justice performs executive functions for the Smithsonian Institution, 20 U.S.C. § 42, affects his characterization as a member of the Judicial Branch of the Government. Nor does the performance of similar functions by three Members of the Senate and three Members of the House, ibid., affect their characterization as members of the Legislative Branch of Government.

least clear that, in most, if not all, of his statutory responsibilities, the Comptroller General is properly characterized as an agent of the Congress.[7]

III

[The conclusion that the Act confers executive power on the Comptroller General] is not only far from obvious but also rests on the unstated and unsound premise that there is a definite line that distinguishes executive power from legislative power. . . . [A]s our cases demonstrate, a particular function, like a chameleon, will often take on the aspect of the office to which it is assigned. For this reason, "[w]hen any Branch acts, it is presumptively exercising the power the Constitution has delegated to it." INS v. Chadha, 462 U.S., at 951.

. . .

The powers delegated to the Comptroller General by § 251 of the Act before us today have a similar chameleon-like quality. The District Court persuasively explained why they may be appropriately characterized as executive powers. But, when that delegation is held invalid, the "fallback provision" provides that the report that would otherwise be issued by the Comptroller General shall be issued by Congress itself. In the event that the resolution is enacted, the congressional report will have the same legal consequences as if it had been issued by the Comptroller General. In that event, moreover, surely no one would suggest that Congress had acted in any capacity other than "legislative." Since the District Court expressly recognized the validity of what it described as the " 'fallback' deficit reduction process," Synar v. United States, 626 F.Supp. 1374, 1377 (1986), it obviously did not doubt the constitutionality of the performance by Congress of the functions delegated to the Comptroller General. . . . [W]hatever the label given the functions to be performed by the Comptroller General under § 251—or by the Congress under § 274—the District Court had no difficulty in concluding that Congress could delegate the performance of those functions to another branch of the Government. If the delegation to a stranger is permissible, why may not Congress delegate the same responsibilities to one of its own agents? That is the central question before us today.

7. Despite the suggestions of the dissents, it is quite obvious that the Comptroller General, and the General Accounting Office, have a fundamentally different relationship with Congress than do independent agencies like the Federal Trade Commission. Rather than an independent agency, the Comptroller General and the GAO are functionally equivalent to congressional agents such as the Congressional Budget Office, the Office of Technology Assessment, and the Library of Congress' Congressional Research Service. As the statutory responsibilities make clear, like those congressional agents, the Comptroller General and the General Accounting Office function virtually as a permanent staff for Congress. . . . [T]o contend that the Comptroller General's numerous statutory responsibilities to serve Congress directly are somehow like an independent agency's obligations to report to Congress and to implement legislatively mandated standards simply misconceives the actual duties of the Comptroller General and the General Accounting Office. It also ignores the clear import of the legislative history of these entities.

IV

Congress regularly delegates responsibility to a number of agents who provide important support for its legislative activities. Many perform functions that could be characterized as "executive" in most contexts—the Capitol Police can arrest and press charges against law breakers, the Sergeant at Arms manages the congressional payroll, the Capitol Architect maintains the buildings and grounds, and its Librarian has custody of a vast number of books and records. Moreover, the Members themselves necessarily engage in many activities that are merely ancillary to their primary lawmaking responsibilities—they manage their separate offices, they communicate with their constituents, they conduct hearings, they inform themselves about the problems confronting the Nation, and they make rules for the governance of their own business. The responsibilities assigned to the Comptroller General in the case before us are, of course, quite different from these delegations and ancillary activities.

The Gramm-Rudman-Hollings Act assigns to the Comptroller General the duty to make policy decisions that have the force of law. . . . Article I of the Constitution specifies the procedures that Congress must follow when it makes policy that binds the Nation: its legislation must be approved by both Houses of Congress and presented to the President. . . . If Congress were free to delegate its policymaking authority to one of its components, or to one of its agents, it would be able to evade "the carefully crafted restraints spelled out in the Constitution." Chadha, at 959. That danger—congressional action that evades constitutional restraints—is not present when Congress delegates lawmaking power to the executive or to an independent agency.

The distinction between the kinds of action that Congress may delegate to its own components and agents and those that require either compliance with Article I procedures or delegation to another Branch pursuant to defined standards is reflected in the practices that have developed over the years regarding congressional resolutions. The *joint* resolution, which is used for "special purposes and . . . incidental matters," 7 Deschler's Precedents of the House of Representatives, 334 (1977), makes binding policy and "requires an affirmative vote by both Houses and submission to the President for approval"—the full Article I requirements. A *concurrent* resolution, in contrast, makes no binding policy; it is "a means of expressing fact, principles, opinions, and purposes of the two Houses," Jefferson's Manual and Rules of the House of Representatives 176 (1983), and thus does not need to be presented to the President. It is settled, however, that if a resolution is intended to make policy that will bind the Nation and thus is "legislative in its character and effect," S.Rep. No. 1335, 54th Cong., 2d Sess., 8 (1897)—then the full Article I requirements must be observed. For "the nature or substance of the resolution, and not its form, controls the question of its disposition."

In my opinion, Congress itself could not exercise the Gramm-Rudman-Hollings functions through a concurrent resolution. The fact that the fallback provision in § 274 requires a joint resolution rather than a concurrent resolution indicates that Congress endorsed this view. I think it equally clear that Congress may not simply delegate those functions to an agent such as the Congressional Budget Office. Since I am persuaded that the Comptroller General is also fairly deemed to be an agent of Congress, he too cannot exercise such functions. . . .

I concur in the judgment.

JUSTICE WHITE, dissenting.

The Court, acting in the name of separation of powers, takes upon itself to strike down the Gramm-Rudman-Hollings Act, one of the most novel and far-reaching legislative responses to a national crisis since the New Deal. The basis of the Court's action is a solitary provision of another statute that was passed over sixty years ago and has lain dormant since that time. . . . Twice in the past four years I have expressed my view that the Court's recent efforts to police the separation of powers have rested on untenable constitutional propositions leading to regrettable results. See Northern Pipeline Construction Co. v. Marathon Pipe Line Co., 458 U.S. 50, 92–118 (1982) (White, J., dissenting); INS v. Chadha, 462 U.S. 919, 967–1003, (White, J., dissenting). Today's result is even more misguided. As I will explain, the Court's decision rests on a feature of the legislative scheme that is of minimal practical significance and that presents no substantial threat to the basic scheme of separation of powers. In attaching dispositive significance to what should be regarded as a triviality, the Court neglects what has in the past been recognized as a fundamental principle governing consideration of disputes over separation of powers:

> "The actual art of governing under our Constitution does not and cannot conform to judicial definitions of the power of any of its branches based on isolated clauses or even single Articles torn from context. While the Constitution diffuses power the better to secure liberty, it also contemplates that practice will integrate the dispersed powers into a workable government." Youngstown Sheet & Tube Co. v. Sawyer, 343 U.S. 579, 635 (1952) (Jackson, J., concurring).

I

. . .

Before examining the merits of the Court's argument, I wish to emphasize what it is that the Court quite pointedly and correctly does *not* hold: namely, that "executive" powers of the sort granted the Comptroller by the Act may only be exercised by officers removable at will by the President. The Court's apparent unwillingness to accept this argument, which has been tendered in this Court by the Solicitor

General,[8] is fully consistent with the Court's longstanding recognition that it is within the power of Congress under the "Necessary and Proper" Clause, Art. I, § 8, to vest authority that falls within the Court's definition of executive power in officers who are not subject to removal at will by the President and are therefore not under the President's direct control. See, e.g., Humphrey's Executor v. United States, 295 U.S. 602 (1935); Wiener v. United States, 357 U.S. 349 (1958).[9] In an earlier day, in which simpler notions of the role of government in society prevailed, it was perhaps plausible to insist that all "executive" officers be subject to an unqualified presidential removal power, see Myers v. United States, 272 U.S. 52 (1926); but with the advent and triumph of the administrative state and the accompanying multiplication of the tasks undertaken by the Federal Government, the Court has been virtually compelled to recognize that Congress may reasonably deem it "necessary and proper" to vest some among the broad new array of governmental functions in officers who are free from the partisanship that may be expected of agents wholly dependent upon the President.

The Court's recognition of the legitimacy of legislation vesting "executive" authority in officers independent of the President does not imply derogation of the President's own constitutional authority—indeed, duty—to "take Care that the Laws be faithfully executed," Art. II, § 3, for any such duty is necessarily limited to a great extent by the content of the laws enacted by the Congress. As Justice Holmes put it, "The duty of the President to see that the laws be executed is a duty that does not go beyond the laws or require him to achieve more than Congress sees fit to leave within his power." Myers v. United States, 272 U.S., at 177 (Holmes, J., dissenting). Justice Holmes perhaps overstated his case, for there are undoubtedly executive functions that, regardless of the enactments of Congress, must be performed by officers subject to removal at will by the President. Whether a particular function falls within this class or within the far larger class that may be relegated to independent officers "will depend upon the character of the office." Humphrey's Executor, 295 U.S., at 631. In determining

---

8. The Solicitor General appeared on behalf of the "United States," or, more properly, the Executive departments, which intervened to attack the constitutionality of the statute that the Chief Executive had earlier endorsed and signed into law.

9. Although the Court in Humphrey's Executor characterized the powers of the Federal Trade Commissioner whose tenure was at issue as "quasi-legislative" and "quasi-judicial," it is clear that the FTC's power to enforce and give content to the Federal Trade Commission Act's proscription of "unfair" acts and practices and methods of competition is in fact "executive" in the same sense as is the Comptroller's authority under Gramm-Rudman—

that is, it involves the implementation, (or the interpretation and application) of an act of Congress. Thus, although the Court in Humphrey's Executor found the use of the labels "quasi-legislative" and "quasi-judicial" helpful in "distinguishing" its then-recent decision in Myers v. United States, 272 U.S. 52 (1926), these terms are hardly of any use in limiting the holding of the case; as Justice Jackson pointed out, "[t]he mere retreat to the qualifying 'quasi' is implicit with confession that all recognized classifications have broken down, and 'quasi' is a smooth cover which we draw over our confusion as we might use a counterpane to conceal a disordered bed." FTC v. Ruberoid Co., 343 U.S. 470, 487–488 (Jackson, J., dissenting).

whether a limitation on the President's power to remove an officer performing executive functions constitutes a violation of the constitutional scheme of separation of powers, a court must "focu[s] on the extent to which [such a limitation] prevents the Executive Branch from accomplishing its constitutionally assigned functions." Nixon v. Administrator of General Services, 433 U.S. 425, 443 (1977). "Only where the potential for disruption is present must we then determine whether that impact is satisfied by an overriding need to promote objectives within the constitutional authority of Congress." Ibid. This inquiry is, to be sure, not one that will beget easy answers; it provides nothing approaching a bright-line rule or set of rules. Such an inquiry, however, is necessitated by the recognition that "formalistic and unbending rules" in the area of separation of powers may "unduly constrict Congress' ability to take needed and innovative action pursuant to its Article I powers." Commodity Futures Trading Commission v. Schor, [p. 107 above, at 111].

It is evident (and nothing in the Court's opinion is to the contrary) that the powers exercised by the Comptroller General under the Gramm-Rudman Act are not such that vesting them in an officer not subject to removal at will by the President would in itself improperly interfere with Presidential powers. . . . Rather, the result of such a delegation, from the standpoint of the President, is no different from the result of more traditional forms of appropriation: under either system, the level of funds available to the Executive branch to carry out its duties is not within the President's discretionary control. To be sure, if the budget-cutting mechanism required the responsible officer to exercise a great deal of policymaking discretion, one might argue that having created such broad discretion Congress had some obligation based upon Art. II to vest it in the Chief Executive or his agents. In Gramm-Rudman, however, Congress has done no such thing; instead, it has created a precise and articulated set of criteria designed to minimize the degree of policy choice exercised by the officer executing the statute and to ensure that the relative spending priorities established by Congress in the appropriations it passes into law remain unaltered. . . . [I]t is eminently reasonable and proper for Congress to vest the budget-cutting authority in an officer who is to the greatest degree possible nonpartisan and independent of the President and his political agenda and who therefore may be relied upon not to allow his calculations to be colored by political considerations. . . .

II

. . . [T]he question remains whether . . . the fact that the officer to whom Congress has delegated the authority to implement the Act is removable by a joint resolution of Congress should require invalidation of the Act. . . . I cannot accept . . . that the exercise of authority by an officer removable for cause by a joint resolution of Congress is analogous to the impermissible execution of the law by Congress itself, nor would I hold that the congressional role in the removal process renders the Comptroller an "agent" of the Congress, incapable of receiving "executive" power.

In Buckley v. Valeo, the Court held that Congress could not reserve to itself the power to appoint members of the Federal Election Commission, a body exercising "executive" power. Buckley, however, was grounded on a textually based separation of powers argument whose central premise was that the Constitution requires that all "Officers of the United States" (defined as "all persons who can be said to hold an office under the government," 424 U.S., at 126) whose appointment is not otherwise specifically provided for elsewhere in its text be appointed through the means specified by the Appointments Clause, Art. II, § 2, cl. 2—that is, either by the President with the advice and consent of the Senate or, if Congress so specifies, by the President alone, by the courts, or by the head of a department. The Buckley Court treated the Appointments Clause as reflecting the principle that "the Legislative Branch may not exercise executive authority," 424 U.S., at 119 (citing Springer v. Philippine Islands, 277 U.S. 189 (1928)), but the Court's holding was merely that Congress may not direct that its laws be implemented through persons who are its agents in the sense that it chose them; the Court did not pass on the legitimacy of other means by which Congress might exercise authority over those who execute its laws. Because the Comptroller is not an appointee of Congress but an officer of the United States appointed by the President with the advice and consent of the Senate, Buckley neither requires that he be characterized as an agent of the Congress nor in any other way calls into question his capacity to exercise "executive" authority. See 424 U.S., at 128, n. 165.

.　.　.

The deficiencies in the Court's [reliance on its Chadha decision] are apparent. First, the Court baldly mischaracterizes the removal provision when it suggests that it allows Congress to remove the Comptroller for "executing the laws in any fashion found to be unsatisfactory"; in fact, Congress may remove the Comptroller only for one or more of five specified reasons, which "although not so narrow as to deny Congress any leeway, circumscribe Congress' power to some extent by providing a basis for judicial review of congressional removal." Ameron, Inc. v. United States Army Corps of Engineers, 787 F.2d 875, 895 (CA3 1986) (Becker, J., concurring in part). Second, and more to the point, the Court overlooks or deliberately ignores the decisive difference between the congressional removal provision and the legislative veto struck down in Chadha: under the Budget and Accounting Act, Congress may remove the Comptroller only through a joint resolution, which by definition must be passed by both Houses and signed by the President.[10]

---

10. The legislative history indicates that the inclusion of the President in the removal process was a deliberate choice on the part of the Congress that enacted the Budget and Accounting Act. The previous year, legislation establishing the position of Comptroller General and providing for removal by *concurrent* resolution—that is, by a resolution not presented to the President—had been vetoed by President Wilson on the ground that granting the sole power of removal to the Congress would be unconstitutional. See 59 Cong.Rec. 8609–8610 (1920). That Congress responded by providing for removal through joint resolution clearly evinces congressional intent that

In other words, a removal of the Comptroller under the statute *satisfies the requirements of bicameralism and presentment laid down in Chadha*. . . .

That a joint resolution removing the Comptroller General would satisfy the requirements for legitimate legislative action laid down in Chadha does not fully answer the separation of powers argument, for it is apparent that even the results of the constitutional legislative process may be unconstitutional if those results are in fact destructive of the scheme of separation of powers. Nixon v. Administrator of General Services, 433 U.S. 425 (1977). The question to be answered is whether the threat of removal of the Comptroller General for cause through joint resolution as authorized by the Budget and Accounting Act renders the Comptroller sufficiently subservient to Congress that investing him with "executive" power can be realistically equated with the unlawful retention of such power by Congress itself; more generally, the question is whether there is a genuine threat of "encroachment or aggrandizement of one branch at the expense of the other," Buckley v. Valeo, 424 U.S., at 122. Common sense indicates that the existence of the removal provision poses no such threat to the principle of separation of powers.

The statute does not permit anyone to remove the Comptroller at will; removal is permitted only for specified cause, with the existence of cause to be determined by Congress following a hearing. Any removal under the statute would presumably be subject to post-termination judicial review to ensure that a hearing had in fact been held and that the finding of cause for removal was not arbitrary.[11] These procedural and substantive limitations on the removal power militate strongly against the characterization of the Comptroller as a mere agent of Congress by virtue of the removal authority. . . . More importantly, the substantial role played by the President in the process of removal through joint resolution . . . obviates the possibility that the Comptroller will perceive himself as so completely at the mercy of Congress that he will function as its tool.[12] If the Comptroller's conduct in office is not so unsatisfactory to the President as to convince the latter that removal is required under the statutory standard, Congress will have no independent power to coerce the Comptroller unless it can muster a two-thirds majority in both Houses—a feat of bipartisanship more difficult than that required to impeach and convict. The incremental *in terrorem* effect of the possibility of congressional removal in the face

removal take place only through the legislative process, with Presidential participation.

11. Cf. Humphrey's Executor v. United States, 295 U.S. 602 (1935), in which the Court entertained a challenge to Presidential removal under a statute that similarly limited removals to specified cause.

12. The Court cites statements made by supporters of the Budget and Accounting Act indicating their belief that the Act's removal provisions would render the Comptroller subservient to Congress by giving Congress "absolute control of the man's destiny in office." Ante, at 3190. The Court's scholarship, however, is faulty: at the time all of these statements were made—including Representative Sisson's statement of May 3, 1921—the proposed legislation provided for removal by concurrent resolution, with no Presidential role. See 61 Cong.Rec. 983, 989–992, 1079–1085 (1921).

of a presidential veto is therefore exceedingly unlikely to have any discernible impact on the extent of congressional influence over the Comptroller.[13]

The practical result of the removal provision is not to render the Comptroller unduly dependent upon or subservient to Congress, but to render him one of the most independent officers in the entire federal establishment. Those who have studied the office agree that the procedural and substantive limits on the power of Congress and the President to remove the Comptroller make dislodging him against his will practically impossible. . . . [O]f the six Comptrollers who have served since 1921, none has been threatened with, much less subjected to, removal. Recent students of the office concur that "[b]arring resignation, death, physical or mental incapacity, or extremely bad behavior, the Comptroller General is assured his tenure if he wants it, and not a day more." F. Mosher, The GAO 242 (1979).[14] The threat of "here-and-now subservience" is obviously remote indeed.[15]

. . .

The majority's contrary conclusion rests on the rigid dogma that, outside of the impeachment process, any "direct congressional role in the removal of officers charged with the execution of the laws . . . is inconsistent with separation of powers." Reliance on such an unyielding principle to strike down a statute posing no real danger of aggrandizement of congressional power is extremely misguided and insensitive to our constitutional role. . . . [T]he role of this Court should be limited to determining whether the Act so alters the balance of authority among the branches of government as to pose a genuine threat to the basic division between the lawmaking power and the power to execute the law. Because I see no such threat, I cannot join the Court in striking down the Act.

13. . . . Of course, if it were demonstrable that the Constitution specifically limited Congress' role in removal to the impeachment process, the insignificance of the marginal increase in congressional influence resulting from the provision authorizing removal through joint resolution would be no answer to a claim of unconstitutionality. But no such limit appears in the Constitution: the Constitution merely provides that all officers of the United States may be impeached for high crimes and misdemeanors, and nowhere suggests that impeachment is the sole means of removing such officers.

. . .

14. Professor Mosher's reference to the fact that the Comptroller is limited to a single term highlights an additional source of independence: unlike an officer with a fixed term who may be reappointed to office, the Comptroller need not concern himself with currying favor with the Senate in order to secure its consent to his reappointment.

15. . . . Justice Stevens' position is puzzling, to say the least. It seems to rest on the view that an officer required to perform certain duties for the benefit of Congress somehow becomes a part of Congress for all purposes. But it is by no means true that an officer who must perform specified duties for some other body is under that body's control or acts as its agent when carrying out other, unrelated duties. . . . [D]uties toward Congress are imposed on a variety of agencies, including the Federal Trade Commission; and certainly it cannot credibly be maintained that by virtue of those duties the agencies become branches of Congress, incapable of wielding governmental power except through the legislative process. Indeed, the President himself is under numerous obligations, both statutory and constitutional, to provide information to Congress, see e.g., Art. II, § 3, cl. 1; surely the President is not thereby transformed into an arm or agency of the Congress.

I dissent.

JUSTICE BLACKMUN, dissenting.

. . . [A]n attempt by Congress to participate *directly* in the removal of an executive officer—other than through the constitutionally prescribed procedure of impeachment—might well violate the principle of separation of powers by assuming for Congress part of the President's constitutional responsibility to carry out the laws. In my view, however, that important and difficult question need not be decided in this case, because no matter how it is resolved the plaintiffs, now appellees, are not entitled to the relief they have requested. Appellees have not sought invalidation of the 1921 provision that authorizes Congress to remove the Comptroller General by joint resolution; indeed, it is far from clear they would have standing to request such a judgment. The only relief sought in this case is nullification of the automatic budget-reduction provisions of the Deficit Control Act . . . . I cannot see the sense of invalidating legislation of this magnitude in order to preserve a cumbersome, 65-year-old removal power that has never been exercised and appears to have been all but forgotten until this litigation.[16]

. . .

In the absence of express statutory direction, I think it is plain that, as both Houses urge, invalidating the Comptroller General's functions under the Deficit Control Act would frustrate congressional objectives far more seriously than would refusing to allow Congress to exercise its removal authority under the 1921 law. . . . Congress has never attempted to use this cumbersome procedure, and the Comp-

---

16. For the reasons identified by the District Court, I agree that the Deficit Control Act does not violate the nondelegation doctrine. See 626 F.Supp. 1374, 1382–1391 (DC 1986).

Justice Stevens concludes that the delegation effected under § 251 contravenes the holding of INS v. Chadha, 462 U.S. 919 (1983), that Congress may make law only "in conformity with the express procedures of the Constitution's prescription for legislative action: passage by a majority of both Houses and presentment to the President." Id., at 958. I do not agree. We made clear in Chadha that the bicameralism and presentation requirements prevented Congress from *itself* exercising legislative power through some kind of procedural shortcut, such as the one-House veto challenged in that case. But we also made clear that our holding in no way questioned "Congress' authority to delegate portions of its power to administrative agencies." . . .

I do not think that danger is present here, either. The Comptroller General is not Congress, nor is he a part of Congress; "irrespective of Congress' designation," he is an officer of the United States, ap-

pointed by the President. Buckley v. Valeo, 424 U.S. 1, 128, n. 165 (1976). In this respect the Comptroller General differs critically from, for example, the Director of the Congressional Budget Office, who is appointed by Congress, see 2 U.S.C. § 601(a)(2), and hence may not "exercis[e] significant authority pursuant to the laws of the United States," Buckley v. Valeo, supra, at 126; see U.S. Const., Art. II, § 2, cl. 2. The exercise of rulemaking authority by an independent agency such as the Federal Trade Commission does not offend Chadha, even though the Commission could be described as an "agent" of Congress because it "carr[ies] into effect legislative policies embodied in the statute in accordance with the legislative standard therein prescribed." Humphrey's Executor v. United States, 295 U.S. 602, 628 (1935). I do not see why the danger of "congressional action that evades constitutional restraints" becomes any more pronounced when a statute delegates power to a presidentially appointed agent whose primary duties require him to provide services to Congress. . . .

troller General has shown few signs of subservience.[17] . . . [T]here is little evidence that Congress as a whole was very concerned in 1921—much less in 1985 or during the intervening decades—with its own ability to control the Comptroller General. The committee reports on the 1921 Act and its predecessor bills strongly suggest that what was critical to the legislators was not the Comptroller General's subservience to Congress, but rather his independence from the President. The debates over the Deficit Control Act contain no suggestion that the Comptroller General was chosen for the tasks outlined in § 251 because Congress thought it could count on him to do its will; instead, the Comptroller General appears to have been selected precisely because of his independence from both the Legislature and the Executive. By assigning the reporting functions to the Comptroller General, rather than to the Congressional Budget Office or to the Office of Management and Budget, Congress sought to create "a wall . . . that takes these decisions out of the hands of the President *and the Congress.*" 131 Cong.Rec. H9846 (Nov. 6, 1985) (remarks of Rep. Gephardt) (emphasis added); see also, e.g., id., at H11894 (Dec. 11, 1985) (remarks of Rep. Weiss); id., at E5622 (Dec. 12, 1985) (remarks of Rep. Bedell).

. . .

I do not claim that the 1921 removal provision is a piece of statutory deadwood utterly without contemporary significance. But it comes close. Rarely if ever invoked even for symbolic purposes, the removal provision certainly pales in importance beside the legislative scheme the Court strikes down today—an extraordinarily far-reaching response to a deficit problem of unprecedented proportions. Because I believe that the constitutional defect found by the Court cannot justify the remedy it has imposed, I respectfully dissent.

NOTES

(1) Compare the opinion written by the same Court on the same day in CFTC v. Schor, p. 107 above. Clearly enough, the Court believes that what it decides here (as in Northern Pipeline, p. 117 above and Chadha, p. 164 above) does not threaten the striking diversity of arrangements by which the government's work is done—even, it appears, other aspects of the work of the GAO. See Ameron, Inc. v. United States Army Corps of Engineers, 787 F.2d 875 (3d Cir.1986), rehearing en banc ordered. Can you find a textual or analytic basis for this confidence?

---

17. "All of the comptrollers general have treasured and defended the independence of their office, not alone from the president but also from the Congress itself. . . . Like the other institutions in the government, GAO depends upon Congress for its powers, its resources, and its general oversight. But it also possesses continuing legal powers, of both long and recent standing, that Congress has granted it and that it can exercise in a quite independent fash-

ion. And the comptroller general, realistically speaking, is immune from removal during his fifteen-year term for anything short of a capital crime, a crippling illness, or insanity." F. Mosher, A Tale of Two Agencies 158 (1984). See also, e.g., Ameron, Inc. v. U.S. Army Corps of Engineers, 787 F.2d 875, 885–887 (CA3 1986); F. Mosher, The GAO 2, 240–244 (1979); H. Mansfield, The Comptroller General 75–76 (1939).

(2) All the opinions in Bowsher refer frequently to MYERS v. UNITED STATES, 272 U.S. 52 (1926) and HUMPHREY'S EXECUTOR (RATHBUN) v. UNITED STATES, 295 U.S. 602 (1935), two cases often invoked as a pair. The circumstances of those cases—the first concerned with congressional reservation of the right to participate in removal of a postmaster; the second, with the effect of a fixed term of office on the President's removal authority over a Federal Trade Commissioner [1]—adequately appear from the several opinions. What does not appear as clearly is the emphasis in both opinions on a radical separation of powers within government, with a concomitant need to place agencies in one or another branch, maximally free from intrusion by the others. For the Myers Court, "the reasonable construction of the Constitution must be that the branches should be kept separate in all cases in which they were not expressly blended, and the Constitution should be expounded to blend them no more than it affirmatively requires." From placement of the Post Office Department in the executive branch and the absence of any constitutional provision for congressional participation in removal, all else followed. For the Humphrey's Executor Court, "[t]he fundamental necessity of maintaining each of the three general departments of government entirely free from the control or coercive influence, direct or indirect, of either of the others, has often been stressed, and is hardly open to serious question." The legislative history of the Federal Trade Commission Act established a purpose that "the commission was not to be subject to anybody in the government but . . . only to the people of the United States, . . . separate and apart from any existing department of the government—not subject to the orders of the President."

The Court described the FTC's functions as follows:

1. The FTC could direct cessation of unfair methods of competition in commerce, after full-dress adjudicatory hearings;

2. It could conduct investigations culminating in a report to the Congress with recommendations for legislation; [2] and

3. It could act "as a master in chancery" in antitrust suits brought by the Attorney General and referred to it by a district court. [3]

It was acutely conscious of the extent to which the Commission acted in circumstances calling for judicial impartiality and the removal from politics that might tend to protect it.

The Solicitor General, at the bar, . . . with commendable candor, agreed that his view . . . necessitated a like view in respect of

1. The Supreme Court intimated as early as Marbury v. Madison, 5 U.S. (1 Cranch) 137 (1803) that congressionally fixed terms of office for some federal officials must be respected. See also United States v. Perkins, 116 U.S. 483 (1886) (Civil Service).

2. The brief which Humphrey's executor filed with the Court indicated that 50% of the FTC's budget was spent for this function.

3. The Court noted that the President was also authorized to direct investigations, but passed over that inconvenient attachment to the executive branch as "so obviously collateral to the main design of the act as not to detract. . . ." Id. at 628 n. 1.

the Interstate Commerce Commission and the Court of Claims. We are thus confronted with the serious question, whether . . . the judges of the legislative Court of Claims, exercising judicial power, continue in office only at the pleasure of the President.

A Federal Trade Commissioner "occupies no place in the executive department and . . . exercises no part of the executive power vested by the Constitution in the President." The Commission, it concluded, was "an agency of the legislative or judicial department of the government," exercising in those contexts only an "executive function—as distinguished from executive power in the constitutional sense." "Such a body cannot in any proper sense be characterized as an arm or an eye of the executive. Its duties are performed without executive leave and, in the contemplation of the statute, must be free from executive control. In administering the provisions of the statute in respect of 'unfair methods of competition'—that is to say in filling in and administering the details embodied by that general standard—the commission acts in part quasi-legislatively and in part quasi-judicially."

(3) BUCKLEY v. VALEO, 424 U.S. 1 (1976), also widely referred to in Bowsher, suggested the possibility of a less formal approach. Buckley presented a series of challenges to the Federal Election Act and to the Federal Election Commission the Act created and empowered; significant for our purposes was a separation-of-powers challenge to a provision for direct legislative appointment of some members of the Commission, which consisted of eight members. The Secretary of the Senate and the Clerk of the House of Representatives were ex officio members of the Commission without the right to vote; two members were to be appointed by the President pro tempore of the Senate "upon the recommendations of the majority leader of the Senate and the minority leader of the Senate"; two more, in like manner, by the Speaker of the House of Representatives; and the remaining two members, by the President. Each of the six voting members of the Commission was to be confirmed by the majority of both Houses of Congress, and each of the three appointing authorities was forbidden to choose both of their appointees from the same political party. This Commission was authorized, inter alia, both to conduct investigations—the activity described as "quasi-legislative" in Humphrey's Executor—and to engage in extensive rulemaking, a quasi-legislative activity that had not been at issue in that case. Were the FEC only empowered to conduct investigations, the Court reasoned, the appointment provisions would not have been objectionable; such powers are "in the same general category as . . . Congress might delegate to one of its own committees." But rulemaking, enforcement, and the Commission's other responsibilities represented "the performance of a significant governmental duty exercised pursuant to a public law," and were therefore to be exercised only by officers of the United States—by persons subject to appointment by the President (with or without senatorial assent) or by a head of one of "the executive departments."

The opinion is not always clear about how it sees the mass of government outside the legislative branch. At some points, it speaks confidently of the "three essential branches of Government" among which all powers are distributed, and writes of functions in "the administration and enforcement of public law" as if it were describing activities of one—the executive—of those three branches. At other points it seems somewhat more hesitant about the independent regulatory commissions, as when it refers to "Heads of 'Departments' . . . [which] are themselves in the Executive Branch or at least have some connection with that branch." All that was necessary was to decide that Congress could not vest in itself appointment power for the head of an agency that would be exercising a "significant governmental duty . . . pursuant to a public law." Just as the Court in Humphrey's Executor, to place the FTC beyond the President's removal claim, seems to have thought it enough for its purposes to show that the FTC's functions were not executive, the Buckley Court found it sufficient to characterize the FEC's functions as "not legislative" to remove it from Congress' appointments claim.

(4) The Bowsher opinion suggests yet another arena of "control" over agency action, one enormously important to the practical achievement of governmental tasks—the appropriations process. That appropriations questions rarely reach lawyers' offices should not conceal their significance. Regulation depends on the provision of resources to achieve it—and will be shaped by the character of resources provided. The effectiveness of a Fair Labor Standards Act or Occupational Safety and Health Act may depend substantially on the number of inspectors provided to assure observance, and that number in turn will influence the enforcement approaches it is possible to take. Over two decades ago a Federal Trade Commissioner complained that presidential power over finances was used as an instrument of policy control: "[OMB] has the authority to tell the Federal Trade Commission how much to spend on enforcing the Wool Products Labeling Act. Perhaps this method of administration relieves Congress of the burdensome duty of detailed oversight over independent agencies. On the other hand, it leaves the door wide open for administrative repeal of congressional action through the funding process without benefit of legislation." [4] Presidentially sponsored budget reductions were a primary means by which the Reagan administration sought to cut back regulation in the 1980's; and the forced reductions to be imposed by the deficit reduction legislation at issue in Bowsher were seen as having a particularly strong impact in the regulatory arena.

On the Presidential side, the OMB's influence on the budgeting process is one of the major sources of its political power. OMB Circular A–11, annually revised, provides thickly for information and supporting materials OMB will require; overall target figures for the national budget, hammered out in public and in private, signal the general constraints agencies must face as they attempt to set their own priorities and plans for the coming year. Shaping the budget request, deciding what items will be emphasized and what dropped during a

4. A. MacIntyre, The Status of Regulatory Independence, 29 Fed.B.J. 1 (1960). Compare National Treasury Employees   Union v. Devine, 733 F.2d 114 (D.C.Cir. 1984).

fiscal year to begin a year after the request is made,[5] has a strong influence on agency planning—is indeed the medium by which the possibilities of the coming year tend to be defined. And that process in turn is shaped by OMB's predictions, whether volunteered or made in response to inquiry, what sorts of initiatives are likely to be smiled upon.

In Congress, the appropriations process engages the attention of two legislative oversight agencies (the CBO and the GAO) as well as numerous committees and subcommittees in each house.[6] The appropriations subcommittees, in particular, tend to develop a specialized awareness of the problems of the departments and agencies whose estimates come before them. Each subcommittee has a permanent staff to aid it in its supervision of administrative programs for which funds are sought. While appropriations itself is an annual process, the interest of the subcommittees and their staffs is in fact constant. A rich political science and economics literature examine the resulting interactions, largely in the context of spending programs such as the Department of Defense rather than regulatory programs.[7]

Not until 1974 were moves made toward coordinating the work of the many virtually independent principalities (that is, the appropriations subcommittees) whose hands were on the purse strings. In that year the Congressional Budget Office as well as House and Senate Budget Committees were created by statute. They have the duty of setting the outer boundaries of spending, in the light of the revenues the committees deem appropriate to anticipate.[8] The Budget Committees have been diligent, far ranging in their inquiries, and seemingly effective in restraining open-ended appropriations and incautious exuberance, at least to the extent of arousing in their colleagues' consciousness an awareness of "targets" and "priorities" for spending.[9] Never-

5. That is, OMB required agencies to submit figures [or data] for Fiscal 1985 appropriations—the budget year commencing October 1, 1984—in September of 1983.

6. See W. Wander, F. Hebert and G. Copeland, Congressional Budgeting: Politics, Process and Power (1984); A. Schick, The Budget as an Instrument of Presidential Power, in L. Salamon, ed., Goverance: The Reagan Era and Beyond (1985). An earlier account appears in A. Schick, The First Five Years of Congressional Budgeting, in R. Penner, The Congressional Budget Process After Five Years 3 (1981).

7. "When we see a public agency spending inordinate amounts of public funds to pave over certain congressional districts, we are not observing an out of control agency. We are observing an agency that is paying off the members who nurture it." M. Fiorina, Congressional Control on the Bureaucracy: A Mismatch of Incentives and Capabilities, in L. Dodd and B. Oppenheimer, Congress Reconsidered 332 (1981); R.D. Arnold, Congress and the Bureaucracy: A Theory of Influence (1979); M. Fi-

orina and R. Noll, Voters, Legislators, and Bureaucracy: Institutional Design in the Public Sector, 68 Am.Ec.Rev. 256 (1978 Papers and Proceedings); K. Shepsle, The Failure of Congressional Budgeting, Occasional Papers of the Center for the Study of American Business No. 46 (1982).

8. 88 Stat. 297, 13 U.S.C. §§ 1301–1353. When the measure was approved in the Senate, Senator Sam Erwin called it "one of the most important pieces of legislation in my [20 years] in the Senate [and] I do not say that lightly." N.Y. Times, Mar. 23, 1974, 1:1.

9. A lively, realistic account of early unsuccessful efforts in the Senate to disregard the previously agreed upon "targets" will be found in B. Asbell, The Senate Nobody Knows 142–163, 268–279 (1978); and see also L. Fisher, Congressional Budget Reform: The First Two Years, 14 Harv. J.Legis. 413 (1977). J. Ellwood & J. Thurber, The Politics of the Congressional Budget Process Re-examined, in L. Dodd & B. Oppenheimer, eds., Congress Reconsidered 246 (1981). More critical recent as-

theless, the appropriations subcommittees have continued to have substantive as well as fiscal influence on public administration, and "those who wanted the congressional budget to be a contest over national priorities have been greatly disappointed." [10]

Expenditure controls are at best indirect mechanisms for dealing with regulators. Regulators do require resources to operate, but the fiscal resources they consume are neither a significant proportion of the federal budget nor an appropriate measure of their impact on those they regulate or the overall economy. Virtually all regulatory costs are paid by the private sector, in responding to regulation, and these expenses of compliance are not a real constraint on regulators (although enforcement expense may be). Just as steelmakers will not spontaneously place economic values on the air and water they use, and so may have to be constrained to conserve and/or protect those "free" resources by law, regulators will not spontaneously place economic values on compliance efforts. For this reason, it is argued, their allocation of the total resources involved in regulation may not be efficient. Of course, if one accepts the proposition that the unregulated economy is not necessarily the most efficient one, one could believe that regulation generates economic as well as social values. These benefits, too, are not internalized by regulatory bureaucracies.

One suggested response for such observations is to undertake a "regulatory budget." Under such a scheme, an agency, or perhaps government as a whole, would be assigned an annual amount of costs it would be permitted to impose on the private economy through regulation. Government could not then choose to impose a $200,000 cost of compliance *here* without foregoing like impositions *there*. By such a means, it is urged, the overall inflationary impact of regulation on the economy could be constrained. Estimates of the costs of regulatory compliance ranging from 60 billion to 200 billion dollars [11] establish, at the same moment, the significance of the problem and the difficulty of establishing a common metric. No such measure is now in place, although Section 6(a)(6) of E.O. 12291 envisions preliminary efforts in that direction. Some assessors of the prospects are enthusiastic; [12] others suggest that practical problems of measurement, [13] the expense in time and money of administration, and the opportunities created for diversionary argument conjoin to establish its unworkability, wholly apart from any abstract merit in the idea. [14] Executive Order 12,498,

sessment of the difficulty of overcoming the impact of geographic self-interest may be found in Penner, ed., The Congressional Budget Process After Five Years (1981) and K. Shepsle, The Failure of Congressional Budgeting, n. 7 above.

10. A. Schick, note 6, supra, at 27 (1981). The time taken by the budget process, nonetheless, is counted by many among the factors distracting Congress from primary legislative action.

11. S. Breyer, Regulation and Its Reform 2 (1982).

12. E.g., W.K. Viscusi, Presidential Oversight: Controlling the Regulators, 2 J.Pol.Anal. & Mgmt 157 (1983); and R. Litan & W. Nordhaus, Reforming Federal Regulations (1983).

13. Who estimates costs? On what basis? Subject to what checking? See the experience of overestimated costs reported by W.K. Viscusi in Cotton Dust Regulation: An OSHA Success Story? 4 J.Pol.Anal. & Man. 325 (1985).

14. E.g., L. Lave, The Strategy of Social Regulation 21–23 (1981).

while intended to foster priority setting for regulation, makes no provision for quantification.

Chapter III

THE EXERCISE OF ADMINISTRATIVE POWER: RULEMAKING AND ADJUDICATION

SECTION 1. THE DISTINCTION BETWEEN RULEMAKING ("QUASI LEGISLATIVE") AND ADJUDICATORY ("QUASI JUDICIAL") ADMINISTRATIVE ACTION

a. The Constitution

LONDONER v. DENVER
Supreme Court of the United States, 1908.
210 U.S. 373.

MR. JUSTICE MOODY delivered the opinion of the court.

The plaintiffs in error began this proceeding in a state court of Colorado to relieve lands owned by them from an assessment of a tax for the cost of paving a street upon which the lands abutted. The relief sought was granted by the trial court, but its action was reversed by the Supreme Court of the State. . . . The Supreme Court held that the tax was assessed in conformity with the constitution and laws of the State, and its decision on that question is conclusive.

. . .

The tax complained of was assessed under the provisions of the charter of the city of Denver, which confers upon the city the power to make local improvements and to assess the cost upon property specially benefited. . . .

It appears from the charter that, in the execution of the power to make local improvements and assess the cost upon the property specially benefited, the main steps to be taken by the city authorities are plainly marked and separated: 1. The board of public works must transmit to the city council a resolution ordering the work to be done and the form of an ordinance authorizing it and creating an assessment district. This it can do only upon certain conditions, one of which is that there shall first be filed a petition asking the improvement, signed by the owners of the majority of the frontage to be assessed. 2. The passage of that ordinance by the city council, which is given authority to determine conclusively whether the action of the board was duly taken. 3. The assessment of the cost upon the landowners after due notice and opportunity for hearing.

209

In the case before us the board took the first step by transmitting to the council the resolution to do the work and the form of an ordinance authorizing it. It is contended, however, that there was wanting an essential condition of the jurisdiction of the board, namely, such a petition from the owners as the law requires. The trial court found this contention to be true. But, as has been seen, the charter gave the city council the authority to determine conclusively that the improvements were duly ordered by the board after due notice and a proper petition. In the exercise of this authority the city council, in the ordinance directing the improvement to be made, adjudged, in effect, that a proper petition had been filed. . . . The state Supreme Court held that the determination of the city council was conclusive that a proper petition was filed, and that decision must be accepted by us as the law of the State. The only question for this court is whether the charter provision authorizing such a finding, without notice to the landowners, denies to them due process of law. We think it does not. The proceedings, from the beginning up to and including the passage of the ordinance authorizing the work did not include any assessment or necessitate any assessment, although they laid the foundation for an assessment, which might or might not subsequently be made. Clearly all this might validly be done without hearing to the landowners, provided a hearing upon the assessment itself is afforded. The legislature might have authorized the making of improvements by the city council without any petition. If it chose to exact a petition as a security for wise and just action it could, so far as the Federal Constitution is concerned, accompany that condition with a provision that the council, with or without notice, should determine finally whether it had been performed. This disposes of the first assignment of error, which is overruled. . . .

. . .

The fifth assignment, though general, vague and obscure, fairly raises, we think, the question whether the assessment was made without notice and opportunity for hearing to those affected by it, thereby denying to them due process of law. The trial court found as a fact that no opportunity for hearing was afforded, and the Supreme Court did not disturb this finding. The record discloses what was actually done, and there seems to be no dispute about it. After the improvement was completed the board of public works, in compliance with § 29 of the charter, certified to the city clerk a statement of the cost, and an apportionment of it to the lots of land to be assessed. Thereupon the city clerk, in compliance with § 30, published a notice stating, inter alia, that the written complaints or objections of the owners, if filed within thirty days, would be "heard and determined by the city council before the passage of any ordinance assessing the cost." Those interested, therefore, were informed that if they reduced their complaints and objections to writing, and filed them within thirty days, those complaints and objections would be heard, and would be heard before any assessment was made. . . . Resting upon the assurance that they would be heard, the plaintiffs in error filed within the thirty days the following paper:

"Denver, Colorado, January 13, 1900.

"To the Honorable Board of Public Works and the Honorable Mayor and City Council of the City of Denver:

"The undersigned, by Joshua Grozier, their attorney, do hereby most earnestly and strenuously protest and object to the passage of the contemplated or any assessing ordinance against the property in Eighth Avenue Paving District No. 1, so called, for each of the following reasons, to wit:

"1st. That said assessment and all and each of the proceedings leading up to the same were and are illegal, voidable and void, and the attempted assessment if made will be void and uncollectible.

"2nd. That said assessment and the cost of said pretended improvement should be collected, if at all, as a general tax against the city at large and not as a special assessment.

"3d. That property in said city not assessed is benefited by the said pretended improvement and certain property assessed is not benefited by said pretended improvement and other property assessed is not benefited by said pretended improvement to the extent of the assessment; that the individual pieces of property in said district are not benefited to the extent assessed against them and each of them respectively; that the assessment is arbitrary and property assessed in an equal amount is not benefited equally; that the boundaries of said pretended district were arbitrarily created without regard to the benefits or any other method of assessment known to law; that said assessment is outrageously large.

". . .

"6th. Because of non-compliance by the contractor with his contract and failure to complete the work in accordance with the contract; because the contract for said work was let without right or authority; because said pretended district is incomplete and the work under said contract has not been completed in accordance with said contract; because items too numerous to mention, which were not a proper charge in the said assessment, are included therein.

". . .

"8th. Because the city had no jurisdiction in the premises. No petition subscribed by the owners of a majority of the frontage in the district to be assessed for said improvements was ever obtained or presented.

". . .

"Wherefore, because of the foregoing and numerous other good and sufficient reasons, the undersigned object and protest against the passage of the said proposed assessing ordinance."

This certainly was a complaint against and objection to the proposed assessment. Instead of affording the plaintiffs in error an opportunity to be heard upon its allegations, the city council, without notice to them, met as a board of equalization, not in a stated but in a specially called session, and, without any hearing, adopted the following resolution:

"Whereas, complaints have been filed by the various persons and firms as the owners of real estate included within the Eighth Avenue Paving District No. 1, of the city of Denver against the proposed assessments on said property for the cost of said paving, . . . and Whereas, no complaint or objection has been filed or made against the apportionment of said assessment made by the board of public works of the city of Denver, but the complaints and objections filed deny wholly the right of the city to assess any district or portion of the assessable property of the city of Denver; therefore, be it

"Resolved, by the city council of the city of Denver, sitting as a board of equalization, that the apportionments of said assessment made by said board of public works be, and the same are hereby, confirmed and approved."

Subsequently, without further notice or hearing, the city council enacted the ordinance of assessment whose validity is to be determined in this case. The facts out of which the question on this assignment arises may be compressed into small compass. The first step in the assessment proceedings was by the certificate of the board of public works of the cost of the improvement and a preliminary apportionment of it. The last step was the enactment of the assessment ordinance. From beginning to end of the proceedings the landowners, although allowed to formulate and file complaints and objections, were not afforded an opportunity to be heard upon them. Upon these facts was there a denial by the State of the due process of law guaranteed by the Fourteenth Amendment to the Constitution of the United States?

In the assessment, apportionment and collection of taxes upon property within their jurisdiction the Constitution of the United States imposes few restrictions upon the States. In the enforcement of such restrictions as the Constitution does impose this court has regarded substance and not form. But where the legislature of a State, instead of fixing the tax itself, commits to some subordinate body the duty of determining whether, in what amount, and upon whom it shall be levied, and of making its assessment and apportionment, due process of law requires that at some stage of the proceedings before the tax becomes irrevocably fixed, the taxpayer shall have an opportunity to be heard, of which he must have notice, either personal, by publication, or by a law fixing the time and place of the hearing. It must be remembered that the law of Colorado denies the landowner the right to object in the courts to the assessment, upon the ground that the objections are cognizable only by the board of equalization.

If it is enough that, under such circumstances, an opportunity is given to submit in writing all objections to and complaints of the tax to the board, then there was a hearing afforded in the case at bar. But we think that something more than that, even in proceedings for taxation, is required by due process of law. Many requirements essential in strictly judicial proceedings may be dispensed with in proceedings of this nature. But even here a hearing in its very essence demands that he who is entitled to it shall have the right to support his allegations by argument however brief, and, if need be, by proof, however informal. Pittsburg &c. Railway Co. v. Backus, 154 U.S. 421, 426; Fallbrook Irrigation District v. Bradley, 164 U.S. 112, 171, et seq. It is apparent that such a hearing was denied to the plaintiffs in error. The denial was by the city council, which, while acting as a board of equalization, represents the State. The assessment was therefore void, and the plaintiffs in error were entitled to a decree discharging their lands from a lien on account of it. . . . Judgment reversed.

THE CHIEF JUSTICE and MR. JUSTICE HOLMES dissent.

BI-METALLIC INVESTMENT CO. v. STATE BD. OF EQUALIZATION OF COLORADO
Supreme Court of the United States, 1915.
239 U.S. 441.

MR. JUSTICE HOLMES delivered the opinion of the court.

This is a suit to enjoin the State Board of Equalization and the Colorado Tax Commission from putting in force, and the defendant Pitcher as assessor of Denver from obeying, an order of the boards increasing the valuation of all taxable property in Denver forty per cent. The order was sustained and the suit directed to be dismissed by the Supreme Court of the State. 56 Colo. 512, 138 P. 1010. See 56 Colo. 343, 138 P. 509. The plaintiff is the owner of real estate in Denver and brings the case here on the ground that it was given no opportunity to be heard and that therefore its property will be taken without due process of law, contrary to the Fourteenth Amendment of the Constitution of the United States. That is the only question with which we have to deal. . . .

For the purposes of decision we assume that the constitutional question is presented in the baldest way—that neither the plaintiff nor the assessor of Denver, who presents a brief on the plaintiff's side, nor any representative of the city and county, was given an opportunity to be heard, other than such as they may have had by reason of the fact that the time of meeting of the boards is fixed by law. On this assumption it is obvious that injustice may be suffered if some property in the county already has been valued at its full worth. But if certain property has been valued at a rate different from that generally prevailing in the county the owner has had his opportunity to protest and appeal as usual in our system of taxation, Hagar v. Reclamation District, 111 U.S. 701, 709, 710, so that it must be assumed that the property owners in the county all stand alike. The question then is whether all individuals have a constitutional right to be heard before a matter can be decided in which all are equally concerned—here, for instance, before a superior board decides that the local taxing officers have adopted a system of undervaluation throughout a county, as notoriously often has been the case. The answer of this court in the State Railroad Tax Cases, 92 U.S. 575, at least as to any further notice, was that it was hard to believe that the proposition was seriously made.

Where a rule of conduct applies to more than a few people it is impracticable that every one should have a direct voice in its adoption. The Constitution does not require all public acts to be done in town meeting or an assembly of the whole. General statutes within the state power are passed that affect the person or property of individuals, sometimes to the point of ruin, without giving them a chance to be heard. Their rights are protected in the only way that they can be in a complex society, by their power, immediate or remote, over those who make the rule. If the result in this case had been reached as it might have been by the State's doubling the rate of taxation, no one would suggest that the Fourteenth Amendment was violated unless every person affected had been allowed an opportunity to raise his voice against it before the body entrusted by the state constitution with the power. In considering this case in this court we must assume that the proper state machinery has been used, and the question is whether, if the state constitution had declared that Denver had been undervalued as compared with the rest of the State and had decreed that for the current year the valuation should be forty per cent higher, the objection now urged could prevail. It appears to us that to put the question is to answer it. There must be a limit to individual argument in such matters if government is to go on. In Londoner v. Denver, 210 U.S. 373, 385, a local board had to determine "whether, in what amount, and upon whom" a tax for paving a street should be levied for special benefits. A relatively small number of persons was concerned, who were exceptionally affected, in each case upon individual grounds, and it was held that they had a right to a hearing. But that decision is far from reaching a general determination dealing only with the principle upon which all the assessments in a county had been laid.

Judgment affirmed.

NOTES

(1) Would the case for a constitutional right to participate in a rulemaking process be stronger if premised on the political rights protected elsewhere in the Constitution? O'Connor, J., speaking for the Court in MINNESOTA STATE BOARD FOR COMMUNITY COLLEGES v. KNIGHT, 465 U.S. 271, 283–287 (1984):

"The Constitution does not grant to members of the public generally a right to be heard by public bodies making decisions of policy. . . .

"Policymaking organs in our system of government have never operated under a constitutional constraint requiring them to afford every interested member of the public an opportunity to present testimony before any policy is adopted. Legislatures throughout the nation, including Congress, frequently enact bills on which no hearings have been held or on which testimony has been received from only a select group. Executive agencies likewise make policy decisions of widespread application without permitting unrestricted public testimony. Public officials at all levels of government daily make policy decisions based only on the advice they decide they need and choose to hear. To recognize a constitutional right to participate directly in government policymaking would work a revolution in existing government practices.

"Not least among the reasons for refusing to recognize such a right is the impossibility of its judicial definition and enforcement. Both federalism and separation-of-powers concerns would be implicated in the massive intrusion into state and federal policymaking that recognition of the claimed right would entail. Moreover, the pragmatic considerations identified by Justice Holmes in Bi-Metallic Investment Co. v. State Board of Equalization are as weighty today as they were in 1915. Government makes so many policy decisions affecting so many people that it would likely grind to a halt were policymaking constrained by constitutional requirements on whose voices must be heard. 'There must be a limit to individual argument in such matters if government is to go on.' Absent statutory restrictions, the state must be free to consult or not to consult whomever it pleases.

"However wise or practicable various levels of public participation in various kinds of policy decisions may be, this Court has never held, and nothing in the Constitution suggests it should hold, that government must provide for such participation. In Bi-Metallic the Court rejected due process as a source of an obligation to listen. Nothing in the First Amendment or in this Court's case law interpreting it suggests that the rights to speak, associate, and petition require government policymakers to listen or respond to individuals' communications on public issues. . . . No other constitutional provision has been advanced as a source of such a requirement. Nor, finally, can the structure of government established and approved by the Constitution provide the source. It is inherent in a republican form of government that direct public participation in government policymaking is limited. See The Federalist No. 10 (Madison). Disagreement with public policy and disapproval of officials' responsiveness, as Justice Holmes suggested in Bi-Metallic, supra, is to be registered principally at the polls."

(2) Compare BURR v. NEW ROCHELLE MUNICIPAL HOUSING AUTHORITY, 479 F.2d 1165 (2d Cir.1973). On June 24, 1971, the Authority sent its 520 tenants notice of the imposition of a service charge of $2.00 per room per month for each apartment, effective August 1, 1971. Some of the tenants instituted an action against the Authority; the district court held that the plaintiffs "had a right under the due process clause of the Fourteenth Amendment to notice and a full adversary hearing before being required" to pay the service charge. On appeal, the Second Circuit, per Hays, J., stated that since " 'the interest at stake' (see Board of Regents of State Colleges v. Roth, 408 U.S. 564 (1972)) was of such a nature as to be within the protection of the Fourteenth Amendment, the remaining question is the extent of the procedural safeguards required by the concept of due process. . . .

"Balancing the interests of the Authority in a summary procedure against the interests of the tenants and the type of procedure necessary to protect these interests, we hold that due process does not require an adversary hearing before a general rent increase or service charge can be imposed. . . . We feel that the interests of the tenants, while concededly important, can be protected through a less formal procedure.

"Notice of a proposed increase in rent shall be served well in advance of the date for the increase. Opportunity for filing written objections shall be given. There need be no opportunity for oral presentation. The tenants or their representatives shall have the right to submit any material they consider relevant to disprove the need for the rent increase. Finally, the Review Board upon reaching a decision shall issue a statement outlining the reasons for either approving or rejecting the requested rent increase. The tenants may of course be represented by counsel."

(3) In considering the desirability of Justice Holmes' distinction, one must not forget (as he did not) that the general statutes which he says can be passed without a hearing, can by their very force, and without any further process, "affect the person or property of individuals, sometimes" (to use his flinty phrase) "to the point of ruin." Very particular rights can thus be lost with no individualized participation. For example, in 1971, Indiana enacted a statute which provided that ownership of subsurface mineral interests—those severed from the ownership of the surface land—would lapse and revert to the owner of the surface rights if for 20 years they had not been used. This statutory lapse could be avoided by separately recording the subsurface interest, and a two-year grace period was allowed from the date of the statute during which old and not-used interests could be recorded. After the two years had passed, various surface owners filed declaratory judgment actions to have subsurface rights which had not been used or recorded formally extinguished. Held, in Texaco, Inc. v. Short, 454 U.S. 516 (1982): the loss of property rights occasioned by the self-executing features of the act was not unconstitutional. The state has power to make ownership of property conditional on obligations such as those here present; "[g]enerally, a legislature need do nothing more than enact and publish the law, and afford the citizenry a reasonable opportunity to familiarize itself with its terms and to comply"; there is no obligation on the state or anyone else to give specific property holders notice of the specific impact of the statute before their property rights could be affected. Of course, the subsurface owners were entitled to notice of the declaratory judgment action, but by then the statute had automatically done its work. Four justices dissented.

(4) R. CRAMTON, A COMMENT ON TRIAL-TYPE HEARINGS IN NUCLEAR POWER PLANT CITING, 58 Va.L.Rev. 585, 591–93 (1972):

"An initial problem is to determine by what standards a given procedure should be judged. What are the criteria for evaluating procedural systems?

"Procedures, for the most part, are a means to an end—the accomplishment of social purposes. But at the same time procedures in themselves may create or destroy important values. The usual statement of these values, in terms of 'fairness,' 'due process,' and the like suffers from undue generality, since the content of these value-laden words shifts from time to time and from person to person.

"The distinction between rulemaking and adjudication also provides little help. While the idea that trials are appropriate only for 'adjudicative facts' is suggestive, it begs the hard question because the identification of 'adjudicative facts' is so subjective and flexible. We are reduced to a basic notion that in a society committed to a representative form of government, private persons should have a meaningful opportunity to participate in government decisions which directly affect them, especially when governmental action is based on individual rather than on general considerations.

"Beyond the fundamental principle of meaningful party participation, any evaluation of administrative procedures must rest on a judgment which balances the advantages and disadvantages of each procedural system. In striking this balance, I believe that the following formulation of competing considerations is more helpful than 'fairness' or 'due process': the extent to which the procedure furthers the accurate selection and determination of relevant facts and issues, the efficient disposition of business, and, when viewed in the light of the statutory objectives, its acceptability to the agency, the participants, and the general public.

"The first consideration, *accuracy*, serves as a short-hand reference to the rational aspects of a decision-making process. The ascertainment of truth, or, more realistically, as close an approximation of reality as human frailty permits, is a major goal of most decision-making. There are better and worse ways, in various contexts, of gathering relevant information, selecting or formulating controlling principles, and applying the correct principles to the probable facts. Accuracy, moreover, is not only a facet of each case but an aggregative or system characteristic of uniform and consistent results that give equal treatment to similarly situated persons. Accurate results in a particular instance ('justice in the individual case') may be less important in many areas than a high degree of consistency in the decision of a large number of cases.

"The second consideration, *efficiency*, emphasizes the time, effort, and expense of elaborate procedures. The work of the world must go on, and endless nit-picking, while it may produce a more nearly ideal solution, imposes huge costs and impairs other important values. In the polycentric administrative case, the efficiency of trial procedures meets the severest test. This criterion, unlike the others, is capable of quantitative statement since time and effort may usually be stated in dollar terms. Concern with public costs and expenditures must not be allowed to obscure the fact that the private costs of administrative delay are usually far higher than the total of governmental costs.

"The final consideration, *acceptability*, emphasizes the indispensable virtues of procedures that are considered fair by those whom they affect, as well as by the general public. Usually this translates into meaningful participation in the decisional process. The authority of decisions in a society resting on the consent of the governed is based on their general acceptability. Moreover, if procedures are deemed fair by those immediately affected, their cooperation and assistance can be obtained, with the result that administrative action will be better informed and thought out."

BOWLES v. WILLINGHAM
Supreme Court of the United States, 1944.
321 U.S. 503.

[This case arose out of the efforts made to deal with rampant inflation in housing costs in areas heavily affected by World War II defense activities. The Emergency Price Control Act of 1942 authorized the Price Administrator, within "defense-rental areas," to "establish such maximum rent or maximum rents . . . as in his judgment will be generally fair and equitable and will effectuate the purposes of this Act." On June 30, 1942, the Administrator issued Maximum Rent Regulation No. 26, effective July 1, 1942. The Regulation provided that the maximum rental for housing accommodations rented on April 1, 1941, should be the rent charged on that date; for housing accommodations not rented on April 1, 1941, but rented between that date and the effective date of the Regulation, the maximum rental should be the rent first charged after April 1, 1941; but in that case, the Rent Director (in whom the Administrator had vested his duties under the Regulation) might order a decrease on his own initiative on the ground, among others, that the rent was higher than that generally prevailing in the area for comparable housing accommodations on April 1, 1941.

Another OPA Regulation provided that whenever the Rent Director proposed to decrease a specific rental, he should, before taking such action, serve a notice upon the landlord stating the proposed action and the grounds therefor. If the landlord objected to the proposed action, he could apply to the Regional Administrator for review of the action; if the Regional Administrator refused the relief requested by the landlord, the latter could file a protest with the Price Administrator for review of the Regional decision. (Or the landlord could file a protest directly with the Price Administrator to set aside or modify the Rent Director's determination.)

Protestants were to file with their protests "affidavits setting forth in full the evidence . . . upon which the protestant relies in support of the facts alleged in the protest." The Administrator could then grant or deny the protest or set the matter down for an oral hearing. A protestant's request for an oral hearing was to be "accompanied by a showing as to why the filing of affidavits or other written evidence and briefs will not permit the fair and expeditious disposition of the protest." § 1300.229 of OPA Revised Procedural Regulation No. 3 (July 1, 1943).

If the Price Administrator did not grant the relief requested by the landlord, the latter could secure judicial review of the Price Administrator's action in the "Emergency Court of Appeals" created by section 204 of the Act. The scope of review of the court was as follows: "No . . . . regulation, order, or price schedule shall be enjoined or set aside in whole or in part, unless the complainant establishes to the satisfaction of the court that the regulation, order, or price schedule is not in accordance with law or is arbitrary or capricious." The judgment or order of the Emergency Court of Appeals was subject to review by the Supreme Court on petition for writ of certiorari. The Act also provided that no other court, "Federal, State, or Territorial, shall have jurisdiction or power to consider the validity of any such regulation, order or price schedule or to stay, restrain, enjoin, or set aside, in whole or in part . . . any provision of any such regulation, order, or price schedule. . . . " [1]

In the instant case, Mrs. Kate C. Willingham owned three apartments in Macon, Georgia. The apartments had not been rented on April 1, 1941; they were first rented on July 1 and August 1, 1941, for a total rental of $137.50 per month. In June, 1943, the Rent Director gave written notice to Mrs. Willingham that he proposed to reduce the maximum rental for the apartments to a total of $90.00 per month on the ground that the rents first charged after April 1, 1941, were in excess of those generally prevailing in the area for comparable accommodations on April 1, 1941. Mrs. Willingham filed objections to that proposed action together with supporting affidavits. The Rent Director thereupon advised her that he would proceed to issue an order reducing the rents. Before that was done, Mrs. Willingham filed a petition in the Superior Court of Bibb County, Georgia, praying that the Rent Director be restrained from issuing the proposed orders. The state court issued, ex parte, a temporary injunction and show cause order. Thereupon the Price Administrator brought this suit in the federal District Court to restrain Mrs. Willingham from further prosecution of the state proceedings and from violation of the Act, and to restrain the sheriff of Bibb County from executing any orders in the state proceedings. The District Court dismissed the Administrator's suit, holding that the regulations and order in question and the provisions of the Act on which they rested were unconstitutional.]

MR. JUSTICE DOUGLAS delivered the opinion of the Court. . . .

It is finally suggested that the Act violates the Fifth Amendment because it makes no provision for a hearing to landlords before the order or regulation fixing rents becomes effective. Obviously, Congress would have been under no necessity to give notice and provide a hearing before it acted, had it decided to fix rents on a national basis the same as it did for the District of Columbia. See 55 Stat. 788. We agree with the Emergency Court of Appeals (Avant v. Bowles, 139 F.2d 702) that Congress need not make that requirement when it delegates the task to an administrative agency. In Bi-Metallic Investment Co. v. State Board, 239 U.S. 441, a suit was brought by a taxpayer and landowner to enjoin a Colorado Board from putting in effect an order which increased the valuation of all taxable property in Denver 40 per cent. Such action, it was alleged, violated the Fourteenth Amendment as the plaintiff was given no opportunity to be heard. Mr. Justice

1. [Ed.] The instructive story of the Emergency Court of Appeals and its exclusive jurisdiction is well told in N. Nathanson, The Emergency Court of Appeals, in Problems in Price Control: Legal Phases (1947).

Holmes, speaking for the Court, stated, page 445 of 239 U.S.: "Where a rule of conduct applies to more than a few people, it is impracticable that every one should have a direct voice in its adoption. The Constitution does not require all public acts to be done in town meeting or an assembly of the whole. General statutes within the state power are passed that affect the person or property of individuals, sometimes to the point of ruin, without giving them a chance to be heard. Their rights are protected in the only way that they can be in a complex society, by their power, immediate or remote, over those who make the rule." We need not go so far in the present case. Here Congress has provided for judicial review of the Administrator's action. To be sure, that review comes after the order has been promulgated; and no provision for a stay is made. But as we have held in Yakus v. United States, 321 U.S. 414, that review satisfies the requirements of due process. As stated by Mr. Justice Brandeis for a unanimous Court in Phillips v. Commissioner, 283 U.S. 589, 596, 597, "Where only property rights are involved, mere postponement of the judicial enquiry is not a denial of due process, if the opportunity given for the ultimate judicial determination of the liability is adequate. . . . Delay in the judicial determination of property rights is not uncommon where it is essential that governmental needs be immediately satisfied."

Language in the cases that due process requires a hearing before the administrative order becomes effective (Morgan v. United States, 304 U.S. 1, 19, 20; Opp Cotton Mills, Inc. v. Administrator, 312 U.S. 126, 152, 153) is to be explained on two grounds. In the first place the statutes there involved required that procedure.

Secondly, as we have held in Yakus v. United States, supra, Congress was dealing here with the exigencies of war time conditions and the insistent demands of inflation control. Cf. Porter v. Investors' Syndicate, 286 U.S. 461, 471. Congress chose not to fix rents in specified areas or on a national scale by legislative fiat. It chose a method designed to meet the needs for rent control as they might arise and to accord some leeway for adjustment within the formula which it prescribed. At the same time the procedure which Congress adopted was selected with the view of eliminating the necessity for "lengthy and costly trials with concomitant dissipation of the time and energies of all concerned in litigation rather than in the common war effort." S.Rep. No. 931, 77th Cong., 2d Sess., p. 7. To require hearings for thousands of landlords before any rent control order could be made effective might have defeated the program of price control. Or Congress might well have thought so. National security might not be able to afford the luxuries of litigation and the long delays which preliminary hearings traditionally have entailed.

We fully recognize . . . that "even the war power does not remove constitutional limitations safeguarding essential liberties." . . . But where Congress has provided for judicial review after the regulations or orders have been made effective it has done all that due process under the war emergency requires.

Other objections are raised concerning the regulations or orders fixing the rents. But these may be considered only by the Emergency Court of Appeals on the review provided by § 204. Yakus v. United States, supra.[2]

Reversed.

[The concurring opinion of Justice Rutledge and the dissenting opinion of Justice Roberts are omitted.][3]

NOTES

(1) The distinction between making a rule and adjudicating a case is one of the most basic in all of jurisprudence. Here are some materials (not necessarily from administrative law sources) that bear on the question, how is the distinction to be drawn:

a. *The element of prospectivity:*

Holmes, J., in Prentis v. Atlantic Coast Line Co., 211 U.S. 210, 226 (1908):

"A judicial inquiry investigates, declares and enforces liabilities as they stand on present or past facts and under laws supposed already to exist. That is its purpose and end. Legislation on the other hand looks to the future and changes existing conditions by making a new rule to be applied thereafter to all or some part of those subject to its power.

2. [Ed.] The Government's brief in the Bowles case contains the following paragraph: "The exigencies of the Price Control Act as an essential wartime measure were regarded by Congress as precluding the holding of formal hearings before the issuance of price or rent regulations. Congress did, however, provide in Sections 203 and 204 of the Act a comprehensive procedure for the adjustment and review of maximum rent regulations and orders issued under the Act. . . . We shall not undertake to discuss here the adequacy of the protest and review procedure available to challenge a basic regulation. That procedure was not availed of in the present case; in any event, its operations are more fully discussed in the Government's brief [in the Yakus case]." pp. 34–36.

The opinion of Chief Justice Stone in the Yakus case states: "Nor can we say that the administrative hearing provided by the statute will prove inadequate. We hold in Bowles v. Willingham . . . that in the circumstances to which this Act was intended to apply, the failure to afford a hearing prior to the issue of a price regulation does not offend against due process. While the hearing on a protest may be restricted to the presentation of documentary evidence, affidavits and briefs, the Act contemplates, and the Administrator's regulations provide for, a full oral hearing upon a showing that written evidence and briefs 'will not permit the fair and expedi-

tious disposition of the protest'. . . . In advance of application to the Administrator for such a hearing we cannot well say whether its denial in any particular case would be a denial of due process." 321 U.S. at 436.

3. [Ed.] Magruder, J., in 150 East 47th Street Corp. v. Creedon, 162 F.2d 206, 210 (Em.Ct.App.1947): "[T]here is no statutory requirement of a hearing either before the issuance of a general rent regulation or before the issuance of an individual rent reduction order pursuant to adjustment provisions of the regulation. In Bowles v. Willingham, 1944, 321 U.S. 503, 519–521, the court held that the Act was not in violation of the Fifth Amendment for failure to make provision for a hearing to landlords before an order or regulation fixing rents becomes effective. It held that the provision for subsequent administrative review by protest under § 203, followed by judicial review in this court under § 204(a), satisfied the requirements of due process. But the Supreme Court's discussion was focused on the legislative character of the basic rent regulation, affecting thousands of persons. A proceeding looking to an individual reduction order, in which the standards set forth in an adjustment provision of the regulation are applied to a particular set of facts relating to a single landlord, is quasi-judicial in character . . . ."

The establishment of a rate is the making of a rule for the future, and therefore is an act legislative not judicial in kind. . . . "

Clark, J., in Linkletter v. Walker, 381 U.S. 618, 619–20, 628–29 (1965):

"In Mapp v. Ohio, 367 U.S. 643 (1961), we held that the exclusion of evidence seized in violation of the search and seizure provisions of the Fourth Amendment was required of the States by the Due Process Clause of the Fourteenth Amendment. In so doing we overruled Wolf v. Colorado, 338 U.S. 25 (1949), to the extent that it failed to apply the exclusionary rule to the States. This case presents the question of whether this requirement operates retrospectively upon cases finally decided in the period prior to Mapp. . . .

"[T]he accepted rule today is that in appropriate cases the Court may in the interest of justice make the rule prospective.

"Once the premise is accepted that we are neither required to apply, nor prohibited from applying, a decision retrospectively, we must then weigh the merits and demerits in each case by looking to the prior history of the rule in question, its purpose and effect, and whether retrospective operation will further or retard its operation. We believe that this approach is particularly correct with reference to the Fourth Amendment's prohibitions as to unreasonable searches and seizures. Rather than 'disparaging' the Amendment we but apply the wisdom of Justice Holmes that '[t]he life of the law has not been logic: it has been experience.' Holmes, The Common Law 5 (Howe ed. 1963)."

P.J. Mishkin, Foreword: The High Court, The Great Writ, and the Due Process of Time and Law, 79 Harv.L.Rev. 56, 60 (1965):

"[I]t is the basic role of courts to decide disputes after they have arisen. That function requires that judicial decisions operate (at least ordinarily) with retroactive effect. In turn, unless those decisions (at least ordinarily) reflect preexisting rules or values, such retroactivity would be intolerable.

". . .

"The essential function of courts which requires that the normal mode of judicial operation be retroactive has implications for our present problem. For that function also requires that the structure of judicial institutions be built so as to respond effectively to demands for retroactive adjudication of past disputes. Adaptation to any other role must be secondary. Thus, the severe limits on and the restricted forms of participation in the judicial process (parties must have specific interests in a particular actual dispute, and may present only formal evidence and arguments of counsel), the modes of the process itself (insulation from political pressure; reasoned argument and opinions), and the nature of available relief (responding to the past history of the parties) all make most sense in the context of resolving past disputes. The relevance of this observation to our present concern lies in the limited adaptability of these institutions to a regime of prospective lawmaking. . . ."

b. *The element of generality:*

R.F. Fuchs, Procedure in Administrative Rule-Making, 52 Harv.L. Rev. 259, 263–64 (1938):

"The most obvious definition of rule-making and the one most often employed in the literature of administrative law asserts simply that it is the function of laying down general regulations as distinguished from orders that apply to named persons or to specific situations. Most acts of legislatures, although by no means all, establish rights and duties with respect either to people generally or to classes of people or situations that are defined but not enumerated. Conversely, the judgments of courts usually are addressed to particular individuals or to situations that are definitely specified. Similarly, administrative action can be classified into general regulations, including determinations whose effect is to bring general regulations into operation, and orders or acts of specific application.

". . . [I]t is feasible to distinguish a general regulation from an order of specific application on the basis of the manner in which the parties subject to it are designated. If they are named, or if they are in effect identified by their relation to a piece of property or transaction or institution which is specified, the order is one of specific application. If they are not named, but the order applies to a designated class of persons or situations, the order is a general regulation or a rule."

J. Dickinson, Administrative Justice and the Supremacy of Law 17–20 (1927):

"Our constitutional distinction between 'legislative,' 'executive' and 'judicial' powers draws the courts frequently into discussions in which the 'legislative' or 'executive' aspect of an administrative act is generally emphasized at the expense of the 'judicial.' Thus, for example, the act of a public-utilities commission in fixing a rate has been held to be 'legislative' for constitutional purposes.

"From one aspect of juristic analysis, legislative it no doubt is— that is, from the aspect of its future operation and its applicability to a whole class of cases. But the writ of mandamus is future in its operation, and yet is not for that reason regarded as legislative; and if we examine rate-fixing from the standpoint of the general applicability of the resulting rate to an indefinite number of future cases as a class, we observe the significant peculiarity that, while the rate applies indifferently, indeed, as against all future shippers, it applies only to the particular carrier or carriers who were parties to the hearing and other proceedings before the commission, and for whom, as the outcome of those proceedings, the rate is prescribed. From the standpoint of shippers, therefore, the rate may no doubt be regarded as legislation, but from the standpoint of the carriers it seems quite as truly adjudication. Even with respect to the shippers, however, it may be likened to the procedure whereby an injunction is obtained against a group of persons designated by a class-description and not named personally in the bill. If the latter procedure is judicial, there is certainly an element of adjudication in administrative rate-fixing; and that is all I wish to insist on here. There is no intention to deny that rate-fixing involves as one of its elements the exercise of a function which may as well as not be called 'legislative.' The whole discussion should go to demonstrate the futility of trying to classify a particular exercise of administrative power as either wholly legislative or wholly judicial. The tendency of the administrative procedure is to foreshorten both functions into a continuous governmental act."

c. *The element of "the rule of law":*

F.A. Hayek, The Constitution of Liberty 153–54 (1960):

"The conception of freedom under the law that is the chief concern of this book rests on the contention that when we obey laws, in the sense of general abstract rules laid down irrespective of their application to us, we are not subject to another man's will and are therefore free. It is because the lawgiver does not know the particular cases to which his rules will apply, and it is because the judge who applies them has no choice in drawing the conclusions that follow from the existing body of rules and the particular facts of the case, that it can be said that laws and not men rule. Because the rule is laid down in ignorance of the particular case and no man's will decides the coercion used to enforce it, the law is not arbitrary. This, however, is true only if by 'law' we mean the general rules that apply equally to everybody. This generality is probably the most important aspect of that attribute of law which we have called its 'abstractness.' As a true law should not name any particulars, so it should especially not single out any specific persons or group of persons. . . . "

R.M. Unger, Knowledge and Politics 89–90 (1975)[†]

". . . To understand the nature of adjudication one must distinguish two different ways of ordering human relations. One way is to establish rules to govern general categories of acts and persons, and then to decide particular disputes among persons on the basis of the established rules. This is legal justice. The other way is to determine goals and then, quite independently of rules, to decide particular cases by a judgment of what decision is most likely to contribute to the predetermined goals, a judgment of instrumental rationality. This is substantive justice.

"In the situation of legal justice, the laws are made against the background of the ends they are designed to promote, even if the sole permissible end is liberty itself. Only after the rules have been formulated do decisions 'under the rules' become possible. Hence, the possibility of some sort of distinction between legislation and adjudication is precisely what defines legal justice. The main task of the theory of adjudication is to say when a decision can truly be said to stand 'under a rule,' if the rule we have in mind is the law of the state, applied by a judge. Only decisions 'under a rule' are consistent with freedom; others constitute arbitrary exercises of judicial power.

"Decisions made under rules must be capable of a kind of justification different from the justification for the rules themselves. The task of judging is distinct from that of lawmaking. Usually, the separation of functions will be accompanied and strengthened by a separation of powers: the person of the lawmaker will not be the same as the person of the law applier. . . .

"There are legal systems in which the line between legislation and adjudication is hazy from the start. This is especially true in a tradition of judge-made law like the Anglo-American common law. A system in which judges both make the law and apply it is not self-evidently inconsistent with a situation of legal justice as long as some screen can be interposed between reasons for having a rule and reasons for applying it to a particular case. . . .

"In substantive justice each decision is justified because it is the one best calculated to advance some accepted objective. The relation between a particular decision and the objective is that of a means to an end. For example, given the goal of increasing national production, a certain bargain should be enforced because its performance will increase output.

"The distinctive feature of substantive justice is the nonexistence of any line between legislation and adjudication. In the pure case of substantive justice, there is neither rulemaking nor rule applying, because rather than prescriptive rules there are only choices as to what should be accomplished and judgments of instrumental rationality about how to get it done. . . . "

(2) The Administrative Procedure Act draws the distinction between rulemaking and adjudication by means of the following set of interlocking definitions (5 U.S.C. § 551(4)–(7)):

(4) "rule" means the whole or a part of an agency statement of general or particular applicability and future effect designed to implement, interpret, or prescribe law or policy or describing the organization, procedure, or practice requirements of an agency and includes the approval or prescription for the future of rates, wages, corporate or financial structures or reorganization thereof, prices, facilities, appliances, services or allowances therefor or of valuations, costs, or accounting, or practices bearing on any of the foregoing;

(5) "rule making" means agency process for formulating, amending, or repealing a rule;

(6) "order" means the whole or a part of a final disposition, whether affirmative, negative, injunctive, or declaratory in form, of an agency in a matter other than rule making but including licensing;

(7) "adjudication" means agency process for the formulation of an order.

b. The Procedural Models of the Administrative Procedure Act

INTRODUCTORY NOTES

(1) Mr. Justice Jackson's opinion in Wong Yang Sung v. McGrath, 339 U.S. 33 (1950), began as follows: "This *habeas corpus* proceeding involves a single ultimate question—whether administrative hearings in deportation cases must conform to requirements of the Administrative Procedure Act of June 11, 1946." In the course of answering that question, he described the Act as follows:

"The Administrative Procedure Act of June 11, 1946, supra, is a new, basic and comprehensive regulation of procedures in many agencies, more than a few of which can advance arguments that its generalities should not or do not include them. Determination of questions of its coverage may well be approached through consideration of its purposes as disclosed by its background.

"Multiplication of federal administrative agencies and expansion of their functions to include adjudications which have serious impact on private rights has been one of the dramatic legal developments of the past half-century. Partly from restriction by statute, partly from judicial self-restraint, and partly by necessity—from the nature of their multitudinous and semilegislative or executive tasks—the decisions of administrative tribunals were accorded considerable finality, and especially with respect to fact finding. The conviction developed, particularly within the legal profession, that this power was not sufficiently safeguarded and sometimes was put to arbitrary and biased use.

"Concern over administrative impartiality and response to growing discontent was reflected in Congress as early as 1929, when Senator Norris introduced a bill to create a separate administrative court. Fears and dissatisfactions increased as tribunals grew in number and jurisdiction, and a succession of bills offering various remedies appeared in Congress. Inquiries into the practices of state agencies, which tended to parallel or follow the federal pattern, were instituted in several states, and some studies noteworthy for thoroughness, impartiality and vision resulted.

"The Executive Branch of the Federal Government also became concerned as to whether the structure and procedure of these bodies was conducive to fairness in the administrative process. President Roosevelt's Committee on Administrative Management in 1937 recommended complete separation of adjudicating functions and personnel from those having to do with investigation or prosecution. The President early in 1939 also directed the Attorney General to name 'a committee of eminent lawyers, jurists, scholars, and administrators to review the entire administrative process in the various departments of the executive Government and to recommend improvements, including the suggestion of any needed legislation.'

"So strong was the demand for reform, however, that Congress did not await the Committee's report but passed what was known as the Walter-Logan bill, a comprehensive and rigid prescription of standardized procedures for administrative agencies. This bill was vetoed by President Roosevelt December 18, 1940, and the veto was sustained by the House. But the President's veto message made no denial of the need for reform. Rather it pointed out that the task of the Committee, whose objective was 'to suggest improvements to make the process more workable and more just,' had proved 'unexpectedly complex.' The President said, 'I should desire to await their report and recommendations before approving any measure in this complicated field.'

"The committee divided in its views and both the majority and the minority submitted bills which were introduced in 1941. A subcommittee of the Senate Judiciary Committee held exhaustive hearings on three proposed measures, but, before the gathering storm of national emergency and war, consideration of the problem was put aside. Though bills on the subject reappeared in 1944, they did not attract much attention.

"The McCarran-Sumners bill, which evolved into the present Act, was introduced in 1945. Its consideration and hearing, especially of agency interests, was painstaking. All administrative agencies were invited to submit their views in writing. A tentative revised bill was then prepared and interested parties again were invited to submit criticisms. The Attorney General named representatives of the Department of Justice to canvass the agencies and report their criticisms, and submitted a favorable report on the bill as finally revised. It passed both Houses without opposition and was signed by President Truman June 11, 1946.

"The Act thus represents a long period of study and strife; it settles long-continued and hard-fought contentions, and enacts a formula upon which opposing social and political forces have come to rest. It contains many compromises and generalities and, no doubt, some ambiguities. Experience may reveal defects. But it would be a disservice to our form of government and to the administrative process itself if the courts should fail, so far as the terms of the Act warrant, to give effect to its remedial purposes where the evils it was aimed at appear." [1]

(2) The cases which follow explore the procedural alternatives for agency action established by the Administrative Procedure Act. The opinions will be hard to follow without a sense of the statute itself. It is set out in Appendix A, page 1209 within.

When the statute was new, the Yale Law Journal published a chart of its basic structure. (The Federal Administrative Procedure Act: Codification or Reform, 56 Yale L.J. 670, 705 (1947).) With the thought that what was helpful to practitioners when the statute was first passed

---

1. [Ed.] For a spirited recounting of the same events, see W. Gellhorn, The Administrative Procedure Act: The Beginnings, 72 Va.L.Rev. 219 (1986).

will also be helpful to students making their first pass at the statute, here (with slight modifications) is that chart:

CHART OF ADMINISTRATIVE PROCEDURE ACT [2]

	Rule Making	Adjudication
Informal	All: publication—sec. 552(a)(1); petitions to alter rules—sec. 553(e). Substantive only: notice, participation, statement of "basis and purpose," 30-day delay between publication and taking effect—sec. 553.	
Formal	Notice—section 553(b); hearing—sec. 556; intermediate and final decision—sec. 557; 30-day delay between publication and taking effect—sec. 553(d); publication—sec. 552(a)(1); petitions to alter rules—sec. 553(e).	Notice, informal settlement; separation of functions—sec. 554; hearing—sec. 556; intermediate and final decision—sec. 557; declaratory orders—section 554(e).

Needless to say, the statute in its entirety is more complex. If you want to try tracking down one of its wrinkles, you might try looking at the particular provisions for initial licensing, described in sections 554(d), 556(d), and 557(b), or you might consider whether section 555(e) could be used to provide some structure for "informal adjudication."

UNITED STATES v. FLORIDA EAST COAST RAILWAY CO.
Supreme Court of the United States, 1973.
410 U.S. 224.

MR. JUSTICE REHNQUIST delivered the opinion of the Court.

Appellees, two railroad companies, brought this action in the District Court for the Middle District of Florida to set aside the incentive per diem rates established by appellant Interstate Commerce Commission in a rule-making proceeding. Incentive Per Diem Charges—1968, Ex parte No. 252 (Sub-No. 1), 337 I.C.C. 217 (1970). They challenged the order of the Commission on both substantive and procedural grounds. The District Court sustained appellees' position that the Commission had failed to comply with the applicable provisions of the Administrative Procedure Act, 5 U.S.C. § 551 et seq., and

---

2. As you will also learn, provisions in the APA can be referred to either by the section numbers in the Act itself (in the right hand column in the appendix) or by the section numbers as codified in Title 5, United States Code (the regular section headings in the appendix). The chart as published did the first, but it has been revised to conform to the second form, which is more commonly used in judicial opinions today. Provisions relating to administrative law judges have been omitted.

therefore set aside the order without dealing with the railroads' other contentions. The District Court held that the language of § 1(14)(a) [1] of the Interstate Commerce Act, 49 U.S.C. § 1(14)(a), required the Commission in a proceeding such as this to act in accordance with the Administrative Procedure Act, 5 U.S.C. § 556(d), and that the Commission's determination to receive submissions from the appellees only in written form was a violation of that section because the appellees were "prejudiced" by that determination within the meaning of that section.

Following our decision last Term in United States v. Allegheny-Ludlum Steel Corp., 406 U.S. 742 (1972), we noted probable jurisdiction, 407 U.S. 908 (1972), and requested the parties to brief the question of whether the Commission's proceeding was governed by 5 U.S.C. § 553, or by §§ 556 and 557, of the Administrative Procedure Act. . . .

I. BACKGROUND OF CHRONIC FREIGHT CAR SHORTAGES

This case arises from the factual background of a chronic freight-car shortage on the Nation's railroads. . . . Judge Simpson, writing for the District Court in this case, noted that "[f]or a number of years portions of the nation have been plagued with seasonal shortages of freight cars in which to ship goods." 322 F.Supp. 725, 726 (MD Fla. 1971). Judge Friendly, writing for a three-judge District Court in the Eastern District of New York in the related case of Long Island R. Co. v. United States, 318 F.Supp. 490, 491 (EDNY 1970), described the Commission's order as "the latest chapter in a long history of freight-car shortages in certain regions and seasons and of attempts to ease them." Congressional concern for the problem was manifested in the enactment in 1966 of an amendment to § 1(14)(a) of the Interstate Commerce Act, enlarging the Commission's authority to prescribe per diem charges for the use by one railroad of freight cars owned by another. . . .

1. Section 1(14)(a) provides:

"The Commission may, after hearing, on a complaint or upon its own initiative without complaint, establish reasonable rules, regulations, and practices with respect to car service by common carriers by railroad subject to this chapter, including the compensation to be paid and other terms of any contract, agreement, or arrangement for the use of any locomotive, car, or other vehicle not owned by the carrier using it (and whether or not owned by another carrier), and the penalties or other sanctions for nonobservance of such rules, regulations, or practices. In fixing such compensation to be paid for the use of any type of freight car, the Commission shall give consideration to the national level of ownership of such type of freight car and to other factors affecting the adequacy of the national freight car supply, and shall, on the basis of such consideration, determine whether compensation should be computed solely on the basis of elements of ownership expense involved in owning and maintaining such type of freight car, including a fair return on value, or whether such compensation should be increased by such incentive element or elements of compensation as in the Commission's judgment will provide just and reasonable compensation to freight car owners, contribute to sound car service practices (including efficient utilization and distribution of cars), and encourage the acquisition and maintenance of a car supply adequate to meet the needs of commerce and the national defense. The Commission shall not make any incentive element applicable to any type of freight car the supply of which the Commission finds to be adequate and may exempt from the compensation to be paid by any group of carriers such incentive element or elements if the Commission finds it to be in the national interest."

The Commission in 1966 commenced an investigation, Ex parte No. 252, Incentive Per Diem Charges, "to determine whether information presently available warranted the establishment of an incentive element increase, on an interim basis, to apply pending further study and investigation." 332 I.C.C. 11, 12 (1967). Statements of position were received from the Commission staff and a number of railroads. Hearings were conducted at which witnesses were examined. In October 1967, the Commission rendered a decision discontinuing the earlier proceeding, but announcing a program of further investigation into the general subject.

In December 1967, the Commission initiated the rule-making procedure giving rise to the order that appellees here challenge. It directed Class I and Class II line-haul railroads to compile and report detailed information with respect to freight-car demand and supply at numerous sample stations for selected days of the week during 12 four-week periods, beginning January 29, 1968.

Some of the affected railroads voiced questions about the proposed study or requested modification in the study procedures outlined by the Commission in its notice of proposed rulemaking. In response to petitions setting forth these carriers' views, the Commission staff held an informal conference in April 1968, at which the objections and proposed modifications were discussed. Twenty railroads, including appellee Seaboard, were represented at this conference, at which the Commission's staff sought to answer questions about reporting methods to accommodate individual circumstances of particular railroads. The conference adjourned on a note that undoubtedly left the impression that hearings would be held at some future date. A detailed report of the conference was sent to all parties to the proceeding before the Commission.

The results of the information thus collected were analyzed and presented to Congress by the Commission during a hearing before the Subcommittee on Surface Transportation of the Senate Committee on Commerce in May 1969. Members of the Subcommittee expressed dissatisfaction with the Commission's slow pace in exercising the authority that had been conferred upon it by the 1966 Amendments to the Interstate Commerce Act. . . .

The Commission, now apparently imbued with a new sense of mission, issued in December 1969 an interim report announcing its tentative decision to adopt incentive per diem charges on standard boxcars based on the information compiled by the railroads. The substantive decision reached by the Commission was that so-called "incentive" per diem charges should be paid by any railroad using on its lines a standard boxcar owned by another railroad. Before the enactment of the 1966 amendment to the Interstate Commerce Act, it was generally thought that the Commission's authority to fix per diem payments for freight car use was limited to setting an amount that reflected fair return on investment for the owning railroad, without any regard being had for the desirability of prompt return to the owning line or for the encouragement of additional purchases of freight cars by the railroads as a method of investing capital. The Commission concluded, however, that in view of the 1966 amendment it could impose additional "incentive" per diem charges to spur prompt return of existing cars and to make acquisition of new cars financially attractive to the railroads. It did so by means of a proposed schedule that established such charges on an across-the-board basis for all common carriers by railroads subject to the Interstate Commerce Act. Embodied in the report was a proposed rule adopting the Commission's tentative conclusions and a notice to the railroads to file [written] statements of position within 60 days, . . . [and stating that] "any party requesting oral hearing shall set forth with specificity the need therefor and the evidence to be adduced."

Both appellee railroads filed statements objecting to the Commission's proposal and requesting an oral hearing, as did numerous other railroads. In April 1970, the Commission, without having held further "hearings," issued a supplemental report making some modifications in the tentative conclusions earlier reached, but overruling in toto the requests of appellees.

The District Court held that in so doing the Commission violated § 556(d) of the Administrative Procedure Act, and it was on this basis that it set aside the order of the Commission.

II. APPLICABILITY OF ADMINISTRATIVE PROCEDURE ACT

In United States v. Allegheny-Ludlum Steel Corp., supra, we held that the language of § 1(14)(a) of the Interstate Commerce Act authorizing the Commission to act "after hearing" was not the equivalent of a requirement that a rule be made "on the record after opportunity for an agency hearing" as the latter term is used in § 553(c) of the Administrative Procedure Act.[2] Since the 1966 amendment to § 1(14)

2. [Ed.] The Allegheny-Ludlum case involved "car service rules" promulgated by the ICC which imposed a general requirement that unloaded freight cars be returned in the direction of the owning railroad. Most of Justice Rehnquist's unanimous opinion dealt with the railroads' contention that the rules were not reasonable and therefore were substantively invalid. His opinion also rejected the argument that the rules were procedurally defective:

". . . Appellees claim that the Commission's procedure here departed from the provisions of 5 U.S.C. §§ 556 and 557 of the Act. Those sections, however, govern a rule-making proceeding only when 5 U.S.C. § 553 so requires. The latter section, dealing generally with rule-making, makes applicable the provisions of §§ 556 and 557 only 'when rules are required by statute to be made on the record after opportunity for an agency hearing. . . . ' The Esch Act, authorizing the Commission 'after hearing, on a complaint or upon its own initiative without complaint, [to] establish

reasonable rules, regulations, and practices with respect to car service . . . .' 49 U.S.C. § 1(14)(a), does not require that such rules 'be made on the record.' 5 U.S.C. § 553. That distinction is determinative for this case. 'A good deal of significance lies in the fact that some statutes do expressly require determinations on the record' 2 K. Davis, Administrative Law Treatise, § 13.08 p. 225 (1958). Sections 556 and 557 need be applied 'only where the agency statute, in addition to providing a hearing, prescribes explicitly that it be "on the record".' Siegel v. Atomic Energy Commission, 400 F.2d 778, 785 (1968); Joseph E. Seagram & Sons Inc. v. Dillon, 311 F.2d 497, 500 n. 9 (1965). Cf. First National Bank of McKeesport v. First Federal Savings and Loan Assn., 225 F.2d 33 (1955). We do not suggest that only the precise words 'on the record' in the applicable statute will suffice to make §§ 556 and 557 applicable to rulemaking proceedings, but we do hold that the language of the Esch Car Service Rules Act is insufficient to invoke these sections.

(a), under which the Commission was here proceeding, does not by its terms add to the hearing requirement contained in the earlier language, the same result should obtain here unless that amendment contains language that is tantamount to such a requirement. Appellees contend that such language is found in the provisions of that Act requiring that:

> [T]he Commission shall give consideration to the national level of ownership of such type of freight car and to other factors affecting the adequacy of the national freight car supply, and shall, on the basis of such consideration, determine whether compensation should be computed. . . .

While this language is undoubtedly a mandate to the Commission to consider the factors there set forth in reaching any conclusion as to imposition of per diem incentive charges, it adds to the hearing requirements of the section neither expressly nor by implication. We know of no reason to think that an administrative agency in reaching a decision cannot accord consideration to factors such as those set forth in the 1966 amendment by means other than a trial-type hearing or the presentation of oral argument by the affected parties. Congress by that amendment specified necessary components of the ultimate decision, but it did not specify the method by which the Commission should acquire information about those components.

Both of the district courts that reviewed this order of the Commission concluded that its proceedings were governed by the stricter requirements of §§ 556 and 557 of the Administrative Procedure Act, rather than by the provisions of § 553 alone.[3] The conclusion of the District Court for the Middle District of Florida, which we here review, was based on the assumption that the language in § 1(14)(a) of the Interstate Commerce Act requiring rulemaking under that section to be done "after hearing" was the equivalent of a statutory requirement that the rule "be made on the record after opportunity for an agency hearing." Such an assumption is inconsistent with our decision in Allegheny-Ludlum, supra.

"Because the proceedings under review were an exercise of legislative rulemaking power rather than adjudicatory hearings as in Wong Yang Sung v. McGrath, 339 U.S. 33 (1950), and Ohio Bell Telephone Co. v. Public Utilities Comm'n, 301 U.S. 292 (1937); and because 49 U.S.C. § 1(14)(a) does not require a determination 'on the record' the provisions of 5 U.S.C. §§ 556, 557, were inapplicable."

3. Both district court opinions were handed down before our decision in United States v. Allegheny-Ludlum Steel Corp., 406 U.S. 742 (1972). . . .

The dissenting opinion of Mr. Justice Douglas relies in part on indications by the Commission that it proposed to apply the more stringent standards of §§ 556 and 557 of the Administrative Procedure Act to these proceedings. This Act is not legislation that the Interstate Commerce Commission, or any other single agency, has primary responsibility for administering. An agency interpretation involving, at least in part, the provisions of that Act does not carry the weight, in ascertaining the intent of Congress, that an interpretation by an agency "charged with the responsibility" of administering a particular statute does.

Moreover, since any agency is free under the Act to accord litigants appearing before it more procedural rights than the Act requires, the fact that an agency may choose to proceed under §§ 556 and 557 does not carry the necessary implication that the agency felt it was required to do so.

The District Court for the Eastern District of New York reached the same conclusion by a somewhat different line of reasoning. That court felt that because § 1(14)(a) of the Interstate Commerce Act had required a "hearing," and because that section was originally enacted in 1917, Congress was probably thinking in terms of a "hearing" such as that described in the opinion of this Court in the roughly contemporaneous case of ICC v. Louisville & Nashville R. Co., 227 U.S. 88, 93 (1913). The ingredients of the "hearing" were there said to be that "[a]ll parties must be fully apprised of the evidence submitted or to be considered, and must be given opportunity to cross-examine witnesses, to inspect documents and to offer evidence in explanation or rebuttal." Combining this view of congressional understanding of the term "hearing" with comments by the Chairman of the Commission at the time of the adoption of the 1966 legislation regarding the necessity for "hearings," that court concluded that Congress had in effect, required that these proceedings be "on the record after opportunity for an agency hearing" within the meaning of § 553(c) of the Administrative Procedure Act.

Insofar as this conclusion is grounded on the belief that the language "after hearing" of § 1(14)(a), without more, would trigger the applicability of §§ 556 and 557, it, too, is contrary to our decision in Allegheny-Ludlum, supra. The District Court observed that it was "rather hard to believe that the last sentence of § 553(c) was directed only to the few legislative sports where the words 'on the record' or their equivalent had found their way into the statute book." 318 F.Supp., at 496. This is, however, the language which Congress used, and since there are statutes on the books that do use these very words, see, e.g., the Fulbright Amendment to the Walsh-Healey Act, 41 U.S.C. § 43a, and 21 U.S.C. § 371(e)(3), the regulations provision of the Food and Drug Act, adherence to that language cannot be said to render the provision nugatory or ineffectual. We recognized in Allegheny-Ludlum that the actual words "on the record" and "after . . . hearing" used in § 553 were not words of art, and that other statutory language having the same meaning could trigger the provisions of §§ 556 and 557 in rulemaking proceedings. But we adhere to our conclusion, expressed in that case, that the phrase "after hearing" in § 1(14)(a) of the Interstate Commerce Act does not have such an effect.

III. "HEARING" REQUIREMENT OF § 1(14)(A) OF THE INTERSTATE COMMERCE ACT

Inextricably intertwined with the hearing requirement of the Administrative Procedure Act in this case is the meaning to be given to the language "after hearing" in § 1(14)(a) of the Interstate Commerce Act. Appellees, both here and in the court below, contend that the Commission procedure here fell short of that mandated by the "hearing" requirement of § 1(14)(a), even though it may have satisfied § 553 of the Administrative Procedure Act. The Administrative Procedure Act states that none of its provisions "limit or repeal additional requirements imposed by statute or otherwise recognized by law." 5 U.S.C. § 559. Thus, even though the Commission was not required to comply with §§ 556 and 557 of that Act, it was required to accord the "hearing" specified in § 1(14)(a) of the Interstate Commerce Act. Though the District Court did not pass on this contention, it is so closely related to the claim based on the Administrative Procedure Act that we proceed to decide it now.

If we were to agree with the reasoning of the District Court for the Eastern District of New York with respect to the type of hearing required by the Interstate Commerce Act, the Commission's action might well violate those requirements, even though it was consistent with the requirements of the Administrative Procedure Act.

The term "hearing" in its legal context undoubtedly has a host of meanings. Its meaning undoubtedly will vary, depending on whether it is used in the context of a rulemaking-type proceeding or in the context of a proceeding devoted to the adjudication of particular disputed facts. It is by no means apparent what the drafters of the Esch Car Service Act of 1917, which became the first part of § 1(14)(a) of the Interstate Commerce Act, meant by the term. Such an intent would surely be an ephemeral one if, indeed, Congress in 1917 had in mind anything more specific than the language it actually used, for none of the parties refer to any legislative history that would shed light on the intended meaning of the words "after hearing." What is apparent, though, is that the term was used in granting authority to the Commission to make rules and regulations of a prospective nature.

. . .

Under these circumstances, confronted with a grant of substantive authority made after the Administrative Procedure Act was enacted, we think that reference to that Act, in which Congress devoted itself exclusively to questions such as the nature and scope of hearings, is a satisfactory basis for determining what is meant by the term "hearing" used in another statute. Turning to that Act, we are convinced that the term "hearing" as used therein does not necessarily embrace either the right to present evidence orally and to cross-examine opposing witnesses, or the right to present oral argument to the agency's decisionmaker.

Section 553 excepts from its requirements rulemaking devoted to "interpretative rules, general statements of policy, or rules of agency organization, procedure, or practice," and rulemaking "when the agency for good cause finds . . . that notice and public procedure thereon are impracticable, unnecessary, or contrary to the public interest." This exception does not apply, however, "when notice or hearing is required by statute"; in those cases, even though interpretative rulemaking be involved, the requirements of § 553 apply. But since these requirements themselves do not mandate any oral presentation, see Allegheny-Ludlum, supra, it cannot be doubted that a statute that requires a "hearing" prior to rulemaking may in some circumstances be satisfied by procedures that meet only the standards of § 553. . . .

Similarly, even where the statute requires that the rulemaking procedure take place "on the record after opportunity for an agency hearing," thus triggering the applicability of § 556, subsection (d) provides that the agency may proceed by the submission of all or part of the evidence in written form if a party will not be "prejudiced thereby." Again, the Act makes it plain that a specific statutory mandate that the proceedings take place on the record after hearing may be satisfied in some circumstances by evidentiary submission in written form only.

We think this treatment of the term "hearing" in the Administrative Procedure Act affords a sufficient basis for concluding that the requirement of a "hearing" contained in § 1(14)(a), in a situation where the Commission was acting under the 1966 statutory rulemaking authority that Congress had conferred upon it, did not by its own force require the Commission either to hear oral testimony, to permit cross-examination of Commission witnesses, or to hear oral argument. Here, the Commission promulgated a tentative draft of an order, and accorded all interested parties 60 days in which to file statements of position, submissions of evidence, and other relevant observations. The parties had fair notice of exactly what the Commission proposed to do, and were given an opportunity to comment, to object, or to make some other form of written submission. The final order of the Commission indicates that it gave consideration to the statements of the two appellees here. Given the "open-ended" nature of the proceedings, and the Commission's announced willingness to consider proposals for modification after operating experience had been acquired, we think the hearing requirement of § 1(14)(a) of the Act was met.

Appellee railroads cite a number of our previous decisions dealing in some manner with the right to a hearing in an administrative proceeding. Although appellees have asserted no claim of constitutional deprivation in this proceeding, some of the cases they rely upon expressly speak in constitutional terms, while others are less than clear as to whether they depend upon the Due Process Clause of the Fifth and Fourteenth Amendments to the Constitution, or upon generalized principles of administrative law formulated prior to the adoption of the Administrative Procedure Act.

Morgan v. United States, 304 U.S. 1 (1938), is cited in support of appellees' contention that the Commission's proceedings were fatally deficient. That opinion describes the proceedings there involved as "quasi-judicial," id., at 14, and thus presumably distinct from a rulemaking proceeding such as that engaged in by the Commission here. But since the order of the Secretary of Agriculture there challenged did involve a form of ratemaking, the case bears enough resemblance to the facts of this case to warrant further examination of appellees' contention. The administrative procedure in Morgan was held to be defective primarily because the persons who were to be affected by the Secretary's order were found not to have been adequately apprised of what the Secretary proposed to do prior to the time that he actually did it. . . .

The proceedings before the Secretary of Agriculture had been initiated by a notice of inquiry into the reasonableness of the rates in question, and the individuals being regulated suffered throughout the proceeding from its essential formlessness. The Court concluded that this formlessness denied the individuals subject to regulation the "full hearing" that the statute had provided.

Assuming, *arguendo,* that the statutory term "full hearing" does not differ significantly from the hearing requirement of § 1(14)(a), we do not believe that the proceedings of the Interstate Commerce Commission before us suffer from the defect found to be fatal in Morgan. Though the initial notice of the proceeding by no means set out in detail what the Commission proposed to do, its tentative conclusions and order of December 1969, could scarcely have been more explicit or detailed. All interested parties were given 60 days following the issuance of these tentative findings and order in which to make appropriate objections. Appellees were "fairly advised" of exactly what the Commission proposed to do sufficiently in advance of the entry of the final order to give them adequate time to formulate and to present objections to the Commission's proposal. Morgan, therefore, does not aid appellees.

ICC v. Louisville & Nashville R. Co., 227 U.S. 88 (1913), involved what the Court there described as a "quasi-judicial" proceeding of a quite different nature from the one we review here. The provisions of the Interstate Commerce Act, as amended, and of the Hepburn Act, in effect at the time that case was decided, left to the railroad carriers the "primary right to make rates," 227 U.S., at 92, but granted to the Commission the authority to set them aside, if after hearing, they were shown to be unreasonable. The proceeding before the Commission in that case had been instituted by the New Orleans Board of Trade complaint that certain class and commodity rates charged by the Louisville & Nashville Railroad from New Orleans to other points were unfair, unreasonable, and discriminatory. The type of proceeding there, in which the Commission adjudicated a complaint by a shipper that specified rates set by a carrier were unreasonable, was sufficiently different from the nationwide incentive payments ordered to be made by all railroads in this proceeding so as to make the Louisville & Nashville opinion inapplicable in the case presently before us.

The basic distinction between rulemaking and adjudication is illustrated by this Court's treatment of two related cases under the Due Process Clause of the Fourteenth Amendment. [The Court restated Londoner v. Denver and Bi-Metallic Investment Co. v. State Board of Equalization.]

Later decisions have continued to observe the distinction adverted to in Bi-Metallic Investment Co., supra. In Ohio Bell Telephone Co. v. Public Utilities Comm'n, 301 U.S. 292, 304–305 (1937), the Court noted the fact that the administrative proceeding there involved was designed to require the utility to refund previously collected rate charges. The Court held that in such a proceeding the agency could not, consistently with due process, act on the basis of undisclosed evidence that was never made a part of the record before the agency. The case is thus more akin to Louisville & Nashville R. Co., supra, than it is to this case. FCC v. WJR, 337 U.S. 265 (1949), established that there was no across-the-board constitutional right to oral argument in every administrative proceeding regardless of its nature. While the line dividing them may not always be a bright one, these decisions represent a recognized distinction in administrative law between proceedings for the purpose of promulgating policy-type rules or standards, on the one hand, and proceedings designed to adjudicate disputed facts in particular cases on the other.

Here, the incentive payments proposed by the Commission in its tentative order, and later adopted in its final order, were applicable across the board to all of the common carriers by railroad subject to the Interstate Commerce Act. No effort was made to single out any particular railroad for special consideration based on its own peculiar circumstances. Indeed, one of the objections of appellee Florida East Coast was that it and other terminating carriers should have been treated differently from the generality of the railroads.[4] But the fact that the order may in its effects have been thought more disadvantageous by some railroads than by others does not change its generalized nature. Though the Commission obviously relied on factual inferences as a basis for its order, the source of these factual inferences was apparent to anyone who read the order of December 1969. The factual inferences were used in the formulation of a basically legislative-type judgment, for prospective application only, rather than in adjudicating a particular set of disputed facts.

The Commission's procedure satisfied both the provisions of § 1(14)(a) of the Interstate Commerce Act and of the Administrative Procedure Act, and were not inconsistent with prior decisions of this Court. We, therefore, reverse the judgment of the District Court, and remand the case so that it may consider those contentions of the parties that are not disposed of by this opinion.

It is so ordered.

MR. JUSTICE POWELL took no part in the consideration or decision of this case.

MR. JUSTICE DOUGLAS, with whom MR. JUSTICE STEWART concurs, dissenting.

[The dissenting opinion of Justice Douglas, with whom Justice Stewart concurred, is omitted. Justice Douglas urged that it was not "within our traditional concepts of due process to allow an administrative agency to saddle anyone with a new rate, charge, or fee without a full hearing [including] the right to present oral testimony, cross examine witnesses, and to present oral argument"; that sections 556 and 557 were applicable; and that the provision in section 556(d) authorizing submission of evidence in written form did not apply, because the railroads were "prejudiced" by the Commission's failure to

---

4. [Ed.] The action taken by the ICC related only to standard box cars, and did not reach the more expensive refrigerated box cars needed for shipment of Florida produce but not for many shipments in the return direction. Thus Florida East Coast not only faced a special burden as a termi-nating carrier of "turning around" cars coming to it from elsewhere in the country; but the cars in which it was most interested and in which it had most heavily invested, would not be speeded back to it, in return.

provide a proper hearing. United States v. Allegheny-Ludlum Steel Corp. was distinguished on the ground that "unlike those we considered in Allegheny-Ludlum, these rules involve the creation of a new financial liability."]

NOTES

(1) In Incentive Per Diem Charges—1968, Ex parte No. 252 (Sub. No. 1), 337 I.C.C. 217, 219 (1970), the Commission said, in part:

No party has been prejudiced by the submission here of all the evidence in written form; and the verified statements and the replies thereto received by this agency accord the parties a hearing under section 556 of that act.

(2) In 1947, shortly after the APA was enacted, the Department of Justice, primarily for the benefit of other government agencies, prepared an Attorney General's Manual on the Administrative Procedure Act. This manual has since been described by Justice Rehnquist (in the Vermont Yankee case reproduced within) as "a contemporaneous interpretation" of the APA to which the Court has "given some deference . . . because of the role played by the Department of Justice in drafting the legislation." Here is what the manual had to say about the "Florida East Coast Railway" problem:

"*Formal rule making.* Section 4(b) [i.e., 5 U.S.C., section 553(c)] provides that 'Where rules are required by statute to be made on the record after opportunity for an agency hearing, the requirements of sections 7 [i.e., section 556] and 8 [i.e., section 557] shall apply in place of the provisions of this subsection.' Thus, where a rule is required by some other statute to be issued on the basis of a record after opportunity for an agency hearing, the public rule making proceedings must consist of hearing and decision in accordance with sections 7 and 8. . . .

"Statutes rarely require hearings prior to the issuance of rules of general applicability. Such requirements, where they exist, appear in radically different contexts. The Federal Food, Drug and Cosmetic Act (21 U.S.C. 801) is almost unique in that it specifically provides that agency action issuing, amending or repealing specified classes of substantive rules may be taken only after notice and hearing, and that 'The Administrator shall base his order only on substantial evidence of record at the hearing and shall set forth as part of the order detailed findings of fact on which the order is based.' Upon review in a circuit court of appeals, a transcript of the record is filed, and 'the findings of the Administrator as to the facts, if supported by substantial evidence, shall be conclusive' (21 U.S.C. 871). It is clear that such rules are 'required by statute to be made on the record after opportunity for an agency hearing'. . . .

"Statutes authorizing agencies to prescribe future rates (i.e., rules of either general or particular applicability) for public utilities and common carriers typically require that such rates be established only after an opportunity for a hearing before the agency. Such statutes rarely specify in terms that the agency action must be taken on the basis of the 'record' developed in the hearing. However, where rates or prices are established by an agency after a hearing required by statute, the agencies themselves and the courts have long assumed that the agency's action must be based upon the evidence adduced at the hearing. Sometimes the requirement of decision on the record is readily inferred from other statutory provisions defining judicial review. . . .

"The Interstate Commerce Commission and the Secretary of Agriculture may, after hearing, prescribe rates for carriers and stockyard agencies, respectively. Both types of rate orders are reviewable under the Urgent Deficiencies Act of 1913 (28 U.S.C. 47). Nothing in the Interstate Commerce Act, the Packers and Stockyards Act, or the Urgent Deficiencies Act requires in terms that such rate orders be 'made on the record', or provides for the filing of a transcript of the administrative record with the reviewing court, or defines the scope of judicial review. However, both of these agencies and the courts have long assumed that such rate orders must be based upon the record made in the hearing; furthermore, it has long been the practice under the Urgent Deficiencies Act to review such orders on the basis of the administrative record which is submitted to the reviewing court. It appears, therefore, that rules (as defined in section 2(c)) which are issued after a hearing required by statute, and which are reviewable under the Urgent Deficiencies Act on the basis of the evidence adduced at the agency hearing, must be regarded as 'required by statute to be made on the record after opportunity for an agency hearing'.

"With respect to the types of rule making discussed above, the statutes not only specifically require the agencies to hold hearings but also, specifically, or by clear implication, or by established administrative and judicial construction, require such rules to be formulated upon the basis of the evidentiary record made in the hearing. In these situations, the public rule making procedures required by section 4(b) will consist of a hearing conducted in accordance with sections 7 and 8.

"There are other statutes which require agencies to hold hearings before issuing rules, but contain no language from which the further requirement of decision 'on the record' can be inferred, nor any provision for judicial review on the record. . . . For example, the Federal Seed Act (7 U.S.C. 1561) simply provides that 'prior to the promulgation of any rule or regulation under this chapter, due notice shall be given by publication in the Federal Register of intention to promulgate and the time and place of a public hearing to be held with reference thereto, and no rule or regulation may be promulgated until after such hearing'. . . . In this type of statute, there is no requirement, express or implied, that rules be formulated 'on the record'.

"There is persuasive legislative history to the effect that the Congress did not intend sections 7 and 8 to apply to rule making where the substantive statute merely required a hearing. In 1941, a subcommittee of the Senate Committee on the Judiciary held hearings on S. 674 (77th Cong., 1st sess.) and other administrative procedure bills. Section 209(d) of S. 674 provided with respect to rule making that 'where legislation specifically requires the holding of hearings prior to the making of rules, formal rulemaking hearings shall be held'. Mr. Ashley Sellers, testifying on behalf of the Department of Agriculture, called the subcommittee's attention to the fact that in various statutes, such as the Federal Seed Act, in which the Congress had required hearings to be held prior to the issuance of rules, the obvious purpose 'was simply to require that the persons interested in the proposed rule should be permitted to express their views'. Mr. Sellers drew a sharp distinction between such hearing requirements and the formal rule making requirements of the Federal Food, Drug and Cosmetic Act. Since this situation was thus specifically called to the subcommittee's attention, it is a legitimate inference that with respect to rule making the present dual requirement, i.e., 'after opportunity for an agency hearing' *and* 'on the record', was intended to avoid the application of formal procedural requirements in cases where the Congress intended only to provide an opportunity for the expression of views."

(3) Acting as a consultant to the Administrative Conference of the United States, Professor Robert W. Hamilton studied the functioning of agencies which administered statutes that required rules to be made on the record after opportunity for agency hearing. He concluded:

"The actual agency experience with these procedural requirements raises serious doubts about their desirability. At best, some agencies have learned to live with them, even though preferable procedures are probably available. At worst, these procedures have warped regulatory programs or resulted in virtual abandonment of them. It is surprising to discover that most agencies required to conduct formal hearings in connection with rulemaking in fact did not do so during the previous five years. . . . Thus, the primary impact of these procedural requirements is often not, as one might otherwise have expected, the testing of agency assumptions by cross-examination, or the testing of agency conclusions by courts on the basis of substantial evidence of record. Rather these procedures either cause the abandonment of the program (as in the Department of Labor), the development of techniques to reach the same regulatory goal but without a hearing (as FDA is now trying to do), or the promulgation of noncontroversial regulations by a process of negotiation and compromise (as FDA historically has done and Interior is encouraged to do). In practice, therefore, the principal effect of imposing rulemaking on a record has often been the dilution of the regulatory process rather than the protection of persons from arbitrary action. . . .

"[It] seems desirable to recommend in fairly general terms that agencies should seek to substitute less formal procedures for formal evidentiary hearings, to the extent it is practical to do so under current statutory requirements, and to recommend, again in general terms, that, where appropriate, agencies seek legislative amendments to permit the use of such procedures. The foregoing study reveals that trial-type procedures work best in connection with narrowly defined factual issues. The basic problem with formal rulemaking on a record is that it mandates such procedures in broad classes of proceedings, without regard to the existence of such issues. Ultimately, therefore, the goal should be the complete elimination of mandatory trial-type procedures in rulemaking." R.W. Hamilton, Procedures for the Adoption of Rules of General Applicability: The Need for Procedural Innovation in Administrative Rulemaking, 60 Calif.L.Rev. 1276, 1312–1313 (1972).

(4) For a careful, critical discussion of the principal case, see N.L. Nathanson, Probing the Mind of the Administrator: Hearing Variations and Standards of Judicial Review Under the Administrative Procedure Act and Other Federal Statutes, 75 Col.L.Rev. 721 (1975).

SEACOAST ANTI–POLLUTION LEAGUE v. COSTLE
United States Court of Appeals, First Circuit, 1978.
572 F.2d 872, cert. denied 439 U.S. 824 (1978).

Before COFFIN, CHIEF JUDGE, CAMPBELL and BOWNES, CIRCUIT JUDGES.

COFFIN, CHIEF JUDGE.   . . .

The Public Service Company of New Hampshire (PSCO) filed an application with the EPA for permission to discharge heated water into the Hampton-Seabrook Estuary which runs into the Gulf of Maine.
. . .

Section 301(a) of the Federal Water Pollution Control Act of 1972 (FWPCA) 33 U.S.C. § 1311(a), prohibits the discharge of any pollutant unless the discharger, the point source operator, has obtained an EPA permit. Heat is a pollutant. 33 U.S.C. § 1362(6). Section 301(b) directs the EPA to promulgate effluent limitations. The parties agree that the cooling system PSCO has proposed does not meet the EPA standards because PSCO would utilize a once-through open cycle system—the water would not undergo any cooling process before being returned to the sea. Therefore, in August, 1974, PSCO applied not only for a discharge permit under § 402 of the FWPCA, 33 U.S.C. § 1312, but also an exemption from the EPA standards pursuant to § 316 of the FWPCA, 33 U.S.C. § 1326. Under § 316(a) a point source operator who "after opportunity for public hearing, can demonstrate to the satisfaction of the Administrator" that the EPA's standards are "more stringent than necessary to assure the projection [sic] and propagation of a balanced, indigenous population of shellfish, fish, and wildlife in and on the body of water" may be allowed to meet a lower standard. Moreover, under § 316(b) the cooling water intake structure must "reflect the best technology available for minimizing adverse environmental impact."

[The Regional Administrator of the EPA denied PSCO's application. PSCO appealed to the Administrator of the EPA who reversed the Regional Administrator's decision. The Seacoast Anti-Pollution League and the Audubon Society of New Hampshire petitioned for review.]

Petitioners assert that the proceedings by which the EPA decided this case contravened certain provisions of the APA governing adjudicatory hearings, 5 U.S.C. §§ 554, 556, and 557. Respondents answer that the APA does not apply to proceedings held pursuant to § 316 or § 402 of the FWPCA, 33 U.S.C. §§ 1326, 1342.

The dispute centers on the meaning of the introductory phrases of § 554(a) of the APA: "This section applies . . . in every case of adjudication required by statute to be determined on the record after opportunity for an agency hearing. . . ." Both § 316(a) and § 402(a) (1) of the FWPCA provide for public hearings, but neither states that the hearing must be "on the record". We are now the third court of appeals to face this issue. The Ninth Circuit and the Seventh Circuit have each found that the APA does apply to proceedings pursuant to § 402. Marathon Oil Co. v. EPA, 564 F.2d 1253 (9th Cir.1977); United States Steel Corp. v. Train, 556 F.2d 822 (7th Cir.1977). We agree.

At the outset we reject the position of intervenor PSCO that the precise words "on the record" must be used to trigger the APA. The Supreme Court has clearly rejected such an extreme reading even in the context of rule making under § 553 of the APA. See United States v. Florida East Coast Ry. Co., 410 U.S. 224, 245 (1973); United States v. Allegheny-Ludlum Steel Corp., 406 U.S. 742, 757 (1972). Rather, we think that the resolution of this issue turns on the substantive nature of the hearing Congress intended to provide.

We begin with the nature of the decision at issue. The EPA Administrator must make specific factual findings about the effects of discharges from a specific point source. On the basis of these findings the Administrator must determine whether to grant a discharge permit to a specific applicant. Though general policy considerations may influence the decision, the decision will not make general policy. Only the rights of the specific applicant will be affected. "As the instant proceeding well demonstrates, the factual questions involved in the issuance of section 402 permits will frequently be sharply disputed. Adversarial hearings will be helpful, therefore, in guaranteeing both reasoned decisionmaking and meaningful judicial review. In summary, the proceedings below were conducted in order 'to adjudicate disputed facts in particular cases,' not 'for the purposes of promulgating policy-type rules or standards.'" Marathon Oil Co., supra at 1262.

This is exactly the kind of quasi-judicial proceeding for which the adjudicatory procedures of the APA were intended. As the Supreme Court has said, "Determination of questions of [the Administrative Procedure Act's] coverage may well be approached through consideration of its purposes as disclosed by its background." Wong Yang Sung v. McGrath, 339 U.S. 33, 36 (1950). One of the developments that prompted the APA was the "[m]ultiplication of federal administrative agencies and expansion of their functions to include adjudications which have serious impact on private rights." Id., 339 U.S. at 36–37. This is just such an adjudication. The panoply of procedural protections provided by the APA is necessary not only to protect the rights of an applicant for less stringent pollutant discharge limits, but is also needed to protect the public for whose benefit the very strict limitations have been enacted. If determinations such as the one at issue here are not made on the record, then the fate of the Hampton-Seabrook

Estuary could be decided on the basis of evidence that a court would never see or, what is worse, that a court could not be sure existed. We cannot believe that Congress would intend such a result.

Our holding does not render the opening phrases of § 554 of the APA meaningless. We are persuaded that their purpose was to exclude "governmental functions, such as the administration of loan programs, which traditionally have never been regarded as adjudicative in nature and as a rule have never been exercised through other than business procedures." Attorney General's Manual on the Administrative Procedure Act 40 (1947). Without some kind of limiting language, the broad sweep of the definition of "adjudication", defined principally as that which is not rule making, 5 U.S.C. § 551(6), (7), would include such ordinary procedures that do not require any kind of hearing at all. In short, we view the crucial part of the limiting language to be the requirement of a statutorily imposed hearing. We are willing to presume that, unless a statute otherwise specifies, an adjudicatory hearing subject to judicial review must be on the record. The legislative history of the APA [1] and its treatment in the courts [2] bear us out.

This rationale and conclusion also are supported by our holding in South Terminal Corp. v. EPA, 504 F.2d 646, 660 (1st Cir.1971) ("public hearing" not tantamount to "on the record"), and the other rule making cases cited to us for similar propositions.[3] The presumption in rule making cases is that formal, adjudicatory procedures are not necessary. A hearing serves a very different function in the rule making context. Witnesses may bring in new information or different points of view, but the agency's final decision need not reflect the public input. The witnesses are not the only source of the evidence on which the Administrator may base his factual findings. For these reasons, we place less importance on the absence of the words "on the record" in the adjudicatory context. "It is believed that with respect to adjudication the specific statutory requirement of a hearing, without anything more, carries with it the further requirement of decision on the basis of the evidence adduced at the hearing. With respect to rule making, it was concluded, supra, that a statutory provision that rules be issued after a hearing, without more, should not be construed as requiring agency action 'on the record', but rather as merely requiring an

1. For instance, one of the Senate documents explained the opening phrases of § 554 as follows: "Limiting application of the sections to those cases in which statutes require a hearing is particularly significant, because there are excluded the great mass of administrative routine as well as pensions, claims, and a variety of similar matters in which Congress has usually intentionally or traditionally refrained from requiring an administrative hearing. Senate Comparative Print of June 1945, p. 7 (Sen.Doc. p. 22)." Attorney General's Manual, supra, 41. We note that this document looks to whether or not an adjudicative hearing is provided, not to whether the hearing must be on the record. . . .

2. See, e.g., Wong Yang Sung v. McGrath, 339 U.S. 33, 50 (1950) (whether a hearing required by the Constitution triggers the APA); Citizens to Preserve Overton Park v. Volpe, 401 U.S. 402 (1971) (whether in the context of the particular statute a hearing is designed to produce a record that is to be the basis of agency action).

3. United States v. Florida East Coast Ry., supra; United States v. Allegheny-Ludlum Steel Corp., supra. The Supreme Court explicitly confined its holding to rule making cases.

opportunity for the expression of views. That conclusion was based on the legislative nature of rule making, from which it was inferred, unless a statute requires otherwise, that an agency hearing on proposed rules would be similar to a hearing before a legislative committee, with neither the legislature nor the agency being limited to the material adduced at the hearing. No such rationale applies to administrative adjudication. In fact, it is assumed that where a statute specifically provides for administrative adjudication (such as the suspension or revocation of a license) after opportunity for an agency hearing, *such specific requirement for a hearing ordinarily implies the further requirement of decision in accordance with evidence adduced at the hearing.* Of course, the foregoing discussion is inapplicable to any situation in which the legislative history or the context of the pertinent statute indicates a contrary congressional intent." Attorney General's Manual, supra, 42–43 (footnote and citation to statutory history omitted) (emphasis added). Here the statute certainly does not indicate that the determination need *not* be on the record, and we find no indication of a contrary congressional intent. Therefore, we will judge the proceedings below according to the standards set forth in §§ 554, 556, and 557 of the APA. . . .

NOTES

(1) When the court ruled on the particular procedural contentions at issue in the principal case, it remanded the proceeding to the EPA Administrator because (1) in considering some of PSCO's submissions without allowing cross-examination, the administrator had not made the determination required by the last sentence of 5 U.S.C. § 556(d); and because (2) a panel of agency experts which the Administrator consulted concerning thermal tolerances of marine wildlife based their analysis on extra-record information, which led the Administrator to do likewise, thus violating 5 U.S.C. § 556(e). The court's discussion of the later point is reprinted at page 834, below.

(2) R.J. PIERCE, JR., S.A. SHAPIRO, AND P.R. VERKUIL, ADMINISTRATIVE LAW AND PROCESS 300 (1985):

"The court's distinction [in Seacoast Anti-Pollution League] between rulemaking and adjudication makes good sense for two reasons. First, the general analogies reflected in the APA between rulemaking and legislating, on one side, and between adjudication and judicial trial, on the other, support the inference that Congress intended to require proceedings of a very different nature when it used an ambiguous term like hearing with reference to each.

"Second, the consequences of a holding that Congress did not intend to require trial-type procedures varies substantially, depending on whether that holding applies to a rulemaking or an adjudication."

(3) UNITED STATES LINES, INC. v. FEDERAL MARITIME COMMISSION, 584 F.2d 519 (D.C.Cir.1978). Section 15 of the Shipping Act requires common carriers by water to file with the FMC copies of all anticompetitive agreements. "The Commission shall by order, after notice and hearing, disapprove, cancel or modify any agreement . . . that it finds to be

unjustly discriminatory or unfair as between carriers . . . or to operate to the detriment of the commerce of the United States, or to be contrary to the public interest, or to be in violation of this chapter, and shall approve all other agreements." Agreements so approved are exempt from the antitrust laws.

Two carriers whose Joint Service Agreement had been approved by the FMC applied for approval of an amendment to permit a third carrier to become a party to the Agreement. This proposal was published in the Federal Register, and an opportunity was afforded interested persons to submit comments and requests for hearing. United States Lines, Inc. (USL), a competitor of the applicants, submitted comments and requested a hearing. The FMC did not grant a hearing but instead approved the immediate inclusion of the third carrier and ordered an investigation and hearing on the question whether the Joint Service Agreement (which was about to expire) should be extended. USL sought review contending in part that FMC's failure to comply with sections 556 and 557 of the APA required reversal. In rejecting this argument, Chief Judge Wright's opinion stated that although "what is involved here appears quasi-adjudicatory in nature [in that] the agency is required to adjudicate the rights of certain named parties to an exemption from the antitrust laws," section 15 does not require a hearing on the record after an opportunity for an agency hearing:

"The Shipping Act does not itself specify the type of hearing required prior to approval under Section 15; it states only that the Commission decision is to be made 'after notice and hearing.' 46 U.S.C. § 814 (1970). Petitioner has argued that the hearing provided by the FMC must comply with the procedural requirements of Sections 556 and 557 of the Administrative Procedure Act governing formal agency hearings. These provisions apply, by the terms of the APA, when a 'hearing on the record' is required by statute. 5 U.S.C. §§ 553(c), 554(c) (2) (1976). While the exact phrase 'on the record' is not an absolute prerequisite to application of the formal hearing requirements, the Supreme Court has made clear that these provisions do not apply unless Congress has clearly indicated that the 'hearing' required by statute must be a trial-type hearing on the record. See United States v. Florida East Coast R. Co., 410 U.S. 224, 234–238 (1973); United States v. Allegheny-Ludlum Steel Co., 406 U.S. 742, 756–758 (1972).

"In this case the Shipping Act itself does not provide for a hearing 'on the record,' and nothing in the terms of the statute or its legislative history indicates that a trial-type hearing, complete with all of the procedures specified in Sections 556 and 557, was intended in all Section 15 cases. Indeed, we have held before that there is room for agency flexibility in structuring Section 15 hearings in light of the circumstances of the case and the nature of the issues involved. 'The requirement of a hearing in a proceeding before an administrative agency may be satisfied by something less time-consuming than courtroom drama.' Marine Space Enclosures, Inc. v. FMC, supra, 420 F.2d at 589. Such flexibility is particularly important where, as is the case with Agreement 9902–5, the Commission sets certain issues for further investigation and trial-type hearing while granting approval of the agreement pendente lite. Clearly, if such approval could not be granted by the Commission on the basis of something less than a full trial-type hearing, the pendente lite authority would effectively be paralyzed.

"We conclude, therefore, that Section 15 hearings are not required by statute to be conducted in accordance with Sections 556 and 557 of the APA. The Commission thus enjoys substantial flexibility to structure the hearings it must provide depending on the nature of the case and the issues requiring resolution. But that freedom is not absolute. The Shipping Act does require that there be a 'hearing,' and that statutory requirement, like the requirement of comment in notice and comment rulemaking, imposes certain minimum constraints on the procedure followed by the agency." [1]

(4) Both the Seacoast Anti-Pollution League case and the United States Lines case continue to be cited by courts of appeals to support determinations concerning the coverage of section 554. For those who like to read tea-leaves from the top, Justice Brennan's apparently favorable treatment of the Seacoast Anti-Pollution League case in a footnote in Steadman v. SEC, 450 U.S. 91, 96–97 n. 13 (1981) can be consulted.

(5) Section 554(a) applies "in every case of adjudication required by statute to be determined on the record after opportunity for an agency hearing" etc. Seacoast Anti-Pollution League turned on the question what statutory language in a substantive statute is sufficient to satisfy this test. Can section 554 ever be made applicable to adjudication by some legal text other than a statute?

In WONG YANG SUNG v. MCGRATH, 339 U.S. 33, 50 (1950) (an excerpt from which appears at the beginning of this section), the Supreme Court thought it clear that Section 554 did not apply to "hearings which administrative agencies may hold by regulation, rule, custom, or special dispensation"; or, in short, to "hearings of less than statutory authority." The actual issue raised by the case, however, concerned a hearing "of more than statutory authority," a deportation hearing not expressly required by the Immigration Act but rather superimposed onto the deportation process by the due process clause of the Constitution. The Court held that section 554 did apply to deportation proceedings. "We would hardly attribute to Congress a purpose to be less scrupulous about the fairness of a hearing necessitated by the Constitution than one granted by it as a matter of expediency."

The Court's confidence about Congress' specific purposes was apparently misplaced, for the specific holding of Wong Yang Sung (that administrative law judges, rather than persons given other departmental duties, must be employed in deportation hearings) was promptly reversed by legislation. See Marcello v. Bonds, 349 U.S. 302 (1955). Wong Yang Sung continues to be cited for the general proposition that aliens have due process rights in deportation hearings. However, the

1. [Ed.] The case is also considered infra p. 929.

"due process explosion" of the 1970's, explored in Chapter IV below, has repeatedly required the Supreme Court and lower federal courts to say what procedures fairness requires for hearings necessitated by the Constitution, and these inquiries today are made without apparent regard to the federal or state character of the agency under an obligation to hear. In federal due process cases, that is, the APA is rarely consulted as a source of governing procedure. See Note, The Requirement of Formal Adjudication Under Section 5 of the Administrative Procedure Act, 12 Harv.J.Legis. 194 (1975). In practice, then, Wong Yang Sung appears to have fallen into obscurity, and the APA's prescriptions have been limited to those highly visible regulatory proceedings that seem to have been the focus of Congress' consideration in 1946. For an unusually self-conscious discussion, see Clardy v. Levi, 545 F.2d 1241 (9th Cir. 1976).

(6) The APA contains provisions which prescribe procedures for formal rulemaking (§§ 553, 556 and 557) and formal adjudication (§§ 554, 556 and 557); and section 553 sets forth requirements for informal rulemaking. But there is no comparable APA section which establishes procedures for informal adjudication. The Report of the Attorney General's Committee on Administrative Procedure (1941) devoted an entire chapter to "Informal Methods of Adjudication," and emphasized that "informal procedures constitute the vast bulk of administrative adjudication and are truly the lifeblood of the administrative process." Id. at 35. But the bill recommended by the Committee to implement "those of its principal recommendations . . . which it believes susceptible of legislative treatment," id. at 191, did not contain provisions to govern informal adjudication.

The omission was not accidental. The chairman of the Committee, Dean G. Acheson, stated in his testimony before the Subcommittee of the Senate Committee on the Judiciary: "We discovered that, in the working of Government, 92 to 94 percent of all of the cases are disposed of by informal administrative proceedings and only a small minority by actual formal proceedings. . . . Since it was true, as I have pointed out that the vast bulk of these proceedings are informal, it was perfectly clear to us that one of our objectives was not to formalize administrative procedure. You can do that quite easily just by insisting that every kind of procedure shall take a certain form. It was perfectly clear to us that that was not the thing to do; that that would not be of service to the citizen; that it would not be of service to the Government and it was an entirely futile thing to do so we had that negative at the start." Hearings Before Subcom. of Comm. on the Judic. on S.674, S.675 and S.918, 77th Cong. 1st Sess. 804 (1941).

Since there is no applicable APA model, the procedures governing informal adjudication by federal agencies will be those (1) established by the agencies in the exercise of their discretion, or (2) prescribed by statute, or (3) required by the Constitution, or (if this is a different category) (4) imposed by the judiciary. Aspects of these subjects are considered later in this volume.

Of course, once something is done, it may not seem so forbidding. The Model State Administrative Procedure Act does set out models for informal adjudication, see pages 1278ff. below; it may well be asked whether a statutory formulation is not better than the hodge-podge of "sources of the law" present in the federal system.

VERMONT YANKEE NUCLEAR POWER CORP. v. NATURAL RESOURCES DEFENSE COUNCIL, INC.

Supreme Court of the United States, 1978.
435 U.S. 519.

MR. JUSTICE REHNQUIST delivered the opinion of the Court.

In 1946, Congress enacted the Administrative Procedure Act, which as we have noted elsewhere was not only "a new, basic and comprehensive regulation of procedures in many agencies," Wong Yang Sung v. McGrath, 339 U.S. 33 (1950), but was also a legislative enactment which settled "long-continued and hard-fought contentions, and enacts a formula upon which opposing social and political forces have come to rest." Id., at 40. Section 4 of the Act, 5 U.S.C. § 553 (1976 ed.), dealing with rulemaking, requires in subsection (b) that "notice of proposed rule making shall be published in the Federal Register . . . ," describes the contents of that notice, and goes on to require in subsection (c) that after the notice the agency "shall give interested persons an opportunity to participate in the rule making through submission of written data, views, or arguments with or without opportunity for oral presentation. After consideration of the relevant matter presented, the agency shall incorporate in the rules adopted a concise general statement of their basis and purpose." Interpreting this provision of the Act in United States v. Allegheny-Ludlum Steel Corp., 406 U.S. 742 (1972), and United States v. Florida East Coast R. Co., 410 U.S. 224 (1973), we held that generally speaking this section of the Act established the maximum procedural requirements which Congress was willing to have the courts impose upon agencies in conducting rulemaking procedures.[1] Agencies are free to grant additional procedural rights in the exercise of their discretion, but reviewing courts are generally not free to impose them if the agencies have not chosen to grant them. This is not to say necessarily that there are no circumstances which would ever justify a court in overturning agency action because of a failure to employ procedures beyond those required by the statute. But such circumstances, if they exist, are extremely rare.

Even apart from the Administrative Procedure Act this Court has for more than four decades emphasized that the formulation of procedures was basically to be left within the discretion of the agencies to which Congress had confided the responsibility for substantive judg-

---

1. While there was division in this Court in United States v. Florida East Coast R. Co. with respect to the constitutionality of such an interpretation in a case involving ratemaking, which Mr. Justice Douglas and Mr. Justice Stewart felt was "adjudicatory" within the terms of the Act, the cases in the Court of Appeals for the District of Columbia Circuit which we review here involve rulemaking procedures in their most pristine sense.

ments. In FCC v. Schreiber, 381 U.S. 279, 290 (1965), the Court explicated this principle, describing it as "an outgrowth of the congressional determination that administrative agencies and administrators will be familiar with the industries which they regulate and will be in a better position than federal courts or Congress itself to design procedural rules adapted to the peculiarities of the industry and the tasks of the agency involved."

. . .

It is in the light of this background of statutory and decisional law that we granted certiorari to review two judgments of the Court of Appeals for the District of Columbia Circuit because of our concern that they had seriously misread or misapplied this statutory and decisional law cautioning reviewing courts against engrafting their own notions of proper procedures upon agencies entrusted with substantive functions by Congress. We conclude that the Court of Appeals has done just that in these cases, and we therefore remand them to it for further proceedings. . . .

I

A

Under the Atomic Energy Act of 1954, as amended, 42 U.S.C. § 2011 et seq., the Atomic Energy Commission [2] was given broad regulatory authority over the development of nuclear energy. Under the terms of the Act, a utility seeking to construct and operate a nuclear power plant must obtain a separate permit or license at both the construction and the operation stage of the project. In order to obtain the construction permit, the utility must file a preliminary safety analysis report, an environmental report, and certain information regarding the antitrust implications of the proposed project. This application then undergoes exhaustive review by the Commission's staff and by the Advisory Committee on Reactor Safeguards (ACRS), a group of distinguished experts in the field of atomic energy. Both groups submit to the Commission their own evaluations, which then become part of the record of the utility's application. The Commission staff also undertakes the review required by the National Environmental Policy Act of 1969 (NEPA), 42 U.S.C. § 4321 et seq., and prepares a draft environmental impact statement, which, after being circulated for comment, is revised and becomes a final environmental impact statement. Thereupon a three-member Atomic Safety and Licensing Board conducts a public adjudicatory hearing, and reaches a decision which can be appealed to the Atomic Safety and Licensing Appeal Board, and currently, in the Commission's discretion, to the Commission itself. The final agency decision may be appealed to the courts of appeals. The same sort of process occurs when the utility applies for a license to

2. The licensing and regulatory functions of the Atomic Energy Commission (AEC) were transferred to the Nuclear Regulatory Commission (NRC) by the Energy Reorganization Act of 1974, 42 U.S.C. § 5801 et seq. (1970 ed., Supp. V). Hereinafter both the AEC and NRC will be referred to as the Commission.

operate the plant, except that a hearing need only be held in contested cases and may be limited to the matters in controversy.

These cases arise from two separate decisions of the Court of Appeals for the District of Columbia Circuit. In the first, the court remanded a decision of the Commission to grant a license to petitioner Vermont Yankee Nuclear Power Corp. to operate a nuclear power plant. Natural Resources Defense Council v. NRC, 178 U.S.App.D.C. 336, 547 F.2d 633 (1976). In the second, the court remanded a decision of that same agency to grant a permit to petitioner Consumers Power Co. to construct two pressurized water nuclear reactors to generate electricity and steam. Aeschliman v. NRC, 178 U.S.App.D.C. 325, 547 F.2d 622 (1976).[3]

B

In December 1967, after the mandatory adjudicatory hearing and necessary review, the Commission granted petitioner Vermont Yankee a permit to build a nuclear power plant in Vernon, Vt. Thereafter, Vermont Yankee applied for an operating license. Respondent Natural Resources Defense Council (NRDC) objected to the granting of a license, however, and therefore a hearing on the application commenced on August 10, 1971. Excluded from consideration at the hearings, over NRDC's objection, was the issue of the environmental effects of operations to reprocess fuel or dispose of wastes resulting from the reprocessing operations.[4] This ruling was affirmed by the Appeal Board in June 1972.

In November 1972, however, the Commission, making specific reference to the Appeal Board's decision with respect to the Vermont Yankee license, instituted rulemaking proceedings "that would specifically deal with the question of consideration of environmental effects associated with the uranium fuel cycle in the individual cost-benefit analyses for light water cooled nuclear power reactors." The notice of proposed rulemaking offered two alternatives, both predicated on a report prepared by the Commission's staff entitled Environmental Survey of the Nuclear Fuel Cycle. The first would have required no quantitative evaluation of the environmental hazards of fuel reprocessing or disposal because the Environmental Survey had found them to be slight. The second would have specified numerical values for the environmental impact of this part of the fuel cycle, which values would then be incorporated into a table, along with the other relevant factors, to determine the overall cost-benefit balance for each operating license.

---

3. [Ed.] Both decisions were written by Chief Judge David Bazelon.

4. The nuclear fission which takes place in light-water nuclear reactors apparently converts its principal fuel, uranium, into plutonium, which is itself highly radioactive but can be used as reactor fuel if separated from the remaining uranium and radioactive waste products. Fuel reprocessing refers to the process necessary to recapture usable plutonium. Waste disposal, at the present stage of technological development, refers to the storage of the very long lived and highly radioactive waste products until they detoxify sufficiently that they no longer present an environmental hazard. There are presently no physical or chemical steps which render this waste less toxic, other than simply the passage of time.

Much of the controversy in this case revolves around the procedures used in the rulemaking hearing which commenced in February 1973. In a supplemental notice of hearing the Commission indicated that while discovery or cross-examination would not be utilized, the Environmental Survey would be available to the public before the hearing along with the extensive background documents cited therein. All participants would be given a reasonable opportunity to present their position and could be represented by counsel if they so desired. Written and, time permitting, oral statements would be received and incorporated into the record. All persons giving oral statements would be subject to questioning by the Commission. At the conclusion of the hearing, a transcript would be made available to the public and the record would remain open for 30 days to allow the filing of supplemental written statements. More than 40 individuals and organizations representing a wide variety of interests submitted written comments. On January 17, 1973, the Licensing Board held a planning session to schedule the appearance of witnesses and to discuss methods for compiling a record. The hearing was held on February 1 and 2, with participation by a number of groups, including the Commission's staff, the United States Environmental Protection Agency, a manufacturer of reactor equipment, a trade association from the nuclear industry, a group of electric utility companies, and a group called Consolidated National Intervenors which represented 79 groups and individuals including respondent NRDC.

After the hearing, the Commission's staff filed a supplemental document for the purpose of clarifying and revising the Environmental Survey. Then the Licensing Board forwarded its report to the Commission without rendering any decision. The Licensing Board identified as the principal procedural question the propriety of declining to use full formal adjudicatory procedures. The major substantive issue was the technical adequacy of the Environmental Survey.

In April 1974, the Commission issued a rule which adopted the second of the two proposed alternatives described above. The Commission also approved the procedures used at the hearing,[5] and indicated that the record, including the Environmental Survey, provided an "adequate data base for the regulation adopted." Finally, the Commission ruled that to the extent the rule differed from the Appeal Board decisions in Vermont Yankee "those decisions have no further precedential significance," but that since "the environmental effects of the uranium fuel cycle have been shown to be relatively insignificant,

---

5. The Commission stated:

"In our view, the procedures adopted provide a more than adequate basis for formulation of the rule we adopted. All parties were fully heard. Nothing offered was excluded. The record does not indicate that any evidentiary material would have been received under different procedures. Nor did the proponent of the strict 'adjudicatory' approach make an offer of proof—or even remotely suggest—what

substantive matters it would develop under different procedures. In addition, we note that 11 documents including the Survey were available to the parties several weeks before the hearing, and the Regulatory staff, though not requested to do so, made available various drafts and handwritten notes. Under all of the circumstances, we conclude that adjudicatory type procedures were not warranted here."

. . . . it is unnecessary to apply the amendment to applicant's environmental reports submitted prior to its effective date or to Final Environmental Statements for which Draft Environmental Statements have been circulated for comment prior to the effective date."

Respondents appealed from both the Commission's adoption of the rule and its decision to grant Vermont Yankee's license to the Court of Appeals for the District of Columbia Circuit.

C

[The description of the Consumers Power Co. case is omitted.]

D

With respect to the challenge of Vermont Yankee's license, the court first ruled that in the absence of effective rulemaking proceedings,[6] the Commission must deal with the environmental impact of fuel reprocessing and disposal in individual licensing proceedings. The court then examined the rulemaking proceedings and, despite the fact that it appeared that the agency employed all the procedures required by 5 U.S.C. § 553 (1976 ed.) and more, the court determined the proceedings to be inadequate and overturned the rule. Accordingly, the Commission's determination with respect to Vermont Yankee's license was also remanded for further proceedings.[7]

[The description of the Court of Appeals' reasons for remanding in the Consumers Power Co. case is omitted.]

II

A

Petitioner Vermont Yankee first argues that the Commission may grant a license to operate a nuclear reactor without any consideration of waste disposal and fuel reprocessing. We find, however, that this issue is no longer presented by the record in this case. The Commission does not contend that it is not required to consider the environ-

6. In the Court of Appeals no one questioned the Commission's authority to deal with fuel cycle issues by informal rulemaking as opposed to adjudication. Neither does anyone seriously question before this Court the Commission's authority in this respect.

7. After the decision of the Court of Appeals the Commission promulgated a new interim rule pending issuance of a final rule. 42 Fed.Reg. 13803 (1977). . . .

As we read the opinion of the Court of Appeals, its view that reviewing courts may in the absence of special circumstances justifying such a course of action impose additional procedural requirements on agency action raises questions of such significance in this area of the law as to warrant our granting certiorari and deciding the case. Since the vast majority of challenges to administrative agency action are brought to the Court of Appeals for the District of Columbia Circuit, the decision of that court in this case will serve as precedent for many more proceedings for judicial review of agency actions than would the decision of another Court of Appeals. Finally, this decision will continue to play a major role in the instant litigation regardless of the Commission's decision to press ahead with further rulemaking proceedings. . . .

mental impact of the spent fuel processes when licensing nuclear power plants. . . . Thus, at this stage of the proceedings the only question presented for review in this regard is whether the Commission may consider the environmental impact of the fuel processes when licensing nuclear reactors. In addition to the weight which normally attaches to the agency's determination of such a question, other reasons support the Commission's conclusion.

Vermont Yankee will produce annually well over 100 pounds of radioactive wastes, some of which will be highly toxic. The Commission itself, in a pamphlet published by its information office, clearly recognizes that these wastes "pose the most severe potential health hazard. . . . " Many of these substances must be isolated for anywhere from 600 to hundreds of thousands of years. It is hard to argue that these wastes do not constitute "adverse environmental effects which cannot be avoided should the proposal be implemented," or that by operating nuclear power plants we are not making "irreversible and irretrievable commitments of resources." . . . For these reasons we hold that the Commission acted well within its statutory authority when it considered the back end of the fuel cycle in individual licensing proceedings.

B

We next turn to the invalidation of the fuel cycle rule. But before determining whether the Court of Appeals reached a permissible result, we must determine exactly what result it did reach, and in this case that is no mean feat. Vermont Yankee argues that the court invalidated the rule because of the inadequacy of the procedures employed in the proceedings. Respondents, on the other hand, labeling petitioner's view of the decision a "straw man," argue to this Court that the court merely held that the record was inadequate to enable the reviewing court to determine whether the agency had fulfilled its statutory obligation. But we unfortunately have not found the parties' characterization of the opinion to be entirely reliable. . . .

After a thorough examination of the opinion itself, we conclude that while the matter is not entirely free from doubt, the majority of the Court of Appeals struck down the rule because of the perceived inadequacies of the procedures employed in the rulemaking proceedings. The court first determined the intervenors' primary argument to be "that the decision to preclude 'discovery or cross-examination' denied them a meaningful opportunity to participate in the proceedings as guaranteed by due process." The court then went on to frame the issue for decision thus:

> Thus, we are called upon to decide whether the procedures provided by the agency were sufficient to ventilate the issues.

The court conceded that absent extraordinary circumstances it is improper for a reviewing court to prescribe the procedural format an agency must follow, but it likewise clearly thought it entirely appropriate to "scrutinize the record as a whole to insure that genuine opportunities to participate in a meaningful way were provided. . . . " The court also refrained from actually ordering the agency to follow any specific procedures, but there is little doubt in our minds that the ineluctable mandate of the court's decision is that the procedures afforded during the hearings were inadequate. This conclusion is particularly buttressed by the fact that after the court examined the record, particularly the testimony of Dr. Pittman, and declared it insufficient, the court proceeded to discuss at some length the necessity for further procedural devices or a more "sensitive" application of those devices employed during the proceedings. The exploration of the record and the statement regarding its insufficiency might initially lead one to conclude that the court was only examining the sufficiency of the evidence, but the remaining portions of the opinion dispel any doubt that this was certainly not the sole or even the principal basis of the decision. Accordingly, we feel compelled to address the opinion on its own terms, and we conclude that it was wrong.

In prior opinions we have intimated that even in a rulemaking proceeding when an agency is making a " 'quasi-judicial' " determination by which a very small number of persons are " 'exceptionally affected, in each case upon individual grounds,' " in some circumstances additional procedures may be required in order to afford the aggrieved individuals due process.[8] United States v. Florida East Coast R. Co., 410 U.S., at 242, 245, quoting from Bi-Metallic Investment Co. v. State Board of Equalization, 239 U.S. 441, 446 (1915). It might also be true, although we do not think the issue is presented in this case and accordingly do not decide it, that a totally unjustified departure from well-settled agency procedures of long standing might require judicial correction.

But this much is absolutely clear. Absent constitutional constraints or extremely compelling circumstances the "administrative agencies 'should be free to fashion their own rules of procedure and to pursue methods of inquiry capable of permitting them to discharge their multitudinous duties.' " FCC v. Schreiber, 381 U.S., at 290, quoting from FCC v. Pottsville Broadcasting Co., 309 U.S., at 143. . . .

We have continually repeated this theme through the years, most recently in FPC v. Transcontinental Gas Pipe Line Corp., 423 U.S. 326 (1976), decided just two Terms ago. . . .

Respondent NRDC argues that § 4 of the Administrative Procedure Act, 5 U.S.C. § 553 (1976 ed.), merely establishes lower procedural bounds and that a court may routinely require more than the minimum

---

8. Respondent NRDC does not now argue that additional procedural devices were required under the Constitution. Since this was clearly a rulemaking proceeding in its purest form, we see nothing to support such a view. See United States v. Florida East Coast R. Co., 410 U.S. 224, 244–245 (1973); Bowles v. Willingham, 321 U.S. 503 (1944); Bi-Metallic Investment Co. v. State Board of Equalization, 239 U.S. 441 (1915).

when an agency's proposed rule addresses complex or technical factual issues or "Issues of Great Public Import."

We have, however, previously shown that our decisions reject this view. We also think the legislative history, even the part which it cites, does not bear out its contention. The Senate Report explains what eventually became § 4 thus:

> This subsection states . . . the minimum requirements of public rule making procedure short of statutory hearing. Under it agencies might in addition confer with industry advisory committees, consult organizations, hold informal "hearings," and the like. Considerations of practicality, necessity, and public interest . . . will naturally govern the agency's determination of the extent to which public proceedings should go. Matters of great import, or those where the public submission of facts will be either useful to the agency or a protection to the public, should naturally be accorded more elaborate public procedures. S.Rep. No. 752, 79th Cong., 1st Sess., 14–15 (1945).

The House Report is in complete accord. . . . And the Attorney General's Manual on the Administrative Procedure Act 31, 35 (1947), a contemporaneous interpretation previously given some deference by this Court because of the role played by the Department of Justice in drafting the legislation, further confirms that view. In short, all of this leaves little doubt that Congress intended that the discretion of the *agencies* and not that of the courts be exercised in determining when extra procedural devices should be employed.

There are compelling reasons for construing § 4 in this manner. In the first place, if courts continually review agency proceedings to determine whether the agency employed procedures which were, in the court's opinion, perfectly tailored to reach what the court perceives to be the "best" or "correct" result, judicial review would be totally unpredictable. And the agencies, operating under this vague injunction to employ the "best" procedures and facing the threat of reversal if they did not, would undoubtedly adopt full adjudicatory procedures in every instance. Not only would this totally disrupt the statutory scheme, through which Congress enacted "a formula upon which opposing social and political forces have come to rest," Wong Yang Sung v. McGrath, 339 U.S., at 40, but all the inherent advantages of informal rulemaking would be totally lost.

Secondly, it is obvious that the court in these cases reviewed the agency's choice of procedures on the basis of the record actually produced at the hearing, and not on the basis of the information available to the agency when it made the decision to structure the proceedings in a certain way. This sort of Monday morning quarterbacking not only encourages but almost compels the agency to conduct all rulemaking proceedings with the full panoply of procedural devices normally associated only with adjudicatory hearings.

Finally, and perhaps most importantly, this sort of review fundamentally misconceives the nature of the standard for judicial review of an agency rule. The court below uncritically assumed that additional procedures will automatically result in a more adequate record because it will give interested parties more of an opportunity to participate in and contribute to the proceedings. But informal rulemaking need not be based solely on the transcript of a hearing held before an agency. Indeed, the agency need not even hold a formal hearing. See 5 U.S.C. § 553(c) (1976 ed.). Thus, the adequacy of the "record" in this type of proceeding is not correlated directly to the type of procedural devices employed, but rather turns on whether the agency has followed the statutory mandate of the Administrative Procedure Act or other relevant statutes. If the agency is compelled to support the rule which it ultimately adopts with the type of record produced only after a full adjudicatory hearing, it simply will have no choice but to conduct a full adjudicatory hearing prior to promulgating every rule. In sum, this sort of unwarranted judicial examination of perceived procedural shortcomings of a rulemaking proceeding can do nothing but seriously interfere with that process prescribed by Congress.

Respondent NRDC also argues that the fact that the Commission's inquiry was undertaken in the context of NEPA somehow permits a court to require procedures beyond those specified in § 4 of the APA when investigating factual issues through rulemaking. The Court of Appeals was apparently also of this view, indicating that agencies may be required to "develop new procedures to accomplish the innovative task of implementing NEPA through rulemaking." But we search in vain for something in NEPA which would mandate such a result. We have before observed that "NEPA does not repeal by implication any other statute." Aberdeen & Rockfish R. Co. v. SCRAP, 422 U.S. 289, 319 (1975). In fact, just two Terms ago, we emphasized that the only procedural requirements imposed by NEPA are those stated in the plain language of the Act. Kleppe v. Sierra Club, 427 U.S. 390, 405–406 (1976). Thus, it is clear NEPA cannot serve as the basis for a substantial revision of the carefully constructed procedural specifications of the APA.

In short, nothing in the APA, NEPA, the circumstances of this case, the nature of the issues being considered, past agency practice, or the statutory mandate under which the Commission operates permitted the court to review and overturn the rulemaking proceeding on the basis of the procedural devices employed (or not employed) by the Commission so long as the Commission employed at least the statutory *minima*, a matter about which there is no doubt in this case.

There remains, of course, the question of whether the challenged rule finds sufficient justification in the administrative proceedings that it should be upheld by the reviewing court. Judge Tamm, concurring in the result reached by the majority of the Court of Appeals, thought that it did not. There are also intimations in the majority opinion which suggest that the judges who joined it likewise may have thought the administrative proceedings an insufficient basis upon which to predicate the rule in question. We accordingly remand so that the Court of Appeals may review the rule as the Administrative Procedure Act provides. We have made it abundantly clear before that when there is a contemporaneous explanation of the agency decision, the validity of that action must "stand or fall on the propriety of that finding, judged, of course, by the appropriate standard of review. If that finding is not sustainable on the administrative record made, then the Comptroller's decision must be vacated and the matter remanded to him for further consideration." Camp v. Pitts, 411 U.S. 138, 143 (1973). See also SEC v. Chenery Corp., 318 U.S. 80 (1943). The court should engage in this kind of review and not stray beyond the judicial province to explore the procedural format or to impose upon the agency its own notion of which procedures are "best" or most likely to further some vague, undefined public good.

III

[The Court's analysis of the companion case is omitted, except for the peroration, which follows:]

All this leads us to make one further observation of some relevance to this case. To say that the Court of Appeals' final reason for remanding is insubstantial at best is a gross understatement. Consumers Power first applied in 1969 for a construction permit—not even an operating license, just a construction permit. The proposed plant underwent an incredibly extensive review. The reports filed and reviewed literally fill books. The proceedings took years, and the actual hearings themselves over two weeks. To then nullify that effort seven years later because one report refers to other problems, which problems admittedly have been discussed at length in other reports available to the public, borders on the Kafkaesque. Nuclear energy may some day be a cheap, safe source of power or it may not. But Congress has made a choice to at least try nuclear energy, establishing a reasonable review process in which courts are to play only a limited role. The fundamental policy questions appropriately resolved in Congress and in the state legislatures are *not* subject to reexamination in the federal courts under the guise of judicial review of agency action. Time may prove wrong the decision to develop nuclear energy, but it is Congress or the States within their appropriate agencies which must eventually make that judgment. In the meantime courts should perform their appointed function. NEPA does set forth significant substantive goals for the Nation, but its mandate to the agencies is essentially procedural. It is to insure a fully informed and well-considered decision, not necessarily a decision the judges of the Court of Appeals or of this Court would have reached had they been members of the decisionmaking unit of the agency. Administrative decisions should be set aside in this context, as in every other, only for substantial procedural or substantive reasons as mandated by statute, Consolo v. FMC, 383 U.S. 607, 620 (1966), not simply because the court is unhappy with the result reached. And a single alleged oversight on a peripheral issue, urged by parties who never fully cooperated or indeed raised the issue below, must not be made the basis for overturning a decision properly made after an otherwise exhaustive proceeding.

Reversed and remanded.

MR. JUSTICE BLACKMUN and MR. JUSTICE POWELL took no part in the consideration or decision of these cases.

NOTES

(1) Despite the title of the principal case, the Nuclear Regulatory Commission was of course a party to the proceeding—nominally as a respondent, though arguing in support of the petitioner utilities. For further events in this effort to litigate the life cycle of nuclear wastes, see Baltimore Gas & Electric Co. v. Natural Resources Defense Council, Inc., 462 U.S. 87 (1983), reversing Natural Resources Defense Council, Inc. v. NRC., 685 F.2d 459 (D.C.Cir.1982), which, on remand from Vermont Yankee, had held a revised fuel cycle rule to be in violation of NEPA and arbitrary and capricious.

(2) Justice Rehnquist's statement of the case seems (at least to one of the editors of this casebook) to obscure what plaintiffs thought was worth fighting about. Here is another description of the factual context, taken from one of the many articles Vermont Yankee provoked (A. SCALIA, VERMONT YANKEE: THE APA, THE D.C. CIRCUIT, AND THE SUPREME COURT, 1978 THE SUPREME COURT REVIEW 345, 352–54):

"The principal issue in Vermont Yankee was the validity of a rule adopted by the Atomic Energy Commission assigning a series of numerical values to the environmental effects of the nuclear fuel cycle, which would thereafter be factored into the cost-benefit analyses in licensing proceedings for individual reactors. Those assigned values amounted to a determination that the environmental effects were 'insignificant.' It was essentially that determination that the environmentalist petitioners were seeking to overturn in the Court of Appeals. The rulemaking procedures used by the Commission had included oral comment, but no discovery or cross-examination. The Court of Appeals characterized as the 'primary argument' of the petitioners the assertion that:

> the decision to preclude "discovery or cross-examination" denied them a meaningful opportunity to participate in the proceedings guaranteed by due process. They do not question the Commission's authority to proceed by informal rulemaking, as opposed to adjudication. They rely instead on the line of cases indicating that in particular circumstances procedures in excess of the bare minima prescribed by the Administrative Procedure Act, 5 U.S.C. § 553, may be required.

"The crucial factual issue in the case was the adequacy of existing high-level waste disposal techniques. The only supporting evidence on this point was a 20-page statement by the director of the Commission's Division of Waste Management and Transportation, which statement had been read during the oral hearings and was subsequently incorporated into the Environmental Survey published after the comment period. On several important points it was strikingly devoid of detail and constituted little more than 'conclusory reassurances.' Although, in the Court's view, 'the vagueness of the presentation regarding waste disposal made detailed criticism of its specifics impossible,' the petitioners had offered 'a number of more general comments concerning the Commission's approach,' including failure to distinguish between design objectives and performance objectives, failure to consider actual experience with waste disposal, and the unjustified assumption that organized human supervision necessary to continued maintenance of the proposed disposal techniques would be available 'in perpetuity.' The Commission's statement of basis and purpose for the rule did not respond specifically to any of these objections.

"The Court of Appeals set aside the portions of the rule pertaining to waste disposal and reprocessing issues."

(3) Writing a year before the Vermont Yankee decision, Professor Richard Stewart saw in a "requirement of reasoned elaboration" (including a requirement of responding to contrary arguments and evidence) and an expanded concept of agency records the basis for a "paper hearing" that "combines many of the advantages of a trial-type adversary process (excepting oral testimony and cross-examination) while avoiding undue delay and cost."

"The development of a 'paper hearing' procedure and the related requirement that the Agency explain in detail the bases for its decision have contributed significantly to the improvement of EPA decisionmaking [1] because the Agency must be prepared to expose the factual and methodological bases for its decision and face judicial review on a record that encompasses the contentions and evidence of the Agency and its opponents, including responses by the Agency to criticism of its decision.

"Far more controversial are occasional court decisions that have gone beyond the requirements of detailed explanation and a 'paper hearing' to require, on a largely ad hoc basis, that EPA grant a limited trial-type hearing on specified issues. . . . A review of the actual procedures utilized by the parties upon remand in these and similar decisions indicated that the industries challenging EPA's position did

1. Former EPA attorney William F. Pedersen, in his article, Formal Records and Informal Rulemaking, 85 Yale L.J. 38 (1975), chronicles the development of EPA "paper hearing" procedures and explains how such procedures, when combined with careful judicial review, contribute to improved Agency decisions. . . .

Based on his own study of EPA decisions during his service over the past year as a member of the Committee on Environmental Decisionmaking, the author is firmly persuaded that the development of "paper hearing" procedures, combined with judicial willingness to scrutinize the grounds and evidence underlying EPA decisions, have contributed substantially to improve the quality of EPA decisionmaking. The reader is invited to make a personal assessment by comparing the adequacy of reasons and supporting evidence in early EPA decisions, such as those involved in Kennecott Copper Co. v. EPA, 462 F.2d 846 (D.C. Cir.1972), or South Terminal Corp. v. EPA, 504 F.2d 646 (1st Cir.1973), with those in later decisions, such as Ethyl Corp. v. EPA, 541 F.2d 1 (D.C.Cir.), cert. denied, 96 S.Ct. 2663 (1976).

not, in the end, insist upon the use of trial-type procedures; technical issues were instead thrashed out through exchange of documents and informal meetings between technical experts.[2]

". . . Recognition of a 'paper hearing' procedure as a third standard model of administrative decision is likely to represent a better solution to the inadequacies of the two traditional paradigms (notice-and-comment procedures and adjudicatory procedures) than a series of ad hoc responses. The development of 'paper hearing' procedures at other agencies, and proposals by commentators, legislators, and the Administrative Conference, indicate that the 'paper hearing' model may well be widely imitated and eventually accepted as a procedural *tertium quid*." (R. Stewart, The Development of Administrative and Quasi-Constitutional Law in Judicial Review of Environmental Decisionmaking: Lessons From the Clean Air Act, 62 Iowa L.Rev. 713, 731–33 (1977)).

Does Vermont Yankee condemn Professor Stewart's *tertium quid*? Do you agree with his assessment, in the wake of that decision, that "Vermont Yankee fails to confront the problem of how best to generate the record which it recognizes is necessary to permit adequate judicial review of agency rulemaking.

". . . By condemning hybrid rulemaking procedural requirements, such as the 'paper hearing,' without providing administrators and lower courts alternative criteria to judge, or methods to ensure, the adequacy of administrative records, Vermont Yankee creates uncertainty and encourages ad hoc judicial remands—the very failings for which Justice Rehnquist criticized the court of appeals.

"The . . . best approach is for courts to provide guidance for administrators and litigants by requiring the use of hybrid procedures likely in most cases to produce an adequate record for judicial review." (R. Stewart, Vermont Yankee and the Evolution of Administrative Procedure, 91 Harv.L.Rev. 1805, 1817–19 (1978)).

(4) C. Byse, Vermont Yankee and the Evolution of Administrative Procedure: A Somewhat Different View, 91 Harv.L.Rev. 1823, 1828–29 (1978):

"If the court is convinced that an adequate record for review can best be achieved by utilization of an additional procedural device, why should it not save everyone's time and energy by ordering the agency to utilize that device?

"There are at least three answers to such an argument. First, although the reviewing court may have convinced itself that an additional procedural device is indispensable, its conviction may well be erroneous. A particular procedural device is a means to an end, not the end itself. If the court has explained in what ways the record is inadequate, very likely there will be various means by which it can be made adequate. By prescribing a particular procedure the court pre-

---

2. Williams, "Hybrid Rulemaking" Under the Administrative Procedure Act: A Legal and Empirical Analysis, 42 U.Chi.L. Rev. 401, 434–35 (1975).

vents the agency, which has the firstline responsibility and experience in administering the statute, from utilizing that experience to provide the needed record in the most cost-effective fashion.

"Second, even if the judicially prescribed procedural device might, in some abstract sense, be thought to be the indispensable *modus operandi,* is it necessary or appropriate for the court to *order* the agency? I think not. If, as I believe and courts occasionally proclaim, courts and agencies constitute a "partnership" in furtherance of the public interest and are "collaborative instrumentalities of justice," the judicial partner should be mindful of the sensitivities and responsibilities of the administrative partner; to the extent possible, the relationship should be one of collaboration, not command. This is not simply a matter of etiquette or abstract *noblesse oblige.* Rather it relates to an important aspect of our legal system that is sometimes overlooked, namely, that although the judiciary has a duty to uphold the law, it also has a duty to recognize and defer to the responsibilities of other components of government, including the administrative component. . . .

"Third, and most important, in enacting APA section 553 in 1946, Congress established a new general model of rulemaking procedure. There is no suggestion in the legislative history of the section that it was declaratory of the common law or that it was a delegation of power to the courts to develop desirable procedural models. On the contrary, the legislative history indicates that the question whether additional procedural devices are to be employed is an *agency* question, not a *judicial* question: '[c]onsiderations of practicality, necessity, and public interest . . . will naturally govern the *agency's* determination of the extent to which public proceedings should go.' "

(5) In VERMONT YANKEE: THE APA, THE D.C. CIRCUIT, AND THE SUPREME COURT, 1978 THE SUPREME COURT REVIEW 345, then Professor (now "The Honorable") Antonin Scalia suggested that Vermont Yankee was most fundamentally an attempt to restore order to administrative law by insisting on the primacy of the APA. In particular, he saw it as a response not only to judicially crafted hybrid rulemaking, but to the trend, which had accelerated in the early 1970's, to legislate particular procedural provisions to accompany each new (or modified) statutory grant of authority to an agency.

"It is important to appreciate that, however little support the D.C. Circuit's approach to the APA could find in the opinions of the Supreme Court, it was fast becoming an accepted part of administrative law theory and practice. Not only did the agencies, for obvious reasons, design their procedures with the D.C. Circuit's philosophy in mind, but the academic community had, by and large, accepted and validated the development. It was no longer regarded as a contradiction in terms but was entirely comprehensible and acceptable to write of 'on-the-record section 553 proceedings,' or of 'Hybrid Rulemaking under the Administrative Procedure Act.' And—perhaps most irreversible of all—the students of administrative law and recent law school graduates on the staffs of the congressional committees had begun to embody this new learning in legislation. Thus, the procedural provisions of the FTC Improvement Act applicable to (what it calls) 'informal hearing[s]' conducted 'in accordance with section 553' read as though they were composed by the D.C. Circuit with some assistance from Prof. K.C. Davis." [These provisions require an oral hearing; a verbatim transcript; an opportunity for all interested persons to make oral submissions, and to make rebuttal submissions and conduct cross-examination with respect to "disputed issues of material fact"; and "substantial evidence" judicial review.]

His article ended with the following analysis:

"What this discussion of the legislative process was meant to emphasize is the fundamental point that one of the functions of procedure is to limit power—not just the power to be unfair, but the power to act in a political mode, or the power to act at all. Such limitation is sometimes an incidental result of pursuing other functions, such as efficiency and fairness; but it may be an end in itself.

" . . .

"The procedural foundations of the judicial process were laid long ago, and the basic role of the courts seems firmly established by both tradition and constitutional prescription. There is little legislative inclination, therefore, to adjust upward and downward the power of the courts, and even less inclination to achieve this by fiddling with procedures. Not so with the agencies. Their powers are for the most part neither constitutionally prescribed nor well established, and their procedures are only recently formed. Thus, the tendency to alter procedures as a means of altering power is immeasurably stronger.

"Of course, once it is accepted that procedures are to be used as a means of expanding or restricting the power to act, the idea of any genuinely stable APA based on fairness and efficiency alone becomes visionary. It also becomes unrealistic to expect the framework of any such superstatute to contain only a few options of procedure among which later legislation must choose—such as the stark choice between formal and informal rulemaking offered under the current APA. . . . The degrees of activism and of political decision making which the Congress expects from (or, more precisely, which the legislative struggle finally induces its divergent factions to accord to) the FTC, the ICC, the INS, the FDA, and the CPSC may vary enormously—and so will the procedures which reflect those expectations.

"One can argue that things should be otherwise. That the Congress should be induced to forswear the use of procedures as a means of restricting power, and to pursue that goal, when desired, by some more sensible means (such as cutting budgets) or by some other equally senseless means (such as blindfolding every third bureaucrat). If such congressional self-denial were achieved, one might think a truly stable framework of administrative procedure could be established. There are two problems, however: one practical, one theoretical. As a practical matter, both the Congress and the lobbyists who appear before it would be foolhardy from a selfish standpoint—and perhaps even from the standpoint of the public interest—to abandon a compromise device which is so well insulated from effective criticism. . . . While 'hybrid rulemaking' may no longer be devised by the courts under the APA, it will continue to flourish in a multiplicity of special statutes that modify the APA's dispositions, at least so long as the APA itself provides so few variants (and those based on considerations of fairness and efficiency alone) from which to select.

"And there is a theoretical reason why this ought to be so. Congress can, indeed, refrain from making use of the connection between procedure and power, but it cannot make that connection itself disappear. Thus, to the extent that the choice of procedures is left to the agencies themselves, to that same extent the agencies are left to determine a substantial aspect of their own power. . . .

"It seems to me, therefore, that if the continuing fragmentation of mandated administrative procedure is to be abated, what is called for is a more modest expectation of what the APA can and should achieve, and a design that will accord with the realities. . . . I would settle for an APA that contains not merely three but ten or fifteen basic procedural formats—an inventory large enough to provide the basis for a whole spectrum of legislative compromises without the necessity for shopping elsewhere. . . . The alternatives, it seems [to] me, are a continuation of ad hoc statutory variations and—whether or not the D.C. Circuit's judicial improvisation can be controlled—an acceleration of our rush away from the kind of fundamental statute Vermont Yankee seeks to preserve."

(6) If it is viewed as a directive to the lower courts to change their ways, has Vermont Yankee succeeded? Subsequent district and circuit court cases are collected and discussed in A.S. Neely, Vermont Yankee Nuclear Power Corp. v. Natural Resources Defense Council, Inc.: Response and Reaction in the Federal Judiciary, 14 U.Balt.L.Rev. 256 (1985). For the moment, it will suffice to report Professor Neely's conclusion, which is that "[o]verall, in the area of informal rulemaking, the leadership of the Court has been moderately effective. To the extent that Vermont Yankee's lead has been ineffective in establishing the intended judicial role in the review of rulemaking, the reason may be the ambiguities of the decision itself as much as perceived arrogance or intransigence in the lower federal judiciary."

(7) In considering what procedures are best suited to rulemaking, it is worth remembering that quite a lot goes on before the notice of proposed rulemaking is issued. In Chapter II, page 147, above, we saw that by operation of Executive Orders 12291 and 12498, there is substantial involvement of the executive branch as a whole, and in Chapter I, page 34 above, we read William Pedersen's description of the lengthy process of consultation within an agency prior to sending out the formal notice of informal rulemaking. Roughly contemporaneous

with Pedersen's article, the EPA published a chart of the processes it uses to develop proposed regulations (43 Fed.Reg. 29892 (1978)):

STAGES IN THE DEVELOPMENT OF SIGNIFICANT EPA REGULATIONS

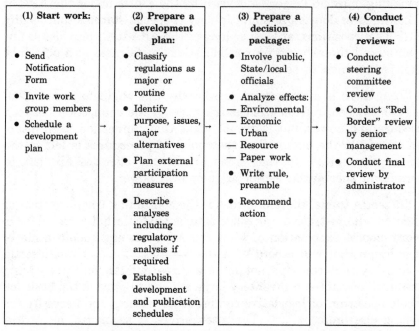

(1) Start work:	(2) Prepare a development plan:	(3) Prepare a decision package:	(4) Conduct internal reviews:
• Send Notification Form • Invite work group members • Schedule a development plan	• Classify regulations as major or routine • Identify purpose, issues, major alternatives • Plan external participation measures • Describe analyses including regulatory analysis if required • Establish development and publication schedules	• Involve public, State/local officials • Analyze effects: — Environmental — Economic — Urban — Resource — Paper work • Write rule, preamble • Recommend action	• Conduct steering committee review • Conduct "Red Border" review by senior management • Conduct final review by administrator

What may perhaps be surprising is that these pre-public rulemaking procedures are by no means secret. The Regulatory Flexibility Act, 5 U.S.C. § 602, requires agencies to publish regulatory agendas; these are combined and published semiannually in a "Unified Agenda of Federal Regulations." This is a substantial document: the Unified Agenda of April 21, 1986, ran from 51 Fed.Reg. 13801 to 51 Fed.Reg. 14974. It lists not only regulations that have been "noticed," but also actions for which a notice is soon to be sent out ("Proposed Rule Stage") and even actions agencies plan to undertake to decide whether to initiate rulemaking ("Prerule Stage"). As part of each item, including those in the "prerule stage," there is an identified "agency contact" with name, address, and phone number. There is, in short, a public invitation to those who are interested (and knowledgable) to contact the agency long before the beginning of the rulemaking proceeding as it appears in litigated cases.

PACIFIC GAS & ELECTRIC CO. v. FEDERAL POWER COMM.

United States Court of Appeals, District of Columbia Circuit, 1974.
506 F.2d 33.

[In 1973, without complying with section 553 of the Administrative Procedure Act, the FPC issued Order No. 467 which set forth a "statement of policy" on priority schedules to be followed by pipeline companies in curtailing supplies of natural gas to customers when curtailment became necessary because of shortages in supplies of natural gas. At the time, shortages were already acute and yet further discrepancies between supplies and demands were strongly feared by many persons, in and out of government. The Order provided that curtailment priorities would be based on use rather than on prior contractual commitments, listed nine categories of use, and required that "full curtailment of the lower priority volumes be accomplished before curtailment of any higher priority volumes is commenced." The Order also stated that "exceptions to those priorities may be permitted" upon a "finding of extraordinary circumstances after a hearing initiated by a petition" pursuant to the Commission's Rules of Practice. However, "barring such circumstances, our review . . . convinces us that the priorities-of-deliveries . . . should be applied to all . . . pipeline curtailment." Customers of pipeline companies petitioned for review of the Order, arguing, inter alia, that the Order was in effect a substantive rule which the Commission should have promulgated pursuant to section 553 of the APA.]

Before BAZELON, CHIEF JUDGE, and MACKINNON, CIRCUIT JUDGE, and A. SHERMAN CHRISTENSEN, U.S. SENIOR DISTRICT JUDGE FOR THE DISTRICT OF UTAH.

MACKINNON, CIRCUIT JUDGE. . . .

The critical distinction between a substantive rule and a general statement of policy is the different practical effect that these two types of pronouncements have in subsequent administrative proceedings. . . . A properly adopted substantive rule establishes a standard of conduct which has the force of law. In subsequent administrative proceedings involving a substantive rule, the issues are whether the adjudicated facts conform to the rule and whether the rule should be waived or applied in that particular instance. The underlying policy embodied in the rule is not generally subject to challenge before the agency.

A general statement of policy, on the other hand, . . . is not finally determinative of the issues or rights to which it is addressed. The agency cannot apply or rely upon a general statement of policy as law because a general statement of policy only announces what the agency seeks to establish as policy. A policy statement announces the agency's tentative intentions for the future. When the agency applies the policy in a particular situation, it must be prepared to support the policy just as if the policy statement had never been issued. An agency cannot escape its responsibility to present evidence and reasoning supporting its substantive rules by announcing binding precedent in the form of a general statement of policy.

Often the agency's own characterization of a particular order provides some indication of the nature of the announcement. The agency's express purpose may be to establish a binding rule of law, not subject to challenge in particular cases. On the other hand the agency may intend merely to publish a policy guideline that is subject to complete attack before it is finally applied in future cases. When the agency states that in subsequent proceedings it will thoroughly consider not only the policy's applicability to the facts of a given case but also the underlying validity of the policy itself, then the agency intends to treat the order as a general statement of policy. . . .

The tentative effect of a general statement of policy has ramifications in subsequent judicial review proceedings as well as in administrative proceedings. Because a general statement of policy is adopted without public participation, the scope of review may be broader than the scope of review for a substantive rule. The rulemaking process prescribed by the APA insures a thorough exploration of the relevant issues. The public is notified of the proposed rule and interested parties submit arguments supporting their positions. The rulemaking process culminates in the agency applying its experience and expertise to the issues. A court reviewing a rule that was adopted pursuant to this extensive rulemaking process will defer to the agency's judgment if the rule satisfies the minimal criterion of reasonableness. . . .

But when an agency promulgates a general statement of policy, the agency does not have the benefit of public exploration of the issues. Judicial review may be the first stage at which the policy is subjected to full criticism by interested parties. Consequently a policy judgment expressed as a general statement of policy is entitled to less deference than a decision expressed as a rule or an adjudicative order. Although the agency's expertise and experience cannot be ignored, the reviewing court has some leeway to assess the underlying wisdom of the policy and need not affirm a general statement of policy that merely satisfies the test of reasonableness. . . .

The FPC of course was under no compulsion to issue Order No. 467. The Commission issued the policy statement because the curtailment plans being submitted reflected sharp differences in philosophy which necessitated Commission guidance in the curtailment area. In the absence of such a policy statement, the Commission could have proceeded on an ad hoc basis and tentatively approved curtailment plans filed under section 4 of the Act which the Commission found to be just and reasonable. In following such a course the only difference from the present situation would be that the Commission would be acting under a secret policy rather than under the publicized guidelines of Order No. 167. The argument that an agency must follow rulemaking procedures when it elects to formulate policy by a substantive rule has no application in this case. Order No. 467 does not establish a substantive rule. Although the Commission is free to initiate a rulemaking proceeding to establish a binding substantive rule, the Commission apparently intends to establish its curtailment policies by proceeding through individual adjudications. Order No. 467 merely announces the general policy which the Commission hopes to establish in subsequent proceedings. . . .

Petitioners contend that Order No. 467 has an immediate and significant practical effect by shifting the burden of proof in curtailment cases from the pipeline companies to their customers because the order "established a presumption that the curtailment rules prescribed are consistent with the Natural Gas Act in any and all situations . . . ." Under section 4 of the Natural Gas Act a pipeline company filing a new curtailment plan has the burden of proving that its plan is reasonable and fair. . . . Petitioners maintain that by stating that tariffs which conform to the proposed plan will be permitted to become effective, Order No. 467 relieves the pipeline companies of their burden of justifying their plans. However, the language of Order No. 467 is as follows: "Proposed tariff sheets which conform to the policies expressed in [Order No. 467] will be accepted for filing, and permitted to become effective, *subject to the rights of intervenors to hearing and adjudication of any claim of preference, discrimination, unjustness or unreasonableness* of the provisions contained in the proposed tariff sheets, and subject to the further right of anyone adversely affected to seek individualized special relief because of extraordinary circumstances." 49 F.P.C. at 585 (emphasis added).

We interpret the italicized proviso to mean that in appropriate cases the Commission will conduct a section 4 proceeding to consider a challenge to the underlying validity of a curtailment plan, even though the plan conforms to Order No. 467. Section 4 renders unlawful curtailment plans which are preferential, discriminatory, unreasonable or unfair and provides for a hearing concerning the lawfulness of newly filed curtailment plans. . . . The Commission has processed curtailment plans under section 4 in the past, and the Supreme Court recently emphasized that section 4 is by far the most appropriate mechanism for evaluating such plans. . . . We expect the Commission generally to continue processing curtailment plans in section 4 proceedings, in which the pipeline company has the burden of proof, and to refrain from treating Order No. 467 as anything more than a general statement of policy. . . .

We conclude that Order No. 467 is a general statement of policy and that it was therefore unnecessary for the Commission to conduct rulemaking proceedings under the Administrative Procedure Act.

. . .

NOTES

(1) Legislative rules mark the tip of an iceberg of governmental formulations of policy. Staff manuals, regulatory guides, and interpretive rules abound in Washington. Some agencies adopt the more important of these formulations employing procedures which permit some public participation; understandable pressures from interested outsiders are that more should (or in some cases must) do so.

(2) The principal alternative to the analysis presented in Pacific Gas & Electric is known as the "substantial impact" test: this test determines whether § 553 procedures have to be used by looking at the substantiality of the impact of the rule on the interests of private parties. See, e.g., Pickus v. United States Bd. of Parole, 507 F.2d 1107 (D.C.Cir.1974), holding that "guidelines" specifying the factors relevant to the discretionary decision whether to parole a federal prisoner were not exempt from the § 553 process. Recent cases from the D.C. Circuit have said that after Vermont Yankee the substantial practical impact of a rule does not by itself make the rule "legislative," or call for the

imposition of notice-and-comment procedures. E.g., Cabais v. Egger, 690 F.2d 234, 237 (D.C.Cir.1982); American Postal Workers Union v. United States Postal Service, 707 F.2d 548, 560, 565 n. 11 (D.C.Cir.1983), cert. denied 465 U.S. 1100 (1984). For a suggestion that the "substantial impact" test may still be alive in some of the circuits, see Note, The Substantial Impact Test: Victim of the Fallout From Vermont Yankee, 53 G.Wash.L.Rev. 118 (1985).

(3) Agencies of course have discretion to add to minimal procedural requirements, and there is legislative history encouraging them not to use the exemptions of Section 553 to the fullest extent. In 1976, the Administrative Conference of the United States issued Recommendation 76–5, Interpretive Rules of General Applicability and Statements of General Policy, 1 CFR § 305.76–5, which reads as follows:

"RECOMMENDATION

"1. Before an agency issues, amends, or repeals an interpretive rule of general applicability or a statement of general policy which is likely to have substantial impact on the public, the agency normally should utilize the procedures set forth in Administrative Procedure Act subsections 553(b) and (c), by publishing the proposed interpretive rule or policy statement in the FEDERAL REGISTER, with a concise statement of its basis and purpose and an invitation to interested persons to submit written comments, with or without opportunity for oral presentation. If it is impracticable, unnecessary, or contrary to the public interest to use such procedures the agency should so state in the interpretive rule or policy statement, with a brief statement of the reasons therefor.

" '2. Where there has been no prepromulgation notice and opportunity for comment, the publication of an interpretive rule of general applicability or a statement of general policy, even one made effective immediately, should include a statement of its basis and purpose and an invitation to interested persons to submit written comments, with or without opportunity for oral presentation, within a following period of not less than thirty days. The agency should evaluate the rule or statement in the light of comments received. Not later than sixty days after the close of the comment period, the agency should indicate in the FEDERAL REGISTER its adherence to or alteration of its previous action, responding as may be appropriate to significant comments received. An agency may omit these post-adoption comment procedures when it incorporates in the interpretive rule or policy statement a declaration, with a brief statement of reasons, that such procedures would serve no public interest or would be so burdensome as to outweigh any foreseeable gain."

This recommendation was largely based on M. Asimow, Public Participation in the Adoption of Interpretive Rules and Policy Statements, 75 Mich.L.Rev. 520 (1977). For a similar approach regarding another of the exemptions from Section 553, see Recommendation No. 83–2, The "Good Cause" Exemption From APA Rulemaking Requirements, 1 CFR § 305.83–2.

(4) For discussion of each of the possible exemptions from section 553, a good place to start is Administrative Conference of the United States, A Guide to Federal Agency Rulemaking 24ff. (1983).

SECTION 2. AGENCY DISCRETION IN CHOOSING A PROCEDURAL MODE

An administrative agency may utilize a variety of informal methods in developing or implementing the substantive policies committed to its care. "For example, the 'lifted eyebrow,' backed by a veiled or express threat of prosecution, of nonrenewal of a license, or of publicity, can be an effective means of declaring and applying a given policy free from the restraints of judicial review. There is also the private ruling or advisory opinion, which may or may not receive general publicity and may or may not be binding on the agency. Speeches and press releases are frequently resorted to for the announcement of important policies or views. But indispensable, wide-spread, and perhaps abused as such relatively informal methods may be, there often comes a time when a policy must be exposed to the rigors of more formal procedures.
. . . " D.L. Shapiro, The Choice of Rulemaking or Adjudication in the Development of Administrative Policy, 78 Harv.L.Rev. 921, 923–924 (1965).[1]

When that time comes, the agency often will be confronted with a choice between adopting a substantive rule pursuant to section 553 of the APA or issuing an order pursuant to the more formal adjudicative procedures of sections 554, 556 and 557.[2] In this section of the materials, we examine the factors governing the choice between rulemaking and adjudication and the respective roles of the agency and the reviewing court in making the choice.

A threshold issue is whether the agency has in fact been vested with both substantive rulemaking and adjudicatory authority, for if it lacks either authority, quite clearly it has no power to make a choice. For example, section 13(a)(10) of the Fair Labor Standards Act of 1938 provides that its provisions—which establish minimum wages and maximum hours—shall not be applicable "to any individual employed within the area of production (as defined by the Administrator), engaged in handling . . . agricultural or horticultural commodities for market. . . . " See Addison v. Holly Hill Fruit Products, Inc., 322

---

1. For additional discussion, see R. Fuchs, Development and Diversification in Administrative Rule Making, 72 Nw.L.Rev. 83 (1977); G. Robinson, The Making of Administrative Policy: Another Look at Rulemaking and Adjudication and Administrative Procedure Reform, 118 U.Pa.L. Rev. 485 (1970). And see B. Boyer, Alternatives to Administrative Trial-Type Hearings for Resolving Complex Scientific, Economic, and Social Issues, 71 Mich.L.Rev. 111 (1972); M. Dakin, Ratemaking as Rulemaking—The New Approach at the FPC: Ad Hoc Rulemaking in the Ratemaking Process, 1973 Duke L.J. 41.

2. This statement of the dichotomy— i.e., informal rulemaking versus formal adjudication under the APA—does not exhaust the possibilities, for in some instances, a rule—e.g., if it were "interpretative," § 553(b)(3)(A)—or an adjudication—e.g., if it involved "the selection of an employee," § 554(a)(2)—would be exempt from the cited APA sections; and, of course, there are statutes which require, even in rulemaking, formal, or at least hybrid, proceedings.

U.S. 607 (1944), infra p. 396. The Administrator of the FLSA is given
substantive rulemaking power in specific instances—to define areas of
production, for example. But the Act does not confer on him authority
to adjudicate alleged violations; instead it vests that authority in the
federal courts. It is thus apparent that the Administrator of the FLSA
does not have a choice between rulemaking and adjudication.

In other situations, resolution of the authority issue is more difficult. A leading case is National Petroleum Refiners Ass'n. v. Federal
Trade Comm., 482 F.2d 672 (D.C.Cir.1973), cert. denied 415 U.S. 951
(1974). Section 5 of the Federal Trade Commission Act directed the
Commission to "prevent persons, partnerships, or corporations . . .
from using unfair methods of competition in commerce and unfair or
deceptive acts or practices in commerce." Section 5(b) of the Act
specified that the Commission was to accomplish this goal by means of
issuance of a complaint, a hearing, findings as to the facts, and issuance
of a cease and desist order. Section 6(g) of the Act stated that the
Commission may "[f]rom time to time . . . classify corporations and
. . . make rules and regulations for the purpose of carrying out the
provisions of . . . this title." Although a number of commentators
indicated that this general grant of power did not authorize substantive
rulemaking but instead was "confined essentially to matters of interpretation, procedure, and internal organization," Shapiro, supra at 961
n. 153, the Commission relied on section 6(g) in 1971 to adopt a Trade
Regulation Rule which provided that failure to post octane numbers on
pumps at service stations would be an unfair method of competition
constituting a violation of Section 5 of the Act. Plaintiffs instituted an
action in the district court, contending that the commission lacked
authority to issue the rule. The district court examined the legislative
history of the statute and concluded that section 6(g) "conveys only the
authority to make . . . rules and regulations in connection with [the
Commission's] housekeeping chore[s] and investigative responsibilities"
and "does not confer upon the . . . Commission the authority to
promulgate Trade Regulation Rules that have the effect of substantive
law." National Petroleum Refiners Ass'n. v. Federal Trade Comm., 340
F.Supp. 1343 (D.C.D.C.1972).

The court of appeals reversed in an opinion by Judge Wright, for
himself, and Chief Judge Bazelon and Judge Robinson. The court's
lengthy opinion emphasized the benefits of rulemaking which are that
it serves "the purpose of shortening and simplifying the adjudicative
process and of clarifying the law in advance," avoids retroactive imposition of a "new and unexpected liability," gives "any agency an invaluable resource-saving flexibility in carrying out [regulatory] tasks . . .
[and] opens up the process of agency policy innovation to a broad range
of criticism, advice and data that is ordinarily less likely to be forthcoming in adjudication. Moreover, the availability of notice before
promulgation and wide public participation in rulemaking avoids the
problem of singling out a single defendant among a group of competitors for initial imposition of a new and inevitably costly legal obliga-

tion. . . . " 482 F.2d 679, 681, 683.[3] The opinion also examined the legislative history of section 6(g), reviewed several of the leading cases upholding an agency's use of rulemaking, stressed the need to "interpret liberally broad grants of rulemaking authority like the one we construe here" and concluded, "[W]e must respectfully register our disagreement with the District Court's painstaking opinion. As we read the statute, the Commission is authorized to issue Trade Regulation Rules. We therefore reverse and remand." (Congress more explicitly granted this authority, and more definitely cabined it, in the FTC Improvement Act of 1975.)

If, as often will be the case, the threshold issue of the existence of both adjudicatory and rulemaking powers is decided affirmatively, the agency must then address possible constraints on its action: May or must it utilize rulemaking? May or must it utilize adjudication?

SECURITIES & EXCHANGE COMM. v. CHENERY CORP.

Supreme Court of the United States, 1947.
332 U.S. 194.

[The Securities and Exchange Commission was empowered to approve the reorganization of a public utility holding company if it found that the reorganization would be "fair and equitable to the persons affected thereby." [1] In the present instance, the Commission had disapproved a plan that in its judgment did not meet this test.]

MR. JUSTICE MURPHY delivered the opinion of the Court.

This case is here for the second time. In S.E.C. v. Chenery Corporation, 318 U.S. 80, we held that an order of the Securities and Exchange Commission could not be sustained on the grounds upon which that agency acted. We therefore directed that the case be

---

3. Compare G. Robinson, supra note 1 at 535: "[R]ulemaking procedures are inherently no more productive of effective policy-making than are adjudicatory proceedings."

1. Section 11(e) of the Public Utility Holding Company Act provided:

"In accordance with such rules and regulations or order as the Commission may deem necessary or appropriate in the public interest or for the protection of investors or consumers, any registered holding company or any subsidiary company of a registered holding company may, at any time after January 1, 1936, submit a plan to the Commission for the divestment of control, securities, or other assets, or for other action by such company or any subsidiary company thereof for the purpose of enabling such company or any subsidiary company thereof to comply with the provisions of subsection (b) of this section. If, after notice and opportunity for hearing, the Commission shall find such plan, as

submitted or as modified, necessary to effectuate the provisions of subsection (b) of this section and fair and equitable to the persons affected by such plan, the Commission shall make an order approving such plan. . . ."

Section 11(b), referred to in section 11(e), read in part:

"It shall be the duty of the Commission, as soon as practicable after January 1, 1938:

(1) To require by order, after notice and opportunity for hearing, that each registered holding company, and each subsidiary company thereof, shall take such action as the Commission shall find necessary to limit the operations of the holding-company system of which such company is a part to a single integrated public-utility system, and to such other businesses as are reasonably incidental, or economically necessary or appropriate to the operations of such integrated public-utility system. . . ."

remanded to the Commission for such further proceedings as might be appropriate. On remand, the Commission reexamined the problem, recast its rationale and reached the same result. The issue now is whether the Commission's action is proper in light of the principles established in our prior decision.

When the case was first here, we emphasized a simple but fundamental rule of administrative law. That rule is to the effect that a reviewing court, in dealing with a determination or judgment which an administrative agency alone is authorized to make, must judge the propriety of such action solely by the grounds invoked by the agency. If those grounds are inadequate or improper, the court is powerless to affirm the administrative action by substituting what it considers to be a more adequate or proper basis. To do so would propel the court into the domain which Congress has set aside exclusively for the administrative agency.

We also emphasized in our prior decision an important corollary of the foregoing rule. If the administrative action is to be tested by the basis upon which it purports to rest, that basis must be set forth with such clarity as to be understandable. It will not do for a court to be compelled to guess at the theory underlying the agency's action; nor can a court be expected to chisel that which must be precise from what the agency has left vague and indecisive. In other words, "We must know what a decision means before the duty becomes ours to say whether it is right or wrong." . . .

Applying this rule and its corollary, the Court was unable to sustain the Commission's original action. The Commission had been dealing with the reorganization of the Federal Water Service Corporation (Federal), a holding company registered under the Public Utility Holding Company Act of 1935, 49 Stat. 803. During the period when successive reorganization plans proposed by the management were before the Commission, the officers, directors and controlling stockholders of Federal purchased a substantial amount of Federal's preferred stock on the over-the-counter market. Under the fourth reorganization plan, this preferred stock was to be converted into common stock of a new corporation; on the basis of the purchases of preferred stock, the management would have received more than 10% of this new common stock. It was frankly admitted that the management's purpose in buying the preferred stock was to protect its interest in the new company. It was also plain that there was no fraud or lack of disclosure in making these purchases.

But the Commission would not approve the fourth plan so long as the preferred stock purchased by the management was to be treated on a parity with the other preferred stock. It felt that the officers and directors of a holding company in process of reorganization under the Act were fiduciaries and were under a duty not to trade in the securities of that company during the reorganization period. 8 S.E.C. 893, 915–921. And so the plan was amended to provide that the preferred stock acquired by the management, unlike that held by others, was not to be converted into the new common stock; instead, it was to be surrendered at cost plus dividends accumulated since the purchase dates. As amended, the plan was approved by the Commission over the management's objections. 10 S.E.C. 200.

The Court interpreted the Commission's order approving this amended plan as grounded solely upon judicial authority. The Commission appeared to have treated the preferred stock acquired by the management in accordance with what it thought were standards theretofore recognized by courts. If it intended to create new standards growing out of its experience in effectuating the legislative policy, it failed to express itself with sufficient clarity and precision to be so understood. Hence the order was judged by the only standards clearly invoked by the Commission. On that basis, the order could not stand. The opinion pointed out that courts do not impose upon officers and directors of a corporation any fiduciary duty to its stockholders which precludes them, merely because they are officers and directors, from buying and selling the corporation's stock. Nor was it felt that the cases upon which the Commission relied established any principles of law or equity which in themselves would be sufficient to justify this order.

The opinion further noted that neither Congress nor the Commission had promulgated any general rule proscribing such action as the purchase of preferred stock by Federal's management. And the only judge-made rule of equity which might have justified the Commission's order related to fraud or mismanagement of the reorganization by the officers and directors, matters which were admittedly absent in this situation.

After the case was remanded to the Commission, Federal Water and Gas Corp. (Federal Water), the surviving corporation under the reorganization plan, made an application for approval of an amendment to the plan to provide for the issuance of new common stock of the reorganized company. This stock was to be distributed to the members of Federal's management on the basis of the shares of the old preferred stock which they had acquired during the period of reorganization, thereby placing them in the same position as the public holders of the old preferred stock. The intervening members of Federal's management joined in this request. The Commission denied the application in an order issued on February 7, 1945. Holding Company Act Release No. 5584. That order was reversed by the Court of Appeals, 154 F.2d 6, which felt that our prior decision precluded such action by the Commission.

The latest order of the Commission definitely avoids the fatal error of relying on judicial precedents which do not sustain it. This time, after a thorough reexamination of the problem in light of the purposes and standards of the Holding Company Act, the Commission has concluded that the proposed transaction is inconsistent with the standards of §§ 7 and 11 of the Act. It has drawn heavily upon its accumulated experience in dealing with utility reorganizations. And it has expressed its reasons with a clarity and thoroughness that admit of no doubt as to the underlying basis of its order.

The argument is pressed upon us, however, that the Commission was foreclosed from taking such a step following our prior decision. It is said that, in the absence of findings of conscious wrongdoing on the part of Federal's management, the Commission could not determine by an order in this particular case that it was inconsistent with the statutory standards to permit Federal's management to realize a profit through the reorganization purchases. All that it could do was to enter an order allowing an amendment to the plan so that the proposed transaction could be consummated. Under this view, the Commission would be free only to promulgate a general rule outlawing such profits in future utility reorganizations; but such a rule would have to be prospective in nature and have no retroactive effect upon the instant situation.

We reject this contention, for it grows out of a misapprehension of our prior decision and of the Commission's statutory duties. We held no more and no less than that the Commission's first order was unsupportable for the reasons supplied by that agency. But when the case left this Court, the problem whether Federal's management should be treated equally with other preferred stockholders still lacked a final and complete answer. It was clear that the Commission could not give a negative answer by resort to prior judicial declarations. And it was also clear that the Commission was not bound by settled judicial precedents in a situation of this nature. 318 U.S. at page 89. Still unsettled, however, was the answer the Commission might give were it to bring to bear on the facts the proper administrative and statutory considerations, a function which belongs exclusively to the Commission in the first instance. The administrative process had taken an erroneous rather than a final turn. Hence we carefully refrained from expressing any views as to the propriety of an order rooted in the proper and relevant considerations. See Siegel v. Federal Trade Commission, 327 U.S. 608, 613, 614.

When the case was directed to be remanded to the Commission for such further proceedings as might be appropriate, it was with the thought that the Commission would give full effect to its duties in harmony with the views we had expressed. . . . This obviously meant something more than the entry of a perfunctory order giving parity treatment to the management holdings of preferred stock. The fact that the Commission had committed a legal error in its first disposition of the case certainly gave Federal's management no vested right to receive the benefits of such an order. See Federal Communications Commission v. Pottsville Broadcasting Co., 309 U.S. 134, 145. After the remand was made, therefore, the Commission was bound to deal with the problem afresh, performing the function delegated to it by Congress. It was again charged with the duty of measuring the proposed treatment of the management's preferred stock holdings by relevant and proper standards. Only in that way could the legislative policies embodied in the Act be effectuated.

The absence of a general rule or regulation governing management trading during reorganization did not affect the Commission's duties in relation to the particular proposal before it. The Commission was asked to grant or deny effectiveness to a proposed amendment to Federal's reorganization plan whereby the management would be accorded parity treatment on its holdings. It could do that only in the form of an order, entered after a due consideration of the particular facts in light of the relevant and proper standards. That was true regardless of whether those standards previously had been spelled out in a general rule or regulation. Indeed, if the Commission rightly felt that the proposed amendment was inconsistent with those standards, an order giving effect to the amendment merely because there was no general rule or regulation covering the matter would be unjustified.

It is true that our prior decision explicitly recognized the possibility that the Commission might have promulgated a general rule dealing with this problem under its statutory rule-making powers, in which case the issue for our consideration would have been entirely different from that which did confront us. 318 U.S. at pages 92, 93. But we did not mean to imply thereby that the failure of the Commission to anticipate this problem and to promulgate a general rule withdrew all power from that agency to perform its statutory duty in this case. To hold that the Commission had no alternative in this proceeding but to approve the proposed transaction, while formulating any general rules it might desire for use in future cases of this nature, would be to stultify the administrative process. That we refuse to do.

Since the Commission, unlike a court, does have the ability to make new law prospectively through the exercise of its rule-making powers, it has less reason to rely upon ad hoc adjudication to formulate new standards of conduct within the framework of the Holding Company Act. The function of filling in the interstices of the Act should be performed, as much as possible, through this quasi-legislative promulgation of rules to be applied in the future. But any rigid requirement to that effect would make the administrative process inflexible and incapable of dealing with many of the specialized problems which arise. See Report of the Attorney General's Committee on Administrative Procedure in Government Agencies, S.Doc. No. 8, 77th Cong., 1st Sess., p. 29. Not every principle essential to the effective administration of a statute can or should be cast immediately into the mold of a general rule. Some principles must await their own development, while others must be adjusted to meet particular, unforeseeable situations. In performing its important functions in these respects, therefore, an administrative agency must be equipped to act either by general rule or by individual order. To insist upon one form of action to the exclusion of the other is to exalt form over necessity.

In other words, problems may arise in a case which the administrative agency could not reasonably foresee, problems which must be solved despite the absence of a relevant general rule. Or the agency may not have had sufficient experience with a particular problem to warrant rigidifying its tentative judgment into a hard and fast rule. Or the problem may be so specialized and varying in nature as to be impossible of capture within the boundaries of a general rule. In those

situations, the agency must retain power to deal with the problems on a
case-to-case basis if the administrative process is to be effective. There
is thus a very definite place for the case-by-case evolution of statutory
standards. And the choice made between proceeding by general rule or
by individual, ad hoc litigation is one that lies primarily in the informed discretion of the administrative agency. See Columbia Broadcasting System v. United States, 316 U.S. 407, 421.

Hence we refuse to say that the Commission, which had not
previously been confronted with the problem of management trading
during reorganization, was forbidden from utilizing this particular
proceeding for announcing and applying a new standard of conduct.
. . . That such action might have a retroactive effect was not
necessarily fatal to its validity. Every case of first impression has a
retroactive effect, whether the new principle is announced by a court or
by an administrative agency. But such retroactivity must be balanced
against the mischief of producing a result which is contrary to a
statutory design or to legal and equitable principles. If that mischief is
greater than the ill effect of the retroactive application of a new
standard, it is not the type of retroactivity which is condemned by law.
See Addison v. Holly Hill Co., 322 U.S. 607, 620.

And so in this case, the fact that the Commission's order might
retroactively prevent Federal's management from securing the profits
and control which were the objects of the preferred stock purchases
may well be outweighed by the dangers inherent in such purchases
from the statutory standpoint. If that is true, the argument of retroactivity becomes nothing more than a claim that the Commission lacks
power to enforce the standards of the Act in this proceeding. Such a
claim deserves rejection.

The problem in this case thus resolves itself into a determination of
whether the Commission's action in denying effectiveness to the proposed amendment to the Federal reorganization plan can be justified on
the basis upon which it clearly rests. As we have noted, the Commission avoided placing its sole reliance on inapplicable judicial precedents. Rather it has derived its conclusions from the particular facts in
the case, its general experience in reorganization matters and its
informed view of statutory requirements. It is those matters which are
the guide for our review.

The Commission concluded that it could not find that the reorganization plan, if amended as proposed, would be "fair and equitable to the
persons affected [thereby]" within the meaning of § 11(e) of the Act,
under which the reorganization was taking place. Its view was that
the amended plan would involve the issuance of securities on terms
"detrimental to the public interest or the interest of investors" contrary
to §§ 7(d)(6) and 7(e), and would result in an "unfair or inequitable
distribution of voting power" among the Federal security holders within the meaning of § 7(e). It was led to this result "not by proof that the
interveners [Federal's management] committed acts of conscious wrongdoing but by the character of the conflicting interests created by the

interveners' program of stock purchases carried out while plans for reorganization were under consideration."

.   .   .

The scope of our review of an administrative order wherein a new principle is announced and applied is no different from that which pertains to ordinary administrative action. The wisdom of the principle adopted is none of our concern. .   .   . Our duty is at an end when it becomes evident that the Commission's action is based upon substantial evidence and is consistent with the authority granted by Congress.

.   .   .

We are unable to say in this case that the Commission erred in reaching the result it did. The facts being undisputed, we are free to disturb the Commission's conclusion only if it lacks any rational and statutory foundation. In that connection, the Commission has made a thorough examination of the problem, utilizing statutory standards and its own accumulated experience with reorganization matters. In essence, it has made what we indicated in our prior opinion would be an informed, expert judgment on the problem. It has taken into account "those more subtle factors in the marketing of utility company securities that gave rise to the very grave evils which the Public Utility Holding Company Act of 1935 was designed to correct" and has relied upon the fact that "Abuse of corporate position, influence, and access to information may raise questions so subtle that the law can deal with them effectively only by prohibitions not concerned with the fairness of a particular transaction."

.   .   .

The Commission's conclusion here rests squarely in that area where administrative judgments are entitled to the greatest amount of weight by appellate courts. It is the product of administrative experience, appreciation of the complexities of the problem, realization of the statutory policies, and responsible treatment of the uncontested facts. It is the type of judgment which administrative agencies are best equipped to make and which justifies the use of the administrative process. .   .   . Whether we agree or disagree with the result reached, it is an allowable judgment which we cannot disturb.

Reversed.

MR. JUSTICE BURTON concurs in the result.

THE CHIEF JUSTICE and MR. JUSTICE DOUGLAS took no part in the consideration or decision of this case.

MR. JUSTICE JACKSON, dissenting. The Court by this present decision sustains the identical administrative order which only recently it held invalid. S.E.C. v. Chenery Corp., 318 U.S. 80. As the Court correctly notes, the Commission has only "recast its rationale and reached the same result." (Par. 1.)[2] There being no change in the order, no additional evidence in the record and no amendment of relevant legislation, it is clear that there has been a shift in attitude

2. For convenience of reference, I have numbered consecutively the paragraphs of the Court's opinion, and cite quotations accordingly.

between that of the controlling membership of the Court when the case was first here and that of those who have the power of decision on this second review.[3]

I feel constrained to disagree with the reasoning offered to rationalize this shift. It makes judicial review of administrative orders a hopeless formality for the litigant, even where granted to him by Congress. It reduces the judicial process in such cases to a mere feint. While the opinion does not have the adherence of a majority of the full Court, if its pronouncements should become governing principles they would, in practice, put most administrative orders over and above the law.

. . .

The essential facts are few and are not in dispute. This corporation filed with the Securities and Exchange Commission a voluntary plan of reorganization. While the reorganization proceedings were pending sixteen officers and directors bought on the open market about 7½% of the corporation's preferred stock. Both the Commission and the Court admit that these purchases were not forbidden by any law, judicial precedent, regulation or rule of the Commission. Nevertheless, the Commission has ordered these individuals to surrender their shares to the corporation at cost, plus 4% interest, and the Court now approves that order.

It is helpful, before considering whether this order is authorized by law, to reflect on what it is and what it is not. It is not conceivably a discharge of the Commission's duty to determine whether a proposed plan of reorganization would be "fair and equitable." It has nothing to do with the corporate structure, or the classes and amounts of stock, or voting rights or dividend preferences. It does not remotely affect the impersonal financial or legal factors of the plan. It is a personal deprivation denying particular persons the right to continue to own their stock and to exercise its privileges. Other persons who bought at the same time and price in the open market would be allowed to keep and convert their stock. Thus, the order is in no sense an exercise of the function of control over the terms and relations of the corporate securities.

Neither is the order one merely to regulate the future use of property. It literally takes valuable property away from its lawful owners for the benefit of other private parties without full compensation and the Court expressly approves the taking. It says that the stock owned by these persons is denied conversion along with similar stock owned by others; "instead, it was to be surrendered at cost plus dividends accumulated since the purchase dates." (Par. 5.) It should be noted that this formula was subsequently altered to read "cost plus 4% interest." That this basis was less than its value is recognized

3. [Ed.] Chenery I was a 4–3 decision. Frankfurter, J., wrote the opinion for himself, Stone, C.J., and Roberts and Jackson, JJ. Black, J., with whom concurred Reed and Murphy, JJ., dissented; Douglas, J., took no part and there was a vacancy on the Court caused by the resignation of Byrnes, J. By the time Chenery II was before the court, Stone had been replaced by Vinson, Roberts by Burton, and the Byrnes vacancy had been filled by Rutledge.

. . . . Admittedly, the value above cost, and interest on it, simply is taken from the owners, without compensation. No such power has ever been confirmed in any administrative body.

It should also be noted that neither the Court nor the Commission purports to adjudge a forfeiture of this property as a consequence of sharp dealing or breach of trust. . . . "It was frankly admitted that the management's purpose in buying the preferred stock was to protect its interest in the new company. It was also plain that there was no fraud or lack of disclosure in making these purchases." (Par. 4.) . . .

The reversal of the position of this Court is due to a fundamental change in prevailing philosophy. The basic assumption of the earlier opinion as therein stated was, "*But before transactions otherwise legal can be outlawed or denied their usual business consequences, they must fall under the ban of some standards of conduct prescribed by an agency of government authorized to prescribe such standards. . . .*" S.E.C. v. Chenery Corp., 318 U.S. 80, 92, 93. The basic assumption of the present opinion is stated thus: "*The absence of a general rule or regulation governing management trading during reorganization did not affect the Commission's duties in relation to the particular proposal before it.*" (Par. 13.) This puts in juxtaposition the two conflicting philosophies which produce opposite results in the same case and on the same facts. The difference between the first and the latest decision of the Court is thus simply the difference between holding that administrative orders must have a basis in law and a holding that absence of a legal basis is not ground on which courts may annul them.

As there admittedly is no law or regulation to support this order, we perused the Court's opinion diligently to find on what grounds it is now held that the Court of Appeals, on pain of being reversed for error, was required to stamp this order with its approval. We find but one. That is the principle of judicial deference to administrative experience. That argument is five times stressed in as many different contexts . . . .

What are we to make of this reiterated deference to "administrative experience" when in another context the Court says, "Hence, we refuse to say that the Commission, *which had not previously been confronted with the problem of management trading during reorganization,* was forbidden from utilizing this particular proceeding for announcing and applying *a new standard of conduct.*"? (Par. 17.) (Emphasis supplied.)

The Court's reasoning adds up to this: The Commission must be sustained because of its accumulated experience in solving a problem with which it had never before been confronted!

Of course, thus to uphold the Commission by professing to find that it has enunciated a "new standard of conduct" brings the Court squarely against the invalidity of retroactive law-making. But the Court does not falter. "That such action might have a retroactive effect was not necessarily fatal to its validity." (Par. 17.) "But such retroactivity must be balanced against the mischief of producing a result which is contrary to a statutory design or to legal and equitable principles." (Par. 17.) Of course, if what these parties did really was condemned by "statutory design" or "legal and equitable principles," it could be stopped without resort to a new rule and there would be no retroactivity to condone. But if it had been the Court's view that some law already prohibited the purchases, it would hardly have been necessary three sentences earlier to hold that the Commission was not prohibited "from utilizing this particular proceeding for announcing and applying a *new standard of conduct.*" (Par. 17.) (Emphasis supplied.)

I give up. Now I realize fully what Mark Twain meant when he said, "The more you explain it, the more I don't understand it."

. . .

I suggest that administrative experience is of weight in judicial review only to this point—it is a persuasive reason for deference to the Commission in the exercise of its discretionary powers under and within the law. It cannot be invoked to support action outside of the law. And what action is, and what is not, within the law must be determined by courts, when authorized to review, no matter how much deference is due to the agency's fact finding. . . .

The truth is that in this decision the Court approves the Commission's assertion of power to govern the matter without law, power to force surrender of stock so purchased whenever it will, and power also to overlook such acquisitions if it so chooses. The reasons which will lead it to take one course as against the other remain locked in its own breast, and it has not and apparently does not intend to commit them to any rule or regulation. This administrative authoritarianism, this power to decide without law, is what the Court seems to approve in so many words: "This absence of a general rule or regulation governing management trading during reorganization did not affect the Commission's duties. . . . " (Par. 13.) This seems to me to undervalue and to belittle the place of law, even in the system of administrative justice. It calls to mind Mr. Justice Cardozo's statement that "Law as a guide to conduct is reduced to the level of mere futility if it is unknown and unknowable."

. . .

I have long urged, and still believe, that the administrative process deserves fostering in our system as an expeditious and nontechnical method of applying law in specialized fields. I can not agree that it be used, and I think its continued effectiveness is endangered when it is used, as a method of dispensing with law in those fields.

Mr. Justice Frankfurter joins in this opinion.

NATIONAL LABOR RELATIONS BOARD v. BELL AEROSPACE COMPANY

Supreme Court of the United States, 1974.
416 U.S. 267.

Mr. Justice Powell delivered the opinion of the Court.

[Bell Aerospace Co. refused to bargain with the elected representative of the 25 buyers at one of its facilities, claiming they were "managerial employees" and therefore outside of the collective bargaining process established by the National Labor Relations Act. The National Labor Relations Board found that the buyers, who enjoyed substantial discretion in their work of procuring items needed by the company, were protected by the Act, so that the company's refusal to bargain was an unfair labor practice. The finding was controversial in two respects. First, while the Board now said that Congress intended to exclude from the Act only those managers involved in formulating and implementing labor relations policies, a long line of its own prior decisions supported the interpretation that *all* "managerial employees," and not just those with a potential conflict of interest on union matters, lay beyond the Board's jurisdiction. Second, even if buyers (or some types of buyers) need not be characterized as "managerial employees," a related line of Board decisions had long treated them that way; even assuming the Board had the authority to change this aspect of its "law," it could be argued that change in such a long-standing approach was required to be effected by rulemaking operating only prospectively, rather than by adjudication. The United States Court of Appeals for the Second Circuit denied enforcement to the Board's order. It acknowledged that there was substantial evidence that the company's buyers were not sufficiently high in the managerial hierarchy to constitute true "managerial employees." Nevertheless, the court denied enforcement for two reasons. First, it was not certain that the Board's decision rested on a factual determination that these buyers were not true "managerial employees" rather than on "its new, and in our view, erroneous holding that it was free to regard *all* managerial employees as covered by the Act unless their duties met" the conflict-of-interest touchstone. Second, although the Board was not precluded from holding that buyers, or some types of buyers, were not "managerial employees," the court thought that, in view of the Board's long line of cases holding the contrary, it could not accomplish this change of position by adjudication.]

II

We begin with the question whether all "managerial employees," rather than just those in positions susceptible to conflicts of interest in labor relations, are excluded from the protections of the Act.[1] . . .

1. Section 2(3) of the Act defines the term "employee" as follows:

"The term 'employee' shall include any employee . . . but shall not include any individual employed as an agricultural laborer, or in the domestic service of any family or person at his home, or any individual employed by his parent or spouse, or any individual having the status of an independent contractor, or any individual employed as a supervisor. . . ." Supervisory employees are expressly excluded from the protections of the Act. That term is defined in § 2(11):

"The term 'supervisor' means any individual having authority, in the interest of the employer, to hire, transfer, suspend, lay off, recall, promote, discharge, assign, reward, or discipline other employees, or responsibility to direct them, or to adjust their grievances, or effectively to recommend such action, if in connection with the foregoing the exercise of such authority is not of a merely routine or clerical nature but requires the use of independent judgment."

In sum, the Board's early decisions, the purpose and legislative history of the Taft-Hartley Act of 1947, the Board's subsequent and consistent construction of the Act for more than two decades, and the decisions of the courts of appeals all point unmistakably to the conclusion that "managerial employees" are not covered by the Act. We agree with the Court of Appeals below that the Board "is not now free" to read a new and more restrictive meaning into the Act.

In view of our conclusion, the case must be remanded to permit the Board to apply the proper legal standard in determining the status of these buyers. SEC v. Chenery Corp., 318 U.S. 80, 85 (1943). We express no opinion as to whether these buyers fall within the category of "managerial employees."

III

The Court of Appeals also held that, although the Board was not precluded from determining that buyers or some types of buyers were not "managerial employees," it could do so only by invoking its rulemaking procedures under § 6 of the Act, 29 U.S.C. § 156.[2] We disagree.

At the outset, the precise nature of the present issue must be noted. The question is not whether the Board should have resorted to rulemaking, or in fact improperly promulgated a "rule," when in the context of the prior representation proceeding it held that the Act covers all "managerial employees" except those meeting the new "conflict of interest in labor relations" touchstone. Our conclusion that the Board applied the wrong legal standard makes consideration of that issue unnecessary. Rather, the present question is whether on remand the Board must invoke its rulemaking procedures if it determines, in light of our opinion, that these buyers are not "managerial employees" under the Act. The Court of Appeals thought that rulemaking was required because any Board finding that the company's buyers are not "managerial" would be contrary to its prior decisions and would presumably be in the nature of a general rule designed "to fit all cases at all times."

A similar issue was presented to this Court in its second decision in SEC v. Chenery Corp., 332 U.S. 194 (1947) (Chenery II). . . . The Court concluded that "the choice made between proceeding by general rule or by individual, ad hoc litigation is one that lies primarily in the informed discretion of the administrative agency."

2. Section 6 provides:

"The Board shall have authority from time to time to make, amend, and rescind, in the manner prescribed by the Administrative Procedure Act, such rules and regulations as may be necessary to carry out the provisions of this subchapter." . . .

Sections 9(c)(1) and (2) of the National Labor Relations Act (NLRA) empower the Board to investigate petitions involving questions of unit representation, to conduct hearings on such petitions, to direct representation elections, and to certify the results thereof. 29 U.S.C. §§ 159(c)(1) and (2). Board determinations on such representation questions would appear to constitute "orders" within the meaning of the APA. See 5 U.S.C. §§ 551(6), (7).

The NLRA does not specify in what instances the Board must resort to rulemaking.

And in NLRB v. Wyman-Gordon Co., 394 U.S. 759 (1969), the Court upheld a Board order enforcing an election list requirement first promulgated in an earlier adjudicative proceeding . . . The plurality opinion of Mr. Justice Fortas, joined by The Chief Justice, Mr. Justice Stewart, and Mr. Justice White, recognized that "[a]djudicated cases may and do . . . serve as vehicles for the formulation of agency policies, which are applied and announced therein," and that such cases "generally provide a guide to action that the agency may be expected to take in future cases." . . . The concurring opinion of Mr. Justice Black, joined by Mr. Justice Brennan and Mr. Justice Marshall, also noted that the Board had both adjudicative and rulemaking powers and that the choice between the two was "within its informed discretion."

The views expressed in Chenery II and Wyman-Gordon make plain that the Board is not precluded from announcing new principles in an adjudicative proceeding and that the choice between rulemaking and adjudication lies in the first instance within the Board's discretion. Although there may be situations where the Board's reliance on adjudication would amount to an abuse of discretion or a violation of the Act, nothing in the present case would justify such a conclusion. Indeed, there is ample indication that adjudication is especially appropriate in the instant context. As the Court of Appeals noted, "[t]here must be tens of thousands of manufacturing, wholesale and retail units which employ buyers, and hundreds of thousands of the latter." Moreover, duties of buyers vary widely depending on the company or industry. It is doubtful whether any generalized standard could be framed which would have more than marginal utility. The Board thus has reason to proceed with caution, developing its standards in a case-by-case manner with attention to the specific character of the buyers' authority and duties in each company. The Board's judgment that adjudication best serves this purpose is entitled to great weight.

The possible reliance of industry on the Board's past decisions with respect to buyers does not require a different result. It has not been shown that the adverse consequences ensuing from such reliance are so substantial that the Board should be precluded from reconsidering the issue in an adjudicative proceeding. Furthermore, this is not a case in which some new liability is sought to be imposed on individuals for past actions which were taken in good-faith reliance on Board pronouncements. Nor are fines or damages involved here. In any event, concern about such consequences is largely speculative, for the Board has not yet finally determined whether these buyers are "managerial."

It is true, of course, that rulemaking would provide the Board with a forum for soliciting the informed views of those affected in industry and labor before embarking on a new course. But surely the Board has discretion to decide that the adjudicative procedures in this case may also produce the relevant information necessary to mature and fair consideration of the issues. Those most immediately affected, the buyers and the company in the particular case, are accorded a full opportunity to be heard before the Board makes its determination.

The judgment of the Court of Appeals is therefore affirmed in part and reversed in part, and the cause remanded to that court with directions to remand to the Board for further proceedings in conformity with this opinion.

It is so ordered.

MR. JUSTICE WHITE, with whom MR. JUSTICE BRENNAN, MR. JUSTICE STEWART, and MR. JUSTICE MARSHALL join, dissenting in part.

I concur in Part III of the Court's opinion insofar as it holds that the Board was not required to resort to rulemaking in deciding this case, but I dissent from its holding in Part II that managerial employees as a class are not "employees" within the meaning of the National Labor Relations Act.

.   .   .

The Board's decisions in this area have not established a cohesive and precise pattern of rulings. It is often difficult to tell whether an individual decision is based on the propriety of excluding certain employees from a particular bargaining unit or whether the worker under consideration is thought to be outside the scope of the Act. But this Court has consistently said that it will accept the Board's determination of whether a particular individual is an "employee" under the Act if that determination "has 'warrant in the record' and a reasonable basis in law," NLRB v. Hearst Publications, Inc., 322 U.S. 111, 131 (1944); NLRB v. United Insurance Co., 390 U.S. 254, 260 (1968). There is no reason here to hamstring the Board and deny a broad category of employees those protections of the Act which neither the statutory language nor its legislative history requires simply because the Board at one time interpreted the Act—erroneously it seems to me—to exclude all managerial as well as supervisory employees.

I respectfully dissent.

NOTES

(1) Judge Friendly's opinion in the court below, holding that the Board could not now allow buyers to be organized under the NLRA except by conducting a rulemaking proceeding, included the following thoughts, 475 F.2d at 496–97:

"The Board was prescribing a new policy, not just with respect to 25 buyers in Wheatfield, N.Y., but in substance, to use Mr. Justice Douglas' phrase, 'to fit all cases at all times.' There must be tens of thousands of manufacturing, wholesale and retail units which employ buyers, and hundreds of thousands of the latter. Yet the Board did not even attempt to inform industry and labor organizations, by means providing some notice though not in conformity with section 4, of its proposed new policy and to invite comment thereon, as it has sometimes done in the past, see Peck, The Atrophied Rule-Making Powers of the National Labor Relations Board, 70 Yale L.J. 729, 756–757 (1961). .   .   . Although policy-making by adjudication often cannot be avoided in unfair labor practice cases, since the parties have already acted and the Board must decide one way or the other, there is no such problem in a representation case. Finally, the argument for rule-making is especially strong when the Board is proposing to reverse a long-standing and oft-repeated policy on which industry and labor have relied. To be sure, the change of policy here in question did not expose an employer to new and unexpected liability. . . . The point rather is that when the Board has so long been committed to a position, it should be particularly sure that it has all available information before adopting another, in a setting where nothing stands in the way of a rule-making proceeding except the Board's congenital disinclination to follow a procedure which, as said in Texaco, Inc. v. FPC, 412 F.2d 740, 744 (3 Cir.1969), 'enables the agency promulgating the rule to educate itself before establishing rules and procedures which have a substantial impact on those regulated,' . . . ."

In a note, he also reported the following, 475 F.2d at 495 n. 14:

"At argument we asked counsel for the Board to advise us in writing whether it had ever engaged in the rule-making on substantive matters contemplated by § 4 of the Administrative Procedure Act, 5 U.S.C. § 553. In a memorandum dated February 12, 1973, counsel advised us that the Board has recently concluded one such proceeding by promulgating a standard for the exercise of jurisdiction over private colleges and universities. Also in the summer of 1972 the Board published notices of proposed rule-making on the questions whether to assert jurisdiction over the horseracing and dogracing industries and over symphony orchestras and, if so, what the standard should be."

Regarding the Labor Board's systematic use of adjudication rather than rulemaking, see Bernstein, The NLRB's Adjudication-Rule Making Dilemma under the Administrative Procedure Act, 79 Yale L.J. 571 (1970).

(2) ROBERT A. GORMAN, BASIC TEXT ON LABOR LAW 18–20 (1976): Following upon Justice Powell's observation that "this is not a case in which some new liability is sought to be imposed on individuals for past actions which were taken in good faith reliance on Board pronouncements," Professor Gorman writes:

"There have, however, been cases in which a retroactive application of a principle announced in unfair labor practice proceedings has indeed resulted in the imposition of significant liability for conduct which was 'lawful when engaged in.' Some courts on review have held that the Board exceeds its powers in imposing such liability, the suggestion being (either explicit or implied) that the Board should have invoked rulemaking which would then have resulted in a general mandate prospective only. For example, in NLRB v. E & B Brewing Co. [, 276 F.2d 594 (6th Cir.1960), cert. denied 366 U.S. 908 (1961)], the union and the employer had entered into an agreement requiring that all hiring be done through a union-operated hiring hall, an agreement which was lawful when executed. The Board subsequently tightened its requirements for hiring-hall legality, declared this particular agreement not to meet those requirements and found both company and union to have violated the law and thus responsible for reinstatement and backpay. The court of appeals set aside the Board's order, finding it 'arbitrary, capricious, and an abuse of discretion,' and concluding that 'The Board's doctrine would retroactively invalidate every union contract which contains an exclusive hiring hall provision. If the Board's order stands, it is doubtful if even the Board can say how many hundreds or thousands of employers and unions are, as of now, guilty of similar unfair labor practices.' The court held this impact to be unjustified by any public interest in retroactive application. In a similar case, NLRB v. Local 176, Carpenters (Dimeo Constr. Co.) [, 276 F.2d 538 (1st Cir.1960)], a 'retroactive' order requiring the union to disgorge all dues collected from employees under its hiring-hall arrangement was overturned by the court as 'an ex post facto penalty.'

"The problem of the propriety of such retroactive orders has become more significant since the Supreme Court decision in NLRB v. Wyman-Gordon Co. [394 U.S. 759 (1969)], because that decision rather clearly discourages the Board from applying only prospectively new principles announced in adjudicatory proceedings. Now, in spite of arguable unfair surprise, the Board may choose to apply new doctrine retroactively to avoid the appearance of rulemaking. A conspicuous example of such arguably unfair retroactive application is found in Laidlaw Corp. v. NLRB [, 414 F.2d 99 (7th Cir.1969), cert. denied 397 U.S. 920 (1970)], in which the Board reversed its traditional position and held that a striker, lawfully replaced, was entitled to have his job back after applying for reinstatement if, even though there were no jobs available on the date of his application, an equivalent position opened up subsequently. Although the company's denial of reinstatement when a job came open was on advice of counsel and in accordance with the law at the time of the company's action, the Board not only applied the new principle to the company and found a violation of section 8(a)(3) but also required reinstatement and backpay. Rejecting the company's argument that the imposition of backpay running back to the denial of reinstatement was unduly harsh, the court of appeals balanced the hardship to the employer against the need to vindicate the rights of the employees and concluded: 'Unless the disadvantaged strikers are compensated, they will have been penalized for exercising statutorily protected rights and the effects of discouraging future such exercises will not be completely dissipated. In these circumstances, it was not arbitrary or capricious for the Board to conclude that complete vindication of employee rights should take precedence over the employer's reliance on prior Board law.'

"The question then rose whether other respondents, who also relied on the pre-Laidlaw privilege not to reinstate after the date of application, should be subjected to a backpay order. The Board has imposed such liability, and has met with a somewhat mixed but generally supportive reaction in the courts of appeals. Two major decisions conclude that the Board imposition of backpay was in the context of a valid adjudication and thus that it was not necessary to utilize the rulemaking procedure, and also that the Board in its adjudication could within its discretion find the hardship to the company outweighed by the interests of the employees in restitution for a statutory violation. American Mach. Corp. v. NLRB [, 424 F.2d 1321 (5th Cir.1970)]; H. &

F. Binch Co. v. NLRB [, 456 F.2d 357 (2d Cir.1972)]. Both courts noted that the change in the law represented by Laidlaw was not entirely unforeseeable at the time the company acted, in view of an earlier decision of the Supreme Court in a somewhat similar setting, in NLRB v. Fleetwood Trailer Co. [, 389 U.S. 375 (1967)]. Another court of appeals, however, although agreeing that the Board had the discretion to impose backpay for a period subsequent to Fleetwood, held—in light of the lack of any evidence of anti-union animus on the part of the company—that the Board's award of backpay running any earlier must be overturned. In finding such an award to be inequitable, the court considered the following factors: '(1) whether the particular case is one of first impression, (2) whether the new rule represents an abrupt departure from well established practice or merely attempts to fill a void in an unsettled area of the law, (3) the extent to which the party against whom the new rule is applied relied on the former rule, (4) the degree of the burden which a retroactive order imposes on a party, and (5) the statutory interest in applying a new rule despite the reliance of a party on the old standard.' Retail Union v. NLRB (Coca-Cola Bottling Works, Inc.) [, 466 F.2d 380 (D.C.Cir.1972)]."

FORD MOTOR COMPANY v. FEDERAL TRADE COMMISSION

United States Court of Appeals, Ninth Circuit, 1981.
673 F.2d 1008, cert. denied 459 U.S. 999 (1982).

Before GOODWIN, KENNEDY, and ALARCON, CIRCUIT JUDGES.

GOODWIN, CIRCUIT JUDGE.

Francis Ford, Inc. petitions this court to review an F.T.C. order finding it in violation of § 5 of the F.T.C. Act, 15 U.S.C. § 45 (unfair trade practices). We have reviewed the petition, and set aside the order.

Francis Ford, Inc. is an Oregon automobile dealership. Its practice in repossessing cars has been to credit the debtor for the wholesale value of the car, charge him for indirect expenses (i.e., overhead and lost profits) as well as direct expenses (i.e., refurbishing) associated with repossession and resale, and sell the repossessed vehicle at retail keeping the "surplus." In doing so, Francis Ford claims it is doing what is commonly done throughout its industry.

The F.T.C. does not approve of the described practice. Nor does it approve of a number of other credit practices now commonly in use in a wide variety of industries. See its investigations of the credit business, and its recent attempted rulemaking. In re Proposed Trade Regulation Rule: Credit Practices, 40 Fed.Reg. 16,347 (1975).

In order to attack Francis Ford's practice, the F.T.C. began in 1976 an adjudicatory action against Ford Motor Co., Ford Credit Co., and Francis Ford, Inc. The commission alleged that the respondents had violated § 5 of the F.T.C. Act by failing to give defaulting customers more than wholesale value for their repossessed cars, and by improperly charging them with indirect expenses such as overhead and lost profits. Parallel proceedings were commenced against Chrysler Corp.

and General Motors, their finance subsidiaries, and two dealers. The National Association of Car Dealers sought to intervene to protect the interests of its members but was not allowed to do so. Eventually, all the respondents except Francis Ford settled with the F.T.C.

Shortly after the consent decrees were entered, the administrative law judge held that Francis Ford's credit practices had violated § 5 of the F.T.C. Act, but that the commission had failed to establish that Francis Ford's acts were substantially injurious to its customers. Both Francis Ford and complaint counsel for the F.T.C. appealed to the full commission. The commission deleted the portion of the order favorable to Francis Ford, and affirmed the administrative law judge's decision. The order directed Francis Ford to cease its present credit practices, and to adopt the F.T.C.'s view of proper credit practices under ORS 79.5040 (U.C.C. § 9–504).

The narrow issue presented here is whether the F.T.C. should have proceeded by rulemaking in this case rather than by adjudication. The Supreme Court has said that an administrative agency, such as the F.T.C., "is not precluded from announcing new principles in the adjudicative proceeding and that the choice between rulemaking and adjudication lies in the first instance within the [agency's] discretion." NLRB v. Bell Aerospace Co., 416 U.S. 267, 294 (1974). See also, Securities Comm'n v. Chenery Corp., 332 U.S. 194, 202–203 (1947). But like all grants of discretion, "there may be situations where the [agency's] reliance on adjudication would amount to an abuse of discretion . . . ." Bell Aerospace Co., 416 U.S. at 294. The problem is one of drawing the line. On that score the Supreme Court has avoided blackletter rules. Lower courts have been left, therefore, with the task of dealing with the problem on a case-by-case basis.

The Ninth Circuit recently made such an attempt in Patel v. Immigration & Naturalization Serv., 638 F.2d 1199 (9th Cir.1980). In Patel, the Immigration and Naturalization Service, by an administrative adjudication, added a requirement to a regulation governing permanent immigration to this country. The court disallowed the requirement because the requirement changed past practices through the "prospective pronouncement of a broad, generally applicable requirement, amount[ing] to 'an agency statement of general or particular applicability and future effect.'" . . . The thrust of the Patel holding, therefore, is that agencies can proceed by adjudication to enforce discrete violations of *existing* laws where the effective scope of the rule's impact will be relatively small; but an agency must proceed by rule-making if it seeks to change the law and establish rules of widespread application.

In the present case, the F.T.C., by its order, has established a rule that would require a secured creditor to credit the debtor with the "best possible" value of the repossessed vehicle, and forbid the creditor from charging the debtor with overhead and lost profits. The administrative decision below so holds. Framed according to Patel, the precise issue therefore is whether this adjudication changes existing law, and has widespread application. It does, and the matter should be addressed by rulemaking.

The F.T.C. admits that industry practice has been to do what Francis Ford does—credit the debtor with the wholesale value and charge the debtor for indirect expenses. But the F.T.C. contends that Francis Ford's particular practice violates state law (ORS 79.5040); that the violation will not be reached by the proposed trade rule on credit practices; and that this adjudication will have only local application. The arguments are not persuasive.

By all accounts this adjudication is the first agency action against a dealer for violating ORS 79.5040 by doing what Francis Ford does. Although the U.C.C. counterpart of ORS 79.5040 is enacted in 49 states, nearly word for word, we have been cited to no case which has interpreted the provision to require a secured creditor to credit the debtor for the "best possible price" and not charge him for overhead and lost profits. It may well be that Oregon courts will interpret U.C.C. § 9–504 in the manner advocated by the F.T.C. if the question is put to them. But it is speculation to contend, as does the F.T.C. here, that Francis Ford is in violation of *existing* Oregon law. One of the basic characteristics of law is that potential violators have, or can obtain, notice of it. No notice of the F.T.C.'s view of the law has been pointed out to us.

The F.T.C. could have formulated its position on U.C.C. § 9–504 and its application to the credit practices of car dealerships in its proposed trade rule on credit practices. It did not do so. The pending rulemaking proceeding and this adjudication seek to remedy, more or less, the same credit practices. Although the former is directed against the practices, inter alia, of car dealers in their accounting of deficiencies, and the latter is directed against a car dealer by reason of his practices in failing to account for surpluses, both matters are covered by U.C.C. § 9–504. If the rule for deficiencies is thought by the F.T.C. to be "appropriately addressed by rulemaking," it should also address the problem of accounting for surpluses by a rulemaking proceeding, and not by adjudication.

Ultimately, however, we are persuaded to set aside this order because the rule of the case made below will have general application. It will not apply just to Francis Ford. Credit practices similar to those of Francis Ford are widespread in the car dealership industry; and the U.C.C. section the F.T.C. wishes us to interpret exists in 49 states. The F.T.C. is aware of this. It has already appended a "Synopsis of Determination" to the order, apparently for the purpose of advising other automobile dealerships of the results of this adjudication. To allow the order to stand as presently written would do far more than remedy a discrete violation of a singular Oregon law as the F.T.C. contends; it would create a national interpretation of U.C.C. § 9–504 and in effect enact the precise rule the F.T.C. has proposed, but not yet promulgated.

Under these circumstances, the F.T.C. has exceeded its authority by proceeding to create new law by adjudication rather than by rulemaking.

The order is vacated.

ORDER

The panel voted to deny the petition for rehearing and to reject the suggestion for rehearing en banc.

The full court having been advised of the suggestion for an en banc rehearing, a judge in active service requested that a vote be taken on the suggestion for rehearing en banc. Fed.R.App.P. 35(b). Upon the vote of the eligible judges in active service, a majority voted against en banc rehearing.

The petition for rehearing is denied and the suggestion for rehearing en banc is rejected.

REINHARDT, CIRCUIT JUDGE, dissenting from denial of rehearing en banc:

I dissent from the court's refusal to rehear this case en banc.

. . .

The panel's opinion pays lip service at most to the basic principle of administrative law that "the choice between rulemaking and adjudication lies in the first instance within the Board's discretion." NLRB v. Bell Aerospace Co., 416 U.S. 267. While repeating the rule, the panel opinion gives it no weight and no significance, and the panel fails to state explicitly that the agency abused its discretion.

. . .

Since the call for an en banc vote failed to muster the support of an absolute majority of the active members of this court who were eligible to vote, it would appear that a number of my colleagues are not as concerned as I am with the conflict between the broad, generalized statement in the panel's opinion and our own prior precedents which carefully apply the applicable line of Supreme Court cases in this area. My colleagues may believe that the broad, generalized statement is limited by the specific explanations subsequently offered in the panel's opinion. Specifically, they may feel that the opinion stands only for the proposition that an administrative agency decision which creates a new and different national interpretation of the uniform law (in this case the Uniform Commercial Code) applicable in all of the states of this nation is beyond an agency's decision making powers, at least where the agency has proposed a rule which would have that effect but has not yet enacted it. If this is my colleagues' view, the damage caused by the panel's opinion will be minor and temporary. I think we would be better served, however, if we would clarify the law of the circuit now, through the en banc procedure, rather than allow the unnecessary confusion which will inevitably exist in the field of administrative law pending the time that we explain the limitations of the majority's opinion in our subsequent decisions. . . .

NOTES

(1) The court's suggestion that "[t]o allow the order to stand . . . would create a national interpretation of U.C.C. § 9–504" needs a bit of explanation. Strictly speaking, the FTC is not in the business of interpreting state statutes; its business is to enforce, by rule or order, the Federal Trade Commission Act, which outlaws "unfair or deceptive acts or practices in or affecting commerce," 15 U.S.C. § 45(a)(1). Inevitably, and indeed quite purposefully, such enforcement often results in finding to be unlawful some practices that are quite permissible at common law or, more to present purposes, that are allowed under the Uniform Commercial Code.

As the court mentions, the FTC attached to its decision in Ford Motor a "synopsis of determination." Amendments to the FTC Act passed in 1975 included a provision permitting the FTC to bring a district court action to obtain a civil penalty from any person who committed an act or practice that had been found by the Commission to be "unfair or deceptive" in a cease and desist order proceeding, whether or not the person was the person subject to the order, if the person sued had "actual knowledge that such act or practice is unfair or deceptive and is unlawful" under the statute. 15 U.S.C. § 45(m)(1)(B) Since the Commission would know, or could discover, almost every participant in the affected industry, its circulation of a synopsis of an adjudicatory decision could have nearly the same impact as might be achieved by enacting a rule, since it would create actual knowledge of what the Commission had found to be unfair and deceptive.

Finally, it is worth mentioning that every state has a state "unfair or deceptive acts or practices" statute which typically (although not universally) makes FTC law at least persuasive authority as to what is permitted under state law. See National Consumer Law Center, Unfair and Deceptive Acts and Practices Sec. 1.1 (1982 and 1985 Supp.) So, in effect, if the FTC determines that creditors can in fact do only so-and-so (whatever U.C.C. § 9–504 might appear to permit), that determination becomes not only the law applied by a federal agency, but the law applicable in most, if not all, state courts as well.

(2) CASENOTE, 58 Wash.L.Rev. 633, 644–46 (1983):

". . . [T]he Ford case does not invoke any of the policy concerns that courts and commentators have suggested would make adjudication an abuse of discretion. One important policy concern is the retroactive effect of adjudication. Retroactivity may cause substantial hardship for a party if it results in significant penalties being imposed. Such punitive retroactivity was not present in Ford. . . .

"Another important policy concern is the anti-competitive effect of ordering a party to cease a practice in which its competitors remain free to engage. This concern, like the others, does not apply to Ford. Not only have the three major United States automobile manufacturers ordered their dealers to comply with the FTC consent order, but the FTC has sought to notify all dealers of the new requirements through publication of a "Synopsis of Determinations," which was attached to the FTC Ford order. The FTC thus ordered Francis Ford to comply with a refund technique similar to that which all dealers will have to follow in the future.

"Yet another important policy concern is that adjudication does not afford interested non-parties notice of, and an opportunity to comment on, the proposed rule prior to its adoption. By limiting effective participation by broad segments of the public, adjudication may prevent an agency from hearing the full range of divergent interests represented by the general public. This reasoning, however, overlooks common agency practices for permitting public participation in adjudications. These practices range from accepting informal statements or amicus briefs to allowing interested persons full intervention as parties. . . .

"Meaningful outside involvement did occur in Ford. The National Automobile Dealers Association (NADA), which represents approximately 20,000 automobile dealers, participated vigorously in the Ford proceedings. It is likely that the FTC afforded significantly more weight to NADA's arguments than it would have to the comments of individual dealers. Furthermore, in this case all the parties likely to appear in a rulemaking proceeding on repossession surpluses have appeared in the adjudication proceeding."

(3) DAVID SHAPIRO, THE CHOICE OF RULEMAKING OR ADJUDICATION IN THE DEVELOPMENT OF ADMINISTRATIVE POLICY, 78 Harv.L.Rev. 921, 926–27 (1965):

"Implicit in some criticism of the failure to utilize the rulemaking process is the view that the lack of regulations is equivalent to a lack of clearly articulated standards to guide those subject to the agency's jurisdiction. And closely paralleling this view is the occasional suggestion that in the absence of regulations, the agency must ordinarily start from scratch in establishing its case in each adjudicatory proceeding even though similar issues have been resolved in prior adjudications. It should therefore be emphasized, . . . that the choice between rulemaking and adjudication is not necessarily the choice between the articulation of a rule and an ad hoc approach in which each case is governed only by a general statutory provision. Agencies, like courts, frequently evolve detailed and precise rules in the course of adjudication. . . . Rules declared in adjudication have varied in form from the imposition of minimum time limits for the observance of statutory obligations to the declaration of presumptions that are based on prior experience and that shift to the respondent the burden of going forward. The soundness and lawfulness of any given rule may be subject to challenge, but the existence of general authority to act in this manner can hardly be questioned, and it is evident that the effect of such a rule is to narrow and simplify the issues requiring resolution in subsequent cases.

"Nevertheless, the process of adjudication, including the decision whether or not to prosecute, is often used without any effort to clarify and elaborate general statutory standards, while the rulemaking process has no real function except elaboration. It is possible to have a regulation providing that each case will turn on its own facts, but the regulation would serve virtually no purpose unless perhaps it was designed to announce that more specific proposals had been considered and rejected."

(4) PETER STRAUSS, RULES, ADJUDICATIONS, AND OTHER SOURCES OF LAW IN AN EXECUTIVE DEPARTMENT: REFLECTIONS ON THE INTERIOR DEPARTMENT'S ADMINISTRATION OF THE MINING LAW, 74 Colum.L.Rev. 1231, 1245–47, 1274–75 (1974):

"The failure to use rulemaking is far less a product of conscious departmental choice than a result of impediments to the making of rules created by the Department's internal procedures. The channels which lead to rulemaking, and to a lesser extent other forms of legislative policy statement such as production of the Manual, are so clogged with obstacles, and the flow through them so sluggish, that staff members hesitate to use them. Several years may elapse between the initial movement towards a rule and its final promulgation. And like an adult game of "Telephone," Department personnel complain, what is suggested at the outset for possible rulemaking is often unrecognizable when and if a formal proposal ultimately emerges. Absent commitment at the highest levels, the process is one that is easily blocked at almost any stage by determined opposition. As a result, rulemaking may be consciously avoided by an individual with an idea for policy change when other means for achieving the same policy ends appear to be available.

". . . The procedures themselves do not reflect any policy determination as to when rulemaking is the preferred mode of policy articulation, unless general disfavor can be inferred from the obstacles imposed.

"The search for mandatory controls over the allocation of the policymaking function between rulemaking and adjudication remains illusory. . . . Yet whether or not controls are applied, there remains a body of belief that for some purposes rules are the superior vehicle. Where clear, accessible rules are possible, it disserves the public to compel it to disentangle a web of sometimes obscure and hidden law sources. Only lawyers stand to gain, if anyone does, from needless complexity. Broader participation in the formulation of policy is encouraged in the rulemaking context; it both assures direct policy control and reduces somewhat the impact of new law on settled expectations. . . .

"In the Department of the Interior, however, and perhaps elsewhere, the concept of "allocation" suggests processes which do not occur. Coordination, unified control over the choice of policymaking technique, much less its outcome, is simply lacking. The principal determinants in the largely unconscious mechanisms by which issues find their way into one or another process are inertia and rulemaking procedures so choked as to be virtually impassable. . . ."

(5) NOTE, NLRB RULEMAKING: POLITICAL REALITY VERSUS PROCEDURAL FAIRNESS, 89 Yale L.J. 982, 995–96 (1980):

"The advantages of adjudicatory lawmaking for an agency concerned with congressional review are substantial. Adjudicatory lawmaking permits the agency to adopt rules without clearly articulating its policies and their implications. By developing a rule gradually over several years, the agency can in effect 'hide the ball.' In leaving its doctrine ambiguous, often seemingly restricted to the facts of a certain case, the Board can legislate in controversial areas without giving critics a clear and final rule to attack.

"Adjudication also gives the agency the opportunity to avoid clarifying the many issues underlying the rule. Unlike the rulemaking process, in which an agency is required to specify the analytical and empirical grounds for its decision, adjudication permits major policy changes to be made with little or no explanation. Indeed, it is a common criticism of the [Labor] Board that it often will announce such changes in an apparently innocuous manner, frequently limiting its analytical discussion to one or two paragraphs. The Board thereby not only avoids antagonizing powerful interests that may disagree with its assumptions regarding industrial relations, but also prevents attacks on the validity of a rule's empirical and analytical foundation.

"Perhaps the greatest advantage of adjudication in avoiding congressional scrutiny is that it presents no firm and final resolution of a policy issue, but only an incremental and ambiguous step. Unlike a promulgated rule, which generally represents a firm statement of agency policy that can be amended only through new rulemaking proceedings, a rule announced in an adjudicatory proceeding may appear as only a step in the gradual evolution of a general doctrine. It is difficult for a congressional committee to justify spending valuable time on a matter for which the agency has announced no clear and final standard. By the time a doctrine is fully developed, however, it often has been incorporated into the system too completely to arouse much organized opposition.[1]"

(6) The principal case is unusual in federal jurisprudence; it is by no means unique. See, e.g., First Bancorporation v. Board of Gover-

---

1. [Ed.] The different rules applicable to Congressional oversight of formal adjudication and informal rulemaking also serve to insulate adjudication, see pp. 957ff. within.

nors, 728 F.2d 434 (10th Cir.1984). As to the perhaps greater willingness to require rulemaking in state administrative law, see Arthur
Bonfield, State Administrative Rule Making 97–140 (1986). Professor
Bonfield's argument is based in part on sections 2–104(3) and 2–104(4)
of the 1981 Model State APA, reproduced within at page 1252.

HECKLER, SECRETARY OF HEALTH AND HUMAN SERVICES v. CAMPBELL

Supreme Court of the United States, 1983.
461 U.S. 458.

JUSTICE POWELL delivered the opinion of the Court.

The issue is whether the Secretary of Health and Human Services
may rely on published medical-vocational guidelines to determine a
claimant's right to Social Security disability benefits.

I

The Social Security Act defines "disability" in terms of the effect a
physical or mental impairment has on a person's ability to function in
the workplace. It provides disability benefits only to persons who are
unable "to engage in any substantial gainful activity by reason of any
medically determinable physical or mental impairment." 42 U.S.C.
§ 423(d)(1)(A). And it specifies that a person must "not only [be]
unable to do his previous work but [must be unable], considering his
age, education, and work experience, [to] engage in any other kind of
substantial gainful work which exists in the national economy, regardless of whether such work exists in the immediate area in which he
lives, or whether a specific job vacancy exists for him, or whether he
would be hired if he applied for work." 42 U.S.C. § 423(d)(2)(A).

In 1978, the Secretary of Health and Human Services promulgated
regulations implementing this definition. The regulations recognize
that certain impairments are so severe that they prevent a person from
pursuing any gainful work. See 20 CFR § 404.1520(d) (1982). A
claimant who establishes that he suffers from one of these impairments
will be considered disabled without further inquiry. If a claimant
suffers from a less severe impairment, the Secretary must determine
whether the claimant retains the ability to perform either his former
work or some less demanding employment. If a claimant can pursue
his former occupation, he is not entitled to disability benefits. If he
cannot, the Secretary must determine whether the claimant retains the
capacity to pursue less demanding work.

The regulations divide this last inquiry into two stages. First, the
Secretary must assess each claimant's present job qualifications. The
regulations direct the Secretary to consider the factors Congress has
identified as relevant: physical ability, age, education, and work experience. Second, she must consider whether jobs exist in the national

economy that a person having the claimant's qualifications could perform.

Prior to 1978, the Secretary relied on vocational experts to establish the existence of suitable jobs in the national economy. After a claimant's limitations and abilities had been determined at a hearing, a vocational expert ordinarily would testify whether work existed that the claimant could perform. Although this testimony often was based on standardized guides, vocational experts frequently were criticized for their inconsistent treatment of similarly situated claimants. To improve both the uniformity and efficiency [1] of this determination, the Secretary promulgated medical-vocational guidelines as part of the 1978 regulations. See 20 CFR pt. 404, subpt. P, app. 2 (1982).

These guidelines relieve the Secretary of the need to rely on vocational experts by establishing through rulemaking the types and numbers of jobs that exist in the national economy. They consist of a matrix of the four factors identified by Congress—physical ability, age, education, and work experience [2]—and set forth rules that identify whether jobs requiring specific combinations of these factors exist in significant numbers in the national economy. [3] Where a claimant's qualifications correspond to the job requirements identified by a rule, [4] the guidelines direct a conclusion as to whether work exists that the claimant could perform. If such work exists, the claimant is not considered disabled.

II

In 1979, Carmen Campbell applied for disability benefits because a back condition and hypertension prevented her from continuing her

---

1. The Social Security hearing system is "probably the largest adjudicative agency in the western world." J. Mashaw, C. Goetz, F. Goodman, W. Schwartz, P. Verkuil, & M. Carrow, Social Security Hearings and Appeals xi (1978). Approximately 2.3 million claims for disability benefits were filed in fiscal year 1981. Department of Health and Human Services, Social Security Annual Report to the Congress for Fiscal Year 1981, pp. 32, 35 (1982). More than a quarter of a million of these claims required a hearing before an administrative law judge. Id., at 38. The need for efficiency is self-evident.

2. Each of these four factors is divided into defined categories. A person's ability to perform physical tasks, for example, is categorized according to the physical exertion requirements necessary to perform varying classes of jobs—i.e., whether a claimant can perform sedentary, light, medium, heavy, or very heavy work. Each of these work categories is defined in terms of the physical demands it places on a worker, such as the weight of objects he must lift

and whether extensive movement or use of arm and leg controls is required.

3. For example, Rule 202.10 provides that a significant number of jobs exist for a person who can perform light work, is closely approaching advanced age, has a limited education but who is literate and can communicate in English, and whose previous work has been unskilled.

4. The regulations recognize that the rules only describe "major functional and vocational patterns." If an individual's capabilities are not described accurately by a rule, the regulations make clear that the individual's particular limitations must be considered. Additionally, the regulations declare that the administrative law judge will not apply the age categories "mechanically in a borderline situation," 20 CFR § 404.1563(a) (1982), and recognize that some claimants may possess limitations that are not factored into the guidelines. Thus, the regulations provide that the rules will be applied only when they describe a claimant's abilities and limitations accurately.

work as a hotel maid. After her application was denied, she requested a hearing de novo before an Administrative Law Judge.[5] He determined that her back problem was not severe enough to find her disabled without further inquiry, and accordingly considered whether she retained the ability to perform either her past work or some less strenuous job. He concluded that even though Campbell's back condition prevented her from returning to her work as a maid, she retained the physical capacity to do light work. In accordance with the regulations, he found that Campbell was 52 years old, that her previous employment consisted of unskilled jobs, and that she had a limited education. He noted that Campbell, who had been born in Panama, experienced difficulty in speaking and writing English. She was able, however, to understand and read English fairly well. Relying on the medical-vocational guidelines, the Administrative Law Judge found that a significant number of jobs existed that a person of Campbell's qualifications could perform. Accordingly, he concluded that she was not disabled.

This determination was upheld by both the Social Security Appeals Council, and the District Court for the Eastern District of New York. The Court of Appeals for the Second Circuit reversed.

. . . The court found that the medical-vocational guidelines did not provide the specific evidence that it previously had required [of "specific alternative occupations available in the national economy that would be suitable for the claimant," "supported by a job description clarifying the nature of the job, [and] demonstrating that the job does not require exertion or skills not possessed by the claimant."] It explained that in the absence of such a showing, "the claimant is deprived of any real chance to present evidence showing that she cannot in fact perform the types of jobs that are administratively noticed by the guidelines." . . .

We granted certiorari to resolve a conflict among the Courts of Appeals. We now reverse.

III

. . . .

A

The Court of Appeals . . . remanded for the Secretary to put into evidence "particular types of jobs suitable to the capabilities of Ms. Campbell." The court's requirement that additional evidence be introduced on this issue prevents the Secretary from putting the guidelines to their intended use and implicitly calls their validity into question. Accordingly, we think the decision below requires us to consider wheth-

5. The Social Security Act provides each claimant with a right to a *de novo* hearing. . . .

er the Secretary may rely on medical-vocational guidelines in appropriate cases.

The Social Security Act directs the Secretary to "adopt reasonable and proper rules and regulations to regulate and provide for the nature and extent of the proofs and evidence and the method of taking and furnishing the same" in disability cases. 42 U.S.C. § 405(a). . . .

We do not think that the Secretary's reliance on medical-vocational guidelines is inconsistent with the Social Security Act. It is true that the statutory scheme contemplates that disability hearings will be individualized determinations based on evidence adduced at a hearing. See 42 U.S.C. § 423(d)(2)(A) (specifying consideration of each individual's condition); 42 U.S.C. § 405(b) (disability determination to be based on evidence adduced at hearing). But this does not bar the Secretary from relying on rulemaking to resolve certain classes of issues. The Court has recognized that even where an agency's enabling statute expressly requires it to hold a hearing, the agency may rely on its rulemaking authority to determine issues that do not require case-by-case consideration. See FPC v. Texaco Inc., 377 U.S. 33, 41–44 (1964); United States v. Storer Broadcasting Co., 351 U.S. 192, 205 (1956). A contrary holding would require the agency continually to relitigate issues that may be established fairly and efficiently in a single rulemaking proceeding.

The Secretary's decision to rely on medical-vocational guidelines is consistent with Texaco and Storer. As noted above, in determining whether a claimant can perform less strenuous work, the Secretary must make two determinations. She must assess each claimant's individual abilities and then determine whether jobs exist that a person having the claimant's qualifications could perform. The first inquiry involves a determination of historic facts, and the regulations properly require the Secretary to make these findings on the basis of evidence adduced at a hearing. We note that the regulations afford claimants ample opportunity both to present evidence relating to their own abilities and to offer evidence that the guidelines do not apply to them.[6] The second inquiry requires the Secretary to determine an issue that is not unique to each claimant—the types and numbers of jobs that exist in the national economy. This type of general factual issue may be resolved as fairly through rulemaking as by introducing the testimony of vocational experts at each disability hearing.

As the Secretary has argued, the use of published guidelines brings with it a uniformity that previously had been perceived as lacking. To require the Secretary to relitigate the existence of jobs in the national

---

6. Both FPC v. Texaco Inc., 377 U.S. 33, 40 (1964), and United States v. Storer Broadcasting Co., 351 U.S. 192, 205 (1956), were careful to note that the statutory scheme at issue allowed an individual applicant to show that the rule promulgated should not be applied to him. The regula-tions here provide a claimant with equal or greater protection since they state that an administrative law judge will not apply the rules contained in the guidelines when they fail to describe a claimant's particular limitations.

economy at each hearing would hinder needlessly an already overburdened agency. We conclude that the Secretary's use of medical-vocational guidelines does not conflict with the statute, nor can we say on the record before us that they are arbitrary and capricious.

B

We now consider Campbell's argument that the Court of Appeals properly required the Secretary to specify alternative available jobs. Campbell contends that such a showing informs claimants of the type of issues to be established at the hearing and is required by both the Secretary's regulation, 20 CFR § 404.944 (1980), and the Due Process Clause.

By referring to notice and an opportunity to respond, the decision below invites the interpretation given it by respondent. But we do not think that the decision fairly can be said to present the issues she raises. . . . Rather the court's reference to notice and an opportunity to respond appears to be based on a principle of administrative law— that when an agency takes official or administrative notice of facts, a litigant must be given an adequate opportunity to respond. See 5 U.S.C. § 556(e); McDaniel v. Celebrezze, 331 F.2d 426 (CA4 1964).

This principle is inapplicable, however, when the agency has promulgated valid regulations. Its purpose is to provide a procedural safeguard: to ensure the accuracy of the facts of which an agency takes notice. But when the accuracy of those facts already has been tested fairly during rulemaking, the rulemaking proceeding itself provides sufficient procedural protection.

IV

The Court of Appeals' decision would require the Secretary to introduce evidence of specific available jobs that respondent could perform. It would limit severely her ability to rely on the medical-vocational guidelines. We think the Secretary reasonably could choose to rely on these guidelines in appropriate cases rather than on the testimony of a vocational expert in each case. Accordingly, the judgment of the Court of Appeals is

Reversed.

JUSTICE BRENNAN, concurring.

I join the Court's opinion. It merits comment, however, that the hearing respondent received . . . reflects poorly on the Administrative Law Judge's adherence to what Chief Judge Godbold has called his "duty of inquiry". . . . The Administrative Law Judge's "duty to inquire" takes on special urgency where, as here, the claimant has little education and limited fluency in English, and, given that the claimant already has a right to a hearing, the additional cost of pursuing relevant issues at the hearing is minimal.

In order to find that respondent was not disabled, the Secretary had to determine that she had the physical capacity to do "light work," a determination that required a finding that she was capable of frequent lifting or carrying of objects weighing up to 10 pounds and sometimes lifting up to 20 pounds. The hearing record included one disinterested doctor's report of a medical examination of respondent that concluded with the unexplained statement "Patient may return to light-duty work," a subsequent report by a second disinterested doctor stating that respondent could lift and carry only "up to 10 pounds." In finding that respondent could perform "light work," the Administrative Law Judge rejected the second doctor's report as "without basis." Yet he failed entirely to adduce evidence relevant to this issue at respondent's hearing. At several points during the hearing, respondent stated that she could not lift things, but the Administrative Law Judge did not question her on the subject at all,[7] nor did he make any inquiry whether by "light-duty work" the first doctor meant the same thing as the Secretary's term "light work."

. . . The Secretary has since determined that respondent is in fact disabled, based on consideration of severe emotional complications not explored at all by the Administrative Law Judge in the hearing that led to her petition for review in this case.[8]

This issue was not presented to the Court of Appeals, nor passed upon by it. . . .

[Justice Marshall filed a similar opinion, disagreeing with Justice Brennan only in that he concluded that the issue had been raised in the court of appeals and so warranted a remand for further proceedings.]

NOTES

(1) The rules at issue in Heckler v. Campbell appear at 20 CFR Pt. 404, Subpt. P, App. 2 (1984), where they are set forth in various tables, one for each category of "residual functional capacity." Here is one of the tables; as you can see, each line is, in legal effect, a separate rule.

7. The following colloquy appears on the record:

"Q. Can you bend?

"A. I cannot bend. The doctor warned me not to lift weights.

"Q. Uh-huh.

"A. And—

"Q. I notice you have stood up several times since you've been in here."

At no point did the Administrative Law Judge so much as ask respondent how she did her shopping, or any other question that might have elicited information on the crucial question of how much she could regularly lift.

8. The decision appears to have rested on evidence similar to the evidence in the record at the hearing in this case, except that the Administrative Law Judge took note that respondent was "an obese, sad individual, who had marked difficulties in sitting, standing, and walking," and he found that her back disorder was "complicated by a severe emotional overlay."

TABLE NO. 2—RESIDUAL FUNCTIONAL CAPACITY: MAXIMUM SUSTAINED WORK CAPABILITY LIMITED TO LIGHT WORK AS A RESULT OF SEVERE MEDICALLY DETERMINABLE IMPAIRMENT(S)

Rule	Age	Education	Previous work experience	Decision
202.01	Advanced age	Limited or less	Unskilled or none	Disabled.
202.02	...do	...do	Skilled or semiskilled—skills not transferable.	Do.
202.03	...do	...do	Skilled or semiskilled—skills transferable [1].	Not disabled.
202.04	...do	High school graduate or more—does not provide for direct entry into skilled work [2].	Unskilled or none	Disabled.
202.05	...do	High school graduate or more—provides for direct entry into skilled work [2]	...do	Not disabled.
202.06	...do	High school graduate or more—does not provide for direct entry into skilled work [2]	Skilled or semiskilled—skills not transferable.	Disabled.
202.07	...do	...do	Skilled or semiskilled—skills transferable [2].	Not disabled.
202.08	...do	High school graduate or more—provides for direct entry into skilled work [2].	Skilled or semiskilled—skills not transferable.	Do.
202.09	Closely approaching advanced age.	Illiterate or unable to communicate in English.	Unskilled or none	Disabled.
202.10	...do	Limited or less—At least literate and able to communicate in English.	...do	Not disabled.
202.11	...do	Limited or less	Skilled or semiskilled—skills not transferable.	Do.
202.12	...do	...do	Skilled or semiskilled—skills transferable.	Do.
202.13	...do	High school graduate or more...	Unskilled or none	Do.
202.14	...do	...do	Skilled or semiskilled—skills not transferable.	Do.
202.15	...do	...do	Skilled or semiskilled—skills transferable.	Do.
202.16	Younger individual	Illiterate or unable to communicate in English.	Unskilled or none	Do.
202.17	...do	Limited or less—At least literate and able to communicate in English.	...do	Do.
202.18	...do	Limited or less	Skilled or semiskilled—skills not transferable.	Do.
202.19	...do	...do	Skilled or semiskilled—skills transferable.	Do.
202.20	...do	High school graduate or more...	Unskilled or none	Do.
202.21	...do	...do	Skilled or semiskilled—skills not transferable.	Do.
202.22	...do	...do	Skilled or semiskilled—skills transferable.	Do.

[1] See 202.00(f).
[2] See 202.00(c).

(2) COLIN DIVER, THE OPTIMAL PRECISION OF ADMINISTRATIVE RULES, 93 Yale L.J. 65, 89–91 (1983):

"The grid rule is the latest stage in a relentless progression toward transparency and complexity in the disability standard. The factor most obviously responsible for this trend is transaction costs. The volume of determinations is immense and was, until recently, growing at a rapid rate. The number of hearings is still growing. Moreover, although the average cost of processing all DI claims is modest ($171 in 1978), the cost per contested claim is a good deal higher. The total administrative cost of the disability insurance system in 1978 was $327 million.

"Raw numbers like these fail to do full justice to the importance of transaction costs. A 'hidden' transaction cost in any benefits system is the impact of delay on deserving applicants. The 551,500 applicants who received a favorable decision in 1976, for example, had to wait an average of 105 days for the award. The human costs of anxiety and deprivation from such delays are enormous.

"A second hidden transaction cost is the difficulty of controlling subordinate decisionmakers. A substantial degree of de facto decentralization is unavoidable in so enormous an operation. But the structure of the DI program promotes decentralization with a vengeance. Initial decisions (which become final determinations in the eighty-five percent of cases not appealed to SSA) are made by officers of fifty autonomous state agencies who are subject only to indirect supervision by SSA. These state agencies themselves are often administratively decentralized and rely heavily on consulting physicians and vocational experts. Within SSA, decisions are made by a cadre of about seven hundred fiercely independent Administrative Law Judges (ALJ's) who preside at hearings where there are usually no representatives of SSA present. Any decisionmaking apparatus so fragmented—especially one which affects such large sums of money and so many people—cries out for tight, centralized control. Recent studies documenting inconsistencies among state agencies and ALJ's have intensified pressures for reform.

"Demands for tighter supervision naturally focus attention on the clarity of substantive standards. The utility of conventional management control devices like reporting systems, performance appraisal, and quality review ultimately depends on the transparency of the underlying standards to be applied. It is one thing to document inconsistency in results by comparing two individuals' resolutions of a hypothetical case. But it is very difficult to remedy that inconsistency without having clear criteria. Without the dramatic increase in regulatory objectivity, SSA's massive quality control program and its impressive quantitative gains would be almost unthinkable."

(3) GIBSON V. HECKLER, 762 F.2d 1516 (11th Cir.1985): Gibson was disabled by a back injury; the ALJ found that "as a result of his back problem Gibson could neither sit nor stand for more than four hours in an eight-hour work day." Held: the application of the grids to deny disability payments in this case was impermissible; case remanded to the agency for individualized fact-finding. The grid variables of sedentary/light/medium work did not take into account the need to locate jobs that could be done partly standing and partly sitting. "[A]ny use of the grids as a measure of Gibson's ability to work would be inappropriate since Gibson's sit/stand limitation renders the residual functional capacity variable grossly over-inclusive."

(4) JERRY MASHAW, CONFLICT AND COMPROMISE AMONG MODELS OF ADMINISTRATIVE JUSTICE, 1981 Duke L.J. 181, 202–05:

"Consider, for example, cases in which parties challenge the method an agency or legislature has used to decide particular issues. Such a challenge might be framed as an attack on agency rulemaking power, as a protest against the use or development of 'bright line' standards in the course of adjudication, as an attack on the adequacy of rulemaking processes, or as a claim to procedural due process. At the heart of each controversy, whatever its formulation, lies a conflict between the bureaucratic-rationality model's view of adjudication as a straightforward fact-finding process, emphasizing accuracy and efficiency, and the moral-judgment model's view of adjudication as a value-realizing process tied inextricably to the deservedness of the affected parties.

"In cases such as National Petroleum Refiners Association v. FTC,[1] United States v. Storer Broadcasting Co.,[2] and FPC v. Texaco, Inc.,[3] the complaining parties attacked the power of the agency to adopt rules that restricted the scope of inquiry in subsequent adjudicatory proceedings. In National Petroleum the Federal Trade Commission had adopted a rule requiring station owners to post octane ratings for gasolines on all retail gas pumps. In Storer Broadcasting the Federal Communications Commission had adopted a rule prohibiting owners of five communications outlets from obtaining other outlets. In Texaco the Federal Power Commission had adopted a rule that certain clauses in contracts for the sale of natural gas would preclude the issuance of certificates for interstate pipeline transmission of the gas. Affected parties in all three cases claimed that they were statutorily entitled to a trial-type hearing about whether their practices or proposed operations were 'unfair,' 'deceptive,' or not in the 'public interest' under the relevant legislative language. It followed, they argued, that the agencies could not foreclose full adjudicatory explorations of the fairness or suitability of the behavior in question by rulemaking. The reviewing courts disagreed and stated that effective administration may demand the particularization of general standards through rulemaking. To find that the agencies lacked the asserted rulemaking power, the courts reasoned, would interfere with the efficient discharge of their regulatory tasks.

" . . .

"We may contrast the preceding cases with a line of cases that are considerably less deferential to the agency's or legislature's choice of decision-making procedure. These contrary cases are the "irrebuttable presumption"[4] cases, and include Bell v. Burson,[5] Stanley v. Illinois,[6] and Cleveland Board of Education v. LaFleur.[7] In Bell, for example, Georgia had adopted legislation barring from the highways persons who had been involved in accidents and had no liability insurance. The plaintiff, a driver suspended under the statute, claimed that the state had deprived him of due process of law by adjudicating his fault, or fitness to retain his license, without a hearing. The Supreme Court agreed. In Stanley, Illinois law provided that children of unwed fathers become wards of the state upon the mother's death, thereby

1.   482 F.2d 672 (D.C.Cir.1973), cert. denied, 415 U.S. 951 (1974).

2.   351 U.S. 192 (1956).

3.   377 U.S. 33 (1964).

4.   In such cases the complaining parties assert that legislative rules require the finding of facts that, at least to them, are untrue. The legislation has thus created an "irrebuttable presumption" that precludes the party from obtaining a fair hearing on a material issue of fact.

5.   402 U.S. 535 (1971).

6.   405 U.S. 645 (1972).

7.   414 U.S. 632 (1974).   See also Vlandis v. Kline, 412 U.S. 441 (1973).

presuming that the father was unfit to raise the children. The Court held that due process requires an individual determination of an unwed father's fitness. Similarly, in LaFleur the Court held unlawful a school-board rule requiring all pregnant teachers to take maternity leave five months before the expected birth. The Court held that a pregnant teacher was entitled to an individual determination of her continuing fitness to teach.

". . .

"Of course, the irrebuttable-presumption decisions not only fail to comport with cases like Storer Broadcasting; they also do not fit the general mold of constitutional law doctrine. If a bright-line rule may not replace a general principle unless the rule perfectly effectuates the principle, then most legislation and regulation, state and federal, is unconstitutional. Apparently recognizing this, the Court appears to have abandoned irrebuttable-presumption analysis without ever cogently explaining the grounds for either its original use or its ultimate rejection. Yet the juxtaposition of the traditional administrative law jurisprudence and the irrebuttable-presumption cases cries out for some meaningful response. When is it necessary to engage in an individual inquiry into deservedness, and when may a rule transform the adjudicatory inquiry into an efficient, fact-seeking one?

"We may make some progress in understanding these two seemingly incompatible lines of decisions by characterizing them in terms of a competition between our bureaucratic-rationality and moral-judgment models of justice. If the adjudication purports to allocate benefits and burdens on the basis of individual deservedness, the moral-judgment model is more appealing. If the decision process does not directly or impliedly raise deservedness issues, a rule-bound and fact-oriented bureaucratic process will suffice. . . . "

(5) How important is the point made in footnote 6 of Heckler v. Campbell as reproduced above? F.C.C. v. WNCN LISTENERS GUILD, 450 U.S. 582 (1981): The FCC is empowered by statute to approve an application for transfer or renewal of a radio license only if "the public interest, convenience and necessity" will be served. In informal rulemaking, the Commission determined (contrary to prior authority) that a desirable diversity of entertainment formats was best promoted by market (rather than regulatory) forces, and accordingly that a station's change in format was not a material factor to be considered by the Commission in making its renewal or transfer determinations. Seven to two, *held*: the rule (which the commission called a "Policy Statement") is sustained. Justices Marshall and Brennan, in dissent, urged that the question was not whether market forces would in general do the job, but rather whether opportunity must be left open to show in particular cases that they would not work. They continued, 450 U.S. at 608–611:

"The problem with the particular Policy Statement challenged here, however, is that it lacks the flexibility we have required of such general regulations and policies. See, e.g., United States v. Storer

Broadcasting Co., [351 U.S. 192 (1956)]; National Broadcasting Co. v. United States, [319 U.S. 190 (1943)]. The Act imposes an affirmative duty on the Commission to make a particularized 'public interest' determination for each application that comes before it. As we explained in National Broadcasting Co. v. United States, the Commission must, in each case, 'exercise an ultimate judgment whether the grant of a license would serve the "public interest, convenience, or necessity." ' The Policy Statement completely forecloses any possibility that the Commission will re-examine the validity of its general policy on format changes as it applies to particular situations. Thus, even when it can be conclusively demonstrated that a particular radio market does not function in the manner predicted by the Commission, the Policy Statement indicates that the Commission will blindly assume that a proposed format change is in the 'public interest.' . . .

"Moreover, our cases have indicated that an agency's discretion to proceed in complex areas through general rules is intimately connected to the existence of a 'safety valve' procedure that allows the agency to consider applications for exemptions based on special circumstances.

"This 'safety valve' feature is particularly essential where, as here, the agency's decision that a general policy promotes the public interest is based on predictions and forecasts that by definition lack complete factual support. . . .

"In my judgment, this requirement of flexibility compels the Commission to provide a procedure through which listeners can attempt to show that a particular radio market differs from the Commission's paradigm, and thereby persuade the Commission to give particularized consideration to a proposed format change."

For the majority, however, the essential question was whether the Policy Statement was consistent with the Act. Having found that it was, the Court was apparently unconcerned with the "safety valve" issue. Justice White's opinion was content merely to note that previous cases had come to the Court with a waiver mechanism attached; the Court had not held that an agency may never adopt a rule that lacks one. 450 U.S. at 601 n. 44.

ALLISON v. BLOCK
United States Court of Appeals, Eighth Circuit, 1983.
723 F.2d 631.

Before LAY, CHIEF JUDGE, and HEANEY and ARNOLD, CIRCUIT JUDGES.

HEANEY, CIRCUIT JUDGE.

In 1978, Congress enacted 7 U.S.C. § 1981a, an amendment to the Consolidated Farm and Rural Development Act of 1961 (CFRDA). Two years thereafter, Roger and Shirley Allison defaulted on farm loans granted to them by the Farmers Home Administration (FmHA) of the United States Department of Agriculture (USDA) under the CFRDA. . . . The district court enjoined foreclosure on the Allisons' farm until the Secretary complied with the letter and spirit of section 1981a. We affirm.

I

BACKGROUND

The Allisons own and operate a farm in Howard County, Missouri. On December 20, 1977, they obtained FmHA financing under the CFRDA in the amount of $103,800, secured by a deed of trust on their realty. Because of adverse weather conditions in 1977 and low grain and livestock prices in 1978, they failed to turn a profit on the operation of the farm during those years. . . . On August 24, 1979, the Allisons received a $190,000 reorganization loan, secured by a deed of trust on their farm. On April 28, 1980, they received a $29,750 operating loan, secured by a deed of trust and liens on their equipment, livestock, supplies, and inventory.

Adverse weather and economic conditions continued to hamper the Allisons' farming operations. In 1979, a dry planting season followed by an early frost reduced their crop yield significantly. In 1980, a severe drought contributed to an eighty-seven percent reduction in corn yield and a sixty-eight percent reduction in bean yield. Following these losses, the Allisons became delinquent on their FmHA loan payments.

. . .

On May 14, 1981, the FmHA accelerated the Allisons' indebtedness, as to both principal and interest, for failure to make timely payments and failure to pay real estate taxes. It notified them that their loans, which were classified as emergency (EM) and economic emergency (EE) loans, would be foreclosed unless the total indebtedness was paid by June 15, 1981. The Allisons appealed the acceleration notice to the FmHA District Director and Assistant Administrator; both upheld the decision. The Allisons then brought their final administrative appeal before the Administrator of the FmHA (Administrator). Pending this appeal, Roger Allison read in a farming magazine about possible loan deferral relief under federal statute and requested such relief from the Administrator. On August 10, 1982, the Program Assistant to the Administrator denied the Allisons' appeal, rejecting the alternatives of consolidation, rescheduling, reamortization, or deferral because the Allisons "did not have the potential to generate sufficient farm income to repay family living and farm operating expenses plus debt service even if a deferral had been granted."

On October 27, 1982, the Allisons filed the present action requesting declaratory and injunctive relief from the acceleration of their loans and foreclosure on their property. They alleged that the Secretary's failure to promulgate adequate procedural and substantive regulations creating a program for loan deferrals under 7 U.S.C. § 1981a (1982) violated that statute, amounted to a denial of equal protection and due process, and constituted an abuse of administrative discretion. . . .[1]

---

1. The district court found it unnecessary to reach the constitutional claims raised by the Allisons because of the statutory violation. We also decline to meet the constitutional issues.

II

STATUTORY REQUIREMENTS

. . . The gist of [the Secretary's] argument is that section 1981a merely created an additional power to be wielded at the discretion of the agency, or placed in the Secretary's "back pocket" for safekeeping. We reject this argument and affirm the district court. The full text of section 1981a is as follows:

> In addition to any other authority that the Secretary may have to defer principal and interest and forego foreclosure, the Secretary may permit, at the request of the borrower, the deferral of principal and interest on any outstanding loan made, insured, or held by the Secretary under this chapter, or under the provisions of any other law administered by the Farmers Home Administration, and may forego foreclosure of any such loan, for such period as the Secretary deems necessary upon a showing by the borrower that due to circumstances beyond the borrower's control, the borrower is temporarily unable to continue making payments of such principal and interest when due without unduly impairing the standard of living of the borrower. The Secretary may permit interest that accrues during the deferral period on any loan deferred under this section to bear no interest during or after such period: Provided, That if the security instrument securing such loan is foreclosed such interest as is included in the purchase price at such foreclosure shall become part of the principal and draw interest from the date of foreclosure at the rate prescribed by law.

The Secretary would have us hold that this statute requires no adjudicatory or regulatory administrative action because it creates no administrative procedural requirements nor any substantive right to relief from loan acceleration or foreclosure. We refuse to so hold. . . .

A. Procedural Requirements

Section 1981a expressly conditions the Secretary's authority to grant relief to CFRDA borrowers upon two actions by the borrower: (1) a request for such relief; and (2) a showing that, because of circumstances beyond the borrower's control, he or she is temporarily unable to continue payments of principal and interest without unduly impairing his or her standard of living. Following such a request and showing, the Secretary "may permit" deferral of payments of principal and interest and "may forego" foreclosure.

We agree with several federal district courts . . . that . . . Congress intended the Secretary to give notice of the availability of section 1981a relief to all CFRDA borrowers subject to loan acceleration or foreclosure and to establish a uniform procedure under which borrowers can make the requisite request and prima facie showing. The requirement of a request by the borrower prior to consideration for section 1981a relief presupposes that the borrower has knowledge of the availability of such relief. Notice to the borrower is therefore indispensable. In like manner, the requirement of a showing of prima facie eligibility is necessarily premised upon the expectation that some procedure will be provided under which the borrower may make the requisite showing. Thus, the rudimentary elements of adequate notice and an opportunity to be heard are embodied in the language of section 1981a.

Furthermore, the legislative history underlying the statute supports the conclusion that the Secretary is required to give notice to defaulting CFRDA borrowers and to create a procedure for asserting section 1981a claims. . . .

In addition to the official reports preceding section 1981a, comments made during the 1978 debates on the statute reflect a congressional intent that the Secretary develop an effective program offering deferral relief to defaulting farmers. . . .

. . . [A]lthough Congress gave the Secretary discretion in the final decision regarding the deferral of individual loans, the legislators did not intend for the Secretary to place section 1981a in his "back pocket;" there was never any question that Congress intended the development of a loan deferral program governed by uniform procedures.

Against this backdrop of statutory language and legislative history, we cannot accept the Secretary's assertion that Congress left the implementation of section 1981a a matter of unfettered administrative discretion. The cases principally relied on by the Secretary, Heim v. United States, 680 F.2d 564 (8th Cir.1982), and Rank v. Nimmo, 677 F.2d 692 (9th Cir.), cert. denied, 459 U.S. 907 (1982), are not controlling. In Heim, we upheld the Secretary's exercise of administrative discretion in denying funds to eradicate tuberculosis in the plaintiff's elk herd under the federal Tuberculosis Eradication Program. We stated that the Secretary's decision "that appropriated funds are better spent on cattle and swine than on elk . . . [was not] arbitrary, capricious, or contrary to law." We were not asked in Heim to decide whether the Secretary could have refused to develop a bovine tuberculosis eradication program altogether.

. . .

We therefore affirm the injunction against foreclosure of the Allisons' farm until the Secretary has complied with his responsibilities to provide adequate notice and procedures under which the Allisons may make the requisite prima facie showing and otherwise demonstrate their eligibility for a section 1981a deferral. Because the Allisons already have notice of the existence of section 1981a, the Secretary may fulfill the notice requirement of the statute in this case by giving the Allisons personal notice of the proper procedures once established.

B. Substantive Standards

Good faith consideration of the section 1981a deferral alternative by the Secretary requires the existence of some substantive standards which, if met, entitle the borrower to relief. Because any other construction would render the statute mere procedural "window-dressing," a result abhorrent to the language and purpose of the 1978 agricultural credit legislation and absurd as a matter of policy, we hold that section 1981a also requires the development of substantive standards at the agency level to guide the Secretary's discretion in making individual deferral decisions.

We cannot accept the Secretary's implicit assertion that the discretion to decide individual cases includes the authority to decide, without formal rulemaking, that—regardless of a borrower's request and prima facie showing, and the particular facts of the case—no CFRDA borrower is eligible for section 1981a deferral relief. . . .

Section 1981a expressly creates prima facie substantive standards of eligibility for deferral relief—"that due to circumstances beyond the borrower's control, the borrower is temporarily unable to continue making payments of . . . principal and interest when due without unduly impairing the standard of living of the borrower." Besides contemplating the existence of a procedure under which the borrower may make the prima facie showing, these preliminary substantive standards limit the number of borrowers eligible for section 1981a relief, indicating Congress's expectation that at least some of those borrowers would in fact merit such relief. Indeed, the title to section 1981a, as presented to Congress and codified as enacted, refers to a "moratorium and policy on foreclosures." Congress surely would not consider an empty procedural shell, with no substantive measure of relief, to be a policy at all.

Furthermore, the legislative history behind section 1981a exhibits Congress's intent that the Secretary respect the substantive standards explicitly set forth, and establish whatever other standards consistent with and necessary to the statute, in administering the emergency loan deferral program. The congressional debates all revolve around the structure and content of the "program" authorized by section 1981a, a strange term if the Secretary could merely make a decision unsupported by administrative investigation or public comment that no borrower deserves the relief which Congress authorized. . . .

We do not decide in what manner the Secretary must develop the substantive standards applicable to section 1981a deferral requests. The District of Columbia Circuit noted under similar circumstances:

> If regulations of general applicability were formulated, it would of course be possible to explain individual decisions by reference to the appropriate regulation. It may well be, however, that standards . . . can best be developed piecemeal, as the Secretary evaluates [particular cases]. Even so, he has an obligation to articulate the criteria that he develops in making each individual decision. We cannot assume, in the absence of adequate explanation, that proper standards are implicit in every exercise of administrative discretion.

Environmental Defense Fund, Inc. v. Ruckelshaus, 439 F.2d 584, 596 (D.C.Cir.1971). Although we believe that formal rulemaking would better insure a uniform set of substantive standards to govern section 1981a requests, we recognize that the Secretary may decide to develop the criteria through adjudicative processes which give some precedential effect to prior FmHA loan deferral decisions. The fact remains at present, however, that the Secretary has chosen neither a process of reasoned decisionmaking to safeguard against an abuse of section 1981a discretion nor the publication of uniform regulations to be used as substantive standards to guide the exercise of that discretion. See . . . 2 K. Davis, Administrative Law Treatise § 7:26, at 128–132 (2d ed. 1979). We cannot accept this complete abdication of the Secretary's responsibilities under section 1981a.

For purposes of the present appeal, we affirm the injunction against foreclosure on the Allison's farm not only pending proper notice of the procedures developed to process section 1981a requests, as previously discussed, but also pending publication of uniform substantive regulations or a reasoned decision on their particular request consistent with section 1981a requests nationwide.[2] We emphasize that, should the Secretary decide to develop substantive criteria through case-by-case adjudication, he cannot achieve this goal by considering each case in isolation. The Supreme Court succinctly stated, "No matter how rational or consistent with congressional intent a particular decision might be, the determination of eligibility cannot be made on an ad hoc basis by the dispenser of the funds." Morton v. Ruiz, 415 U.S. 199, 232 (1974). Thus, even if the Secretary does not publish formal findings of fact and conclusions of law in each case, he must clearly articulate the reasons for each section 1981a decision in a manner susceptible to judicial review for an abuse of discretion.

III

CONCLUSION

We realize that the plight of many farmers throughout the nation is so bleak that the forbearance of creditors will not save their operations. We are also aware, however, that the agricultural industry is especially vulnerable to the changing winds of time, nature, fate, and the economy; farmers of skill, perseverance, and dedication are no less vulnerable. Congress in 1978 clearly expressed its intent to assist farmers blown astray by these winds by granting those who could show that their inability to meet their financial obligations was temporary more time to repay their debts to the government. It commissioned the Secretary to implement this intent not as a private banker, but as a public broker. We view the Secretary's conscious disregard of section 1981a as contrary to that commission, and therefore affirm the injunction on foreclosure of the Allisons' farm until the intent of Congress becomes the action of the Secretary.

2. To the extent that the Secretary argues that the FmHA in fact made a reasoned decision to deny deferral relief to the Allisons, we affirm the district court's holding that the reasons given for that denial were "conclusory, unsupported, and contradictory," and the decision was thus an abuse of discretion.

NOTES

(1) Why shouldn't the Secretary be able to act like a private banker?

(2) The court says that the Secretary may develop law either through adjudicative processes that include a system of precedent or through "formal rulemaking." Despite the language, "formal rulemaking" probably only means organized, public rulemaking; presumably "informal rulemaking" under the APA would suffice. As to section 553(a)(2), making informal rulemaking proceedings unnecessary "to the extent that there is involved . . . a matter relating to . . . public property, loans, grants, benefits, or contracts," apparently the Department of Agriculture had publicly stated that it would not rely on that provision in matters relating to loans. See Curry v. Block, 738 F.2d 1556, 1564 (11th Cir.1984).

(3) The § 1981a program—or non-program—has been litigated in a whole series of "v. Block" cases. In Matzke v. Block, 732 F.2d 799 (10th Cir.1984), the court went beyond the principal case to say that "the rulemaking procedure must be utilized." When the matter got to the eleventh circuit, Curry v. Block, 738 F.2d 1556 (11th Cir.1984), the court wrote, 738 F.2d at 1563: "Thus far, the circuits have split over the method by which the Secretary shall establish a deferral relief program. The Eighth Circuit has concluded, at least with respect to substantive eligibility criteria, that, although formal rulemaking would be preferable, the Secretary may utilize adjudicative processes; on the other hand, the Tenth Circuit has concluded that the Secretary must employ rulemaking procedure. We agree with the Tenth Circuit that the urgent need Congress perceived for deferral relief to farmers and the national scope of the problems presented in this litigation render 'it . . . a bit late to begin the accumulation of decisional guides.' "

(4) In support of its claim that the Secretary must generate some law, and not rely on mere discretion, in the operation of the deferral program, the Allison court cites 2 K. Davis, Administrative Law Treatise § 7.26, at 128–132 (2d ed. 1979). Here are some excerpts from Professor Davis' treatment:

"§ 7.26. Required Rules: Discretion Unguided by Rules or Precedents

"The law may be in the early stages of a massive movement toward judicially required rulemaking that will reduce discretion that is unguided by rules or precedents. Under the new law, agencies that use systems of precedents are still generally free to choose between adjudication and rulemaking, but agencies without systems of precedents may be judicially required to use their rulemaking power to provide guiding standards.

"When the Supreme Court said in SEC v. Chenery Corp., 332 U.S. 194, 203 (1947), that the SEC could make new law either by adjudication or by rulemaking, it had in mind, as it said, that the alternative to rulemaking was 'case-by-case evolution of statutory standards.' The alternative to rulemaking that it had in mind was not unguided discretion to make a determination that would not be treated as a precedent. In formal adjudications the SEC writes reasoned opinions that are likely to be used as precedents. The problem of required rulemaking is altogether different for informal adjudication or other informal action by an agency that does not write reasoned opinions and has no system of precedents.

" . . .

"Several rather solid legal theories are available to support a judicial requirement of rulemaking to guide discretionary action, and all of them in combination are quite powerful. The non-delegation doctrine was used over a period of four or five decades to require statutory standards; now that the nondelegation doctrine has largely failed, courts may substitute a requirement of administrative standards or rules for the former requirement of statutory standards. . . . A second theory that supports a judicial requirement of rules or standards is simply that in some circumstances the lack of rules or standards is so unreasonable that due process is denied. . . . A third theory builds on the void for vagueness doctrine. In holding a vagrancy ordinance unconstitutional, the Supreme Court said: 'Where, as here, there are no standards governing the exercise of discretion granted by the ordinance, the scheme permits and encourages arbitrary and discriminatory enforcement.' Papachristou v. City of Jacksonville, 405 U.S. 156, 170 (1972). . . . The fourth method, which has much to commend it, is simply that of evolving common law or equitable considerations, based on judicial understanding of fairness and propriety. Whether a court says so or not, due process may be in the background, or unstated intent of the legislative body in the basic statute could be deemed the basis for the decision."

(5) The Supreme Court case that is usually cited as supporting this "trend," (if trend it be) is MORTON v. RUIZ, 415 U.S. 199 (1974). Ruiz and his family, Papago Indians, moved 15 miles off the Papago reservation so that he could live and work at the Phelps-Dodge copper mines at Ajo, Arizona. They maintained close ties with the reservation and, said the Court, "have not been assimilated into the dominant culture." Twenty-seven years after the Ruizes moved, the miners went on strike; the state of Arizona refused general assistance to striking workers; and Ruiz applied for general assistance from the Bureau of Indian Affairs. The sole ground for denying his application was that, although he lived near the reservation, the BIA's internal "Manual" limited general assistance benefits to "Indians living on reservations and in jurisdictions under the Bureau of Indian Affairs in Alaska and Oklahoma."

"This case," wrote Justice Blackmun for a unanimous Court (415 U.S. at 201), "presents a narrow but important issue in the administration of the federal general assistance program for needy Indians:

Are general assistance benefits available only to those Indians living *on* reservations in the United States (or in areas regulated by the Bureau of Indian Affairs in Alaska and Oklahoma), and are they thus unavailable to Indians (outside Alaska and Oklahoma) living *off,* although near, a reservation? "

The statutory basis for the program was, it turned out, phrased in extraordinarily general language; the appropriations acts which funded the program year-by-year were similarly vague. The government placed its reliance on that fact that the BIA's formal budget requests always stated that "[g]eneral assistance will be provided to needy Indians on reservations." But the Court was not impressed because, as it showed by quoting page on page of the agency's testimony before Congress, in considering who was "on" a reservation and who was "off," the agency had always represented that "near" equalled "on." The "history clearly shows that Congress was led to believe that the programs were being made available to those unassimilated needy Indians living near the reservation as well as to those living 'on.'"

In one sense, this was (after some 30 pages of discussion) the end of the case. The BIA's central claim had been that, given the agency's budget requests, Congress itself had appropriated funds only for those living directly on reservations; this claim had failed; there was little doubt that if those "near" reservations would qualify, the Ruizes would. Instead of stopping there, however, Justice Blackmun went on to consider whether the agency's Manual, which limited benefits to those "on" reservations, might itself have some binding legal effect.

He began with the following two paragraphs, which contain the language for which Morton v. Ruiz is usually (as in the Allison case) cited:

"Having found that the congressional appropriation was intended to cover welfare services at least to those Indians residing 'on or near' the reservation, it does not necessarily follow that the Secretary is without power to create reasonable classifications and eligibility requirements in order to allocate the limited funds available to him for this purpose. See Dandridge v. Williams, 397 U.S. 471 (1970); Jefferson v. Hackney, 406 U.S. 535 (1972). Thus, if there were only enough funds appropriated to provide meaningfully for 10,000 needy Indian beneficiaries and the entire class of eligible beneficiaries numbered 20,000, it would be incumbent upon the BIA to develop an eligibility standard to deal with this problem, and the standard, if rational and proper, might leave some of the class otherwise encompassed by the appropriation without benefits. But in such a case the agency must, at a minimum, let the standard be generally known so as to assure that it is being applied consistently and so as to avoid both the reality and the appearance of arbitrary denial of benefits to potential beneficiaries.

"Assuming, arguendo, that the Secretary rationally could limit the 'on or near' appropriation to include only the smaller class of Indians who lived directly "on" the reservation plus those in Alaska and Oklahoma, the question that remains is whether this has been validly accomplished. The power of an administrative agency to administer a congressionally created and funded program necessarily requires the formulation of policy and the making of rules to fill any gap left, implicitly or explicitly, by Congress. In the area of Indian affairs, the

Executive has long been empowered to promulgate rules and policies, and the power has been given explicitly to the Secretary and his delegates at the BIA. This agency power to make rules that affect substantial individual rights and obligations carries with it the responsibility not only to remain consistent with the governing legislation, but also to employ procedures that conform to the law. No matter how rational or consistent with congressional intent a particular decision might be, the determination of eligibility cannot be made on an ad hoc basis by the dispenser of the funds." 415 U.S. at 230–232.

But, if ad hoc means for Justice Blackmun what it usually means, it is a little hard to see how having field personnel operate under a rule in a departmental manual automatically generates ad hoc behavior, since it might well lead (and presumably was intended to lead) to consistency; and if Justice Blackmun wished to make something of the possibility that in this type of situation the BIA had not in practice applied its own rule even-handedly, perhaps because the case-by-case decisions were made by ordinary bureaucrats, without a mechanism for reporting them, he certainly did not say so. Instead, when it came time to decide the case at hand, he denied legal force to the Manual's language for two other reasons. First, the rule had not been published in the Federal Register as required by the Agency's own regulations, and by the APA, 5 U.S.C. § 552(a)(1), which accordingly made it "ineffective so far as extinguishing rights of those otherwise within the class of beneficiaries contemplated by Congress is concerned." Second, the rule did not represent a persuasive authority as to the proper interpretation of otherwise vague statutory language because it was the contrary of what the BIA had itself represented to Congress.

At the end, the Court held that the Ruizes were entitled to assistance. As to the dimensions of the class entitled to relief, that "will be determined, to the extent necessary, by the District Court on remand of the case. Whether other persons qualify for general assistance will be left to cases that arise in the future." Presumably the "cases" the Court had in mind were in-court proceedings.

(6) Professor Davis suggests that what we might call the "Allison v. Block" approach can be grounded in constitutional requirements of due process. The case probably most often cited for this proposition is Holmes v. New York City Housing Authority, 398 F.2d 262 (2d Cir. 1968). Each year the Authority received approximately 90,000 applications for public housing, out of which it could select only 10,000 families for admission. In federally-aided projects, it was required to follow an objective scoring system to choose among applicants. For projects built with state and local money, however, there was no similar regulation. Plaintiffs alleged that they had applied for public housing, that they had never been advised of their eligibility or ineligibility, and that applications filed with the Authority were not processed according to any reasonable, or even ascertainable, system. On interlocutory appeal, the question was whether their complaint stated a federal, which is to say constitutional, cause of action. Anderson, J.:

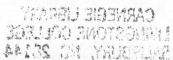

"One charge made against the defendant, which has merit at least in connection with state-aided projects where the Authority has adopted no standards for selection among non-preference candidates, is that it thereby failed to establish the fair and orderly procedure for allocating its scarce supply of housing which due process requires. It hardly need be said that the existence of an absolute and uncontrolled discretion in an agency of government vested with the administration of a vast program, such as public housing, would be an intolerable invitation to abuse. See Hornsby v. Allen, 326 F.2d 605, 609–610 (5 Cir.1964). For this reason alone due process requires that selections among applicants be made in accordance with 'ascertainable standards,' id. at 612, and, in cases where many candidates are equally qualified under these standards, that further selections be made in some reasonable manner such as 'by lot or on the basis of the chronological order of application.' Hornsby v. Allen, 330 F.2d 55, 56 (5 Cir.1964) (on petition for rehearing). Due process is a flexible concept which would certainly also leave room for the employment of a scheme such as the 'objective scoring system' suggested in the resolution adopted by the Authority for federal-aided projects."

SECTION 3. PARTY PARTICIPATION IN CHOOSING A PROCEDURAL MODE

To speak a bit over-simply, the preceding section revolved around the question whether it is the agencies or the courts that choose the structure for administrative proceedings. Now we turn to the question whether "outsiders" can influence the overall shape of a proceeding. A private party might think that it can present its case better in a more formal proceeding; or it might fear that its point of view will not be heard at all in a proceeding from which it has been excluded. Or it might not care about rational persuasion, and only be interested in collecting as many procedural weapons as it can to use to influence the course of governmental action. Whatever the reason, it is certainly not sufficient to think that only courts and agencies are involved in the process.

a. Party Initiation of Formal Proceedings [1]

The organic statute establishing an administrative agency will typically provide that the power to investigate evils and bring administrative charges looking to their cessation belongs with the agency itself. For example, the Federal Trade Commission Act provides that complaints are issued "[w]henever the Commission shall have reason to believe that any . . . person . . . has been or is using any unfair method of competition or unfair or deceptive act or practice in or affecting commerce. . . . " 15 U.S.C. § 45(b). The public authority

---

1. It is perhaps worth noting that what is here being discussed is the initiation by a private party of an agency proceeding. There is, of course, another large body of law dealing with the question whether a private party can sue directly in court to enforce through judicial processes a regulatory statute. See, e.g., Middlesex Cty. Sewerage Auth. v. National Sea Clammers Association, 453 U.S. 1 (1981). That is a different question, although many similar policy concerns are implicated.

is given control of the enforcement practice of the agency. Indeed, the FTC Act also provides that the agency can issue a complaint only after finding that "a proceeding by it . . . would be to the interest of the public," id., and the courts have said that this language prevents the initiation of a hearing to vindicate a purely "private" right. See, e.g., Montgomery Ward Co. v. F.T.C., 379 F.2d 666, 672 (7th Cir.1967).

The typical statutory pattern is not, however, the only statutory pattern. The Interstate Commerce Act, for example—at least as it stood prior to deregulation—gave the Commission rate-making authority. Proceedings to have a rate declared "unjust or unreasonable or unjustly discriminatory or unduly preferential" could be started by the Commission on its own initiative, or they could be started by a complaint filed by "[a]ny person, firm, corporation, company, or association, or any mercantile, agricultural, or manufacturing society or other organization, or any body politic or municipal organization, or any common carrier." 49 U.S.C. §§ 13, 15.

But where the statute does place the power to initiate proceedings solely with a public authority, do private parties have any way to require the agency to begin? In the archetypical case, the enforcement of the criminal law, the usual response is that "the exercise of prosecutorial discretion is not subject to judicial review."[2] The proposition reflects both formal constraints of the separation of powers—the reluctance of courts to interfere in executive functions—and the related recognition that a prosecutor must be free to deploy her limited resources in accordance with public, rather than private, priorities.

2. Even as regards the criminal law, of course, the proper scope for unreviewable prosecutorial discretion is debatable. For a large scope (H. Friendly, Review [of K. Davis, Police Discretion (1975)], 44 U.Chi. L.Rev. 255, 257–78 (1976)):

"We are told that '[a] limited judicial review of the kind that is customary with respect to other administrative action is clearly desirable. Members of the bar are likely to be almost unanimous in that judgment.' The second sentence is certainly correct; members of the bar are attracted to judicial review with a fervor reminiscent of goats in rut. But review by what standards and at the suit of whom? In states with full enforcement statutes, the appropriate legal standard would seem to be full enforcement—which nobody wants. Even in states without such enactments, are the courts to tell the police, save in cases where the rules are racially or religiously discriminatory on their face, just how far the police shall enforce or not enforce admittedly governing and valid criminal statutes? Quo warranto? Furthermore, who has standing to invoke this strange exercise of judicial power? I know of no principle, absent a charge of discrimination on the basis of race or religion, that would

entitle a person selected for enforcement to complain that others equally guilty were not. These are not 'rules' governing the conduct of citizens; they are instructions from one policeman to others."

For a reduced scope of unreviewable discretion: A. Goldstein, The Passive Judiciary (1981): "The most important consequence of judicial review—if it is reinforced by occasional denial of motions to dismiss or rejection of guilty pleas—is that it would make the prosecutor more accountable. He would have to explain and justify his departures from the formal rules, and his explanations would become subject to verification. . . . . [T]he objective should not be to deny discretion to the prosecutor but rather to require that he share with the courts a responsibility for the public interest in criminal law.

". . . It does not serve the cause of legality to permit officials to ignore the legislature, or to have legislatures act on the assumption that their statutes will be ignored or discounted. . . . And it is not genuinely helpful to prosecutors to burden them with so heavy a responsibility for defining and administering criminal law. . . ."

Should the result be any different for more particular regulatory schemes?

In DUNLOP v. BACHOWSKI, 421 U.S. 560 (1975), also discussed at pp. 472 and 997 below, Bachowski had lost a union election under circumstances which he believed entitled him to have it set aside. The governing statute confers on the Secretary of Labor exclusive enforcement authority, in order to protect the apparent victors from frivolous litigation, and to assure a quick, definitive settlement to any dispute. Bachowski complained to the Secretary, who found after an investigation that action to set the results aside would not be warranted. He gave only a brief explanation of his views and Bachowski sought to have his actions declared arbitrary and capricious, and to require that an action be instituted. One question the Court was obliged to decide was whether the Secretary's decision was protected from review by its prosecutorial character; it disposed of that question summarily: "We agree with the Court of Appeals, for the reasons stated in its opinion, 502 F.2d at 86–88, that there is no merit in the Secretary's contention that his decision is an unreviewable exercise of prosecutorial discretion." Those pages of 502 F.2d state as follows:

"The Secretary contends that his decision whether to bring suit under § 402 of the L–MRDA is an exercise of prosecutorial discretion which is unreviewable and cannot be compelled by a court. Not every refusal by a Government official to take action to enforce a statute, however, is unreviewable. See Adams v. Richardson, 480 F.2d 1159 (1973).[3] Although the Secretary's decision to bring suit bears some similarity to the decision to commence a criminal prosecution, the principle of absolute prosecutorial discretion is not applicable to the facts of this case.

"To begin with, we believe that the doctrine of prosecutorial discretion, should be limited to those civil cases which, like criminal prosecutions, involve the vindication of societal or governmental interest, rather than the protection of individual rights. The Confiscation Cases, [74 U.S. (7 Wall.) 454 (1869)], on which the Secretary primarily relies, were suits to confiscate property used in aid of rebellion; there

3. [Ed.] In the Adams case, black students, citizens and taxpayers sued the Secretary of HEW and the Director of HEW's Office of Civil Rights alleging that the defendants had been derelict in their duty to enforce Title VI of the Civil Rights Act of 1964 in that they had not taken appropriate action to end segregation in public educational institutions receiving federal funds. The district court ordered the defendants to "(1) institute compliance procedures against ten state-operated systems of higher education, (2) commence enforcement proceedings against seventy-four secondary and primary school districts found either to have reneged on previously approved desegregation plans or to be otherwise out of compliance with Title VI, (3) commence enforcement proceedings against forty-two districts previously

deemed by HEW to be in presumptive violation of the Supreme Court's ruling in Swann v. Charlotte-Mecklenburg Bd. of Educ., 402 U.S. 1 (1971), (4) demand of eighty-five other secondary and primary districts an explanation of racial disproportion in apparent violation of [the law], (5) implement an enforcement program to secure Title VI compliance with respect to vocational and special schools, (6) monitor all school districts under court desegregation orders to the extent that HEW resources permit, and (7) make periodic reports to [plaintiff] on their activities in each of the above areas."

The court of appeals, en banc, modified the injunction concerning higher education and affirmed the remainder of the order.

was little question that they were 'for the benefit of the United States,' rather than on behalf of any aggrieved individuals. However, the legislative history of the L–MRDA demonstrates a deep concern with the interest of individual union members, as well as the general public, in the integrity of union elections. Thus, in seeking to remedy violations of the Act, the Secretary acts not only for the benefit of the country as a whole, but also on behalf of those individuals whose rights have been infringed. To grant the Secretary absolute discretion in this situation seems particularly inappropriate, for if he wrongfully refuses to file suit, individual union members are left without a remedy.

"Furthermore, as Professor Davis has observed, perhaps the most convincing reason for the unreviewability of prosecutorial discretion is that a prosecutor 'may be actuated by many considerations that are beyond the judicial capacity to supervise.' Davis, Administrative Law Treatise, § 28.16 at 984 (1970 Supp.). The factors to be considered by the Secretary, however, are more limited and clearly defined: § 482(b) of the L–MRDA provides that after investigating a complaint, he must determine whether there is probable cause to believe that violations of § 481 have occurred affecting the outcome of the election. Where a complaint is meritorious and no settlement has been reached which would remedy the violations found to exist, the language and purpose of § 402(b) indicate that Congress intended the Secretary to file suit. Thus, apart from the possibility of settlement, the Secretary's decision whether to bring suit depends on a rather straightforward factual determination, and we see nothing in the nature of that task that places the Secretary's decision 'beyond the judicial capacity to supervise.' " [4]

The Supreme Court carefully avoided, as unnecessary to its immediate conclusion, any discussion of the remedial authority a district court might have if, after affording the Secretary a chance for explanation, it found "that the Secretary's statement of reasons on its face renders necessary the conclusion that his decision not to sue is so irrational as to constitute the decision arbitrary and capricious." 421 U.S. at 575. The discipline of public explanation itself, the Court appeared to believe, would tend to prevent such an outcome.

The Court's action was strongly objected to by Justice Rehnquist, who thought the requirement of a statement of reasons had been conceded by the government and was in any event properly based on Section 555(e). Whether a statement thus provided could form the basis for judicial review for arbitrariness or capriciousness presented wholly

---

4. Recent literature abundantly concerns prosecutorial discretion; Professor Kenneth Davis has been a noteworthy contributor. See his Discretionary Justice: A Preliminary Survey (1969); An Approach to Legal Control of the Police, 52 Tex.L. Rev. 703 (1974); Police Discretion (1975); Discretionary Justice in Europe and America (1976).

See also, e.g., W.R. LaFave, The Prosecutor's Discretion in the United States, 18 Am.J.Comp.L. 532 (1970); R. Neumann, Jr., The New Era of Administrative Regularization: Controlling Prosecutorial Discretion Through the Administrative Procedure Act, 3 U.Dayton L.Rev. 23 (1978); J. Rosenblum, A New Look at the General Counsel's Unreviewable Discretion Not to Issue a Complaint Under the NLRA, 86 Yale L.J. 1349 (1977); J. Vorenberg, Decent Restraint of Prosecutorial Discretion, 94 Harv.L.Rev. 1521 (1981).

different issues; in his view, the Secretary's decision constituted "agency action . . . committed to agency discretion by law," 5 U.S.C. § 701(a)(2), and hence exempt from review. "The exclusivity of the Secretary's role in the enforcement of Title IV rights is no accident. It represents a conscious legislative compromise adopted to balance two important but conflicting interests: vindication of the rights of union members and freedom of unions from undue harassment. This Court has recognized unreviewable discretion both in the labor area, Vaca v. Sipes, 386 U.S. 171, 182 (1967), and in other civil areas. The Confiscation Cases, 7 Wall. 454 (1869); FTC v. Klesner, 280 U.S. 19, 25 (1929). The Court of Appeals sought to distinguish this line of cases on the grounds that it involved 'vindication of societal or governmental interest, rather than the protection of individual rights,' 502 F.2d, at 87. While the Secretary points out the artificiality of this purported distinction . . . a more basic response is that such considerations provide no basis for contravention of legislative intent:

> Congress for reasons of its own decided upon the method for the protection of the "right" which it created. It selected the precise machinery and fashioned the tool which it deemed suited to that end. . . . All constitutional questions aside, it is for Congress to determine how the rights which it creates shall be enforced.

Switchmen's Union v. National Mediation Board, 320 U.S. 297, 301 (1943)." 421 U.S. at 597.

The law of Dunlop v. Bachowski was restated, or revised, in Justice Rehnquist's opinion for the Court in HECKLER V. CHANEY, 470 U.S. 821 (1985), which is set out at p. 1021, below as an example of agency action committed to agency discretion. Important here are the opinion's broad conclusion and the distinction made of Dunlop v. Bachowski. The broad principle: "an agency's decision not to prosecute or enforce, whether through civil or criminal process, is a decision generally committed to an agency's absolute discretion." 470 U.S. at 831. And the distinction:

". . . Congress may limit an agency's exercise of enforcement power if it wishes, either by setting substantive priorities, or by otherwise circumscribing an agency's power to discriminate among issues or cases it will pursue. . . .

"Dunlop v. Bachowski, 421 U.S. 560 (1975) . . . presents an example of statutory language which supplied sufficient standards to rebut the presumption of unreviewability. [This Court] rejected the Secretary's argument that the statute precluded judicial review, and in a footnote it stated its agreement with the conclusion of the Court of Appeals that the decision was not 'an unreviewable exercise of prosecutorial discretion.' 421 U.S., at 567, n. 7. . . . The Court of Appeals, in turn, had found the 'principle of absolute prosecutorial discretion' inapplicable, because the language of the LMRDA indicated that the Secretary was required to file suit if certain 'clearly defined' factors were present. The decision therefore was not 'beyond the judicial capacity to supervise.'

"Dunlop is thus consistent with a general presumption of un-reviewability of decisions not to enforce. The statute being administered quite clearly withdrew discretion from the agency and provided guidelines for exercise of its enforcement power. . . ." 470 U.S. at 833–34.

b. Party Initiation of Rulemaking

Congress can command rulemaking proceedings if it wants to. While passing the Magnuson-Moss Warranty Act, for example, Congress directed the FTC (15 U.S.C. § 2309(b)): "The Commission shall initiate within one year after the date of the enactment of this Act a rulemaking proceeding dealing with warranties and warranty practices in connection with the sale of used motor vehicles. . . . " One would not expect there to have to be a private lawsuit to get such a statute implemented. Where Congress has provided (as it occasionally has) not just for proceedings to start, but for rules on specific topics to be issued by a given date, it has sometimes apparently authorized private parties to sue to enforce that mandate; in such a case, of course, litigation may ensue. See, e.g., Natural Resources Defense Council v. Train, 510 F.2d 692 (D.C.Cir.1974).

But, to take a somewhat more usual case, what if Congress simply makes a fairly broad delegation and provides that the agency will make rules to fill in the interstices? In PULIDO V. HECKLER, 758 F.2d 503 (10th Cir.1985), plaintiffs sued to compel the Department of Health and Human Services to conduct a notice-and-comment rulemaking proceeding. The subject of the proposed rule was the criteria to be used in deciding when claimants for various social security benefits would be entitled to be reimbursed for the travel expenses involved in attending various hearings; provisions of the Social Security Act authorized such payments to be made. "It is true," said the court, "that, as a general rule, an administrative agency is not required to promulgate detailed rules interpreting every statutory provision that may be relevant to its actions. See . . . SEC v. Chenery Corp., 332 U.S. 194 (1947). A statute may, however, impose a duty to do so." Here, the statute specifically stated, for example, that there would be no reimbursement for first-class travel "unless the use of first-class accommodations is required (as determined under regulations of the Secretary) because of such person's health condition. . . . "

But what of the many aspects of reimbursement concerning which there was no such specific command? As to these, the statute stated the Secretary's authority to make rules as follows:

> The Secretary shall have full power and authority to make rules and regulations and to establish procedures, not inconsistent with the provisions of this title, which are necessary or appropriate to carry out such provisions, and shall adopt reasonable and proper rules and regulations to regulate and provide for the nature and extent of the proofs and evidence and the method of taking and furnishing the same in order to establish the right to benefits hereunder. 42 U.S.C. § 405(a).

Attending a hearing, said the court, was part of the process of furnishing proof and, more to present purposes, the statutory term "shall adopt" was meant to be mandatory.

Finally, the Secretary argued that even if she were under a duty to promulgate regulations, the timing of the proceeding was within her discretion. "The relevant provisions of the Social Security Act," responded the court, "were enacted in 1980—more than four years ago. Whatever discretion the Secretary may have had, a delay of more than four years is contrary to the purposes of the Act, and impermissibly abuses that discretion." Accordingly, "we find it necessary to have a timetable established to ensure that the regulations mandated by the statute are, indeed, promulgated."

It may seem that the Tenth Circuit in Pulido was willing to go rather far in finding that the Secretary's rulemaking authority was mandatory. It still may not be, from the point of view of some parties, far enough. What can be done if, in the delegation of rulemaking authority, there is no "shall" in sight?

Section 553(e) of the Administrative Procedure Act requires each agency to "give an interested person the right to petition for the issuance, amendment, or repeal of a rule." And Section 555(e) provides that "Prompt notice shall be given of the denial in whole or in part of a written application, petition, or other request of an interested person made in connection with any agency proceeding. Except in affirming a prior denial or when the denial is self-explanatory, the notice shall be accompanied by a brief statement of the grounds for denial."

Who is "an interested person" mentioned in both of these provisions? The Attorney General's Manual on the Administrative Procedure Act, p. 38, describes her as one "whose interests are or will be affected" by the proposed action, which suggests that the limitation is one unlikely often to deter the imaginative petitioner.

The procedures of Section 553(e) are often invoked by members of the public seeking to prompt regulatory action. The rulemaking docket of the Nuclear Regulatory Commission, for example, showed some 35 petitions pending as of March 31, 1978; seventeen of these had been submitted by licensees or bodies clearly associated with licensee interests, thirteen by citizen action groups or environmental litigators, and the remainder by state or federal authorities. The subjects ranged from the technical to the broadly social, with no necessary correlation as to petitioner; in most cases comments had been sought through the Federal Register and other means, but usually no more than a dozen were received. For those cases in which outcomes were noted, denials and favorable outcomes were about evenly matched. A roughly contemporaneous Senate committee survey of nine agencies found that about 28% of all rulemaking petitions had consumer group origins, as against 66% from industry and 5% from government.[1]

---

1. III Study on Federal Regulation pursuant to S.Res. 71, 95th Cong., 1st Sess. (1977) p. 15. The Committee found that participation in rulemaking, as distinct from initiation, was more weighted to regulated interests, with no other organized public participation in more than half of the rulemakings the agencies had identified as their most significant; where participation did occur, other-than-industry in-

WWHT, INC. v. FEDERAL COMMUNICATIONS COMMISSION

United States Court of Appeals, District of Columbia Circuit, 1981.
656 F.2d 807.

[In 1968 the FCC established a system of over-the-air subscription television (STV), using scrambled signals. At the same time, it issued a notice of a proposed rule which would have required cable television systems to carry the signals of local subscription television stations, just as they were already required to do with regard to conventional broadcasting. Comments were filed by interested persons but the Commission took no action until September 21, 1978, when it terminated the rulemaking proceeding without adopting the proposed rule. In its order of termination, the Commission stated in part: "The comments filed in this Docket are now stale and a number of changes in the nature of our regulations have been made since the proceeding was commenced so that the record does not provide an adequate basis for the adoption of rules. . . . We are aware that there are parties interested in an expedited resolution of this proceeding through the adoption of rules. However, the lack of adequate comment in the record presents a procedural barrier to that action. At this point we believe the most efficacious procedure for those desiring further action would be the filing of petitions for rulemaking setting forth the rule changes requested and the public interest justification therefore. Our decision terminating this proceeding is not intended to foreclose the possibility of a new proceeding being commenced if that appears warranted." On the following day Blonder-Tongue Laboratories, Inc. (BTL) petitioned the Commission to institute a rulemaking proceeding to require cable television systems to carry STV signals. Suburban Broadcasting Corporation (Suburban) filed a request for a declaration that the existing rules of the Commission already required cable carriage of subscription television signals. Comments in support of the petitions were filed by various STV licensees, the Motion Picture Association of America, and two sports leagues. Opposing comments were filed by several cable TV associations.

The Commission denied the petition for rulemaking. 77 F.C.C.2d 523 (1980). Its opinion and order discussed the pro and con comments and concluded that BTL's "petition for rulemaking and the associated comments . . . leave us in essentially the same position we were in when the earlier [1968] proceeding was terminated [in 1978]. . . . [The] reasons advanced in the petition and comments . . . do not persuade us that the rule suggested should be proposed by the Commission for adoption. In particular the suggested parallel with the conventional station carriage rules ignores the very significant economic and technical differences between the two types of services. At the outset, there is no evidence and barely even a suggestion in the comments that cable carriage is fundamental to the survival or economic success of STV stations. . . . It was this concern . . . which provided the

terests rarely exceeded 25% of identifiable commenters and often represented a far smaller proportion. At 13–14. No legal barrier to such participation exists.

most fundamental basis for the mandatory carriage rules when they were first adopted for conventional television broadcasting stations."

Other reasons cited by the Commission included: (1) the carriage rules for conventional television broadcasting were premised on the Commission's view that the carriage requirements imposed no substantial burden on the ordinary CATV operator while the same had not been established with respect to the carriage of the subscription programming of STV stations; (2) the transmission of "scrambled transmissions" would impose burdens on cable operators not associated with the carriage of conventional stations; (3) STV service would be purchased by only a fraction of total subscribers but all subscribers would be required to bear the cost of carriage; and (4) the requested rule "would involve a costly redundancy of transmission paths with the same signal going to the same subscriber locations both over-the-air and by cable." The Commission concluded that, although competition might be "more acute" if cable operators were required to carry STV transmissions, it is "appropriate that STV operators and cable television operators be left free to bargain in their own best interests for cable carriage."

The Commission also denied Suburban's request for a declaratory ruling that the existing rules of the Commission required cable carriage STV signals, stating that it had publicly, and consistently for twelve years "not intended or enforced its rules to require cable carriage of scrambled programming of STV stations." But to make the text of the cable carriage rules unambiguous, the commission issued an "Editorial Amendment" to state explicitly that they "shall not operate to require carriage of any subscription television broadcast program."

BTL and other STV broadcasters petitioned for review of the Commission's orders, alleging that the conclusions reached by the Commission were neither factually supported by the record nor legally supported by the language of the Commission's rules.]

Before ROBINSON, CHIEF JUDGE, and MACKINNON and EDWARDS, CIRCUIT JUDGES.

HARRY T. EDWARDS, CIRCUIT JUDGE:

This case raises the questions of whether, and under what circumstances, a reviewing court may require an agency to institute rulemaking proceedings after the agency has denied a petition for rulemaking.

.   .   .

For the reasons hereafter enumerated, we hold that, except where there is evidence of a "clear and convincing legislative intent to negate review," Natural Resources Defense Council v. S.E.C., 606 F.2d 1031, 1043 (D.C.Cir.1979), an agency's denial of a rulemaking petition is subject to judicial review. However, we believe that the decision to institute rulemaking is one that is largely committed to the discretion of the agency, and that the scope of review of such a determination must, of necessity, be very narrow.

With these standards in mind, we cannot find that judgment of the Commission in Signal Carriage Rules-STV was arbitrary, capricious, an abuse of discretion, or otherwise not in accordance with law; we therefore affirm the order of the Commission denying the petition for rulemaking. As for the order in Editorial Amendment, we find that the Commission reasonably concluded that existing regulations did not require cable carriage of STV transmissions, and that it properly adopted an "interpretative rule" to this effect.[1]

. . . .

II. INFORMAL RULEMAKING UNDER THE ADMINISTRATIVE PROCEDURE ACT

A. Petitions for Rulemaking

Section 4 of the Administrative Procedure Act, 5 U.S.C. § 553 (1976), sets out the procedures to be followed by administrative agencies in informal rulemaking. . . .

With respect to petitions for rulemaking, section 4(d) of the APA provides that:

> Each agency shall give an interested person the right to petition for the issuance, amendment, or repeal of a rule.

5 U.S.C. § 553(e). In the legislative history accompanying 4(d), it was stated that this section "requires agencies to receive and consider requests" for rulemaking.[2]

Although the legislative history accompanying section 4(d) makes it plain that an agency must receive and respond to petitions for rulemaking, it is equally clear from the legislative history that Congress did not intend to compel an agency to undertake rulemaking merely because a petition has been filed. When petitions for rulemaking are filed, section 4(d) requires the agency to

> fully and promptly consider them, take such action as may be required, and . . . notify the petitioner in case the request is denied. The agency may either grant the petition, undertake public rule making proceedings . . . or deny the petition.

S.Rep.No.752, 79th Cong., 1st Sess. (1945), reprinted in Legislative History, at 185, 201 (1946). In its report on the APA, the Senate Judiciary Committee emphasized that

> [t]he mere filing of a petition does not require an agency to grant it, or to hold a hearing, or engage in any other public rule making proceedings. The refusal of an agency to grant the petition or to hold rule making proceedings, therefore, would not per se be subject to judicial reversal. However, the facts or considerations brought to the attention of an agency by such a petition might be such as to require the agency to act to

---

1. Since the order in the Commission's Editorial Amendment represented an "interpretative rule," it was exempt, under 5 U.S.C. § 553(b), from the usual rulemaking notice and comment procedures of the Administrative Procedure Act.

2. "Senate Judiciary Committee Print, June 1945," reprinted in Administrative Procedure Act: Legislative History, 79th Cong. 1944–46, S.Doc.No. 248, 79th Cong., 2d Sess. 11, 21 (1946) [hereafter "Legislative History"].

prevent the rule from continuing or becoming vulnerable upon judicial review. . . .

Id. at 201-02.[3]

The Attorney General's Manual on the APA confirms these interpretations of the APA. See United States Dep't of Justice, Attorney General's Manual on the Administrative Procedure Act at 38-39 (1947). The Manual parallels the language of the Senate Report, indicating that an agency is not required to grant a petition for rulemaking merely because it is filed, and that prompt notice should be given when a petition is denied. With respect to the particular procedures followed by each agency in receiving and disposing of petitions for rulemaking, the Manual refers to the rules promulgated by each agency pursuant to 5 U.S.C. § 553.

Under existing rules of the FCC, any interested party may petition the Commission for "the issuance, amendment or repeal" of a rule or regulation. 47 C.F.R. § 1.401(a) (1979). When a petition is filed, the Commission is to determine whether the petition "discloses sufficient reasons in support of the action requested to justify the institution of a rulemaking proceeding." 47 C.F.R. § 1.407 (1979). In cases where the Commission determines that rulemaking is not warranted, the "petition for rule making will be denied and the petitioner will be notified of the Commission's action with the grounds therefor." Id.

No serious questions have been raised in this case with respect to the *procedures* followed by the FCC in receiving and responding to the petition for rulemaking. Indeed, it is clear from the record of the agency proceedings that no procedural infirmity can be cited.

B. Judicial Review of Agency Action on Petitions for Rulemaking

Section 10 of the Administrative Procedure Act, 5 U.S.C. §§ 701-706 (1976), governs judicial review of agency actions. Under 5 U.S.C. § 702, any person adversely affected by agency action is entitled to judicial review, except where the statute under which the action was taken precludes judicial review, or where the action is committed to agency discretion by law. 5 U.S.C. § 701(a). While there is no claim in this case that judicial review is barred by some statutory preclusion, there is a question as to whether the Commission's denial of the petition for rulemaking was an "agency action committed to agency discretion by law." 5 U.S.C. § 701(a)(2).

The 1947 Attorney General's Manual interpreted section 4(d), 5 U.S.C. § 553(e), of the APA to preclude judicial review of the denial of a petition to promulgate a rule or amendment, or of an agency's refusal

---

3. It is also evident, from both the legislative history of the APA and the text of the Act itself, that an agency is required to give "prompt notice," along with a brief explanation, whenever petitions for rulemaking are denied. 5 U.S.C. § 555(e) provides:

Prompt notice shall be given of the denial in whole or in part of a written appli-

cation, petition, or other request of an interested person made in connection with any agency proceeding. Except in affirming a prior denial or when the denial is self-explanatory, the notice shall be accompanied by a brief statement of the grounds for denial.

to institute rulemaking proceedings. While we agree that judicial intrusion into an agency's exercise of discretion in the discharge of its essentially legislative rulemaking functions should be severely circumscribed, we reject the suggestion that agency denials of requests for rulemaking are exempt from judicial review.

Except where there is evidence of a "clear and convincing legislative intent to negate review," Natural Resources Defense Council v. S.E.C., 606 F.2d 1031, 1043 (D.C.Cir.1979), agency denials of petitions for rulemaking may be made the subject of judicial review. We have no doubt that, except in the rarest of cases, the decision to institute rulemaking is one that is largely committed to agency discretion; however, this begs the question with respect to judicial review.

. . .

In Natural Resources Defense Council, this court stated that 5 U.S.C. § 701(a) "creates a strong presumption of reviewability that can be rebutted only by a clear showing that judicial review would be inappropriate." 606 F.2d at 1043. The court referred to language in Senate Committee Report No. 752, reprinted in Legislative History, at 185, 201, noting that "[t]he refusal of an agency to grant the petition or to hold rule making proceedings . . . would not per se be subject to judicial *reversal*," and concluded that the language implied that judicial review *would* sometimes be available when agencies refuse to institute rulemaking proceedings. 606 F.2d at 1043, n.14. The NRDC court also noted that, notwithstanding the role played by the Justice Department in drafting the APA, the Attorney General's Manual was not entitled to particular deference, "to the extent that it is inconsistent with the Senate Report." Id.

. . .

In the context of the instant case, petitioners have alleged that the FCC abused its discretion when it denied the request for rulemaking. This contention presents an issue that is plainly cognizable under 5 U.S.C. § 706(2)(A) of the APA. Although we believe that the *scope* of review must of necessity be narrow, we nevertheless hold that this court has jurisdiction to review the issue posed by petitioners.

III. THE LAW IN THIS CIRCUIT ON THE SCOPE OF REVIEW

A. Scope of Review of Agency Decisions Not to Promulgate Rules

The most comprehensive statement by this court as to the availability and scope of review of an agency's decision to deny a petition for rulemaking can be found in the thoughtful opinion by Judge McGowan in Natural Resources Defense Council, Inc. v. S.E.C., 606 F.2d 1031 (D.C.Cir.1979). Appellants in NRDC challenged the Commission's failure to promulgate rules requiring regulated corporations to make comprehensive disclosures of their environmental and equal employment policies. . . .

. . . . [T]he court in NRDC separated out the aspects of appellees' claim that were essentially procedural from those addressed more to the policy determinations reflected in the Commission's action.[4] The substantive aspects of appellees' claim challenged the rationality of the SEC's ultimate decision *not* to adopt the environmental and equal employment rules proposed by appellees. In analyzing the reviewability of the decision to reject the proposed rules, the court noted that the Commission possessed "broad discretionary powers to promulgate (or not promulgate)" rules of disclosure, and that the NEPA did not go so far as to *require* agencies to promulgate specific rules. Id. at 1045. Nevertheless, even though the "pragmatic calculus" inclined against reviewability of the SEC's decision, the court concluded that, in light of the strong presumption of reviewability,

> in a context like the present one, in which the agency has in fact held extensive rulemaking proceedings narrowly focused on the particular rules at issue, and has explained in detail its reasons for not adopting those rules, we believe that the questions posed will be amenable to at least a minimal level of judicial scrutiny.

Id. at 1047.

The court in NRDC also discussed the possibility of some minor interference with the agency's performance of its statutory mission. Specifically, the court referred to the diversion of scarce institutional resources to defend in court a decision not to adopt proposed rules that an agency had already determined, in its expert judgment, to be not even worth the effort already expended. Id. at 1045. However, this factor was considered less compelling in NRDC, where the SEC had evidenced its view that the proposed rules were sufficiently meritorious to warrant further investigation via the institution of rulemaking proceedings. In other words, the greater the agency's investment of resources in considering the issues raised by the petition, and the more complete the record compiled during the course of the agency's consideration, "the more likely it is that the ultimate decision not to take action will be a proper subject of judicial review." Id. at 1047, n.19. Where, as in this case, the agency simply declines to initiate any rulemaking procedures, the court in NRDC intimated that the scope of judicial review should be *extremely limited*, if permitted at all. Id. at 1045–46.

Finally, with respect to an agency decision not to promulgate a certain rule, the court stated:

> An agency's discretionary decision *not* to regulate a given activity is inevitably based, in large measure, on factors not inherently susceptible to judicial resolution—e.g., internal management considerations as to budget and personnel; evaluations of its own competence; weighing of competing policies within a broad statutory framework. Further, even if an agency considers a particular problem worthy of regulation, it

---

4. The court in NRDC identified both procedural and substantive challenges. The court found, with "little difficulty," that the procedural aspects of appellees' claim—those grounded in the Commission's alleged failure to comply with certain procedures mandated by the National Environmental Policy Act (NEPA)—were a proper subject for judicial review. 606 F.2d at 1044.

may determine for reasons lying within its special expertise that the time for action has not yet arrived. The area may be one of such rapid technological development that regulations would be outdated by the time they could become effective, or the scientific state of the art may be such that sufficient data are not yet available on which to premise adequate regulations. The circumstances in the regulated industry may be evolving in a way that could vitiate the need for regulation, or the agency may still be developing the expertise necessary for effective regulation.

Id. at 1046 (citations omitted).

Obviously, the case for reviewability of the order before us is even less compelling than that in NRDC. The agency in NRDC suggested the *possibility* that the proposed rules there were of some merit when it granted the petition and instituted rulemaking proceedings. In the case before us, however, the Commission, after some preliminary consideration of the proposed rule, concluded that further deliberations would be unwarranted.

While it is clear that the applicable scope of review of discretionary agency decisions not to promulgate certain rules can be found under section 10(e)(2)(A) of the APA, 5 U.S.C. § 706(2)(A), the parameters of the "arbitrary and capricious" standard of review will vary with the context of the case. . . .

In determining the scope of review in this case, . . . we adhere to Judge McGowan's suggestion that, where the proposed rule pertains to a matter of policy within the agency's expertise and discretion, the scope of review should "perforce be a narrow one, limited to ensuring that the Commission has adequately explained the facts and policy concerns it relied on and to satisfy ourselves that those facts have some basis in the record." 606 F.2d at 1053. We also recognize that where the agency decides not to proceed with rulemaking, the "record" for purposes of review need only include the petition for rulemaking, comments pro and con where deemed appropriate, and the agency's explanation of its decision to reject the petition. Obviously, the "record" in a case such as the one before us will not resemble the records compiled in cases like NRDC, and National Black Media Coalition v. FCC, 589 F.2d 578 (D.C.Cir.1978), where rulemaking procedures were actually initiated.

B. Judicially Imposed Rulemaking

Because of the broad discretionary powers possessed by administrative agencies to promulgate (or not promulgate) rules, and the narrow scope of review to which the exercise of that discretion is subjected, there are very few cases in which courts have forced agencies to institute rulemaking proceedings on a particular issue after it has declined to do so. As was recognized in Action for Children's Television, [v. F.C.C., 564 F.2d 458, 479 (D.C.Cir.1977)]:

As a corollary of [the agency's] broad general discretion, the Commission has considerable latitude in responding to requests to institute proceedings or to promulgate rules, even though it possesses the authority to do so should it see fit. "Administrative rule making does not ordinarily comprehend any rights in private parties to compel an agency to institute such proceedings or promulgate rules." Rhode Island Television Corp. v. FCC, 116 U.S.App.D.C. 40, 44, 320 F.2d 762, 766 (1963).

It is only in the rarest and most compelling of circumstances that this court has acted to overturn an agency judgment not to institute rulemaking.

In Geller v. FCC, 610 F.2d 973 (D.C.Cir.1979), we ordered the Commission to make a fresh determination as to whether regulations promulgated pursuant to an agreement reached in 1972 continued to serve the public interest long after the predicate for the agreement had ceased to exist. The regulations in issue had been promulgated initially to reflect a "consensus agreement" reached by parties affected by the Commission's cable television policies in their efforts to facilitate the passage of new copyright legislation. After the new copyright legislation was passed in 1976, petitioner had requested the Commission to reexamine the regulations to determine their continuing validity. The Commission refused to conduct such a proceeding on the ground that petitioner had introduced no evidence to aid in its determination of whether the rules continued to serve the public interest. The court reversed the Commission's order, finding the Commission's exercise of discretion *not* to institute rulemaking proceedings to be "plainly misguided" 610 F.2d at 979. The court in Geller ruled that an agency "cannot sidestep a reexamination of particular regulations when abnormal circumstances make that course imperative." Id. (footnote omitted). The rule that emerges from Geller, then, is a limited one: that an agency may be forced by a reviewing court to institute rulemaking proceedings if a significant factual predicate of a prior decision on the subject (either to promulgate or not to promulgate specific rules) has been removed.

This court found equally compelling the circumstances in NAACP v. FPC, 520 F.2d 432 (D.C.Cir.1975), aff'd, 425 U.S. 662 (1976), and in National Organization for Reform of Marijuana Laws v. Ingersoll, 497 F.2d 654 (D.C.Cir.1974). In NAACP, this court vacated the Commission's order dismissing petitioner's request for rulemaking on the ground that the Commission was mistaken in concluding that it lacked jurisdiction to promulgate regulations concerning employment discrimination by its regulatees. Similarly, in National Organization for Reform of Marijuana Laws, we remanded an order of the Bureau of Narcotics and Dangerous Drugs that rejected outright a rulemaking petition on the ground that the Bureau was not authorized to institute proceedings for a rule that would be inconsistent with United States treaty obligations under the Single Convention on Narcotics Drugs, 1961, 18 U.S.T. 1407 (1967). 497 F.2d at 656. The opinion noted that "rejection" of a party's *filing* is a "peremptory" action, soundly used only in cases where there is a "procedural defect or failure to comply with a clear-cut requirement of law." Id. at 659. The court in NORML then stated that, if in fact the Bureau's assessment of the rule sought by petitioners was correct, the agency's determination should be reflected in a denial of the petition on the merits. Id.

It is significant that in neither NAACP nor NORML did the court compel the agency to actually institute rulemaking proceedings. Rather, each agency was required on remand to *reconsider* its denial of the petition, in light of the correct interpretation of the law as enunciated by the court.[5]

IV. DISPOSITION OF THIS CASE

As we have already noted in part "II.A." of this opinion, no serious questions have been raised in this case with respect to the procedures followed by the FCC in receiving and responding to the petition for rulemaking. Our review of the record indicates that no procedural infirmity mars the actions of the agency below.

We are left then, with a challenge to the factual and policy determinations of the Commission. We note at the outset that the interest sought to be protected by petitioners is primarily economic; in particular, petitioners, STV broadcasters, seek the protections of the mandatory cable carriage rules which have been afforded conventional broadcasters. Such an interest, without more, does not present the unusual or compelling circumstances that are required in order to justify a judgment by this court overturning a decision of the Commission not to proceed with rulemaking.

For us to seriously indulge petitioners' claims in this case would be to ignore the institutional disruption that would be visited on the Commission by our second-guessing its "expert" determination not to pursue a particular program or policy at a given time. It would also require us to ignore the plain fact that the policy determinations made by the Commission in this case—as to the relative merits of mandatory cable carriage of STV signals—raise issues that are not well-suited for determination by this court. These considerations lead us to conclude that our review of the Commission's actions should be *extremely narrow,* consistent with the views heretofore expressed. The Commission's substantive determinations are essentially legislative in this case and are thus committed to the discretion of the agency.

Nevertheless, as we have already held, the Commission is required to give some explanation for its actions. Such an explanation enables a reviewing court to satisfy itself that the agency's action was neither arbitrary, nor capricious, nor an abuse of discretion, nor otherwise contrary to statutory, procedural or constitutional requirements.

Having considered the record in this case, we are satisfied that the orders of the Commission must be affirmed. The Commission adequately explained the facts and policy concerns it relied on, and there is nothing to indicate that the opinions of the Commission are unlawful, arbitrary, capricious or wholly irrational. Therefore, the judgment of

---

5. Other instances in which this court had required rulemaking proceedings are distinguishable by virtue of statutorily imposed rulemaking requirements. See e. g., Environmental Defense Fund v. HEW, 428 F.2d 1083 (D.C.Cir.1970).

the Commission not to proceed with rulemaking at this time must be left undisturbed.

For all of the foregoing reasons, the orders of the Commission are hereby affirmed.

NOTES

(1) Present consideration of the reviewability of denials of rulemaking petitions will have to take into account the Supreme Court's decision in Heckler v. Chaney, discussed at p. 319 above. Prior Supreme Court opinions have at least twice indicated that some review is possible, since they have assumed that such a petition would be the appropriate means to frame an issue the Court found not presented in the proceeding before it.[6]

(2) For a general discussion of private rights to initiate agency action of all sorts, see R. Stewart and C. Sunstein, Public Programs and Private Rights, 95 Harv.L.Rev. 1193, 1267–89 (1982).

c. Intervention in Ongoing Proceedings

Very often, the question is not whether there is going to be a proceeding, but what the shape of it will be. If the agency conducts an informal rulemaking, any question about party structure almost answers itself. Section 553(c) provides that "the agency shall give interested persons an opportunity to participate," and it seems to be universally understood that anyone who claims to be interested is interested for this purpose; or at least, an attempt to exclude anyone under this language has never been litigated. If, instead, the agency conducts a formal proceeding, the initial participants will be, in APA language, the "agency" and "parties," a closed set. Of course, in the common case of an adjudication to determine contested facts and not much more, no one else will want to join the sole or few parties the agency will itself want to involve so that they will be directly bound by the decision. The case likely to provoke contest is when the agency, using the discretion we have seen it has, chooses to use a restricted, formal proceeding to consider an issue which non-participants fear will have great consequences for them. Sometimes the agency itself understands the large scope of what it is doing, and invites others to participate, or at least to kibitz as amici curiae. But the agency may not understand what is at stake, or may not be forward enough in its proposal for participation.

At that point, the question of petitioning for intervention has arisen.

The typical setting for intervention in agency proceedings is like that in which intervention occurs in judicial proceedings. The agency's statute or, more likely,[1] its procedural rules will state some governing

---

6. Flint Ridge Development Co. v. Scenic Rivers Ass'n of Okl., 426 U.S. 776 (1976) [at n. 14]; Simon v. Eastern Kentucky Welfare Rights Organization, 426 U.S. 26 (1975) (concurrence).

1. Specific statutory requirements concerning intervention are rare. They usually pertain to participation by public bodies—as, for example, the command of the Public Utilities Holding Company Act that,

criteria, often in terms reminiscent of Fed.R.Civ.P. 24, governing entry to the proceeding. These may require a written petition stating the bases on and purposes for which intervention is sought, and identify as relevant to disposition of the petition such matters as timeliness, the character of the petitioner's interest (in itself and as it may be affected by the proceeding), and the extent to which that interest either establishes a right to participate, suggests an ability to assist in developing a sound record, or forebodes unmanageable enlargement of issues or delay.[2]

Section 6(a) of the Administrative Procedure Act, 5 U.S.C. § 555(b) provides, "So far as the orderly conduct of public business permits, an interested person may appear before an agency or its responsible employees for the presentation, adjustment, or determination of an issue, request, or controversy in a proceeding, whether interlocutory, summary, or otherwise, or in connection with an agency function." Professor David L. Shapiro has properly cautioned that this provision "should not and need not be interpreted, as it has on occasion, to afford any 'interested person' a right of intervention in agency proceedings. Such a person 'may appear' only '[s]o far as the orderly conduct of public business permits.' He is not given an absolute, or even a conditional, right to be a party. Agency procedures short of intervention, which permit a person to present written statements, to offer evidence, or in some instances to cross-examine, may in many cases fully satisfy the provision in section 6(a) for an opportunity to be heard." D.L. Shapiro, Some Thoughts on Intervention Before Courts, Agencies, and Arbitrators, 81 Harv.L.Rev. 721, 766 (1968).

In considering the question of intervention, keep in mind that more consequences may flow from permission to intervene at a hearing than from recognition of standing to seek review of the result. In this connection Professor Jaffe has noted that courts and lawyers often "assume without much reflection that standing to appeal does involve a right to administrative hearing; and statutes—such as the Communications Act—which specifically entitle 'parties in interest' to a hearing

in any case brought under that law, the Securities and Exchange Commission admit as a party "any interested State, State commission, State securities commission, municipality or other political subdivision of a State." For the most part, the statutes are drawn very loosely—as, for instance, the Federal Trade Commission Act and the Packers and Stockyards Act, which say merely that any person "upon good cause shown may be allowed" to intervene. Or they are entirely silent, thus leaving the matter, in the first instance, to the agency's discretion as reflected in its procedural rules or practices.

2. Writing in 1977, the staff of the Senate Committee on Governmental Affairs found that agency rules typically left administrative law judges wide discretion on these matters, but that agencies generally "consider their attitudes on citizens group intervention to be open-minded. . . . Surely it is difficult to imagine a more all-

encompassing standard than that of the Civil Aeronautics Board:

'(1) The nature of the petitioner's right under the statute to be made a party to the proceeding; (2) the nature and extent of the property, financial or other interests of the petitioner; (3) the effect of the order which may be entered in the proceeding on petitioner's interest; (4) the availability of other means whereby the petitioner's interest may be protected; (5) the extent to which petitioner's interest will be represented by existing parties; (6) the extent to which petitioner's participation may reasonably be expected to assist in the development of a sound record; and (7) the extent to which participation of the petitioner will broaden the issue or delay the proceeding.' "

Public Participation in Regulatory Agency Proceedings, III Study on Federal Regulation pursuant to S.Res. 71, Sen Comm. on Governmental Affairs, 95th Cong., 1st Sess. (1977), pp. 46–47.

and 'aggrieved persons' to appeal are read together as similar in content."[3] But as Professor Davis has accurately observed, the factors bearing upon participation at the stage of administrative hearing and at the stage of judicial review are by no means the same, nor are the statutory provisions concerning intervention usually couched in the same language as those concerning judicial review. "The central problem of intervention is usually the disadvantage to the tribunal and to other parties of extended cross-examination; judicial review involves no such problem. Adequate protection for interests obliquely affected may often be afforded through limited participation; no such compromise concerning judicial review is customary. No constitutional restrictions affect intervention; standing to obtain review is substantially affected by the constitutional requirement of case or controversy. Intervention means mere participation in a proceeding already initiated by others; obtaining judicial review normally means instituting an entirely new judicial proceeding."[4]

Probably the leading case on judicial control of participation in agency proceedings is OFFICE OF COMMUNICATION OF UNITED CHURCH OF CHRIST v. FCC, 359 F.2d 994 (D.C.Cir.1966). Under Section 309(d) of the Federal Communications' Act, 47 U.S.C. § 309(d) any "party in interest" may file a petition to deny another's license application, and have an evidentiary hearing on the petition. Who is a "party in interest"? UCC filed a petition to deny the application of television station WLBT (of Jackson, Miss.) for renewal of its license. UCC claimed to represent a variety of listener interests in balanced presentations, especially in fairer treatment of issues of interest to the black community. The FCC found that these interests did *not* confer party status but nonetheless considered UCC's contentions informally. It concluded that serious questions had been presented and, by a divided vote, determined not to conduct a hearing but to grant a conditional license renewal limited to one year, rather than the customary three years—in effect, a probationary grant.

On appeal, UCC contended that it had a right to a hearing which this amicus curiae status could not satisfy. Judge (later Chief Justice) Burger, for the court of appeals, agreed. "All parties seem to consider that the same standards are applicable to determining standing before the Commission and standing to appeal a commission order to this

---

3. L. Jaffe, Judicial Control of Administrative Action 535 (1965).

4. 3 Davis, Administrative Law Treatise 241 (1958); Koniag, Inc. v. Andrus, 580 F.2d 601 (D.C.Cir.1978).

See also D. Shapiro, supra, 81 Harv.L. Rev. at 767: ". . . [J]ust as the right to review does not follow automatically from one's status as a party before the agency, the right to be a party should not be an ineluctable consequence of the right to obtain review. The analogy is admittedly far from perfect, and fails altogether in the instance of a statute like the Natural Gas Act under which *only* parties before the

agency may seek review. But, absent such a provision, it is certainly possible that A's interests could be adequately represented before the agency by B, a party to the proceedings; under these circumstances A would have no right to intervene, but he might be entitled to appeal if he were adversely affected by a final order. Similarly, one who would be aggrieved by an adverse order and entitled to appeal might legitimately be given a sufficient opportunity to appear before the agency through some form of participation short of full intervention."

court. We have, therefore, used the cases dealing with standing in the two tribunals interchangeably." The court then noted that although up to that time courts had "granted standing to intervene only to those alleging electrical interference . . . or alleging some economic injury," the concept of standing is "practical and functional" and "we can see no reason to exclude those with such an obvious and acute concern as the listening audience." The court then turned to the argument that the Commission could be relied upon to represent and protect the interests of the listening public:

> The theory that the Commission can always effectively represent the listener interests in a renewal proceeding without the aid and participation of legitimate listener representatives fulfilling the role of private attorneys general is one of those assumptions we collectively try to work with so long as they are reasonably adequate. When it becomes clear, as it does to us now, that it is no longer a valid assumption which stands up under the realities of actual experience, neither we nor the Commission can continue to rely on it. The gradual expansion and evolution of concepts of standing in administrative law attests that experience rather than logic or fixed rules has been accepted as the guide.

The court explicitly recognized that its holding would create problems for the Commission in that under the holding the number of interveners could be increased. Said Judge Burger, "The competing consideration is that experience demonstrates consumers are generally among the best vindicators of the public interest." In addition, the Commission need not allow itself to be overwhelmed by purely captious or obstructive protests. It "should be accorded broad discretion in establishing and applying rules for such public participation, including rules for determining which community representatives are to be allowed to participate and how many are reasonably required to give the Commission the assistance it needs in vindicating the public interest.[1]" Petitions and briefs can be consolidated and there is always the "restraining factor . . . [of] the expense of participation in the administrative process, an economic reality which will operate to limit the number of those who will seek participation. . . .

"[W]e do not now hold that all of the Appellants have standing to challenge WLBT's renewal. [W]e limit ourselves to holding that the Commission must allow standing to one or more of them as responsible representatives to assert and prove the claims they have urged in their petition." The court closed its discussion of this issue with the state-

---

1. Professor Jaffe concedes there are strong reasons to reject public or listener standing but he believes "it does have much to commend it" in certain areas if put in terms of "jurisdiction subject to judicial discretion to be exercised with due regard for the character of the interests and the issues involved in each case." Jaffe, Standing to Secure Judicial Review: Private Actions, 75 Harv.L.Rev. 255, 282 (1961). "There are many persons . . . who feel that neither the industry nor the FCC can be trusted to protect the listener interest. If this is so, the public action is appropriate. But a frank recognition that the action is a public action and not a private remedy would allow us to introduce the notion of discretion at both the administrative and judicial levels." Id. at 284.

ment, "[W]e . . . emphasize that intervention on behalf of the public is not allowed to press private interest but only to vindicate the broad public interest relating to a licensee's performance of the public trust inherent in every license."   See also Scenic Hudson Preservation Conference v. FPC, 354 F.2d 608 (2d Cir.1965), cert. denied 384 U.S. 941 (1966).

By 1973, one practitioner before agencies in Washington could assert that "today, at least in my experience, intervention is seldom denied." [2]

Commenting on this trend in 1975, Professor Richard Stewart wrote (The Reformation of American Administrative Law, 88 Harv.L. Rev. 1667, 1760–62):

"The expansion of the traditional model to afford participation rights in the process of agency decision and judicial review to a wide variety of affected interests must ultimately rest on the premise that such procedural changes will be an effective and workable means of assuring improved agency decisions.   Advocates of extended access believe that an enlarged system of formal proceedings can, by securing adequate consideration of the interests of all affected persons, yield outcomes that better serve society as a whole. . . .

"Although the courts have displayed caution in expanding and reworking administrative law doctrine to ensure the representation of all affected interests, the thrust of decisions over the past decade supports the assessment of the Court of Appeals for the District of Columbia Circuit that: 'In recent years, the concept that public participation in decisions which involve the public interest is not only valuable but indispensable has gained increasing support.' The principle of interest group representation in agency adjudication has been warmly endorsed by commentators and by the Administrative Conference of the United States. Such participation, it is claimed, will not only improve the quality of agency decisions and make them more responsive to the needs of the various participating interests, but is valuable in itself because it gives citizens a sense of involvement in the process of government, and increases confidence in the fairness of government decisions.

"Not only is the expansion of participation rights applauded, but it is urged that resources be made available to facilitate the representation of otherwise unrepresented interests by private attorneys and by governmental agencies such as a proposed federal consumer advocate agency. Such proposals follow logically from the premise that justice results when all interests are considered.

"The time has come for a critical assessment of this prescription for asserted biases and inadequacies in agency decisions. The judges' incipient transformation of administrative law into a scheme of interest representation is responding to powerful needs that have been neglected by other branches of government. There are serious perceived

2. A. Butzel, Intervention and Class Actions Before the Agencies and the Courts, 25 Ad.L.Rev. 135, 136 (1973).

inadequacies in agency performance, and this perception must be addressed if attitudes towards government are not to degenerate into cynicism or despair. Moreover, the realities of agency performance may often indeed be far short of what is desirable or even tolerable. But whether a judicially implemented system of interest representation is an adequate or workable response to these needs is a question deserving the most careful consideration."

NATIONAL WELFARE RIGHTS ORGANIZATION v. FINCH, 429 F.2d 725 (D.C.Cir.1970) illustrates both the fears an agency may have concerning outsiders' seizure of the regulatory initiative by intervention, and the difficulty a court may have in fully endorsing those fears. Pending before the Secretary of HEW were hearings he had initiated to determine whether Nevada and Connecticut were in conformity with specified federal standards governing Social Security Act payments to the states. Had he concluded not, those payments would have ceased. The initiation of the hearings, in itself an unusual step, created substantial pressure to settle. The NWRO and other welfare organizations, responding to a public notice of the hearings, then sought unsuccessfully to intervene, asserting that the interests of their welfare recipient members in welfare administration entitled them to full participatory rights. Department officials took the position that they could attend the hearing and submit views, orally and in writing; but that they would not be given party status. After failing to secure injunctive relief in district court, the would-be intervenors prevailed in the court of appeals, before a panel consisting of Judges Bazelon, Wright and McGowan.

No specific statute provided for intervention, but Judge Wright for the court, found the "congressional silence" not controlling. Noting the broadening recognition of participatory rights, particularly in the standing cases to be taken up in Chapter IX, Section 3 within, the court readily concluded the NWRO would be able to secure review of the Secretary's ultimate conclusion.

"The right of judicial review cannot be taken as fully realized, however, if appellants are excluded from participating in the proceeding to be reviewed. . . . [W]ithout participation . . . , issues which appellants here might wish to raise about the character of the state's plans may have been foreclosed as a topic for review. . . . As intervenors in conformity hearings appellants may serve the public interest in the maintenance of an efficient state-federal cooperative welfare system. . . .

"It is true that increased participation through intervention creates problems for both the tribunal and other parties; multiple and extended cross-examination may be deleterious to the administrative process. . . . Certainly keeping conformity hearings manageable may be a legitimate interest, but as this court set out in Virginia Petroleum Jobbers Ass'n v. F.P.C., 265 F.2d 364, 367 n. 1 (1959):

'. . . Efficient and expeditious hearings should be achieved, not by excluding parties who have a right to participate, but by controlling the proceeding so that all participants are required to adhere to the issues and to refrain from introducing cumulative or irrelevant evidence.'

The threat of hundreds of intervenors in conformity hearings is more apparent than real. The expense of participation, particularly for welfare beneficiaries, is a factor limiting participation; legal and related expenses can be burdensome. . . .

"In finding that appellants may intervene . . . we contemplate enlargement of the rights of participation already accorded them only to the extent of an additional right to present live witnesses and to cross-examine witnesses for other parties.[1] We do not hold that this intervenor status creates in appellants a right to participate in any way in the Secretary's informal efforts . . . to bring a state into conformity, nor do we limit his right to terminate a hearing, once called or begun, upon a determination by him that it is no longer necessary because he believes that conformity has been achieved. In such event, appellants are free to question that determination either indirectly by proceeding against the state, or directly against the Secretary by a suit asserting that he is acting beyond, or in conflict with, his statutory authority. In order to enhance orderly procedures regarding any such litigation as may ensue, the Secretary should provide the parties to a conformity hearing with a preliminary statement of his purpose to terminate the hearing, along with a statement of his reasons for termination and a copy of the proposed state plan on which the state and he have settled. The parties should then be afforded the opportunity to submit, for the Secretary's consideration and for the record, their views as to, or any information bearing upon, the merits of the proposed plan and the reasons for terminating the conformity hearing."

———

The issues posed by intervention to an agency—or, as you will, the policy-forcing advantages offered by intervention to a would-be intervenor—are particularly dramatic when there would likely be no formal hearing at all in the absence of the intervention sought. The issuance of a renewed broadcast license, or of a license to export nuclear fuels to a foreign land, are often matters of routine—handled on the papers by agency staff with little if any involvement from the top. Dispute is often missing between applicant and agency. Still, these applications may be matters respecting which, by statute, rule, or implication, "any interested person" may seek a hearing; if successful, the would-be intervenor may have converted a paper-processing routine into a careful consideration of major issues of regulatory policy.

1. To the extent that appellees are apprehensive of chaos and confusion as an incident to this enlarged right, we remind that they have already recognized the right of appellants to be present at the hearings and to be heard through counsel. Reliance for proper control of the hearings and the orderly compilation of the hearing record must, of course, be on the hearing examiner. He is fully authorized to be the arbiter of the relevance of proffered testimony and of the proper scope of cross-examination, and to insist that all parties address themselves to the business at hand with dignity and dispatch.

IN THE MATTER OF EDLOW INTERNATIONAL CO.

United States Nuclear Regulatory Commission, 1976.

3 N.R.C. 563.

[In 1963, the United States and India entered into an Agreement for Cooperation for Civil Uses of Atomic Energy, under which two nuclear power reactors were authorized for export from the United States to India; they were constructed at Tarapur, near Bombay. The United States also agreed to supply fuel for the reactors, and the Indian government in turn agreed that the reactors would "be operated on no other [nuclear fuel] than that made available by the United States." Art. II(A) of the Agreement of August 8, 1963, T.I.A.S. 5446. Shipments of fuel were made from time to time, in each instance pursuant to an export license obtained from the Nuclear Regulatory Commission (NRC) or its predecessor agency, the Atomic Energy Commission, by the transporter of the fuel. These license applications were routinely processed on the papers, and without formal public notice. The explosion by the Indian government of a nuclear device during 1974 raised significant questions respecting the appropriateness of continuing to supply nuclear fuel to India, but the AEC continued to do so when assured, by diplomatic means, that Tarapur fuels had not been used to produce the explosives and that these fuels would be devoted exclusively to the use of the Tarapur facility. The Indian government did not, however, undertake to discontinue the development of nuclear devices using materials derived from other sources and for this reason continuing supply remained controversial, within and without the government. A Freedom of Information Act request brought into public view the application papers for pending nuclear fuel export license applications, including two for the Tarapur reactors.]

OPINION

On March 2, 1976, joint petitions were filed with the Nuclear Regulatory Commission on behalf of three organizations (Natural Resources Defense Council, Inc.; the Sierra Club; and the Union of Concerned Scientists) for leave to intervene and for a hearing on two pending licensing applications concerning the export of special nuclear material to India. . . .

As part of the continuing fuel supply arrangements under the United States/Indian Agreement for Cooperation of August 8, 1963 (T.I. A.S. 5546), the Commission has received several presentations concerning the Tarapur Atomic Power Stations [TAPS]. As it does for all nations to which special nuclear materials may be exported, the Commission has received a regular flow of State Department cable traffic bearing on the supply of U.S. nuclear material to India. Further, the NRC has had frequent contacts with cognizant Executive Branch agencies on the Indian situation, and the Commissioners have engaged in numerous discussions among themselves and with the Staff on these matters. In conjunction with the licensing of fuel for use at TAPS, four classified briefings have been received on the Commission level between

September, 1975, and February, 1976, from the State Department and other agencies, including the Central Intelligence Agency and the Energy Research and Development Administration. Written questions supplementing those routinely posed by the Commission in conjunction with fuel export license applications pursuant to Executive Order 11902 have also been submitted to the State Department. Written submissions from Executive Branch agencies have been received and, unless classified, are part of the public docket in this matter. Thus, the written submissions and oral presentations in connection with the present proceeding supplement an already extensive consideration of the issues involved in licensing exports for use at Tarapur.

. . .

I.   Standing to intervene as a matter of right

The Sierra Club is a non-profit conservation organization, incorporated in the State of California, with a membership of approximately 156,000 persons in the United States and 100 foreign countries. The Club's corporate purposes are "[t]o protect and conserve the natural resources of the Sierra Nevada, the United States and the World; to undertake and publish scientific and educational studies concerning all aspects of man's environment and the natural eco-systems of the World; and to educate the people of the United States and the World to the need to preserve and restore the quality of that environment and the integrity of those eco-systems." The Natural Resources Defense Council, Inc. (NRDC), is a non-profit, public benefit organization incorporated in the State of New York, with a membership of over 22,000 persons in the United States and foreign countries. NRDC's objectives are to "maintain and enhance environmental quality"; to "monitor federal agencies to ensure that environmental values are fully considered in decision-making"; and to advance its environmental goals by participating in agency proceedings and by undertaking lawsuits. The Union of Concerned Scientists (UCS) is a non-profit corporation incorporated in the District of Columbia by "a coalition of scientists, engineers and other professionals concerned about the impact of advanced technology on society." It is not a membership organization. Its purpose is "to coordinate scientific analysis and research of public policy and technological issues."

The petitions to intervene filed on behalf of these organizations, if granted, would require the holding of an adjudicatory, or trial-type, hearing subject to appropriate modifications made in accordance with Administrative Procedure Act's "foreign policy" exception. 5 U.S.C. § 554(a)(4). Grant of the petitions as a matter of right turns on petitioners' standing to participate and the standing question, in turn, is framed by Section 189(a) of the Atomic Energy Act of 1954, 42 U.S.C. § 2239(a), which provides in pertinent part that: "[i]n any proceeding under this Act, for the granting . . . of any license . . . the Commission shall grant a hearing upon the request of any person whose interest may be affected by the proceeding, and shall admit any such person as a party to such proceeding." The Tarapur application is one "for granting . . . of any license." Thus, petitioners to establish

a right to the hearing they request must show they possess standing—
that is, an "interest" which may be "affected" by the proceeding.
. . .

First, as a general proposition, the Commission relies principally on
judicial precedents in deciding issues of standing to intervene. We
recognize that standing requirements in the federal courts need not be
the model for those applicable to administrative proceedings. For
example, the constitutional requirement for a "case or controversy"
under Article III does not apply to NRC licensing proceedings. Nevertheless, administrative agencies have generally accepted the standards
announced by the federal courts as useful guides in determining the
kinds of interests a petitioner must establish to sustain a claim for
participation in a proceeding as a matter of right. This Commission
and its predecessor, the Atomic Energy Commission, are no exception to
this practice. . . . Indeed, each of the three participants in these
proceedings makes detailed reference to judicial decisions on the question of standing. We have found particularly useful the United States
Supreme Court's discussion of prudential concepts of standing and their
relationship to constitutional standards. See, e.g., Warth v. Seldin, 422
U.S. 490, 500 (1975); United States v. Richardson, 418 U.S. 166, 179–80,
188–193 (Powell J., concurring). Adjudication in the administrative
context has liabilities as well as advantages, especially for setting
policy. The functional need for well-defined and specific interests,
which will lend concrete adversity to the decision-making process,
applies as directly to our licensing review as it would to a federal
lawsuit.

Second, we have concluded as a matter of policy that an expansive
rule of standing would be undesirable in the export licensing context,
which involves sensitive questions of the nation's conduct of foreign
policy. These matters have traditionally been viewed as appropriately
resolved in settings other than a public, adversary adjudication. See,
Pauling v. McNamara, 331 F.2d 796 (D.C.Cir.1964). The accommodation of deeply felt national interests requires a process of international
negotiation, clarification and adjustment which does not fit an adjudicatory format or timetable.[1] Given such considerations, "oversight" of

1. [Ed.] Among these complexities were
the following: the reactors supply a significant proportion of electricity to a relatively
industrialized portion of India otherwise
dependent on hydroelectric power derived
from inconstant monsoon rains, and alternative nuclear fuels are both forbidden by
the Agreement for Cooperation and not
readily available; if such fuels were to be
made available, in all likelihood this could
only be through the Russian government,
which has for many years been in competition with the United States for influence in
India. The human as well as the diplomatic consequence of an embargo, or even of
delay to the point of exhausting existing
supplies, could thus be considerable. The
principal arguments for the embargo were
instrumental ones—that is, to create a lever by which to persuade the Indian government to give up nuclear explosives development—since the Tarapur facilities
themselves had not been implicated in the
1974 explosion; other reactors and Indian
source material had been used for this
purpose. But the materials at Tarapur
could supply the source for a number of
nuclear devices if the Indian government
were to believe itself freed of the obligation
under the Agreement for Cooperation and
the 1974 understanding to withhold *that*
material from such use; and they might so
regard a breach by the United States of its
promise to supply.

When the Congress enacted the Nuclear
Non-Proliferation Act, P.L. 95–242, 42
U.S.C. § 2155, in 1977, it required no fur-

the Commission's policies and practices is most appropriately performed by the Congress, through the Joint Committee on Atomic Energy and other concerned committees. It might be noted in this connection that, during the past year the Commission has testified and provided briefings concerning its nuclear export activities on numerous occasions before several Congressional committees.

Petitioners' reliance on such cases as Office of Communications of the United Church of Christ v. FCC, 359 F.2d 994 (D.C.Cir.1966) for the proposition that "it may be in the public interest for the Commission to permit intervention, even when judicial doctrines of standing would not authorize it" is misplaced. . . . In the United Church of Christ case, the Court of Appeals allowed a petition by members of the listening public to intervene in proceedings for renewal of a broadcast license. The proceeding there saw the FCC in its central licensing function, comparable to a [domestic nuclear power plant licensing] proceeding before this agency, and a function in which adjudication was the expected and appropriate mode of decision. The petitioners there, representatives and residents of local viewers, had a direct and personal stake in the outcome which sharply differentiated them from the nation's citizenry as a whole. Here, adjudication is not a normal mode, in part because of the foreign relations considerations. Also, . . . the petitioners here do not represent a discrete group alleging a specific identifiable injury. The interests they claim to represent are those of the nation as a whole, which we, no less than the Congress and the Executive Branch, are sworn by oath to uphold. In these circumstances, the need for separate representation and for adjudication rather than political oversight is not established. Schlesinger v. Reservists To Stop The War, 418 U.S. 208, 217–219 (1974).

The same reasoning leads us to conclude that Congress has not granted an express right of action to citizens who can claim an undifferentiated risk to themselves in the context of export license proceedings. While for domestic licensing our licensing boards have recognized claims of risk which may be considered somewhat remote as a basis for intervention, we believe it inappropriate and unnecessary to give the notion of "interest" which "may be affected" under Section 189(a), a broadly permissive reading here. Not every risk with which the Commission is substantially concerned is, perforce, one which must be deemed to create standing in some member of the public. When Section 189(a) was written, in 1954, established tests of citizen standing, in both administrative and judicial proceedings, were constrained to

ther procedures than the NRC had afforded in the reported case, but enacted specific and rather stringent non-proliferation standards to be employed by the Commission in considering proposed export licenses. At the same time, it provided that the President could override a Commission refusal to license particular shipments, on making a finding that national interest urgently so required and on laying his judgment before Congress for a period during which it, in turn, might be disapproved.

When the NRC failed to approve the first application sought for Tarapur under the new statutory regime, 7 NRC 436 (1978), President Carter—himself a strong advocate of non-proliferation measures—immediately invoked his override authority; and the Congress, in turn, permitted that decision to license the shipment to take effect. E.O. 12055, 43 Fed.Reg. 18157 (Apr. 27, 1978); N.Y. Times, Wed. June 21, 1978, A4:4.

their traditional, rather narrow, dimensions. See, Davis, Administrative Law Treatise, Vol. 3, Chapter 22—Standing (1958), esp. § 22.08. In the domestic reactor licensing proceedings, the Atomic Energy Act, as amended, and its legislative history contemplate hearings as an important aspect of the licensing process, and our boards' practice reflects this fact. There is nothing in the legislative history of the Atomic Energy Act, as amended, or in its implementation, which suggests that, in the export licensing context, any but the usual rules of standing, as they have evolved since 1954, are to be applied.

The continuing validity of this view is supported by the practices of the Atomic Energy Commission in administering the export license program, and by the fact that Congress did not address itself to these issues when the Nuclear Regulatory Commission was established.

. . .

IV. Discretionary hearing procedures

. . . Even if petitioners were entitled to a hearing as of right, the Commission does not believe that full adjudicatory procedures . . . would be appropriate in considering discrete nuclear materials licenses. In recognition of the sensitive and complex foreign policy issues raised, modification of adjudicatory procedures in such circumstances is authorized by the foreign affairs exemption to the Administrative Procedure Act, 5 U.S.C. § 554(a)(4), and would be undertaken in advance of a formal hearing. . . .

The practical difficulties of conducting an adjudicatory hearing should not be overlooked. An adjudicatory proceeding would produce a rather disjointed record. Questioning of witnesses could be expected to alternate frequently between public matters and confidential ones. Either the consideration of confidential responses would have to be postponed to a later time, or an executive session of the hearing would have to be convened, with the consequent inconvenience to parties, witnesses and public observers. Although cross-examination may be an effective tool where factual matters are in dispute, the issues here relate primarily to matters of law and policy. Even were that not the case, we believe that resulting delay, fragmentation of the record, and the inappropriateness of adversary confrontation concerning sensitive foreign relations matters all argue against using a trial-type approach.

A legislative format permits a more rational scheduling of witnesses, and a more ordered public record. Hearings more closely related to those typically used by legislative bodies will meet the petitioners' objective of presenting information and analyses regarding the issues involved in these two licenses before an appropriate government body. Even in this context, if a participant feels there are questions which need to be asked of the Executive Branch or other participants, those may be submitted to the Commission for possible use after review for relevance, materiality, and the likelihood that a full response would require reference to confidential information.

An open legislative type hearing can be conducted without prejudicing the important national interests on which export licensing determinations are based. Foreign nations that rely on the U.S. to supply their legitimate nuclear needs are accustomed to Congressional hearings on nuclear export and nonproliferation issues. Adjudicatory procedures are well suited to the resolution of concrete, factual disputes; broad public interests can be aired more appropriately and more effectively in an open public hearing of the type conducted by Congressional committees when they deal with similar issues. . . .

NOTES

(1) The Edlow decision was appealed to the D.C. Circuit, and argued in December, 1976. In the meantime, a two-day hearing was held along the suggested lines, with petitioners presenting views and testimony and suggesting questions to be directed to the Department of State. Subsequently, Congress enacted the law described at n. 1 to the decision above; and the President specifically authorized continuation of these shipments. In July, 1978, the court of appeals found the decision to have become moot. Natural Resources Defense Council v. United States Nuclear Regulatory Comm., 580 F.2d 698 (D.C.Cir.1978).

(2) Edlow appears to presuppose the general validity of the approach taken in the United Church of Christ and National Welfare Rights Organization cases. Current evaluation of the continuing viability of judicially enforced "interest representation" has to take into account Justice O'Connor's opinion for a unanimous Supreme Court in Block v. Community Nutrition Institute, 467 U.S. 340 (1984).[2] There, the Court held that a consumer's group was precluded from seeking judicial review of a milk marketing order promulgated by the Secretary of Agriculture under the Agriculture Marketing Agreement Act of 1937. In the course of its opinion, the Court said (467 U.S. at 346–47):

> The . . . statutory scheme, . . . , makes . . . clear Congress' intention to limit the classes entitled to participate in the development of market orders. The Act contemplates a cooperative venture among the Secretary, handlers, and producers the principal purposes of which are to raise the price of agricultural products and to establish an orderly system for marketing them. Handlers and producers—but not consumers—are entitled to participate in the adoption and retention of market orders. The Act provides for agreements among the Secretary, producers, and handlers, for hearings among them, and for votes by producers and handlers. Nowhere in the Act, however, is there an express provision for participation by consumers in any proceeding. In a complex scheme of this type, the omission of such a provision is sufficient reason to believe that Congress intended to foreclose consumer participation in the regulatory process.

The consumers group had not sought to participate in the administrative proceeding, rendering this passage simple dictum. Yet, if they *had* sought that opportunity, should the author of United Church of

2. The opinion is more fully set out below at p. 997.

Christ have agreed that the absence of "an express provision for participation" gave "sufficient reason to believe" that Congress intended to "foreclose consumer participation"?

And here is one final point for the future. As was said above, in informal rulemaking there is no need to petition to be let in, because there is no wall to keep one out. In recent years, there have been several proposals that agencies should at least experiment with rulemaking procedures that would encourage parties to be more cooperative, and less antagonistic, than they often now are; the suggested cure is negotiation. Note, Rethinking Regulation: Negotiation as an Alternative to Traditional Rulemaking, 94 Harv.L.Rev. 1871 (1981); P. Harter, Negotiating Regulations: A Cure for Malaise, 71 Geo.L.J. 1 (1982). Inherently, if rules are going to be negotiated, there will have to be a more-or-less restrictive rule that determines who is entitled to participate; and that will raise in rulemaking questions of intervention similar to those we have just been investigating. Consider, in this light, the proposal of the Administrative Conference that agencies experiment in having affected interests participate directly in developing proposed rules.

ADMINISTRATIVE CONFERENCE OF THE UNITED STATES, PROCEDURES FOR NEGOTIATING PROPOSED REGULATIONS (RECOMMENDATION NO. 82–4):

RECOMMENDATION

1. Agencies should consider using regulatory negotiation, as described in this recommendation, as a means of drafting for agency consideration the text of a proposed regulation. . . .

2. Congress should facilitate the regulatory negotiation process by passing legislation explicitly authorizing agencies to conduct rulemaking proceedings in the manner described in this recommendation. . . .

3. In legislation authorizing regulatory negotiation, Congress should authorize agencies to designate a "convenor" to organize the negotiations in a particular proceeding. The convenor should be an individual, government agency, or private organization, neutral with respect to the regulatory policy issues under consideration. If the agency chooses an individual who is an employee of the agency itself, that person should not be associated with either the rulemaking or enforcement staff. The convenor would be responsible for (i) advising the agency as to whether, in a given proceeding, regulatory negotiation is feasible and is likely to be conducive to the fairer and more efficient conduct of the agency's regulatory program, and (ii) determining, in

consultation with the agency, who should participate in the negotiations.

4. An agency considering use of regulatory negotiation should select and consult with a convenor at the earliest practicable time about the feasibility of its use. The convenor should conduct a preliminary inquiry to determine whether a regulatory negotiating group should be empanelled to develop a proposed rule relating to the particular topic. The convenor should consider the risks that negotiation procedures would increase the likelihood of a consensus proposal that would limit output, raise prices, restrict entry, or otherwise establish or support unreasonable restraints on competition. Other factors bearing on this decision include the following:

(a) The issues to be raised in the proceeding should be mature and ripe for decision. . . .

(b) The resolution of issues should not be such as to require participants in negotiations to compromise their fundamental tenets, since it is unlikely that agreement will be reached in such circumstances. . . .

(c) The interests significantly affected should be such that individuals can be selected who will adequately represent those interests. Since negotiations cannot generally be conducted with a large number of participants, there should be a limited number of interests that will be significantly affected by the rule and therefore represented in the negotiations. A rule of thumb might be that negotiations should ordinarily involve no more than 15 participants.

(d) There should be a number of diverse issues that the participants can rank according to their own priorities and on which they might reach agreement by attempting to optimize the return to all the participants.

(e) No single interest should be able to dominate the negotiations.
. . .

(f) The participants in the negotiations should be willing to negotiate in good faith to draft a proposed rule.

(g) The agency should be willing to designate an appropriate staff member to participate as the agency's representative, but the representative should make clear to the other participants that he or she cannot bind the agency.

5. If the convenor determines that regulatory negotiation would be appropriate, it would recommend this procedure to the agency. If the agency and the convenor agree that regulatory negotiation is appropriate, the convenor should be responsible for determining preliminarily the interests that will likely be substantially affected by a proposed rule, the individuals that will represent those interests in negotiations, the scope of issues to be addressed, and a schedule for completing the work. . . .

. . .

7. To ensure that the appropriate interests have been identified and have had the opportunity to be represented in the negotiating

group, the agency should publish in the FEDERAL REGISTER a notice that it is contemplating developing a rule by negotiation and indicate in the notice the issues involved and the participants and interests already identified. If an additional person or interest petitions for membership or representation in the negotiating group, the convenor, in consultation with the agency, should determine (i) whether that interest would be substantially affected by the rule, (ii) if so, whether it would be represented by an individual already in the negotiating group, and (iii) whether, in any event, the petitioner should be added to the negotiating group, or whether interests can be consolidated and still provide adequate representation.

. . .

9. It may be that, in particular proceedings, certain affected interests will require reimbursement for direct expenses to be able to participate at a level that will foster broadly-based, successful negotiations. Unlike intervenors, the negotiating group will be performing a function normally performed within the agency, and the agency should consider reimbursing the direct expenses of such participants. . . . Congress should clarify the authority of agencies to provide such financial resources.

. . .

11. The goal of the negotiating group should be to arrive at a consensus on a proposed rule. Consensus in this context means that each interest represented in the negotiating group concurs in the result, unless all members of the group agree at the outset on another definition. . . . The participants may, of course, be unable to reach a consensus on a proposed rule, and, in that event, they should identify in the report both the areas in which they are agreed and the areas in which consensus could not be achieved. This could serve to narrow the issues in dispute, identify information necessary to resolve issues, rank priorities, and identify potentially acceptable solutions.

. . .

13. The agency should publish the negotiated text of the proposed rule in its notice of proposed rulemaking. If the agency does not publish the negotiated text as a proposed rule, it should explain its reasons. The agency may wish to propose amendments or modifications to the negotiated proposed rule, but it should do so in such a manner that the public at large can identify the work of the agency and of the negotiating group.

14. The negotiating group should be afforded an opportunity to review any comments that are received in response to the notice of proposed rulemaking so that the participants can determine whether their recommendations should be modified. The final responsibility for issuing the rule would remain with the agency.

NOTES

(1) P. HARTER, REGULATORY NEGOTIATION: THE EXPERIENCE SO FAR, Winter 1984 Resolve 1:

"In 1978, the Occupational Safety and Health Administration (OSHA) of the U.S. Department of Labor issued a standard governing occupational exposures to benzene. It was challenged by industry, and the case wound up in the Supreme Court as the first of two in which the role of costs in OSHA health regulations was considered. The Court invalidated the standard and sent it back for further work. OSHA committed itself to publishing a proposed rule by the end of 1983 and a final rule by summer 1984. . . .

"Simultaneously with announcing its commitment to this schedule, OSHA retained Gerald Cormick and this author through the Mediation Institute in Seattle to conduct a feasibility analysis to determine whether it would be appropriate to develop the rule through regulatory negotiation. To that end, meetings were held with the interests that had played a major role in the earlier, particularly bitter rule-making proceeding. . . .

"Although in the abstract the issues met the criteria for regulatory negotiation quite well, one overriding problem caused the consultants to recommend against using a negotiated rule-making process: no one wanted to interfere with the short timetable OSHA had allowed itself. Hence, using the regulatory negotiation process was inappropriate unless the chances of success were greater than they appeared to be at that time. In addition, there was considerable disquiet about whether it would be appropriate to use negotiation to develop a health standard and a healthy skepticism over whether it would work.

"On the other hand, it appeared to the conveners that the parties did indeed have a great deal to discuss. They proposed a joint meeting to determine whether additional meetings would be fruitful, what the ground rules for such meetings would be, and what items could be placed on an agenda for discussion. The meeting took place with four industry associations (and member companies) and four unions represented. OSHA made a presentation but did not attend as a participant. . . .

"At this first joint meeting, the unions presented an outline of the policies that they thought were needed in the benzene standard, and the ideas were discussed fully and openly. At the next meeting, the industry groups made a similar presentation. Both meetings reflected considerable thought and preparation, and the level of the discussion was high.

"The group actually addressed the issues at the third meeting, covering perhaps half the issues involved in the standard. The parties resolved their differences on many of the issues and narrowed their disagreement on others. . . . At the time this article was written, the group was making a significant effort, and indeed was making progress, to reach consensus on the whole standard. . . .

"The group is also grappling with the question of precisely what effect a consensus position would have and how binding it would be and on whom. Hence, it is too early to tell whether the effort will succeed in developing a final recommendation to OSHA. Whether or not that happens, the parties have made substantial progress in addressing what had been a bitter issue. Both sides have commented to this author that they have found the process helpful and worthwhile.

"...

"... [I]t would have been highly unlikely that an OSHA health standard could have been negotiated before the role of costs was clarified, at least somewhat, by the Supreme Court. Otherwise, a fundamental tenet to all the parties would have been a matter of negotiation. But, since that has been confronted in litigation, developing the standard itself has not forced the parties to compromise their beliefs, although some parties may come close. . . ."

(2) In late 1985, the Administrative Conference reported that initial experience with four efforts to negotiate rules "has shown that the original recommendation was basically sound"; ACUS did make some further recommendations on ways to make the process successful. Procedures for Negotiating Proposed Regulations (Recommendation No. 85–51), 50 Fed.Reg. 52895 (1985).*

(3) Multi-party negotiation is, of course, a technique which can be used for more than rulemaking. For another possible application, see Negotiated Cleanup of Hazardous Waste Sites under CERCLA (Recommendation No. 84–4) 1 CFR § 305.84–4, and the report of the study on which the ACUS recommendation was based, F.R. Anderson, Negotiation and Informal Agency Action: The Case of Superfund (1985 Duke L.J. 261.)

SECTION 4. SCOPE OF REVIEW OF ADMINISTRATIVE ACTION

Chapter II of this book deals with legislative and executive control of administrative action. The first three sections of this chapter (as well as subsequent materials) consider the manner in which agencies exercise their powers. In this section we direct explicit attention to a topic which interrelates with most of the other aspects of the subject and which, therefore, already has been implicitly involved in some of the preceding materials. The topic is judicial review of the substance of administrative action, a key aspect of which is the "scope of review": when review does occur, how closely does the court inquire—how much is essentially left to the agency, how much is essentially decided by the court?[1] Allocating functions and responsibility between court and agency is unquestionably important, not a mere matter of organization charts or division of labor. "The availability of judicial review is the necessary condition, psychologically if not logically, of a system of administrative power which purports to be legitimate, or legally valid."[2]

* For further consideration of "alternative dispute resolution" techniques as applied to administrative problems, see S. Goldberg, E. Green, and F. Sander, Dispute Resolution (1985), esp. at 403–442.

1. Other aspects of judicial review are treated in Chapter 9—whether it is available; if so, what legal methods are used, when and at whose behest.

2. L. Jaffe, Judicial Control of Administrative Action 320 (1965). And: "Congress has been willing to delegate its legislative powers broadly—and courts have upheld such delegation—because there is court review to assure that the agency exercises the delegated power within statutory limits. . . . " Ethyl Corp. v. EPA, 541 F.2d

The relationship between courts and agencies has been described in a "comforting metaphor" as one of "collaboration" or "partnership." [3] But what does the partnership agreement provide? Inescapably, it is interpreted by the courts. They speak in terms of scope of review, but there is disagreement about whether such terms reflect criteria that actually determine when judges refrain from reversing agency action they disagree with—or are used instead as a verbal facade manipulated to declare deference only when judges agree with the agency's result or care little about it.

If we envision scope as a spectrum, there is agreement about the end-points. At one extreme, the administrative determination is conclusive, that is, the reviewing court must accept the administrative decision; this is in fact no review at all, and is extremely rare in American law.[4] At the other extreme, "de novo" review gives the administrative determination no effect, that is, the court exercises its own judgment wholly independent of the agency's decision; although not as rare as no review at all, de novo review is not widely used. Between those extremes occurs the overwhelming bulk of judicial review, with a range of degrees of judicial aggressiveness or restraint, described by formulaic phrases such as "clearly erroneous," "substantial evidence on the whole record," and "arbitrary and capricious" or "an abuse of discretion", each purportedly describing a "differential deferential role." [5]

Judges and brief-writers in thousands of cases go on at length, especially in recent decades, about which scope is applicable or how it should be applied. At risk of overstating positions, we may categorize four divergent views about what all that writing means. We might call one view "realist" (some might call it nihilist):

1, 68 (D.C.Cir.1976, Leventhal, J., concurring), cert. denied 426 U.S. 941 (1976).

3. W. Gardner, Federal Courts and Agencies: An Audit of the Partnership Books, 75 Colum.L.R. 800, 820 (1975). Frequent recent references to "partnership" stem from Greater Boston Television Corp. v. FCC, 444 F.2d 841, 851–52 (D.C.Cir.1970), cert. denied 403 U.S. 923 (1971). However comforting the metaphor, Judge Friendly observed wryly concerning "partnership" pronouncements by the D.C. Circuit, "There is little doubt who is considered to be the senior partner." H. Friendly, "Some Kind of Hearing," 123 U.Pa.L.Rev. 1267, 1311 n. 221 (1975).

Judge Wald uses another analogy for her court's relationship with the FCC, over 90% of whose court of appeals cases come to the D.C. Circuit: "To some degree, we and you are like a tired middle-aged couple: Committed to our conjugal duty, devoted to each other deep down, yes—but passionately aroused, most of the time, no. You need to put back the romance, the excitement, into our relationship. Nearly 20 cases a month, 8 months a year, an extra hundred motions to dismiss appeals, stay orders, and remand records thrown in and we're staring at administrative law burnout. Your brief, your argument, your appeal have to be something special. . . . " Remarks before Federal Communications Bar Association, April 7, 1984, p. 4.

4. See Chapter 9, section 2.

5. The last phrase is Professor Rosenblum's, On Teaching and Decision Making About Administrative Law, 1983 A.B.F.R.J. 771, 775. Compare the recent developments about scope of review in Constitutional Law, where "strict scrutiny" as distinct from "mere rationality" applies to review of statutes said to affect "fundamental rights," and intermediate levels are also invoked. There too we find discussion both of what is the appropriate scope of review and of whether scope matters or is only facade. See G. Gunther, Constitutional Law Cases and Materials, 457–8, 472–5, 516, 588–591 (11th ed. 1985).

At best concepts such as "substantial evidence" tend to be little more than convenient labels attached to results reached without their aid. . . . [We suspect] that the rules governing judicial review have no more substance at the core than a seedless grape. . . . Nevertheless, despite this recognition of the essential meaninglessness of the accepted formulae of judicial review, the rules unaccountably command endless attention in the classroom and legal literature.[6]

A second view may be called "reductionist":

The scope of review varies all the way from total unreviewability to *de novo* review, but the dominant scope of review is in the middle: *Courts usually substitute judgment on the kind of questions of law that are within their special competence, but on other questions they limit themselves to deciding reasonableness; they do not clarify the meaning of reasonableness but retain full discretion in each case to stretch it in either direction.* The italicized statement is in general an adequate summary of the main idea of the law of scope of review and may be more reliable than the many complexities and refinements that are constantly repeated in judicial opinions.[7]

A third view may be called "formalist," attaching much weight to which formula is employed and making many refinements in how the formulas should apply to different actions or issues under review. By no means is formalism removed from realities: many statutes reflect legislative struggles over what scope of review formula should be used, and one of the fullest Congressional efforts regarding Administrative Law in this generation has involved an effort to amend the APA's provisions on scope.[8]

A fourth view, finally, might be labeled "pragmatic." Scope must be dealt with, *first* because different statutes use the language of scope to fill in the "partnership agreement" between different agencies and the courts: if the formulaic phrases are used to allocate functions and degrees of responsibility, then whether one is involved in legislating, administering or litigating, one needs a working sense of what the statutory language calls for. *Second,* reflecting such statutes and much judge-made law, there is a vast body of judicial opining on scope: "we should not assume that our judges are dissemblers"[9] and certainly the opinions must be susceptible to analysis if one is to say how existing law may bear on a new matter. *Third,* a number of well-recognized factors operate to invoke more deferential or more aggressive review;

6. E. Gellhorn and G. Robinson, Perspectives in Administrative Law, 75 Colum.L.Rev., 771, 780–781 (1975). Also:

"[T]he suspicion has arisen, certainly among practitioners who can say such things, that the grand synthesizing principle that tells us whether the courts will dig deeply or bow cursorily depends exclusively on whether the judge agrees with the result of the administrative decision." W. Rodgers, "Judicial Review of Risk Assess-

ment: The Role of Decision Theory in Unscrambling the *Benzene* Decision," 11 Env. L. 301, 302 (1981).

7. 5 K. Davis, Administrative Law Treatise 332 (2d ed. 1984).

8. See p. 401 on the Bumpers Amendment.

9. C. Byse, Scope of Review in Informal Rulemaking, 33 Ad.L.Rev. 183, 193 (1981).

awareness of these factors helps greatly in analyzing precedent and predicting results. *Last,* going beyond (or to a different level of) pragmatism, if neither formulas nor discoverable factors are operating with reasonable consistency, then the "senior partner" is intervening as it freely chooses whenever it freely chooses, an assertion about the judiciary that is at once both unrealistic and in a democracy, unacceptable.

Your goal ought not to be to emerge with a few generalizations that might be used like cookie-cutters; that cannot be expected, considering the variety of problems in which there is argument over scope, or the leeway the most formalist of judges enjoys even when the appropriate scope is clear.[10] What scope doctrine exists to do is to set or affect judges' moods in reviewing agency action.

Indeed, the importance of "mood" is undeniable. It has long been acknowledged that the intensity of review is affected by a number of unarticulated factors such as "the character of the administrative agency, the nature of the problems with which it deals, the nature and consequences of the administrative action, the confidence which the agency has won, the degree to which the review would interfere with the agency's functions or burden the courts, the nature of the proceedings before the administrative agency, and similar factors." Report of the Attorney General's Committee on Administrative Procedure 91 (1941). Moreover, "courts develop reputations on various issues. Some, such as the First, Second, and D.C. Circuits, are seen as particularly hospitable to environmental groups. Industry is more likely to receive a sympathetic hearing in the Fourth, Ninth, or Tenth Circuits, or in its favorite district court, the Eastern District of Louisiana. . . . It is, in short, misleading to speak of 'the courts' as a unified entity." [11]

Despite the existence of these (and other) "unarticulated factors" which contribute to a sensitive if at times unruly judicial role, it is well to recall the warning of Second Circuit Judge Irving R. Kaufman: "[E]ven after rendering the agency that which is plainly the agency's, the courts are regularly confronted by difficult cases which cannot be avoided. . . . Some contend that over many years and after many cases, a judge develops a disciplined instinct for right, a kind of 'finely

---

10. "Although the standard of review may dictate the rhetorical guise, it generally cannot eliminate the risk [that the court will substitute its judgment for the agency's]. Indeed, the only kind of review that does not entail that risk is no review, and that is the one 'standard' clearly incompatible with the will of Congress." M. Garland, Deregulation and Judicial Review, 98 Harv.L.Rev. 505, 558 (1985).

11. R. Melnick, Regulation and the Courts, 70 (1983).

The old Fifth Circuit had a long record of reversing the NLRB notably more than other circuits, which may have reflected the South's somewhat different labor relations scene. In 1965–7, the Fifth Circuit's NLRB affirmance rate was 52%, compared to 63% for the D.C. Circuit and 68% for the Second Circuit, the only ones studied. J. Howard, Courts of Appeals in the Federal Judicial System (1981), 52, 322–330. Notably, Professor Howard found, judges' votes on deferral to the agency in labor-management cases (or indeed in most categories of cases) showed very little correlation with their political orientation, and only slightly more correlation with their "judicial role perceptions" ("innovator, realist or interpreter"). Howard, supra, 173–7.

honed' expertise in generalism, in fundamental concepts of fairness, due process and plain common sense which must ultimately govern in even the most complex of factual disputes. This overriding sense of judicialness may compensate for the judge's lack of detailed expert knowledge of nuclear physics or computer technology or statistical analysis. . . . I am no exponent of what Max Weber once referred to as 'Khadi justice,' in which the great caliph would sit on his cushion and decide each case intuitively, without regard to precedents or reasoned elaboration of law. Like cases must be treated alike, even if the 'bad fellows' occasionally emerge triumphant." I. Kaufman, Judicial Review of Agency Action: A Judge's Unburdening, 45 N.Y.U. 201 (1970).

And, finally, recall that "the statute under which an agency operates is not the whole law applicable to its operation. An agency is not an island entire of itself. It is one of the many rooms in the magnificent mansion of the law. The very subordination of the agency to judicial jurisdiction is intended to proclaim the premise that each agency is to be brought into harmony with the totality of the law. . . . " L. Jaffe, Judicial Control of Administrative Action 590 (1965).

Whenever the scope of review is at issue, the first step is to say precisely what error the complaining party claims the agency committed. Next is the inquiry about the "partnership agreement": so far as the relevant statute indicates, just what is the extent of the power delegated to the agency for the function under review? Much turns on precisely what agency function is under review: Is it adjudicating or rule-making—and in either case, is it on a formal record or not? If rule-making, was it pursuant to an express grant of power (e.g., a statute saying . . . "area of production (as defined by the Administrator)" [12]), or was it pursuant to a general grant of power to "make rules to carry out the purposes of this Act"? Was the agency finding a fact, making a prediction, exercising discretion, applying the statute to the situation, construing aspects of the statute not affected by the particular situation—or deciding its procedure for performing such functions?

Courts have not customarily analyzed scope problems in such terms. Traditionally, the focus has been on fitting the questions presented on review into hoary categories, "questions of fact", as to which review is almost always limited; or "questions of law," as to which review is usually independent; sometimes a third category, "mixed questions," as to which review is most simply described as mixed; and recently more significant, a fourth category of "judgmental questions", getting limited review. We will examine how well such categories work and whether we can find any pattern of analysis that works better.

a. What is a "Question of Fact"?

No two terms of legal science have rendered better service than "law" and "fact". They are basic assumptions; irreduci-

12. See Addison v. Holly Hill Fruit   below.
Products, Inc., 322 U.S. 607 (1944), p. 396

ble minimums and the most comprehensive maximums at the same instant. They readily accommodate themselves to any meaning we desire to give them. In them and their kind a science of law finds its strength and durability. They are the creations of centuries. What judge has not found refuge in them? The man who could succeed in defining them would be a public enemy. L. Green, Judge and Jury, 270–1 (1930).

Despite that admonition, these phrases are so central that we need a sense of how they are used.[1] In a case involving an appeal from an order of the Federal Communications Commission denying an application for a radio station construction permit, the Court said:

"In discussing . . . findings of fact, it will be helpful to spell out the process which a commission properly follows in reaching a decision. The process necessarily includes at least four parts: (1) evidence must be taken and weighed, both as to its accuracy and credibility; (2) from attentive consideration of this evidence a determination of facts of a basic or underlying nature must be reached; (3) from these basic facts the ultimate facts, usually in the language of the statute, are to be inferred, or not, as the case may be; (4) from this finding the decision will follow by the application of the statutory criterion. For example, before the Communications Commission may grant a construction permit it must, under the statute, be convinced that the public interest, convenience or necessity will be served. An affirmative or negative finding on this topic would be a finding of ultimate fact. This ultimate fact, however, will be reached by inference from basic facts, such as, for example, the probable existence or nonexistence of electrical interference, in view of the number of other stations operating in the area, their power, wave length, and the like. These basic facts will themselves appear or fail to appear, as the case may be, from the evidence introduced when attentively considered. Thus, upon the issue of electrical interference evidence may be introduced concerning power and wave length of a proposed station and of existing stations, and expert opinion based upon this evidence may be offered as to the likelihood of interference; and expert opinion based on evidence of field measurements of signal strength of existing stations may also be offered. This testimony may conflict. It is the Commission's duty to find from such evidence the basic facts as to the operation of the proposed and present stations in respect of power, wave length, and the like, and whether or not electrical interference will result from the operation of the proposed station, and then to find as an ultimate fact whether public interest, convenience, or necessity will be served by granting or not granting the application." Saginaw Broadcasting Co. v. Federal Communications Commission, 96 F.2d 554, 559–560 (D.C.Cir.1938).

1. The infinitely frequent uses of these phrases by courts is almost equalled by the number of articles noting the courts' difficulties. Our courts are not alone: "There can hardly be a subject on which the [British] courts act with such total lack of consistency as the difference between fact and law." H. Wade, Administrative Law 817 (5th ed.1982). It has often been recognized that inconsistency in language may be far greater than in actual resolution of problems. A thorough recent treatment is R. Levin, Identifying Questions of Law in Administrative Law, 74 Geo. L.J. 1 (1985).

Do "ultimate facts" belong together with "basic facts"? Professor Jaffe brings out what turns on—or determines—these categorizations:

"It is often said that in many situations it is difficult, perhaps indeed impossible to make a clean distinction between fact and law; that the difference is one of degree, that the relation of fact and law can be described as a spectrum with finding of fact shading imperceptibly into conclusion of law. It is sometimes said that a question is fact or law depending on whether the court chooses to 'treat' it as one or the other. If, for example, a court holds that the failure of a motorist to stop, look, and listen before crossing a railroad track is negligence per se, the question by the very force of the decision is or has become one of law; if the court, however, permits a jury to decide the question it is 'treated' as a question of fact or a 'mixed' question of law and fact. This method of statement when used by some reflects a postulate that a court has the duty to decide all questions of law; therefore if it chooses not to decide a question, the postulate can be fulfilled only if the question is denominated as one of fact or, at least, as 'mixed.' In this view it is difficult to analyze the nature of the question, since it turns on a guess as to how the court will act. This analytic confusion complicates description of what the court is doing and conceals the true character of this aspect of judicial review. *If we admit that the administrative as well as the judiciary can, and within limits should, make law, our analytic problem is much simplified.* Nor should it be supposed that such an analysis is intended to aggrandize the administrative at the expense of the judiciary, or to imperil the traditional 'rule of law.' Indeed, the contrary is true. The device of characterizing a question as one of fact or as 'mixed' permits a court to pretend that it *must* affirm the administrative action if it is 'supported by evidence' or is 'reasonable.' But if the question is analyzed and faced as one of law the court cannot thus avoid its responsibility. True, the basic and ineradicable difficulty still obtains, namely: whether it is or is not a case for the exercise of the judicial law-making power. But, at least, the problem cannot be brushed off or obscured by a pretense that the court is without power to intervene.

"How then do we distinguish fact from law? *It will be more meaningful, I think, to put the question: how do we distinguish a finding of fact from a conclusion of law?* In this way we emphasize that we are concerned with the function and the functioning of the decisional process: what is the officer doing, we ask, when he 'finds' a fact and how does this action differ from his making a conclusion of law? Thus we may perhaps avoid the unanchored abstractness of distinguishing between fact and law *simpliciter. A finding of fact is the assertion that a phenomenon has happened or is or will be happening independent of or anterior to any assertion as to its legal effect.* It can, for example, be made by a person who is ignorant of the applicable law. Thus a statute may provide compensation for injuries arising out of and during the course of employment. It has been found that an employee while at work has been intentionally hit on the head by a fellow employee. This is a finding of fact. It owes nothing to the compensation statute. If, however, it is asserted that the injury arose out of the employment and is therefore compensable, the assertion is something more than a finding of fact; it is, in our view, a conclusion of law. The assertion cannot be derived by one who is ignorant of the applicable statutes. It is, unless it is a purely arbitrary exercise of power, an assertion that the purpose of the statute will be served by awarding compensation. L. Jaffe, Judicial Control of Administrative Action 546–48 (1965).

Is Jaffe saying that "mixed" questions belong with "questions of fact" and so get equally limited review? What of the question whether a contract was formed?[2] Judge Friendly said that under Jaffe's view adhering to "Holmes' narrow definition of 'fact' . . . the making of a contract would be a question of law, not of fact." NLRB v. Marcus Trucking Co., 286 F.2d 583 (2d Cir.1961). Professor Jaffe responded: "I would demur to his conclusion that under my view 'the making of a contract' is necessarily a question of law. That depends on whether what is at issue are the events, the intentions, etc., which are asserted to constitute a contract. If so, the questions are questions of fact. . . . I do, however, agree with him that if the conclusion to be drawn from the facts involves no more than applying the statute with no further and explicit questions raised as to its 'meaning', the reviewing court should accept it, but not because it is a finding of fact. Rather, in my view, . . . a law-applying judgment is *presumptively* within the area of the agency's discretion. . . . " Jaffe, supra, 549–50.

Before we can consider "mixed questions," consider how "questions of fact" are reviewed.

b. Review of Questions of Fact

Before considering the judicial role in reviewing agency fact-finding, it may be helpful to recall that appellate courts long have been reviewing facts found by trial courts. Courts of appeal review factual findings in non-jury decisions under the "clearly erroneous" standard—a standard which itself has been the source of controversy.[1]

In review of Federal agency action, treatment of "questions of fact" is usually governed by section 706 of the APA: de novo review in a

2. What of questions of contract interpretation? For unusually helpful discussion, see Judge Newman's concurrence in Antilles S.S. Co. v. Members of American Hull Ass'n, 733 F.2d 195, 202 (2d Cir.1984).

1. See Anderson v. Bessemer City, 470 U.S. 564 (1985).

Roughly contemporaneous with Universal Camera Corp. v. NLRB, the next principal case, Judge Jerome Frank of the Second Circuit wrote: "[E]vidence sufficient to support a jury verdict or an administrative finding may not suffice to support a trial judge's finding. . . . "We must sustain a general or a special jury verdict when there is some evidence which the jury might have believed, and when a reasonable inference from that evidence will sup-port the verdict, regardless of whether that evidence is oral or by deposition. In the case of findings by an administrative agency, the usual rule is substantially the same as that in the case of a jury, the findings being treated like a special verdict . . . . A wag might say that a verdict is entitled to high respect because the jurors are inexperienced in finding facts, an administrative finding is given high respect because the administrative officers are specialists (guided by experts) in finding a particular class of facts, but, paradoxically, a trial judge's finding has far less respect because he is blessed neither with jurors' inexperience nor administrative officers' expertness." Orvis v. Higgins, 180 F.2d 537, 539, 540 n. 7 (2d Cir. 1950).

limited category of cases; "substantial evidence" review of decisions made in on-the-record proceedings; and review for arbitrariness, capriciousness, or abuse of discretion in cases not otherwise provided for. The first, by definition, is hardly review as such. Our consideration of the last, characteristic of informal proceedings, is postponed to the end of this section. We turn now to the substantial evidence problem.

Over a half century ago, in reviewing a rate reduction order issued by the Interstate Commerce Commission (the Act had no provision on scope), the Supreme Court stated that a court would "not consider the expediency or wisdom of the order, or whether, on like testimony, it would have made a similar ruling. . . . [The Commission's] conclusion, of course, is subject to review, but when supported by evidence is accepted as final; not that its decision, involving as it does so many and such vast public interests, can be supported by a mere scintilla of proof—but the courts will not examine the facts further than to determine whether there was substantial evidence to sustain the order." ICC v. Union Pacific Ry. Co., 222 U.S. 541, 547–548 (1912).[2]

Over the years, substantial evidence came to be the dominant though not universal formula for the scope of review of administrative findings of fact in on-the-record proceedings.[3] As early as the Federal Trade Commission Act of 1914, Congress provided explicitly: "Findings of fact, if supported by substantial evidence, shall be conclusive."[4] Even when Congress omits the word "substantial," courts often fill in, as when the Supreme Court said: "[T]he statute, in providing that 'the findings of the [National Labor Relations] Board as to the facts, if supported by evidence, shall be conclusive' means supported by substantial evidence." Consolidated Edison Co. v. NLRB, 305 U.S. 197, 229 (1938).

But without question, "there is often greater difficulty in applying the [substantial evidence] test than in formulating it." Stork Restaurant, Inc. v. Boland, 282 N.Y. 256, 26 N.E.2d 247, 255 (1940). When the APA was adopted in 1946, lively debate began about what if any change the Act made in the scope of judicial review of administrative findings of fact. The major if not definitive answer came five years later. The

---

2. Judge Learned Hand described substantial evidence memorably: "the kind of evidence on which responsible persons are accustomed to rely in serious affairs." NLRB v. Remington Rand, Inc., 94 F.2d 862, 873 (2d Cir.1938).

3. As the Uniform Law Commissioners said in 1981, "an increasing number of states, either by express language or by judicial interpretation," have adopted the substantial evidence test. Comment on Model State APA § 5–116. The 1981 revision of the Model Act (see Appendix B, infra) prescribes substantial evidence for review of determinations of fact, as had the 1946 Model Act; but the 1961 revision used the "clearly erroneous" test.

In 1958, after several years of controversy, the Food, Drug and Cosmetic Act, 21

U.S.C. § 348, was amended to require a company seeking to use a food additive to petition for permission; previously, use was legal unless the FDA disapproved it. A petition was to be denied if a "fair evaluation of the data" did not establish that the use would be "safe." (The agency was to consider probable consumption, cumulative effects and "safety factors which in the opinion of experts are generally recognized as appropriate for the use of animal experimentation data.") If reviewed, the findings were to be upheld "if based upon a fair evaluation of the entire record." How does such review differ from review under the substantial evidence test?

4. 38 Stat. 717, 15 U.S.C. § 41.

case involved review of a National Labor Relations Board decision about whether a supervisory employee had been fired because he had testified supporting the union's position in an NLRB representation proceeding, or solely because subsequently he had accused the personnel manager of drunkenness. The trial examiner, crediting the employer's testimony, found that antiunion animus had not entered into the discharge and recommended dismissing the complaint. The Board made the opposite finding in a divided opinion, holding the discharge to be an unfair labor practice. The Second Circuit also divided, affirming per Judge Learned Hand but with express misgivings about the Board's assessment of the evidence. The Supreme Court granted certiorari.

UNIVERSAL CAMERA CORP. v. NATIONAL LABOR RELATIONS BOARD

Supreme Court of the United States, 1951.
340 U.S. 474.

MR. JUSTICE FRANKFURTER delivered the opinion of the Court.

The essential issue raised by this case and its companion, National Labor Relations Board v. Pittsburgh Steamship Co., 340 U.S. 498, infra, is the effect of the Administrative Procedure Act and the legislation colloquially known as the Taft-Hartley Act, 5 U.S.C. § 1001 et seq.; 29 U.S.C. § 141 et seq., on the duty of Courts of Appeals when called upon to review orders of the National Labor Relations Board.

The Court of Appeals for the Second Circuit . . . decreed full enforcement of the order. 2 Cir., 179 F.2d 749. Because the views of that court regarding the effect of the new legislation on the relation between the Board and the Courts of Appeals in the enforcement of the Board's orders conflicted with those of the Court of Appeals for the Sixth Circuit [1] we brought both cases here. . . . The clash of opinion obviously required settlement by this Court.

I

Want of certainty in judicial review of Labor Board decisions partly reflects the intractability of any formula to furnish definiteness of content for all the impalpable factors involved in judicial review. But in part doubts as to the nature of the reviewing power and uncertainties in its application derive from history, and to that extent an elucidation of this history may clear them away.

The Wagner Act provided: "The findings of the Board as to the facts, if supported by evidence, shall be conclusive." . . . . This Court read "evidence" to mean "substantial evidence," . . . and we said that "[s]ubstantial evidence is more than a mere scintilla. It means such relevant evidence as a reasonable mind might accept as adequate to support a conclusion." Consolidated Edison Co. v. National Labor

1. National Labor Relations Board v. Pittsburgh Steamship Co., 180 F.2d 731; Id., 340 U.S. 498. The Courts of Appeals of five circuits have agreed with the Court of Appeals for the Second Circuit that no material change was made in the reviewing power. . . .

Relations Board, 305 U.S. 197, 229. Accordingly, it "must do more than create a suspicion of the existence of the fact to be established. . . . it must be enough to justify, if the trial were to a jury, a refusal to direct a verdict when the conclusion sought to be drawn from it is one of fact for the jury." . . .

The very smoothness of the "substantial evidence" formula as the standard for reviewing the evidentiary validity of the Board's findings established its currency. But the inevitably variant applications of the standard to conflicting evidence soon brought contrariety of views and in due course bred criticism. Even though the whole record may have been canvassed in order to determine whether the evidentiary foundation of a determination by the Board was "substantial," the phrasing of this Court's process of review readily lent itself to the notion that it was enough that the evidence supporting the Board's result was "substantial" when considered by itself. It is fair to say that by imperceptible steps regard for the fact-finding function of the Board led to the assumption that the requirements of the Wagner Act were met when the reviewing court could find in the record evidence which, when viewed in isolation, substantiated the Board's findings. . . . This is not to say that every member of this Court was consciously guided by this view or that the Court ever explicitly avowed this practice as doctrine. What matters is that the belief justifiably arose that the Court had so construed the obligation to review.

Criticism of so contracted a reviewing power reinforced dissatisfaction felt in various quarters with the Board's administration of the Wagner Act in the years preceding the war. The scheme of the Act was attacked as an inherently unfair fusion of the functions of prosecutor and judge. Accusations of partisan bias were not wanting. The "irresponsible admission and weighing of hearsay, opinion, and emotional speculation in place of factual evidence" was said to be a "serious menace." No doubt some, perhaps even much of the criticism was baseless and some surely was reckless. What is here relevant, however is the climate of opinion thereby generated and its effect on Congress. Protests against "shocking injustices" and intimations of judicial "abdication"[2] with which some courts granted enforcement of the Board's orders stimulated pressures for legislative relief from alleged administrative excesses.

The strength of these pressures was reflected in the passage in 1940 of the Walter-Logan Bill. It was vetoed by President Roosevelt, partly because it imposed unduly rigid limitations on the administrative process, and partly because of the investigation into the actual operation of the administrative process then being conducted by an

---

2. In National Labor Relations Board v. Standard Oil Co., 2 Cir., 138 F.2d 885, 887, Judge Learned Hand said, "We understand the law to be that the decision of the Board upon that issue is for all practical purposes not open to us at all; certainly not after we have once decided that there was 'substan- tial' evidence that the 'disestablished' union was immediately preceded by a period during which there was a 'dominated' union. . . . [W]e recognize how momentous may be such an abdication of any power of review. . . ."

experienced committee appointed by the Attorney General, [chaired by Dean Acheson and directed by Walter Gellhorn]. It is worth noting that despite its aim to tighten control over administrative determinations of fact, the Walter-Logan Bill contented itself with the conventional formula that an agency's decision could be set aside if "the findings of fact are not supported by substantial evidence."

The final report of the Attorney General's Committee was submitted in January, 1941. The majority concluded that "[d]issatisfaction with the existing standards as to the scope of judicial review derives largely from dissatisfaction with the fact-finding procedures now employed by the administrative bodies." Departure from the "substantial evidence" test, it thought, would either create unnecessary uncertainty or transfer to courts the responsibility for ascertaining and assaying matters the significance of which lies outside judicial competence. Accordingly, it recommended against legislation embodying a general scheme of judicial review.

Three members of the Committee [dissented:] the "present system or lack of system of judicial review" led to inconsistency and uncertainty. They reported that under a "prevalent" interpretation of the "substantial evidence" rule "if what is called 'substantial evidence' is found anywhere in the record to support conclusions of fact, the courts are said to be obliged to sustain the decision without reference to how heavily the countervailing evidence may preponderate—unless indeed the stage of arbitrary decision is reached. Under this interpretation, the courts need to read only one side of the case and, if they find any evidence there, the administrative action is to be sustained and the record to the contrary is to be ignored." Their view led them to recommend that Congress enact principles of review applicable to all agencies not excepted by unique characteristics. One of these principles was expressed by the formula that judicial review could extend to "findings, inferences, or conclusions of fact unsupported, upon the whole record, by substantial evidence." So far as the history of this movement for enlarged review reveals, the phrase "upon the whole record" makes its first appearance in this recommendation of the minority of the Attorney General's Committee. This evidence of the close relationship between the phrase and the criticism out of which it arose is important, for the substance of this formula for judicial review found its way into the statute books when Congress with unquestioning—we might even say uncritical—unanimity enacted the Administrative Procedure Act.

One is tempted to say "uncritical" because the legislative history of that Act hardly speaks with that clarity of purpose which Congress supposedly furnishes courts in order to enable them to enforce its true will. On the one hand, the sponsors of the legislation indicated that they were reaffirming the prevailing "substantial evidence" test. But with equal clarity they expressed disapproval of the manner in which the courts were applying their own standard. The committee reports of both houses refer to the practice of agencies to rely upon "suspicion, surmise, implications, or plainly incredible evidence," and indicate that courts are to exact higher standards "in the exercise of their independent judgment" and on consideration of "the whole record."

Similar dissatisfaction with too restricted application of the "substantial evidence" test is reflected in the legislative history of the Taft-Hartley Act. The bill as reported to the House provided that the "findings of the Board as to the facts shall be conclusive unless it is made to appear to the satisfaction of the court either (1) that the findings of fact are against the manifest weight of the evidence, or (2) that the findings of fact are not supported by substantial evidence." The bill left the House with this provision. Early committee prints in the Senate provided for review by "weight of the evidence" or "clearly erroneous" standards. But, as the Senate Committee Report relates, "it was finally decided to conform the statute to the corresponding section of the Administrative Procedure Act where the substantial evidence test prevails. In order to clarify any ambiguity in that statute, however, the committee inserted the words 'questions of fact, if supported by substantial evidence *on the record considered as a whole.* . . .'"[3]

This phraseology was adopted by the Senate. The House conferees agreed. They reported to the House: "It is believed that the provisions of the conference agreement relating to the courts' reviewing power will be adequate to preclude such decisions as those in N.L.R.B. v. Nevada Consol. Copper Corp., 316 U.S. 105 and in the . . . Hearst, and Le Tourneau, etc. cases, . . . without unduly burdening the courts." The Senate version became the law.

It is fair to say that in all this Congress expressed a mood. And it expressed its mood not merely by oratory but by legislation. As legislation that mood must be respected, even though it can only serve as a standard for judgment and not as a body of rigid rules assuring sameness of application. Enforcement of such broad standards implies subtlety of mind and solidity of judgment. But it is not for us to question that Congress may assume such qualities in the federal judiciary.

From the legislative story we have summarized, two concrete conclusions do emerge. One is the identity of aim of the Administrative Procedure Act and the Taft-Hartley Act regarding the proof with which the Labor Board must support a decision. The other is that now Congress has left no room for doubt as to the kind of scrutiny which a court of appeals must give the record before the Board to satisfy itself that the Board's order rests on adequate proof.

It would be mischievous word-playing to find that the scope of review under the Taft-Hartley Act is any different from that under the Administrative Procedure Act. The Senate Committee which reported the review clause of the Taft-Hartley Act expressly indicated that the

3. . . . Senator Taft gave this explanation to the Senate of the meaning of the section: "In the first place, the evidence must be substantial; in the second place, it must still look substantial when viewed in the light of the entire record. That does not go so far as saying that a decision can be reversed on the weight of the evidence. It does not go quite so far as the power given to a circuit court of appeals to review a district-court decision, but it goes a great deal further than the present law, and gives the court greater opportunity to reverse an obviously unjust decision on the part of the National Labor Relations Board."

two standards were to conform in this regard, and the wording of the two Acts is for purposes of judicial administration identical. And so we hold that the standard of proof specifically required of the Labor Board by the Taft-Hartley Act is the same as that to be exacted by courts reviewing every administrative action subject to the Administrative Procedure Act.

Whether or not it was ever permissible for courts to determine the substantiality of evidence supporting a Labor Board decision merely on the basis of evidence which in and of itself justified it, without taking into account contradictory evidence or evidence from which conflicting inferences could be drawn, the new legislation definitively precludes such a theory of review and bars its practice.[4] The substantiality of evidence must take into account whatever in the record fairly detracts from its weight. This is clearly the significance of the requirement in both statutes that courts consider the whole record. . . .

To be sure, the requirement for canvassing "the whole record" in order to ascertain substantiality does not furnish a calculus of value by which a reviewing court can assess the evidence. Nor was it intended to negative the function of the Labor Board as one of those agencies presumably equipped or informed by experience to deal with a specialized field of knowledge, whose findings within that field carry the authority of an expertness which courts do not possess and therefore must respect. Nor does it mean that even as to matters not requiring expertise a court may displace the Board's choice between two fairly conflicting views, even though the court would justifiably have made a different choice had the matter been before it de novo. Congress has merely made it clear that a reviewing court is not barred from setting aside a Board decision when it cannot conscientiously find that the evidence supporting that decision is substantial when viewed in the light that the record in its entirety furnishes, including the body of evidence opposed to the Board's view.

There remains, then, the question whether enactment of these two statutes has altered the scope of review other than to require that substantiality be determined in the light of all that the record relevantly presents. A formula for judicial review of administrative action may afford grounds for certitude but cannot assure certainty of application. Some scope for judicial discretion in applying the formula can be avoided only by falsifying the actual process of judging or by using the formula as an instrument of futile casuistry. It cannot be too often repeated that judges are not automata. The ultimate reliance for the fair operation of any standard is a judiciary of high competence and

4. [Ed.] Judge Breyer gives this example: "[I]f I see water pouring down outside the window, I can reasonably infer that it is raining, although my inference in part depends upon the absence of evidence that there are small boys with a garden hose standing on the roof. Add to the record, however, the facts there are such small boys and the sun is shining, and my inference of rain becomes unreasonable. If I try to support it by pointing out an *absence* of evidence, in the record that the hose was turned on, I am still acting unreasonably. Because of the *facts* involved, a conclusion based in part upon the record's silence is reasonable in the first instance but not in the second. Most silences in an administrative record are of this factual sort. . . ." NLRB v. Transportation Mgt. Corp., 674 F.2d 130, 132 n. 1 (1st Cir. 1982) (concurring opinion), reversed 462 U.S. 393 (1983).

character and the constant play of an informed professional critique upon its work.

Since the precise way in which courts interfere with agency findings cannot be imprisoned within any form of words, new formulas attempting to rephrase the old are not likely to be more helpful than the old. There are no talismanic words that can avoid the process of judgment. The difficulty is that we cannot escape, in relation to this problem, the use of undefined defining terms.

Whatever changes were made by the Administrative Procedure and Taft-Hartley Acts are clearly within this area where precise definition is impossible. Retention of the familiar "substantial evidence" terminology indicates that no drastic reversal of attitude was intended.

But a standard leaving an unavoidable margin for individual judgment does not leave the judicial judgment at large even though the phrasing of the standard does not wholly fence it in. The legislative history of these Acts demonstrates a purpose to impose on courts a responsibility which has not always been recognized. Of course it is a statute and not a committee report which we are interpreting. But the fair interpretation of a statute is often "the art of proliferating a purpose", . . . revealed more by the demonstrable forces that produced it than by its precise phrasing. The adoption in these statutes of the judicially-constructed "substantial evidence" test was a response to pressures for stricter and more uniform practice, not a reflection of approval of all existing practices. To find the change so elusive that it cannot be precisely defined does not mean it may be ignored. We should fail in our duty to effectuate the will of Congress if we denied recognition to expressed Congressional disapproval of the finality accorded to Labor Board findings by some decisions of this and lower courts, or even of the atmosphere which may have favored those decisions.

We conclude, therefore, that the Administrative Procedure Act and the Taft-Hartley Act direct that courts must now assume more responsibility for the reasonableness and fairness of Labor Board decisions than some courts have shown in the past. Reviewing courts must be influenced by a feeling that they are not to abdicate the conventional judicial function. Congress has imposed on them responsibility for assuring that the Board keeps within reasonable grounds. That responsibility is not less real because it is limited to enforcing the requirement that evidence appear substantial when viewed, on the record as a whole, by courts invested with the authority and enjoying the prestige of the Courts of Appeals. The Board's findings are entitled to respect; but they must nonetheless be set aside when the record before a Court of Appeals clearly precludes the Board's decision from being justified by a fair estimate of the worth of the testimony of witnesses or its informed judgment on matters within its special competence or both.

From this it follows that enactment of these statutes does not require every Court of Appeals to alter its practice. Some—perhaps a majority—have always applied the attitude reflected in this legislation.

To explore whether a particular court should or should not alter its practice would only divert attention from the application of the standard now prescribed to a futile inquiry into the nature of the test formerly used by a particular court.

Our power to review the correctness of application of the present standard ought seldom to be called into action. Whether on the record as a whole there is substantial evidence to support agency findings is a question which Congress has placed in the keeping of the Courts of Appeals. This Court will intervene only in what ought to be the rare instance when the standard appears to have been misapprehended or grossly misapplied.

II

Our disagreement with the view of the court below that the scope of review of Labor Board decisions is unaltered by recent legislation does not of itself, as we have noted, require reversal of its decision. The court may have applied a standard of review which satisfies the present Congressional requirement.

The decision of the Court of Appeals is assailed on two grounds. It is said (1) that the court erred in holding that it was barred from taking into account the report of the examiner on questions of fact insofar as that report was rejected by the Board, and (2) that the Board's order was not supported by substantial evidence on the record considered as a whole, even apart from the validity of the court's refusal to consider the rejected portions of the examiner's report.

The latter contention is easily met. It is true that two of the earlier decisions of the court below were among those disapproved by Congress. But this disapproval, we have seen, may well have been caused by unintended intimations of judicial phrasing. And in any event, it is clear from the court's opinion in this case that it in fact did consider the "record as a whole," and did not deem itself merely the judicial echo of the Board's conclusion. The testimony of the company's witnesses was inconsistent, and there was clear evidence that the complaining employee had been discharged by an officer who was at one time influenced against him because of his appearance at the Board hearing. On such a record we could not say that it would be error to grant enforcement.

The first contention, however, raises serious questions to which we now turn.

III

The Court of Appeals deemed itself bound by the Board's rejection of the examiner's findings because the court considered these findings not "as unassailable as a master's." [5] They are not. Section 10(c) of the Labor Management Relations Act provides that "If upon the pre-

5. Rule 53(e)(2), Fed.Rules Civ.Proc., gives finality to the findings of a master unless they are clearly erroneous.

ponderance of the testimony taken the Board shall be of the opinion that any person named in the complaint has engaged in or is engaging in any such unfair labor practice, then the Board shall state its findings of fact . . . ” 61 Stat. 147, 29 U.S.C.A. § 160(c). The responsibility for decision thus placed on the Board is wholly inconsistent with the notion that it has power to reverse an examiner's findings only when they are "clearly erroneous." Such a limitation would make so drastic a departure from prior administrative practice that explicitness would be required.

The Court of Appeals concluded from this premise "that, although the Board would be wrong in totally disregarding his findings, it is practically impossible for a court, upon review of those findings which the Board itself substitutes, to consider the Board's reversal as a factor in the court's own decision. This we say, because we cannot find any middle ground between doing that and treating such a reversal as error, whenever it would be such, if done by a judge to a master in equity." 179 F.2d at 753. Much as we respect the logical acumen of the Chief Judge of the Court of Appeals, we do not find ourselves pinioned between the horns of his dilemma.

We are aware that to give the examiner's findings less finality than a master's and yet entitle them to consideration in striking the account, is to introduce another and an unruly factor into the judgmatical process of review. But we ought not to fashion an exclusionary rule merely to reduce the number of imponderables to be considered by reviewing courts.

The Taft-Hartley Act provides that "The findings of the Board with respect to questions of fact if supported by substantial evidence on the record considered as a whole shall be conclusive." § 160(e). Surely an examiner's report is as much a part of the record as the complaint or the testimony. According to the Administrative Procedure Act, "All decisions (including initial, recommended, or tentative decisions) shall become a part of the record . . . ” § 8(b). We found that this Act's provision for judicial review has the same meaning as that in the Taft-Hartley Act. The similarity of the two statutes in language and purpose also requires that the definition of "record" found in the Administrative Procedure Act be construed to be applicable as well to the term "record" as used in the Taft-Hartley Act.

It is therefore difficult to escape the conclusion that the plain language of the statute directs a reviewing court to determine the substantiality of evidence on the record including the examiner's report. The conclusion is confirmed by the indications in the legislative history that enhancement of the status and function of the trial examiner was one of the important purposes of the movement for administrative reform.

This aim was set forth by the Attorney General's Committee on Administrative Procedure: "In general, the relationship upon appeal between the hearing commissioner and the agency ought to a considerable extent to be that of trial court to appellate court. Conclusions, interpretations, law, and policy should, of course, be open to full review.

On the other hand, on matters which the hearing commissioner, having heard the evidence and seen the witnesses, is best qualified to decide, the agency should be reluctant to disturb his findings unless error is clearly shown."

Apparently it was the Committee's opinion that these recommendations should not be obligatory. For the bill which accompanied the Final Report required only that hearing officers make an initial decision which would become final in the absence of further agency action, and that agencies which differed on the facts from their examiners give reasons and record citations supporting their conclusion. This proposal was further moderated by the Administrative Procedure Act. It permits agencies to use examiners to record testimony but not to evaluate it, and contains the rather obscure provision that an agency which reviews an examiner's report has "all the powers which it would have in making the initial decision."

But this refusal to make mandatory the recommendations of the Attorney General's Committee should not be construed as a repudiation of them. Nothing in the statutes suggests that the Labor Board should not be influenced by the examiner's opportunity to observe the witnesses he hears and sees and the Board does not. Nothing suggests that reviewing courts should not give to the examiner's report such probative force as it intrinsically commands. To the contrary, § 11 of the Administrative Procedure Act contains detailed provisions designed to maintain high standards of independence and competence in examiners. Section 10(c) of the Labor Management Relations Act requires that examiners "shall issue . . . a proposed report, together with a recommended order". Both statutes thus evince a purpose to increase the importance of the role of examiners in the administrative process. High standards of public administration counsel that we attribute to the Labor Board's examiners both due regard for the responsibility which Congress imposes on them and the competence to discharge it.

The committee reports also make it clear that the sponsors of the legislation thought the statutes gave significance to the findings of examiners. . . .

We do not require that the examiner's findings be given more weight than in reason and in the light of judicial experience they deserve. The "substantial evidence" standard is not modified in any way when the Board and its examiner disagree. We intend only to recognize that evidence supporting a conclusion may be less substantial when an impartial, experienced examiner who has observed the witnesses and lived with the case has drawn conclusions different from the Board's than when he has reached the same conclusion. The findings of the examiner are to be considered along with the consistency and inherent probability of testimony. The significance of his report, of course, depends largely on the importance of credibility in the particular case. To give it this significance does not seem to us materially more difficult than to heed the other factors which in sum determine whether evidence is "substantial."

The direction in which the law moves is often a guide for decision of particular cases, and here it serves to confirm our conclusion.

However halting its progress, the trend in litigation is toward a rational inquiry into truth, in which the tribunal considers everything "logically probative of some matter requiring to be proved." Thayer, A Preliminary Treatise on Evidence, 530. . . . Machinery for discovery of evidence has been strengthened; the boundaries of judicial notice have been slowly but perceptibly enlarged. It would reverse this process for courts to deny examiners' findings the probative force they would have in the conduct of affairs outside a courtroom.

We therefore remand the cause to the Court of Appeals. On reconsideration of the record it should accord the findings of the trial examiner the relevance that they reasonably command in answering the comprehensive question whether the evidence supporting the Board's order is substantial. But the court need not limit its reexamination of the case to the effect of that report on its decision. We leave it free to grant or deny enforcement as it thinks the principles expressed in this opinion dictate.

Judgment vacated and cause remanded.

MR. JUSTICE BLACK and MR. JUSTICE DOUGLAS concur with parts I and II of this opinion but as to part III agree with the opinion of the court below.

NOTES

(1) For this and the following case, it may be useful to have some understanding of the NLRB and its processes. The excerpt from Cox, Bok and Gorman, p. 38 above, outlines the adjudication process and may profitably be reread at this point; the position of the administrative law judge is treated, generally, at p. 862 below.

Judge Richard Posner of the Seventh Circuit, calling for a different review process, gives this picture of the current one: "Decisions by administrative law judges are appealed to the Board, which invariably issues some type of opinion. But usually the opinion is a paragraph of boilerplate with at most a footnote making one or two minor modifications in the administrative law judge's decision. As a result of this perfunctory administrative review process, federal judicial review of Labor Board decisions means, in the vast majority of cases, federal judicial review of decisions of administrative law judges—to whose decisions the principles of administrative review require the courts of appeals to give as much and maybe more deference than to decisions of federal district judges.[1] I realize that the Board's members have a far heavier caseload than any federal appellate judges do, but it would be easier and cheaper for Congress to establish within the Board a tier of

1. [Ed.] NLRB cases alone are a major segment of all judicial review, since Board orders carry no sanctions and if efforts to secure voluntary compliance fail, the Board must seek enforcement in a court of appeals (or the respondent may seek review). Of all administrative appeals since 1970, in the average year 34% in the Courts of Appeals are from the NLRB. Annual Reports of the Director of the Administrative Office of the U.S. Courts. Of course these cases may present issues other than whether there was substantial evidence, but in some circuits judges "commonly complained that too many [NLRB] appeals involved merely factual issues." One judge of the 5th Circuit, asked what mandatory appeals he would like to be rid of, said "I'd pick the most important one of all—labor—the most colossal waste of

credible appellate judges who would write opinions in all but frivolous cases than to continue expanding the federal courts so that they can keep up with a rising workload of administrative-review cases." R. Posner, The Federal Courts, 161 (1985).[2]

(2) *The standard Congress chose:* "Congress was very deliberate in adopting [the substantial evidence] standard of review. It frees the reviewing courts of the time-consuming and difficult task of weighing the evidence, it gives proper respect to the expertise of the administrative tribunal and it helps promote the uniform application of the statute." Consolo v. FMC, 383 U.S. 607, 620 (1966).

So much is clear from the APA's legislative history rejecting more intense review under the "weight of evidence" standard. But reviewing courts would be even freer and uniformity even greater if judicial review of findings of fact were barred, or narrowed to some standard like "no basis in fact".[3] Judicial review of facts does not bring "cosmic truth," and review is not the only safeguard: Congress required the NLRB to conduct hearings on the record, providing some assurance not only that parties would be able to bring forward evidence and attack opposing evidence, but also that Board decisions would more likely be thorough and reasoned treatment of those records. Presumably Congress believed that safeguard not effective enough unless reinforced by judicial review sufficiently intense and sufficiently likely to be invoked to keep the Board thorough and reasoned.

The APA's "whole record" requirement resulted from congressional criticism of decisions like one Justice Frankfurter discussed in "[o]ne of the most amusing passages in the argument of [Universal Camera,

---

time. The aperture of review is so narrow. To call upon us to read thousands of pages is the most colossal waste of time I know. If Congress wants an independent review of facts, let it create one with powers of certified legal questions to us. I don't want to be a fact finder." J. Howard, Courts of Appeals in the Federal Judicial System, 46, 287 (1981).

The next largest agency source for the courts of appeals in recent years has been the Immigration and Naturalization Service, averaging 13% of all appeals. The largest category in the district courts involves Social Security.

2. Since "time is of the essence in implementing NLRB remedies," since expedition is a standard reason for establishing many agencies, and since in thinking about judicial review one must remember the delay it imposes, consider:

DELAY IN PROCESSING UNFAIR LABOR PRACTICE CHARGES,
1970–1980 (all times in days)

Year	Filing to Complaint	Complaint to Close of Hearing	Close of Hearing to ALJ Decision	ALJ to Board Decision	Filing to Board Decision	Bd. Decis. to C.A. Opinion
1970	57	58	84	124	348	—
1975	54	55	72	134	332	359
1980	46	155	158	133	484	485

P. Weiler, Promises to Keep: Securing Workers' Rights to Self-Organization under the NLRA, 96 Harv.L.Rev. 1769, 1795–6 (1983).

3. That was the scope of review of local draft board classification decisions under the Military Selective Service Act of 1967. That formulation derived from Estep v. United States, 327 U.S. 114 (1946), holding that the statutory provision making draft board decisions "final" meant "no basis in fact." The narrow scope has been acknowledged but some classifications still overturned because of inadequate explanation or procedural defects, e.g. Clay a.k.a. Ali v. United States, 403 U.S. 698 (1971).

after Government counsel tried] to convince the Court that it had always been doing its duty by 'the whole record.' Mr. Justice Frankfurter . . . answered: 'One of them, if I may intervene, is a decision of this Court in the Nevada Copper case, which was a per curiam decision . . . and in that case this Court said, "since upon an examination of the record we cannot say that the finding of fact of the Board is without support in the evidence"—that means if I find something in the evidence which supports it, my case is at an end. That is what I thought I had been doing.'

"Mr. Stern: 'I cannot contradict your Honor. The Court itself thus reveals that many of us were in error as to what we thought it had been doing.'" L. Jaffe, Judicial Review: "Substantial Evidence on the Whole Record," 64 Harv.L.Rev. 1223, 1235–36 (1951).

While the "whole record" requirement does not mean judges must read every page rather than merely the portions counsel cite, review of complex matters (particularly rule-making) often involves massive records presenting considerable problems when judges find it necessary to go beyond counsel's selections. See, e.g., p. 845 below.

(3) It is the lower courts that apply the substantial evidence standard, as Justice Frankfurter pointed out in Camera and emphasized the same day in a companion case (NLRB v. Pittsburgh S.S. Co., 340 U.S. 498, 502–3 (1951)). As you might imagine, the Supreme Court never reviews the substantial evidence test's applications, as such, although it may consider whether a court of appeals properly understood the test.[4]

On remand in Universal Camera, Judge Learned Hand of the Second Circuit concluded: "[U]pon a re-examination of the record as a whole, and upon giving weight to the examiner's findings—now in compliance with the Court's directions as we understand them—we think that our first disposition of the appeal was wrong, and we hold

---

4. An example is FCC v. Allentown Broadcasting Corp., 349 U.S. 358 (1955), reversing 222 F.2d 781 (D.C.Cir.1954). The FCC had reached a different judgment than its trial examiner, who had based her reasoning in part on her conclusions that one party's witnesses had been evasive, not candid. The court of appeals, vacating the FCC, opined that it would require "very substantial preponderance" to allow the Commission to overturn the examiner's findings on veracity.

The Supreme Court reversed the court of appeals, emphasizing that the question is *not* whether an agency has "erred" in "overruling" an examiner's findings but whether its *own* findings command substantial support on a record which includes the examiner's view. The Court said:

"The Court of Appeals' conclusion of error as to evasiveness relies largely on its understanding that the Examiner's findings based on demeanor of a witness are not to be overruled by a Board without a 'very substantial preponderance in the testimony as recorded'. . . . We think this attitude goes too far. It seems to adopt for examiners of administrative agencies the 'clearly erroneous' rule of the Fed.Rules Civ.Proc., 52(a), applicable to courts. In Universal Camera . . . we said, as to the Labor Management Relations Act hearings:

"'. . . The responsibility for decision . . . placed on the Board is wholly inconsistent with the notion that it has power to reverse an examiner's findings only when they are "clearly erroneous." Such a limitation would make so drastic a departure from prior administrative practice that explicitness would be required.'

"That comment is here applicable. See also [APA § 8]."

The Court then remanded so that the court of appeals, properly instructed, could make the substantial evidence determination.

that the Board should have dismissed the complaint." Judge Frank, concurring, included these thoughts:

"An examiner's finding binds the Board only to the extent that it is a 'testimonial inference,' or 'primary inference', i.e., an inference that a fact to which a witness orally testified is an actual fact because the witness so testified and because observation of the witness induces a belief in that testimony. The Board, however, is not bound by the examiner's 'secondary inferences,' or 'derivative inferences', i.e., facts to which no witness orally testified but which the examiner inferred from facts orally testified by witnesses whom the examiner believed. The Board may reach its own 'secondary inferences' and we must abide by them unless they are irrational; in that way, the Board differs from a trial judge (in a jury-less case) who hears and sees the witnesses, for although we are usually bound by his 'testimonial inferences' we need not accept his 'secondary inferences' even if rational, but where other rational 'secondary inferences' are possible, we may substitute our own." NLRB v. Universal Camera Corp., 190 F.2d 429 (2d Cir.1951).

(4) In considering the working of the "substantial evidence" test, does the relationship it supposes between trial and appellate tribunals give pause? The relationship between an agency and its administrative law judge is discussed further in Chapter 8, Section 2 below. Here, consider observations made by Judge John Gibbons of the Third Circuit about the proposition that courts of appeal should find facts de novo on appeal from non-jury findings by a district court when the state of the record permits (for example, because it is largely documentary): "The concurrence of several judges in a factual inference possibly increases the likelihood of achieving truth in the cosmic sense. . . . [But] the primary function of appellate courts is the correction of errors of law. The primary function of the trial court is to make a record and from it to determine the relevant facts.

" 'Even in instances where an appellate court is in as good a position to decide as the trial court, it should not disregard the trial court's finding, for to do so impairs confidence in the trial courts and multiplies appeals with attendant expense and delay.' In addition to encouraging the filing of appeals, the majority's rule has the disadvantage of increasing the already considerable burden on this court with respect to those that are filed. . . .

"The 'we are in as good a position as the trial court' rationale is, of course, a possible model for an appellate court system. But it is a model which imposes enormous costs without commensurate social benefits. The judicial process is at best a less than scientific method of determining the facts. The process is at its least scientific in determining such facts as subjective motivation. All that can be expected is the opportunity to present to a neutral factfinder the parties' respective versions, under rules designed to assure a measure of fairness, and to let that factfinder draw inferences. Since certainty is impossible no matter how often the process is repeated, society's interest emphasizes finality at that point. The clearly erroneous standard accepts the strong interest in finality, while the majority's 'we are in as good a position as the trial court' rule ignores it. The late Judge Charles E. Clark, who drafted Rule 52(a), recognized that society's interest in finality outweighed any competing interest in allowing even those philosopher kings with whom he sat on the Second Circuit to perform anew the task of drawing inferences." Davis v. United States Steel Supply, 32 Fed.Rules Serv.2d 727, 739–40 (3d Cir.1981) (Gibbons, J., dissenting), vacated, see 688 F.2d 166, 178 (3d Cir.1982).

As to application of the "clearly erroneous" standard, Judge Gibbons' view has substantially prevailed. See Anderson v. Bessemer City, 470 U.S. 564, ___ (1985).

PENASQUITOS VILLAGE, INC. v. NLRB
United States Court of Appeals, Ninth Circuit, 1977.
565 F.2d 1074.

Before DUNIWAY, CHOY and WALLACE, CIRCUIT JUDGES.

WALLACE, CIRCUIT JUDGE:

The National Labor Relations Board (the Board), reversing the decision of an administrative law judge, held that Penasquitos Village, Inc. and affiliated companies (Penasquitos) had engaged in coercive interrogation of employees in violation of section 8(a)(1) of the National Labor Relations Act (the Act), 29 U.S.C. § 158(a)(1), and had wrongfully discharged employees in violation of section 8(a)(3) of the Act.

[Two separate incidents were involved. In one, Zamora, a supervisory employee, was alleged to have threatened and coercively questioned three employees, including one Cuevas. Conflicting versions of the conversations on which the charge was based were testified to; the ALJ had believed Zamora's side of the story. He also believed Zamora's account of the events that led to the discharge of Rios and Martinez, two workers who had been involved in union organization efforts.]

I

. . . . The most difficult problem facing the reviewing court arises when, as in this case, the Board and the administrative law judge disagree on the facts. . . . [W]e have found no decision, nor has one been cited to us, sustaining a finding of fact by the Board which rests *solely* on testimonial evidence discredited either expressly or by clear implication by the administrative law judge. A typical case demonstrating the need for independent, credited evidence is Amco Electric v. NLRB, 358 F.2d 370 (9th Cir.1966). There the legality of a discharge turned on a narrow question of fact: Did the discharged employee use the company's car radio to give orders to another employee or merely to contact the union steward? The trial examiner (now referred to as an administrative law judge) discredited the testimony of both the discharged employee and the employee receiving the call. The Board, however, disagreed and accepted the discharged employee's version. In refusing to enforce the Board's order against the company, we stated: "Considering the record as a whole *the only evidence* which we believe supports the Board's findings is the [discredited] testimony of the [discharged employee]. While the Board is not bound by the credibility determinations of the trial examiner, nevertheless the probative weight which may be properly given to testimony is severely reduced when an impartial experienced examiner who has observed the witnesses and lived with the case has drawn different conclusions." (Emphasis added; footnote omitted). . . .

The cases also demonstrate that even when the record contains independent, credited evidence supportive of the Board's decision, a reviewing court will review more critically the Board's findings of fact if they are contrary to the administrative law judge's factual conclusions. . . . All aspects of the witness's demeanor—including the expression of his countenance, how he sits or stands, whether he is inordinately nervous, his coloration during critical examination, the modulation or pace of his speech and other non-verbal communication—may convince the observing trial judge that the witness is testifying truthfully or falsely. These same very important factors, however, are entirely unavailable to a reader of the transcript, such as the Board or the Court of Appeals. But it should be noted that the administrative law judge's opportunity to observe the witnesses' demeanor does not, by itself, require deference with regard to his or her derivative inferences. Observation of demeanor makes weighty only the observer's testimonial inferences.

Deference is accorded the Board's factual conclusions for a different reason—Board members are presumed to have broad experience and expertise in labor-management relations. . . . Further, it is the Board to which Congress has delegated administration of the Act. The Board, therefore, is viewed as particularly capable of drawing inferences from the facts of a labor dispute. Accordingly, it has been said that a Court of Appeals must abide by the Board's derivative inferences, if drawn from not discredited testimony, unless those inferences are "irrational" . . . .

. . .

[In part IIA of his opinion, Judge Wallace reviewed the Board's conclusions that Zamora had engaged in threats and coercive interrogations. Here, "clear-cut questions of credibility" governed; the ALJ had disbelieved witnesses who testified to coercive behavior and had believed Zamora, and Judge Wallace was unpersuaded by the Board's reasons for disagreeing. In part IIB of the opinion, he turned to the discharges of Rios and Martinez, found discriminatory by the Board but not by the ALJ.]

B

In this case, the administrative law judge and the Board disagreed on Penasquitos' motive. Whether, in light of this disagreement, the Board's conclusion is sustainable because it is based on substantial evidence is an extremely close question. We conclude, however, that the Board's finding of improper motive cannot be sustained, primarily because a significant number of the Board's derivative inferences were drawn from discredited testimony.

The keystone of the administrative law judge's finding of proper motive was his conviction that Zamora told the truth. Zamora testified that he observed Rios and Martinez working slowly and watching several women sunbathe in bikinis some distance from the employees' worksite. Upset with their performance, Zamora approached Rios and Martinez and stated that "if you want to see girls wearing bikinis there were some better ones at the beach." Zamora then left, verified with his superior that he had authority to fire, returned and discharged the two men. At the hearing before the administrative law judge, Martinez admitted that he was working at a slow pace on the day he was fired.

The administrative law judge relied on other evidence also. Several months prior to the discharge, Zamora and another supervisor watched for 5 or 10 minutes while Rios and two other employees stood under a tree, doing no work. When Zamora approached and demanded an explanation, the employees stated that they had no work to do and were waiting for quitting time. Zamora then suspended them—a fact initially denied by the mendacious Rios during cross-examination but later clearly established.

In reaching a contrary conclusion regarding Zamora's motive, the Board relied on a variety of inferences. First, the Board transferred to Zamora's action in discharging Rios and Martinez the anti-union animus it found in his alleged threats and unlawful interrogations. But, as we concluded in part IIA, supra, that finding of anti-union animus was not supported by substantial evidence. The Board also ascribed an improper motive to Zamora for the discharge because of . . . alleged statements[; but] the witnesses testifying about that incident were not credited by the administrative law judge, thus vitiating the inference the Board attempted to draw from it.

The Board also relied on the fact that Martinez and Rios had signed authorization cards for the union and that Cuevas had informed Zamora that those two, among others, were the leaders of the organizing effort. But against this must be placed the credited testimony of Zamora that he was unconcerned about who was doing the organizing because "I thought they were all in the Union . . . ."

The Board drew two inferences, however, from uncontroverted facts. First, the discharge was abrupt. Rios and Martinez received no warning prior to their discharge that a failure to speed up their work would result in termination. Second, the discharge came only two days after the Board's Regional Director issued a Decision and Direction of Election ordering an election among the Penasquitos employees under Zamora's supervision. These derivative inferences undoubtedly carry weight, which is not diminished by the fact that the administrative law judge drew a contrary inference from the timing of the discharge. As noted before, special deference is accorded the Board when, in the application of its expertise and experience, it derives such inferences from the facts of a labor dispute.

But in this case, credibility played a dominant role. The administrative law judge's testimonial inferences reduce significantly the substantiality of the Board's contrary derivative inferences. Particularly, removing the Board's finding of anti-union animus based upon alleged unlawful threats and interrogations, leaves poorly substantiated the Board's other conclusion that the discharges were improperly motivated. Considering the record as a whole, we conclude that the Board's conclusion that Penasquitos committed unlawful labor practices is not supported by substantial evidence and must, therefore, be set aside.

Enforcement Denied, Order Set Aside

DUNIWAY, CIRCUIT JUDGE (concurring in part and dissenting in part):

I concur in the result reached in part II A of Judge Wallace's opinion, but I have some reservations about the rationale by which that result is reached. I dissent from part II B of the opinion. . . .

I

My reservations relate to Judge Wallace's adoption of the dichotomy between "credibility determinations based on demeanor . . . *testimonial inferences*" and those based on "inferences drawn from the evidence itself—. . . *derivative inferences*. . . . " This distinction he finds in a concurring opinion of Judge Frank in NLRB v. Universal Camera Corp. Judge Wallace is careful to emphasize that the administrative law judge's determinations of credibility are not conclusive, but I am concerned lest the dichotomy that he adopts may result in future decisions that are merely mechanical applications of labels, which hinder rather than help the intelligent and principled application or growth of the law. . . .

The notion that special deference is owed to the determination of a trier of fact, . . . is deeply imbedded in the law. . . . As a generalization, it is unassailable.

In his opinion, Judge Wallace fleshes it out. . . . Here is where I begin to have difficulty. I venture to suggest that, as to every one of the factors that Judge Wallace lists, one trier of fact may take it to indicate that the witness is truthful and another may think that it shows that the witness is lying.

I am convinced, both from experience as a trial lawyer and from experience as an appellate judge, that much that is thought and said about the trier of fact as a lie detector is myth or folklore. Every trial lawyer knows, and most trial judges will admit, that it is not unusual for an accomplished liar to fool a jury (or, even, heaven forbid, a trial judge) into believing him because his demeanor is so convincing. The expression of his countenance may be open and frank; he may sit squarely in the chair, with no squirming; he may show no nervousness; his answers to questions may be clear, concise and audible, and given without hesitation; his coloration may be normal—neither pale nor flushed. In short, he may appear to be the trial lawyer's ideal witness. He may also be a consummate liar. In such a case, the fact finder may fit Iago's description of Othello:

The Moor is of a free and open nature,

That thinks men honest that but seem to be so;

And will as tenderly be led by the nose as asses are.

(Othello, Act 1, Sc. 3, l. 405–8)

On the other hand, another fact finder seeing and hearing the same witness may conclude that he is just too good a testifier, that he is an expert actor, and that he is also a liar.

Conversely, many trial lawyers, and some trial judges, will admit that the demeanor of a perfectly honest but unsophisticated or timid witness may be—or can be made by an astute cross-examiner to be—such that he will be thought by the jury or the judge to be a liar. He may be unable to face the cross-examiner, the jury, or the judge; he may slouch and squirm in the chair; he may be obviously tense and nervous; his answers to questions may be indirect, rambling, and inaudible; he may hesitate before answering; he may alternately turn pale and blush. In short, he may, to the trier of fact, be a liar, but in fact be entirely truthful. Again, however, another fact finder, seeing and hearing the same witness, may attribute his demeanor to the natural timidity of the average not very well educated and non-public sort of person when dragged to court against his will and forced to testify and face a hostile cross-examiner, and conclude that the witness is telling the truth.

.   .   .

I write to suggest that Judge Wallace's dichotomy should not be taken to protect the myth and folklore behind an almost impenetrable wall. I do not want fact finders to believe that to make their findings almost totally unassailable they need only use the right incantation: "I don't (or I do) believe him because of his demeanor," or "on the basis of testimonial inferences."

I doubt if there are many cases in which the fact finder relies on demeanor alone. There may not be any; I hope that there are none. I think that in every case in which he thinks about what he is doing, the fact finder should and does consider both the demeanor of the witness and what he says—the content of his testimony—and weighs those factors in relation to the fact finder's knowledge of life's realities, the internal consistency of what the witness is saying, and its consistency, or lack of it, with the other evidence in the case, testimonial, documentary, and physical. The fact finding as to credibility of the witness should be, and is, based on all of these things.   .   .   .

II

Having stated my doubts about Judge Wallace's dichotomy, I nevertheless agree with the result that he reaches in part II A of his opinion. The evidence as a whole, including the credibility rulings of the administrative law judge, seems to me too thin to be called substantial support for the Board's findings. I therefore concur in the result stated in part II A.

III

I do not concur in part II B. As Judge Wallace observes, the question is "extremely close." In such a case, I give more weight to the experience and expertise of the Board than he does. I refer particularly to the two uncontradicted facts, the abruptness and the timing of the discharges. I cannot say that the inferences that the Board drew from these facts are "irrational" or "tenuous" or "unwarranted" or "arbitrary."

I would enforce that part of the Board's order that deals with the discharges of Rios and Martinez.

CHOY, CIRCUIT JUDGE (concurring):

I concur in the results reached by Judge Wallace in both parts II A and II B.

However, I share the concern that Judge Duniway feels about Judge Wallace's treatment of demeanor evidence and testimonial inferences. I, therefore, concur in Judge Duniway's eloquent exposition of his reservations contained in part I of his concurring and dissenting opinion.

NOTES

(1) Compare UNITED STATES EX REL. EXARCHOU v. MURFF, 265 F.2d 504 (2d Cir.1959). Exarchou, who conceded that he was a deportable alien, sought discretionary relief from the Immigration and Naturalization Service. In order to be eligible for relief, Exarchou had to prove that he was of good moral character. The Special Inquiry Officer who heard the case found that Exarchou had not sustained this burden. The facts were that Exarchou had become estranged from his wife in 1954, and she obtained a divorce on the grounds of desertion in the fall of 1956. Shortly after he and his wife separated, Exarchou resided for a time at the home of a divorcee who lived with her two sons and her mother. Exarchou testified that, although he occasionally took this woman dancing in the evening and contributed money toward the rent of her home, their relationship was merely one of friendship and was not adulterous. She refused to answer questions at the hearing upon Fifth Amendment grounds. There was no testimony contradicting his claim, although in a letter written by his first wife when, in the words of the court, "domestic ties between them were strained," there were some rambling accusations. The Special Inquiry Officer's report stated in part:

"I think I can best sum up my impressions of the respondent by saying that he tells an interesting, almost fantastic, story. Certainly not one that I consider credible. In fact, I do not believe it. The respondent would have me believe that he continued this so-called platonic relationship with this woman out of the goodness of his heart and out of his sympathy for her at a time when he was admittedly separated from his own wife. . . . Even were it the truth, and as I say I do not believe it, it seems to me that a married man is not free to carry on such a relationship and still be considered one of good character. The mores of our times may well be most liberal but I do not think they have reached that degree of liberality as yet."

Exarchou's petition for a writ of habeas corpus was dismissed by the district court. The court of appeals reversed in an unanimous opinion written by Chief Judge Clark. The court first noted that, as the Immigration Service conceded, no inference could legally be drawn from the refusal of the divorcee to testify at the hearing.[1] Second, "We do not believe weight should attach" to the wife's accusatory letter, because of the circumstances under which it was written. Therefore, "the Service was thrown back completely on Exarchou's own testimony as to his conduct during the period in question. Perhaps the most doubtful fact here was the amount of money he admitted to having paid the woman, more than would be a reasonable rent under the circumstances. But he seems generally to have been free with his money. Beyond this his denials of adulterous conduct were steady, persistent, and unshaken. They would appear consistent with the surrounding facts and circumstances he disclosed. When he stayed with her he slept on a sofa in the living room. She slept in her bedroom on the second floor with a small son aged seven at the time of the hearing, and the other two bedrooms were occupied one by her mother and the other by her elder son of college age. Thus opportunity would seem not wholly propitious. . . . [We cannot go] so far as to hold that any stay under the roof of a married lady inevitably signifies adultery."

The Service in this case has "convicted relator necessarily wholly on his statement and through application of a rigid rule of presumption. But presumptions as to facts should be only a reasonable substitute for definite proof. In other words, they should point to probabilities. Here we think the result departs from that standard."

"It is of course true that questions of a witness' credibility must be left to the administrative fact finder. Ng Fung Ho v. White, 259 U.S. 276. Here, however, the Special Inquiry Officer's report demonstrates an incredulity not of the witness, but of the story itself. The Officer simply did not believe it possible that a man who behaved like relator could not have been committing adultery. We do not think this finding of impossibility accords with the facts of human life. Moreover, we are disturbed by the insistence in the decision upon the *appearance* of good moral character. The statute makes good character itself, not a reputation for it, the finding necessary to the Service's decision. . . . Thus we cannot accept the Service's alternative conclusion that, even if Exarchou truthfully described his conduct, 'a married man is not free to carry on such a relationship and still be considered one of good character.'

1. [Ed.] "Actually," said Judge Clark "the record indicates that avoidance of embarrassment was probably a stronger factor in her refusal than fear of self-incrimination. She had remarried by the time of the hearing and stated frankly that she was annoyed at being drawn into the proceedings and had sought and obtained advice as to means—which she took—to eliminate herself from a dispute in which she had no concern or interest."

"We conclude only that Exarchou has sustained his burden of establishing good moral character under § 19(c) of the Immigration Act of 1917, former 8 U.S.C. § 155(c), and is entitled to further consideration of his application. . . . " Has the court here permitted its administration of the scope of review to be influenced by the importance of the personal interests involved? Would that be appropriate? Compare NLRB v. Walton Mfg. Co., 369 U.S. 404 (1962): "There is no place in the statutory scheme for one test of the evidence in reinstatement cases and another test in other cases."

(2) Industrial Union Department, AFL–CIO v. Hodgson, p. 481 below.

(3) Related to scope but distinct from it is the *standard of proof* by which the agency is to find facts initially. "The difference is most graphically illustrated in a criminal case [where the offense must be proved] beyond a reasonable doubt. [If the correct standard] was imposed at trial, judicial review is generally limited to ascertaining whether the evidence relied upon by the trier of fact was of sufficient quality and substantiality to support the rationality of the judgment. In other words, an appellate court in a criminal case ordinarily does not ask itself whether it believes that the evidence at the trial established guilt beyond a reasonable doubt, but whether the judgment is supported by substantial evidence." WOODBY v. INS, 385 U.S. 276, 282 (1966). Woodby, one of two leading cases on standard of proof, involved deportation proceedings against a resident alien wife of an American soldier who, after she was deserted, engaged briefly in prostitution and claimed a defense of duress; the Government contended that the prostitution, deportable conduct, continued after any duress. No statute defined the applicable burden of proof. A divided Supreme Court required "clear, unequivocal and convincing evidence;" the dissenters would have required only "reasonable, substantial and probative evidence."[2]

What standard of proof is called for in formal proceedings by APA § 556(d)? "Except as otherwise provided by statute, the proponent of a rule or order has the burden of proof. . . . A sanction may not be imposed or rule or order issued except on consideration of the whole record or those parts thereof cited by a party *and supported and in accordance with the reliable, probative, and substantial evidence.*" In STEADMAN v. SEC, 450 U.S. 91 (1981), the SEC had held (as it had since at least 1938) that the preponderance-of-the-evidence standard of proof sufficed to establish violations of the antifraud and related securities law provisions, and so to support an order permanently barring the long-time head of several investment companies from any association with any such companies. Respondent argued that such severe sanctions required a clear-and-convincing standard. The courts of appeals had been divided. Seven Justices held that the "somewhat opaque" language of § 556(c), in light of legislative history, adopted the tradi-

---

2. Subsequently, it has become clear that the Woodby standard rested on only administrative common law: Congress' 1961 lowering of the standard in denaturalization cases to a mere preponderance of evidence was upheld, with four dissents that it was unconstitutional. Vance v. Terrazas, 444 U.S. 252 (1980). The majority expressly noted Woodby and said that deportation was *a fortiori* within congressional power to set the proof standard. Among the dissenters was Woodby's author, Justice Stewart.

tional standard the SEC used. Two dissenters argued that at common law, fraud had to be proved by clear and convincing evidence and there was no indication that Congress intended to change the standard of proof. How would you vote; and would your vote be affected by the fact that since 1943, courts have held that fraud under the securities statutes covers more conduct than common law fraud covered?

(4) A second issue distinct from but often discussed, as here, in conjunction with scope of review of factual determinations, is who bears the *burden* of meeting the standard of proof when the agency is finding facts and drawing conclusions, for example, in a "dual motivation" discharge case at the NLRB? Although § 556(d)'s first sentence, just quoted, seems clear, the Supreme Court recently relied on strong legislative history and an earlier court of appeals decision to reach the conclusion that "the term 'burden of proof' was not employed in any strict sense, but rather as synonymous with the 'burden of going forward'." [3]

NLRB v. TRANSPORTATION MGT. CORP., 462 U.S. 393, 404 (1983), concerned the NLRB's treatment of "dual motivation" discharges. In 1980, the NLRB adopted this allocation of burden of proof: the General Counsel carried the burden of persuasion that antiunion animus motivated or substantially contributed to an employer's decision to discharge an employee; but even if some such motivation was proved, an employer could escape an unfair labor practice finding if it persuaded the Board that the employee would have been fired anyway—that is, the employer carried the burden of proving an affirmative defense. The courts of appeals divided on the Board's authority to do that: some said the Board could not impose on a company the burden of proving itself 'innocent' of a violation, but only a burden of coming forward with enough evidence to undercut the General Counsel's position. Thus, said those courts of appeals, if the evidence was in equipoise, the employer would win. The Supreme Court upheld the Board.

Underlying the dispute was an issue that will deeply concern us in the next segment of this casebook: how much respect was due the NLRB's *legal* judgment. Judge Stephen Breyer of the First Circuit, concurring below, had written that the allocation of burden of proof was not a question on which a court should defer to agency views. "Whether the Board can impose such an overall burden on the employer is a pure question of law. . . . The fact that the agency might find such burden shifting administratively useful would be significant had Congress intended to delegate such authority to the agency, but that is not the case here.

"[I]t is worth recalling that one major purpose underlying court review of administrative agency decisions is that of keeping agency action within statutory bounds laid down by Congress—including those statutory qualifications that limit the agency's more important basic mission. To do so, Congress has entrusted courts with primary respon-

---

3. Environmental Defense Fund v. EPA, 548 F.2d 998, 1015 (D.C.Cir.1976, supplemental opinion 1977), cert. denied sub nom. Velsicol Chemical Corp. v. EPA, 431 U.S. 925 (1977), holding that in a proceeding concerning the EPA's refusal to register an insecticide, fungicide or rodenticide, EPA staff bore the burden of producing evidence of unsafety, but the manufacturer bore the ultimate burden of proving safety.

sibility for determining questions of law related to the agency's mission. And, to prevent the agencies from extending that mission or escaping statutory limitations through one-sided fact-finding, Congress has required the courts to make certain that factual findings are supported by 'substantial evidence' on the basis of the 'whole record'. This historic division of tasks between court and agency, and the major purpose underlying it, suggests why it is desirable to require the Board to certify that, after hearing both sides, it still believes the evidence in the record by a preponderance shows a violation of the statute: Doing so forces the agency to focus directly on what Congress told it to do; it prevents the agency from retreating behind the opaque language of 'burden of proof;' and it simplifies the work of a reviewing court, which could otherwise be uncertain as to when it could, and when it could not, properly overturn an agency decision. (Compare the difficulty of deciding whether there is substantial evidence on the record as a whole that the employer has not *proved* that the bad motive did *not* move him.)" 674 F.2d at 133, 134.

Unanimously reversing, the Supreme Court said that the Board's was at least a permissible construction of the Act and fair as well, considering that in such cases the General Counsel had proved the employer a wrongdoer. The Court said the Board could have adhered to (a) its early position that dual motivation was a flat violation; or (b) its position in the 1940's that sometimes it might not be; or (c) the position of some courts that antiunion animus is a "but for" cause; or (d) the position that there was a violation if antiunion animus was involved at all, but the employer could affect the remedy by proving dual motivation; or last, (e) the position upheld here, that there was no violation if the employer could prove the affirmative defense. In short, the statute gave the Board enough leeway on declaring the law on dual motivation cases, for it to allocate the burden of proof as it deemed appropriate.

(5) The materials to this point have all dealt with review of factual determinations made in on-the-record proceedings and subject to the substantial evidence test. The important questions of reviewing factual determinations made in conjunction with informal adjudications and rulemakings, and the special problem of "constitutional" or "jurisdictional" facts, are taken up at later stages.

c.　Review of "Mixed Questions" and "Questions of Law"

Whatever the problems of reviewing findings of fact, scope is more controverted by far when other kinds of "questions" are under review. What is—or should be—the scope of review of an agency's (a) application of a statutory term to undisputed facts (or to facts supported by substantial evidence in the whole record), or (b) interpretation of a statutory term, or (c) exercise of judgment or discretion?

The traditional method has been first to state that questions of "law" are subject to full or independent judicial review and that questions of "fact" are subject to limited judicial review; second, to classify the question at issue as "fact" or "law," depending on whether the scope of review should be independent or limited; and third, to downplay or ignore on *what* that last, key choice depends.

Yet, as one of your editors once remarked to the judges most concerned with these issues, "the phrases 'questions of fact' and 'questions of law' are not only misleading, but also tend to invite focus on the wrong factors. The inquiry, when deciding what is the appropriate scope of review, of course should be not into the nature of the issue to be decided, e.g., fact or law, but rather should focus upon how much of the resolution of the issue is to be by the judge, how much by the agency. Thus, we should speak of fact-finding, which obviously is mainly for the administrator; law-declaring, which has to do with general construction of a statute wholly independently of the particular controversy at bar, which will be mainly, and very often entirely, for our best experts at such matters as statutory construction, you judges; and the last function, spoken of in the familiar but muddling way as 'mixed question,' is what I call law-applying, or applying a statute or other item of law to the particular facts at bar, a function which in the normal course is mainly for the agency because in the normal course, the decisions will have little bearing on any other decision. That is, it's part of the normal particularized administration of the statute and its resolution belongs mainly to the body with the first-line responsibility for that administration." [1]

(i) Some Historical Building Blocks

On the same day as it decided Universal Camera, the Supreme Court announced the following opinion:

O'LEARY v. BROWN–PACIFIC–MAXON, INC.
Supreme Court of the United States, 1951.
340 U.S. 504.

MR. JUSTICE FRANKFURTER delivered the opinion of the Court.

In this case we are called upon to review an award of compensation under the Longshoremen's and Harbor Workers' Compensation Act of March 4, 1927 as amended. The award was made on a claim arising from the accidental death of an employee of Brown-Pacific-Maxon, Inc., a government contractor operating on the island of Guam. Brown-Pacific maintained for its employees a recreation center near the shoreline, along which ran a channel so dangerous for swimmers that its use was forbidden and signs to that effect erected. John Valak, the employee, spent the afternoon at the center, and was waiting for his employer's bus to take him from the area when he saw or heard two men, standing on the reefs beyond the channel, signaling for help. Followed by nearly twenty others, he plunged in to effect a rescue. In attempting to swim the channel to reach the two men he was drowned.

A claim was filed by his dependent mother, based on the Longshoremen's Act and on an Act of August 16, 1941, extending the

---

1. R. Schotland, Scope of Review of Administrative Action—Remarks Before the   D.C. Circuit Judicial Conference, 34 Fed. B.J. 54, 58 (1975).

compensation provisions to certain employment in overseas possessions. In due course of the statutory procedure, the Deputy Commissioner found as a "fact" that "at the time of his drowning and death the deceased was using the recreational facilities sponsored and made available by the employer for the use of its employees and such participation by the deceased was an incident of his employment, and that his drowning and death arose out of and in the course of said employment . . . ." Accordingly, he awarded a death benefit of $9.38 per week. Brown-Pacific and its insurance carrier thereupon petitioned the District Court under § 21 of the Act to set aside the award. That court denied the petition on the ground that "there is substantial evidence . . . to sustain the compensation order." On appeal, the Court of Appeals for the Ninth Circuit reversed. It concluded that "The lethal currents were not a part of the recreational facilities supplied by the employer and the swimming in them for the rescue of the unknown man was not recreation. It was an act entirely disconnected from any use for which the recreational camp was provided and not in the course of Valak's employment." 182 F.2d 772, 773. We granted certiorari, 340 U.S. 849, because the case brought into question judicial review of awards under the Longshoremen's Act in light of the Administrative Procedure Act.

The Longshoremen's and Harbor Workers' Act authorizes payment of compensation for "accidental injury or death arising out of and in the course of employment". As we read its opinion the Court of Appeals entertained the view that this standard precluded an award for injuries incurred in an attempt to rescue persons not known to be in the employer's service, undertaken in forbidden waters outside the employer's premises. We think this is too restricted an interpretation of the Act. Workmen's compensation is not confined by common-law conceptions of scope of employment. The test of recovery is not a causal relation between the nature of employment of the injured person and the accident. Nor is it necessary that the employee be engaged at the time of the injury in activity of benefit to his employer. All that is required is that the "obligations or conditions" of employment create the "zone of special danger" out of which the injury arose. A reasonable rescue attempt, like pursuit in aid of an officer making an arrest, may be "one of the risks of the employment, an incident of the service, foreseeable, if not foreseen, and so covered by the statute." Matter of Babington v. Yellow Taxi Corp., 250 N.Y. 14, 17, 164 N.E. 726, 727. This is not to say that there are not cases "where an employee even with the laudable purpose of helping another, might go so far from his employment and become so thoroughly disconnected from the service of his employer that it would be entirely unreasonable to say that injuries suffered by him arose out of and in the course of his employment." Matter of Waters v. William J. Taylor Co., 218 N.Y. at page 252, 112 N.E. at page 728. We hold only that rescue attempts such as that before us are not necessarily excluded from the coverage of the Act as the kind of conduct that employees engage in as frolics of their own.

The Deputy Commissioner treated the question whether the particular rescue attempt described by the evidence was one of the class covered by the Act as a question of "fact." Doing so only serves to illustrate once more the variety of ascertainments covered by the blanket term "fact." Here of course it does not connote a simple, external, physical event as to which there is conflicting testimony. The conclusion concerns a combination of happenings and the inferences drawn from them. In part at least, the inferences presuppose applicable standards for assessing the simple, external facts. Yet the standards are not so severable from the experience of industry nor of such a nature as to be peculiarly appropriate for independent judicial ascertainment as "questions of law."

Both sides conceded that the scope of judicial review of such findings of fact is governed by the Administrative Procedure Act. The standard, therefore, is that discussed in Universal Camera. It is sufficiently described by saying that the findings are to be accepted unless they are unsupported by substantial evidence on the record considered as a whole. The District Court recognized this standard.

When this Court determines that a Court of Appeals has applied an incorrect principle of law, wise judicial administration normally counsels remand of the cause to the Court of Appeals with instructions to reconsider the record. Compare Universal Camera. In this instance, however, we have a slim record and the relevant standard is not difficult to apply; and we think the litigation had better terminate now. Accordingly we have ourselves examined the record to assess the sufficiency of the evidence.

We are satisfied that the record supports the Deputy Commissioner's finding. The pertinent evidence was presented by the written statements of four persons and the testimony of one witness. It is, on the whole, consistent and credible. From it the Deputy Commissioner could rationally infer that Valak acted reasonably in attempting the rescue, and that his death may fairly be attributable to the risks of the employment. We do not mean that the evidence compelled this inference; we do not suggest that had the Deputy Commissioner decided against the claimant, a court would have been justified in disturbing his conclusion. We hold only that on this record the decision of the District Court that the award should not be set aside should be sustained.

Reversed.

MR. JUSTICE MINTON, with whom MR. JUSTICE JACKSON and MR. JUSTICE BURTON join, dissenting.

Liability accrues in the instant case only if the death arose out of and in the course of the employment. This is a statutory provision common to all Workmen's Compensation Acts. There must be more than death and the relationship of employee and employer. There must be some connection between the death and the employment. Not in any common-law sense of causal connection but in the common-sense, everyday, realistic view. The Deputy Commissioner knew that, so he found as a *fact* that "at the time of his drowning and death the deceased was using the recreational facilities sponsored and made available by the employer for the use of its employees and such participation by the deceased was an incident of his employment. . . . " This finding is false and has no scintilla of evidence or inference to support it.

I am unable to understand how this Court can say this is a fact based upon evidence. It is undisputed upon this record that the deceased, at the time he met his death, was outside the recreational area in the performance of a voluntary act of attempted rescue of someone unknown to the record. There can be no inference of liability here unless liability follows from the mere relationship of employer and employee. The attempt to rescue was an isolated, voluntary act of bravery of the deceased in no manner arising out of or in the course of his employment. The only relation his employment had with the attempted rescue and the following death was that his employment put him on the Island of Guam.

I suppose the way to avoid what we said today in Universal Camera is to find facts where there are no facts, on the whole record or any piece of it. It sounds a bit hollow to me for the Court, as it does, to quote from the New York case of Matter of Waters "where an employee, even with the laudable purpose of helping another, might go so far from his employment and become so thoroughly disconnected from the service of his employer that it would be entirely unreasonable to say that injuries suffered by him arose out of and in the course of his employment." This would seem to indicate that we are leaving some place for voluntary acts of the employees outside the course of their employment from which the employer may not be liable. There surely are such areas, but this case does not recognize them. The employer is liable in this case because he is an employer.

I would affirm the judgment of the Court of Appeals.

NATIONAL LABOR RELATIONS BOARD v. HEARST PUBLICATIONS, INC.

Supreme Court of the United States, 1944.
322 U.S. 111.

MR. JUSTICE RUTLEDGE delivered the opinion of the Court.[1]

These cases arise from the refusal of respondents, publishers of four Los Angeles daily newspapers, to bargain collectively with a union representing newsboys who distribute their papers on the streets of that city. Respondents' contention that they were not required to bargain because the newsboys are not their "employees" within the meaning of that term in the National Labor Relations Act, 29 U.S.C. section 152,[2] presents the important question which we granted certio-

1. As noted in Universal Camera, when the APA was passed in 1946, the House conferees said its provisions on review would "preclude" various decisions, specifically including Hearst. Certainly if this case had come up after 1946, some of its phrasing would have differed. Would any-thing else differ? As we will shortly see, the Supreme Court has treated Hearst as unimpaired by passage of the APA.

2. Section 2(3) of the Act provides that "The term 'employee' shall include any employee, and shall not be limited to the

rari to resolve . . . [T]he Board made findings of fact and concluded that the regular full-time newsboys selling each paper were employees within the Act and that questions affecting commerce concerning the representation of employees had arisen. It designated appropriate units and ordered elections. 28 N.L.R.B. 1006. At these the union was selected as their representative by majorities of the eligible newsboys.

After the union was appropriately certified, 33 N.L.R.B. 941, 36 N.L.R.B. 285, the respondents refused to bargain with it. Thereupon proceedings under Section 10, 49 Stat. 453–455, 29 U.S.C. § 160, were instituted, a hearing was held and respondents were found to have violated Section 8(1) and (5) of the Act, 49 Stat. 452, 453, 29 U.S.C. § 158(1), (5). They were ordered to cease and desist from such violations and to bargain collectively with the union upon request. 39 N.L. R.B. 1245, 1256.

Upon respondents' petitions for review and the Board's petitions for enforcement, the Circuit Court of Appeals, one judge dissenting, set aside the Board's orders. Rejecting the Board's analysis, the court independently examined the question whether the newsboys are employees within the Act, decided that the statute imports common-law standards to determine that question, and held the newsboys are not employees. 136 F.2d 608. . . .

The papers are distributed to the ultimate consumer through a variety of channels, including . . . newsboys who sell on the streets of the city and its suburbs. . . .

The newsboys work under varying terms and conditions. They may be "bootjackers," selling to the general public at places other than established corners, or they may sell at fixed "spots." They may sell only casually or part-time, or full-time; and they may be employed regularly and continuously or only temporarily. The units which the Board determined to be appropriate are composed of those who sell full-time at established spots. Those vendors, misnamed boys, are generally mature men, dependent upon the proceeds of their sales for their sustenance, and frequently supporters of families. Working thus as news vendors on a regular basis, often for a number of years, they form a stable group with relatively little turnover, in contrast to schoolboys and others who sell as bootjackers, temporary and casual distributors.

[The Court then set forth several paragraphs of detail about the newsboys' supervision, compensation and conditions of work.]

In this pattern of employment the Board found that the newsboys are an integral part of the publishers' distribution system and circulation organization. And the record discloses that the newsboys and checkmen feel they are employees of the papers and respondents' supervisory employees, if not respondents themselves, regard them as such.

In addition to questioning the sufficiency of the evidence to sustain these findings, respondents point to a number of other attributes

employees of a particular employer, unless the Act explicitly states otherwise. . . . ."

characterizing their relationship with the newsboys and urge that on the entire record the latter cannot be considered their employees. They base this conclusion on the argument that by common-law standards the extent of their control and direction of the newsboys' working activities creates no more than an "independent contractor" relationship and that common-law standards determine the "employee" relationship under the Act. . . .

I

The principal question is whether the newsboys are "employees." Because Congress did not explicitly define the term, respondents say its meaning must be determined by reference to common-law standards. In their view "common-law standards" are those the courts have applied in distinguishing between "employees" and "independent contractors" when working out various problems unrelated to the Wagner Act's purposes and provisions.

The argument assumes that there is some simple, uniform and easily applicable test which the courts have used, in dealing with such problems, to determine whether persons doing work for others fall in one class or the other. Unfortunately this is not true. Only by a long and tortuous history was the simple formulation worked out which has been stated most frequently as "the test" for deciding whether one who hires another is responsible in tort for his wrongdoing. But this formula has been by no means exclusively controlling in the solution of other problems. And its simplicity has been illusory because it is more largely simplicity of formulation than of application. Few problems in the law have given greater variety of application and conflict in results than the cases arising in the borderland between what is clearly an employer-employee relationship and what is clearly one of independent entrepreneurial dealing. This is true within the limited field of determining vicarious liability in tort. It becomes more so when the field is expanded to include all of the possible applications of the distinction.

It is hardly necessary to stress particular instances of these variations or to emphasize that they have arisen principally, first, in the struggle of the courts to work out common-law liabilities where the legislature has given no guides for judgment, more recently also under statutes which have posed the same problem for solution in the light of the enactment's particular terms and purposes. It is enough to point out that, with reference to an identical problem, results may be contrary over a very considerable region of doubt in applying the distinction, depending upon the state or jurisdiction where the determination is made; and that within a single jurisdiction a person who, for instance, is held to be an "independent contractor" for the purpose of imposing vicarious liability in tort may be an "employee" for the purposes of particular legislation, such as unemployment compensation. . . .

Mere reference to these possible variations as characterizing the application of the Wagner Act in the treatment of persons identically situated in the facts surrounding their employment and in the influences tending to disrupt it, would be enough to require pause before accepting a thesis which would introduce them into its administration. This would be true, even if the statute itself had indicated less clearly than it does the intent they should not apply.

Two possible consequences could follow. One would be to refer the decision of who are employees to local state law. The alternative would be to make it turn on a sort of pervading general essence distilled from state law. Congress obviously did not intend the former result. It would introduce variations into the statute's operation as wide as the differences the forty-eight states and other local jurisdictions make in applying the distinction for wholly different purposes. Persons who might be "employees" in one state would be "independent contractors" in another. . . . Persons working across state lines might fall in one class or the other, possibly both, depending on whether the Board and the courts would be required to give effect to the law of one state or of the adjoining one, or to that of each in relation to the portion of the work done within its borders.

Both the terms and the purposes of the statute, as well as the legislative history, show that Congress had in mind no such patchwork plan for securing freedom of employees' organization and of collective bargaining. The Wagner Act is federal legislation, administered by a national agency, intended to solve a national problem on a national scale. . . .

II

Whether, given the intended national uniformity, the term "employee" includes such workers as these newsboys must be answered primarily from the history, terms and purposes of the legislation. The word "is not treated by Congress as a word of art having a definite meaning . . . ." Rather "it . . . must be read in the light of the mischief to be corrected and the end to be attained." South Chicago Coal & Dock Co. v. Bassett, 309 U.S. 251 . . . . .

Congress, on the one hand, was not thinking solely of the immediate technical relation of employer and employee. It had in mind at least some other persons than those standing in the proximate legal relation of employee to the particular employer involved in the labor dispute. It cannot be taken, however, that the purpose was to include all other persons who may perform service for another or was to ignore entirely legal classifications made for other purposes. Congress had in mind a wider field than the narrow technical legal relation of "master and servant," as the common law had worked this out in all its variations, and at the same time a narrower one than the entire area of rendering service to others. The question comes down therefore to how much was included of the intermediate region between what is clearly and unequivocally "employment," by any appropriate test, and what is as clearly entrepreneurial enterprise and not employment. . . .

Congress . . . sought to find a broad solution, one that would bring industrial peace by substituting, so far as its power could reach, the rights of workers to self-organization and collective bargaining for the industrial strife which prevails where these rights are not effectively established. Yet only partial solutions would be provided if large segments of workers about whose technical legal position such local differences exist should be wholly excluded from coverage by reason of such differences. Yet that result could not be avoided, if choice must be made among them and controlled by them in deciding who are "employees" within the Act's meaning. Enmeshed in such distinctions, the administration of the statute soon might become encumbered by the same sort of technical legal refinement as has characterized the long evolution of the employee-independent contractor dichotomy in the courts for other purposes. The consequences would be ultimately to defeat, in part at least, the achievement of the statute's objectives. Congress no more intended to import this mass of technicality as a controlling "standard" for uniform national application than to refer decision of the question outright to the local law.

The Act, as its first section states, was designed to avert the "substantial obstructions to the free flow of commerce" which result from "strikes and other forms of industrial strife or unrest" by eliminating the causes of that unrest. It is premised on explicit findings that strikes and industrial strife themselves result in large measure from the refusal of employers to bargain collectively and the inability of individual workers to bargain successfully for improvements in their "wages, hours, or other working conditions" with employers who are "organized in the corporate or other forms of ownership association." Hence the avowed and the interrelated purposes of the Act are to encourage collective bargaining and to remedy the individual worker's inequality of bargaining power by "protecting the exercise . . . of full freedom of association, self-organization, and designation of representatives of their own choosing, for the purpose of negotiating the terms and conditions of their employment or other mutual aid or protection." 49 Stat. 449, 450.

The mischief at which the Act is aimed and the remedies it offers are not confined exclusively to "employees" within the traditional legal distinctions separating them from "independent contractors." Myriad forms of service relationship, with infinite and subtle variations in the terms of employment, blanket the nation's economy. Some are within this Act, others beyond its coverage. Large numbers will fall clearly on one side or on the other, by whatever test may be applied. But intermediate there will be many, the incidents of whose employment partake in part of the one group, in part of the other, in varying proportions of weight. And consequently the legal pendulum, for purposes of applying the statute, may swing one way or the other, depending upon the weight of this balance and its relation to the special purpose at hand.

. . . Interruption of commerce through strikes and unrest may stem as well from labor disputes between some who, for other purposes, are technically "independent contractors" and their employers as from disputes between persons who, for those purposes, are "employees" and their employers. . . . Inequality of bargaining power in controversies over wages, hours and working conditions may as well characterize the status of the one group as of the other. The former, when acting alone, may be as "helpless in dealing with an employer," as "dependent . . . on his daily wage" and as "unable to leave the employ and to resist arbitrary and unfair treatment" as the latter. For each, "union . . . [may be] essential to give . . . opportunity to deal on equality with their employer." And for each, collective bargaining may be appropriate and effective for the "friendly adjustment of industrial disputes arising out of differences as to wages, hours, or other working conditions." 49 Stat. 449. In short, when the particular situation of employment combines these characteristics, so that the economic facts of the relation make it more nearly one of employment than of independent business enterprise with respect to the ends sought to be accomplished by the legislation, those characteristics may outweigh technical legal classification for purposes unrelated to the statute's objectives and bring the relation within its protections. . . .

It is not necessary in this case to make a completely definitive limitation around the term "employee." That task has been assigned primarily to the agency created by Congress to administer the Act. Determination of "where all the conditions of the relation require protection" involves inquiries for the Board charged with this duty. Everyday experience in the administration of the statute gives it familiarity with the circumstances and backgrounds of employment relationships in various industries, with the abilities and needs of the workers for self organization and collective action, and with the adaptability of collective bargaining for the peaceful settlement of their disputes with their employers. The experience thus acquired must be brought frequently to bear on the question who is an employee under the Act. Resolving that question, like determining whether unfair labor practices have been committed, "belongs to the usual administrative routine" of the Board. Gray v. Powell, 314 U.S. 402, 411 . . . . .

In making that body's determinations as to the facts in these matters conclusive, if supported by evidence, Congress entrusted to it primarily the decision whether the evidence establishes the material facts. Hence in reviewing the Board's ultimate conclusions, it is not the court's function to substitute its own inferences of fact for the Board's, when the latter have support in the record. . . . Undoubtedly questions of statutory interpretation, especially when arising in the first instance in judicial proceedings, are for the courts to resolve, giving appropriate weight to the judgment of those whose special duty is to administer the questioned statute. Norwegian Nitrogen Products Co. v. United States, 288 U.S. 294. But where the question is one of specific application of a broad statutory term in a proceeding in which the agency administering the statute must determine it initially, the reviewing court's function is limited. Like the commissioner's determination under the Longshoremen's & Harbor Workers' Act, that a man is not a "member of a crew" or that he was injured "in the course of his employment" and the Federal Communications Commission's determination that one company is under the "control" of another, the Board's determination that specified persons are "employees" under this Act is to be accepted if it has "warrant in the record" and a reasonable basis in law.

In this case the Board found that the designated newsboys work continuously and regularly, rely upon their earnings for the support of themselves and their families, and have their total wages influenced in large measure by the publishers who dictate their buying and selling prices, fix their markets and control their supply of papers. Their hours of work and their efforts on the job are supervised and to some extent prescribed by the publishers or their agents. Much of their sales equipment and advertising materials is furnished by the publishers with the intention that it be used for the publisher's benefit. Stating that "the primary consideration in the determination of the applicability of the statutory definition is whether effectuation of the declared policy and purposes of the Act comprehend securing to the individual the rights guaranteed and protection afforded by the Act," the Board concluded that the newsboys are employees. The record sustains the Board's findings and there is ample basis in the law for its conclusion.

. . .

MR. JUSTICE REED concurs in the result. . . .

Reversed and remanded.

MR. JUSTICE ROBERTS: . . . I think it plain that newsboys are not "employees" of the respondents within the meaning and intent of the National Labor Relations Act. When Congress, in § 2(3) said: "The term 'employee' shall include any employee, . . . " it stated as clearly as language could do it that the provisions of the Act were to extend to those who, as a result of decades of tradition which had become part of the common understanding of our people, bear the named relationship. Clearly also Congress did not delegate to the National Labor Relations Board the function of defining the relationship of employment so as to promote what the Board understood to be the underlying purpose of the statute. The question who is an employee, so as to make the statute applicable to him, is a question of the meaning of the Act and, therefore, is a judicial and not an administrative question.

. . .

NOTES

(1) GRAY v. POWELL, 314 U.S. 402 (1941), cited by the Court on p. 388 supra, is sometimes regarded as the leading case for the proposition that courts, rather than exercising an independent judgment when reviewing an administrative application of a statutory term to undisputed facts, should affirm the administrative decision if it has a rational basis—a proposition sometimes referred to as "the doctrine of Gray v. Powell."

The case involved the Bituminous Coal Act, which set restrictions on the marketing of coal that did not "apply to coal consumed by the producer" of the coal. One who claimed an exemption as a producer was to apply to the administrative agency, which would either grant it or conduct a hearing; an order denying the application was reviewable in a court of appeals and the findings of the agency "as to the facts, if supported by substantial evidence, shall be conclusive."

An exemption was sought for a coal-burning railway which secured about half its coal by renting coal lands with a right to mine, paying per-ton royalties to the landowners (with a set annual minimum sum), hiring contractors to mine without supervision by the railroad, and taking delivery of all the mines' output. The agency held that the railroad was not a "producer," the court of appeals reversed and a divided Supreme Court reinstated the agency order.

"In a matter left specifically by Congress to the determination of an administrative body, as the question of exemption was here, . . . the function of review placed upon the courts . . . is fully performed when they determine that there has been a fair hearing, with notice and an opportunity to present the circumstances and arguments to the decisive body, and an application of the statute in a just and reasoned manner. . . .

"Such a determination as is here involved belongs to the usual administrative routine. . . .

"Where as here a determination has been left to an administrative body, this delegation will be respected and the administrative conclusion left untouched. Certainly a finding on Congressional reference that an admittedly constitutional act is applicable to a particular situation does not require such further scrutiny. Although we have here no dispute as to the evidentiary facts, that does not permit a court to substitute its judgment for that of the Director. United States v. Louisville & Nashville R.R., 235 U.S. 314, 320.[1] . . . It is not the province of a court to absorb the administrative functions to such an extent that the executive or legislative agencies become mere fact-finding bodies deprived of the advantages of prompt and definite action. . . .

"The separation of production and consumption is complete when a buyer obtains supplies from a seller totally free from buyer connection. Their identity is undoubted when the consumer extracts coal from its own land with its own employees. Between the two extremes are the innumerable variations that bring the arrangements closer to one pole or the other of the range between exemption and inclusion. To determine upon which side of the median line the particular instance falls calls for the expert, experienced judgment of those familiar with the

1. [Ed.] The question in the Louisville & Nashville case was whether the railroad, by granting reshipping privileges at Nashville, while refusing such privileges at Atlanta, had violated the section of the Interstate Commerce Act which prohibited any "undue or unreasonable preference." The court below held that since the facts were undisputed, the question was one of law which it should decide independently. The Supreme Court reversed, "[F]rom the beginning the very purpose for which the Commission was created was to bring into existence a body which from its peculiar character would be most fitted to primarily decide whether from facts, disputed or undisputed, in a given case preferences or discrimination existed. . . . [I]f the view of the statute upheld below be sustained, the Commission would become but a mere instrument for the purpose of taking testimony to be submitted to the courts for their ultimate action."

industry. Unless we can say that a set of circumstances deemed by the Commission to bring them within the concept 'producer' is so unrelated to the tasks entrusted by Congress to the Commission as in effect to deny a sensible exercise of judgment, it is the Court's duty to leave the Commission's judgment undisturbed." [2]

(2) NATHANIEL L. NATHANSON, ADMINISTRATIVE DISCRETION IN THE INTERPRETATION OF STATUTES, 3 Vand.L.Rev. 470, 473–75 (1950): "But the real issue in the Gray case could scarcely be appreciated if attention were centered exclusively on the exemption clause set forth above. Whether there was a rational basis for the administrative application of term 'producer' itself depended upon a broader issue of statutory interpretation; namely, whether the regulatory provisions of the statute authorizing maximum and minimum prices could be applied to deliveries of coal which involved no change in its ownership. If price regulation under the statute was necessarily limited in its application to sales in the usual sense of the word, the denial of the exemption served no useful purpose; but if transfers such as occurred between the contractor and Seaboard were within the scope of the Act, the denial might well be essential to prevent the development of an obvious and widespread pattern of evasion. If the opinion of the Court had resolved this basic question in the same way it resolved the issue of the particular application of the producer-consumer clause, by reliance upon a principle of limited review, it might have been justly charged with substituting administrative for judicial interpretation of statutes. But Mr. Justice Reed, writing for the Court, did no such thing; instead, he faced and resolved the fundamental question with the conventional tools of statutory interpretation, analysis of language, consideration of objectives, and recognition of the unfortunate consequences to those objectives if the more limited interpretation were adopted. But even after the resolution of this question, there still remained an area for administrative discretion in passing upon applications for exemption.

. . .

"The foregoing analysis of Gray v. Powell suggests a pattern which is in general applicable to several other instances where the principle of limited judicial review of questions of law has been invoked. In National Labor Relations Board v. Hearst Publications, Inc., for example . . . ."

(3) PACKARD MOTOR CAR CO. v. NLRB, 330 U.S. 485 (1947), often considered in tandem with Hearst, presented a problem about what the Court called a "naked question of law"—whether foremen could organize for collective bargaining under the NLRA. The Act provided that " 'employee' shall include any employee" and also that " 'employer' includes any person acting in the interest of an employer, directly or indirectly . . . ."

Packard's 1100 foremen wanted to organize as a unit of the Foremen's Assn. of America, representing supervisory employees exclu-

---

2. [Ed.] L. Jaffe, Judicial Review: Questions of Law, 69 Harv.L.Rev. 239, 363 (1955): "[P]roperly understood the doctrine　　in Gray v. Powell is as traditional as it is sound."

sively.[3] The foremen supervised Packard's 32,000 rank-and-file workers, represented by the United Auto Workers; foremen were relatively highly paid and responsible for maintaining quantity and quality of production under overall control by management; foremen could not hire or fire but could discipline and recommend promotion, demotion, etc. The NLRB decided the foremen were "employees", and then decided that they constituted an appropriate bargaining unit. Packard refused to bargain, claiming foremen were not "employees".

The Court affirmed the Board, none of the Justices deferring to the Board on this "tremendously important" policy affecting industry nation-wide, but a majority agreeing with the Board about how the Act treated foremen. (Hearst was cited only once, by the dissent, and only for the proposition that "the term 'employee' must be considered in the context of the Act.") The only mention of deference to the Board was by Justice Jackson, writing for the Court, who described the NLRB's views on this issue as vacillating and said this:

"If we were obliged to depend upon administrative interpretation for light in finding the meaning of the statute, the inconsistency of the Board's decisions would leave us in the dark. But there are difficult questions of policy involved in these [10 Board] cases which, together with changes in Board membership, account for the contradictory views that characterize their history in the Board. Whatever special questions there are in determining the appropriate bargaining unit for [these] foremen are for the Board, and the history of the issue in the Board shows the difficulty of the problem committed to its discretion. We are not at liberty to be governed by those policy considerations. . . ."

Can you reconcile with Hearst the proposition that deciding whether the NLRA excluded the meaning given the term "employee" by the Board in Packard presented a "naked question of law"?

SKIDMORE v. SWIFT & CO.
Supreme Court of the United States, 1944.
323 U.S. 134.

MR. JUSTICE JACKSON delivered the opinion of the Court.

Seven employees of the Swift and Company packing plant at Fort Worth, Texas, brought an action under the Fair Labor Standards Act, to recover overtime, liquidated damages, and attorneys' fees, totalling approximately $77,000. The District Court rendered judgment denying this claim wholly, and the Circuit Court of Appeals for the Fifth Circuit affirmed. 136 F.2d 112.

It is not denied that the daytime employment of these persons was working time within the Act. Two were engaged in general fire hall duties and maintenance of fire-fighting equipment of the Swift plant. The others operated elevators or acted as relief men in fire duties.

3. The statutory exclusion of "supervisory employees" from the Act mentioned in NLRB v. Bell Aerospace Co., p. 280 above, was added by the Taft-Hartley Act of 1947, shortly after the Packard decision.

They worked from 7:00 a.m. to 3:30 p.m., with a half-hour lunch period, five days a week. They were paid weekly salaries.

Under their oral agreement of employment, however, petitioners undertook to stay in the fire hall on the Company premises, or within hailing distance, three and a half to four nights a week. This involved no task except to answer alarms, either because of fire or because the sprinkler was set off for some other reason. No fires occurred during the period in issue, the alarms were rare, and the time required for their answer rarely exceeded an hour. For each alarm answered the employees were paid in addition to their fixed compensation an agreed amount, fifty cents at first, and later sixty-four cents. The Company provided a brick fire hall equipped with steam heat and air-conditioned rooms. It provided sleeping quarters, a pool table, a domino table, and a radio. The men used their time in sleep or amusement as they saw fit, except that they were required to stay in or close by the fire hall and be ready to respond to alarms. It is stipulated that "they agreed to remain in the fire hall and stay in it or within hailing distance, subject to call, in event of fire or other casualty, but were not required to perform any specific tasks during these periods of time, except in answering alarms." The trial court found the evidentiary facts as stipulated; it made no findings of fact as such as to whether under the arrangement of the parties and the circumstances of this case, which in some respects differ from those of the Armour case [Armour & Co. v. Wantock et al., 323 U.S. 126], the fire hall duty or any part thereof constituted working time. It said, however, as a "conclusion of law" that "the time plaintiffs spent in the fire hall subject to call to answer fire alarms does not constitute hours worked, for which overtime compensation is due them under the Fair Labor Standards Act, as interpreted by the Administrator and the Courts," and in its opinion [53 F.Supp. 1020, 1021] observed, "of course we know pursuing such pleasurable occupations or performing such personal chores does not constitute work." The Circuit Court of Appeals affirmed.

For reasons set forth in the Armour case, 323 U.S. 126, decided herewith we hold that no principle of law found either in the statute or in Court decisions precludes waiting time from also being working time. We have not attempted to, and we cannot, lay down a legal formula to resolve cases so varied in their facts as are the many situations in which employment involves waiting time. Whether in a concrete case such time falls within or without the Act is a question of fact to be resolved by appropriate findings of the trial court. . . . This involves scrutiny and construction of the agreements between the particular parties, appraisal of their practical construction of the working agreement by conduct, consideration of the nature of the service, and its relation to the waiting time, and all of the surrounding circumstances. Facts may show that the employee was engaged to wait, or they may show that he waited to be engaged. His compensation may cover both waiting and task, or only performance of the task itself. Living quarters may in some situations be furnished as a facility of the task and in another as a part of its compensation. The law does not impose an arrangement upon the parties. It imposes upon the courts the task of finding what the arrangement was.

We do not minimize the difficulty of such an inquiry where the arrangements of the parties have not contemplated the problem posed by the statute. But it does not differ in nature or in the standards to guide judgment from that which frequently confronts courts where they must find retrospectively the effect of contracts as to matters which the parties failed to anticipate or explicitly to provide for.

Congress did not utilize the services of an administrative agency to find facts and to determine in the first instance whether particular cases fall within or without the Act. Instead, it put this responsibility on the courts. . . . But it did create the office of Administrator, impose upon him a variety of duties, endow him with powers to inform himself of conditions in industries and employments subject to the Act, and put on him the duties of bringing injunction actions to restrain violations. Pursuit of his duties has accumulated a considerable experience in the problems of ascertaining working time in employments involving periods of inactivity and a knowledge of the customs prevailing in reference to their solution. From these he is obliged to reach conclusions as to conduct without the law, so that he should seek injunctions to stop it, and that within the law, so that he has no call to interfere. He has set forth his views of the application of the Act under different circumstances in an interpretative bulletin and in informal rulings. They provide a practical guide to employers and employees as to how the office representing the public interest in its enforcement will seek to apply it. Wage and Hour Division, Interpretative Bulletin No. 13.

The Administrator thinks the problems presented by inactive duty require a flexible solution, rather than the all-in or all-out rules respectively urged by the parties in this case, and his Bulletin endeavors to suggest standards and examples to guide in particular situations. In some occupations, it says, periods of inactivity are not properly counted as working time even though the employee is subject to call. Examples are an operator of a small telephone exchange where the switchboard is in her home and she ordinarily gets several hours of uninterrupted sleep each night; or a pumper of a stripper well or watchman of a lumber camp during the off season, who may be on duty twenty-four hours a day but ordinarily "has a normal night's sleep, has ample time in which to eat his meals, and has a certain amount of time for relaxation and entirely private pursuits." Exclusion of all such hours the Administrator thinks may be justified. In general, the answer depends "upon the degree to which the employee is free to engage in personal activities during periods of idleness when he is subject to call and the number of consecutive hours that the employee is subject to call without being required to perform active work." "Hours worked are not limited to the time spent in active labor but include time given by the employee to the employer. . . . "

The facts of this case do not fall within any of the specific examples given, but the conclusion of the Administrator, as expressed in the brief amicus curiae, is that the general tests which he has suggested point to the exclusion of sleeping and eating time of these employees from the work week and the inclusion of all other on-call time: although the employees were required to remain on the premises during the entire time, the evidence shows that they were very rarely interrupted in their normal sleeping and eating time, and these are pursuits of a purely private nature which would presumably occupy the employees' time whether they were on duty or not and which apparently could be pursued adequately and comfortably in the required circumstances; the rest of the time is different because there is nothing in the record to suggest that, even though pleasurably spent, it was spent in the ways the men would have chosen had they been free to do so.

There is no statutory provision as to what, if any, deference courts should pay to the Administrator's conclusions. And, while we have given them notice, we have had no occasion to try to prescribe their influence. The rulings of this Administrator are not reached as a result of hearing adversary proceedings in which he finds facts from evidence and reaches conclusions of law from findings of fact. They are not, of course, conclusive, even in the cases with which they directly deal, much less in those to which they apply only by analogy. They do not constitute an interpretation of the Act or a standard for judging factual situations which binds a district court's processes, as an authoritative pronouncement of a higher court might do. But the Administrator's policies are made in pursuance of official duty, based upon more specialized experience and broader investigations and information than is likely to come to a judge in a particular case. They do determine the policy which will guide applications for enforcement by injunction on behalf of the Government. Good administration of the Act and good judicial administration alike require that the standards of public enforcement and those for determining private rights shall be at variance only where justified by very good reasons. The fact that the Administrator's policies and standards are not reached by trial in adversary form does not mean that they are not entitled to respect. This Court has long given considerable and in some cases decisive weight to Treasury Decisions and to interpretative regulations of the Treasury and of other bodies that were not of adversary origin.

We consider that the rulings, interpretations and opinions of the Administrator under this Act, while not controlling upon the courts by reason of their authority, do constitute a body of experience and informed judgment to which courts and litigants may properly resort for guidance. The weight of such a judgment in a particular case will depend upon the thoroughness evident in its consideration, the validity of its reasoning, its consistency with earlier and later pronouncements, and all those factors which give it power to persuade, if lacking power to control.

The court in the Armour case weighed the evidence in the particular case in the light of the Administrator's rulings and reached a result consistent therewith. The evidence in this case in some respects, such as the understanding as to separate compensation for answering alarms, is different. Each case must stand on its own facts. But in this case, although the District Court referred to the Administrator's Bulletin, its evaluation and inquiry were apparently restricted by its notion that waiting time may not be work, an understanding of the law which we hold to be erroneous. Accordingly, the judgment is reversed and the cause remanded for further proceedings consistent herewith.

Reversed.

NOTES

(1) Justice Jackson's penultimate paragraph is quoted probably as much as any statement on scope of review. Just how much deference does it call for? "Courteous regard"?[1] Could we not use the same language to describe the weight a court attaches to a litigant's brief, or at least an "institutional" litigant possessing a "body of experience and informed judgment" (General Motors? the New York Stock Exchange?)? Yet how else describe the deference due an agency to which Congress has given no authority to adjudicate or make binding rules?

"A rule-making power had been contained in the Act as originally introduced. The issuance of 'interpretative bulletins' by the Wage and Hour Division stemmed from the failure of Congress to include a rule-making provision in the Act. The bulletins were the creature of necessity. . . . [and] self-denying as witnessed by the following typical statement:

'. . . interpretations announced by the Administrator, except in certain specific instances where the statute directs the Administrator to make various regulations and definitions, serve only to indicate the construction of the law which will guide the Administrator in the performance of his administrative duties, unless he is directed otherwise by the authoritative rulings of the courts, or unless he shall subsequently decide that a prior interpretation is incorrect.'

". . . The interpretative bulletins are not binding on industry; they are merely legal advice—good, perhaps the best. While industry is advised to comply, if in doubt, the employer is not immune if, in reliance upon an interpretative bulletin, he concludes that the Act is not applicable to him. He may be subsequently prosecuted under Section 16(a), sued by an employee under Section 16(b), or enjoined under Section 17." S. Herman, The Administration and Enforcement of the Fair Labor Standards Act, 6 Law and Contemp.Prob. 368, 378–80 (1939).[2]

(2) ADDISON v. HOLLY HILL FRUIT PRODUCTS, INC., 322 U.S. 607 (1944). A suit was brought by employees of a citrus fruit cannery

---

1. C. Diver, Statutory Interpretation in the Administrative State, 133 U.Pa.L.Rev. 549, 565 (1985).

2. [Ed.] For a discussion of a proposal that Congress should adopt "more inclusive legislation to protect people who rely on official advice," see F. Newman, Should Official Advice be Reliable?—Proposals as to Estoppel and Related Doctrines in Administrative Law, 53 Colum.L.Rev. 374 (1953). See also M. Asimow, Advice to the Public from Federal Administrative Agencies 63–68 (1973). And see section on Estopping the Government, p. 522 below.

employing 200 workers, for wage payments under the Fair Labor Standards Act of 1938. The court below had held that the company's employees were not covered by the Act because they were exempted by a provision that the statute was not applicable "to any individual employed within the area of production (as defined by the Administrator), engaged in handling . . . agricultural or horticultural commodities for market . . . ." The court below reached its conclusion by holding that a portion of the definition of "area of production" made by the Administrator of the Wage and Hour Division was invalid and that the remaining portion exempted these employees. Specifically, the Administrator had defined "area of production" to exempt canning operations if the cannery obtains its raw materials exclusively from farms in the neighborhood *"and the number of employees engaged in those operations in that establishment does not exceed seven."*

Said Justice Frankfurter: "The textual meaning of 'area of production' . . . calls for delimitation of territory in relation to the complicated economic factors that operate between agricultural labor conditions and the labor market of enterprises concerned with agricultural commodities and more or less near their production. The phrase is the most apt designation of a zone within which economic influences may be deemed to operate and outside of which they lose their force. In view, however, of the variety of agricultural conditions and industries throughout the country, the bounds of these areas could not be defined by Congress itself. Neither was it deemed wise to leave such economic determination to the contingencies and inevitable diversities of litigation. And so Congress left the boundary-making to the experienced and informed judgment of the Administrator. Thereby Congress gave the Administrator appropriate discretion to assess all the factors relevant to the subject matter, that is, the fixing of minimum wages and maximum hours.

"In delimiting the area the Administrator may properly weigh and synthesize all such factors. So long as he does that and no more, judgment belongs to him and not to the courts. For Congress has cast upon him the authority and the duty to define the 'area of production' of agricultural commodities with reference to which exemption in subsidiary employments may operate. But if Congress intended to allow the Administrator to discriminate between smaller and bigger establishments within the zone of agricultural production, Congress wholly failed to express its purpose. Where Congress wanted to make exemption depend on size, as it did in two or three instances not here relevant, it did so by appropriate language. . . . Congress referred to quantity when it desired to legislate on the basis of quantity.

". . . The determination of the extent of authority given to a delegated agency by Congress is not left for the decision of him in whom authority is vested.

". . . [T]he ultimate question is what has Congress commanded, when it has given no clue to its intentions except familiar English words and no hint by the draftsmen of the words that they meant to use them in any but an ordinary sense. The idea which is now sought to be read into the grant by Congress to the Administrator to define 'the area of production' beyond the plain geographic implications of that phrase is not so complicated nor is English speech so poor that words were not easily available to express the idea or at least to suggest it. After all, legislation when not expressed in technical terms is addressed to the common run of men and is therefore to be understood according to the sense of the thing, as the ordinary man has a right to rely on ordinary words addressed to him." The Court held invalid the limitation as to the number of employees within the defined area, over three dissents.

(ii) Perspectives on Approach to Scope

(1) In his opinion in NLRB v. Marcus Trucking Co., 286 F.2d 583 (2d Cir.1961), Judge Henry Friendly attempted to domesticate the distinction between questions of fact and questions of law. The cases, he wrote, "seem to fall into three major groupings, although, as would be expected, the lines between them are fuzzy:

"(a) Cases, typified by Consolidated Edison Co. of N.Y. v. N.L.R.B., 1938, 305 U.S. 197, 229; N.L.R.B. v. Southern Bell T. & T. Co., 1943, 319 U.S. 50, 60, and Corn Products Refining Co. v. F.T.C., 1945, 324 U.S. 726, 739 [discrimination], where the chief problem is the propriety of an administrative conclusion that raw facts, undisputed or within the agency's power to find, fall under a statutory term as to whose meaning, at least in the particular case, there is little dispute;

"(b) Cases where there is dispute both as to the propriety of the inferences drawn by the agency from the raw facts and as to the meaning of the statutory term, e.g., Rochester Tel. Corp. v. United States, 1939, 307 U.S. 125 [control]; O'Leary v. Brown-Pacific-Maxon, Inc., 1951, 340 U.S. 504 [course of employment];

"(c) Cases where the only or principal dispute relates to the meaning of the statutory term, e.g., Gray v. Powell, 1941, 314 U.S. 402 [producer]; Davies Warehouse Co. v. Bowles, 1944, 321 U.S. 144 [public utility]; N.L.R.B. v. Hearst Publications, Inc., 1944, 322 U.S. 111, 130–131, and Packard Motor Car Co. v. N.L.R.B., 1947, 330 U.S. 485 [employee]; Social Security Board v. Nierotko, 1946, 327 U.S. 358 [back pay]; N.L.R.B. v. Highland Park Mfg. Co., 1951, 341 U.S. 322 [national or international labor organization]."

Do you agree with that categorization? In O'Leary, did the Court apply the same scope of review to "the inferences drawn by the agency from the raw facts" and to "the meaning of the statutory term"? Would Professor Nathanson approve submerging the different treatment of different issues in Gray v. Powell? Is it right to say the issue in Hearst concerned, primarily, the meaning of the term "employee"? Where should Skidmore be placed in this catalog?

(2) At least as early as the seminal 1958 casebook by Professors Henry Hart and Albert Sacks, The Legal Process: Basic Problems in the Making and Application of Law, the traditional approach was shown to suffer two flaws more serious than fuzziness: it uses labels which turn out to be wholly conclusory, and it draws us into an effort to

identify the kind of issue being reviewed instead of into the problem at hand, which is to determine what decisionmaker—as between judge and jury, trial court and appellate, or court and agency—should bear how much of the responsibility for final resolution of the issue. Id. at 369–83. Drawing on Hart and Sacks, Professor Henry Monaghan describes three different functions in legal decisions: "Law declaration involves formulating a proposition [that] affects not only the [immediate] case . . . but all others that fall within its terms. In a strict sense, then, law declaration yields only what we commonly think of as 'law'— conclusions about the existence and content of governing legal rules, standards, and principles. The important point about law is that it yields a proposition that is *general* in character.

"Fact identification, by contrast, is a case-specific inquiry into *what happened here*. It is designed to yield only assertions that can be made without *significantly* implicating the governing legal principles. Such assertions, for example, generally respond to inquiries about who, when, what, and where—inquiries that can be made 'by a person who is ignorant of the applicable law'. . . . [T]he question is 'not whether the fact exists in an absolute sense but whether the evidence is adequate to justify the exercise of [the decisionmaker's] power'. This means that while what happened may be viewed as a question of fact, the legal sufficiency of the evidence may be viewed as the equivalent of a question of law.

"Law application, the third function, is residual in character. It involves relating the legal standard of conduct to the facts established by the evidence. If all legal propositions could be formulated in great detail, this function would be rather mechanical and require no distinctive consideration. But such is not the case. Linking the rule to the conduct is a complex psychological process, one that often involves judgment. Thus, law application frequently entails some attempt to elaborate the governing norm. But in contrast to the generalizing feature of law declaration, law application is situation-specific; any ad hoc norm elaboration is, in theory, like a ticket good for a specific trip only. Moreover, in this kind of situation, specific norm elaboration is generally invisible. By definition, when law application occurs, further explicit norm elaboration ceases. And any implicit norm elaboration may be buried in a general verdict and in the decisionmaker's resolution of the controversy over the facts. The typical jury verdict in a negligence case provides a good example." H. Monaghan, Constitutional Fact Review, 85 Colum.L.Rev. 229, 235–36 (1985).

By replacing the labels "question of fact," "mixed" and "question of law" with "fact finding, law applying and law declaring," we shift from trying to analyze the nature of the question being decided (why was the employee fired? are newsboys employees? are foremen?), to focusing on which body has what responsibility for deciding that question. Changing the labels is not a necessary but a helpful first step toward bringing out not only what is the allocation, but also why.[1]

1. In a recent decision addressing the scope of review in habeas corpus proceedings, the court made the following pertinent observation:

(3) Our natural yearning for generalization and categorization [2] to help resolve particular cases might lead us to say that law applying in the ordinary administrative routine is reviewed like fact finding and for essentially the same reasons, while law declaring and unusual law applying are reviewed independently. But note that most of the cases on scope considered so far involve on-the-record adjudication. Can we find as much relative clarity in review of aspects of informal adjudication, formal and informal rulemaking, discretionary treatment of waivers or sanctions, agencies' prescription of their own procedures, etc.?

One approach to analysis of scope is to consider review of each form of agency action separately[3]; that has much merit because reviewing courts are always aware of, and results may be determined by, discrete aspects of the particular form of action under review. A second approach is to retain acute awareness of the form under review but focus primarily on the particular issues that are allegedly reversible error, usually categorized as one of the traditional "questions." A merit of this second approach is that courts reviewing one kind of agency action regularly use language originated in review of another kind. For example, the dominant standard of review of informal rulemaking derives from review of informal adjudication, Citizens to Preserve Overton Park, Inc. v. Volpe, 401 U.S. 402 (1971), considered fully later. Thus, despite the limitations of the traditional categorization, that tradition is live enough that statutes use, and cases tend to cluster by those categories so that we may use them even as we seek to go beyond them to bring out which scope is being used, why, and of course, how sound we find it.

"At least in those instances in which Congress has not spoken and in which the issue falls somewhere between a pristine legal standard and a simple historical fact, the fact/law distinction at times has turned on a determination that, as a matter of sound administration of justice, one judicial actor is better positioned than another to decide the issue in question."

Miller v. Fenton, 106 S.Ct. 445, 452 (1985).

2. "Confronted with disturbing variety, we often feel a tension from which a generalization, an abstraction, relieves us. It serves as a de-problemizer, aiding us to pass from an unstable, problematical, situation to a more stable one. It satisfies a craving, meets what Emerson called "the insatiable demand of harmony in man," a demand which translates itself into the so-called "law" of "the least effort." But the solution of a problem through the invention of a new generalization is no final solution: The new generalization breeds new problems. Stressing a newly perceived likeness between many particular happenings which had theretofore seemed unlike, it may blind us to continuing unlikenesses. Hypnotized by a label which emphasizes identities, we may be led to ignore differences. In all fields of thought

that evil is encountered. Nowhere can it do more harm than in democratic government—and in democratic courthouse government in particular." Guiseppi v. Walling, 144 F.2d 608, 618–9 (2d Cir.1944; Frank, J.).

3. Commenting on a state statute calling for reviewing courts to treat "separately . . . disputed issues of agency procedure, interpretations of law, determinations of fact or policy within the agency's exercise of delegated discretion, Oregon Supreme Court Justice Hans Linde and Professor Donald Brodie wrote: "The key . . . is the directive that '[t]he reviewing court shall deal *separately*. . . .' This provision goes a long way toward satisfying the need to articulate the basis of arguments and of decisions on review." They noted another "important innovation" in the statute's "deliberate omission of the accordion-like terms 'arbitrary', 'capricious,' and 'abuse.' In place of these familiar epithets, the statute requires the reviewing court to analyze the component elements of agency actions which involve discretion." State Court Review of Administrative Action: Prescribing the Scope of Review, 1977 Ariz.St.L.J. 537, 558–60.

Whatever administrative form of action is under review, much language in cases and commentary suggests that we can readily generalize about review of any "pure questions of law," or law-declaring, by the agency. This follows, it is said, from Marbury v. Madison's establishing that it is the "duty of the judicial department to say what the law is." [4] More directly, APA § 706 opens: "To the extent necessary to decision and when presented, the reviewing court shall decide all relevant questions of law, interpret constitutional and statutory provisions, and determine the meaning or applicability of the terms of an agency action." [5] But, where does that leave such a "question of law" as whether Congress has delegated to an agency the responsibility (within, say, the limits of a sound discretion) to decide how a particular statutory term shall be construed? Or, whether the complexity of a statutory scheme and the need for uniform and informed national implementation require the courts to defer to agency judgment as to matters of interpretation not clearly resolved by a statute's language or history?

(4) Senator Dale Bumpers' (Dem. Ark.) proposal to amend the APA provisions on scope of review to provide that courts must "*independently* decide all relevant questions of law" has attracted wide support in recent years. In 1975, he told the Senate: "[T]he courts have abdicated a large measure of their traditional power to interpret and apply the laws of Congress. . . . The courts, it seems, have forgotten that Congress is the creator, and the agency the creature, of legislation. No person should be judge in his own cause, and neither should any agency determine the limits of its own power.

"Perhaps the leading case stating this accepted doctrine is NLRB v. Hearst. . . . The Supreme Court . . . did not itself construe the words of the statute. Instead, it simply accepted the statutory interpretation of the Labor Board on the ground that it had 'warrant in the record' and 'a reasonable basis in law'. . . . I have no quarrel with the particular interpretation of the word 'employee' involved in Hearst. Undoubtedly the Labor Board's interpretation of the statute in that instance was correct, and the Supreme Court properly approved it. The point for present purposes is simply that the Board in effect determined the limits of its own authority, even though in theory it has only so much power as has been delegated to it by Congress. . . .

4. Fine analyses of this proposition are H. Monaghan, Marbury and the Administrative State, 83 Colum.L.Rev. 1 (1983) and R. Levin, Identifying Questions of Law in Administrative Law, 74 Geo.L.J. 1 (1985). The Marbury phrase is incanted so frequently as to seem our lawyers' or judges' national anthem, but the portion of Marbury noting a realm of non-reviewable executive discretion lags in visibility; and all but lost from sight is United States v. Vowell, 9 U.S. (5 Cranch) 368 (1809), in which the Court, per Chief Justice Marshall, expressly noted the deference due a long-standing (relatively) Treasury Department interpretation of a statute.

Consider also: "In an age that freely accepts explicit delegations of broad rulemaking authority, the degree of lawmaking discretion implicit in a deferential standard of review will scarcely raise an eyebrow." C. Diver, Statutory Interpretation in the Administrative State, 133 U.Pa. L.Rev. 549, 569 (1985).

5. Note also the 1981 Revised Model State APA § 5–116(c)(4): agency action is to be set aside if the "agency has erroneously interpreted or applied the law." The Uniform Law Commissioners' accompanying commentary says there should be less deference for "interpretations" of law than for "applications."

"A good deal of this looseness in judicial review can be accounted for by the fashionableness in legal circles of one word: discretion. Agencies, it is said, have been delegated the power by Congress to work out the details of public policy, and their judgment should not be disturbed so long as it is within their 'discretion,' or so long as their discretion is not 'abused.' Although this doctrine in its beginnings was healthy, designed to prevent unnecessary judicial interference with social policies adopted by the Congress, it has long since exceeded proper boundaries. . . . " 121 Cong.Rec. 29957 (Sept. 24, 1975).

Do you agree with Senator Bumpers' reading of Hearst? If the ascription to Congress of having delegated "discretion" to the agencies is accurate (is it?), what would be the most appropriate response from the courts? From Congress?

(5) LOUIS L. JAFFE, JUDICIAL CONTROL OF ADMINISTRATIVE ACTION 572, 573, 576 * (1965): ". . . I would urge that there is a presumption (subject to rebuttal by reference to statutory history, custom in legislative drafting) that a rule-making or order-making agency with a specialized jurisdiction is meant to have some discretion, some policy-making function.

"It is at this point that we come to the heart of the difficulty. *Discretion, as we have said, is not self-defining; it does not arise parthenogenetically from 'broad' phrases.* Its contour is determined by the courts, which must define its scope and its limit. Put in terms of judicial review: why do courts in some cases pronounce the law and in some not? Put in terms of administrative power: why are agencies in some cases permitted to make law and in some not? *The answer, I submit, should run primarily and presumptively in terms of clear statutory purpose, or as Professor Fuller would say, 'the intention of the statute.'* The phrase 'clear purpose' has certain doubtful connotations. The word 'clear' suggests a clarity, an objectivity of application which quite evidently is not present in these situations. What it means very simply—if simplicity has not by this time been quite frightened away— is that where the *judges* are themselves *convinced* that certain reading, or application, of the statute is the *correct* —or the only *faithful* — reading or application, they should intervene and so declare. . . .

"[T]he legislature in realizing its purposes has chosen to work through an administrative agency, and so (presumptively, as we have said) to confer on it some policy-making function. This discretion should normally be permitted to function short of the point where the court is *convinced* that the purpose of the statute is contradicted. The court, we have said, should test each exercise of power in terms of statutory purpose. But in a great many cases the court will grant that any one or two or more proposed answers is consistent with the statute. In such a situation its function is complete when it decides that the administrative answer is reasonable, unless the presumption yields to certain considerations discussed below. . . .

". . . A judge may say: 'There is more than one sensible construction of this statute, but this construction appears to me to be the correct one.' If this is what he thinks, he should not defer either to his colleagues or to the agency. Such a view better explains the decisions, particularly those in which majority and minority judges both write persuasive opinions concerning which *reasoning* men disagree. Such a view comports better with a confident and responsible judiciary; if a judge may vote as he sees the law only on condition that he first conclude that the opposition is 'unreasonable,' he, if sensitive or modest, may be finally reduced to mere deference or frustration.

"It will no doubt be urged against a test in terms of purpose that it gives no predictive clue to the likely result in a new case because there is no rule for the ascertainment of purpose. That is indeed true, as it is of all statutory interpretation. The test channels the search for an answer but the answer ultimately depends on the appreciation of the particular judge. Furthermore, though the purpose test be the primary or basic criterion there are additional considerations which determine its application; some of these considerations are implied in the test of statutory purpose, some operate outside of it. Among them are (1) the degree to which the framing of a rule appears to depend on expertise, (2) the clarity with which a rule can be made to emerge and be given a stable form and content, (3) the importance of the rule in the statutory and administrative scheme, (4) the possible psychological advantage of judicial as compared with administrative pronouncement and (5) the role of the court as the guardian of the integrity of the legal system. Thus there will be cases where though the rule to be laid down or the decision to be made does not clearly emerge from a study of the statute, nevertheless the court will—indeed should—take upon itself the power and responsibility for decision. . . . In exercising that power the above considerations will be relevant, but not all the relevant considerations can be explicitly formulated."

(6) That "study of the statute" may be illuminating but not dispositive is memorably noted by FELIX FRANKFURTER and NATHANIEL L. NATHANSON, FORBIDDEN DIALOGUE: STANDARDS OF JUDICIAL REVIEW OF ADMINISTRATIVE ACTION, 1963 Sup.Ct.Rev. 206, 208: "F.F.: . . . Can one interpret statutes without being guided by assumptions drawn from experience and refined by rationalization and articulation? Is every statute to be approached as if it were something naked, unique and entirely unanticipated, with no guides to judgment but the words of the particular statute and its own peculiar history? Is that the sterility to which you would condemn one of the most delicate of the lawyer's arts?"

(7) ROBERT L. STERN, REVIEW OF FINDINGS OF ADMINISTRATORS, JUDGES AND JURIES: A COMPARATIVE ANALYSIS, 58 Harv.L.Rev. 70, 105–107 (1944): ". . . When Congress establishes an administrative agency and lays down general standards for it to follow, the agency has the function of filling in the interstices which have been deliberately left open. The duty of the courts in reviewing the administrative decision

for error of law is to see that the agency has stayed within the bounds for the exercise of discretion fixed by Congress, and that it has applied the statutory standards and no others. As long as the agency does so, the courts are not to substitute their judgment, even though the administrative determination has a general applicability beyond the facts of the particular case. . . .

"From the above analysis, it would seem that the function of the reviewing court in determining the 'law' in this field is to search for legislative intention, which of course would include an intention to vest the administrator with discretionary power, and then to decide whether the administrative ruling is consistent with it. The legislative intent may have been expressed either in terms of a broad delegation of power or a very narrow one. As an illustration of the latter, legislative history might indicate specifically that the Labor Board was or was not to have authority to issue a certain kind of order, or might refer to a particular company as illustrative of the type not intended to be included in a statutory exemption. In such a case, there might be little room for administrative judgment. On the other hand, Congress may have intended the agency to determine the 'sub-principle' within the statutory framework. The vital factor is the intention of Congress, not the generality of the administrative application. This does not mean that the court reviewing for error of law under a statute does not lay down general rules. Of course it does; in interpreting the act it prescribes the important principles which the administrative body is to follow. But the court is not called upon to act independently on every issue which may have general significance because of that fact alone."

(8) What if analysis of the statutory scheme alone leaves one utterly uncertain whether or how much to defer to the agency? Professor Kenneth Davis urges an approach which has been cited often and which, although he addresses it to only law-applying, may warrant consideration more broadly: "[T]he chief guide . . . should be comparative qualifications." He argues that courts are the experts "on many types of issues, including constitutional law, common law, ethics, overall philosophy of law and government, procedural fairness, judge-made law developed through statutory interpretation, most analysis of legislative history, and problems transcending the field of the particular agency." 5 K. Davis, Administrative Law Treatise (2d ed.1984), 393.

Professor Colin Diver finds it "difficult to tease a general presumption" in favor of courts or agencies on grounds of relative competence in finding statutory meaning: courts may be more neutral, agencies more knowledgeable about circumstances surrounding enactment. To the extent that statutory interpretation is "unavoidably an act of creating meaning," his allocation of roles emphasizes consideration of geographical uniformity, continuity over time, harmony with related policies, integration of policy and enforcement, and expedition of implementation. C. Diver, Statutory Interpretation in the Administrative State, 133 U.Pa.L.Rev. 549, 574, 582, 585 (1985).

(iii) Contemporary Cases

Armed with the foregoing, consider now the following, more recent cases. Note that (characteristically for the current day) the matters under review are much less likely to arise out of on-the-record adjudication. Not only are rulemaking and other forms of informal action more frequently at issue, but the stakes to the participants (and the economy) are higher: rather than a cease and desist order concerning a few "employees," a rule having multi-million dollar consequences for industry and irreversible impact on the environment. Do, or ought, these new parameters invoke greater judicial care, and if so, to what extent?

Whether one expects to emerge from the cases with usable formulas or generalizations, or comes to believe that scope has indeed "no more substance at the core than a seedless grape"; or is instead convinced that judges would not go on so about scope if there were nothing to it, and that we must discover what makes them readier to review sometimes and readier to defer other times since the differences cannot turn all (or even much) of the time on sheer personal predilection—whatever one's view so far, analysis of the following cases should begin as suggested frequently above: in each case, consider first precisely what agency error is alleged, and second, what does the statutory scheme indicate or suggest should be left to the agency, what should not?

CHEVRON, U.S.A., INC. v. NATURAL RESOURCES DEFENSE COUNCIL, INC.

Supreme Court of the United States, 1984.
467 U.S. 837.

Justice STEVENS delivered the opinion of the Court.

In the Clean Air Act Amendments of 1977, Pub.L. 95–95, 91 Stat. 685, Congress enacted certain requirements applicable to States that had not achieved the national air quality standards established by the Environmental Protection Agency (EPA) pursuant to earlier legislation. The amended Clean Air Act required these "nonattainment" States to establish a permit program regulating "new or modified major stationary sources" of air pollution. Generally, a permit may not be issued for a new or modified major stationary source unless several stringent conditions are met. The EPA regulation promulgated to implement this permit requirement allows a State to adopt a plantwide definition of the term "stationary source." Under this definition, an existing plant that contains several pollution-emitting devices may install or modify one piece of equipment without meeting the permit conditions if the alteration will not increase the total emissions from the plant. The question presented by this case is whether EPA's decision to allow States to treat all of the pollution-emitting devices within the same industrial grouping as though they were encased within a single "bubble" is based on a reasonable construction of the statutory term "stationary source."

I

The EPA regulations containing the plantwide definition of the term stationary source were promulgated on October 14, 1981. 46 Fed. Reg. 50766. Respondents filed a timely petition for review in the United States Court of Appeals for the District of Columbia Circuit pursuant to 42 U.S.C. § 7607(b)(1). The Court of Appeals set aside the regulations. Natural Resources Defense Council, Inc. v. Gorsuch, 685 F.2d 718 (1982).

The court observed that the relevant part of the amended Clean Air Act "does not explicitly define what Congress envisioned as a 'stationary source', to which the permit program . . . should apply," and further stated that the precise issue was not "squarely addressed in the legislative history." In light of its conclusion that the legislative history bearing on the question was "at best contradictory," it reasoned that "the purposes of the nonattainment program should guide our decision here." [1] Based on two of its precedents concerning the applicability of the bubble concept to certain Clean Air Act programs, the court stated that the bubble concept was "mandatory" in programs designed merely to maintain existing air quality, but held that it was "inappropriate" in programs enacted to improve air quality. Since the purpose of the permit program—its "raison d'etre," in the court's view—was to improve air quality, the court held that the bubble concept was inapplicable in this case under its prior precedents. It therefore set aside the regulations embodying the bubble concept as contrary to law. We . . . now reverse.

The basic legal error of the Court of Appeals was to adopt a static judicial definition of the term stationary source when it had decided that Congress itself had not commanded that definition. . . .

II

When a court reviews an agency's construction of the statute which it administers, it is confronted with two questions. First, always, is the question whether Congress has directly spoken to the precise question at issue. If the intent of Congress is clear, that is the end of the matter; for the court, as well as the agency, must give effect to the unambiguously expressed intent of Congress.[2] If, however, the court determines Congress has not directly addressed the precise question at issue, the court does not simply impose its own construction on the statute, as would be necessary in the absence of an administrative

---

1. The court remarked in this regard:

"We regret, of course, that Congress did not advert specifically to the bubble concept's application to various Clean Air Act programs, and note that a further clarifying statutory directive would facilitate the work of the agency and of the court in their endeavors to serve the legislators' will."

2. The judiciary is the final authority on issues of statutory construction and must reject administrative constructions which are contrary to clear congressional intent. See, e.g., FEC v. Democratic Senatorial Campaign Committee, 454 U.S. 27, 32 (1981) [citing cases]. If a court, employing traditional tools of statutory construction, ascertains that Congress had an intention on the precise question at issue, that intention is the law and must be given effect.

interpretation. Rather, if the statute is silent or ambiguous with respect to the specific issue, the question for the court is whether the agency's answer is based on a permissible construction of the statute.[3]

"The power of an administrative agency to administer a congressionally created . . . program necessarily requires the formulation of policy and the making of rules to fill any gap left, implicitly or explicitly, by Congress." Morton v. Ruiz, 415 U.S. 199, 231 (1974). If Congress has explicitly left a gap for the agency to fill, there is an express delegation of authority to the agency to elucidate a specific provision of the statute by regulation. Such legislative regulations are given controlling weight unless they are arbitrary, capricious, or manifestly contrary to the statute. Sometimes the legislative delegation to an agency on a particular question is implicit rather than explicit. In such a case, a court may not substitute its own construction of a statutory provision for a reasonable interpretation made by the administrator of an agency.

We have long recognized that considerable weight should be accorded to an executive department's construction of a statutory scheme it is entrusted to administer, and the principle of deference to administrative interpretations "has been consistently followed by this Court whenever decision as to the meaning or reach of a statute has involved reconciling conflicting policies, and a full understanding of the force of the statutory policy in the given situation has depended upon more than ordinary knowledge respecting the matters subjected to agency regulations. See e.g., Labor Board v. Hearst Publications, Inc., 322 U.S. 111; Securities & Exchange Comm'n v. Chenery Corp., 332 U.S. 194.

". . . If this choice represents a reasonable accommodation of conflicting policies that were committed to the agency's care by the statute, we should not disturb it unless it appears from the statute or its legislative history that the accommodation is not one that Congress would have sanctioned." United States v. Shimer, 367 U.S. 374, 382, 383 (1961).

In light of these well-settled principles it is clear that the Court of Appeals misconceived the nature of its role in reviewing the regulations at issue. Once it determined, after its own examination of the legislation, that Congress did not actually have an intent regarding the applicability of the bubble concept to the permit program, the question before it was not whether in its view the concept is "inappropriate" in the general context of a program designed to improve air quality, but whether the Administrator's view that it is appropriate in the context of this particular program is a reasonable one. Based on the examination of the legislation and its history which follows, we agree with the Court of Appeals that Congress did not have a specific intention on the applicability of the bubble concept in these cases, and conclude that the

---

3. The court need not conclude that the agency construction was the only one it permissibly could have adopted to uphold the construction, or even the reading the court would have reached if the question initially had arisen in a judicial proceeding.

EPA's use of that concept here is a reasonable policy choice for the agency to make.

III

[The Court then reviewed the legislative history at length, remarking that the issue before it concerned "one phrase" of a "small portion" of "a lengthy, detailed, technical, complex, and comprehensive response to a major social issue," the Clean Air Act Amendments of 1977, that in turn was only part of a much larger statutory scheme under EPA's administration. "The legislative history of the portion of the 1977 Amendments dealing with nonattainment areas," it remarked, "does not contain any specific comment on the 'bubble concept' or the question whether a plantwide definition of a stationary source is permissible under the permit program. It does, however, plainly disclose that in the permit program Congress sought to accommodate the conflict between the economic interest in permitting capital improvements to continue and the environmental interest in improving air quality."

[Turning to the administrative history of implementation, the Court noted that EPA had at first proposed interpretations like that under challenge.]

VI

In August 1980, however, the EPA adopted a regulation that, in essence, applied the basic reasoning of the Court of Appeals in this case. The EPA took particular note of the two then-recent Court of Appeals decisions, which had created the bright-line rule that the bubble concept should be employed in a program designed to maintain air quality but not in one designed to enhance air quality. Relying heavily on those cases, EPA adopted a dual definition of "source" for nonattainment areas that required a permit whenever a change in either the entire plant, or one of its components, would result in a significant increase in emissions even if the increase was completely offset by reductions elsewhere in the plant. . . .

In 1981 a new administration took office and initiated a "Government-wide reexamination of regulatory burdens and complexities." In the context of that review, the EPA reevaluated the various arguments that had been advanced in connection with the proper definition of the term "source" and concluded that the term should be given the same definition in both nonattainment areas and PSD [preventing significant deterioration] areas.

In explaining its conclusion, the EPA first noted that the definitional issue was not squarely addressed in either the statute or its legislative history and therefore that the issue involved an agency "judgment as how to best carry out the Act." It then set forth several reasons for concluding that the plantwide definition was more appropriate. . . .

VII

. . .

Based on our examination of the legislative history, we agree with the Court of Appeals that it is unilluminating. The general remarks pointed to by respondents "were obviously not made with this narrow issue in mind and they cannot be said to demonstrate a Congressional desire . . . ." Jewell Ridge Coal Corp. v. Mine Workers, 325 U.S. 161, 168–169 (1945) . . . . We find that the legislative history as a whole is silent on the precise issue before us. It is, however, consistent with the view that the EPA should have broad discretion in implementing the policies of the 1977 Amendments.

More importantly, that history plainly identifies the policy concerns that motivated the enactment; the plantwide definition is fully consistent with one of those concerns—the allowance of reasonable economic growth—and, whether or not we believe it most effectively implements the other, we must recognize that the EPA has advanced a reasonable explanation for its conclusion that the regulations serve the environmental objectives as well. Indeed, its reasoning is supported by the public record developed in the rulemaking process, as well as by certain private studies.[4]

Our review of the EPA's varying interpretations of the word "source"—both before and after the 1977 Amendments—convince us that the agency primarily responsible for administering this important legislation has consistently interpreted it flexibly—not in a sterile textual vacuum, but in the context of implementing policy decisions in a technical and complex arena. The fact that the agency has from time to time changed its interpretation of the term source does not, as respondents argue, lead us to conclude that no deference should be accorded the agency's interpretation of the statute. An initial agency interpretation is not instantly carved in stone. On the contrary, the agency, to engage in informed rulemaking, must consider varying interpretations and the wisdom of its policy on a continuing basis. Moreover, the fact that the agency has adopted different definitions in different contexts adds force to the argument that the definition itself is flexible, particularly since Congress has never indicated any disapproval of a flexible reading of the statute.

Significantly, it was not the agency in 1980, but rather the Court of Appeals that read the statute inflexibly to command a plantwide definition for programs designed to maintain clean air and to forbid such a definition for programs designed to improve air quality. The distinction the court drew may well be a sensible one, but our labored

---

4. "Economists have proposed that economic incentives be substituted for the cumbersome administrative-legal framework. The objective is to make the profit and cost incentives that work so well in the marketplace work for pollution control. . . . [The 'bubble' or 'netting' concept] is a first attempt in this direction. By giving a plant manager flexibility to find the places and processes within a plant that control emissions most cheaply, pollution control can be achieved more quickly and cheaply." L. Lave & G. Omenn, Cleaning the Air: Reforming the Clean Air Act 28 (1981) (footnote omitted).

review of the problem has surely disclosed that it is not a distinction that Congress ever articulated itself, or one that the EPA found in the statute before the courts began to review the legislative work product. We conclude that it was the Court of Appeals, rather than Congress or any of the decisionmakers who are authorized by Congress to administer this legislation, that was primarily responsible for the 1980 position taken by the agency.

Policy

. . .

In this case, the Administrator's interpretation represents a reasonable accommodation of manifestly competing interests and is entitled to deference: the regulatory scheme is technical and complex, the agency considered the matter in a detailed and reasoned fashion, and the decision involves reconciling conflicting policies. Congress intended to accommodate both interests, but did not do so itself on the level of specificity presented by this case. Perhaps that body consciously desired the Administrator to strike the balance at this level, thinking that those with great expertise and charged with responsibility for administering the provision would be in a better position to do so; perhaps it simply did not consider the question at this level; and perhaps Congress was unable to forge a coalition on either side of the question, and those on each side decided to take their chances with the scheme devised by the agency. For judicial purposes, it matters not which of these things occurred.

Judges are not experts in the field, and are not part of either political branch of the Government. Courts must, in some cases, reconcile competing political interests, but not on the basis of the judges' personal policy preferences. In contrast, an agency to which Congress has delegated policy-making responsibilities may, within the limits of that delegation, properly rely upon the incumbent administration's views of wise policy to inform its judgments. While agencies are not directly accountable to the people, the Chief Executive is, and it is entirely appropriate for this political branch of the Government to make such policy choices—resolving the competing interests which Congress itself either inadvertently did not resolve, or intentionally left to be resolved by the agency charged with the administration of the statute in light of everyday realities.

When a challenge to an agency construction of a statutory provision, fairly conceptualized, really centers on the wisdom of the agency's policy, rather than whether it is a reasonable choice within a gap left open by Congress, the challenge must fail. In such a case, federal judges—who have no constituency—have a duty to respect legitimate policy choices made by those who do. The responsibilities for assessing the wisdom of such policy choices and resolving the struggle between competing views of the public interest are not judicial ones: "Our Constitution vests such responsibilities in the political branches." TVA v. Hill, 437 U.S. 153, 195 (1978).

. . . [R]eversed.

JUSTICE MARSHALL and JUSTICE REHNQUIST did not participate in the consideration or decision of these cases.

JUSTICE O'CONNOR did not participate in the decision of these cases.[5]

NOTES

(1) BOARD OF GOVERNORS, FEDERAL RESERVE SYSTEM V. DIMENSION FINANCIAL CORP., 106 S.Ct. 681 (1986) may serve as Packard to Chevron's Hearst. The Federal Reserve Board (FRB) had adopted a legislative rule extending its regulation of "banks" to institutions offering services like traditional checking accounts and commercial loans—but not quite. For example, checking accounts impose on banks a legal obligation to pay funds represented by a properly presented check; the look-alike NOW accounts are subject to a seldom-exercised right of the bank to require notice of withdrawal prior to presentation. The FRB's regulatory jurisdiction is limited to banks, as defined in a statutory provision that had been the subject of careful congressional attention and revision over the years: Section 2(c) of the Bank Holding Company Act defines "bank" as any institution "which (1) accepts deposits that the depositor has a legal right to withdraw on demand, and (2) engages in the business of making commercial loans." 12 U.S.C. § 1841(c). The FRB's rule, to reach these "non-bank banks," had redefined a "bank" as any institution that (1) accepts deposits that "as a matter of practice" are payable on demand and (2) engages in the business of making "any loan other than a loan to an individual for personal, family, household, or charitable purposes," including "the purchase of retail installment loans or commercial paper, certificates of deposit, bankers' acceptances, and similar money market instruments."

Overturning the regulation, Chief Justice Burger said for a unanimous Court, inter alia:

"By the 1966 amendments to § 2(c), Congress expressly limited the Act to regulation of institutions that accept deposits that 'the depositor has a legal right to withdraw on demand.' 12 U.S.C. § 1841(c). The Board would now define 'legal right' as meaning the same as 'a matter of practice.' But no amount of agency expertise—however sound may be the result—can make the words 'legal right' mean a right to do something 'as a matter of practice.' A *legal* right to withdraw on demand means just that: a right to withdraw deposits without prior notice or limitation. Institutions offering NOW accounts do not give the depositor a legal right to withdraw on demand; rather, the institution itself retains the ultimate legal right to require advance notice of withdrawal. The Board's definition of 'demand deposit,' therefore, is not an accurate or reasonable interpretation of § 2(c).

[A similar, slightly more complex, rebuff was given to the effort to bring "commercial loan substitutes" within the statutory term "commercial loans."]

5. [Ed.] For insightful analysis and perspective, see J. Delong, The Bubble Case, Ad.Law News, Fall 1984, 1.

"Unable to support its new definitions on the plain language of § 2(c), the Board contends that its new definitions fall within the 'plain purpose' of the Bank Holding Company Act. Nonbank banks must be subject to regulation, the Board insists, because 'a statute must be read with a view to the "policy of the legislation as a whole" and cannot be read to negate the plain purpose of the legislation.' The plain purpose of the legislation, the Board contends, is to regulate institutions 'functionally equivalent' to banks. . . .

"The 'plain purpose' of legislation, however, is determined in the first instance with reference to the plain language of the statute itself. Application of 'broad purposes' of legislation at the expense of specific provisions ignores the complexity of the problems Congress is called upon to address and the dynamics of legislative action. Congress may be unanimous in its intent to stamp out some vague social or economic evil; however, because its Members may differ sharply on the means for effectuating that intent, the final language of the legislation may reflect hard fought compromises. Invocation of the 'plain purpose' of legislation at the expense of the terms of the statute itself takes no account of the processes of compromise and, in the end, prevents the effectuation of congressional intent.

"Without doubt there is much to be said for regulating financial institutions that are the functional equivalent of banks. NOW accounts have much in common with traditional payment-on-demand checking accounts; indeed we recognize that they generally serve the same purpose. Rather than defining 'bank' as an institution that offers the functional equivalent of banking services, however, Congress defined with specificity certain transactions that constitute banking subject to regulation. The statute may be imperfect, but the Board has no power to correct flaws that it perceives in the statute it is empowered to administer. Its rulemaking power is limited to adopting regulations to carry into effect the will of Congress as expressed in the statute.[1] . . . "

How could you reconcile *this* unanimous expression of views about the role of the Court in the process of statutory interpretation, and the significance of the political processes of Congress in legislating, with the views unanimously expressed two years earlier in Chevron?

(2) C. DIVER, STATUTORY INTERPRETATION IN THE ADMINISTRATIVE STATE, 133 U.Pa.L.Rev. 549, 562 * (1985): ". . . [T]he prevailing judicial orthodoxy . . . consists of three tenets:

1. The process of effectuating Congressional intent at times may yield anomalies. In TVA v. Hill, 437 U.S. 153 (1978), for example, we were confronted with the explicit language of a statute that in application produced a curious result. Noting that nothing prohibited Congress from passing unwise legislation, we upheld the enforcement of the statute as Congress had written it. Congress swiftly granted relief to the petitioner in Hill; but did so in a fashion that could not have been tailored by the courts. See Pub.L. 95–632, § 5, 92 Stat. 3760.

* Copyright © 1985 by the University of Pennsylvania Law Review. Reprinted with permission.

"(1) Only if the statute's 'plain' meaning (as illuminated by judicial examination of its text and history) fails to solve the riddle is an inquiry into deference appropriate.[2]

"(2) The decision whether to grant deference depends on various attributes of the agency's legal authority and functions and of the administrative interpretation at issue.[3]

"(3) The consequence of granting deference is to convert the court's task from determining whether the contested interpretation is correct to determining whether it is 'reasonable.' "

(3) Chevron raises several questions. It has the attraction of simplifying matters: once one finds a statute reveals "no intent" on a substantive question, defer to the agency—presumably without needing to consider the various factors brought out by Professor Diver. But why should "no intent" be read as an intent to leave the matter to the agency? Isn't Congress entitled to assume, when it has difficulty in treating a question, that on a matter of statutory construction the courts will defer much, little or none depending on what is the precise question and whether—in light of various factors—court or agency should decide? If the Chevron approach is followed, and if one assumes that in our increasingly complex world there likely will be increasing difficulty in answering questions or indicating preferences when initially drafting a statute, how should Congress respond? Should it make up its mind more often? Explicitly assign resolution of "no-intent" questions *always* to the courts? Leave these matters to the agencies? Or prefer a multi-factor analysis under judicial administration? Is it

2. [Ed.] As Professor Diver notes, despite repeated mention of the "plain meaning" rule, the Court neither takes statutory words narrowly nor out of context, and rarely if ever ignores legislative history. See 133 U.Pa. at 556. The "rule," if there ever was one, has long been dead except as an empty phrase. See A. Murphy, Old Maxims Never Die: The "Plain-Meaning Rule" and Statutory Interpretation in the "Modern" Federal Courts, 75 Colum.L.Rev. 1299 (1975); see also P. Wald, Some Observations on the Use of Legislative History in the 1981 Supreme Court Term, 68 Iowa L.Rev. 195 (1983). Nonetheless, as the previous note case illustrates, it does treat language as having a determinate *range* of possible meaning. See also United States v. Locke, 471 U.S. 84 (1985) ("prior to December 31" not met by December 31 filing.)

3. A partial list of the factors cited by the Court would include: (1) whether the agency construction was rendered contemporaneously with the statute's passage, see, e.g., Norwegian Nitrogen Prods. Co. v. United States, 288 U.S. 294, 315 (1933); (2) whether the agency's construction is of longstanding application, see, e.g., NLRB v. Bell Aerospace Co. 416 U.S. 267, 275 (1974); (3) whether the agency has maintained its position consistently (even if infrequently),

see, e.g., Haig v. Agee, 453 U.S. 280, 293 (1981); (4) whether the public has relied on the agency's interpretation, see, e.g., Udall v. Tallman, 380 U.S. 1, 18 (1965); (5) whether the interpretation involves a matter of "public controversy," see, e.g., United States v. Rutherford, 442 U.S. 544 (1979) [whether Food and Drug Administration could bar use of Laetrile by terminally ill cancer patients, as a "new drug" neither approved under nor exempt from statute]; (6) whether the interpretation is based on "expertise" or involves a "technical and complex" subject, see, e.g., Aluminum Co. of Am. v. Central Lincoln People's Util. Dist., [467 U.S. 380 (1984)]; (7) whether the agency has rulemaking authority, see, e.g., FCC v. National Citizens Comm. for Broadcasting, 436 U.S. 775, 793 (1978); (8) whether agency action is necessary to set the statute in motion, see, e.g., Ford Motor Co. v. Milhollin, 444 U.S. 555, 565–66 (1980); (9) whether Congress was aware of the agency interpretation and failed to repudiate it, see, e.g., Zemel v. Rusk, 381 U.S. 1, 11 (1965); and (10) whether the agency has expressly addressed the application of the statute to its proposed action, see, e.g., Investment Co. Inst. v. Camp, 401 U.S. 617, 627–28 (1971).

proper for the courts—do they even have the right?—to tell Congress
that except to the extent it indicates intent, it should not expect the
courts to oversee the agencies' constructions?

(4) STATE, DEPT. OF INSURANCE V. INSURANCE SERVICES OFFICE, 434 So.
2d 908 (Fla. 1st DCA 1983) contained an opinion suggestive of one kind
of reason why the last question might be answered in the affirmative.
The case involved an appeal from an order of the centralized Division of
Administrative Hearings holding invalid an Insurance Department rule
implementing a statute providing this: "No insurer shall, with respect
to premiums charged for automobile insurance, unfairly discriminate
solely on the basis of age, sex, marital status, or scholastic achievement." The statute provided also that in promulgating rules identifying prohibited practices, the Department "may not enact a rule which
shall enlarge upon or extend" the statute. The three-judge panel
divided, two agreeing that the Department's rule invalidly extended the
statute, and the chief judge dissenting at length that there were 12
reasonable constructions of "unfairly discriminate," some involving no
"extension," and so proper deference called for upholding the Department's construction. He said: "At this stage in the maturity of our
judicial system, a modest disclaimer of judicial hegemony in matters of
statutory interpretation would seem to be required by a decent respect
for the executive as a coordinate branch of government, made more
responsive to the public, and more disciplined, by APA processes. But
if neither those considerations nor our decisions endorsing them convince us of that, we should be persuaded to that end by the needs of our
own institution, this court, for adjudicative processes that operate with
fair uniformity. For as we judges grow more numerous, forty-six and
counting in the appellate courts of Florida, and twelve on this court
alone, the folly of three judges or a majority of them declaring the 'one
right answer' to a question of statutory interpretation, when the
executive branch has spoken another permissible answer through
rulemaking, becomes more evident and more dangerous. . . .

"[T]o a great but incalculable degree, the numerousness of judges
from whom the decisive judgment must come adds to the problem of
legitimacy. Consider first the array of *twelve permissible interpretations* [of the statute]:

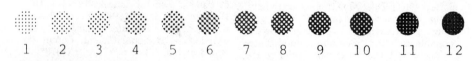

"Consider next the array of *twelve judges,* each conscientious and
fully informed, but each with different perceptions in matters of choice:

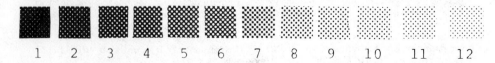

"If my colleagues are judges 2 and 5, say, and I am judge 10, then their judgment calls for *Sixth* override mine for *Tenth*. But if the panel were instead judges 2, 10 and 11, would the same 'one right answer' prevail?

"As the number of judges increases on a court that decides in shifting panels of three, certain destructive tendencies, among them the fragmentation of principle and the ascendancy of preference, are set loose. Remembering Edinburgh's court of session, which he saw abolished in the year 1808 after three centuries as a Scottish institution, Henry Cockburn wrote:

> [I]t was extinguished at last by defects which no modern tribunal could survive. Its radical defect was its numerousness. A bench of fifteen judges can only be 'a learned crowd.'

". . . These perils of judicial numerousness are by no means peculiar to Scotland, or to courts of the early 1800's. [Judge Tjoflat] of the multifarious and recently bifurcated United States court of appeals for the fifth circuit recently commented upon the modern perils of numerousness of appellate judges: 'This tremendous potential for instability in the rule of law creates a great deal of litigation. So you have a situation where you add judges to dispose of more cases, and at the court of appeals level, at least, the new judges may well cause more litigation than they can terminate.'

"For this court of twelve, the proper response to the modern perils of numerousness is neither bifurcation nor handwringing; rather, the proper response is coherence, which is to be achieved only by sublimating preference to principle and, in cases of this sort, by acknowledging the rightful power of the executive branch to select the most propitious of several permissible statutory interpretations, broadly conceived. In this we not only acknowledge the executive's rightful place in government, depending on the legislature and the electorate to apply corrective forces where necessary. By our deference we also resist the seductive notion, fatal to a court of many judges, that our individual judgment calls, the small preferences of each of us, are infallible." 434 So.2d at 927–29.

(5) Here are four excerpts from the Courts of Appeals, expressing further thoughts on factors judges might employ in policing a sophisticated allocation of responsibility between agency and court:

(i) HI-CRAFT CLOTHING CO. v. NLRB, 660 F.2d 910, 915–16 (3d Cir. 1981): (1) Whether the issue falls outside the agency's area "and is one in which the courts have a special competence, i.e., the common law or the constitutional law."; (2) "When the agency diet is food for the courts on a regular basis, there is little reason for judges to subordinate their own competence to administrative 'expertness.' For example, the issues in social security disability cases are hardly unfamiliar to judges who try or review personal injury tort cases on a regular basis. Recognition that an agency is not the exclusive repository of technical expertise may, in part, account for the Supreme Court's reluctance on occasion to accept the SEC's interpretation of the Securities Acts, a field in which the courts are often the forum for disputes between private litigants." (3) "Another important facet of administrative interpretation comes to the fore when the agency construes its own authorization statute. There the Court has been less inclined to be influenced by administrative constructions. . . . When the agency has participated in the legislative activity leading to its authorization, generally more respect will be accorded the administrative interpretation."

(ii) BETHLEHEM STEEL CORP. v. EPA, 723 F.2d 1303, 1309 (7th Cir. 1983): "[W]here a statute strikes a political balance but administration of the statute is entrusted to an agency that may not embody that balance, it is dangerous to defer automatically to the agency's view. An agency that may be dominated by one faction in the legislative struggle that led to enactment of a compromise is not authorized to hand that faction a victory that was denied it in the legislative arena through the efforts of another faction. The court must enforce the compromise, not the maximum position of one of the interest groups among which the compromise was struck."

(iii) MAYBURG v. SECRETARY OF HHS, 740 F.2d 100, 105–7 (1st Cir. 1984): "[W]e must ask *why* courts should ever defer, or give special weight, to an agency's interpretation of a statute's meaning. And, here there are at least two types of answers. : . . First, one might argue that specialized agencies, at least sometimes, know better than the courts what Congress actually intended the words of the statute to mean. Thus, in Skidmore v. Swift [supra p. 392].

"Second, a court might give special weight to an agency's interpretation of a statute because Congress intended it to do just that. . . . But, if Congress is silent, courts may still infer . . . by asking what a sensible legislator would have expected given the statutory circumstances. The less important the question of law, the more interstitial its character, the more closely related to the everyday administration of the statute and to the agency's (rather than the court's) administrative or substantive expertise, the less likely it is that Congress (would have) 'wished' or 'expected' the courts to remain indifferent to the agency's views. Conversely, the larger the question, the more its answer is likely to clarify or stabilize a broad area of law, the more likely Congress intended the courts to decide the question themselves."

(iv) NATURAL RESOURCES DEFENSE COUNCIL v. EPA, 725 F.2d 761, 767 (D.C.Cir.1984): "[T]he case law under the [APA] has not crystallized around a single doctrinal formulation which captures the extent to which courts should defer to agency interpretations of law. Instead, two 'opposing platitudes' exert countervailing 'gravitational pulls' on the law. At one pole stands the maxim that courts should defer to 'reasonable' agency interpretative positions, see Udall v. Tallman, 380 U.S. 1 (1965), a maxim increasingly prevalent in recent decisions. . . . Pulling in the other direction is the principle that courts remain the final arbiters of statutory meaning; . . . that principle, too, is embossed with recent approval. See e.g., FEC v. Democratic Senatorial Campaign Comm., 454 U.S. 27, 32 (1981)."

FORD MOTOR CREDIT CO. v. MILHOLLIN
Supreme Court of the United States, 1980.
444 U.S. 555.

MR. JUSTICE BRENNAN delivered the opinion of the Court. The issue for decision in this case is whether the Truth in Lending Act (TILA), 82 Stat. 146, as amended, 15 U.S.C. § 1601 et seq., requires that the existence of an acceleration clause always be disclosed on the face of a credit agreement. The Federal Reserve Board [FRB] staff has consistently construed the statute and regulations as imposing no such uniform requirement. Because we believe that a high degree of deference to this administrative interpretation is warranted, we hold that TILA does not mandate a general rule of disclosure for acceleration clauses.

I

The [respondents] in this case purchased automobiles from various dealers, financing their purchases through standard retail installment contracts that were assigned to petitioner Ford Motor Credit Co. (FMCC), a finance company. Each contract provided that respondents were to pay a precomputed finance charge. As required by TILA and [FRB] Regulation Z, which implements the Act, the front page of each contract disclosed and explained certain features of the agreement. Among these disclosures was a paragraph informing the buyer that he

> may prepay his obligation under this contract in full at any time prior to maturity of the final installment hereunder, and, if he does so, shall receive a rebate of the unearned portion of the Finance Charge computed under the sum of the digits method. . . .

The face of the contract also stated that temporary default on a particular installment would result in a predetermined delinquency charge. Not mentioned on the disclosure page was a clause in the body of the contract giving the creditor a right to accelerate payment of the entire debt upon the buyer's default.[1]

[The respondents won in the district court and the Ninth Circuit affirmed on the narrow ground that under Regulation Z, "[t]he creditor must disclose whether a rebate of unearned interest will be made upon acceleration and also disclose the method by which the amount of unearned interest will be computed if the debt is accelerated." In so holding, that court rejected a contrary FRB interpretation with which five other courts of appeals had agreed.]

---

1. "In the event Buyer defaults in any payment . . . Seller shall have the right to declare all amounts due or to be- come due hereunder to be immediately due and payble. . . . "

II

[TILA] has the broad purpose of promoting "the informed use of credit" by assuring "meaningful disclosure of credit terms" to consumers. [The Act's principal means were disclosure and uniformity for methods of determining charges.] Because of their complexity and variety, however, credit transactions defy exhaustive regulation by a single statute. Congress therefore delegated expansive authority to the [FRB] to elaborate and expand the legal framework governing commerce in credit. Mourning v. Family Publications Service, Inc., 411 U.S. 356 (1973). The Board executed its responsibility by promulgating Regulation Z, 12 CFR part 226 (1979), which at least partly fills the statutory gaps. Even Regulation Z, however, cannot speak explicitly to every credit disclosure issue. At the threshold, therefore, interpretation of TILA and Regulation Z demands an examination of their express language; absent a clear expression, it becomes necessary to consider the implicit character of the statutory scheme. For the reasons following we conclude that the issue of acceleration disclosure is not governed by clear expression in the statute or regulation, and that it is appropriate to defer to the [FRB] and staff in determining what resolution of that issue is implied by [TILA].

Respondents have advanced two theories to buttress their claim that the Act and regulation expressly mandate disclosure of acceleration clauses. In the District Court, they contended that acceleration clauses were comprehended by the general statutory prescription that a creditor shall disclose "default, delinquency, or similar charges payable in the event of late payments," 15 U.S.C. §§ 1638(a)(9), 1639(a)(7), and were included within the provision of Regulation Z requiring disclosure of the "amount, or method of computing the amount, of any default, delinquency, or similar charges payable in the event of late payments," 12 CFR § 226.8(b)(4) (1979). Before this Court, respondents follow the Court of Appeals in arguing that 12 CFR § 226.8(b)(7) may be the source of an obligation to disclose procedures governing the rebate of unearned finance charges that accrue under acceleration. That section commands

> [i]dentification of the method of computing any unearned portion of the finance charge in the event of prepayment in full of an obligation which includes precomputed finance charges and a statement of the amount or method of computation of any charge that may be deducted from the amount of any rebate of such unearned finance charge that will be credited to an obligation or refunded to the customer.

A fair reading of the pertinent provisions does not sustain respondents' contention that acceleration clauses are within their terms.

An acceleration clause cannot be equated with a "default, delinquency, or similar charg[e]," subject to disclosure under 15 U.S.C. §§ 1638(a)(9), 1639(a)(7), and 12 CFR § 226.8(b)(4). The prerogative of acceleration affords the creditor a mechanism for collecting the outstanding portion of a debt on which there has been a partial default. In itself, acceleration entails no monetary penalty, although a creditor may independently impose such a penalty, for example, by failing to rebate unearned finance charges. A "default, delinquency, or similar *charg[e]*," on the other hand, self-evidently refers to a specific assessable sum. Thus, within the trade, delinquency charges are understood to be "the *compensation* a creditor receives on a precomputed contract for the debtor's delay in making timely installment payments," 1 CCH Consumer Credit Guide ¶¶ 4230, 4231 (1977) (emphasis added). Acceleration is not compensatory; a creditor accelerates to avoid further delay by demanding immediate payment of the outstanding debt.

The language employed in TILA §§ 1638(a)(9) and 1639(a)(7), and in 12 CFR § 226.8(b)(4) (1979), confirms the interpretation of "charges" as specific penalty sums. The statutory provisions speak of "charges *payable* in the event of late payments." (Emphasis added.) Even if one considers the burdensomeness of acceleration as a form of "charge" upon the debtor, it would hardly make sense to speak of that burden as "payable" to the creditor. Similarly Regulation Z orders disclosure of the "*amount, or method of computing the amount,* of any default, delinquency, or similar charges. . . . " (Emphasis added.) That command has no sensible application to the remedy of acceleration. In short, we would have to stretch these provisions beyond their obvious limits to construe them as a mandate for the disclosure of acceleration clauses.[2]

The prepayment rebate disclosure regulation, 12 CFR § 226.8(b)(7) (1979), also fails to afford direct support for an invariable specific acceleration disclosure rule [and] squares with the position of the [FRB] staff that specific disclosure of acceleration rebate policy is only necessary when that policy varies from the custom with respect to voluntary prepayment rebates. FRB Official Staff Interpretation No. FC–0054, 12 CFR part 226 Appendix, p. 627 (1979).

III

Notwithstanding the absence of an express statutory mandate that acceleration procedures be invariably disclosed, the Court of Appeals has held that the "creditor must [always] disclose whether a rebate of unearned interest will be made upon acceleration and also disclose the method by which the amount of unearned interest will be computed if the debt is accelerated." In so deciding, the Court of Appeals explicitly rejected the view of the [FRB] staff that the right of acceleration need *not* be disclosed, and that rebate practice under acceleration must be disclosed only if it differs from the creditor's rebate policy with respect to voluntary prepayment. FRB Official Staff Interpretation No. FC–0054, supra; see FRB Public Information Letter No. 851, [1974–1977 Transfer Binder] CCH Consumer Credit Guide ¶ 31,173; FRB Public

---

2. Seven of the Courts of Appeals, including that for the Ninth Circuit, have refused to treat acceleration *simpliciter* as a "charge" within 15 U.S.C. § 1638(a)(9) and 12 CFR § 226.8(b)(4) (1979).

Information Letter No. 1208, id., ¶ 31,647; FRB Public Information Letter No. 1324, 5 CCH Consumer Credit Guide ¶ 31,827 (1979).[3] Rather, [the Court of Appeals] declared that it would "choose the direction that makes more sense to us in trying to achieve the congressional purpose of providing meaningful disclosure to the debtor about the costs of his borrowing."

It is a commonplace that courts will further legislative goals by filling the interstitial silences within a statute or a regulation. Because legislators cannot foresee all eventualities, judges must decide unanticipated cases by extrapolating from related statutes or administrative provisions. But legislative silence is not always the result of a lack of prescience; it may instead betoken permission or, perhaps, considered abstention from regulation. In that event, judges are not accredited to supersede Congress or the appropriate agency by embellishing upon the regulatory scheme. Accordingly, caution must temper judicial creativity in the face of legislative or regulatory silence.

At the very least, that caution requires attentiveness to the views of the administrative entity appointed to apply and enforce a statute. And deference is especially appropriate in the process of interpreting [TILA] and Regulation Z. Unless demonstrably irrational, [FRB] staff opinions construing the Act or Regulation should be dispositive for several reasons.

The Court has often repeated the general proposition that considerable respect is due " 'the interpretation given [a] statute by the officers or agency charged with its administration.' " Zenith Radio Corp. v. United States, 437 U.S. 443, 450 (1978), quoting Udall v. Tallman, 380 U.S. 1, 16 (1965). An agency's construction of its own regulations has been regarded as especially due that respect. See Bowles v. Seminole Rock Co., 325 U.S. 410, 413–414 (1945) ["the ultimate criterion is the administrative interpretation, which becomes of controlling weight unless it is plainly erroneous or inconsistent with the regulation."]. This traditional acquiescence in administrative expertise is particularly apt under TILA, because the [FRB] has played a pivotal role in "setting [the statutory] machinery in motion. . . . " Norwegian Nitrogen Products Co. v. United States, 288 U.S. 294, 315 (1933). As we emphasized in Mourning, Congress delegated broad administrative lawmaking power to the [FRB] when it framed TILA. The Act is best construed by those who gave it substance in promulgating regulations thereunder.[4]

---

3. [T]he Court of Appeals spurned these administrative opinions as a source of interpretive guidance on the ground that the several letters were "conflicting signals." As we read the Staff Opinion and Letters, however, they are fundamentally consistent, if somewhat inartfully drafted. The staff's position in each appears to be that separate disclosure of acceleration rebate practices is unnecessary when those practices parallel voluntary prepayment rebate policy. On the other hand, where acceleration rebates are less than voluntary pre-

payment rebates, acceleration policy must be separately explained under § 226.8(b)(4) and, perhaps as well, under § 226.8(b)(7). Neither the Opinion nor the Letters suggest that acceleration rebate policy must be separately disclosed in all instances.

4. To be sure, the administrative interpretations proffered in this case were issued by the Federal Reserve staff rather than the Board. But to the extent that deference to administrative views is bottomed on respect for agency expertise, it is

Furthermore, Congress has specifically designated the [FRB] and staff as the primary source for interpretation and application of truth-in-lending law. Because creditors need sure guidance through the "highly technical" [TILA], S.Rep. No. 93–278, p. 13 (1973), legislators have twice acted to promote reliance upon Federal Reserve pronouncements. In 1974, TILA was amended to provide creditors with a defense from liability based upon good-faith compliance with a "rule, regulation, or interpretation" of the [FRB] itself. 15 U.S.C. § 1640(f). The explicit purpose of the amendment was to relieve the creditor of the burden of choosing "between the Board's construction of the Act and the creditor's own assessment of how a court may interpret the Act." S.Rep. No. 93–278, supra, at 13. The same rationale prompted a further change in the statute in 1976, authorizing a liability defense for "conformity with any interpretation or approval by an official or employee of the Federal Reserve System duly authorized by the Board to issue such interpretations or approvals. . . . " § 1640(f); see 122 Cong.Rec. 2836 (1976).[5]

The enactment and expansion of § 1640(f) has significance beyond the express creation of a good-faith immunity.[6] That statutory provision signals an unmistakable congressional decision to treat administrative rulemaking and interpretation under TILA as authoritative. Moreover, language in the legislative history evinces a decided preference for resolving interpretive issues by uniform administrative decision, rather than piecemeal through litigation. Courts should honor that congressional choice. Thus, while not abdicating their ultimate

unrealistic to draw a radical distinction between opinions issued under the imprimatur of the Board and those submitted as official staff memoranda. . . . At any rate, it is unnecessary to explore the Board/staff difference at length, because Congress has conferred special status upon official staff interpretations. See 15 U.S.C. § 1640(f). . . . [That section: "No provision of this section . . . imposing any liability shall apply to any act done or omitted in good faith in conformity with any rule, regulation, or interpretation thereof by the Board or in conformity with any interpretation or approval by an official or employee of the Federal Reserve System duly authorized by the Board to issue such interpretations or approvals under such procedures as the Board may prescribe therefor, notwithstanding that after such act or omission has occurred, such rule, regulation, interpretation, or approval is amended, rescinded, or determined by judicial or other authority to be invalid for any reason."]

5. Title 12 CFR § 226.1(d) (1979) authorizes the issuance of official staff interpretations that trigger the application of § 1640(f). Official interpretations are published in the Federal Register, and opportunity for public comment may be request-

ed. 12 CFR § 226.1(d). Unofficial interpretations have no special status under § 1640(f). ["Unofficial staff interpretations, called 'Public Information Letters,' were issued at the discretion of the staff. Official staff interpretations, on the other hand, were issued only pursuant to specified procedures, which included an opportunity for public comment on the proposed interpretation. These FRB, official staff, and unofficial staff interpretations constituted a formidable body of material: between 1968 and 1980, the Board and its staff issued more than 60 Board Interpretations, 160 official staff interpretations, and 1300 unofficial staff interpretations." Greenfield, Consumer Transactions (1983), 128.]

6. Although FMCC claims that its pre-1976 disclosure comported with Official Staff Interpretations No. FC–0054 (issued in 1977), it has not argued before this Court that it is entitled to the immunity afforded by the 1976 amendment to § 1640(f). We need not decide, therefore, whether the 1976 amendment may be invoked with respect to contracts formed before its enactment or whether conformity with a subsequently issued official staff interpretation constitutes "compliance" within the terms of § 1640(f).

judicial responsibility to determine the law, cf. generally SEC v. Chenery Corp., 318 U.S. 80, 92–94 (1943), judges ought to refrain from substituting their own interstitial lawmaking for that of the Federal Reserve, so long as the latter's lawmaking is not irrational.

Finally, wholly apart from jurisprudential considerations or congressional intent, deference to the Federal Reserve is compelled by necessity; a court that tries to chart a true course to the Act's purpose embarks upon a voyage without a compass when it disregards the agency's views. The concept of "meaningful disclosure" that animates TILA cannot be applied in the abstract. *Meaningful* disclosure does not mean *more* disclosure. Rather, it describes a balance between "competing considerations of complete disclosure . . . and the need to avoid [informational overload]." And striking the appropriate balance is an empirical process that entails investigation into consumer psychology and that presupposes broad experience with credit practices. Administrative agencies are simply better suited than courts to engage in such a process.

The [FRB] staff treatment of acceleration disclosure rationally accommodates the conflicting demands for completeness and for simplicity. In determining that acceleration rebate practices need be disclosed only when they diverge from other prepayment rebates practices, the Federal Reserve has adopted what may be termed a "bottom-line" approach: that the most important information in a credit purchase is that which explains differing net charges and rates. . . . Although the staff might have decided that acceleration rebates are so analytically distinct from identical voluntary prepayment rebates as to warrant separate disclosure, it was reasonable to conclude, alternatively, that ordinary consumers would be concerned chiefly about differing financial consequences. Faced with an apparent lacuna in the express prescriptions of TILA and Regulation Z, the Court of Appeals had no ground for displacing the Federal Reserve staff's expert judgment. . . .

Reversed and remanded.

MR. JUSTICE BLACKMUN, with whom THE CHIEF JUSTICE joins, concurring.

I join the Court's opinion but write separately because I do not fully agree . . . that the [FRB]'s approach to the disclosure of acceleration rebates is [as logical as] other alternatives it might have chosen. In particular . . . I think the interpretation adopted by the Fifth Circuit . . . which requires disclosure of the creditor's right to retain finance charges upon acceleration when it differs from the right to such charges upon prepayment, may prove to be a sounder and more durable application of the statute than the position currently adopted by the Board. Nevertheless, I agree with the Court that the Board's approach is reasonable. In order to uphold the Board's position, "we need not find that its construction is the only reasonable one, or even that it is the result we would have reached had the question arisen in the first instance in judicial proceedings." Udall v. Tallman, 380 U.S. 1, 16

(1965). Accordingly, I agree that the courts should not add to the disclosure obligations that the Board has outlined through its staff opinions.[7]

NOTES

(1) BATTERTON v. FRANCIS, 432 U.S. 416 (1977) involved the Health, Education and Welfare Secretary's regulation determining what constituted "unemployment" for purposes of eligibility for benefits under the Aid to Families with Dependent Children–Unemployed Fathers statute which said: "unemployment (as determined in accordance with standards prescribed by the Secretary). . . . " In the course of upholding the regulation (over four dissents arguing that the statute precluded the particular determination), the Court said:

"Ordinarily, administrative interpretations of statutory terms are given important but not controlling significance. This was the Court's approach, for example, when it had under consideration the question whether the term 'wages' in Title II of the Social Security Act included a backpay award [ordered by the NLRB]. Social Security Board v. Nierotko, 327 U.S. 358, 369 (1946).[1]

"Unlike the statutory term in Title II, however, Congress in § 407(a) expressly *delegated* to the Secretary the power to prescribe standards for determining what constitutes 'unemployment' for purposes of AFDC–UF eligibility. In a situation of this kind, Congress entrusts to the Secretary, rather than to the courts, the primary responsibility of interpreting the statutory term. In exercising that

---

7. [Ed.] "The original statute and regulations were quite complex. Compliance was exceptionally difficult, perhaps even impossible, and trivial violations resulted in substantial losses for creditors. So in 1980 Congress enacted the Truth-in-Lending Simplification and Improvement Act. The main reforms of this legislation are a reduction in the information creditors must disclose, a contraction of civil liability for failure to disclose the required information, and a command to the FRB to promulgate model disclosure forms for creditors to use. . . .

"Pursuant to the 1980 amendments, the FRB comprehensively revised Regulation Z. In connection with this revision the staff adopted a lengthy "Official Staff Commentary" to replace the official Board Interpretations, the official staff interpretations, and the unofficial staff interpretations. . . . The Board and its staff contemplate the issuance of no further interpretations, relying instead on periodic revision of Regulation Z and the Official Staff Commentary." M. Greenfield, Consumer Transactions (1983), 128, 131.

1. The Court there explained:

'Administration, when it interprets a statute so as to make it apply to particular circumstances, acts as a delegate to the legislative power. Congress might have declared that "back pay" awards under the Labor Act should or should not be treated as wages. Congress might have delegated to the Social Security Board to determine what compensation paid by employers to employees should be treated as wages. Except as such interpretative power may be included in the agencies' administrative functions, Congress did neither. An agency may not finally decide the limits of its statutory power. That is a judicial function. Congress used a well understood word—"wages"—to indicate the receipts which were to govern taxes and benefits under the Social Security Act. There may be borderline payments to employees on which courts would follow administrative determination as to whether such payments were or were not wages under the act.

'We conclude, however, that the [Social Security] Board's interpretation of this statute to exclude back pay goes beyond the boundaries of administrative routine and the statutory limits.' 327 U.S., at 369 (footnote omitted).

responsibility, the Secretary adopts regulations with legislative effect. A reviewing court is not free to set aside those regulations simply because it would have interpreted the statute in a different manner.[2]
. . .

"The regulation at issue in this case is therefore entitled to more than mere deference or weight. It can be set aside only if the Secretary exceeded his statutory authority or if the regulation is 'arbitrary, capricious, an abuse of discretion, or otherwise not in accordance with law.' 5 U.S.C. §§ 706(2)(A), (C)."

(2) Should deference to agency constructions of their own regulations differ from statutory construction? The most frequently cited case is UDALL V. TALLMAN, 380 U.S. 1 (1965), involving the Interior Secretary's authority to issue oil and gas leases under an Executive Order and the Secretary's own 1948 order saying which wildlife refuge lands could be developed for oil and gas. After much Departmental consideration and House and Senate committees' rejection of a bill to halt such leasing, in 1956 leases were issued after another House committee hearing had culminated in the committee chairman's informing the Department that the committee unanimously approved issuance. Subsequently, when a statute was passed to broaden the Secretary's authority to issue leases in a related area, the Senate Report noted the issuance of the leases at issue in this case. By the time of this case, 700,000 acres had been leased and tens of millions of dollars spent in development. Upholding the Secretary's construction of the Executive Order and his own 1948 order and thus upholding the leases, the Court said:

"When faced with a problem of statutory construction, this Court shows great deference to the interpretation given the statute by the officers or agency charged with its administration. 'To sustain the Commission's application of this statutory term, we need not find that its construction is the only reasonable one, or even that it is the result we would have reached had the question arisen in the first instance in judicial proceedings.' See also e.g., Gray v. Powell, 314 U.S. 402. 'Particularly is this respect due when the administrative practice at stake "involves a contemporaneous construction of a statute by the men charged with the responsibility of setting its machinery in motion, of making the parts work efficiently and smoothly while they are yet untried and new."' Power Reactor Development Co. v. International Union of Electricians, 367 U.S. 396, 408. When the construction of an

---

2. Legislative, or substantive, regulations are 'issued by an agency pursuant to statutory authority and . . . implement the statute, as for example, the proxy rules issued by the Securities and Exchange Commission. . . . Such rules have the force and effect of law.' U.S. Dept. of Justice, Attorney General's Manual on the Administrative Procedure Act 30 n. 3 (1947).

By way of contrast, a court is not required to give effect to an interpretative regulation. Varying degrees of deference are accorded to administrative interpretations, based on such factors as the timing and consistency of the agency's position, and the nature of its expertise. See General Electric Co. v. Gilbert, 429 U.S. 125, 141–145 (1976); Morton v. Ruiz, 415 U.S. 199, 231–237 (1974); Skidmore v. Swift & Co. . . . . .

"Findings," in general usage, refers to conclusions about the facts in controversy; "reasons" usually refers to the considerations of law or policy that led the agency to assign the stated consequences to the facts it had found. The 1981 Revised Model State Administrative Procedure Act, as proposed by the National Conference of Commissioners on Uniform State Laws, requires far more than its predecessor: Final orders in adjudications "must include, separately stated, findings of fact, conclusions of law, and policy reasons for the decision if it is an exercise of the agency's discretion, for all aspects of the order, including the remedy prescribed and, if applicable, the action taken on a petition for stay of effectiveness. Findings of fact, if set forth in language that is no more than mere repetition or paraphrase of the relevant provision of law, must be accompanied by a concise and explicit statement of the underlying facts of record to support the findings. . . . " § 4–215(c).[3] As if all this general statutory bombardment were not enough, innumerable particularly applicable statutes specify that findings must be stated by administrators who make decisions of one kind or another.

Presumably these sweeping commands are meant to accomplish something more than mere formalization: American society, struggling to stay afloat in a sea of words, will not gain from adding whereases and hereinbefore-mentioneds. Judge Henry Friendly has written that a statement of findings and reasons is "almost essential if there is to be judicial review," and is "desirable on many other grounds. The necessity for justification is a powerful preventive of wrong decisions. The requirement also tends to effectuate intra-agency uniformity, and would be particularly important in this regard if the hearing board were composed of individuals drawn from outside the agency. A statement of reasons may even make a decision somewhat more acceptable to a losing claimant." [4]

(1) NEW JERSEY BELL TELEPHONE CO. v. COMMUNICATIONS WORKERS OF AMERICA, 5 N.J. 354, 75 A.2d 721 (1950). A New Jersey statute authorized the Governor to seize a public utility in event of a strike. The matters in dispute were then to be submitted to a Board of Arbitration which, after hearing, was to "make written findings of fact . . . and promulgate a written decision and order upon the . . . issues presented. . . . " The Board was to "base its findings of fact, decision and order upon the following factors: (1) The interests and welfare of the public. (2) Comparison of wages, hours and condition of employment . . . in similar or comparable work" and (3) "in industries in general and in public utilities in particular throughout the nation" and in New Jersey. (4) "The security and tenure of employment . . . in the industry." (5) Such other factors as are traditionally taken into consideration in making collective bargaining agreements or

interested person," § 555(e) requires that denial of the request, in whole or in part, must be followed by "prompt notice . . . accompanied by a brief statement of the grounds for denial." See p. 472 below.

See p. 472 below.

3. The 1961 Act's corresponding provision required that each decision in a contested case shall contain separately stated "findings of fact and conclusions of law," the findings of fact to "be accompanied by a concise and explicit statement of the underlying facts supporting the findings."

4. Some Kind of Hearing, 123 U.Pa.L. Rev. 1267, 1292 (1975).

arbitration decisions. "The findings of fact, decision and order of the board shall be made within thirty days after submission of the issues . . . and shall forthwith be filed by such board with the Governor. . . . "

A telephone strike led to seizure under the statute and ultimately to a hearing, and decision by a Board of Arbitration. The arbitrators awarded a wage increase of fifty cents. The arbitrators declared that they had been "impressed" by the fact that wage increases had been given since August 1946 to "large numbers of workers in industry in general . . . and public utilities in particular." As to the amounts of those increases, "we find guidance in the statistics furnished by the Bureau of Labor Statistics and the Bureau of National Affairs," as well as recent wage settlements affecting bus drivers in New Jersey and utility workers in New York. "Our conclusion is that wage increases are justified . . . in the amount of 50 cents. . . . " The quoted fragments do not constitute the totality of the "findings" made by the Board, but they fairly reflect the tone of the document. Would you find them sufficient?

The court set aside the award, saying that these findings do not embody "sufficient factual data for us to determine whether the Board's conclusions are predicated upon facts or speculation, and if upon facts, what facts." . . . Then the court quoted extensively from Saginaw Broadcasting Co. v. Federal Communications Commission, 96 F.2d 554, 559 (D.C.Cir.), cert. denied 305 U.S. 613 (1938), including this:

" 'The requirement that courts, and commissions acting in a quasi-judicial capacity, shall make findings of fact, is a means provided by Congress for guaranteeing that cases shall be decided according to the evidence and the law, rather than arbitrarily or from extra-legal considerations; and findings of fact serve the additional purpose, where provisions for review are made, of apprising the parties and the reviewing tribunal of the factual basis of the action of the court or commission, so that the parties and the reviewing tribunal may determine whether the case has been decided upon the evidence and the law or, on the contrary, upon arbitrary or extra-legal considerations. . . . The requirement of findings is thus far from a technicality. On the contrary, it is to insure against Star Chamber methods, to make certain that justice shall be administered according to the facts and law.' "

The New Jersey court remarked that the Board, which has alone been statutorily empowered to find facts in the complex and specialized field of employer-employee relations, had not made the essential findings upon which its conclusion supposedly rested. How then could the court perform its own task of review, ascertaining whether the findings were supported by substantial evidence and whether the Board, in making them, proceeded upon a correct legal theory? So the case had to be sent back to the Board of Arbitration for a better decision.

(2) ELITE DAIRY PRODUCTS, INC. v. TEN EYCK, 271 N.Y. 488, 3 N.E.2d 606 (1936). The Commissioner of Agriculture denied an application for a "license to purchase, handle, sell or distribute milk." Before the

denial a hearing had been had before a field employee of the Department of Agriculture and Markets. The statute stated that no license should be granted "unless the commissioner is satisfied that the applicant is qualified by character, experience, financial responsibility and equipment to properly conduct the proposed business, that the issuance of the license will not tend to a destructive competition in a market already adequately served, and that issuance of the license is in the public interest." *Held:* the order of denial must be annulled because no findings accompanied it, and the proceeding should be remitted to the commissioner for further proceedings. "The applicant is entitled to opportunity to challenge a determination against him. He is denied a right to engage in a business from which he may not be lawfully excluded if he complies with the conditions properly imposed by the Legislature and which must be applicable to all persons in similar situation. The conditions imposed by the Legislature are separable. Failure to show compliance with any one condition may be fatal. Then the applicant is entitled to findings which will show the particular matter determined against him. . . . Only after the commissioner has made findings of fact can the court decide whether the findings are sustained by the evidence and whether the Legislature had power to decree that facts so found should be ground for a denial of a license."

(3) SCHAFFER TRANSPORTATION CO. v. UNITED STATES, 355 U.S. 83 (1957). Schaffer, a motor carrier, had been authorized to transport granite from South Dakota quarries. The present case, a "leading case" in the field of findings, grew out of Schaffer's application for an extension of its "certificate of public necessity and convenience" to permit it to transport granite from Vermont quarries to various midwestern and southern states. The applicable statute provided in part as follows: ". . . a certificate shall be issued to any qualified applicant . . . if it is found that the applicant is fit, willing, and able properly to perform the service proposed . . . and that the proposed service, to the extent to be authorized by the certificate, is or will be required by the present or future public convenience and necessity; otherwise such application shall be denied.

A Division of the ICC reported that Schaffer's proposed service would be faster and cheaper than existing rail service for less-than-carload shipments. According to the Division's report, small shippers had suffered delays that would be diminished if truck delivery were available. "Then, too," the Division added, "the lack of truck service has impeded shippers' ability to increase their sales and expand their markets in this area. By use of the proposed service, certain other benefits also would accrue to the shippers or dealers. For example, the latter would be able to maintain lower inventories, receive their freight faster and more frequently, and, thus, be able better to meet erection deadlines, especially during the peak seasons. Furthermore, the amount of crating now necessary would be reduced with resultant savings in time and money."

These factors led the Division to approve Schaffer's application. But on the same record the full Commission (with four dissents) ordered that it be denied. The lower court sustained the Commission's denial of Schaffer's request for added authorization, but the Supreme Court reversed and directed remand to the Commission for further consideration. Chief Justice Warren acknowledged that the Commission had been given wide authority, but whatever the Commission chooses to do must be harmonious with the National Transportation Policy.

That policy, embodied in 54 Stat. 899, was *"to provide for fair and impartial regulation of all modes of transportation . . . , so administered as to recognize and preserve the inherent advantages of each,"* while at the same time promoting safe, cheap service, avoiding destructive competition, encouraging fair wages and good working conditions, washing behind the ears, and honoring thy father and thy mother—"all to the end of developing, coordinating and preserving a national transportation system by water, highway, and rail as well as other means, adequate to meet the needs of the commerce of the United States, of the Postal Service, and of the national defense."

In the present instance, the Commission's discussion of the case showed that the ICC focused its main attention upon the adequacy of the existing rail service (which the ICC thought reasonably good) and upon the motives of those who supported Schaffer's application whose main purpose, the Commission concluded, was "to obtain lower rates rather than improved service"). Nowhere, so far as the Court could discern, had the ICC evaluated the "inherent advantages" of the trucking service Schaffer wanted to provide. The Court thought that the Commission had failed to assess the "critical factor" of whether motor service would have an inherent advantage over rail service, even if the latter were (as the Commission had here found to be the case) "reasonably adequate." The adequacy of existing rail service is relevant but, as the Court said, must be examined comparatively, not as an isolated matter "when the interests of competition are being reconciled with the policy of maintaining a sound transportation system." The record "does not disclose the factors the Commission compared in concluding that existing rail service is 'reasonably adequate.' For example, the Commission has not determined whether there are benefits that motor service would provide which are not now being provided by the rail carriers, whether certification of a motor carrier would be 'unduly prejudicial' to the existing carriers, and whether on balance the public interest would be better served by additional competitive service. To reject a motor carrier's application on the bare conclusion that existing rail service can move the available traffic, without regard to the inherent advantages of the proposed service, would give one mode of transportation unwarranted protection from competition from others."

As to the second apparent ground of the ICC's decision—namely, that Schaffer's supporters were motivated by the prospect of obtaining lower rates—the Court thought that the Commission erred in discounting such testimony. The Chief Justice's opinion says: "The ability of one mode of transportation to operate with a rate lower than competing types of transportation is precisely the sort of 'inherent advantage' that the congressional policy requires the Commission to recognize. . . . [A] rate benefit attributable to differences between the two modes of transportation is an 'inherent advantage' of the competing type of carrier and cannot be ignored by the Commission."

What, then, should be the disposition of the case? Said the Chief Justice: "We do not minimize the complexity of the task the Commission faces in evaluating and balancing the numerous considerations that collectively determine where the public interest lies in a particular situation. And we do not suggest that the National Transportation Policy is a set of self-executing principles that inevitably point the way to a clear result in each case. On the contrary, those principles overlap and may conflict, and where this occurs, resolution is the task of the agency that is expert in the field." The Court cannot tell the Commission what its decision should be, but "the Commission must proceed further in light of what we have said."[5]

(4) Note how in the preceding case the issue of adequately detailed *findings of fact* has merged with the issue of *adequate explanation of reasoning or policy.*

As to the former, a general conclusion—similar to a jury's general verdict—does not suffice, according to USV Pharmaceutical Corp. v. Secretary of Health, Education, and Welfare, 466 F.2d 455 (D.C.Cir. 1972), because it does not enable a reviewing court "to determine whether the decision reached by an administrative agency follows as a matter of law from the facts stated as its basis, and whether the facts so found have any substantial support in the evidence." The finding the court believed to be deficient in that case was, simply, that a drug which purported to control serious blood disorders would not be approved for distribution because "there is a lack of substantial evidence that [it] will have the effect it . . . is represented to have under the conditions of use prescribed, recommended, or suggested in the labeling thereof."

Suppose, for a moment, that a drug distributor had been sued, in either a civil action for damages or in a criminal proceeding, for selling a worthless drug and had insisted, by way of defense, upon the drug's worth. Suppose further that a trial jury had brought in a general verdict against the seller. Would the verdict have been set aside because, on appeal, a court could not have related the evidence in the record to each of the particular segments of the broadly stated conclusion reached by the jurors? How significant is the fact that in the jury case the judge must have delivered a charge to the jury, telling the

---

5. [Ed.] Justice Frankfurter dissented because he thought that Congress had meant to allow the Commission to exercise "the widest areas for judgment," drawing upon its own "massive experience," and with very little room for judicial review in cases of this type. But even he stated that "the Court's decision may serve a useful purpose if it will lead the . . . Commission, despite its enormous volume of business, to a more detailed and illuminating formulation of the reasons for the judgment that it reaches even in that class of cases where Congress has relied on the Commission's discretion in enforcing the most broadly expressed congressional policy. Since the orders in such cases also fall under judicial scrutiny, it is desirable to insist upon precision in the findings and the reasons for the Commission's action."

jurors about the subordinate issues which they should consider (and, by hypothesis, do conscientiously consider) on the way to arriving at their ultimate verdict?[6]

Concerning adequate explanation of reasoning or policy, do you find persuasive the suggestion of Judge Harold Leventhal that the need for findings is substantially explained by the failures of the delegation doctrine? "If the nondelegation doctrine is a dim though still flickering star in the firmament of administrative law, the requirement of reasoned decisionmaking is a brilliant sun. Under that requirement an agency must develop standards and adhere to them without discrimination; it may reserve the latitude to change standards deliberately, but not to ignore them casually or haphazardly." H. Leventhal, Review of K. Davis, Administrative Law of the Seventies, 44 U.Chi.L.Rev. 260, 263 (1976).

Cases like Schaffer illustrate how an administrative agency's stated findings may reveal not an "arbitrary" judgment, but merely a mistaken judgment—"mistaken" in the sense that the agency has misconceived the significance of the statute it has attempted to apply, that is, has committed a substantial legal error. In this way, the reviewing court is able to perceive that an arguably correct administrative decision was in fact incorrect, in the sense that the agency had failed to do the entire job entrusted to its judgment. If the administrative conclusion had been stated baldly, without explanation of the reasons on which it was based, then the reviewing court would have been in no position to know whether or not the agency had turned its mind to all the issues the court now says should be taken into account.[7]

AND HOW ELABORATE MUST FINDINGS AND REASONS BE TO ACHIEVE ADEQUACY?

Statutory requirements like the Administrative Procedure Act commonly seem to demand of agency opinion writers a compulsive attention to detail. One hundred printed pages to show "findings and conclusions, and the reasons and basis therefor, on *all* the material issues of fact, law or discretion presented" is a not uncommon, if sometimes apparently unread, consequence.[1]

---

6. The possible utility of special verdicts—that is, detailed findings concerning the issues the judge has identified as significant—has been discussed for many years. See, e.g., H. Trubitt, Patchwork Verdicts, Different-Jurors Verdicts, and American Jury Theory: Whether Verdicts Are Invalidated By Juror Disagreement on Issues, 36 Okla.L.Rev. 473, 496–505 (1983); L. Finz, Does the Trend in Our Substantive Law Dictate an Expanded Use of the Special Verdict? 37 Alb.L.Rev. 229 (1973); C. Wright, The Use of Special Verdicts in Federal Court, 38 F.R.D. 199 (1966); see also Judge Frank's substantial discussion in Skidmore v. B. & O. R.R., 167 F.2d 54 (2d Cir.), cert. denied 335 U.S. 816 (1948).

7. See e.g., FCC v. RCA Communications, Inc., 346 U.S. 86 (1953); ASG Industries, Inc. v. United States, 548 F.2d 147 (6th Cir.1977); Citizen's Ass'n v. Zoning Comm., 477 F.2d 402 (D.C.Cir.1973); Continental Air Lines v. CAB, 443 F.2d 745 (D.C. Cir.1971). Compare C. Byse, Requirement of Findings and Reasons in Formal Proceedings in Administrative Law, 26 Am.J. Comp.L. 393 (1978).

1. In Economou v. United States Dept. of Agriculture, 494 F.2d 519 (2d Cir.1974), the court reversed in four sentences an administrative opinion of some 120 pages, following on a fifteen-hour oral argument before the Judicial Officer of the Department of Agriculture. In a subsequent, un-

When put to it, courts are frequently less demanding than such statutory phrases suggest, stressing simply the need to understand the administrative decision. That is to say, they require not some stylistic organization of the agency's utterance, but, rather, a communication (in whatever form) of precisely what has been decided, so that even if "the findings of the Commission . . . leave much to be desired . . . the path which it followed can be discerned. And we do not believe its findings are so vague and obscure as to make the judicial review contemplated by the Act a perfunctory process." Colorado Interstate Gas Co. v. Federal Power Commission, 324 U.S. 581 (1945).

If the issue to be decided has been clearly delineated from the start, a finding may sometimes be implied by the very fact of decision. Mason v. Lit Realty Co., 6 A.D.2d 715, 226 N.Y.S.2d 895 (3d Dept.1962), illustrates this possibility. An apartment house doorman was injured while lifting a heavy box of books from a tenant's closet shelf. He sought an award of workmen's compensation. Neither the fact of the injury nor its gravity had been controverted. But the employer, asserting that the claimant had not been acting in the course of his employment when the accident occurred, denied liability. Testimony was taken concerning the claimant's duties, the employer's "rules," the alleged instructions to the claimant to be courteous and helpful to the tenants, the employer's alleged knowledge that the claimant often did odd jobs for tenants. The Workmen's Compensation Board's decision was favorable to the claimant. It was attacked as defective because it lacked any specific finding by the Board. As to this, the court said: "While we do not approve of this procedure, we find that the issues here involved are so limited and so clearly defined as to permit no doubt as to the basis of the board's determination. Remittal would thus serve no useful purpose."

In other cases, the character of a controversy may seem to require especially full findings—as, for example, when an ALJ, review board and commission have been in apparent, but not fully explained, disagreement over the meaning of governing policy. This is not the Universal Camera question whether internal disagreement affects the deference due the agency decision; but rather, the question whether fuller explanation is needed to meet the APA requirements. See, e.g., Ventura Broadcasting Co. v. FCC, 765 F.2d 184 (D.C.Cir.1985), reversing for fuller explanation a comparative licensing decision in which the ALJ was reversed by the FCC's Review Board, which was reversed by the full Commission, all turning on reading of precedents of both the Review Board and the Commission.

related case, the Judicial Officer was driven to speculate that the court had either neglected to consider the governing statute, declined to immerse itself in the record, or reached decision on some cloaked basis it was unable or unwilling to articulate. In re Jake Muehlenthaler, 37 Agric. Decisions 313 (1978). Excessive attention to detail in opinion writing may, indeed, be as destructive to judicial review and administrative efficiency as slothful terseness. See J. Wold, Going Through The Motions: The Monotony of Appellate Court Decisionmaking, 62 Judicature 58 (Aug. 1978).

Is the reason for this reversal the court's need for a clearer path *in this case,* or the belief that the agency's law—evidently in disarray on the point, given the confusion—needs to be settled for the benefit of future litigants? The latter is, to be sure, an additional function findings and reasons serve; yet the courts themselves have indicated by their behavior that the general claim of the legal community for explanation is not as commanding as that of the parties. Even in the United States courts of appeals, we no longer enjoy a uniform practice of published, or even written, opinions: In 1982, the District of Columbia Circuit made 627 decisions (on the merits, as distinct from stays, motions, etc.), disposing of 51% by order of judgment alone or with a brief, unpublished and unciteable memorandum; in 1983, 33% of that court's 533 decisions were so treated. But the practice is not without criticism.[2]

In the particular case of agency findings, one important function served may be to reduce the influence of "post hoc rationalizations" by counsel and to promote, however marginally, the responsibility of those actually responsible for decision.[3] "Congress has delegated to the administrative official and not to appellate counsel the responsibility for elaborating and enforcing statutory commands." FTC v. Sperry & Hutchinson Co., 405 U.S. 233, 246 (1972).[4] Of course, that official is unlikely to write the elaboration personally; that will often be done by an office of opinion-writers, who may even share the General Counsel's office with the agency's litigators. But at least it receives the official's approval and stands for his thought process, as an agency brief does not.[5] Granted that one may be dealing with a justification for the decision rather than an explanation of the steps a decision-maker's mind moved through to reach the result—just as a description of a scientific discovery explains what has been found, not why the scientist was interested in the problem, nor his step-by-step path to discovery [6]—

---

2. National Classification Committee v. United States, 765 F.2d 164, 173 n. 2 (D.C. Cir.1985) (separate statement of Judge Wald), pp. 1, 2: "Specifically it is argued that unpublished opinions: result in less carefully prepared or soundly reasoned opinions; reduce judicial accountability; increase the risk of nonuniformity; allow difficult issues to be swept under the carpet; and result in a body of 'secret law' practically inaccessible to many lawyers. Furthermore, there is no uniformly enforced or practiced guidelines [sic] for making the publication decision; hence judges exercise considerable discretion in deciding when an opinion should be published, i.e., when an opinion will become law."

Justices Frankfurter and Stevens have commented on the "practical considerations" that justify the Supreme Court's not explaining denials of certiorari. State v. Baltimore Radio Show, Inc., 338 U.S. 912, 918 (1950); Singleton v. Commissioner, 439 U.S. 940 (1978).

3. Judge Leventhal described counsel's post-hoc explanations, as "repair carpentry," WNCN Listeners Guild v. FCC, 610 F.2d 838, 860 (D.C.Cir.1979) (concurring), reversed, FCC v. WNCN Listeners Guild, 450 U.S. 582 (1981). But Judge Wald has said: "I'll even offer you a tip: although the court won't let 'post hoc rationalizations of counsel' substitute for reasoned decision by the agency, we *do* read those alleged 'post hoc rationalizations,' and in close cases if they are persuasive and consistent with a terse agency decision, we are rather unlikely totally to disregard them." Remarks to Federal Communications Bar Association, April 7, 1984, p. 12.

4. See, to the same effect, Chenery I, p. 271 above, and Burlington Truck Lines v. United States, 371 U.S. 156 (1962).

5. On the process of decision, see Chapter 8, Section 2 infra.

6. See R. Wasserstrom, The Judicial Decision, 25–30, 92–97 (1961); and M. Boudin, Memoirs in a Classical Style (in

still it is worth insisting that the justification be contemporary with the decision, and subscribed by the responsible person.

After all has been said about the need for agency findings or other indication of its reasoning, judges, being usually reasonable people, will measure that need in the light of realities. An agency making only a relatively few decisions, but those few of large public importance, may be held to a more stringent standard of explicitness than applies to a quite different agency. Sheer dimensions of workload inevitably affect expectations, for example, of a state workmen's compensation board or unemployment insurance appeals tribunal rendering literally thousands of judgments annually in appeals growing out of many tens of thousands of decisions by hearing officers.

The tension between workload—not merely from the officials' point of view, but also in terms of impact on affected citizens—and the value of articulating decisions is posed sharply in recent Seventh Circuit opinions about how full an ALJ's findings must be when denying claims for Social Security disability. In STEPHENS v. HECKLER, 766 F.2d 284 (7th Cir.1985), Judge Frank Easterbrook wrote for the court: "The court review judgments, not opinions. The statute requires us to review the quality of the evidence, which must be 'substantial,' not the quality of the ALJ's literary skills. The ALJs work under great burdens. Their supervisors urge them to work quickly. When they slow down to write better opinions, that holds up the queue and prevents deserving people from receiving benefits. Cf. Heckler v. Day, 467 U.S. 104 (1984) (discussing delay in the process). When they process cases quickly, they necessarily take less time on opinions. When a court remands a case with an order to write a better opinion, it clogs the queue in two ways—first because the new hearing on remand takes time, second because it sends the signal that ALJs should write more in each case (and thus hear fewer cases).

"The ALJ's opinion is important not in its own right but because it tells us whether the ALJ has considered all the evidence. . . . If a sketchy opinion assures us that the ALJ considered the important evidence, and the opinion enables us to trace the path of the ALJ's reasoning, the ALJ has done enough. . . . A more extensive requirement sacrifices on the altar of perfectionism the claims of other people stuck in the queue. . . . "

Judge Joel Flaum, concurring, added: ". . . . I write separately to underscore that the ALJ in this case clearly met the existing standards that this circuit has heretofore established for the proper evaluation of Social Security disability cases, and to express disagreement with the majority's unduly restrictive view of the roles of the ALJs and the courts in adjudicating disability claims. . . . The majority's analysis in this regard makes the common and, I believe, erroneous assumption that an ALJ opinion that satisfies [our] simple requirement [of a 'minimal level of articulation'] must be lengthier, or must take longer

honor of Henry J. Friendly), 133 U.Pa.L. Rev. 1 (1984). See also J. Noonan, Persons and Masks of the Law, Chapter 4: The Passengers of Palsgraf (1976).

to formulate, than one that does not. . . . I believe that the tenor—if not the substance—of the majority's remarks might convey an inappropriate message concerning this court's view of the roles that Congress has assigned both to the ALJs and to the courts in the adjudication of disability claims." [7]

d. Exercise of Judgment and Discretion

The next case is as much-cited as any we encounter, a Baedecker on judicial review (although not error-free even about the APA provisions it discusses). Consider what administrative procedures were provided; before whom; what was the "administrative record"; how and by whom was the question of authorizing use of Overton Park acted upon in the Department; and, what do you suppose any "administrative record" contained regarding the two statutory directives at issue.

CITIZENS TO PRESERVE OVERTON PARK, INC. v. VOLPE
Supreme Court of the United States, 1971.
401 U.S. 402.

Opinion of the Court by MR. JUSTICE MARSHALL announced by MR. JUSTICE STEWART.

The growing public concern about the quality of our natural environment has prompted Congress in recent years to enact legislation designed to curb the accelerating destruction of our country's natural beauty. We are concerned in this case with § 4(f) of the Department of Transportation Act of 1966, as amended, and § 18(a) of the Federal-Aid Highway Act of 1968, 82 Stat. 823, 23 U.S.C. § 138 [1] . . . .

Petitioners, private citizens as well as local and national conservation organizations, contend that the Secretary [of Transportation] has violated these statutes by authorizing the expenditure of federal funds for the construction of a six-lane interstate highway through a public park in Memphis, Tennessee. Their claim was rejected by the District Court, which granted the Secretary's motion for summary judgment, and the Court of Appeals for the Sixth Circuit affirmed. After oral

---

7. In his remarkable study, Bureaucratic Justice 141, 143 (1983), Professor Jerry Mashaw reminds us that an ALJ's opinion speaks to applicants as well as to courts: "The technical soundness of medical and vocational judgments is not particularly meaningful to people who have concluded from concrete and often bitter and demoralizing experience that they cannot work. . . . [The agency] must contend in addition with the difficulties of communicating to an audience that has modest interpretative skills and a strong incentive to feel aggrieved."

1. [Each section says:] "It is hereby declared to be the national policy that special effort should be made to preserve the natural beauty of the countryside and public park and recreation lands, wildlife and waterfowl refuges, and historic sites. . . . After [August 23, 1968], the Secretary shall not approve any program or project which requires the use of any publicly owned land from a public park, recreation area, or wildlife and waterfowl refuge of national, State, or local significance as determined by the Federal, State, or local officials having jurisdiction thereof, or any land from an historic site of national, State or local significance as so determined by such officials unless (1) there is no feasible and prudent alternative to the use of such land, and (2) such program includes all possible planning to minimize harm to such park, recreational area, wildlife and waterfowl refuge, or historic site resulting from such use."

argument, this Court granted a stay that halted construction and, treating the application for the stay as a petition for certiorari, granted review. 400 U.S. 939. We now reverse the judgment below and remand for further proceedings in the District Court.

Overton Park is a 342-acre city park located near the center of Memphis. The park contains a zoo, a nine-hole municipal golf course, an outdoor theater, nature trails, a bridle path, an art academy, picnic areas, and 170 acres of forest. The proposed highway, which is to be a six-lane, high-speed, expressway, will sever the zoo from the rest of the park. Although the roadway will be depressed below ground level except where it crosses a small creek, 26 acres of the park will be destroyed. . . .

Although the route through the park was approved by the Bureau of Public Roads in 1956 and by the Federal Highway Administrator in 1966, the enactment of § 4(f) . . . prevented distribution of federal funds for the section of the highway designated to go through Overton Park until the Secretary of Transportation determined whether the requirements of § 4(f) had been met. . . . In April 1968, the Secretary announced that he concurred in the judgment of local officials that I–40 should be built through the park. . . . Final approval for the project—the route as well as the design—was not announced until November 1969, after Congress had reiterated in § 138 of the Federal-Aid Highway Act that highway construction through public parks was to be restricted. [The Secretary's approval of federal funds for the highway was not] accompanied by a statement of the Secretary's factual findings. He did not indicate why he believed there were no feasible and prudent alternative routes or why design changes could not be made to reduce the harm to the park.

Petitioners contend that the Secretary's action is invalid without such formal findings and that the Secretary did not make an independent determination but merely relied on the judgment of the Memphis City Council. . . .[2]

Respondents argue that it was unnecessary for the Secretary to make formal findings, and that he did, in fact, exercise his own independent judgment which was supported by the facts. In the District Court, respondents introduced affidavits, prepared specifically

---

2. [Ed.] The judgment of the Memphis City Council had been obtained pursuant to a statutory provision requiring consultation with local officials. In conducting these consultations, the Secretary had insisted that the Council consider only issues of community values and not costs—as the federal government would pay most of the expenses—and he regarded this instruction as an important means of implementing § 4(f). Those local hearings were widely reported in the Memphis press, and the issues were hotly debated. One outcome of *that* process was that the city used the money it received for the 26 acres of Over-

ton Park needed for the highway to buy several hundred acres of land for parks to be located throughout the city. Creation of the new parks was complete at the time of the lawsuit.

Although the interpretation to be given § 4(f) is not, as such, a matter of administrative law interest, one might ask: could the Court have interpreted the provision for local consultation—likely, as here, to lead to local political responsibility informed by parkland values—as bearing on the meaning to be given § 4(f)?

for this litigation, which indicated that the Secretary had made the decision and that the decision was supportable. These affidavits were contradicted by affidavits introduced by petitioners. . . .

The District Court and the Court of Appeals found that formal findings by the Secretary were not necessary and refused to order the deposition of the former Federal Highway Administrator because those courts believed that probing of the mental processes of an administrative decisionmaker was prohibited. And, believing that the Secretary's authority was wide and reviewing courts' authority narrow in the approval of highway routes, the lower courts held that the affidavits contained no basis for a determination that the Secretary had exceeded his authority.

We agree that formal findings were not required. But we do not believe that in this case judicial review based solely on litigation affidavits was adequate.

A threshold question—whether petitioners are entitled to any judicial review—is easily answered. Section 701 of the Administrative Procedure Act . . . provides that the action of "each authority of the Government of the United States," which includes the Department of Transportation, is subject to judicial review except where there is a statutory prohibition on review or where "agency action is committed to agency discretion by law." In this case, there is no indication that Congress sought to prohibit judicial review and there is most certainly no "showing of 'clear and convincing evidence' of a . . . legislative intent" to restrict access to judicial review. Abbott Laboratories v. Gardner, 387 U.S. 136, 141 (1967), [p. 1105 within] . . .

Similarly, the Secretary's decision here does not fall within the exception for action "committed to agency discretion." This is a very narrow exception.[3] Berger, Administrative Arbitrariness and Judicial Review, 65 Col.L.Rev. 55 (1965). The legislative history of the Administrative Procedure Act indicates that it is applicable in those rare instances where "statutes are drawn in such broad terms that in a given case there is no law to apply." S.Rep. No. 752, 79th Cong., 1st Sess., 26 (1945).

Section 4(f) of the Department of Transportation Act and § 138 of the Federal-Aid Highway Act are clear and specific directives. . . . [Their] language is a plain and explicit bar to the use of federal funds for construction of highways through parks—only the most unusual situations are exempted.

Despite the clarity of the statutory language, respondents argue that the Secretary has wide discretion. They recognize that the requirement that there be no "feasible" alternative route admits of little administrative discretion. For this exemption to apply the Secretary must find that as a matter of sound engineering it would not be feasible to build the highway along any other route. Respondents argue, however, that the requirement that there be no other "prudent" route

---

3. [Ed.] See the discussion at p. 1021 ff. below.

requires the Secretary to engage in a wide-ranging balancing of compet-ing interests.　They contend that the Secretary should weigh the detriment resulting from the destruction of parkland against the cost of other routes, safety considerations, and other factors, and determine on the basis of the importance that he attaches to these other factors whether, on balance, alternative feasible routes would be "prudent."

But no such wide-ranging endeavor was intended.　It is obvious that in most cases considerations of cost, directness of route, and community disruption will indicate that parkland should be used for highway construction whenever possible.　Although it may be neces-sary to transfer funds from one jurisdiction to another, there will always be a smaller outlay required from the public purse when parkland is used since the public already owns the land and there will be no need to pay for right-of-way.　And since people do not live or work in parks, if a highway is built on parkland no one will have to leave his home or give up his business.　Such factors are common to substantially all highway construction.　Thus, if Congress intended these factors to be on an equal footing with preservation of parkland there would have been no need for the statutes.

Congress clearly did not intend that cost and disruption of the community were to be ignored by the Secretary.　But the very exis-tence of the statutes [4] indicates that protection of parkland was to be given paramount importance.　The few green havens that are public parks were not to be lost unless there were truly unusual factors present in a particular case or the cost or community disruption resulting from alternative routes reached extraordinary magnitudes. If the statutes are to have any meaning, the Secretary cannot approve the destruction of parkland unless he finds that alternative routes present unique problems.

Plainly, there is "law to apply" and thus the exemption for action "committed to agency discretion" is inapplicable.　But the existence of judicial review is only the start: the standard for review must also be determined.　For that we must look to § 706 of the Administrative Procedure Act .　.　.　. [A] "reviewing court shall .　.　. hold unlawful and set aside agency action, findings, and conclusions found" not to meet six separate standards.　In all cases agency action must be set aside if the action was "arbitrary, capricious, an abuse of discretion, or otherwise not in accordance with law" or if the action failed to meet statutory, procedural, or constitutional requirements.　5 U.S.C.

---

4. The legislative history of both § 4(f) of the Department of Transportation Act .　.　. and § 138 of the Federal-Aid High-way Act .　.　. is ambiguous.　The legisla-tive committee reports tend to support re-spondents' view that the statutes are merely general directives to the Secretary requiring him to consider the importance of parkland as well as cost, community disruption, and other factors.　See, e.g., S.Rep. No. 1340, 90th Cong., 2d Sess., 19; H.R.Rep. No. 1584, 90th Cong., 2d Sess., 12.

Statements by proponents of the statutes as well as the Senate committee report on § 4(f) indicate, however, that the Secretary was to have limited authority.　See, e.g., 114 Cong.Rec. 24033–24037; S.Rep. No. 1659, 89th Cong., 2d Sess., 22.　See also H.R.Conf.Rep. No. 2236, 89th Cong., 2d Sess., 25.　Because of this ambiguity it is clear that we must look primarily to the statutes themselves to find the legislative intent.

§§ 706(2)(A), (B), (C), (D). In certain narrow, specifically limited situations, the agency action is to be set aside if the action was not supported by "substantial evidence." And in other equally narrow circumstances the reviewing court is to engage in a de novo review of the action and set it aside if it was "unwarranted by the facts."

Petitioners argue that the Secretary's approval of the construction of [the highway] through Overton Park is subject to one or the other of these latter two standards of limited applicability. First, they contend that the "substantial evidence" standard of § 706(2)(E) must be applied. In the alternative, they claim that § 706(2)(F) applies and that there must be a de novo review to determine if the Secretary's action was "unwarranted by the facts." Neither of these standards is, however, applicable.

Review under the substantial-evidence test is authorized only when the agency action is taken pursuant to a rulemaking provision of the Administrative Procedure Act itself, 5 U.S.C. § 553 (Supp. V), or when the agency action is based on a public adjudicatory hearing. See 5 U.S.C. §§ 556, 557. The Secretary's decision to allow the expenditure of federal funds to build [the highway] through Overton Park was plainly not an exercise of a rulemaking function. And the only hearing that is required by either the Administrative Procedure Act or the statutes regulating the distribution of federal funds for highway construction is a public hearing conducted by local officials for the purpose of informing the community about the proposed project and eliciting community views on the design and route. 23 U.S.C. § 128. The hearing is nonadjudicatory, quasi-legislative in nature. It is not designed to produce a record that is to be the basis of agency action—the basic requirement for substantial-evidence review.

Petitioners' alternative argument also fails. De novo review of whether the Secretary's decision was "unwarranted by the facts" is authorized by § 706(2)(F) in only two circumstances. First, such de novo review is authorized when the action is adjudicatory in nature and the agency factfinding procedures are inadequate. And, there may be independent judicial factfinding when issues that were not before the agency are raised in a proceeding to enforce nonadjudicatory agency action. Neither situation exists here.

Even though there is no de novo review in this case and the Secretary's approval of the route . . . does not have ultimately to meet the substantial-evidence test, the generally applicable standards of § 706 require the reviewing court to engage in a substantial inquiry. Certainly, the Secretary's decision is entitled to a presumption of regularity. See, e.g., Pacific States Box & Basket Co. v. White, 296 U.S. 176, 185 (1935). But that presumption is not to shield his action from a thorough, probing, in-depth review.

The court is first required to decide whether the Secretary acted within the scope of his authority. This determination naturally begins with a delineation of the scope of the Secretary's authority and discretion. L. Jaffe, Judicial Control of Administrative Action 359 (1965).

As has been shown, Congress has specified only a small range of choices that the Secretary can make. Also involved in this initial inquiry is a determination of whether on the facts the Secretary's decision can reasonably be said to be within that range. The reviewing court must consider whether the Secretary properly construed his authority to approve the use of parkland as limited to situations where there are no feasible alternative routes or where feasible alternative routes involve uniquely difficult problems. And the reviewing court must be able to find that the Secretary could have reasonably believed that in this case there are no feasible alternatives or that alternatives do involve unique problems.

Scrutiny of the facts does not end, however, with the determination that the Secretary has acted within the scope of his statutory authority. Section 706(2)(A) requires a finding that the actual choice made was not "arbitrary, capricious, an abuse of discretion, or otherwise not in accordance with law." To make this finding the court must consider whether the decision was based on a consideration of the relevant factors and whether there has been a clear error of judgment. . . . Although this inquiry into the facts is to be searching and careful, the ultimate standard of review is a narrow one. The court is not empowered to substitute its judgment for that of the agency.

The final inquiry is whether the Secretary's action followed the necessary procedural requirements. Here the only procedural error alleged is the failure of the Secretary to make formal findings and state his reason for allowing the highway to be built through the park.

Undoubtedly, review of the Secretary's action is hampered by his failure to make such findings, but the absence of formal findings does not necessarily require that the case be remanded to the Secretary. Neither the Department of Transportation Act nor the Federal-Aid Highway Act requires such formal findings. Moreover, the Administrative Procedure Act requirements that there be formal findings in certain rulemaking and adjudicatory proceedings do not apply to the Secretary's action here. See 5 U.S.C. §§ 553(a)(2), 554(a). And, although formal findings may be required in some cases in the absence of statutory directives when the nature of the agency action is ambiguous, those situations are rare. Plainly, there is no ambiguity here; the Secretary has approved the construction of [the highway] through Overton Park and has approved a specific design for the project. . . .

Moreover, there is an administrative record that allows the full, prompt review of the Secretary's action that is sought without additional delay which would result from having a remand to the Secretary.

That administrative record is not, however, before us. The lower courts based their review on the litigation affidavits that were presented. These affidavits were merely "post hoc" rationalizations, Burlington Truck Lines v. United States, 371 U.S. 156, 168–169 (1962), which have traditionally been found to be an inadequate basis for review. Burlington Truck Lines v. United States, supra; SEC v. Chenery Corp.,

318 U.S. 80, 87 (1943). And they clearly do not constitute the "whole record" compiled by the agency: the basis for review required by § 706 of the Administrative Procedure Act.

Thus it is necessary to remand this case to the District Court for plenary review of the Secretary's decision. That review is to be based on the full administrative record that was before the Secretary at the time he made his decision. But since the bare record may not disclose the factors that were considered or the Secretary's construction of the evidence it may be necessary for the District Court to require some explanation in order to determine if the Secretary acted within the scope of his authority and if the Secretary's action was justifiable under the applicable standard.

The court may require the administrative officials who participated in the decision to give testimony explaining their action. Of course, such inquiry into the mental processes of administrative decisionmakers is usually to be avoided. United States v. Morgan, 313 U.S. 409, 422 (1941). And where there are administrative findings that were made at the same time as the decision, as was the case in Morgan, there must be a strong showing of bad faith or improper behavior before such inquiry may be made. But here there are no such formal findings and it may be that the only way there can be effective judicial review is by examining the decisionmakers themselves. See Shaughnessy v. Accardi, 349 U.S. 280 (1955).

The District Court is not, however, required to make such an inquiry. It may be that the Secretary can prepare formal findings including the information required by DOT Order 5610.1 that will provide an adequate explanation for his action. Such an explanation will, to some extent, be a "post hoc rationalization" and thus must be viewed critically. If the District Court decides that additional explanation is necessary, that court should consider which method will prove the most expeditious so that full review may be had as soon as possible.

Reversed and remanded.

[Justice Black, with whom Justice Brennan concurred, dissented on the ground that "it is our duty" to remand this case to the Secretary so he can "give this whole matter the hearing it deserves in full good-faith obedience to the Act of Congress." Justice Blackmun, although joining in the Court's opinion and judgment, filed a brief concurring opinion. Justice Douglas did not participate.][5]

5. On remand, the district court conducted a 25-day trial that included affidavits of the Secretary and testimony of subordinates, and held: (1) Secretary Volpe had never actually made a route or corridor determination which was required by section 4 of the Department of Transportation Act and (2) even if the Secretary had made such a determination, his determination was based on an incorrect view of the applicable law. Accordingly, in January 1972, the district court remanded the case to the Secretary to make a route determination in accordance with the applicable law. 335 F.Supp. 873. The Secretary rendered his decision in January 1973. He stated in part: "On the basis of the record before me and in light of guidance provided by the Supreme Court, I find that an Interstate highway as proposed by the State through Overton Park cannot be approved. . . . I cannot find . . . that there are no prudent and feasible alternatives to the use of parkland nor that the broader environmental protection objectives of the NEPA and the Federal-Aid

NOTES

(1) Overton Park came before the Court in a rush: a motion for stay was treated by the Court as a petition for certiorari and granted December 7, 1970; petitioner's brief was required to be filed December 21, 1970; the government's, January 4, 1971; and oral argument was heard January 11. The opinion was handed down in early March. For all that, it has had tremendous influence; as of May 30, 1986, a Lexis search found 1,674 mentions of "Citizens to Preserve Overton Park" in the federal courts.

The central question briefed and argued, of course, was the meaning of § 4(f). Note that the Court remarks (n. 4, above) that the legislative history is ambiguous and that the Court gives no significance whatever to the provisions for involving local officials. Ought it to have paid some attention to the interpretation given the statute by the official (the Secretary) charged with its implementation? Why or why not? If your answer is, in part, because of his failure formally to declare what his interpretation was, as he might have done in an opinion or rule, does that suggest a significant cost of his failure to make findings, from the Secretary's perspective? If the Secretary *did* misinterpret the statute, shouldn't the court simply have remanded the case for a fresh Secretarial decision under an informed interpretation? Or was it another result of the Secretary's failure to find, that the Court had to treat as possible (despite his lawyers' arguments) that the Secretary had *correctly* interpreted the statute so that the issue *now* on judicial review was whether he had properly applied it.

(2) CAMP v. PITTS, 411 U.S. 138 (1973) was a major (although less frequently cited) sequel to Overton Park: An application to organize a new national bank was denied by the Comptroller of the Currency; no hearing or findings were required, but a brief explanation was given by letter.[1] Upon the applicants' suit for review, the district court reviewed the administrative record of information from bank examiners and other interested parties, and granted summary judgment for the Comptroller. The court of appeals reversed and remanded for trial de novo because the Comptroller had "inadequately and inarticulately resolved the [respondents'] presentation." The court directed that in the District Court, respondents "will open the trial with proof of their applica-

Highway Act have been met, nor that the existing proposal would comply with FHWA standards on noise."

The State of Tennessee then sought review in the district court, contending that the Secretary was required either to approve the Overton Park route or to specify an alternate route. The district court agreed with the State but its decision was reversed by the Sixth Circuit. Citizens to Preserve Overton Park, Inc. v. Brinegar, 494 F.2d 1212 (6th Cir.1974), cert. denied 421 U.S. 991 (1975).

1. The letter read in part:

"On each application we endeavor to develop the need and convenience factors in conjunction with all other banking factors and in this case we were unable to reach a favorable conclusion as to the need factor. The record reflects that this market area is now served by the Peoples Bank with deposits of $7.2MM, The Bank of Hartsville with deposits of $12.8MM, The First Federal Savings and Loan Association with deposits of $5.4MM, The Mutual Savings and Loan Association with deposits of $8.2MM and the Sonoco Employees Credit Union with deposits of $6.5MM. The aforementioned are as of December 31, 1968."

tion and compliance with the statutory inquiries, and proffer of any other relevant evidence." Then, "[t]estimony may . . . be adduced by the Comptroller or intervenors manifesting opposition, if any, to the new bank." On the basis of the record thus made, the District Court was instructed to make its own findings of fact and conclusions of law in order to determine "whether the [respondents] have shown by a preponderance of evidence that the Comptroller's ruling is capricious or an abuse of discretion." 463 F.2d, at 634.

The Supreme Court reversed per curiam, closing as follows:

". . . It is quite plain from our decision in Citizens to Preserve Overton Park v. Volpe, 401 U.S. 402 (1971), that de novo review is appropriate only where there are inadequate factfinding procedures in an adjudicatory proceeding, or where judicial proceedings are brought to enforce certain administrative actions. Neither situation applies here. The proceeding in the District Court was obviously not brought to enforce the Comptroller's decision, and the only deficiency suggested in agency action or proceedings is that the Comptroller inadequately explained his decision. As Overton Park demonstrates, however, that failure, if it occurred in this case, is not a deficiency in factfinding procedures such as to warrant the de novo hearing ordered in this case.

"The appropriate standard for review was, accordingly, whether the Comptroller's adjudication was arbitrary, capricious, an abuse of discretion, or otherwise not in accordance with law, as specified in 5 U.S.C. § 706(2)(A). In applying that standard, the focal point for judicial review should be the administrative record already in existence, not some new record made initially in the reviewing court.

"   . . .

"If, as the Court of Appeals held and as the Comptroller does not now contest, there was such failure to explain administrative action as to frustrate effective judicial review, the remedy was not to hold a de novo hearing but, as contemplated by Overton Park, to obtain from the agency, either through affidavits or testimony, such additional explanation of the reasons for the agency decision as may prove necessary. We add a caveat, however. Unlike Overton Park, in the present case there was contemporaneous explanation of the agency decision. The explanation may have been curt, but it surely indicated the determinative reason for the final action taken: the finding that a new bank was an uneconomic venture in light of the banking needs and the banking services already available in the surrounding community. The validity of the Comptroller's action must, therefore, stand or fall on the propriety of that finding, judged, of course, by the appropriate standard of review. If that finding is not sustainable on the administrative record made, then the Comptroller's decision must be vacated and the matter remanded to him for further consideration. See SEC v. Chenery Corp., 318 U.S. 80 (1943). . . .[2]

2. [Ed.] See K. Scott, In Quest of Reason: The Licensing Decisions of Federal Banking Agencies, 42 U.Chi.L.Rev. 235 (1975); C. Murphy, What Reason for the Quest: A Response to Professor Scott, 42 U.Chi.L.Rev. 299 (1975).

(3) *A note on organization.* Overton Park, embracing so much, points in many directions: What is the nature of the record in informal administrative proceedings? How does review of questions of fact on the administrative record of an informal proceeding differ in practice from "substantial evidence" review? When findings are supplied in informal proceedings, how closely is the agency's reasoning to be examined? Under what, if any, circumstances is it appropriate to look behind the surface of that reasoning to see what "really" happened? Each of these questions, moreover, can be viewed from the perspective of a court—that is, "scope"—or from the perspective of agency behavior, as such. Obviously the two are interrelated; it will already have occurred to you that a case like Overton Park will teach an agency much about how it ought to behave.

The pages following examine, largely from the judicial perspective, the matters of "record," "factual review," and the problems of reviewing agency exercises of discretion under complex statutory schemes; some corresponding problems at the agency level will be found in Chapters 7 and 8.

(i) Is There a Record in Proceedings Not on the Record?

The great bulk of administrative decision-making, whether adopting rules, setting policies, administering grants or contracts, initiating enforcement activity, or the like, is not required to be done on *the* record, though it doubtless occurs on the basis of *a* record of some character. External submissions may be received, as in the case of informal rulemaking. Staff members or other government agencies supply analyses, recommendations, and pressures. Institutional and personal memories, consciously invoked or unconsciously influential, contribute as well. Decisions may accumulate across a series of desks as analyses are made and options are incrementally refined. For this type of decision-making, you will recall, the Supreme Court said in Overton Park that, if possible, review (as the Court described it) was "to be based on the full administrative record that was before the Secretary at the time he made his decision."

What are the contents of this "full administrative record"? For "on-the-record" proceedings, the answer to that question is supplied in substantial part by the APA. Sections 556(e) and 557 define "the exclusive record" as comprising transcript, exhibits, papers filed in the proceeding, formal rulings and decisions (which are to follow a stated format), and records of forbidden ex parte communications.[1] Confinement of decision to that record is secured by APA provisions concerning the required impartiality of the hearer of fact; constraints on private communication within the agency by staff immediately associated with presentation of the agency's "case"; a recommended decision which is

---

1. For a lively dispute whether, even in this context, a court could properly examine materials beyond the record certified to it by an agency, see San Luis Obispo Mothers for Peace v. NRC, 751 F.2d 1287 (D.C.Cir.1984), 789 F.2d 26 (D.C.Cir. en banc 1986), noted at p. 791 below.

part of the record, and perhaps is not to be supplemented off the record; a prohibition on private approaches to the decision-maker by the parties; and so forth.[2] No comparable provisions appear in the APA respecting informal proceedings, or any "record" that may be generated in them, although § 553 does provide for *agency* "consideration of the relevant matter presented."

WILLIAM F. PEDERSEN, JR.,* FORMAL RECORDS AND INFORMAL RULEMAKING **
85 Yale Law Journal 59–65 (1975).

[Portions of the article describing the internal workings of informal rulemaking at the EPA are set out at p. 34 above.]

In the review of agency actions less formal than full-scale adjudication, the guidelines followed in recent years have been those laid down in the Overton Park case . . . . [T]he Court must have meant that the documents actually presented to the Secretary for his consideration would constitute the record. But this is based on the false assumption that all documents critical in reaching a given agency decision are in fact placed "before" the head of the agency, and that the internal procedures of the agency are firmly enough established and well enough observed to make location of these documents a rather ministerial act. Since these assumptions are not true, the only way to assemble a record that gives the court a picture of what the agency actually thought and considered is through an ad hoc effort to reconstruct what happened in a particular case. To do this, the documents that have passed through the formal internal procedures of the agency must be examined. But since these *formal* procedures are scarcely the exclusive vehicles for considering issues within an agency, much else must be included as well. I call this effort at post hoc reconstruction of what actually happened a "historical" approach to compiling a record.

Courts and commentators have often endorsed a historical approach. It does not correspond, however, to the way records for decision and judicial review are generated in trial courts and agency adjudication. [A] record is normally defined as the material which has been accepted under a given obligatory set of procedures. I call this a "procedural" approach to compiling the record. A trial court record is "procedural" since it consists of everything that has been properly placed in evidence under defined rules of admissibility during the course of the trial. . . . The Administrative Conference of the United States has recommended[1] that the record for judicial review of informal rulemaking should consist of (1) the notice of proposed rulemaking and any documents referred to in it; (2) the comments and documents

---

2. These issues, and corresponding issues concerning informal proceedings, are addressed in Chapter 8.

* Former Deputy General Counsel, Environmental Protection Administration.

** Copyright and reprinted by permission of the author, the Yale Law Journal, and Fred B. Rothman & Co.

1. Recommendation No. 74–4, Preenforcement judicial review of rules of general applicability, 1 C.F.R. § 305.74–4 (1975) (adopted May 30–31, 1974).

submitted by interested persons; (3) transcripts of any hearings held in the course of the rulemaking; (4) reports of any advisory committees; (5) the agency's concise general statement or final order and any documents referred to in it; *and* (6) other factual information "not included in the foregoing that was considered by the authority responsible for promulgation of the rule or that is proffered by the agency as pertinent to the rule."

The first five items cause no difficulty. Both under a historical approach to the record and under a procedural approach, they would certainly be included. But the first clause of the sixth recommendation comes down squarely on the side of the historical approach by explicitly recognizing the agency's right to include in the record whatever documents it "considered"—even if they arose outside the APA notice and comment procedures.[2] In addition, in defining the record as what was considered by the "authority responsible for promulgation of the rule," the Administrative Conference misstates the nature of rulemaking. Only a very few, highly controversial issues can hope to receive detailed personal attention from the administrator of a busy agency, be he or she ever so competent. In all other cases, no single authority passes judgment on the rule. Different parts of the agency work on different parts of the rule, or on the same part from different angles—and the rule emerges. It follows from the lack of any meaningful central "authority" that the phrase "considered by the authority" also loses meaning, and sets no clear boundary to the size or content of the record. Given the diffuse nature of rulemaking, it will be a rare document that cannot claim to have been considered somewhere to some extent by someone in connection with the rulemaking, and a document almost as rare that will have received the personal attention of the administrator.

The other test suggested by the Administrative Conference for including documents in the record—whether they are "proffered by the agency as pertinent to the rule"—is even worse. It breaks free of the restriction implicit even in the historical approach that the record certified to the court should reflect what the agency *actually* weighed and evaluated in some manner at the time of the rulemaking. Indeed, it would apparently allow the agency to include whatever it thinks would help support its actions once litigation has begun.[3] . . .

NOTES

(1) By the time Mr. Pedersen wrote, a number of developments had occurred that promoted both the growth and the regularization of records in informal proceedings generally—and in important rulemak-

2. Indeed the recommendation could be read as refusing to adopt the rule laid down in Portland Cement Ass'n v. Ruckelshaus, 486 F.2d 375 (D.C.Cir.1973), that highly relevant factual materials be disclosed to interested parties for comment before the agency may rely on them. [Ed.: See p. 480 below.]

3. The cases have long since established that an agency action may not be upheld for reasons put forward for the first time by counsel during judicial review, rather than by the agency itself. Burlington Truck Lines v. United States, 371 U.S. 156, 168–69 (1962) . . . .

ings, in particular. Overton Park itself was one. The government's brief in that case, as the opinion tells us, refers self-confidently to an "administrative record" that, on remand, proved a mirage. Twenty-five trial days and extensive documentary discovery stood witness to the elusiveness of collecting the data that had lain before—and in the backs of the minds of—the many functionaries of the Department of Transportation who shared responsibility for that decision.[1]

Second, the Freedom of Information Act, discussed in Chapter 6, Section 1 below, had given counsel the means to collect their own records. A request for "all studies in the agency's possession that it has considered or is considering in connection with the rule proposed at 34 Fed.Reg. 6419" suddenly promised to identify the previously unattainable. Participants were not only in a position to know a good deal more about internal deliberations, but also able to assure that this data would be placed before a court. The Government in the Sunshine Act may offer like opportunities with respect to agencies headed by multi-member commissions.[2]

Finally, for these purposes, there were the developments already addressed under the rubric "paper hearing," p. 259 above. While general consideration of this development is best postponed, it is appropriate to note here the development of a strong requirement that, as part of the "paper hearing" process, an agency must share the important elements of its data base by placing them in the rulemaking record—and doing so in time for an informal response to be made. "It is not consonant with the purpose of a rulemaking proceeding to promulgate rules on the basis of inadequate data, or on data that, to a critical degree, is known only to the agency." Portland Cement Ass'n v. Ruckleshaus, 486 F.2d 375, 393 (D.C.Cir.1973), cert. denied 417 U.S. 921 (1974). "[A]lthough we recognize that an agency may resort to its own expertise outside the record in an informal rulemaking procedure, we do not believe that when the pertinent research material is readily available and the agency has no special expertise on the precise parameters involved, there is any reason to conceal the scientific data relied upon from the interested parties. . . . If the failure to notify interested persons of the scientific research upon which the agency was relying actually prevented the presentation of relevant comment, the agency may be held not to have considered all 'the relevant factors.' We can think of no sound reason for secrecy or reluctance to expose to public view (with an exception for trade secrets or national security) the ingredients of the deliberative process. Indeed, the FDA's own regulations now specifically require that every notice of proposed rulemaking contain 'references to all data and information on which the Commissioner relies for the proposal (copies or a full list of which shall be a part of the administrative file on the matter . . .).' 21 C.F.R. § 10.040(b)(1) (1977). And this is, undoubtedly, the trend. See, e.g.,

---

1. See Citizens to Preserve Overton Park v. Volpe, 335 F.Supp. 873 (W.D.Tenn. 1972), commented on at 2 E.L.R. 10011 (1972).

2. See Chapter 6, Section 2 below, especially San Luis Obispo Mothers for Peace v. NRC, p. 791 below.

National Nutritional Foods v. Weinberger, 512 F.2d 688 (2d Cir.), cert. denied, 423 U.S. 827 (1975) . . . . One cannot ask for comment on a scientific paper without allowing the participants to read the paper. Scientific research is sometimes rejected for diverse inadequacies of methodology; and statistical results are sometimes rebutted because of a lack of adequate gathering technique or of supportable extrapolation. Such is the stuff of scientific debate. . . . " United States v. Nova Scotia Food Products Corp., 568 F.2d 240 (2d Cir.1977).

(2) Does it matter in what context the "record" question arises? UNITED STATES v. NOVA SCOTIA FOOD PRODUCTS CORP., 568 F.2d 240 (2d Cir.1977), quoted as well in the previous note and at p. 482 below, arose in an action brought in 1975 to enforce a Food and Drug Administration regulation setting standards for the processing of smoked fish. The rule had been adopted in 1970 to safeguard against botulism poisoning in all smoked fish, a purpose which the court found to be within the FDA's authority. Those challenging the rule were smokers of whitefish, and asserted that application of a portion of the rule (concerning the duration and temperature of the smoking process) to whitefish would prevent the production of marketable fish. (The rule covered a variety of topics, and applied generally to all smoked fish, see 417 F.Supp. 1364 (E.D.N.Y.1976)). Judge Murray Gurfein, writing for the Second Circuit, said on this aspect:

"The question of what is an adequate 'record' in informal rulemaking has engaged the attention of commentators for several years. The extent of the administrative record required for judicial review of informal rulemaking is largely a function of the scope of judicial review. Even when the standard of review is whether the promulgation of the rule was 'arbitrary, capricious, an abuse of discretion, or otherwise not in accordance with law,' as specified in 5 U.S.C. § 706(2)(A), judicial review must nevertheless, be based on the 'whole record' (id.). . . .

"With respect to the content of the administrative 'record,' the Supreme Court has told us that in informal rulemaking, 'the focal point for judicial review should be the administrative record already in existence, not some new record made initially in the reviewing court.' See Camp v. Pitts, 411 U.S. 138, 142 (1973).

"No contemporaneous record was made or certified [at the time of the rulemaking]. When, during the enforcement action, the basis for the regulation was sought through pretrial discovery, the record was created by searching the files of the FDA and the memories of those who participated in the process of rulemaking. This resulted in what became Exhibit D at the trial of the injunction action. Exhibit D consists of (1) Tab A containing the comments received from outside parties during the administrative 'notice-and-comment' proceeding and (2) Tabs B through L consisting of scientific data and the like upon which the Commissioner now says he relied but which were not made known to the interested parties.

"Appellants object to the exclusion of evidence in the District Court 'aimed directly at showing that the scientific evidence relied upon by the FDA was inaccurate and not based upon a realistic appraisal of the true facts. Appellants attempted to introduce scientific evidence to demonstrate that in fixing the processing parameters FDA relied upon tests in which ground fish were injected with many millions of botulism [*sic*] spores and then tested for outgrowth at various processing levels whereas the spore levels in nature are far less and outgrowth would have been prevented by far less stringent processing parameters.' (Br. p. 33). The District Court properly excluded the evidence.

"In an enforcement action, we must rely exclusively on the record made before the agency to determine the validity of the regulation. The exception to the exclusivity of that record is that 'there may be independent judicial fact-finding when issues that were not before the agency are raised in a proceeding to *enforce* non-adjudicatory agency action.' Overton Park, supra, 401 U.S. at 415 (1971). (Emphasis added.)

"Though this is an enforcement proceeding and the question is close, we think that the 'issues' were fairly before the agency and hence that de novo evidence was properly excluded by Judge Dooling. Camp v. Pitts, supra."

Do you agree? How would you respond to the following argument: The whole point about decisions not required to be made "on the record" is that the agency can draw on conversations, staff knowledge, meetings and other sources not readily aggregated into a file drawer and labelled "record." When a rule is adopted, memory of these matters is fresh and materials that may have been relied on have not been redistributed through the agency's files. It is not that hard for the agency, indeed it is appropriate to require it, to bring these sources together for submission to a reviewing court when the basis for its rulemaking judgments are promptly challenged. An enforcement proceeding, however, as in the Nova Scotia case, may lie years in the future. By that time the momentary mental organization of the agency will have dissipated. To require *then* an organized agency record is to convert all rulemaking, for review purposes, into proceedings in which the agency's informal knowledge and processes cannot be used.

Further aspects of this problem are developed in Chapter 8, at pp. 881–905 below.

(3) Mr. Peder... ...shadowed enactment of Section 307(d) of the Clean Air Act, 42 U.S.C. § 7607(a). That section adopts a "procedural record" approach requiring EPA to include in the record "all data information and documents" on which the rule relies and envisioning that participants would have an opportunity to comment on all significant factual material relied on by the agency. Its special requirements often influence judicial consideration of record issues in EPA rulemaking.[3] What do you see as the possible advantages

3. See, e.g., Sierra Club v. Costle, 657 F.2d 298, 398 (D.C.Cir.1981) ("If . . . documents . . . upon which EPA intended to rely had been entered on the docket too

and disadvantages of this approach? [4] Consider the following proposal, limited to informal rulemaking; which in 1982 a similar bill won unanimous approval in the U.S. Senate.

S. 1080
98th Cong., 1st Sess. 1983.

.   .   .

[§ 553(f):] The agency shall maintain a file for each rule making proceeding conducted pursuant to this section and shall maintain a current index to such file. The file and the material excluded from the file pursuant to paragraph (3) of this subsection shall constitute the rule making record for purposes of judicial review. Except as provided in paragraph (3) of this subsection, the file shall be made available to the public beginning on the date on which the agency makes an initial publication concerning the rule. The file shall include—

(A)(i) the notice of proposed rule making and any supplement to or modification or revision of such notice; and

(ii) any advance notice of proposed rule making;

(B) copies of all written comments received on the proposed rule;

(C) a transcript of any public hearing conducted in the rule making;

(D) copies, or an identification of the place at which copies may be obtained, of all data, methodologies, reports, studies, scientific evaluations, or other similar information described by the agency in its Notice of Proposed Rulemaking as material on which the agency plan substantially to rely in the rule making; and of other factual and methodological materials not [so] described .   .   . that pertains directly to the rule making and that the agency considered in connection with the rule making, or that was prepared by or for the agency in connection with the rule making;

(E) any statement, description, analysis, or any other material that the agency is required to make public in connection with the rule making, including any preliminary or final regulatory analysis issued by the agency .   .   . ;

late for any meaningful public comment .   .   . , then both the structure and spirit of section 307 would have been violated."); Lead Industries Assoc. v. EPA, 647 F.2d 1130 (D.C.Cir.), cert. den. 449 U.S. 1042 (1980) (statutory specification of contents of rulemaking record limits court in considering additional material on appeal).

4. The Administrative Conference recommendations Mr. Pederson criticizes at p. 446 were the result of Conference deliberations on a report published as P. Verkuil, Judicial Review of Informal Rulemaking, 60 Va.L.Rev. 185 (1974), in which he remarked: "[Recent] cases have contributed important parts to the rulemaking model. By defining the whole record to include the notice of rulemaking, all comments submitted by interested persons, and important factual information relied upon by the agency in formulating the rule, the courts are reflecting what seems to be congressional inclinations as well. And while there is some danger that defining the whole record in this way may back informal rulemaking into the 'on the record' posture of formal rulemaking, there still is room for agency expertise to roam. All that is required is for the agency to say where it has been. .   .   . "

(F) copies of all written material pertaining to the rule, including any drafts of the proposed and the final rule, submitted by the agency to the President or his designee directed by the President to review proposed or final rules for their regulatory impact; and

(G) a written explanation of the specific reasons for any significant changes made by the agency in the drafts of the proposed or final rule which respond to any comment received by the agency on the draft proposed rule, the proposed rule, the draft final rule, or the final rule, made by the President or his designee directed by the President to review proposed or final rules for their regulatory impact.

(2) The agency shall place the materials described in clauses (A) through [(G) above] in the file required by such paragraph as soon as practicable after such materials become available to the agency.

(3) The file required by paragraph (1) of this subsection need not include any material that need not be made available to the public under section 552 of this title [the Freedom of Information Act] if the agency includes in such file a statement that notes the existence of such material and the basis upon which the material is exempt from public disclosure under such section. The agency may not substantially rely on any such material in formulating a rule unless it makes the substance of such material available for adequate comment by interested persons. The agency may use summaries, aggregations of data, or other appropriate mechanisms so as to protect the confidentiality of such material to the maximum extent possible.

(4) No court shall hold unlawful or set aside an agency rule because of a violation of paragraph (1) of this subsection unless the court finds that such violation has precluded fair public consideration of a material issue of the rule making taken as a whole. Judicial review of compliance or noncompliance with paragraph (1) of this subsection shall be limited to review of action or inaction on the part of an agency.

STEVEN STARK * and SARAH WALD,** SETTING NO RECORDS: THE FAILED ATTEMPTS TO LIMIT THE RECORD IN REVIEW OF ADMINISTRATIVE ACTION †

36 Ad.L.Rev. 333 (1984).

sion to allow off-road vehicles in national seashores and parks, they circumscribe their inquiry to what they commonly describe as "review on the record." By this, courts generally mean that they never examine an agency determination from scratch or *de novo,* but limit their review to those documents which the agency examined when it made its original decision. . . . [A]n examination of the concept of review on the record in the courts surprisingly reveals that the doctrine no

* Lecturer on Law, Harvard Law School.

** Ass't. Sec'y. of Consumer Affairs and Business Regulation, Commonwealth of Massachusetts.

† Reprinted with permission.

longer exists in any coherent form, although judges and analysts pretend that it is still viable. Faced with the difficulty of defining the record in specific cases, courts have developed so many unwritten exceptions to the doctrine of record review, that industrious advocates now can introduce any evidence they choose in cases reviewing informal administrative action. . . .

In . . . Citizens of Overton Park v. Volpe and Camp v. Pitts, the Supreme Court set up severe obstacles to challenging parties who want to introduce evidence of their own to supplement the record as defined by the agency. In both cases, the rationale seemed to be that expanding the definition of what constitutes the record would expand the nature of judicial review beyond its proper scope. . . .

Because the Court rejected almost any submission of evidence by challenging plaintiffs in these two cases, it implied that the definition of what constitutes the record on review of informal agency action was quite narrow. The practical effect of these two decisions meant that even in cases where an agency failed to explain its original decisions adequately, the agency would be given another chance to explain its actions on review by a court, with no evidentiary rebuttal from the challenging party. . . .

These two decisions also limited the scope of discovery. Since little or no extra-record evidence would be admissible, challenging parties most likely could not search for such evidence through discovery under the relevancy standard of the Federal Rules of Civil Procedure. . . .

Presented with the Overton Park-Camp formula, some circuit courts soon announced their allegiance to a concept of judicial review based solely on the administrative record which the agency claimed existed at the time the agency made its decision. But because of its inherent contradictions, the rule soon proved impossible to apply. Thus, in many cases where a circuit court announced its allegiance to this rule, the court then broke the rule by allowing evidence from outside the administrative record as defined by the agency.[1] . . .

Briefly, the exceptions which have developed to allow extra-record evidence are the following: (1) when agency action is not adequately explained in the record before the court; (2) when the agency failed to consider factors which are relevant to its final decision; (3) when an agency considered evidence which it failed to include in the record; (4) when a case is so complex that a court needs more evidence to enable it to understand the issues clearly; (5) in cases where evidence arising after the agency action shows whether the decision was correct or not; (6) in cases where agencies are sued for a failure to take action; (7) in cases arising under the National Environmental Policy Act; and (8) in cases where relief is at issue, especially at the preliminary injunction stage. . . . [W]ith so many broad exceptions to the stated rule of

1. For examples of courts acknowledging the rule of limited record review, then recognizing exceptions, see, e.g., Public Power Council v. Johnson, 674 F.2d 791 (9th Cir.1982); Asarco, Inc. v. EPA, 616 F.2d 1153 (9th Cir.1980); County of Suffolk v. Secretary of the Interior, 562 F.2d 1368 (2d Cir.1977).

review on the record, lawyers challenging agency action should be able to find an exception applicable to their case. But even if a court should disagree, the procedure a court must follow to evaluate such a claim virtually guarantees that the court will examine the evidence anyway. Having examined the questioned evidence, it becomes difficult for the court to keep the evidence out of the record, or to make rigid distinctions between what belonged in a voluminous record and what did not.

This tendency of courts to accept evidence once it has examined it is apparent in Asarco, Inc. v. EPA, 616 F.2d 1153 (9th Cir.1980), a recent Ninth Circuit case. . . . There, the district court had considered extra-record testimony and documents designed to illuminate the necessity of an air pollution order requiring the plaintiffs to install a sampling station in a 1,000 foot stack at a copper smelter. After a hearing, the district court found that the order requiring stack-testing was arbitrary and capricious because the evidence did not support the scientific conclusion that certain chemical reactions occurred.

On appeal, the court of appeals found that the district court had gone too far in considering the extensive extra-record testimony. However, the court of appeals went on to look closely at the extra-record testimony of each expert in order to analyze whether the testimony fit a record exception. While the court ruled that much of the evidence should have been excluded, the court did admit some of the evidence. The court then invalidated EPA's action, based on the administrative record, supplemented by proper explanatory evidence established in the district court. What changed the court's mind? Was it the properly submitted evidence or was it the evidence which should have been excluded? It is difficult to say.

Furthermore, the exceptions provide a sound justification for a wide scope of discovery in cases challenging informal administrative action. In the absence of these exceptions, the government could argue that because no extra-record evidence is admissible, the plaintiffs should be permitted little discovery about the contents of the record because it cannot possibly lead to admissible evidence. The fact that some extra-record evidence is admissible cuts off a blanket refusal by the agency to produce documents concerning the decision and, in fact,

[A]cceptance of a broader definition of the record in cases reviewing informal agency decisions does not have to imply an illegitimate role for courts. . . . When, as here, many of the procedural protections of the APA are inapplicable, courts have a responsibility to undertake a more searching review of the record and merits in order to assure that agency action is lawful. Without a broader concept of record review in these cases, courts would give agencies unreviewable authority to make the important decisions which affect the lives of all Americans. To do that would be to undermine the nature and purpose of judicial review itself.

NOTE

The last paragraphs of the preceding article open up the question of inquiring into a decision-maker's mental processes. Whatever might be said about the need for broad exposure of an agency's data base, the agency thought process has generally been regarded as privileged.[1] Indeed, in concluding that "the court may require the administrative officials who participated in the decision to give testimony explaining their actions" in the absence of contemporaneous findings, the Court in Overton Park threatened to reopen a chasm many had thought bridged over. The process threatened to bring into public view pre-decisional advice to the Secretary ordinarily regarded as privileged, as part of the "full administrative record that was before the Secretary at the time he made his decision."[2] Whether or not "formal findings" were "required" by Overton Park, surely there was profound impetus to making them in the Court's observation that, "where there are administrative findings that were made at the same time as the decision, as was the case in [UNITED STATES v. MORGAN, 313 U.S. 409 (1941)], there must be a strong showing of bad faith or improper behavior before such inquiry may be made." See also Camp v. Pitts, p. 443 above.

The Morgan case was the fourth in a series involving the validity of an order of the Secretary of Agriculture fixing the maximum rates to be charged by market agencies for buying and selling livestock at the Kansas City Stockyards. In the first of the Morgan cases, discussed within at pp. 882–902,[3] the market agencies had alleged, "on information and belief," that the Secretary had been irresponsible in the manner in which he reached his decision, and the Court found this allegation sufficient to withstand a motion to dismiss. Upon remand to the District Court, the plaintiff filed more than a hundred interrogatories, asking the Secretary about his time expenditure in studying this and that part of the record, about his reading of the briefs, about his consideration of one or another approach to the problem of fixing rates for services, and so on. Many hours were then spent in his office, while depositions were taken; Secretary Wallace is said to have felt that he had been rather roughly handled by the lawyers. Apart from his wounded sensibilities, the sheer burdensomeness of responding to hec-

1. Aspects of this problem are treated in connection with the Freedom of Information Act's Exemption 5 (pp. 735–48 below), the Government in the Sunshine Act (p. 780 ff. below) and the problem of political pressure (p. 957 ff. below).

2. See the discussion of Exemption 5 of the Freedom of Information Act, 5 U.S.C. § 552(b)(5), at pp. 735–48 below.

3. Morgan II, 304 U.S. 1 (1937), having to do with the filing of an intermediate report, is set out at p. 886. Morgan III, 307 U.S. 183 (1939), involved the propriety of the District Court's retaining control over impounded moneys that represented the difference between the rates the commission merchants (the market agencies) had charged their clients and the rates the Secretary had sought to establish. After his defeats in Morgan I and Morgan II, the Secretary decided to begin the proceedings afresh; to that end, he set aside his original rate order pending the creation of a new one. The District Court, over the Secretary's objection, then proposed to pay over to the commission merchants the impounded moneys held by the court. But the Supreme Court said that the District Court should keep the moneys until the case was really at an end.

toring questions about how a decision had been arrived at seemed more likely to impede the administrative process than to illuminate it.[4] Time spent by adjudicators in explaining what they had done in past cases must be drawn from the time available for working on the new cases that remain to be adjudicated.

Uncertainty about the permissibility of exploratory expeditions into the decision-maker's methods and mentality continued for five years, when the same case came back to the Court for the fourth time. Morgan IV involved the validity of a rate order promulgated by the Secretary to supplement the one that had initiated the litigation. In sustaining the Secretary's final order, the Court, in an opinion by Mr. Justice Frankfurter, sought to put at rest for the federal courts the question of whether the mental processes of an administrative tribunal are to be probed in later judicial proceedings. Said the Court: "Over the Government's objection the district court authorized the market agencies to take the deposition of the Secretary. The Secretary thereupon appeared in person at the trial. He was questioned at length regarding the process by which he reached the conclusions of his order, including the manner and extent of his study of the record and his consultation with subordinates. His testimony shows that he dealt with the enormous record in a manner not unlike the practice of judges in similar situations, and that he held various conferences with the examiner who heard the evidence. Much was made of his disregard of a memorandum from one of his officials who, on reading the proposed order, urged considerations favorable to the market agencies. But the short of the business is that the Secretary should never have been subjected to this examination. The proceeding before the Secretary 'has a quality resembling that of a judicial proceeding'. Morgan v. United States, 298 U.S. 468, 480. Such an examination of a judge would be destructive of judicial responsibility. Just as a judge cannot be subjected to such a scrutiny, . . . so the integrity of the administrative process must be equally respected. . . . It will bear repeating that although the administrative process has had a different development and pursues somewhat different ways from those of courts, they are to be deemed collaborative instrumentalities of justice and the appropriate independence of each should be respected by the other."

The Supreme Court's characterization of subsequent developments

quires a "strong showing of bad faith or improper behavior"—captures their flavor if not the precise facts. Usual expressions by reviewing courts were that an agency's recital "that it has considered the evi-

4. It also ran counter, one may add, to the teaching of a much earlier case, Chicago, Burlington & Quincy Ry. Co. v. Babcock, 204 U.S. 585 (1907): Railroad companies attacked tax assessments against them, asserting that they were fraudulent and had been influenced by political duress. The members of the assessing board were called as witnesses and were cross-examined as to the mental operations which led to the assessments. This was held by the Supreme Court, speaking through Mr. Justice Holmes, to be improper; the board members were entitled to the immunity of a jury or an umpire, if not to "the possibly higher immunities of a judge."

dence and rendered a decision according to its responsibilities [could not] be overcome by speculative allegations." Braniff Airways, Inc. v. CAB, 379 F.2d 453 (D.C.Cir.1967); and see B. Schwartz, Institutional Administrative Decisions and the Morgan Cases: A Reexamination, 4 J.Pub.Law 49, 63, 65 (1955).[5]

What constitutes a speculative allegation, however, cannot always be anticipated before judgment. In S.D. Warren Co. v. NLRB, 342 F.2d 814 (1st Cir.1965), the absence of two material exhibits from the record of an earlier proceeding—probably innocent, but suggestive that the case may have been decided on an incomplete record—led to a request for affidavits from Board members whether they had in fact received and considered the exhibits. Singer Sewing Machine Co. v. NLRB, 329 F.2d 200 (4th Cir.1964), directed an inquiry into the behavior of one of the Board's regional directors on the strength of the company's offer to prove by testimony of managerial employees and a union business agent that the director had taken an impermissible approach; the mental process rule must give way, the court said, when a prima facie showing of misconduct has been made, citing a case having to do with interrogation of jurors after discovery of evidence of their misconduct.[6] And in United Savings Bank v. Saxon, 209 F.Supp. 319 (D.D.C.1962),

5. In National Nutritional Foods Ass'n v. FDA, 491 F.2d 1141, 1145–46 (2d Cir.), cert. denied 419 U.S. 874 (1974), it was asserted that Commissioner of Food and Drugs could not possibly have given personal attention to highly controversial regulations he signed within thirteen days of taking office, particularly in light of the other business he dispatched during that period; and on that ground, leave to take his deposition was sought. Rather than demonstrate the bad faith necessary to justify further inquiry, the court thought the case's facts "vividly illustrate the necessity of adhering to the presumption of regularity with respect to the participation of the officer authorized to sign administrative orders, especially in the context of the promulgation of legislative rules as distinguished from adjudication. . . . Petitioners do not contest that predecessors of Commissioner Schmidt, notably Commissioner Edwards, took an active part in the development of the regulations. All would have been well, apparently, if Commissioner Edwards had continued to serve. But because he resigned in April 1973 and Commissioner Schmidt did not take office until mid-July, promulgation must wait until the new Commissioner could personally familiarize himself with 1,000 pages of formal exceptions, 20,000 letters, and the staff's views about them, and read the relevant portions of the record (or summaries of them). . . . With the enormous increase in delegation of lawmaking power which Congress has been obliged to make to agencies, both independent and in the

executive branch, and in the complexity of life, government would become impossible if courts were to insist on anything of the sort. It would suffice under the circumstances that Commissioner Schmidt considered the summaries of the objections and of the answers contained in the elaborate preambles and conferred with his staff about them. There is no reason why he could not have done this even in the limited time available, . . . although we do not envy him the task. In any event, absent the most powerful preliminary showing to the contrary, effective government requires us to presume that he did. It was his special insight into the workings of the administrative process, as it was and might become, that enabled Mr. Justice Frankfurter in Morgan IV to persuade the Court to retreat from Morgan I. This is no time for an attempt to regain territory so wisely yielded." See Note, 50 Wash.L.Rev. 739 (1975).

6. Commenting on this case, 78 Harv.L. Rev. 655, 657 (1965) says: "Unfortunately, the court gave no explanation of its terms, but it seems that prima facie is not used in its more usual sense to mean sufficient evidence to establish misconduct if not rebutted, but is rather used to mean enough evidence to make it reasonable to conclude that there had been misconduct. In this respect, the court is adopting a more liberal position than its language alone would indicate." See also KFC National Management Corp. v. NLRB, 497 F.2d 298 (2d Cir.1974).

the Comptroller of the Currency had given permission to Tinker National Bank to open a branch in competition with Union Savings. Union Savings alleged "on information and belief" that this had been done "on the basis of ex parte representations by the Tinker National Bank and a 'personal relationship' between the president of said Bank and the defendant Saxon, and in violation of Title 12 U.S.C. § 36, and § 4.5(a) of the Rules and Regulations of the Bureau of Comptroller of the Currency." On no further showing than this, Judge Walsh declared: "Certainly, this court does not encourage the procedure of taking the oral deposition of the head of an agency of the United States Government, and under normal circumstances would not allow such procedure. The court recognizes that such an official's time and the exigencies of his everyday business would be severely impeded if every plaintiff filing a complaint against an agency head, in his official capacity, were allowed to take his oral deposition. Such procedure would be contrary to the public interest. . . . In the instant case, however, plaintiffs allege actions personal to the defendant and in violation of the United States Code. Therefore, under the circumstances of this case, and restricted solely to the facts of this case, the court is of the opinion that justice and reason require that plaintiff be allowed to take the oral deposition of the defendant, but such deposition should be limited to the procedural action taken by the defendant as to the subject matter of this case, and not the workings of his (Saxon's) mind."

Notable recent refusals to inquire were made in Sierra Club v. Costle, 657 F.2d 298 (D.C.Cir.1981), p. 963 below; and in San Luis Obispo Mothers for Peace v. NRC, 751 F.2d 1287 (D.C.Cir.1984), 789 F.2d 26 (D.C.Cir. en banc 1986), p. 791 below.

(ii) Review of Factual Determinations in Proceedings Not Required to Be Decided on the Record

ASSOCIATION OF DATA PROCESSING SERVICE ORGANIZATIONS, INC. v. BOARD OF GOVERNORS OF THE FEDERAL RESERVE SYSTEM

United State Court of Appeals, District of Columbia Circuit, 1984.
745 F.2d 677.

by designation.

SCALIA, CIRCUIT JUDGE:

The Association of Data Processing Service Organizations, Inc. ("ADAPSO"), a national trade association representing the data processing industry, and two of its members petition this court for review of two orders of the Board of Governors of the Federal Reserve System, pursuant to 12 U.S.C. § 1848 (1982). In No. 82–1910, they seek review of the Board's July 9, 1982 order approving Citicorp's application to establish a subsidiary, Citishare, to engage in certain data processing and transmission services. In No. 82–2108, they seek review of the Board's August 23, 1982 order, entered after notice and comment rulemaking, amending those portions of Regulation Y which dealt with the performance of data processing activities by bank holding companies. We consolidated the two appeals.

The Bank Holding Company Act of 1956 requires all bank holding companies to seek prior regulatory approval before engaging in non-banking activities. The restrictions do not apply to:

> activities . . . which the Board after due notice and opportunity for hearing has determined (by order or regulation) to be so closely related to banking or managing or controlling banks as to be a proper incident thereto. . . . In determining whether a particular activity is a proper incident to banking or managing or controlling banks the Board shall consider whether its performance by an affiliate of a holding company can reasonably be expected to produce benefits to the public, such as greater convenience, increased competition, or gains in efficiency, that outweigh possible adverse effects, such as undue concentration of resources, decreased or unfair competition, conflicts of interests, or unsound banking practices.

12 U.S.C. § 1843(c)(8). Section 1848, the source of our review authority, provides that "[t]he findings of the Board as to the facts, if supported by substantial evidence, shall be conclusive."

On February 23, 1979, Citicorp applied for authority to engage . . . in the processing and transmission of banking, financial, and economic related data through timesharing, electronic funds transfer, home banking and other techniques. . . . The Board published notice of Citicorp's application, which was protested by ADAPSO, and set it for formal hearing. Before the hearing was held, Citicorp amended its application to add certain activities and to request amendment of Regulation Y to permit the activities it had specified. The Board published an Amended Order for Hearing and invited public comments and participation. A formal hearing was held before an Administrative Law Judge in which the merits of both the application and the proposed rule were considered. [M]ore than sixty companies and individuals submitted written comments on the proposed rule. [T]he ALJ decided that the activities proposed by Citicorp were closely related to banking and would produce benefits to the public which would outweigh their costs [and] also recommended amendments to Regulation Y that would permit those activities contained in the Citicorp application. On July 9, 1982, the Board adopted the ALJ's recommendation to approve the Citicorp application, with certain restrictions. On August 23, 1982, the Board adopted the ALJ's recommended amendments to Regulation Y, again with certain restrictions. ADAPSO, and two of its members, participants in the actions below, filed these petitions for review.

I. Standard of Review

We are faced at the outset with a dispute regarding the proper standard of review. These consolidated appeals call for us to review both an on-the-record adjudication and an informal notice and comment rulemaking. Petitioners contend that the substantial evidence standard, which presumably authorizes more rigorous judicial review, should govern our review of both orders. The Board agrees, noting that § 1848 applies a substantial evidence standard to factual determinations. . . . Intervenor Citicorp contends that while the substantial evidence standard should govern review of the Citicorp order, Regulation Y should be upset only if arbitrary or capricious. . . . The parties' submissions on this point reflect considerable confusion, which is understandable when one examines decisions defining the standard of review under this statute. . . . The courts of appeals, however, have applied the substantial evidence standard of § 1848 to Board adjudications such as the authorization in the first order here under review, while applying the arbitrary or capricious standard, despite § 1848, to Board rules, including specifically amendments of Regulation Y. In fact one appellate opinion has, like this one, addressed precisely the situation in which *both* an adjudicatory authorization *and* an amendment of Regulation Y were at issue in the same case—and applied the § 1848 substantial evidence standard to the former but the arbitrary or capricious to the latter. This would make a lot of sense if, as the Board has argued in some cases, § 1848 in its totality applies only to adjudication rather than rulemaking, since it is limited to "orders" of the Board, a word which the [APA] defines to mean the product of an adjudication. [APA] § 551(4), (6). Such a technical interpretation of the provision, however, has been uniformly and quite correctly rejected. That leaves the courts with the difficult task of explaining why the last sentence of § 1848, unlike all the rest of it, should be deemed to apply only to adjudication and not to rulemaking. Difficult, because there is nothing in either the text [1] or the legislative history of the section to suggest such a result. The courts applying the arbitrary or capricious standard to Board rulemaking . . . dispose of this problem either by totally ignoring it, or by noting that the parties "do not appear to contest" the point, or by the *ipse dixit* that "[w]e interpret [the last sentence of § 1848] to apply to findings of fact 'on the record' in an adjudicatory hearing as contrasted with a rulemaking proceeding".

We think that there is no basis for giving the last sentence of § 1848 anything less than the general application given to the rest of ~~~~~~~~~~~~ . . . [A]ts uich application to the requirement of factual

---

1. 12 U.S.C. § 1848 reads as follows:

"Any party aggrieved by an order of the Board under this chapter may obtain a review of such order in the United States Court of Appeals within any circuit wherein such party has its principal place of business or in the Court of Appeals in the District of Columbia by filing in the court, within thirty days after the entry of the Board's order, a petition praying that the order of the Board be set aside. A copy of such petition shall be forthwith transmit-

ted to the Board by the clerk of the court, and thereupon the Board shall file in the court the record made before the Board. . . . Upon the filing of such petition the court shall have the jurisdiction to affirm, set aside, or modify the order of the Board and to require the Board to take such action with regard to the matter under review as the court deems proper. The finding of the Board as to the facts, if supported by substantial evidence, shall be conclusive."

support the substantial evidence test and arbitrary or capricious test are one and the same. The former is only a specific application of the latter. . . . The "scope of review" provisions of the APA, § 706(2), are cumulative. Thus, an agency action which is supported by the required substantial evidence may in another regard be "arbitrary, capricious, an abuse of discretion, or otherwise not in accordance with law"—for example, because it is an abrupt and unexplained departure from agency precedent. Paragraph (A) of subsection 706(2)—the "arbitrary or capricious" provision—is a catch-all, picking up administrative misconduct not covered by the other more specific paragraphs. Thus, in those situations where paragraph (E) has no application (informal rulemaking, for example, which is not governed by §§ 556 and 557 to which paragraph (E) refers), paragraph (A) takes up the slack, so to speak, enabling the courts to strike down, as arbitrary, agency action that is devoid of needed factual support. When the arbitrary or capricious standard is performing that function of assuring factual support, there is no *substantive* difference between what it requires and what would be required by the substantial evidence test, since it is impossible to conceive of a "nonarbitrary" factual judgment supported only by evidence that is not substantial in the APA sense—i.e., not " 'enough to justify, if the trial were to a jury, a refusal to direct a verdict when the conclusion sought to be drawn . . . is one of fact for the jury' ".

We have noted on several occasions that the distinction between the substantial evidence test and the arbitrary or capricious test is "largely semantic", and have indeed described that view as "the emerging consensus of the Court of Appeals". . . . The distinctive function of paragraph (E)—what it achieves that paragraph (A) does not—is to require substantial evidence to be found *within the record of closed-record proceedings* to which it exclusively applies. The importance of that requirement should not be underestimated. It is true that, as the Supreme Court said in Camp v. Pitts, 411 U.S. 138, 142, even informal agency action (not governed by paragraph (E)) must be reviewed only on the basis of "the administrative record already in existence." But that is quite a different and less onerous requirement, meaning only that whether the administrator was arbitrary must be determined on the basis of what he had before him when he acted, and not on the basis of "some new record made initially in the reviewing court," id. That "administrative record" might well include crucial material that was neither shown to nor known by the private parties in the proceeding— as indeed appears to have been the situation in Camp v. Pitts itself. It is true that, in informal rulemaking, at least the most critical factual material that is used to support the agency's position on review must have been made public in the proceeding and exposed to refutation. That requirement, however, does not extend to all data, and it only applies in rulemaking and not in other informal agency action, since it derives not from the arbitrary or capricious test but from the command of 5 U.S.C. § 553(c) that "the agency . . . give interested persons an opportunity to participate in the rule making." See Portland Cement Association v. Ruckelshaus, 486 F.2d 375, 393 n. 67 (D.C.Cir.1973).

Consolidated cases such as those before us here—involving simultaneous review of a rule (whose factual basis is governed only by paragraph (A)'s catch-all control against "arbitrary or capricious" action) and of a formal adjudication dealing with the same subject (whose factual basis is governed by paragraph (E)'s requirement of substantial evidence)—demonstrate why the foregoing interpretation of the two standards is the only interpretation that makes sense. If the standards were substantively different . . . the Citicorp order, authorizing one bank holding company's data processing services, would be subject to more rigorous judicial review of factual support than the Regulation Y order which, due to its general applicability, would affect the operations of every bank holding company in the nation. Or, to put the point another way: If the Board had never issued any Regulation Y, and simply determined in the context of a particular application that the provision of timesharing services is "closely related" to banking, that determination, which could be reconsidered and revised in the context of the next adjudication, would require more factual support than the same determination in a rulemaking, which would have immediate nationwide application and, until amended by further rulemaking, would have to be applied to all subsequent applications.

This seemingly upside-down application of varying standards is not an issue in the present case since, as we have observed, § 1848 makes it clear that only *one* standard, the substantial evidence test—applies to review of all Board actions. The relevance of the foregoing discussion here is to determine what that standard *means*. What we have said suggests that the normal (APA) meaning of the "substantial evidence" terminology connotes a substantive standard no different from the arbitrary or capricious test. One cannot dismiss out of hand, however, the possibility that, in this particular statute, a different meaning was intended—in which case that different standard would govern review of both rulemaking and adjudication. A number of "substantial evidence" review provisions have been attached to rulemaking authority, particular in recent years. See, e.g., 29 U.S.C. § 655(f) (1982) (Occupational Safety and Health Act); 30 U.S.C. § 816(a) (1982) (Federal Coal Mine Health and Safety Act); 15 U.S.C. § 1193(e)(3) (1982) (Flammable Fabrics Act); 15 U.S.C. § 57a(e)(3)(A) (1982) (FTC Improvement.

. . . . It is conceivable that some of these were intended, as the Fifth Circuit found with regard to such a provision in the Consumer Product Safety Act, 15 U.S.C. § 2060 (1982), to require the courts "to scrutinize [agency] actions more closely than an 'arbitrary or capricious' standard would allow." Aqua Slide 'N' Dive Corp. v. CPSC, 569 F.2d 831, 837 (5th Cir.1978). Congress's unpropitious use of the "substantial evidence" APA language for such a purpose is plausible, since the standard has acquired a reputation for being more stringent.[2] One

---

2. The reason for this reputation, one may surmise, is that under the APA the substantial evidence test applies almost exclusively to formal adjudication (formal rulemaking is rare), which is, by contrast to rulemaking, characteristically long on

should not be too quick, however, to impute such a congressional intent. There is surely little appeal to an ineffable review standard that lies somewhere in-between the quantum of factual support required to go to a jury (the traditional "substantial evidence" test) and the "preponderance of the evidence" standard that would apply in de novo review. . . . The Supreme Court has evidently rejected the notion that [§ 1848] alters normal APA review requirements, since the Court's opinions reviewing Board action deem the provision unworthy of mention, and specifically accord the Board "the greatest deference." We hold, therefore, that the § 1848 "substantial evidence" requirement applicable to our review here demands a quantum of factual support no different from that demanded by the substantial evidence provision of the APA, which is in turn no different from that demanded by the arbitrary or capricious standard. . . .

NOTES

(1) ETHYL CORP. v. ENVIRONMENTAL PROTECTION AGENCY, 541 F.2d 1 (D.C.Cir.1975), cert. denied 426 U.S. 941 (1976). Section 211(c)(1)(A) of the Clean Air Act authorizes the Administrator of EPA to promulgate regulations that "control or prohibit the manufacture, introduction into commerce, offering for sale, or sale of any fuel or fuel additive for use in a motor vehicle or motor vehicle engine (A) if any emission products of such fuel or fuel additive will endanger the public health or welfare. . . ." Acting pursuant to this authority, the Administrator determined that leaded gasoline automotive emissions present "a significant risk of harm" to the public health, thereby endangering it within the contemplation of the statute. Based on this determination, the Administrator issued regulations requiring annual reductions in the lead content of leaded gasoline.

Various manufacturers of lead additives and refiners of gasoline petitioned for review. A panel of the court, one judge dissenting, ordered the regulations set aside. A petition for a rehearing en banc was granted, the judgment and opinions of the panel were vacated, and the case was reargued before the nine judges of the court. The result was a 5–4 affirmance of the EPA action. Judge Wright wrote the majority opinion. His discussion of the "Standard of Review" included this:

"In promulgating the low-lead regulations under Section 211, EPA engaged in informal rule-making. As such, since the statute does not indicate otherwise, its procedures are conducted pursuant to [APA] § 553 . . .. Our review of the evidence is governed by APA § 706(2) (A)–(D), which requires us to strike 'agency action, findings, and conclusions' that we find to be 'arbitrary, capricious, an abuse of discretion, or otherwise not in accordance with law. . . . ' This standard of review is a highly deferential one. It presumes agency action to be valid. Moreover, it forbids the court's substituting its judgment for

facts and short on policy—so that the inadequacy of factual support is typically the central issue in the judicial appeal and is the most common reason for reversal.

that of the agency and requires affirmance if a rational basis exists for the agency's decision.

"This is not to say, however, that we must rubberstamp the agency decision as correct. To do so would render the appellate process a superfluous (although time-consuming) ritual. Rather, the reviewing court must assure itself that the agency decision was 'based on a consideration of the relevant factors . . . .' Moreover, it must engage in a 'substantial inquiry' into the facts, one that is 'searching and careful.' This is particularly true in highly technical cases such as this one. 'A court does not depart from its proper function when it undertakes a study of the record, hopefully perceptive, even as to the evidence on technical and specialized matters, for this enables the court to penetrate to the underlying decisions of the agency, to satisfy itself that the agency has exercised a reasoned discretion, with reasons that do not deviate from or ignore the ascertainable legislative intent.' Greater Boston Television Corp. v. FCC, 444 F.2d 841, 850 (D.C.Cir.1970), cert. denied 403 U.S. 923 (1971).[1]

"There is no inconsistency between the deferential standard of review and the requirement that the reviewing court involve itself in even the most complex evidentiary matters; rather, the two indicia of arbitrary and capricious review stand in careful balance. The close scrutiny of the evidence is intended to educate the court. It must understand enough about the problem confronting the agency to comprehend the meaning of the evidence relied upon and the evidence discarded; the questions addressed by the agency and those bypassed; the choices open to the agency and those made. The more technical the case, the more intensive must be the court's effort to understand the evidence, for without an appropriate understanding of the case before it the court cannot properly perform its appellate function. But that function must be performed with conscientious awareness of its limited nature. The enforced education into the intricacies of the problem before the agency is not designed to enable the court to become a superagency that can supplant the agency's expert decision-maker. To the contrary, the court must give due deference to the agency's ability to rely on its own developed expertise. The immersion in the evidence is designed *solely* to enable the court to determine whether the agency decision was rational and based on consideration of the relevant factors.

long as this test is met. . . .

"Thus, after our careful study of the record, we must take a step back from the agency decision. We must look at the decision not as the chemist, biologist or statistician that we are qualified neither by training nor experience to be, but as a reviewing court exercising our narrowly defined duty of holding agencies to certain minimal standards of rationality. 'Although [our] inquiry into the facts is to be searching

---

1. While Greater Boston Television Corp. v. FCC, was a substantial evidence case, its statement of the proper scope of a reviewing court's inquiry into the evidence has been adopted by . . . informal rulemaking cases [decided by this Circuit.]

and careful, the ultimate standard of review is a narrow one.' We must affirm unless the agency decision is arbitrary or capricious." [2]

Judge Wright for the majority and Judge Wilkey for the minority presented detailed analyses of the evidence concerning the health consequences of airborne lead. Judge Bazelon, with whom Judge McGowan concurred, wrote in part as follows:

"I agree with the court's construction of the statute that the Administrator is called upon to make 'essentially legislative policy judgments' in assessing risks to public health. But I cannot agree that this automatically relieves the Administrator's decision from the 'procedural . . . rigor proper for questions of fact.' Quite the contrary, this case strengthens my view that [3] '. . . in cases of great technological complexity, the best way for courts to guard against unreasonable or erroneous administrative decisions is not for the judges themselves to scrutinize the technical merits of each decision. Rather, it is to establish a decision-making process that assures a reasoned decision that can be held up to the scrutiny of the scientific community and the public.' This record provides vivid demonstration of the dangers implicit in the contrary view, ably espoused by Judge Leventhal, which would have judges 'steeping' themselves 'in technical matters to determine whether the agency "has exercised a reasoned discretion." ' It is one thing for judges to scrutinize FCC judgments concerning diversification of media ownership to determine if they are rational. But I doubt judges contribute much to improving the quality of the difficult decisions which must be made in highly technical areas when they take it upon themselves to decide, as did the panel in this case, that 'in assessing the scientific and medical data the Administrator made clear errors of judgment.' The process [of] making a de novo evaluation of the scientific evidence inevitably invites judges of opposing views to make plausible-sounding, but simplistic, judgments of the relative weight to be afforded various pieces of technical data. . . .

"Because substantive review of mathematical and scientific evidence by technically illiterate judges is dangerously unreliable, I continue to believe we will do more to improve administrative decision-making by concentrating our efforts on strengthening administrative procedures. . . . "

Judge Leventhal answered in part as follows:[3a]

"Taking [Chief Judge Bazelon's] opinion in its fair implication, as a signal to judges to abstain from any substantive review, it is my view that while giving up is the easier course, it is not legitimately open to us at present. In the case of legislative enactments, the sole responsibility of the courts is constitutional due process review. In the case of

2. [Ed.] Most of Judge Wright's extensive documentation is omitted. Citizens to Preserve Overton Park was referred to or quoted twelve times.

3. International Harvester Co. v. Ruckelshaus, 478 F.2d 615, 652 (D.C.Cir.1973) (Bazelon, C.J., concurring).

3a. [Ed. Another Bazelon-Leventhal exchange is found in their separate statements in Friends of the Earth v. U.S. Atomic Energy Comm., 485 F.2d 1031, 1032–1035 (D.C.Cir.1973).]

agency decision-making the courts have an additional responsibility set by Congress. Congress has been willing to delegate its legislative powers broadly—and courts have upheld such delegation—because there is court review to assure that the agency exercises the delegated power within statutory limits, and that it fleshes out objectives within those limits by an administration that is not irrational or discriminatory. Nor is that envisioned judicial role ephemeral, as Overton Park [4] makes clear. . . .

"The aim of the judges is not to exercise expertise or decide technical questions, but simply to gain sufficient background orientation. Our obligation is not to be jettisoned because our initial technical understanding may be meagre when compared to our initial grasp of FCC or freedom of speech questions. When called upon to make de novo decisions, individual judges have had to acquire the learning pertinent to complex technical questions in such fields as economics, science, technology and psychology. Our role is not as demanding when we are engaged in review of agency decisions, where we exercise restraint, and affirm even if we would have decided otherwise so long as the agency's decisionmaking is not irrational or discriminatory.

"The substantive review of administrative action is modest, but it cannot be carried out in a vacuum of understanding. Better no judicial review at all than a charade that gives the imprimatur without the substance of judicial confirmation that the agency is not acting unreasonably. Once the presumption of regularity in agency action [5] is challenged with a factual submission, and even to determine whether such a challenge has been made, the agency's record and reasoning has to be looked at. If there is some factual support for the challenge, there must be either evidence or judicial notice available explicating the agency's result, or a remand to supply the gap. . . .

"On issues of substantive review, on conformance to statutory standards and requirements of rationality, the judges must act with restraint. Restraint, yes, abdication, no."

(2) WILLIAM F. PEDERSEN, JR., FORMAL RECORDS AND INFORMAL RULEMAKING, 85 Yale L.J. 38, 59* (1975):

"[D]etailed factual review of regulations by those with the power to change them takes place in two forums only—at the level of the office of primary interest and working group inside EPA

. . . understand the technical complexities of a regulation. So to a great extent will members of the industry being regulated. But the review process within the agency and the executive branch does not spur a working group to make sure that the final

---

4. [Overton Park] requires the reviewing court to scrutinize the facts and consider whether the agency decision was "based on a consideration of the relevant factors" in the context of nonformalized, discretionary executive decisionmaking. A fortiori, at least that rigor of review should apply to more formal decisionmaking processes like informal rulemaking.

5. Pacific States Box and Basket Co. v. White, 296 U.S. 176 (1935).

* Reprinted by permission of the author, The Yale Law Journal Company and Fred B. Rothman & Co.

regulation adequately reflects these complexities. To the extent that internal review is the only review worried about, comments by the affected industry or (to pick a less frequent case) by environmental groups may not be given the kind of detailed consideration they deserve. Since the higher levels of review are unwilling or unable to consider the more complex issues, the best hope for detailed, effective review of complex regulations is the judiciary.

"Judge Leventhal's opinions in International Harvester Co. v. Ruckelshaus [6] and Portland Cement Association v. Ruckelshaus,[7] and Judge Bell's opinion in Texas v. EPA [8] represent a factual probing several times more detailed than the regulations at issue had received since they were first written. . . . "

(3) Ethyl Corp. was decided three years before Vermont Yankee Nuclear Power Corp. v. NRDC, p. 248 above, which at the least decided this debate in favor of Judge Leventhal. A post-Vermont Yankee example of factual review may be found in the D.C. Circuit's 125-page opinion in Sierra Club v. Costle, relevant excerpts of which, for these purposes, are set out beginning on page 845 below.

(iii) Review of Findings and Reasons in Informal Adjudication

INDEPENDENT U.S. TANKER OWNERS COMMITTEE v. LEWIS

United States Court of Appeals, District of Columbia Circuit, 1982.
690 F.2d 908

[Under the relevant federal statutes the U.S. merchant marine fleet is divided into two distinct segments. The first, the "Jones Act" fleet is owned and operated by United States citizens and by statute is given the exclusive right to engage in domestic trade, which is defined as trade "between points in the United States, including Districts, Territories and possessions. . . . " Unlike the Jones Act fleet, which is not subsidized, U.S. carriers engaged in foreign trade are heavily subsidized by the government. A condition of the subsidy is that the carrier will operate only in foreign trade. However, the statute provides that the Maritime Administration (MarAd) may consent to the operation of a subsidized vessel in the domestic trade for up to six months in any twelve-month period whenever it determines that such "transfer is necessary or appropriate to carry out the purposes of this chapter." Proportional repayment of the subsidy is required whenever such consent is granted.

In the 1970's, conditions in the international oil market coupled with overbuilding caused a virtual collapse of the world tanker market. World-scale rates were well below the break-even costs of U.S. tankers, subsidized or not. The domestic market, on the other hand, especially

---

6. 478 F.2d 615 (D.C.Cir.1973).

7. 486 F.2d 375 (D.C.Cir.1973), cert. denied, 417 U.S. 921 (1974).

8. 499 F.2d 289 (5th Cir.1974).

West Coast/Panama Canal trade from Alaska was flourishing. As a result, there was persistent pressure from subsidized vessels for permission to enter the domestic market on a permanent basis in exchange for a total repayment of any construction subsidies received.

MarAd's response was to grant a series of requests for repayment and permission to engage in domestic trade; competitors brought suit challenging MarAd's authority to do so. The district court upheld MarAd's power. The D.C. Circuit reversed; relying on the total absence of any authorization in either the Act or the legislative history, the court held that MarAd could not lift the domestic restrictions for any period longer than the six months allowed in the Act. The Supreme Court reversed, citing MarAd's broad contracting powers and the absence of anything in the Act prohibiting MarAd from permanently lifting the restriction.

Thereafter MarAd published an interim rule which stated that applications for repayment and permission to enter the domestic trade would be granted in "exceptional circumstances." [1] After MarAd had approved such an application, its action was challenged by the U.S. Tanker Owners Committee, composed of owners of nonsubsidized tanker vessels engaged in domestic trade, particularly in carrying crude oil from Alaska to points in the U.S. The district court granted summary judgment for MarAd.]

Before TAMM and WILKEY, CIRCUIT JUDGES, and SENIOR CIRCUIT JUDGE FAIRCHILD, sitting by designation.

WILKEY, CIRCUIT JUDGE: . . . . Our responsibility in reviewing this informal adjudication [2] is essentially two-fold. First, we must review the record to ensure that MarAd's decision is not "arbitrary, capricious, an abuse of discretion, or otherwise not in accordance with law." The critical elements of such review are clear. While MarAd's decision is "entitled to a presumption of regularity," the presumption "is not to shield . . . action from a thorough, probing, in-depth review." [3] Thus, though we are not permitted to substitute our judgment for MarAd's, our inquiry must be "searching and careful," [4] and we must ensure "both that [MarAd] has adequately considered all relevant factors . . . . and that it has demonstrated 'a rational connection between the facts found and the choices made.' " [5]

---

among others" to be considered in determining whether exceptional circumstances existed:

(1) The purposes and policy of the Act.

(2) The economic impact on the U.S.–flag foreign and domestic tanker fleets.

(3) The economic impact on shipbuilding in the U.S.

(4) The financial situation of the applicant and its related companies.

(5) The financial interest of the Government including Title XI obligations.

adjudication is informal because no requirement of a hearing "on the record" is to be found in the Maritime Act nor reasonably inferred from its legislative history. See 5 U.S.C. § 554 (1976).

3. Citizens to Preserve Overton Park, Inc. v. Volpe, 401 U.S. 402, 415.

4. Id. at 416.

5. Home Box Office, Inc. v. FCC, 567 F.2d 9, 35 (per curiam), cert. denied, 434 U.S. 829 [set out at p. 921 below].

Our second obligation is to examine the procedures MarAd employed in reaching its decision to ensure that they comply with the APA and any applicable statutory or constitutional requirements. The critical elements of this review, however, are far from clear. The APA rulemaking requirements of notice, an opportunity for comment, and a concise general statement of basis and purpose do not extend to informal adjudication. And where, as here, MarAd's authorization to accept repayment applications is inferred from rather than found in the Maritime Act, there are no statutorily mandated procedures to which the court can turn. Yet, some minimum procedures are necessary to provide a record adequate for the court to perform its review.

The distinct and steady trend of the courts has been to demand in informal adjudications procedures similar to those already required in informal rulemaking.[6] Courts have required *some explanation* for agency action [7] and, to ensure the adequacy of that explanation, some opportunity for interested parties to be informed of and comment upon the relevant evidence before the agency.[8] Thus, despite the Supreme Court's dictum in Vermont Yankee Nuclear Power Corp. v. Natural Resources Defense Council, Inc.,[9] that courts may not add to the procedural requirements of the APA except in "extremely rare" circumstances, we are justified in demanding some sort of procedures for notice, comment, and a statement of reasons as a necessary means of carrying out our responsibility for a thorough and searching review.

This demand is further bolstered and given a more concrete form by the interim rule adopted by MarAd. It states the procedures MarAd must follow in considering applications for total repayment of unamortized CDS for tankers of at least 100,000 DWT.

> With respect to any such request received, the Board will publish a notice in the Federal Register, providing opportunity for comment by interested parties. After the Board has acted upon any such application, the Board will publish a concise written explanation for its action.
>
> . . .

We must, therefore, ensure not only that MarAd's decision was not arbitrary or capricious, but also, as a related task, that MarAd made available for comment all relevant evidence and produced an adequate explanation for its action, canvassing the competing comments received and explaining why it resolved the differences as it did.

[The court then examined MarAd's decisional process and concluded that it was defective. Some indication of the court's analysis is suggested by the following:] [W]here an agency's analytic task *begins* rather than ends with a set of forecasts, sound practice would seem to dictate disclosure of those forecasts so that interested parties can

---

6. K. Davis, Administrative Law Treatise § 14.24 (2d ed. 1980).

7. Dunlop v. Bachowski, 421 U.S. 560, 571–72 (1975); Citizens to Preserve Overton Park, Inc. v. Volpe, 401 U.S. 402, 420.

8. U.S. Lines v. FMC, 584 F.2d 519, 534 (1978) [noted at p. 244 above].

9. 435 U.S. 519, 524 (1978) [set out at p. 248 above].

comment upon the conclusions properly to be drawn from them. We do not wish to lay too much stress upon the particular point. But the failing is part of an overall picture of totally unacceptable agency practice: A staff report was produced. It differed in fundamental respects from prior staff reports to which interested parties directed their comments. (*Misdirected* their comments, we now should say.) MarAd relied on the report in making a decision with substantial economic consequences. But the decision was published without any explanation. The report remained buried in the bowels of the agency.

All standards of fairness and due process in administrative law preclude such behavior. And the only way to ensure that it will not continue is to refuse to accept the decision resulting from it.

. . .

NOTES

(1) Do you agree that adoption of a judicial requirement of findings and reasons is consistent with Vermont Yankee? With Overton Park? Note that whether required or not, findings are a common element of federal informal adjudication. See p. 474 below. The leading authority on English administrative law has noted the strong case to be made for the giving of reasons as an important element of administrative justice. . . . "[T]he giving of reasons is required by the ordinary man's sense of justice and is also a healthy discipline for all who exercise power over others." [10] Professor Kenneth Davis, long a vigorous proponent of findings requirements as one means of controlling informal agency action, wrote in 1970 about a striking example arising out of "the informal handling of applications by the Immigration and Naturalization Service. About 700,000 applications are disposed of each year, of which 35,000 are denied. Almost all are handled without hearings. Some of the questions involved are of great moment to particular aliens. The author of the Treatise suggested to the Commissioner and other top officers of the Immigration Service in 1964 that an alien should always be entitled to have a written reason for the denial of a written application, as required by APA § 555(e). The initial response to this proposal was that it might require a doubling of the staff of some seven thousand and that the proposal was totally impractical. But on further study the Service found the idea of practical application it prepared printed cards, listing all the usual reasons for denials. The officer was required to check the applicable reason and to give the card to the alien. This was a great gain. The alien now knows whether he should take some action to change his circumstances and file another application, whether the denial is based on a mistaken impression of the facts, and whether he should fight the case further by going to a superior officer. Furthermore, if the facts are in the file, a superior officer has the means of checking the officer's judgment. The new system has caused no increase in the size of the

10. H.W.R. Wade, Administrative Law 463–64 (4th ed. 1977).

staff." Admin.L.Treatise 562 (1970 Supp.); see also A. Sofaer, Judicial Control of Informal Discretionary Adjudication and Enforcement, 72 Colum.L.Rev. 1293 (1972).

More subtle issues may be presented when one is considering *how* a findings requirement might be rationalized and developed. In his 1978 Supplement, Professor Davis wrote that courts should not go far in imposing constitutional due process requirements depriving "the legislative body of power to determine whether and when findings and reasons should be required (Davis, Admin.L. Treatise § 16.00–09). In his 1980 edition, he urges courts to press forward: "[T]he method of the common law . . . is [by] far the best. It has every advantage and no disadvantage. It allows courts to focus on the needs of justice and the needs of administrative effectiveness, and it permits the law to develop on the basis of increasing experience. It does not cut into legislative power to determine the question in particular instances." 3 Davis, K., Admin.L. Treatise 121 (1980).

(2) Is it a reason to oppose a findings requirement, or at least temper its enforcement, that it may tend to produce excessive bureaucratic requirements or intrusive review? The Supreme Court has refused to require federal mine inspectors to accompany proposed penalty assessments with findings and reasons; a hearing was available on demand, and the Court thought "effective enforcement of the Act would be weakened if the Secretary were required to make findings of fact for every penalty assessment," even those cases in which miners agreed to pay the proposed penalty. National Independent Coal Operators Ass'n v. Kleppe, 423 U.S. 388, 399 (1976). Consider also Judge Antonin Scalia's dissenting views in Steger v. Defense Investigative Service Dept. of Defense, 717 F.2d 1402, 1407, 1409 (D.C.Cir.1983). The majority, per curiam, had found a failure of explanation by the Merit System Protection Board of its decision to reject an application for attorney's fees on behalf of a successful litigant, and Judge Scalia responded: "I dissent because I believe the majority has applied a microscope to an inquiry which Congress meant to be conducted with the naked eye. . . . The majority opinion, as I understand it, does not [disagree that this case *could* be distinguished from the Board's prior precedent], but reverses the Board for not expressly stating that this was the reason the earlier . . . cases were inapplicable. That imposes a degree of refinement which I find inappropriate for such discretionary decisions. I think it no more arbitrary for the Board to fail to distinguish its arguably but not clearly inconsistent precedent when it makes fee-award determinations, than it is arbitrary for us to fail to do so when we award or deny attorneys' fees . . . or when we deny a motion for stay. . . . For agencies, no less than for courts, it is unnecessary to provide the same high degree, not merely of consistency, but of *explicit justification* for all determinations. . . . To require that the agency not merely allude to those grounds (which it *did* here) but also identify them as the specific reason for departing from arguably applicable precedent, is to impose intricacies of process reserved for more important and less discretionary determinations. In

holding otherwise, the court continues the progressive complication of agency process and encourages the progressive trivialization of the business of appellate courts."[11]

(3) DUNLOP v. BACHOWSKI, 421 U.S. 560 (1975), cited in the principal case and also discussed at pp. 317 and 997 herein, concerned a findings requirement based on statute, but seemed to speak more broadly. Bachowski, an unsuccessful candidate for a union office, filed a complaint with the Secretary of Labor alleging that the winner had violated § 401 of the Labor-Management Reporting and Disclosure Act of 1959 (LMRDA), thereby invoking Section 402 of the Act which requires the Secretary to investigate the complaint and decide whether to bring a court action to set aside the election.[12] After investigating, the Secretary informed Bachowski by letter that "based upon the investigative findings, it has been determined . . . that civil action to set aside the election is not warranted." Bachowski then brought an action against the Secretary seeking a declaration that the action of the Secretary was arbitrary and capricious and an order that the Secretary "file suit to set aside the election."

The Court in an opinion by Justice Brennan held that the Secretary's statement of reasons for not bringing the action, contained in his letter to Bachowski, was insufficient [13]:

"Two conclusions follow from [a] survey of our decisions: (1) since the statute relies upon the special knowledge and discretion of the Secretary for the determination of both the probable violation and the probable effect, clearly the reviewing court is not authorized to substitute its judgment for the decision of the Secretary not to bring suit; (2)

11. [Ed.] "What good is an official explanation if there is no opportunity to challenge the truthfulness of the explanation or the accuracy of its supporting facts? What good is the right to challenge the explanation without sufficient time to prepare the challenge?" R. Smolla, The Reemergence of the Right-Privilege Distinction in Constitutional Law: The Price of Protesting Too Much, 35 Stan.L.Rev. 69, 115 (1982).

12. Section 402(b), 29 U.S.C. § 482(b) provides:

complaint and, if he finds probable cause to believe that a violation of this subchapter has occurred and has not been remedied, he shall, within sixty days after the filing of such complaint, bring a civil action against the labor organization as an entity in the district court of the United States in which such labor organization maintains its principal office to set aside the invalid election, if any, and to direct the conduct of an election or hearing and vote upon the removal of officers under the supervision of the Secretary. . . ." That is the sole channel of redress open to such a complainant; before resorting to it, the complainant had to exhaust available remedies within the union. "A review of the legislative history shows that Congress made suit by the Secretary the exclusive post-election remedy for two principal reasons: (1) to protect unions from frivolous litigation and unnecessary judicial interference with their elections, and (2) to centralize in a single proceeding such litigation as might be warranted with respect to a single election." Trbovich v. United Mine Workers, 404 U.S. 528, 532 (1972).

13. [Ed.] The court had previously the Secretary's contention that his decision is an unreviewable exercise of prosecutorial discretion." 421 U.S. at 567 n. 7.

The Third Circuit had held that the doctrine of "absolute prosecutorial discretion . . . should be limited to those civil cases which, like criminal prosecutions, involve the vindication of societal or governmental interest, rather than the protection of individual rights. . . . To grant the Secretary absolute discretion in this situation seems particularly inappropriate; for if he wrongfully refuses to file suit, individual union members are left without a remedy." 502 F.2d 79, 86–88 (3d Cir.1974).

therefore, to enable the reviewing court intelligently to review the Secretary's determination, the Secretary must provide the court and the complaining witness with copies of a statement of reasons supporting his determination. '[W]hen action is taken by [the Secretary] it must be such as to enable a reviewing Court to determine with some measure of confidence whether or not the discretion, which still remains in the Secretary, has been exercised in a manner that is neither arbitrary nor capricious. . . . [I]t is necessary for [him] to delineate and make explicit the basis upon which discretionary action is taken, particularly in a case such as this where the decision taken consists of a failure to act after the finding of union election irregularities.'

"Moreover, a statement of reasons serves purposes other than judicial review. Since the Secretary's role as lawyer for the complaining union member does not include the duty to indulge a client's usual prerogative to direct his lawyer to file suit, we may reasonably infer that Congress intended that the Secretary supply the member with a reasoned statement why he determined not to proceed. . . . Finally, a 'reasons' requirement promotes thought by the Secretary and compels him to cover the relevant points and eschew irrelevancies, and as noted by the Court of Appeals in this case, the need to assure careful administrative consideration 'would be relevant even if the Secretary's decision were unreviewable.' . . .

"The necessity that the reviewing court refrain from substitution of its judgment for that of the Secretary thus helps define the permissible scope of review. Except in what must be the rare case, the court's review should be confined to examination of the 'reasons' statement, and the determination whether the statement, without more, evinces that the Secretary's decision is so irrational as to constitute the decision arbitrary and capricious. . . . The full trappings of adversary trial-type hearings would be defiant of congressional objectives not to permit individuals to block or delay resolution of post-election disputes, but rather 'to settle as quickly as practicable the cloud on the incumbents' titles to office.'

"Thus, the Secretary's letter of November 7, 1973, may have sufficed as a 'brief statement of the grounds for denial' for the purposes of the Administrative Procedure Act, 5 U.S.C. § 555(e), but plainly it did not suffice as a statement of reasons required by the LMRDA. For a statement of reasons must be adequate to enable the court to determine whether the Secretary's decision was reached for an impermissible reason or for no reason at all. For this essential purpose, although detailed findings of fact are not required, the statement of reasons should inform the court and the complaining union member of both the grounds of decision and the essential facts upon which the Secretary's inferences are based. . . .

"There remains the question of remedy. When the district court determines that the Secretary's statement of reasons adequately demonstrates that his decision not to sue is not contrary to law, the complaining union member's suit fails and should be dismissed. . . .

Where the statement inadequately discloses his reasons, the Secretary may be afforded opportunity to supplement his statement. . . . The court must be mindful, however, that endless litigation concerning the sufficiency of the written statement is inconsistent with the statute's goal of expeditious resolution of post-election disputes."[14] Justice Rehnquist, believing a § 555(e) statement sufficient, dissented.

(4) Section 555(e)'s requirement of a "brief statement of the grounds for denial" of a "request made in connection with any agency proceeding" has had little formative impact. Many agencies provide opportunities for complaints to be heard, but whether the section applies to such self-initiated matters (rather than to requests received in the course of a proceeding already initiated) is uncertain. The Attorney General's Manual (p. 70) took the view that Section 555(e) "has no application to matters which do not relate to rule making, adjudication or licensing [i.e., 'any agency proceeding']." Bachowski and recent court of appeals readings, however, suggest that the "brief statement of the grounds for denial" may be generally required in response to requests for action, whether received in or out of existing proceedings.[15] Even without the requirement, sound practice would counsel some form of statement to explain a response to requests seriously made. Usually, however, such requests are not made to—or at least expected to be answered by—the agency heads themselves; some functionary or officer within the staff receives the complaint or petition, determines what to do with it, and supplies any statement of reasons for his decision. The question then arises whether there is any

14. [Ed.] On remand, complainant argued that this was a "rare case" warranting full trial to review the Secretary's decision, but the district court held the Secretary's statement not "on its face plainly questionable." However, a supplemental statement was ordered because the statement did not explain a significant aspect of the Secretary's method of treating the "infected" vote in the election. Bachowski v. Brennan, 405 F.Supp. 1227 (W.D.Pa.1975). When that explanation was filed, the court found the method irrational and remanded the matter to the Secretary. 413 F.Supp. 147 (W.D.Pa.1976).

Bachowski v. Usery, 545 F.2d 363 (3d Cir. 1976). Subsequently, the district court's decision has been called the only one that found the Secretary's statement arbitrary, criticized as substitution of judgment, and not followed when the Secretary's "irrational" method was challenged again, Sadlowski v. Marshall, 464 F.Supp. 858 (D.D.C.1979).

15. Nine Justices agreed, and the government conceded, that the 555(e) obligation applied in Bachowski, which involved neither rulemaking, Section 554 adjudication, nor licensing proceedings; no proceeding existed when Bachowski sought to

invoke the Secretary's aid. Most cases relying on this section were challenges to Board of Parole decisions, before a 1976 statute imposed explicit findings requirements for those decisions, see e.g., King v. United States, 492 F.2d 1337 (7th Cir.1974). But the section has also been the basis of requiring findings from the Bureau of Prisons when denying a para-legal access to prison; from the FCC when refusing to reconsider a decision; and from the Air Force when denying an honorable discharge. See Roelofs v. Secretary of Air Force, 628 F.2d 594, 559–600 (D.C.Cir.1980)

simple but fundamental requirement that an agency or official set forth its reasons, a requirement that is essential to 'the integrity of the Administrative process,' for it tends to require 'the agency to focus on the values served by its decision . . . hence releasing the clutch of unconscious preference and irrelevant prejudice.' "); and Kalista v. Secretary of Navy, 560 F.Supp. 608 (D.Colo.1983). Whether the requirement extends to requests for action which less directly affects the requester's interests— for example, a citizen's demand that enforcement action be taken by the EPA against an alleged polluter—is not settled by the cases.

internal mechanism for appealing to higher authority. Where such internal mechanisms exist at all, they may not reach to the top of the agency; or if they do reach that far, they are likely to be highly discretionary—both to avoid premature involvement of the agency heads and to protect their limited time from being swallowed up in the resolution of a series of relatively slight disputes. This fact is significant for the invocation of judicial review of the decision made, if not the obligation to state reasons. In Kixmiller v. SEC, 492 F.2d 641 (D.C.Cir. 1974), the Commission declined to review its staff's decision to recommend that no adverse action be taken if a proposed course of conduct was carried out. In consequence, the court found, there was no "order" of the Commission to be reviewed. Thus an unsuccessful effort to provoke agency action should usually be explained; but whether that explanation can be made the object of judicial oversight may depend on whose explanation is given.[16] A further obstacle to review arises when the decision made, as in Bachowski, concerns initiation of an agency proceeding. On the "presumption of unreviewability" of such decisions absent special statute see Heckler v. Chaney, p. 1021 below.

e. "Hard Look" Review and Informal Rulemaking in the High Technology Era

"Hard look" review of agency rulemaking warrants discrete treatment: its emergence and development have been major features of administrative law in the '70's and '80's. Significant pieces of that development have already been seen: Overton Park, p. 436 above, as an expression of a review function that could be, at once, both "narrow" and "probing," "searching," and "careful"; and Ethyl Corporation, p. 463, reflecting judicial awareness that the factual premises for rules that might govern the lives and safety of thousands, and impose millions in costs, warranted substantial efforts at judicial understanding even though they arose from informal proceedings; again the Ethyl case, reflecting the vigorous debate that divided the D.C. Circuit during the '70's between solutions that stressed the technological unsophistication of judges and consequent need for added agency procedures (Judge David Bazelon), and those that insisted judges must do what they can on review to understand the premises of agency action and secure rational agency outcomes (Judge Harold Leventhal); and, finally, Vermont Yankee Nuclear Power Corp., p. 248 above, suggesting at the least that Judge Bazelon had lost that debate.

Vermont Yankee might have been taken as well—might it still be taken?—to suggest that Judge Leventhal, too, had lost, for the "hard look" carried its own baggage of apparently procedural requirements not obvious on the face of APA § 553: an expanded notion of the "record"; a requirement that the agency reveal its data base in time for responsive comment to it; a burden of explanation that reaches well

---

16. See National Automatic Laundry and Cleaning Council v. Shultz, 443 F.2d 689 (D.C.Cir.1971), set out at p. 1124 with-in; National Urban League v. Office of Comptroller of the Currency, (D.D.C.1978) [43 P. & F.Ad.L.2d 117].

beyond what might ordinarily be inferred from § 553's provision for a "concise general statement of [a rule's] basis and purpose." The pages following present materials in addition to those already seen, more or less in chronological order, from which the student will be able to make her own assessment.[1] We start, however, with Judge Leventhal's statement in GREATER BOSTON TELEVISION CORP. v. FCC, 444 F.2d 841, 850–53 (D.C.Cir.1970), cert. denied 403 U.S. 923 (1971)—a statement that, although uttered in an on-the-record proceeding, has proved enormously influential in judicial review of informal determinations:

"Approaching this case as we have with full awareness of and responsiveness to the court's 'supervisory' function in review of agency decision, it may be appropriate to take note of the salient aspects of that review. It begins at the threshold, with enforcement of the requirement of reasonable procedure, with fair notice and opportunity to the parties to present their case. It continues into examination of the evidence and agency's findings of facts, for the court must be satisfied that the agency's evidentiary fact findings are supported by substantial evidence, and provide rational support for the agency's inferences of ultimate fact. Full allowance must be given not only for the opportunity of the agency, or at least its examiners, to observe the demeanor of the witnesses, but also for the reality that agency matters typically involve a kind of expertise—sometimes technical in a scientific sense, sometimes more a matter of specialization in kinds of regulatory programs. Expert discretion is secured, not crippled, by the requirements for substantial evidence, findings and reasoned analysis. Expertise is strengthened in its proper role as the servant of government when it is denied the opportunity to 'become a monster which rules with no practical limits on its discretion.' Burlington Truck Lines v. United States, 371 U.S. 156, 167 (1962). A court does not depart from its proper function when it undertakes a study of the record, hopefully perceptive, even as to the evidence on technical and specialized matters, for this enables the court to penetrate to the underlying decisions of the agency, to satisfy itself that the agency has exercised a reasoned discretion, with reasons that do not deviate from or ignore the ascertainable legislative intent. 'The deference owed to an expert tribunal cannot be allowed to slip into a judicial inertia.' Hellenic Lines Ltd., Aktiengesellschaft v. FMC, 390 U.S. 261, 272 (1968).

In saturating the agency with law and the legislative mandate, the function of the court is not merely to find facts and make judgments, but also to serve in the public interest. The function of the court is to assure that the agency has given reasoned consideration to all the material facts and issues, with insistence that the agency articulate with reasonable clarity its reasons for decision, and identify the significance of the crucial facts, a course that tends to assure that the agency's policies effectuate general standards, applied without unreasonable discrimination. . . .

1. The question returns, as well, in later chapters. See, in particular, Chapter 7, Section 4 and Chapter 8, Sections 3 and 4.

"Its supervisory function calls on the court to intervene not merely in case of procedural inadequacies, or bypassing of the mandate in the legislative charter, but more broadly if the court becomes aware, especially from a combination of danger signals, that the agency has not really taken a 'hard look' at the salient problems, and has not genuinely engaged in reasoned decision-making. If the agency has not shirked this fundamental task, however, the court exercises restraint and affirms the agency's action even though the court would on its own account have made different findings or adopted different standards. Nor will the court upset a decision because of errors that are not material, there being room for the doctrine of harmless error. If satisfied that the agency has taken a hard look at the issues with the use of reasons and standards, the court will uphold its findings, though of less than ideal clarity, if the agency's path may reasonably be discerned, though of course the court must not be left to guess as to the agency's findings or reasons.

"The process thus combines judicial supervision with a salutary principle of judicial restraint, an awareness that agencies and courts together constitute a 'partnership' in furtherance of the public interest, and are 'collaborative instrumentalities of justice.' The court is in a real sense part of the total administrative process, and not a hostile stranger to the office of first instance. This collaborative spirit does not undercut, it rather underlines the court's rigorous insistence on the need for conjunction of articulated standards and reflective findings, in furtherance of even handed application of law, rather than impermissible whim, improper influence, or misplaced zeal. Reasoned decision promotes results in the public interest by requiring the agency to focus on the values served by its decision, and hence releasing the clutch of unconscious preference and irrelevant prejudice. It furthers the broad public interest of enabling the public to repose confidence in the process as well as the judgments of its decision-makers.

"There was once a day when a court upheld the 'sensible judgments' of a board, say of tax assessors, on the ground that they 'express an intuition of experience which outruns analysis.' There may still exist narrow areas where this approach persists, partly for historic reasons.

"Generally, however, the applicable doctrine that has evolved with the enormous growth and significance of administrative determination in the past forty or fifty years has insisted on reasoned decision-making.

. . . .

"Judicial vigilance to enforce the Rule of Law in the administrative process is particularly called upon where . . . the area under consideration is one wherein the Commission's policies are in flux. An agency's view of what is in the public interest may change, either with or without a change in circumstances. But an agency changing its course must supply a reasoned analysis indicating that prior policies and standards are being deliberately changed, not casually ignored, and if an agency glosses over or swerves from prior precedents without discussion it may cross the line from the tolerably terse to the intolerably mute.

"The net result of our study and reflection in this case is our conclusion that the record findings and opinions before us, while not without problems, reveal in essence that the Commission has been diligent to take a hard look at the problem areas, and to set forth with clarity grounds of reasoned decision which we think permissible."

(1) PACIFIC STATES BOX & BASKET CO. v. WHITE, 296 U.S. 176 (1935) concerned a rule of the Oregon Division of Plant Industry fixing official standards for containers used to package raspberries and strawberries, standards which could not be met by the fruit baskets petitioner made. The circumstances suggested, but no finding stated, that the Oregon board might have found that use of a single container type (among the 34 available) would enhance consumer protection against short measures. Acknowledging that no such finding would be required of a legislature, petitioner urged that findings were constitutionally requisite for the actions of administrators wielding delegated powers. A unanimous court, speaking through Justice Brandeis, found that that contention was "without support in authority or reason, and rests upon misconception. Every exertion of the police power, either by the legislature or by an administrative body, is an exercise of delegated power. . . . Where the regulation is within the scope of authority legally delegated, the presumption of the existence of facts justifying its specific exercise attaches alike to statutes . . . and to orders of administrative bodies. . . . [T]he statute did not require special findings; doubtless because the regulation authorized was general legislation, not an administrative order in the nature of a judgment directed against an individual concern."

(2) Committee Reports accompanying the Administrative Procedure Act explained the requirement of a "concise general statement" as follows: "The agency must analyze and consider all relevant matter presented. The required statement . . . should not only relate to the data so presented but with reasonable fullness explain the actual basis and objective of the rule." Sen.Doc. No. 248, 79th Cong., 2d Sess. 201, 259 (1946). The Attorney General's Manual on the Administrative Procedure Act 32 (1947) expressed the opinion that these statements would be important as an aid to interpretation, but that "findings of fact and conclusions of law are not necessary. Nor is there required an elaborate analysis of the rules or of the considerations upon which the rules were issued. Rather, the statement is intended to advise the public of the general basis and purpose of the rules." As late as the 1970 Supplement to his Treatise, Professor Davis found no occasion in _____ _____ ____ _____ ____ _____ findings in rulemaking;

adopted without such a statement, if the basis and purpose
to the reviewing court. Hoving Corp. v. FTC, 290 F.2d 803 (2d Cir. 1961); contra, Tabor v. Joint Bd. for the Enrollment of Actuaries, 566

F.2d 705 (D.C.Cir.1977). Compare K. Davis, Administrative Law Treatise §§ 6.10 and 16.00 (Supp.1970), with id., § 6.12 (2d Ed.1978).

(3) AUTOMOTIVE PARTS & ACCESSORIES v. BOYD, 407 F.2d 330, 338 (D.C.Cir.1968), the first challenge to implementation of the National Traffic and Motor Vehicle Safety Act, cautioned "against an overly literal reading of the statutory terms 'concise' and 'general.' These adjectives must be accommodated to the realities of judicial scrutiny. . . . We do not expect the agency to discuss every item of fact or opinion included in the submissions made to it in informal rule making. We do expect that, if the judicial review which Congress has thought it important to provide is to be meaningful, the 'concise general statement of . . . basis and purpose' mandated by [APA § 553(c)] will enable us to see what major issues of policy were ventilated by the informal proceedings and why the agency reacted to them as it did."

(4) CITIZENS TO PRESERVE OVERTON PARK, INC. v. VOLPE, p. 436 above.

(5) In KENNECOTT COPPER CORP. v. ENVIRONMENTAL PROTECTION AGENCY, 462 F.2d 846 (D.C.Cir.1972), the court considered a challenge to a rule setting national air quality standards limiting common industrial wastes, sulfur oxides, to 60 micrograms per cubic meter; the statute authorizing the limit required that it "shall accurately reflect the latest scientific knowledge useful in indicating the kind and extent of all identifiable effects on public health or welfare which may be expected from the presence of such pollutant in the ambient air, in varying quantities." 42 U.S.C. § 1857c–3(a)(2). In adopting the standard, the administrator said only that it was "requisite to protect the public welfare from any known or anticipated adverse effects associated with the presence of air pollutants in the ambient air." He referred to a bulky set of Air Quality Criteria for Sulfur Oxides, previously published by the government, and intended to reflect existing scientific knowledge concerning health and other effects to be expected from the presence of the oxides. But the summary of that document referred to no figure lower than 85 micrograms per cubic meter as having a demonstrable effect. The government argued that lower figures could be found in the body of the criteria document; or, alternatively, that the chosen level (60) could be supported as leaving a margin for error.

"This court has been assigned special responsibility for determining challenges to EPA's air quality standards. . . . Inherent in the responsibility entrusted to this court is a requirement that we be given sufficient indication of the basis on which the Administrator reached the 60 figure so that we may consider whether it embodies an abuse of discretion or error of law. . . .

"We are not to be taken as specifying that the agency must provide the same articulation as is required for orders or regulations issued after evidentiary hearings. We are keenly aware of the need to avoid procedural strait jackets that would seriously hinder this new agency in the discharge of the novel, sensitive and formidable, tasks entrusted to it by Congress. This concern is emphasized by the fact that in the 1970 Amendments Congress was significantly concerned with expedition and avoidance of previous cumbersome and time-consuming procedures in effect under prior law.

"The provision by Congress of only informal rule-making, as a preliminary to the issuance of standards, and the contemplation of expedition, yield as reasonable corollaries some latitude in the requirement for delineation of approach. While the provision in § 4 of the APA for a "concise general statement" of the basis and purpose of regulations is not to be interpreted overliterally, the regulation before us contains sufficient exposition of the purpose and basis of the regulation as a whole to satisfy this legislative minimum. . . .

"There are contexts, however, contexts of fact, statutory framework and nature of action, in which the minimum requirements of the Administrative Procedure Act may not be sufficient. In the interest of justice, cf. 28 U.S.C. § 2106, and in aid of the judicial function, centralized in this court, of expeditious disposition of challenges to standards, the record is remanded for the Administrator to supply an implementing statement that will enlighten the court as to the basis on which he reached the 60 standard from the material in the Criteria."

(6) In PORTLAND CEMENT ASS'N v. RUCKELSHAUS, 486 F.2d 375, 393–94 (D.C.Cir.1973), cert. denied 417 U.S. 921 (1974), other clean air standards—on this occasion concerning the control of cement dust—were at issue. When proposed, the rule had been accompanied by a Background Document disclosing some information about the tests employed in reaching the (then) proposal, but no specific information about methodology. In the wake of the Kennecott decision, EPA published a supplemental statement conveying more information about those tests, to facilitate the review process already under way. One of the intervenor cement companies then successfully moved to have the court's review postponed while it submitted to the EPA its additional comments on the newly revealed matter—comments embodied in a report by its expert, Ralph Striker, sharply critical of the methodology the EPA had employed. The court thought this "opportunity to make further comment necessary to sound execution of our judicial review function," noting that "Obviously, a prerequisite to the ability to make meaningful comment is to know the basis upon which the rule is proposed." The court continued, "the fact that the agency chose to perform additional tests and release the results indicates that it did not believe possible agency consideration was frozen. It is not consonant with the purpose of a rule-making proceeding to promulgate rules on the basis of inadequate data, or on data that . . . [are] known only to the agency.

"*2. The EPA response to the remand* . . . made no written
. . . . . . additional comments made by petitioners. As the

without response. . . . .
unless we hear EPA's response to his comments, and the record must be remanded again, for that purpose.

"We are not establishing any broad principle that EPA must respond to every comment made by manufacturers on the validity of its standards or the methodology and scientific basis for their formulation. In the case of the Striker presentation, however, our prior remand reflects this court's view of the significance, or at least potential significance, of this presentation. . . .

"This agency, particularly when its decisions can literally mean survival of persons or property, has a continuing duty to take a 'hard look' at the problems involved in its regulatory task, and that includes an obligation to comment on matters identified as potentially significant by the court order remanding for further presentation. Manufacturers' comments must be significant enough to step over a threshold requirement of materiality before any lack of agency response or consideration becomes of concern. . . . "

Following the remand on this issue (and others), the Administrator reaffirmed his regulation, with an enlarged response, and was upheld in having done so. Portland Cement Ass'n v. Train, 513 F.2d 506 (D.C. Cir.1975), cert. denied 423 U.S. 1025 (1975).

(7) INDUSTRIAL UNION DEPARTMENT, AFL–CIO v. HODGSON, 499 F.2d 467 (D.C.Cir.1974) was an early D.C. Circuit encounter with a statutory requirement of "substantial evidence" review for informal rulemaking. The court found the challenge daunting: "Congress—with no apparent awareness of anomaly—has explicitly combined an informal agency procedure with a standard of review traditionally conceived of as suited to formal adjudication or rulemaking. The federal courts, hard pressed as they are by the flood of new tasks imposed upon them by Congress, surely have some claim to be spared additional burdens deriving from the illogic of legislative compromise. At the least, it would have been helpful if there had been some recognition by Congress that the quick answer it gave to a legislative stalemate posed serious problems for a reviewing court, and that there would inevitably have to be some latitude accorded it to surmount those problems consistently with the legislative purposes. The duty remains, in any event, to decide the case before us in accordance with our statutory mandate, however dimly the rationale, if any, underlying it can be perceived. . . . "

In the course of responding to this challenge, the court voiced thoughts that have had a broader influence: "[I]n some degree the record approaches the form of one customarily conceived of as appropriate for substantial evidence review. In other respects, it does not. . . . From extensive and often conflicting evidence, the Secretary in this case made numerous factual determinations. With respect to some of those questions, the evidence was such that the task consisted primarily of evaluating the data and drawing conclusions from it. The court can review that data in the record and determine whether it reflects substantial support for the Secretary's findings. But some of the questions involved in the promulgation of these standards are on the frontiers of scientific knowledge, and consequently as to them insufficient data is presently available to make a fully informed factual determination. Decision making must in that circumstance depend to a greater extent upon policy judgments and less upon purely factual analysis. Thus, in addition to currently unresolved factual issues, the formulation of standards involves choices that by their nature require basic policy determinations rather than resolution of factual controversies. . . . Regardless of the manner in which the task of judicial review is articulated, policy choices of this sort are not susceptible to the same type of verification or refutation by reference to the record as are some factual questions. Consequently, the court's approach must necessarily be different no matter how the standards of review are labeled. That does not mean that such decisions escape exacting scrutiny, for, as this court has stated in a similar context: 'This exercise need be no less searching and strict in its weighing of whether the agency has performed in accordance with the Congressional purposes, but, because it is addressed to different materials, it inevitably varies from the adjudicatory model. The paramount objective is to see whether the agency, given an essentially legislative task to perform, has carried it out in a manner calculated to negate the dangers of arbitrariness and irrationality in the formulation of rules for general application in the future.' Automotive Parts and Accessories Ass'n v. Boyd, 407 F.2d 330, 338 (D.C.Cir.1968). . . .

"What we are entitled to at all events is a careful identification by the Secretary, when his proposed standards are challenged, of the reasons why he chooses to follow one course rather than another. Where that choice purports to be based on the existence of certain determinable facts, the Secretary must, in form as well as substance, find those facts from evidence in the record. By the same token, when the Secretary is obliged to make policy judgments where no factual certainties exist or where facts alone do not provide the answer, he should so state and go on to identify the considerations he found persuasive."

(8) ETHYL CORP. v. EPA, p. 463 above.

(9) UNITED STATES v. NOVA SCOTIA FOOD PRODUCTS CORP., 568 F.2d 240 (2d Cir.1977)[2] concerned, in part, the adequacy of the FDA's "concise general statement" accompanying its standards for the handling of smoked fish to safeguard against botulism poisoning. The rule was a general one, covering many topics and extending without differentiation to all species of smoked fish. Comments had urged a different approach in one respect (duration and temperature of smoking) for whitefish—whose marketability, it was asserted, would be destroyed by the generally required approach:

"It is not in keeping with the rational process to leave vital questions, raised by comments which are of cogent materiality, completely unanswered. The agencies certainly have a good deal of discre-

... ~~but the~~ agencies do not have quite

_____

2. Other portions of the opinion are set out at pp. 449–50 above.

not purport to transfer its legislative power to the unbounded discretion of the regulatory body.' F.C.C. v. RCA Communications, Inc., 346 U.S. 86, 90 (1953) (Frankfurter, J.). . . .

"The Secretary was squarely faced with the question whether it was necessary to formulate a rule with specific parameters that applied to all species of fish, and particularly whether lower temperatures with the addition of nitrite and salt would not be sufficient. Though this alternative was suggested by an agency of the federal government, its suggestion, though acknowledged, was never answered.

"Moreover, the comment that to apply the proposed T–T–S requirements to whitefish would destroy the commercial product was neither discussed nor answered. We think that to sanction silence in the face of such vital questions would be to make the statutory requirement of a 'concise general statement' less than an adequate safeguard against arbitrary decision-making. . . .

"It is easy enough for an administrator to ban everything. In the regulation of food processing, the worldwide need for food also must be taken into account in formulating measures taken for the protection of health. In the light of the history of smoked whitefish to which we have referred,[3] we find no articulate balancing here sufficient to make the procedure followed less than arbitrary."

(10) VERMONT YANKEE NUCLEAR POWER CORP. v. NRDC, p. 248 above.

(11) NATIONAL LIME ASSOCIATION v. EPA, 627 F.2d 416 (D.C.Cir. 1980): "The rigorousness of the review in which this court has engaged in previous [decisions on EPA new source performance standards, NSPS]—known to some as the 'hard look' standard—has already been described. . . . Both decisions reviewing the NSPS and those reviewing other administrative determinations under the Clean Air Act evince a concern that variables be accounted for, that the representativeness of test conditions be ascertained, that the validity of tests be assured and the statistical significance of results determined. Collectively, these concerns have sometimes been expressed as a need for 'reasoned decision-making' and sometimes as a need for adequate 'methodology.' However expressed, these more substantive concerns have been coupled with a requirement that assumptions be stated, that process be revealed, that the rejection of alternate theories or abandonment of alternate courses of action be explained and that the rationale for the ultimate decision be set forth in a manner which permits the public to exercise its statutory prerogative of comment and the courts to exercise their statutory responsibility upon review. The standard we

---

3. "The history of botulism occurrence in whitefish, as established in the trial record, which we must assume was available to the FDA in 1970, is as follows. Between 1899 and 1964 there were only eight cases of botulism reported as attributable to hot-smoked whitefish. In all eight instances, vacuum-packed whitefish was involved. All of the eight cases occurred in 1960 and 1963. The industry has abandoned vacuum-packing, and there has not been a single case of botulism associated with commercially prepared whitefish since 1963, though 2,750,000 pounds of whitefish are processed annually. . . ."

apply here is neither more rigorous nor more deferential than the standard applied in these earlier cases."

(12) What is the impact of the "hard look" approach? Reversal rates would suggest, "not very much." It remains undeniable that the "ultimate standard of review," to use the Overton Park phrase, is "a narrow one" for these matters so laden with policy and administrative judgment, although nose-counts show more reversals than before, say, 1970.[4] But perhaps that is the product of the agencies learning well what will be expected, as much as it is limited judicial carry-through. "It is a great tonic," wrote William Pedersen in the article we have already much quoted in these pages, "to discover that even if a regulation can be slipped or wrestled through various layers of internal or external review [inside the bureaucracy] without significant change, the final and most prestigious reviewing forum of all—a circuit court of appeals—will inquire into the minute details of methodology, data sufficiency and test procedure and will send the regulations back if these are lacking. The effect of such judicial opinions within the agency reaches beyond those who were concerned with the specific regulations reviewed. They serve as a precedent for future rulewriters and give those who care about well-documented and well-reasoned decisionmaking a lever with which to move those who do not." [5] Formal Records and Informal Rulemaking, 85 Yale L.J. 38, 60 * (1975).

A perspective similar as to result, but perhaps less pleased, was offered by Douglas M. Costle, Pedersen's boss during the Carter administration: "Under the Toxic Substances Control Act, EPA was required to write a Pre-Manufacture Notification rule; in essence, this requires a company to notify us before moving from development to large-scale production of a chemical. The proposed rule brought forth 192 commentors at 29 public meetings, and 300 pages of comment raising 400

---

4. In fiscal 1982, the courts of appeals nationally averaged an 87.4% affirmance rate on direct appeals from agencies; the D.C. Circuit's was 91.5%, in contrast to 87% in fiscal 1981 and 80% in fiscal 1976. "Pragmatically, too, we are aware that never in recent memory has a circuit court been reversed for upholding an agency rule. . . . " Wald, Remarks to Administrative Conference of the U.S., July 7, 1983, p. 2 (giving data also to show that the authorship and participation in reversals by her court were "spread evenly among the judges"). And see M. Garland, Deregulation and Judicial Review, 98 Harv.L.Rev. 505, 540–41 (1985).

5. [Ed.] In 1984, Judge Wald said this to the Federal Communications Bar Association: "The majority of agency reversals in
. . . ~~-ding to my reckoning, are~~
~~c— arbitrary —— .~~
we can't understand the agency's rationale, once we understand it, it doesn't make

sense, or it does not take account of prominent considerations that it should. This comes down to a problem of communication. It may be that, in fact, the agency does have good reasons for what it does, but internal or even external politics or inadvertence or sheer weariness prevent the drafts from saying what these good reasons are. Having worked in government agencies myself, I suspect that often the battle to get the policy through is so overwhelming that once victory is sure, the effort flags to rationalize that policy in a succinct but comprehensive way. Or else, there are reasons, sometimes having nothing to do with the case, that impede the agency from making a complete statement of the real basis for its actions, otherwise known as—we got our head handed to us at the White House." Remarks, Apr. 7, 1984, p. 7.

The Yale Law Journal Company, B. Rothman & Co.

discrete issues, *each* requiring an EPA response. Our defense comprised 300 pages of response, 800 pages of economic analysis performed at a cost of $600,000, and 500 pages of related analysis on regulatory impact. . . . " Brave New Chemical: The Future Regulatory History of Phlogiston, 33 Ad.L.Rev. 195, 199, 200 (1981).

The most extensive example this casebook offers of "hard look" in action, excerpts from the D.C. Circuit's 1981 125-page opinion in Sierra Club v. Costle, pp. 845 and 963 below, makes clear that even to obtain an affirmance, agency and court must labor exceedingly hard—and, given the stakes, one need not mean by such a statement, too hard.

Because EPA has operated since 1977 under special and demanding procedures, defined by the Clean Air Act Amendments of 1977, it would be possible to believe that "hard look" is in fact a localized phenomenon. Vermont Yankee might be thought to underscore that view, given the doubt it cast on judicial extension of the APA's specific provisions. Yet, the "hard look" was developed under the APA and has continued to be applied, in a variety of situations, without hesitation on Vermont Yankee grounds.

One might also think that "hard look" would be especially *un*likely to show up in the context of *de*regulation. Deregulation, this argument would run, "vindicates the societal interest in individual autonomy. . . . [T]he *substantive* inertia of our laws . . . favors not the status quo but private autonomy." Agency action eliminating "burdens upon private parties—like an agency's failure to impose burdens in the first place—must fall within that portion of the scale giving the administrator broadest leeway, and the courts the narrowest scope of review." [6] Further, it might be argued, deregulation is analogous to agency inaction in that each results in an unregulated scene. Courts typically treat challenges to inaction as unreviewable or entitled to particularly great deference because, among other reasons, of the limited record to review and the acute problem of second-guessing an agency's judgment on allocating its resources.[7] It would make little sense to deny great deference to formal agency steps that conserve or redirect agency resources, since crucial budget and staffing decisions about what resources are to be available never even get to court.

A contrary argument is of course possible, and had in fact been used in the court of appeals opinion reviewed in the case immediately following: that agencies may be held responsible to enacted policy and, while flexible, must make their own judgments on the merits, not merely reflect shifting political balances unless those are firm and strong enough to legislate new directions. Any change from a "settled course of behavior" is to be taken as a "danger signal" invoking close

6. Active Judges and Passive Restraints, Regulation, July-Aug. 1982, 10, 11, 13; also see M. Garland, Deregulation and Judicial Review, 98 Harv.L.Rev. 505, 508, n. 4 (1985); C. Sunstein, Deregulation and the Hard-Look Doctrine, 1983 Sup.Ct. Rev. 177; and J. O'Reilly, Judicial Review of Agency Deregulation: Alternatives and Problems for the Courts, 37 Vand.L.Rev. 509 (1984).

7. See Heckler v. Chaney, 470 U.S. 821 (1985), set out at p. 1021 within. For a contrary argument, see an excellent student note, Judicial Review of Administrative Inaction, 83 Columb.L.Rev. 627 (1983).

scrutiny as to whether there is justifying change in underlying social and economic circumstances, or new data or reconsideration on the merits—or only nothing new but an election. Agency discretion must operate, that is, under the rule of law.

Consider, then, the following decision, reviewed under the APA:

MOTOR VEHICLE MANUFACTURERS ASSOCIATION OF THE UNITED STATES, INC.

v.

STATE FARM MUTUAL AUTOMOBILE INSURANCE COMPANY

Supreme Court of United States, 1983.
463 U.S. 29.

JUSTICE WHITE delivered the opinion of the Court.

The development of the automobile gave Americans unprecedented freedom to travel, but exacted a high price for enhanced mobility. Since 1929, motor vehicles have been the leading cause of accidental deaths and injuries in the United States. In 1982, 46,300 Americans died in motor vehicle accidents and hundreds of thousands more were maimed and injured. While a consensus exists that the current loss of life on our highways is unacceptably high, improving safety does not admit to easy solution. In 1966, Congress decided that at least part of the answer lies in improving the design and safety features of the vehicle itself. But much of the technology for building safer cars was undeveloped or untested. Before changes in automobile design could be mandated, the effectiveness of these changes had to be studied, their costs examined, and public acceptance considered. This task called for considerable expertise and Congress responded by enacting the National Traffic and Motor Vehicle Safety Act of 1966, 15 U.S.C. § 1381.

. . .

The Act, created for the purpose of "reduc[ing] traffic accidents and deaths and injuries to persons resulting from traffic accidents," § 1381, directs the Secretary of Transportation or his delegate to issue motor vehicle safety standards that "shall be practicable, shall meet the need for motor vehicle safety, and shall be stated in objective terms." § 1392(a). In issuing these standards, the Secretary is directed to consider "relevant available motor vehicle safety data," whether the proposed standard "is reasonable, practicable and appropriate" for the particular type of motor vehicle, and the "extent to which such standards will contribute to carrying out the purposes" of the Act. §§ 1392(f)(1), (3), (4).

The Act also authorizes judicial review under [APA § 706] of all "orders establishing, amending, or revoking a Federal motor vehicle safety standard," § 1392(b). Under this authority, we review today whether NHTSA acted arbitrarily and capriciously in revoking the requirement in Motor Vehicle Safety Standard 208 that new motor vehicles produced after September 1982 be equipped with passive restraints to protect the safety of the occupants of the vehicle in the event of a collision. . . .

I

The regulation whose recission is at issue bears a complex and convoluted history. Over the course of approximately 60 rulemaking notices, the requirement has been imposed, amended, rescinded, reimposed, and now rescinded again.

As originally issued by the Department of Transportation in 1967, Standard 208 simply required the installation of seatbelts in all automobiles. It soon became apparent that the level of seatbelt use was too low to reduce traffic injuries to an acceptable level. The Department therefore began consideration of "passive occupant restraint systems"— devices that do not depend for their effectiveness upon any action taken by the occupant except that necessary to operate the vehicle. Two types of automatic crash protection emerged: automatic seatbelts and airbags. The automatic seatbelt is a traditional safety belt, which when fastened to the interior of the door remains attached without impeding entry or exit from the vehicle, and deploys automatically without any action on the part of the passenger. The airbag is an inflatable device concealed in the dashboard and steering column. It automatically inflates when a sensor indicates that deceleration forces from an accident have exceeded a preset minimum, then rapidly deflates to dissipate those forces. The life-saving potential of these devices was immediately recognized, and in 1977, after substantial on-the-road experience with both devices, it was estimated by NHTSA that passive restraints could prevent approximately 12,000 deaths and over 100,000 serious injuries annually.

In 1969, the Department formally proposed a standard requiring the installation of passive restraints . . . and in 1972, the agency amended the Standard to require full passive protection for all front seat occupants of vehicles manufactured after August 15, 1975. In the interim, vehicles built between August 1973 and August 1975 were to carry either passive restraints or lap and shoulder belts coupled with an "ignition interlock" that would prevent starting the vehicle if the belts were not connected. On review, the agency's decision to require passive restraints was found to be supported by "substantial evidence" and upheld. Chrysler Corp. v. Department of Transportation, 472 F.2d 659 (CA6 1972).

In preparing for the upcoming model year, most car makers chose the "ignition interlock" option, a decision which was highly unpopular, and led Congress to amend the Act to prohibit a motor vehicle safety standard from requiring or permitting compliance by means of an ignition interlock or a continuous buzzer designed to indicate that safety belts were not in use. Motor Vehicle and Schoolbus Safety Amendments of 1974. The 1974 Amendments also provided that any safety standard that could be satisfied by a system other than seatbelts would have to be submitted to Congress where it could be vetoed by concurrent resolution of both Houses.

The effective date for mandatory passive restraint systems was extended for a year until August 31, 1976. But in June 1976, Secretary of Transportation William Coleman, Jr., initiated a new rulemaking on the issue. After hearing testimony and reviewing written comments, Coleman extended the optional alternatives indefinitely and suspended the passive restraint requirement.[1] Although he found passive restraints technologically and economically feasible, the Secretary based his decision on the expectation that there would be widespread public resistance to the new systems. He instead proposed a demonstration project involving up to 500,000 cars installed with passive restraints, in order to smooth the way for public acceptance of mandatory passive restraints at a later date.

Coleman's successor as Secretary of Transportation disagreed. Within months of assuming office, Secretary Brock Adams decided that the demonstration project was unnecessary. He issued a new mandatory passive restraint regulation [that] mandated the phasing in of passive restraints beginning with large cars in model year 1982 and extending to all cars by model year 1984. The two principal systems that would satisfy the Standard were airbags and passive belts; the choice of which system to install was left to the manufacturers. In Pacific Legal Foundation v. Department of Transportation, 593 F.2d 1338, cert. denied, 444 U.S. 830 (1979), the Court of Appeals upheld Modified Standard 208 as a rational, nonarbitrary regulation consistent with the agency's mandate under the Act. The Standard also survived scrutiny by Congress, which did not exercise its authority under the legislative veto provision of the 1974 Amendments. . . .

Over the next several years, the automobile industry geared up to comply with Modified Standard 208. . . . In February 1981, however, Secretary of Transportation Andrew Lewis reopened the rulemaking due to changed economic circumstances and, in particular, the difficulties of the automobile industry. Two months later, the agency ordered a one-year delay in the application of the Standard to large cars, extending the deadline to September 1982 and at the same time, proposed the possible rescission of the entire Standard. After receiving written comments and holding public hearings, NHTSA issued a final rule (Notice 25) that rescinded the passive restraint requirement contained in Modified Standard 208.

---

1. [Ed.] In a step unprecedented except by his own similar actions on several other matters (e.g., landing rights in the United States for supersonic airliners), Secretary Coleman personally presided over these hearings. Persons familiar with the hearings were impressed or amazed at this leading lawyer's complete preparation and command of all material. The final decision was directly his own to a degree that is becoming rare even among leading judges. When one of your editors asked ex-Secretary Coleman how other high officials could possibly find the time to perform as he had, the response was: "Fewer cocktail parties."

II

In a statement explaining the rescission, NHTSA maintained that it was no longer able to find, as it had in 1977, that the automatic restraint requirement would produce significant safety benefits. . . . In 1977, the agency had assumed that airbags would be installed in 60% of all new cars and automatic seatbelts in 40%. By 1981 it became apparent that automobile manufacturers planned to install the automatic seatbelts in approximately 99% of the new cars. For this reason, the lifesaving potential of airbags would not be realized. Moreover, it now appeared that the overwhelming majority of passive belts planned to be installed by manufacturers could be detached easily and left that way permanently. Passive belts, once detached, then required "the same type of affirmative action that is the stumbling block to obtaining high usage levels of manual belts." For this reason, the agency concluded that there was no longer a basis for reliably predicting that the Standard would lead to any significant increased usage of restraints at all.

In view of the possibly minimal safety benefits, the automatic restraint requirement no longer was reasonable or practicable in the agency's view. The requirement would require approximately $1 billion to implement and the agency did not believe it would be reasonable to impose such substantial costs on manufacturers and consumers without more adequate assurance that sufficient safety benefits would accrue. In addition, NHTSA concluded that automatic restraints might have an adverse effect on the public's attitude toward safety. Given the high expense and limited benefits of detachable belts, NHTSA feared that many consumers would regard the Standard as an instance of ineffective regulation, adversely affecting the public's view of safety regulation and, in particular, "poisoning . . . popular sentiment toward efforts to improve occupant restraint systems in the future." . . . . [The court of appeals reversed.]

III

Unlike the Court of Appeals, we do not find the appropriate scope of judicial review to be the "most troublesome question" in [this case]. Both the [1966] Act and the 1974 Amendments concerning occupant crash protection standards indicate that motor vehicle safety standards are to be promulgated under the informal rulemaking procedures of [the APA]. The agency's action in promulgating such standards therefore may be set aside if found to be "arbitrary, capricious, an abuse of discretion, or otherwise not in accordance with law." [APA] § 706(2) (A). . . . . [T]he rescission or modification of an occupant-protection standard is subject to the same test. Section 103(b) of the Act states that the procedural and judicial review provisions of the Administrative Procedure Act "shall apply to all orders establishing, amending, or revoking a Federal motor vehicle safety standard," and suggests no difference in the scope of judicial review depending upon the nature of the agency's action.

Petitioner Motor Vehicle Manufacturers Association (MVMA) . . . contend[s] that the rescission of an agency rule should be judged by the same standard a court would use to judge an agency's refusal to promulgate a rule in the first place—a standard petitioner believes considerably narrower than the traditional arbitrary-and-capricious test. . . . Moreover, the revocation of an extant regulation is substantially different than a failure to act. Revocation constitutes a reversal of the agency's former views as to the proper course. A "settled course of behavior embodies the agency's informed judgment that, by pursuing that course, it will carry out the policies committed to it by Congress. There is, then, at least a presumption that those policies will be carried out best if the settled rule is adhered to." Atchison, T. & S.F.R. Co. v. Wichita Bd. of Trade, 412 U.S. 800, 807–808 (1973). Accordingly, an agency changing its course by rescinding a rule is obligated to supply a reasoned analysis for the change beyond that which may be required when an agency does not act in the first instance.

In so holding, we fully recognize that "[r]egulatory agencies do not establish rules of conduct to last forever," American Trucking Assns., Inc. v. Atchison, T. & S.F.R. Co., 387 U.S. 397, 416 (1967), and that an agency must be given ample latitude to "adapt their rules and policies to the demands of changing circumstances." Permian Basin Area Rate Cases, 390 U.S. 747, 784 (1968). But the forces of change do not always or necessarily point in the direction of deregulation. In the abstract, there is no more reason to presume that changing circumstances require the rescission of prior action, instead of a revision in or even the extension of current regulation. If Congress established a presumption from which judicial review should start, that presumption—contrary to petitioners' views—is not *against* safety regulation, but *against* changes in current policy that are not justified by the rulemaking record. While the removal of a regulation may not entail the monetary expenditures and other costs of enacting a new standard, and, accordingly, it may be easier for an agency to justify a deregulatory action, the direction in which an agency chooses to move does not alter the standard of judicial review established by law.

The Department of Transportation . . . argues that under [the "arbitrary and capricious" standard], a reviewing court may not set aside an agency rule that is rational, based on consideration of the relevant factors, and within the scope of the authority delegated to the agency by the statute. We do not disagree with this formulation.[2] The scope of review under the "arbitrary and capricious" standard is

2. The Department of Transportation suggests that the arbitrary-and-capricious standard requires no more than the minimum rationality a statute must bear in order to withstand analysis under the Due Process Clause. We do not view as equivalent the presumption of constitutionality afforded legislation drafted by Congress and the presumption of regularity afforded an agency in fulfilling its statutory mandate.

narrow and a court is not to substitute its judgment for that of the agency. Nevertheless, the agency must examine the relevant data and articulate a satisfactory explanation for its action including a "rational connection between the facts found and the choice made." Burlington Truck Lines, Inc. v. United States, 371 U.S. 156, 168. . . . Normally, an agency rule would be arbitrary and capricious if the agency has relied on factors which Congress has not intended it to consider, entirely failed to consider an important aspect of the problem, offered an explanation for its decision that runs counter to the evidence before the agency, or is so implausible that it could not be ascribed to a difference in view or the product of agency expertise. The reviewing court should not attempt itself to make up for such deficiencies; we may not supply a reasoned basis for the agency's action that the agency itself has not given. SEC v. Chenery Corp., 332 U.S. 194, 196 (1947). . . . For purposes of this case, it is also relevant that Congress required a record of the rulemaking proceedings to be compiled and submitted to a reviewing court, § 1394, and intended that agency findings under the Act would be supported by "substantial evidence on the record considered as a whole. . . ."

. . .

V

The ultimate question before us is whether NHTSA's rescission of the passive restraint requirement of Standard 208 was arbitrary and capricious. . . .

A

The first and most obvious reason for finding the rescission arbitrary and capricious is that NHTSA apparently gave no consideration whatever to modifying the Standard to require that airbag technology be utilized. Standard 208 sought to achieve automatic crash protection by requiring automobile manufacturers to install either of two passive restraint devices: airbags or automatic seatbelts. There was no suggestion in the long rulemaking process that led to Standard 208 that if only one of these options were feasible, no passive restraint standard should be promulgated. Indeed, the agency's original proposed standard contemplated the installation of inflatable restraints in all cars. Automatic belts were added [in 1971] as a means of complying with the Standard because they were believed to be as effective as airbags in achieving the goal of occupant crash protection. . . . At that time, the passive belt approved by the agency could not be detached. Only later, at a manufacturer's behest, did the agency approve of the detachability feature—and only after assurances that the feature would not compromise the safety benefits of the restraint. Although it was then foreseen that 60% of the new cars would contain airbags and 40% would have automatic seatbelts, the ratio between the two was not significant as long as the passive belt would also assure greater passenger safety.

The agency has now determined that the detachable automatic belts will not attain anticipated safety benefits because so many individuals will detach the mechanism. Even if this conclusion were acceptable in its entirety, . . . standing alone it would not justify any more than an amendment of Standard 208 to disallow compliance by means of the one technology which will not provide effective passenger protection. . . . Given the effectiveness ascribed to airbag technology by the agency, the mandate of the Act to achieve traffic safety would suggest that the logical response to the faults of detachable seatbelts would be to require the installation of airbags. At the very least this alternative way of achieving the objectives of the Act should have been addressed and adequate reasons given for its abandonment. But the agency not only did not require compliance through airbags, it also did not even consider the possibility in its 1981 rulemaking. Not one sentence of its rulemaking statement discusses the airbags-only option. . . . [W]hat we said in Burlington Truck Lines, Inc. v. United States, 371 U.S., at 167, is apropos here: "There are no findings and no analysis here to justify the choice made, no indication of the basis on which the [agency] exercised its expert discretion. We are not prepared to and the Administrative Procedure Act will not permit us to accept such . . . practice. . . . Expert discretion is the lifeblood of the administrative process, but 'unless we make the requirements for administrative action strict and demanding, *expertise,* the strength of modern government, can become a monster which rules with no practical limits on its discretion.' " We have frequently reiterated that an agency must cogently explain why it has exercised its discretion in a given manner, Atchison, T. & S.F.R. Co. v. Wichita Bd. of Trade, 412 U.S. [800,] 806 [3] . . . and we reaffirm this principle again today.

The automobile industry has opted for the passive belt over the airbag, but surely it is not enough that the regulated industry has eschewed a given safety device. For nearly a decade, the automobile industry waged the regulatory equivalent of war against the airbag and lost—the inflatable restraint was proven sufficiently effective. Now the automobile industry has decided to employ a seatbelt system which will not meet the safety objectives of Standard 208. This hardly constitutes cause to revoke the Standard itself. Indeed, the Act was necessary because the industry was not sufficiently responsive to safety concerns. . . . .

[P]etitioners recite a number of difficulties that they believe would be posed by a mandatory airbag standard. These range from questions concerning the installation of airbags in small cars to that of adverse public reaction. But these are not the agency's reasons for rejecting a mandatory airbag standard. Not having discussed the possibility, the agency submitted no reasons at all. . . .

Petitioners also invoke our decision in Vermont Yankee . . . as though it were a talisman under which any agency decision is by definition unimpeachable. Specifically, it is submitted that to require

3. [Ed.] See p. 513, below.

an agency to consider an airbags-only alternative is, in essence, to dictate to the agency the procedures it is to follow. Petitioners both misread Vermont Yankee and misconstrue the nature of the remand that is in order. . . . We do not require today any specific procedures which NHTSA must follow. Nor do we broadly require an agency to consider all policy alternatives in reaching decision. It is true that a rulemaking "cannot be found wanting simply because the agency failed to include every alternative device and thought conceivable by the mind of man . . . regardless of how uncommon or unknown that alternative may have been. . . . " 435 U.S., at 551. But the airbag is more than a policy alternative to the passive restraint Standard; it is a technological alternative within the ambit of the existing Standard. We hold only that given the judgment made in 1977 that airbags are an effective and cost-beneficial life-saving technology, the mandatory passive restraint rule may not be abandoned without any consideration whatsoever of an airbags-only requirement.

B

Although the issue is closer, we also find that the agency was too quick to dismiss the safety benefits of automatic seatbelts. NHTSA's critical finding was that, in light of the industry's plans to install readily detachable passive belts, it could not reliably predict "even a 5 percentage point increase as the minimum level of expected usage increase." The Court of Appeals rejected this finding because there is "not one iota" of evidence that Modified Standard 208 will fail to increase nationwide seatbelt use by at least 13 percentage points, the level of increased usage necessary for the Standard to justify its cost. Given the lack of probative evidence, the court held that "only a well-justified refusal to seek more evidence could render rescission non-arbitrary." 680 F.2d, at 232.

Petitioners object to this conclusion. In their view, "substantial uncertainty" that a regulation will accomplish its intended purpose is sufficient reason, without more, to rescind a regulation. We agree with petitioners that just as an agency reasonably may decline to issue a safety standard if it is uncertain about its efficacy, an agency may also revoke a standard on the basis of serious uncertainties if supported by the record and reasonably explained. Rescission of the passive restraint requirement would not be arbitrary and capricious simply because there was no evidence in direct support of the agency's conclusion. It is not infrequent that the available data does not settle a regulatory issue and the agency must then exercise its judgment in moving from the facts and probabilities on the record to a policy conclusion. Recognizing that policymaking in a complex society must account for uncertainty, however, does not imply that it is sufficient for an agency to merely recite the terms "substantial uncertainty" as a justification for its actions. [T]he agency must explain the evidence which is available, and must offer a "rational connection between the facts found and the choice made." Burlington Truck Lines, Inc. v. United States, supra, 371 U.S. at 168. Generally, one aspect of that explanation would be a justification for rescinding the regulation before engaging in a search for further evidence. . . .

We start with the accepted ground that if used, seatbelts unquestionably would save many thousands of lives and would prevent tens of thousands of crippling injuries. Unlike recent regulatory decisions we have reviewed, Industrial Union Dept. v. American Petroleum Institute, 448 U.S. 607 (1980); American Textile Mfrs. Institute, Inc. v. Donovan, 452 U.S. 490 (1981), the safety benefits of wearing seatbelts are not in doubt, and it is not challenged that were those benefits to accrue, the monetary costs of implementing the standard would be easily justified. We move next to the fact that there is no direct evidence in support of the agency's finding that detachable automatic belts cannot be predicted to yield a substantial increase in usage. The empirical evidence on the record, consisting of surveys of drivers of automobiles equipped with passive belts, reveals more than a doubling of the usage rate experienced with manual belts.[4] Much of the agency's rulemaking statement—and much of the controversy in this case—centers on the conclusions that should be drawn from these studies. The agency maintained that the doubling of seatbelt usage in these studies could not be extrapolated to an across-the-board mandatory standard because the passive seatbelts were guarded by ignition interlocks and purchasers of the tested cars are somewhat atypical.[5] Respondents insist these studies demonstrate that Modified Standard 208 will substantially increase seatbelt usage. We believe that it is within the agency's discretion to pass upon the generalizability of these field studies. This is precisely the type of issue which rests within the expertise of NHTSA, and upon which a reviewing court must be most hesitant to intrude.

But accepting the agency's view of the field tests on passive restraints indicates only that there is no reliable real-world experience that usage rates will substantially increase. To be sure, NHTSA opines that "it cannot reliably predict even a 5 percentage point increase as the minimum level of expected increased usage." But this and other statements that passive belts will not yield substantial increases in seatbelt usage apparently take no account of the critical difference between detachable automatic belts and current manual belts. A detached passive belt does require an affirmative act to reconnect it, but—unlike a manual seatbelt—the passive belt, once reattached, will

4. Between 1975 and 1980, Volkswagen sold approximately 350,000 Rabbits equipped with detachable passive seatbelts that were guarded by an ignition interlock. General Motors sold 8,000 1978 and 1979 Chevettes with a similar system, but eliminated the ignition interlock on the 13,000 Chevettes sold in 1980. NHTSA found that belt usage in the Rabbits averaged 34% for manual belts and 84% for passive belts. RIA, at IV–52, App 108. For the 1978–1979 Chevettes, NHTSA calculated 34% usages for manual belts and 72% for passive belts. On 1980 Chevettes, the agency found these figures to be 31% for manual belts and 70% for passive belts.

5. "NHTSA believes that the usage of automatic belts in Rabbits and Chevettes would have been substantially lower if the automatic belts in those cars were not equipped with a use-inducing device inhibiting detachment." Notice 25, 46 Fed.Reg. at 53422 (1981). [Ed. The "atypicality" was also that small car owners use seatbelts more than others do; and most owners with passive belts in these cars had voluntarily paid extra for them.]

continue to function automatically unless again disconnected. Thus, inertia—a factor which the agency's own studies have found significant in explaining the current low usage rates for seatbelts [6]—works in *favor* of, not *against,* use of the protective device. Since 20% to 50% of motorists currently wear seatbelts on some occasions, there would seem to be grounds to believe that seatbelt use by occasional users will be substantially increased by the detachable passive belts. Whether this is in fact the case is a matter for the agency to decide, but it must bring its expertise to bear on the question. . . .

The agency also failed to articulate a basis for not requiring nondetachable belts under Standard 208. It is argued that the concern of the agency with the easy detachability of the currently favored design would be readily solved by a continuous passive belt, which allows the occupant to "spool out" the belt and create the necessary slack for easy extrication from the vehicle. The agency did not separately consider the continuous belt option, but treated it together with the ignition interlock device in a category it titled "Option of Adoption of Use-Compelling Features." The agency was concerned that use-compelling devices would "complicate extrication of [an] occupant from his or her car." "[T]o require that passive belts contain use-compelling features," the agency observed, "could be counterproductive [given] . . . widespread, latent and irrational fear in many members of the public that they could be trapped by the seatbelt after a crash." In addition, based on the experience with the ignition interlock, the agency feared that use-compelling features might trigger adverse public reaction.

By failing to analyze the continuous seatbelts in its own right, the agency has failed to offer the rational connection between facts and judgment required to pass muster under the arbitrary-and-capricious standard. . . . NHTSA did not suggest that the emergency release mechanisms used in nondetachable belts are any less effective for emergency egress than the buckle release system used in detachable belts. In 1978, when General Motors obtained the agency's approval to install a continuous passive belt, it assured the agency that nondetachable belts with spool releases were as safe as detachable belts with buckle releases. NHTSA was satisfied that this belt design assured easy extricability: "[t]he agency does not believe that the use of [such] release mechanisms will cause serious occupant egress problems. . . . " While the agency is entitled to change its view on the acceptability of continuous passive belts, it is obligated to explain its reasons for doing so.

---

6. NHTSA commissioned a number of surveys of public attitudes in an effort to better understand why people were not using manual belts and to determine how they would react to passive restraints. The surveys reveal that while 20% to 40% of the public is opposed to wearing manual belts, the larger proportion of the population does not wear belts because they for-got or found manual belts inconvenient or bothersome. In another survey, 38% of the surveyed group responded that they would welcome automatic belts, and 25% would "tolerate" them. NHTSA did not comment upon these attitude surveys in its explanation accompanying the rescission of the passive restraint requirement.

The agency also failed to offer any explanation why a continuous passive belt would engender the same adverse public reaction as the ignition interlock, and, as the Court of Appeals concluded, "every indication in the record points the other way." We see no basis for equating the two devices: the continuous belt, unlike the ignition interlock, does not interfere with the operation of the vehicle. More importantly, it is the agency's responsibility, not this Court's, to explain its decision.

VI

"An agency's view of what is in the public interest may change, either with or without a change in circumstances. But an agency changing its course must supply a reasoned analysis. . . ." Greater Boston Television Corp. v. FCC, 444 F.2d 841, 852 (1970), cert. denied 403 U.S. 923 (1971). We do not accept all of the reasoning of the Court of Appeals but we do conclude that the agency has failed to supply the requisite "reasoned analysis" in this case. Accordingly, we vacate the judgment of the Court of Appeals and remand the case to that court with directions to remand the matter to the NHTSA for further consideration consistent with this opinion.

So ordered.

JUSTICE REHNQUIST, with whom the CHIEF JUSTICE, JUSTICE POWELL, and JUSTICE O'CONNOR join, concurring in part and dissenting in part.

I join parts, I, II, III, IV, and V–A of the Court's opinion. In particular, I agree that, since the airbag and continuous spool automatic seatbelt were explicitly approved in the Standard the agency was rescinding, the agency should explain why it declined to leave those requirements intact. In this case, the agency gave no explanation at all. . . .

I do not believe, however, that NHTSA's view of detachable automatic seatbelts was arbitrary and capricious. . . . [T]he agency's explanation, while by no means a model, is adequate. The agency acknowledged that there would probably be some increase in belt usage, but concluded that the increase would be small and not worth the cost of mandatory detachable automatic belts. . . .

The agency's changed view of the standard seems to be related to the election of a new President of a different political party. It is readily apparent that the responsible members of one administration may consider public resistance and uncertainties to be more important than do their counterparts in a previous administration. A change in administration brought about by the people casting their votes is a perfectly reasonable basis for an executive agency's reappraisal of the costs and benefits of its programs and regulations. As long as the agency remains within the bounds established by Congress,[7] it is enti-

---

7. Of course, a new administration may not refuse to enforce laws of which it does not approve, or to ignore statutory standards in carrying out its regulatory func- tions. But in this case, as the Court correctly concludes . . . Congress has not required the agency to require passive restraints.

tled to assess administrative records and evaluate priorities in light of the philosophy of the administration.

NOTES

(1) C. SUNSTEIN, DEREGULATION AND THE HARD-LOOK DOCTRINE, 1983 Sup.Ct.Rev. 177, 207. "Investigation of alternatives . . . can be costly. Airbags raise a host of questions different from those involved in the decision whether to require detachable belts. To resolve these questions, a substantial investment of resource may be required. Why should it not be sufficient for the agency to note that fact, to point to the various demands on its budget, to rescind the (by hypothesis) defective existing rule, and to say that it would be preferable to take up the question of airbags at some later date?"

(2) In addition to what the case says about scope of review, consider what it indicates about the substance of this regulatory program. Take it as given that seatbelts are a key safety-promoting device. As early as one year after the 1966 enactment of this program, common lap-belts were required. 32 F.R. 2415 (1967). In 1984, New York passed the first mandatory seatbelt law. To: The same year, NHTSA required either enactment of such laws in two-thirds of the states or else mandatory passive restraints, to be effective in 1990—already extended to 1993, 24 years after their first formal proposal requiring such restraints. What lesson is to be found here about auto safety regulation, or regulation more generally? That without the 1969–84 rulemaking efforts, seatbelts would be used even less? That if the public is divided or not greatly concerned and the regulated industry "wages war" against the proposed rules, then regardless of the merits, great delay or defeat is inescapable? That the agency failed, either because of its own limitations or the state of the art, to establish the merits clearly enough? That the 1972 requirement of an "ignition interlock" and 1974 Congressional override showed the agency's political incapacity in terms of their judgment or "muscle" or both? That the Nixon-Ford Administration or at least NHTSA, and the Carter Administration or at least DOT, had a safety orientation that never took effect (on passive restraints) because the inescapable lead-time let political and/or economic circumstances change? That to think of whether NHTSA in 1981 was faithful to a 1966 statute is to ignore the "play in the joints of government" that is inevitable—and desirable? Or, that to evaluate the level of success of a regulatory effort requires so much knowledge of the substance and relevant externalities, and such judgment about the particular politics, that we should not sit in judgment on this effort without more information—if so, what kind of information? But between the information we do have and assumptions to fill any gaps, can we draw from this regulatory effort any useful inferences about regulation generally?

(3) Would any purpose be served by adding the following language to § 553(c)—another provision of the consensus Senate administrative

procedure reform bill, S. 1080, p. 451 above—to require a statement of basis and purpose to include:

"(A) an explanation of the need for, objectives of, and statutory authority for the rule;

"(B) a discussion of any significant issues raised by the comments on the proposed rule, including a description of the reasonable alternatives to the rule proposed by the agency and by interested persons, and the reasons why each such alternative was rejected; and

"(C) an explanation of how the factual conclusions upon which the rule is based are substantially supported in the rule making file maintained pursuant to subsection (f) of this section."

(4) CENTER FOR AUTO SAFETY v. PECK, 751 F.2d 1336 (D.C.Cir.1985), upheld NHTSA's reducing the minimum performance standard for auto bumpers from having to withstand impact speed of 5 m.p.h., to only 2.5 m.p.h., over a lengthy and detailed dissent by Judge Wright. Judge Scalia's opinion began by noting the "recent reminder" from the Supreme Court's State Farm decision that review is to be narrow. Judge Scalia examined in close detail, however, (a) the various accident data (including some he derived from comments in the rulemaking record) to evaluate how well they took into account that in some prior years bumper heights had been standardized; (b) the difficulties of developing further data; (c) the significance of strong bumpers in "crash energy management"; and (d) the cost analyses, including 1) relationship between bumper weight and fuel costs; 2) impact on repair costs; 3) validity of relying on test conditions to establish real costs; 4) validity of methodology; 5) costs of time lost at accidents, in obtaining repair estimates and repair, and in losing the car during repair; 6) original purchase costs; and last, 7) comparison of such costs among alternatives.

One would need to read not only the 55 pages of opinions but at least the record, to decide whether one agrees with Judge Wright that the majority had "abandoned entirely its mandate of rigorous judicial review." But considering the modesty of the matter at issue and the review given, this summary alone should make clear the distance we have come from the era of Pacific States Box and Basket, p. 478 above.

NOTE ON THE SPECIAL PROBLEM OF PREDICTIONS AND GAMBLES

Particularly in scientific and technological matters, "uncertainty" is a major element in administrative judgment. Events conspire to demand action before knowledge is complete. How ought uncertainty be managed by agencies, and their acknowledgement of it be treated by courts on review? Given, for example, that enormous commitments of social resources may be made, or lives may be exposed to harm, on the basis of the judgments made? Space permits no more than a brief sampling, beginning with a 1951 decision (occasionally cited in the preceding materials) that will present more of a contrast if you pay attention to expectations about the agency's underlying effort, rather than the result.[1]

(1) RADIO CORP. OF AMERICA v. UNITED STATES, 341 U.S. 412 (1951) upheld the FCC's order prescribing standards for color television transmission, in effect accepting the color television broadcasting system proposed by CBS and rejecting RCA's. (There was no dispute that a single system had to be selected. The Korean War halted CBS's implementation of its victory, and after a few years RCA developed a superior system and prevailed.) The three-judge district court's affirmance was so far from a "hard look" as to include this: "[W]e have been unable to free our minds of the question as to why we should devote the time and energy which the importance of the case merits, realizing as we must that the controversy can only be finally terminated by a decision of the Supreme Court. This is so because any decision we make is appealable to that court as a matter of right . . . ."

The Supreme Court affirmed in seven pages (which included giving the background, and noting that the FCC hearing transcript was 9,717 pages). The Court held that the wisdom of the action was debatable but "not arbitrary or against the public interest as a matter of law." Justice Frankfurter filed a "dubitante" opinion, including this: "I am no friend of judicial intrusion into the administrative process. . . . [But] what may be an obvious matter of judgment for the Commission in one situation may so profoundly affect the public interest in another as not to be a mere exercise of conventional discretion. . . . What the Commission here decided is that it could not wait, or the American public could not wait, a little while longer, with every prospect of a development which, when it does come, concededly will promote the public interest more than the incompatible system now authorized. Surely what constitutes the public interest on an issue like this is not one of those expert matters as to which courts should properly bow to the Commission's expertness. In any event, nothing was submitted to us on argument, nor do I find anything in the Commission's brief of 150 pages, which gives any hint as to the public interest that brooks no delay in getting color television even though the method by which it will get it is intrinsically undesirable, inevitably limits the possibilities of an improved system or, in any event, leads to potential great economic waste. The only basis for this haste is that the desired better method has not yet proved itself and in view of past failures there is no great assurance of early success. And so, since a system of color television, though with obvious disadvantages, is available, the requisite public interest which must control the Commission's authorization is established. I do not agree." 341 U.S. at 422–25.

(2) FCC v. NATIONAL CITIZENS COMMITTEE FOR BROADCASTING, 436 U.S. 775, 813–14 (1978): The Supreme Court unanimously reversed a circuit court decision that the FCC's record was incomplete when it adopted rules limiting newspaper-broadcaster combinations, in order to

---

1. The materials of Chapter 7, Section 4 also bear here.

promote diversification of media ownership. "[T]o the extent that factual determinations were involved in the Commission's decision to 'grandfather' most existing combinations, they were primarily of a judgmental or predictive nature—e.g., whether a divestiture requirement would result in trading of stations with out-of-town owners; whether new owners would perform as well as existing crossowners, either in the short run or in the long run; whether losses to existing owners would result from forced sales; whether such losses would discourage future investment in quality programming; and whether new owners would have sufficient working capital to finance local programming. In such circumstances complete factual support in the record for the Commission's judgment or prediction is not possible or required; 'a forecast of the direction in which future public interest lies necessarily involves deductions based on the expert knowledge of the agency'. . . . "

(3) BALTIMORE GAS & ELECTRIC CO. v. NRC, 462 U.S. 87 (1983), the second appearance of the Vermont Yankee dispute in the Supreme Court, unanimously upheld the NRC's decision that licensing of nuclear power plants could proceed in the face of high uncertainty, fully acknowledged, about the environmental effects of nuclear waste disposal. The NRC had responded to Vermont Yankee I as follows: Licensing boards dealing with particular applications could take evidence about the health and other effects of nuclear plant operation, but were to assume that waste fuel could be adequately disposed of and would not harm the environment. The Commission acknowledged uncertainty because of the remote possibility that water might enter a waste depository, resulting in release of radioactive materials; but it predicted that bedded-salt repositories would be satisfactory and it found the evidence "tentative but favorable" that such sites would be found. Further, the NRC found any undue optimism in those assumptions offset by related assumptions that were probably conservative in nature. The NRC said: "On the individual reactor licensing level, where the proceedings deal with fuel cycle issues only peripherally, the Commission sees no advantage in having licensing boards repeatedly weigh for themselves the effect of uncertainties on the selection of fuel cycle impacts for use in cost-benefit balancing. This is a generic question properly dealt with in the rulemaking. . . . The Commission concludes, having noted that uncertainties exist, that for the limited purpose of the fuel cycle rule it is reasonable to base impacts on the assumption which the Commission believes the probabilities favor, i.e., that bedded-salt repository sites can be found which will provide effective isolation of radioactive waste from the biosphere." 44 Fed. Reg. 45362, 45369 (1979).

A divided court of appeals, per Judge Bazelon, found the NRC's treatment both arbitrary and violative of NEPA, NRDC v. United States NCR, 685 F.2d 459 (D.C.Cir.1982). If the NRC's "zero-release assumption" was viewed as a finding of fact, it was arbitrary because admittedly surrounded with uncertainty. If instead the assumption was viewed as a "decisionmaking device" permitting the Commission to use generic rulemaking to evaluate environmental impacts common to all licensing decisions, the Commission was preventing factors relevant under NEPA from affecting individual licensing decisions, thus violating NEPA and also arbitrary. Dissenting, Judge Wilkey said that "the effect of the majority's analysis is to state that it is error for the Commission to proceed in the face of admitted uncertainties." 685 F.2d at 540.

Per Justice O'Connor, the Supreme Court spoke unanimously: "[N]o one suggests that the uncertainties are trivial or the potential effects insignificant if time proves the zero-release assumption to have been seriously wrong. After confronting the issue, though, the Commission has determined that the uncertainties concerning the development of nuclear waste storage facilities are not sufficient to affect the outcome of any individual licensing board.

"It is clear that the Commission, in making this determination, has made the careful consideration and disclosure required by NEPA. The sheer volume of proceedings before the Commission is impressive. Of far greater importance, the Commission's Statement of Consideration announcing the final . . . rule shows that it has digested this mass of material and disclosed all substantial risks. . . . Our only task is to determine whether the Commission has considered the relevant factors and articulated a rational connection between the facts found and the choice made." 462 U.S. 87, 98–99, 105.[2]

(4) D. SCROGGINS, EPA HEALTH RISK POLICY WILL HAVE BROAD IMPACT, Legal Times,[*] July 15, 1985, 19: "EPA is in the final stages of promulgating generic risk assessments guidelines to set general criteria for the adequacy of the risk assessments that the agency uses as a basis for its environmental regulatory programs. In response to the EPA administrator's request, EPA's prestigious and independent Science Advisory Board (SAB) formally reviewed the proposed guidelines and advised EPA of the necessity to incorporate in the guidelines a basic requirement for full disclosure of the uncertainties in all risk assessments. . . .

"Currently, virtually all health risk assessments present only the upper limit extreme of an estimated range of risk and fail to disclose that the actual risk could lie anywhere between this upper limit and zero. The SAB has advised EPA that every risk assessment must contain specific language stating the uncertainties and the range in the estimates of health risk, including both the upper and lower limits, rather than just the upper limits that currently are used.

---

2. The NRC was also upheld in refusing to hold a hearing on how an emergency evacuation plan would be affected if an earthquake occurred at about the same time as a nuclear accident at a plant. A majority of five judges affirmed because they found the likelihood of such a concurrence of events was 1 in 35,750,000 during the life of the plant. The four dissenters said the relevant figure was the likelihood of a significant earthquake, about 1 in 275 per year; and that in any event, the Commission had not quantified the probabilities as did the majority's "post-hoc rationalization for the agency's decision." San Luis Obispo Mothers For Peace v. NRC, 789 F.2d 26, 52 n. 10 (D.C.Cir. en banc 1986).

* Reprinted with permission.

"For example, rather than stating that the risk posed by industrial emissions of a certain cancer-causing substance is '10 cancer deaths per year,' the risk assessment would now read explicitly that 'the real risk is unknown, but is estimated to lie between an upper limit of 10 cancer deaths per year and lower limit of zero.' Whenever possible, the presentation of 'most likely or best estimates of risk for use in risk management' also would be required. . . .

"Some activist groups strongly urge agencies to rely upon risk assessments . . . not to disclose the uncertainties and range associated with the estimates of risk in promulgating regulations. . . . For example, in recent comments submitted to EPA regarding the agency's proposed withdrawal of benzene regulations because the health risks were determined to be insignificant, one such organization argued that public health agencies such as EPA should respond to even one 'statistical' death with the same urgency with which a police department would respond to 'a tip that a dangerous person has threatened to shoot randomly into a Times Square crowd until he kills one person. . . . '

"While full disclosure of uncertainties associated with risk assessments is a fundamental requirement for scientific adequacy, risk assessments intended for use in governmental regulations have rarely included this information. The recognition that a regulation—perhaps costing society hundreds of millions of dollars—was prompted by a calculated health risk that is as likely to be zero as it is to be the upper limit number and hinges upon unproven theoretical assumptions, may be disquieting to policy-makers and risk assessors, as well as to the parties directly affected. As a consequence, risk numbers that are in fact only the extreme upper limit of the estimated range of risk tend to assume a false appearance of precision and certainty, taking on a life of their own in the press and in the minds of the public. More importantly, however, they create a faulty predicate for rulemaking.

"The failure of current risk assessments to lay out openly and candidly the full range of scientific information available, including the uncertainty information, is precisely what renders the final regulatory actions based upon such risk assessments legally vulnerable. While courts are reluctant to substitute their judgment as to how various factors should be weighed in reaching an agency's regulatory decisions, they are nevertheless quick to condemn as arbitrary and capricious agency decisions based on less than full consideration of all the relevant information. . . .

"The hotly contested litigation concerning EPA's regulations to limit emissions of airborne radioactive particles ('radionuclides') . . . pointedly illustrates the value of a risk assessment that fully discloses uncertainties to the risk manager. Administrator Alvin L. Alm recently asserted that industrial emissions of radionuclides pose a health risk that is 'miniscule' when compared with other exposures to radiation. Harvard Law Professor Richard B. Stewart has also observed that in light of the 'quite trivial' risks posed by radionuclide emissions, '[t]he entire exercise represents a serious misallocation of administrative resources.'

"On the other hand, however, several activist groups have voiced outrage at the agency's consideration of the significance of risk. In the words of one group, 'The decision not to set standards that would reduce public exposure to known causes of cancer is a decision to abandon the war on cancer.' "

(5) M. SHAPIRO, ADMINISTRATIVE DISCRETION: THE NEXT STAGE, 92 Yale L.J. 1487, 1507 (1983): "Courts cannot take a hard look at materials they cannot understand nor be partners to technocrats in a realm in which only technocrats speak the language."

f. Respecting Choices of Sanctions and Means of Enforcement

Enforcement by agencies is a form of discretionary activity obviously having major significance yet drawing relatively little academic attention. This likely is merely an example of our pattern of preoccupation with what rights are or should be recognized, leaving too little time to consider problems of enforcing rights. Also, as a classic realm of agency discretion, questions of enforcement produce fewer judicial opinions, which in itself doubtless accounts for some of our under-attention to the area. We have been considering, if you will, judicial review of quasi-judicial and quasi-legislative action. Enforcement may be deemed committed to the executive branch by the President's duty to "take Care that the Laws be faithfully executed", Art. II, Section 3.[1] The doctrine of prosecutorial discretion may rest on that (and similar state constitutional provisions); notably, no federal agency can invoke criminal process except through the Department of Justice. Decisions on whether to enforce, how frequently, and against whom to proceed, even when made by agencies, in the context of civil not criminal law, appear to be unusually secure from judicial inquiry.[2]

"In designing the most appropriate means to enforce the law, agency discretion is at its zenith and judicial power at its nadir." American Trucking Associations, Inc. v. ICC, 697 F.2d 1146, 1153 (D.C. Cir.1983) (Scalia, J.).

One might believe, however, that judicial controls might be more aggressive at the nether end of the administrative process, where sanctions are decided upon. Here, large issues of resource allocation or priority setting are less likely to be presented. Particular decisions have been made, which *could* be explained; and the subjects of those decisions may have a plausible claim to make that they are being imposed upon in some disproportionate way. To be sure, we do not ordinarily provide for appellate judicial review of criminal sentences— the closest analog—but that practice itself has been the subject of

1. See generally Wayte v. United States, 105 S.Ct. 1524 (1985), recognizing the possibility of a constitutional (equal protection) constraint.

2. See the materials on public participation in the initiation of administrative proceedings, p. 315 above, and Heckler v. Chaney, set out at p. 1021 below.

trenchant criticism [3] and recent reform.[4] Consider how far the tools we have been examining are, or might profitably be, employed in the cases following:

(1) BUTZ v. GLOVER LIVESTOCK COMMISSION CO., 411 U.S. 182 (1973). Glover, a livestock marketing business, registered under the Packers and Stockyards Act, was found (after a hearing) to have incorrectly weighed cattle which had been consigned to it for sale and, consequently, to have underpaid the consignors whose interests it was ostensibly serving. The Judicial Officer of the Agriculture Department (acting for Secretary Butz) entered an order to desist from violations of this kind and to keep correct accounts in the future. In addition, the Judicial Officer suspended Glover's registration, saying that though imposing sanctions "is not a pleasant task," he had concluded that twenty days' suspension should be imposed "in view of the previous warnings given respondent."

The Court of Appeals upheld the cease and desist order, but set aside the suspension because, first, in the past suspension had occurred only for "intentional and flagrant" violations of law rather than for merely careless violations as Glover's were deemed to be, and therefore the present suspension ran counter to the policy of achieving "uniformi-

3. "It is an anomaly that a judicial system which has developed so scrupulous a concern for the protection of a criminal defendant throughout every other stage of the proceedings against him should have so neglected this most important dimension of fundamental justice." Shepard v. United States, 257 F.2d 293, 294 (6th Cir.1958) (Stewart, J.). See also M. Frankel, Criminal Sentences (1973) and Remarks on Criminal Code Reform Act, 80 F.R.D. 152 (1977); R. Labbe, Appellate Review of Sentences: Penology on the Judicial Doorstep, 68 J. Crim. L. & Crim. 122 (1977).

4. The Comprehensive Crime Control Act of 1984, P.L. 98–473, 98 Stat. 1976, established a Sentencing Commission of seven members, three of whom will be sitting Federal judges selected by the President from a list of six recommended by the Judicial Conference; the Attorney General (or designee) is to be a nonvoting member. 28 U.S.C. § 991(a). The Commission is to issue guidelines (through informal rulemaking process, APA § 553; § 944(w)) on whether and how much to fine, imprison, or use probation; whether multiple sentences should be concurrent or consecutive, etc.; and is also to issue general policy statements. § 994(a). The statute specifies seven factors to be considered in establishing categories of offenses and 11 for categories of defendants. § 994(c), (d).

Sentencing courts are also given factors to consider and are directed to sentence within the range set forth in the applicable Commission guidelines unless aggravating or mitigating circumstances exist. The

judge is to state in open court the reasons for imposing the particular sentence and, if the sentence is within a guideline range, why it is imposed "at a particular point within the range"; and if not in a guideline range, "the specific reason for the imposition. . . . " § 3553. Last, both defendant and prosecution can appeal a sentence; on defendant's appeal a sentence can only be affirmed or lowered, on government appeal only affirmed or raised. § 3742. The House Report said: "It is an anomaly to provide for appellate correction of prejudicial trial errors and not to provide for appellate correction of incorrect or unreasonable sentences. . . . "

"Appellate review of sentences is essential to assure that the guidelines are applied properly and to provide case law development of the appropriate reasons for sentencing outside the guidelines. This, in turn, will assist the Sentencing Commission in refining the sentencing guidelines as the need arises." H.Rep. No. 98–1030, 98th Cong.2d Sess. 150–51 (1984).

Compare United States v. Ely, 719 F.2d 902, 907 (7th Cir.1983), cert. denied 465 U.S. 1037 (1984) ("[W]e are unwilling to broaden the extremely narrow scope of appellate review of sentences. All other considerations to one side, Judge Friendly's warning, which is even more timely today than when delivered a decade ago, that a general power of appellate review of sentences would end the federal appellate court system as we know it, must give us pause. Friendly, Federal Jurisdiction: A General View 36 (1973).") (Posner, J.).

ty of sanctions for similar violations"; second, the damaging publicity surrounding these proceedings and the cease and desist order would, the court believed, suffice to discourage the misbehavior which the Agriculture Department was seeking to eliminate.

The Supreme Court reversed, saying flatly that "the setting aside of the suspension was an impermissible judicial intrusion into the administrative domain." Nowhere in the statute could the Court find a requirement of "uniformity of sanctions for similar violations." On the contrary, the Act authorizes the Secretary to suspend any violator "for a reasonable specified period." Moreover, the statute does not say that the suspension is appropriate only when misconduct has been "intentional and flagrant." Rather, the broad grant of authority implies a legislative purpose to permit the Secretary to impose suspension in order to deter repeated violations, whether they were intentional or merely negligent. "The employment of a sanction within the authority of an administrative agency is thus not rendered invalid in a particular case because it is more severe than sanctions imposed in other cases. FCC v. WOKO, 329 U.S. 223, 227–228 (1946)." Nor was the suspension order so unjustified in fact as to constitute an abuse of the Secretary's discretion. "The Judicial Officer rested the suspension on his view of its necessity in light of respondent's disregard of previous warnings. The facts found concerning the previous warnings and respondent's disregard of these warnings were sustained by the Court of Appeals as based on ample evidence. In that circumstance, the overturning of the suspension authorized by the statute was an impermissible intrusion into the administrative domain." And as to the Court of Appeals' belief that damaging publicity plus the cease-and-desist order would suffice, the Supreme Court said that the Court below had "clearly exceeded its function of judicial review. The fashioning of an appropriate and reasonable remedy is for the Secretary, not the court. The court may decide only whether under the pertinent statute and relevant facts, the Secretary made 'an allowable judgment in [his] choice of the remedy.' Jacob Siegel Co. v. FTC, 327 U.S. 608, 612 (1946)."

Justices Stewart and Douglas dissented. The majority view, they asserted, "moves administrative decision-making one step closer to unreviewability, an odd result at a time when serious concern is being expressed about the fairness of agency justice. Second, the Court serves notice upon the federal judiciary to be wary indeed of venturing to correct administrative arbitrariness."

(2) JACOB SIEGEL CO. v. FTC, 327 U.S. 608 (1946), involved a manufacturer of overcoats marketed under the name Alpacuna; they contained alpaca, mohair, wool and cotton, but no vicuna, one of the finest and costliest of fabrics. The Commission found respondent had made various misrepresentations, *not* including any representation that the coats contained vicuna; however, it did find the name Alpacuna deceptive because many consumers would be misled into believing the coats contain vicuna. The Commission's order forbade using "Alpacuna" or any other "word which in whole or in part is indicative of the word, 'vicuna,' to designate or describe" the non-vicuna coats.

The Federal Trade Commission Act made unlawful "unfair methods of competition in commerce, and unfair or deceptive acts or practices in commerce"; it provided that when the Commission's cease and desist orders were challenged in the courts, the findings of the Commission "as to the facts, if supported by evidence, shall be conclusive"; and it provided also that the court "shall have power to make and enter . . . a decree affirming, modifying, or setting aside the order of the Commission, and enforcing the same to the extent that such order is affirmed. . . ."

A unanimous Supreme Court, per Justice Douglas, remanded the Commission's order for proceedings in conformity with the following: "The Commission has wide discretion in its choice of a remedy deemed adequate to cope with the unlawful practices in this area of trade and commerce. Here, as in the case of orders of other administrative agencies under comparable statutes . . . judicial review is limited. It extends no further than to ascertain whether the Commission made an allowable judgment in its choice of the remedy. As applied to this particular type of case, it is whether the Commission abused its discretion in concluding that no change 'short of the excision' of the trade name would give adequate protection. . . . The issue is stated that way for the reason that we are dealing here with trade names which . . . are valuable business assets. The fact that they were adopted without fraudulent design or were registered as trade-marks does not stay the Commission's hand. . . . But the policy of the law to protect them as assets of a business indicates that their destruction "should not be ordered if less drastic means will accomplish the same result. . . . " The problem is to ascertain whether that policy and the other policy of preventing unfair or deceptive trade practices can be accommodated. That is a question initially and primarily for the Commission. . . .

"But in the present case, we do not reach the question whether the Commission would be warranted in holding that no qualifying language . . . would eliminate the deception which it found lurking in the word Alpacuna. For the Commission seems not to have considered whether in that way the ends of the Act could be satisfied and the trade name at the same time saved. We find no indication that the Commission considered the possibility of such an accommodation. It indicated that prohibition of the use of the name was in the public interest since the cease and desist order prohibited the further use of the name.[5] But we are left in the dark whether some change of name short of excision would in the judgment of the Commission be adequate. Yet that is the test . . . Its application involves the exercise of an informed, expert

5. "This appears not from the opinion but from the paragraph following the order entered by the Commission:

'Commissioner Freer dissents from so much of the order as wholly prohibits the continued use of the trade name 'Alpacuna' for the reason that this trade name, which has been in use for more than thirteen years, is a valuable business asset, and is neither deceptive per se, nor is the testimony concerning its tendency or capacity to deceive sufficiently clear and convincing as to render such prohibition of its use necessary in the public interest.

'A majority of the Commission do not agree with either Commissioner Freer's statements of fact or his conclusions of law.' "

judgment. The Commission is entitled not only to appraise the facts of the particular case and the dangers of the marketing methods employed . . . Its expert opinion is entitled to great weight in the reviewing courts. But the courts are not ready to pass on the question whether the limits of discretion have been exceeded in the choice of the remedy until the administrative determination is first made.[6]"

(3) "Review of the factual determination that a violation occurred is normal grist for the courts; review of the length of highly discretionary a [sic] sentence of disqualification is not." H.R.Rep. No. 464, 95th Cong., 1st Sess. 397–98 (1977). That statement, made in the course of amending the Food Stamp Act of 1964, was provoked by division among courts of appeals about what responsibility they were given by this statutory provision: the "validity" of an "administrative action" of the Secretary of Agriculture disqualifying a grocer or wholesaler from participating in the food stamp program was to be "determined" by trial de novo in district court, 7 U.S.C. § 2022(c). (There was no evidentiary hearing at the administrative level.) Is the de novo review limited to the finding of violations, or does it include the sanction imposed? Before 1977, two courts of appeals extended de novo review to include the sanction; two other courts reviewed the sanction only for abuse of discretion—they included a requirement of explanation. See Wolff v. United States Dept. of Agriculture, 455 F.Supp. 169 (E.D.Mo. 1978).[7]

Does concern for consistency suggest fuller or lesser review of the sanctions? "The agency, in contrast to a court, deals with the relationship of penalty to violation on a frequent basis. If the myriad federal and state courts [the statute authorizes challenges there too] were to determine the penalty, uniformity and coherence of administration would be difficult to achieve." Kulkin v. Bergland, 626 F.2d 181, 185

---

6. [Ed.] On remand, the Commission modified its order to permit the word "Alpacuna" to refer to Siegel's nonvicuna costs "if in immediate connection and conjunction therewith, wherever used, there appear words clearly and conspicuously designating all the constituent materials or fibers therein contained. . . . "

In Warner-Lambert Co. v. FTC, 562 F.2d 749, 763 (D.C.Cir.1977), the Trade Commission, having found advertisements for Listerine to have been misleading, ordered its manufacturer to take a variety of corrective steps, including publication of the statement, "Contrary to prior advertising, Listerine will not help prevent colds or sore throats or lessen their severity." The court modified the order by eliminating the confessional element, finding that the remedy, generally, was "well calculated to assure that the disclosure will reach the public. It will necessarily attract the notice of readers, viewers, and listeners, and be plainly conveyed. Given these safeguards, we believe the preamble 'Contrary to prior advertising' is not necessary. It

can serve only two purposes: either to attract attention that a correction follows or to humiliate the advertiser. The Commission claims only the first purpose for it, and this we think is obviated by the other terms of the order. The second purpose, if it were intended, might be called for in an egregious case of deliberate deception, but this is not one. While we do not decide whether petitioner proffered its cold claims in good faith or bad, the record compiled could support a finding of good faith. On these facts, the confessional preamble to the disclosure is not warranted."

7. Despite this discussion in the House Report, the 1977 amendments did not in fact change the statute; one court of appeals, which had previously extended de novo review, acknowledged the legislative history but noted that "what Congress intended to do is thus plain enough, but what it actually did do is another matter entirely." Hough v. United States Dept. of Agriculture, 707 F.2d 866, 868 n. 1 (5th Cir. 1983).

(1st Cir.1980) (concluding that the "Butz v. Glover Livestock Commission Co. standard controls," and reviewing only for abuse of discretion).

(4) The appearance of disparity or surprising harshness doubtless fuels court intervention. Professor Frederick H. Thomforde, Jr.'s three articles respecting the invocation of sanctions by the Securities & Exchange Commission [8] reveal geographic and other patterns of sanctioning and enforcement choices hard to square with rational enforcement policy; he concludes one article with a forthright call for enhanced control:

"It is sometimes suggested that requiring agencies to supply reasons for their discretionary decisions and subjecting those decisions to review would impose unnecessary costs upon the agency. When essential questions are raised that challenge the inherent fairness of our system of adjudication, however, arguments and equations about costs and benefits must themselves be weighed against the costs to a just legal system. In the case of the SEC, a requirement of standards and reasons would not place a substantial new burden upon the agency; the agency not only already has rule-making authority and rule-making mechanisms, but already formulates specific reasoned opinions that purport to justify its sanctions in light of the statutorily imposed public interest standard. If judicial scrutiny of the agency's standards and reasons imposes a cost upon the agency, that expense is balanced by the potential cost to offenders who may have been sanctioned arbitrarily." 74 Mich.L.Rev. at 758.

(5) FTC v. UNIVERSAL-RUNDLE CORP., 387 U.S. 244 (1967): In 1960, the FTC issued a complaint against Universal-Rundle for giving some of its plumbing-fixture customers discounts that it withheld from their competitors, thus allegedly lessening competition in violation of the Clayton Act. The discounts went to purchasers of full truckloads. The proceedings dragged on for four years without Universal-Rundle mentioning its own competitors. However, one month after the FTC ordered it to cease and desist from giving truckload discounts, Universal-Rundle asked the Commission to stay the order and "investigate and institute whatever proceedings are deemed appropriate . . . to correct the industry-wide practice by plumbing fixture manufacturers of granting discounts in prices on truckload shipments." Universal-Rundle submitted affidavits that (1) competitors offered even larger discounts than it had done, (2) Universal-Rundle was in sixth place among seven main plumbing manufacturers, and (3) its five larger competitors had made money and Universal-Rundle had lost money during each of the past three years. The Company's vice president for marketing declared on information and belief that Universal-Rundle would suffer heavily if it alone were ordered to cease and desist.

The FTC denied the stay and said that a general allegation of wrongdoing by competitors was insufficient basis to begin an industry-

8. F. Thomforde, Controlling Administrative Sanctions, 74 Mich.L.Rev. 709 (1976); Patterns of Disparity in SEC Administrative Sanctioning Practice, 42 Tenn.L.Rev. 465 (1975); Negotiating Administrative Settlements in SEC Broker-Dealer Disciplinary Proceedings, 52 NYU L.Rev. 237 (1977).

wide proceeding or to withhold enforcement of the order against Universal-Rundle's demonstrated wrongdoing. Moreover, the Commission added, truckload discounts are not illegal per se, but only when they create the proscribed anti-competitive effects found in this instance. On appeal, the denial of the stay was set aside; the court did not reach the merits of the cease and desist order, but remanded to the Commission with instructions to conduct an inquiry, since Universal-Rundle's evidentiary offering showed the denial of the stay was an abuse of discretion. The Supreme Court summed up the court of appeals' premises: "(1) The 'Commission has directed its attack against a general practice which is prevalent in the industry'; (2) enforcement would lead to the 'sacrifice' of one of the 'smallest participants' in the industry; and, consequently, (3) approval of the enforcement sanctions would be contrary to the purposes of the Clayton Act since 'the giants in the field would be the real benefactors [sic]—not the public.'"

The Supreme Court, reversing unanimously, said that whether to postpone enforcement of a case and desist order " 'depends upon a variety of factors peculiarly within the expert understanding of the Commission.' Thus, 'although an allegedly illegal practice may appear to be operative throughout an industry, whether such appearances reflect fact' is a question 'that call[s] for discretionary determination by the administrative agency.' Because these determinations require the specialized experienced judgment of the Commission, they cannot be overturned by the courts 'in the absence of a patent abuse of discretion.' " The Court pointed out that Universal-Rundle had not shown that its competitors offered discounts that had an anti-competitive effect (as its discounts had) and further, that its vice-president's "unsupported speculation" about the order's impact on Universal-Rundle was insufficient. But, the Court went on, even if the competitors' practices were the same and enforcement would cause the company substantial financial injury, "as we stated in Moog Industries [v. FTC], 355 U.S. [411 (1958)] at 413:

> It is clearly within the special competence of the Commission to appraise the adverse effect on competition that might result from postponing a particular order prohibiting continued violations of the law. Furthermore, the Commission alone is empowered to develop the enforcement policy best calculated to achieve the ends contemplated by Congress and to allocate its available funds and personnel in such a way as to execute its policy efficiently and economically.

"On the other hand, as the Moog Industries case also indicates, the Federal Trade Commission does not have unbridled power to institute proceedings which will arbitrarily destroy one of many law violators in an industry. This is not such a case. The Commission's refusal to withhold enforcement of the cease-and-desist order against respondent was based upon a reasonable evaluation of the merits of the petition for a stay; thus it was not within the scope of the reviewing authority of the court below to overthrow the Commission's determination. Consequently, we reverse the judgment below, set aside the stay, and remand the cause for further proceedings consistent with this opinion." [9]

Is this the "rule or order" question, p. 209 above, in another guise?

(6) The preceding cases have considered assertedly excessive severity in administrative judgment. What of assertedly excessive administrative gentleness? INTERNATIONAL UNION OF ELECTRICAL WORKERS v. NLRB (TIIDEE PRODUCTS, INC.), 426 F.2d 1243 (D.C.Cir.), cert. denied 400 U.S. 950 (1970), involved a Board order that the employer cease interfering with employee rights, reinstate improperly discharged employees with back pay, and bargain collectively. The union sought review of that order as inadequate, arguing that there should be compensatory relief because the refusal to bargain was so clearly unjustified. The court, agreeing that the refusal was "brazen," also agreed that effective relief required compensating the party wronged and withholding from the wrongdoer the "fruits of its violation. . . . [I]t profited through the delay that review entails: all during this litigation it has not had to bargain. . . . " It was the Board's statutory duty " 'to take such affirmative action . . . as will effectuate the policies' " of the labor relations act; but the court could not "discern, and the Board has not explained, on what basis it could or did conclude that its order under review is designed 'to insure meaningful bargaining.' Counsel for the Board tells us that the prospective order to bargain entered in this case is what is conventionally entered by the Board. . . . There is a presumption that favors the Board, with its expertise, in its selection of remedies. . . . That presumption is given full effect when the Board makes a conscious selection of remedies to effectuate the Act, provided reasons for its conclusion are stated or may fairly be discerned. That is not the situation in the case before us." The court remanded for the Board to order damages measured by wages the parties would have agreed to if they had bargained (with future pay to be set by bargaining); and also for the Board to determine whether the employer should have to pay the union dues for the "lost" period. Unless compensatory relief was ordered for refusals to bargain that were "palpably without merit," the court said, the Board was only encouraging frivolous litigation before it and in the reviewing courts.

"No serious objection may be lodged against the make-whole relief because it adds elements of novelty to the Board's lexicon of orders. In

---

9. [Ed.] Compare Professor Colin Diver's observation, addressing agency practice under the 266 statutes permitting discretionary remission of civil penalties— remissions he found commonly unexplained, and made in the absence of announced standards:

"Unless we are satisfied to think of parties subjected to such penalties as fortunate to receive any mercy and not entitled to complain of inconsistency, here too there seems need not merely for findings and reasons, but for a foundation of general standards to draw upon to produce findings and reasons. We return to Judge Friendly's wise simplicity: 'checking a list on a card' may go far to increase the likelihood of like treatment for like cases, even if fuller findings and reasons are not feasible."

C. Diver, Civil Money Penalties, 79 Colum.L.Rev. 1435, 1443 (1979). See also P. Schuck, When the Exception Becomes the Rule: Regulatory Equity and the Formulation of Energy Policy through an Exceptions Process, 1984 Duke L.J. 163; and A. Aman, Administrative Equity: An Analysis of Exceptions to Administrative Rules, 1982 Duke L.J. 277.

the pithy words of Judge, now Chief Justice, Burger: 'In the evolution of the law of remedies some things are bound to happen for the "first time." ' "

(7) R. SHEP MELNICK, REGULATION AND THE COURTS: THE CASE OF THE CLEAN AIR ACT * (1983) reminds us that our picture of judicial oversight is incomplete if we think only of what courts choose to do, as distinct from the question of *which* courts the legislature chooses for the overseeing. For example, the EPA's rules are reviewed in courts of appeals, but its enforcement efforts begin in district courts. "Enforcement cases contrast sharply with [cases on review of rules].[10] Here the EPA faces industry lawyers, not environmentalists. District courts, not appellate courts, constitute the principal forum. Policy emerges from the accumulation of rulings on many small cases rather than from landmark decisions. And most important, the pattern of judicial action has been to weaken, not strengthen, environmental regulations. . . . District courts, in fact, have demonstrated a nearly limitless capacity to review the peculiar circumstances of individual facilities. The fact that courts have chosen to investigate cost and feasibility in this context, though, has important policy consequences. Here industry litigants far outnumber environmentalists. The interest of the citizens who breathe polluted air seems speculative and ephemeral when compared with the interest of local breadwinners who could lose their jobs, especially if the injured breathers live hundreds of miles downwind. Moreover, consideration of cost on a case-by-case basis rules out the possibility that a cleanup burden found unreasonable by a judge will be redistributed to other polluters. And finally, judges have not used the adjudicatory process to examine how this system affects the EPA's treatment of those thousands of cases that never come to court. Adjudication in this setting magnifies the benefits of leniency and ignores its costs.

"It is the courts' decentralized structure that accommodates both their detailed review of the circumstances of each polluter and their inconsistent evaluation of the costs and benefits of regulation. It is only a slight exaggeration to say that trial judges and appellate judges see the entire regulatory world differently. The former not only directly observe the effect of imposing strict regulations, but share responsibility for imposing these burdens on local citizens. The latter, more removed from local concerns, better able to place responsibility for enforcement on others, and more likely to be inspired by statements about broad public goals, value uniformity more than flexibility. To the trial judge justice requires being responsive to the peculiar needs of individual citizens and localities. To the appellate judge it means consistent, unbending application of the laws and the intent of Congress.

* Reprinted from Regulation and the Courts: The Case of the Clean Air Act, by R. Shep Melnick. Copyright © 1983 The Brookings Institution.

10. "Section 307 requires challenges to rules of 'national applicability' to go directly to the D.C. Circuit Court. Section 304 allows citizens to bring 'nondiscretionary duty' cases to any federal district court, including the one in the District of Columbia. Judges in these courts see many more administrative law cases than do other judges. They are neither cowed by federal administrators nor fearful of a powerful federal government."

". . . Trial courts can listen to witnesses, review depositions, conduct inspections, and meet frequently with the parties before them. Appellate courts can seldom do more than listen to the arguments of the parties' attorneys and examine the formal record established by the agency or the court below. . . . Thus, in enforcement cases there is a rough proportion between the court's ability to review evidence and the complexity of the issue involved. In other cases the issues are far more complex and the capacity of the courts to investigate them more restricted." (pp. 353–55, 362, 369–70).

g. Standards to Which Government May Be Held? The Problems of Consistency, Res Judicata, Nonacquiescence, and Equitable Estoppel

(i) Requirement of Consistency

(1) DAVIS v. COMMISSIONER, 69 T.C. 716 (1978): The Internal Revenue Service had disallowed part of a small charitable deduction Professor Kenneth Davis claimed for books received from West Publishing Co., used, and then donated to the University of Chicago Law Library. Contesting the IRS position, Davis obtained via discovery IRS "letter rulings" (without identification of taxpayers involved) issued to Members of Congress who received free copies of the Congressional Record, gave them to charitable organizations and deducted the value of the gifts.[1] After receiving four such rulings, Davis sought via additional discovery all pertinent letter rulings in the IRS's "reference" file to support his position that the IRS must act evenhandedly. Discovery was denied because the rulings bore "too nebulous a relationship to the specific substantive issues." As another Tax Court judge said two years earlier in a similar effort by the professor over a different deduction, "It has long been the position of this Court that our responsibility is to apply the law to the facts of the case . . . before us; how the Commissioner may have treated other taxpayers has generally been considered irrelevant in making that determination. . . . Any change in that position would have widespread ramifications in the administration and application of the Federal tax laws and in the conduct of our work. . . . Over 11,000 new cases were commenced in this Court in the past year, and although many of those cases are settled, the Court still has a herculean task to keep abreast of its caseload. Were we to embrace the principles urged by Mr. Davis, the task would be magnified. Every trial would be extended, for it would

1. The IRS issues letter rulings with less structured review than "revenue rulings," which are officially published and on which all taxpayers are encouraged to rely. The IRS considers itself bound by revenue rulings until revoked, but bound by letter rulings only as to the addressee taxpayer. However, since decisions under the Freedom of Information Act and a 1976 Tax Code amendment, letter rulings have been publicly available; one legal service publishes all of them, roughly 16,000 in 1983. The IRS files letter rulings in two categories, an unindexed "historical" file kept for four years, and a "reference" file kept about 40 years along with court decisions and revenue rulings, organized by code sections and used by IRS personnel when preparing other letter rulings or revenue rulings. See L. Zelenak, Should Courts Require the Internal Revenue Service to be Consistent? 38 Tax L.Rev. 411 (1985).

then become necessary to allow the petitioner to inquire into the Commissioner's treatment of other similarly situated taxpayers. Moreover, any decision to require the publication of all letter rulings involves a weighing of the advantages to be secured by such publication against the possible adverse effect on the rulings practice. . . . [T]he notion of equal justice has strong appeal in our society and might lead to the conclusion that his position should ultimately be adopted. Yet, a full appreciation of the ramifications of this matter makes abundantly clear that it should be approached cautiously." Davis v. Commissioner, 65 T.C. 1014, 1022–23 (1976).

(2) We will return to this apparent justification for arbitrariness shortly, but not before noting that certain steps to promote consistency are clearly feasible, like requiring reasoned treatment of precedent. ATCHISON, TOPEKA & SANTA FE RY. CO. v. WICHITA BD. OF TRADE, 412 U.S. 800 (1973), remanded to the ICC its approval of a new charge for a service (in-transit inspection of grain) which previously had been included in the line-haul rates. The ICC had not repudiated or adequately distinguished its prior cases establishing the rule that "it will not allow a separate charge for an accessorial service previously performed as part of the line-haul rates without substantial evidence that such an additional charge is justified measured against the overall services rendered and the overall reasonableness of the increased line-haul rate resulting therefrom."

Justice Marshall explained: ". . . A settled course of behavior embodies the agency's informed judgment that, by pursuing that course, it will carry out the policies committed to it by Congress.

"There is, then, at least a presumption that those policies will be carried out best if the settled rule is adhered to. From this presumption flows the agency's duty to explain its departure from prior norms. . . . The agency may flatly repudiate those norms, deciding, for example, that changed circumstances mean that they are no longer required in order to effectuate congressional policy. Or it may narrow the zone in which some rule will be applied, because it appears that a more discriminating invocation of the rule will best serve congressional policy. Or it may find that, although the rule in general serves useful purposes, peculiarities of the case before it suggest that the rule not be applied in that case. Whatever the ground for the departure from prior norms, however, it must be clearly set forth so that the reviewing court may understand the basis of the agency's action and so may judge the consistency of that action with the agency's mandate."

(3) Just as precedent must be followed, distinguished or discarded, an agency must comply with its own rules or explain noncompliance even though the initial adoption of the rule may have been voluntary. The most famous example is a dramatic part of the Watergate events, NADER v. BORK, 366 F.Supp. 104 (D.D.C.1973). On June 4, 1973, the day he designated Archibald Cox as Special Prosecutor, Watergate Special Prosecution Force, Attorney General Elliot L. Richardson issued a regulation which gave the Special Prosecutor broad power to investigate and prosecute offenses arising out of the Watergate break-in, the

1972 Presidential election, and allegations involving the President, members of the White House staff or presidential appointees. Specifically, the Special Prosecutor was charged with responsibility to conduct court proceedings and to determine whether or not to contest assertions of Executive privilege. He was to remain in office until a date mutually agreed upon between the Attorney General and himself, and the regulation stated: "The Special Prosecutor will not be removed from his duties except for extraordinary improprieties on his part." 38 F.R. 14688. In the evening of October 20, 1973 (as a part of what has been termed the "Saturday Night Massacre" which included the resignation of Attorney General Elliot Richardson and next-in-line William Ruckelshaus), Acting Attorney General Robert H. Bork, pursuant to instructions from President Nixon, discharged Mr. Cox. There was no suggestion that Mr. Cox had been guilty of any "extraordinary impropriety."

Judge Gesell held the discharge illegal. Although without the regulation the Attorney General "would have had the authority to fire Mr. Cox at any time and for any reason . . . , he chose to limit his own authority in this regard by promulgating the Watergate Special Prosecutor regulation. . . . It is settled beyond dispute that under such circumstances an agency regulation has the force and effect of law and is binding upon the body that issues it. Accardi v. Shaughnessy, 347 U.S. 260 (1954). . . .

"[T]he Supreme Court has twice held that an Executive department may not discharge one of its officers in a manner inconsistent with its own regulations concerning such discharge. See Vitarelli v. Seaton, 359 U.S. 535 (1959); Service v. Dulles, [354 U.S. 363 (1957)].[2] The firing of Archibald Cox in the absence of a finding of extraordinary impropriety was in clear violation of an existing Justice Department regulation having the force of law and was therefore illegal."

After the discharge of Cox, Leon Jaworski was appointed Special Prosecutor. He secured issuance of a subpoena duces tecum ordering President Nixon to produce certain tape recordings and documents

---

2. [Ed.] In the Vitarelli case an employee of the Department of Interior, who could have been discharged at any time without cause, was dismissed by the Secretary "in the interests of national security." The Court held the discharge illegal because the Secretary did not afford the employee the procedural protections prescribed in Departmental regulations to govern dismissals on security grounds. The specific provisions of the regulations which were violated were (1) the statement of charges was not "as specific and detailed as security considerations . . . permit," (2) "reasonable restrictions [were not] imposed as to relevancy, competency, and materiality of matters considered," and (3) the employee was not afforded the right "to cross-examine any witness offered in support of the charges."

The Service case involved the dismissal of an employee by the Secretary of State under the so-called McCarran Rider, which provided that the Secretary could terminate the employment of any employee "whenever he shall deem such termination necessary or advisable in the interests of the United States." The discharge was held to be unlawful because of noncompliance with a departmental regulation establishing standards and procedures to be followed in effecting McCarran Rider dismissals. The specific provisions violated were (1) if, as here, the Deputy Under Secretary of State made a determination favorable to the employee, that determination is final and not subject to reversal by the Secretary, and (2) the Secretary failed to make a decision, as required by the regulations, "on all the evidence and after consideration of the complete file, arguments, briefs, and testimony presented."

relating to the President's conversations with aides and advisers. The President's motion to quash the subpoena was denied by the district court and the President appealed to the court of appeals; the Supreme Court granted a before-judgment petition for certiorari.

In United States v. Nixon, 418 U.S. 683 (1974), the President argued that under "the firmly established doctrine of separation of powers, the Judiciary is without jurisdiction to intervene in the solely intra-executive dispute presented here . . . [because the] ultimate authority over all executive branch decisions is, under Article II of the Constitution, vested exclusively in the President of the United States," Brief for Respondent 27–28, and therefore there was no justiciable case or controversy. A unanimous opinion by Chief Justice Burger rejected the argument:

"Our starting point is the nature of the proceeding for which the evidence is sought—here a pending criminal prosecution. It is a judicial proceeding in a federal court alleging violation of federal laws and is brought in the name of the United States as sovereign. Under the authority of Art. II, § 2, Congress has vested in the Attorney General the power to conduct the criminal litigation of the United States Government. It has also vested in him the power to appoint subordinate officers to assist him in the discharge of his duties. Acting pursuant to those statutes, the Attorney General has delegated the authority to represent the United States in these particular matters to a Special Prosecutor with unique authority and tenure. The regulation gives the Special Prosecutor explicit power to contest the invocation of executive privilege in the process of seeking evidence deemed relevant to the performance of these specially delegated duties.

"So long as this regulation is extant it has the force of law. In United States ex rel. Accardi v. Shaughnessy, 347 U.S. 260 (1954), regulations of the Attorney General delegated certain of his discretionary powers to the Board of Immigration Appeals and required that Board to exercise its own discretion on appeals in deportation cases. The Court held that so long as the Attorney General's regulations remained operative, he denied himself the authority to exercise the discretion delegated to the Board even though the original authority was his and he could reassert it by amending the regulations. Service v. Dulles, 354 U.S. 363, 388 (1957), and Vitarelli v. Seaton, 359 U.S. 535 (1959), reaffirmed the basic holding of Accardi.

"Here, as in Accardi, it is theoretically possible for the Attorney General to amend or revoke the regulation defining the Special Prosecutor's authority. But he has not done so. So long as this regulation remains in force the Executive Branch is bound by it . . . ."[3]

---

3. [Ed.] Of course non-compliance with a rule may be explained satisfactorily or found to be nonprejudicial. See e.g. American Far Lines v. Black Ball Freight Service, 397 U.S. 532 (1970). And see United States v. Caceres, 440 U.S. 741 (1979) (reversing, in prosecution for bribing an IRS agent, lower courts' order to suppress tape recordings made by IRS in violation of its own internal regulation, since violation was "purely one of form" and was pursuant to erroneous but not unreasonable construction of the regulation). See generally P. Raven–Hansen, Regulatory Estoppel: When Agencies Break Their Own "Laws," 64 Tex.L.Rev. 1 (1985).

(4) But the isolable and clear problems of assuring reasoned treatment of precedents or of rules do not raise the most difficult problems of consistency. Major regulatory programs have been profoundly attacked for inconsistency that seemed to reflect fundamental inability or unwillingness to establish policy; for various reasons, those programs are now history.[4] Very different but also daunting problems of treating like cases alike exist in mass administrative justice, such as the 2,071,901 Social Security disability determinations and reviews decided in 1985 (in contrast to 339,718 civil and criminal matters decided that year by all Article III judges). These are the problems invoked by the Tax Court's reference in the Davis case, p. 513 above, to its own caseload and (indirectly) to the thousands of IRS employees struggling daily to achieve uniform implementation of the nation's tax laws. Agree as we all might that the observation that "government is at its most arbitrary when it treats similarly situated people differently"[5] is "the most basic principle of jurisprudence",[6] situations such as these present enormous difficulties in achieving—or for that matter deciding how to measure our achievement of—that agreed goal.[7]

Professor Jerry Mashaw's continuing writings on Social Security disability administration, encountered frequently in these pages, provide a useful illustration. His first study, completed in 1978, produced a damning indictment from a perspective much like Professor Davis': individual cases were being decided without discernible pattern. "The inconsistency of the disability process is patent. Indeed, it is widely believed that the outcome of cases depends more on who decides the case than on what the facts are."[8] But now consider the three models of Mashaw's "Bureaucratic Justice," set out at p. 656 below. The model of individual justice condemns these outcomes, but for the model of bureaucratic rationality the issues are whether *gross* errors have been avoided and marginal errors *evenly distributed* (that is, about as many wrongful grants as wrongful denials) at reasonable cost; that will maximize the extent to which programmatic purposes are achieved and, thus, overall fairness is accomplished. For the "similarly situated" people at the margin of eligibility, inconsistent treatment is a necessary cost of a workable scheme; all that can be asked—that the judgment on eligibility not be "too wrong"—has been achieved. Thus, too, devices like the Heckler v. Campbell grid, p. 295 above, with its obvious costs in individual justice balanced by gains in efficiency and elimination of broad disparity in decision.[9]

4. See H. Friendly, The Federal Administrative Agencies: The Need for Better Definition of Standards, 74 (1962) (criticizing CAB); S. Breyer and R. Stewart, Administrative Law and Regulatory Policy (1985) (ch. 5.B.4., "requiring Consistency in Agency Adjudication: The FCC and Allocation in the 'Public Interest' ").

5. Etelson v. Office of Personnel Mgt., 684 F.2d 918, 926 (D.C. Cir.1982).

6. H. Friendly, Indiscretion About Discretion, 31 Emory L.J. 747, 758 (1982).

7. You may find it useful here to reread R. Kagan, Regulatory Justice, p. 40 above.

8. Mashaw, Goetz, Goodman, Schwartz, Verkuil and Carrow, Social Security Hearings and Appeals: A Study of the Social Security Administration Hearing System xxi (1978).

9. See also D. Gifford, Need Like Cases be Decided Alike? Mashaw's Bureaucratic Justice, 1983 Am. Bar F. Res. J. 985, 989.

(ii) Res Judicata, Collateral Estoppel, and Nonacquiescence

"The federal courts have traditionally adhered to the related doctrines of res judicata and collateral estoppel. Under res judicata, a final judgment on the merits of an action precludes the parties or their privies from relitigating issues that were or could have been raised in that action. . . . Under collateral estoppel, once a court has decided an issue of fact or law necessary to its judgment, that decision [is conclusive in subsequent suits based] on a different cause of action involving a party to the first case. Montana v. United States, 440 U.S. 147, 153.[1] As this Court and other courts have often recognized, res judicata and collateral estoppel relieve parties of the cost and vexation of multiple lawsuits, conserve judicial resources, and, by preventing inconsistent decisions, encourage reliance on adjudication." Allen v. McCurry, 449 U.S. 90, 94 (1980).

There was a time when the Supreme Court appeared to disfavor applying such principles to administrative determinations, but in United States v. Utah Construction & Mining Co., 384 U.S. 394, 422 (1966), the Court stated: "When an administrative agency is acting in a judicial capacity and resolves disputed issues of fact properly before it which the parties have had an adequate opportunity to litigate, the courts have not hesitated to apply res judicata to enforce repose." [2]

1. [Ed.] "A survey of relevant informed opinion reveals little agreement as to how the doctrines should be defined, how they differ from each other, or how the two may be reliably differentiated in any but the most commonplace situations. . . . In an effort to organize and simplify this body of law, the Restatement (Second) of Judgments [now speaks of res judicata as 'claim preclusion' and collateral estoppel as 'issue preclusion.'] Unfortunately this did little to dispel the confusion because the two new terms are invariably defined in terms of the old. . . . The problem was never really one of difficult terminology but rather one of inadequately delineated concepts. What generally travels under the name of res judicata is a preclusion problem where the alignment of parties, facts, and allegations is exceedingly close; collateral estoppel is generally applied when the alignment is less tight—when the same legal issues arise in connection with a different subject matter or different parties. . . . [W]e think the choice of label is of little import. . . . " Clark-Cowlitz Joint Operating Agency v. FERC, 775 F.2d 366, 373–74 (D.C. Cir.1985), vacated and rehearing en banc ordered, 787 F.2d 674 (D.C.Cir.1986).

2. The 1980 Restatement of Judgments comments on the changes in administrative adjudication over the last 50 years (pp. 269–71) and has a wholly new section: "§ 83. Adjudicative Determination by Administrative Tribunal

"[A] valid and final adjudicative determination by an administrative tribunal has the same effects under the rules of res judicata, subject to the same exceptions and qualifications, as a judgment of a court . . . [if] the proceeding resulting in the determination entailed the essential elements of adjudication . . . [unless] the scheme of remedies permits assertion of the second claim notwithstanding the adjudication of the first claim . . . [or unless] according preclusive effect to determination of the issue would be incompatible with a legislative policy that:

"(a) The determination of the tribunal adjudicating the issue is not to be accorded conclusive effect in subsequent proceedings; or

"(b) The tribunal in which the issue subsequently arises be free to make an independent determination of the issue in question."

[Ed.] Traditional rules of res judicata require: (1) A final decision had been reached; (2) the claim in both proceedings is the same; (3) the parties are the same or in "privity"; (4) the tribunal had jurisdiction of the parties and the claim; and with respect to collateral estoppel or issue preclusion, (5) the issue had actually been litigated.

"[A]dministrative res judicata . . . is applied with less rigidity than its judicial counterpart." Parker v. Califano, 644 F.2d 1199, 1202 (6th Cir.1981) (mental illness

(1) An agency's power to change action taken previously will be governed, in the first instance, by any applicable statutory provision concerning reconsideration or modification. In Banks v. Chicago Grain Trimmers Ass'n, Inc., 390 U.S. 459 (1968), the claimant discovered new evidence after a death benefit had been denied under the Longshoremen's and Harbor Workers' Compensation Act. Her second claim succeeded and was upheld because the Act expressly authorized reconsidering a compensation claim within one year after its rejection "on the ground of a change of conditions or because of a mistake in a determination of fact." But it hardly seems surprising that when FERC granted a license to build a small hydroelectric power plant and the time for review had passed, the Commission could not reopen the matter even though it sought a comparative evaluation of all applications filed for the same stretch of river. Hirschey v. FERC, 701 F.2d 215 (D.C.Cir.1983).

(2) On the same day in early 1984, the Supreme Court decided the following two cases testing how, if at all, the interests in repose that would bar relitigation by a private party apply to the Government. UNITED STATES v. STAUFFER CHEMICAL CO., 464 U.S. 165 (1984), involved the EPA's effort to use private contractors as well as its own employees to inspect private facilities. Stauffer refused to allow the contractors to enter its plant in Tennessee. Two weeks earlier, it had refused entry to its plant in Wyoming, then won a Tenth Circuit decision that EPA lacked authority for inspections by private contractors. Thereafter, the refusal to allow entry into the Tennessee plant was also upheld, by the Sixth Circuit, on various grounds.

In the Supreme Court, the Government argued first that even if relitigation against Stauffer were barred in the Tenth Circuit, to bar relitigation in the Sixth, which had not previously taken a position, would freeze the development of the law. Second, that even if relitigation were barred in both the Tenth Circuit and in circuits with no previous position, relitigation should be allowed in circuits which already had a *contrary* position. Specifically, the Ninth Circuit (in a case not involving Stauffer) had upheld the very statutory authority the Tenth Circuit had rejected, and the Government argued it would be unjust for Stauffer to enjoy in the Ninth Circuit one rule while its competitors there were under another.

All Justices agreed that relitigation against Stauffer was barred in the Tenth and Sixth Circuits, although Justice White found the Sixth a "harder question." As for whether EPA could relitigate against Stauffer in the Ninth Circuit, Justice White would allow it and eight Justices said only "the issue . . . is not before the court." 464 U.S. at 175.

UNITED STATES v. MENDOZA, 464 U.S. 154 (1984), involved a petition for naturalization, denied by the INS. A district court reversed on the ground that Mendoza's legal argument had prevailed against the Government a few years earlier, by another district court in a case to which Mendoza had not been a party. The Government did not appeal that

impairing claimant's understanding of remedies to pursue after denial could pre-   vent application of res judicata or raise claim of lack of due process).

earlier decision because the new Carter Administration's INS Commissioner chose "a course of compassion and amnesty." If Mendoza had been a party to the earlier case, clearly the Government would be bound. Or if the earlier case had been between two private parties and Mendoza was now litigating against one of them, clearly Mendoza could bar his adversary from relitigating any issue necessarily decided in the earlier suit.

The Court unanimously (per Justice Rehnquist) decided to allow relitigation. First, government litigation frequently involves issues best resolved by allowing "thorough development" through "litigation in multiple forums", not by "freezing the first final decision", 464 U.S. at 160, 163. Second, Supreme Court certiorari practice relies on the benefit of "percolation" and conflicts among the circuits. Third, unlike private litigants, the government considers a variety of factors in deciding whether to appeal, including resource allocation and possible policy changes as administrations change. Moreover, control of litigation is an executive branch responsibility.[3]

(3) If Mendoza had held the government bound, a single district court's ruling would establish nationwide law. With so sweeping a rule rejected, is the government free to ignore a ruling in similar cases within the same jurisdiction, or should the government comply although not actually bound except as to successful appellants? Stare decisis presses for compliance; but pressing for agency freedom to decide whether to comply is the executive responsibility to carry out a national program efficiently. Mendoza added fuel to an existing heated controversy over some agencies' (not including the INS) claim of freedom to "nonacquiesce" in lower-court decisions. When, for example, courts of appeals decided that disability benefits cannot be terminated without evidence of improved medical condition, the Social Security Administration claimed the right[4] to limit those decisions to the successful appellants, and to proceed with its termination policy unchanged even within those circuits, fully recognizing that it would be reversed each time a termination was appealed.[5]

The SSA's nonacquiescence policy placed it in conflict on one issue with every circuit court (except one which had not ruled at all), and with several circuits on another.[6] In none of those cases did SSA seek Supreme Court review. One circuit judge was provoked to analogize

3. For critical discussion of the Mendoza decision, see Note, Collateral Estoppel and Nonacquiescence: Precluding Government Relitigation in the Pursuit of Litigant Equality, 99 Harv.L.Rev. 847 (1986).

4. The right was said to be supported by the Mendoza decision. Senate Finance Committee Hearings, Social Security Administration's Nonacquiescence Policy, Social Security Disability Insurance Program, 98th Cong., 2d Sess., 117–21 (1984) (statement of Caroline Kuhl, Deputy Asst. A.G., Civil Div., Dep't. of Justice).

5. It has long been understood that a court of appeals decision does not govern outside the circuit. Any resulting lack of national uniformity seems unavoidable until inter-circuit conflicts are resolved either by the Supreme Court (or a new court devoted to such matters, as Congress has been considering), or by statute, or of course by the courts of appeals coming into agreement. See S. Eichel, "Respectful Disagreement"; Nonacquiescence by Federal Administrative Agencies in United States Courts of Appeals Precedents, 18 Col.J.Law & Soc.Probs. 463, 466, n. 22 (1985).

6. H.R.Rep. No. 98–618, 98th Cong., 2d Sess., at 24 (1984).

SSA's policy to the pre-Civil War southern states' doctrine of nullification of federal authority; [7] the number of disability appeals to the courts soared; [8] and after substantial media coverage and Congressional hearings, Congress agreed with the courts of appeals and changed SSA policy—but without resolving the agency's right to refuse to comply with judicial decisions (except as to the parties) even within a court's jurisdiction. [9] The House bill would have required SSA to comply with a prior court of appeals decision within the circuit until it got Supreme Court review; the Senate would have required SSA to notify Congress and insert in the Federal Register explanation of any nonacquiescence. The conferees dropped both provisions, cautioning against any inference that they approved of nonacquiescence, but finding "legal and Constitutional issues" that "can only be settled by the Supreme Court." [10] The conferees noted "congressional intent that the Secretary resolve policy conflicts promptly in order to achieve consistent uniform administration of the program" by seeking Supreme Court or congressional resolution, rather than relitigation costly to both the government and beneficiaries.

The SSA's widespread and sustained nonacquiescence has been the most dramatic challenge to the court-agency partnership, but other agencies, particularly the NLRB and IRS, have long asserted similar rights. [11] For the latter agencies, however, liberal venue provisions render unpredictable which court of appeals will review a case, so that nonacquiescence seems inevitable unless all possible reviewing courts are in agreement. Moreover, if the NLRB or IRS refuses to seek review of an unfavorable decision, review is still likely at the behest of the losing union or employer or taxpayer. But for SSA, the venue of appeals is predictable; if that agency neither appeals nor acquiesces, Supreme Court review will not occur; and disability claimants cannot easily take any appeals.

In defense of intra-circuit nonacquiescence, the main argument is this: complying with different rules in different circuits reduces uniformity and increases administrative burdens; the agency is responsible for efficiently conducting a national program; and only Congress, the Supreme Court, and the agency are authoritative. Would you go beyond that to argue that the executive's responsibility to "take care" authorizes it to ignore even en banc court of appeals decisions, or even

7. Lopez v. Heckler, 713 F.2d 1432, 1441 (9th Cir.1983) (Pregerson, J.).

8. H.R.Rep., supra n. 6, at 23.

9. Social Security Disability Benefits Reform Act of 1984, P.L. 98–640.

10. House Conf.Rpt. 98–1039, 98th Cong., 2d Sess., at 38–9 (1984).

11. The NLRB since at least the early 1970's has claimed the right to nonacquiesce within a circuit, occasionally even on direct remand, and has been strongly criticized by several courts of appeals. See Note, Administrative Agency Intracircuit Nonacquiescence, 85 Colum.L.Rev. 582,

587–8 (1985). However, Judge Skelly Wright approvingly quoted an earlier case that " 'assumed without deciding' " that an agency was " 'free to decline to follow decisions of the courts of appeals with which it disagrees, even in cases arising in those circuits.' " Yellow Taxi Co. v. NLRB, 721 F.2d 366, 384 (D.C.Cir.1983) (concurring) (quoting S & H Riggers & Erectors, Inc. v. OSHRC, 659 F.2d 1273, 1278–79 (5th Cir.1981)).

The IRS's nonacquiescence practice is even older, but has escaped criticism, 85 Colum.L.Rev. at 588–9. In 1980–81, OSHA and FCC also nonacquiesced, id. at 584.

all circuits together? [12]　Or to the contrary, would you agree with the repeated recital of the Marbury litany that since it "is emphatically the province and duty of the judicial department to say what the law is",[13] the executive is constitutionally bound to comply with lower courts' decisions within their jurisdiction?　Or last, is freedom to nonacquiesce simply a question of Congressional intent, program by program?　Even that view raises separation of powers issues: can Congress direct the executive that it must appeal or else treat court decisions as if they are statutes binding all within the jurisdiction?

　　Certainly there are pragmatic problems to intra-circuit nonacquiescence, and perhaps also professional responsibility and constitutional ones.　Encouraging repetitive litigation burdens the agency, the private parties and the courts.[14]　Stare decisis exists in large part to avoid just such burdens.　Relitigation may be justifiable if the law is unsettled or circumstances have changed, but relitigation in the face of settled dispositive decisions may even be a violation of counsel's duty of good faith and ethical conduct.　Judge Jack Weinstein "argue[s] that the statutes and rules governing the ethical obligations of government attorneys support independent decision-making by them", and applauded the U.S. Attorney for the Southern District of New York for refusing to comply with SSA's nonacquiescence to Second Circuit precedents.[15]　Moreover, desirable as is national uniformity, what of uniformity within a circuit as between persons who pursue appeals and those who do not?　Even if equal protection law would allow, how desirable is a "distinction between those beneficiaries with the resources and fortitude to pursue their claims, and those who accept the government's original denial in good faith or because they lack the means to appeal their case"?[16]　"Particularly with respect to the type of

---

12.　See Kuehner v. Schweiker, 717 F.2d 813, 818 (3d Cir.1983) (noting that "the Secretary may feel [he is] free to express nonacquiescence" in a precedent that had been followed en banc, and referring to the costs resulting from only *non*acquiescence), vacated for remand to agency pursuant to Social Security Disability Benefits Reform Act of 1984, 469 U.S. 977 (1984).

13.　Marbury v. Madison, 5 U.S. (1 Cranch) 137, 177 (1803), relied upon by cases cited in Stieberger v. Heckler, 615 F.Supp. 1315, 1353–58 (S.D.N.Y.1985), vacated in light of intervening decision, 801 F.2d 29 (2d Cir.1986).

14.　For example, the U.S. Postal Service's immunity from state garnishment proceedings was addressed 20 times in district courts and seven times in courts of appeals before the Supreme Court decided it.　Brief of Appellant at 7, Franchise Tax Bd. v. United States Postal Serv., 467 U.S. 512 (1984) (upholding garnishment and noting the "nearly universal conclusion" of the lower courts).　See A. L. Levin and S. Leeson, Issue Preclusion Against the United States Government, 70 Iowa L.Rev. 113 (1984).

Not all repetitive litigation is fruitless. On several different matters, the NLRB lost in many circuits before it prevailed in the Supreme Court.　See Eichel, supra n. 5, at 480–483.

15.　J. Weinstein and G. Crosthwait, Some Reflections on Conflicts Between Government Attorneys and Clients, 1 Touro L.Rev. 1, 6, 8 (1985).　Model Code of Professional Responsibility Ethical Consideration 7–14 says that a government attorney with discretionary power over the conduct of litigation "should refrain from . . . continuing litigation that is obviously unfair."　And see Fed.R.Civ.P. 11 (attorney certifies that all papers filed with a court are "well grounded in fact and . . . warranted by existing law").　U.S. Attorney General Cushing said over 100 years ago that "in the performance of . . . his duty . . . [a government attorney] is not counsel giving advice to the government as his client, but a public officer, acting judicially, under all the solemn responsibilities of conscience and of legal obligation."　Weinstein and Crosthwait, at 12.

16.　H.R.Rep., supra n. 6, at 25.　The equal protection issue is raised in

individuals [in disability matters], whose resources, health and prospective longevity are, by definition, relatively limited, such a dual system of justice is prejudicial and unfair." [17]

Even if public officials are entitled to relitigate issues when there is reason to believe different rulings may result, what practice is sound when a court of appeals has ruled in a way which the agency believes both wrong and a serious administrative problem, once rehearing or en banc consideration have been denied or have sustained the original ruling? [18] More often than not, even if Supreme Court or Congressional review is sought, it will be denied or long delayed. How should administrators and Congress resolve this dilemma?

(iii) Estopping the Government

Professor Michael Asimow ended his 1973 study of "The Reliability of Government Advice" (Chapter 3, on Advice to the Public from Federal Administration Agencies, 68) as follows: "The present case law

Stieberger v. Heckler, supra n. 13, at 1362–63.

A possibly potent inhibition against unwarranted repetitive litigation is the Equal Access to Justice Act, P.L. 96–481 (1980), made permanent by P.L. 99–80 (1985), providing that a court could award reasonable fees and costs to a prevailing party (other than the U.S.) in any civil action by or against the U.S. "unless the court finds that the position of the United States was substantially justified . . . ." Judge Weinstein applied the Act to award fees after reversing a denial of disability benefits, Zimmerman v. Schweiker, 575 F.Supp. 1436 (E.D.N.Y.1983).

17. Lopez v. Heckler, supra n. 7, at 1440. If an agency is free to nonacquiesce within a circuit, a class action might be brought on behalf of, e.g., all disability recipients subject to termination proceedings. Lopez, such a suit, raised complexities of defining the class and the appropriate relief. Preliminary injunction granted, 572 F.Supp. 26 (C.D.Cal.1983), partial stay denied 713 F.2d 1432 (9th Cir.1983); partial stay granted by Circuit Justice Rehnquist 463 U.S. 1328 (1983); application to vacate stay denied, 464 U.S. 879 (1983); preliminary injunction affirmed in part, reversed in part 725 F.2d 1489 (9th Cir.1984); vacated and remanded for reconsideration in light of 1984 amendments 469 U.S. 1082 (1984); definition of the class clarified 106 F.R.D. 268 (C.D.Cal.1984); stay pending appeal denied 753 F.2d 1464 (9th Cir.1985). In 1985, one court of appeals reversed class relief enjoining nonacquiescence because, it said, granting such relief would be like carrying out the 1984 House bill that Congress had not adopted (see n. 10, supra). Hyatt v. Heckler, 757 F.2d 1455, 1459–60 (4th Cir.1985), vacated for reconsideration in light of Bowen v. New York, 106 S.Ct. 2022 (1986), 106 S.Ct. 2886 (1986).

During oral argument in a later class action in New York, the district judge directed SSA counsel to secure a review of the nonacquiescence policy "by officials at the highest levels of HHS," and in June 1985 a new policy, more restrained in its assertion of nonacquiescence, was adopted. But the court was left with "serious reservations," certified a class and granted a preliminary injunction, Stieberger v. Heckler, supra n. 13, at 1322, 1367–74.

In 1979, the Secretary argued against class relief "because he will appeal adverse decisions or abide them within the jurisdiction of the courts rendering them", but lost, Califano v. Yamasaki, 442 U.S. 682, 699 (1979). Sometimes courts refuse class certification as unnecessary precisely because "public officials, mindful of their responsibilities, will apply the determination here made equally to all persons similarly situated." Feld v. Berger, 424 F.Supp. 1356, 1363 (S.D.N.Y.1976), and see cases cited in Note, supra n. 11, at 596, n. 96.

18. That assumes no constitutional compulsion; but is there any? Justice Rehnquist, when granting a partial stay in Lopez v. Heckler, seemed to doubt the constitutional grounds for challenging nonacquiescence, 463 U.S. at 1336. Writing separately when Justice Rehnquist's stay was upheld, Justice Stevens, joined by Justice Blackmun, seemed to agree with Justice Rehnquist, 464 U.S. at 883. Justice Brennan, joined by Justice Marshall, remarked in the course of dissent that "it is clear to me that it is the Secretary who has not paid due respect to a coordinate branch of government by expressly refusing to implement the binding decisions of the Ninth Circuit." 464 U.S. at 887.

involving estoppel of the government presents an uninspiring picture of injustice, anachronism, and rampant confusion. It would be difficult to discover anything comparable. At the same time, the personnel of almost every government agency represents that the reliance interest of private parties who had been misled by poor advice would always be protected. The fact that such a policy seems to be practical suggests that the case law is in drastic need of reconsideration." Since that time, many cases have arisen but enough confusion remains that we should consider whether statutory clarification would help and, however one answers that, what a statute might provide. Can we provide a more reliable and practical procedure for securing trustworthy advice from the government than section 554(e) of the APA, merely authorizing issuance of a declaratory order? Since additional statutory aid is hardly a novel idea,[1] our main task is to bring out the factors that determine when "the public interest in ensuring that the Government can enforce the law free from estoppel might be outweighed by the countervailing interest of citizens in some minimum standard of decency, honor and reliability in their dealings with their Government." Heckler v. Community Health Services, 467 U.S. 51, 60–61 (1984).[2]

PORTMANN v. UNITED STATES,

United States Court of Appeals, 7th Circuit, 1982.
674 F.2d 1155.

Before CUMMINGS, CHIEF JUDGE, CUDAHY, CIRCUIT JUDGE, and SENIOR JUDGE CAMPBELL, sitting by designation.

CUDAHY, CIRCUIT JUDGE:

[Plaintiff Michele Portmann, a free lance graphic arts designer, paid the U.S. Postal Service $31 to send three small packages of color film separations, taken from photographs of the works of Salvador Dali, from Illinois to New York. She alleges (and the Government says it has no basis to confirm or deny) that she told the clerk the packages' contents and their great value and he assured her that $31 for "Express Mail" and "Document Reconstruction Insurance" guaranteed insurance against loss up to $50,000. She designated values of $1,000, $2,000, and $3,000 on package three, which was lost in the mail. When she claimed indemnity, the Service said the contents were "merchandise," not "nonnegotiable documents" eligible for the insurance she had, and so the insurance liability was limited to $500. (Shortly after she sued, the Service amended its regulations "to clarify insurance coverage and improve customer understanding and administration of insurance claims.") The district court granted summary judgment (a) upholding the Government's application of the regulations and (b) rejecting Portmann's argument that the Service could be bound by the erroneous representation of an employee. The court of appeals agreed as to (a) and went on:]

The doctrine of equitable estoppel precludes a litigant from asserting a claim or defense which might otherwise be available to him against another party who has detrimentally altered her position in reliance on the former's misrepresentation or failure to disclose some material fact. See . . . Note, Equitable Estoppel of the Government, 47 Brooklyn L.Rev. 423, 424

1. See M. Asimow, supra, and F. Newman, Should Official Advice be Reliable? Proposals as to Estoppel and Related Doctrines in Administrative Law, 53 Colum.L. Rev. 374, 389 (1953).

2. The case is noted at p. 529 below.

(1981). In the United States, the traditional view has been that equitable estoppel will not lie against the Government or any of its agencies. Originally, this view rested largely on considerations of sovereign immunity. . . . Once it was conceded that the government could not be held liable for the wrongful acts of its agents, it followed, as a logical corollary, that the government could not be estopped by the misrepresentations or material omissions of its employees.[1]

As the doctrine of sovereign immunity eroded, it became necessary to offer other justifications for the government's exemption from equitable estoppel. One such justification invoked a separation of powers rationale; proponents argued that permitting equitable estoppel against the government would, in effect, allow government employees to "legislate" by misinterpreting or ignoring an applicable statute or regulation. Judicial validation of such unauthorized "legislation," it was claimed, would infringe upon Congress' exclusive constitutional authority to make law.[2] Although this rationale has some logical appeal, applied literally and generally, it would seem to preclude *any* application of estoppel against the government including its use in areas such as government procurement contracts and legal proceedings—areas in which the government has long been held subject to estoppel principles.[3] Moreover, such a rigid separation of powers analysis contrasts sharply with the more realistic and flexible judicial approach to separation of powers problems in other areas such as legislative delegation. In any event, reliance on a separation of powers rationale to preclude estoppel against the government is considerably less persuasive where only an agency's own regulations are at stake than it would be where adherence to government misinformation threatens to contravene an explicit statutory requirement. See Note, Equitable Estoppel of the Government, 79 Colum.L.Rev. 551, 565–66 (1979). . . .

In addition to invoking a separation of powers rationale, some courts and commentators have relied on public policy considerations to support the no-estoppel rule, drawing in particular on several early Supreme Court opinions in which the Court expressed concern that holding the government bound by the improper acts of its agents might promote fraud and collusion, or lead to the severe depletion of the public treasury at the hands of a few enterprising individuals. Critics of this "traditional" view, however, have

1. As Professor Davis has noted:

"Sovereign immunity from contract and tort liability naturally carried with it sovereign immunity from equitable estoppel. A Supreme Court which was freely asserting that 'The government is not responsible for . . . the wrongful acts of its officers,' could hardly assert that the government was estopped on account of representations by its officers." 2 K. Davis, Admin. Law Treatise (1958), § 17.01 at 492 (quoting Hart v. United States, 95 U.S. 316, 318 (1877)).

2. Pursuant to this rationale, many courts have explained their refusal to allow estoppel against the government by underscoring "the duty of all courts to observe the conditions defined by Congress for charging the public treasury," Federal Crop Insurance Corp. v. Merrill, 332 U.S. 380, 385 (1947), and by emphasizing the need to prevent the frustration of federal statutes. See e.g., Schweiker v. Hansen, 450 U.S. 785 (1981); Goldberg v. Weinberger, 546 F.2d 477 (2d Cir.1976), cert. denied, 431 U.S. 937 (1977).

3. See, e.g., Russell Corp. v. United States, 537 F.2d 474, 484 (Ct.Cl.1976), cert. denied, 429 U.S. 1073 (1977) (doctrine of equitable estoppel will be applied, in appropriate case, to prevent United States from denying existence of a contractual agreement); Roberts v. United States, 357 F.2d 938, 946–47 (Ct.Cl. 1966) ("When the Government is acting in its proprietary capacity, it may be estopped by an act of waiver in the same manner as a private contractor.") . . .

pointed out that the incidence of "improper collusions" has historically been exceedingly small and that large sums of money are not often at stake in estoppel cases.[4] Finally, some courts and commentators have argued that allowing estoppel against the government might interfere with agency flexibility in changing rules and implementing new policies.[5] More modern decisions, however, have discredited this rationale, and have noted that a concern for administrative efficiency should not permit the government to deal unfairly or capriciously with its citizens. . . .

With the growth of the federal government and the broadening of government interaction with private parties, many courts have reconsidered their reluctance to apply the doctrine of equitable estoppel against the government. One widely applied judicial technique for limiting the no-estoppel rule posits a distinction between the "sovereign" (or governmental) and the "proprietary" (or nongovernmental) functions of federal agencies. Under this approach, activities by the government undertaken primarily for the commercial benefit of the government or an individual government agency are subject to estoppel while actions involving the exercise of exclusively governmental or sovereign powers are not.[6] The sovereign/ proprietary distinction has proven to be particularly useful in cases involving government contracts. With respect to 'proprietary' contracts— that is, essentially commercial transactions involving the purchase or sale of goods or services—courts have tended to find no significant obstacles to the use of estoppel based on the conduct of government agents acting within the scope of their actual or apparent authority. On the other hand, government transactions found to be exercises of "sovereign" responsibilities, including a diverse range of loan agreements, subsidies and direct grants have continued to be evaluated according to the traditional rule.[7] Such a distinction between the sovereign and proprietary functions of government has served as a shorthand reminder that "protection of the public welfare and deference to Congressional desires are much more apt to outweigh hardships to private individuals in the equitable balance when estoppel is asserted against sovereign acts," than when purely commercial federal interests are at stake.

Despite its practical appeal, an analysis focusing solely on a sovereign vs. proprietary distinction has several significant shortcomings. First, the line between sovereign and proprietary functions is somewhat artificial and difficult to apply. For example, even routine operational contracts of federal agencies may be conditioned on a variety of special requirements

4. [T]o the extent that a deterrent against public fraud is required, it is supplied by the severe criminal sanctions imposed for defrauding the government. . . .

5. . . . In response to this argument, it has been noted that if the public is given sufficient notice of changes in agency rules and policies, no estoppel could be based on adherence to an old rule, since no justifiable reliance could be shown. . . .

6. Characteristic "sovereign" activities traditionally not subject to estoppel include criminal prosecutions. . . interpretation of tax statutes. . . and enforcement of health and safety regulations. . . . [Ed. But see United States v. Pennsylvania Industrial Chemical Corp., 411 U.S. 655 (1973) (Corps of Engineer regulations construing statute may have deprived defendant of fair warning that conduct consistent with regulations might violate statute) and Buccaneer Point Estates, Inc. v. United States, 729 F.2d 1297 (11th Cir. 1984) (developer justifiably relied on Corps of Engineers letter as to where it could build).]

7. See, e.g.. . . Gressley v. Califano, 609 F.2d 1265 (7th Cir.1979) (federal disability benefits); Hicks v. Harris, 606 F.2d 65 (5th Cir.1979) (student loans). . . .

imposed by Congress or the Executive for the promotion of national policy goals, thus adding a "sovereign" element to an otherwise purely commercial transaction.[8] Second, although there is some early Supreme Court authority to support the distinction, more recent Supreme Court decisions have either left the issue open . . . or rejected the sovereign vs. proprietary dichotomy altogether. See Federal Crop Ins. Corp. v. Merrill. . . . Finally, exclusive reliance on such a single factor analysis may mask or contradict more basic constitutional, practical and equitable considerations that should be relevant to determining the availability of estoppel in any particular case. Thus, while we believe that the "proprietary" or commercial character of the government activity at issue in the instant case militates in favor of allowing an estoppel claim, we do not view this factor as determinative in all situations.

The Supreme Court decision most often cited as authority for refusing to apply estoppel against the government . . . is Federal Crop Insurance Corp. v. Merrill [see note following, p. 528. The court distinguished that case: 1) Since only the Government provided the type of insurance at issue there, Merrill had no alternative even if he had been accurately informed; Portmann alleged she would have simply used a private carrier offering full insurance. 2) The crop insurance regulation was clear; this one was so unclear that reliance was reasonable. 3) Crop insurance payments came from the Treasury; all postal operations are funded almost entirely by postal revenues.].

In its more recent decisions, the Supreme Court has backed away from its suggestion in Merrill that equitable estoppel may never be asserted against the federal government. In Montana v. Kennedy, 366 U.S. 308 (1961), the Court rejected an alien's attempt to resist deportation on equitable estoppel grounds, but remarked in dicta that the misconduct of which the petitioner complained was insufficient to estop the government. . . . Twelve years later, in United States Immigration & Naturalization Service v. Hibi, 414 U.S. 5 (1973) (per curiam), the Supreme Court, referring to the Montana dictum, observed that the Montana court did not pass on the question "whether 'affirmative misconduct' on the part of the Government might estop it from denying citizenship. . . ." The Court in Hibi, however, again rejected petitioner's citizenship claim, holding that the governmental action complained of could not be characterized as "affirmative misconduct," and, thus, that estoppel would not lie against the government. In retrospect, Hibi was not a strong case for invoking estoppel against the government, since not all the requisite elements of an equitable estoppel were present.[9]

---

8. . . . Exec.Order No. 11246, as amended, 3 C.F.R. 339 (1964–65 Comp.) (affirmative action requirements for federal contractors).

9. For a classic and oft-cited statement of the requirements of an equitable estoppel, see J. Pomeroy, Equity Jurisprudence § 805 at 191–92:

"1. There must be conduct—acts, language, or silence—amounting to a representation or a concealment of material facts. 2. These facts must be known to the party estopped at the time of his said conduct, or at least the circumstances must be such that knowledge of them is necessarily imputed to him. 3. The truth concerning these facts must be unknown to the other party claiming

[In the 1981 case of Schweiker v. Hansen, briefly described in note 2 following this case, the] Court noted that in several of the cases it distinguished, "the government had entered into written agreements which supported the claims of estoppel," and that in others, "estoppel did not threaten the public fisc," as the Court felt it would in Schweiker. The instant case arguably exhibits both of these distinguishing characteristics.

In sum, we find nothing in any of the Supreme Court's estoppel decisions which clearly forecloses the availability of estoppel in the instant case. . . .

Our conclusion that equitable estoppel may be available against the government in the instant case is supported by numerous decisions [and also] by the somewhat unique, quasi-private status of the United States Postal Service. In enacting the Postal Reorganization Act of 1970, Congress intended to "[c]onvert the Post Office Department into an *independent establishment* within the Executive Branch of the Government," unencumbered by direct political pressure and capable of delivering the mail in an efficient and "business like" manner. H.R.Rep. No. 1104, 91st Cong., 2d Sess. 1104. . . . To effectuate this goal, Congress clothed the Service with broad and extensive powers, including the ability "to sue and be sued in its official name," 39 U.S.C. § 401(1), the power "to enter into and perform contracts, execute instruments, and determine the character of, and necessity for, its expenditures," § 401(1), and the authority to "settle and compromise claims by or against it." . . . In addition, by establishing a special self-sustaining Postal Service Fund within the Treasury Department, and by entrusting the Service with broad financing powers, Congress meant to put the Postal Service on an independent financial basis, requiring only transitional appropriations through the Congressional budgetary process. . . .

In light of these considerations, virtually all courts that have considered the question have concluded that the Postal Service is not immune, as is the federal government generally, from commercial or judicial garnishment proceedings. . . .

In transporting Ms. Portmann's separation negatives, the Service was not performing an inherently sovereign or peculiarly governmental function. Instead, it was competing directly for plaintiff's business with a number of private express mail carriers. . . .

In addition, we think we would do the Postal Service no competitive favor by conferring on it an absolute immunity from estoppel in the circumstances of this case. [T]he dubious privilege of not being bound by the representations of its employees in routine commercial transactions would seem to further reflect on the Service's already tarnished reputation as a provider of regular and express mail service. . . .

the benefit of the estoppel, at the time when such conduct was done, and at the time when it was acted upon by him. 4. The conduct must be done with the intention, or at least with the expectation, that it will be acted upon by the other party, and, thus relying, he must be led to act upon it. 5. He must in fact act upon it in such a manner as to change his position for the worse. . . . "

NOTES

(1) FEDERAL CROP INSURANCE CORP. v. MERRILL, 332 U.S. 380 (1947) arose when plaintiff, a farmer, insured his 400-acre "reseeded" wheat crop after the Government corporation's agent told him it was insurable; later, drought took most of the crop. A regulation, of which plaintiff and the agent were unaware, barred insurance for reseeded wheat; the corporation refused to pay, and was upheld, Justice Frankfurter writing:

"The case no doubt presents phases of hardship . . . [W]e assume that recovery could be had against a private insurance company. But the Corporation is not a private insurance company. . . . [A]nyone entering into an arrangement with the Government takes the risk of having accurately ascertained that he who purports to act for the Government stays within the bounds of his authority.

"If the Federal Crop Insurance Act had by explicit language prohibited the insurance of spring wheat which is reseeded on winter wheat acreage, the ignorance of such a restriction, either by the respondents or the Corporation's agent, would be immaterial and recovery could not be had against the Corporation for loss of such reseeded wheat. Congress could hardly define the multitudinous details appropriate for the business of crop insurance when the Government entered it. Inevitably 'the terms and conditions' upon which valid governmental insurance can be had must be defined by the agency acting for the Government. And so Congress has legislated in this instance, as in modern regulatory enactments it so often does, by conferring the rule-making power upon the agency created for carrying out its policy. . . . Just as everyone is charged with knowledge of the United States Statutes at Large, Congress has provided that the appearance of rules and regulations in the Federal Register gives legal notice of their contents.

"Accordingly, the Wheat Crop Insurance Regulations were binding on all who sought to come within the Federal Crop Insurance Act, regardless of actual knowledge of what is in the Regulations or of the hardship resulting from innocent ignorance. The oft-quoted observation in Rock Island, Arkansas & Louisiana Railroad Co. v. United States, 254 U.S. 141, 143, that 'Men must turn square corners when they deal with the Government,' [Justice Holmes] does not reflect a callous outlook. It merely expresses the duty of all courts to observe the conditions defined by Congress for charging the public treasury. The 'terms and conditions' defined by the Corporation, under authority of Congress, for creating liability on the part of the Government preclude recovery for the loss of the reseeded wheat no matter with what good reason the respondents thought they had obtained insurance from the Government." [1]

(2) SCHWEIKER v. HANSEN, 450 U.S. 785 (1981) arose when a Social Security Administration employee erroneously told plaintiff she was not eligible for "mother's insurance benefits" and so she filed no application.

---

1. [Ed.] Four justices dissented. Justice Jackson complained that it would be an absurdity to expect a farmer to know what was in the Federal Register. "If he were to peruse this voluminous and dull publication . . . , he would never need crop insurance, for he would never get time to plant any crops."

The Act required applications; a regulation required written applications; and an agency handbook instructed employees to advise applicants to file written applications if uncertain of eligibility; but plaintiff was not so advised. After she did file about a year later and began receiving benefits, she sued for retroactive benefits, claiming estoppel, but lost. "This Court has never decided what type of conduct by a Government employee will estop the Government from insisting upon compliance with valid regulations governing the distribution of welfare benefits. In two cases involving denial of citizenship, the Court has declined to decide whether even 'affirmative misconduct' would estop the Government from denying citizenship, for in neither case was 'affirmative misconduct' involved. . . . [W]e are convinced that [the] conduct [here is] less than 'affirmative misconduct' . . . [A]t worst, [the] conduct did not cause respondent to take action . . . or fail to take action . . . that respondent could not correct at any time.

"Similarly, there is no doubt that [the employee] failed to follow the Claims Manual . . . a 13-volume handbook for internal use by thousands of SSA employees, including the hundreds of employees who received untold numbers of oral inquiries like respondent's each year. . . . [If this conduct estops] the Government [then it] is put 'at risk that every alleged failure by an agent to follow instructions to the last detail in one of a thousand cases will deprive it of the benefit of the written application requirement which experience has taught to be essential to the honest and effective administration of the Social Security Laws.' " Justices Marshall and Brennan dissented.

(3) HECKLER v. COMMUNITY HEALTH SERVICES, 467 U.S. 51 (1984) rejected claims of equitable estoppel made by a provider of health care services, on lines that may crack the "seemingly monolithic structure" Professor Asimow noted in 1973.[2] The basis for rejecting the claim was that no private party would be found estopped on the facts. Writing for seven Justices, Justice Stevens described two earlier decisions as resting "on the premise that when the Government acts in misleading ways, it may not enforce the law if to do so would harm a private party as a result of governmental deception." (Justice Rehnquist's dissent, joined by the Chief Justice, said those decisions were "not traditional equitable estoppel cases," but one a criminal case without fair warning, the other a "rather cryptic opinion.") And, while the dissent said the Court's course of decisions had "left open the possibility of estoppel against the Government only in a rather narrow possible range of circumstances," the majority quoted a 1961 dissent by Justice Black: " 'Our Government should not by picayunish haggling over the scope of its promise, permit one of its arms to do that which, by any fair construction, the Government has given its word that no arm will do. It is no less good morals and good law that the Government should turn square corners in dealing with the people than that the people should turn square corners in dealing with their government.' " Also quoted was Justice Jackson's dissent in Federal Crop Insurance: " 'It is very well to say that those who deal with the Government should turn square

---

2. M. Asimow, p. 522 above at 37. See also   When Agencies Break Their Own "Laws," 64
P. Raven-Hansen, Regulatory Estoppel: Tex.L.Rev. 1 (1985).

corners. But there is no reason why square corners should constitute a one-way street.' "   467 U.S. at 61 n. 13.

h. The Special Problem of "Constitutional" or "Jurisdictional" Facts

We have seen that courts generally accept administrative findings of fact supported by evidence sufficient to satisfy the applicable standard, "substantial evidence" or "arbitrary, capricious. . . ." We have seen also that "specific application of broad statutory terms" sometimes enjoys similar deference, at least when it "belongs to the usual administrative routine" of the agency—and sometimes not. What review should be given determinations with constitutional implications? For example, the first amendment protects an employer's expression of views to his employees to discourage a union organizing effort, but that is deemed not to include expression constituting a "threat of reprisal or force or promise of benefit," 29 U.S.C. § 158(c). How closely should a court review the NLRB's conclusions as to what the employer said, what impact resulted, and whether the statements were an unfair labor practice or protected free speech? There is no question that declaring the first amendment's legal content or any other question of constitutional *law,* is wholly up to the courts; it is hard to imagine any factor that would suggest any degree of deference to any agency on such matters.[1] How then allocate responsibility for *applying* the first amendment in the union organizing dispute, or even the responsibility for finding facts as to what happened? "Of course, many lawyers would insist that who finds the facts is far more important than who applies the law, and at least a plurality of the present Court endorses that view."[2]

In constitutional litigation wholly unrelated to the administrative process, the Supreme Court and other appellate courts in some circumstances appraise independently the factual foundations of decisions under review. For example, in defamation suits by "public figures," a finding of "actual malice" is necessary to lift the first amendment's protection; the Supreme Court recently divided 6–3 on whether such a finding so implicates the first amendment that it must be subject to the Court's independent review of the trial judge, or is ordinary fact-finding governed by Rule 52(a).[3]

---

1. See H. Monaghan, Marbury and the Administrative State, 83 Colum.L.Rev. 1 (1983).

2. H. Monaghan, Constitutional Fact Review, 85 Colum.L.Rev. 229, 255, n. 141 (1985), referring to Northern Pipeline Constr. Co. v. Marathon Pipe Line Co., 458 U.S. 50, 84–86 (1982). This article valuably illuminates review in both constitutional cases and related administrative ones.

3. Bose Corp. v. Consumers Union of U.S., Inc., 466 U.S. 485 (1984), holding that independent review was required:

"Regarding certain largely factual questions in some areas of the law, the stakes—in terms of impact on future cases and future conduct—are too great to entrust them final-

ly to the judgment of the trier of fact." 104 S.Ct. at 1960, n. 17.

For many years, it was clear that federal courts independently reviewed challenges to state criminal convictions asserting, e.g., that a confession was coerced or that racial discrimination was systematically employed in selecting juries where the trial occurred, see Ashcraft v. Tennessee, 322 U.S. 143 (1944) and Norris v. Alabama, 294 U.S. 587 (1935). However, significant changes have occurred in the state courts and views of them as well as in administration of federal habeas corpus jurisdiction. Since 1966, a presumption of correctness has been required by statute for state court findings of fact in criminal cases so long as the state proceedings satisfy seven conditions, e.g., they are "evidenced by a

Should similar treatment apply to the NLRB's finding that an employer's statement was coercive—or to an agency's rate order challenged as so deficient as to be unconstitutionally confiscatory?

The question first became prominent in OHIO VALLEY WATER COMPANY v. BEN AVON BOROUGH, 253 U.S. 287 (1920).[4] That case involved a run-of-the-mill ratemaking proceeding, but the company, claiming that under-valuation of its property had led to a confiscatorily low rate, won reversal of the rate in trial court. The state supreme court reviewed the evidence at great length and held that the commission's findings were all amply supported by evidence, declared that the trial court had merely substituted its judgment for the commission's, and reinstated the rate. The U.S. Supreme Court reversed in a four-page opinion by Justice McReynolds, including the assertion that "if the owner claims confiscation of his property will result, the State must provide a fair opportunity for submitting that issue to a judicial tribunal for determination upon its own independent judgment as to both law and facts; otherwise the order is void because in conflict with the due process clause. . . . " The decision (Justices Brandeis, Holmes and Clark dissenting) at once drew voluminous critical comment along these lines: The Court seemingly reasoned that since the rate order was a substitute for what the legislature itself could have done by statute, and since a statute could have been challenged as confiscatory in an independent judicial proceeding, therefore the rate order must also be subject to independent review. Such reasoning was questionable on several counts. First, if a statute is attacked as unconstitutional, the attack must occur in an independent judicial trial of some sort because no other trial-type hearing had produced a record and findings based on that record. But when the legislature delegates rate-making functions to an administrative commission, the commission does produce record and findings and so might well be subject to review different from review of a statute's unconstitution-ality. Second, if a court, in making an "independent determination" of the facts in a rate case, decides what is the correct view of the facts (as apparently Justice McReynolds required), then it assumes more responsibil-ity than if it were reviewing a statute imposing the same rate, when the court would ask only whether the legislature had acted reasonably. If the legislature chose to delegate the job of fixing rates to a body more "expert" than itself or the courts, it seemed anomalous to end up with more active judicial review. Last, if the court was to exercise its own "independent judgment as to both law and facts," would it not duplicate much or all of the proceeding already conducted administratively?

written finding, written opinion, or other reliable and adequate written indicia," are "fairly supported by the record," and there was a full fair hearing, 28 U.S.C. § 2254(d)(8).

4. Earlier, the Court had held that due process required judicial review of a claim that administratively prescribed rates were confiscatory, but had not indicated what the scope of review would be. Chicago, Milwaukee & St. Paul Ry. v. Minnesota, 134 U.S. 418 (1890). And in 1908, the Court per Justice Holmes said this:

"Whether [the railroads'] property was taken unconstitutionally depends upon the valuation of the property, the income to be derived from the proposed rate and the pro-portion between the two—pure matters of fact. . . . They are not to be forbidden to try those facts before a court of their own choosing if otherwise competent." Prentis v. Atlantic Coast Line, 211 U.S. 210, 228 (dictum).

Professor Monaghan stresses that "Ben Avon need not have spawned constitutional fact review outside of the rate setting context. . . . It is enough to note that Ben Avon's independent judgment rule could have been limited to cases in which the agency was performing what were then understood as 'legislative' functions.

"That the Supreme Court would not view constitutional fact review so narrowly became quickly apparent. NG FUNG HO v. WHITE,[5] decided only two years after Ben Avon, sanctioned constitutional fact review in the context of what was clearly 'adjudicative' action by an administrative agency. At issue were habeas challenges to administrative deportation warrants. Petitioners insisted that their deportation was improper because they were United States citizens. Administrative rejection of petitioners' claims was not conclusive on the courts, said Justice Brandeis, because citizenship is 'an essential jurisdictional fact.' Deportation works an obvious and grievous loss of liberty, and '[a]gainst the danger of such deprivation without the sanction afforded by judicial proceedings,' the due process clause 'affords protection.' This, the Court insisted, was not novel doctrine. 'The difference in security of judicial over administrative action has been adverted to by this court.' "[6]

In later years Justice Brandeis himself made a determined if not altogether convincing attempt to explain away Ng Fung Ho. On one occasion he summarized the holding as follows (dissenting opinion in Crowell v. Benson, 285 U.S. 22 at 90 n. 26 (1932)): "In Ng Fung Ho . . . the statute authorized the deportation only of aliens, without provision for judicial review of the executive order. . . . Upon application for a writ of habeas corpus, by a person arrested who claimed to be a citizen, it was held that he was entitled to a judicial determination of that claim. No question arose as to whether Congress might validly have provided for review exclusively upon the record made in the executive department; nor as to the scope of review which might have been permissible upon such record." And in his concurring opinion in St. Joseph Stock Yards Co. v. United States, 298 U.S. 38 at 77 (1936), Justice Brandeis sought to limit the significance of Ng Fung Ho by stressing a supposed distinction "between the right of liberty of person and other constitutional rights."[7] It appears that

---

5. 259 U.S. 276 (1922).

6. Monaghan, supra n. 2, at 252–3. Professor Monaghan points out that "Constitutional fact review had its antecedents in the doctrine of jurisdictional fact, which the English superior courts, particularly King's Bench, developed to confine administrative agencies and inferior courts within their delegated authority. The jurisdictional fact concept emerged as a construct for partitioning functions between agencies and the superintending courts; 'ordinary facts' could be left for final administrative determination, but the superior courts would render independent judgment upon those 'facts' governing the agency's 'jurisdiction.' And though the distinction between ordinary and jurisdictional fact was not, and could not be, expressed with logical precision, it was not on that account empty. Its basis seems to have been intuitive

and functional, a device employed to permit judicial control of administrative action to prevent what, in terms of the statutory scheme under review, would be viewed as an important error." Id. at 249.

7. Justice Brandeis had said in Ng that "To deport one who . . . claims to be a citizen, obviously deprives him of liberty. . . . It may result also in loss of both property and life; or of all that makes life worth living." 259 U.S. at 284.

It was in his Crowell dissent that Justice Brandeis made clear what he deemed the relevant limit on Congress's power to rely on adjudication by agencies instead of courts:

"If there be any controversy to which the judicial power extends that may not be subjected to the conclusive determination of administrative bodies or federal legislative

Justice Brandeis regretted having written Ng Fung Ho in "the unmitigated language of jurisdictional fact," [8] possibly launching an expandable concept.

Expand it did, in a case with major significance in some regards although dormant or dead in others. CROWELL v. BENSON, 285 U.S. 22 (1932), has already been considered, p. 105 above, in connection with the Article III question of what adjudicative functions may be assigned to bodies or officers other than Article III courts and judges. Left unaddressed in those pages were the portions of Crowell indicating that de novo review was required on constitutional questions bearing on the agency's jurisdiction. Crowell, recall, involved a proceeding under the Longshoremen's and Harbor Workers' Act, a federal workmen's compensation law covering certain maritime employment. A compensation commissioner had made an award after finding that the claimant's injury occurred while performing services on navigable waters and that the claimant was an employee. The Court upheld that assignment of responsibility—and thus the general practice of administrative adjudication.

"To hold otherwise would be to defeat the obvious purpose of the legislation to furnish a prompt, continuous, expert and inexpensive method for dealing with a class of questions of fact which are peculiarly suited to examination and determination by an administrative agency specially assigned to that task. . . . [T]he efficacy of the plan depends upon the finality of the determinations of fact with respect to the circumstances, nature, extent and consequences of the employee's injuries and the amount of compensation that should be awarded. [Such questions of fact belong] to the contemplated routine of administration. . . . "

However—"What has been said thus far relates to the determination of claims of employees within the purview of the Act. A different question is presented where the determinations of fact are fundamental or 'jurisdictional,' in the sense that their existence is a condition precedent to the operation of the statutory scheme. These fundamental requirements are that the injury occur upon the navigable waters of the United States and that the relation of master and servant exist. These conditions are indispensable to the application of the statute, not only because the Congress has so provided explicitly . . . but also because the power of the Congress to enact the legislation turns upon the existence of these conditions.

"In amending and revising the maritime law, the Congress cannot reach beyond the constitutional limits which are inherent in the admiralty and maritime jurisdiction. . . . Unless the injuries to which the Act relates occur upon the navigable waters of the United States, they

courts, it is not because of any prohibition against the diminution of the jurisdiction of the federal district courts as such, but because, under certain circumstances, the constitutional requirement of due process is a requirement of judicial process." 285 U.S. at 87.

Justice Brandeis's view that a claim of U.S. citizenship by a person subject to deportation is so special as to warrant de novo review has been reaffirmed by the Court, and in 1961 Congress kept such cases in district court with de novo review when other deportation cases were moved to the courts of appeals for review on the administrative record. See Agosto v. INS, 436 U.S. 748 (1978).

8. L. Jaffe, Judicial Control of Administrative Action, 637.

fall outside that jurisdiction. . . . Not only is navigability itself a question of fact, as waters that are navigable in fact are navigable in law, but, where navigability is not in dispute, the locality of the injury, that is, whether it has occurred upon the navigable waters of the United States, determines the existence of the congressional power to create the liability prescribed by the statute. . . .

"In relation to these basic facts, the question is not the ordinary one as to the propriety of provision for administrative determinations. Nor have we simply the question of due process in relation to notice and hearing. It is rather a question of the appropriate maintenance of the Federal judicial power in requiring the observance of constitutional restrictions. It is the question whether the Congress may substitute for constitutional courts, in which the judicial power of the United States is vested, an administrative agency—in this instance a single deputy commissioner—for the final determination of the existence of the facts upon which the enforcement of the constitutional rights of the citizen depend. The recognition of the utility and convenience of administrative agencies for the investigation and finding of facts within their proper province, and the support of their authorized action, does not require the conclusion that there is no limitation of their use, and that the Congress could completely oust the courts of all determinations of fact by vesting the authority to make them with finality in its own instrumentalities or in the Executive Department. That would be to sap the judicial power as it exists under the Federal Constitution, and to establish a government of a bureaucratic character alien to our system, wherever fundamental rights depend, as not infrequently they do depend, upon the facts and finality as to facts becomes in effect finality in law. . . .

"Assuming that the Federal court may determine for itself the existence of these fundamental or jurisdictional facts . . . Upon what record is the determination to be made? There is no provision of the statute which seeks to confine the court in such a case to the record before the deputy commissioner or to the evidence which he has taken. . . . We think that the essential independence of the exercise of the judicial power of the United States in the enforcement of constitutional rights requires that the Federal court should determine such an issue upon its own record and the facts elicited before it. . . .

"It cannot be regarded as an impairment of the intended efficiency of an administrative agency that it is confined to its proper sphere, but it may be observed that the instances which permit of a challenge to the application of the statute, upon the grounds we have stated, appear to be few. Out of the many thousands of cases which have been brought before the deputy commissioners throughout the country, a review by the courts has been sought in only a small number, and an inconsiderable proportion of these appear to have involved the question whether the injury occurred within the maritime jurisdiction or whether the relation of employment existed. . . . "

This aspect of Crowell generated a larger amount of contemporary comment than any case since Ben Avon; and the comment was almost exclusively a blend of alarm and indignation. What was going to become of the already well established workmen's compensation agencies? If "jurisdictional facts" were to be triable de novo, what would be the point of having an administrative process? Would not duplicate trials of issues of fact serve simply to destroy the already impecunious claimants of workmen's compensation? If the existence of the master-servant relationship were to be deemed "jurisdictional," why would not many other facts (such as the fact of the injury itself) be deemed jurisdictional? And how could the theory of the necessary trial de novo be confined to workmen's compensation cases? Suppose, for example, that a building inspection department were authorized to order structural changes in a building found to be a fire hazard. Would not the existence of a fire hazard have to be re-tried before a judge, since, presumably, authority could not be validly conferred on an administrative agency to order structural changes, and the cost of the changes could be challenged as an unconstitutional taking, if no dangerous condition made them necessary?

The late John Dickinson, in one of the ablest analyses of the case,[9] noted the kinship between the "independent judgment" about confiscation, laid down as a necessity in the Ben Avon case, and the trial de novo of jurisdictional facts laid down as a necessity in Crowell.

"There can be little doubt," he said, "that the rule of the Ben Avon case rests at bottom on unconscious acceptance of the particular brand of philosophy designated as 'naive realism.' It rests on the assumption that the existence of a fact is something absolute and fixed, and capable of being apprehended rightly or wrongly, correctly or incorrectly. The legal authority of the administrative body is consequently regarded as depending on the *real* or *actual* presence of a fact, independently of anyone's correct or incorrect apprehension of it, or conclusion about it. From this point of view, the reasonableness or lack of reasonableness of the administrative body's conclusion makes obviously no difference." The trouble with this attitude is that the court has no other access to the fact itself than does the administrative body; its "finding" is, after all, only its conclusion and no more identical with the fact itself than is the administrative finding. "If it is thus understood that conclusion is merely being checked against conclusion, it should be enough for the reviewing tribunal to pass on whether the conclusion below was reasonable."

One Crowell requirement, an independent record made in court, was interred only four years later by the Chief Justice himself in St. Joseph Stock Yards Co. v. United States, 298 U.S. 38, 53 (1936): "[T]his judicial duty to exercise an independent judgment does not require or justify disregard of the weight which may properly attach to findings upon hearing and evidence. On the contrary, the judicial duty is performed in the light of the proceedings already had and may be greatly facilitated by the assembling and analysis of the facts in the course of the legislative determination. Judicial judgment may be none the less appropriately independent because informed and aided by the sifting procedure of an expert legislative agency."

---

9. J. Dickinson, Crowell v. Benson: Judicial Review of Administrative Determinations of Questions of "Constitutional Fact," 80 U.Pa.L.Rev. 1055, 1074 (1932).

Aside from that cut-back on Crowell, St. Joseph was read to have reaffirmed Crowell's requirement of independent judgment; and because it was a rate case (under the Packers and Stockyards Act), it was seen to reaffirm Ben Avon as well.   The Court clearly spoke of a judicial duty of independent judgment, explaining: "Legislative agencies, with varying qualifications, work in a field peculiarly exposed to political demands. Some may be expert and impartial, others subservient. It is not difficult for them to observe the requirements of law in giving a hearing and receiving evidence. But to say that their findings of fact may be made conclusive where constitutional rights of liberty and property are involved, although the evidence clearly establishes that the findings are wrong and constitutional rights have been invaded, is to place those rights at the mercy of administrative officials and seriously to impair the security inherent in our judicial safeguards. That prospect, with our multiplication of administrative agencies, is not one to be lightly regarded."   Id. at 52.

However, the Court's description of how independent judgment would operate made it seem little different from the substantial evidence standard: "[A]s the question is whether the legislative action has passed beyond the lowest limit of the permitted zone of reasonableness into the forbidden reaches of confiscation, judicial scrutiny must of necessity take into account the entire legislative process, including the reasoning and findings upon which the legislative action rests. We have said that 'in a question of ratemaking there is a strong presumption in favor of the conclusions reached by an experienced administrative body after a full hearing.' . . . The established principle which guides the court in the exercise of its judgment on the entire case is that the complaining party carries the burden of making a convincing showing and that the court will not interfere with the exercise of the rate-making power unless confiscation is clearly established. . . . [A]s the ultimate determination whether or not rates are confiscatory ordinarily rests upon a variety of subordinate or primary findings of fact as to particular elements, such findings made by a legislative agency after hearing will not be disturbed save as in particular instances they are plainly shown to be overborne." Id. at 53, 54. Moreover, while the Court did review the evidence very closely and find it sufficient to uphold the order, it affirmed a district court which had explicitly deemed the substantial evidence rule applicable.[10]

10. Greater doubt about the independent judgment rule, at least in review of rate-making, arose from two cases soon after St. Joseph, in which orders limiting oil production were challenged as confiscatory, the lower courts exercised independent judgment—and were reversed, without the majority or dissent even citing St. Joseph or Ben Avon. Railroad Commission v. Rowan & Nichols, 310 U.S. 573 (1940) and 311 U.S. 570 (1941).

Professor W. Summers, in "Does the Regulation of Oil Production Require the Denial of Due Process and the Equal Protection of the Laws?" 19 Tex.L.Rev. 1 (1940), slashingly attacked the first Rowan & Nichols decision, saying that Justice Frankfurter had simply misunderstood the technical aspects of the proration issues with which he had dealt. In an answering article, Professor K.C. Davis, "Judicial Emasculation of Administrative Action and Oil Proration: Another View," 19 Tex.L.Rev. 29 (1940), drew a different conclusion from it: "When so able a judge has difficulty in stating the technical problem accurately perhaps the lesson we may learn is that the solution of the problem requires technical specialists who may devote full time to such problems, not judges who are expected to be jacks-of-all-trades."

Subsequent changes in constitutional doctrine applicable to rate-making have left Ben Avon and St. Joseph all but overruled.[11] But where does that leave the requirement of de novo review for constitutional facts? The jurisdictional facts at issue in Crowell, and similar constitutional-jurisdictional facts, seem no longer deemed constitutional facts and are not accorded de novo review.[12]

Interestingly, however, while that aspect of Crowell never drew more than the most restricted following and is as strong an example as can be found of being overruled by being ignored,[13] the idea remains that an agency's determinations of its own jurisdiction should receive no deference on review: it is one of the leading proposals in Senator Bumpers' effort to amend the APA provisions on scope (see p. 401 above).

But the concept of independent review of constitutional fact questions seems vigorous in at least first amendment litigation not involving administrative action, and perhaps in review of administrative action as well.[14] Consider again the situation with which this note opened: when

11. In FPC v. Hope Natural Gas Co., 320 U.S. 591 (1944), the Court held that the method of valuation used in connection with rate-making was not a reviewable issue; the only question open to judicial consideration was the reasonableness of the final result, thus shrinking the area of dispute about "confiscation" to the vanishing point.

While Ben Avon was followed in some States—eight, as of a 1971 study—there too it has withered. L. Glick, Independent Judicial Review of Administrative Rate-making. The Rise and Demise of the Ben Avon Doctrine, 40 Ford.L.Rev. 305, 313 n. 34 (1971); see New York Telephone Co. v. Public Service Commission, 36 A.D.2d 261, 320 N.Y.S.2d 280 (3d Dept. 1971) (specifically rejects Ben Avon), modified on other grounds, 29 N.Y.2d 164, 324 N.Y.S.2d 53, 272 N.E.2d 554 (1971); Public Service Comm. v. General Telephone Co., 555 S.W.2d 395 (Tenn.1977) ("the Supreme Court has abandoned the independent judgment rule of Ben Avon . . . [and we] reject [that] rule as controlling Tennessee constitutional law").

12. Northern Pipeline Construction Co. v. Marathon Pipe Line Co., 458 U.S. 50, 82 n. 34 (1982) (plurality opinion).

E.g., in 1938 in Myers v. Bethlehem Shipbuilding Corporation, page 1082 below, the Court held that the "jurisdictional fact" of whether the corporation's business affected interstate commerce must first be tried before the administrative agency, with subsequent judicial review of the record made in the administrative hearing. Nowhere did the Court manifest any sense that opportunity must be given for trial de novo of the jurisdictional fact, or that the scope of review need be any more extensive than was ordinarily provided. See also National La-

bor Relations Board v. Hearst Publications, Inc., page 383 above.

13. The Act at issue in Crowell, as amended in 1972, makes two notable changes from the original scheme of a decision by a deputy commissioner and review in district court. First, the deputy commissioner's or ALJ's decision is reviewed by a Department of Labor Benefits Review Board and sustained if supported by substantial evidence. Second, the Review Board's decision can be reviewed in a court of appeals; the statute does not specify the standard of review there, but it has been held that if the Board reversed the initial decision, the question in court is not whether there was substantial evidence to support the Board, but whether there was substantial evidence to support the initial decision. The Black Lung Benefits Act incorporates the same regime. See Old Ben Coal Co. v. Prewitt, 755 F.2d 588 (7th Cir.1985). Thus, since the 1972 amendments, Crowell's specific holding on de novo review seems interred even more deeply than when Professor Schwartz wrote Does the Ghost of Crowell v. Benson Still Walk? 98 U.Pa.L.Rev. 163 (1949).

14. See A Quaker Action Group v. Hickel, 421 F.2d 1111 (D.C.Cir.1969) (refusing to limit review to whether National Park Service was "wholly irrational" in denying permits for demonstrations in Lafayette Park to groups of more than 500 and groups of more than 100 on the White House sidewalk.)

"The expertise of those entrusted with the protection of the President does not qualify them to resolve First Amendment issues, the traditional province of the judiciary. A balancing of First Amendment freedoms against the requirements of Presidential safety may be left to other agencies in

the NLRB determines that an employer's statements were coercive and so not protected by the first amendment, what if any deference should be given by a reviewing court? The Supreme Court perhaps straddled: "[W]e do note that an employer's free speech right to communicate his views to his employees is firmly established and cannot be infringed by a union or the Board. . . . Any assessment of the precise scope of employer expression, of course, must be made in the context of its labor relations setting. Thus, an employer's rights cannot outweigh the equal rights of the employees to associate freely. . . .

"Petitioner argues that the line between so-called permitted predictions and proscribed threats is too vague to stand up under traditional First Amendment analysis and that the Board's discretion to curtail free speech rights is correspondingly too uncontrolled. It is true that a reviewing court must recognize the Board's competence in the first instance to judge the impact of utterances made in the context of the employer-employee relationship. . . . But an employer, who has control over that relationship and therefore knows it best, cannot be heard to complain that he is without an adequate guide for his behavior. . . ." NLRB v. Gissel Packing Co., 395 U.S. 575, 617, 620 (1969). Will—should—such situations draw independent review? If so, could the NLRB reduce such review by using rulemaking to resolve aspects of problems like Gissel Packing, since both Crowell and Northern Pipeline not only involved adjudication, but stressed Article III? Is especially full review likelier for first amendment problems? Review of the vast litigation over whether administrative procedures satisfy due process requirements would reveal few instances of deference to administrators (of course there is deference to the legislature). The same is true of the fourth amendment and agencies' power to investigate or to require information.

To the extent that we see judicial review of administrative action continue any significant degree of independent scrutiny for constitutional "facts," will not that review likely be much closer on application of law to the facts, rather than on the basic fact findings? [15] Here too, allocating responsibility for different aspects of decisions may be guided by the familiar rough rule of thumb of what belongs "to the contemplated routine of administration."

the first instance. But absent a compelling showing—which has not been begun here—that courts cannot evaluate the questions of fact involved in estimating danger to the President, the final judgment must rest with the courts." Id. at 1118.

See also Porter v. Califano, 592 F.2d 770 (5th Cir.1979) (claim of suspended federal employee that punishment occurred because of protected free speech requires full hearing and independent judgment, requiring reversal since district court may have relied on agency findings or deferred to agency rulings, error under APA § 706(2)(B)); and Meehan v. Macy, 392 F.2d 822 (D.C.Cir. 1968) (court's duty to review for substantial evidence supporting discharge of civil servant "must not be scanted" when underlying issue involves free speech, and evidence found in opinion by Leventhal, J., to "not ring out with requisite clarity," over dissent by Tamm, J., who cited precedent that such cases are always reviewed narrowly, but did not mention free speech element).

15. Professor Monaghan notes that even in Bose, supra n. 3, "appellate judges may accept the historical facts found in the court below, but they may not defer to the first amendment law application conclusions . . . no matter how reasonable." Monaghan, supra n. 2, at 229–30.

i. Conclusion

Evaluation of judicial review of agency action involves not merely scope of review but also aspects developed more fully in Chapter 9: the delay inherent in review; the unevenness with which review is invoked by various affected groups; the unevenness in which types of matters are susceptible to review; and the sporadic and incomplete nature of review in terms of the overall programs of which it is only a part. Therefore, any evaluation at this point is itself incomplete but is nonetheless worthwhile if understood as an interim stocktaking subject to later modification of tone, shape and depth. And here as so often, the limits of generalized statement or generalized inference from particularized statement remind us why, for lawyers, it is a cliche to say, "It depends".

(1) JERRY MASHAW, BUREAUCRATIC JUSTICE: MANAGING SOCIAL SECURITY DISABILITY CLAIMS (1983), 7–9. "[In 1978, my] colleagues and I found that the tens of thousands of judicial review proceedings that have been held since the disability program's inception have either had no perceptible impact on its functioning or have made it worse. . . .

"Why should anyone believe that particular issues raised in episodic litigation between parties having peculiar litigating interests should provide the judiciary with sufficient information for it to understand the administrative, political, social, economic, or scientific reality of a congressional-administrative program, much less provide an opportunity to take effective action to mold that reality in desirable forms? That the courts generally do not hold such a belief is a testament to their wisdom. That they sometimes act as if they did is perhaps a result of our general tendency to exert unreasonable pressure on all public institutions. If we demand persistently enough that the judges pull our chestnuts out of the fire, they will sometimes try."

(2) LANCE LIEBMAN AND RICHARD STEWART, BUREAUCRATIC VISION (Review of Mashaw's Bureaucratic Justice), 96 Harv.L.Rev. 1952, 1959–63 * (1983): "Mashaw first asserts that judicial review has had only a minor impact on the bulk of administrative decisions in the SSD program. . . . Second, he argues that this result is desirable, or at least necessary. . . .

"Despite his broadside attack on judicial review, Mashaw takes no more than a glance at the court decisions that have confronted systemic issues about the procedural functioning of the program. . . . With some exceptions, those decisions have upheld the SSA's management practices against statutory and constitutional challenges. . . .

"Mashaw's principal target is 'retail' judicial reversal of random individual cases. Assume that no change in the bureaucratic regimen will follow such reversals. Should judicial review nonetheless still be available? The argument for retaining such review is that the Social Security system encourages and depends on a widespread public belief that benefits are individual entitlements that must be honored through appropriate procedures. . . .

"But there are, as Mashaw shows, powerful objections to providing such an opportunity. Most of those who press their claims through the ALJs or the courts will get on the disability rolls or successfully resist removal from them. . . . Available data show, not surprisingly, that white applicants and applicants who are better off are more likely to appeal. . . . This disparity in results seems unjust, particularly when one considers that ability to maneuver one's way through the system is being rewarded in a program created for the *disabled.* . . . Mashaw thus implicitly suggests that judicial review be abolished not only because it is expensive and does not improve the routine operations of the system, but also because on balance it produces less justice than do bureaucratic measures designed to promote consistency and equity. . . .

"Even if the constitutional issues are put to one side, Mashaw's readiness to jettison ALJ and judicial review raises doubts not easily silenced. If there were no ALJ or federal judicial review, would the SSA continue to operate with a high degree of competence and public confidence? Would Social Security participants continue to trust and rely on the program? . . . Is it acceptable, in a nation more suspicious of bureaucratic administration than are other industrial democracies, that such decisions be placed in the hands of persons whose main claim to this power is that they passed a civil service test?"

(3) R. SHEP MELNICK, REGULATION AND THE COURTS: THE CASE OF THE CLEAN AIR ACT 151–3, 294–8, 342–3, 347–8, 350, 356–7, 359, 367, 372–3, 388–9 * (1983) studied the impact of judicial review through six case studies arising under that Act. While Melnick found court action "counterproductive" in only one of his six studies, he points up strengths and weaknesses that inhibit any simple overall conclusion "pro" or "con" review.

The Melnick roster, in summary: First, in 1972 and 1974, early in EPA history, two courts of appeals read an ambiguous statute as setting specific goals, which later the EPA and Congress did come to favor and incorporate in 1977 amendments. "[W]hile the President and Congress engaged [in 1973–4] in a partisan, crisis-oriented battle over environmental and energy policies in the hectic months after the 1973 oil embargo, the courts took a more long-range perspective on the issues before them . . . [T]he courts' independence allowed them to focus the EPA's attention on a serious environmental problem (atmospheric loading) that threatened to become forgotten amid the chorus of demands for an immediate response to the energy crisis. Mounting evidence of the damage caused by acid rain makes the courts look farsighted indeed. Moreover, by taking the matter out of the hands of EPA engineers, the courts helped political executives in the agency see the policy significance of decisions that had previously been justified on narrow technical grounds. Generalists on the bench helped generalists in the agency get control over specialists nominally under the latter's control." But, "counterbalancing these advantages of court intervention", the courts'

---

* Reprinted from Regulation and the Courts: The Case of the Clean Air Act, by   R. Shep Melnick. Copyright © 1983 The Brookings Institution.

reading of the legislative history of the 1970 Act shifted who had won in the political process. Also, the courts' "solution" to the key problem of smokestack height limits was "an extreme rule that revealed [the courts'] primitive understanding of the issues. . . . The adjudicatory process clearly failed to provide . . . an adequate understanding. . . . The policy arguments of the litigants and the courts were as rudimentary as their arguments on legislative intent were misleading. . . . Moreover, to the extent that adjudication addressed policy issues at all, it focused entirely on identifying problems rather than reviewing possible solutions. The court apparently determined that atmospheric loading and degradation of air quality in pristine western areas were serious problems and ordered the EPA to find a solution. [T]he courts' independence from bureaucratic responsibilities brought with it lack of concern for administrative feasibility. . . . Similarly, independence from political pressure led the courts to underestimate—or perhaps to dismiss cavalierly—the substantial costs, environmental as well as economic, imposed by this immense program." In addition, the decisions led environmentalists to support a cumbersome approach and resist innovations, which has delayed more effective pollution control.

Going on to another case study: "Most writers who have evaluated the courts' performance in reviewing national air quality standards have praised the judiciary for improving the EPA's technical analysis and expanding public participation. . . . [But] many jurists and scholars have warned that the adjudicatory process is not capable of explaining complex scientific issues to generalist judges. However, the number of occasions on which judges have misread scientific evidence is extremely small. By overturning only those decisions based on glaring error, the courts have managed to avoid becoming enmeshed in disputes between experts. Judges appear to recognize their own limitations when reviewing clinical, epidemiological, and toxicological studies.

"What the adjudicatory process has not seemed to convey to key federal judges, though, is the fact that health effects thresholds [1] do not exist for most pollutants. While most scientists agree on this and congressional committees have conceded that the health effects threshold is little more than a myth, the courts continue to insist upon a 'health only' approach that rests on the threshold assumption. [B]y insisting upon a 'health only' approach, the courts have helped reduce national standards to the status of long-term targets. Standards that seem excessively demanding to state and local administrators, congressmen and presidents, and members of the public directly affected by regulatory programs are harder to enforce than standards that seem more reasonable. . . . By itself, announcing rights does not protect rights. Warnings about the imminent demise of the species do not improve the species' chances of survival if they contribute to the public's perception of the federal government as a bureaucratic Chicken Little.

"[Also,] by ruling that the EPA cannot consider cost in standard setting the courts have preserved the myth of thresholds and have thus

1. [Ed.] That is, levels above 0% and beneath which it can confidently be ex- pected that human health will not be affected.

muddled the public debate over how to deal with the problem of risk. Regulators inevitably consider cost. But presently they cannot explain how they do so. . . .

"If the courts have had an unfortunate effect on standard setting, it is not because they have misinterpreted scientific evidence, but rather because they have been guided by an idea—a judicially protected, quasi-constitutional 'right' to health—that is incompatible with the medical evidence on the effects of pollution. No amount of documentation, no number of 'hard looks,' no corps of science clerks will solve the courts' problem until judges reexamine the views on public health and the regulatory process that guide their laborious review of air quality standards."

Speaking generally: "To a large extent the debate over judicial activism has focused on the ability of the adjudicatory process to supply generalist judges with information sufficient for solving complex social problems. The case studies in this book have provided evidence on both sides of the controversy. In several instances judges failed to understand issues of central importance to the case before them. In others the courts' disciplined analysis of evidence helped educate the EPA as well as the bench. . . . Like other institutions, courts both make mistakes and learn from their mistakes.

"Surprisingly, the issues that judges either overlooked or misunderstood were not particularly technical ones. . . . Despite the technical complexity of most clean air issues, the case studies in this book show that what the courts need most is a better understanding of *administrative* issues, not technical ones. The courts have gotten into trouble when they have relied on general impressions and sketchy evidence to conclude that an environmental or administrative problem exists and then issued haphazard instructions on how the EPA should deal with it.

"To perform competently the tasks they have taken on, judges must learn more about the nature of the problem they seek to cure, the policy options open to administrators, and the constraints on those who must carry out their orders. Judges can take a major step in this direction by starting to think about specific remedies as soon as they consider possible interpretations of the law. Linking abstract legal terms to concrete administrative action will help them recognize the difficulties they create for administrators when they issue vague directives such as 'prevent significant deterioration,' 'prohibit dispersion,' or 'implement transportation controls.' . . .

"Greater specificity in court orders will, of course, reduce administrative flexibility. But presumably courts overrule agency decisions only when agencies have exceeded the outer bounds of their discretion. If the agency has done something wrong, the court should be able to specify what that wrong is and how the agency should correct it. . . . By paying more attention to remedies, judges will also put themselves in closer touch with nonlawyers in the agency and reduce the power of agency attorneys. . . . This diminishes the likelihood that courts and agency attorneys will set goals that other agency officials know cannot be achieved.

"Thinking about remedies and soliciting the opinions of those with administrative responsibilities will, no doubt, increase judges' deference to administrators.

Last: "[I]ndependence proved to be a mixed blessing for the courts in this series of cases [about transportation controls]. Freedom from political pressure allowed the courts to insist that the law be carried out regardless of cost. But here, as in many other areas, administrators needed more than a push from the judiciary to overcome the many objections. . . . They needed cooperation from those outside the agency. . . .

"It is clear what judges are free *from:* political accountability, administrative responsibilities, the norms of specialized professions. One expects that freedom from these constraints will lead judges to take a broad view of the public interest. Adopting this broad view, though, takes more than independence; it takes broad familiarity with both policy debates and the political process. Seeing different parts of the whole, most judges have adopted partial views of what the public interest requires. . . . The judiciary as a whole has not reconciled the divergent points of view adopted by its component parts. Nor have the courts forced Congress to reconcile the competing demands it makes of the EPA. . . .

"The courts have the option of refusing to play the middleman between congressional and agency advocates of programs without political support. They can simply refuse to hear cases in which plaintiffs without traditional standing ask the courts to initiate new programs disliked by agency officials. This would permit agencies to allocate their scarce resources—especially political capital—to those programs they view as most productive. If Congress is dissatisfied, it can communicate this directly to the agency in oversight and confirmation hearings, in the authorization and appropriations process, and in its rewriting of the law. Agencies are hardly immune from such political pressure. The greater the support for the program within Congress, the more costly resistance becomes for the agency. Thus the withdrawal of the courts would not leave agencies uncontrolled, but would encourage congressional advocates of administrative programs to build legislative coalitions instead of legislative histories.

"This book has called into question the conventional wisdom on the effect of these court decisions on pollution control policy. Looking beyond formal court records and the avowed purposes of judicial actions, one discovers a multitude of unintended and undesirable consequences of court action. Just as studies of policy implementation by bureaucracies have revealed the difficulties administrators have in turning statutory mandates into concerted action, analysis of the implementation of court decisions shows that judges frequently issue commands ignored or modified by others, pursue inconsistent policies, and generally 'muddle through.' . . . "

(4) LOUIS JAFFE, JUDICIAL CONTROL OF ADMINISTRATIVE ACTION 321 (1965): "[T]here is in our society a profound, tradition-taught reliance on the courts as the ultimate guardian and assurance of the limits set upon executive power by the constitutions and legislatures."

Chapter IV

THE CONSTITUTIONAL REQUIREMENT OF AN OPPORTUNITY TO BE HEARD

"No freeman shall be taken and imprisoned or disseized or exiled or in any way destroyed, nor will we go upon him nor send upon him, except by the lawful judgment of his peers and by the law of the land." Section XXXIX, Magna Carta (1215)

"No person shall be . . . deprived of life, liberty, or property, without due process of law. . . ." Amendment V, United States Constitution (1791)

". . . [N]or shall any State deprive any person of life, liberty, or property, without due process of law. . . ." Amendment XIV, United States Constitution (1868)

"Many controversies have raged about the cryptic and abstract words of the Due Process Clause but there can be no doubt that at a minimum they require that deprivation of life, liberty or property by adjudication be preceded by notice and opportunity for hearing appropriate to the nature of the case." Mullane v. Central Hanover Bank & Trust Co., 339 U.S. 306, 313 (1950).

INTRODUCTORY NOTE

The lawyer—and especially the law student—may be forgiven for thinking that everywhere she or he turns, a due process clause lies in wait. In a recent case, Justice Stevens explained that this clause in the fourteenth amendment

"is the source of three different kinds of constitutional protection. First, it incorporates specific protections defined in the Bill of Rights. Thus, the State, as well as the Federal Government, must comply with the commands in the First and Eighth Amendments; so too, the State must respect the guarantees in the Fourth, Fifth, and Sixth Amendments. Second, it contains a substantive component, sometimes referred to as 'substantive due process,' which bars certain arbitrary government actions 'regardless of the fairness of the procedures used to implement them.' Third, it is a guarantee of fair procedure, sometimes referred to as 'procedural due process': the State may not execute, imprison, or fine a defendant without giving him a fair trial, nor may it take property without providing appropriate procedural safeguards. . . ."

Daniels v. Williams, 106 S.Ct. 662, 677–78 (1986) (concurring opinion).

For present purposes, we must make even a further division. As a "guarantee of fair procedure," the due process clause of either the fifth or fourteenth amendments has application to judicial proceedings as well as administrative ones. Thus, it is a question of due process how far a state court's extra-territorial jurisdiction extends (see, e.g., International Shoe Co. v. Washington, 326 U.S. 310 (1945)) or what procedures must be followed before a court's writ of garnishment may issue (see, e.g., North Georgia Finishing, Inc. v. Di–Chem, Inc., 419 U.S. 601 (1975)) or what notice will suffice to give a court the power to adjudicate a defendant's rights (see, e.g., Mullane v. Central Hanover Bank & Trust Co., 339 U.S. 306 (1950)). Our purpose in looking at the cases reproduced in this chapter, however, will be to consider the operation of due process as a guarantee of fair administrative procedure.

Is that a separable topic? Are the cases which follow recognizably bound together by their concern with administrative justice in the twentieth century? Or are they just a part of a gangly sprawl of doctrine which has substantive as well as procedural components, judicial as well as administrative applications, and which partakes of all the deep disputes which characterize constitutional law?

SECTION 1. SOME OLD LEARNING

LONDONER v. DENVER
Supreme Court of the United States, 1908.
210 U.S. 373.

(Reprinted p. 209, supra)

BI–METALLIC INVESTMENT CO. v. STATE BD. OF EQUALIZATION OF COLORADO
Supreme Court of the United States, 1915.
239 U.S. 441.

(Reprinted p. 213, supra)

NORTH AMERICAN COLD STORAGE CO. v. CHICAGO
Supreme Court of the United States, 1908.
211 U.S. 306.

[Section 1161 of the Revised Municipal Code of the City of Chicago read as follows:

"Every person being the owner . . . of any . . . cold storage house . . . where any meat, fish, poultry, game, vegetables, fruit, or other perishable article adapted or designed to be used for human food shall be stored or kept . . . shall put, preserve and keep such article of food supply in a clean and wholesome condition, and shall not allow the same, nor any part thereof, to become putrid, decayed, poisoned, infected, or in any other manner rendered or made unsafe or unwholesome for human food; and it shall be the duty of the meat and food inspectors and other duly authorized employes of the health department of the city to enter any and all such premises above specified at any time of any day and to forthwith seize, condemn and destroy any such putrid, decayed, poisoned and infected food, which any such inspector may find in and upon said premises."

Under this ordinance officials of the city ordered complainant, a cold storage company, to deliver up to them, for purposes of destruction, forty-seven barrels of poultry which allegedly had become putrid. This the plaintiff refused to do. Thereupon defendants threatened to destroy summarily such of complainant's goods as they deemed unfit for human consumption. They further announced that no deliveries to or from the warehouse would be allowed until their original order had been complied with; and they threatened to imprison anyone attempting to make such deliveries. By these means complainant's business was completely halted. Complainant applied for an injunction enjoining both the stoppage of deliveries and the threatened destruction of the allegedly putrid poultry. On demurrer the lower court dismissed the bill.]

MR. JUSTICE PECKHAM . . . delivered the opinion of the court. . . .

Holding there was jurisdiction in the court below, we come to the merits of the case. The action of the defendants, which is admitted by the demurrer, in refusing to permit the complainant to carry on its ordinary business until it delivered the poultry, would seem to have been arbitrary and wholly indefensible. Counsel for the complainant, however, for the purpose of obtaining a decision in regard to the constitutional question as to the right to seize and destroy property without a prior hearing, states that he will lay no stress here upon that portion of the bill which alleges the unlawful and forcible taking possession of complainant's business by the defendants. He states in his brief as follows:

"There is but one question in this case, and that question is, Is section 1161 of the Revised Municipal Code of Chicago in conflict with the due process of law provision of the Fourteenth Amendment, in this, that it does not provide for notice and an opportunity to be heard before the destruction of the food products therein referred to?" . . .

The general power of the State to legislate upon the subject embraced in the above ordinance of the city of Chicago, counsel does not deny. Nor does he deny the right to seize and destroy unwholesome or putrid food, provided that notice and opportunity to be heard be given the owner or custodian of the property before it is destroyed. We are of opinion, however, that provision for a hearing before seizure and condemnation and destruction of food which is unwholesome and unfit for use, is not necessary. . . . The right to so seize and destroy is, of course, based upon the fact that the food is not fit to be eaten. Food that is in such a condition, if kept for sale or in danger of being sold, is in itself a nuisance, and a nuisance of the most dangerous kind, involving, as it does, the health, if not the lives, of persons who may eat it. A determination on the part of the seizing officers that food is in an unfit condition to be eaten is not a decision which concludes the owner. The ex parte finding of the health officers as to the fact is not in any way binding upon those who own or claim the right to sell the food. If a party cannot get his hearing in advance of the seizure and destruction he has the right to have it afterward, which right may be claimed upon the trial in an action brought for the destruction of his property, and in that action those who destroyed it can only successfully defend if the jury shall find the fact of unwholesomeness as claimed by them. . . .

Miller v. Horton, 152 Massachusetts, 540, is in principle like the case before us. It was an action brought for killing the plaintiff's horse. The defendants admitted the killing but justified the act under an order of the board of health, which declared that the horse had the glanders, and directed it to be killed. The court held that the decision of the board of health was not conclusive as to whether or not the horse was diseased, and said that: "Of course there cannot be a trial by jury before killing an animal supposed to have a contagious disease, and we assume that the legislature may authorize its destruction in such emergencies without a hearing beforehand. But it does not follow that it can throw the loss upon the owner without a hearing. If he cannot be heard beforehand he may be heard afterward. The statute may provide for paying him in case it should appear that his property was not what the legislature had declared to be a nuisance and may give him his hearing in that way. If it does not do so, the statute may leave those who act under it to proceed at their peril, and the owner gets his hearing in an action against them."

. . .

Complainant, however, contends that there was no emergency requiring speedy action for the destruction of the poultry in order to protect the public health from danger resulting from consumption of such poultry. It is said that the food was in cold storage, and that it would continue in the same condition it then was for three months, if properly stored, and that therefore the defendants had ample time in which to give notice to complainant or the owner and have a hearing of the question as to the condition of the poultry, and as the ordinance provided for no hearing, it was void. But we think this is not required. The power of the legislature to enact laws in relation to the public health being conceded, as it must be, it is to a great extent within legislative discretion as to whether any hearing need be given before the destruction of unwholesome food which is unfit for human consumption. If a hearing were to be always necessary, even under the circumstances of this case, the question at once arises as to what is to be done with the food in the meantime. Is it to remain with the cold storage company, and if so under what security that it will not be removed? To be sure that it will not be removed during the time necessary for the hearing, which might frequently be indefinitely prolonged, some guard would probably have to be placed over the subject-matter of investigation, which would involve expense, and might not even then prove effectual. What is the emergency which would render a hearing unnecessary? We think when the question is one regarding the destruction of food which is not fit for human use the emergency must be one which would fairly appeal to the reasonable discretion of the legislature as to the necessity for a prior hearing, and in that case its decision would not be a subject for review by the courts. As the owner of the food or its custodian is amply protected against the party seizing the food, who must in a subsequent action against him show as a fact that it was within the statute, we think that due process of law is not denied the owner or custodian by the destruction of the food alleged to be unwholesome and unfit for human food without a preliminary hearing. . . .

Even if it be a fact that some value may remain for certain purposes in food that is unfit for human consumption, the right to destroy it is not on that account taken away. The small value that might remain in said food is a mere incident, and furnishes no defense to its destruction when it is plainly kept to be sold at some time as food. . . .

Affirmed.

MR. JUSTICE BREWER dissents.

NOTE

How far does the Cold Storage principle go? In PHILLIPS v. COMMISSIONER, 283 U.S. 589 (1931), a tax was assessed against a company which had already dissolved and distributed its assets. The Commissioner then sent a notice to Phillips, a stockholder and one of the transferrees of the company's assets, assessing the uncollected tax (which was smaller than the distribution he had received) against him. Prior to a then-recent statutory amendment, the liability of a transferree had had to be established not by the Commissioner's assessment, but by suit brought against the transferree in court. "The contention mainly urged is that the summary procedure permitted by the [new statute] violates the Constitution because it does not provide for a judicial determination of the transferee's liability at the outset." But, in the words of Justice Brandeis for a unanimous Court, "The right of the United States to collect its internal revenue by summary administrative proceedings has long been settled. Where, as here, adequate opportunity is afforded for a later judicial determination of the legal rights, summary proceedings to secure prompt performance of pecuniary obligations to the government have been consistently sustained."

And then, in words which were subsequently quoted in other cases, this passage, 283 U.S. at 596–97:

"Where only property rights are involved, mere postponement of the judicial enquiry is not a denial of due process, if the opportunity given for the ultimate judicial determination of the liability is adequate. Delay in the judicial determination of property rights is not uncommon where it is essential that governmental needs be immediately satisfied. For the protection of public health, a State may order the summary destruction of property by administrative authorities without antecedent notice or hearing. North American Cold Storage Co. v. Chicago, 211 U.S. 306; . . . Because of the public necessity, the property of citizens may be summarily seized in war-time. And at any time, the United States may acquire property by eminent domain, without paying, or determining the amount of the compensation before the taking. . . . "

For a thoughtful discussion, see J. Freedman, Summary Action by Administrative Agencies, 40 U.Chi.L.Rev. 1 (1972).

BAILEY v. RICHARDSON

United States Court of Appeals, District of Columbia Circuit, 1950.
182 F.2d 46, aff'd by an equally divided Court, 341 U.S. 918 (1951).

Before EDGERTON, PRETTYMAN and PROCTOR, CIRCUIT JUDGES.

PRETTYMAN, CIRCUIT JUDGE.

[Plaintiff sued officials in the Federal Security Agency and the Civil Service Commission; the district court granted defendants' summary judgment motion.

After having been employed in the civil service for eight years, plaintiff was discharged "due to reduction in force"; a year later, she was reinstated. Civil Service Regulations made reinstatement subject to various conditions, including disqualification if "On all the evidence, reasonable grounds exist for belief that the person involved is disloyal to the Government of the United States."

Two months after her reinstatement, plaintiff received a letter from the Commission's "Loyalty Board"; it said, in part:

"[A]n investigation of you has been conducted under the provisions of Executive Order 9835, which established the Federal Employees Loyalty Program. This investigation disclosed information which, it is believed, you should have an opportunity to explain or refute.

"The questions in the attached Interrogatory are based on the information received, and are to be answered in writing in sufficient detail to present fairly your explanation or answers thereto. . . .

"You are further advised that you have the right, upon request, to an administrative hearing on the issues in the case before the Regional Loyalty Board. You may appear personally before the Board and be represented by counsel or representative of your own choice; and you may present evidence in your behalf. . . . "

The interrogatory further stated that the Commission had received information that Ms. Bailey was or had been a Communist party member and that she was or had been a member of two other organizations "declared by the Attorney General to come within the purview" of the Loyalty Program.]

Miss Bailey answered the interrogatories directly and specifically, denying each item of information recited therein as having been received by the Commission, except that she admitted past membership for a short time in the American League for Peace and Democracy. She vigorously asserted her loyalty to the United States. She requested an administrative hearing. A hearing was held before the Regional Board. She appeared and testified and presented other witnesses and numerous affidavits. No person other than those presented by her testified.

On November 1, 1948, the Regional Board advised the Federal Security Agency, in which Miss Bailey was employed, that:

"As a result of such investigation and after a hearing before this Board, it was found that, on all the evidence, reasonable grounds exist for belief that Miss Bailey is disloyal to the Government of the United States.

"Therefore, she has been rated ineligible for Federal employment; she has been barred from competing in civil service examinations for a period of three years, and your office is instructed to separate her from the service." . . .

Miss Bailey appealed to the Loyalty Review Board and requested a hearing. Hearing was held before a panel of that Board. Miss Bailey appeared, testified, and presented affidavits. No person other than Miss Bailey testified, and no affidavits other than hers were presented on the record.

On February 9, 1949, the Chairman of the Loyalty Review Board advised the Federal Security Agency that the finding of the Regional Board was sustained. . . .

The case presented for Miss Bailey is undoubtedly appealing. She was denied reinstatement in her former employment because Government officials found reasonable ground to believe her disloyal. She was not given a trial in any sense of the word, and she does not know who informed upon her. Thus viewed, her situation appeals powerfully to our sense of the fair and the just. But the case must be placed in context and in perspective.

The Constitution placed upon the President and the Congress, and upon them alone, responsibility for the welfare of this country in the arena of world affairs. It so happens that we are presently in an adversary position to a government whose most successful recent method of contest is the infiltration of a government service by its sympathizers. This is the context of Miss Bailey's question.

The essence of her complaint is not that she was denied reinstatement; the complaint is that she was denied reinstatement without revelation by the Government of the names of those who informed against her and of the method by which her alleged activities were detected. So the question actually posed by the case is whether the President is faced with an inescapable dilemma, either to continue in Government employment a person whose loyalty he reasonably suspects or else to reveal publicly the methods by which he detects disloyalty and the names of any persons who may venture to assist him.

. . .

The presentation of appellant's contentions is impressive. Each detail of the trial which she unquestionably did not get is depicted separately, in a mounting cumulation into analogies to the Dreyfus case and the Nazi judicial process. Thus, a picture of a simple black-and-white fact—that appellant did not get a trial in the judicial sense—is drawn in bold and appealing colors. But the question is not whether she had a trial. The question is whether she should have had one.

If the whole of this case were as appellant pictures it, if we had only to decide the question which she states and as she states it, our task would indeed be simple and attractively pleasant. But it is not so. We are dealing with a major clash between individual and public interests. We must ascertain with precision whether individual rights are involved, and we must then weigh the sum of those rights, if there be any, against the inexorable necessities of the Government. We must examine not only one side of the controversy but both sides.

[The court first determined that the plaintiff was not entitled either by executive order or statute to more process than she received. It then determined that the portion of the government's orders which barred the plaintiff from federal service for three years hence were invalid as constituting a "punishment" which could be meted out only through compliance with the Sixth Amendment. Mere dismissal from employment, however, was not such a "punishment."]

Fifth Amendment.

It is next said on behalf of appellant that the due process clause of the Fifth Amendment requires that she be afforded a hearing of the quasi-judicial type before being dismissed. The due process clause provides: "No person shall * * * be deprived of life, liberty, or property, without due process of law; * * *." It has been held repeatedly and consistently that Government employ is not "property" and that in this particular it is not a contract. We are unable to perceive how it could be held to be "liberty". Certainly it is not "life". So much that is clear would seem to dispose of the point. In terms the due process clause does not apply to the holding of a Government office.

Other considerations lead to the same conclusion. Never in our history has a Government administrative employee been entitled to a hearing of the quasi-judicial type upon his dismissal from Government service. That record of a hundred and sixty years of Government administration is the sort of history which speaks with great force. It is pertinent to repeat in this connection that the [1913] Act, sponsored and enacted by advocates of a merit classified government service, expressly denies the right to such a hearing. Moreover, in the acute and sometimes bitter historic hundred-year contest over the wholesale summary dismissal of Government employees, there seems never to have been a claim that, absent congressional limitation, the President was without constitutional power to dismiss without notice, hearing or evidence; except for the question as to officials appointed with the advice and consent of the Senate. . . .

In the absence of statute or ancient custom to the contrary, executive offices are held at the will of the appointing authority, not for life or for fixed terms. If removal be at will, of what purpose would process be? To hold office at the will of a superior and to be removable therefrom only by constitutional due process of law are opposite and inherently conflicting ideas. Due process of law is not applicable unless one is being deprived of something to which he has a right.

Constitutionally, the criterion for retention or removal of subordinate employees is the confidence of superior executive officials. Confidence is not controllable by process. What may be required by acts of the Congress is another matter, but there is no requirement in the Constitution that the executive branch rely upon the services of persons in whom it lacks confidence. . . .

We hold that the due process of law clause of the Fifth Amendment does not restrict the President's discretion or the prescriptive power of Congress in respect to executive personnel.

We do not reach the question whether, if the due process of law clause does apply, it requires more than this appellant was given. . . .

[The court proceeded to consider plaintiff's first amendment claims, and held that nothing in the Constitution prevented dismissal of government employees because of their political affiliations; absent statutory protection, Republican Presidents were entitled to dismiss Democrats, and so forth. Finally, it reached the contention that the allegation of *disloyalty* was, after all, different in kind.]

It is said on behalf of appellant that disloyalty is akin to treason and that dismissal is akin to conviction. Forthwith it is asserted that Miss Bailey has been convicted of disloyalty. As we have seen, nothing resembling a conviction from the legal standpoint has been visited upon her. She was merely refused Government employment for reasons satisfactory to the appointing authorities.

But it is said that the public does not distinguish, that she has been stigmatized and her chance of making a living seriously impaired. . . . But it has long been established that if the Government, in the exercise of a governmental power, injures an individual, that individual has no redress. Official action beyond the scope of official authority can be prevented or nullified by the courts, and so official action which violates a constitutional right of an individual can be rectified. But if no constitutional right of the individual is being impinged and officials are acting within the scope of official authority, the fact that the individual concerned is injured in the process neither invalidates the official act nor gives the individual a right to redress. . . .

. . .

The case will be remanded to the District Court with instructions to enter a decree holding invalid those sections of the orders of the Loyalty Boards and the Federal Security Agency which would bar Miss Bailey from employment for three years, and holding valid those sections which accomplished her removal from the rolls and from office in the classified civil service.

Reversed in part, affirmed in part, and remanded with instructions.

[Judge Edgerton dissented on the grounds that the Executive Order establishing the Loyalty Program entitled plaintiff to more process than she got; that "dismissal for disloyalty is punishment and requires all the safeguards of a judicial trial"; and that her dismissal constituted an abridgement of the Freedom of Speech. His highly charged statement of the facts included the following description of Ms. Bailey's second administrative "hearing":]

Appellant appeared and testified before a panel of the Loyalty Review Board. She submitted her own affidavit and the affidavits of some 70 persons who knew her, including bankers, corporate officials, federal and state officials, union members, and others. Again no one testified against her. She proved she had publicly and to the knowledge of a number of the affiants taken positions inconsistent with Communist sympathies. She showed not only by her own testimony but by that of other persons that she favored the Marshall Plan, which the Communist Party notoriously opposed, and that in 1940, during the Nazi-Soviet Pact, she favored Lend-Lease and was very critical of the Soviet position. In her union she urged its officers to execute noncommunist affidavits, opposed a foreign policy resolution widely publicized as pro-Russian, and favored what was then the official CIO resolution on foreign policy.

Against all this, there were only the unsworn reports in the secret files to the effect that unsworn statements of a general sort, purporting to connect appellant with Communism, had been made by unnamed persons. Some if not all of these statements did not purport to be based on knowledge, but only on belief. Appellant sought to learn the names of the informants or, if their names were confidential, then at least whether they had been active in appellant's union, in which there were factional quarrels. The Board did not furnish or even have this information. Chairman Richardson said: "I haven't the slightest knowledge as to who they were or how active they have been in anything." All that the Board knew or we know about the informants is that unidentified members of the Federal Bureau of Investigation, who did not appear before the Board, believed them to be reliable. To quote again from the record: "Chairman Richardson: I can only say to you that five or six of the reports come from informants certified to us by the Federal Bureau of Investigation as experienced and entirely reliable." . . .

On such material, the Review Board sustained the action of the Regional Board and directed the Federal Security Agency to dismiss the appellant. . . .

NOTES

(1) In JOINT ANTI-FASCIST REFUGEE COMMITTEE v. McGRATH, 341 U.S. 123 (1951), three organizations challenged their being designated as "Communist" by the Attorney General under another aspect of the same Loyalty Program. On the day that the Bailey case was affirmed by an equally divided Court without opinion, the Supreme Court held, 5–3, that the organizations had stated a cause of action. This time there were a riot of opinions, each of the justices in the majority writing separately. Some of the opinions went off on procedural points not here important; at the other extreme, Justice Black wrote that in his view the executive had no authority, with or without a hearing, to promulgate "officially prepared and proclaimed governmental blacklists." As regards procedural due process, the most comprehensive (and

famous) opinion was that of Justice Frankfurter.[1] Here are some excerpts, 341 U.S. at 160 ff.:

". . . Petitioners are organizations which, on the face of the record, are engaged solely in charitable or insurance activities. They have been designated "communist" by the Attorney General of the United States. This designation imposes no legal sanction on these organizations other than that it serves as evidence in ridding the Government of persons reasonably suspected of disloyalty. It would be blindness, however, not to recognize that in the conditions of our time such designation drastically restricts the organizations, if it does not proscribe them. . . . Yet, designation has been made without notice, without disclosure of any reasons justifying it, without opportunity to meet the undisclosed evidence or suspicion on which designation may have been based, and without opportunity to establish affirmatively that the aims and acts of the organization are innocent. It is claimed that thus to maim or decapitate, on the mere say-so of the Attorney General, an organization to all outward-seeming engaged in lawful objectives is so devoid of fundamental fairness as to offend the Due Process Clause of the Fifth Amendment.

". . . 'Due process,' unlike some legal rules, is not a technical conception with a fixed content unrelated to time, place and circumstances. Expressing as it does in its ultimate analysis respect enforced by law for that feeling of just treatment which has been evolved through centuries of Anglo-American constitutional history and civilization, 'due process' cannot be imprisoned within the treacherous limits of any formula. Representing a profound attitude of fairness between man and man, and more particularly between the individual and government, 'due process' is compounded of history, reason, the past course of decisions, and stout confidence in the strength of the democratic faith which we profess. Due process is not a mechanical instrument. It is not a yardstick. It is a process. It is a delicate process of adjustment inescapably involving the exercise of judgment by those whom the Constitution entrusted with the unfolding of the process.

". . . The precise nature of the interest that has been adversely affected, the manner in which this was done, the reasons for doing it, the available alternatives to the procedure that was followed, the protection implicit in the office of the functionary whose conduct is challenged, the balance of hurt complained of and good accomplished— these are some of the considerations that must enter into the judicial judgment.

". . .

"This Court is not alone in recognizing that the right to be heard before being condemned to suffer grievous loss of any kind, even though it may not involve the stigma and hardships of a criminal conviction, is a principle basic to our society. . . . Congress has often entrusted, as it may, protection of interests which it has created to administrative

---

1. Judge Henry Friendly called this concurrence "still the finest exposition of the need for a 'hearing.'" "Some Kind of Hearing," 123 U.Pa.L.Rev. 1267, 1277 (1975).

agencies rather than to the courts. But rarely has it authorized such agencies to act without those essential safeguards for fair judgment which in the course of centuries have come to be associated with due process. . . .

"The heart of the matter is that democracy implies respect for the elementary rights of men, however suspect or unworthy; a democratic government must therefore practice fairness; and fairness can rarely be obtained by secret, one-sided determination of facts decisive of rights.

". . .

"Man being what he is cannot safely be trusted with complete immunity from outward responsibility in depriving others of their rights. At least such is the conviction underlying our Bill of Rights. That a conclusion satisfies one's private conscience does not attest its reliability. The validity and moral authority of a conclusion largely depend on the mode by which it was reached. Secrecy is not congenial to truth-seeking and self-righteousness gives too slender an assurance of rightness. No better instrument has been devised for arriving at truth than to give a person in jeopardy of serious loss notice of the case against him and opportunity to meet it. Nor has a better way been found for generating the feeling, so important to a popular government, that justice has been done.

". . .

"We are not here dealing with the grant of Government largess. We have not before us the measured action of Congress, with the pause that is properly engendered when the validity of legislation is assailed. The Attorney General is certainly not immune from the historic requirements of fairness merely because he acts, however conscientiously, in the name of security. Nor does he obtain immunity on the ground that designation is not an 'adjudication' or a 'regulation' in the conventional use of those terms. Due process is not confined in its scope to the particular forms in which rights have heretofore been found to have been curtailed for want of procedural fairness. Due process is perhaps the most majestic concept in our whole constitutional system. While it contains the garnered wisdom of the past in assuring fundamental justice, it is also a living principle not confined to past instances. . . ."

The dissenters, in an opinion by Justice Reed, took a different view of the organizations' claims that they had been denied due process, 341 U.S. at 202–03:

"The contention can be answered summarily by saying that there is no deprivation of any property or liberty of any listed organization by the Attorney General's designation. It may be assumed that the listing is hurtful to their prestige, reputation and earning power. It may be such an injury as would entitle organizations to damages in a tort action against persons not protected by privilege. This designation, however, does not prohibit any business of the organizations, subject them to any punishment or deprive them of liberty of speech or other freedom. The cases relied upon in the briefs and opinions of the majority as requiring notice and hearing before valid action can be taken by administrative officers are where complainant will lose some property or enforceable civil or statutory right by the action taken or proposed. '[A] mere abstract declaration' by an administrator regarding the character of an organization, without the effect of forbidding or compelling conduct on the part of complainant, ought not to be subject to judicial interference. That is, it does not require notice and hearing."

(2) Holmes, J., in McAuliffe v. Mayor of New Bedford, 155 Mass. 216, 220 (1892): "[T]here is nothing in the Constitution . . . to prevent the city from attaching obedience to this rule [which prohibited police officers from soliciting money for political purposes] as a condition to the office of policeman, and making it part of the good conduct required. The petitioner may have a constitutional right to talk politics, but he has no constitutional right to be a policeman. There are few employments for hire in which the servant does not agree to suspend his constitutional right of free speech, as well as of idleness, by the implied terms of his contract. The servant cannot complain, as he takes the employment on the terms which are offered him."

Jackson, J., concurring in Joint Anti-Fascist Refugee Committee v. McGrath, 341 U.S. 123, 185 (1951): "The fact that one may not have a legal right to get or keep a government post does not mean that he can be adjudged ineligible illegally."

Is Jackson's statement the antithesis of Holmes'? Or does it proceed by granting Holmes' premises and then avoiding their effect?

(3) In "Cracks in 'The New Property': Adjudicative Due Process in the Administrative State," 62 Corn.L.Rev. 445 (1977), W. Van Alstyne speaks of "the complete extinction of the 'right-privilege' distinction," claiming that "[v]irtually its last significant appearance came in 1950, in Bailey v. Richardson."

CAFETERIA & RESTAURANT WORKERS UNION
v. McELROY

Supreme Court of the United States, 1961.
367 U.S. 886.

Mr. Justice Stewart delivered the opinion of the Court.

In 1956 the petitioner Rachel Brawner was a shortorder cook at a cafeteria operated by her employer, M & M Restaurants, Inc., on the premises of the Naval Gun Factory in the city of Washington. She had worked there for more than six years, and from her employer's point of view her record was entirely satisfactory.

The Gun Factory was engaged in designing, producing, and inspecting naval ordnance, including the development of weapons systems of a highly classified nature. . . . [T]he installation was under the command of Rear Admiral D.M. Tyree, Superintendent. . . . Identification badges were issued to persons authorized to enter the premises by

the Security Officer, a naval officer subordinate to the Superintendent.
. . . Rachel Brawner had been issued such a badge.

The cafeteria where she worked was operated by M & M under a contract. . . . Section 5(b) of the contract provided:

". . . In no event shall the Concessionaire engage, or continue to engage, for operations under this Agreement, personnel who . . .

"(iii) fail to meet the security requirements or other requirements under applicable regulations of the Activity, as determined by the Security Officer of the Activity."

On November 15, 1956, Mrs. Brawner was required to turn in her identification badge because of . . . [a] determination that she had failed to meet the security requirements of the installation. The Security Officer's determination was subsequently approved by Admiral Tyree, who cited § 5(b)(iii) of the contract as the basis for his action. At the request of the petitioner Union, which represented the employees at the cafeteria, M & M sought to arrange a meeting with officials of the Gun Factory "for the purpose of a hearing regarding the denial of admittance to the Naval Gun Factory of Rachel Brawner." This request was denied by Admiral Tyree on the ground that such a meeting would "serve no useful purpose."

Since the day her identification badge was withdrawn Mrs. Brawner has not been permitted to enter the Gun Factory. M & M offered to employ her in another restaurant which the company operated in the suburban Washington area, but she refused on the ground that the location was inconvenient.

The petitioners brought this action . . . seeking, among other things, to compel the return to Mrs. Brawner of her identification badge, so that she might be permitted to enter the Gun Factory and resume her former employment. [The court of appeals affirmed the district court's grant of summary judgment for the defendants.]

As the case comes here, two basic questions are presented. Was the commanding officer of the Gun Factory authorized to deny Rachel Brawner access to the installation in the way he did? If he was so authorized, did his action in excluding her operate to deprive her of any right secured to her by the Constitution?

I.

[The Court answered its first question affirmatively.]

II.

The question remains whether Admiral Tyree's action in summarily denying Rachel Brawner access to the site of her former employment violated the requirements of the Due Process Clause of the Fifth Amendment. This question cannot be answered by easy assertion that, because she had no consitutional right to be there in the first place, she was not deprived of liberty or property by the Superintendent's action. "One may not have a constitutional right to go to Baghdad, but the Government may not prohibit one from going there unless by means consonant with due process of law." Homer v. Richmond, 110 U.S. App. D.C. 226, 229, 292 F.2d 719, 722. It is the petitioners' claim that due process in this case required that Rachel Brawner be advised of the specific grounds for her exclusion and be accorded a hearing at which she might refute them. We are satisfied, however, that under the circumstances of this case such a procedure was not constitutionally required.

The Fifth Amendment does not require a trial-type hearing in every conceivable case of government impairment of private interest. . . . The very nature of due process negates any concept of inflexible procedures universally applicable to every imaginable situation. " '[D]ue process,' unlike some legal rules, is not a technical conception with a fixed content unrelated to time, place and circumstances." It is "compounded of history, reason, the past course of decisions. . . . " Joint Anti-Fascist Comm. v. McGrath, 341 U.S. 123, 162–163 (concurring opinion).

. . . [C]onsideration of what procedures due process may require under any given set of circumstances must begin with a determination of the precise nature of the government function involved as well as of the private interest that has been affected by governmental action. Where it has been possible to characterize that private interest (perhaps in oversimplification) as a mere privilege subject to the Executive's plenary power, it has traditionally been held that notice and hearing are not constitutionally required.

What, then, was the private interest affected by Admiral Tyree's action in the present case? It most assuredly was not the right to follow a chosen trade or profession. Rachel Brawner remained entirely free to obtain employment as a short-order cook or to get any other job, either with M & M or with any other employer. All that was denied her was the opportunity to work at one isolated and specific military installation.

Moreover, the governmental function operating here was not the power to regulate or license, as lawmaker, an entire trade or profession, or to control an entire branch of private business, but, rather, as proprietor, to manage the internal operation of an important federal military establishment. In that proprietary military capacity, the Federal Government, as has been pointed out, has traditionally exercised unfettered control.

. . .

The Court has consistently recognized that an interest closely analogous to Rachel Brawner's, the interest of a government employee in retaining his job, can be summarily denied. It has become a settled principle that government employment, in the absence of legislation, can be revoked at the will of the appointing officer. This principle was reaffirmed quite recently in Vitarelli v. Seaton, 359 U.S. 535. There we pointed out that Vitarelli, an Interior Department employee who had not qualified for statutory protection under the Civil Service Act, "could have been summarily discharged by the Secretary at any time without the giving of a reason. . . . " 359 U.S., at 539.

It is argued that this view of Rachel Brawner's interest is inconsistent with our decisions in United Public Workers v. Mitchell, 330 U.S. 75, and Wieman v. Updegraff, 344 U.S. 183. . . . Those cases demonstrate only that the state and federal governments, even in the exercise of their internal operations, do not constitutionally have the complete freedom of action enjoyed by a private employer. But to acknowledge that there exist constitutional restraints upon state and federal governments in dealing with their employees is not to say that all such employees have a constitutional right to notice and a hearing before they can be removed. We may assume that Rachel Brawner could not constitutionally have been excluded from the Gun Factory if the announced grounds for her exclusion had been patently arbitrary or discriminatory—that she could not have been kept out because she was a Democrat or a Methodist. It does not follow, however, that she was entitled to notice and a hearing when the reason advanced for her exclusion was, as here, entirely rational and in accord with the contract with M & M.

Finally, it is to be noted that this is not a case where government action has operated to bestow a badge of disloyalty or infamy, with an attendant foreclosure from other employment opportunity. See Joint Anti-Fascist Comm. v. McGrath, 341 U.S. 123, 140–141; cf. Bailey v. Richardson, 86 U.S.App.D.C. 248, 182 F.2d 46, aff'd by an equally divided Court, 341 U.S. 918. All this record shows is that, in the opinion of the Security Officer of the Gun Factory, concurred in by the Superintendent, Rachel Brawner failed to meet the particular security requirements of that specific military installation. There is nothing to indicate that this determination would in any way impair Rachel Brawner's employment opportunities anywhere else. As pointed out by Judge Prettyman, speaking for the Court of Appeals, "Nobody has said that Brawner is disloyal or is suspected of the slightest shadow of intentional wrongdoing. 'Security requirements' at such an installation, like such requirements under many other circumstances, cover many matters other than loyalty." For all that appears, the Security Officer and the Superintendent may have simply thought that Rachel Brawner was garrulous, or careless with her identification badge.

For these reasons, we conclude that the Due Process Clause of the Fifth Amendment was not violated in this case.

Affirmed.

MR. JUSTICE BRENNAN, with whom THE CHIEF JUSTICE, MR. JUSTICE BLACK and MR. JUSTICE DOUGLAS join, dissenting.

. . .

I read the Court's opinion to acknowledge that petitioner's status as an employee at the Gun Factory was an interest of sufficient definiteness to be protected by the Federal Constitution from some kinds of governmental injury. . . . In other words, if petitioner Brawner's badge had been lifted avowedly on grounds of her race, religion, or political opinions the Court would concede that some constitutionally protected interest—whether "liberty" or "property" it is unnecessary to state—had been injured. But, as the Court says, there has been no such open discrimination here. The expressed ground of exclusion was the obscuring formulation that petitioner failed to meet the "security requirements" of the naval installation where she worked. I assume for present purposes that separation as a "security risk," if the charge is properly established, is not unconstitutional. But the Court goes beyond that. It holds that the mere assertion by government that exclusion is for a valid reason forecloses further inquiry. That is, unless the government official is foolish enough to admit what he is doing—and few will be so foolish after today's decision—he may employ "security requirements" as a blind behind which to dismiss at will for the most discriminatory of causes.

Such a result in effect nullifies the substantive right—not to be arbitrarily injured by Government—which the Court purports to recognize. What sort of right is it which enjoys absolutely no procedural protection? I do not mean to imply that petitioner could not have been excluded from the installation without the full procedural panoply of first having been subjected to a trial, with cross-examination and confrontation of accusers, and proof of guilt beyond a reasonable doubt. I need not go so far in this case. For under today's holding petitioner is entitled to no process at all. She is not told what she did wrong; she is not given a chance to defend herself. She may be the victim of the basest calumny, perhaps even the caprice of the government officials in whose power her status rested completely. In such a case, I cannot believe that she is not entitled to some procedures. "[T]he right to be heard before being condemned to suffer grievous loss of any kind, even though it may not involve the stigma and hardships of a criminal conviction, is a principle basic to our society." Joint Anti-Fascist Refugee Comm. v. McGrath, 341 U.S. 123, 168 (1951) (concurring opinion.) . . .

One further circumstance makes this particularly a case where procedural requirements of fairness are essential. Petitioner was not simply excluded from the base summarily, without a notice and chance to defend herself. She was excluded as a "security risk," that designation most odious in our times. The Court consoles itself with the speculation that she may have been merely garrulous, or careless with her identification badge, and indeed she might, although she will never find out. But, in the common understanding of the public with whom petitioner must hereafter live and work, the term "security risk" carries a much more sinister meaning. . . .

It may be, of course, that petitioner was justly excluded from the Gun Factory. But, in my view, it is fundamentally unfair, and therefore violative of the Due Process Clause of the Fifth Amendment, to deprive her of a valuable relationship so summarily.

NOTE

In DIXON v. ALABAMA STATE BOARD OF HIGHER EDUCATION, 294 F.2d 150 (5 Cir., 1961), cert. denied 368 U.S. 930 (1961), the issue was "whether due process requires notice and some opportunity for hearing before students at a tax-supported college are expelled for misconduct." In a case growing out of expulsions which had followed various sit-ins and demonstrations, and decided shortly after Cafeteria Workers, the

Fifth Circuit, 2–1, said it does. Cafeteria Workers was relied on in order to establish the importance of looking at both the private interest at stake and the governmental power being exercised, and in order to downplay the significance of the proposition that the right to attend a public college is not in itself a constitutional right. But Cafeteria Workers was distinguished as "a case where the governmental power was almost absolute and the private interest was slight." Here, "the precise nature of the private interest involved . . . is the right to remain at a public institution of higher learning in which the plaintiffs were students in good standing. It requires no argument to demonstrate that education is vital and, indeed, basic to civilized society." On the other side, "[i]n the disciplining of college students there are no considerations of immediate danger to the public, or of peril to the national security, which should prevent the [defendant] from exercising at least the fundamental principles of fairness by giving the accused students notice of the charges and an opportunity to be heard in their own defense." A "full-dress judicial hearing, with the right to cross-examine witnesses" was not, however, required.

SECTION 2.   THE EXPLOSION

GOLDBERG v. KELLY
Supreme Court of the United States, 1970.
397 U.S. 254.

Mr. Justice Brennan delivered the opinion of the Court.

The question for decision is whether a State that terminates public assistance payments to a particular recipient without affording him the opportunity for an evidentiary hearing prior to termination denies the recipient procedural due process in violation of the Due Process Clause of the Fourteenth Amendment.

This action was brought in the District Court for the Southern District of New York by residents of New York City receiving financial aid under the federally assisted program of Aid to Families with Dependent Children (AFDC) or under New York State's general Home Relief program.[1] Their complaint alleged that the New York State and New York City officials administering these programs terminated, or were about to terminate, such aid without prior notice and hearing, thereby denying them due process of law.[2] At the time the suits were

---

1. AFDC was established by the Social Security Act of 1935. It is a categorical assistance program supported by federal grants-in-aid but administered by the States according to regulations of the Secretary of Health, Education, and Welfare.

Home Relief is a general assistance program financed and administered solely by New York state and local governments. . . . .

2. Two suits were brought and consolidated in the District Court. The named plaintiffs were 20 in number, including intervenors. Fourteen had been or were about to be cut off from AFDC, and six

from Home Relief. During the course of this litigation most, though not all, of the plaintiffs either received a "fair hearing" or were restored to the rolls without a hearing. However, even in many of the cases where payments have been resumed, the underlying questions of eligibility that resulted in the bringing of this suit have not been resolved. For example, Mrs. Altagracia Guzman alleged that she was in danger of losing AFDC payments for failure to cooperate with the City Department of Social Services in suing her estranged husband. She contended that the departmental policy requiring such cooperation

filed there was no requirement of prior notice or hearing of any kind before termination of financial aid. However, the State and city adopted procedures for notice and hearing after the suits were brought, and the plaintiffs, appellees here, then challenged the constitutional adequacy of those procedures.

The State Commissioner of Social Services amended the State Department of Social Services' Official Regulations to require that local social services officials proposing to discontinue or suspend a recipient's financial aid do so according to a procedure that conforms to either subdivision (a) or subdivision (b) of § 351.26 of the regulations as amended. . . .

Pursuant to subdivision (b), the New York City Department of Social Services promulgated Procedure No. 68–18. A caseworker who has doubts about the recipient's continued eligibility must first discuss them with the recipient. If the caseworker concludes that the recipient is no longer eligible, he recommends termination of aid to a unit supervisor. If the latter concurs, he sends the recipient a letter stating the reasons for proposing to terminate aid and notifying him that within seven days he may request that a higher official review the record, and may support the request with a written statement prepared personally or with the aid of an attorney or other person. If the reviewing official affirms the determination of ineligibility, aid is stopped immediately and the recipient is informed by letter of the reasons for the action. Appellees' challenge to this procedure emphasizes the absence of any provisions for the personal appearance of the recipient before the reviewing official, for oral presentation of evidence, and for confrontation and cross-examination of adverse witnesses. However, the letter does inform the recipient that he may request a post-termination "fair hearing." [3] This is a proceeding before an independent state hearing officer at which the recipient may appear personally, offer oral evidence, confront and cross-examine the witnesses against him, and have a record made of the hearing. If the recipient prevails at the "fair hearing" he is paid all funds erroneously withheld. A recipient whose aid is not restored by a "fair hearing" decision may have judicial review. The recipient is so notified.

I

The constitutional issue to be decided, therefore, is the narrow one whether the Due Process Clause requires that the recipient be afforded an evidentiary hearing *before* the termination of benefits. The District

was inapplicable to the facts of her case. The record shows that payments to Mrs. Guzman have not been terminated, but there is no indication that the basic dispute over her duty to cooperate has been resolved, or that the alleged danger of termination payments has been removed. Home Relief payments to Juan DeJesus were terminated because he refused to accept counseling and rehabilitation for drug addiction. Mr. DeJesus maintains that he does not use drugs. His payments were restored the day after his complaint was filed. But there is nothing in the record to indicate that the underlying factual dispute in his case has been settled. . . .

3. . . . In both AFDC and Home Relief the "fair hearing" must be held within 10 working days of the request, with decision within 12 working days thereafter. It was conceded in oral argument that these time limits are not in fact observed.

Court held that only a pre-termination evidentiary hearing would satisfy the constitutional command, and rejected the argument of the state and city officials that the combination of the post-termination "fair hearing" with the informal pre-termination review disposed of all due process claims. The court said: "While post-termination review is relevant, there is one overpowering fact which controls here. By hypothesis, a welfare recipient is destitute, without funds or assets. . . . Suffice it to say that to cut off a welfare recipient in the face of . . . 'brutal need' without a prior hearing of some sort is unconscionable, unless overwhelming considerations justify it." Kelly v. Wyman, 294 F.Supp. 893, 899, 900 (1968). The court rejected the argument that the need to protect the public's tax revenues supplied the requisite "overwhelming consideration." . . . Although state officials were party defendants in the action, only the Commissioner of Social Services of the City of New York appealed. . . . We affirm.

Appellant does not contend that procedural due process is not applicable to the termination of welfare benefits. Such benefits are a matter of statutory entitlement for persons qualified to receive them.[4] Their termination involves state action that adjudicates important rights. The constitutional challenge cannot be answered by an argument that public assistance benefits are "a 'privilege' and not a 'right.'" Shapiro v. Thompson, 394 U.S. 618, 627 n. 6 (1969). Relevant constitutional restraints apply as much to the withdrawal of public assistance benefits as to disqualification for unemployment compensation, Sherbert v. Verner, 374 U.S. 398 (1963); or to denial of a tax exemption, Speiser v. Randall, 357 U.S. 513 (1958); or to discharge from public employment, Slochower v. Board of Higher Education, 350 U.S. 551 (1956).[5] The extent to which procedural due process must be afforded the recipient is influenced by the extent to which he may be "condemned to suffer grievous loss," Joint Anti-Fascist Refugee Committee v. McGrath, 341 U.S. 123, 168 (1951) (Frankfurter, J., concurring), and depends upon whether the recipient's interest in avoiding that loss outweighs the governmental interest in summary adjudica-

---

4. It may be realistic today to regard welfare entitlements as more like "property" than a "gratuity." Much of the existing wealth in this country takes the form of rights that do not fall within traditional common-law concepts of property. It has been aptly noted that

"[s]ociety today is built around entitlement. The automobile dealer has his franchise, the doctor and lawyer their professional licenses, the worker his union membership, contract, and pension rights, the executive his contract and stock options; all are devices to aid security and independence. Many of the most important of these entitlements now flow from government: subsidies to farmers and businessmen, routes for airlines and channels for television stations; long term contracts for defense, space, and education; social security pensions for individuals. Such

sources of security, whether private or public, are no longer regarded as luxuries or gratuities; to the recipients they are essentials, fully deserved, and in no sense a form of charity. It is only the poor whose entitlements, although recognized by public policy, have not been effectively enforced." Reich, Individual Rights and Social Welfare: The Emerging Legal Issues, 74 Yale L.J. 1245, 1255 (1965). See also Reich, The New Property, 73 Yale L.J. 733 (1964).

5. See also Goldsmith v. United States Board of Tax Appeals, 270 U.S. 117 (1926) (right of a certified public accountant to practice before the Board of Tax Appeals); Hornsby v. Allen, 326 F.2d 605 (C.A. 5th Cir.1964) (right to obtain a retail liquor store license); Dixon v. Alabama State Board of Education, 294 F.2d 150 (C.A. 5th Cir.), cert. denied, 368 U.S. 930 (1961) (right to attend a public college).

tion. Accordingly, as we said in Cafeteria & Restaurant Workers Union v. McElroy, 367 U.S. 886, 895 (1961), "consideration of what procedures due process may require under any given set of circumstances must begin with a determination of the precise nature of the government function involved as well as of the private interest that has been affected by governmental action."

It is true, of course, that some governmental benefits may be administratively terminated without affording the recipient a pre-termination evidentiary hearing.[6] But we agree with the District Court that when welfare is discontinued, only a pre-termination evidentiary hearing provides the recipient with procedural due process. For qualified recipients, welfare provides the means to obtain essential food, clothing, housing, and medical care. Thus the crucial factor in this context—a factor not present in the case of the blacklisted government contractor, the discharged government employee, the taxpayer denied a tax exemption, or virtually anyone else whose governmental entitlements are ended—is that termination of aid pending resolution of a controversy over eligibility may deprive an *eligible* recipient of the very means by which to live while he waits. Since he lacks independent resources, his situation becomes immediately desperate. His need to concentrate upon finding the means for daily subsistence, in turn, adversely affects his ability to seek redress from the welfare bureaucracy.

Moreover, important governmental interests are promoted by affording recipients a pre-termination evidentiary hearing. From its founding the Nation's basic commitment has been to foster the dignity and well-being of all persons within its borders. We have come to recognize that forces not within the control of the poor contribute to their poverty. This perception, against the background of our traditions, has significantly influenced the development of the contemporary public assistance system. Welfare, by meeting the basic demands of subsistence, can help bring within the reach of the poor the same opportunities that are available to others to participate meaningfully in the life of the community. At the same time, welfare guards against the societal malaise that may flow from a widespread sense of unjustified frustration and insecurity. Public assistance, then, is not mere charity, but a means to "promote the general Welfare, and secure the Blessings of Liberty to ourselves and our Posterity." The same governmental interests that counsel the provision of welfare, counsel as well

---

6. One Court of Appeals has stated: "In a wide variety of situations, it has long been recognized that where harm to the public is threatened, and the private interest infringed is reasonably deemed to be of less importance, an official body can take summary action pending a later hearing." R.A. Holman & Co. v. SEC, 112 U.S.App. D.C. 43, 47, 299 F.2d 127, 131, cert. denied, 370 U.S. 911 (1962) (suspension of exemption from stock registration requirement). See also, for example, Ewing v. Mytinger & Casselberry, Inc., 339 U.S. 594 (1950) (seizure of mislabeled vitamin product); North American Cold Storage Co. v. Chicago, 211 U.S. 306 (1908) (seizure of food not fit for human use). . . . In Cafeteria & Restaurant Workers Union v. McElroy, [367 U.S. 886, 896 (1961)] summary dismissal of a public employee was upheld because "[i]n [its] proprietary military capacity, the Federal Government . . . has traditionally exercised unfettered control," and because the case involved the Government's "dispatch of its own internal affairs."

its uninterrupted provision to those eligible to receive it; pre-termination evidentiary hearings are indispensable to that end.

Appellant does not challenge the force of these considerations but argues that they are outweighed by countervailing governmental interests in conserving fiscal and administrative resources. These interests, the argument goes, justify the delay of any evidentiary hearing until after discontinuance of the grants. Summary adjudication protects the public fisc by stopping payments promptly upon discovery of reason to believe that a recipient is no longer eligible. Since most terminations are accepted without challenge, summary adjudication also conserves both the fisc and administrative time and energy by reducing the number of evidentiary hearings actually held.

We agree with the District Court, however, that these governmental interests are not overriding in the welfare context. The requirement of a prior hearing doubtless involves some greater expense, and the benefits paid to ineligible recipients pending decision at the hearing probably cannot be recouped, since these recipients are likely to be judgment-proof. But the State is not without weapons to minimize these increased costs. Much of the drain on fiscal and administrative resources can be reduced by developing procedures for prompt pre-termination hearings and by skillful use of personnel and facilities. Indeed, the very provision for a post-termination evidentiary hearing in New York's Home Relief program is itself cogent evidence that the State recognizes the primacy of the public interest in correct eligibility determinations and therefore in the provision of procedural safeguards. Thus, the interest of the eligible recipient in uninterrupted receipt of public assistance, coupled with the State's interest that his payments not be erroneously terminated, clearly outweighs the State's competing concern to prevent any increase in its fiscal and administrative burdens. As the District Court correctly concluded, "[t]he stakes are simply too high for the welfare recipient, and the possibility for honest error or irritable misjudgment too great, to allow termination of aid without giving the recipient a chance, if he so desires, to be fully informed of the case against him so that he may contest its basis and produce evidence in rebuttal." 294 F.Supp., at 904–905.

II

We also agree with the District Court, however, that the pre-termination hearing need not take the form of a judicial or quasi-judicial trial. We bear in mind that the statutory "fair hearing" will provide the recipient with a full administrative review.[7] Accordingly, the pre-termination hearing has one function only: to produce an initial determination of the validity of the welfare department's grounds for discontinuance of payments in order to protect a recipient against an erroneous termination of his benefits. Thus, a complete record and a comprehensive opinion, which would serve primarily to

---

7. Due process does not, of course, require two hearings. If, for example, a State simply wishes to continue benefits until after a "fair" hearing there will be no need for a preliminary hearing.

facilitate judicial review and to guide future decisions, need not be provided at the pre-termination stage. We recognize, too, that both welfare authorities and recipients have an interest in relatively speedy resolution of questions of eligibility, that they are used to dealing with one another informally, and that some welfare departments have very burdensome caseloads. These considerations justify the limitation of the pre-termination hearing to minimum procedural safeguards, adapted to the particular characteristics of welfare recipients, and to the limited nature of the controversies to be resolved. We wish to add that we, no less than the dissenters, recognize the importance of not imposing upon the States or the Federal Government in this developing field of law any procedural requirements beyond those demanded by rudimentary due process.

"The fundamental requisite of due process of law is the opportunity to be heard." Grannis v. Ordean, 234 U.S. 385, 394 (1914). The hearing must be "at a meaningful time and in a meaningful manner." Armstrong v. Manzo, 380 U.S. 545, 552 (1965). In the present context these principles require that a recipient have timely and adequate notice detailing the reasons for a proposed termination, and an effective opportunity to defend by confronting any adverse witnesses and by presenting his own arguments and evidence orally. These rights are important in cases such as those before us, where recipients have challenged proposed terminations as resting on incorrect or misleading factual premises or on misapplication of rules or policies to the facts of particular cases.[8]

We are not prepared to say that the seven-day notice currently provided by New York City is constitutionally insufficient per se, although there may be cases where fairness would require that a longer time be given. Nor do we see any constitutional deficiency in the content or form of the notice. New York employs both a letter and a personal conference with a caseworker to inform a recipient of the precise questions raised about his continued eligibility. Evidently the recipient is told the legal and factual bases for the Department's doubts. This combination is probably the most effective method of communicating with recipients.

The city's procedures presently do not permit recipients to appear personally with or without counsel before the official who finally determines continued eligibility. Thus a recipient is not permitted to present evidence to that official orally, or to confront or cross-examine adverse witnesses. These omissions are fatal to the constitutional adequacy of the procedures.

The opportunity to be heard must be tailored to the capacities and circumstances of those who are to be heard. It is not enough that a welfare recipient may present his position to the decision maker in writing or secondhand through his caseworker. Written submissions

---

8. This case presents no question requiring our determination whether due process requires only an opportunity for written submission, or an opportunity both for written submission and oral argument, where there are no factual issues in dispute or where the application of the rule of law is not intertwined with factual issues. See FCC v. WJR, 337 U.S. 265, 275–277 (1949).

are an unrealistic option for most recipients, who lack the educational attainment necessary to write effectively and who cannot obtain professional assistance. Moreover, written submissions do not afford the flexibility of oral presentations; they do not permit the recipient to mold his argument to the issues the decision maker appears to regard as important. Particularly where credibility and veracity are at issue, as they must be in many termination proceedings, written submissions are a wholly unsatisfactory basis for decision. The secondhand presentation to the decisionmaker by the caseworker has its own deficiencies; since the caseworker usually gathers the facts upon which the charge of ineligibility rests, the presentation of the recipient's side of the controversy cannot safely be left to him. Therefore a recipient must be allowed to state his position orally. Informal procedures will suffice; in this context due process does not require a particular order of proof or mode of offering evidence.

In almost every setting where important decisions turn on questions of fact, due process requires an opportunity to confront and cross-examine adverse witnesses. What we said in Greene v. McElroy, 360 U.S. 474, 496–497 (1959), is particularly pertinent here:

"Certain principles have remained relatively immutable in our jurisprudence. One of these is that where governmental action seriously injures an individual, and the reasonableness of the action depends on fact findings, the evidence used to prove the Government's case must be disclosed to the individual so that he has an opportunity to show that it is untrue. While this is important in the case of documentary evidence, it is even more important where the evidence consists of the testimony of individuals whose memory might be faulty or who, in fact, might be perjurers or persons motivated by malice, vindictiveness, intolerance, prejudice, or jealousy. . . . "

Welfare recipients must therefore be given an opportunity to confront and cross-examine the witnesses relied on by the department.

"The right to be heard would be, in many cases, of little avail if it did not comprehend the right to be heard by counsel." Powell v. Alabama, 287 U.S. 45, 68–69 (1932). We do not say that counsel must be provided at the pre-termination hearing, but only that the recipient must be allowed to retain an attorney if he so desires. Counsel can help delineate the issues, present the factual contentions in an orderly manner, conduct cross-examination, and generally safeguard the interests of the recipient. We do not anticipate that this assistance will unduly prolong or otherwise encumber the hearing. . . .

Finally, the decisionmaker's conclusion as to a recipient's eligibility must rest solely on the legal rules and evidence adduced at the hearing. To demonstrate compliance with this elementary requirement, the decision maker should state the reasons for his determination and indicate the evidence he relied on, though his statement need not amount to a full opinion or even formal findings of fact and conclusions of law. And, of course, an impartial decision maker is essential. We agree with the District Court that prior involvement in some aspects of a case will not necessarily bar a welfare official from acting as a decision maker. He should not, however, have participated in making the determination under review.

Affirmed.

MR. JUSTICE BLACK, dissenting.

. . .

The more than a million names on the relief rolls in New York, and the more than nine million names on the rolls of all the 50 States were not put there at random. The names are there because state welfare officials believed that those people were eligible for assistance. Probably in the officials' haste to make out the lists many names were put there erroneously in order to alleviate immediate suffering, and undoubtedly some people are drawing relief who are not entitled under the law to do so. Doubtless some draw relief checks from time to time who know they are not eligible, either because they are not actually in need or for some other reason. Many of those who thus draw undeserved gratuities are without sufficient property to enable the government to collect back from them any money they wrongfully receive. But the Court today holds that it would violate the Due Process Clause of the Fourteenth Amendment to stop paying those people weekly or monthly allowances unless the government first affords them a full "evidentiary hearing" even though welfare officials are persuaded that the recipients are not rightfully entitled to receive a penny under the law. In other words, although some recipients might be on the lists for payment wholly because of deliberate fraud on their part, the Court holds that the government is helpless and must continue, until after an evidentiary hearing, to pay money that it does not owe, never has owed, and never could owe. I do not believe there is any provision in our Constitution that should thus paralyze the government's efforts to protect itself against making payments to people who are not entitled to them.

. . . The Court, however, relies upon the Fourteenth Amendment and in effect says that failure of the government to pay a promised charitable instalment to an individual deprives that individual of *his own property*, in violation of the Due Process Clause of the Fourteenth Amendment. It somewhat strains credulity to say that the government's promise of charity to an individual is property belonging to that individual when the government denies that the individual is honestly entitled to receive such a payment.

. . . Although the majority attempts to bolster its decision with limited quotations from prior cases, it is obvious that today's result does not depend on the language of the Constitution itself or the principles of other decisions, but solely on the collective judgment of the majority as to what would be a fair and humane procedure in this case.

This decision is thus only another variant of the view often expressed by some members of this Court that the Due Process Clause forbids any conduct that a majority of the Court believes "unfair," "indecent," or "shocking to their consciences." See, e.g., Rochin v. California, 342 U.S. 165, 172 (1952). Neither these words nor any like them appear anywhere in the Due Process Clause.

. . . The procedure required today as a matter of constitutional law finds no precedent in our legal system. Reduced to its simplest terms, the problem in this case is similar to that frequently encountered when two parties have an ongoing legal relationship that requires one party to make periodic payments to the other. Often the situation arises where the party "owing" the money stops paying it and justifies his conduct by arguing that the recipient is not legally entitled to payment. The recipient can, of course, disagree and go to court to compel payment. But I know of no situation in our legal system in which the person alleged to owe money to another is required by law to continue making payments to a judgment-proof claimant without the benefit of any security or bond to insure that these payments can be recovered if he wins his legal argument. . . .

The Court apparently feels that this decision will benefit the poor and needy. In my judgment the eventual result will be just the opposite. While today's decision requires only an administrative, evidentiary hearing, the inevitable logic of the approach taken will lead to constitutionally imposed, time-consuming delays of a full adversary process of administrative and judicial review. In the next case the welfare recipients are bound to argue that cutting off benefits before judicial review of the agency's decision is also a denial of due process. Since, by hypothesis, termination of aid at that point may still "deprive an *eligible* recipient of the very means by which to live while he waits," I would be surprised if the weighing process did not compel the conclusion that termination without full judicial review would be unconscionable. After all, at each step, as the majority seems to feel, the issue is only one of weighing the government's pocketbook against the actual survival of the recipient, and surely that balance must always tip in favor of the individual. . . . [T]he inevitable result of such a constitutionally imposed burden will be that the government will not put a claimant on the rolls initially until it has made an exhaustive investigation to determine his eligibility. While this Court will perhaps have insured that no needy person will be taken off the rolls without a full "due process" proceeding, it will also have insured that many will never get on the rolls, or at least that they will remain destitute during the lengthy proceedings followed to determine initial eligibility.

For the foregoing reasons I dissent from the Court's holding. The operation of a welfare state is a new experiment for our Nation. For this reason, among others, I feel that new experiments in carrying out a welfare program should not be frozen into our constitutional structure. They should be left, as are other legislative determinations, to the Congress and the legislatures that the people elect to make our laws.

[Wheeler v. Montgomery, 397 U.S. 280 (1970), a companion case involving the validity of California welfare termination procedures, was decided on the basis of Goldberg. Chief Justice Burger, joined by Justice Black, wrote a dissenting opinion applicable to both Goldberg and Wheeler. Although agreeing "in large part with Mr. Justice Black's views," the Chief Justice added: (1) Since HEW has recently adopted new procedural regulations which "go far beyond the result reached today," the Court should "hold the heavy hand of constitutional adjudication and allow evolutionary" administrative experimentation. (2) "[N]ew layers of procedural protection may become an intolerable drain on the very funds earmarked for food, clothing, and other living essentials."

Justice Stewart dissented in a brief opinion: "Although the question is for me a close one, I do not believe that the procedures that New York and California now follow in terminating welfare payments are violative of the United States Constitution. See Cafeteria & Restaurant Workers Union v. McElroy, 367 U.S. 886, 894–897."]

NOTES

(1) Speaking in 1975, the late Judge Henry Friendly said that since Goldberg "we have witnessed a due process explosion in which the Court has carried the hearing requirement from one new area of government action to another. . . . [I]ndeed, we have witnessed a greater expansion of procedural due process in the last five years than in the entire period since ratification of the Constitution." H. Friendly, "Some Kind of Hearing," 123 U.Pa.L.Rev. 1267, 1268, 1273 (1975). Writing 10 years later, Professor Jerry Mashaw made roughly the same point. Using LEXIS and WESTLAW data bases, he concluded that "federal court complaints of procedural due process deprivation in the 1970's showed a 350 percent increase over the 1960's. The increase in litigation of all kinds was only 70 percent. Procedural due process cases were increasing five times as fast as litigation generally." J. Mashaw, Due Process in the Administrative State 9–10 (1985). However, he also noted: "[J]ust looking at the numbers the Supreme Court seems to be attempting to dampen plaintiffs' enthusiasm. From 1970 to 1975 the Court ruled favorably on administrative due process claims 56 percent of the time. From 1976 to 1982 that percentage was cut almost exactly in half to 29 percent." Id. at 30, n. 80.

(2) Footnote 4 in the above-edited Goldberg opinion quotes from an article by Charles Reich, and makes reference to his famous earlier work, "THE NEW PROPERTY," 73 Yale L.J. 733 (1964). Here are some excerpts from that work:

". . . [P]roperty performs the function of maintaining independence, dignity and pluralism in society by creating zones within which the majority has to yield to the owner. Whim, caprice, irrationality and 'antisocial' activities are given the protection of law; the owner may do what all or most of his neighbors decry. The Bill of Rights also serves this function, but while the Bill of Rights comes into play only at extraordinary moments of conflict or crisis, property affords day-to-day protection in the ordinary affairs of life. Indeed, in the final analysis the Bill of Rights depends upon the existence of private property. Political rights presuppose that individuals and private groups have the will and the means to act independently. But so long as individuals are motivated largely by self-interest, their well-being must first be independent. Civil liberties must have a basis in property, or bills of rights will not preserve them. . . .

"Because it is so hard to confine relevance and discretion, procedure offers a valuable means for restraining arbitrary action. This was recognized in the strong procedural emphasis of the Bill of Rights, and it is being recognized in the increasingly procedural emphasis of administrative law. The law of government largess has developed with little regard for procedure. Reversal of this trend is long overdue. . . .

"Finally, it must be recognized that we are becoming a society based upon relationship and status—status deriving primarily from source of livelihood. Status is so closely linked to personality that destruction of one may well destroy the other. Status must therefore be surrounded with the kind of safeguards once reserved for personality. Eventually those forms of largess which are closely linked to status must be deemed to be held as of right." Id. at 771, 783, 785.

Could the plaintiffs' success in Goldberg be seen as congruent not only with a "new property" but also with the last half-century's developments in contract law—in particular, with the increasing recognition that serious and foreseeable reliance will bind what would under traditional doctrine be considered merely a gratuitous, and therefore unenforceable, promise? Or is the search for common-law analogues for positive claims against the government misleading?

(3) As the dissenters emphasize, the decision in Goldberg v. Kelly has to mesh not only with legal concepts but also with practical realities. Consider the following excerpts:

(a) DANIEL J. BAUM, THE WELFARE FAMILY AND MASS ADMINISTRATIVE JUSTICE 36–40, 50–51 (1974):[†] "Consider the enormity in sheer volume of [the] task in a city such as New York. There are approximately 1.5 million persons dependent on categorical aids in the state of New York. Most of these fall within AFDC, and most of the recipients, a total of 1.2 million, are resident in New York City. On a monthly average in the city, about 20,000 AFDC cases are terminated, and another 20,000 are reduced. To handle this flow, the city Human Resources Administration employs an income maintenance staff of 2,500 and another 500 supervisors. And, said the unit head of that staff, 'there are always between 150 and 200 vacancies which we are now trying to fill as fast as we can'. . . .

"[W]ithout in any way imputing bad intent on the part of the city Human Resources Administration, there is no small question as to whether that agency can comply with the Court's order and the HEW regulations concerning advance notice. . . . 12,000 notices of intent to reduce or terminate benefits are sent monthly. This figure must be contrasted with the monthly terminations numbering 20,000 plus the monthly reductions numbering 20,000. It is true that notice need not be sent under certain very limited conditions. It is at least questionable whether those conditions justifying not sending notices existed in all or most of the 28,000 monthly cases (i.e., the difference between 12,000 and 40,000).

"At the problem's root are the difficulties raised by a high volume of cases and quality and quantity of staff. Centralization with a pyramid structure for review will backlog work. Decentralization, even with a mobile review staff, makes it hard for orders and policies to be passed down, received, understood, and acted upon. Moreover, there is the added difficulty of institutional motivation. To some extent the incentives operating upon a welfare agency are not geared to maximizing recipient benefits. Often they are geared, even as official policy, toward effecting welfare savings, sometimes articulated as 'taking the cheaters off of the rolls'. In such a setting one can safely say that there may be absolute disincentives operating on eligibility technicians, income maintenance specialists, and their supervisors to give an overly high priority in providing recipients advance notice of benefit reduction or termination. . . .

"For New York, as for every other state, the hearings are state, not local, proceedings. . . . In New York City, fair hearings are held at the massive World Trade Center. . . . The hearings are scheduled at half-hour intervals, but rarely does the examiner meet the schedule. Usually all hearings docketed for 2 p.m. are carried over to the next day. The result tends to bring a police court environment; a sense of hurry pervades the hearings. Claimants certainly are not made to feel that an informal process has been designed to provide for a full, relaxed opportunity to present their case. Nor is the city pleased. It is pressured to prepare its case on short notice. Then it is faced with delay and lost manpower because of the wait to be heard.

"At the hearing itself the examiner takes notes. These, together with a proposed decision, are sent to a fair hearing unit within the state welfare department. There the decision is reviewed and often rewritten to comport with one of numerous forms developed by the state.

"The decision itself is to be rendered within 60 days following request for a fair hearing. Based upon the sheer volume of litigation, it is not surprising that decision time lags somewhat behind that 60-day deadline. In the interim, of course, the city must continue to pay benefits. . . .

"Fair hearings . . . presently cover all categorical aid programs and medical assistance. AFDC accounted for the largest number of requests for hearings, 44.1 percent; the adult categories accounted for 47.5 percent; and medical assistance for 8.4 percent. Requests for hearings did not always result in fair hearings taking place. Twelve states, including California and New York, reported that *more than one-half* of their hearing requests were disposed of without a formal hearing. The nature of that disposition generally, and by a considerable margin, was not in favor of the claimant. Indeed, where the matter was disposed of without hearing, the largest category was that of 'request withdrawn', though this did not always mean a decision against the claimant. Where the matter went to hearing the claimant generally, and by a considerable margin, lost. The hearing decision ratio on a national basis for the reporting period January-June 1971 was about three to one against the claimant."

(b) JERRY L. MASHAW, DUE PROCESS IN THE ADMINISTRATIVE STATE 33–34 (1985):[†]

"Goldberg required that recipients be provided a relatively full trial-type hearing (timely and specific notice, oral presentation of evidence and cross-examination, a neutral hearing officer, assistance of counsel, and a decision based wholly on the evidence produced at the hearing) before benefits could be terminated. The ruling presented welfare administrators with a significant problem. First, if a substantial percentage of the recipients noticed for termination exercised their appeal rights, the welfare departments would simply be unable to process the cases without a large infusion of funds for administration. Because of the complexity of welfare decision making, adequate preparation of cases to prove the correctness of termination decisions was likely to be quite costly. But the alternative would be even more expensive—leaving substantial numbers of ineligible persons on the rolls.

"These administrative difficulties reinforced a political difficulty. Welfare rolls were already increasing rapidly. State legislators were unwilling to provide more funds either for well-constructed hearings or for welfare benefits. A strategy was needed that would preserve fiscal integrity and produce defensible decisions.

"A number of tactical moves ultimately comprised the grand design. One was to tighten up and slow down the initial eligibility determination process. Another was to generalize and objectify the substantive eligibility criteria so that messy subjective judgments about individual cases would not have to be made and defended. This move led to the realization that professional social welfare workers were no longer needed. Costs could be reduced further by lowering the quality of the staff and by depersonalizing staff-claimant encounters. If these reactions were not sufficient to restore fiscal balance, then payment levels could be reduced or allowed to remain stable in the face of rising prices. A tougher stance was also to be taken with respect to work requirements and prosecution of absent parents. Moreover, because hearings presumably protected the claimants' interests, internal audit procedures were skewed to ignore nonpayment and underpayment problems and concentrate on preventing over-payments and payments to ineligibles.

"If this story of welfare since Goldberg v. Kelly is generally accurate, then the legal reconceptualization of welfare recipients as rights-bearing citizens entitled to quasi-judicial processes for the protection of their rights has had very substantial effects. . . ."

(c) The Goldberg opinion, in a few pages, identifies ten different procedures as minimally required by due process for the programs there considered. The following tables, compiled from P. Verkuil, A Study of Informal Adjudication Procedures, 43 U.Chi.L.Rev. 739 (1976), give

---

the results of a survey, taken a few years later, of forty-two federal programs of various sorts, to determine the extent to which similar procedures were being employed in making *final* "administrative decisions that [were] not governed by statutory procedures, but which nevertheless affect[ed] an individual's rights, obligations or opportunities," id. at 739 n. 1.

TABLE 1

Element of Hearing	Number of programs providing
Timely and adequate notice	40
Confronting adverse witnesses	10
Oral presentation of argument	21
Oral presentation of evidence	12
Cross-examination of adverse witnesses	9
Disclosure of opposing evidence	10
Right to retain and be represented by an attorney	16
Determination on the record	8
Statement of reasons and evidence relied on	37
Impartial decisionmaker	38

TABLE 2

Number of Goldberg rights recognized	10	9	8	7	6	5	4	3	2	1	0
TOTAL	2	5	2	4	1	1	9	13	3		2
Grant programs	2	1					6	8			
Licensing		1	2	3	1	1	1	2			1
Inspection		1							3		1
Planning				1			2	3			
Other		2									

(4) In considering the reach of Justice Black's arguments, one legal issue that has to be faced is whether applicants for benefits (as distinguished from present recipients who are threatened with termination of benefits) are also entitled to some sort of hearing. On the one hand, there are factual issues to be resolved even at the beginning if one wants to make an accurate assessment of entitlement; on the other hand, it is generally thought to be more grievous to take away something someone already has than merely to fail to give it in the first place. In GRIFFETH v. DETRICH, 603 F.2d 118 (9th Cir.1979), the plaintiffs challenged the constitutionality of the procedures used in San Diego County for reviewing applications for general relief. The district court held that applicants for such benefits had no protected interest. The Court of Appeals concluded otherwise, and remanded for a consideration of whether the actual procedures used were "due" or not; its opinion emphasized that under state law the provision of general relief to qualified persons was mandatory and not discretionary. A petition for certiorari was filed, and denied sub nom Peer v. Griffeth, 445 U.S. 970 (1980). Justice Rehnquist dissented from the denial of the

petition, stating that is his view the court below "has taken a significant step in this case to expand the ruling of this Court in Goldberg v. Kelly, 397 U.S. 254 (1970), a step that I believe merits plenary consideration by the full Court." [9] In 1985, in Walters v. National Ass'n of Radiation Survivors, reprinted below at p. 645, the Court, in an opinion by Justice Rehnquist, was careful to note that it has never held that applicants for benefits have procedural due process hearing rights, and that the case before it also did not call for a resolution of the issue. 470 U.S. at ____, n. 8.

(5) As another example of the circa 1970 "due process explosion," consider WISCONSIN v. CONSTANTINEAU, 400 U.S. 433 (1971). The police chief of Hartford, Wisconsin, had a notice posted in all retail liquor stores in the town forbidding sale of liquor to the plaintiff. He acted under a statute authorizing such "posting," without notice or hearing, of any person who "by excessive drinking" produced various results, such as exposing his family to want. Held: the statute was unconstitutional on its face. "Where a person's good name, reputation, honor, or integrity is at stake because of what the government is doing to him, notice and an opportunity to be heard are essential. 'Posting' under the Wisconsin act may to some be merely the mark of illness, to others it is a stigma, an official branding of a person. The label is a degrading one. . . . Only when the whole proceedings leading to the pinning of an unsavory label on a person are aired can oppressive results be prevented."

SECTION 3. THE NEW LEARNING

BOARD OF REGENTS OF STATE COLLEGES v. ROTH
Supreme Court of the United States, 1972.
408 U.S. 564.

MR. JUSTICE STEWART delivered the opinion of the Court.

In 1968 the respondent, David Roth, was hired for his first teaching job as assistant professor of political science at Wisconsin State University-Oshkosh. He was hired for a fixed term of one academic year. The notice of his faculty appointment specified that his employment would begin on September 1, 1968, and would end on June 30, 1969.[1]

9. [Ed.] See also Gregory v. Pittsfield, 470 U.S. 1018 (1985), Justice O'Connor (joined by Justices Brennan and Marshall) dissenting from denial of certiorari: "The conclusion of the Supreme Judicial Court [of Maine] that an applicant for general assistance does not have an interest protected by the Due Process Clause is unsettling in its implication that less fortunate persons in our society may arbitrarily be denied benefits that a state has granted as a matter of right. . . . Although this Court has never addressed the issue whether applicants for general assistance have a protected property interest, see Peer v. Griffeth, 445 U.S. 970 (1980) (Rehnquist, J., dissenting from denial of certiorari), the weight of authority among lower courts is contrary to the conclusion of the Supreme Judicial Court."

1. The respondent had no contract of employment. Rather, his formal notice of appointment was the equivalent of an employment contract.

The notice of his appointment provided that: "David F. Roth is hereby appointed to the faculty of the Wisconsin State University Position number 0262. (Location:) Oshkosh as (Rank:) Assistant Professor of (Department:) Political Science this (Date:) first day of (Month:) September (Year:) 1968." The notice went on to specify that the respondent's "appointment basis" was for the "academic year." And it provided that "[r]egulations governing tenure are in

The respondent completed that term. But he was informed that he would not be rehired for the next academic year.

The respondent had no tenure rights to continued employment. Under Wisconsin statutory law a state university teacher can acquire tenure as a "permanent" employee only after four years of year-to-year employment. Having acquired tenure, a teacher is entitled to continued employment "during efficiency and good behavior." A relatively new teacher without tenure, however, is under Wisconsin law entitled to nothing beyond his one-year appointment. There are no statutory or administrative standards defining eligibility for re-employment. State law thus clearly leaves the decision whether to rehire a nontenured teacher for another year to the unfettered discretion of university officials.

The procedural protection afforded a Wisconsin State University teacher before he is separated from the University corresponds to his job security. As a matter of statutory law, a tenured teacher cannot be "discharged except for cause upon written charges" and pursuant to certain procedures. A nontenured teacher, similarly, is protected to some extent *during* his one-year term. Rules promulgated by the Board of Regents provide that a nontenured teacher "dismissed" before the end of the year may have some opportunity for review of the "dismissal." But the Rules provide no real protection for a nontenured teacher who simply is not re-employed for the next year. He must be informed by February 1 "concerning retention or non-retention for the ensuing year." But "no reason for non-retention need be given. No review or appeal is provided in such case."

In conformance with these Rules, the President of Wisconsin State University-Oshkosh informed the respondent before February 1, 1969, that he would not be rehired for the 1969–1970 academic year. He gave the respondent no reason for the decision and no opportunity to challenge it at any sort of hearing.

The respondent then brought this action in Federal District Court alleging that the decision not to rehire him for the next year infringed his Fourteenth Amendment rights. He attacked the decision both in substance and procedure. First, he alleged that the true reason for the decision was to punish him for certain statements critical of the University administration, and that it therefore violated his right to freedom of speech.[2] Second, he alleged that the failure of University officials to give him notice of any reason for nonretention and an opportunity for a hearing violated his right to procedural due process of law.

accord with Chapter 37.31, Wisconsin Statutes. The employment of any staff member for an academic year shall not be for a term beyond June 30th of the fiscal year in which the appointment is made."

2. While the respondent alleged that he was not rehired because of his exercise of free speech, the petitioners insisted that the non-retention decision was based on other, constitutionally valid grounds. The District Court came to no conclusion whatever regarding the true reason for the University President's decision. "In the present case," it stated, "it appears that a determination as to the actual bases of [the] decision must await amplification of the facts at trial. . . . Summary judgment is inappropriate." 310 F.Supp. 972, 982.

The District Court granted summary judgment for the respondent on the procedural issue, ordering the University officials to provide him with reasons and a hearing. The Court of Appeals, with one judge dissenting, affirmed this partial summary judgment. We granted certiorari. The only question presented to us at this stage in the case is whether the respondent had a constitutional right to a statement of reasons and a hearing on the University's decision not to rehire him for another year. We hold that he did not.

I

The requirements of procedural due process apply only to the deprivation of interests encompassed by the Fourteenth Amendment's protection of liberty and property. When protected interests are implicated, the right to some kind of prior hearing is paramount.[3] But the range of interests protected by procedural due process is not infinite.

The District Court decided that procedural due process guarantees apply in this case by assessing and balancing the weights of the particular interests involved. It concluded that the respondent's interest in re-employment at Wisconsin State University-Oshkosh outweighed the University's interest in denying him re-employment summarily. Undeniably, the respondent's re-employment prospects were of major concern to him—concern that we surely cannot say was insignificant. And a weighing process has long been a part of any determination of the *form* of hearing required in particular situations by procedural due process.[4] But, to determine whether due process requirements apply in the first place, we must look not to the "weight" but to the *nature* of the interest at stake. We must look to see if the interest is within the Fourteenth Amendment's protection of liberty and property.

"Liberty" and "property" are broad and majestic terms. They are among the "[g]reat [constitutional] concepts . . . purposely left to gather meaning from experience. . . . [T]hey relate to the whole domain of social and economic fact, and the statesmen who founded this Nation knew too well that only a stagnant society remains unchanged." National Ins. Co. v. Tidewater Co., 337 U.S. 582, 646 (Frankfurter, J.,

---

3. Before a person is deprived of a protected interest, he must be afforded opportunity for some kind of a hearing, "except for extraordinary situations where some valid governmental interest is at stake that justifies postponing the hearing until after the event." Boddie v. Connecticut, 401 U.S. 371, 379. "While '[m]any controversies have raged about . . . the Due Process Clause,' . . . . it is fundamental that except in emergency situations (and this is not one) due process requires that when a State seeks to terminate [a protected] interest . . . , it must afford 'notice and opportunity for hearing appropriate to the nature of the case' *before* the termination becomes effective." Bell v. Burson, 402 U.S. 535, 542. For the rare and extraordinary situations in which we have held that deprivation of a protected interest need not be preceded by opportunity for some kind of hearing, see, e.g., Central Union Trust Co. v. Garvan, 254 U.S. 554, 566; Phillips v. Commissioner of Internal Revenue, 283 U.S. 589, 597; Ewing v. Mytinger & Casselberry, Inc., 339 U.S. 594.

4. "The formality and procedural requisites for the hearing can vary, depending upon the importance of the interests involved and the nature of the subsequent proceedings." Boddie v. Connecticut, supra, at 378. See, e.g., Goldberg v. Kelly, 397 U.S. 254, 263; Hannah v. Larche, 363 U.S. 420. The constitutional requirement of opportunity for *some* form of hearing before deprivation of a protected interest, of course, does not depend upon such a narrow balancing process.

dissenting). For that reason, the Court has fully and finally rejected the wooden distinction between "rights" and "privileges" that once seemed to govern the applicability of procedural due process rights.[5] The Court has also made clear that the property interests protected by procedural due process extend well beyond actual ownership of real estate, chattels, or money. By the same token, the Court has required due process protection for deprivations of liberty beyond the sort of formal constraints imposed by the criminal process.

Yet, while the Court has eschewed rigid or formalistic limitations on the protection of procedural due process, it has at the same time observed certain boundaries. For the words "liberty" and "property" in the Due Process Clause of the Fourteenth Amendment must be given some meaning.

II

"While this Court has not attempted to define with exactness the liberty . . . guaranteed [by the Fourteenth Amendment], the term has received much consideration and some of the included things have been definitely stated. Without doubt, it denotes not merely freedom from bodily restraint but also the right of the individual to contract, to engage in any of the common occupations of life, to acquire useful knowledge, to marry, establish a home and bring up children, to worship God according to the dictates of his own conscience, and generally to enjoy those privileges long recognized . . . as essential to the orderly pursuit of happiness by free men." Meyer v. Nebraska, 262 U.S. 390, 399. In a Constitution for a free people, there can be no doubt that the meaning of "liberty" must be broad indeed.

There might be cases in which a State refused to re-employ a person under such circumstances that interests in liberty would be implicated. But this is not such a case.

The State, in declining to rehire the respondent, did not make any charge against him that might seriously damage his standing and associations in his community. It did not base the nonrenewal of his contract on a charge, for example, that he had been guilty of dishonesty, or immorality. Had it done so, this would be a different case. For "[w]here a person's good name, reputation, honor, or integrity is at stake because of what the government is doing to him, notice and an opportunity to be heard are essential." Wisconsin v. Constantineau, 400 U.S. 433, 437 . . . . See Cafeteria Workers v. McElroy, 367 U.S. 886, 898. In such a case, due process would accord an opportunity to refute the charge before University officials.[6] In the present case,

---

5. In a leading case decided many years ago, the Court of Appeals for the District of Columbia Circuit held that public employment in general was a "privilege," not a "right," and that procedural due process guarantees therefore were inapplicable. Bailey v. Richardson, 86 U.S.App.D.C. 248, 182 F.2d 46, aff'd by an equally divided Court, 341 U.S. 918. The basis of this holding has been thoroughly undermined in the ensuing years. For, as Mr. Justice Blackmun wrote for the Court only last year, "this Court now has rejected the concept that constitutional rights turn upon whether a governmental benefit is characterized as a 'right' or as a 'privilege.'" Graham v. Richardson, 403 U.S. 365, 374.

6. The purpose of such notice and hearing is to provide the person an opportunity

however, there is no suggestion whatever that the respondent's "good name, reputation, honor, or integrity" is at stake.

Similarly, there is no suggestion that the State, in declining to re-employ the respondent, imposed on him a stigma or other disability that foreclosed his freedom to take advantage of other employment opportunities. The State, for example, did not invoke any regulations to bar the respondent from all other public employment in state universities. Had it done so, this, again, would be a different case. For "[t]o be deprived not only of present government employment but of future opportunity for it certainly is no small injury . . . ." Joint Anti-Fascist Refugee Committee v. McGrath, supra, at 185 (Jackson, J., concurring). The Court has held, for example, that a State, in regulating eligibility for a type of professional employment, cannot foreclose a range of opportunities "in a manner . . . that contravene[s] . . . Due Process," Schware v. Board of Bar Examiners, 353 U.S. 232, 238, and, specifically, in a manner that denies the right to a full prior hearing. Willner v. Committee on Character, 373 U.S. 96, 103. See Cafeteria Workers v. McElroy, supra, at 898. In the present case, however, this principle does not come into play.[7]

To be sure, the respondent has alleged that the nonrenewal of his contract was based on his exercise of his right to freedom of speech. But this allegation is not now before us. The District Court stayed proceedings on this issue, and the respondent has yet to prove that the decision not to rehire him was, in fact, based on his free speech activities.[8]

Hence, on the record before us, all that clearly appears is that the respondent was not rehired for one year at one university. It stretches

to clear his name. Once a person has cleared his name at a hearing, his employer, of course, may remain free to deny him future employment for other reasons.

7. The District Court made an *assumption* "that non-retention by one university or college creates concrete and practical difficulties for a professor in his subsequent academic career." 310 F.Supp., at 979. And the Court of Appeals based its affirmance of the summary judgment largely on the premise that "the substantial adverse effect non-retention is likely to have upon the career interests of an individual professor" amounts to a limitation on future employment opportunities sufficient to invoke procedural due process guarantees. 446 F.2d, at 809. But even assuming, *arguendo,* that such a "substantial adverse effect" under these circumstances would constitute a state-imposed restriction on liberty, the record contains no support for these assumptions. There is no suggestion of how nonretention might affect the respondent's future employment prospects. Mere proof, for example, that his record of nonretention in one job, taken alone, might make him somewhat less attractive to some other employers would

hardly establish the kind of foreclosure of opportunities amounting to a deprivation of "liberty."

8. See n. 2, supra. The Court of Appeals, nonetheless, argued that opportunity for a hearing and a statement of reasons were required here "as a *prophylactic* against non-retention decisions improperly motivated by exercise of protected rights." 446 F.2d, at 810 (emphasis supplied). While the Court of Appeals recognized the lack of a finding that the respondent's non-retention was based on exercise of the right of free speech, it felt that the respondent's interest in liberty was sufficiently implicated here because the decision not to rehire him was made "with a background of controversy and unwelcome expressions of opinion." . . .

In the respondent's case, however, the State has not directly impinged upon interests in free speech or free press in any way comparable to a seizure of books or an injunction against meetings. Whatever may be a teacher's rights of free speech, the interest in holding a teaching job at a state university, *simpliciter,* is not itself a free speech interest.

the concept too far to suggest that a person is deprived of "liberty" when he simply is not rehired in one job but remains as free as before to seek another. Cafeteria Workers v. McElroy, supra, at 895–896.

III

The Fourteenth Amendment's procedural protection of property is a safeguard of the security of interests that a person has already acquired in specific benefits. These interests—property interests—may take many forms.

Thus, the Court has held that a person receiving welfare benefits under statutory and administrative standards defining eligibility for them has an interest in continued receipt of those benefits that is safeguarded by procedural due process. Goldberg v. Kelly, 397 U.S. 254. Similarly, in the area of public employment, the Court has held that a public college professor dismissed from an office held under tenure provisions, Slochower v. Board of Education, 350 U.S. 551, and college professors and staff members dismissed during the terms of their contracts, Wieman v. Updegraff, 344 U.S. 183, have interests in continued employment that are safeguarded by due process. Only last year, the Court held that this principle "proscribing summary dismissal from public employment without hearing or inquiry required by due process" also applied to a teacher recently hired without tenure or a formal contract, but nonetheless with a clearly implied promise of continued employment. Connell v. Higginbotham, 403 U.S. 207, 208.

Certain attributes of "property" interests protected by procedural due process emerge from these decisions. To have a property interest in a benefit, a person clearly must have more than an abstract need or desire for it. He must have more than a unilateral expectation of it. He must, instead, have a legitimate claim of entitlement to it. It is a purpose of the ancient institution of property to protect those claims upon which people rely in their daily lives, reliance that must not be arbitrarily undermined. It is a purpose of the constitutional right to a hearing to provide an opportunity for a person to vindicate those claims.

Property interests, of course, are not created by the Constitution. Rather, they are created and their dimensions are defined by existing rules or understandings that stem from an independent source such as state law—rules or understandings that secure certain benefits and that support claims of entitlement to those benefits. Thus, the welfare recipients in Goldberg v. Kelly, supra, had a claim of entitlement to welfare payments that was grounded in the statute defining eligibility for them. The recipients had not yet shown that they were, in fact, within the statutory terms of eligibility. But we held that they had a right to a hearing at which they might attempt to do so.

Just as the welfare recipients' "property" interest in welfare payments was created and defined by statutory terms, so the respondent's "property" interest in employment at Wisconsin State University-Oshkosh was created and defined by the terms of his appointment. Those terms secured his interest in employment up to June 30, 1969.

But the important fact in this case is that they specifically provided that the respondent's employment was to terminate on June 30. They did not provide for contract renewal absent "sufficient cause." Indeed, they made no provision for renewal whatsoever.

Thus, the terms of the respondent's appointment secured absolutely no interest in re-employment for the next year. They supported absolutely no possible claim of entitlement to re-employment. Nor, significantly, was there any state statute or University rule or policy that secured his interest in re-employment or that created any legitimate claim to it.[9] In these circumstances, the respondent surely had an abstract concern in being rehired, but he did not have a *property* interest sufficient to require the University authorities to give him a hearing when they declined to renew his contract of employment.

IV

Our analysis of the respondent's constitutional rights in this case in no way indicates a view that an opportunity for a hearing or a statement of reasons for nonretention would, or would not, be appropriate or wise in public colleges and universities. For it is a written Constitution that we apply. Our role is confined to interpretation of that Constitution.

We must conclude that the summary judgment for the respondent should not have been granted, since the respondent has not shown that he was deprived of liberty or property protected by the Fourteenth Amendment. The judgment of the Court of Appeals, accordingly, is reversed and the case is remanded for further proceedings consistent with this opinion.

It is so ordered.[10]

. . .

MR. JUSTICE MARSHALL, dissenting.

. . .

While I agree with Part I of the Court's opinion, setting forth the proper framework for consideration of the issue presented, and also with those portions of Parts II and III of the Court's opinion that assert that a public employee is entitled to procedural due process whenever a State stigmatizes him by denying employment, or injures his future employment prospects severely, or whenever the State deprives him of

9. To be sure, the respondent does suggest that most teachers hired on a year-to-year basis by Wisconsin State University-Oshkosh are, in fact, rehired. But the District Court has not found that there is anything approaching a "common law" of re-employment, see Perry v. Sindermann, post, so strong as to require University officials to give the respondent a statement of reasons and a hearing on their decision not to rehire him.

10. [Ed.] See the Chronicle of Higher Education, Nov. 26, 1973, p. 3, col. 1:

"David F. Roth . . . has been awarded $6,746 in damages in federal district court. . . . A six-person jury found that Mr. Roth's constitutional right to free speech was violated by [Wisconsin State University at Oshkosh]. . . . Judge Doyle also has yet to rule on requests from Mr. Roth for reinstatement in his position at Oshkosh. . . . Even if Judge Doyle orders his reinstatement, Mr. Roth is not likely to return to Oshkosh, since he now teaches at Purdue University."

a property interest, I would go further than the Court does in defining the terms "liberty" and "property."

. . .

In my view, every citizen who applies for a government job is entitled to it unless the government can establish some reason for denying the employment. This is the "property" right that I believe is protected by the Fourteenth Amendment and that cannot be denied "without due process of law." And it is also liberty—liberty to work— which is the "very essence of the personal freedom and opportunity" secured by the Fourteenth Amendment.

. . .

Employment is one of the greatest, if not the greatest, benefits that governments offer in modern-day life. When something as valuable as the opportunity to work is at stake, the government may not reward some citizens and not others without demonstrating that its actions are fair and equitable. And it is procedural due process that is our fundamental guarantee of fairness, our protection against arbitrary, capricious, and unreasonable government action.

. . .

We have often noted that procedural due process means many different things in the numerous contexts in which it applies. See, e.g., Goldberg v. Kelly, 397 U.S. 254 (1970); Bell v. Burson, 402 U.S. 535 (1971). Prior decisions have held that an applicant for admission to practice as an attorney before the United States Board of Tax Appeals may not be rejected without a statement of reasons and a chance for a hearing on disputed issues of fact; that a tenured teacher could not be summarily dismissed without notice of the reasons and a hearing; that an applicant for admission to a state bar could not be denied the opportunity to practice law without notice of the reasons for the rejection of his application and a hearing; and even that a substitute teacher who had been employed only two months could not be dismissed merely because she refused to take a loyalty oath without an inquiry into the specific facts of her case and a hearing on those in dispute. I would follow these cases and hold that respondent was denied due process when his contract was not renewed and he was not informed of the reasons and given an opportunity to respond.

. . .

[Justices Burger, White, Blackmun, and Rehnquist joined Justice Stewart. Justice Powell took no part in the case. Justices Brennan and Douglas were, like Justice Marshall, dissenters; their opinions have not been reproduced. Finally, Chief Justice Burger also filed a concurring opinion, reproduced following the next case.]

PERRY v. SINDERMANN

Supreme Court of the United States, 1972.
408 U.S. 593.

MR. JUSTICE STEWART delivered the opinion of the Court.

From 1959 to 1969 the respondent, Robert Sindermann, was a teacher in the state college system of the State of Texas. After teaching for two years at the University of Texas and for four years at San Antonio Junior College, he became a professor of Government and Social Science at Odessa Junior College in 1965. He was employed at the college for four successive years, under a series of one-year contracts. He was successful enough to be appointed, for a time, the cochairman of his department.

During the 1968–1969 academic year, however, controversy arose between the respondent and the college administration. The respondent was elected president of the Texas Junior College Teachers Association. In this capacity, he left his teaching duties on several occasions to testify before committees of the Texas Legislature, and he became involved in public disagreements with the policies of the college's Board of Regents. In particular, he aligned himself with a group advocating the elevation of the college to four-year status—a change opposed by the Regents. And, on one occasion, a newspaper advertisement appeared over his name that was highly critical of the Regents.

Finally, in May 1969, the respondent's one-year employment contract terminated and the Board of Regents voted not to offer him a new contract for the next academic year. The Regents issued a press release setting forth allegations of the respondent's insubordination.[1] But they provided him no official statement of the reasons for the nonrenewal of his contract. And they allowed him no opportunity for a hearing to challenge the basis of the nonrenewal.

The respondent then brought this action in Federal District Court. He alleged primarily that the Regents' decision not to rehire him was based on his public criticism of the policies of the college administration and thus infringed his right to freedom of speech. He also alleged that their failure to provide him an opportunity for a hearing violated the Fourteenth Amendment's guarantee of procedural due process. The petitioners—members of the Board of Regents and the president of the college—denied that their decision was made in retaliation for the respondent's public criticism and argued that they had no obligation to provide a hearing. On the basis of these bare pleadings and three brief affidavits filed by the respondent, the District Court granted summary judgment for the petitioners. It concluded that the respondent had "no cause of action against the [petitioners] since his contract of employment terminated May 31, 1969, and Odessa Junior College has not adopted the tenure system."

1. The press release stated, for example, that the respondent had defied his superiors by attending legislative committee meetings when college officials had specifically refused to permit him to leave his classes for that purpose.

The Court of Appeals reversed the judgment of the District Court. First, it held that, despite the respondent's lack of tenure, the nonrenewal of his contract would violate the Fourteenth Amendment if it in fact was based on his protected free speech. Since the actual reason for the Regents' decision was "in total dispute" in the pleadings, the court remanded the case for a full hearing on this contested issue of fact. Second, the Court of Appeals held that, despite the respondent's lack of tenure, the failure to allow him an opportunity for a hearing would violate the constitutional guarantee of procedural due process if the respondent could show that he had an "expectancy" of re-employment. It, therefore, ordered that this issue of fact also be aired upon remand. We granted a writ of certiorari, and we have considered this case along with Board of Regents v. Roth.

I

The first question presented is whether the respondent's lack of a contractual or tenure right to re-employment, taken alone, defeats his claim that the nonrenewal of his contract violated the First and Fourteenth Amendments. We hold that it does not.

For at least a quarter-century, this Court has made clear that even though a person has no "right" to a valuable governmental benefit and even though the government may deny him the benefit for any number of reasons, there are some reasons upon which the government may not rely. It may not deny a benefit to a person on a basis that infringes his constitutionally protected interests—especially, his interest in freedom of speech. For if the government could deny a benefit to a person because of his constitutionally protected speech or associations, his exercise of those freedoms would in effect be penalized and inhibited. This would allow the government to "produce a result which [it] could not command directly." Speiser v. Randall, 357 U.S. 513, 526. Such interference with constitutional rights is impermissible.

. . .

Thus, the respondent's lack of a contractual or tenure "right" to re-employment for the 1969–1970 academic year is immaterial to his free speech claim. . . .

In this case, of course, the respondent has yet to show that the decision not to renew his contract was, in fact, made in retaliation for his exercise of the constitutional right of free speech. . . .

But we agree with the Court of Appeals that there is a genuine dispute as to "whether the college refused to renew the teaching contract on an impermissible basis—as a reprisal for the exercise of constitutionally protected rights." . . .

For this reason we hold that the grant of summary judgment against the respondent, without full exploration of this issue, was improper.

II

The respondent's lack of formal contractual or tenure security in continued employment at Odessa Junior College, though irrelevant to his free speech claim, is highly relevant to his procedural due process claim. But it may not be entirely dispositive.

We have held today in Board of Regents v. Roth that the Constitution does not require opportunity for a hearing before the nonrenewal of a nontenured teacher's contract, unless he can show that the decision not to rehire him somehow deprived him of an interest in "liberty" or that he had a "property" interest in continued employment, despite the lack of tenure or a formal contract. In Roth the teacher had not made a showing on either point to justify summary judgment in his favor.

Similarly, the respondent here has yet to show that he has been deprived of an interest that could invoke procedural due process protection. As in Roth, the mere showing that he was not rehired in one particular job, without more, did not amount to a showing of a loss of liberty.[2] Nor did it amount to a showing of a loss of property.

But the respondent's allegations—which we must construe most favorably to the respondent at this stage of the litigation—do raise a genuine issue as to his interest in continued employment at Odessa Junior College. He alleged that this interest, though not secured by a formal contractual tenure provision, was secured by a no less binding understanding fostered by the college administration. In particular, the respondent alleged that the college had a de facto tenure program, and that he had tenure under that program. He claimed that he and others legitimately relied upon an unusual provision that had been in the college's official Faculty Guide for many years:

> *Teacher Tenure:* Odessa College has no tenure system. The Administration of the College wishes the faculty member to feel that he has permanent tenure as long as his teaching services are satisfactory and as long as he displays a cooperative attitude toward his co-workers and his superiors, and as long as he is happy in his work.

Moreover, the respondent claimed legitimate reliance upon guidelines promulgated by the Coordinating Board of the Texas College and University System that provided that a person, like himself, who had been employed as a teacher in the state college and university system for seven years or more has some form of job tenure. Thus, the respondent offered to prove that a teacher with his long period of service at this particular State College had no less a "property" interest in continued employment than a formally tenured teacher at other colleges, and had no less a procedural due process right to a

---

2. The Court of Appeals suggested that the respondent might have a due process right to some kind of hearing simply if he *asserts* to college officials that their decision was based on his constitutionally protected conduct. We have rejected this approach in Board of Regents v. Roth.

statement of reasons and a hearing before college officials upon their decision not to retain him.

We have made clear in Roth that "property" interests subject to procedural due process protection are not limited by a few rigid, technical forms. Rather, "property" denotes a broad range of interests that are secured by "existing rules or understandings." A person's interest in a benefit is a "property" interest for due process purposes if there are such rules or mutually explicit understandings that support his claim of entitlement to the benefit and that he may invoke at a hearing.

A written contract with an explicit tenure provision clearly is evidence of a formal understanding that supports a teacher's claim of entitlement to continued employment unless sufficient "cause" is shown. Yet absence of such an explicit contractual provision may not always foreclose the possibility that a teacher has a "property" interest in re-employment. For example, the law of contracts in most, if not all, jurisdictions long has employed a process by which agreements, though not formalized in writing, may be "implied." 3 A. Corbin on Contracts §§ 561–572A (1960). Explicit contractual provisions may be supplemented by other agreements implied from "the promisor's words and conduct in the light of the surrounding circumstances." Id., at § 562. And, "[t]he meaning of [the promisor's] words and acts is found by relating them to the usage of the past." Ibid.

A teacher, like the respondent, who has held his position for a number of years, might be able to show from the circumstances of this service—and from other relevant facts—that he has a legitimate claim of entitlement to job tenure. . . . This is particularly likely in a college or university, like Odessa Junior College, that has no explicit tenure system even for senior members of its faculty, but that nonetheless may have created such a system in practice. See C. Byse & L. Joughin, Tenure in American Higher Education 17–28 (1959).[3]

In this case, the respondent has alleged the existence of rules and understandings, promulgated and fostered by state officials, that may justify his legitimate claim of entitlement to continued employment absent "sufficient cause." We disagree with the Court of Appeals insofar as it held that a mere subjective "expectancy" is protected by procedural due process, but we agree that the respondent must be given an opportunity to prove the legitimacy of his claim of such entitlement in light of "the policies and practices of the institution." 430 F.2d, at 943. Proof of such a property interest would not, of course, entitle him to reinstatement. But such proof would obligate college officials to grant a hearing at his request, where he could be informed of the grounds for his nonretention and challenge their sufficiency.

3. We do not now hold that the respondent has any such legitimate claim of entitlement to job tenure. For "[p]roperty interests . . . are not created by the Constitution. Rather, they are created and their dimensions are defined by existing rules or understandings that stem from an independent source such as state law . . . ." Board of Regents v. Roth, at 577. If it is the law of Texas that a teacher in the respondent's position has no contractual or other claim to job tenure, the respondent's claim would be defeated.

Therefore, while we do not wholly agree with the opinion of the Court of Appeals, its judgment remanding this case to the District Court is

Affirmed.[4]

.   .   .

MR. CHIEF JUSTICE BURGER, concurring.

I concur in the Court's judgments and opinions in Sindermann and Roth, but there is one central point in both decisions that I would like to underscore since it may have been obscured in the comprehensive discussion of the cases. That point is that the relationship between a state institution and one of its teachers is essentially a matter of state concern and state law. The Court holds today only that a state-employed teacher who has a right to re-employment under state law, arising from either an express or implied contract, has, in turn, a right guaranteed by the Fourteenth Amendment to some form of prior administrative or academic hearing on the cause for nonrenewal of his contract. Thus, whether a particular teacher in a particular context has any right to such administrative hearing hinges on a question of state law. . . .

[Justices Burger, White, Blackmun and Rehnquist joined Justice Stewart. Justice Powell took no part in the case. Justices Brennan, Douglas, and Marshall agreed with Part I of the Court's opinion, but also voted "to direct the District Court to enter summary judgment for respondent entitling him to a statement of reasons why his contract was not renewed and a hearing on disputed issues of fact."]

NOTES

(1) If the constitutional phrase "deprive any person of life, liberty, or property" "must be given some meaning" (Justice Stewart's phrase), is the Court's meaning in these cases any stronger textually than the meaning asserted by the older cases the Court rejects? Is not a distinction between "rights," if they can be thought to exist prior to government action, and "privileges," which depend on government grant and therefore cannot be (as against the government) within the term "deprive," a perfectly good reading of the text? If the reason for rejecting a distinction between "rights" and "privileges" is that "only a stagnant society remains unchanged," as the Roth opinion suggests, then why do we have to give a doctrinal significance to each element of the constitutional text? If we are going to give a doctrinal meaning to each textual word, is there any warrant for the Court's quite different treatment of "liberty" and "property"?

---

4. [Ed.] See the Odessa American, Nov. 12, 1972, p. 1, col. 1: "Robert P. Sindermann flew to Odessa Saturday and picked up the $48,000 check made out to him by Odessa College in settlement of his lawsuit stemming from the college's refusal to rehire him in 1969. . . .

"The 43-year-old former Odessa College government teacher said one of the conditions of the settlement was that the college offered to reinstate him. 'I have politely declined the invitation,' Sindermann grinned."

(2) FRANK I. MICHELMAN, FORMAL AND ASSOCIATIONAL AIMS IN PROCE-
DURAL DUE PROCESS, in Due Process, Nomos XVIII 126–129 (J.R. Pen-
nock and J.W. Chapman eds. 1977):[†]

"One familiar notion of due process is that of an obligation on the
part of those who make decisions about the concerns of other individuals to engage in explanatory procedures—procedures in which agents
state reasons for their decisions and affected individuals are allowed to
examine and contest the proffered reasons. . . .

"Explanatory procedures may be either formal or nonformal. A
procedure is formal insofar as it focuses on the question of legal
justification—and lays the agent's decision open to reversal by an
arbiter or judge in case the agent can point to no true ground which
justifies the action under some legally valid precept. A nonformal
procedure does not aim at such third-party review of challenged action
for legal adequacy. In a nonformal procedure, the individual questions
the validity of the agent's precept (if at all) under some criterion other
than legality—prudence, morality, fairness, or whatever; or he may do
neither, merely hearing the agent out and accepting or concurring in
the action. . . .

"An obvious purpose of formal explanatory procedures is vindication of the private claims of individuals to have what belongs to them
under the law. What of nonformal, including quasi-formal, procedures?
What compelling purposes might they serve? Such procedures seem
responsive to demands for *revelation* and *participation.* They attach
value to the individual's *being told why* the agent is treating him
unfavorably and to his *having a part in the decision.* The individual
may have various reasons for wanting to be told why, even if he makes
no claim to legal protection, and even if no further participation is
allowed him. Some of those reasons may pertain to external consequences: the individual may wish to make political use of the information, or use it to help ward off harm to his reputation. Yet the
information may also be wanted for introspective reasons—because, for
example, it fills a potentially destructive gap in the individual's conception of himself. Similarly, the individual may have various reasons for
wanting an opportunity to discuss the decision with the agent. Some
pertain to external consequences: the individual might succeed in
persuading the agent away from the harmful action. But again a
participatory opportunity may also be psychologically important to the
individual: to have played a part in, to have made one's apt contribution to, decisions which are about oneself may be counted important
even though the decision, as it turns out, is the most unfavorable one
imaginable and one's efforts have not proved influential.

"A demand for nonformal procedures might issue from a certain
kind of ideal conception of social relations and political arrangements,
expressing revulsion against the thought of life in a society that accepts
it as normal for agents representing the society to make and act upon

decisions about other members without full and frank interchange with those other members, a kind of accountability to them even if not legal accountability. A nonformal view of an explanatory procedure would thus recognize a communal or fraternal aspect of social life of which a purely formal view, strictly concerned with ensuring that the private entitlements of individuals will be respected, may remain oblivious.

". . . [E]xplanatory procedures of the sort we tend to associate with due process can and sometimes do simultaneously serve both the proprietary aims of formality and the relational aims implied by revelation and participation. In any explanatory procedure, formal or not, the affected individual obtains a more-or-less trenchant statement of the official's reasons for treating him unfavorably and has an opportunity to participate in a determination or the appropriateness of those reasons—at least under the criterion of legality, and perhaps also under criteria of prudence or fairness. . . . "

(3) WILLIAM VAN ALSTYNE, CRACKS IN "THE NEW PROPERTY": ADJUDICATIVE DUE PROCESS IN THE ADMINISTRATIVE STATE, 62 Corn.L.Rev. 445, 484 (1977):

"The concept of public sector status as property both overstates and understates the problem. It overstates the problem by carrying with it additional notions of personal entitlement and of sinecurism that no constitutional court since Lochner should desire to encourage. At the same time, it understates the problem by ignoring a vast number of situations in which it is impossible to describe the relationship as one giving rise to property, but in which the government's procedural grossness is nevertheless profoundly unfair and objectionable."

(4) Some examples of the Roth and Sindermann "property" test in action:

(a) BISHOP v. WOOD, 426 U.S. 341 (1976). Bishop was discharged without hearing from being a policeman in Marion, N.C. He had been employed for nearly three years; after the first six months he had been a "permanent employee." A city ordinance provided that "If a permanent employee fails to perform work up to the standard of the classification held, or continues to be negligent, inefficient, or unfit to perform his duties, he may be dismissed by the City manager." Under state law, however, at least as construed by a United States District Judge sitting in North Carolina, even with this language Bishop "held his position at the will and pleasure of the city." Held: In the circumstances, the Supreme Court would defer to the trial judge's interpretation of state law; given that interpretation, Bishop's discharge deprived him of no property interest protected by the Fourteenth Amendment. Several justices strongly dissented, finding this interpretation by a federal judge incredible.

(b) BARRY v. BARCHI, 443 U.S. 55 (1979). Barchi was licensed under New York law to train horses for harness racing. One of his horses placed second; was tested; and was found to have been given a stimulant. Despite protestations of innocence, Barchi was suspended for fifteen days. By state law, his only opportunity for a hearing would come at some unspecified time after suspension. "It is conceded," wrote Justice White, "that, under New York law, Barchi's license could have been suspended only upon a satisfactory showing that his horse had been drugged and that he was at least negligent in failing to prevent the drugging. As a threshold matter, therefore, it is clear that Barchi had a property interest in his license sufficient to invoke the protection of the Due Process clause." Id. at 2649. In the circumstances, interim suspension without an evidentiary hearing was justified, but the state's scheme was constitutionally infirm for failure to assure a prompt post-suspension hearing.

(c) EIDSON v. PIERCE, 745 F.2d 453 (7th Cir.1984). Under Section 8 of the United States Housing Act, private landlords agree to rent to low-income families in exchange for a federal government undertaking to pay the difference between what the tenants can afford and the fair market rent. There are fewer Section 8 housing units than there are applicants for them. In these consolidated cases, landlords refused to rent to plaintiffs because of poor references from prior landlords, poor credit records, and the like. Plaintiffs sued for, among other things, the right to a procedure in which they could establish their eligibility for Section 8 housing. Held: plaintiffs had no protected property interest. While federal law requires landlords to favor certain classes of prospective tenants—for example, those who have been involuntarily displaced—it also looks to the landlord to exercise discretion and judgment in choosing particular tenants. Thus, even if the plaintiffs established, say, that the credit information was wrong, they would still not be entitled to any Section 8 housing, for the landlord would still be free to accept or reject their application. Similarly, since the Section 8 program establishes no preferences by which to allocate its scarce benefits among eligible class members, hearings would not enhance accurate implementation of the program's goals. In sum, "a legitimate claim of entitlement is created only when the statutes or regulations in question establish a framework of factual conditions delimiting entitlements which are capable of being explored at a due process hearing." 745 F.2d at 459–460.

In reaching this result, the Seventh Circuit explicitly rejected what appears to be the directly contrary holding of the Ninth Circuit in RESSLER v. PIERCE, 692 F.2d 1212 (9th Cir.1982). Same program; same problem; held: rejected applicants for subsidized housing under the Section 8 program are entitled to notice and an informal hearing to be conducted by a HUD employee. Section 8 was intended to benefit a definable class of persons, and landlords exercise only a limited discretion in choosing from among that class; these restrictions give applicants a sufficient property interest under the Roth test to entitle them to due process protection.

Losing counsel in Eidson, the later case, did not petition the Supreme Court to hear the case and resolve this conflict.

Is the problem here one which could only arise in the course of applying for benefits? Or do these cases raise an issue akin to the problem presented when third parties try to enforce ordinary contracts claiming to be intended, and not merely incidental, beneficiaries of the arrangement? If the latter, the problem is one which could be presented even by those already benefiting from a program. Compare Grace Towers Tenants Ass'n v. Grace Housing Development Fund, Inc., 538 F.2d 491 (2d Cir.1976).

(5) In Roth, Justice Stewart claims that "the Court has fully and finally rejected the wooden distinction between 'rights' and 'privileges' that once seemed to govern the applicability of procedural due process rights." In 1950, in one application of "the wooden distinction," the Supreme Court had said that "[a]dmission of aliens to the United States is a privilege granted by the sovereign" and accordingly "[w]hatever the procedure authorized by Congress is, it is due process as far as an alien denied entry is concerned." United States ex rel. Knauff v. Shaughnessy, 338 U.S. 537, 542, 544 (1950). Despite Justice Stewart's claim, this particular application survived Roth. LANDON v. PLASENCIA, 459 U.S. 21, 32 (1982): "This Court has long held that an alien seeking initial admission to the United States requests a privilege and has no constitutional rights regarding his application, for the power to admit or exclude aliens is a sovereign prerogative. See, e.g., United States ex rel. Knauff v. Shaughnessy. . . ." For discussion of these cases, see Developments in the Law: Immigration Policy and the Rights of Aliens, 96 Harv.L.Rev. 1286, 1318–1324 (1983).

MEACHUM v. FANO
Supreme Court of the United States, 1976.
427 U.S. 215.

MR. JUSTICE WHITE delivered the opinion of the Court.

The question here is whether the Due Process Clause of the Fourteenth Amendment entitles a state prisoner to a hearing when he is transferred to a prison the conditions of which are substantially less favorable to the prisoner, absent a state law or practice conditioning such transfers on proof of serious misconduct or the occurrence of other events. We hold that it does not.

I

[After nine fires occurred at the medium-security prison where respondents were incarcerated, respondents were notified that the authorities had information of their bad behavior and that there would be proceedings leading to their possible transfer to a maximum-security institution.]

Individual classification hearings were held, each respondent being represented by counsel. Each hearing began by the reading of a prepared statement by the Classification Board. The Board then heard, in camera and out of the respondents' presence, the testimony of petitioner Meachum, the Norfolk prison superintendent, who repeated the information that had been received from informants. Each respondent was then told that the evidence supported the allegations contained in the notice but was not then—or ever—given transcripts or summaries of Meachum's testimony before the Board. Each respondent was allowed to present evidence in his own behalf; and each denied involvement in the particular infraction being investigated.

Some respondents submitted supportive testimony or written statements from correction officers. A social worker also testified in the presence of each respondent, furnishing the respondent's criminal and custodial record, including prior rule infractions, if any, and other aspects of his performance and "general adjustment" at Norfolk.

[The Board recommended various transfers which, after internal review in the Corrections Department, were mostly carried out.]

. . . No respondent was subjected to disciplinary punishment upon arrival at the transfer prison. None of the transfers ordered entailed loss of good time or disciplinary confinement.

Meanwhile respondents had brought this action under 42 U.S.C. § 1983 . . . alleging that respondents were being deprived of liberty without due process of law in that petitioners had ordered them transferred to a less favorable institution without an adequate factfinding hearing. They sought an injunction setting aside the ordered transfer, declaratory relief, and damages. . . .

[The District Court held in favor of the prisoners, and a divided panel of the Court of Appeals affirmed.]

II

. . . We reject at the outset the notion that *any* grievous loss visited upon a person by the State is sufficient to invoke the procedural protections of the Due Process Clause. In Board of Regents v. Roth, 408 U.S. 564 (1972), a university professor was deprived of his job, a loss which was surely a matter of great substance, but because the professor had no property interest in his position, due process procedures were not required in connection with his dismissal. We there held that the determining factor is the nature of the interest involved rather than its weight.

Similarly, we cannot agree that *any* change in the conditions of confinement having a substantial adverse impact on the prisoner involved is sufficient to invoke the protections of the Due Process Clause. The Due Process Clause by its own force forbids the State from convicting any person of crime and depriving him of his liberty without complying fully with the requirements of the Clause. But given a valid conviction, the criminal defendant has been constitutionally deprived of his liberty to the extent that the State may confine him and subject him to the rules of its prison system so long as the conditions of confinement do not otherwise violate the Constitution. . . .

Neither, in our view, does the Due Process Clause in and of itself protect a duly convicted prisoner against transfer from one institution to another within the state prison system. Confinement in any of the State's institutions is within the normal limits or range of custody which the conviction has authorized the State to impose. That life in one prison is much more disagreeable than in another does not in itself signify that a Fourteenth Amendment liberty interest is implicated when a prisoner is transferred to the institution with the more severe rules.

. . .

Wolff v. McDonnell [418 U.S. 539 (1974)], on which the Court of Appeals heavily relied, is not to the contrary. Under that case, the Due Process Clause entitles a state prisoner to certain procedural protections when he is deprived of good-time credits because of serious misconduct. But the liberty interest there identified did not originate in the Constitution, which "itself does not guarantee good-time credit for satisfactory behavior while in prison." Id., at 557. The State itself, not the Constitution, had "not only provided a statutory right to good time but also specifies that it is to be forfeited only for serious misbehavior." Ibid. We concluded:

> [A] person's liberty is equally protected, even when the liberty itself is a statutory creation of the State. The touchstone of due process is protection of the individual against arbitrary action of government, Dent v. West Virginia, 129 U.S. 114, 123 (1889). Since prisoners in Nebraska can only lose good-time credits if they are guilty of serious misconduct, the determination of whether such behavior has occurred becomes critical, and the minimum requirements of procedural due process appropriate for the circumstances must be observed. Id., at 558.

The liberty interest protected in Wolff had its roots in state law, and the minimum procedures appropriate under the circumstances were held required by the Due Process Clause "to insure that the state-created right is not arbitrarily abrogated." Id., at 557. This is consistent with our approach in other due process cases such as Goss v. Lopez, 419 U.S. 565 (1975); Board of Regents v. Roth; Perry v. Sindermann; Goldberg v. Kelly.

Here, Massachusetts law conferred no right on the prisoner to remain in the prison to which he was initially assigned, defeasible only upon proof of specific acts of misconduct. Insofar as we are advised, transfers between Massachusetts prisons are not conditioned upon the occurrence of specified events. On the contrary, transfer in a wide variety of circumstances is vested in prison officials. The predicate for invoking the protection of the Fourteenth Amendment as construed and applied in Wolff v. McDonnell is totally nonexistent in this case.

. . .

A prisoner's behavior may precipitate a transfer; and absent such behavior, perhaps transfer would not take place at all. But, as we have said, Massachusetts prison officials have the discretion to transfer prisoners for any number of reasons. Their discretion is not limited to instances of serious misconduct. As we understand it no legal interest or right of these respondents under Massachusetts law would have been violated by their transfer whether or not their misconduct had been proved in accordance with procedures that might be required by the Due Process Clause in other circumstances. Whatever expectation the prisoner may have in remaining at a particular prison so long as he behaves himself, it is too ephemeral and insubstantial to trigger procedural due process protections as long as prison officials have discretion to transfer him for whatever reason or for no reason at all.

Holding that arrangements like this are within reach of the procedural protections of the Due Process Clause would place the Clause astride the day-to-day functioning of state prisons and involve the judiciary in issues and discretionary decisions that are not the business of federal judges. We decline to so interpret and apply the Due Process Clause. The federal courts do not sit to supervise state prisons, the administration of which is of acute interest to the States. . . .

The judgment of the Court of Appeals accordingly is

Reversed.

MR. JUSTICE STEVENS, with whom MR. JUSTICE BRENNAN and MR. JUSTICE MARSHALL join, dissenting.

The Court's rationale is more disturbing than its narrow holding. If the Court had merely held that the transfer of a prisoner from one penal institution to another does not cause a sufficiently grievous loss to amount to a deprivation of liberty within the meaning of the Due Process Clause of the Fourteenth Amendment, I would disagree with the conclusion but not with the constitutional analysis. The Court's holding today, however, appears to rest on a conception of "liberty" which I consider fundamentally incorrect.

The Court indicates that a "liberty interest" may have either of two sources. According to the Court, a liberty interest may "originate in the Constitution," or it may have "its roots in state law." Apart from those two possible origins, the Court is unable to find that a person has a constitutionally protected interest in liberty.

If man were a creature of the State, the analysis would be correct. But neither the Bill of Rights nor the laws of sovereign States create the liberty which the Due Process Clause protects. The relevant constitutional provisions are limitations on the power of the sovereign to infringe on the liberty of the citizen. The relevant state laws either create property rights, or they curtail the freedom of the citizen who must live in an ordered society. Of course, law is essential to the exercise and enjoyment of individual liberty in a complex society. But it is not the source of liberty, and surely not the exclusive source.

I had thought it self-evident that all men were endowed by their Creator with liberty as one of the cardinal unalienable rights. It is that basic freedom which the Due Process Clause protects, rather than the particular rights or privileges conferred by specific laws or regulations.

. . .

. . . I think it clear that even the inmate retains an unalienable interest in liberty—at the very minimum the right to be treated with dignity—which the Constitution may never ignore.

. . .

That does not mean, of course, that every adversity amounts to a deprivation within the meaning of the Fourteenth Amendment. There must be grievous loss, and that term itself is somewhat flexible. I would certainly not consider every transfer within a prison system, even to more onerous conditions of confinement, such a loss. . . .

In view of the Court's basic holding, I merely note that I agree with the Court of Appeals that the transfer involved in this case was sufficiently serious to invoke the protection of the Constitution.

I respectfully dissent.

NOTES

(1) "The federal courts do not sit to supervise state prisons, the administration of which is of acute interest to the States." Is it legally relevant that the institution whose operation was in question in Meachum was a prison system? Is it legally relevant that it was a state system? Or has Justice White simply tossed in an interesting, but legally irrelevant, comment?

(2) Accepting the futility of a court-enforced nondelegation doctrine, Professor Davis has long urged that "the non-delegation doctrine should gradually grow into a broad requirement extending beyond the subject of delegation—that officers with discretionary power must do about as much as feasible to structure their discretion through appropriate safeguards and to confine and guide their discretion through standards, principles, and rules. . . . " K. DAVIS, 1 ADMINISTRATIVE LAW TREATISE, (2d ed., 1978) 207–08. If structuring discretion is a central concern of administrative law, does the Meachum case set up perverse incentives for administrative agencies?

(3) The Supreme Court has many times considered the due process rights of prisoners in one context or another. Wolff v. McDonnell, one of the earlier cases, is discussed in the principal opinion. Here are two later cases, each decided in light of Meachum:

(a) VITEK v. JONES, 445 U.S. 480 (1980). Jones, convicted of robbery, burned himself severely while in prison, and was transferred to a state mental hospital. Under Nebraska's statutes, this transfer had to be based on a finding made by a physician or psychologist that a prisoner "suffers from a mental disease or defect" not properly treatable in the prison. In an opinion for the court written by Justice White, *held*: Jones was entitled to a hearing consistent with due process before being transferred. (1) Prisoners in Nebraska have an "objective expectation" based on state statute and practice that transfer to a mental hospital will occur only if they are found mentally ill; this expectation constitutes a "liberty interest" sufficient to implicate the fourteenth amendment. (2) Even absent the Nebraska statute, the potentially stigmatizing consequences of transfer to a mental hospital coupled with possible subjection to mandatory behavior modification treatment serve to put Jones' transfer outside the "range of confinement" justified by the initial criminal trial and sentence, and therefore call for an additional hearing. Four justices dissented on grounds of mootness or ripeness.

(b) OLIM v. WAKINEKONA, 461 U.S. 238 (1983). Plaintiff, who was moved from a state prison in Hawaii to one in California, claimed that the officials who were responsible for ordering the transfer were biased against him. The merits of that claim were never reached, however, for the Court held that he lacked an interest protected by the due process clause. (1) Interstate transfer of prisoners is widely authorized by state and federal statutes, and not uncommon; unlike the situation in Vitek, confinement in a prison in another state is within the range of custody authorized by the initial conviction. (2) Although the state conceded for purposes of argument that plaintiff suffered a grievous loss when he was transferred, nothing in the applicable statutes or regulations limited the unfettered discretion of prison officials to order the transfer. (3) The fact that state law did require a kind of hearing before a prisoner could be transferred (which plaintiff allegedly did not receive) did not make a federal case of the matter. Blackmun, J: "Process is not an end in itself. Its constitutional purpose is to protect a substantive interest to which the individual has a legitimate claim of entitlement. . . . The State may choose to require procedures for reasons other than protection against deprivation of substantive rights, of course, but in making that choice the State does not create an independent substantive right." Id. at 250. Justices Brennan, Marshall, and Stevens, all part of the Vitek majority, dissented.[1]

(4) What drives Justice White to ground liberty in positive texts? Reminding us of the overall constitutional law context of this line of cases, Richard B. Stewart and Cass R. Sunstein, Public Programs and Private Rights, 95 Harv.L.Rev. 1193, 1257–58, suggest the following:

"A formal definition of entitlements was not inevitable. The Court might have sought to identify those interests that are as central to individual well-being in contemporary society as were the interests protected at common law in a different era. The judicial discretion inherent in any such task has been a major factor in the Court's refusal to follow a functional approach. Moreover, if courts were to select certain 'important' interests as those deserving due process protection, they might be driven to give those interests substantive as well as procedural protection; procedural rights alone might be of little value if administrators were free to decide cases as they pleased as long as procedural formalities were observed. A functional approach could thus invite courts to rule the welfare state through a new form of substantive due process."

MATHEWS v. ELDRIDGE
Supreme Court of the United States, 1976.
424 U.S. 319.

MR. JUSTICE POWELL delivered the opinion of the Court.

The issue in this case is whether the Due Process Clause of the Fifth Amendment requires that prior to the termination of Social Security disability benefit payments the recipient be afforded an opportunity for an evidentiary hearing.

1. For a general discussion of the prisoner due process cases, see Susan N. Herman, The New Liberty: The Procedural Due Process Rights of Prisoners and Others Under the Burger Court, 59 N.Y. U.L.Rev. 482 (1984).

I

Cash benefits are provided to workers during periods in which they are completely disabled under the disability insurance benefits program created by the 1956 amendments to Title II of the Social Security Act. 42 U.S.C. § 423.[1] Respondent Eldridge was first awarded benefits in June 1968. In March 1972, he received a questionnaire from the state agency charged with monitoring his medical condition. Eldridge completed the questionnaire, indicating that his condition had not improved and identifying the medical sources, including physicians, from whom he had received treatment recently. The state agency then obtained reports from his physician and a psychiatric consultant. After considering these reports and other information in his file the agency informed Eldridge by letter that it had made a tentative determination that his disability had ceased in May 1972. The letter included a statement of reasons for the proposed termination of benefits, and advised Eldridge that he might request reasonable time in which to obtain and submit additional information pertaining to his condition.

In his written response, Eldridge disputed one characterization of his medical condition and indicated that the agency already had enough evidence to establish his disability.[2] The state agency then made its final determination that he had ceased to be disabled in May 1972. This determination was accepted by the Social Security Administration (SSA), which notified Eldridge in July that his benefits would terminate after that month. The notification also advised him of his right to seek reconsideration by the state agency of this initial determination within six months.

Instead of requesting reconsideration Eldridge commenced this action challenging the constitutional validity of the administrative procedures established by the Secretary of Health, Education, and Welfare for assessing whether there exists a continuing disability.
. . . .

The District Court concluded that the administrative procedures pursuant to which the Secretary had terminated Eldridge's benefits abridged his right to procedural due process. The court viewed the interest of the disability recipient in uninterrupted benefits as indistin-

---

1. The program is financed by revenues derived from employee and employer payroll taxes. It provides monthly benefits to disabled persons who have worked sufficiently long to have an insured status, and who have had substantial work experience in a specified interval directly preceding the onset of disability. Benefits also are provided to the worker's dependents under specified circumstances. When the recipient reaches age 65 his disability benefits are automatically converted to retirement benefits. In fiscal 1974 approximately 3,700,000 persons received assistance under the program. Social Security Administration, The Year in Review 21 (1974).

2. Eldridge originally was disabled due to chronic anxiety and back strain. He subsequently was found to have diabetes. The tentative determination letter indicated that aid would be terminated because available medical evidence indicated that his diabetes was under control, that there existed no limitations on his back movements which would impose severe functional restrictions, and that he no longer suffered emotional problems that would preclude him from all work for which he was qualified. In his reply letter he claimed to have arthritis of the spine rather than a strained back.

guishable from that of the welfare recipient in Goldberg. . . . [T]he Court of Appeals for the Fourth Circuit affirmed. . . .

II

[The courts have jurisdiction.]

III

A

. . . . The Secretary does not contend that procedural due process is inapplicable to terminations of Social Security disability benefits. . . . . Rather, the Secretary contends that the existing administrative procedures, detailed below, provide all the process that is constitutionally due before a recipient can be deprived of that interest. . . . Eldridge agrees that the review procedures available to a claimant before the initial determination of ineligibility becomes final would be adequate if disability benefits were not terminated until after the evidentiary hearing stage of the administrative process. The dispute centers upon what process is due prior to the initial termination of benefits, pending review.

In recent years this Court increasingly has had occasion to consider the extent to which due process requires an evidentiary hearing prior to the deprivation of some type of property interest even if such a hearing is provided thereafter. In only one case, Goldberg v. Kelly, has the Court held that a hearing closely approximating a judicial trial is necessary. In other cases requiring some type of pretermination hearing as a matter of constitutional right the Court has spoken sparingly about the requisite procedures. . . . More recently, in Arnett v. Kennedy, 416 U.S. 134, we sustained the validity of procedures by which a federal employee could be dismissed for cause. They included notice of the action sought, a copy of the charge, reasonable time for filing a written response, and an opportunity for an oral appearance. Following dismissal, an evidentiary hearing was provided.

These decisions underscore the truism that " '[d]ue process,' unlike some legal rules, is not a technical conception with a fixed content unrelated to time, place and circumstances." Cafeteria Workers v. McElroy, 367 U.S. 886, 895 (1961). . . . . Accordingly, resolution of the issue whether the administrative procedures provided here are constitutionally sufficient requires analysis of the governmental and private interests that are affected. Arnett v. Kennedy, supra, at 167–168 (POWELL, J., concurring in part); Goldberg v. Kelly, supra, at 263–266; Cafeteria Workers v. McElroy, supra, at 895. More precisely, our prior decisions indicate that identification of the specific dictates of due process generally requires consideration of three distinct factors: First, the private interest that will be affected by the official action; second, the risk of an erroneous deprivation of such interest through the procedures used, and the probable value, if any, of additional or substitute procedural safeguards; and finally, the Government's interest, including the function involved and the fiscal and administrative burdens that the additional or substitute procedural requirement would entail. See, e.g., Goldberg v. Kelly, supra, at 263–271.

We turn first to a description of the procedures for the termination of Social Security disability benefits, and thereafter consider the factors bearing upon the constitutional adequacy of these procedures.

B

The disability insurance program is administered jointly by state and federal agencies. State agencies make the initial determination whether a disability exists, when it began, and when it ceased. The standards applied and the procedures followed are prescribed by the Secretary, who has delegated his responsibilities and powers under the Act to the SSA.

In order to establish initial and continued entitlement to disability benefits a worker must demonstrate that he is unable

> to engage in any substantial gainful activity by reason of any medically determinable physical or mental impairment which can be expected to result in death or which has lasted or can be expected to last for a continuous period of not less than 12 months . . . . 42 U.S.C. § 423(d)(1)(A).

To satisfy this test the worker bears a continuing burden of showing, by means of "medically acceptable clinical and laboratory diagnostic techniques," § 423(d)(3), that he has a physical or mental impairment of such severity that

> he is not only unable to do his previous work but cannot, considering his age, education, and work experience, engage in any other kind of substantial gainful work which exists in the national economy, regardless of whether such work exists in the immediate area in which he lives, or whether a specific job vacancy exists for him, or whether he would be hired if he applied for work. § 423(d)(2)(A).

. . .

The continuing-eligibility investigation is made by a state agency acting through a "team" consisting of a physician and a nonmedical person trained in disability evaluation. The agency periodically communicates with the disabled worker, usually by mail—in which case he is sent a detailed questionnaire—or by telephone, and requests information concerning his present condition, including current medical restrictions and sources of treatment, and any additional information that he considers relevant to his continued entitlement to benefits.

Information regarding the recipient's current condition is also obtained from his sources of medical treatment. If there is a conflict between the information provided by the beneficiary and that obtained from medical sources such as his physician, or between two sources of treatment, the agency may arrange for an examination by an independent consulting physician. Whenever the agency's tentative assessment of the beneficiary's condition differs from his own assessment, the beneficiary is informed that benefits may be terminated, provided a summary of the evidence upon which the proposed determination to terminate is based, and afforded an opportunity to review the medical reports and other evidence in his case file. He also may respond in writing and submit additional evidence.

The state agency then makes its final determination, which is reviewed by an examiner in the SSA Bureau of Disability Insurance. If, as is usually the case, the SSA accepts the agency determination it notifies the recipient in writing, informing him of the reasons for the decision, and of his right to seek de novo reconsideration by the state agency.[3] Upon acceptance by the SSA, benefits are terminated effective two months after the month in which medical recovery is found to have occurred.

If the recipient seeks reconsideration by the state agency and the determination is adverse, the SSA reviews the reconsideration determination and notifies the recipient of the decision. He then has a right to an evidentiary hearing before an SSA administrative law judge. The hearing is non-adversary, and the SSA is not represented by counsel. As at all prior and subsequent stages of the administrative process, however, the claimant may be represented by counsel or other spokesmen. If this hearing results in an adverse decision, the claimant is entitled to request discretionary review by the SSA Appeals Council, and finally may obtain judicial review.

Should it be determined at any point after termination of benefits, that the claimant's disability extended beyond the date of cessation initially established, the worker is entitled to retroactive payments. If, on the other hand, a beneficiary receives any payments to which he is later determined not to be entitled, the statute authorizes the Secretary to attempt to recoup these funds in specified circumstances.

C

Despite the elaborate character of the administrative procedures provided by the Secretary, the courts below held them to be constitutionally inadequate, concluding that due process requires an evidentiary hearing prior to termination. In light of the private and governmental interests at stake here and the nature of the existing procedures, we think this was error.

Since a recipient whose benefits are terminated is awarded full retroactive relief if he ultimately prevails, his sole interest is in the uninterrupted receipt of this source of income pending final administrative decision on his claim. His potential injury is thus similar in nature to that of the welfare recipient in Goldberg, see 397 U.S., at 263–264, [and] the nonprobationary federal employee in Arnett, see 416 U.S., at 146 . . . .

Only in Goldberg has the Court held that due process requires an evidentiary hearing prior to a temporary deprivation. It was empha-

---

3. The reconsideration assessment is initially made by the state agency, but usually not by the same persons who considered the case originally. R. Dixon, Social Security Disability and Mass Justice 32 (1973). Both the recipient and the agency may adduce new evidence.

sized there that welfare assistance is given to persons on the very margin of subsistence . . . . Eligibility for disability benefits, in contrast, is not based upon financial need.[4] Indeed, it is wholly unrelated to the worker's income or support from many other sources, such as earnings of other family members, workmen's compensation awards, tort claims awards, savings, private insurance, public or private pensions, veterans' benefits, food stamps, public assistance, or the "many other important programs, both public and private, which contain provisions for disability payments affecting a substantial portion of the work force . . . ." Richardson v. Belcher, 404 U.S., at 85–87 (Douglas, J., dissenting).

As Goldberg illustrates, the degree of potential deprivation that may be created by a particular decison is a factor to be considered in assessing the validity of any administrative decisionmaking process. The potential deprivation here is generally likely to be less than in Goldberg, although the degree of difference can be overstated. As the District Court emphasized, to remain eligible for benefits a recipient must be "unable to engage in substantial gainful activity." Thus, in contrast to the discharged federal employee in Arnett, there is little possibility that the terminated recipient will be able to find even temporary employment to ameliorate the interim loss.

As we recognized last Term in Fusari v. Steinberg, 419 U.S. 379, 389 (1975), "the possible length of wrongful deprivation of . . . benefits [also] is an important factor in assessing the impact of official action on the private interests." The Secretary concedes that the delay between a request for a hearing before an administrative law judge and a decision on the claim is currently between 10 and 11 months. Since a terminated recipient must first obtain a reconsideration decision as a prerequisite to invoking his right to an evidentiary hearing, the delay between the actual cutoff of benefits and final decision after a hearing exceeds one year.

In view of the torpidity of this administrative review process and the typically modest resources of the family unit of the physically disabled worker [5] the hardship imposed upon the erroneously terminated disability recipient may be significant. Still, the disabled worker's need is likely to be less than that of a welfare recipient. In addition to the possibility of access to private resources, other forms of government assistance will become available where the termination of disability benefits places a worker or his family below the subsistence level. In view of these potential sources of temporary income, there is less reason here than in Goldberg to depart from the ordinary principle,

---

4. The level of benefits is determined by the worker's average monthly earnings during the period prior to disability, his age, and other factors not directly related to financial need . . . .

5. Amici cite statistics compiled by the Secretary which indicate that in 1965 the mean income of the family unit of a disabled worker was $3,803, while the median income for the unit was $2,836. The mean liquid assets—i.e., cash, stocks, bonds—of these family units was $4,862; the median was $940. These statistics do not take into account the family unit's nonliquid assets—i.e., automobile, real estate, and the like. Brief for AFL–CIO et al. as Amici Curiae App. 4a.

established by our decisions, that something less than an evidentiary hearing is sufficient prior to adverse administrative action.

D

An additional factor to be considered here is the fairness and reliability of the existing pretermination procedures, and the probable value, if any, of additional procedural safeguards. Central to the evaluation of any administrative process is the nature of the relevant inquiry. See . . . Friendly, Some Kind of Hearing, 123 U.Pa.L.Rev. 1267, 1281 (1975). In order to remain eligible for benefits the disabled worker must demonstrate by means of "medically acceptable clinical and laboratory diagnostic techniques," 42 U.S.C. § 423(d)(3), that he is unable "to engage in any substantial gainful activity by reason of any *medically determinable* physical or mental impairment. . . ." § 423(d)(1)(A) (emphasis supplied). In short, a medical assessment of the worker's physical or mental condition is required. This is a more sharply focused and easily documented decision than the typical determination of welfare entitlement. In the latter case, a wide variety of information may be deemed relevant and issues of witness credibility and veracity often are critical to the decisionmaking process. Goldberg noted that in such circumstances "written submissions are a wholly unsatisfactory basis for decision." 397 U.S., at 269.

By contrast, the decision whether to discontinue disability benefits will turn, in most cases, upon "routine, standard, and unbiased medical reports by physician specialists," Richardson v. Perales, 402 U.S., at 404, concerning a subject whom they have personally examined.[6] In Richardson the Court recognized the "reliability and probative worth of written medical reports," emphasizing that while there may be "professional disagreement with the medical conclusions" the "specter of questionable credibility and veracity is not present." To be sure, credibility and veracity may be a factor in the ultimate disability assessment in some cases. But procedural due process rules are shaped by the risk of error inherent in the truthfinding process as applied to the generality of cases, not the rare exceptions. The potential value of an evidentiary hearing, or even oral presentation to the decisionmaker, is substantially less in this context than in Goldberg.

The decision in Goldberg also was based on the Court's conclusion that written submissions were an inadequate substitute for oral presentation because they did not provide an effective means for the recipient

6. The decision is not purely a question of the accuracy of a medical diagnosis since the ultimate issue which the state agency must resolve is whether in light of the particular worker's "age, education, and work experience" he cannot "engage in any . . . substantial gainful work which exists in the national economy. . . ." 42 U.S.C. § 423(d)(2)(A). Yet information concerning each of these worker characteristics is amenable to effective written presentation. The value of an evidentiary hearing, or even a limited oral presentation, to an accurate presentation of those factors to the decisionmaker does not appear substantial. Similarly, resolution of the inquiry as to the types of employment opportunities that exist in the national economy for a physically impaired worker with a particular set of skills would not necessarily be advanced by an evidentiary hearing. Cf. 1 K. Davis, Administrative Law Treatise § 7.06, p. 429 (1958). The statistical information relevant to this judgment is more amenable to written than to oral presentation.

to communicate his case to the decisionmaker. Written submissions were viewed as an unrealistic option, for most recipients lacked the "educational attainment necessary to write effectively" and could not afford professional assistance. In addition, such submissions would not provide the "flexibility of oral presentations" or "permit the recipient to mold his argument to the issues the decision maker appears to regard as important." 397 U.S., at 269. In the context of the disability-benefits-entitlement assessment the administrative procedures under review here fully answer these objections.

The detailed questionnaire which the state agency periodically sends the recipient identifies with particularity the information relevant to the entitlement decision, and the recipient is invited to obtain assistance from the local SSA office in completing the questionnaire. More important, the information critical to the entitlement decision usually is derived from medical sources, such as the treating physician. Such sources are likely to be able to communicate more effectively through written documents than are welfare recipients or the lay witnesses supporting their cause. The conclusions of physicians often are supported by X-rays and the results of clinical or laboratory tests, information typically more amenable to written than to oral presentation. Cf. W. Gellhorn & C. Byse, Administrative Law—Cases and Comments 860–863 (6th ed. 1974).

A further safeguard against mistake is the policy of allowing the disability recipient's representative full access to all information relied upon by the state agency. In addition, prior to the cutoff of benefits the agency informs the recipient of its tentative assessment, the reasons therefor, and provides a summary of the evidence that it considers most relevant. Opportunity is then afforded the recipient to submit additional evidence or arguments, enabling him to challenge directly the accuracy of information in his file as well as the correctness of the agency's tentative conclusions. These procedures, again as contrasted with those before the Court in Goldberg, enable the recipient to "mold" his argument to respond to the precise issues which the decisionmaker regards as crucial.

Despite these carefully structured procedures, amici point to the significant reversal rate for appealed cases as clear evidence that the current process is inadequate. Depending upon the base selected and the line of analysis followed, the relevant reversal rates urged by the contending parties vary from a high of 58.6% for appealed reconsideration decisions to an overall reversal rate of only 3.3%. Bare statistics rarely provide a satisfactory measure of the fairness of a decisionmaking process. Their adequacy is especially suspect here since the administrative review system is operated on an open-file basis. A recipient may always submit new evidence, and such submissions may result in additional medical examinations. Such fresh examinations were held in approximately 30% to 40% of the appealed cases in fiscal 1973, either at the reconsideration or evidentiary hearing stage of the administrative process. In this context, the value of reversal rate statistics as one means of evaluating the adequacy of the pretermination process is diminished. Thus, although we view such information as relevant, it is certainly not controlling in this case.

E

In striking the appropriate due process balance the final factor to be assessed is the public interest. This includes the administrative burden and other societal costs that would be associated with requiring, as a matter of constitutional right, an evidentiary hearing upon demand in all cases prior to the termination of disability benefits. The most visible burden would be the incremental cost resulting from the increased number of hearings and the expense of providing benefits to ineligible recipients pending decision. No one can predict the extent of the increase, but the fact that full benefits would continue until after such hearings would assure the exhaustion in most cases of this attractive option. Nor would the theoretical right of the Secretary to recover undeserved benefits result, as a practical matter, in any substantial offset to the added outlay of public funds. The parties submit widely varying estimates of the probable additional financial cost. We only need say that experience with the constitutionalizing of government procedures suggests that the ultimate additional cost in terms of money and administrative burden would not be insubstantial.

Financial cost alone is not a controlling weight in determining whether due process requires a particular procedural safeguard prior to some administrative decision. But the Government's interest, and hence that of the public, in conserving scarce fiscal and administrative resources is a factor that must be weighed. At some point the benefit of an additional safeguard to the individual affected by the administrative action and to society in terms of increased assurance that the action is just, may be outweighed by the cost. Significantly, the cost of protecting those whom the preliminary administrative process has identified as likely to be found undeserving may in the end come out of the pockets of the deserving since resources available for any particular program of social welfare are not unlimited. See Friendly, supra, 123 U.Pa.L.Rev., at 1276, 1303.

But more is implicated in cases of this type than ad hoc weighing of fiscal and administrative burdens against the interests of a particular category of claimants. The ultimate balance involves a determination as to when, under our constitutional system, judicial-type procedures must be imposed upon administrative action to assure fairness. . . . The judicial model of an evidentiary hearing is neither a required, nor even the most effective, method of decisionmaking in all circumstances. The essence of due process is the requirement that "a person in jeopardy of serious loss [be given] notice of the case against him and opportunity to meet it." Joint Anti-Fascist Comm. v. McGrath, 341 U.S., at 171–172 (Frankfurter, J., concurring). All that is necessary is that the procedures be tailored, in light of the decision to be made, to "the capacities and circumstances of those who are to be heard," Goldberg v. Kelly, 397 U.S., at 268–269 (footnote omitted) to insure that they are given a meaningful opportunity to present their case. In assessing what process is due in this case, substantial weight must be given to the good-faith judgments of the individuals charged by Congress with the administration of social welfare programs that the procedures they have provided assure fair consideration of the entitlement claims of individuals. This is especially so where, as here, the prescribed procedures not only provide the claimant with an effective process for asserting his claim prior to any administrative action, but also assure a right to an evidentiary hearing, as well as to subsequent judicial review, before the denial of his claim becomes final.

We conclude that an evidentiary hearing is not required prior to the termination of disability benefits and that the present administrative procedures fully comport with due process.

The judgment of the Court of Appeals is

Reversed.

MR. JUSTICE STEVENS took no part in the consideration or decision of this case.

MR. JUSTICE BRENNAN, with whom MR. JUSTICE MARSHALL concurs, dissenting. . . .

[T]he Court's consideration that a discontinuance of disability benefits may cause the recipient to suffer only a limited deprivation is no argument. It is speculative. Moreover, the very legislative determination to provide disability benefits, without any prerequisite determination of need in fact, presumes a need by the recipient which is not this Court's function to denigrate. Indeed, in the present case, it is indicated that because disability benefits were terminated there was a foreclosure upon the Eldridge home and the family's furniture was repossessed, forcing Eldridge, his wife, and their children to sleep in one bed. Finally, it is also no argument that a worker, who has been placed in the untenable position of having been denied disability benefits, may still seek other forms of public assistance.

NOTES

(1) JERRY L. MASHAW, THE SUPREME COURT'S DUE PROCESS CALCULUS FOR ADMINISTRATIVE ADJUDICATION IN MATHEWS v. ELDRIDGE: THREE FACTORS IN SEARCH OF A THEORY OF VALUE, 44 U.Chi.L.Rev. 28, 48–49 (1976):[†]

"The utilitarian calculus is not, however, without difficulties. The Eldridge Court conceives of the values of procedure too narrowly: it views the sole purpose of procedural protections as enhancing accuracy, and thus limits its calculus to the benefits or costs that flow from correct or incorrect decisions. No attention is paid to 'process values' that might inhere in oral proceedings or to the demoralization costs that may result from the grant-withdrawal-grant-withdrawal sequence to which claimants like Eldridge are subjected. Perhaps more important, as the Court seeks to make sense of a calculus in which accuracy is the sole goal of procedure, it tends erroneously to characterize disability hearings as concerned almost exclusively with medical im-

† Reprinted by permission of the publisher and author.

pairment and thus concludes that such hearings involve only medical evidence, whose reliability would be little enhanced by oral procedure. As applied by the Eldridge Court the utilitarian calculus tends, as cost-benefit analyses typically do, to 'dwarf soft variables' and to ignore complexities and ambiguities.

"The problem with a utilitarian calculus is not merely that the Court may define the relevant costs and benefits too narrowly. However broadly conceived, the calculus asks unanswerable questions. For example, what is the social value, and the social cost, of continuing disability payments until after an oral hearing for persons initially determined to be ineligible? Answers to those questions require a technique for measuring the social value and social cost of government income transfers, but no such technique exists. Even if such formidable tasks of social accounting could be accomplished, the effectiveness of oral hearings in forestalling the losses that result from erroneous terminations would remain uncertain. In the face of these pervasive indeterminacies the Eldridge Court was forced to retreat to a presumption of constitutionality.

"Finally, it is not clear that the utilitarian balancing analysis asks the constitutionally relevant questions. The due process clause is one of those Bill of Rights protections meant to insure individual liberty in the face of contrary collective action. Therefore, a collective legislative or administrative decision about procedure, one arguably reflecting the intensity of the contending social values and representing an optimum position from the contemporary social perspective, cannot answer the constitutional question of whether due process has been accorded. A balancing analysis that would have the Court merely redetermine the question of social utility is similarly inadequate. There is no reason to believe that the Court has superior competence or legitimacy as a utilitarian balancer except as it performs its peculiar institutional role of insuring that libertarian values are considered in the calculus of decision."

(2) In the years following the decision in Mathews v. Eldridge, Professor Mashaw published a series of influential works, of increasing generality, that appeared to draw impetus, if not from Mathews, then from the problems of administering the statutory scheme to which it relates. J. Mashaw, C. Goetz, F. Goodman, W. Schwartz, P. Verkuil and M. Carrow, Social Security Hearings and Appeals: A Study of the Social Security Administration Hearing System (1978); J. Mashaw, Bureaucratic Justice (1983); J. Mashaw, Due Process in the Administrative State (1985). The second of these works draws attention to the proposition that both the program and appropriate controls for its functioning can be viewed from several coherent, and competing, perspectives. Consider the following excerpt (from pages 21–25, 31), knowing that a small piece cannot do justice to a work students repeatedly describe to one of your editors as a candidate for "mandatory reading in this course":[†]

"There is a substantial critical literature on the administration of disability benefits under Titles II and XVI of the Social Security Act. One strand of the commentary is concerned that the disability program fails to provide adequate service to claimants and beneficiaries. This view at least implicitly characterizes the program's purposes as paternalistic and therapeutic, purposes that would seem to require a major role for health care, vocational, social service, and other professionals in program administration. The failure of the bureaucratic decision process to emphasize the role of professional judgment and to adopt a service orientation is seen as the program's major deficiency.

"A second, more 'legalistic' perspective is concerned primarily with the capacity of individual claimants to assert and defend their rights to disability benefits. This literature is concerned with such problems as the inadequacy of the notices of denial sent to rejected applicants; the need for representation of claimants in disability hearings; the lack of adversarial testing of the evidence provided by participants in the adjudicatory process; the substantial reversal rate of those cases that are heard orally by independent administrative law judges and on review in federal courts. In sum, the concern is with the failure of the disability decision process to provide the essential ingredients of judicial trials.

"A third strand of the critical literature chides SSA for failing to manage the adjudication of claims in ways that produce predictable and consistent outcomes. The concern is that the system may be out of control, and the suggestions for reform are essentially managerial: SSA should provide more complete and objective criteria for the exercise of adjudicatory discretion; greater control should be gained over the internal routines of the disability decision services in the states; the system of management oversight and statistical quality assurance should be strengthened. In short, the system is viewed in bureaucratic terms and criticized for its inadequate management controls.

"This pattern of criticism is curious. First, why is the disability program's adjudicatory function viewed in such divergent ways? Is the disagreement about the program's purposes or about the appropriate means for achieving those purposes or both? Second, why does the criticism tend to fall into the described pattern? What unifies each perspective? Something specific to this program? Or some more general notions about administrative justice? Third, why, given the continuous and repetitive nature of the criticism—some of it from powerful political actors—has the program not been modified to eliminate the problems that one or all of the critics perceive?

"In reflecting on these curiosities I have come to some hypotheses that seem to have interesting implications, not just for the disability program but for the evaluation of administrative adjudication generally. First, these criticisms reflect distinct conceptual models of administrative justice. Second, each of the models is coherent and attractive. But, third, the models, while not mutually exclusive, are highly competitive: the internal logic of any one of them tends to drive the characteristics of the others from the field as it works itself out in concrete situations.

"If these hypotheses are correct, then it may also follow that the best system of administrative adjudication may be the one most open to criticism. A compromise that seeks to preserve the values and to respond at once to the insights of all of these conceptions of justice will, from the perspective of each separate conception, appear incoherent and unjust. The best system of administrative adjudication that can be devised may fall tragically short of our inconsistent ideals.

". . .

"The three strands in the critical literature on the disability program suggest three types of justice arguments: (1) that decisions should be accurate and efficient concrete realizations of the legislative will; (2) that decisions should provide appropriate support or therapy from the perspective of relevant professional cultures; and (3) that decisions should be fairly arrived at when assessed in the light of traditional processes for determining individual entitlements. Elaboration of these arguments in the context of the disability program produces three distinct models of administrative justice; models that I shall denominate *bureaucratic rationality, professional treatment,* and *moral judgment.*"

(3) Justice Powell's opinion twice cites a then-recent and now-famous article by the late Court of Appeals Judge HENRY J. FRIENDLY, "SOME KIND OF HEARING," 123 U.Pa.L.Rev. 1267 (1975). In this article, Judge Friendly focused on the question: "If a Hearing, What Kind of Hearing." Although he admitted that a test which balanced the importance of the private interest and the usefulness of a particular safeguard against the burden of providing additional process seemed "uncertain and subjective," he thought that "the more elaborate specification of the relevant factors may help to produce more principled and predictable decisions." He then endeavored to "compile one list enumerating factors that have been considered to be elements of a fair hearing, roughly in order of priority, and another that arrays various types of government action that have been urged to call for a hearing, starting with the most serious."

Here is Judge Friendly's list compiled "roughly in order of priority" of the elements of a fair hearing:

1. An Unbiased Tribunal

2. Notice of the Proposed Action and the Grounds Asserted for It

3. An Opportunity to Present Reasons Why the Proposed Action Should Not be Taken

4. The Right to Call Witnesses

5. The Right To Know the Evidence Against One

6. The Right To Have Decision Based Only on the Evidence Presented

7. Counsel

8. The Making of a Record

9. A Statement of Reasons

10. Public Attendance

11. Judicial Review

(For his discussion of the seriousness of various types of governmental actions, see id. at 1295 ff.)

Judge Friendly closed his article with the thought that "in the mass justice area" the Supreme Court had too easily accepted the idea that the adversary model was the only model, and had encouraged the lower courts to follow suit by "pulling practically all the procedural stops in Goldberg" when in fact all that was there needed was an opportunity for oral presentation and some testing of the credibility of "tipsters."

(4) Justice Powell's three-factored framework for deciding what process is due is presented in Mathews as an authoritative restatement of prior law. Even the two dissenting justices quarreled essentially only about the weight to be accorded various facts. As one would imagine—and as some of the subsequent cases in this part of the book will show—Mathews is often treated as the leading case on this part of the law. However, some of the Court's subsequent cases concerned with what process is due have not been decided by application of the Mathews framework.

In BOARD OF CURATORS OF THE UNIVERSITY OF MISSOURI v. HOROWITZ, 435 U.S. 78 (1978), the plaintiff was dismissed from medical school in her last year for failure to perform adequately in her clinical rotations. She had been placed on probation after her next-to-last year, based on faculty members' assessments of her performance, and she was notified of her deficiencies by letter and orally by the Dean. In the middle of her last year she again met with the Dean, who discussed with her her failure to come up to standard. Finally, before dismissing her the school arranged for her clinical performance to be evaluated separately by seven practicing physicians who each spent a substantial amount of time with her.

In a separate opinion—speaking only for himself—Justice Marshall applied the Mathews framework to these facts. The private interest was a weighty one, since the evidence was that the plaintiff stood to lose not only a place at this medical school, but perhaps all chance of further medical education or employment. There was some risk of error since faculty evaluations of personal hygiene or patient rapport were not based on hard evidence. And the interest of the school in summary proceedings did not seem great. Plaintiff, said Justice Marshall, was entitled to more than an informal give-and-take with the Dean before dismissal. However, the "appeals" process of getting outside evaluations, although not a procedural protection typical of the traditional adversary system, was well suited to the problem. Accordingly, overall, plaintiff got as much procedural protection as the Constitution required.

Justice Rehnquist's opinion for the Court—speaking for five justices—took quite another tack, although with the same result on the facts presented. Dismissal from school for academic reasons is far different from a disciplinary determination. Many years of precedent in lower and state courts have drawn the distinction. Academic dismissal is subjective and evaluative rather than primarily factual. "Like the decision of an individual professor as to the proper grade for a student in his course, the determination whether to dismiss a student for academic reasons requires an expert evaluation of cumulative information and is not readily adapted to the procedural tools of judicial or administrative decisionmaking." Accordingly, "we decline to ignore the historic judgment of educators and thereby formalize the academic dismissal process by requiring a hearing." Apparently even an informal give-and-take was not constitutionally required. Mathews v. Eldridge was mentioned only in a footnote.

Other Justices simply noted that whether the Court's opinion or Justice Marshall's opinion was correct, the outcome was the same.

For another example of the Court's deference to the substantive professional judgments made about students' academic abilities, see Regents of the University of Michigan v. Ewing, 106 S.Ct. 507 (1985).

INGRAHAM v. WRIGHT
Supreme Court of the United States, 1977.
430 U.S. 651.

MR. JUSTICE POWELL delivered the opinion of the Court.

[Plaintiffs James Ingraham and Roosevelt Andrews, eighth and ninth graders at Drew Junior High in Dade County, Fla., sued various school officials. After plaintiffs' evidence was in, the district court dismissed the case.]

Petitioners' evidence may be summarized briefly. In the 1970–1971 school year many of the 237 schools in Dade County used corporal punishment as a means of maintaining discipline pursuant to Florida legislation and a local School Board regulation. . . . The authorized punishment consisted of paddling the recalcitrant student on the buttocks with a flat wooden paddle measuring less than two feet long, three to four inches wide, and about one-half inch thick. The normal punishment was limited to one to five "licks" or blows with the paddle and resulted in no apparent physical injury to the student. School authorities viewed corporal punishment as a less drastic means of discipline than suspension or expulsion. . . .

. . . The evidence, consisting mainly of the testimony of 16 students, suggests that the regime at Drew was exceptionally harsh. The testimony of Ingraham and Andrews, in support of their individual claims for damages, is illustrative. Because he was slow to respond to his teacher's instructions, Ingraham was subjected to more than 20 licks with a paddle while being held over a table in the principal's office. The paddling was so severe that he suffered a hematoma requiring medical attention and keeping him out of school for several days. Andrews was paddled several times for minor infractions. On two occasions he was struck on his arms, once depriving him of the full use of his arm for a week.

The District Court made no findings on the credibility of the students' testimony. Rather, assuming their testimony to be credible, the court found no constitutional basis for relief.

. . .

A panel of the Court of Appeals voted to reverse. . . . Upon rehearing, the en banc court rejected these conclusions and affirmed the judgment of the District Court. . . .

We granted certiorari, limited to the questions of cruel and unusual punishment and procedural due process.

II

In addressing the scope of the Eighth Amendment's prohibition on cruel and unusual punishment, this Court has found it useful to refer to "[t]raditional common-law concepts," Powell v. Texas, 392 U.S. 514, 535 (1968) (plurality opinion), and to the "attitude[s] which our society has traditionally taken." Id., at 531. So, too, in defining the requirements of procedural due process under the Fifth and Fourteenth Amendments, the Court has been attuned to what "has always been the law of the land," United States v. Barnett, 376 U.S. 681, 692 (1964), and to "traditional ideas of fair procedure." Greene v. McElroy, 360 U.S. 474, 508 (1959). We therefore begin by examining the way in which our traditions and our laws have responded to the use of corporal punishment in public schools.

The use of corporal punishment in this country as a means of disciplining schoolchildren dates back to the colonial period. . . . Professional and public opinion is sharply divided on the practice, and has been for more than a century. . . .

At common law a single principle has governed the use of corporal punishment since before the American Revolution: Teachers may impose reasonable but not excessive force to discipline a child. . . . The prevalent rule in this country today privileges such force as a teacher or administrator "reasonably believes to be necessary for [the child's] proper control, training, or education." Restatement (Second) of Torts § 147(2) (1965); see id., § 153(2). To the extent that the force is excessive or unreasonable, the educator in virtually all States is subject to possible civil and criminal liability.

. . .

III

. . . . An examination of the history of the [Eighth] Amendment and the decisions of this Court construing the proscription against cruel and unusual punishment confirms that it was designed to protect those convicted of crimes. We adhere to this longstanding limitation and hold that the Eighth Amendment does not apply to the paddling of children as a means of maintaining discipline in public schools.

. . .

IV

The Fourteenth Amendment prohibits any state deprivation of life, liberty, or property without due process of law. Application of this prohibition requires the familiar two-stage analysis: We must first ask whether the asserted individual interests are encompassed within the Fourteenth Amendment's protection of "life, liberty or property"; if protected interests are implicated, we then must decide what procedures constitute "due process of law." Following that analysis here, we find that corporal punishment in public schools implicates a constitutionally protected liberty interest, but we hold that the traditional common-law remedies are fully adequate to afford due process.

A

"[T]he range of interests protected by procedural due process is not infinite." Board of Regents v. Roth, [408 U.S.,] at 570. We have repeatedly rejected "the notion that *any* grievous loss visited upon a person by the State is sufficient to invoke the procedural protections of the Due Process Clause." Meachum v. Fano, 427 U.S., at 224. Due process is required only when a decision of the State implicates an interest within the protection of the Fourteenth Amendment. And "to determine whether due process requirements apply in the first place, we must look not to the 'weight' but to the *nature* of the interest at stake." Roth, at 570–571.

The Due Process Clause of the Fifth Amendment, later incorporated into the Fourteenth, was intended to give Americans at least the protection against governmental power that they had enjoyed as Englishmen against the power of the Crown. The liberty preserved from deprivation without due process included the right "generally to enjoy those privileges long recognized at common law as essential to the orderly pursuit of happiness by free men." Meyer v. Nebraska, 262 U.S. 390, 399 (1923). Among the historic liberties so protected was a right to be free from, and to obtain judicial relief for, unjustified intrusions on personal security.

While the contours of this historic liberty interest in the context of our federal system of government have not been defined precisely, they always have been thought to encompass freedom from bodily restraint and punishment. It is fundamental that the state cannot hold and physically punish an individual except in accordance with due process of law.

This constitutionally protected liberty interest is at stake in this case. There is, of course, a de minimis level of imposition with which the Constitution is not concerned. But at least where school authorities, acting under color of state law, deliberately decide to punish a child for misconduct by restraining the child and inflicting appreciable physical pain, we hold that Fourteenth Amendment liberty interests are implicated.[1]

---

1. Unlike Goss v. Lopez, this case does not involve the state-created property interest in public education. The purpose of corporal punishment is to correct a child's

B

"[T]he question remains what process is due." Morrissey v. Brewer, [408 U.S.] at 481. Were it not for the common-law privilege permitting teachers to inflict reasonable corporal punishment on children in their care, and the availability of the traditional remedies for abuse, the case for requiring advance procedural safeguards would be strong indeed. But here we deal with a punishment—paddling—within that tradition, and the question is whether the common-law remedies are adequate to afford due process.

. . . Whether in this case the common-law remedies for excessive corporal punishment constitute due process of law must turn on an analysis of the competing interests at stake, viewed against the background of "history, reason, [and] the past course of decisions." The analysis requires consideration of three distinct factors: "First, the private interest that will be affected . . . ; second, the risk of an erroneous deprivation of such interest . . . and the probable value, if any, of additional or substitute procedural safeguards; and finally, the [state] interest, including the function involved and the fiscal and administrative burdens that the additional or substitute procedural requirement would entail." Mathews v. Eldridge, 424 U.S. 319, 335 (1976).

1

Because it is rooted in history, the child's liberty interest in avoiding corporal punishment while in the care of public school authorities is subject to historical limitations. . . .

The concept that reasonable corporal punishment in school is justifiable continues to be recognized in the laws of most States. . . .

This is not to say that the child's interest in procedural safeguards is insubstantial. . . .

We turn now to a consideration of the safeguards that are available under applicable Florida law.

2

Florida has continued to recognize, and indeed has strengthened by statute, the common-law right of a child not to be subjected to excessive corporal punishment in school. Under Florida law the teacher and principal of the school decide in the first instance whether corporal punishment is reasonably necessary under the circumstances in order

behavior without interrupting his education. That corporal punishment may, in a rare case, have the unintended effect of temporarily removing a child from school affords no basis for concluding that the practice itself deprives students of property protected by the Fourteenth Amendment.

Nor does this case involve any state-created interest in liberty going beyond the Fourteenth Amendment's protection of freedom from bodily restraint and corporal punishment. Cf. Meachum v. Fano.

to discipline a child who has misbehaved. But they must exercise prudence and restraint. For Florida has preserved the traditional judicial proceedings for determining whether the punishment was justified. If the punishment inflicted is later found to have been excessive—not reasonably believed at the time to be necessary for the child's discipline or training—the school authorities inflicting it may be held liable in damages to the child and, if malice is shown, they may be subject to criminal penalties.[2]

Although students have testified in this case to specific instances of abuse, there is every reason to believe that such mistreatment is an aberration. . . . Moreover, because paddlings are usually inflicted in response to conduct directly observed by teachers in their presence, the risk that a child will be paddled without cause is typically insignificant. . . .

In those cases where severe punishment is contemplated, the available civil and criminal sanctions for abuse—considered in light of the openness of the school environment—afford significant protection against unjustified corporal punishment. Teachers and school authorities are unlikely to inflict corporal punishment unnecessarily or excessively when a possible consequence of doing so is the institution of civil or criminal proceedings against them.[3]

It still may be argued, of course, that the child's liberty interest would be better protected if the common-law remedies were supplemented by the administrative safeguards of prior notice and a hearing. . . . But where the State has preserved what "has always been the law of the land," United States v. Barnett, 376 U.S. 681 (1964), the case for administrative safeguards is significantly less compelling.[4] . . .

2. . . . Both the District Court and the Court of Appeals expressed the view that the common-law tort remedy was available to the petitioners in this case. And petitioners conceded in this Court that a teacher who inflicts excessive punishment on a child may be held both civilly and criminally liable under Florida law.

In view of the statutory adoption of the common-law rule, and the unanimity of the parties and the courts below, the doubts expressed in Mr. Justice White's dissenting opinion as to the availability of tort remedies in Florida can only be viewed as chimerical. . . .

3. The low incidence of abuse, and the availability of established judicial remedies in the event of abuse, distinguish this case from Goss v. Lopez, 419 U.S. 565 (1975). The Ohio law struck down in Goss provided for suspensions from public school of up to 10 days without "any written procedure applicable to suspensions." Id., at 567. Although Ohio law provided generally for administrative review, the Court assumed that the short suspensions would not be stayed pending review, with the result that

the review proceeding could serve neither a deterrent nor a remedial function. 419 U.S., at 581 n. 10. In these circumstances, the Court held the law authorizing suspensions unconstitutional for failure to require "that there be at least an informal give-and-take between student and disciplinarian, preferably prior to the suspension. . . . " Id., at 584. The subsequent civil and criminal proceedings available in this case may be viewed as affording substantially greater protection to the child than the informal conference mandated by Goss.

4. "[P]rior hearings might well be dispensed with in many circumstances in which the state's conduct, if not adequately justified, would constitute a common-law tort. This would leave the injured plaintiff in precisely the same posture as a common-law plaintiff, and this procedural consequence would be quite harmonious with the substantive view that the fourteenth amendment encompasses the same liberties as those protected by the common law." Monaghan, Of "Liberty" and "Property," 62 Cornell L.Rev. 405, 431 (1977) (footnote omitted). . . .

3

But even if the need for advance procedural safeguards were clear, the question would remain whether the incremental benefit could justify the cost. Acceptance of petitioners' claims would work a transformation in the law governing corporal punishment in Florida and most other States. Given the impracticability of formulating a rule of procedural due process that varies with the severity of the particular imposition, the prior hearing petitioners seek would have to precede *any* paddling, however moderate or trivial.

Such a universal constitutional requirement would significantly burden the use of corporal punishment as a disciplinary measure. . . . Teachers, properly concerned with maintaining authority in the classroom, may well prefer to rely on other disciplinary measures— which they may view as less effective—rather than confront the possible disruption that prior notice and a hearing may entail.[5] Paradoxically, such an alteration of disciplinary policy is most likely to occur in the ordinary case where the contemplated punishment is well within the common-law privilege.[6]

. . .

"At some point the benefit of an additional safeguard to the individual affected . . . and to society in terms of increased assurance that the action is just, may be outweighed by the cost." Mathews v. Eldridge, 424 U.S., at 348. We think that point has been reached in this case. In view of the low incidence of abuse, the openness of our schools, and the common-law safeguards that already exist, the risk of error that may result in violation of a schoolchild's substantive rights can only be regarded as minimal. Imposing additional administrative safeguards as a constitutional requirement might reduce that risk marginally, but would also entail a significant intrusion into an area of primary educational responsibility. We conclude that the Due Process Clause does not require notice and a hearing prior to the imposition of corporal punishment in the public schools, as that practice is authorized and limited by the common law.

. . .

Affirmed.

MR. JUSTICE WHITE, with whom MR. JUSTICE BRENNAN, MR. JUSTICE MARSHALL, and MR. JUSTICE STEVENS join, dissenting.

Today the Court holds that corporal punishment in public schools, no matter how severe, can never be the subject of the protections afforded by the Eighth Amendment. It also holds that students in the public school systems are not constitutionally entitled to a hearing of any sort before beatings can be inflicted on them. . . .

---

5. If a prior hearing, with the inevitable attendant publicity within the school, resulted in rejection of the teacher's recommendation, the consequent impairment of the teacher's ability to maintain discipline in the classroom would not be insubstantial.

6. The effect of interposing prior procedural safeguards may well be to make the punishment more severe by increasing the anxiety of the child. For this reason, the school authorities in Dade County found it desirable that the punishment be inflicted as soon as possible after the infraction.

I

. . .

The issue presented in this phase of the case is limited to whether corporal punishment in public schools can *ever* be prohibited by the Eighth Amendment. . . . Where corporal punishment becomes so severe as to be unacceptable in a civilized society, I can see no reason that it should become any more acceptable just because it is inflicted on children in the public schools.

II

The majority concedes that corporal punishment in the public schools implicates an interest protected by the Due Process Clause. . . . The question remaining, as the majority recognizes, is what process is due.

The reason that the Constitution requires a State to provide "due process of law" when it punishes an individual for misconduct is to protect the individual from erroneous or mistaken punishment that the State would not have inflicted had it found the facts in a more reliable way. In Goss v. Lopez, 419 U.S. 565 (1975), the Court applied this principle to the school disciplinary process, holding that a student must be given an informal opportunity to be heard before he is finally suspended from public school.

> *Disciplinarians, although proceeding in utmost good faith, frequently act on the reports and advice of others;* and the controlling facts and the nature of the conduct under challenge are often disputed. *The risk of error is not at all trivial,* and it should be guarded against if that may be done without prohibitive cost or interference with the educational process. Id., at 580. (Emphasis added.)

To guard against this risk of punishing an innocent child, the Due Process Clause requires, not an "elaborate hearing" before a neutral party, but simply "an informal give-and-take between student and disciplinarian" which gives the student "an opportunity to explain his version of the facts." Id., at 580, 582, 584.

The Court now holds that these "rudimentary precautions against unfair or mistaken findings of misconduct," id., at 581, are not required if the student is punished with "appreciable physical pain" rather than with a suspension, even though both punishments deprive the student of a constitutionally protected interest. . . .

[The Florida] tort action is utterly inadequate to protect against erroneous infliction of punishment for two reasons. First, under Florida law, a student . . . has no remedy at all for punishment imposed on the basis of mistaken facts [7] . . . . The "traditional common-law

---

7. The majority's assurances to the contrary, it is unclear to me whether and to what extent Florida law provides a damages action against school officials for excessive corporal punishment. Giving the majority the benefit of every doubt, I think it is fair to say that the most a student punished on the basis of mistaken allegations of misconduct can hope for in Florida is a recovery for unreasonable or bad-faith

remedies" on which the majority relies, thus do nothing to protect the student from the danger that concerned the Court in Goss—the risk of reasonable, good-faith mistake in the school disciplinary process.

Second, and more important, even if the student could sue for good-faith error in the infliction of punishment, the lawsuit occurs after the punishment has been finally imposed. The infliction of physical pain is final and irreparable; it cannot be undone in a subsequent proceeding. There is every reason to require, as the Court did in Goss, a few minutes of "informal give-and-take between student and disciplinarian" as a "meaningful hedge" against the erroneous infliction of irreparable injury. 419 U.S., at 583–584.

The majority's conclusion that a damages remedy for excessive corporal punishment affords adequate process rests on the novel theory that the State may punish an individual without giving him any opportunity to present his side of the story, as long as he can later recover damages from a state official if he is innocent. . . . There is no authority for this theory, nor does the majority purport to find any, in the procedural due process decisions of this Court. . . .

I would reverse the judgment below.

Mr. Justice Stevens, dissenting.

. . . Notwithstanding my disagreement with the Court's holding . . . my respect for Mr. Justice Powell's reasoning in Part IV–B of his opinion for the Court prompts these comments.

The constitutional prohibition of state deprivations of life, liberty, or property without due process of law does not, by its express language, require that a hearing be provided *before* any deprivation may occur. To be sure, the timing of the process may be a critical element in determining its adequacy—that is, in deciding what process is due in a particular context. Generally, adequate notice and a fair opportunity to be heard in advance of any deprivation of a constitutionally protected interest are essential. The Court has recognized, however, that the wording of the command that there shall be no deprivation "without" due process of law is consistent with the conclusion that a postdeprivation remedy is sometimes constitutionally sufficient.

When only an invasion of a property interest is involved, there is a greater likelihood that a damages award will make a person completely whole than when an invasion of the individual's interest in freedom from bodily restraint and punishment has occurred. In the property context, therefore, frequently a postdeprivation state remedy may be all the process that the Fourteenth Amendment requires. It may also be true—although I do not express an opinion on the point—that an adequate state remedy for defamation may satisfy the due process requirement when a State has impaired an individual's interest in his reputation. On that hypothesis, the Court's analysis today gives rise to the thought that Paul v. Davis, 424 U.S. 693, may have been correctly

error. But I strongly suspect that even
this remedy is not available.

. . . .

decided on an incorrect rationale. Perhaps the Court will one day agree with Mr. Justice Brennan's appraisal of the importance of the constitutional interest at stake in id., at 720–723, 734 (dissenting opinion), and nevertheless conclude that an adequate state remedy may prevent every state-inflicted injury to a person's reputation from violating 42 U.S.C. § 1983.

NOTES

(1) As the opinions in Ingraham indicate, the case was written against the background of GOSS v. LOPEZ, 419 U.S. 565 (1975), the Court's first brush with the procedures applicable to school discipline. There, an Ohio statute authorized the suspension of a student for up to 10 days without requiring any process other than the principal's sending of a letter to the student's parents explaining why the action had been taken. *Held*: the statute was unconstitutional. State law which provides for public education—and, indeed, requires student attendance—provides an entitlement sufficient to implicate the fourteenth amendment, and deprivation of that entitlement for up to 10 days is not de minimis. In addition, a suspension can tarnish a student's reputation, thus depriving him or her of a liberty interest. As to the process required, the Goss majority departed strikingly from the Goldberg formula. As Justice White's opinion in Ingraham indicates, all that is constitutionally required, in light of the interests implicated, the desire to avoid error, and the functional requisites of the institutional setting, is "an informal give-and-take between student and disciplinarian." The student should be "given oral or written notice of the charges against him and, if he denies them, an explanation of the evidence the authorities have and an opportunity to present his side of the story." Where there is an immediate threat of institutional disruption, the school can remove first as long as it discusses immediately afterward.

The dissent in Goss contended first, that any possible deprivation under the statute would not be serious enough to implicate constitutional guarantees; and second, that it was wrong to refashion school discipline according to an adversarial model, however rudimentary, because providing a traditional structure of discipline was part of the educational mission of the school.

The Goss decision is greatly admired by some, notably by Professor K. C. Davis. In the current edition of his Treatise he devotes a section to "The Goss Principle" (2 Administrative Law Treatise § 13:2 (1979)), which he states thusly: "In some circumstances due process does not require trial procedure but forbids resolving a question of adjudicative fact against a party without first allowing him to respond informally to a summary of adverse evidence." Professor Davis continues:

> The Goss principle is a true fundamental. As it develops further and as its many applications proliferate, judges and lawyers will soon look back in wonder that the legal system was for so long without it. Many of the most fundamental ideas, after their creators have invented them and after they have become widely understood and integrated into the legal

system, appear to be so obvious that their development seems in retrospect to have been inevitable. The Goss principle is one of those fundamental ideas. The Court's enunciation of it is a long step forward in the development of procedural justice.

In Professor Davis' view, The Goss "principle" "will surely survive the setback it suffered in the Ingraham case." 2 Administrative Law Treatise § 13:3 at 481 (1979).

Goss was a 5–4 decision. Justice White delivered the majority opinion, with Douglas, Brennan, Stewart and Marshall joining. Justice Powell wrote the dissent; Burger, Blackmun, and Rehnquist joined him. Ingraham was a 5–4 decision. Justice Powell's majority opinion was joined by Burger, Stewart, Blackmun and Rehnquist; Justice White's dissent by Brennan, Marshall, and Stevens. Justice Stewart thus cast the swing vote.

(2) ROBERT A. BURT, THE CONSTITUTION OF THE FAMILY, 1979 THE SUPREME COURT REVIEW 329, 341–42:

"[I]n Ingraham v. Wright, Mr. Justice Powell identified a problem of central concern to him. . . . : 'If a prior hearing, with the inevitable attendant publicity within the school, resulted in rejection of the teacher's recommendation, the consequent impairment of the teacher's ability to maintain discipline in the classroom would not be insubstantial.' . . .

"It would be unfair, however, to portray the Court in Ingraham or its conservative nucleus as intending to condone or encourage brutality by teachers, parents, or judges. This nucleus intends to encourage an unquestioning attitude toward, and a reciprocally firm and self-confident attitude by, constituted authority. An idealized image of conflict-free interpersonal relations appears to lie beneath this intention. Mr. Justice Powell reveals this in his Goss v. Lopez dissent: 'The role of the teacher in our society historically has been an honored and respected one, rooted in the experience of decades that has left for most of us warm memories of our teachers, especially those of the formative years of primary and secondary education.' It might thus appear an insult to these honored memories if the Supreme Court were now to abandon '[our reliance] for generations upon the experience, good faith and dedication of those who staff our public schools.' "

Is it legitimate, in considering the reach of constitutional due process, to take into account the degree to which an extension of procedural rights will alter institutional power relationships? Is it responsible not to consider these possible consequences?

(3) Justice Stevens' remarks at the end of Ingraham are directed at a famous, perhaps infamous, and certainly remarkable case decided the previous term, PAUL v. DAVIS, 424 U.S. 693 (1976). Davis, a newspaper photographer, was included in a flier listing and containing pictures of purported "Active Shoplifters," which was circulated by Paul, a police chief. In fact, Davis had been arrested a year-and-a-half before, had pleaded not guilty at his arraignment, and had not been further prosecuted. Alleging that he had been branded without having ever

been tried, and that his future employment opportunities would be impaired, Davis filed suit under 42 U.S.C. § 1983 and the fourteenth amendment. In an opinion by Justice Rehnquist, for the same five justices who constituted the Ingraham majority, *held*: no cause of action for violation of fourteenth amendment rights had been stated; hence there had been no deprivation of a constitutional right for the purposes of § 1983; hence the case should be dismissed.

Most of Justice Rehnquist's opinion was devoted to showing that the interest in reputation asserted by Davis was not "liberty" or "property." Given statements decrying the official stigmatization of a person's good name which stretched back at least as far as Joint Anti-Fascist Refugee Comm. v. McGrath, this involved some fancy footwork. For example, Wisconsin v. Constantineau, the 1971 case which had held that "posting" of persons for excessive drinking was unconstitutional without notice and hearing, was distinguished as turning not on the stigma of being called a drunkard, but rather on losing the right to purchase liquor. (To see how this claim was reconciled with the Constantineau Court's statement that "[w]here a person's good name, reputation, honor, or integrity is at stake because of what the government is doing to him, notice and an opportunity to be heard are essential," consult 424 U.S. at 708.)

Justice Rehnquist also developed the point, less clearly relevant, but perhaps more powerful, that what Davis alleged was simply a common law defamation—but brought in federal court as a constitutional law matter. "Respondent's [plaintiff's] construction would seem almost necessarily to result in every legally cognizable injury which may have been inflicted by a state official acting under 'color of law' establishing a violation of the Fourteenth Amendment." Even this, however, did not impress the dissenters, who thought that the intentional action of the police officers in this case constituted (if the allegations were true) an abuse of official position by a local official, precisely the sort of thing the federal courts acting under the fourteenth amendment were supposed to be concerned about.

Paul v. Davis received largely negative reviews in the academic press. See, e.g., David Shapiro, Mr. Justice Rehnquist: A Preliminary View, 90 Harv.L.Rev. 293, 324–328 (1976). Of particular importance was the extended discussion in HENRY MONAGHAN, OF "LIBERTY" AND "PROPERTY," 62 Corn.L.Rev. 405 (1977). The Paul opinion's treatment of precedent, said Professor Monaghan, was "wholly startling." Moreover, even if the constitutional status of the interest in reputation were an open question, Justice Rehnquist's discussion was wide of the mark. "[I]t is an unsettling conception of 'liberty' that protects an individual against state interference with his access to liquor but not with his reputation in the community." More broadly, defamation is a serious assault on personal identity, and "the Court's conclusion that such an assault implicates no constitutionally protected interest stands wholly at odds with our ethical, political, and constitutional assumption about the worth of each individual."

And then Professor Monaghan went further, and attempted to reconstruct Paul v. Davis by focusing on the process due rather than the interest protected. The Court's problem, he said, grew out of its insistence in Goldberg on prior hearings. Common-law plaintiffs sue in court after being injured, and in many cases common-law-like interests protected against the state could be treated procedurally the same way. "This view, if accepted, would have disposed of the procedural due process objection in Paul." Without discussing Paul v. Davis in terms, this part of Professor Monaghan's article turns up in the majority opinion in Ingraham as a footnote (footnote 4 in the above-edited version). The same sort of argument is presented by Justice Stevens in his discussion of the Paul case. (Justice Stevens had not participated in the actual decision.)

(4) To understand fully the field of forces to which Paul and Ingraham are a response, something more must be said concerning the federalism aspects of the matter.

42 U.S.C. § 1983 provides as follows:

Every person who, under color of any statute, ordinance, regulation, custom, or usage, of any State or Territory or the District of Columbia, subjects, or causes to be subjected, any citizen of the United States or other person within the jurisdiction thereof to the deprivation of any rights, privileges, or immunities secured by the Constitution and laws, shall be liable to the party injured in an action at law, suit in equity, or other proper proceeding for redress. . . .

As can be seen, this statute provides an express federal remedy for the deprivation of constitutional (or other federal) rights, when such deprivation occurs "under color of" state law. In Monroe v. Pape, 365 U.S. 167 (1961), the Supreme Court sustained a complaint, in federal court against local police officers, which alleged that they had without lawful grounds invaded plaintiff's home, searched it, and made an arrest. The fourth amendment's guarantee against unreasonable searches and seizures was applicable to the states through the fourteenth amendment, so that plaintiff had alleged a deprivation of constitutional right. As to the deprivation being "under color of" state law, it was sufficient that the police officers had acted as if officially authorized. The fact that what they had done in reality violated state law, so that there would be a state remedy, made no difference. The federal remedy was additional to the state remedy, and could be used directly.

Section 1983 might have been more narrowly confined, given its origins in the post-Civil-War efforts to establish racial equality. Once it is interpreted to give a direct federal cause of action which encompasses the full range of an individual's federal rights against a state, does it inevitably put pressure on what the content of those rights can be? Some have so claimed. "Although the Court has formally adhered to Monroe by not requiring exhaustion of state judicial remedies in section 1983 cases, on other issues the Court has relied on state remedies to curtail section 1983's scope. . . . [I]n Ingraham v. Wright . . . the Court relied on the availability of state remedies to restrict the scope of section 1983, by restricting the content of the Constitution." T. Eisenberg, Section 1983: Doctrinal Foundations and an Empirical Study, 67 Corn.L.Rev. 482, 514 (1982). See also E. Travis and B. Adams, The Supreme Court's Shell Game: The Confusion of Jurisdiction and Substantive Rights in Section 1983 Litigation, 24 Bos.Coll.L.Rev. 635 (1983).

Is a fear of the federal courts' intruding overly on state institutions a good reason to change substantive law applicable to both state and federal governments? Or is the Ingraham principle in fact only applicable to state remedies for state torts?

(5) "The respondent is an inmate at the Nebraska Penal and Correctional Complex who ordered by mail certain hobby materials valued at $23.50. The hobby materials were lost and respondent brought suit under 42 U.S.C. § 1983 to recover their value. At first blush one might well inquire why respondent brought an action in federal court to recover damages of such a small amount for negligent loss of property, but because 28 U.S.C. § 1343, the predicate for . . . jurisdiction . . . contains no minimum dollar limitation, he was authorized by Congress to bring his action . . . if he stated a claim for relief under 42 U.S.C. § 1983. Respondent claimed that his property was negligently lost by prison officials. . . . More specifically, he claimed that he had been deprived of property without due process of law."

Thus begins Justice Rehnquist's opinion in PARRATT v. TAYLOR, 451 U.S. 527 (1981). Has a cause of action been stated? No. Why not? Well—

(a) The problem is not that § 1983 does not apply. Section 1983, says the Court, is not limited to intentional deprivations of constitutional rights, and indeed imposes no state of mind requirement beyond whatever might be imposed on the cause of action by the underlying constitutional claim.

(b) The problem is not that there is no "property." A hobby kit worth $23.50 is property.

(c) The problem is not that there is no "deprivation." The loss of the hobby kit, even though negligently caused, amounts to a deprivation.

(d) The problem is, the State of Nebraska provides a tort claims procedure. Post-deprivation remedies can satisfy the due process clause (citing, e.g., North American Cold Storage Co. v. Chicago and Phillips v. Commissioner). Since the alleged deprivation resulted from the random and unauthorized act of a state official, and not from an established procedure, it is difficult to see how a useful pre-deprivation hearing could be held. The hearing must be post-, and constitutionally can be post- if it is meaningful. "This analysis is also quite consistent with the approach taken by this Court in Ingraham v. Wright." Under Nebraska law, "[t]he remedies provided could have fully compensated the respondent for the property loss he suffered, and we hold that they are sufficient to satisfy the requirements of due process."

(e) Besides, "To accept respondent's argument that the conduct of the state officials in this case constituted a violation of the Fourteenth Amendment would almost necessarily result in turning every alleged injury which may have been inflicted by a state official acting under 'color of law' into a violation of the Fourteenth Amendment cognizable under § 1983."

But what if the state's officers are shielded from suit by sovereign (or official) immunity? Do we then say that the application of that sovereign immunity doctrine in state court violates due process? Or do we then say that the state provides no process which is due, and allow the federal cause of action to proceed?

Neither.

Prisoner Daniels slipped on a pillow left on a stairway in the prison; he alleged it had been negligently left there by a correctional officer. Virginia state law might have given the defendant a sovereign immunity defense. Prisoner Davidson was assaulted and injured by another inmate; he proved at trial negligence on the part of prison officials who failed to prevent the attack after he had notified them of its possibility. New Jersey law distinctly provided that "[n]either a public entity nor a public employee is liable for . . . any injury caused by . . . a prisoner to any other prisoner." *Held*, in cases considered as a pair: neither prisoner had a remedy under the due process clause. DANIELS v. WILLIAMS, 106 S.Ct. 662 (1986); DAVIDSON v. CANNON, 106 S.Ct. 668 (1986). The statement in Parratt that a loss of property negligently caused by prison officials constituted a "deprivation" had been ill-considered and, on reflection, was overruled. Justice Rehnquist, who had also written the opinion in Parratt, explained as follows, 106 S.Ct. at 665–66:

". . . Historically, this guarantee of due process has been applied to *deliberate* decisions of government officials to deprive a person of life, liberty or property. No decision of this Court before Parratt supported the view that negligent conduct by a state official, even though causing injury, constitutes a deprivation under the Due Process Clause. This history reflects the traditional and common-sense notion that the Due Process Clause, like its forebear in the Magna Carta, see Corwin, The Doctrine of Due Process of Law Before the Civil War, 24 Harv.L.Rev. 366, 368 (1911), was '"intended to secure the individual from the arbitrary exercise of the powers of government,"' Hurtado v. California, 110 U.S. 516, 527 (1884) (quoting Bank of Columbia v. Okely, 4 Wheat. 235, 244 (1819)). . . . By requiring the government to follow appropriate procedures when its agents decide to 'deprive any person of life, liberty, or property,' the Due Process Clause promotes fairness in such decisions. . . .

"We think that the actions of prison custodians in leaving a pillow on the prison stairs, or mislaying an inmate's property, are quite remote from the concerns just discussed. Far from an abuse of power, lack of due care suggests no more than a failure to measure up to the conduct of a reasonable person. To hold that injury caused by such conduct is a deprivation within the meaning of the Fourteenth Amendment would trivialize the centuries-old principle of due process of law.

"The Fourteenth Amendment is a part of a constitution generally designed to allocate governing authority among the branches of the Federal Government and between that Government and the States, and to secure certain individual rights against both State and Federal Government. When dealing with a claim that such a document creates a right in prisoners to sue a government official because he negligently created an unsafe condition in the prison, we bear in mind Chief Justice Marshall's admonition that 'we must never forget, that it is a *constitution* we are expounding,' McCulloch v. Maryland, 4 Wheat. 316, 407 (1819) (emphasis in original). Our Constitution deals with the large concerns of the governors and the governed, but it does not purport to supplant traditional tort law in laying down rules of conduct to regulate liability for injuries that attend living together in society. . . ."

The breadth of this reasoning was challenged by Justice Blackmun, 106 S.Ct. at 671–77. He agreed that "deprivation" of a liberty interest under the fourteenth amendment generally requires something more than a "mere infringement," and that negligent activity would not ordinarily amount to the abuse of state power necessary to implicate the due process clause. This statement, however, was a "rule of thumb" and not a "dogma." In some cases, governmental negligence could represent an abuse of power, and indeed, Davidson's case was one of those cases. By enforcing the rules of prison life, the state stripped Davidson of all means of self-protection. Having done so, it assumed a responsibility to protect him. Negligence in the performance of this special responsibility was a deprivation of liberty for constitutional purposes. Accordingly, Justice Blackmun concurred in the Daniels case but dissented in Davidson. Indeed, all nine Justices concurred in the Daniels result.

(6) What if the claim is that an official *intentionally* destroyed a prisoner's property? In HUDSON v. PALMER, 468 U.S. 517 (1984), it was held that if the intentional act is random and unauthorized, the reasoning and result of the Parratt case apply. Once again, it seems hard to see how a meaningful pre-deprivation remedy can be constructed; if the state provides a post-deprivation remedy for the tort, and does not shield its officers behind sovereign immunity, it provides the process that is due.

And what if the state does purport to shield its officers even for intentional torts? Nothing said in Justice Rehnquist's opinions for the Court in Daniels and Davidson would suggest that due process would in that circumstance be satisfied. However, Justice Stevens, concurring, and writing only for himself in those cases, stated that the proper analysis was not that negligence did not constitute a "deprivation," but rather that even the application of a sovereign immunity doctrine might not prevent a state court system from providing adequate process. "[T]he mere fact that a State elects to provide some of its agents with a sovereign immunity defense in certain cases does not justify the conclusion that its remedial system is constitutionally inadequate." 106

S.Ct. at 681. This argument might carry over from negligent deprivations to at least some intentional ones. For an authority suggesting the contrary of Justice Stevens' proposition, however, see General Oil Co. v. Crain, 209 U.S. 211, 226–27 (1908).

(7) MEMPHIS LIGHT, GAS & WATER DIVISION v. CRAFT, 436 U.S. 1 (1978). A utility run by a municipality, which under state law can terminate a customer's service only for cause, must, prior to termination, (1) give notice not merely of the proposed termination but of the availability of a procedure for protesting the termination as unjustified; and (2) provide an opportunity for the customer to meet with an employee of the utility empowered to hear arguments why termination should not take place and to resolve the dispute. The utility contended that the availability under state law of actions to enjoin an unjustified termination, to compel a refund of any overcharge, and to get damages for any harm caused by an unjustified termination, was more than enough court process to cure any defect in the utility's own procedures. The Court, in an opinion by Justice Powell, refused to extend Ingraham to this situation. There was a real need for process prior to termination, since utility services were essential, and the probability of error was not insubstantial. While judicial process for an injunction was theoretically available before any service was stopped, the disputes likely to arise would typically not justify hiring a lawyer. Accordingly, it was only the informal administrative hearing that constituted the process that was due.[1]

SCHWEIKER v. McCLURE
Supreme Court of the United States, 1982.
456 U.S. 188.

MR. JUSTICE POWELL delivered the opinion of the Court.

The question is whether Congress, consistently with the requirements of due process, may provide that hearings on disputed claims for certain Medicare payments be held by private insurance carriers, without a further right of appeal.

I

Title XVIII of the Social Security Act, 42 U.S.C. § 1395 et seq., commonly known as the Medicare program, is administered by the Secretary of Health and Human Services. It consists of two parts. Part A, which is not at issue in this case, provides insurance against the cost of institutional health services, such as hospital and nursing home fees. Part B is entitled "Supplementary Medical Insurance Benefits for the Aged and Disabled." It covers a portion (typically 80%) of the cost of certain physician services, outpatient physical therapy, x-rays, laboratory tests, and other medical and health care. Only persons 65 or

---

1. Justice Stevens, joined by Chief Justice Burger and Justice Rehnquist, dissented. Justice Stevens thought that the record did not disclose either any threat to health or safety or a failure on the part of the utility to respond once the customer secured counsel. "A potential loss of utility service sufficiently grievous to qualify as a constitutional deprivation can hardly be too petty to justify invoking the aid of counsel or the judiciary. Conversely, routine billing disputes too petty for the bench or the bar can hardly merit extraordinary constitutional protection."

older or disabled may enroll, and eligibility does not depend on financial need. Part B is financed by the Federal Supplementary Medical Insurance Trust Fund. This Trust Fund in turn is funded by appropriations from the Treasury, together with monthly premiums paid by the individuals who choose voluntarily to enroll in the Part B program. Part B consequently resembles a private medical insurance program that is subsidized in major part by the federal government.

Part B is a social program of substantial dimensions. More than 27 million individuals presently participate, and the Secretary pays out more than $10 billion in benefits annually. In 1980, 158 million Part B claims were processed. In order to make the administration of this sweeping program more efficient, Congress authorized the Secretary to contract with private insurance carriers to administer on his behalf the payment of qualifying Part B claims. (In this case, for instance, the private carriers that performed these tasks in California for the Secretary were Blue Shield of California and the Occidental Insurance Company.) The congressional design was to take advantage of such insurance carriers' "great experience in reimbursing physicians." H.R. Rep. No. 213, 89th Cong., 1st Se?s., 46 (1965).

The Secretary pays the participating carriers' costs of claims administration. In return, the carriers act as the Secretary's agents. They review and pay Part B claims for the Secretary according to a precisely specified process. Once the carrier has been billed for a particular service, it decides initially whether the services were medically necessary, whether the charges are reasonable, and whether the claim is otherwise covered by Part B. If it determines that the claim meets all these criteria, the carrier pays the claim out of the government's Trust Fund—not out of its own pocket.

Should the carrier refuse on behalf of the Secretary to pay a portion of the claim, the claimant has one or more opportunities to appeal. First, all claimants are entitled to a "review determination," in which they may submit written evidence and arguments of fact and law. A carrier employee, other than the initial decisionmaker, will review the written record de novo and affirm or adjust the original determination. If the amount in dispute is $100 or more, a still-dissatisfied claimant then has a right to an oral hearing. An officer chosen by the carrier presides over this hearing. The hearing officers "do not participate personally, prior to the hearing [stage], in any case [that] they adjudicate." . . .

Hearing officers receive evidence and hear arguments pertinent to the matters at issue. As soon as practicable thereafter, they must render written decisions based on the record. Neither the statute nor the regulations make provision for further review of the hearing officer's decision. . . .

II

[The district court had held plaintiffs entitled to a de novo hearing before a Social Security ALJ, such as the ALJ's used to administer Part A appeals.]

III

A

The hearing officers involved in this case serve in a quasi-judicial capacity, similar in many respects to that of administrative law judges. As this Court repeatedly has recognized, due process demands impartiality on the part of those who function in judicial or quasi-judicial capacities. We must start, however, from the presumption that the hearing officers who decide Part B claims are unbiased. . . .

Fairly interpreted, the factual findings made in this case do not reveal any disqualifying interest under the standard of our cases. The District Court relied almost exclusively on generalized assumptions of possible interest, placing special weight on the various connections of the hearing officers with the private insurance carriers. The difficulty with this reasoning is that these connections would be relevant only if the carriers themselves are biased or interested. We find no basis in the record for reaching such a conclusion. As previously noted, the carriers pay all Part B claims from federal, and not their own, funds. Similarly, the salaries of the hearing officers are paid by the federal government. Further, the carriers operate under contracts that require compliance with standards prescribed by the statute and the Secretary. In the absence of proof of financial interest on the part of the carriers, there is no basis for assuming a derivative bias among their hearing officers.

B

Appellees further argued, and the District Court agreed, that due process requires an additional administrative or judicial review by a government rather than a carrier-appointed hearing officer. Specifically, the District Court ruled that "[e]xisting Part B procedures might remain intact so long as aggrieved beneficiaries would be entitled to appeal carrier appointees' decisions to Part A administrative law judges." . . .

We may assume that the District Court was correct in viewing the private interest in Part B payments as "considerable," though "not quite as precious as the right to receive welfare or social security benefits." 503 F.Supp. at 416. We likewise may assume, in considering the third Mathews factor, that the additional cost and inconvenience of providing administrative law judges would not be unduly burdensome.

We focus narrowly on the second Mathews factor that considers the risk of erroneous decision and the probable value, if any, of the additional procedure. The District Court's reasoning on this point consisted only of this sentence:

"In light of [appellees'] undisputed showing that carrier-appointed hearing officers receive little or no formal training and are not required to satisfy any threshold criteria such as having a law degree, it must be assumed that additional safeguards would reduce the risk of erroneous deprivation of Part B benefits." 503 F.Supp., at 416 (footnote omitted).

Again, the record does not support these conclusions. The Secretary has directed carriers to select as a hearing officer

"an attorney or other *qualified* individual with the ability to conduct formal hearings and with a general understanding of medical matters and terminology. The [hearing officer] must have a *thorough knowledge* of the Medicare program and the statutory authority and regulations upon which it is based, as well as rulings, policy statements, and general instructions pertinent to the Medicare Bureau." App., 22, quoting Department of Health and Welfare Services, Medicare Part B Carriers Manual, p. 12–21 (emphasis added).

The District Court did not identify any specific deficiencies in the Secretary's selection criteria. By definition, a "qualified" individual already possessing "ability" and "thorough knowledge" would not require further training. The court's further general concern that hearing officers "are not required to satisfy any threshold criteria" overlooks the Secretary's quoted regulation. Moreover, the District Court apparently gave no weight to the qualifications of hearing officers about whom there is information in the record. Their qualifications tend to undermine rather than to support the contention that accuracy of Part B decisionmaking may suffer by reason of carrier appointment of unqualified hearing officers.[1]

"[D]ue Process is flexible and calls for such procedural protections as the particular situation demands." Morrissey v. Brewer, 408 U.S. 471, 481 (1972). We have considered appellees' claims in light of the strong presumption in favor of the validity of congressional action and consistently with this Court's recognition of "congressional solicitude for fair procedure. . . ." Califano v. Yamasaki, 442 U.S. 682, 693 (1979). Appellees simply have not shown that the procedures prescribed by Congress and the Secretary are not fair or that different or additional procedures would reduce the risk of erroneous deprivation of Part B benefits.

IV

The judgment of the District Court is reversed and the case is remanded for judgment to be entered for the Secretary.

So ordered.

NOTES

(1) GRAY PANTHERS v. SCHWEIKER, 652 F.2d 146 (D.C.Cir.1980), reconsidered after remand 716 F.2d 23 (D.C.Cir.1983), treats a problem not presented in the principal case, the procedures required to be employed in handling claims for which less than $100 is in controversy.

1. The record contains information on nine hearing officers. Two were retired administrative law judges with 15 to 18 years of judging experience, five had extensive experience in medicine or medical insurance, one had been a practicing attorney for 20 years, and one was an attorney with 42 years experience in the insurance industry who was self-employed as an insurance adjuster. . . .

The lengthy opinions, not easily compressed, exemplify the difficulties courts encounter in applying the Mathews v. Eldridge criteria in concrete cases. In the first opinion, Judge Wald writing, the court concluded that, while the statute did not provide for an oral hearing for such claimants, the constitution required one:

"To date, the Supreme Court has never expressly approved as meeting due process hearing requirements a procedure in which a claimant has been finally deprived of the right to government benefits without affording that individual an opportunity to appeal personally and orally to the decisionmaker. . . . Ambiguities which are not readily apparent on the face of a document can be disclosed and clarified with a few moments of oral exchange between the individual and the decisionmaker. . . . An oral hearing requirement . . . serves to ensure that decisionmakers recognize that their decisions affect the lives of human beings, a fact that is often obscured by a jumble of papers and depersonalized identification numbers. . . . [And] no other procedure so effectively fosters a belief that one has been dealt with fairly, even if there remains a disagreement with the result. . . .

"We are convinced that simplified, streamlined, informal oral procedures are available which would be responsive to the concerns of Congress for efficiency and low cost yet which would provide claimants with the right to participate in decisions affecting their interests in cases where such participation is critical. . . ."

The case was remanded with directions to the parties to assist the district court in framing an order that would meet these criteria. When the case returned two years later the court, Judge Mikva now writing, found that work not yet complete. In part that was due to the government's failure fully to cooperate in the remanded proceedings. But in part it stemmed from the difficulty of constructing procedures that would be effective and yet reasonable in cost.

"As a compromise, the Department has proposed a toll-free telephone system through which beneficiaries eventually would be able to speak with a carrier employee who is familiar with the particular facts of their disputed claim. . . . We believe that the toll-free telephone system proposed by the Secretary—when combined with . . . improved notice . . . and the full written review procedures that currently exist—meets the dictates of due process for most of the claims at issue in this litigation. [A] face-to-face meeting with the decisionmaker is not required for every claim. The telephone system will give many beneficiaries a chance to communicate orally with a carrier employee who is familiar with their particular claim, thereby improving the process somewhat for those beneficiaries who have trouble when they rely solely on written submissions or for whom a telephone is the most accessible means of communication.

"Finally, the Gray Panthers argue that the proposed telephone system is overly burdensome on the elderly and infirm population with which we are concerned. Not only is it expected that 40% of the beneficiaries attempting to reach the toll-free number will receive a busy signal on their first try, but special problems exist for many beneficiaries trying to use a telephone because they have difficulty hearing or trouble comprehending a fast-paced telephone conversation. We do not mean to denigrate the concerns that the Gray Panthers raise—indeed, in response to these criticisms, we expect good faith efforts to be made by the Secretary to improve the telephone system in all ways that are feasible and practicable. But however much we might prefer, as a policy matter, to have face-to-face hearings mandated for all beneficiaries, we cannot say that the flexible requirements of due process are not satisfied by the complete procedural system that soon will be in place—including an improved written notice, the toll-free telephone system, and full written review procedures."

(2) In SUPERINTENDENT, MASS. CORR. INSTITUTION, WALPOLE v. HILL, 105 S.Ct. 2768 (1985), the Supreme Court weighed the arguments pro and con and decided that the decision of a prison disciplinary board to revoke an inmate's "good time" credits has to be supported by "some evidence" but does not have to meet "any other standard greater than some evidence."

CLEVELAND BOARD OF EDUCATION v. LOUDERMILL
Supreme Court of the United States, 1985.
470 U.S. 532.

JUSTICE WHITE delivered the opinion of the Court.

In these cases we consider what pretermination process must be accorded a public employee who can be discharged only for cause.

I

In 1979 the Cleveland Board of Education . . . hired respondent James Loudermill as a security guard. On his job application, Loudermill stated that he had never been convicted of a felony. Eleven months later, as part of a routine examination of his employment records, the Board discovered that in fact Loudermill had been convicted of grand larceny in 1968. By letter dated November 3, 1980, the Board's Business Manager informed Loudermill that he had been dismissed because of his dishonesty in filling out the employment application. Loudermill was not afforded an opportunity to respond to the charge of dishonesty or to challenge his dismissal. On November 13, the Board adopted a resolution officially approving the discharge.

Under Ohio law, Loudermill was a "classified civil servant." Ohio Rev.Code Ann. § 124.11 (1984). Such employees can be terminated only for cause, and may obtain administrative review if discharged. § 124.34 (1984). Pursuant to this provision, Loudermill filed an appeal with the Cleveland Civil Service Commission on November 12. The Commission appointed a referee, who held a hearing on January 29, 1981. Loudermill argued that he had thought that his 1968 larceny conviction was for a misdemeanor rather than a felony. The referee recommended reinstatement. On July 20, 1981, the full Commission heard argument and orally announced that it would uphold the dismissal. Proposed findings of fact and conclusions of law followed on

August 10, and Loudermill's attorneys were advised of the result by mail on August 21.

Although the Commission's decision was subject to judicial review in the state courts, Loudermill instead brought the present suit in the Federal District Court for the Northern District of Ohio. The complaint alleged that § 124.34 was unconstitutional on its face because it did not provide the employee an opportunity to respond to the charges against him prior to removal. As a result, discharged employees were deprived of liberty and property without due process. The complaint also alleged that the provision was unconstitutional as applied because discharged employees were not given sufficiently prompt post-removal hearings.

Before a responsive pleading was filed, the District Court dismissed for failure to state a claim on which relief could be granted. See Fed. Rule Civ. Proc. 12(b)(6). . . .

The other case before us [involving Richard Donnelly, a bus mechanic for the Parma, Ohio, Board of Education] arises on similar facts and followed a similar course. [After "a year of wrangling," Donnelly was reinstated, but without backpay.]

. . . [T]he cases were consolidated for appeal. A divided panel of the Court of Appeals for the Sixth Circuit reversed in part and remanded. . . . [I]t concluded that the compelling private interest in retaining employment, combined with the value of presenting evidence prior to dismissal, outweighed the added administrative burden of a pretermination hearing. With regard to the alleged deprivation of liberty, and Loudermill's 9-month wait for an administrative decision, the court affirmed the District Court, finding no constitutional violation.

. . .

We . . . now affirm in all respects.

II

Respondents' federal constitutional claim depends on their having had a property right in continued employment. If they did, the State could not deprive them of this property without due process.

Property interests are not created by the Constitution, "they are created and their dimensions are defined by existing rules or understandings that stem from an independent source such as state law. . . . " Board of Regents v. Roth. The Ohio statute plainly creates such an interest. Respondents were "classified civil service employees," Ohio Rev.Code Ann. § 124.11 (1984), entitled to retain their positions "during good behavior and efficient service," who could not be dismissed "except . . . for . . . misfeasance, malfeasance, or nonfeasance in office," § 124.34. . . .

The Parma Board argues, however, that the property right is defined by, and conditioned on, the legislature's choice of procedures for its deprivation. The Board stresses that in addition to specifying the grounds for termination, the statute sets out procedures by which termination may take place.[1] The procedures were adhered to in these cases. According to petitioner, "[t]o require additional procedures would in effect expand the scope of the property interest itself."

This argument, which was accepted by the District Court, has its genesis in the plurality opinion in Arnett v. Kennedy, 416 U.S. 134 (1974). Arnett involved a challenge by a former federal employee to the procedures by which he was dismissed. The plurality reasoned that where the legislation conferring the substantive right also sets out the procedural mechanism for enforcing that right, the two cannot be separated:

"The employee's statutorily defined right is not a guarantee against removal without cause in the abstract, but such a guarantee as enforced by the procedures which Congress has designated for the determination of cause.

". . . [W]here the grant of a substantive right is inextricably intertwined with the limitations on the procedures which are to be employed in determining that right, a litigant in the position of appellee must take the bitter with the sweet." Id., at 152–154.

This view garnered three votes in Arnett, but was specifically rejected by the other six Justices. See id., at 166–167 (Powell, J., joined by Blackmun, J.,); id., at 177–178, 185 (White, J.,); id., at 211 (Marshall, J., joined by Douglas and Brennan, JJ.). Since then, this theory has at times seemed to gather some additional support. See Bishop v. Wood, 426 U.S. 341, 355–361 (1976) (White, J., dissenting); Goss v. Lopez, 419 U.S., at 586–587 (Powell, J., joined by Burger, C.J., and Blackmun and Rehnquist, JJ., dissenting). More recently, however, the Court has clearly rejected it. In Vitek v. Jones, 445 U.S. 480, 491 (1980), we pointed out that "minimum [procedural] requirements [are] a matter of federal law, they are not diminished by the fact that the State may have specified its own procedures that it may deem adequate for determining the preconditions to adverse official action." This conclusion was reiterated in Logan v. Zimmerman Brush Co., 455 U.S. 422, 432 (1982). . . .

In light of these holdings, it is settled that the "bitter with the sweet" approach misconceives the constitutional guarantee. If a clearer holding is needed, we provide it today. The point is straight-forward: the Due Process Clause provides that certain substantive rights—life, liberty, and property—cannot be deprived except pursuant to constitutionally adequate procedures. The categories of substance and procedure are distinct. Were the rule otherwise, the Clause would be reduced to a mere tautology. "Property" cannot be defined by the

1. After providing for dismissal only for cause, § 124.34 states that the dismissed employee is to be provided with a copy of the order of removal giving the reasons therefor. Within 10 days of the filing of the order with the director of administrative services, the employee may file a written appeal with the state personnel board of review or the Commission. "In the event such an appeal is filed, the board or commission shall forthwith notify the appointing authority and shall hear, or appoint a trial board to hear, such appeal within thirty days from and after its filing with the board or commission, and it may affirm, disaffirm, or modify the judgment of the appointing authority." Either side may obtain review of the Commission's decision in the state court of common pleas.

procedures provided for its deprivation any more than can life or
liberty. The right to due process "is conferred, not by legislative grace,
but by constitutional guarantee. While the legislature may elect not to
confer a property interest in [public] employment, it may not constitutionally authorize the deprivation of such an interest, once conferred,
without appropriate procedural safeguards." Arnett v. Kennedy, 416
U.S., at 167 (Powell, J., concurring in part and concurring in result in
part).

In short, once it is determined that the Due Process Clause applies,
"the question remains what process is due." Morrissey v. Brewer, 408
U.S. 471, 481 (1972). The answer to that question is not to be found in
the Ohio statute.

III

An essential principle of due process is that a deprivation of life,
liberty, or property "be preceded by notice and opportunity for hearing
appropriate to the nature of the case." Mullane v. Central Hanover
Bank & Trust Co., 339 U.S. 306, 313 (1950). We have described "the
root requirement" of the Due Process Clause as being "that an individual be given an opportunity for a hearing *before* he is deprived of any
significant property interest." Boddie v. Connecticut, 401 U.S. 371, 379
(1971).[2] This principle requires "some kind of a hearing" prior to the
discharge of an employee who has a constitutionally protected property
interest in his employment. Even decisions finding no constitutional
violation in termination procedures have relied on the existence of
some pretermination opportunity to respond. For example, in Arnett
six Justices found constitutional minima satisfied where the employee
had access to the material upon which the charge was based and could
respond orally and in writing and present rebuttal affidavits. . . .

The need for some form of pretermination hearing, recognized in
these cases, is evident from a balancing of the competing interests at
stake. These are the private interests in retaining employment, the
governmental interest in the expeditious removal of unsatisfactory
employees and the avoidance of administrative burdens, and the risk of
an erroneous termination. See Mathews v. Eldridge.

First, the significance of the private interest in retaining employment cannot be gainsaid. We have frequently recognized the severity
of depriving a person of the means of livelihood. While a fired worker
may find employment elsewhere, doing so will take some time and is
likely to be burdened by the questionable circumstances under which
he left his previous job.

Second, some opportunity for the employee to present his side of
the case is recurringly of obvious value in reaching an accurate decision. Dismissals for cause will often involve factual disputes. Cf.
Califano v. Yamasaki, 442 U.S. 682, 686 (1979). Even where the facts
are clear, the appropriateness or necessity of the discharge may not be;

2. There are, of course, some situations
in which a post-deprivation hearing will
satisfy due process requirements. See
. . . North American Cold Storage Co. v.
Chicago, 211 U.S. 306 (1908).

in such cases, the only meaningful opportunity to invoke the discretion of the decisionmaker is likely to be before the termination takes effect. See Goss v. Lopez . . . .[3]

The cases before us illustrate these considerations. Both respondents had plausible arguments to make that might have prevented their discharge. The fact that the Commission saw fit to reinstate Donnelly suggests that an error might have been avoided had he been provided an opportunity to make his case to the Board. As for Loudermill, given the Commission's ruling we cannot say that the discharge was mistaken. Nonetheless, in light of the referee's recommendation, neither can we say that a fully informed decisionmaker might not have exercised its discretion and decided not to dismiss him, notwithstanding its authority to do so. In any event, the termination involved arguable issues,[4] and the right to a hearing does not depend on a demonstration of certain success.

The governmental interest in immediate termination does not outweigh these interests. As we shall explain, affording the employee an opportunity to respond prior to termination would impose neither a significant administrative burden nor intolerable delays. Furthermore, the employer shares the employee's interest in avoiding disruption and erroneous decisions; and until the matter is settled, the employer would continue to receive the benefit of the employee's labors. It is preferable to keep a qualified employee on than to train a new one. A governmental employer also has an interest in keeping citizens usefully employed rather than taking the possibly erroneous and counter-productive step of forcing its employees onto the welfare rolls. Finally, in those situations where the employer perceives a significant hazard in keeping the employee on the job,[5] it can avoid the problem by suspending with pay.

IV

The foregoing considerations indicate that the pretermination "hearing," though necessary, need not be elaborate. . . . Under state

---

3. This is not to say that where state conduct is entirely discretionary the Due Process Clause is brought into play. See Meachum v. Fano, 427 U.S. 215, 228 (1976). Nor is it to say that a person can insist on a hearing in order to argue that the decisionmaker should be lenient and depart from legal requirements. See Dixon v. Love, 431 U.S. 105 (1977). The point is that where there is an entitlement, a prior hearing facilitates the consideration of whether a permissible course of action is also an appropriate one. . . .

4. Loudermill's dismissal turned not on the objective fact that he was an ex-felon or the inaccuracy of his statement to the contrary, but on the subjective question whether he had lied on his application form. His explanation for the false statement is plausible in light of the fact that

he received only a suspended 6-month sentence and a fine on the grand larceny conviction.

5. In the cases before us, no such danger seems to have existed. . . . As for Loudermill, petitioner states that "to find that we have a person who is an ex-felon as our security guard is very distressful to us." Tr. of Oral Arg. 19. But the termination was based on the presumed misrepresentation on the employment form, not on the felony conviction. In fact, Ohio law provides that an employee "shall not be disciplined for acts," including criminal convictions, occurring more than two years previously. See Ohio Admin.Code § 124-3-04 (1979). Petitioner concedes that Loudermill's job performance was fully satisfactory.

law, respondents were later entitled to a full administrative hearing and judicial review. The only question is what steps were required before the termination took effect.

In only one case, Goldberg v. Kelly, has the Court required a full adversarial evidentiary hearing prior to adverse governmental action. However, as the Goldberg Court itself pointed out, that case presented significantly different considerations than are present in the context of public employment. Here, the pretermination hearing need not definitively resolve the propriety of the discharge. It should be an initial check against mistaken decisions—essentially, a determination of whether there are reasonable grounds to believe that the charges against the employee are true and support the proposed action.

The essential requirements of due process, and all that respondents seek or the Court of Appeals required, are notice and an opportunity to respond. . . . The tenured public employee is entitled to oral or written notice of the charges against him, an explanation of the employer's evidence, and an opportunity to present his side of the story. To require more than this prior to termination would intrude to an unwarranted extent on the government's interest in quickly removing an unsatisfactory employee.

V

Our holding rests in part on the provisions in Ohio law for a full post-termination hearing. In his cross-petition Loudermill asserts, as a separate constitutional violation, that his administrative proceedings took too long.[6] . . . At some point, a delay in the post-termination hearing would become a constitutional violation. . . . A 9-month adjudication is not . . . unconstitutionally lengthy per se. Yet Loudermill offers no indication that his wait was unreasonably prolonged other than the fact that it took nine months. The chronology of the proceedings set out in the complaint, coupled with the assertion that nine months is too long to wait, does not state a claim of a constitutional deprivation.[7]

VI

We conclude that all the process that is due is provided by a pretermination opportunity to respond, coupled with post-termination administrative procedures as provided by the Ohio statute. Because respondents allege in their complaints that they had no chance to respond, the District Court erred in dismissing for failure to state a

---

6. Loudermill's hearing before the referee occurred two and one-half months after he filed his appeal. The Commission issued its written decision six and one-half months after that. . . .

Section 124.34 provides that a hearing is to be held within 30 days of the appeal, though the Ohio courts have ruled that the time limit is not mandatory. The statute does not provide a time limit for the actual decision.

7. The cross-petition also argues that Loudermill was unconstitutionally deprived of liberty because of the accusation of dishonesty that hung over his head during the administrative proceedings. As the Court of Appeals found, 721 F.2d, at 563, n. 18, the failure to allege that the reasons for the dismissal were published dooms this claim. See Bishop v. Wood, 426 U.S. 341, 348 (1976).

claim. The judgment of the Court of Appeals is affirmed, and the case is remanded for further proceedings consistent with this opinion.

So ordered.

JUSTICE MARSHALL, concurring in Part II and concurring in the judgment.

. . . Because the Court holds that the respondents were due all the process they requested, I concur in the judgment of the Court.

I write separately, however, to reaffirm my belief that public employees who may be discharged only for cause are entitled, under the Due Process Clause of the Fourteenth Amendment, to more than respondents sought in this case. I continue to believe that *before the decision is made to terminate an employee's wages,* the employee is entitled to an opportunity to test the strength of the evidence "by confronting and cross-examining adverse witnesses and by presenting witnesses on [their] own behalf, whenever there are substantial disputes in testimonial evidence," Arnett v. Kennedy, 416 U.S. 134, 214 (1974) (Marshall, J., dissenting). . . .

To my mind, the disruption caused by a loss of wages may be so devastating to an employee that, whenever there are substantial disputes about the evidence, additional pre-deprivation procedures are necessary to minimize the risk of an erroneous termination. That is, I place significantly greater weight than does the Court on the public employee's substantial interest in the accuracy of the pre-termination proceeding. After wage termination, the employee often must wait months before his case is finally resolved, during which time he is without wages from his public employment. By limiting the procedures due prior to termination of wages, the Court accepts an impermissibly high risk that a wrongfully discharged employee will be subjected to this often lengthy wait for vindication, and to the attendant and often traumatic disruptions to his personal and economic life.

. . .

JUSTICE BRENNAN, concurring in part and dissenting in part.

[Justice Brennan dissented from Part V of the Court's opinion; he claimed that Loudermill's complaint was sufficient to tender an issue concerning the constitutionality of the nine month delay.]

JUSTICE REHNQUIST, dissenting.

In Arnett v. Kennedy, six Members of this Court agreed that a public employee could be dismissed for misconduct without a full hearing prior to termination. A plurality of Justices agreed that the employee was entitled to exactly what Congress gave him, and no more. The Chief Justice, Justice Stewart, and I said:

"Here appellee did have a statutory expectancy that he not be removed other than for 'such cause as will promote the efficiency of [the] service.' But the very section of the statute which granted him that right, a right which had previously existed only by virtue of administrative regulation, expressly provided also for the procedure by which 'cause' was to be determined, and expressly omitted the procedural guarantees which appellee insists are mandated by the Constitution. Only by bifurcating the very sentence of the Act of Congress which conferred upon appellee the right not to be removed save for cause could it be said that he had an expectancy of that substantive right without the procedural limitations which Congress attached to it. In the area of federal regulation of government employees, where in the absence of statutory limitation the governmental employer has had virtually uncontrolled latitude in decisions as to hiring and firing, Cafeteria Workers v. McElroy, 367 U.S. 886, 896–897 (1961), we do not believe that a statutory enactment such as the Lloyd-La Follette Act may be parsed as discretely as appellee urges. . . . Where the focus of legislation was thus strongly on the procedural mechanism for enforcing the substantive right which was simultaneously conferred, we decline to conclude that the substantive right may be viewed wholly apart from the procedure provided for its enforcement. . . ."

. . . . [I]n one legislative breath Ohio has conferred upon civil service employees such as respondents in this case a limited form of tenure during good behavior, and prescribed the procedures by which that tenure may be terminated. Here, as in Arnett, "[t]he employee's statutorily defined right is not a guarantee against removal without cause in the abstract, but such a guarantee as enforced by the procedures which [the Ohio legislature] has designated for the determination of cause." 416 U.S. at 152 (opinion of Rehnquist, J.). . . . We ought to recognize the totality of the State's definition of the property right in question, and not merely seize upon one of several paragraphs in a unitary statute to proclaim that in that paragraph the State has inexorably conferred upon a civil service employee something which it is powerless under the United States Constitution to qualify in the next paragraph of the statute. This practice ignores our duty under Roth to rely on state law as the source of property interests for purposes of applying the Due Process Clause of the Fourteenth Amendment. While it does not impose a federal definition of property, the Court departs from the full breadth of the holding in Roth by its selective choice from among the sentences the Ohio legislature chooses to use in establishing and qualifying a right.

Having concluded by this somewhat tortured reasoning that Ohio has created a property right in the respondents in this case, the Court naturally proceeds to inquire what process is "due" before the respondents may be divested of that right. This customary "balancing" inquiry conducted by the Court in this case reaches a result that is quite unobjectionable, but it seems to me that it is devoid of any principles which will either instruct or endure. The balance is simply an ad hoc weighing which depends to a great extent upon how the Court subjectively views the underlying interests at stake. The results in previous cases and in this case have been quite unpredictable. To paraphrase Justice Black, today's balancing act requires a "pretermination opportunity to respond" but there is nothing that indicates what tomorrow's will be. Goldberg v. Kelly, 397 U.S. 254, 276 (1970) (Black, J., dissenting). The results from today's balance certainly do not jibe with the result in Goldberg or Mathews v. Eldridge, 424 U.S. 319

(1976).[8] The lack of any principled standards in this area means that these procedural due process cases will recur time and again. Every different set of facts will present a new issue on what process was due and when. One way to avoid this subjective and varying interpretation of the Due Process Clause in cases such as this is to hold that one who avails himself of government entitlements accepts the grant of tenure along with its inherent limitations.

Because I believe that the Fourteenth Amendment of the United States Constitution does not support the conclusion that Ohio's effort to confer a limited form of tenure upon respondents resulted in the creation of a "property right" in their employment, I dissent. . . .

NOTES

(1) As the Loudermill opinions show, a nearly identical case was decided by the Court a decade before. ARNETT v. KENNEDY, 416 U.S. 134 (1974). Arnett differed from Loudermill in three respects. First, Kennedy was a federal employee, and the statute in question was a federal statute. For all that anybody writes in Loudermill, this point appears to be irrelevant. Second, although the federal statute did not provide for an evidentiary hearing until after dismissal, it did give the employee 30 days notice of the reasons for his proposed discharge; a chance to respond, including a chance to submit affidavits in his favor; and an opportunity to appear personally before the official who had the authority to make the final decision. Some of the Justices' votes turned on these features of the statute. Third, the most important ground for Kennedy's dismissal was that he had slandered the very person authorized to conduct the pretermination proceeding. Accordingly, even if the federal scheme was generally acceptable, its application in the particular case could be questioned.

The plurality opinion in Arnett was written by Justice Rehnquist for himself and Justices Burger and Stewart; he sustained the procedures used in the discharge on the ground "that where the grant of a

---

8. Today the balancing test requires a pretermination opportunity to respond. In Goldberg we required a full-fledged trial-type hearing, and in Mathews we declined to require any pretermination process other than those required by the statute. At times this balancing process may look as if it were undertaken with a thumb on the scale, depending upon the result the Court desired. For example, in Mathews we minimized the importance of the benefit to the recipient, stating that after termination he could always go on welfare to survive. Today, however, the Court exalts the recipient's interest in retaining employment; not a word is said about going on welfare. Conversely, in Mathews we stressed the interests of the State, while today, in a footnote, the Court goes so far as to denigrate the State's interest in firing a school security guard who had lied about a prior felony conviction.

Today the Court purports to describe the State's interest but does so in a way that is contrary to what the State has asserted in its briefs. The description of the State's interests looks more like a make-weight to support the Court's result. The decision whom to train and employ is strictly a decision for the State. The Court attempts to ameliorate its ruling by stating that a State may always suspend an employee with pay, in lieu of a predischarge hearing, if it determines that he poses a threat. This does less than justice to the State's interest in its financial integrity and its interest in promptly terminating an employee who has violated the conditions of his tenure, and ignores Ohio's current practice of paying back wages to wrongfully-discharged employees.

substantive right is inextricably intertwined with the limitations on the procedures what are to be employed in determining that right, a litigant . . . must take the bitter with the sweet." The majority was formed by the concurrence in the result of Justices Powell and Blackmun. They, however, justified their votes on the ground that the procedures provided by the statute represented "a reasonable accommodation of the competing interests" and thus provided due process. Justice White, the author of Loudermill, agreed with Justices Powell and Blackmun on that point, but thought that in the particular case the employee was entitled to have a different person decide prior to termination. Justice Douglas dissented on a first amendment ground. Finally, Justice Marshall, with whom Justices Douglas and Brennan joined, dissented on grounds very similar to those stated in his Loudermill opinion.

(2) The "bitter with the sweet" theory provoked a great deal of law review commentary. Here are some samples:

(a) L. Tribe, Structural Due Process, 10 Harv.C.R.C.L.L.Rev. 269, 278–280 (1975):

"It seems evident that a theory of 'differential reliance' underlies the Court's distinction between the substantive content of an entitlement and the procedures provided for its protection in cases like Arnett . . . : an employee . . . seeking to avoid certain adverse consequences may justifiably rely, in shaping his primary conduct, on the statutes and contract provisions spelling out the events which trigger those consequences. But no parallel accommodation of behavior can realistically be expected to flow from the definition, in the same source of law, of truncated procedures for determining whether the triggering event has occurred."

(b) H. Monaghan, of "Liberty" and "Property," 62 Corn.L.Rev. 405, 438–39 (1977):

". . . The thrust of [Justice Rehnquist's] analysis, however, is to break down any distinction between substance and procedure and to assert that, in some contexts at least, procedural safeguards are themselves indispensable aspects of the 'property' itself. There is probably nothing inherently illogical in this approach. 'Property' may be viewed as merely a series of discrete rights and powers, the property teacher's 'bundle of sticks.' And there is no a priori reason to exclude 'procedural sticks' from the bundle. But our legal traditions strongly oppose this mode of analysis. In countless contexts we distinguish between substance and procedure, and subject the procedural aspects of 'property' rights to independent constitutional scrutiny. Moreover, the fundamental premises behind the treating of 'entitlements' as property argue against disregarding distinctions between substance and procedure."

(c) R. Smolla, The Reemergence of the Right-Privilege Distinction in Constitutional Law: The Price of Protesting Too Much, 35 Stan.L.Rev. 69, 75 (1982):

"Clearly the strongest motive force behind entitlement theory, however, is deference to majoritarian sovereignty. In its most extreme form entitlement doctrine rejects the existence of a dichotomy between 'substantive' and 'procedural' aspects of an interest in largess. It is possible to treat the creation of a welfare program or a parole system as purely political affairs, as matters of legislative choice beyond the pale of judicial review, while nonetheless arguing that minimum procedural integrity in the administration of those programs is a matter of constitutional right. Entitlement theory in its purest form repudiates that division, and proceeds instead on the assumption that the procedural accoutrements that accompany an interest in largess are among the defining characteristics of the interest itself. Under this theory the level of procedural protection that surrounds a government job, for example, is a political expression of the importance of the job to the body politic; as such it is as much a matter of legislative prerogative as the level of salary assigned to that class of job holder."

(d) F. EASTERBROOK, SUBSTANCE AND DUE PROCESS, 1982 THE SUPREME COURT REVIEW 85, 112:

"Substance and process are intimately related. The procedures one uses determine how much substance is achieved, and by whom. Procedural rules usually are just a measure of how much the substantive entitlements are worth, of what we are willing to sacrifice to see a given goal attained. The body that creates a substantive rule is the logical judge of how much should be spent to avoid errors in the process of disposing of claims to that right. The substantive rule itself is best seen as a promised benefit coupled with a promised rate of mistake: the legislature sets up an $X\%$ probability that a person will receive a certain boon. The Court cannot logically be reticent about revising the substantive rules but unabashed about rewriting the procedures to be followed in administering those rules. . . . "

Can you distinguish (like the majority in Loudermill) a property right from the procedures which provide a remedy for its violation? If you can, can you (again like the majority) assess its importance to its holder (in order to conduct the Mathews balancing test) without referring to the importance which you believe it is accorded by state or federal non-constitutional law? If you can do both of these things, why do you care whether non-constitutional law has recognized the property right in the first place?

On the other hand, if you do care, why do you not also care about the procedures non-constitutional law has provided for protecting the right?

(3) As stated in a standard British treatise, H.W.R. WADE, ADMINISTRATIVE LAW 413 (5 ed. 1982),[†] the concept of "natural justice" "plays much the same part in British law as does 'due process of law' in the Constitution of the United States." Here are some excerpts from Wade's discussion of the British doctrine (414–18, footnotes omitted):

"In its broadest sense natural justice may mean simply 'the natural sense of what is right and wrong', and even in its technical sense it is now often equated with 'fairness'. . . .

"But in administrative law natural justice is a well defined concept which comprises two fundamental rules of fair procedure: that a man may not be a judge in his own cause; and that a man's defence must always be fairly heard. In courts of law and in statutory tribunals it can be taken for granted that these rules must be observed. But so universal are they, so 'natural', that they are not confined to judicial power. They apply equally to administrative power . . . . It is in their application to ordinary administrative power that public authorities are prone to overlook them, for example where a police authority is dismissing a constable or a minister is confirming a housing scheme. Cases of this kind have multiplied in recent years, as the courts have developed their rules and the range of administrative powers has increased. Natural justice has become one of the most active departments of administrative law.

". . .

"The rules requiring impartial adjudicators and fair hearings can be traced back to medieval precedents, and, indeed, they were not unknown in the ancient world. In their medieval guise they were regarded as part of the immutable order of things, so that in theory even the power of the legislature could not alter them. This theory lingered into the seventeenth and faintly even into the eighteenth century, though by then it was incompatible with the modern theory of parliamentary sovereignty which was supplanting the old ideas. It reached its high-water mark in Dr. Bonham's case (1610), where Chief Justice Coke went so far as to say that the court could declare an Act of Parliament void if it made a man judge in his own cause, or was otherwise 'against common right and reason'. This was one of his grounds for disallowing the claim of the College of Physicians to fine and imprison Dr. Bonham, a doctor of physic of Cambridge University, for practising in the City of London without the licence of the College of Physicians. The statute under which the College acted provided that fines should go half to the king and half to the College, so that the College had a financial interest in its own judgment and was judge in its own cause.

"No modern judge could repeat this exploit, for to hold an Act of Parliament void is to blaspheme against the doctrine of parliamentary sovereignty. . . . Natural justice, natural law, the law of God and 'common right and reason' were all aspects of the old concept of fundamental and unalterable law. They no longer represent any kind of limit to the power of statute. Natural justice has had to look for a new foothold, and has found it as a mode not of destroying enacted law but of fulfilling it. Its basis now is in the rules of interpretation. The courts may presume that Parliament, when it grants powers, intends them to be exercised in a right and proper way. Since Parliament is very unlikely to make provision to the contrary, this allows considerable scope for the courts to devise a set of canons of fair administrative procedure, suitable to the needs of the time."

When Justice Rehnquist writes: "Where the focus of legislation was thus strongly on the procedural mechanism for enforcing the substantive right which was simultaneously conferred, we decline to conclude that the substantive right may be viewed wholly apart from the procedure provided for its enforcement," is he in effect adopting the tradition (and the limits) of "natural justice"? If so, is it an adequate answer to him to say that the American understanding of constitutional norms, growing from a written constitution, is different from the British one? Or can he legitimately respond that if the legislature has distinctly and definitely focused on the administrative process to be used, each citizen has received all the process he is "due" in the legislative process? Or do we fear that the legislative assessment of what "fairness" requires will be distorted by "extraneous" "political" considerations? Compare, in this regard, Justice Rehnquist's opinion in the Vermont Yankee case, reprinted in Chapter 3, part 1.

(4) While the topic of "natural justice" is before us, a brief excursion into the concept's current place in American law may be justified. For a plaintiff to prevail under either of the due process clauses, she must show that the defendant's action is, or fairly represents, governmental action. This requirement of the fifth and fourteenth amendments—the "state action" requirement—is more commonly confronted in equal protection jurisprudence, but it is fully applicable to due process issues as well. See, e.g., Jackson v. Metropolitan Edison Co., 419 U.S. 345 (1974) (a "private" electric utility does not have to observe due process before terminating service); Rendell-Baker v. Kohn, 457 U.S. 830 (1982) (a "private" school does not have to observe due process before discharging teachers). In ordinary administrative law matters the defendant will incontestably be or represent the government, and the details of the doctrine need not concern us here. (For further reading, see L. Tribe, American Constitutional Law Ch. 18 (1978) and K. Davis, 5 Admin. Law Treatise § 27:35 (2 ed. 1984).)

What is worth remembering is that "natural justice" is a common law principle; accordingly, even if "state action" cannot be shown, a common law claim in the nature of a due process claim can still be stated. There are many English cases; probably the leading cases in this country are Falcone v. Middlesex County Medical Society, 34 N.J. 582, 170 A.2d 791 (1961) and Pinsker v. Pacific Coast Society of Orthodontists, 12 Cal.3d 541, 116 Cal.Rptr. 245, 526 P.2d 253 (1974), both dealing with the membership-determining procedures of private professional organizations. A more recent example is Curran v. Mount Diablo Council of the Boy Scouts of America, 147 Cal.App.3d 712, 195 Cal.Rptr. 325 (1983), appeal dismissed 104 S.Ct. 3574 (1984), holding, among other things, that expulsion of an Eagle Scout from the Boy Scouts on grounds of his homosexuality, without holding a hearing on the issue of whether there was likely to be "any significant harm to the association," violated "the common law right of fair procedure." For commentary, see Z. Chafee, Jr., The Internal Affairs of Associations Not For Profit, 43 Harv.L.Rev. 993 (1930); Developments in the Law: Judicial Control of Actions of Private Associations, 76 Harv.L.Rev. 983 (1963); Comment, Judicial Intervention in Admission Decisions of Private Professional Associations, 49 U.Chi.L.Rev. 840 (1982).

(5) What should the Court do if the legislative qualifications on the property right are apparently "substantive?" Under the Medicare and Medicaid programs, aged, disabled, and poor persons are entitled to receive certain nursing home care. Under the same programs, a nursing home is entitled to receive reimbursement for furnishing that care if it is certified as a "skilled nursing facility." 42 U.S.C. § 1396(a) (23) provides for the intersection of these entitlements by stipulating that a patient may get nursing home care "from any institution . . . qualified to perform the . . . services . . . who undertakes to provide him such services." Is the patient entitled to a hearing before the government "decertifies" the nursing home, with the consequence that the patient must uproot and go elsewhere? For an aged or infirm person, such a move may be very traumatic—but has there been a deprivation of property?

In O'BANNON v. TOWN COURT NURSING CENTER, 447 U.S. 773 (1980), seven Justices held that patients in a nursing home had no due process right to a hearing before the home was decertified. Six joined the opinion of Justice Stevens, which rested on two points. First, the substantive entitlement of the patients was not the "right to remain in the home of one's choice absent specific cause for transfer," as the court of appeals had suggested, but rather a "right to continued benefits to pay for care in the qualified institution of his choice," with "no enforceable expectation of continued benefits to pay for care in an institution that has been determined to be unqualified." Second, the decision to decertify is not a direct withdrawal of benefits, and indeed may well be in the patients' interests; the possible "indirect and incidental" impact of the government's enforcement action does not amount to a deprivation of a protected interest. Justice Blackmun rejected this analysis, but reached the same result. He drew the scope of the protected entitlement on the basis of what he considered to be the relevant constitutional policies. The factors he considered vital were (1) the nursing home itself had been given substantial procedural protection, and shared many interests with the patients; (2) the nursing home was the source of the patients' benefits; (3) a large number of patients were involved in each home (here citing Bi-Metallic Co. v. Colorado and Bowles v. Willingham); and (4) the patients were not being singled out on the basis of their own particular "fault." Justice Brennan dissented; Justice Marshall did not participate.

(6) As the Loudermill opinion indicates at note 3, the question of whether there is a right to a hearing on a matter involving discretionary judgment has been somewhat unsettled. In addition to the materials already included in this chapter—for example, Justice Frankfurter's opinion in Joint Anti-Fascist Committee v. McGrath, and the Roth and Meachum cases—consider CALIFANO v. YAMASAKI, 442 U.S. 682 (1979). Section 204(a) of the Social Security Act authorizes recovery of overpayments erroneously made under the old-age, survivors, or disability insurance programs. Section 204(b) reads:

> In any case in which more than the correct amount of payment
> has been made, there shall be no adjustment of payments to, or

recovery by the United States from, any person who is without fault if such adjustment or recovery would defeat the purpose of this subchapter or would be against equity and good conscience.

Held: as a matter of statutory construction (under the principle of "assum[ing] a congressional solicitude for fair procedure, absent explicit statutory language to the contrary"), a "prerecoupment oral hearing" is required whenever a recipient requests a waiver of a proposed recoupment.

". . . The Court previously has noted that a 'broad "fault" standard is inherently subject to factual determination and adversarial input.' Mitchell v. W.T. Grant Co., 416 U.S. 600, 617 (1974). As the Secretary's regulations make clear, 'fault' depends on an evaluation of 'all pertinent circumstances' including the recipient's 'intelligence . . . and physical and mental condition' as well as his good faith. We do not see how these can be evaluated absent personal contact between the recipient and the person who decides his case. Evaluating fault, like judging detrimental reliance, usually requires an assessment of the recipient's credibility, and written submissions are a particularly inappropriate way to distinguish a genuine hard luck story from a fabricated tall tale. See Goldberg v. Kelly." Id. at 696–97.

For further discussion, see L. Cooper, Goldberg's Forgotten Footnote: Is There a Due Process Right to a Hearing Prior to Termination of Welfare Benefits When The Only Issue Raised is a Question of Law?, 64 Minn.L.Rev. 1107 (1980).

WALTERS v. NATIONAL ASSOCIATION OF RADIATION SURVIVORS
Supreme Court of the United States, 1985.
413 U.S. 305.

JUSTICE REHNQUIST delivered the opinion of the Court.

. . .

I

Congress has by statute established an administrative system for granting service-connected death or disability benefits to veterans. See 38 U.S.C. § 301 et seq. The amount of the benefit award is not based upon need, but upon service connection—that is, whether the disability is causally related to an injury sustained in the service—and the degree of incapacity caused by the disability. A detailed system has been established by statute and Veterans Administration (VA) regulation for determining a veteran's entitlement, with final authority resting with an administrative body known as the Board of Veterans' Appeals (BVA). . . . The controversy in this case centers on the opportunity for a benefit applicant or recipient to obtain legal counsel to aid in the presentation of his claim to the VA. Section 3404(c) of Title 38 provides:

> The Administrator shall determine and pay fees to agents or attorneys recognized under this section in allowed claims for monetary benefits under laws administered by the Veterans' Administration. Such fees—
>
> . . .
>
> (2) shall not exceed $10 with respect to any one claim. . . .

Section 3405 provides criminal penalties for any person who charges fees in excess of the limitation of § 3404.

Appellees here are two veterans organizations, three individual veterans, and a veteran's widow. The two veterans organizations are the National Association of Radiation Survivors, an organization principally concerned with obtaining compensation for its members for injuries resulting from atomic bomb tests, and Swords to Plowshares Veterans Rights Organization, an organization particularly devoted to the concerns of Vietnam veterans. . . .

. . . In 1978, the year covered by the report of the Legal Services Corporation to Congress that was introduced into evidence in the District Court, approximately 800,000 claims for service-connected disability or death and pensions were decided by the 58 regional offices of the VA. Slightly more than half of these were claims for service-connected disability or death, and the remainder were pension claims. Of the 800,000 total claims in 1978, more than 400,000 were allowed, and some 379,000 were denied. Sixty-six thousand of these denials were contested at the regional level; about a quarter of these contests were dropped, 15% prevailed on reconsideration at the local level, and the remaining 36,000 were appealed to the BVA. At that level some 4,500, or 12%, prevailed, and another 13% won a remand for further proceedings. Although these figures are from 1978, the statistics in evidence indicate that the figures remain fairly constant from year to year.

As might be expected in a system which processes such a large number of claims each year, the process prescribed by Congress for obtaining disability benefits does not contemplate the adversary mode of dispute resolution utilized by courts in this country. It is commenced by the submission of a claim form to the local veterans agency, which form is provided by the VA either upon request or upon receipt of notice of the death of a veteran. Upon application a claim generally is first reviewed by a three-person "rating board" of the VA regional office—consisting of a medical specialist, a legal specialist, and an "occupational specialist." A claimant is "entitled to a hearing at any time on any issue involved in a claim. . . . " Proceedings in front of the rating board "are ex parte in nature"; no government official appears in opposition. The principal issues are the extent of the claimant's disability and whether it is service-connected. The panel is required by regulation "to assist a claimant in developing the facts pertinent to his claim," and to consider any evidence offered by the claimant. In deciding the claim the panel generally will request the applicant's armed service and medical records, and will order a medical examination by a VA hospital. Moreover, the board is directed by regulation to resolve all reasonable doubts in favor of the claimant.

After reviewing the evidence the board renders a decision either denying the claim or assigning a disability "rating" pursuant to detailed regulations developed for assessing various disabilities. Money benefits are calculated based on the rating. The claimant is notified of the board's decision and its reasons, and the claimant may then initiate an appeal by filing a "notice of disagreement" with the local agency. If the local agency adheres to its original decision it must then provide the claimant with a "statement of the case"—a written description of the facts and applicable law upon which the panel based its determination—so that the claimant may adequately present his appeal to the BVA. Hearings in front of the BVA are subject to the same rules as local agency hearings—they are ex parte, there is no formal questioning or cross-examination, and no formal rules of evidence apply. The BVA's decision is not subject to judicial review. 38 U.S.C. § 211(a).[1]

The process is designed to function throughout with a high degree of informality and solicitude for the claimant. There is no statute of limitations, and a denial of benefits has no formal res judicata effect . . . . Perhaps more importantly for present purposes, however, various veterans organizations across the country make available trained service agents, free of charge, to assist claimants in developing and presenting their claims. These service representatives are contemplated by the VA statute, 38 U.S.C. § 3402, and they are recognized as an important part of the administrative scheme. Appellees' counsel agreed at argument that a representative is available for any claimant who requests one, regardless of the claimant's affiliation with any particular veterans group.[2]

[The district court held that appellees had a strong likelihood of showing that the administrative scheme violated the due process clause, and entered a "preliminary injunction" enjoining the enforcement of 38 U.S.C. § 3404–3405. The aid of the service representatives was unsatisfactory, said the trial court, because a heavy case load and lack of legal training led to inadequate research and failure to develop the facts, it was "standard practice . . . to submit merely a one to two page hand written brief."

In reaching its conclusions the court relied heavily on the problems presented by what it described as "complex cases" which apparently included those in which a disability was slow-developing and therefore difficult to find service-connected, as well as other cases involving difficult matters of medical judgment. There were no findings as to what proportion of the VA caseload "complex cases" comprised. The evidence suggested, said Justice Rehnquist, "that the sum total of such claims is extremely small; in 1982, for example, roughly 2% of the BVA caseload consisted of "agent orange" or "radiation" claims, and what evidence there is suggests that the percentage of such claims in the regional offices was even less—perhaps as little as 3 in 1000."]

1. [Ed.] § 211 is considered in chapter 9, § 2, p. 1009 below.

2. The VA statistics show that 86% of all claimants are represented by service representatives, 12% proceed pro se, and 2% are represented by lawyers. . . .

II

. . .

[The Supreme Court concluded that it had jurisdiction under 28 U.S.C. § 1252 over this appeal from a preliminary injunction.]

III

. . .

Appellees' first claim, accepted by the District Court, is that the statutory fee limitation, as it bears on the administrative scheme in operation, deprives a rejected claimant or recipient of "life, liberty or property, without due process of law," U.S. Const., Amnt. V, by depriving him of representation by expert legal counsel.[3] . . .

These general principles are reflected in the test set out in Mathews, which test the District Court purported to follow . . . . In applying this test we must keep in mind, in addition to the deference owed to Congress, the fact that the very nature of the due process inquiry indicates that the fundamental fairness of a particular procedure does not turn on the result obtained in any individual case; rather, "procedural due process rules are shaped by the risk of error inherent in the truth-finding process as applied to the generality of cases, not the rare exceptions." 424 U.S. at 344.

The government interest, which has been articulated in congressional debates since the fee limitation was first enacted in 1862 during the Civil War, has been this: that the system for administering benefits should be managed in a sufficiently informal way that there should be no need for the employment of an attorney to obtain benefits to which a claimant was entitled, so that the claimant would receive the entirety of the award without having to divide it with a lawyer. This purpose is reinforced by a similar absolute prohibition on compensation of any service organization representative. While Congress has recently considered proposals to modify the fee limitation in some respects, a Senate Committee report in 1982 highlighted that body's concern "that any changes relating to attorneys' fees be made carefully so as not to induce unnecessary retention of attorneys by VA claimants and not to disrupt unnecessarily the very effective network of nonattorney resources that has evolved in the absence of significant attorney involvement in VA claims matters." S.Rep. No. 97–466, p. 49 (1982). Although this same Report professed the Senate's belief that the original stated interest in protecting veterans from unscrupulous lawyers was "no longer tena-

---

3. The District Court held that applicants for benefits, no less than persons already receiving them, had a "legitimate claim of entitlement" to benefits if they met the statutory qualifications. The court noted that this Court has never so held, although this Court has held that a person receiving such benefits has a "property" interest in their continued receipt. See Atkins v. Block, — U.S. —, —, 105 S.Ct. 2520, — (1985); Mathews v. El-

dridge, 424 U.S. 319 (1976). Since at least one of the claimants here alleged a diminution of benefits already being received, however, we must in any event decide whether "due process" under the circumstances includes the right to be represented by employed counsel. In light of our decision on that question, we need not presently define what class would be entitled to the process requested.

ble," the Senate nevertheless concluded that the fee limitation should with a limited exception remain in effect, in order to "protect claimants' benefits" from being unnecessarily diverted to lawyers.

In the face of this congressional commitment to the fee limitation for more than a century, the District Court had only this to say with respect to the governmental interest:

> The government has neither argued nor shown that lifting the fee limit would harm the government in any way, except as the paternalistic protector of claimants' supposed best interests. To the extent the paternalistic role is valid, there are less drastic means available to ensure that attorneys' fees do not deplete veterans' death or disability benefits.

It is not for the District Court or any other federal court to invalidate a federal statute by so cavalierly dismissing a long-asserted congressional purpose. If "paternalism" is an insignificant government interest, then Congress first went astray in 1792, when by its Act of March 23 of that year it prohibited the "sale, transfer or mortgage . . . of the pension . . . [of a] soldier . . . before the same shall become due." Ch. 11, § 6, 1 Stat. 245. Acts of Congress long on the books, such as the Fair Labor Standards Act, might similarly be described as "paternalistic"; indeed, this Court once opined that "[s]tatutes of the nature of that under review, limiting the hours in which grown and intelligent men may labor to earn their living, are mere meddlesome interferences with the rights of the individual. . . . " Lochner v. New York, 198 U.S. 45, 61 (1905). That day is fortunately long gone, and with it the condemnation of rational paternalism as a legitimate legislative goal.

There can be little doubt that invalidation of the fee limitation would seriously frustrate the oft repeated congressional purpose for enacting it. Attorneys would be freely employable by claimants to veterans benefits, and the claimant would as a result end up paying part of the award, or its equivalent, to an attorney. But this would not be the only consequence of striking down the fee limitation that would be deleterious to the congressional plan.

A necessary concomitant of Congress' desire that a veteran not need a representative to assist him in making his claim was that the system should be as informal and nonadversarial as possible. This is not to say that complicated factual inquiries may be rendered simple by the expedient of informality, but surely Congress desired that the proceedings be as informal and nonadversarial as possible. The regular introduction of lawyers into the proceedings would be quite unlikely to further this goal. . . .

. . .

Thus, even apart from the frustration of Congress' principal goal of wanting the veteran to get the entirety of the award, the destruction of the fee limitation would bid fair to complicate a proceeding which Congress wished to keep as simple as possible. It is scarcely open to doubt that if claimants were permitted to retain compensated attorneys the day might come when it could be said that an attorney might indeed be necessary to present a claim properly in a system rendered more adversary and more complex by the very presence of lawyer representation. It is only a small step beyond that to the situation in which the claimant who has a factually simple and obviously deserving claim may nonetheless feel impelled to retain an attorney simply because so many other claimants retain attorneys. And this additional complexity will undoubtedly engender greater administrative costs, with the end result being that less government money reaches its intended beneficiaries.

We accordingly conclude that under the Mathews v. Eldridge analysis great weight must be accorded to the government interest at stake here. The flexibility of our approach in due process cases is intended in part to allow room for other forms of dispute resolution. . . . It would take an extraordinarily strong showing of probability of error under the present system—and the probability that the presence of attorneys would sharply diminish that possibility—to warrant a holding that the fee limitation denies claimants due process of law. We have no hesitation in deciding that no such showing was made out on the record before the District Court. . . .

. . . In this case we are fortunate to have statistics that bear directly on this question, which statistics were addressed by the District Court. These unchallenged statistics chronicle the success rates before the BVA depending on the type of representation of the claimant, and are summarized in the following figures taken from the record.

Ultimate Success Rates Before the Board of Veterans Appeals by Mode of Representation

American Legion	16.2%
American Red Cross	16.8%
Disabled American Veterans	16.6%
Veterans of Foreign Wars	16.7%
Other non-attorney	15.8%
No representation	15.2%
Attorney/Agent	18.3%

The District Court opined that these statistics were not helpful, because in its view lawyers were retained so infrequently that no body of lawyers with an expertise in VA practice had developed, and lawyers who represented veterans regularly might do better than lawyers who represented them only pro bono on a sporadic basis. . . .

We think the District Court's analysis of this issue totally unconvincing, and quite lacking in the deference which ought to be shown by any federal court in evaluating the constitutionality of an Act of Congress. We have the most serious doubt whether a competent lawyer taking a veteran's case on a pro bono basis would give less than his best effort, and we see no reason why experience in developing facts as to causation in the numerous other areas of the law where it is relevant would not be readily transferable to proceedings before the VA. . . .

The District Court's treatment of the likely usefulness of attorneys is on the same plane with its efforts to quantify the likelihood of error under the present system. The court states several times in its opinion that lawyers could provide more services than claimants presently receive—a fact which may freely be conceded—but does not suggest how the availability of these services would reduce the likelihood of error in the run-of-the-mine case. Simple factual questions are capable of resolution in a nonadversarial context, and it is less than crystal clear why *lawyers* must be available to identify possible errors in *medical* judgment. The availability of particular lawyers' services in so-called "complex" cases might be more of a factor in preventing error in such cases, but on this record we simply do not know how those cases should be defined or what percentage of all of the cases before the VA they make up. Even if the showing in the District Court had been much more favorable, appellees still would confront the constitutional hurdle posed by the principle enunciated in cases such as Mathews to the effect that a process must be judged by the generality of cases to which it applies, and therefore process which is sufficient for the large majority of a group of claims is by constitutional definition sufficient for all of them. But here appellees have failed to make the very difficult factual showing necessary.

    . . .

We have in previous cases, of course, not only held that the Constitution permits retention of an attorney, but that on occasion it requires the Government to provide the services of an attorney. [The Court then discussed a series of precedents concerning the provision of counsel in criminal and other sanctioning proceedings.]

But where, as here, the only interest protected by the Due Process Clause is a property interest in the continued receipt of government benefits, which interest is conferred and terminated in a non-adversary proceeding, these precedents are of only tangential relevance. Appellees rely on Goldberg v. Kelly, 397 U.S. 254 (1970), in which the Court held that a welfare recipient subject to possible termination of benefits was entitled to be represented by an attorney. . . .

We think that the benefits at stake in VA proceedings, which are not granted on the basis of need, are more akin to the social security benefits involved in Mathews than they are to the welfare payments upon which the recipients in Goldberg depended for their daily subsistence. Just as this factor was dispositive in Mathews in the Court's determination that no evidentiary hearing was required prior to a temporary deprivation of benefits, so we think it is here determinative of the right to employ counsel. . . .

This case is further distinguishable from our prior decisions because the process here is not designed to operate adversarially. . . .

    . . . Especially in light of the government interests at stake, the evidence adduced before the District Court as to success rates in claims handled with or without lawyers shows no such great disparity as to warrant the inference that the congressional fee limitation under consideration here violates the Due Process Clause of the Fifth Amendment. What evidence we have been pointed to in the record regarding complex cases falls far short of the kind which would warrant upsetting Congress' judgment that this is the manner in which it wishes claims for veterans benefits adjudicated. Schweiker v. McClure. The District Court abused its discretion in holding otherwise.

IV

[In the final portion of its opinion, the Court rejected the argument that the fee limitation violated First Amendment rights.]

Reversed.

JUSTICE O'CONNOR, with whom JUSTICE BLACKMUN joins, concurring.

. . . I agree that the record before us is insufficient to evaluate the claims of any individuals or identifiable groups. I write separately to note that such claims remain open on remand.

The grant of appellate jurisdiction under § 1252 does not give the Court license to depart from established standards of appellate review. This Court, like other appellate courts, has always applied the "abuse of discretion" standard on review of a preliminary injunction. . . . In order to justify the sort of categorical relief the District Court afforded here, the fee limitation must pose a risk of erroneous deprivation of rights in the generality of cases reached by the injunctive relief. Cf. Mathews v. Eldridge, 424 U.S. 319, 344 (1976). Given the nature of the typical claim and the simplified Veterans Administration procedures, the record falls short of establishing any likelihood of such sweeping facial invalidity.

. . .

Nevertheless, it is my understanding that the Court, in reversing the lower court's preliminary injunction, does not determine the merits of the respondents' individual "as applied" claims. The complaint indicates that respondents challenged the fee limitation both on its face and as applied to them, and sought a ruling that they were entitled to a rehearing of claims processed without assistance of an attorney. . . .

The merits of these claims are difficult to evaluate on the record of affidavits and depositions developed at the preliminary injunction stage. Though the Court concludes that denial of expert representation is not "per se unconstitutional," given the availability of service representatives to assist the veteran and the Veterans Administration Board's emphasis on nonadversarial procedures, "[o]n remand, the District Court is free to and should consider any individual claims that [the procedures] did not meet the standards we have described in this opinion." Parham v. J.R., 442 U.S., at 616–617 (1979).

JUSTICE BRENNAN, with whom JUSTICE MARSHALL joins, dissenting.

. . .

[Justice Brennan's opinion was devoted to arguing that the Court did not have jurisdiction directly to review the preliminary injunction decision of the district court. He also thought that the opinion of Justice Rehnquist (but not Justice O'Connor) lost sight of the fact that the trial court had only opined on the "likelihood" of the outcome on the merits, in a proceeding in which the factual record had not been fully developed.]

JUSTICE STEVENS, with whom JUSTICE BRENNAN and JUSTICE MARSHALL join, dissenting.

The Court does not appreciate the value of individual liberty. It may well be true that in the vast majority of cases a veteran does not need to employ a lawyer, and that the system of processing veterans benefit claims, by and large, functions fairly and effectively without the participation of retained counsel. Everyone agrees, however, that there are at least some complicated cases in which the services of a lawyer would be useful to the veteran and, indeed, would simplify the work of the agency by helping to organize the relevant facts and to identify the controlling issues. What is the reason for denying the veteran the right to counsel of his choice in such cases? The Court gives us two answers: First, the paternalistic interest in protecting the veteran from the consequences of his own improvidence, and second, the bureaucratic interest in minimizing the cost of administering the benefit program. I agree that both interests are legitimate, but neither provides an adequate justification for the restraint on liberty imposed by the $10-fee limitation.

. . . .

I

The first fee limitation—$5 per claim—was enacted in 1862. That limitation was repealed two years later and replaced by the $10-fee limitation, which has survived ever since. The limitation was designed to protect the veteran from extortion or improvident bargains with unscrupulous lawyers. Obviously, it was believed that the number of scoundrels practicing law was large enough to justify a legislative prohibition against charging excessive fees.

At the time the $10-fee limitation was enacted, Congress presumably considered that fee reasonable. The legal work involved in preparing a veteran's claim consisted of little more than filling out an appropriate form, and, in terms of the average serviceman's base pay, a $10 fee then was roughly the equivalent of a $580 fee today. At its inception, therefore, the fee limitation had neither the purpose nor the effect of precluding the employment of reputable counsel by veterans. Indeed, the statute then, as now, expressly contemplated that claims for veterans benefits could be processed by "agents or attorneys."

The fact that the statute was aimed at unscrupulous attorneys is confirmed by the provision for criminal penalties. . . . Thus, the law that was enacted in 1864 to protect veterans from unscrupulous lawyers—those who charge excessive fees—effectively denies today's veteran access to *all* lawyers who charge reasonable fees for their services.

II

. . . .

In my opinion, the bureaucratic interest in minimizing the cost of administration is nothing but a red herring. Congress has not prohibited lawyers from participating in the processing of claims for benefits and there is no reason why it should. The complexity of the agency procedures can be regulated by limiting the number of hearings, the time for argument, the length of written submissions, and in other ways, but there is no reason to believe that the *agency's* cost of administration will be increased because a claimant is represented by counsel instead of appearing pro se. The informality that the Court emphasizes is desirable because it no doubt enables many veterans, or their lay representatives, to handle their claims without the assistance of counsel. But there is no reason to assume that lawyers would add confusion rather than clarity to the proceedings. As a profession, lawyers are skilled communicators dedicated to the service of their clients. Only if it is assumed that the average lawyer is incompetent or unscrupulous can one rationally conclude that the efficiency of the agency's work would be undermined by allowing counsel to participate whenever a veteran is willing to pay for his services. I categorically reject any such assumption.

. . .

Moreover, the growth of the strong system of active service officers who provide excellent representation at no cost to claimants is significant because it has virtually eliminated the danger that a claimant will be tempted to waste money on unnecessary legal services. . . . [T]he availability of such competent, free representation is not a reason for denying a claimant the right to employ counsel of his own choice in an appropriate case.

III

The Court correctly notes that the presumption of constitutionality that attaches to every Act of Congress requires the challenger to bear the burden of demonstrating its invalidity. Before attempting to do so, I must comment on two aspects of the Court's rhetoric: Its references to the age of the statute and to the repudiation of Lochner v. New York, 198 U.S. 45 (1905).

The fact that the $10-fee limitation has been on the books since 1864 does not, in my opinion, add any force at all to the presumption of validity. Surely the age of the de jure segregation at issue in Brown v. Board of Education, 347 U.S. 483 (1954), or the age of the gerry-mandered voting districts at issue in Baker v. Carr, 369 U.S. 186 (1962), provided no legitimate support for those rules. In this case, the passage of time, instead of providing support for the fee limitation, has effectively eroded the one legitimate justification that formerly made the legislation rational. The age of the statute cuts against, not in favor of, its validity.

It is true that the statute that was incorrectly invalidated in Lochner provided protection for a group of workers, but that protection was a response to the assumed disparity in the bargaining power of employers and employees, and was justified by the interest in protecting the health and welfare of the protected group. It is rather misleading to imply that a rejection of the Lochner holding is an endorsement of rational paternalism as a legitimate legislative goal. But in any event, the kind of paternalism reflected in this statute as it operates today is irrational. It purports to protect the veteran who has little or no need for protection and it actually denies him assistance in cases in which the help of his own lawyer may be of critical importance.

But the statute is unconstitutional for a reason that is more fundamental than its apparent irrationality. What is at stake is the right of an individual to consult an attorney of his choice in connection with a controversy with the Government. In my opinion that right is firmly protected by the Due Process Clause of the Fifth Amendment and by the First Amendment.

. . .

The fundamental error in the Court's analysis is its assumption that the individual's right to employ counsel of his choice in a contest with his sovereign is a kind of second-class interest that can be assigned a material value and balanced on a utilitarian scale of costs and benefits. . . . [W]e are not considering a procedural right that would involve any cost to the Government. We are concerned with the individual's right to spend his own money to obtain the advice and assistance of independent counsel in advancing his claim against the Government.

. . . If the Government, in the guise of a paternalistic interest in protecting the citizen from his own improvidence, can deny him access to independent counsel of his choice, it can change the character of our free society. Even though a dispute with the sovereign may only involve property rights, or as in this case a statutory entitlement, the citizen's right of access to the independent, private bar is itself an aspect of liberty that is of critical importance in our democracy. Just as I disagree with the present Court's crabbed view of the concept of "liberty," so do I reject its apparent unawareness of the function of the independent lawyer as a guardian of our freedom.[4]

. . . [T]he citizen's right to consult an independent lawyer and to retain that lawyer to speak on his or her behalf is an aspect of liberty that is priceless. It should not be bargained away on the notion that a totalitarian appraisal of the mass of claims processed by the Veterans' Administration does not identify an especially high probability of error.

. . .

I respectfully dissent.

NOTES

(1) If not the adversarial system, then what? Reconsider the excerpts from J. Mashaw, Bureaucratic Justice (1983), pp. 608–609

---

4. That function was, however, well understood by Jack Cade and his followers, characters who are often forgotten and whose most famous line is often misunderstood. Dick's statement ("The first thing we do, let's kill all the lawyers") was spoken by a rebel, not a friend of liberty. See

W. Shakespeare, King Henry VI, pt. II, Act IV, scene 2, line 72. As a careful reading of that text will reveal, Shakespeare insightfully realized that disposing of lawyers is a step in the direction of a totalitarian form of government.

above. Part of Professor Mashaw's argument is that traditional, individualized adjudication (although it sometimes takes place without formal adversarial process) is part of the moral judgment model, because in our culture individually adjudicated cases inevitable spill over beyond the mere application of existing rules to found facts (the bureaucratic rationality model) and begin to address broader, more diffuse, questions of moral entitlement. Such cases lead, in Professor Mashaw's phrase, to a "contextual exploration of individual deservingness." As against this, he suggests we could have—and to some extent do have—programs which emphasize the application of professional judgment in a service relationship, or programs which emphasize cost-effective rational decisionmaking. Professor Mashaw makes a strong case for (as his title says) bureaucratic justice; for a thoughtful review, see L. Liebman and R. Stewart, 96 Harv.L.Rev. 1952 (1983) (reprinted in part at page 539 above).

(2) Justice O'Connor suggests that plaintiffs are entitled to have the statutory procedure tested "as applied" for consistency with the due process clause. Is an "as applied" test consistent with the method of Mathews v. Eldridge?

(3) Reconsider the note materials following Goldberg v. Kelly, pp. 572ff above. Can one easily dismiss the claim that regular use of attorneys might catalyze a fundamental change in the character and costs of VA Administration? Does Justice Stevens' dissent stand or fall on the contention that there will be no additional cost of administration to the agency? Or is there an appropriate doctrinal limitation to matters that are properly subjected to cost-benefit analysis, and those that are beyond that criterion?

(4) Admitting that he had not always followed his own counsel of restraint, Justice Powell wrote, in 1982 (Logan v. Zimmerman Brush Co., 455 U.S. 422, 443 n.* (concurring opinion)):

It is necessary for this Court to decide cases during almost every Term on due process and equal protection grounds. Our opinions in these areas often are criticized, with justice, as lacking consistency and clarity. Because these issues arise in varied settings, and opinions are written by each of nine Justices, consistency of language is an ideal unlikely to be achieved. Yet I suppose we would all agree—at least in theory—that unnecessarily broad statements of doctrine frequently do more to confuse than to clarify our jurisprudence.

As you finish this chapter, do you agree?

For some recent efforts to reconstruct this body of law, see R. Smolla, The Reemergence of the Right-Privilege Distinction in Constitutional Law: The Price of Protesting Too Much, 35 Stan.L.Rev. 69 (1982); E. Rubin, Due Process and the Administrative State, 72 Cal.L.Rev. 1044 (1984); and J. Mashaw, Due Process in the Administrative State (1985).

Chapter V

AGENCY ACQUISITION OF INFORMATION

Although the Administrative Procedure Act is chiefly concerned with rulemaking and adjudication, the citizen's most common contact with administrative agencies arises when they are acquiring information—the raw materials from which policy or action, in whatever shape, will be fashioned. Information may be required in the course of adjudication or rulemaking, in advance of either of these activities, or in the service of other agency business: staff action on requests for governmental action, such as licensing or public grants; identifying industry problems or policy issues which may require agency response; monitoring circumstances in which enforcement activity may be required; preparing for dealings with the legislature or the executive on issues of policy or oversight involving matters within the agency's responsibility. Much such information can readily be obtained from governmental materials already at hand, or may be voluntarily produced by private sources once apprised of the agency's need. Sometimes, however, disclosure must be commanded rather than simply requested. Once legal compulsion enters, our compound wish for a government that is at the same time effective, not excessively costly, and "safe" produces tensions and conundrums of what are by now perhaps a familiar sort.

Working through these materials one will find a number of not readily reconciled themes. On the one hand, government must have information to carry out the substantive laws. As in other settings, it needs powers adequate to deal with social bad apples, and a legal system that eludes ready manipulation by them to escape detection or correction. As a general proposition, too, the citizens who pay the cost of government share with it an interest in reducing both the costs it encounters and the costs it imposes on others in achieving its substantive ends. On the other hand, to be safe from excessive, not to say tyrannical government, and to pursue all those aspects of life that have little or nothing to do with government, citizens need privacy—breathing room. Under the Fourth Amendment one's person, house, papers and effects are not to be invaded without reason—generally, as demonstrated to a neutral magistrate—and under the Fifth Amendment, one may not be compelled to self-incrimination. Data may also have a commercial value one would not readily share, especially with one's competitors but even with a government whose interest and ability to avoid leaks may be less than one's own. And, in a computerized age, how much internal sharing of information held in one or another part of government, lowering the time and money costs of information collection, can be done without threatening to overwhelm individual privacy? Finally, beyond individual concerns for personal privacy lie general political concerns of a sort encountered also in other aspects of this course: to what extent ought control over information acquisition to lie in Congress, President, and/or the courts? Such controls regularly entail costs as well as benefits.

The materials that follow are intended to illuminate these tensions in the context of the variety of information-acquiring techniques government employs. Administrative agencies having to command disclosure do so: (1) by requiring information in application forms or in reports; (2) by themselves inspecting records or premises; (3) by issuing subpoenas which direct the recipient to testify or to produce documents it possesses. The means of compelling obedience are also varied. An applicant may find an agency's staff unwilling to accept a license application until he has provided the information which makes it, in the staff's view, complete. Failure to make a required report (or the making of false statements) may have negative consequences for an existing or hoped-for relationship with the agency, or may lead the agency to impose a civil penalty. Collection of a civil penalty, however, may require judicial enforcement, and disobeying an administrative command to supply information, or the providing of erroneous information, often has no legal consequence until the agency brings an independent judicial proceeding seeking issuance of a warrant or an order to produce, enforcement of a subpoena, or imposition of a penal sanction prescribed by statute. The varieties of, and limits on, agency powers to mandate disclosure are the subject of the paragraphs that follow.

SECTION 1. REQUIRED FORMS AND REPORTS

Experience with required forms and reports is as close at hand as an application for welfare benefits, a pharmacist's prescription records, or the filing of an annual tax return. For citizens and regulated entities alike, the burdens of such reporting are substantial. The Federal Government's periodic Guide to Record Keeping Requirements spanned 103 fine print pages of the Federal Register in 1977 [1]; in the same year, a Commission on Federal Paperwork, in its Final Summary Report, estimated the annual costs of federal paperwork alone at about $500 per person, or more than $100 billion. The nation's 10,000 largest firms were thought to spend an amount which aggregates more than one million times their number. While the costs of preparing the environmental and technical analyses required for regulatory approval of a single large electric generating facility ran to eight figures,[2] the

1. 42 Fed.Reg. 29182 ff.

2. "The paperwork in licensing a single nuclear power plant frequently exceeds 15,000 pages and may cost $15 million to the utility applying for the license. This paperwork takes the form of reports, questions and answers pertaining to these reports, and transcripts of public hearings. Most of the applicant-prepared material is printed in batches of 300–500 copies for distribution to the Nuclear Regulatory Commission, other Federal agencies, State agencies, and interested members of the

public. The cost of paperwork relative to the importance of a nuclear plant to the applicant is always small. . . .

. . . The first [economic concern for a utility planning a nuclear plant] is expanding electric generating capacity and the possible cost advantage of nuclear over other fuels; second is the length of time to bring a plant into operation and the unpredictability of this period. The third concern is paperwork per se. This ranking of concerns becomes clear from a review of

Commission found that the greatest impact fell on individuals, small businessmen, farmers, smaller organizations and institutions and local government units. As the very existence of the Commission suggests, the cumulating, expensive, sometimes duplicative and even psychologically disturbing character of the paperwork burden produced demands for limitations or controls.

Any effort at control, however, quickly confronts the reality that much of the government's curiosity is firmly rooted in the programs it seeks to administer. Information is required to assure that the rules of government programs are being respected; to permit intelligent decisions about the future course of policy; to understand the workings and needs of that part of the private sector being subject to regulation; and to inform the public about matters of common concern. Thus, the Commission found much of the burden to be "necessary and important in achieving national goals" [3]; Herbert Kaufman, a respected analyst of governmental functioning, argues:

"Maybe we could suppress [red tape] if it were merely the nefarious work of a small group of villains or if it were a waste product easily separated from the things we want of government, but it is neither. Anyway, if we did do away with it, we would be appalled by the resurgence of the evils and follies it currently prevents. . . . We are ambivalent about the appropriate trade-offs between discretion and constraint, each of us demanding the former for ourselves and the latter for our neighbors. Under these conditions, learning to live with it is the only thing to do.

"Learning to live with it does not mean accepting all its manifestations and worst features, however. Rather, it means systematically laboring to minimize its net costs. What we need is a detached clinical approach rather than heated attacks, the delicate wielding of a scalpel rather than furious flailing about with a meat ax.

"Dealing with bits and pieces of the problem will not yield dramatic results. Indeed, since there is little prospect of 'breakthroughs,' . . . since the world is growing more complex and interdependent all the time, an inexorable increase must be expected in the number of requirements and prohibitions with which we will have to put up. The best we can hope for is that the rate of growth will be sufficiently controlled to allow us to adjust to these additional irritants." [4]

The principal general control over agency reporting requirements is the Paperwork Reduction Act of 1980, P.L. 96–511, 44 U.S.C. §§ 3501–3520. This act centralizes control over information requirements in the presidency (through an Office of Information and Regulatory Affairs in the Office of Management and Budget) to a degree that is quite striking when compared to the level of statutory recognition generally given presidential direction of agency affairs. An agency

the licensing process." Commission on Federal Paperwork, Energy 61 (1977).

3. Commission of Federal Paperwork, Final Summary Report 5 (1977). See also Comment, Red Tape and National Informa-

tion Policy: The Commission on Federal Paperwork, 26 Am.U.L.Rev. 1208 (1977).

4. H. Kaufman, Red Tape: Its Origins, Uses, and Abuses 97–98 (1977).

seeking to collect information by identical questions or requirements posed to more than ten sources must first seek OMB's approval, which may be withheld or made subject to a condition that the information be obtained through a central collection agency able to coordinate this request with those of other agencies interested in similar data. Agencies remain freer to pursue their own course if they adopt information requirements following APA rulemaking procedures;[5] yet having to engage in that process obviously enhances political as well as public controls. If the agency does *not* follow rulemaking procedures, the OMB itself determines "whether the collection of information is necessary for the proper performance of the functions of the agency, including whether the information will have practical utility," and may conduct informal hearings to that end. 44 U.S.C. § 3508. No one need comply with an information request required to be, but not, approved in this manner. 44 U.S.C. § 3508. And OMB's decisions are generally protected from judicial review of any kind. 44 U.S.C. § 3504(h)(9). Even the independent regulatory commissions are subject to this constraint, although a commission may override OMB by a publicly explained majority vote. 44 U.S.C. § 3507(c).

Here is a presidential political control and coordination mechanism of surprising strength, endorsed by the Congress as other centralized controls[6] have yet to be and explicitly protected from judicial review. While OMB's function is focussed on coordination and cost-reduction, and the statute explicitly disclaims any purpose to enlarge its authority over an agency's "substantive policies and programs," 44 U.S.C. § 3518(e), compliance with that limitation is itself in the hands of the White House and Executive Office Building. Is this a salutary recognition of the need for presidential coordination of law enforcement and of the benefits of sharing information across government (including the need to avoid the costs of duplicative information demands from a variety of agencies largely unaware of each others' activities)? Or is it an invitation to covert undermining of agency functioning by influential regulated interests invited to make use of White House friends in opposing the information requirements that attend regulatory initiatives? Or is it a thoughtless step toward national data banks subversive of important privacy values? Readers will judge for themselves. The function is one not likely to come to nearly so much public attention as its importance deserves,[7] and reports to date, even from skeptical quarters, are inconclusive.[8]

---

5. Under the terms of the statute, OMB may block such proposals only if it comments publicly in the rulemaking and the agency then responds to the comments in a manner OMB's Director finds "unreasonable." 44 U.S.C. § 3504(h)(5)(c).

6. For example, regulatory analysis procedures, see p. 147 above.

7. "Paperwork reduction is what newspaper editors call a 'three-bowler.' (It has so little sex appeal that a reader's face will plop into his cereal bowl three times before he finishes the story in the morning pa-

per.) That may be one reason why paperwork legislation got farther than the administration's regulatory reform bill. In any case, all the tools are finally in place, and a fascinating experiment in government management is under way." R. Neustadt, "Taming the Paperwork Tiger," Regulation p. 32 (Jan./Feb. 1981)

8. S. & M. Tolchin, Dismantling America 67 (1983). At legislative oversight hearings held early in 1984, an OMB official announced that despite 400 million "burden hours" of paperwork eliminated in

We turn now from the general controls of the Paperwork Reduction Act to those that may be invoked by individuals facing particular information requests. To a substantial extent, the information requirements imposed by forms and reports are the product of statute or associated rulemaking, enforceable through the withholding of administrative benefits, the imposition of administrative sanctions, or civil or criminal action. A court assessing the propriety of an administrative sanction, or enforcing its own remedy, will not inquire into the appropriateness of an information requirement whose lawfulness has once been established; although issues of application may be raised, the correctness of coercion in general is rarely in doubt, and the agency thus need invoke no judicial process to make the coercion effective.

a. Reports Required of Institutional Respondents

Constitutional controls. For corporations and unincorporated associations, at least, the Constitution offers little hope for a successful challenge to an agency requirement that information be provided in forms or reports. A requirement that information of arguable utility to a lawful regulatory program be collected or submitted is unlikely to be found outside the constitutional power of either federal or state government to impose. Whalen v. Roe, 429 U.S. 589 (1977).[9] Nor may a corporation or unincorporated association refuse to provide information, the tendency of which may be to incriminate it. Although the Fifth Amendment protects "any person" against both the deprivation of property without due process of law and self-incrimination, and corporate *property* is thus protected, the Supreme Court has consistently held since Hale v. Henkel, 201 U.S. 43 (1906), that only individuals asserting personal rights may invoke the privilege to deflect government informational demands. As Justice Marshall wrote for the Court in Bellis v.

the preceding two years, over two billion hours would still be spent by the private sector in responding to federal paperwork in the coming year. Subcomm. on Information Management and Regulatory Affairs, Senate Committee on Governmental Affairs, Hearings on S. 2433 Paperwork Reduction Act Amendments of 1984, 98th Cong., 2nd Sess. (Comm. Print 1984). For a thorough review, and a strong call to consolidate analysis of paperwork requirements with other regulatory reform measures, see W. Funk, The Paperwork Reduction Act: Paperwork Reduction Meets Administrative Law (Admin.Conf.1986).

9. The question whether the Constitution constrains government disclosure of information once collected, where individual rights of privacy are adversely affected, was specifically not addressed by the Court, and was the occasion for sharply disagreeing individual concurrences by Justices Brennan and Stewart. Cf. pp. 772–780 infra; K. Greenawalt, Legal Protections of Privacy, Final Report to the Office of Telecommunications Policy (1976);

Industrial Foundation of the South v. Texas Industrial Accident Board, 540 S.W.2d 668 (1976), cert. den. 430 U.S. 931 (1977). Statutory constraints on federal disclosure of information provided in confidence are discussed at pp. 763–780 infra.

Such constraints may appear the more important when one confronts the holding in California Bankers Ass'n v. Shultz, 416 U.S. 21 (1974), that the keeping of records may be required even when the primary purpose of the obligation is to assist regulation of one other than the record keeper. That case concerned the requirement of the Bank Secrecy Act of 1970, 12 U.S.C. 1829b, and implementing regulations, that federally insured banks make and preserve microfilm records of their customers' checks. Noting that "provisions requiring reporting or recordkeeping by the paying institution . . . are by no means unique," as under the Internal Revenue Code, the Court readily found sufficient connection between the banks and the checks required to be reported to pass constitutional muster. At 47–49.

United States, 417 U.S. 85 (1974), [involving the records of a very small law firm,] the inapplicability of the privilege for corporate books and papers "can easily be understood as a recognition that corporate records do not contain the requisite element of privacy or confidentiality essential for the privilege to attach." [10]

Similar reasoning led the Supreme Court to find little footing in the Fourth Amendment's prohibitions against "unreasonable searches and seizures" for organizations attempting to defeat an obligation to report information of arguable regulatory significance. United States v. Morton Salt Co., 338 U.S. 632 (1950) concerned the Federal Trade Commission's requirement for the filing of periodic "compliance reports," which would permit the Commission to assess the company's obedience to governing law and Commission directive. The Court found it unnecessary to examine whether Fourth Amendment claims were at all available, observing with reference to Hale v. Henkel that ". . . neither incorporated nor unincorporated associations can plead an unqualified right to conduct their affairs in secret.

"While they may and should have protection from unlawful demands made in the name of public investigation, corporations can claim no equality with individuals in the enjoyment of a right to privacy. They are endowed with public attributes. They have a collective impact upon society, from which they derive the privilege of acting as artificial entities. . . . Favors from government often carry with them an enhanced measure of regulation. Even if one were to regard the request for information in the case as caused by nothing more than official curiosity, nevertheless law-enforcing agencies have a legitimate right to satisfy themselves that corporate behavior is consistent with the law and the public interest." 338 U.S. at 652: see also Pacific Coast European Conference v. Federal Maritime Comm., 359 F.2d 416 (9th Cir.1966); United States v. St. Regis Paper Co., 285 F.2d 607 (2d Cir.1960), aff'd 368 U.S. 208 (1961).[11]

Statutory and administrative controls. Absent significant constitutional controls, then, the principal checks on administrative information requirements are legislative and administrative. But ultra vires arguments, while available here as elsewhere in administrative law, are particularly likely to be unpersuasive when measured against an agency's assessment of its own information needs. An agency's compliance with the Paperwork Reduction Act will only strengthen that judicial disposition.

SUPERIOR OIL CO. v. FEDERAL ENERGY REGULATORY COMM., 563 F.2d 191 (5th Cir.1977) concerned an information requirement adopted by rule, and certified for use under a precursor of the Paperwork Reduc-

---

10. See R. Heidt, The Conjurer's Circle: The Fifth Amendment Privilege in Civil Cases, 91 Yale L.J. 1062 (1982); K. Greenawalt and E. Noam, "Confidentiality Claims of Business Organizations," in Business Disclosure, Government's Need to Know 378 (H. Goldschmid, ed. 1979).

11. Note carefully the context of this quotation. As Section 2, within, demon-

strates, such sentiments have been rejected in applying the Fourth Amendment to physical inspections of corporate premises. This apparent skew has been examined in an excellent student Note, Reasonable Relation Reassessed: The Examination of Private Documents by Federal Regulatory Agencies, 56 N.Y.U.L.Rev. 742 (1981).

tion Act. The Federal Power Commission, whose functions have since been assumed by FERC, decided it needed information independent of summaries prepared by natural gas producers themselves (through their trade association, the American Gas Association) to support effective regulation of their pricing and interstate sale of natural gas. Through APA rulemaking, it first proposed and then adopted a new Form 64 as one of three new data collection instruments designed to furnish it with an independent source of raw data. Many critical comments were filed during the rulemaking. "The producers objected to Form 64 on the grounds, among others, that it was duplicative, burdensome, required the submission of unavailable data, and failed to provide that the information submitted would be kept confidential and that both the questionnaire and the directions accompanying it were unclear. . . . While rejecting or not discussing some suggestions, the FPC did modify Form 64 in several significant ways." With the assurance of "sensitivity to producer concerns" it thought was given by these modifications, the court easily upheld the rule.

"The congressional delegation of power to regulate the interstate sale of natural gas for resale has long been held to encompass the power to fix the price at which such sales shall be made. For effective and meaningful price regulation, the FPC must be able to insure the integrity of its information about producer expenditure for exploration and development which are critical components of cost and essential for determining a just and reasonable rate. . . . [I]f the FPC lacked the power to compel both statutory natural gas companies and their controlled affiliates to disclose the affiliates' exploration and development expenditures, it would be unable to prevent the artificial shifting of properties among affiliates and powerless to accomplish the primary purposes of the Act. . . . When information is 'essential to effective rate making,' the FPC is authorized to procure it."

IN RE: FTC LINE OF BUSINESS REPORT LITIGATION, 595 F.2d 685 (D.C. Cir.1978), cert. denied 439 U.S. 958 (1978), concerned an information requirement imposed by an FTC order.[12] Enforcement of such an order may be obtained by an administrative finding of default, which begins the running of a $100/day civil penalty,[13] or by a summary judicial enforcement proceeding similar to that for enforcement of a subpoena.[14]

---

12. Under Section 6(b) of the Federal Trade Commission Act, 15 U.S.C. § 46(b), the FTC may ". . . require, by general or special orders, persons, partnerships, and corporations, engaged in or whose business affects commerce, . . . to file with the Commission in such form as the Commission may prescribe annual or special reports or answers in writing to specific questions, furnishing to the Commission such information as it may require as to the organization, business, conduct, practices, management, and relation to other corporations, partnerships, and individuals of the respective persons, partnerships and corporations filing such reports or answers in writing. Such reports and answers shall be made under oath, or otherwise, as the Commission may prescribe. . . . "

13. 15 U.S.C. § 50. The penalty must be collected through judicial proceedings, but continues to cumulate from the agency's declaration of default unless judicially stayed. Genuine Parts Co. v. Federal Trade Commission, 445 F.2d 1382 (5th Cir. 1971). The issues for judicial decision in a collection proceeding are essentially the same as they would be in a proceeding brought by the agency to compel submission of the required information.

14. 15 U.S.C. § 49. Subpoena enforcement is treated within, at pp. 718–724.

The dispute had its source in the FTC's efforts to understand the increasing importance of conglomerate enterprise in the American economy. Through a series of required reports, collected and used only for statistical purposes, the FTC had been collecting economic information about corporate performance since the mid–1940's. When reporting firms typically engaged in only one line of business, say steel manufacture, this information could readily be segregated on the basis of industrial groups, and used to acquire insights into their competitive functioning. With the formation of conglomerates, whose corporate statistics might mix apples with mattress pads and truck bodies, this was no longer possible. In order to restore the utility of the information it sought—and, it could be argued, require of conglomerates the same information about their individual lines of business as a corporation engaged in only a single line of business would necessarily supply—the FTC began in 1970 to attempt to require the nation's largest business enterprises to report business statistics on a "line of business" basis.[15]

Resistance to this effort was substantial, beginning during OMB review of the proposed new reporting forms [16] and spilling over into the Congress and then the courts.[17] Concerns beyond natural instincts to preserve corporate privacy appear to have animated this resistance. Although the FTC's data needs more or less fit readily available data for single-line corporations, there need be no such congruence between what the FTC believes it should know about individual lines of a conglomerate's business and the accounting data the conglomerate maintains for its own use; thus, the FTC's demands were said to impose substantial added expense, while producing information lacking in business utility (since not thought to be needed by the businesses themselves). "Perhaps it is no more ridiculous," one critic wrote, "to ask whether more required financial disclosure is better than less than it is to ask whether a woman's place is always in the home, or whether smoke pouring out of factory chimneys necessarily is a sign of progress and prosperity." [18] Beyond cost and futility were concerns that the information would be used in ways harmful to the providers: if the FTC

15. For a valuable general account see H. Goldschmid, ed., Business Disclosure: Government's Need to Know (1979).

16. This review occurred under the Federal Reports Act of 1942, the precursor of the Paperwork Reduction Act.

17. The FTC substantially changed what it proposed to require, as opportunities for comment, oral arguments, and advice were received. Yet grounds also existed for the view that "[m]any respondents spend tremendous time and effort . . . fighting reporting requirements rather than working with the agencies to constructively solve problems raised by the reporting requirements." Letter from Chairman, FTC, in Commission on Federal Paperwork, Segmented Financial Reporting 106 (1977); and see Note, The FTC's Annual Line of Business Reporting Pro-

gram, 1975 Duke L.J. 389. That opportunities for participation may be used for opposition as well as constructive criticism will not strike anyone as unusual or shocking, although it doubtless contributed to a sense of frustration on the part of government officials anxious to get on with matters of importance, and skepticism about some of the "help" being offered.

18. G.J. Benston, An Appraisal of the Costs and Benefits of Government-Required Disclosure: SEC and FTC Requirements 41 L. & Contemp.Prob. 30, 32 (1977); for another highly critical view, see W. Breit and K. Elzinger, Information for Antitrust and Business Activity: Line of Business Reporting in K. Clarkson and T. Muris, eds., The Federal Trade Commission since 1970, Economic Regulation and Bureaucratic Behavior (1981).

could or would not protect the information from disclosure to others, competitive harm might result; and even within the FTC, data respecting particular conglomerate enterprises acquired for statistical purposes by the Commission's Bureau of Economics, could be especially useful to the Bureau of Competition, whose responsibilities extend to the enforcement of antitrust laws and which for years had been seeking to develop information and standards for understanding and possibly resisting particular conglomerate mergers. Recipients of the line-of-business forms already in litigation with the FTC respecting particular competitive issues objected to the possibility that the information they were asked to supply might be brought into their litigation by the Commission's complaint counsel (prosecutor) without having gone through the usual forms of discovery in that litigation.

The Court of Appeals directed compliance with the FTC's order. It was unimpressed that the Commission had not employed Section 553 rulemaking procedures (the FTC, GAO and OMB had each provided opportunities for comment in fact), since "[i]nvestigative acts, specifically including report orders, are encompassed in Section 6(b) of the APA, [5 U.S.C. § 555(c)], which states 'process, requirement of a report, inspection, or other investigative act or demand may not be issued, made, or enforced except as authorized by law.'" The court observed that the FTC had proceeded as authorized by its own organic statute, and had made all required consultations, and that investigation is an agency activity separate and apart from adjudication and rulemaking.[19] That the Commission in fact provided multiple opportunities for access to its decisionmaking, the court opined, was wholly a matter for its discretion. The court readily found that the information sought was "relevant" to a lawful agency purpose, and that the corporations had failed to establish excessive burdensomeness: even "assuming the accuracy of the most extravagant cost estimates, the costs of compliance were de minimis relative to the overall corporate operating budget." As for the fears the corporations had expressed regarding the confidentiality with which the information would be held, the court noted statutory provisions and regulatory actions generally protective of confidentiality, but then concluded that the issue was misplaced in an action seeking to enforce an order to produce information; the enforcement proceeding is properly concerned only with the agency's right to collect the information in question, not with determining all uses to which it might be put.

The question of preventing release of sensitive information to the public is best taken up in connection with the Freedom of Information and Privacy Acts, considered in Chapter VI.[20] The problem of transfer

---

19. See also United States v. W.H. Hodges & Co., Inc., 533 F.2d 276, 278 (5th Cir.1976); Montship Lines, Ltd. v. Federal Maritime Bd., 295 F.2d 147 (D.C.Cir.1961).

20. Should the fact that records being sought are medical records warrant refusal of enforcement for privacy reasons even if disclosure outside government is not threatened? Compare Hawaii Psychiatric

Soc. v. Ariyoshi, 481 F.Supp. 1028 (D.Hawaii 1979) (denying enforcement to subpoena for psychiatric records in conjunction with Medicaid investigation) with General Motors Corp. v. Director of NIOSH, 636 F.2d 163 (6th Cir.1980), cert. denied 454 U.S. 877 (1981) (enforcing subpoena for medical records on occupational safety and health inquiry) and United

of information within government warrants a few words here. Both government efficiency and holding down private costs of compliance with information requests argue for sharing, and transfer of information from one agency to another is unrestricted in the absence of special statutes.[21] Sometimes, as is the case with census materials, legislators might choose to restrict transfer in order to encourage private cooperation with the information gatherers. Does the larger vulnerability to enforcement action that results from transferability itself warrant restrictions, in "fairness" to the potential object of regulation? That argument was unavailingly made in Shell Oil Co. v. Department of Energy, 477 F.Supp. 413 (D.Del.1979), affirmed 631 F.2d 231 (3d Cir. 1980), cert. denied, 450 U.S. 1024 (1981), which concerned a reporting regime much like the FTC's Line of Business report—intended primarily for use in formulating energy policy, but subject to sharing with the FTC and the Department of Justice's Antitrust Division. Dissenting from denial of the petition for certiorari, Justice Powell wrote:

> The dissemination of this extraordinary volume of data to those prosecutorial government agencies raises a serious question as these agencies may thereby obtain information that statutory and constitutional safeguards would bar them from obtaining directly in antitrust enforcement action. The likelihood that rights of potential antitrust defendants will be violated increases as DOE demands increasingly more data from companies subject to its regulation and then disseminates the information to prosecutorial agencies. Congress has given DOE an investigative power that appears to be intrusive as well as excessively burdensome in its own right. But that power should not become a blanket discovery authority for the use of the Department of Justice and the Federal Trade Commission without the safeguards provided by law against abuse of legal rights.

Are these arguments persuasive? Note a series of cases in which the Supreme Court has interpreted the Federal Rules of Criminal Procedure to restrict agency access to grand jury materials sharply. United States v. Sells Engineering, Inc., 463 U.S. 418 (1983); United States v. Baggot, 463 U.S. 476 (1983). Characterizing the government's claim in Sells as one to "rummage through the records of any grand jury in the country, simply by right of office," the Court appears hostile to the claims for efficiency in this context.[22] Note, too, that in 1980 Congress amended the Federal Trade Commission Act to prevent line-of-business reports from individual firms for other than statistical purposes. "In-

States v. Westinghouse Electric Corp., 638 F.2d 570 (3d Cir.1980) (enforcing NIOSH subpoena subject to notification of individual employees).

21. R. Stevenson, Panel Discussion Agency Release and Sharing of Information, 34 Ad.L.Rev. 159, 160 (1982); Emerson Electric Co. v. Schlesinger, 609 F.2d 898 (8th Cir.1979). The Census Act and The Right to Financial Privacy Act of 1978 (12 U.S.C.) §§ 3401, 3412 (bank records) are perhaps the most prominent statutes restricting intergovernmental transfers. See Carey v. Klutznick, 653 F.2d 732 (2d Cir. 1981), cert. denied 455 U.S. 999 (1982).

22. The context differs from agency information acquiring in arguably significant ways: The grand jury can bring greater coercive force to bear, and is not subject to the various controls that operate on agencies' investigative power.

formation for carrying out specific law enforcement responsibilities" was to be obtained using procedures appropriate to that end. Sec. 4, Federal Trade Commission Improvement Act of 1980, 94 Stat. 375, amending 15 U.S.C. § 46.

b. Reports Required of Individuals

Unlike corporations and unincorporated associations, individuals subjected to reporting requirements—taxpayers, small businessmen, applicants for welfare—*do* have a Fifth Amendment claim not to be required to incriminate themselves. Since most business regulation is enforced by criminal penalties, albeit often minor ones, there might appear to be substantial obstacles to effective reporting obligations. Suppose, for example, truck drivers are required to keep a log of their daily activities, showing what they are doing for each quarter hour of the day, in order to police adherence to rules restricting driving hours, and violation of those rules is an offense: may truck drivers refuse to complete the forms, asserting a privilege against self-incrimination?

(1) In SHAPIRO v. UNITED STATES, 335 U.S. 1 (1948), the Court was concerned with sales records, incriminating under the Price Control Act then in force, which the Administrator had required to be preserved and made available for inspection pursuant to statutory authority to require any dealer in commodities to keep records and other documents. Shapiro was the individual proprietor of an unincorporated wholesale grocery business. Five members of the Court subscribed to the views, stated by Chief Justice Vinson, that the records he had been required to keep were not within the Amendment's purpose:

"It may be assumed at the outset that there are limits which the government cannot constitutionally exceed in requiring the keeping of records which may be inspected by an administrative agency and may be used in prosecuting statutory violations committed by the recordkeeper himself. But no serious misgiving that those bounds have been overstepped would appear to be evoked when there is a sufficient relation between the activity sought to be regulated and the public concern so that the government can constitutionally regulate or forbid the basic activity concerned, and can constitutionally require the keeping of particular records, subject to inspection by the Administrator. It is not questioned here that Congress has constitutional authority to prescribe commodity prices as a war emergency measure, and that the licensing and record-keeping requirements of the Price Control Act represent a legitimate exercise of that power. Accordingly, the principle enunciated in [Wilson v. United States, 221 U.S. 361 (1911)], and reaffirmed as recently as [Davis v. United States, 328 U.S. 582 (1946)], is clearly applicable here: namely, that the privilege which exists as to private papers cannot be maintained in relation to 'records required by law to be kept in order that there may be suitable information of transactions which are the appropriate subjects of governmental regulation, and the enforcement of restrictions validly established.'

". . . The record involved in the case at bar was a sales record required to be maintained under an appropriate regulation, its relevance to the lawful purpose of the Administrator is unquestioned, and the transaction which it recorded was one in which the petitioner could lawfully engage solely by virtue of the license granted to him under the statute."

Justice Frankfurter vigorously dissented:

"The Court this day decides that when Congress prescribes for a limited Governmental purpose, enforceable by appropriate sanctions, the form in which some records are to be kept, not by corporations but by private individuals, in what in everyday language is a private and not a Governmental business, Congress thereby takes such records out of the protection of the Constitution against self-incrimination and search and seizure. . . .

"The underlying assumption of the Court's opinion is that all records which Congress in the exercise of its constitutional powers may require individuals to keep in the conduct of their affairs, because those affairs also have aspects of public interest, become 'public' records in the sense that they fall outside the constitutional protection of the Fifth Amendment. The validity of such a doctrine lies in the scope of its implications. The claim touches records that may be required to be kept by federal regulatory laws, revenue measures, labor and census legislation in the conduct of business which the understanding and feeling of our people still treat as private enterprise, even though its relations to the public may call for governmental regulation, including the duty to keep designated records.

"If the records in controversy here are in fact *public,* in the sense of publicly owned, or governmental, records, their non-privileged status follows. . . . No one has a private right to keep for his own use the contents of such records. But the notion that whenever Congress requires an individual to keep in a particular form his own books dealing with his own affairs his records cease to be his when he is accused of crime, is indeed startling. . . .

"Different considerations control where the business of an enterprise is, as it were, the public's. Clearly the records of a business licensed to sell state-owned property are public records . . . And the records of a public utility, apart from the considerations relevant to corporate enterprise, may similarly be treated as public records. . . . This has been extended to the records of 'occupations which are malum in se, or so closely allied thereto, as to endanger the public health, morals or safety.' . . .

"Here the subject matter of petitioner's business was not such as to render it public. Surely, there is nothing inherently dangerous, immoral, or unhealthy about the sale of fruits and vegetables. Nor was there anything in his possession or control of the records to cast a cloud on his title to them. They were the records that he customarily kept. I find nothing in the Act, or in the Court's construction of the Act, that made him a public officer. He was being administered, not administering. Nor was he in any legitimate sense of the word a 'custodian' of the records. I see nothing frivolous in a distinction between the records of an 'unincorporated entrepreneur' and those of a corporation. . . .

The distinction between corporate and individual enterprise is one of the deepest in our constitutional law, as it is for the shapers of public policy.

"The phrase 'required to be kept by law,' then, is not a magic phrase by which the legislature opens the door to in-roads upon the Fifth Amendment. . . . "

Justice Jackson, with whom Justice Murphy agreed, and Justice Rutledge also wrote dissenting opinions.

(2) MARCHETTI v. UNITED STATES, 390 U.S. 39 (1968), involved prosecution for failure to register with the Internal Revenue Service and to provide detailed information in connection with an occupational tax imposed on those who desired to engage in the business of accepting wagers. Payment of the tax did not exempt the taxpayer from federal or state anti-gambling laws. Marchetti argued that the statutory requirements forced him either to violate the law (by not registering) or to incriminate himself by providing evidence of his intended gambling activities. The Government sought to uphold the requirements, relying strongly on the Shapiro case. The Supreme Court sustained Marchetti's position, distinguishing his case from Shapiro's on three grounds:

(a) Marchetti, unlike Shapiro, was not obliged to keep and preserve records "of a kind he has customarily kept," but was, instead, forced to provide information unrelated to any records he might otherwise have maintained;

(b) Whatever "public aspects" may have existed in respect of Shapiro's records, none were present in the information Marchetti was required to give. "The Government's anxiety to obtain information known to a private individual does not without more render that information public; if it did, no room would remain for the application of the Constitutional privilege;"

(c) The record-keeping requirements in Shapiro's case arose in "an essentially non-criminal and regulatory area of activity." The information-giving requirements in Marchetti's case, by contrast, related to a "selective group inherently suspect of criminal activities." Even though the purpose of the United States is to collect revenue rather than to punish gamblers, "the characteristics of the activities about which information is sought, and the composition of the groups to which inquiries are made," differentiate this situation from that in Shapiro's case.[1]

How easy will it be to differentiate between "essentially non-criminal" activities and those which are likely to be engaged in by a

1. In companion cases the Court reemphasized these distinctions. Grosso v. United States, 390 U.S. 62 (1968), involved a different federal tax on gambling activities; Haynes v. United States, 390 U.S. 85 (1968), involved prosecution for failure to register a firearm of an illegal type. See B. Meltzer Required Records, The McCarran Act and The Privilege Against Self-Incrimination, 18 U.Chi.L.Rev. 687 (1951);

J. Mansfield, The Albertson Case: Conflict Between the Privilege Against Self-Incrimination and the Government's Need for Information, 1966 Sup.Ct.Rev. 103; R. McKay, Self-Incrimination and the New Privacy, 1967 Sup.Ct.Rev. 193; see also Note, Business Records and The Fifth Amendment Right Against Self-Incrimination, 38 Ohio St.L.J. 351 (1977).

"selective group inherently suspect"? A grand jury subpoena had called upon process servers to produce records which municipal regulations required to be kept. Fake records created by a process server who engaged in "sewer service" (that is, who certified that he had personally served the process, but who had instead figuratively "tossed the papers into the sewer") would constitute evidence of crime. Was the record-keeping requirement meant to regulate lawful conduct in the public interest or was it, instead, designed as an indirect means of striking at unlawful activity? Application of Nadelson and Wasserman, 353 F.Supp. 971 (S.D.N.Y.1973).

Suppose now the issue is not a record-keeping requirement compelling cooperation in what is arguably the detection of crime, but a requirement enforced by criminal sanction that government be notified when an administrative regulation punishable by civil sanction has been breached. Section 311(b) of the Federal Water Pollution Control Act prohibits discharges of oil into navigable waters, requires reporting such discharges to the government on pain of fine or imprisonment, and imposes a "civil penalty" for violations; the fact that a person has reported a discharge may not, however, be used against the reporter in any criminal case (other than for false statement). Ward reported a discharge from his dwelling facility and was subsequently assessed for a $500 penalty by the Coast Guard. Although the Fifth Circuit characterized the outcome as sufficiently punitive to intrude upon the Fifth Amendment's protection against compulsory self-incrimination, the Supreme Court disagreed; the civil penalty did not trigger constitutional protections applicable to criminal proceedings. United States v. Ward, 448 U.S. 242 (1980).

(3) For a required form which is *not* inherently incriminatory, unlike the form in Marchetti, one cannot assert the privilege by refusing to make any return at all. United States v. Sullivan, 274 U.S. 259 (1927) (income tax return). But if incrimination is then feared as to a particular item, it must be claimed; if a truthful answer is given, it can be used to incriminate, Garner v. United States, 424 U.S. 648 (1976), and even though no answer need have been given, a false answer subjects one to prosecution for having lied to mislead the government. ". . . [I]t cannot be thought that as a general principle of our law a citizen has a privilege to answer fraudulently a question which the Government should not have asked." Bryson v. United States, 396 U.S. 64 (1969). And see Selective Service System v. Minnesota PIRG, 468 U.S. 841 (1984).

(4) The availability of the Fifth Amendment as a defense to government claims for documentary materials was sharply limited by a series of cases in the mid-'70's principally concerning tax investigations. Fisher v. United States, 425 U.S. 391 (1976); California Bankers Ass'n v. Shultz, 416 U.S. 21 (1974); Couch v. United States, 409 U.S. 322 (1973). Thus, if documents are in the physical possession of another, whether by chance or (as in the case of bank records) because the government has compelled that they be maintained, the privilege is unavailable. The decisive question is whether the individual claiming

the privilege is *herself* "required to aid in the discovery, production, or authentication of incriminating evidence." Andresen v. Maryland, 427 U.S. 463, 474 (1976).

For one who *is* required to aid, an early case had suggested the possible existence of a zone of privacy, within which the Fifth Amendment as well as the Fourth would shield an individual from compelled production of personal records. Boyd v. United States, 116 U.S. 616, 630 (1886). In United States v. Doe, 465 U.S. 605 (1984), the defendant had resisted on Fifth Amendment grounds a subpoena requiring him to supply the business records of companies of which he was sole proprietor. No law had compelled the defendant to keep those records (if it had, see Shapiro v. United States, above), and for that reason the Court found the documents themselves beyond the Amendment's protective reach. The Court accepted lower court findings that the very act of producing the document would itself be incriminatory, but thought the government could avoid that problem by making the defendant immune from any evidentiary use *of that act* to establish his guilt. That is, the government would have to forego using the fact that he brought the documents forward; but it could use as evidence whatever was *in* the documents.[2] Does this mean that the contents of private diaries, voluntarily kept, might now fall under a prosecutor's inquiring gaze? Justice O'Connor wrote a separate concurrence for the sole purpose of making "explicit . . . that the Fifth Amendment provides absolutely no protection for the contents of private papers of any kind." Justices Marshall and Brennan noted their equally strong view that "[t]his case presented nothing remotely close to the question that Justice O'Connor eagerly poses and answers. . . . [T]he documents at stake here are business records, which implicate a lesser degree of concern for privacy interests than, for example, personal diaries." How workable do you find a test that makes the Fifth Amendment's application depend on the extent to which particular documents implicate privacy issues? How different is this question from that facing the Court in Shapiro, above?

(5) The availability of Fourth Amendment claims has also been sharply limited. In CALIFORNIA BANKERS ASS'N v. SHULTZ, above, the Supreme Court considered, in part, a requirement by the Secretary of the Treasury, under authority of the Bank Secrecy Act of 1970, 12 U.S. C.A. § 1829b, that financial institutions report a substantial body of identifying data about participants in any bank transaction in currency in an amount exceeding $10,000 (for established customers often engaged in such transactions, such reports need not be made, but the

2. From the government's perspective, might the impairment of value thus entailed be substantial? "What the government would need for authentication [of the documents] is exactly what [Doe] would provide by production—an admission that the subpoenaed documents are records pertaining to his business. . . . " United States v. Fox, 721 F.2d 32 (2d Cir.1983).

How far the result in Doe permits custodians of corporate records to refuse to au-

thenticate them, on Fifth Amendment grounds, has been a lively question. See In re Grand Jury Matter (Brown) 768 F.2d 525 (3d Cir. en banc 1985) (sole stockholder of professional corporation may refuse authentication) and In re Grand Jury Proceedings (Morganstern), 747 F.2d 1098 (6th Cir. en banc 1984) (agent of collective entity required to produce its records may not refuse to produce records even if mere act of production is incriminatory).

names of the customers must be made available to the Secretary on demand). A bank claim that the reporting requirement offended its Fourth Amendment privilege was quickly disposed of on the basis of United States v. Morton Salt Co., discussed briefly at p. 662 above. 416 U.S. at 65–67. A similar claim made by bank depositors was not directly reached, the Court finding no sufficient allegation that these depositors were likely to be involved in the type of transaction required to be reported. At 67–70. Three Justices dissented, finding in this and other aspects of the Act a potent mechanism for invasion of the privacy of bank customers.

The majority had also declined to reach the depositors' claims that provisions of the Act requiring microfilming of their checks and retention of the microfilms by the banks, were offensive to their Fourth Amendment rights. These records were producible only on subpoena, and so, the majority concluded, any dispute about their production was premature. 416 U.S. at 52. No provision of the Act or implementing regulations, however, required notice to depositors that a request for records had been made; the banks were under no obligation to insist upon formal legal process, and might well provide access to such records voluntarily; and, as had been remarked in an earlier case noted by the majority, "[I]t is difficult to see how the summoning of a third party, and the records of a third party, can violate the rights of [another]. . . . " Donaldson v. United States, 400 U.S. 517, 537 (Douglas, J., concurring) (1971), cited at 416 U.S. 53. "Indeed," Justice Marshall observed in dissent, "it is ironic that although the majority deems the bank customers' Fourth Amendment claims premature, it also intimates that once the bank has made copies of a customer's checks, the customer no longer has standing to invoke his Fourth Amendment rights when a demand is made on the bank by the Government for the records." 416 U.S. at 97.

The intimation became holding in UNITED STATES v. MILLER, 425 U.S. 435 (1976), in which a taxpayer learned after indictment that his banks had voluntarily complied with Treasury Department subpoenas to produce records of his accounts required to be maintained by the Bank Secrecy Act. He moved to suppress the information thus produced, but to no avail. No Fourth Amendment interests of the taxpayer were implicated, for "the Fourth Amendment does not prohibit the obtaining of information revealed to a third party and conveyed by him to Government authorities, even if the information is revealed on the assumption that it will be used only for a limited purpose and the confidence placed in the third party will not be betrayed." Although permissive—not mandatory—intervention by the taxpayer might have been possible had the banks insisted upon enforcement of the subpoenas, see Donaldson v. United States, 400 U.S. 517 (1971), their failure to resist, or even to notify Miller of the requests, was without legal consequence.[3] See Note, Formalism, Legal Realism, and Constitution-

---

3. In 1976, Congress revised each of these conclusions for the particular case of tax summonses. Section 7609 of the Internal Revenue Code, enacted as part of the Tax Reform Act of 1976, generally requires third party recordkeepers to notify taxpayers of IRS summonses for their records; the taxpayers then have the right to direct

ally Protected Privacy Under the Fourth and Fifth Amendments, 90 Harv.L.Rev. 945, 946 (1977); J.A. McKenna, The Constitutional Protection of Private Papers: The Role of a Hierarchical Fourth Amendment, 53 Ind.L.J. 55 (1977).

SECTION 2. PHYSICAL INSPECTIONS

Inspection is a widely used governmental technique, capable of serving either as a means for acquiring the information needed for enforcement or other government action, or as a decision mechanism itself, or for both self-informing and decision. The Department of Agriculture's grading of agricultural commodities or a state Motor Vehicle Department's periodic inspection of automobiles represents primarily decisional activity, with the inspector herself resolving the question presented in a way unlikely to be disputed and in any event irresolvable without further inspections. Section 5(a)(3) of the Administrative Procedure Act, 5 U.S.C. § 554(a)(3), recognizes the possibility of using "inspection, tests, or elections" as an alternative to formal adjudication. While theoretical and judicial discussions have been scarce, inspections seem appropriate for any matters that turn "either upon physical facts as to which there is little room for difference of opinion, or else upon technical facts like the quality of tea or the condition of airplanes, as to which administrative hearings have long been thought unnecessary." [1] These issues are considered further in Chapter 7, section 1, below.

Here, we consider the information-gathering aspects of inspections, in particular the question what if any constraints law imposes on the use of inspections as a prelude to the imposition of administrative sanctions, or the withdrawing or withholding of administrative benefits. Examples of this kind of activity also come readily to mind. Complex and hazardous equipment or facilities—airplanes, mines, or nuclear power plants—may be subject to more or less continuous inspection by officials concerned with developing understanding of possible future safety problems and improvements as well as finding immediate safety violations. Meat processing and drug manufacturing plants, milk bottlers and liquor sellers, restaurants, hotels, elevators, electrical wiring,

the recordkeepers not to comply; and they have the right to intervene in any subsequent enforcement proceeding. However, the defenses available in those enforcement proceedings are not enlarged. See generally T. Kummer, Summonses and the 1976 Tax Reform Act, 13 Wake For.L.Rev. 773 (1977).

Title XI of the Financial Institutions Regulatory and Interest Rate Control Act of 1978, P.L. 95–630, 92 Stat. 3641, 12 U.S.C. §§ 3401 ff., makes similar provisions generally to govern federal agencies seeking access to a financial institution's records of an individual's transactions. See also Report, Government Access to Privately-Maintained Financial, Communications Toll and Credit Records, 33 The Rec-

ord 401 (1978). The Supreme Court has held unanimously, however, that such procedures are strictly statutory; there is no constitutional claim to notice of information demands made on third parties. SEC v. Jerry T. O'Brien, Inc., 467 U.S. 735 (1984).

1. Door v. Donaldson, 195 F.2d 764 (D.C.Cir.1952); Attorney General's Comm. on Administrative Procedure, Final Report: Administrative Procedure in Government Agencies, S.Doc. 8, 77th Cong., 1st Sess. 36–38 (1941); see, in particular, the Committee's full description of the procedures for grading under the Grain Standards Act in id., Part 7, S.Doc. 186, 76th Cong., 3d Sess. 15–17 (1940).

fire hazards, and structural conditions in nuclear power plants, factories, and dwelling places—at the federal, state and local level, inspection is a paradigm activity.

Inspection is not only common, but of major significance to governmental action. In 1978, the United States Department of Labor's Bureau of Labor Statistics reported 100,000 persons working as government inspectors with 60% of them working for the federal government.[2] Professor Bernard Schwartz has written in Volume I of his Commentary on the Constitution of the United States—Rights of the Person 204–205 (1977) that "inspection is *the* indispensable law-enforcement device in the urban community. Without inspections, there is no practical way to determine whether undesirable housing conditions or other violations of the standards prescribed exist." Social interdependence necessitates inquiries that, in ancient days, might have been regarded as impertinences. "A man's house may still, in theory, be his castle," Professor Schwartz remarks, "but that castle no longer sits on a hill isolated by a moat. The modern 'castle' is connected to a central water system, a sewage system, a garbage collection system, and, more often than not, to houses on either side.

"The paramount need in the metropolitan agglomerations in which the population is becoming increasingly concentrated is the enforcement of the plethora of health, sanitary, safety, and housing regulations which ensure that living conditions among the nation's urban masses remain tolerable. And over all hangs the problem of urban blight and decay—with the city engaged in an endless effort to maintain existing standards by preventive measures and slum clearance, if

2. Bureau of Labor Statistics, Occupational Outlook Handbook, 1980–81 ed. Inspectors' salaries as often resemble those of government stenographers as they do middle level bureaucrats; and their working conditions—whether the stench of a slaughterhouse or the stooped, damp blackness of a mine—often leave much to be desired. The following table, which appeared in E. Bardach and R.A. Kagan, Going By The Book: The Problem of Regulatory Unreasonableness 161 (1982), suggests both the variety of work involved and the resource constraints under which it most often occurs:

Table 1

Approximate Ratio of Inspectors to Sites to Be Inspected

Agency	Number of Inspectors	Number of Sites (approx.)	Ratio
OSHA and state affiliates	3,300	5,000,000	1:1515
Cal-OSHA elevator unit (elevators, hoists, etc.)	29	32,000	1:1103
San Francisco Bay Area Air Pollution Control District	40		
(significant stationary sources)		10,500	1:263
(establishments)		1,700	1:43
California Motor Safety Unit	14	3,500	1:254
Food and Drug Administration (food processing and storage)	1,000	77,000	1:77
California milk and dairy	110	6,960	1:63
Mine Safety and Health Administration	1,300	22,000	1:17
Nuclear Regulatory Commission	1,564	9,000	1:6

not to raise conditions above the marginal level through schemes of urban renewal."

Yet not all inspections will be seen, particularly by their subjects, as involving benevolent public ends. In part this may be responsive to official attitudes toward function—whether the inspector sees herself as principally concerned with the prevention or correction of undesired conditions, or with the detection and punishment of wrongdoers. If the 1000 or so inspectors of the Department of Labor's Occupational Safety and Health Administration, responsible with a somewhat larger number of state counterparts for working conditions at 5 million business establishments, seem more concerned with ticketing unsafe working conditions than with identifying them for correction, that will have its consequences for the amount of cooperation that can be expected from even the well-intentioned business owner.[4] Yet the difficulties may also arise from less malleable factors—from what seems necessary to maintain honest and efficient functioning among inspectors in the field who have to apply centrally-created policy to the unruly facts of particular circumstances. In considering the following excerpt, ask yourself to what extent the differences described are inevitable, and to what extent they can (and should) be overcome by effective public administration.

4. Two well regarded studies of varying inspectorate styles are S. Kelman, Regulating America, Regulating Sweden: A Comparative Study of Occupational Safety and Health Regulations (1981), and the Bardach and Kagan book next excerpted in the text. While in its early years OSHA emphasized fine-based enforcement, recently it has de-emphasized that. Although federal inspections in fiscal 1983 numbered in excess of 68,000—higher than any year since 1976—only $6,600,000 in fines were assessed, a sharp drop from previous years (e.g., $25,000,000 in 1980); where 15% of citations were contested in 1980, only 3% were contested in 1983. Compare 13 BNA OSHA Rep. 799 (Dec. 22, 1983) with M. Rothstein, OSHA After Ten Years: A Review and Some Proposed Reforms, 34 Vand.L.Rev. 71, 99 n. 164 and 116 n. 278. These changes may be ascribable to OSHA's effort to develop a series of voluntary compliance programs in which employers undertake to assure rapid response to workplace hazards in consultation with OSHA, in return for relative freedom from compliance inspections that could result in lengthy hearings and fines. Rothstein, at 98–110; 48 Fed.Reg. 45411 (Oct. 5, 1983) (consultation agreements), 54546 (Dec. 5, 1983) (Health Policy).

All of this, of course, assumes a purpose of achievement on the part of the public administrators which may sometimes be open to doubt. Initiatives during President Reagan's administration sharply reduced the number of inspectors and changed the character of inspections—reducing repeat visitations, stressing "hazardous worksites" such as construction over manufacturing locations with lower apparent accident rates, and increasing the proportion of inspections examining employer records rather than actual workplace conditions. Presented as efforts to move the American model of confrontation toward the Swedish model of cooperation, these changes were seen by many sympathetic to labor interests in a more cynical light. See, e.g. M. Wines, "Auchter's Record at OSHA leaves Labor Outraged, Business Satisfied," National Journal, Oct. 1, 1983, p. 2008; P. Bollier, "The Emasculation of OSHA," Business and Society Review, Fall 1984, p. 37; A. Szasz, The Reversal of Federal Policy Toward Worker Safety and Health, 50 Science and Society 25 (1986).

EUGENE BARDACH * AND ROBERT A. KAGAN,** GOING BY THE BOOK: THE PROBLEM OF REGULATORY UNREASONABLENESS†

(Temple University Press, Philadelphia, 1982) pp. 4–5.

[To illustrate the skew between what they describe as the "civilian" and "official" views of regulation, the authors composed a dialog between Al Schaefer, the pseudonymous director of workplace safety for a major aluminum manufacturing company and an official of the Occupational Safety and Health Administration (OSHA):]

By all accounts, including those of a labor union safety officer, a regional OSHA official and a plant-level safety engineer with experience in other firms, Schaefer's company seems to have a positive attitude toward worker safety and an aggressive safety program. Still, the corporation's numerous plants have been visited by OSHA inspectors a total of 30 to 50 times a year; the company received an average of 225 citations each year and paid a total of $25,000 in fines over the last seven years. But, argues Schaefer, OSHA inspections have made little positive contribution to safety in his company. "The major problem with OSHA," he says, "is that they mandate safety standards even where they are not the highest priority risk in a particular plant." He gave an example involving an OSHA regulation that called for "alternative means of egress" from public gathering places, such as restaurants. An OSHA inspector applied this rule to the lunchrooms in an aluminum smelting plant. The heart of the smelter is composed of long rows of furnaces (or "pots") in which molten aluminum are transported along these rows by motorized vehicles. Small, airconditioned lunchrooms are adjacent to the "potline" but separated from it by a cinder-block wall; the doors to the lunchroom do not open directly into the potline, but open off side corridors. The lunchrooms had no rear exits.

OSHA said rear exits were required. The only justification OSHA could offer (other than the text of the regulation) was that if the molten aluminum spilled and went into the side corridors and a fire started, workers in the lunchrooms would be trapped.

"Now that citation does not represent a rational assessment of risk." Schaefer says. "Of course, it could happen. Almost anything could happen. Never mind that it's more likely that an earthquake could happen. Never mind that in the 15 years the plant has been operating nothing like that happened, or even any incidents that suggest it might happen."

Besides, he points out, because the lunchrooms are of cinder-block construction, the only thing that could burn is the wooden door. To cut through the other side and install a door, he says, would cost $6,000 per lunchroom, times 10 lunchrooms. "This is a total misapplication of

* Professor, Graduate School of Public Policy, University of California, Berkeley.

** Professor of Political Science, University of California, Berkeley.

resources. I could use that money for real risk reduction in plenty of other places."

To Schaefer, OSHA appeared unreasonable. But was OSHA unreasonable? Although we did not investigate the details of this or several similar instances described by Schaefer, we did interview many regulatory officials from a variety of agencies, including OSHA, and a rebuttal to Schaefer might have sounded like this:

Either directly or through state agencies that enforce the OSHA regulations for us, we regulate worker safety and health in almost five million workplaces. They are extremely varied. If we had rules that were exactly suited to each hazard and each situation in every one of those workplaces, the inspector's manual would have to be transported in a truck. So we have to simplify and standardize, and obviously some cases of overinclusive rules and regulations are going to result. Remember, Al Schaefer or people like him can always file for a variance because the law does give us latitude to waive compliance in cases where equivalent protection is provided by other means.

True, we don't let the inspector at the field level have the discretion to waive compliance. But that is because he would then be susceptible to manipulation, bribery, and perhaps intimidation. Besides, not all 3,000 occupational safety and health inspectors are sufficiently trained or clever or morally upright to be entrusted with discretionary power. It may be somewhat inconvenient for Al Schaefer and others in his position to seek waivers through the proper channels, and in some cases they just might choose to comply with regulatory rules rather than do it, but remember that workers' lives and well-being are at issue. If the system has to make errors, which of course it does, it is better to err on the side of safety. We at OSHA think that, our statutory mandate indicates that Congress thinks that, and public opinion polls suggest that the public overwhelmingly thinks so too.

Who, then, was unreasonable?

NOTES

(1) Measuring the impact of inspection (like any regulatory regime) is both difficult and susceptible to manipulation to suit political purposes. OSHA's inspections (and workplace safety rules), in particular, have often been presented as ineffective or economically unjustified.[1] Finding means of requiring employers to pay the full cost of workplace injuries, it is argued, would provide a more direct and efficient means for reducing the incidence of such injuries than external imposition of rules, inspections, and penalties for violation. Consider in this respect, however, the findings reported in L. ROBERTSON AND J. KEEVE, WORKER INJURIES: THE EFFECTS OF WORKERS' COMPENSATION AND OSHA INSPEC-

---

1. See, e.g., J. Mendeloff, Regulating Safety: An Economic and Political Analysis of Occupational Safety and Health Policy (1979); W. Viscusi, Risk by Choice: Regulating Health and Safety in the Workplace (1983); A. Bartel and L. Thomas, Direct and Indirect Effects of Regulation: A New Look at OSHA's Impact, 28 J.Law & Ec. 1 (1985). A. Szasz, n. 4 p. 675 above, at 30–34. For a somewhat more favorable view of health (as opposed to safety) regulation, See W. Viscusi, Cotton Dust Regulation: An OSHA Success Story? 4 J.Pol.Anal. & Mgmt. 325 (1985).

TIONS, 8 J. Health Politics, Policy and Law 581 (1983). Rising workers' compensation payments, these authors believe, increase the number of claims for workplace injury and in this way obscure the impact of inspections. "Data on days lost due to injury in 167 industrial groupings in 20 states . . . indicate significant reductions of workdays lost in correlation with OSHA inspections, when increases due to Workers' Compensation are controlled."

The authors closely studied three plants of one company, each located in a separate state. There, too, "the enforcement of OSHA standards resulted in significantly reduced injuries and fewer days lost from injury in the year after each inspection. . . . The relatively large reduction in injuries following an OSHA inspection could not have been simply a result of corrections of the relatively few hazards for which citations occurred. . . . A review of correspondence associated with OSHA citations . . . revealed great concern for the cost of any suggestion by OSHA for modification to the workplace, and no reference whatever to the cost in compensation to the workers when hazards result in injuries. . . . Although the standard litany in neoclassic economists' writings on behavior of the firm tells us that managers will act to reduce injuries to the extent that marginal costs of Workers' Compensation and other reductions in profit are offset by the marginal costs of injury reduction, no evidence was found to support such beliefs. Indeed, increasing the costs to the firm of compensable injuries has a multiplier effect on the firm's expenses, with no benefit in reduced injuries: incrementing injury compensation to workers at a rate greater than inflation substantially increased both the number and the cost of injury claims.

. . .

"Total incidence of verifiable injuries was not related to Workers' Compensation, but objectively verifiable time-loss injuries did increase in relation to increased compensation. Although those who believe that degree of worker caution is related to level of compensation may take heart in the latter finding, the lack of correlation to total incidence suggests an alternative explanation: workers may be more demanding of time off for an injury when the compensation is such that they can afford the time off, whereas they might continue to work with a similar injury when compensation is inadequate. . . .

"Both time spent in the workplace and properly disaggregated data lead to our final conclusion: OSHA inspections do appear to work in the short term; and, primarily, they seem to work not by permanently correcting specific safety violations, but by temporarily instilling a greater consciousness of transient factors related to injuries. . . ."

(2) Very much at issue here is the problem of discretion. The "good cop" or the "good inspector" needs substantial freedom of action to be able to bend to circumstances, to counsel as well as command. To the extent legal constraints encourage legalism, they create a setting antithetical to the cooperative endeavor well-motivated safety directors

such as Schaefer say they wish.[2] Yet legal constraints are as necessary to deal with the bad apples—and bad tendencies—in the inspectorate's bin as they are to create the framework within which compliance can be demanded of those who may not be as well motivated as Schaefer's company is supposed to be.[3]

An inspector may appear to be exacting an intolerable price in loss of privacy as a condition of continuing or extending a desired benefit. As in all such matters, the statutes must be looked to in the first instance to define the inspector's authority to "force the door" or to insist on agreement to future inspections as a condition for accepting an application, issuing a license, or otherwise conferring some public benefit. 5 U.S.C. § 555(c). Is a customs agent authorized to disassemble a traveller's suitcase in search of false panels which may be concealing smuggled contraband? Can a city fine a homeowner who refuses a periodic neighborhood fire inspection? May the Nuclear Regulatory Commission require each of its permittees to provide on-site office space and continuous, unimpeded access to its facilities for NRC inspectors as a condition of issuing a desired permit? May a welfare agency restrict its payment of benefits for children to families who agree to occasional "home visits" to assess the quality of the children's environment or for other reasons? Does it matter whether such visits are scheduled or unscheduled, at reasonable hours or in the middle of the night? The Fourth Amendment to the United States Constitution, applicable as well to state and local governments through the Fourteenth Amendment, provides:

> The right of the people to be secure in their persons, houses, papers, and effects, against unreasonable searches and seizures, shall not be violated, and no Warrants shall issue, but upon probable cause, supported by Oath or affirmation, and particularly describing the place to be searched, and the persons or things to be seized.

2. Remarks attributed to a retiring workplace safety engineer in a large steel mill: "I no longer can be considered a progressive saver of people; I respond only to OSHA compliance officers and grievance committeemen. . . . It just ain't the same ballgame. No longer room for imagination, dedication, loyalty to a cause, pride of accomplishment and desire to serve. . . . The brother's keeper philosophy on which our old group lived . . . is no more. It has given way to a posture which asks, 'Is it required by OSHA?' . . . I suppose the best tipoff is that our [new] Safety Director is a lawyer. . . . " Bardach and Kagan, above, p. 323.

3. Comparing the approaches used to obtain compliance with workplace safety rules in Sweden and America, Steven Kelman speculates that the much greater Swedish reliance on persuasion may reflect fundamental differences in social attitude. "Out of the Swedish [political] tradition grows the notion that people ought to defer to the wishes of those in authority. Out of the American liberal tradition grows the notion that it is legitimate for people to define and pursue their own goals, independent of what the state thinks is best for them. . . . The traditional problem of European states with established rulers has been to tame those rulers and let people breathe; that of America with its liberal tradition has been to tame the unruly so that other people can breathe." S. Kelman, Regulating America, Regulating Sweden: A Comparative Study of Occupational Safety and Health Policy 196 (1981); see also S. Kelman, "Enforcement of Occupational Safety and Health Regulations: A Comparison of Swedish and American Practices," in K. Hawkins and J. Thomas, eds., Enforcing Regulation 97 (1984).

Its bearing on questions such as the above is the subject of the materials that follow.

MARSHALL v. BARLOW'S, INC.
Supreme Court of the United States, 1978.
436 U.S. 307.

MR. JUSTICE WHITE delivered the opinion of the Court.

Section 8(a) of the Occupational Safety and Health Act of 1970 (OSHA) [1] empowers agents of the Secretary of Labor (the Secretary) to search the work area of any employment facility within the Act's jurisdiction. The purpose of the search is to inspect for safety hazards and violations of OSHA regulations. No search warrant or other process is expressly required under the Act.

On the morning of September 11, 1975, an OSHA inspector entered the customer service area of Barlow's, Inc., an electrical and plumbing installation business located in Pocatello, Idaho. The president and general manager, Ferrol G. "Bill" Barlow, was on hand; and the OSHA inspector, after showing his credentials, informed Mr. Barlow that he wished to conduct a search of the working areas of the business. Mr. Barlow inquired whether any complaint had been received about his company. The inspector answered no, but that Barlow's, Inc. had simply turned up in the agency's selection process. The inspector again asked to enter the nonpublic area of the business. Mr. Barlow's response was to inquire whether the inspector had a search warrant. The inspector had none. Thereupon, Mr. Barlow refused the inspector admission to the employee area of his business. He said he was relying on his rights as guaranteed by the Fourth Amendment of the United States Constitution.

Three months later, the Secretary petitioned the United States District Court for the District of Idaho to issue an order compelling Mr. Barlow to admit the inspector. The requested order was issued on December 30, 1975, and was presented to Mr. Barlow on January 5, 1976. Mr. Barlow again refused admission, and he sought his own injunctive relief against the warrantless searches assertedly permitted by OSHA. . . .

I

The Warrant Clause of the Fourth Amendment protects commercial buildings as well as private homes. To hold otherwise would belie

---

1. "In order to carry out the purposes of this chapter, the Secretary, upon presenting appropriate credentials to the owner, operator, or agent in charge, is authorized—

"(1) to enter without delay and at reasonable times any factory, plant, establishment, construction site, or other area, workplace or environment where work is performed by an employee of an employer; and

"(2) to inspect and investigate during regular working hours and at other reasonable times, and within reasonable limits and in a reasonable manner, any such place of employment and all pertinent conditions, structures, machines, apparatus, devices, equipment, and materials therein, and to question privately any such employer, owner, operator, agent, or employee." 84 Stat. 1590, 29 U.S.C. § 657(a) (1970).

the origin of that Amendment, and the American colonial experience. An important forerunner of the first 10 Amendments to the United States Constitution, the Virginia Bill of Rights, specifically opposed "general warrants, whereby an officer or messenger may be commanded to search suspected places without evidence of a fact committed." The general warrant was a recurring point of contention in the colonies immediately preceding the Revolution. The particular offensiveness it engendered was acutely felt by the merchants and businessmen whose premises and products were inspected for compliance with the several Parliamentary revenue measures that most irritated the colonists. . . .

This Court has already held that warrantless searches are generally unreasonable and that this rule applies to commercial premises as well as homes. In Camara v. Municipal Court, 387 U.S. 523, 528–529 (1967), we held: "[E]xcept in certain carefully defined classes of cases, a search of private property without proper consent is 'unreasonable' unless it has been authorized by a valid search warrant."

On the same day, we also ruled: "As we explained in Camara, a search of private houses is presumptively unreasonable if conducted without a warrant. The businessman, like the occupant of a residence, has a constitutional right to go about his business free from unreasonable official entries upon his private commercial property. The businessman, too, has that right placed in jeopardy if the decision to enter and inspect for violation of regulatory laws can be made and enforced by the inspector in the field without official authority evidenced by a warrant." See v. City of Seattle, 387 U.S. 541, 543 (1967).

These same cases also held that the Fourth Amendment prohibition against unreasonable searches protects against warrantless intrusions during civil as well as criminal investigations. . . . The reason is found in the "basic purpose of this Amendment . . . [which] is to safeguard the privacy and security of individuals against arbitrary invasions by governmental officials." Camara, supra, 387 U.S., at 528. . . . If the government intrudes on a person's property, the privacy interest suffers whether the government's motivation is to investigate violations of criminal laws or breaches of other statutory or regulatory standards.

. . . [A]n exception from the search warrant requirement has been recognized for "pervasively regulated business[es]," United States v. Biswell, 406 U.S. 311, 316 (1972), and for "closely regulated" industries "long subject to close supervision and inspection." Colonnade Catering Corp. v. United States, 397 U.S. 72, 74, 77 (1970). . . . Certain industries have such a history of government oversight that no reasonable expectation of privacy could exist for a proprietor over the stock of such an enterprise. Liquor (Colonnade) and firearms (Biswell) are industries of this type; when an entrepreneur embarks upon such a business, he has voluntarily chosen to subject himself to a full arsenal of governmental regulation.

. . .

The clear import of our cases is that the closely regulated industry of the type involved in Colonnade and Biswell is the exception. The Secretary would make it the rule. Invoking the Walsh-Healey Act of 1936, 41 U.S.C. § 35 et seq., the Secretary attempts to support a conclusion that all businesses involved in interstate commerce have long been subjected to close supervision of employee safety and health conditions. But . . . it is quite unconvincing to argue that the imposition of minimum wages and maximum hours on employers who contracted with the government under the Walsh-Healey Act prepared the entirety of American interstate commerce for regulation of working conditions to the minutest detail. Nor can any but the most fictional sense of voluntary consent to later searches be found in the single fact that one conducts a business affecting interstate commerce; under current practice and law, few businesses can be conducted without having some effect on interstate commerce.

. . .

II

. . . Because "reasonableness is still the ultimate standard," Camara v. Municipal Court, supra, 387 U.S., at 539, the Secretary suggests that the Court decide whether a warrant is needed by arriving at a sensible balance between the administrative necessities of OSHA inspections and the incremental protection of privacy of business owners a warrant would afford. . . .

The Secretary submits that warrantless inspections are essential to the proper enforcement of OSHA because they afford the opportunity to inspect without prior notice and hence to preserve the advantages of surprise. . . . The risk is that during the interval between an inspector's initial request to search a plant and his procuring a warrant following the owner's refusal of permission, violations . . . could be corrected and thus escape the inspector's notice. To the suggestion that warrants may be issued ex parte and executed without delay and without prior notice, thereby preserving the element of surprise, the Secretary expresses concern for the administrative strain that would be experienced by the inspection system and by the courts, should ex parte warrants issued in advance become standard practice.

We are unconvinced, however, that requiring warrants to inspect will impose serious burdens on the inspection system or the courts, will prevent inspections necessary to enforce the statute, or will make them less effective. In the first place, the great majority of businessmen can be expected in normal course to consent to inspection without warrant; the Secretary has not brought to this Court's attention any widespread pattern of refusal.[2] In those cases where an owner does [refuse to permit an inspector to enter the property or to complete his inspection] . . . the Secretary has also promulgated a regulation providing that . . . the inspector shall attempt to ascertain the reasons for the

---

2. We recognize that today's holding might itself have an impact on whether owners choose to resist requested searches; we can only await the development of evidence not present on this record to determine how serious an impediment to effective enforcement this might be.

refusal and report to his superior, who shall "promptly take appropriate action, including compulsory process, if necessary." 29 CFR § 1903.4. . . .[3]

Nor is it immediately apparent why the advantages of surprise would be lost if, after being refused entry, procedures were available for the Secretary to seek an ex parte warrant and to reappear at the premises without further notice to the establishment being inspected.

Whether the Secretary proceeds to secure a warrant or other process, with or without prior notice, his entitlement to inspect will not depend on his demonstrating probable cause to believe that conditions in violation of OSHA exist on the premises. . . . For purposes of an administrative search such as this, probable cause justifying the issuance of a warrant may be based not only on specific evidence of an existing violation but also on a showing that "reasonable legislative or administrative standards for conducting an . . . inspection are satisfied with respect to a particular [establishment]." Camara v. Municipal Court, supra, at 538. A warrant showing that a specific business has been chosen for an OSHA search on the basis of a general administrative plan for the enforcement of the Act derived from neutral sources such as, for example, dispersion of employees in various types of industries across a given area, and the desired frequency of searches in any of the lesser divisions of the area, would protect an employer's Fourth Amendment rights. . . .

Nor do we agree that the incremental protections afforded the employer's privacy by a warrant are so marginal that they fail to justify the administrative burdens that may be entailed. The authority to make warrantless searches devolves almost unbridled discretion upon executive and administrative officers, particularly those in the field, as to when to search and whom to search. A warrant, by contrast, would provide assurances from a neutral officer that the inspection is reasonable under the Constitution, is authorized by statute, and is pursuant to an administrative plan containing specific neutral criteria. Also, a warrant would then and there advise the owner of the scope and objects of the search, beyond which limits the inspector is not expected to proceed. These are important functions for a warrant to perform, functions which underlie the Court's prior decisions that the Warrant Clause applies to inspections for compliance with regulatory statutes. . . .

III

We hold that Barlow was entitled to a declaratory judgment that the Act is unconstitutional insofar as it purports to authorize inspections without warrant or its equivalent and to an injunction enjoining the Act's enforcement to that extent.[4] The judgment of the District Court is therefore affirmed.

---

3. . . . [Section] 8(a) of the Act purports to authorize inspections without warrant; but . . . it does not forbid the Secretary from proceeding to inspect only by warrant or other process. . . .

4. The injunction entered by the District Court, however, should not be understood to forbid the Secretary from exercising the inspection authority conferred by § 657 pursuant to regulations and judicial

So ordered.

MR. JUSTICE BRENNAN took no part in the consideration or decision of this case.

MR. JUSTICE STEVENS, with whom MR. JUSTICE BLACKMUN and MR. JUSTICE REHNQUIST join, dissenting.

. . .

The Fourth Amendment contains two separate clauses, each flatly prohibiting a category of governmental conduct. The first clause states that the right to be free from unreasonable searches "shall not be violated"; the second unequivocally prohibits the issuance of warrants except "upon probable cause." In this case the ultimate question is whether the category of warrantless searches authorized by the statute is "unreasonable" within the meaning of the first clause.

. . . The routine OSHA inspections are, by definition, not based on cause to believe there is a violation on the premises to be inspected. Hence, if the inspections were measured against the requirements of the Warrant Clause, they would be automatically and unequivocally unreasonable. . . .

. . . "[O]ur constitutional fathers were not concerned about warrantless searches, but about overreaching warrants. It is perhaps too much to say that they feared the warrant more than the search, but it is plain enough that the warrant was the prime object of their concern. Far from looking at the warrant as a protection against unreasonable searches, they saw it as an authority for unreasonable and oppressive searches . . . ." [5]

Since the general warrant, not the warrantless search, was the immediate evil at which the Fourth Amendment was directed, it is not surprising that the Framers placed precise limits on its issuance. The requirement that a warrant only issue on a showing of particularized probable cause was the means adopted to circumscribe the warrant power. . . .

Fidelity to the original understanding of the Fourth Amendment, therefore, leads to the conclusion that the Warrant Clause has no application to routine, regulatory inspections of commercial premises. If such inspections are valid, it is because they comport with the ultimate reasonableness standard of the Fourth Amendment. . . .

The Court's analysis does not persuade me that Congress' determination that the warrantless inspection power as a necessary adjunct of the exercise of the regulatory power is unreasonable. . . . [T]he Court's prediction of the effect a warrant requirement would have on the behavior of covered employers . . . is essentially empirical. On such an issue, I would defer to Congress' judgment regarding the importance of a warrantless search power to the OSHA enforcement scheme.

. . .

process that satisfy the Fourth Amendment.

5. Taylor, Two Studies in Constitutional Interpretation, 41 (1969).

What purposes, then, are served by the administrative warrant procedure? The inspection warrant purports to serve three functions: to inform the employer that the inspection is authorized by the statute, to advise him of the lawful limits of the inspection, and to assure him that the person demanding entry is an authorized inspector. An examination of these functions in the OSHA context reveals that the inspection warrant adds little to the protections already afforded by the statute and pertinent regulations, and the slight additional benefit it might provide is insufficient to identify a constitutional violation or to justify overriding Congress' judgment that the power to conduct warrantless inspections is essential.

. . . Until today we have not rejected a congressional judgment concerning the reasonableness of a category of regulatory inspections of commercial premises. While businesses are unquestionably entitled to Fourth Amendment protection, we have "recognized that a business by its special nature and voluntary existence, may open itself to intrusions that would not be permissible in a purely private context." G.M. Leasing Corp. v. United States, 429 U.S. 338, 353 (1976). . . .

The Court, however, concludes that the deference accorded Congress in Biswell and Colonnade should be limited to situations where the evils addressed by the regulatory statute are peculiar to a specific industry and that industry is one which has long been subject to government regulation. . . . I cannot agree that the respect due the congressional judgment should be so narrowly confined.

. . . The pertinent inquiry is not whether the inspection program is authorized by a regulatory statute directed at a single industry but whether Congress has limited the exercise of the inspection power to those commercial premises where the evils at which the statute is directed are to be found. Thus, in Biswell, if Congress had authorized inspections of all commercial premises as a means of restricting the illegal traffic in firearms, the Court would have found the inspection program unreasonable; the power to inspect was upheld because it was tailored to the subject matter of Congress' proper exercise of regulatory power. Similarly, OSHA is directed at health and safety hazards in the work place, and the inspection power granted the Secretary extends only to those areas where such hazards are likely to be found.

Finally, the Court would distinguish the respect accorded Congress' judgment in Colonnade and Biswell on the ground that businesses engaged in the liquor and firearms industry "accept the burdens as well as the benefits of their trade . . . ." In the Court's view, such businesses consent to the restrictions placed upon them, while it would be fiction to conclude that a businessman subject to OSHA consented to routine safety inspections. . . . In both situations, the validity of the regulations depends not upon the consent of those regulated but on the existence of a federal statute embodying a congressional determination that the public interest in the health of the Nation's work force or the limitation of illegal firearms traffic outweighs the businessman's interest in preventing a government inspector from viewing those areas of his premises which relate to the subject matter of the regulation.

DONOVAN v. DEWEY
Supreme Court of the United States, 1981.
452 U.S. 594.

JUSTICE MARSHALL delivered the opinion of the Court.

. . .

I

The Federal Mine Safety and Health Act of 1977, 30 U.S.C. § 801 et seq., requires the Secretary of Labor to develop detailed mandatory health and safety standards to govern the operation of the Nation's mines. Section 103(a) of the Act, 30 U.S.C. § 813(a) provides that federal mine inspectors are to inspect underground mines at least four times per year and surface mines at least twice a year to insure compliance with these standards, and to make followup inspections to determine whether previously discovered violations have been corrected. This section also grants mine inspectors "a right of entry . . . " and states that "no advance notice of an inspection shall be provided to any person." If a mine operator refuses to allow a warrantless inspection conducted pursuant to § 103(a), the Secretary is authorized to institute a civil action to obtain injunctive or other appropriate relief.

In July 1978, a federal mine inspector attempted to inspect quarries owned by appellee Waukesha Lime and Stone Co. in order to determine whether all 25 safety and health violations uncovered during a prior inspection had been corrected. After the inspector had been on the site for about an hour, Waukesha's president, appellee Douglas Dewey, refused to allow the inspection to continue unless the inspector first obtained a search warrant. The inspector issued a citation to Waukesha for terminating the inspection,[1] and the Secretary subsequently filed this civil action in the District Court for the Eastern District of Wisconsin seeking to enjoin appellees from refusing to permit warrantless searches of the Waukesha facility.

The District Court granted summary judgment in favor of appellees[2].

II

Our prior cases have established that the Fourth Amendment's prohibition against unreasonable searches applies to administrative inspections of private commercial property. Marshall v. Barlow's, Inc., 436 U.S. 307 (1978); See v. City of Seattle, 387 U.S. 541 (1967). However, unlike searches of private homes, which generally must be conducted pursuant to a warrant in order to be reasonable under the

1. In this case, the Administrative Law Judge upheld a $1,000 civil penalty proposed by the Secretary. This decision is currently under review by the Mine Safety and Health Review Commission.

2. Although the District Court limited its holding to the constitutionality of Para.

103(a) as applied to warrantless inspections of stone quarries, the Act makes no distinction as to the type of mine to be inspected, and our conclusions here apply equally to all warrantless inspections authorized by the Act.

Fourth Amendment,[3] legislative schemes authorizing warrantless administrative searches of commercial property do not necessarily violate the Fourth Amendment. See, e.g., United States v. Biswell, 406 U.S. 311 (1972); Colonnade Catering Corp. v. United States, 397 U.S. 72 (1970). The greater latitude to conduct warrantless inspections of commercial property reflects the fact that the expectation of privacy that the owner of commercial property enjoys in such property differs significantly from the sanctity accorded an individual's home . . . . .

The interest of the owner of commercial property is not one in being free from any inspections. Congress has broad authority to regulate commercial enterprises engaged in or affecting interstate commerce, and an inspection program may in some cases be a necessary component of federal regulation. Rather, the Fourth Amendment protects the interest of the owner of property in being free from *unreasonable* intrusions onto his property by agents of the government. . . . Thus, in Colonnade Corp. v. United States, we recognized that because the alcoholic beverage industry had long been "subject to close supervision and inspection," Congress enjoyed "broad power to design such powers of inspection . . . as it deems necessary to meet the evils at hand." 397 U.S., at 76–77. Similarly, in United States v. Biswell, . . . [a]fter describing the strong federal interest in conducting unannounced, warrantless inspections, we noted:

> It is also plain that inspections for compliance with the Gun Control Act pose only limited threats to the dealer's justifiable expectations of privacy. When a dealer chooses to engage in this pervasively regulated business . . . , he does so with the knowledge that his records, firearms, and ammunition will be subject to effective inspection. . . . The dealer is not left to wonder about the purposes of the inspector or the limits of his task. 406 U.S., at 316.

These decisions make clear that a warrant may not be constitutionally required when Congress has reasonably determined that warrantless searches are necessary to further a regulatory scheme and the federal regulatory presence is sufficiently comprehensive and defined that the owner of commercial property cannot help but be aware that his property will be subject to periodic inspections undertaken for specific purposes.

We re-emphasized this exception to the warrant requirement most recently in Marshall v. Barlow's, Inc. In that case, we held that absent consent a warrant was constitutionally required in order to conduct administrative inspections under § 8(a) of the Occupational Safety and Health Act. . . . [That statute] fails to tailor the scope and frequency of such administrative inspections to the particular health and safety concerns posed by the numerous and varied businesses regulated by the statute. . . . Similarly, the Act does not provide any standards to

---

3. Absent consent or exigent circumstances, a private home may not be entered to conduct a search or effect an arrest without a warrant. Steagald v. United States, 451 U.S. 204 (1981). Of course, these same restrictions pertain when commercial property is searched for contraband or evidence of crime. G.M. Leasing Corp. v. United States, 429 U.S. 338, 352–59 (1977).

guide inspectors either in their selection of establishments to be searched or in the exercise of their authority to search.

. . .

In assessing this regulatory scheme, this Court found that the provision authorizing administrative searches "devolves almost unbridled discretion upon executive and administrative officers, particularly those in the field, as to when to search and whom to search" . . . noting that the "reasonableness of a warrantless search . . . will depend upon the specific enforcement needs and privacy guarantees of each statute" and that some statutes "apply only to a single industry, where regulations might already be so pervasive that a Colonnade-Biswell exception to the warrant requirement could apply." Id., at 321.

Applying this analysis to the case before us, we conclude that the warrantless inspections required by the Mine Safety and Health Act do not offend the Fourth Amendment.

. . .

In designing an inspection program, Congress expressly recognized that a warrant requirement could significantly frustrate effective enforcement of the Act. Thus, it provided in § 103(a) of the Act that "no advance notice of an inspection shall be provided to any person." In explaining this provision, the Senate Report notes:

> [I]n [light] of the notorious ease with which many safety or health hazards may be concealed if advance warning of inspection is obtained, a warrant requirement would seriously undercut this Act's objectives. S.Rep. No. 95–181, p. 27 (1977).

We see no reason not to defer to this legislative determination. . . .

Because a warrant requirement clearly might impede the "specific enforcement needs" of the Act, Marshall v. Barlow's, Inc., 436 U.S., at 321, the only real issue before us is whether the statute's inspection program, in terms of the certainty and regularity of its application, provides a constitutionally adequate substitute for a warrant. We believe that it does. Unlike the statute at issue in Barlow's, the Mine Safety and Health Act applies to industrial activity with a notorious history of serious accidents and unhealthful working conditions. The Act is specifically tailored to address those concerns, and the regulation of mines it imposes is sufficiently pervasive and defined that the owner of such a facility cannot help but be aware that he "will be subject to effective inspection." United States v. Biswell, supra, at 316. First, [unlike OSHA,] the Act requires inspection of *all* mines and specifically defines the frequency of inspection. Representatives of the Secretary must inspect all surface mines at least twice annually and all underground mines at least four times annually. Similarly, all mining operations that generate explosive gases must be inspected at irregular 5-, 10-, or 15-day intervals. Moreover, the Secretary must conduct followup inspections of mines where violations of the Act have previously been discovered, and must inspect a mine immediately if notified by a miner or a miner's representative that a violation of the Act or an imminently dangerous condition exists. Second, the standards with which a mine operator is required to comply are all specifically set

forth in the Act or in Title 30 of the Code of Federal Regulations.
. . . Thus, rather than leaving the frequency and purpose of inspections to the unchecked discretion of Government officers, the Act
establishes a predictable and guided federal regulatory presence.
. . .

Finally, the Act provides a specific mechanism for accommodating
any special privacy concerns that a specific mine operator might have.
The Act prohibits forcible entries, and instead requires the Secretary,
when refused entry onto a mining facility, to file a civil action in
federal court to obtain an injunction against future refusals. 30 U.S.C.
§ 818(a). This proceeding provides an adequate forum for the mineowner to show that a specific search is outside the federal regulatory
authority, or to seek from the district court an order accommodating
any unusual privacy interests that the mineowner might have.

Under these circumstances, it is difficult to see what additional
protection a warrant requirement would provide.
. . .

Appellees contend, however, that even if § 103(a) is constitutional
as applied to most segments of the mining industry, it nonetheless
violates the Fourth Amendment as applied to authorize warrantless
inspections of stone quarries . . . which came under federal regulation in 1966, [and] do not have a long tradition of government regulation. To be sure, in Colonnade this Court referred to "the long history
of the regulation of the liquor industry," 397 U.S. at 75 . . . .
However, it is the pervasiveness and regularity of the federal regulation that ultimately determines whether a warrant is necessary to
render an inspection program reasonable under the Fourth Amendment.
. . .

Of course, the duration of a particular regulatory scheme will often
be an important factor . . . [but if it were the only criterion,] new or
emerging industries, including ones such as the nuclear power industry
that pose enormous potential safety and health problems, could never
be subject to warrantless searches even under the most carefully
structured inspection program . . . .

The Fourth Amendment's central concept of reasonableness will
not tolerate such arbitrary results, and we therefore conclude that
warrantless inspection of stone quarries, like similar inspections of
other mines covered by the Act, are constitutionally permissible. The
judgment of the District Court is reversed, and the case is remanded for
further proceedings consistent with this opinion.

So ordered.

JUSTICE STEVENS, concurring.
. . .

I am not persuaded that the *holding* in Barlow's, Inc., requires the
Court to invalidate the program of mine inspections authorized by the
statute we construe today. . . . Because I agree with today's majority that the cases are distinguishable, I need not confront the more

difficult question whether Camara represented such a fundamental misreading of the Fourth Amendment that it should be overruled. I would merely observe that that option is more viable today than when some of the reasoning that would support it could only be found in dissenting opinions, see 387 U.S. at 546–555 (Clark, J., dissenting); 436 U.S., at 325–339 (Stevens, J., dissenting), or in the earlier Court opinion in Frank that had itself been overruled in Camara.

JUSTICE REHNQUIST, concurring in the judgment.

Our prior cases hold that, absent consent or exigent circumstances, the government must obtain a warrant to conduct a search or effect an arrest in a private home. This case, however, involves the search of commercial property. Though the proprietor of commercial property is protected from unreasonable intrusions by governmental agents, the Court correctly notes that "legislative schemes authorizing warrantless administrative searches of commercial property do not necessarily violate the Fourth Amendment."

I do not believe, however, that the warrantless entry authorized by Congress in this case, § 103(a) of the Federal Mine Safety and Health Act of 1977, can be justified by the Court's rationale. . . . I have no doubt that had Congress enacted a criminal statute similar to that involved here—authorizing, for example, unannounced warrantless searches of property reasonably thought to house unlawful drug activity—the warrantless search would be struck down under our existing Fourth Amendment line of decisions. This Court would invalidate the search despite the fact that Congress has a strong interest in regulating and preventing drug related crime and has in fact pervasively regulated such conduct for a far longer period of time than it has regulated mining. . . .

JUSTICE STEWART, dissenting.

In Frank v. Maryland, 359 U.S. 360, the Court concluded that warrantless administrative inspections are not subject to the restrictions that the Fourth and Fourteenth Amendments place upon conventional searches. The Frank decision was overruled eight years later in Camara v. Municipal Court, 387 U.S. 523, over the dissent of three Members of the Court, of whom I was one. . . .

I must, nonetheless, accept the law as it is, and the law is now established that administrative inspections are searches within the meaning of the Fourth Amendment. As such, warrantless administrative inspections of private property without consent, are, like other searches, constitutionally invalid except in a few precisely defined circumstances. Camara, supra, at 528–529.

. . .

Until today, exceptions to the general rule have been found in only two cases. In Colonnade Catering Corp. v. United States, 397 U.S. 72, the Court upheld against constitutional attack a statute that authorized warrantless searches of a liquor licensee's premises by Internal Revenue agents. And in United States v. Biswell, 406 U.S. 311, the Court held that federal Treasury agents could search the premises of a licensed gun dealer to determine whether he was in compliance with the Gun Control Act. . . .

[A]s explained in Barlow's, the Colonnade-Biswell exception is a single and narrow one: the exception applies to businesses that are both pervasively regulated *and* have a long history of regulation. Today the Court conveniently discards the latter portion of the exception.[4] Yet the very rationale for the exception—that the "businessman . . . in effect consents to the restrictions placed upon him"—disappears without it. It can hardly be said that a businessman consents to restrictions on his business when those restrictions are not imposed until *after* he has entered the business. Yet, because it does not overrule Barlow's, that is precisely what the Court says today to many stone quarry operators.

Under the peculiar logic of today's opinion, the scope of the Fourth Amendment diminishes as the power of governmental regulation increases. Yet I would have supposed that the mandates of the Fourth Amendment demand heightened, not lowered, respect, as the intrusive regulatory authority of government expands. . . .

NOTES

(1) CAMARA v. MUNICIPAL COURT, 387 U.S. 523 (1967) and SEE v. SEATTLE, 387 U.S. 541 (1967), were the principal cases relied on in Barlow's. These decisions, also written by Mr. Justice White, have been treated by the Court since their decision as the point of departure for Fourth Amendment analysis, especially in cases not involving a search in aid of imminent criminal prosecution. Camara was the lessee of an apartment not supposed to be used as a personal dwelling but apparently so used; he several times refused entry to a San Francisco public health inspector during daytime hours, and was then prosecuted for impeding a lawful inspection, a violation of the Municipal Code. See, the operator of a commercial warehouse in Seattle, was prosecuted for blocking a Fire Department inspector's access to the warehouse during a routine, periodic canvass of premises subject to the city's Fire Code. In each case, no forcible inspection had been tried. In each, six Justices joined in finding the Warrant clause controlling.

The Camara and See opinions rejected possible lines of distinction between the two fact settings before the Court, and between criminal and administrative searches, that may seem to be attracting renewed attention in the cases just read. Camara concerned the search of what

---

4. The Court's recasting of what the Court said in Barlow's is remarkable. After discussing Colonnade and Biswell, it states that those decisions create an exception to the warrant requirement when "Congress has reasonably determined that warrantless searches are necessary to further a regulatory scheme and the federal regulatory presence is sufficiently comprehensive and defined that the owner of commercial property cannot help but be aware that his property will be subject to periodic inspections undertaken for specific purposes." Ante, at 600. It then says that "this" exception to the warrant requirement was re-emphasized in Barlow's. Ante, at 600.

Nothing of the sort was re-emphasized in Barlow's. Rather, the Court re-emphasized that "[t]he element that distinguishes these enterprises from ordinary businesses is a long tradition of close government supervision, of which any person who chooses to enter such a business must . . . be aware." 436 U.S., at 313. . . .

was apparently, if illegally, a private residence; See, business premises. While acknowledging this difference, the See Court concluded that "the basic component of a reasonable search under the Fourth Amendment—that it not be enforced without a suitable warrant procedure—is applicable in this context, as in others, to business premises as well as to residential premises."[1]

Camara and See both concerned a search which could readily be characterized as facilitative rather than punitive in prospect [2]; but the fact that the Court might "agree that a routine inspection of the physical condition of private property is a less hostile intrusion than the typical policeman's search for the fruits and instrumentalities of crime [does not defeat the warrant requirement].[3] . . . It is surely anomalous to say that the individual and his private property are fully protected by the Fourth Amendment only when the individual is suspected of criminal behavior. For instance, even the most law-abiding citizen has a very tangible interest in limiting the circumstances under which the sanctity of his home may be broken by official authority, for the possibility of criminal entry under the guise of official sanction is a serious threat to personal and family security. . . . [I]nspections of the kind we are here considering do in fact jeopardize self protection interests of the property owner." As Barlow's indicates, the Court did find a variable standard of probable cause appropriate in the administrative search context.

1. "The businessman, like the occupant of a residence, has a constitutional right to go about his business free from unreasonable official entries upon his private commercial property.

". . . Official entry upon commercial property is a technique commonly adopted by administrative agencies at all levels of government to enforce a variety of regulatory laws; thus, entry may permit inspection of the structure in which a business is housed, as in this case, or inspection of business products, or a perusal of financial books and records. This Court has not had occasion to consider the Fourth Amendment's relation to this broad range of investigations. However, we have dealt with the Fourth Amendment issues raised by another common investigative technique, the administrative subpoena of corporate books and records. We find strong support in these subpoena cases for our conclusion that warrants are a necessary and a tolerable limitation on the right to enter upon and inspect commercial premises.

"It is now settled that, when an administrative agency subpoenas corporate books or records, the Fourth Amendment requires that the subpoena be sufficiently limited in scope, relevant in purpose, and specific in directive so that compliance will not be unreasonably burdensome. The agency has the right to conduct all reasonable inspections of such documents which are contemplated by statute, but it must delimit the confines of a search by designating the needed documents in a formal subpoena. In addition, while the demand to inspect may be issued by the agency, in the form of an administrative subpoena, it may not be made and enforced by the inspector in the field, and the subpoenaed party may obtain judicial review of the reasonableness of the demand prior to suffering penalties for refusing to comply." Id.

2. "[T]he health inspector who conducts an inspection, . . . , has no reason to anticipate that he will find particular violations; . . . the absence of instances of non-compliance ought to be a source of satisfaction, rather than of disappointment, to him." F.P. Grad, Public Health Law Manual 76 (1965).

3. As the opinion in Barlow's reflects, the character of the intrusion was conceded by the Camara court to be of high relevance to the magistrate's determination whether "probable cause" had been shown.

"In determining whether a particular inspection is reasonable—and thus in determining whether there is probable cause to issue a warrant for that inspection—the need for the inspection must be weighed in terms of [the] reasonable goals of code enforcement."

Justices Clark, Harlan and Stewart dissented. Like the dissenters in Barlow's they believed that "reasonableness" was the central inquiry, that the searches at issue met that test, and that transforming the question of reasonableness for routine inspections into an issue whether probable cause exists to issue a warrant was an exercise, a "pretense" that would not only destroy the integrity of the search warrant but "degrade the magistrate issuing them and soon bring disrepute not only upon the practice but upon the judicial process." A search warrant, once obtained, they noted, might be less desirable from the public's perspective, as well as expensive and wasteful; aided by a warrant, a forced entry in the night would be lawful, where under the challenged ordinances hours were restricted and enforcement was effected only by the imposition of fines for refusals to admit. They also expressed concern for a factor later noted by the Barlow's minority: that the impact of the holding would be to encourage resistance to essential community undertakings, thus threatening achievement of the statutory ends of improved public health and safety. To date, it may be noted, no such impact has been identified.[4]

(2) The distinction between "closely regulated industries" and "ordinary enterprise," which takes differing shapes in the two principal opinions, has recurred in various settings, with greater or lesser success, throughout American constitutional history. During the years when "substantive due process" considerations were regularly found to govern questions of the permissible scope of state or federal regulation of enterprise, it served to segregate settings in which broad regulation was freely permitted from those in which close constitutional scrutiny would be given. Compare Munn v. Illinois, 94 U.S. 113 (1877) with Allgeyer v. Louisiana, 165 U.S. 578 (1897) and Lochner v. New York, 198 U.S. 45 (1905). The distinction was sharply discredited as a test of regulatory authority by cases decided during the late 1930's and early 1940's, including one upholding the Walsh-Healey Act imposing federal wage and hour standards. United States v. Darby, 312 U.S. 100 (1941); see also Nebbia v. New York, 291 U.S. 502 (1934). As the majority opinion in Barlow's makes clear, the Secretary of Labor had relied on the extensive recognition Darby gave his regulatory power under the Walsh-Healey Act, in arguing that Congress could with equal sweep authorize "reasonable" warrantless searches of commercial establishments as a mechanism to aid enforcement of regulation within its authority to impose. In Shapiro v. United States, noted at p. 667 supra, the Court had rejected Justice Frankfurter's effort to rely on the "closely regulated industry"—"ordinary enterprise" distinction as a basis for recognizing the Fifth Amendment claims of a greengrocer legislatively required to keep what proved to be incriminatory records.

---

4. In the immediate wake of Camara, an enterprising law student found that the San Francisco Department of Public Health was not encountering an aroused citizenry; it had to obtain fewer than five warrants during an eight-month period in which it made more than 32,000 inspections. Note, Search Warrants and Administrative Area Searches, 3 Gonzaga L.Rev. 172, 189n (1968). During the October, 1978 to April, 1980 period, on the other hand, 2.6% of employers (one in forty) demanded warrants. See M. Rothstein, OSHA After Ten Years: A Review and Some Proposed Reforms, 34 Vand.L.Rev. 71, 110 n. 234 (1981).

Does either Barlow's or Dewey describe in workable and persuasive terms the basis on which a setting requiring a warrant can be distinguished from one in which congressional findings suffice? [5]

(3) DOW CHEMICAL CO. V. UNITED STATES, 106 S.Ct. 1819 (1986) challenged the legality of an EPA inspection of a large industrial complex conducted by aerial surveillance, using highly sophisticated photography equipment. The Court split 5–4, with Chief Justice Burger writing for the majority and Justice Powell (with Brennan, Marshall and Blackmun), for the dissent. For the majority, no "search" was involved. Although Dow Chemical had walled the perimeter of its facility to protect its premises from observation and enjoyed state law "trade secrets" in the processes observation might reveal, EPA's aircraft was lawfully in the public navigable airspace, and EPA could photograph whatever it might have been able to observe. Dow's only protection from EPA's photography was to roof its premises; the majority was not impressed that the photography permitted observation far more detailed and sophisticated than the human eye could ever achieve. "From Hester v. United States, 265 U.S. 57 (1924) to Oliver v. United States, 466 U.S. 170 (1984), the Court has drawn a line as to what expectations are reasonable in the open areas beyond the curtilage of a dwelling; . . . 'an individual may not legitimately demand privacy for activities out of doors in fields, except in the [curtilage, the] area immediately surrounding the home.' Oliver at 178. To fall within the open fields doctrine the area 'need be neither "open" nor a "field" as those terms are used in common speech.' Id. at 180, n. 11." Relying in part on the government's "greater latitude to conduct warrantless inspections of commercial property," Dewey, above, the majority found the premises to be more like a "field" than the intensely private area immediately surrounding a private home. "For nearly twenty years," the dissent responded, "the Court has adhered to a standard that ensured that Fourth Amendment rights would retain their vitality as technology expanded the Government's capacity to commit unsuspected intrusions into private areas and activities." Dow had done all that could reasonably be expected of it—from fencing to elaborate security programs—to signal the expected privacy of its facility. Donovan established no general principle of lesser worth for commercial establishments' expectations of privacy; rather, that in some cases a business owner's "reasonable expectation of privacy . . . may be adequately protected by the regulatory scheme itself." Dow had such an expectation, and the majority was insufficiently responsive to the needs modern technology creates to protect it.

(4) Unaddressed in these cases were questions that might arise about the scope of a search, whether or not pursuant to a warrant, or about the consequences of error by a magistrate in issuing a warrant. Suppose, for example, OSHA obtains a warrant on the basis of an

---

5. The Court dispensed with the warrant requirement entirely, while continuing to insist that searches must be "reasonable," in dealing with searches of school children by their teachers. New Jersey v. T.L.O., 105 S.Ct. 733 (1985). What would be "reasonable" grounds for how intrusive a search provided the occasion for a lively dispute between a majority generally impressed with searchers aims and needs, and dissenters focussing on student privacy claims.

employee's complaint about the safety of a particular operation. Once on the premises, may its inspector react to other conditions that come effortlessly to view? Air Pollution Variance Bd. v. Western Alfalfa Corp., 416 U.S. 861 (1974) and Coolidge v. New Hampshire, 403 U.S. 443, 465–466 (1971) suggest it may. May she go further and engage in a general inspection for workplace hazards? That has been the subject of lively dispute; one side argues from administrative convenience, and the reasonableness of believing that particular problems so aggravated as to provoke an apparent act of employee disloyalty may signal more general issues; the other, from traditional understandings of warrants and their purpose, and the possibility that employee complaints may be a vindictive gesture rather than a genuine expression of concern. Compare Donovan v. Sarasota Concrete Co., 693 F.2d 1061 (11th Cir. 1982) (search limited) with Hern Iron Works, Inc. v. Donovan, 670 F.2d 838 (9th Cir.1982), cert. denied, 459 U.S. 830 (1982) (workplace search upheld). If an error has been made in the search or underlying warrant, must the resulting evidence be excluded? Applying the exclusionary rule in OSHA proceedings at all has been characterized as "unsettled and highly controversial;"[6] arguments that exclusion will promote useful inspector discipline are met with the observation that hazardous workplaces then remain. Even if an exclusionary rule applies, may an ALJ receive evidence secured by an inspector who believed in good faith she was acting within her lawful authority? The Supreme Court, over passionate dissents, has recently recognized a "good faith exception" to exclusion for certain errors by magistrates in issuing warrants, concluding after "balancing" the relevant considerations that exclusion in such cases is not needed to promote lawful behavior by police or prosecutors, United States v. Leon, 468 U.S. 897 (1984); for criminal searches made in the absence of a warrant, the exclusionary rule apparently remains in place. For administrative searches, the arguments from the civil, corrective character of the agency's work seem especially strong. Compare Donovan v. Sarasota Concrete, above (supporting exclusion) with Donovan v. Federal Clearing Die Casting Co., 695 F.2d 1020 (7th Cir.1982) (endorsing "good faith" exception). On the same day as Leon, in a case arising in the deportation context, the Supreme Court held, 5–4, that "weigh[ing] the likely social benefits of excluding unlawfully seized evidence against the likely costs," "there is no convincing indication that application of the exclusionary rule in civil deportation hearings will contribute materially to [protect the Fourth Amendment rights of all persons]," given what the Court believed it knew of other administrative practices. Immigration and Naturalization Service v. Lopez-Mendoza, 468 U.S. 1032 (1984).

(5) *Search Warrant v. Subpoena.* Search or inspection procedures occur without prior notice to the party to be inspected. This is in apparently sharp contrast to procedures for compelling production of information by issuance of a subpoena, which is served on the possessor

---

6. Cerro Metal Prods. v. Marshall, 620 F.2d 964, 974 (3d Cir.1980); see C. Trent, OSHA and the exclusionary Rule: Should the Employer Go Free Because the Compliance Officer Has Blundered, 1981 Duke L.J. 667; Comment, OSHA and the exclusionary Rule: The Cost of Constitutional Protection, 19 Wake For.L.Rev. 819 (1983).

of the desired data and typically has no bite until later enforced by judicial decree. The Court in Barlow's emphasized the availability of this surprise element, the ex parte character of the magistrate's review of the request for a search warrant.[7] And in another decision the same Term, involving the search under warrant of a newpaper's offices for photographs thought likely to aid in identifying the perpetrators of a criminal assault, the Court explicitly rejected a lower court decision that would have compelled investigators to use subpoenas—thus giving warning—when seeking evidence from individuals not themselves suspects or demonstrably likely to destroy or damage the evidence being sought:

"The Fourth Amendment has itself struck the balance between privacy and public need, and there is no occasion or justification for a court to revise the Amendment and strike a new balance by denying the search warrant in the circumstances present here and by insisting that the investigation proceed by subpoena duces tecum, whether on the theory that the latter is a less intrusive alternative, or otherwise.

". . . The seemingly blameless third party in possession of the fruits or evidence may not be innocent at all; and if he is, he may nevertheless be so related to or so sympathetic with the culpable that he cannot be relied upon to retain and preserve the articles that may implicate his friends, or at least not to notify those who would be damaged by the evidence that the authorities are aware of its location. In any event, . . . the delay involved in employing the subpoena duces tecum, offering as it does the opportunity to litigate its validity, could easily result in the disappearance of the evidence, whatever the good faith of the third party."

In addition to delay, the Court noted, use of the subpoena route could engender Fifth Amendment claims by the persons to whom the subpoenas were directed—claims unavailable in response to a search. "The burden of overcoming an assertion of the Fifth Amendment privilege, even if prompted by a desire not to cooperate rather than any real fear of self-incrimination, is one which prosecutors would rarely be able to meet in the early stages of an investigation despite the fact they did not regard the witness as a suspect. Even time spent litigating such matters could seriously impede criminal investigations."[8]

7. "Obviously, to permit an employer to appear before the magistrate and contest the issuance of an inspection warrant would conflict with the explicit congressional policy that OSHA inspections be undelayed and without notice." Matter of Worksite Inspection of S.D. Warren, Division of Scott Paper, 481 F.Supp. 491 (D.Me. 1979).

8. [Ed.] Of the eight sitting Justices, only Justice Stevens appeared to take issue with these general conclusions, arguing that the government was required to establish the need for an unannounced search by force as part of its ex parte presentation in support of the warrant. Noting that "only with great reluctance has this Court

approved even the seizure of refrigerators or washing machines without notice and a prior adversary hearing," he found no interest sufficient to support ex parte authorization of inspection of the papers and possessions of individuals not suspected of crime or demonstrably unlikely to honor a subpoena or informal request to produce. For a similar argument, emphasizing special Fourth Amendment concerns for searches touch private papers, see J.A. McKenna. The Constitutional Protection of Private Papers: The Role of a Hierarchical Fourth Amendment, 53 Ind.L.J. 55 (1977).

Justices Stewart and Marshall also dissented, but on the ground that search of a

(6) *The problem of forcible entry.* Zurcher v. The Stanford Daily, 436 U.S. 547 (1978). In the criminal investigation setting of Zurcher, a warrant once obtained may be executed by force. May the administrative inspector armed with a warrant or "reasonable" legislative provision for warrantless search force his way through the doors? In Colonnade Catering Corp. v. United States, 397 U.S. 72 (1970), the Court found that Congress had ample power to authorize warrantless inspection of federally licensed dealers in alcoholic beverages and had done so, but nonetheless excluded evidence seized as a result of a warrantless search because Congress had not expressly provided for forcible entry; it had made refusal to admit the inspectors a criminal offense and that, the Court concluded, was the remedy available. Note that any hearing on an injunction requiring Colonnade Catering to unlock the doors of its warehouse would constitute the prior hearing found uncalled for in Zurcher. The Federal Mine Safety and Health Act of 1977, considered in the Dewey case above, similarly envisions a civil action to force entry if a warrantless search under its provisions is refused. In a pair of OSHA cases, in which warrants had been obtained, the Third Circuit similarly assumed entrance might be refused. At that point the agency could seek a civil contempt order in the issuing court—a prior hearing in which the lawfulness of the search could be determined.[9] Persistence had its price in each case—constituting an offense in Colonnade, and requiring the inspectees to risk civil contempt sanctions in the Third Circuit cases. These costs might have encouraged submitting to the search in the first instance and challenging its legality only later; the possibilities then might include tort relief, the exclusion of evidence unlawfully obtained or, perhaps, an injunction against future repetitions of unlawful behavior. Yet the fact remains that the search itself can be postponed to follow a judicial hearing at which the inspectee will be present and have some opportunity to speak to the issue of lawfulness. How would you balance the possible cost of that delay[10] against the argument that only the urgency of criminal law enforcement or immediate danger to public health or safety could warrant the use of force to open private doors?[11]

newspaper office brought the special values of the First Amendment into play.

9. Babcock & Wilcox Co. v. Marshall, 610 F.2d 1128 (3d Cir.1979); Marshall v. Whittaker Corp. Berwick Forge & Fabricating Co., 610 F.2d 1141 (3d Cir. 1979).

10. In Donovan v. Wollaston Alloys, Inc., 695 F.2d 1 (1st Cir.1982), a warrant was first sought July 31, 1981. Denial of entry led to a U.S. Magistrate's recommendation for a finding of contempt October 7, 1981. That recommendation and the Company's challenges to the warrant were considered by a United States District Court, which on February 16, 1982 upheld the warrant on the merits and directed compliance, but did *not* find contempt. On March 1, 1982, when the search had not yet been permitted, contempt was found

and the company given 48 hours to purge it by permitting the inspection. It continued to refuse, and a $5,000/day penalty set by the court then began for the first time to run. The company sought a stay pending appeal and only complied with the warrant March 12, 1982, one day after that stay was denied by the appellate court and more than seven months after the warrant had issued. It was fined $40,000 for its contempt during the March 3–March 12 period. Donovan v. Wollaston Alloys, 11 OSHC 1587 (D.Mass. June 28, 1983).

11. See Note, Administrative Inspections and the Fourth Amendment—A Rationale, 65 Colum.L.Rev. 288, 294 (1965); W.R. LaFave, Administrative Searches and the Fourth Amendment; The Camara and See Cases, 1967 Sup.Ct.Rev. 1, 31–32.

NOTES ON CONSENT

(1) *Consent as a factual issue.* A search that might otherwise be improper becomes legitimate if it has been made with consent. Consent must, however, be genuine, not coerced or obtained by deception or based on acceptance of an invalid warrant or an invalid statutory command. As was said in Bumper v. North Carolina, 391 U.S. 543 (1968), "When a law enforcement officer claims authority to search a home under a warrant, he announces in effect that the occupant has no right to resist the search. The situation is instinct with coercion—albeit colorably lawful coercion. Where there is coercion there cannot be consent."

But consent to routinized administrative inspection of business premises is much more readily assumed than is a search for evidence of crime. UNITED STATES v. THRIFTIMART, INC., 429 F.2d 1006 (9th Cir.), cert. denied 440 U.S. 926 (1970), is illustrative. There, Food & Drug Administration inspectors routinely inspected four company warehouses, all of which were found to contain insect-infested food. When they had arrived at the warehouses, they had requested permission to enter. In each instance the local manager had said "Go ahead" or words of that nature. The inspectors had not obtained search warrants, nor did the inspectors inform the warehouse managers that they had a right to insist upon a warrant; because the managers had not been apprised that they had a right to refuse entry and since no proof had been offered that they knew they had this right, their consent was not effective to remove the need for a search warrant. The court was not persuaded:

"The issue in this case is whether the body of law that has grown up around the definition of consent to a search in the criminal area should mechanically be applied to the inspection of a warehouse.

"In a criminal search the inherent coercion of the badge and the presence of armed police make it likely that the consent to a criminal search is not voluntary. Further, there is likelihood that confrontation comes as a surprise for which the citizen is unprepared and the subject of a criminal search will probably be uninformed as to his rights and the consequences of denial of entry. Finally, the consent given to a fruitful search in a criminal case is inherently suspect. A criminal with something to hide is not likely to turn it over to the police on request unless he believes that he has no choice. Nor, in the common experience of man, is one embroiled with the law likely to relieve the state of its heavy burden before the magistrate if he knows he need not do so.

"These circumstances are not present in the administrative inspection. The citizen is not likely to be uninformed or surprised. Food inspections occur with regularity. As here, the judgment as to consent to access is often a matter of company policy rather than of local managerial decision. FDA inspectors are unarmed and make their inspections during business hours. Also, the consent to an inspection is not only not suspect but is to be expected. The inspection itself is inevitable.　Nothing is to be gained by demanding a warrant except that the inspectors have been put to trouble—an unlikely aim for the businessman anxious for administrative good will."

(2) *Unconstitutional conditions.*　Consent is sometimes said to have been obtained, not at the office door, but as a consideration for government benefits sought and extended—a license, welfare benefits, or the like.　This, as you recall, was a major theme of both the Dewey opinion and the earlier holdings on which it relied.　As in Dewey, the argument has often been controversial.　The problem, closely allied with that of the closely regulated industry—ordinary enterprise issue discussed at p. 693 above, is that the argument from fictitious consent threatens to place in government's hands an illimitable tool for incursion on private activity.[12]　Cf. the court's rejection, in Cleveland Board of Education v. Loudermill, p. 631 above, of Justice Rehnquist's suggestion in Arnette v. Kennedy that ".　.　. [Where the grant of a substantive right is extricably intertwined with the limitations on the procedures which are to be employed in determining that right, a litigant .　.　. must take the bitter with the sweet."

(3) WYMAN v. JAMES, 400 U.S. 309 (1971).　Is the idea of consent especially attractive where the visit being "consented" to can be thought to bring benefits as well as burdens or potential liability to the subject of the visit?　Test that proposition against the Court's opinion in this case.　Mrs. James, who received welfare on behalf of her son Maurice, was taken off the rolls when she refused to schedule a warrantless visit of her caseworker to her home.　She offered to have an interview elsewhere, but New York's welfare officials asserted that quarterly home visits were a necessary and "rehabilitative" part of the program (to assess the environment in relation to the child's needs). Justice Blackmun wrote the Court's opinion sustaining the State's requirement, which was enforced only by the withholding of benefits from uncooperative families.　Granted that the visit involved the home,

---

12. "It would be a palpable incongruity to strike down an act of state legislation which, by words of express divestment, seeks to strip the citizen of rights guaranteed by the federal Constitution, but to uphold an act by which the same result is accomplished under the guise of a surrender of a right in exchange for a valuable privilege which the state threatens otherwise to withhold. . . . If the state may compel the surrender of one constitutional right as a condition of its favor, it may, in a like manner, compel a surrender of all. It is inconceivable that guarantees embedded in the Constitution of the United States may thus be manipulated out of existence." Frost & Frost Trucking Co. v. Railroad Com., 271 U.S. 583, 593–594 (1926). On the other hand, W. Van Alstyne, the Demise of the Right-Privilege Distinction in Constitutional Law, 81 Harv. L.Rev. 1439, 1448 (1968), has asserted:

"The basic flaw in the doctrine [of unconstitutional conditions] is its assumption

that the same evil results from attaching certain conditions to government-connected activity as from imposing such conditions on persons not connected with government."

See, generally, Note, Administrative Searches and the Implied Consent Doctrine: Beyond the Fourth Amendment, 43 Bklyn.L.Rev. 91 (1976); Comment, Entitlement, Enjoyment, and Due Process of Law, 1974 Duke L.J. 89, 108–112; R. O'Neil, The Price of Dependency 39–57 (1970); Comment, Another Look at Unconstitutional Conditions, 117 U.Pa.L.Rev. 144 (1968); Note, Unconstitutional Conditions, 73 Harv.L.Rev. 1595 (1960); R. Hale, Unconstitutional Conditions and Constitutional Rights, 35 Colum.L.Rev. 321 (1935). And compare F.C.C. v. League of Women Voters of Calif., 468 U.S. 364 (1984) with Selective Service System v. Minnesota PIRG, 468 U.S. 841 (1984).

still, he thought, it was poorly characterized as a search. To be sure, "the caseworker's posture in the home visit is . . . both rehabilitative and investigative. But this latter aspect . . . is given too broad a character and far more emphasis than it deserves if it is equated with a search in the traditional criminal law context. . . . If consent to the visitation is withheld, no visitation takes place. The aid then never begins or merely ceases, as the case may be."

Even if the visit were taken to be a search, it would be "reasonable." Protection of the dependent child creates special claims (the Justice hinted darkly, dehors the record, of possible child abuse); as donor of charity, the state was entitled to "command a gentle means, of limited extent and of practical and considerate application, of achieving that assurance." Mrs. James had reasonable control over the timing of the visit and "no specific complaint of any unreasonable intrusion of her home . . . ."

"The visit . . . is made by a caseworker of some training [13] whose primary objective is, or should be, the welfare, not the prosecution, of the aid recipient. . . . The caseworker is not a sleuth . . . . The home visit is not a criminal investigation . . . ." In such a context, a warrant procedure would be an insulting, counter-productive intrusion.

Justice Douglas, in dissent, wrote in terms of unconstitutional conditions. "Whatever the semantics, the central question is whether the government by force of its largesse has the power to 'buy up' rights guaranteed by the Constitution." Justices Marshall and Brennan, sharing this concern, remarked that the state's own case had emphasized the search characteristics of the visits. "[T]he welfare visit is not some sort of purely benevolent inspection. . . . Of course, caseworkers seek to be friends, but the point is that they are also required to be sleuths. . . . Time and again, in briefs and at oral argument, appellants emphasized the need to enter AFDC homes to guard against welfare fraud and child abuse, both of which are felonies. Even accepting the idea that the visits were rehabilitative," the Justices remarked, a paternalistic notion that a complaining citizen's constitutional rights can be violated so long as the State is somehow helping him is alien to our Nation's philosophy.

Although initially seen as providing the means for ready circumvention of the warrant requirements of Camara and See,[14] Wyman v. James has apparently had little impact, and is rarely cited in the warrantless inspection context. See Zweibon v. Mitchell, 516 F.2d 594,

13. The amicus brief submitted on behalf of the Social Services Employees Union Local 371, AFSCME, AFL–CIO, the bargaining representative for the social service staff employed in the New York City Department of Social Services, recites that "caseworkers are either badly trained or untrained" and that "[g]enerally, a caseworker is not only poorly trained, but also young and inexperienced . . . ." Despite this astonishing description by the union of the lack of qualification of its own members for the work they are employed

to do, we must assume that the caseworker possesses at least some qualifications and some dedication to duty.

14. Note, Administrative Investigations of Welfare Recipients, 22 Case West.Res.L. Rev. 581, 588 (1971); Note, Welfare Home Visits and a Strict Construction of the Fourth Amendment, 66 Nw.U.L.Rev. 714, 734 (1971); compare Note, Wyman v. James: New Restrictions Placed Upon the Individual's Right to Privacy, 21 DePaul L.Rev. 1081 (1972).

632–33, n. 94 (D.C.Cir.1975) cert. denied 425 U.S. 944 (1976). Its critical reception was at best mixed, some reflecting active skepticism about "the benevolent conceits of the welfare home visit at stake," [15] vigorously protesting the opinion's use and misuse of the record, and bitterly attacking its "double standard disfavoring the [poor]"; [16] another, finding support for the result in a "novel element . . . disregarded by the Supreme Court dissenters as it was by the lower court, . . . that the child has an interest in the home-visit that is separate from his mother's. . . . Until the James decision this principle was ignored in relation to welfare mothers, partly, no doubt, because the welfare mother had spokesmen through the National Welfare Rights Organization, other groups, and attorneys, while her child was inarticulate and unrepresented." [17]   A view of the decision that limited its impact to situations involving government action assertedly benefiting *helpless* third parties—as, for example, a manufacturing firm's employees are not—may as readily explain its want of subsequent influence as the hypothesis that the critical reaction has effectively discredited it.

SECTION 3. COMPULSORY PROCESS

Any consideration of agency use of subpoena authority necessarily focuses on the courts. This is so because, in the usual case, obedience to compulsory process issued by an agency can be required only by court order. Though often complied with—to earn good will, for other tactical reasons, or out of ignorance that no obligation has yet attached—an agency subpoena typically has no independent force.[1]

15. R.A. Burt, Forcing Protection on Children and Their Parents: The Impact of Wyman v. James, 69 Mich.L.Rev. 1259 (1971). Professor Burt, who favored a warrant requirement for welfare visitation, acknowledged "some slight reason to believe that welfare families as a group, for whatever cause, are more likely than other families to warrant state intervention to protect young children." However, he doubted that "many welfare recipients need more than money for assistance." Even if they do need services as well as funds and even if "a coerced home visit would ensure acceptance of those services by the recipient or for her children," Professor Burt argued that a warrant requirement would not "interfere with the welfare agency's ability to carry out its avowed beneficent purposes." The judiciary, he contends, "should use its procedural weaponry to assure in some degree that coerced assistance is what it claims to be"—that is, assistance which is "more than merely coercive."

16. A.M. Dershowitz and J.H. Ely, Harris v. New York: Some Anxious Observations on the Candor and Logic of the Emerging Nixon Majority, 80 Yale L.J. 1198, 1223–1224 n. 100 and 1204–1206 nn. 39–40 (1971).

17. N. Dembitz, The Good of the Child Versus the Rights of the Parent, 86 Pol.Sci. Q. 389, 395–6 (1971). The author was an experienced judge of the Family Court of the State of New York, having served previously for many years as counsel to the New York Civil Liberties Union.

1. In an adjudicatory context, agencies may be able to attach procedural consequences, such as limiting rights of cross-examination, to failure by a party to honor a subpoena. NLRB v. C.H. Sprague, 428 F.2d 938 (1st Cir.1970); See pp. 722–725 within. In investigatory contexts, agencies may have authority to withhold future benefits (e.g., additional government contracts) or impose cumulating civil penalties for failures to honor compulsory process. See, e.g., Uniroyal, Inc. v. Marshall, 482 F.Supp. 364 (D.D.C.1979) (debarment). All these measures are to a degree coercive, and effectively shift the burden of seeking relief to the party subject to the information demand. Yet in Federal courts, at least, direct enforcement—the creation of an obligation of response enforcible through imprisonment for civil contempt—remains a strictly judicial matter.

Agency enforcement efforts may take the form of a summary action as authorized by Fed.R.Civ.P. 81(a)(3),[2] an action to collect a sanction prescribed by statute, or the like;[3] but the obligation to respond is determined only upon judicial review of the underlying order.

It does not follow that agencies themselves lack procedures for determining the appropriateness of information demands made by their staffs. Agency rules of procedure for adjudicatory actions frequently incorporate discovery mechanisms analogous to those of the Federal Rules, vesting in Administrative Law Judges controls similar to those exercised by federal district judges with review by the agency heads available as it would be in a court of appeals.[4] Outside of such proceedings, the agency's investigative staff may be generally authorized to issue information demands on their own, subject only to a motion to limit or quash the demand before the agency heads. Internal rules or policies respecting the required specificity or cause for an informational demand may vary with the context, with greater sharpness of inquiry and clarity of purpose insisted upon in enforcement proceedings under way than in the nascent stages of an investigation.

Obviously, lawyers are attentive to such matters as well as the precise terms of any statutory authorization—"exhaustion of remedies" considerations are as likely to prevail with courts in this context as in any other; the existence of an agency mechanism for considering objections to information demands is influential on what, as we shall see, is a highly permissive judicial inquiry; and, consequently, in most circumstances, the administrative remedies are likely to be the only ones tried. At their conclusion, judicial enforcement usually appears inevitable. Nevertheless, to repeat, that enforcement is generally required; and from this fact, and the potential for obstruction and delay it connotes, arise many of the tensions and conclusions reflected in the following materials.

2. Summary proceedings are not to be mistaken for peremptory ones. Informed that subpoena enforcement was being handled as a routine motions matter in district court, the District of Columbia Circuit remarked: "These subpoena enforcement proceedings must be adversarial in character and, as the Fifth Circuit noted, afford 'an adequate opportunity to raise all objections to [the] administrative subpoena.' Atlantic Richfield Company v. Federal Trade Commission, 546 F.2d 646, 650 n. 5 (1977), citing cases. Depending on the circumstances of the case, this adversary proceeding may take the form of an evidentiary hearing, oral arguments without the taking of evidence, or, as is doubtless the appropriate course in many applications for enforcement orders, consideration based on the papers submitted by the parties to the court." FTC v. Atlantic Richfield Co., 567 F.2d 96, 106 n. 22 (D.C.Cir. 1977).

3. The wide differences in enforcement devices were regarded as without "appar-

ent reason" in 1941. Report of the Attorney General's Committee on Administrative Procedure, Sen.Doc. No. 8, 77th Cong., 1st Sess. 414–415 (1941). Decades later the same differences existed, with the same lack of reason in the eyes of highly qualified analysts. See Selected Reports of the Administrative Conference of the United States, Sen.Doc. No. 24, 88th Cong., 1st Sess. 213–219 (1963); See Note, The Argument for Agency Self-Enforcement of Discovery Orders, 83 Colum.L.Rev. 215 (1983).

4. 5 U.S.C. § 556(c). Although the Administrative Procedure Act does not grant subpoena authority to agencies (leaving that to individual enabling statutes), it does provide that where such power exists in adversary proceedings, subpoenas are available to any "party," private litigant or agency counsel, on equal terms. 5 U.S.C. § 555(d). See the note on discovery at the end of this chapter.

a. May a Subpoena be Issued Without "Probable Cause" to Believe It Will Produce Evidence of Wrongdoing?

Years ago the Supreme Court held that the Federal Trade Commission, under the statute then in force, was powerless to compel the production of books and records whose specific relevance could not be forecast. Mr. Justice Holmes, speaking for the Court, said that only "the most explicit language" could lead him to believe that Congress "intended to authorize one of its subordinate agencies to sweep all our traditions into the fire and to direct fishing expeditions into private papers on the possibility that they may disclose evidence of crime." Federal Trade Commission v. American Tobacco Co., 264 U.S. 298, 305–306 (1924). These were ringing words but the insistent "reasonable" pressure of administrative agencies for the information they required to perform their function eroded them away. A prominent step came in a dispute involving a government contractor—a setting in which it might have been thought a bargain had been made, a condition agreed to:

ENDICOTT JOHNSON CORPORATION v. PERKINS, 317 U.S. 501 (1943), involved an investigation under the Walsh-Healey Act, which required manufacturers of supplies for the Government to observe minimum standards as to wages, hours of labor, employment of children, and so on. Secretary of Labor Perkins began an investigation into compliance by the Corporation, a manufacturer of shoes the Government had contracted to buy. Her investigation, however, was directed not at the plants where shoes were made, but at related factories owned by the Corporation—a cardboard carton plant, for example, and a tannery. When Miss Perkins sought information about payrolls in those establishments, the Corporation refused to give it, arguing that its contracts with the Government related only to shoe factories and that the Secretary's investigatory power went no farther.

The Court took the position that the Secretary was empowered to inquire into alleged violations of the contracts the Corporation had made, subject to the provisions of the Walsh-Healey Act. In the course of investigation she would have to determine what employees were covered by the contracts and the Act. Before she could make any order, of course she would also have to find that violations of the Act had occurred. She was not required to pursue inquiry into these issues in any particular sequence. The conduct of investigations had been left up to the Secretary. She could look for evidence of underpayment of wages first and consider the question of jurisdiction afterward, if she chose. And as to the issue of "coverage"—that is, whether the box factory was covered by the shoe manufacturing contracts—this was something for the Secretary, not a court, to decide in the first instance. "The evidence sought by the subpoena," Justice Jackson said, "was not plainly incompetent or irrelevant to any lawful purpose of the Secretary in the discharge of her duties under the Act, and it was the duty of the District Court to order its production for the Secretary's consideration."

What the Court seemed to be saying in this case was that "jurisdiction" to conduct an investigation exists if the inquiry is of the general kind the official is authorized to make. That is to say, the courts must seek to aid, not to block, an investigation that deals with an appropriate *subject matter*. The question to be considered is not whether a particular respondent or a particular bit of desired information is or is not within the investigator's "jurisdiction." The question is, rather, whether the topic to which the inquiry pertains is a topic the official has been empowered to investigate.

OKLAHOMA PRESS PUBLISHING CO. v. WALLING, 327 U.S. 186 (1946), took the proposition beyond the arguably special context of government contracts, and so drove home this lesson beyond dispute. The Fair Labor Standards Act of 1938 set minimum wage and hour standards for businesses affecting interstate commerce. The Wage and Hour Administrator had been authorized, among other things, to "investigate and gather data regarding the wages, hours, and other conditions and practices of employment in any industry subject to this Act, and may enter and inspect such places and such records . . . and investigate such . . . matters as he may deem necessary or appropriate to determine whether any person has violated any provision of this Act." He subpoenaed the Company to give him full payroll data and, also, information about the source of its advertisements and news, the distribution of its papers outside Oklahoma, and so on. The Company refused, saying that it, as a newspaper publisher, was not subject to the Act; and in any event, it added, no reason existed for supposing that it had been violating the statute, so that the Secretary was simply "fishing" for evidence. The Administrator then brought an action in court to secure enforcement of his subpoena. The Supreme Court upheld the subpoena. The following points in Justice Rutledge's opinion deserve note:

(a) The Company argued that a "general fishing expedition," without a prior charge that the Act has been violated, runs afoul of the Fourth Amendment's search and seizure provisions. Simply hunting for evidence on which to base an accusation, the Company said, is the kind of rummaging around in private papers that the Constitution is designed to prevent. "The short answer to the Fourth Amendment objections," Justice Rutledge responded, "is that the records in these cases present no question of actual search and seizure. . . . No officer or other person has sought to enter petitioners' premises against their will, to search them, or to seize or examine their books, records or papers without their assent, otherwise than pursuant to orders of court authorized by law and made after adequate opportunity to present objections, which in fact were made." The Court cautioned against confusing a "figurative" or "constructive" search with an *actual* search and seizure." [5]

(b) The Fifth Amendment's "somewhat related guaranty against self-incrimination" has no bearing on this case because "this privilege

---

5. Compare Justice White's later analysis in the See case, set out at p. 692 n. 1   supra, treating the Fourth Amendment as the governing constitutional text.

gives no protection to corporations or their officers against the production of corporate records pursuant to lawful judicial order. . . . " That is, the privilege against self-incrimination can be claimed only by a natural person concerning his own papers or his own testimony concerning himself.

(c) The Administrator was empowered to investigate not simply to help prove a pending charge or complaint, but to discover and procure evidence "upon which to make one if, in the Administrator's judgment, the facts thus discovered should justify doing so." That is all right, the Court said, so long as the investigator's subpoena is not too indefinite or too broad in what it demands and "if also the inquiry is one the demanding agency is authorized by law to make and the materials specified are relevant." The disclosure sought must not be "unreasonable." A specifically charged violation of law is not a prerequisite of investigation. "It is enough that the investigation be for a lawfully authorized purpose, within the power of Congress to command"—as is true, also, of grand jury investigations and, indeed, of Congressional investigations themselves. A grand jury, as the Supreme Court had occasion to remark in a later case, "can investigate merely on suspicion that the law is being violated, or even just because it wants assurance that it is not." United States v. Morton Salt Co., 338 U.S. 632, 642–43 (1950), noted also at p. 662 above.

(d) In this case, the Administrator was seeking information concerning two issues: Was the Company subject to the Act and, if so, was the Company violating the Act? Both of those were authorized subjects of inquiry. How can those questions be answered until the evidence is at hand and has been studied? And whose job is it to do the studying in the first instance? The Administrator need not allege "probable cause" for believing he knows the answers before he knows the facts.[6]

(e) "Petitioners stress that enforcement will subject them to inconvenience, expense and harassment. . . . There is no harassment when the subpoena is issued and enforced according to law. The Administrator is authorized to enter and inspect, but the Act makes his right to do so subject in all cases to judicial supervision. Persons from whom he seeks relevant information are not required to submit to his demand, if in any respect it is unreasonable or overreaches the authority Congress has given. To it they may make 'appropriate defense' surrounded by every safeguard of judicial restraint."

---

6. And see Securities and Exchange Commission v. Brigadoon Scotch Distributing Co., 480 F.2d 1047 (2d Cir.1973), cert. den. 415 U.S. 915 (1974) enforcing a subpoena issued in an SEC investigation of the offer and sale of whiskey warehouse receipts, possibly in violation of federal antifraud and registration laws. The sellers resisted, saying that they were simply selling title to specific cases of whiskey, and were therefore not dealing in securities at all. Said the court: "The Commission must be free without undue interference or delay to conduct an investigation which will adequately develop a factual basis for a determination as to whether particular activities come within the Commission's regulatory authority." [Subsequently, a federal court held, on the merits, that Scotch whiskey warehouse receipts are indeed "securities" within the meaning of the Securities Act and are therefore subject to SEC registration requirements. SEC v. M.A. Lundy Associates, 362 F.Supp. 226 (D.R.I.1973).]

b. What is the Judicial Role in Proceedings to Enforce Administrative Subpoenas?

In light of this broad language, what objections can be raised against an administrative demand for information? Must a subpoena be obeyed so long as it has a tenuous connection with a subject matter that has been entrusted to administrative concern? Is the court, when it enters its own order directing compliance with a subpoena issued by another agency of government, a mere rubber stamp?

The applicable section of the Federal Administrative Procedure Act—5 U.S.C. § 555(d)—does not greatly help to answer those questions. It says, simply, that if the validity of an administrative subpoena is contested, "the court shall sustain the subpoena or similar process or demand to the extent that it is found to be *in accordance with law.*" [1] The following comments are distilled from judicial holdings rather than from statutory provisions.

(a) *The subpoena must be issued in pursuit of an authorized objective.* An administrator cannot confer power on himself. Hence a respondent may ignore a command to produce evidence or to testify in an investigation that has not been expressly or impliedly authorized by statute; and even if the investigation has been authorized, courts still will not enforce an administrative subpoena whose issuance has not been based on a statute. Serr v. Sullivan, 390 F.2d 619 (3d Cir.1968). This is simply an application of the cautionary reminder in 5 U.S.C. § 555(c) that "Process, requirement of a report, inspection, or other investigative act or demand may not be issued, made, or enforced except as authorized by law." Most of the modern regulatory statutes are so broad, however, that findings of ultra vires are not likely to be frequent.

Regulations as well as statutes may be looked to in determining ultra vires issues, of course. United States v. Frontier Airlines, Inc., 563 F.2d 1008 (10th Cir.1977). And despite the contrary intimations of Endicott Johnson, the question whether a subpoena has been issued in pursuit of an authorized objective seduces occasional courts into determining issues of agency jurisdiction as an element of subpoena enforcement. Thus, the District Court for the District of Columbia examined at length whether "aluminum home wiring" was a "consumer product" within reach of the Consumer Product Safety Commission before enforcing a subpoena calling on manufacturers to provide files bearing on a product widely thought to have created a substantial fire hazard in homes in which it was employed. United States v. Anaconda Co., 445 F.Supp. 486 (D.D.C.1977). The more general view is that "substantive issues which may be raised in defense against an administrative complaint are premature in [a subpoena] enforcement proceeding." FTC v. Texaco, Inc., 555 F.2d 862 (D.C.Cir., en banc), cert. denied 431 U.S. 974 (1977).

---

1. See also p. 702 n. 4 above; In re: FTC Line of Business Report Litigation, noted above at p. 663.

But suppose the subject of the subpoena can demonstrate a specific statutory purpose to exclude it from the permissible scope of investigation? A common carrier subject to the Interstate Commerce Commission, and for that reason statutorily exempt from both FTC regulation of its business practice *and* FTC investigation, was able to defeat on this ground "the strong policy against litigating the issue of coverage . . . in a subpoena enforcement proceeding." The right to be free from investigation could not be vindicated at any later stage in the proceeding; the issue was strictly legal, unlikely to be amplified by the agency's expertise or factual determinations; and the violation of the right, once found to exist, was clear. "If [the carrier's] statutory right to be free from FTC investigation is to have any meaning at all, it must be possible to assert it in response to the agency's attempt to enforce its subpoenas." FTC v. Miller, 549 F.2d 452 (7th Cir.1977); see also FTC v. Feldman, 532 F.2d 1092, 1096 (7th Cir.1976); cf. Leedom v. Kyne, 358 U.S. 184 (1958).

The same conclusion is not reached when the defense is merely that the person to whom the subpoena has been directed is not himself subject to the agency's regulation. For example, in Freeman v. Brown Brothers Harriman & Co., 357 F.2d 741 (2d Cir.1966), cert. den. sub nom. Meyer Zausner Sales, Inc. v. Freeman, 384 U.S. 933 (1966), the Secretary of Agriculture sought information from a bank concerning the account of one of its customers over whom the Secretary concededly had no jurisdiction. The bank refused to divulge the desired data. But the information bore on the possibility that a company (under regulation by the Secretary) had paid unlawful rebates to the bank's depositor. The court held that this was a matter within the Secretary's power to investigate and that the subpoena should therefore be enforced.

A NOTE ON MOTIVE

An occasional basis for declaring an investigation to be ultra vires is the conclusion that it has been undertaken "in bad faith"—that its true motivation is unauthorized or improper. Illustrative is Shasta Minerals & Chemical Co. v. Securities and Exchange Commission, 328 F.2d 285 (10th Cir.1964). The SEC had directed the Company to produce its stockholders' names and addresses, purportedly for use in an investigation into whether the Company was violating various sections of the Securities Act. The Company, resisting efforts to enforce the SEC's subpoena, made allegations from which a conclusion could be drawn that the Commission's staff was systematically harassing and persecuting the Company and its president. The Commission did not deign to refute the allegations, relying on its statutory power to investigate. The District Court rather reluctantly upheld the Commission and ordered the Company to comply with the subpoena. The Court of Appeals had no patience with this approach. The questions of fact raised by the Company, the court said, "are material because they are relevant to the question of whether or not the Commission was acting arbitrarily or in excess of its statutory authority." The SEC had power to investigate alleged violations of the Securities Act, but did not have power to use an investigation as a club. As the Supreme Court has remarked, a court whose process is being invoked to enforce an administrative command should not allow itself to be abused, as it would be if it forced compliance with an administrative summons that "had been issued for an improper purpose, such as to harass the [respondent] or to put pressure on him to settle a collateral dispute, or for any other purpose reflecting on the good faith of the particular investigation." United States v. Powell, 379 U.S. 48, 58 (1964). And see also United States v. Roundtree, 420 F.2d 845 (5th Cir.1969).

As every lawyer soon learns, however, inquiry into motive is among law's most subtle, complex, and difficult tasks. Full-throated pursuit of the question would inevitably require inquiries into internal function which could be disruptive, demeaning, time-consuming, yet unlikely to produce clear-cut outcomes. Given the potential for delay and obstruction which inheres in any opportunity to create litigation on secondary issues, the courts have generally taken a much more restrained approach. In United States v. LaSalle Nat. Bank, 437 U.S. 298 (1978), a special agent of the Internal Revenue Service sought to compel production of a trustee's records of financial transactions involving an individual under investigation for tax fraud. The information sought could have been used in either criminal or civil tax fraud actions. The Supreme Court found it improper to inquire whether the agent's only subjective purpose was to gather evidence for use in a criminal prosecution. Although a summons issued with that sole purpose would not have been issued "in the good faith pursuit of the congressional authorized purposes" of the enabling statute, the Court thought inquiry into an individual agent's personal goals was both too difficult and too likely to disrupt the government's proper investigations. The Court was able to point out a brighter line distinguishing civil from criminal investigations: the decision to refer a case to the Justice Department for criminal prosecution after supervisory review within the Service. Only when the IRS could be shown to have made "an institutional commitment to make the referral" could a court refuse enforcement for want of good faith in use of the summons authority.[2] See also United States v. Tiffany Fine Arts, Inc., 718 F.2d 7 (2d Cir.1983).

The burden of showing an abusive exercise of administrative power, coupled with an effort to abuse judicial process, rests on the

---

2. Note that no question was raised whether Congress *could* authorize use of a summons to secure evidence of crime for use in criminal prosecutions; cf. Zurcher v. The Stanford Daily, noted at p. 696 above. Rather the issue was whether Congress *had* authorized this kind of use, and the Court concluded that it had not. The majority of five was willing to have the district court inquire whether an "institutional commitment" had been made, in order to prevent the Service from delaying submitting a recommendation for criminal prosecution to the Justice Department while it gathered additional evidence; "[s]uch a delay would be tantamount to the use of the summons authority after the recommendation," hence abusive of the Service's limited statutory authorization. Four Justices, led by Justice Stewart, would have authorized no inquiry; they found examination of the " 'institutional good faith' of the entire Internal Revenue Service . . . even less desirable and less rewarding" than establishing the mental processes of an individual agent, and at least equally productive of "endless discovery proceedings and ultimate frustration of the fair administration of the Internal Revenue Code." For them it was sufficient that the reference had not yet in fact been made. See also United States v. Morgan Guaranty Trust Co., 572 F.2d 36 (2d Cir. 1978) cert. den. sub nom. Keech v. U.S., 439 U.S. 822 (1978).

accuser—that is, on the person who resists an outwardly valid demand for information. The practical result of this burden is to limit sharply the occasions in which discovery techniques can be used in building a case against subpoena enforcement. As the Court of Appeal for the District of Columbia remarked in enforcing an SEC subpoena in the face of claims of bad faith on the part of the Commission:

"[D]istrict courts must be cautious in granting such discovery rights, lest they transform subpoena enforcement proceedings into exhaustive inquisitions into the practices of the regulatory agencies. . . . [S]pecial circumstances that raise doubts about the agency's good faith [are necessary; e]ven then, district courts must limit discovery to the minimum. . . . " SEC v. Dresser Industries, Inc., 628 F.2d 1368 (D.C.Cir.1980), cert. denied 449 U.S. 993 (1980). That the agency had undertaken an investigation for its own enforcement purposes parallel to a grand jury's criminal investigation and (as a statute expressly provided) intended to share its findings with the grand jury did not suggest bad faith; that, it appeared, would be shown only if the SEC's own investigation were a sham conducted to evade discovery restrictions in the criminal investigation.[3]

Even when the agency has announced a purpose that the court regards as improper, the court may enforce a subpoena also supported by proper purposes, providing by protective order against the improper use. Thus, in Lynn v. Biderman, 536 F.2d 820 (9th Cir.) cert. denied sub nom. Biderman v. Hills, 429 U.S. 920 (1976), the Administrator of an office within the Department of Housing and Urban Development had demanded customer lists and sales documents from certain real estate developers, announcing his intention to send each customer an official letter informing her of a statutory right to void her contract with the developers and to receive a refund of any moneys paid to them. The court enforced the subpoena, readily finding legitimate purposes and relevance to the inquiry; but it entered a protective order precluding the responsible officials from advising the developers' customers of statutory rights to rescind their contracts and recover back any money they had paid. Any such activity did not reflect a legitimate purpose, in the court's view; while "[i]t is not a ground to deny enforcement of a subpoena that it is being employed for a wrongful purpose if there is also a legitimate purpose," enforcement of the subpoena could be accompanied by a protective order in such a case.[4]

---

3. See also United States v. Hayes, 408 F.2d 932 (7th Cir.), cert. denied 396 U.S. 835 (1969) (the fact that a House Subcommittee had expressed an interest in an internal revenue investigation did not show that the investigation was conducted for an improper purpose). Most judges are sophisticated enough not to indulge sheer conjecture about hidden reasons for an agency's seeking information that is, so far as surface appearances go, pertinent to an investigation. In National Labor Relations Board v. Kingston Trap Rock Co., 222 F.2d 299 (3d Cir.1955), the respondent had ar-

gued that the data demanded by the Board, purportedly for its own use, would in fact be turned over to others; the court was unimpressed, saying (at 302): "The astonishing contention that one may refuse to comply with a proper subpoena because of a self-conjured groundless suspicion that there is a 'danger' that a governmental employee will commit a wrongful act is brazen and insulting."

4. To the same effect, see American Int'l Trading Co. v. Bagley, 536 F.2d 1196 (7th Cir.1976).

(b) *The evidence sought must be germane to a lawful subject of inquiry.* Of course the books and records or other evidence to which an agency seeks access by its compulsory process must be relevant. How can relevance be determined, however, when nobody knows what is in the records until after the records have been produced and have been examined? If in the course of a hearing an objection were voiced to receiving a certain bit of evidence, a ruling would be possible because at that stage of the game one would be able to identify the evidence and to relate it to a well defined context. But when an investigation is still in progress, the precise nature of the evidence has not yet been disclosed and its relationship to other evidence cannot be easily predicted.

Chief Judge Cardozo declared over half a century ago that investigatory power would be crippled if a subpoena were to be quashed "upon forecasts of the testimony and nicely balanced arguments as to its probable importance." Often, he added, the bearing of information cannot be estimated "until it is placed in its setting, a tile in the mosaic. Investigation will be paralyzed if arguments as to materiality or relevance, however appropriate at the hearing, are to be transferred upon a doubtful showing to the stage of a preliminary contest as to the obligation of the writ. . . . *Only where the futility of the process to uncover anything legitimate is inevitable or obvious must there be a halt upon the threshold.*" Matter of Edge Ho Holding Corp., 256 N.Y. 374, 381–382, 176 N.E. 537, 539 (1931). This test of relevance presupposes, of course, that the purpose of the inquiry has been revealed to persons commanded to aid it by producing evidence. Only if they know why evidence has been demanded can they appraise whether the demand will inevitably fail "to uncover anything legitimate" and may therefore be disobeyed.

More recently, agents of the Civil Aeronautics Board sought generally to inspect the files of United Airlines at its executive offices, asserting that their statutory right to "have access to . . . all documents, papers, and correspondence, now or hereafter existing and kept or required to be kept by air carriers" entitled them to inspect without specifying—or indeed having—any particular purpose in doing so. This the Seventh Circuit found insupportable. "[W]hile the expectation of privacy of a regulated carrier is limited, it nevertheless exists. . . . [T]here are internal corporate papers 'that stand at the heart of management effort, and so long as our carrier operations are rooted in private enterprise there is a strong element of privacy in such items [which is] a reason for limiting the occasion of [their] production'. . . . " Concluding that any "general warrant" authority such as the Board claimed would raise serious constitutional questions, and that the circumstances bearing on its statutory inspection rights did not require such a construction of the quoted provision, the court held that reasonable relevance must be established, in the first instance by the Board itself. Since the Board had taken the position that it need not specify its purpose, enforcement was denied. CAB v. United Airlines, Inc., 542 F.2d 394 (7th Cir.1976).[5]

5. This judicial attitude closely resembles that exhibited in cases involving alleg-edly contumacious refusal to answer questions of legislative investigators. A

Once an appropriate purpose has been specified, then the relevance of the subpoenaed material is to be measured against it. Thus, subpoenas issued in investigatory stages need be less sharply defined than subpoenas issued during the course of an adjudication. "[I]n the pre-complaint stage, an investigating agency is under no obligation to propound a narrowly focused theory of a *possible* future case. Accordingly, the relevance of the agency's subpoena request may be measured only against the general purposes of its investigation. The district court is not free to speculate about the possible charges that might be brought in a future complaint, and then to determine the relevance of the subpoena requests by reference to those hypothetical charges . . . [T]he agency is merely exercising its legitimate right to determine the facts, and . . . complaint may not, and need not, ever issue." FTC v. Texaco, Inc., 555 F.2d 862, 874 (D.C.Cir. en banc), cert. denied 431 U.S. 974 (1977). In the case from which this quotation is taken, the FTC was seeking information bearing on the accuracy of reported gas reserves, a matter of obvious sensitivity to the natural gas industry. The gas producers were seeking to confine the inquiry, by arguing that certain of this information had no sufficient relationship to the inquiry as the FTC had defined it. The particular controversy need not be understood to appreciate the import of the relevance requirement: the Commission was obliged to explain its needs to a neutral tribunal (the court) in a manner that plausibly related them to the project it had undertaken, and in a proceeding which permitted the companies an opportunity to argue the contrary.

How, precisely, is this relationship to be determined? In Texaco, the FTC had argued "that the pertinent inquiry is whether the requested material is 'plainly irrelevant' to the investigation." The court responded:

"The 'plainly irrelevant' language is derived, of course, from the Supreme Court's statement in Endicott Johnson that the evidence sought by the subpoena was not 'plainly incompetent or irrelevant' to any lawful purpose of the Secretary. 317 U.S. at 509. The issue before the Endicott Court was the authority of the district court to decide the question of statutory coverage; the appropriate standard of relevance was not directly addressed. In Oklahoma Press and Morton Salt, decided after Endicott, the Court spoke of information 'relevant' and 'reasonably relevant' respectively, to the inquiry. . . . And in See v. City of Seattle, 387 U.S. 541 (1967), the Court noted, citing Morton Salt and Oklahoma Press, that when an administrative agency subpoenas corporate books or records, the subpoena must be 'sufficiently limited in scope, relevant in purpose, and specific in directive so that compliance will not be unreasonably burdensome.' Id. at 544. . . .

"Without deciding whether a 'plainly irrelevant' standard actually is indicative of a more limited power of review, it suffices to dispose of

witness, the Supreme Court has ruled in various contexts, must be clearly informed about the purpose of interrogation before he can be adjudged in contempt for refusal to cooperate; only when he knows why he is being questioned can he form a judgment about the relevance of the questions to which his response has been commanded. See Russell v. United States, 369 U.S. 749 (1962), and cases there cited.

this case that the material sought by FTC is 'reasonably relevant' to a permissible FTC purpose."

A recent student note, Reasonable Relation Reassessed: The Examination of Private Documents by Federal Regulatory Agencies, 56 N.Y.U.L. Rev. 742, 783 (1981), argues that protection for the objects of agency investigations would be enhanced, and the general body of law made more readily comprehensible, if the materiality standards for administrative subpoenas were the same as those now applied to administrative searches. "More specifically, document subpoenas should be enforced only if either of two criteria is met; (1) the agency has some reason, less than criminal probable cause but more than mere conjecture, to believe that a valid regulatory interest would be served by the investigation; or (2) the investigation is part of a general plan of supervision, oversight, or enforcement." Do you agree that this would mark an improvement in understanding?

However "relevance" is understood, bear in mind that it will be determined on the basis of possibilities. The courts are not prone to speculate about whether the materials sought by an administrative subpoena will *in fact* prove to be useful in a suitably identified and lawful investigation. They inquire only into whether the materials *might possibly be useful.* See, e.g., Lee v. Federal Maritime Board, 284 F.2d 577 (9th Cir.1960); United States v. Feaster, 376 F.2d 147 (5th Cir. 1967).

(c) *The demands made must not be unduly vague or unreasonably burdensome.* Related to the issue of relevance and yet somewhat apart from it are the questions of whether an administrative command is sufficiently precise and sufficiently considerate to deserve obedience.

Obviously, obedience is impossible if the command is so loosely formulated that nobody can understand it. But, especially in connection with desired examination of books and records whose precise contents are not yet known, an administrative subpoena can rarely resemble a rifle bullet, aimed at a plainly identified target. If, for example, the Federal Trade Commission were to investigate a rumored unreasonable restraint upon competition, it would be unlikely to be able to frame its subpoena precisely, by saying: "Produce the letter you wrote to Mr. Jones on August 27 in which you proposed to fix prices in order to put Mr. Smith out of business, and your memorandum of August 31 in which you noted Mr. Jones's telephone call in response to your suggestion." After all, if the Commission knew enough to be that specific, it would have little need to investigate further. As a practical matter, therefore, administrative subpoenas are often drawn in sweeping terms. When this occurs, respondents sometimes complain that the materials they are expected to produce have been too loosely identified or, alternatively, have been so comprehensively identified as to create unconscionable burdens.

The judicial response has occasionally been couched in rather gaseous language. Adams v. Federal Trade Commission, 296 F.2d 861, 866 (8th Cir.1961), cert. denied 369 U.S. 864 (1962), is fairly typical: "Initially the administrative agency must exercise its discretion in determining what information it will require in making the investigation, but when the jurisdiction of the court is invoked in an enforcement proceeding, it must be judicially determined whether the agency abused its discretion; in other words, the court must determine whether the subpoena power has been confined to the rudimentary principles of justice."

When, however, the gas is blown away and one looks at what the courts actually do, one realizes that nowadays a subpoena must indeed be almost inconceivably vague or almost inconceivably oppressive in order to run counter to "rudimentary principles of justice." Civil Aeronautics Board v. Hermann, 353 U.S. 322 (1957), involved subpoenas issued in connection with a proceeding to revoke the operating authority of two small air carriers. The subpoenas called for the production of innumerable documents, most of which were generically identified—as, for example, "All bank statements and cancelled checks" and "All correspondence, contracts, agreements and options between any of the following corporations, partnerships and individuals, and between any of them and any other entity acting for or on behalf of any of [the twenty-one companies or persons whose names were then listed]." One of the individuals thus subpoenaed filed an affidavit that according to her best estimate she would have to "search through more than one million documents in order to locate and produce the documents sought." The District Court nevertheless enforced the subpoenas, saying that none of the desired documentary material was plainly immaterial or irrelevant to the proceeding before the Board. The Court of Appeals reversed, on the theory that the utility of the subpoenaed papers should be more closely examined by the trial judge. The Supreme Court, however, agreed with the District Court. The material demanded had been sufficiently identified and the types of documents sought were relevant to the issues before the Board. That sufficed.

In re FTC Line of Business Report Litigation, 595 F.2d 685 (D.C. Cir.), cert. denied 439 U.S. 958 (1978), noted at p. 663 above, enforced information requirements steadfastly resisted in every available arena as imposing massive and unwarranted accounting costs; the respondents were being obliged, they asserted, to create information they did not possess, in accordance with accounting concepts and categories which were meaningless in terms of their internal management and information structure. After noting that "the onus of demonstrating that a request is unduly burdensome is the corporation's," requiring a showing "that compliance threatens to disrupt or unduly hinder the normal operations of a business," the court swept the contention aside.[6]

---

6. Undue burden may also arise from repeated demands for information. For this reason, it is generally a defense that information being sought is already in the government's possession. Suppose, however, that one government agency with appropriate regulatory interests fully considered whether it needed particular information and decided not; and that another agency with similar interests later determined that it did need the same information. The relevance of "collateral estoppel" to subpoena enforcement is extensively treated in FTC v. Texaco, Inc., 555 F.2d 862, 878–880 (D.C.Cir. en banc), cert. denied 431 U.S. 974 (1977) (prior Federal Power Commission decision that similar information was not required for like purpose); and see Note, Administrative Collateral Estoppel: The Case of Subpoenas, 87 Yale L.J. 1247 (1978).

The fact that courts do regularly enforce very sweeping subpoenas does not mean that genuine objections will be altogether ignored. When the burden asserted in defense to a subpoena is not the cost of identifying or gathering the information required for compliance, but the commercial risks involved in providing it, the response may be to consider issuance of a protective order. Thus, when the Federal Trade Commission sought disclosure of the formulae and associated costs for the Kellogg Company's 30 varieties of breakfast cereals in proceedings also involving the other three leading manufacturers of such cereals, Kellogg objected that "disclosure of the information involved would do great injury to Kellogg and to competition in the industry." The Administrative Law Judge to whom these objections were first made accepted Kellogg's view that "the disclosure of alleged trade secrets should be required only if those trade secrets are not only relevant to the issues presented by the complaint, but are also necessary for a proper disposition of this controversy." After need had been specially shown, and Kellogg had been given an opportunity to suggest less threatening alternatives for providing information to satisfy that need, the Administrative Law Judge ordered production of the information; but he entered a protective order in a form Kellogg had suggested, limiting access to counsel of record and their supervisory and clerical employees. In affirming a district court order enforcing the subpoena, the court of appeals found it unnecessary to consider whether a showing of need is required where "trade secret" information is sought; it affirmed the district court's entry of a judicial protective order similar to that which had been entered by the administrative law judge. FTC v. Lonning, 539 F.2d 202 (D.C.Cir.1976); see also FTC v. Owens-Corning Fiberglas Corp., 626 F.2d 966 (D.C.Cir.1980).[7]

Sometimes the courts help to work out an arrangement that minimizes the strain on the respondent. This occurred, for example, in Federal Trade Commission v. Ace Brooks, Inc., Par. 70,164 Trade Cas. (S.D.N.Y.1961), involving a command to appear at the courthouse with masses of documents which might aid an investigation into magazine and book distribution. The respondents failed to comply. When the Commission sought enforcement of its subpoena, the respondents did not challenge the Commission's power, but simply asked that the investigation be transferred from the courthouse to their own offices "to obviate the need for removing voluminous records from their place of business where they are needed." The court thought that this was a reasonable request, and modified the subpoena's command accordingly. The court refused, however, to grant the respondent's additional re-

---

7. The importance of being able to obtain protective orders increased with the emergence of open government statutes such as the Freedom of Information Act, discussed in the following chapter. In the wake of judicial discussions emphasizing that concerns with the possible wrongful distribution of lawfully obtained information do not justify withholding enforcement of FTC subpoenas, e.g., FTC Line of Business Report Litigation noted at p. 663 above, Congress enacted as part of the Federal Trade Commission Improvements Act of 1980 detailed provisions for assuring the confidentiality of information obtained by the FTC using its investigatory powers. See 15 U.S.C. §§ 46 (f) and 57 bm, as amended by Sections 3 and 14 of the FTC Improvements Act of 1980, 94 Stat. 374.

quest that the Commission be required to pay the reasonable cost of producing the subpoenaed records.

Another example is provided by Hunt Foods & Industries, Inc. v. Federal Trade Commission, 286 F.2d 803 (9th Cir.1960), cert. denied 365 U.S. 877 (1961), in which the Commission's subpoena was said to require close examination of 230,000 transactions to determine what documents were to be supplied—a four-year task for twenty employees. Troubled about enforcing so onerous a demand, the District Court asked the Commission what to do. The Commission offered to sample files indicated by the respondent's staff using its own employees, working on the respondent's premises for no more than 760 man-hours. The respondent still objected, but the court had no difficulty in concluding that the subpoena, as now limited by the Commission's promise to do the necessary work, was not overly broad or burdensome.

Of course a respondent who hopes for judicial sympathy should do more than simply make wild charges, unsupported by evidence, that compliance with a subpoena will take away thousands of records in daily use and will be "tantamount to the virtual destruction of a successful business;" howls of that sort are not likely to be any more successful than they were in FTC v. Standard American, Inc., 306 F.2d 231 (3d Cir.1962). Most judges realize, as do most administrative lawyers, that the agency issuing the subpoena will often respond reasonably to a request for adjustments based on genuine business need (and not mere obstruction). They are aware, too, of the difference between trying to work out mutually agreeable compromise, and stringing the agency along in an effort to secure the advantages of delay. See Genuine Parts Co. v. Federal Trade Comm., 445 F.2d 1382 (5th Cir. 1971).

We add, finally, that courts may be more sensitive to the burdensomeness of a demand when administrative subpoenas have been served on non-parties. The legal formulas for subpoena enforcement do not differ as between the target of an investigation and a witness, or other person not himself the object of inquiry. But courts do in fact behave somewhat differently in assessing the burdensomeness of demands on such persons.[8]

(d) *The administrative command must not ignore a privilege to remain uncommunicative.* Chief among the privileges to remain silent is that provided by the Fifth Amendment's assurance that no person

---

8. See Note, Reasonable Relation Reassessed: The Examination of Private Documents by Federal Regulatory Agencies, 56 N.Y.U.L.Rev. 742, 788 (1981). Of course, the conduct of the subject of the subpoena may also be influential. In FTC v. Dresser Industries, Inc., CCH 1977–1 Trade Cases 61,400 (D.D.C. Apr. 26, 1977), the District Court enforced a subpoena issued at the request of the Kaiser Aluminum and Chemical Company in the course of FTC antitrust proceedings to which Kaiser alone was a party. Dresser claimed that compliance would cost it approximately $400,000. But Dresser had rejected modifications Kaiser had offered to lessen the burden of compliance for other firms served with similar subpoenas, which they had accepted. Moreover, Dresser was the dominant firm in the industry in which Kaiser had been charged with violations. The fact that "all the other companies which were subpoenaed, including those with subpoenas virtually identical to that of Dresser, have agreed to comply . . . strains the credibility of Dresser's claim of unreasonable burden."

may be compelled to incriminate himself. This has long been interpreted to mean that a witness may not be forced to respond to a question if his answer could directly incriminate him or if it could provide a link which, joined together with other information, might become part of a chain of evidence against him. The privilege against self incrimination can be claimed as a barrier against demands for documentary materials as well as for testimonial utterance. In administrative proceedings, documents provide the chief testing ground of privilege, because efforts to compel testimony are relatively rare.[9]

Some major limitations on the protection against being forced to produce evidence against oneself have already been discussed in Section 1, above. Another large limitation upon the privilege against self-incrimination is the possibility of statutory grants of immunity against prosecution in respect of matters about which a witness has been compelled to provide evidence.[10] Ullman v. United States, 350 U.S. 422 (1956), held that a witness who had been immunized against prosecution could not refuse to testify because his testimony might expose him to other unhappinesses such as "loss of job, expulsion from labor unions, state registration and investigation statutes, passport eligibility, and general public opprobrium;" the Fifth Amendment protects only against being compelled to incriminate oneself, and if an "immunity bath" has removed the possibility of incrimination, compulsory process may be used to obtain information the witness could otherwise have refused to disclose. The Ullman case was strongly reinforced by Kastigar v. United States, 406 U.S. 441 (1972), and Zicarelli v. New Jersey State Comm. of Investigation, 406 U.S. 472 (1972), both of which upheld immunity statutes. The later cases, moreover, said that the immunization need not extend beyond *using* the compelled testimony or other compelled information against the person who had been required to supply it in criminal proceedings,[11] the person could still be proceeded against if the prosecutorial authorities were able to prove that the evidence they intend to use "is derived from a legitimate source wholly independent of the compelled testimony." Recall, too, that the only matter as to which immunity need be granted is that part of a communication that could not constitutionally be compelled; it was for

9. Do agencies *need* the power to compel testimony, as distinct from documentary material? See F.C. Newman, Federal Agency Investigations: Procedural Rights of the Subpoenaed Witness, 60 Mich.L.Rev. 169, 181–185 (1961).

10. The melange of federal immunity statutes once available has been replaced by a uniform federal codification, 18 U.S.C. § 6001 et seq. For pertinent references see Symposium on Witness Immunity, 67 J.Crim.L. & Crimin. 129 (1976). And see also Note, Immunity Legislation: Making Better Use of a Valuable Law Enforcement Tool, 9 Colum.J.L. & Soc.Prob. 197 (1973).

11. In Burley v. United States Drug Enforcement Administration, 443 F.Supp. 619 (M.D.Tenn.1977), the court refused to enjoin federal agents from supplying the Tennessee Board of Pharmacy with documents provided them in accordance with a grant of use immunity, even though the likely outcome would be the initiation of disciplinary proceedings against the recipient of the immunity. As the court understood it, the possible outcomes of such a proceeding "are not penal in nature but rather in the nature of a civil penalty . . . directed at assuring the fitness of pharmacists to practice in the State of Tennessee. . . . " Absent some indication of a sham set up to circumvent the immunity grant, the grant of use immunity would not prevent the Tennessee Board from relying on the information provided.

this reason that the Court in United States v. Doe, noted above at p. 671, indicated that granting immunity from incriminating use of the fact that a person has produced documents in response to a subpoena, would permit incriminating use of whatever might be *in* those documents.

The emphasis thus far laid on the privilege against self-incrimination should not suggest that it alone is important. The student is no doubt familiar with other testimonial privileges. The law has long believed that confidentiality should be preserved in the lawyer-client, doctor-patient, priest-penitent, and husband-wife relationships; society gains, so it has been supposed, when communications within those relationships can be made freely, without fear that privacy will later be shattered by governmental command. See, e.g., C.A.B. v. Air Transport Ass'n, 201 F.Supp. 318 (D.D.C.1961): "The attorney-client privilege is deeply embedded and is part of the warp and woof of the common law. In order to abrogate it in whole or in part as to any proceeding whatsoever, affirmative legislative action would be required that is free from ambiguity." [12] Considerable doubt exists, nevertheless, as to the force in federal administrative proceedings of these and similar testimonial privileges. They are for the most part products of state statutes, building on a common law base. They have different dimensions in different states, and new privileges grow out of local episodes or pressures (psychologist-patient, accountant-client, news reporter-informant, for example).

No Congressional enactment that confers investigatory power on a federal agency has ever made any reference at all to these privileges, which derive not from the Constitution but from other legislatures' appraisal of competing public policies. Some years ago Judge Learned Hand, in the course of holding that a stockbroker was not privileged to withhold evidence concerning a customer's transactions, simply assumed that "the conduct of investigation [by the Securities and Exchange Commission] is subject to the same testimonial privileges as judicial proceedings." McMann v. Securities and Exchange Comm., 87 F.2d 377, 378 (2d Cir.1973), cert. denied 301 U.S. 684 (1937). In subsequent years most courts have indulged pretty much the same assumption, though its foundation in federal statutes has never been discovered.

The general attitude of the federal courts, perhaps especially in the context of tax enforcement, has been one of inhospitality to privilege claims. In United States v. Arthur Young & Co., 677 F.2d 211 (2d Cir. 1982), reversed 465 U.S. 805 (1984), for example, an accounting firm persuaded the Second Circuit to accept a claim of accounting privilege for workpapers generated during corporate audits required for compliance with federal securities laws. To "protect those who benefit from the enforcement of the securities laws from the grave dangers of inaccuracy and untrustworthiness," it thought, the auditors needed the

---

12. But cf. C.T. McCormick, Evidence 205 (1984): "If one were legislating for a new commonwealth, without history or customs, it would be hard to maintain that a privilege for lawyer-client communications would facilitate more than it would obstruct the administration of justice."

assurance of confidentiality that would prompt "uninhibited disclosure of confidential information such as questionable positions taken on tax returns." Permitting routine IRS summonses for the workpapers generated during the preparation of these statements would compromise the important policies of the securities laws, and so a privilege was to be recognized. The Supreme Court, however, was unimpressed, and unanimously reversed. Corporations were bound by law to reveal to their accountants the matters that would be in the workpapers; their utility to the IRS in revealing "soft spots" in the audited tax returns was undeniable; and the accountant's public function of certifying the probity of corporate financial reports did not create the same claim to confidentiality as the attorney's advocacy role. To similar effect are Ryan v. Commissioner of Internal Revenue, 568 F.2d 531, 542–545 (7th Cir.1977), cert. denied 439 U.S. 820 (1978) (Tax Court held not bound to recognize a claim of marital privilege; a demand for information about business income threatened no harm to family integrity or privacy, especially since use immunity had been granted and the demand was not associated with one spouse's innocent observation of the other's crime) and Couch v. United States, 409 U.S. 322 (1973) ("We note that no confidential accountant-client privilege exists under federal law, and no State-created privilege has been recognized in federal cases"). For further discussion see Note, Privileged Communications before Federal Administrative Agencies, 31 U.Chi.L.Rev. 395 (1964); and compare J.B. Weinstein, Recognition in the United States of the Privileges of Another Jurisdiction, 56 Colum.L.Rev. 535 (1956).

(e) *The administrative command must be issued in proper form.*

Finally, the subpoena must be issued by a person authorized to do so, in proper form. Ordinarily, no such question will arise; for each agency, issuance is a matter of well-established routine generally delegated to staff.

As one able commentator has said: "The attitude of the courts of appeals and the Supreme Court appears to be that so long as respondent has the protection afforded by his right to demand that a district judge pass upon the reasonableness of the demand for information, no harm is done in permitting delegation to staff assistants of power to take action with reference to the issuance, revocation, and applications for enforcement of subpoenas. Indeed, it is suggested that because of their greater familiarity with the details of the cases involved, these staff assistants are in a much better position than are their superior officers to exercise intelligent discretion on the appropriateness of the requested demand." F.E. Cooper, Federal Agency Investigations: Requirements for the Production of Documents, 60 Mich.L.Rev. 187, 204 (1961).

c. The Problem of Enforcing Administrative Subpoenas

The discussion in preceding pages has sought to shed light on the scope of administrative power to demand information, but has not revealed very much about what happens when a valid demand is resisted. As was remarked at the outset of this section, resistance ordinarily begins within the agency itself, where motions to quash or alter information demands may be heard by administrative law judges or—originally or on appeal—by the agency itself. If compliance still is not forthcoming once this process is complete, measures analogous to the discovery sanctions sometimes employed by federal district judges may be available.[1] If direct compulsion is desired, however, that must be sought in court. There, the most common enforcement method is a "two-stage proceeding." The agency applies to a trial judge for an order directing a recalcitrant witness to comply; if the judge determines that the demand is valid, he orders compliance on whatever terms he may see fit. That is the first stage.

Since the subpoena enforcement proceeding is a discrete judicial action in an adversary proceeding, the resulting order is "final," and thus appealable. Compare Reisman v. Caplin, 375 U.S. 440 (1964). Once appeals have been exhausted, if the non-cooperative witness persists in his recalcitrance, a fresh proceeding is commenced to adjudge the respondent to be in contempt of court because he disobeyed the court's order. That is the second stage.

This brief, and not exhaustive,[2] description should make apparent that a person who resolutely seeks to block an investigation can tie up the proceedings for long periods, and have the benefit of many different views of the correctness of the demand made. Compare Penfield Co. v. Securities and Exchange Comm., 330 U.S. 585 (1947). In this respect a witness in an administrative subpoena enforcement proceeding is in a far more comfortable position than is a person who has been ordered by a judge to answer questions put to him by a grand jury or in the course of a trial. In judicial proceedings a judge's direction to be cooperative is not appealable.[3] Instead, a contumacious witness may seek appellate review only after he has been held in contempt and the judge has ordered that he be punished. This makes a potentially uncooperative witness think twice before continuing to be contumacious, because if the appellate court upholds the trial judge, the punishment will follow without more ado. Recall that the same effective compulsion is available in proceedings to enforce administrative search warrants; because they begin as ex parte proceedings, the first stage of judicial enforcement is not seen to result in an appealable order. See p. 695 above. Are these differences warranted, in your view?

Dragging one's heels in administrative proceedings is more than a theoretical possibility. Sometimes it can have serious secondary results. Federal Maritime Comm. v. New York Terminal Conference, 373 F.2d 424 (2d Cir.1967), is illustrative. There, the Commission was

---

1. See pp. 722–725 below.

2. Omitted here, for example, is the possibility that a person anticipating enforcement efforts will herself initiate a judicial action for declaratory judgment or an order to quash—in order, for example, to choose a more desirable venue. Such efforts will be repulsed if an effective administrative remedy is available, American Motors Co. v. FTC, 601 F.2d 1329 (6th Cir.

1979), cert. denied 444 U.S. 941 (1979), but not before additional time has elapsed.

3. See In re Myron Farber, 158 N.J. Super. 488, 386 A.2d 466 (1978) cert. denied sub nom. New York Times v. New Jersey, 439 U.S. 997 (1978) and associated opinions on petition for stay of the contempt order, 98 S.Ct. 3058, 3060, 99 S.Ct. 6, 11; Cobbledick v. United States, 309 U.S. 323 (1940).

investigating whether certain ocean freight rates were exorbitant. In that connection it sought information about an agreement of terminal operators that fixed rates and practices in the Port of New York. During a period of eight months the desired data were withheld on the asserted ground that they did not relate to the Commission's authority. After quickly pointing out the nexus between the subpoenaed material and the agency's statutory responsibilities, the court—in a stinging opinion by Judge Henry Friendly—remarked: "All this is so self-evident that it is difficult to believe that experienced business men and hard-nosed lawyers required judicial instruction." The investigation, the court added, "has thus been stalled in its tracks for eight months, quite needlessly as this opinion shows." The unmeritorious challenge to the subpoena had this immediate consequence: During the period of obstructionist tactics American ocean-borne commerce continued to pay rates for port facilities that had been challenged as yielding an outrageous profit.[4]

Some statutes, hoping to compress everything into a one-stage proceeding, authorize judges to impose a contempt penalty without the preliminary step of ordering compliance. In certain of his activities for example, the Secretary of Labor may simply certify to a district court that somebody has disobeyed the Secretary's lawful order or process; the court is then supposed to conduct a summary hearing concerning the acts complained of "and if the evidence so warrants punish such person in the same manner and to the same extent as for contempt committed before the court, or commit such person upon the same conditions as if the doing of the forbidden act had occurred with reference to the process of or in the presence of the court." 80 Stat. 545, 5 U.S.C. § 8125 (1966). In actuality, the courts behave under these statutes just about as they do in the two-stage proceedings discussed earlier. They consider first whether the administrative process deserves to be enforced; then they direct compliance and stay any penalty pending an appeal; then an appeal is taken if the resistant witness still feels like fighting. See, e.g., United States v. McDonald, 313 F.2d 832 (2d Cir.1963). The validity of one-stage proceedings has been questioned. See R.L. Goldfarb, The Contempt Power 157–158 (1963). The real question is not whether they are valid, but whether they are especially effective. And the answer to that question seems to be negative. Compare J.D. Burroughs, The Use of the Administrative Summons in Federal Tax Investigations, 9 Vill.L.Rev. 371 (1964).

Another approach to securing compliance with administrative subpoenas is to make disobedience a crime or the occasion for imposition of a money penalty. The Federal Trade Commission Act, for instance, authorizes a fine of $1,000 to $5,000 or a year's imprisonment or both for any person who refuses to attend or produce documentary evidence "in obedience to the subpoena or lawful requirement of the commis-

---

4. Of course toleration of obstructionism does not extend to downright destruction of the material sought. See, e.g., FTC v. Gladstone, 450 F.2d 913 (5th Cir.1971) (respondent sentenced to jail for willful criminal contempt, after having removed and destroyed assertedly irrelevant documents contained in files he had been ordered to produce).

sion." The Department of Justice has not been eager to launch criminal prosecutions under this provision, or others like it; the Fourth Amendment overtones of subpoena enforcement have sometimes seemed to require that there be an opportunity for the detached gaze of a magistrate to fall on an information demand before it becomes effective. Civil penalties, over which the agency has greater control, have seen somewhat greater use. Thus, another section of the Act subjects a corporation to a forfeiture of $100, recoverable in a civil suit, for each day of default in filing a required report. In June 1958 informal requests were made for reports. Formal requests followed in January 1959. Nearly three years later, in December 1961, the Supreme Court upheld the propriety of the Commission's command and said that the information should have been given earlier to halt the accumulation of forfeitures. St. Regis Paper Co. v. United States, 368 U.S. 208 (1961).

A finding by the Commission that a corporation is in default in responding to an information demand shifts the burden to the corporation to avoid accumulation of the statutory penalty. This impact has been taken as one circumstance warranting an action for preenforcement review of the information demand at the corporation's initiative. A.O. Smith Corp. v. FTC, 530 F.2d 515 (3d Cir.1976). Moreover, the corporation may seek a stay of the accumulation of the penalties during the review process. Thus, in United States v. Morton Salt Co., 338 U.S. 632, 654 (1950), in which a respondent had complained that forfeitures might accrue over a long period of time, the Court was "not prepared to say that courts would be powerless" to prevent the building up of ruinous penalties pending a good faith test of the validity of an administrative command. This thought was repeated in the St. Regis case (at 226–227). It was acted upon positively in Genuine Parts Co. v. FTC, 445 F.2d 1382 (5th Cir.1971), where the statutory penalty was stayed during lengthy proceedings which the FTC insisted had been brought in bad faith for the purpose of delay alone—a contention the Court of Appeals regarded as "not without support" in the record. One may question whether $100/day, a level set in 1914, will often represent a ruinous penalty to those who vigorously resist FTC information demands; perhaps the more important observation is that a stay is unlikely to be automatic—the resisting corporation will have to travel some distance in convincing the court of its bona fides, if not its prospects of eventual success.[5]

5. The Federal Trade Commission Improvements Act of 1980, 94 Stat. 374, changed the Commission's information practice in a number of respects, but Congress did *not* act favorably on a proposal to increase the daily penalty for noncompliance, extend its application to all forms of compulsory process, and restrict the availability of a stay to cases in which likely success on the merits could be shown. Said the Chairman of the Federal Trade Commission at the time, "the lack of adequate sanctions makes it possible for those subject to compulsory process simply to refuse to comply without any substantial legal or factual justification. These refusals force the Commission to institute enforcement proceedings in the courts, which, while almost invariably resulting in orders requiring compliance, normally take several months and have been known to take years." "Federal Trade Commission Amendments of 1977 and Oversight," Hearings before the Subcommittee on Consumer Protection and Finance, House Committee on Interstate and Foreign Commerce, 95th Cong. 1st Sess. 70 (1977) (Testimony of FTC Chairman Collier).

A third technique is the application by the agency of discovery sanctions analogous to these available in federal civil litigation: a party not complying with the agency's information request may be disabled from either cross-examination or the presentation of evidence on the factual matters that were the subject of the request, or may have a presumption that the information request, if honored, could have shown facts unfavorable to it. An early Supreme Court decision remarked that the inquiry whether a witness before the Commission is bound to answer a particular question propounded to him, or to produce books, papers, etc., in his possession and called for by that body, is one that cannot be committed to a subordinate administrative or executive tribunal for final determination. "Such a body could not, under our system of government, and consistently with due process of law, be invested with authority to compel obedience to its orders by a judgment of fine or imprisonment . . . . [T]he power to impose fine or imprisonment in order to compel the performance of a legal duty imposed by the United States, can only be exerted, under the law of the land, by a competent judicial tribunal having jurisdiction in the premises." [6]

While the inherently judicial character of contempt proceedings has recently been reaffirmed,[7] a rule precluding the introduction of evidence or requiring the drawing of adverse influences might be viewed as much less significant.

Two recent cases limn the controversy. In NLRB v. INTERNATIONAL MEDICATION SYSTEMS, LTD., 640 F.2d 1110 (9th Cir.1981), cert. denied 455 U.S. 1017 (1982), the National Labor Relations Board subpoenaed an employer's personnel records, seeking information on the employer's policy on absenteeism and layoffs. The employer refused to produce the records and the Board did not seek judicial enforcement of the subpoena. Instead, the employer was barred from rebutting the general counsel's evidence on those subjects either by cross-examining witnesses or by presenting its own evidence. Relying heavily on Brimson, the Ninth Circuit reversed, holding that the Board could not "by-pass district court enforcement proceedings," and that challenges to agency subpoenas must be resolved by the judiciary before compliance can be compelled. The court treated the Board's preclusion order as an action

While conceding the appropriateness of requiring a respondent to demonstrate "that it is seeking a 'good faith test' of 'reasonable objections' to a Commission order which 'appears suspect' in order to obtain a stay," ABA representatives responded as vigorously: "A statutory standard is unconstitutional if it has a chilling effect on the ability of a respondent to contest judicially agency process to which there are reasonable objections." Id. at 264–265 (Testimony of C.O. Hobbs).

Such constitutional claims frequently are grounded in decisions pre-dating the Declaratory Judgment Act: Ex parte Young, 209 U.S. 123 (1908); Wadley Southern Ry. Co. v. Georgia, 235 U.S. 651 (1915); Oklahoma Operating Co. v. Love, 252 U.S. 331 (1920); see Comment, Procedures to Challenge the Process of Administrative Agencies, 30 U.Chi.L.Rev. 508 (1963). As a more recent decision has indicated, the argument depends for its force upon the "ruinous" character of the accumulating penalties; the existence of an opportunity to contest validity of the underlying order before the penalties reach the "ruinous" level is sufficient to defeat the constitutional claim. See Brown & Williamson Tobacco Corp. v. Engman, 527 F.2d 1115 (2d Cir. 1975), cert. denied 426 U.S. 911 (1976).

6. ICC v. Brimson, 154 U.S. 447, 485 (1894).

7. Northern Pipeline Constr. Co. v. Marathon Pipeline Co., p. 117 above.

intruding upon the judicial contempt power, and implied that, even absent an outstanding subpoena, administrative discovery sanctions could not be utilized "before the judicial questions have been asked and answered." In ATLANTIC RICHFIELD CO. v. UNITED STATES DEPT. OF ENERGY, 769 F.2d 771 (1984) the D.C. Circuit strongly disagreed, in the course of finding authority for the Department of Energy to issue an order precluding ARCO from entering affirmative defenses in administrative adjudicatory proceedings concerning ARCO's alleged isolation of price controls on petroleum; ARCO had disobeyed a departmental discovery order and contended that the order could only be enforced in independent judicial proceedings:

"Brimson was decided in 1894, long before the advent of the 'modern administrative state.' Although Brimson acknowledged that 'there are matters involving public rights' which are 'susceptible of judicial determination,' yet within the power of Congress to remove from the 'cognizance of the courts of the United States,'[8] it was not until 1932 that, in Crowell v. Benson,[9] the scope of the power became clear. . . . We think the broad congressional power to authorize agencies to adjudicate 'public rights' necessarily carries with it power to authorize an agency to take such procedural actions as may be necessary to maintain the integrity of the agency's adjudicatory proceedings. . . .

"We have sustained, indeed required, the drawing of adverse inferences against persons not complying with discovery orders in adjudicatory proceedings before the National Labor Relations Board.[10] The adverse-inference rule, we said, is a 'well recognized means available for vindicating [an agency's] power to require production of relevant documents short of a subpoena enforcement proceeding.' Collateral enforcement proceedings, we recognized, are 'cumbersome and time-consuming,' and '[t]he adverse inference rule provides a quick, fair method of encouraging parties to come forward with all material relevant to the controversy between them.' . . .

"Until the decision in International Medication Systems, other circuits considering the question had likewise sustained an evidentiary ban in National Labor Relations Board adjudicatory proceedings as a sanction for noncompliance with a Board subpoena.[11] The sanction had been deemed necessary in order to 'maintain[ ] the integrity of the hearing process,' and we consider that need no less compelling in situations such as that now before us.

8. 154 U.S. at 475 quoting Murray's Lessee v. Hoboken Land & Improvement Co., 59 U.S. (18 How.) 272, 284, (1855).

9. 285 U.S. 22 (1932).

10. UAW v. NLRB, 459 F.2d 1329 (D.C. Cir.1972).

11. NLRB v. C.H. Sprague & Son Co., 428 F.2d 938, 942 (1st Cir.1970) (employer who refused to produce concededly relevant information in response to subpoena precluded from "cross examin[ing] witnesses with reference to any matter which could have been produced by complying with the subpoena"); NLRB v. American Art Indus., Inc., 415 F.2d 1223, 1230 (5th Cir.1969), cert. denied 397 U.S. 990 (1970) (employer not allowed "to later produce evidence of a secondary nature to prove what could have been conclusively established if the subpoena had been honored").

"An evidentiary preclusion order falls far short of an effort to exact compliance with the subpoena by a judgment of fine or imprisonment.[12] Furthermore, over the years since Crowell v. Benson, we have increasingly entrusted agencies with decision making affecting many rights and privileges hardly less important than those at stake in discovery rulings. It seems to us incongruous to grant an agency authority to adjudicate—which involves vitally the power to find the material facts—and yet deny authority to assure the soundness of the factfinding process. Without an adequate evidentiary sanction, a party served with a discovery order in the course of an administrative adjudicatory proceeding has no incentive to comply, and ofttimes has every incentive to refuse to comply.[13]

. . .

"Lest it be forgotten, judicial review of the discovery sanction . . . remains available. Should the Federal Energy Regulatory Commission sustain the Department's preclusion order, ARCO is free to challenge the sanction in a federal district court on review of any adverse Commission final order. The court will then determine independently whether, under the particular circumstances, the sanction was justified.[14]

"In our view, evidentiary sanctions for recalcitrance in discovery are part and parcel of the power conferred upon the Secretary of Energy to adjudicate the factual issues related to remedial orders. It follows that such sanctions need not be authorized eo nomine in the Secretary's enabling statute."

A NOTE ON DISCOVERY

Once caught up in agency adjudication, an attorney may be able to turn the agency's investigatory authority to her own use, to prepare her presentation, to anticipate other presentations to be made, and to shape the course of the forthcoming proceedings.

Federal and state rules of civil procedure provide richly for the prehearing stages of trials. Pretrial discovery of evidence within the reach of an adversary party has become a commonplace aspect of modern civil procedure. "In the theory of the federal rulemakers," Professor Maurice Rosenberg has declared, "discovery, in all its forms, is the make-or-break device of the whole system. . . . The experience of a generation shows that discovery has been by long odds the most often used procedural tool in the kit of the federal court practitioner." [1]

Neither the Constitution nor the Administrative Procedure Act has as yet plainly required similar prehearing devices in administrative proceedings. A few agencies, in fact, have no statutory power to issue subpoenas that private parties can use to compel unwilling witnesses to

---

12. But see Note, The Argument for Agency Self-Enforcement of Discovery Orders, 83 Colum.L.Rev. 215, 228–229 n. 62 (1983); Williams, Authority of Federal Agencies to Impose Discovery Sanctions: The FTC—A Case in Point, 65 Geo.L.J. 739, 757–758 (1977).

13. UAW v. NLRB, supra note 10. See also, Note, supra note 12, 83 Colum.L.Rev. at 217–219.

14. We repeat that judicial review at this juncture is limited to the question of whether the Department has power to impose an evidentiary sanction, and does not extend to the question of propriety of any sanction actually imposed.

1. M. Rosenberg, Sanctions to Effectuate Pretrial Discovery, 58 Colum.L.Rev. 480, 480 (1958); and see the same author's Changes Ahead in Federal Pretrial Discovery, 45 Fed.Rules Dec. 481 (1969).

attend at the hearing stage itself, let alone at the prehearing stage; this gap in the administrative armament has not been thought to cause a hearing to lose its essential core of fairness.[2]

Despite the absence of a uniform federal statute or a standardized rule of agency practice in respect of prehearing procedures, numerous agencies in recent years have provided, in somewhat gingerly manner, opportunities akin to those to be found in civil courts. The impetus toward change in that direction came from the Administrative Conference of the United States, which in 1970 recommended fresh attention to nine different aspects of the prehearing phase of formal adjudicatory proceedings: prehearing conferences, depositions, witnesses, written interrogatories, requests for admission, production of documents and tangible things, role of the administrative law judge, protective orders, and subpoenas.[3]

As to each of these, the ACUS recommendations departed from the Federal Rules of Civil Procedure in order, as an accompanying committee report said, "to meet the special needs of administrative proceedings. The administrative process, for instance, must remain relatively inexpensive and speedy. . . . Mechanical provisions must frequently vary between agencies because each agency must structure its discovery rules to meet the peculiar nature of its proceedings. While these recommendations thus allow the individual agencies to fill in many details of discovery, they contemplate that agencies generally will follow federal law on the proper use and scope of these discovery tools where the recommendations themselves do not propose modifications. For instance, agencies should look to the Federal Rules of Civil Procedure and judicial decisions interpreting them for guidance in resolving such issues as the privileges available to litigants, the sufficiency of answers to written interrogatories, and the permissible use of depositions at the hearing itself. It was not felt necessary to refer to these matters in the text of the recommendations because the recommendations concentrate on the modifications which the administrative model for discovery must make in the judicial model. . . . "[4]

Before the ACUS recommendation, only three federal agencies—the Federal Trade Commission, the Federal Communications Commission, and the Federal Maritime Commission—had adopted discovery rules fairly

2. Compare Low Wah Suey v. Backus, 225 U.S. 460 (1911); Missouri ex rel. Hurwitz v. North, 271 U.S. 40 (1926); Ubiotica Corp. v. Food and Drug Administration, 427 F.2d 376 (6th Cir.1970); Brinkley v. Hassig, 130 Kan. 874, 289 P. 64, app. dismissed 282 U.S. 800 (1930); New Products Corp. v. State Highway Comm., 352 Mich. 73, 88 N.W.2d 528 (1958). But cf. Jenkins v. McKeithen, 395 U.S. 411, 429 (1969); and see Connecticut State Public Welfare Department v. HEW, 448 F.2d 209 (2d Cir.1971); Bristol-Myers Co. v. FTC, 469 F.2d 1116 (2d Cir.1972). And see H. Friendly, "Some Kind of Hearing," 123 U.Pa.L.Rev. 1267 (1975), espousing the view that in some instances (prison or school discipline cases, for example) the right to call even voluntary witnesses may be restricted; a fortiori, the right to compel attendance would not be deemed limitless.

In 1974 the Administrative Conference of the United States recommended that the Administrative Procedure Act be amended to give every federal agency subpoena authority in formal proceedings. 1 CFR 305.74–1. The ACUS proposal, supported by the American Bar Association, had not yet been enacted when this book went to press.

3. See ACUS Recommendation No. 70–4. 1 CFR 305.70–4. The study on which the recommendation was based is E. Tomlinson, Discovery in Agency Adjudication, 1971 Duke L.J. 89.

4. Recommendations and Reports of the Admin.Conf. of the U.S., vol. 1, at 579–580 (1970).

closely resembling those embodied in the Federal Rules of Civil Procedure.[5] Subsequently the preponderant number of federal agencies significantly involved in adjudicatory proceedings adopted rules of practice substantially conforming with the Conference recommendation.[6]

Among the states, too, the use of discovery has expanded. A significant number of states have provided general discovery authority for all agencies,[7] and the 1981 draft Model State Administrative Procedure Act contains a provision to that end.[8]

Before joy reign unconfined because benighted administrators have moved (or been forced to move) toward emulating the methods of enlightened judges, it may be well to remember that assertions of discovery abuse and calls for discovery reform have been prominent for some time.[9]   Moreover, a well informed scholar has written, "litigants in the federal courts often can afford to spend several years on discovery because congested court calendars do not permit a speedy trial; agencies cannot afford such delays if they are to enforce the law and

---

5. Of these three, however, only the Federal Maritime Commission allowed private parties routinely to take depositions of agency employees. See Tomlinson, note 3 above, at 107n. The Federal Trade Commission practices have been criticized because they did not wholly adopt the federal rules' approach of leaving discovery under the parties' control; under those rules, "the party seeking discovery need only file notice of his intent, and judicial intervention occurs only if the party against whom recovery is sought resists. If there is a contest, the resisting party has the burden of showing good cause why the discovery should not take place. Under the FTC rules, however, application must be made to the administrative law judge each time a deposition or subpoena for documents is sought. Furthermore, the party . . . must show that the deposition is necessary for purposes of discovery and . . . must show the general relevance of the documents and the reasonableness of the scope of the subpoena." J. Bennett, Post-Complaint Discovery in Administrative Proceedings: The FTC as a Case Study, 1975 Duke L.J. 329, 334. And see H. Shniderman, Securing Adequate Discovery in Administrative Proceedings, 25 Ad.L. Rev. 167 (1973).

6. See M. Paglin. Report on Implementation of Administrative Conference Recommendations 18, 34 (ACUS, May 1976).

7. E.g. West's Ann.Cal.Gov't.Code § 11507.6 (1968); N.Y.—McKinney's State Admin.Proc.Act Sec. 305 (1977); Vernon's Ann.Texas Civ.Stat art. 6252—13a, § 14a (1978); Wyo.Stat. § 16–3–107(a), (h) (1975); Tenn.Code Ann. § 4–5–311 (1982) (Cum. Supp.); Iowa Code Ann. § 17A.13 (1978): Wis.Stat.Ann. 227.08 (West 1982); Fla.Stat. Ann. § 120.58(1)(b) (Harrison's 1978).

8. See Para. 4–210, p. 1269 infra; Adams, State Administrative Procedure: The Role of

Intervention and Discovery in Adjudicatory Hearings, 74 N.W.U.L.Rev. 854 (1980).

9. The president of the A.B.A. declared in 1978: "The reasons for court congestion are many and varied, but one of them is the prolonging of litigation because of the abuse of discovery procedures. It is ironic that discovery has contributed to court congestion because when it was adopted in the 1930s, it was conceived of as a way of expediting litigation." W. Spann, Jr., Reforms Proposed for the Discovery Process, 64 A.B.A.J. 157 (1978). The chairman of the A.B.A. Section of Litigation has chimed in with the following: "One who traces the roots of modern legal processes cannot help but note the role torture has played in the development of criminal and civil procedure. For many centuries it was an established part of the legal process. Now lawyers are questioning whether trial by ordeal still lingers with us, now in the guise of discovery. . . . Indeed, the situation has gotten so out of hand that an eminent former jurist and now trial lawyer, Simon H. Rifkind, has commented: 'I believe it is fair to say that currently the power for the most massive invasion into private papers and private information is available to anyone willing to take the trouble to file a civil complaint.' And Judge Rifkind's experience is not unique. . . . Well-known consumer advocates Ralph Nader and Mark Green, in an article in the New York Times Sunday Magazine of November 20, 1977, discuss the rising concern of clients with high legal fees, a great part of which is attributable to discovery costs. . . . " W. Lundquist and H. Schechter, The New Relevancy: An End to Trial by Ordeal, 64 A.B.A.J. 59, 60 (1978). But see Schroeder and Franke, Discovery Reform: Long Road to Nowheresville, 68 A.B.A.J. 572 (1982).

uphold the public interest." [10]   These cavils do not prove that fuller "judicialization of the administrative process" would be, on balance, a loss rather than a gain. They do, however, suggest caution. The dangers that discovery procedures may add to already swollen expense and already irksome delay are heightened when, as often occurs in administrative matters, numerous parties are involved.

A question somewhat related to prehearing preparation is whether private parties may as a matter of right demand issuance of an agency's subpoenas to appear as a witness or to produce documentary material at the hearing itself. Must those who seek subpoenas instead make some special showing of need and of the relevance of the information whose production is sought to be compelled?

Federal district courts issue their subpoenas "signed and sealed but otherwise in blank" (Fed.Rules of Civ.Proc., Rule 45) to a party who requests them; the party then fills in the blank spaces and serves the subpoenas. Most federal administrative agencies, however, exercise fuller control over private parties' use of compulsory process. The Administrative Procedure Act, 5 U.S.C. § 555(d), provides that when an agency possesses statutory power to issue subpoenas, it shall issue them at a party's request "*and when required by rules of procedure, on a statement or showing of general relevance and reasonable scope of the evidence sought.*" Many rules do provide that this kind of preliminary showing must be made.

A district court's subpoenas, one may perhaps need to be reminded, have force only within the district itself or within a hundred miles of the place of trial. A federal agency's reach, in most instances, is nationwide, thus magnifying the possibility that distant witnesses may be burdened by parties' inconsiderate or possibly malicious use of compulsory process intended to obstruct hearings rather than to instruct hearers.[11] For this reason courts have on the whole quickly rejected parties' attacks on restrictive administrative rules or practices that have had the effect of hampering the private use of subpoenas.[12] Consider, for example, Papercraft Corp. v. FTC, 472 F.2d 927 (7th Cir.1973), involving a respondent's request for 551 subpoenas duces tecum addressed to other companies allegedly engaged in the relevant commerce. The respondent attacked the Commission's refusal to issue the subpoenas. The Commission pointed out that other means of reliably developing necessary industry data were already available. The court agreed with the administrative ruling because, as it said, "the service of so many subpoenas, and the processing of

---

10. Tomlinson, note 3 above, at 106. Compare K. Davis, Administrative Law Treatise, 1970 Supp. 393 (1971): "Judge Irving R. Kaufman quotes the [Davis] Treatise for the proposition that no sound reason can be given for lack of administrative discovery and says: 'I have also been unable to find any sound explanation for this situation.' Kaufman, Have Administrative Agencies Kept Pace with Modern Court-Developed Techniques against Delay?—A Judge's View, 12 Ad.L. Bull. 103, 115 (1959–60)."

11. As to the protections a witness may possibly demand, see F. Newman, Federal Agency Investigations: Procedural Rights of the Subpoenaed Witness, 60 Mich.L.Rev. 169 (1961).

12. See, e.g., Independent Directory Corp. v. FTC, 188 F.2d 468 (2d Cir.1951); Virginia Petroleum Jobbers Ass'n v. FPC, 293 F.2d 527 (D.C.Cir.), cert. denied 368 U.S. 940 (1961); Great Lakes Airlines, Inc. v. CAB, 291 F.2d 354 (9th Cir.), cert. denied 368 U.S. 890 (1961).

the responses, would inevitably tend to delay the proceedings and might unnecessarily require the disclosure of confidential data." [13]

Somewhat different considerations obtain when the issue is determining what information is already in the possession of a governmental agency, whether or not it be charged with the responsibility of adjudicating. Here, the question is not whether the agency has authority to compel disclosure; the question is, rather, whether the government absolutely must expose its files in order to enable an affected party to confront the case against it. When and how this is to be done becomes largely an issue of timing, rather than a simple matter of discovery; it is an element of a claim to know the record on the basis of which decision is being taken, or a claim that "fairness" requires government to disclose what it knows adverse to its own case.[14] Not surprisingly, specific provision is made in some agency rules for disclosure of materials in the agency's possession, provision more generous than those authorizing discovery of materials in the hands of other participants or third parties. E.g., 10 CFR §§ 2.720(h), 2.744, 2.790 (Nuclear Regulatory Commission).[15]

---

13. For additional examples, see American Brake Shoe Co., Docket 8622 (F.T.C.1965) (request to take depositions of 196 persons in nine states, without any showing of relevancy and without any concern for undue burden or delay); NLRB v. Blackstone Mfg. Co., 123 F.2d 633 (2d Cir. 1941) (employer sought to subpoena 121 employees to testify concerning authenticity of their signatures, though a far more convenient means of verification was available—"frivolous and dilatory demands," said the court); San Francisco Mining Exchange, 41 S.E.C. 860 (1964), affirmed 378 F.2d 162 (9th Cir.1967) (the five S.E.C. commissioners and the Commission's secretary were sought as witnesses in a proceeding then before the Commission for adjudication, thus creating "a serious potential for impairment of its impartiality and for harassment and delay of the administrative process"); Coro, Inc. v. FTC, 338 F.2d 149 (1st Cir.1964), cert. denied 380 U.S. 954 (1965) (subpoenas were sought to explore generally into the "policies and practices" of the agency, because the party had a "bare suspicion," unsupported by any specification, that the agency had been acting capriciously). And see Note, Reimbursement of Costs of Compliance with Administrative Subpoenas Duces Tecum, 48 Geo. Wash.L.Rev. 83 (1979).

14. See, e.g., Devine v. Cleland, 616 F.2d 1080 (9th Cir.1980); McCabe v. Department of Registration and Ed., 90 Ill. App.3d 1123, 46 Ill.Dec. 240, 413 N.E.2d

1353 (1980), cert. denied 454 U.S. 838 (1981).

15. In this connection refer to the discussion of Freedom of Information litigation in Chapter VI concerning issues of privilege. Some material in agency files is commercially valuable, supplied under a promise of confidence. Hence, even when administrative agencies have no objection to telling what they know and where they learned it, the source of information may strongly oppose divulgence. A telling study of this complicated problem has been published by the House Committee on Government Operations under the title "Freedom of Information Act Requests for Business Data and Reverse-FOIA Lawsuits," H.Rep. No. 95–1382 (95th Cong.2d Sess. 1978).

Courts have held that the permissible breadth of discovery by a private party to civil litigation involving an administrative agency is governed by the Federal Rules of Civil Procedure, unaffected by the Freedom of Information Act. See Clements Wire & Mfg. Co. v. NLRB, 589 F.2d 894 (5th Cir.1979); NLRB v. Martins Ferry Hospital Ass'n, 649 F.2d 445 (6th Cir.1981), cert. denied 454 U.S. 1083 (1981); Association for Women in Science v. Califano, 566 F.2d 339 (D.C.Cir.1977). And see Note, Discovery of Government Documents and the Official Information Privilege, 76 Colum.L.Rev. 142 (1976).

Chapter VI

OPEN GOVERNMENT

SECTION 1. THE FREEDOM OF INFORMATION ACT

In 1967, Congress enacted a Freedom of Information Act that sought to compel each federal agency to make "promptly available to any person" records that he had identified and requested in accordance with procedures to be amplified in the agency's rules. The act, codified as part of the Administrative Procedure Act, 5 U.S.C. § 552, also expanded previously existing obligations to make public information about agency structure, procedures and governing agency policy. As in the past, rules and organizational information were to be published in the Federal Register; the statute also required, however, that agencies index and make available for public inspection and copying all final opinions and orders in adjudicatory cases, statements of policy and interpretation, and staff manuals and instructions that affect a member of the public. 5 U.S.C. § 552(a)(1, 2). Failure to comply with these publicity requirements deprives the agency of its ability to rely on these possible sources of law, absent actual notice of them to the affected party.[1] These requirements are independent of public request.[2]

The obligation to make agency records available on request has drawn the greatest attention.[3] Note that the statute makes information

1. See Morton v. Ruiz, 415 U.S. 199 (1974). For a suggestion of the practical difficulties sometimes attending these publication, indexing and availability requirements see P.L. Strauss, Procedures of the Department of the Interior with respect to Mining Claims on Public Lands, 3 Recommendations & Reports of the Administrative Conference 451, 553–557 (1974); W. Gardner, The Informal Actions of the Federal Government, 26 Am.U.L.Rev. 799, 808–814 (1977).

2. "The primary purpose of subsection (a)(2) was to compel disclosure of what has been called 'secret law', or as the 1966 House Report put it, agency materials which have 'the force and effect of law in most cases.' H.R.Rept. 1497, 89th Cong., 2d Sess. 7 [1966]. Generally speaking, (a)(2) materials consist of those documents which contain what the agency has treated as authoritative indications of its position on legal or policy questions. It should be noted that some recent court decisions point towards a considerable broadening of the class of documents which meet these criteria." Attorney General's Memoran-

dum on the 1974 Amendments to the Freedom of Information Act 28 (U.S.Dept. of Justice Feb. 1975). See, e.g., Schlefer v. United States, 702 F.2d 233 (D.C.Cir.1983) (index-digests of Chief Counsel Opinions in the Maritime Administration, prepared for internal use and relied upon within the agency); Taxation With Representation Fund v. IRS, 646 F.2d 666 (D.C.Cir.1981) (IRS General Counsel's Memoranda). And see pp. 735–748 within.

3. The volume of litigation and scholarly commentary on the Freedom of Information Act is substantial. The major treatise, looseleaf in two volumes, is J. O'Reilly, Federal Information Disclosure; see also D. O'Brien, The Public's Right to Know (1981); R. Vaughn, A Guide to Practices and Procedure Under the Federal Freedom of Information Act, Privacy Act, Sunshine Act and Advisory Committee Act (1981); and A. Adler and M. Halperin, eds., Litigation under the Amended Federal FOIA (9th ed. 1984). An Annual Development Note has appeared since 1973 in a spring number of the Duke Law Journal; other regular publications include a De-

available to any *person* rather than only to a *party*. Previously, legal procedures to obtain information were limited to official bodies, or to participants in formal agency proceedings (to the extent agency rules might so provide), and information might be withheld "in the public interest," or "for good cause shown," or simply because the person who desired to have it was not "properly and directly concerned." The Act not only opened agency files, as a general rule, to requests for access from anyone who might wish it, but also imposed limits and structure on agencies desiring to maintain some privacy for those files. The obligation "promptly" to disclose was made general and enforceable in district court, in a proceeding to be given precedence on the court's calendar and tried de novo, with "the burden . . . on the agency to sustain its action." 5 U.S.C. § 552(a)(3).[4] Disclosure could be refused only on a determination that the matter in question fell within one or more of nine stated exemptive categories, each identifying a category of government-generated or privately supplied information or views for which confidentiality was thought appropriate. 5 U.S.C. § 552(b)(1–9). These nine exemptions, Judge Patricia Wald wrote recently, "are exclusive and are to be 'narrowly construed.' Yet they squeeze into a short subsection virtually every major dilemma, accommodation, and delicate balance that a modern democratic government faces: claims of national security in Exemption 1; trade secrets and confidential commercial information obtained from private companies in Exemption 4; confidential advice and recommendation underlying the formulation of public policy in Exemption 5; information that impermissibly invades personal privacy in Exemption 6 and investigative records compiled by law enforcement agencies in Exemption 7."[5]

Perhaps for these reasons, although congressional oversight[6] and facilitative coordination by the Department of Justice[7] contributed to speedy implementation of the Act, not all administrators welcomed

partment of Justice circular (FOIA Update, published by the Office of Information and Privacy), a commercial news letter (AC-CESS Reports), and publications of "public interest" suitors (The Freedom of Information Clearinghouse of the Center for the Study of Responsive Law and the University of Missouri Freedom of Information Center). See also Symposium, The Freedom of Information Act a Decade Later, 39 Pub.Ad.Rev. 310 (1979); Note, The Freedom of Information Act: A Seven-year Assessment, 74 Colum.L.Rev. 895 (1974); Project, Government Information Mich.L.Rev. 971 (1975). A. Mathews, The Darker Reaches of Government (1978) (comparative study of U.S.A., U.K., and Rep. So. Africa) and D. Rowat, The Right to Know: Essays on Governmental Policy and Public Access to Information (1981) (Canada) suggest comparative perspectives.

4. The requirement of priority has since been repealed. See p. 734 n. 22 below.

5. P. Wald, The Freedom of Information Act: A Short Case Study in The Perils

and Paybacks of Legislating Democratic Values, 33 Emory L.J. 649, 656–57 (1984).

6. See, e.g., Hearings on H.R. 5425 et al. Before the Subcomm. on Foreign Operations and Government Information of the House Committee on Government Operations, 23d Cong. 1st Sess. (1973).

7. Attorney General's Memorandum on the Public Information Section of the Administrative Procedure Act. U.S. Dept. of Justice, U.S. Gov't Printing Office June 1967. In late 1969 an advisory committee centered in the Office of Legal Counsel, Department of Justice, was formed to help agencies confronted by difficult choices under the FOIA. The advisory group's services have been increasingly utilized. R. Saloschin, The FOIA—A Governmental Perspective, 35 Public Admin.Rev. 10 (1975). The committee was supplanted in the fall of 1978 by an office under the supervision of the Associate Attorney General, now known as the Office of Information and Privacy.

inquiries.[8] Implementation of the Act was particularly disappointing for the press, whose news stories tended to perish while administrative processing of unwelcome requests dragged on. FOIA litigation became commonplace; congressional oversight became increasingly short-tempered with "foot dragging by the Federal bureaucracy" and the difficulties in convincing the "secrecy minded bureaucrat that public records are public property." [9] Delay and resistance were not wholly the product of petty spite; the agencies were unprepared to process the mass of often mammoth and undifferentiated requests which descended upon them,[10] and in general the considerations underlying the several exemptions Congress had recognized produced strong counterforces to the openness theme.[11] These countervailing considerations tended to be recognized and built upon by appellate courts in litigation under the Act, making plain that the release of possibly sensitive information was not a mere clerk's job, readily dispatched in the time previously given to filing records or distributing the day's mail.[12]

The resulting Congressional dissatisfactions produced amendments in 1974 [13] and, to lesser extent, in 1976.[14] Three of the Act's exemp-

8. See, e.g., R. Nader, Freedom From Information: The Act and the Agencies, 5 Harv.Civil Rights—Civil Liberties L.Rev. 1 (1970); L. Huard, The 1966 Public Information Act: An Appraisal without Enthusiasm, 2 Pub.Cont.L.J. 213 (1969).

9. Twenty-first Report by the Committee on Government Operations, H.R.Rep. No. 92–1419, 92d Cong., 2d Sess. (1972) 8–9.

10. "[N]o agency has control of its workload under the Act, which may crest or shift without warning. For example, in 1970 and 1971 the Agriculture Department was deeply involved in controversies over Freedom of Information requests, but in 1973 and 1974 this activity has fallen off sharply at Agriculture, while other agencies are experiencing large increases. Nor have any funds been specifically provided for the agencies or the Justice Department for work under the Act, the theory to date apparently being that this work can somehow be squeezed into the regularly funded activities of the agencies." R. Saloschin, n. 7 above, 35 Public Admin.Rev. at p. 11.

The Agriculture Department's problems are suggested by Freeman v. Seligson, 405 F.2d 1326 (D.C.Cir.1968). In that one case, approximately half a million documents were sought from the Secretary of Agriculture, to assist a trustee in bankruptcy who was exploring whether suits should be brought against persons with whom the bankrupt had done business. The Secretary contended that many of the desired records were protected by one or another privilege against disclosure (such as their being part of investigative files or intra-agency policy discussions). Remanding these contentions for further consideration by the trial court, the Court of Appeals remarked upon "the frequently, and in this case almost certain, laborious page-by-page examination which assertions of privilege will require, certainly of the Secretary and perhaps also of the court." (405 F.2d at 1338, 1339).

11. Compare with Judge Wald's remarks, above, the comments of then Acting Attorney General Bork to the Administrative Conference of the United States in 1973, quoted in R. Saloschin, note 7 above, 35 Public Admin.Rev. at p. 13: "Problems under the Freedom of Information Act, I think, partake of the nature of the most difficult constitutional issues. . . . [The Act's] basic thrust is disclosure and only when another critical value conflicts . . . does the Act permit nondisclosure. That is easy enough to say . . . but the adjustment of those basic and conflicting values in individual cases, I find at least, a nerve-wracking task."

12. Thus, agency and court were obliged to look closely at requested material, to segregate disclosable fact from what might be kept confidential. See Bristol-Myers Co. v. FTC, 424 F.2d 935 (D.C.Cir. 1970), cert. denied 400 U.S. 824 (1970); Vaughn v. Rosen, 484 F.2d 820 (D.C.Cir. 1973), cert. denied 415 U.S. 977 (1973).

13. P.L. 93–502, 94th Cong. 1st Sess. (1974). The legislative history has been compiled in a Freedom of Information Act and Amendments of 1974 (P.L. 93–502) Sourcebook by the Subcomm. on Government Information and Individual Rights of the House Comm. on Government Operations (1975). And see Note, The Freedom of Information Act Amendments of 1974: An Analysis, 26 Syr.L.Rev. 951 (1975).

14. Government in the Sunshine Act. P.L. 94–409, § 5(b), 90 Stat. 1247 (1976); Note,

tions were made more specific, in response to court opinions believed by the Congress to encourage too great a degree of withholding.[15] Congress also adopted a judicially devised solution to the problem presented by a document or file that contains both exempt and disclosable matter. "Any reasonably segregable portion of a record shall be provided to any person requesting such record after deletion of the portions which are exempt under this subsection." 5 U.S.C. § 552(b). (We consider some exemptions in more detail below.)

The 1974 amendments provided for agency, judicial and oversight procedures intended to produce openness, uniformity, ease of access, and speed in the bureaucratic processing of FOIA requests. Under these procedures, to be supplemented by agency rules, an initial request need only "reasonably describe" the records desired; the agency is given ten working days to identify the documents at issue and make an initial decision to release or withhold; this period may be extended for an additional ten days by written notice, but only if the request is voluminous or requires the assistance of field offices or other separate entities; if any information is denied, the requester must be told of his right to appeal to "the head of the agency," in practice often a designated subordinate, who has an additional twenty working days to consider the appeal; a ten day extension is again possible. If one of the specified periods lapses without action being taken, the requester is free to sue, and a court called upon for relief may grant it, even though the agency has not acted, unless the government "can show exceptional circumstances exist and that the agency is exercising due diligence in response to the request. . . . "[16] Any agency denials of information must set out the names and titles of each person responsible for decision. 5 U.S.C. § 552(a)(6). Records to be disclosed must be made "promptly available," at fees which may not exceed the direct costs of

The Effect of the 1976 Amendment to Exemption Three of the Freedom of Information Act, 76 Colum.L.Rev. 1029 (1976).

15. Thus, Environmental Protection Agency v. Mink, 410 U.S. 73 (1973) held that courts were to accept the fact that the government had classified a document "confidential" or "secret" as sufficient to excuse production of the whole document from public disclosure under the first exemption of the Act; in Weisberg v. United States Dept. of Justice, 489 F.2d 1195 (D.C. Cir.1973), cert. denied 416 U.S. 993 (1973), the seventh exemption (for material in investigatory files) was taken to apply to the entire file, which need neither be inspected by the judge or reviewed for the presence of material releasable without harm to investigation interests. Cf. Frankel v. SEC, 460 F.2d 813 (2d Cir.1972), cert. denied 409 U.S. 889 (1972). These interpretations did not survive the 1974 amendments. Cf. NLRB v. Robbins Tire & Rubber Co., 437 U.S. 214 (1978). The 1976 amendment made the FOIA's third exemption, for materials made confidential by statute,

more specific in response to an expansive reading of the exemption given in Administrator, Federal Aviation Administration v. Robertson, 422 U.S. 255 (1975).

16. The FBI, in particular, has been faced with a backlog of thousands of requests. See Open America v. Watergate Special Prosecution Force, 547 F.2d 605 (D.C.Cir.1976), excusing delay for this reason; Note, Developments Under the Freedom of Information Act—1976, 1977 Duke L.J. 532, 533–538, characterized the case as "a broad judicial capitulation to budgetary exigencies . . . ," but a highly regarded committee of attorneys concluded that its approach "best serves the public interest." Committee on Federal Legislation, Assoc. of the Bar of the City of New York, Freedom of Information Reform Act—S.774 (1983) p. 8. One court has held that a demonstration of compelling need can move a request "up the line." Exner v. FBI, 542 F.2d 1121 (9th Cir.1976). See also Crooker v. United States Marshals Service, 577 F.Supp. 1217 (D.D.C.1983).

search and duplication and which should be waived or reduced where "furnishing the information can be considered as primarily benefitting the general public." 5 U.S.C. § 552(a)(3, 4).

The judicial process was equally cabined. To the existing requirement that FOIA suits be given priority on the calendar and in a proceeding de novo, Congress added a thirty day limit on the government's ordinary time to answer; in determining whether the agency has met its burden to sustain its refusal to disclose, the court may examine the documents in camera; if the requester "substantially prevail[s]," [17] the court may assess reasonable attorney fees and costs against the United States; if it also finds that the withholding may have been arbitrary or capricious, its finding initiates a Merit System Protection Board proceeding for possible administrative discipline of the offending official. 5 U.S.C. § 552(a)(4). Finally, an entirely new section of the Act created congressional oversight mechanisms which again suggest that Congress' greater concern is to detect irresponsible denials of access to information, not inappropriate disclosures. 5 U.S.C. § 552(d).

While resistance to governmental disclosure continues, notably in the context of information thought important to national security,[18] one's impression is that information respecting the contents of government files is far more widely available today than it was a decade ago, and that the bureaucracy as a whole is becoming accustomed to the new ethic.[19] Numerous success stories are told, in which use of the Act has contributed significantly to public awareness—ranging from information about the Bay of Pigs invasion to environmental hazards, from

17. See, e.g., Exner v. FBI, 612 F.2d 1202 (9th Cir.1980).

18. The wording of exemption 1 to FOIA permitted President Reagan to accomplish a significant restriction of national defense and foreign policy information without legislative action. The exemption excludes information classified "under criteria established by an Executive order," and Executive Order 12,356, 47 Fed.Reg. 14874 (April 2, 1982) substantially broadened the range of information subject to valid classification. See Note, Developments Under the Freedom of Information Act-1983, 1984 Duke L.J. 377, 386–391.

In 1984, Congress passed the Civil Intelligence Information Act, P.L. 98–477, 98 Stat. 2209, generally excluding defined operational files of the Central Intelligence Agency from the Freedom of Information Act and providing special procedures for judicial review of FOIA denials by the CIA, procedures giving heightened interim protection to the materials at issue. The legislative history of the measure asserts substantial agreement among FOIA proponents as well as CIA officials that the measure's chief impact will be to make it "less burdensome for the CIA to deny access to files that are already exempt"; in that way, the measure was expected to free CIA resources to deal with a two-to-three year backlog of requests that had made the FOIA "all but useless" in dealing with the agency. H.Rep. No. 98–726, 98th Cong. 2d Sess., Pt. I, p. 5, Pt. II, p. 7 (1984).

19. From 1974 to 1981, FOIA requests grew at the rate of 27% per year. W. Casey, Jr., J. Martinson, & L. Moss, Entrepreneurships, Productivity and the FOIA 63 (1983). At the FDA, for example, among the most active of FOIA agencies, 33,587 requests were filed in 1981, and 454 were initially denied; the Department of Health and Human Services as a whole received 50,065 FOIA requests and initially denied 1,173 of them; 155 appeals were taken, and sixty of these were successful, in whole or in part. Annual Report of the Department of Health and Human Services on FOI Activities (1981). A 1975 survey of 9 government agencies showed 90% of requests being granted. Subcomm. on Oversight and Investigations, House Comm. on Interstate and Foreign Commerce, 94th Cong.2d Sess. Report on Federal Regulation and Regulatory Reform 569 (Comm. Print 1976).

consumer protection to inefficiency and corruption.[20] Despite repeated efforts at "reform," Congress has not significantly altered the Act's coverage since 1976.[21] Section 552(a)(4)(D), which gave FOIA review proceedings special priority in federal district court, was formally repealed in 1984 as part of a statute generally repudiating such special provisions and substituting a general "good cause" test for expedition; yet the new statute appears to have given back most of what it took away, specifically identifying as "good cause" a showing that "rights under Section 552 of title 5" would be enhanced by expedition.[22]

In giving FOIA claims such dramatic support, Congress underscores the importance now attached to openness; but the side effects of its judgments on the performance of agency functions may also be worthy of attention. The Chairman of the Securities & Exchanges Commission remarked to a 1976 Conference on Government Information Needs and Business Disclosure that, as a result of the Act, "companies have reassessed their willingness to cooperate with our investigations. More and more our staff comes in and looks but takes no documents out, and even when we subpoena documents that were formerly handed over voluntarily, we find an increasing number of companies resisting our subpoenas because of fears that information in our files may be taken out by FOIA request.

"Eight times this past year we had to go before a U.S. District judge to get an order to secure information from companies who were perfectly willing to give the information to the SEC for our enforcement purposes but who wished the court to condition its availability by instructing the SEC not to make it available to any other parties without first getting the court's approval." [23]

The Chairman was also concerned that "the manpower and monetary resources of the Commission are being diverted from its primary goals to serve what may be best termed as a secondary goal." He thought it took an average of thirty hours to satisfy a Freedom of

---

20. See P. Wald, note 5 above, passim.

21. In 1984 the Senate unanimously passed a bill, S. 774, that would have broadened exemptions 2, 6 and 7, restricted usage of FOIA by felons and non-citizens, provided explicit procedural rights for private submitters of information that becomes subject to a FOIA request, and permitted the government to capture a higher proportion of its search costs and any commercial value of information created at public expense. 130 Cong.Rec. 51794 (Feb. 27, 1984). It died in the House. See Note, Developments Under the Freedom of Information Act—1983, 1984 Duke L.J. 377, 383. In 1986, as part of the anti-drug abuse act of 1986, P.L. 99–570, —— Stat. ——, Congress tightened the seventh exemption (for investigating material) and adapted an elaborate provision on fees for users of the act.

22. P.L. 98–620, Section 401, 98 Stat. 3356, enacting 28 U.S.C. § 1657 and repealing (inter alia) 5 U.S.C. § 552(a)(4)(D) (1984); H.Rep. 98–985, 98th Cong., 2d Sess.

1, 6 (1984) is explicit both that the "ad hoc and random" provisions of United States law granting priority to various sorts of civil actions are to be eliminated, and "that the 'good cause' provision [of 28 U.S.C. § 1657 is to] be liberally construed by the courts in granting requests for expedited consideration under the Freedom of Information Act."

23. An FTC official reported in 1981 that the Commission had found companies under investigation more willing to provide information voluntarily in the wake of a legislative change sharply increasing the protection of business papers in FTC hands from FOIA disclosure. B. Rubin, Spotlight on FTC Experience, 34 Ad.L.Rev. 151, 155 (1982).

The CIA's repeatedly voiced concerns about similar impacts on its intelligence activities contributed to the legislative development described in note 18 above. Neither it nor the FBI appear able, to date, to demonstrate actual compromise of data or informants, however. Wald, note 5 above, 33 Emory L.J. at 672–76.

Information Act request. And, while a House Report had predicted the costs attributable to the bill should not exceed $100,000 a year throughout government, he estimated that in 1975 the SEC alone had spent several hundred thousand dollars.[24]

a. Freedom of Information and Government Need for Confidentiality

5 U.S.C. § 552(b): "This section does not apply to matters that are—

(1)(A) specifically authorized under criteria established by an Executive order to be kept secret in the interest of national defense or foreign policy and (B) are in fact properly classified pursuant to such Executive order;

. . .

(5) inter-agency or intra-agency memorandums or letters which would not be available by law to a party other than an agency in litigation with the agency;

. . .

(7) records or information compiled for law enforcement purposes, but only to the extent that the production of such law enforcement records or information (A) could reasonably be expected to interfere with enforcement proceedings, (B) would deprive a person of a right to a fair trial or an impartial adjudication, (C) could reasonably be expected to constitute an unwarranted invasion of personal privacy, (D) could reasonably be expected to disclose the identity of a confidential source, including a State, local, or foreign agency or authority or any private institution which furnished information on a confidential basis, and, in the case of a record or information compiled by criminal law enforcement authority in the course of a criminal investigation or by an agency conducting a lawful national security intelligence investigation, information furnished by a confidential source, (E) would disclose techniques and procedures for law enforcement investigations or prosecutions, or would disclose guidelines for law enforcement investigations or prosecutions if such disclosure could reasonably be expected to risk circumvention of the law, or (F) could reasonably be expected to endanger the life or physical safety of any individual;*

. . .

Any reasonably segregable portion of a record shall be provided to any person requesting such record after deletion of the portions which are exempt under this subsection."

NATIONAL LABOR RELATIONS BOARD v. SEARS, ROEBUCK & CO.

Supreme Court of the United States, 1975.
421 U.S. 132.

[Sears, Roebuck & Co. had unsuccessfully urged a Regional Director of the Board to file an unfair labor practice complaint against a labor union with which it was engaged in collective bargaining. The Regional Director refused, the company was told, because Sears had delayed taking certain steps in the bargaining; he was guided in his judgment

---

24. H.R.Rep. No. 876, 93d Cong., 2d Sess. 10 (1974). In 1982, the GAO told the House Committee on Government Operations, 2,577 government employees spent 295,312 working days on FOIA matters;   total costs for that year, it told the Senate Committee on Judiciary, exceeded $61 million.

* As amended by the Anti-Drug Abuse Act of 1986, P.L. 99–570, 100 Stat. 3207.

by internal advice received from the General Counsel of the Board. His refusal was appealable to the General Counsel. While preparing its appeal, Sears requested disclosure of various memoranda and indices generated by the Office of the General Counsel in deciding whether or not to issue unfair labor practice complaints. The General Counsel resisted, principally on the ground that the fifth exemption to the FOIA, 5 U.S.C. § 552(b)(5) permitted him to refuse disclosure of "intra-agency memorandums . . . which would not be available by law . . . . in litigation with an agency." Sears brought suit in United States District Court for the District of Columbia, claiming that the documents it sought were disclosable both as "final opinions" or "instructions to staff that affect a member of the public" (5 U.S.C. § 552(a)(2)) and as "identifiable records" not within any exemptive category (5 U.S.C. § 552(a)(3)). After the General Counsel failed in efforts to settle the dispute, the district court granted Sears sweeping relief; the court of appeals affirmed without opinion.][1]

MR. JUSTICE WHITE delivered the opinion of the Court.

. . .

A

The parties are in apparent agreement that Exemption 5 withholds from a member of the public documents which a private party could not discover in litigation with the agency. EPA v. Mink, 410 U.S. 73, 85–86 (1973). Since virtually any document not privileged may be discovered by the appropriate litigant, if it is relevant to his litigation; and since the Act clearly intended to give any member of the public as much right to disclosure as one with a special interest therein, it is reasonable to construe Exemption 5 to exempt those documents, and only those documents, normally privileged in the civil discovery context.[2] The privileges claimed by the government to be relevant to this case are (i) the "generally . . . recognized" privilege for "confidential intra-agen-

---

1. [Ed.] Should NLRB proceedings have been stayed pending judicial decision? In a separate action, the D.C. Circuit had vacated a district court order staying the Labor Board proceedings pending final resolution of the FOIA dispute. Sears, Roebuck and Co. v. NLRB, 473 F.2d 91 (1972), cert. denied, 415 U.S. 950 (1974). The court of appeals had concluded that Sears had not demonstrated "irreparable harm" from being forced to proceed without the documents in question. In fact, Sears persuaded the General Counsel to issue an unfair labor practice complaint, and the resulting proceedings were complete before the Court rendered its decision. Thus the Supreme Court did not have to address the issue. It noted, however, that "Sears' rights under the Act are neither increased nor decreased by reason of the fact that it claims an interest in the Advice and Appeals Memoranda greater than that shared by the average member of the public. The Act is fundamentally designed to inform the public about agency action and not to benefit private litigants." 421 U.S. at 143

n. 10. Following this analysis, courts have generally declined to acknowledge special claims that might arise from use of FOIA for discovery purposes. See New England Apple Council v. Donovan, 725 F.2d 139 (1st Cir.1984); Lead Industries Ass'n v. OSHA, 610 F.2d 70 (2d Cir.1979).

2. The ability of a private litigant to override a privilege claim set up by the Government, with respect to an otherwise disclosable document, may itself turn on the extent of the litigant's need in the context of the facts of his particular case; or on the nature of the case. . . . However, it is not sensible to construe the Act to require disclosure of any document which would be disclosed in the hypothetical litigation in which the private party's claim is the most compelling. Indeed, the House Report says that Exemption 5 was intended to permit disclosure of those intra-agency memoranda which would "routinely be disclosed" in private litigation, H.R.Rep. No. 1497, p. 10, and we accept this as the law.

cy advisory opinions . . . ," disclosure of which would be "injurious to the consultative functions of government . . . ." EPA v. Mink, supra, at 86–87, (sometimes referred to as "executive privilege"), and (ii) the attorney-client and attorney work product privileges generally available to all litigants.

(i)

That Congress had the Government's executive privilege specifically in mind in adopting Exemption 5 is clear . . . . The precise contours of the privilege in the context of this case are less clear, but may be gleaned from expressions of legislative purpose and the prior case law. The cases uniformly rest the privilege on the policy of protecting the "decision making processes of government agencies" . . . and focus on documents "reflecting advisory opinions, recommendations and deliberations comprising part of a process by which governmental decisions and policies are formulated." Carl Zeiss Stiftung v. E.B. Carl Zeiss, Jena, 40 F.R.D., at 324 [D.D.C.1966]. The point, plainly made in the Senate Report, is that the frank discussion of legal and policy matters in writing might be inhibited if the discussion were made public; and that the "decisions" and "policies formulated" would be the poorer as a result. . . . As . . . we have said in an analogous context, "[h]uman experience teaches that those who expect public dissemination of their remarks may well temper candor with a concern for appearances . . . to the *detriment of the decisionmaking process.*" United States v. Nixon, 418 U.S. 683, 705 (1974) (emphasis added).[3]

Manifestly, the ultimate purpose of this long-recognized privilege is to prevent injury to the quality of agency decisions. The quality of a particular agency decision will clearly be affected by the communications received by the decisionmaker on the subject of the decision prior to the time the decision is made. However, it is difficult to see how the quality of a decision will be affected by communications with respect to the decision occurring after the decision is finally reached; and therefore equally difficult to see how the quality of the decision will be affected by forced disclosure of such communications, as long as prior communications and the ingredients of the decisionmaking process are not disclosed. Accordingly, the lower courts have uniformly drawn a distinction between predecisional communications, which are privileged,[4] . . . and communications made after the decision and designed to explain it, which are not.[5] . . . The public is only marginally

---

3. Our remarks in United States v. Nixon were made in the context of a claim of "executive privilege" resting solely on the Constitution of the United States. No such claim is made here and we do not mean to intimate that any documents involved here are protected by whatever constitutional content the doctrine of executive privilege might have.

4. Our emphasis on the need to protect predecisional documents does not mean that the existence of the privilege turns on

the ability of an agency to identify a specific decision in connection with which a memorandum is prepared. Agencies are, and properly should be, engaged in a continuing process of examining their policies; this process will generate memoranda containing recommendations which do not ripen into agency decisions; and the lower courts should be wary of interfering with this process.

5. We are aware that the line between predecisional documents and postdecisional

concerned with reasons supporting a policy which an agency has rejected, or with reasons which might have supplied, but did not supply, the basis for a policy which was actually adopted on a different ground. In contrast, the public is vitally concerned with the reasons which did supply the basis for an agency policy actually adopted. These reasons, if expressed within the agency, constitute the "working law" of the agency and have been held by the lower courts to be outside the protection of Exemption 5. Bannercraft v. Renegotiation Board, 466 F.2d 345, 352 (D.C.Cir.1972). Exemption 5, properly construed, calls for "disclosure of all 'opinions and interpretations'—which embody the agency's effective law and policy, and the withholding of all papers which reflect the agency's group thinking in the process of working out its policy and determining what its law shall be." Davis, The Information Act: A Preliminary Analysis, 34 U.Chi.L.Rev. 761, 797; Note, Freedom of Information Act and the Exemption for Inter-Agency Memoranda, 86 Harv.L.Rev. 1047.

This conclusion is powerfully supported by the other provisions of the Act. The affirmative portion of the Act, expressly requiring indexing of "final opinions," "statements of policy and interpretations which have been adopted by the agency," and "instructions to staff that affect a member of the public," 5 U.S.C. § 552(a)(2), represents a strong congressional aversion to "secret agency law," Davis, supra, at 797; and represents an affirmative congressional purpose to require disclosure of documents which have "the force and effect of law." We should be reluctant therefore to construe Exemption 5 to apply to the documents described in 5 U.S.C. § 552(a)(2); and with respect at least to "final opinions," which not only invariably explain agency action already taken or an agency decision already made, but also constitute "final dispositions" of matters by an agency, we hold that Exemption 5 can never apply.[6]

(ii)

It is equally clear that Congress had the attorney work product privilege specifically in mind when it adopted Exemption 5 and that such a privilege had been recognized in the civil discovery context by the prior case law. . . . Whatever the outer boundaries of the attorney work product rule are, the rule clearly applies to memoranda

---

documents may not always be a bright one. Indeed, even the prototype of the postdecisional document—the "final opinion"— serves the dual function of explaining the decision just made and providing guides for decisions of similar or analogous cases arising in the future. In its latter function, the opinion is predecisional; and the manner in which it is written may, therefore, affect decisions in later cases. For present purposes it is sufficient to note that final opinions are *primarily* postdecisional— looking back on and explaining, as they do, a decision already reached or a policy already adopted—and that their disclosure poses a negligible risk of denying to agency decisionmakers the uninhibited advice which is so important to agency decisions.

6. See Note, 86 Harv.L.Rev. 1047. Technically, of course, if a document could be, for example, both a "final opinion" and an intra-agency memorandum within Exemption 5, it would be nondisclosable, since the Act "does not apply" to documents falling within any of the exemptions.

prepared by an attorney in contemplation of litigation which set forth the attorney's theory of the case and his litigation strategy.

B

Applying these principles to the memoranda sought by Sears, it becomes clear that Exemption 5 does not apply to those Appeals and Advice Memoranda which conclude that no complaint should be filed and which have the effect of finally denying relief to the charging party; but that Exemption 5 does protect from disclosure those Appeals and Advice Memoranda which direct the filing of a complaint and the commencement of litigation before the Board.

(i)

Under the procedures employed by the General Counsel, Advice and Appeals Memoranda are communicated to the Regional Director *after* the General Counsel, through his Advice and Appeals Branches, has decided whether or not to issue a complaint; and represent an explanation to the Regional Director of a legal or policy decision already adopted by the General Counsel. In the case of decisions *not* to file a complaint, the Memoranda effect as "final" a "disposition" as an administrative decision can—representing, as it does, an unreviewable rejection of the charge filed by the private party. Disclosure of these Memoranda would not intrude on predecisional processes, and protecting them would not improve the quality of agency decisions, since when the Memoranda are communicated to the Regional Director, the General Counsel has already reached his decision and the Regional Director who receives them has no decision to make—he is bound to dismiss the charge. Moreover, the General Counsel's decisions not to file complaints together with the Advice and Appeals Memoranda explaining them, are precisely the kind of agency law in which the public is so vitally interested and which Congress sought to prevent the agency from keeping secret.[7]

. . .

For essentially the same reasons, these Memoranda are "final opinions" made in the "adjudication of cases" which must be indexed pursuant to 5 U.S.C. § 552(a)(2)(A). . . .

---

7. The General Counsel argues that he makes no law, analogizing his authority to decide whether or not to file a complaint to a public prosecutor's authority to decide whether a criminal case should be brought, and claims that he does not adjudicate anything resembling a civil dispute. Without deciding whether a public prosecutor makes "law" when he decides not to prosecute or whether memoranda explaining such decisions are "final opinions," it is sufficient to note that the General Counsel's analogy is far from perfect. The General Counsel, unlike most prosecutors, may authorize the filing of a complaint with the Board only if a private citizen files a "charge." Unlike the victim of a crime, the charging party will, if a complaint is filed by the General Counsel, become a party to the unfair labor practice proceeding before the Board. And, if an unfair labor practice is found to exist, the ensuing cease and desist order will, unlike the punishment of the defendant in a criminal case, coerce conduct by the wrongdoer flowing particularly to the benefit of the charging party.

(ii)

Advice and Appeals Memoranda which direct the filing of a complaint, on the other hand, fall within the coverage of Exemption 5. The filing of a complaint does not finally dispose even of the General Counsel's responsibility with respect to the case. The case will be litigated before and decided by the Board; and the General Counsel will have the responsibility of advocating the position of the charging party before the Board. The Memoranda will inexorably contain the General Counsel's theory of the case and may communicate to the Regional Director some litigation strategy or settlement advice. Since the Memoranda will also have been prepared in contemplation of the upcoming litigation, they fall squarely within Exemption 5's protection of an attorney's work product. At the same time, the public's interest in disclosure is substantially reduced by the fact . . . that the basis for the General Counsel's legal decision will come out in the course of litigation before the Board; and that the "law" with respect to these cases will ultimately be made not by the General Counsel but by the Board or the courts.

We recognize that an Advice or Appeals Memorandum directing the filing of a complaint . . . has many of the characteristics of the documents described in 5 U.S.C. § 552(a)(2). Although not a "final opinion" in the "adjudication" of a "case" because it does not effect a "final disposition," the Memorandum does explain a decision already reached by the General Counsel which has real operative effect—it permits litigation before the Board; and we have indicated a reluctance to construe Exemption 5 to protect such documents. We do so in this case only because the decisionmaker—the General Counsel—must become a litigating party to the case with respect to which he has made his decision. The attorney work-product policies which Congress clearly incorporated into Exemption 5 thus come into play and lead us to hold that the Advice and Appeals Memoranda directing the filing of a complaint are exempt whether or not they are, as the District Court held, "instructions to staff that affect a member of the public."

C

Petitioner asserts that the District Court erred in holding that documents incorporated by reference in non-exempt Advice and Appeals Memoranda lose any exemption they might previously have held as "intra-agency" memoranda.[8] We disagree.

The probability that an agency employee will be inhibited from freely advising a decisionmaker for fear that his advice *if adopted,* will become public is slight. First, when adopted, the reasoning becomes that of the agency and becomes *its* responsibility to defend. Second, agency employees will generally be encouraged rather than discouraged by public knowledge that their policy suggestions have been adopted by

---

8. It should be noted that the documents incorporated by reference are, in the main, factual documents which are proba-bly not entitled to Exemption 5 treatment in the first place.

the agency. Moreover, the public interest in knowing the reasons for policy actually adopted by an agency supports the District Court's decision below. Thus, we hold that, if an agency chooses *expressly* to adopt or incorporate by reference an intra-agency memorandum previously covered by Exemption 5 in what would otherwise be a final opinion, that memorandum may be withheld only on the ground that it falls within the coverage of some exemption other than Exemption 5.

The Government also asserts that the District Court's order erroneously requires it to produce or create explanatory material in those instances in which an Appeals Memorandum refers to "the circumstances of the case." We agree. The Act does not compel agencies to write opinions in cases in which they would not otherwise be required to do so. It only requires disclosure of certain documents which the law requires the agency to prepare or which the agency has decided for its own reasons to create . . . .

. . .

Judgment affirmed in part and reversed in part and case remanded.

The CHIEF JUSTICE concurs in the judgment.

MR. JUSTICE POWELL took no part in the consideration or decision of this case.

ARTHUR ANDERSEN & CO. v. INTERNAL REVENUE SERVICE

United States Court of Appeals, District of Columbia Circuit, 1982.
679 F.2d 254.

Before WRIGHT and WALD, CIRCUIT JUDGES, and CELEBREZZE, SENIOR CIRCUIT JUDGE for the Sixth Circuit.

WALD, CIRCUIT JUDGE: . . .

On March 5, 1979, Arthur Andersen & Co., a national public accounting firm, requested of the IRS, pursuant to FOIA and IRS public disclosure rules, "a copy of the Internal Revenue Service file on Revenue Ruling 77–284" and "a copy of any background file documents as defined in Section 301.6110–2(g) related to Revenue Ruling 77–284." On July 20, 1979, the IRS notified Andersen that certain documents in the file would be released but that others were exempt from FOIA disclosure requirements. Following an unsuccessful administrative appeal, Andersen filed a complaint in the district court on March 19, 1980.

On June 11, 1980, the parties . . . agreed to submit the documents to the court for in camera inspection and to each file "position papers" setting forth its case for disclosure or exemption and a reply to the other party's position paper. Andersen further agreed not to pursue discovery and to be bound by the determination of the district court based on these submissions. The court approved the stipulation two days later. . . . On May 21, 1981, the district court . . . ordered disclosure of them all. . . .

Exemption 5 permits an agency to withhold documents that "would not normally be discoverable by a private party in the course of civil litigation with the agency." Jordan v. Department of Justice, supra, 591 F.2d [753,] 772 [(D.C.Cir.1978) (en banc)]. "Congress intended that agencies should not lose the protection traditionally afforded through the evidentiary privileges simply because of the passage of the FOIA." Coastal States Gas Corp. v. Department of Energy, 617 F.2d 854, 862 (D.C.Cir.1980). Among those privileges protected by Exemption 5 is the "executive 'deliberative process' privilege," id., which is "unique to the government." Id. at 866. This privilege covers " 'all papers which reflect the agency's group thinking in the process of working out its policy and determining what its law shall be.' " NLRB v. Sears, Roebuck & Co., supra, 421 U.S. at 153. . . . "[P]redecisional documents are thought generally to reflect the agency 'give-and-take' leading up to a decision that is characteristic of the deliberative process; whereas post-decisional documents often represent the agency's position on an issue, or explain such a position, and thus may constitute the 'working law' of an agency" which Congress intended by FOIA to make accessible to the public. Taxation With Representation Fund v. IRS, 646 F.2d 666, 677 (D.C.Cir.1981). Thus, in general, predecisional communications are likely to qualify as privileged and "communications made after the decision and designed to explain it" are not. NLRB v. Sears, supra, 421 U.S. at 151–52.

. . .

FOIA imposes on the Agency the burden "to sustain its action" in withholding documents. 5 U.S.C. § 552(a)(4)(B). The Agency must thus carry the burden of establishing that documents contain "the ideas and theories which go into the making of the law" and not "the law itself," Sterling Drug, Inc. v. FTC, 450 F.2d 698, 708 (D.C.Cir.1971). This involves showing "what deliberative process is involved, and the role played by the documents in issue in the course of that process." Coastal States, supra, 617 F.2d at 868. To establish that documents do not constitute the "working law" of the agency, the agency must present to the court the "function and significance of the document[s] in the agency's decisionmaking process," Taxation With Representation, supra, 646 F.2d at 678, "the nature of the decisionmaking authority vested in the office or person issuing the disputed document[s]," id. at 679, and the positions in the chain of command of the parties to the documents. Id. at 681.

The procedures by which an agency must ordinarily make such a showing were defined in Vaughn v. Rosen, 484 F.2d 820 (D.C.Cir.1973), cert. denied, 415 U.S. 977 (1974). "[T]o allow the courts to determine the validity of the government's claims without physically examining each document," Coastal States, supra, 617 F.2d at 861, . . . [and b]ecause the party seeking disclosure is ignorant of the contents of withheld documents . . . , Vaughn required that an agency justify withholding of documents through itemized and indexed explanations. Otherwise, the burden of justification would be imposed on the court. As Vaughn explained,

[t]he burden has been placed specifically by statute on the Government. Yet under existing procedures, the Government claims all it need do to fulfill its burden is to aver that the factual nature of the information is such that it falls under one of the exemptions. At this point the opposing party is comparatively helpless to controvert this characterization. If justice is to be done and the Government's characterization adequately tested, the burden now falls on the court system to make its own investigation. This is clearly not what Congress had in mind.

484 F.2d at 825–26.[1]

Here, however, the district court voluntarily assumed, through approval of the stipulation, the obligation of determining from the documents themselves and the "position papers" whether the documents were exempt [and] the issue before us is . . . whether the record evidence shows that the documents were part of a predecisional deliberative process.

The deliberative process from which a proposed revenue ruling emerges is described in the affidavit of Jerome Sebastian of the IRS Office of Chief Counsel, dated July 3, 1979, which explains the "function and significance" of drafts:

> The legal review by the Office of Chief Counsel . . . is only one of several levels of review involved in the consideration of the proposed determination, which generally originates in a division of the Office of the Assistant Commissioner (Technical). After a Technical employee prepares a draft of the proposed determination, it is reviewed at the Branch, and possibly the Division and Assistant Commissioner levels in Technical. Depending on the importance, complexity or sensitivity of the issue involved, the proposed determination may,

---

1. [Ed.] In Coastal States, 617 F.2d at 861, the court had found the Vaughn index inadequate in passages suggesting the dimension of that burden—one justified (in its view) by both the helplessness of the requesting party and the statutory purpose of disclosure:

"In lieu of in camera inspection, DOE submitted an index of the withheld documents, along with affidavits from regional counsel in support of its decision not to release the memoranda. . . .

"A typical line from the index supplied in this case identifies who wrote the memorandum, to whom it was addressed, its date, and a brief description of the memorandum such as 'Advice on audit of reseller whether product costs can include imported freight charges, discounts, or rental fees. Sections 212.93 and 212.92.' DOE claimed this document was 'PD' (predecisional), 'ATWP' (attorney work-product) and that 'some' of it was in an investigatory file. That is all we are told, save for the affidavits submitted by the regional counsel which repeat in conclusory terms that all the documents withheld fall within one or another of the exemptions.

"Such an index is patently inadequate to permit a court to decide whether the exemption was properly claimed. . . .

"Contrast the index submitted by the agency and described in Mead Data Central, Inc. v. U.S. Dep't of the Air Force, 566 F.2d 242 ([D.C.Cir.] 1977), which clearly describes the characteristics of the documents which the agency felt brought them within the exemption claimed, and which was still inadequate to permit the court to determine whether all elements of the privileges were present in each document."

In Mead Data, the test had been stated, in part, as whether "the withheld documents were described in sufficient detail to allow Mead Data to argue effectively against the Department's exemption claims."

but will not necessarily, be referred to higher review levels within the Service, or to the Interpretative Division, Office of Chief Counsel for legal review.

In camera review of the documents supports this description of the process. On their face there appear the number, identities and titles of the various persons in successively higher positions to whom the drafts were submitted for "approval" and the alterations these persons made in the text of the background note and revenue ruling. Thus, the flow of the documents was from subordinate to superior. Because approval was required at each higher level, all the participants up to the Commissioner were without authority to make a final determination. The Sebastian affidavit's description of the process complements the documents to adequately (albeit barely) establish their predecisional and deliberative nature. A comparison of the successive drafts with each other and with the final revenue ruling reveals no policy or reasons explained in these drafts that were not contained in the ruling ultimately published. The inference we draw from this is that these documents could not and do not serve as agency "working law," providing substantive guidance in future decisions. Andersen offers no evidence to the contrary. This contrasts markedly with the documents ordered released in Taxation With Representation, supra, 646 F.2d at 682, which (as revealed through discovery) were indexed, compiled, and consulted as sources of agency law by IRS employees. In this case, there is neither evidence nor a logical inference to be drawn from the documents that they would be so consulted. Nor, in foregoing discovery, can plaintiffs impose on the IRS the obligation to account for the ultimate disposition and use of the disputed documents. It is enough in the context of this case that the uncontradicted evidence shows the documents to be predecisional and deliberative, and thus eligible for Exemption 5 treatments.

. . .

The case is remanded to the district court with directions to enter judgment for the defendants.

NOTES

(1) We met the government's executive privilege, referred to in Sears, in Chapter II, Section 3 at p. 163. The relationship between that privilege and the FOIA warrants brief mention here.

Courts have long recognized two general headings of executive privilege. The first, corresponding roughly to the first exemption of the FOIA, relates to what have been often described as state secrets, matters relating to national security, either military or diplomatic. The second, most sharply reflected in the fifth and seventh exemptions, consists of "official information." The right to disclosure differs markedly with the two classifications. Because they pose patent dangers to the public interest, "disclosures that would impair national security or diplomatic relations are not required by the courts." Environmental Protection Agency v. Mink, 410 U.S. 73 (1973); Halkin v. Helms, 598 F.2d 1 (D.C.Cir.1978), affirmed after remand 690 F.2d 977 (1982). The disclosure of "official information," on the other hand, involves a far lesser danger to the public interest than the disclosure of "state secrets." Correspondingly, closer judicial review of contested documents and judicial balancing of the competing claims have long been accepted practice. See FTC v. Warner Communications, Inc., 742 F.2d 1156 (9th Cir.1984); United States v. Nixon, 418 U.S. 683, 705–707, 710–711 (1974).

At least until 1974, the Freedom of Information Act could be said not to have encroached on the previously recognized dimensions of "executive privilege." The "valid need for protection of communications" was accommodated by the express reference in exemption 5 to materials available through discovery in litigation and by the broad formulation of exemption 7; it was precisely in the discovery context that executive privilege in its broader dimension had been recognized.[1] And the unqualified exemption recognized for national security and foreign affairs information, in exemption 1, permitted the courts to avoid confrontation with the executive branch over information respecting intrinsic executive functions. In Environmental Protection Agency v. Mink, 410 U.S. 73 (1973) the Supreme Court had interpreted that language to make proof of classification in itself sufficient to establish the exemption's availability. The reviewing court was not to examine the document in camera or otherwise review classifiability.[2]

The 1974 amendments specifically overruled the holding in Mink, despite its constitutional overtones. As the statute now reads, the first exemption reaches only national defense or foreign policy matters that are "(A) specifically authorized under criteria established by an Executive order to be kept secret . . . and (B) are in fact properly classified

---

1. See generally, Note, Discovery of Government Documents and the Official Information Privilege, 76 Colum.L.Rev. 142 (1976). This aspect of the privilege has been characterized as having more a common law than a constitutional character, and applied equally to the Congress and the judiciary. A noted legal scholar, once Attorney General of the United States, has observed that "[T]he term executive privilege . . . fails to express the nature of the interests at issue; its emotive value presently exceeds and consumes what cognitive value it might have possessed. The need for confidentiality is old, common to all governments, essential to ours since its formation." E. Levi, Confidentiality and Democratic Government, 30 The Record 323 (1975). There seems little doubt that in its details, if not its core, this aspect of executive privilege is subject to statutory modification. Nixon v. Warner Communications, 435 U.S. 589 (1978); Nixon v. Administrator of General Services, 433 U.S. 425 (1977).

2. Then Professor Abraham Sofaer's painstaking and insightful review of the early sources suggests that this deference to executive branch views mirrors long-standing Congressional practice—a practice made the more striking by Congress' greater responsibilities for such matters: "The information practices observed in early American history, and largely followed today, . . . demonstrate the risks and limited utility of relying on the courts to bring about adjustments in the power of the legislative and executive branches. . . . [T]hey could involve the courts in highly charged conflicts over matters of great political complexity, . . . [forcing the Court] to decide such questions as which branch is the more deserving of its assistance, whether Congress would in fact assure confidentiality, and whether Congress was engaged in an effort to embarrass or obstruct a president rather than in some endeavor felt to be more constructive." A. Sofaer, Executive Power and the Control of Information: Practice Under the Framers, 1977 Duke L.J. 1, 48–53; see also United States v. American Telephone & Telegraph Co., 551 F.2d 384, 391 (D.C. Cir.1976); G. Casper, Constitutional Constraints on the Conduct of Foreign and Defense Policy: A Nonjudicial Model, 43 U.Chi.L.Rev. 463 (1976).

pursuant to such Executive order." Since courts are to try all claims of exemption de novo, with the burden on the agency to sustain its action, is the executive branch now required to provide any classified document a person asks to see under the FOIA to a district court, for its independent judgment whether the document has been properly classified? If the court discovers that some required procedural step was omitted, however sensitive the information, is it then to direct release? Must it inspect the document itself, although assured by affidavit of the appropriate government officer that the necessary judgments have been made, and presented with sufficient information about the document to establish the reasonableness of those judgments?

Concerns such as these contributed to President Ford's veto of the 1974 Amendments—a veto promptly overridden by Congress [3]—and to the passage in 1984 of the Civil Intelligence Act, which excluded certain Central Intelligence Agency files from FOIA review and provided special judicial review procedures.[4] Exemption 1 issues arise with relative infrequency;[5] the President's acknowledged authority to set classification standards gives him substantial authority over the FOIA's reach; and courts faced with such issues have in fact tended to accord substantial weight to executive branch views on classification, and to avoid in camera inspection where circumstances permit judgment on the basis of a sufficiently detailed affidavit. See, e.g., Weissman v. CIA, 565 F.2d 692 (D.C.Cir.1977); Note, 26 U.Kan.L.Rev. 617 (1978).

(2) FEDERAL OPEN MARKET COMMITTEE v. MERRILL, 443 U.S. 340 (1979), concerned the government's effort to keep its monthly decisions about how it would conduct operations in the market for federal securities confidential while those operations were being conducted. Each month, a Committee of members of the Federal Reserve system decides what policies it will follow for the coming month in transacting business in government securities. The policies might be to expand or contract the money supply, or to set tolerance ranges for monetary growth that the Committee will attempt to maintain during the relevant period. While the policies are known to the (limited number of) bank officials who must act to carry them into effect, widespread knowledge might frustrate their accomplishment or heighten speculation. Consequently, the Committee publishes its decisions at the end of the month in which they have been in effect rather than when the decisions are made.

A law student invoked the FOIA to force revelation of the decisions as soon as they were made. By its actions the FOMC recognized that these were decisions required to be made public, he argued, and the FOIA makes no provision for interim confidentiality.

3. Veto of Freedom of Information Act Amendments, 10 Weekly Comp. of Pres. Doc., (Oct. 17, 1974) 1318.

4. See n. 18, p. 733 above.

5. A partial summary of FOIA annual reports for 1981, including both the Department of Defense and the Department of State, indicates that exemption 1 claims accounted for only 6% of all exemptions invoked on initial denial; exemptions 5 and 7 accounted for about half the total and the privacy exemptions, 4 and 6, about one third. Access Reports/FOI, Vol. 8 No. 18, September 15, 1982, at p. 7.

The Court rejected a claim "that Exemption 5 confers general authority upon an agency to delay disclosure of intra-agency memoranda that would undermine the effectiveness of the agency's policy if released immediately." The language of the statute, it reasoned, referred only to litigation privilege. A claim to protect the effectiveness of government action would prove too much, by tending to reinstate the vague "public interest" standard for withholding information, a standard Congress clearly had meant to repudiate.

More successful was the argument that the government would be able to claim in litigation a privilege for "confidential . . . commercial information," Fed.R.Civ.P. 26(c)(7), that could be found to reach the FOMC policy decisions during the period within which they were operative. Limited legislative history had mentioned analogous settings—early disclosure of information that might prejudice government contracting, for example. This persuaded seven Justices that recognition of a privilege for confidential commercial information was appropriate.[6] The case was remanded for a determination by the district court, in the first instance, whether the impact of immediate disclosure of the FOMC decisions warranted the conclusion that a privilege against discovery would ordinarily be recognized in civil litigation.

Subsequent decisions by the Court have underscored the Court's perception that "Exemption 5 simply incorporates civil discovery privileges." United States v. Weber Aircraft Corp., 465 U.S. 792 (1984). In FTC v. Grolier, Inc., 462 U.S. 19 (1983), the question was whether the FOIA exemption for attorneys' work-product ceased with termination of the litigation with which the work was associated; the Court looked to the general rule applicable in civil discovery practice to hold that it did not. In United States v. Weber Aircraft Corp., above, the question was whether a statement made by an Air Force pilot under a promise of confidentiality during a safety investigation was privileged; the Court relied upon "well-settled" prior case law establishing a privilege for "official government information" in civil discovery in holding that it was—in this instance, without regard to the mention of the particular privilege in the legislative history of the FOIA. "[R]espondent's contention that they can obtain through the FOIA material that is normally privileged would create an anomaly in that the FOIA could be used to supplement civil discovery. We have consistently rejected such a construction of the FOIA." At 801.

Does this rather literal approach to the language of Exemption 5 suggest future difficulties? The air crash safety investigation in Weber Aircraft concerned a pilot who was a government employee; the Court did not have to decide whether statements made by civilians would be equally privileged as "official government information" made part of an "intra-agency memorandum." Such statements, of course, are often made. The policy claim that assured confidentiality is essential to obtaining cooperation (and thus promoting safety) is, if anything, stronger for persons not subject to the loyalties and discipline of

---

6. Justices Stevens and Stewart dissented. They found "nothing in any of the nine exemptions to the Act . . . bearing on the situation" and thought a temporary exemption inconsistent with the Act's structure.

government employment. Would recognizing a privilege here present the same risks as the Merrill Court thought would be presented by general recognition of "undermine the effectiveness" arguments? See Brockway v. Department of Air Force, 518 F.2d 1184 (8th Cir.1975), recognizing such a privilege to prevent impairment of deliberative function; Farnsworth v. Proctor & Gamble Co., 758 F.2d 1545 (11th Cir. 1985), withholding from civil discovery names and addresses of persons cooperating in a study by the Center for Disease Control, to avoid inhibition of information-gathering for future studies.

(3) "Secret law" may be more useful as a slogan, signaling the result, than as a shibboleth for distinguishing the necessary-to-be-revealed from the appropriately private. Prosecutorial offices commonly maintain manuals for their staff, detailing enforcement techniques, priorities, and other like matters. In a strong practical sense, these represent the "secret law" of these offices; yet knowledge of such strategies, forced by inevitable shortages of prosecutorial resources, would be of enormous value to would-be law-evaders. Must they be revealed? Section 552(a)(2)(C), the publication requirement, speaks of "*administrative* staff manuals and instructions to staff"; does that exclude "investigative," "law enforcement," or "prosecutorial" staff manuals? The Supreme Court said in a different context that the second exemption to the FOIA, for material "related solely to internal personnel rules and practices," was to apply only in the case of "minor or trivial matters," Department of The Air Force v. Rose, p. 772 within, but reserved the question whether the exemption might also reach documents whose "disclosure may risk circumvention of agency regulation." The several opinions in Crooker v. Bureau of Alcohol, Tobacco & Firearms, 670 F.2d 1051 (D.C.Cir.1981) (en banc) canvas the arguments in detail, concluding (as had all other circuits before it, on varying theories) that disclosure is not required.

BUREAU OF NATIONAL AFFAIRS v. UNITED STATES DEPARTMENT OF JUSTICE

United States Court of Appeals, District of Columbia Circuit, 1984.
742 F.2d 1484.

Before MIKVA and EDWARDS, CIRCUIT JUDGES, and BAZELON, SENIOR CIRCUIT JUDGE.

MIKVA, CIRCUIT JUDGE:

. . .

In 1981, the Bureau of National Affairs (BNA) filed a FOIA request with the Department of Justice (DOJ or the Justice Department) for all records of appointments and meetings between William Baxter, then Assistant Attorney General for Antitrust, and all parties outside the Justice Department. DOJ denied BNA's request on the ground that the materials were not "agency records" subject to disclosure under FOIA. Following exhaustion of its administrative remedies, BNA filed suit in the district court to compel disclosure.[1]

---

1. [Ed.] The court's opinion also dealt with a similar dispute involving OMB papers sought by the Environmental Defense Fund; references to that dispute have been edited out in the interest of conciseness.

Mr. Baxter's appointment materials include two types of documents. The first consists of two sets of desk appointment calendars maintained for Mr. Baxter in 1981 and 1982. One set of calendars was maintained by Mr. Baxter himself; the other was kept by his personal secretary. According to Mr. Baxter, the calendar entries "generally reflect[ed] the location of a meeting or appointment, the people expected to be present, and on occasion, the general purpose of the meeting or appointment." Top level assistants occasionally had access to the calendars so that they would know how to contact Mr. Baxter. The calendars included personal appointments wholly unrelated to the business of the Antitrust Division and did not always reflect changes in appointments or cancellations of meetings.

The other set of documents sought by BNA are the daily agendas which Mr. Baxter's secretary prepared and distributed to top staff within the Antitrust Division so that they would know his schedule on a given day. The staff usually destroyed these agendas at the end of each day, but Mr. Baxter's secretary retained copies for her own files.

. . .

The requirement that materials sought by a private party be "agency records" is jurisdictional—only when an agency withholds an agency record does the district court have authority to compel disclosure.

. . . "As has often been remarked, the Freedom of Information Act, for all its attention to the treatment of 'agency records,' never defines that crucial phrase." McGehee v. Central Intelligence Agency, 697 F.2d 1095, 1106 (D.C.Cir.1983) (footnotes omitted), modified in other respects, 711 F.2d 1076 (1983). Moreover, "the legislative history yields insignificant insight into Congress' conception of the sorts of materials the Act covers." Id. (footnote omitted).

. . .

1. Judicial interpretation of the term "agency records"

The Supreme Court has elaborated on the meaning of the term "agency records" on two occasions. . . . Kissinger v. Reporters Committee for Freedom of the Press, 445 U.S. 136 (1980), involved three separate FOIA requests for the transcripts and summaries of Henry Kissinger's telephone conversations (telephone notes) which were maintained while he was Secretary of State and national security advisor to the President. While still serving in the State Department, Dr. Kissinger transferred the telephone notes from his office to a private location and entered into an agreement deeding those notes to the Library of Congress. Dr. Kissinger treated the notes as his own personal papers. Two of the three FOIA requests in the Kissinger case were filed after the telephone notes had been taken from the State Department. As to those requests, the Court . . . found that . . . the State Department had not "withheld" anything. Because the documents had been removed from the State Department's possession prior to the filing of a FOIA request, "the agency ha[d] neither the custody nor the control to enable it to withhold."

Although the third FOIA request had been filed before the telephone notes were removed from the State Department, the Court concluded nonetheless that the documents sought in that instance were not "agency records." . . . [T]he particular documents requested were notes of telephone conversations that Dr. Kissinger had had while he was in the Office of the President prior to becoming Secretary of State. Because FOIA does not include Presidential assistants in the definition of "agency," the records of those phone conversations were not *"agency"* records. The Court further concluded that the mere physical transfer of those documents to the State Department—an agency clearly covered by FOIA—did not by itself render them "agency records" within the meaning of FOIA. The Court explained:

> The papers were not in the control of the State Department at any time. They were not generated in the State Department. They never entered the State Department's files, and they were not used by the Department for any purpose. If mere physical location of papers and materials could confer status as an "agency record" Kissinger's personal books, speeches, and all other memorabilia stored in his office would have been agency records subject to disclosure under the FOIA.

Thus, in determining whether the documents were "agency records" under FOIA, the Court focused on several factors: whether the documents were (1) in the agency's control; (2) generated within the agency; (3) placed into the agency's files; and (4) used by the agency "for any purpose."

In a second case decided the same day as Kissinger the Court held that data created and held by a private organization to conduct a federally funded study are not "agency records" under FOIA. In Forsham v. Harris, 445 U.S. 169 (1980), petitioners sought disclosure under FOIA of raw data that formed the basis of a study that had been funded entirely through federal grants. Pursuant to federal regulations, the data was available upon request to the agencies that had supplied the funding. The data, therefore, had been "generated, owned and possessed by a privately controlled organization receiving federal study grants," but was available to the federal government. The Court refused to order the agency to exercise its right of access to the data because such an order would compel the agency to "create" a record, a result which the Court held went beyond the reach of the Act.

. . . .

Under the case law, it is clear that, at least in some circumstances, the agency's use of a document is relevant for determining its status as an "agency record." Where, as here, a document is created by an agency employee, consideration of whether and to what extent that employee used the document to conduct agency business is highly relevant for determining whether that document is an "agency record" within the meaning of FOIA. Use alone, however, is not dispositive; the other factors mentioned in Kissinger must also be considered:

whether the document is in the agency's control, was generated within the agency, and has been placed into the agency's files. Our inquiry must therefore focus on the totality of the circumstances surrounding the creation, maintenance, and use of the document to determine whether the document is in fact an "agency record" and not an employee's record that happens to be located physically within an agency.

In particular, the statute cannot be extended to sweep into FOIA's reach personal papers that may "relate to" an employee's work—such as a personal diary containing an individual's private reflections on his or her work—but which the individual does not rely upon to perform his or her duties. In this regard, use of the documents by employees other than the author is an important consideration. An inquiry is therefore required into the purpose for which the document was created, the actual use of the document, and the extent to which the creator of the document and other employees acting within the scope of their employment relied upon the document to carry out the business of the agency.

In adopting this analysis, we reject the government's invitation to hold that the treatment of documents for disposal and retention purposes under the various federal records management statutes determines their status under FOIA. Those statutes prescribe how federal agencies are to create, dispose of, and otherwise manage documents and other material. See, e.g., Federal Records Act of 1950, 44 U.S.C. § 2901 et seq. (1976 & Supp. V 1981); Records Disposal Act, 44 U.S.C. § 3301 et seq. (1976 & Supp. V 1981); Presidential Records Act of 1978, 44 U.S.C. § 2201 (Supp. V 1981). However tempting such a "bright line" test may be, it cannot be used as the divining rod for the meaning of "agency records" under FOIA. . . . Rigid adherence to the records disposal regulations to determine the status of a document under FOIA would contradict the policy of disclosure underlying FOIA. . . .

While holding that FOIA does not require an agency to "create or retain" documents, the Supreme Court expressly left open the question of whether "non-record materials" are "agency records" under the FOIA and thus subject to disclosure. Forsham, 445 U.S. at 183 n. 14. While an agency's treatment of the documents pursuant to its record retention and disposal obligations is relevant for determining the documents' status under FOIA, we refuse to apply a rigid test that removes all non-record materials from FOIA's coverage.

We also note that our analysis is not based upon the rationale set forth in two district court opinions relied upon by the government . . . [concluding] that handwritten notes, that were created by an agency employee and that reflected his impressions of substantive discussions and meetings held in the course of agency business, are not "agency records." Porter County Chapter of the Izaak Walton League of America v. United States Atomic Energy Commission, 380 F.Supp. 630 (N.D.Ind.1974).

The court's analysis in Porter County was based entirely on the *content* of the notes, not on the agency's control, possession or use of the notes. A fair reading of Porter County suggests that the court was applying policies underlying the FOIA exemptions in concluding that the documents were not "agency records." In particular, the court was concerned primarily with the potential chilling effect that disclosure of handwritten notes might have on the activities of government employees:

> Disclosure of such personal documents would invade the privacy of and impede the working habits of individual staff members; it would preclude employees from ever committing any thoughts to writing which the author is unprepared, for whatever reason, to disseminate publicly. Even if the records were "agency records," their disclosure would be akin to revealing the opinions, advice, recommendations and detailed mental processes of government officials. Such notes would not be available by discovery in ordinary litigation.

380 F.Supp. at 633. We question the analysis relied upon by the court in Porter County. The policy concerns underlying the court's opinion are addressed more appropriately to the applicability of particular exemptions, such as Exemption 5, to the requested material. The term "agency records" should not be manipulated to avoid the basic structure of the FOIA: records are presumptively disclosable unless the government can show that one of the enumerated exemptions applies. See Note, The Definition of "Agency Records" Under the Freedom of Information Act, 31 Stan.L.Rev. 1093, 1099 (July, 1979) ("restricting the definition of 'record' to material with a certain content also might be seen as improperly expanding the Act's exemptions.").

In determining the status of the appointment materials requested in these cases, we conclude that it is necessary to look at the circumstances surrounding the creation, maintenance and use of the documents within the agency. In particular, we must focus on the four factors outlined by the Court in Kissinger: whether the document was generated within the agency, has been placed into the agency's files, is in the agency's control, and has been used by the agency for an agency purpose. . . .

2. Appointment materials as "agency records"

. . . [T]hese materials share three common attributes that are relevant for our analysis. First, all of these materials were "generated" within the agencies. They were prepared on government time, at government expense and with government materials, including the blank appointment calendars themselves. [Mr. Baxter's] personal secretar[y] maintained the appointment records as part of [her] official agency duties. Second, the materials have not been placed into agency files. Third, DOJ . . . permit[s its] employees to dispose of these "non-record materials" at their discretion. . . .

Mr. Baxter's secretary at DOJ created daily agendas indicating Mr. Baxter's schedule. She circulated these agendas to certain members of Mr. Baxter's staff. Although the staff threw out the agendas regularly, Mr. Baxter's secretary maintained copies in her desk, apparently in the absence of any instructions to the contrary. The purpose of the agendas was to inform the staff of Mr. Baxter's availability; they facilitated the day-to-day operations of the Antitrust Division.

    . . . [T]he daily agendas are "agency records" within the meaning of FOIA. They were created for the express purpose of facilitating the daily activities of the Antitrust Division. Even though the agendas reflected personal appointments, they were circulated to the staff for a business purpose. The agency can segregate out any notations that refer to purely personal matters. . . .

The appointment calendars are the most difficult to categorize. The purpose of the calendars was to facilitate the individuals' performance of their official duties and to organize both their business and personal activities. . . . [T]he calendars often gave some indication of the topic of a particular meeting, as well as the location and identity of the participants. . . . In the case of Mr. Baxter. . . , immediate staff had access to the calendars to determine the officials' availability. In that sense, the calendars were similar to the daily agendas.

We conclude, however, that these particular appointment calendars are not "agency records." They are distinguishable from the daily agendas in two important respects. First, they were not *distributed* to other employees, but were retained solely for the convenience of the individual officials. Second, the daily agendas were created by Mr. Baxter's secretary *for the express purpose* of informing other staff of Mr. Baxter's whereabouts during the course of a business day so that they could determine Mr. Baxter's availability for meetings. Thus the daily agendas were created for the purpose of conducting agency business. In contrast, the appointment calendars were created for personal convenience. . . .

The inclusion of personal items in the appointment calendars buttresses the conclusion that the calendars were created for. . . personal convenience. . . not for an official agency purpose. The inclusion of personal information does not, by itself, take material outside the ambit of FOIA, for personal information can be redacted from the copies of documents disclosed to a FOIA requester. But the presence of such information may be relevant in determining the author's intended use of the documents at the time he or she created them. . . . FOIA's reach does not extend to such personalized documents absent some showing that the agency itself exercised control over or possession of the documents. . . .

b. Freedom of Information and Private Needs for Confidentiality

5 U.S.C. § 552(b): "This section does not apply to matters that are

    . . .

    (4) trade secrets and commercial or financial information obtained from a person and privileged or confidential;

    . . .

(6) personnel and medical files and similar files the disclosure of which would constitute a clearly unwarranted invasion
of personal privacy; . . . ."

Not all information held in confidence by the government is so held
because of official preferences, legitimate or not, to operate out of the
public eye.

As Chapter 5 develops at length, the government is an insatiable
consumer of information from the private world it seeks to regulate.
Railroad rates cannot be regulated, nuclear power plants licensed, new
drugs authorized, taxes collected, or censuses taken without intimate
knowledge of details of corporate operations, technical fact, and personal life which the private owner would not choose to share with the
world at large. Where the government must solicit cooperation rather
than force disclosure, confidentiality may have to be assured for that
cooperation to be forthcoming. Even if disclosure could be forced or
bargained for, as in rate regulation or technology licensing, sound
public policy may support the conclusion that confidentiality of some
kinds of data should be preserved, to foster innovation, to avoid creating circumstances conducive to unfair competition, or to prevent other
forms of harm. A competitor's intimate knowledge of his rival's costs
or techniques could provide a business edge government might not wish
inadvertently to confer. Broad access to information individuals share
with government for limited civic purposes would be destructive of
privacy values which lie at the core of civilized relationship with
government. Widespread dissemination of information concerning
one's dealings with government can work a gratuitous injury.

(i) Proprietary Information

NATIONAL PARKS AND CONSERVATION ASS'N v. MORTON

United States Court of Appeals, District of Columbia Circuit, 1974.
498 F.2d 765.

[Appellant had sought access to certain agency records concerning
concessions operated in the national parks. The National Park Service
licenses private concessioners to operate within the parks, providing
the millions who annually visit the parks with souvenirs, and other
goods and services. The Service supervises price and quality of service
and periodically sets fees. Concessioners are required to assist in this
examination by submitting detailed financial information to the Service
on a continuing basis. For example, when a concessioner enters a
licensing agreement with the Service, it submits a "Concessioner Opening Balance Sheet," revealing its assets, liabilities, net worth and
additional supporting information. Annually, it must provide a "Concessioner Annual Financial Report," showing balance sheet information
and operating data in detail, and thus giving a complete picture of a
concessioner's operating condition. Another annual form describes all
projects existing or planned for the following year, by location, cost and
occupancy capacity; the "Annual Report of Statistical Information—
Concession Facilities" describes every type of concession facility, by

location, number of rooms and baths, percentage of room occupancy during peak months, trailer site capacity and additional similar information. The Service's own periodic audits of concession operations produce similar though even more detailed financial information. These were the materials the appellant sought. It had lost in district court on the ground that the information sought was exempt from disclosure under Section 552(b)(4) of the FOIA.]

Before BAZELON, CHIEF JUDGE, and WRIGHT and TAMM, CIRCUIT JUDGES.

TAMM, CIRCUIT JUDGE: . . . .

In order to bring a matter (other than a trade secret) within [the fourth] exemption, it must be shown that the information is (a) commercial or financial, (b) obtained from a person, and (c) privileged or confidential. Since the parties agree that the matter in question is financial information obtained from a person and that it is not privileged, the only issue on appeal is whether the information is "confidential" within the meaning of the exemption.

I

Unfortunately, the statute contains no definition of the word "confidential." In the past, our decisions concerning this exemption have been guided by the following passage from the Senate Report, particularly the italicized portion:

"This exception is necessary to protect the confidentiality of information which is obtained by the Government through questionnaires or other inquiries, *but which would customarily not be released to the public by the person from whom it was obtained.*"

S.Rep. No. 813, 89th Cong., 1st Sess. 9 (1965) (emphasis added). We have made it clear, however, that the test for confidentiality is an objective one. Whether particular information would customarily be disclosed to the public by the person from whom it was obtained is not the only relevant inquiry. . . . A court must also be satisfied that non-disclosure is justified by the legislative purpose which underlies the exemption. . . .

The "financial information" exemption recognizes the need of government policymakers to have access to commercial and financial data. Unless persons having necessary information can be assured that it will remain confidential, they may decline to cooperate with officials and the ability of the Government to make intelligent, well informed decisions will be impaired. This concern finds expression in the legislative history as well as the case law. During debate on a predecessor to the bill which was ultimately enacted, Senator Humphrey pointed out that sources of information relied upon by the Bureau of Labor Statistics would be "seriously jeopardized" unless the information collected by the Bureau was exempt from disclosure. He was assured that such information was fully protected under the exemption as it then appeared.[1] Although the exemption now contains the additional qualifying words "commercial or financial" the purpose of protecting government access to necessary data remains. As the Senate Report explains:

"This exception is necessary to protect the confidentiality of information which is obtained by the Government through *questionnaires or other inquiries*. . . ." S.Rep. No. 813, 89th Cong. 1st Sess. 9 (1965) (emphasis added).

The House Report states with respect to Section 552(b)(4):

"It would also include information which is given to an agency in confidence, since a citizen must be able to confide in his Government. Moreover, where the Government has obligated itself in good faith not to disclose documents or information which it receives, it should be able to honor such obligations." H.Rep. No. 1497, 89th Cong. 2d Sess. 10 (1966).

. . .

Apart from encouraging cooperation with the Government by persons having information useful to officials, Section 552(b)(4) serves another distinct but equally important purpose. It protects persons who submit financial or commercial data to government agencies from the competitive disadvantages which would result from its publication. The need for such protection was raised several times during hearings on S. 1666, the predecessor of the bill which became law, . . . which contained no exemption for trade secrets or commercial or financial information. . . . In each of these instances it was suggested that an exemption for "trade secrets" would avert the danger that valuable business information would be made public by agencies which had obtained it pursuant to statute or regulation. A representative of the Department of Justice endorsed this idea at length:

"A second problem area lies in the large body of the Government's information involving private business data and trade secrets, the disclosure of which could severely damage individual enterprise and cause widespread disruption of the channels of commerce. Much of this information is volunteered by employers, merchants, manufacturers, carriers, exporters, and other businessmen and professional people for purposes of market news services, labor and wage statistics, commercial reports, and other Government services which are considered useful to the cooperating reporters, the public and the agencies. Perhaps the greater part of such information is exacted, by statute, in the course of necessary regulatory or other governmental functions.

"Again, not only as a matter of fairness, but as a matter of right, and as a matter basic to our free enterprise system, private business information should be afforded appropriate protection, at least from competitors."

A particularly significant aspect of the latter statement is its recognition of a twofold justification for the exemption of commercial material:

1. [110 Cong.Rec. 17667 (1964).] S. 1666 contained the following version of the exemption: ". . . trade secrets and other information obtained from the public and customarily privileged or confidential . . . ." S.Rep. No. 1219, 88th Cong. 2d Sess. 2. (1964).

(1) encouraging cooperation by those who are not obliged to provide information to the government and (2) protecting the rights of those who must.

After the hearings, the bill was reported with amendments, one of which added the following exemption:

". . . trade secrets and other information obtained from the public and customarily privileged or confidential . . . ." S.Rep. 1219, 88th Cong., 2d Sess. 2 (1964).

Although the bill passed the Senate, Congress adjourned before the House of Representatives had completed action. The bill was reintroduced in the Senate in the following session with only two changes in the fourth exemption:

". . . trade secrets and commercial or financial information obtained from the public and privileged or confidential . . . ."

This version substitutes the words "commercial or financial" for the word "other" and deletes the word "customarily." No explanation was given for either change . . . . The explanation of the fourth exemption was identical to that appearing in the Report on the previous bill except for the following significant addition:

"Specifically [the exemption] would include any commercial, technical, and financial data, submitted by an applicant or a borrower to a lending agency in connection with any loan application or loan." S.Rep. No. 813, 89th Cong. 1st Sess. 9 (1965).

This history firmly supports the inference that Section 552(b)(4) is intended for the benefit of persons who supply information as well as the agencies which gather it.

To summarize, commercial or financial matter is "confidential" for purposes of the exemption if disclosure of the information is likely to have either of the following effects: (1) to impair the Government's ability to obtain necessary information in the future; or (2) to cause substantial harm to the competitive position of the person from whom the information was obtained.

II

The financial information sought by appellant consists of audits conducted upon the books of companies operating concessions in national parks, annual financial statements filed by the concessioners with the National Park Service and other financial information. The district court concluded that this information was of the kind "that would not generally be made available for public perusal." While we discern no error in this finding, we do not think that by itself, it supports application of the financial information exemption. The district court must also inquire into the possibility that disclosure will harm legitimate private or governmental interests in secrecy.

On the record before us the Government has no apparent interest in preventing disclosure of the matter in question. . . . [D]isclosure of this material to the Park Service is a mandatory condition of the concessioners' right to operate in national parks. Since the concessioners are *required* to provide this financial information to the government, there is presumably no danger that public disclosure will impair the ability of the Government to obtain this information in the future.

As we have already explained, however, Section 552(b)(4) may . . . be invoked for the benefit of the person who has provided commercial or financial information if it can be shown that public disclosure is likely to cause substantial harm to his competitive position. Appellant argues that such a showing cannot be made in this case because the concessioners are monopolists, protected from competition during the term of their contracts and enjoying a statutory preference over other bidders at renewal time. In other words, appellant argues that disclosure cannot impair the concessioners' competitive position because they have no competition. While this argument is very compelling, we are reluctant to accept it without first providing appellee the opportunity to develop a fuller record in the district court. It might be shown, for example, that disclosure of information about concession activities will injure the concessioner's competitive position in a non-concession enterprise. In that case disclosure would be improper. This matter is therefore remanded to the district court for the purpose of determining whether public disclosure of the information in question poses the likelihood of substantial harm to the competitive positions of the parties from whom it has been obtained. . . .

NOTES

(1) This case appeared in the court of appeals a second time, National Parks and Conservation Ass'n v. Kleppe, 547 F.2d 673 (D.C. Cir.1976). The court of appeals was satisfied, as to most of the concessioners, that the district court had a sufficient basis in the record on remand to support its conclusion that disclosure would be likely to cause adverse competitive effect; but it did not sustain the district court's inference from these facts as to *some* concessioners that two others who had made no direct proof were also faced with "meaningful competition" and a resulting potential for real harm from disclosure. The case was sent back for a third hearing, at which they could make their own proof of the issue. While the court of appeals thus set its face firmly against conjecture, surmise, and conclusory statement as a means for establishing the availability of an exemption, it indicated that the necessary proof need show only the possibility, not the certainty or actuality of harm, and it rejected the Association's suggestions for elaborate proof of actual harm, remarking that "the costs of obtaining such detailed economic evidence . . . might well preclude a small business from ever seeking to prevent disclosure. . . . " At 681 n. 24. Hearings before a subcommittee of the House Committee on Government Operations on the Business Record Exemption of the Freedom of Information Act (Comm. Print, 95th Cong., 1st Sess. 1977) suggest, perhaps not surprisingly, that this effort to gain the middle ground has proved satisfactory neither to the business community nor to its critics.

(2) What is the effect of the reference to "commercial or financial" information? The legislative history quoted by the court speaks generally of information obtained by the government under a promise of confidence; or, if obtained by compulsion, obtained in circumstances that would lead to an expectation that confidence would be maintained. As the court remarks, the "commercial or financial" limitation was supplied, without explanation, during the course of legislative consideration. This change led Professor Davis to characterize the exemption as "probably the most troublesome provision of the Act." K. Davis, The Information Act: A Preliminary Analysis, 34 U.Chi.L.Rev. 761, 787 (1967). He wished that the exemption had remained as it had been in the earlier Senate version, but did not "see how any court could conscientiously find that an exemption of non-commercial and non-financial information is 'specifically stated' by the statutory words. . . . " At 791.

Thus, where research designs which had been submitted in the expectation of confidence by not-for-profit organizations were sought, they could not be withheld:

". . . [T]he government has been at some pains to argue that biomedical researchers are really a mean-spirited lot who pursue self-interest as ruthlessly as the Barbary pirates did in their own chosen field. Whether this is the sad truth, or whether, as appellee suggests, 'secrecy is antithetical to the philosophical values of science,' is not, however, an issue in this case; the reach of the exemption for 'trade secrets or commercial or financial information' is not necessarily coextensive with the existence of competition in any form.

". . . [I]t defies common sense to pretend that the scientist is engaged in trade or commerce. This is not to say that the scientist may not have a preference for or an interest in nondisclosure of his research design, but only that it is not a trade or commercial interest."

Washington Research Project, Inc. v. Department of Health, Educ. & Welfare, 504 F.2d 238, 244–245 (D.C.Cir.1974), cert. denied 421 U.S. 963 (1975); see also Save the Dolphins v. United States Dept. of Commerce, 404 F.Supp. 407 (N.D.Cal.1975).

(3) What is a "trade secret"? The FOIA does not say. The Restatement of Torts defined it broadly in terms of the holder's commercial advantage—"any formula, pattern, device, or compilation of information which is used in one's business and which gives him an opportunity to obtain an advantage over competitors who do not know or use it." 4 id. § 757 comment b (1939). Precedent under the Federal Trade Secrets Act, a criminal statute forbidding federal agency officials to disclose "trade secrets" except as authorized by law,[1] regarded trade secrets more narrowly—as limited to information actually used in the productive process "for the making, preparing, compounding, treating or processing of articles or materials which are trade commodities." United States ex rel. Norwegian Nitrogen Prod. Co. v. United States Tariff Commission, 6 F.2d 491, 495 (D.C.Cir.1925), vacated as moot, 274

1. The Act is treated in Chrysler Corp.
v. Brown, within p. 763.

U.S. 106 (1927). The difference between the two formulations was highlighted when a public interest group asked the FDA for data resulting from clinical studies of a medical appliance under agency review for certification. PUBLIC CITIZEN HEALTH RESEARCH GROUP V. FDA, 704 F.2d 1280 (D.C.Cir.1983). The manufacturers performing these studies could use them to obtain a competitive advantage (FDA approval), but the data did not concern the manufacturing process as such.

"In deciding between these competing definitions of trade secret, we begin with two observations, each of which suggests that our choice is relatively unconstrained by prior administrative or judicial actions. First, although the FDA has endorsed the Restatement definition and adopted it in its FOIA regulations, we are not bound by the agency's interpretive regulation. Any other conclusion would produce an intolerable situation in which different agencies could adopt inconsistent interpretations of the FOIA and substantially complicate the administration of the Act. The FDA's expertise in this area should not be wholly discounted. See Pharmaceutical Manufacturers Association v. Weinberger, 411 F.Supp. 576, 578 (D.D.C.1976). But Congress has made clear both that the federal courts, and not the administrative agencies, are ultimately responsible for construing the language of the FOIA, and that agencies cannot alter the dictates of the Act by their own express or implied promises of confidentiality.

"Prior judicial decisions also need not detain us unduly. . . . Concededly, the Washington Research Project court did cite the Restatement definition, see 504 F.2d at 245 n. 8, and several other courts have also used this definition in exemption 4 cases. But the courts' application of this broad interpretation of trade secrets has been mechanical, and they have given no consideration to its suitability in FOIA cases. As a result, the persuasive force of these prior decisions is minimal.

"Since we are bound by neither the agency's interpretation nor judicial precedent, we feel free to repudiate the broad Restatement approach and the FDA's regulation as inconsistent with the language of the FOIA and its underlying policies. In our opinion, the term 'trade secrets' in exemption 4 of the FOIA should be defined in its narrower common law sense, which incorporates a direct relationship between the information at issue and the productive process. Accordingly, we define trade secret, solely for the purpose of FOIA exemption 4, as a secret, commercially valuable plan, formula, process, or device that is used for the making, preparing, compounding, or processing of trade commodities and that can be said to be the end project of either innovation or substantial effort. This definition, we believe, hews more closely to the language and legislative intent of the FOIA than does the Restatement approach.

"Several arguments support this conclusion. First, we have found no evidence in the debates and reports leading to the enactment of the FOIA militating in favor of a broad definition of 'trade secrets.' Second, the Restatement definition of trade secrets renders meaningless the second prong of exemption 4. As the House Committee on Government Operations has recognized:

> If a trade secret can be any information used in a business which gives competitive advantage, then there is little or no information left that could qualify as commercial or financial information under the second category of the exemption without also qualifying as a trade secret. *This definition is therefore inconsistent with the language of the act,* as well as with the general approach taken by the courts to the concept of confidential business information.

H.R.Rep. No. 1382, 95th Cong., 2d Sess. 16 (1978) (emphasis added).[2] Tellingly, when asked in the oral argument before this court to specify a category of information that would be included in the 'commercial or financial information' prong of exemption 4 but not in the FDA's definition of trade secrets, counsel for the federal appellees could not give a single example. Third, the Restatement definition, tailored as it is to protecting businesses from breaches of contract and confidence by departing employees and others under fiduciary obligations is ill-suited for the public law context in which FOIA determinations must be made.[3] . . .

"Applying our definition of 'trade secrets' to the records at issue on this appeal, we conclude that they are not protected under the first prong of exemption 4. The relationship of the requested information to the productive process is tangential at best; under no plausible reading of the phrase 'plan, formula, process, or device' could the reports, letters, and memorandums sought by the HRG be said to fall within its ambit."

The court found that the district court had correctly found many of the documents protected as "confidential commercial information" under exemption 4. For other documents, for which this was unclear, it remanded the case to the district court for determination of that issue, identifying as the pivotal question whether the second prong of the National Parks text—the likelihood of causing substantial competitive harm to the supplier of the information—had been met.[4]

2. But see S.Rep. No. 838, 92nd Cong., 2d Sess., pt. II, at 72, reprinted in 1972 U.S.Code Cong. & Ad.News 4023, 4091–92 (giving general approval to Restatement definition of trade secret in legislation also protecting commercial or financial information).

3. "When the question of defining proprietary information appears in the public context of whether health and safety data submitted to an agency should be publicly disclosed, the interests of the public in disclosure and the protection of innovation incentives pose important considerations which the common law definition was not designed to handle. The Restatement approach, with its emphasis on culpability and misappropriation, is ill-equipped to strike an appropriate balance between the competing interests of regulated industries and the general public. Therefore, lumping health and safety testing data with all other types of proprietary information is inherently suspect."

McGarity & Shapiro, The Trade Secret Status of Health and Safety Testing Information: Reforming Agency Disclosure Policies, 93 Harv.L.Rev. 837, 863 (1980). . . .

4. In Ruckelshaus v. Monsanto, 467 U.S. 986 (1984), the Supreme Court accepted the Restatement definition of "trade secret" as expressing Missouri law on the subject, for purposes of its holding that trade secrets could be constitutional "property" whose taking by the federal government must be paid for under the Fifth Amendment. See page 770 within. The

(4) The fourth exemption provides no basis for considering the motive with which information is sought as an element in deciding its availability. The most elevated public interest claimant is no more or less a "person" entitled to demand information under the act than a competitor whose interest is solely in obtaining insights into his adversary's business that may help him gain an advantage in the marketplace. Information is predominantly demanded for the latter purpose.[5] That prospect gives rise to a profound interest on the part of the suppliers of the information to assure that the exemption is asserted when information they have supplied in confidence is sought. Several difficulties can arise in satisfying this interest: (1) The busy government functionary whose desk the request for information crosses may not recognize its implications—he is not thoroughly acquainted with the supplier's business, or likely to be aware of the sophisticated analyses that might be made of apparently harmless data—and so it may be granted before the supplier has a chance even to object. (2) There may be no regular procedure for identifying information believed to be sensitive in advance, so that the functionary becomes aware of a possible claim; and there may be no procedure for notifying the supplier even in those cases in which the problem is recognized. (3) The FOIA serves only to define information an agency *must* disclose on request, and does not in terms oblige the agency to withhold information which could be withheld under one or another exemption but which the agency decides—in the public interest, to avoid litigation, or simply out of error—to make public; indeed, it rather encourages error in the direction of disclosure, not withholding, of information. (4) The agency may disagree with the supplier on the question whether given information fits within the exemption or, agreeing that the exemption does apply, it may nonetheless decide to disclose it. (5) It may be unclear to what extent other law authorizes or prohibits such disclo-

---

Court had no occasion to define "trade secret" for federal purposes.

5. In 1981, it was reported, about one out of each twenty FOIA requests made came from a journalist, scholar or author; four out of five came from businessmen or their lawyers. P. Wald, The Freedom of Information Act: A Short Case Study in the Perils and Paybacks of Legislating Democratic Values, 33 Emory L.J. 648, 665 (1984), citing 1 Freedom of Information Act: Hearings Before the Subcommittee on the Constitution of the Senate Committee on the Judiciary, 97th Cong., 1st Sess. 159, 161 (Jonathan Rose), 776 (Jack Landau) (1981). Of the more than 33,000 requests received by the FDA in that year, to take one example, 31% came from corporations, 8% from law firms, and 47% from FOI service companies requesting materials for corporate clients; 1% came from public interest groups, and 1% from the press. W. Casey, Jr., J. Marthinsen, and L. Moss, Entrepreneurship, Productivity and the FOIA 12 (1983). The FDA reported its total cost for administering its FOIA program in 1981 as $3,442,868; it received $182,262 in fees paid by requesters. Annual Report of the Department of Health and Human Services on Freedom of Information Activities (1981). In a 1983 report to the Chairman of the Senate Subcommittee on the general subject of weakness in FOIA cost-accounting, the General Accounting Office estimated that "additional unreported costs for the FDA were over $1.2 million in 1981." While only 454 denials were made in 1981, Annual Report, "what is sometimes difficult and time consuming is identifying . . . and locating [the] documents. It is not at all uncommon to get a request that runs five or six pages or a request that says 'Let me have everything that you have on saccharin.' As you might imagine there are quite a few pieces of paper running around on saccharin at FDA." Commissioner of the Food and Drug Administration, Donald Kennedy in Hearings, p. 758 supra, at 74.

sures, and what remedies are available to enforce any such prohibitions.

CHRYSLER CORP. v. BROWN
Supreme Court of the United States, 1979.
441 U.S. 281.

[As a major defense contractor, the Chrysler Corporation was required by Executive Orders 11246 and 11375 to observe non-discriminatory ("equal employment opportunity") hiring practices and to furnish reports and other information about its programs to the Department of Defense Logistics Agency (DLA), pursuant to regulations of the Department of Labor's Office of Federal Contract Compliance Programs (OFCCP). Some of the information provided is commercially sensitive data—for example, "manning tables," listing job titles and the number of people performing each job [1]—which might be used by a competitor to its advantage. OFCCP regulations stated that even though such information might be exempt from mandatory disclosure under the FOIA, "records obtained or generated pursuant to Executive Order 11246 (as amended) . . . shall be made available for inspection and copying . . . if it is determined that the requested inspection or copying furthers the public interest and does not impede any of the functions of the OFCC[P] or the Compliance Agencies except in the case of records disclosure of which is prohibited by law." Persons interested in monitoring Chrysler's employment practices filed FOIA requests for reports concerning two of its facilities; pursuant to its regulations, DLA notified Chrysler of the requests and, later, of its intention to honor them. Chrysler then sought to enjoin the release of information which it asserted to be within the protection of the FOIA's fourth exemption. In district court it succeeded on a narrow ground; the Third Circuit reversed, broadly sustaining the government's contentions: that the FOIA creates no right to withholding of information within its exemptions; that other confidentiality statutes create no private right of

---

1. Writing about a claim for similar data from a large insurance firm, a district court observed "The work force analyses, or manning tables, contain a breakdown by specific job categories of the total number of employees in each job category and of the number of women and minorities in each job category. Metropolitan's Department Lists also reveal the number of women, and, in the 1975 Department List, the number of minority group members ("MGMs") employed in each of the Company's specific job categories. The disclosure of this information would cause the companies substantial competitive harm by increasing the companies vulnerability to employee raiding.

"The raiding or proselytizing of employees is a serious problem faced by the insurance industry today, particularly for large companies with sophisticated training programs such as John Hancock, Metropolitan, and Prudential. . . .

"Even with the names and identification numbers of employees deleted, disclosure of the manning tables would significantly enhance a person's ability to locate employees and the companies' vulnerability to raiding . . . . Because the tables provide a breakdown of employees at a particular location by job, grade, sex, and race, these tables provide information on the precise location and availability of many types of employees, such as computer programmers or claims approvers, by sex and race, which does not appear to be currently available to any significant degree. . . . " Metropolitan Life Insurance Co. v. Usery, 426 F.Supp. 150, 160–162 (D.D.C.1976), cert. before judgment denied sub nom. Prudential Ins. Co. v. National Org. for Women, 431 U.S. 924, 2198 (1977), affirmed and remanded sub nom. Nat'l Org. For Women, Washington D.C. Chapter v. Social Security Administration, 736 F.2d 727 (D.C.Cir. 1984). See p. 771 within.

action, and recognize as proper disclosures "authorized by law"; that the OFCCP regulations created any necessary authority to disclose, and were themselves within the Department of Labor's authority to adopt; and that, given authority to disclose, judicial review of the exercise of that authority would be limited to assuring procedural regularity and checking abuses of discretion. Since the administrative record was insufficient to perform such review, the Third Circuit had directed the district court to remand the case to the agency for supplementation. At this point, the Court granted certiorari.]

Mr. Justice Rehnquist delivered the opinion of the Court:

.　.　.

In contending that the FOIA bars disclosure of the requested equal employment opportunity information, Chrysler relies .　.　. specifically on Exemption 4:

"(b) [FOIA] does not apply to matters that are—

.　.　.

"(4) trade secrets and commercial or financial information obtained from a person and privileged or confidential .　.　." 5 U.S.C. § 552(b)(4).

Chrysler contends that the nine exemptions in general, and Exemption 4 in particular, reflect a sensitivity to the privacy interests of private individuals and nongovernmental entities. That contention may be conceded without inexorably requiring the conclusion that the exemptions impose affirmative duties on an agency to withhold information sought. In fact, that conclusion is not supported by the language, logic or history of the Act.

.　.　. By its terms, subsection (b) demarcates the limits of the agency's obligation to disclose; it does not foreclose disclosure.

That the FOIA is exclusively a disclosure statute is, perhaps, demonstrated most convincingly by examining its provision for judicial relief. Subsection (a)(4)(B) gives federal district courts "jurisdiction to enjoin the agency from withholding agency records and to order the production of any agency records improperly withheld from the complainant." 5 U.S.C. § 552(a)(4)(B). That provision does not give the authority to bar disclosure, and thus fortifies our belief that Chrysler, and courts which have shared its view, have incorrectly interpreted the exemption provisions to the FOIA. The Act is an attempt to meet the demand for open government while preserving workable confidentiality in governmental decision-making. Congress appreciated that with the expanding sphere of governmental regulation and enterprise, much of the information within Government files has been submitted by private entities seeking Government contracts or responding to unconditional reporting obligations imposed by law. There was sentiment that Government agencies should have the latitude, in certain circumstances, to afford the confidentiality desired by these submitters. But the congressional concern was with the *agency's* need or preference for confidentiality; the FOIA by itself protects the submitters' interest in confidentiality only to the extent that this interest is endorsed by the agency collecting the information.

Enlarged access to governmental information undoubtedly cuts against the privacy concerns of nongovernmental entities, and as a matter of policy some balancing and accommodation may well be desirable. We simply hold here that Congress did not design the FOIA exemptions to be mandatory bars to disclosure.[2] . . .

Chrysler contends, however, that even if its suit for injunctive relief cannot be based on the FOIA, such an action can be premised on the Trade Secrets Act, 18 U.S.C. § 1905. The Act provides:

"Whoever, being an officer or employee of the United States or of any department or agency thereof, publishes, divulges, discloses, or makes known in any manner or to any extent not authorized by law any information coming to him in the course of his employment or official duties or by reason of any examination or investigation made by, or return, report or record made to or filed with, such department or agency or officer or employee thereof, which information concerns or relates to the trade secrets, processes, operations, style of work, or apparatus, or to the identity, confidential statistical data, amount or source of any income, profits, losses, or expenditures of any person, firm, partnership, corporation, or association; or permits any income return or copy thereof or any book containing any abstract or particulars thereof to be seen or examined by any person except as provided by law; shall be fined not more than $1,000 or imprisoned not more than one year, or both; and shall be removed from office or employment."

There are necessarily two parts to Chrysler's argument: that § 1905 is applicable to the type of disclosure threatened in this case, and that it affords Chrysler a private right of action to obtain injunctive relief.

A

The Court of Appeals held that § 1905 was not applicable to the agency disclosure at issue here because such disclosure was "authorized by law" within the meaning of the Act. The court found the source of that authorization to be the OFCCP regulations that DLA relied on in deciding to disclose information on the Hamtramck and Newark plants. Chrysler contends here that these agency regulations are not "law" within the meaning of § 1905.

2. It is informative in this regard to compare the FOIA with the Privacy Act of 1974, 5 U.S.C. § 552a. In the latter Act Congress explicitly requires agencies to withhold records about an individual from most third parties unless the subject gives his permission. Even more telling is 49 U.S.C. § 1357, a section which authorizes the Administrator of the FAA to take antihijacking measures, including research and development into protection devices.

"Notwithstanding [FOIA], the Administrator shall prescribe such regulations as he may deem necessary to prohibit disclosure of any information obtained or developed in the conduct of research and development activities under this subsection if, in the opinion of the Administrator, the disclosure of such information— . . . .

"(B) would reveal trade secrets or privileged or confidential commercial or financial information obtained from any person . . . ." Id., § 1357(d)(2)(B).

It has been established in a variety of contexts that properly promulgated, substantive agency regulations have the "force and effect of law." This doctrine is so well established that agency regulations implementing federal statutes have been held to pre-empt state law under the Supremacy Clause. It would therefore take a clear showing of contrary legislative intent before the phrase "authorized by law" in § 1905 could be held to have a narrower ambit than the traditional understanding. [Examining the legislative history of the Trade Secrets Act, the Court found no such clear showing. Before turning to the question whether the OFCCP regulations constituted the authorization of law, however, it rejected a government argument that § 1905 was only an anti-leak statute applying to surreptitious, unofficial acts, and was therefore wholly irrelevant to "official" agency actions, taken within channels. That reading, the Court thought, would "require an expansive and unprecedented holding that any agency action directed or approved by an agency head is 'authorized by law' "; such a holding would be contrary to repeated assurances to the Congress that § 1905 reached formal agency action as well as employee skullduggery. The Court then resumed discussion whether the OFCCP regulations provided the required authorization.] . . .

In order for a regulation to have the "force and effect of law," it must have certain substantive characteristics and be the product of certain procedural requisites. The central distinction among agency regulations found in the Administrative Procedure Act (APA) is that between "substantive rules" on the one hand and "interpretive rules, general statements of policy, or rules of agency organization, procedure, or practice" on the other. A "substantive rule" is not defined in the APA, and other authoritative sources essentially offer definitions by negative inference. But in Morton v. Ruiz, 415 U.S. 199 (1974), we noted a characteristic inherent in the concept of a "substantive rule." We described a substantive rule—or a "legislative-type rule,"—as one "affecting individual rights and obligations." This characteristic is an important touchstone for distinguishing those rules that may be "binding" or have the "force of law."

That an agency regulation is "substantive," however, does not by itself give it the "force and effect of law." The legislative power of the United States is vested in the Congress, and the exercise of quasi-legislative authority by governmental departments and agencies must be rooted in a grant of such power by the Congress and subject to limitations which that body imposes. As this Court noted in Batterton v. Francis, 432 U.S. 416, 425 n. 9 (1977):

> Legislative, or substantive, regulations are "issued by an agency pursuant to statutory authority and . . . implement the statute, as, for example, the proxy rules issued by the Securities and Exchange Commission. . . . Such rules have the force and effect of law."

Likewise the promulgation of these regulations must conform with any procedural requirements imposed by Congress. For agency discretion is not only limited by substantive, statutory grants of authority, but also by the procedural requirements which "assure fairness and mature consideration of rules of general application." NLRB v. Wyman-Gordon Co., 394 U.S. 759, 764 (1969). The pertinent procedural limitations in this case are those found in the APA.

The regulations relied on by the Government in this case as providing "authoriz[ation] by law" within the meaning of § 1905 certainly affect individual rights and obligations; they govern the public's right to information in records obtained under Executive Order 11246 and the confidentiality rights of those who submit information to OFCCP and its compliance agencies. It is a much closer question, however, whether they are the product of a congressional grant of legislative authority.

[In an analysis that prompted Justice Marshall to observe in a special concurrence that the validity of OFCCP regulations as a whole was not in question, the Court concluded that Congress had *not* authorized the OFCCP to adopt rules having the force and effect of law on the question of information disclosure. Additionally, the Court found, the Secretary of Labor had not used notice and comment rulemaking procedures in adopting the regulations—thus confirming their character as interpretative regulations, "not the product of procedures which Congress prescribed as necessary prerequisites to giving a regulation the binding effect of law. An interpretative regulation or general statement of agency policy cannot be the 'authoriz[ation] by law' required by § 1905."]

B

We reject, however, Chrysler's contention that the Trade Secrets Act affords a private right of action to enjoin disclosure in violation of the statute. In Cort v. Ash, 422 U.S. 66 (1975), we noted that this Court has rarely implied a private right of action under a criminal statute and where it has done so "there was at least a statutory basis for inferring that a civil cause of action of some sort lay in favor of someone." Nothing in § 1905 prompts such an inference. Nor are other pertinent circumstances outlined in Cort present here. As our review of the legislative history of § 1905—or lack of same—might suggest, there is no indication of legislative intent to create a private right of action. Most importantly, a private right of action under § 1905 is not "necessary to make effective the congressional purpose," J.I. Case Co. v. Borak, 377 U.S. 426, 433 (1964), for we find that review of DLA's decision to disclose Chrysler's employment data is available under the APA.

. . . Section 10(a) of the APA provides that "[a] person suffering legal wrong because of agency action, or adversely affected or aggrieved by agency action . . . , is entitled to judicial review thereof." 5 U.S.C. § 702 (1976). Two exceptions to this general rule of reviewability are set out in § 10. Review is not available where "statutes preclude judicial review" or where "agency action is committed to agency discretion by law." 5 U.S.C. § 701(a)(1), (2) (1976). In Citizens to Preserve Overton Park, Inc. v. Volpe, 401 U.S. 402, 410 (1971), the Court held that the latter exception applies "where 'statutes are drawn in such broad terms that in a given case there is no law to apply.'" Were we simply confronted with the authorization in 5 U.S.C. § 301 to prescribe regulations regarding "the custody, use, and preservation of [agency] records, papers and property," it would be difficult to derive any standards limiting agency conduct which might constitute "law to apply." But . . . § 1905 and any "authoriz[ation] by law" contemplated by that section place substantive limits on agency action. Therefore, we conclude that DLA's decision to disclose the Chrysler reports is reviewable agency action and Chrysler is a person "adversely affected or aggrieved" within the meaning of § 10(a).

Both Chrysler and the Government agree that there is APA review of DLA's decision. They disagree on the proper scope of review. Chrysler argues that there should be de novo review, while the Government contends that such review is only available in extraordinary cases and this is not such a case.

The pertinent provisions of § 10(e) of the APA, 5 U.S.C. § 706 (1976), provide that a reviewing court shall

> "(2) hold unlawful and set aside agency action, findings, and conclusions found to be—

> "(A) arbitrary, capricious, an abuse of discretion, or otherwise not in accordance with law;

> . . .

> "(F) unwarranted by the facts to the extent that the facts are subject to trial de novo by the reviewing court."

For the reasons previously stated, we believe any disclosure that violates § 1905 is "not in accordance with law" within the meaning of 5 U.S.C. § 706(2)(A). De novo review by the District Court is ordinarily not necessary to decide whether a contemplated disclosure runs afoul of § 1905. The District Court in this case concluded that disclosure of some of Chrysler's documents was barred by § 1905, but the Court of Appeals did not reach the issue. We shall therefore vacate the Court of Appeals' judgment and remand for further proceedings consistent with this opinion in order that the Court of Appeals may consider whether the contemplated disclosures would violate the prohibition of § 1905.[3] Since the decision regarding this substantive issue—the scope of § 1905—will necessarily have some effect on the proper form of judicial review pursuant to § 706(2), we think it unnecessary, and therefore

3. Since the Court of Appeals assumed for purposes of argument that the material in question was within an exemption to the FOIA, that court found it unnecessary expressly to decide that issue and it is open on remand. We, of course, do not here attempt to determine the relative ambits of Exemption 4 and § 1905, or to determine whether § 1905 is an exempting statute within the terms of the amended Exemption 3, 5 U.S.C. § 552(b)(3) (1976). Although there is a theoretical possibility that material might be outside Exemption 4 yet within the substantive provisions of § 1905, and that therefore the FOIA might provide the necessary "authoriz[ation] by law" for purposes of § 1905, that possibility is at most of limited practical significance in view of the similarity of language between Exemption 4 and the substantive provisions of § 1905.

unwise, at the present stage of this case for us to express any additional views on that issue.

Vacated and remanded.[4]

NOTES

(1) The problem of submitters' rights in information has been the subject of continuing litigation, commentary, and legislative consideration. Many agencies have adopted rules providing for advance determinations whether information will be treated as proprietary, and/or for notification to information suppliers if requests for possibly proprietary information are received with some opportunity then to participate in agency consideration of the request.[1] When the Food and Drug Administration adopted a rule specifying categories of information that would, or would not, be afforded exemption 4 status in the event of request, and providing for pre-disclosure consultation with the supplier only when the confidentiality of the FOIA-requested information was "uncertain," 21 CFR § 20.45 (1977), the Pharmaceutical Manufacturers' Association argued that the Constitution and federal statutes required consultation in every case. The FDA also provided that a submitter of information could provide its views regarding confidentiality and, if the information was submitted voluntarily rather than in response to obligation, obtain a preliminary determination of its disclosability. 21 CFR § 20.44 (1977). Without deciding whether due process might require some form of procedure, a district court found the FDA's procedures sufficient, citing the agency's experience, its heavy FOIA caseload, and the strict time limits of the Act among the factors making "broad, categorical regulations . . . imperative [and] ad hoc inquiries or item by item consultations . . . impractical." Pharmaceutical Manufacturers' Ass'n v. Weinberger, 411 F.Supp. 576, 579 (D.C.D.C. 1976); see also Westinghouse Electric Corp. v. NRC, 555 F.2d 82 (3d Cir. 1977).

How much proprietary information has in fact been released is a matter of lively dispute. The persistence of an active Freedom of Information Act "industry" and the dominance of commercial factors among users of the Act suggest that valuable ore is in fact being mined and scholarly and professional analyses have generally supported this view—and, correspondingly, legislative provision of formal participatory rights and remedies for submitters.[2] An analysis undertaken for the Administrative Conference of the United States by Professor Russell

---

4. Mr. Justice Marshall's concurrence is omitted.

1. See, e.g., 28 CFR § 16.7 (Department of Justice); 40 CFR § 2.201 ff. (EPA); 21 CFR § 20.44–.45 (FDA); 10 CFR § 2.790 (NRC); 41 CFR § 60 et seq. (OFCCP). Surveys by the Department of Justice's Office of Information Policy reveal little uniformity among the agencies. See, e.g., U.S. Department of Justice FOIA Update, Vol. III, No. 3 ("several agencies still have no formal procedures for providing submitters with full notice and objection rights

and [others that do] do not ensure that they are followed in all instances").

2. In addition to Professor Stevenson's analysis, next cited in the text, see the resulting Administrative Conference Recommendation, ACUS 82–1, 1 CFR § 305.82–1; Symposium, Your Business, Your Trade Secrets and Your Government, 34 Ad.L.Rev. 107 (1982); Note, Reverse-FOIA Litigation, 39 Wash. & Lee L.Rev. 445 (1982); Note, Protecting Confidential Business Information from Federal Agency Disclosure, 80 Colum.L.Rev. 109 (1980);

Stevenson, Jr. found very little evidence of release of commercially valuable information, although Professor Stevenson acknowledged that submitters might not have wanted to call attention to what had been released, or that minor releases, of incremental value, may not have come to attention.[3] Stevenson concluded that "the perception that business secrets are not safe in the hands of the government is itself reason enough to attempt to rationalize agency procedures in order to provide greater guarantees that competitively sensitive information will not improperly be disclosed pursuant to FOIA requests." R. Stevenson, Jr., Protecting Business Secrets Under the Freedom of Information Act: Managing Exemption 4, 34 Ad.L.Rev. 207, 218–222, 261 (1982).

(2) One of the few documented releases of commercially valuable information concerned the formula for an herbicide registered with the Environmental Protection Agency by the Monsanto Corporation. During the pendency of a lawsuit brought by Monsanto to challenge provisions of the Federal Insecticide, Fungicide and Rodenticide Act authorizing EPA to make public or use data submitted by a manufacturer in other proceedings, the EPA mistakenly released the information in response to an FOIA request. Monsanto's lawsuit resulted in a holding by the Supreme Court that trade secrets submitted by manufacturers in an application process might constitute "property" (depending on relevant state law) that the government could not disclose or use for the benefit of others without paying the "just compensation" owing to any person whose property is taken for public use. This conclusion would apply where the trade secrets were "property" under state law *and* federal law created an expectation that submitted information would neither be disclosed nor used in assessing other applicants' submissions to the agency without appropriate compensation. RUCKEL-SHAUS V. MONSANTO CO., 467 U.S. 986 (1984).

When the mistaken FOIA disclosure came to light, Monsanto moved in its proceeding against EPA to prevent competitors from registering pesticides based on the disclosed information. Under the resulting orders, the attorney to whom the material had been disclosed

---

Committee on Fed. Legislation, A Remedy to Prevent Injury From Freedom of Information Act Disclosure, 34 Rec.A.B. City of N.Y. 612 (1979).

Typical of the legislative proposals is S. 774, 98th Cong., 1st Sess., which unanimously passed the Senate in 1984 but then lapsed. See p. 734 n. 21 above. Under the bill, submitters of information who initially designated information as confidential would have been given notice of any request for the information and an opportunity to respond in writing. The submitter would then have been authorized to seek judicial review of any outcome adverse to its position; on review, the court was to determine the applicability of exemption 4 de novo.

3. Those examples that were brought to Professor Stevenson's attention, he concluded, often proved on further analysis not ascribable to maladministration under the Act. Three earlier investigators thought skillful FOIA use produced demonstrable if not dramatic commercial advantages—one competitor learned enough about another's design and testing of an inflatable life raft to be able to design its own; a railroad used ICC statistics to gain a more accurate picture of the age and capacity of its rivals' freight car fleets; others garnered information competition had paid to develop about shared markets. D. Montgomery, A. Peters & C. Weinberg, The Freedom of Information Act: Strategic Opportunities and Threats, 19 Sloan Mgmnt.Rev. 1002 (1978). See also Worthington Compressors, Inc. v. Castle, 662 F.2d 45 (1981), petition for rehearing denied 668 F.2d 1371 (D.C.Cir.1981).

returned the data, affirming that no copies had been retained but refusing on grounds of privilege to identify his client. EPA and Monsanto then entered a consent decree establishing a special review procedure intended to screen applications for new registration to detect any "leakage" that might nonetheless have occurred. The problem now was to protect Monsanto's interest in its proprietary information without compromising the like interests of new applicants who very probably had *not* had the advantage of Monsanto's submissions. See Monsanto Co. v. Ruckelshaus, 753 F.2d 649 (8th Cir.1985).

(3) In the APA review proceeding Chrysler Corp. establishes as the proper vehicle for reverse-FOIA suits, what is the standard of review for an agency's conclusion that given information does not fall within Exemption 4? (The Chrysler case, recall, addressed this question only in the context of the Trade Secret Act.) A conclusion that the exemption does apply would be reviewed de novo; legislative proposals and recommendations for reverse-FOIA procedures generally suggest the same standard should be enacted in providing for review of agency determinations that the exemption does not apply; [4] can that result be reached judicially, under Section 706 of the APA alone? Yes, reasoned Chief Judge Spottswood Robinson, III of the D.C. Circuit in a concurrence in NAT'L ORG. FOR WOMEN, WASHINGTON D.C. CHAPTER v. SOCIAL SECURITY ADMINISTRATION, 736 F.2d 727 (D.C.Cir.1984)—a case whose factual background rather resembles that of Chrysler Corp.[5] As interpreted in Citizens to Preserve Overton Park v. Volpe, p. 436 above, Section 706(2)(F) authorizes de novo review "when the action is adjudicating in nature and the agency factfinding procedures are inadequate." Regarding the proceedings as "adjudicative" in the APA sense, Judge Robinson found the agency procedures inadequate from the submitters' perspective:

"I start with the 'fundamental proposition of administrative law that interested parties must have an effective chance to respond to crucial facts.' This precept finds expression in the familiar requirement of notice of contemplated agency action and opportunity to be heard, and its reach extends to a demand for suitable means of addressing not only the opponent's case but the agency's concerns as well. . . .

"In the litigation at bar, the principal question before OFCCP was the applicability of FOIA's Exemption 4, which ushered in centrally a test distinctly factual in nature: whether disclosure of the sought-after data likely would beget substantial harm to the companies' competitive positions. The agency's regulations confined the companies, in their efforts to establish just such a threat, to written specifications of reasons for confidential treatment. . . . Neither the agency's regulations nor its procedures offered the companies any guidance in focusing their presentations or documentation and, for much of the material implicated, the companies became aware of the agency's objections to their claims only after the agency's final decision to disclose. . . .

4. See p. 769 n. 2 above.   5. See p. 763 n. 1 above.

[T]he companies had no opportunity whatsoever to learn the final decisionmaker's concerns, much less to address them." Judicial review *would* be confined to the administrative record, and "arbitrary, capricious" review, if the agency provided more adequate procedures.

Judges Mikva and McGowan, the other members of the panel, disagreed, believing that agency "procedures must be severely defective before a court proceeding under the APA can substitute de novo review for review of the agency's record. . . .

"[A]lthough we might not describe the agency's procedures as being the most effective or open, they were not closed, unfair, or otherwise inadequate to the task of developing a factual record, as well as a record of submitters' objections, based upon which one could decide rationally whether material is exempt from disclosure. For this reason, we disagree with Chief Judge Robinson's conclusion that de novo review was proper here under the APA."

(ii) Individual Privacy

DEPARTMENT OF THE AIR FORCE v. ROSE

Supreme Court of the United States (1976).
425 U.S. 352.

MR. JUSTICE BRENNAN delivered the opinion of the Court.

Respondents, student editors or former student editors of the New York University Law Review researching disciplinary systems and procedures at the military service academies for an article for the Law Review, were denied access by petitioners to case summaries of honor and ethics hearings, with personal references or other identifying information deleted, maintained in the United States Air Force Academy's Honor and Ethics Code Reading Files, although Academy practice is to post copies of such summaries on 40 squadron bulletin boards throughout the Academy and to distribute copies to Academy faculty and administration officials.[1] . . .

Under the Honor Code enrolled cadets pledge that "We will not lie, steal, or cheat, nor tolerate among us anyone who does." The Honor Code is administered by an Honor Committee composed of Academy cadets. . . . At the [conclusion of an Honor Board Hearing] the Honor Committee Chairman reminds all cadets present at the hearing that all matters discussed at the hearing are confidential and should not be discussed outside the room with anyone other than an Honor Representative. A case summary consisting of a brief statement, usually only one page, of the significant facts is prepared by the Committee. As we have said, copies of the summaries are posted on 40 squadron bulletin boards throughout the Academy, and distributed

---

1. Upon respondent Rose's request for documents, Academy officials gave him copies of the Honor Code, the Honor Reference Manual, Lesson Plans, Honor Hearing Procedures, and various other materials explaining the Honor and Ethics Codes. They denied him access to the case summaries, however, on the grounds that even with the names deleted "[s]ome cases may be recognized by the reader by the circumstances alone without the identity of the cadet given" and "[t]here is no way of determining just how these facts will or could be used."

among Academy faculty and administration officials. Cadets are instructed not to read the summaries, unless they have a need, beyond mere curiosity, to know their contents, and the Reading Files are covered with a notice that they are "for official use only." . . . [I]n guilty cases, the guilty cadet's name is not deleted from the summary, but posting on the bulletin boards is deferred until after the guilty cadet has left the Academy.

[The respondents brought suit under the Freedom of Information Act, but their claims were rejected by the district court on the alternative grounds that the case summaries "related solely to the internal personnel rules and practices" of the Air Force, 5 U.S.C. § 552(b)(2) and that, even as edited, they were "files the disclosure of which would constitute a clearly unwarranted invasion of personal privacy," 5 U.S.C. § 552(b)(6). The Second Circuit reversed, finding the second exemption inapplicable and the sixth exemption potentially avoidable through careful editing by the district court of the case summaries.

In discussing the second exemption (concerning internal personnel rules and practices), the Court resolved conflicting indications in the legislative history by crediting the Senate report—"the only committee report that was before both houses of Congress." On the Senate view of the exemption, it was to apply only in the case of "minor or trivial matters."

"The general thrust of the exemption is simply to relieve agencies of the burden of assembling and maintaining for public inspection matter in which the public could not reasonably be expected to have an interest." Because "the implication for the general public of the Academy's administration of discipline is obvious," and "underscored by the Agency's own proclamations of the importance of cadet-administered Codes to the Academy's educational and training program," the majority reasoned, "the case summaries plainly do not fit that description."]

Additional questions are involved in the determination whether Exemption 6 exempts the case summaries from mandatory disclosure as "personnel and medical files and similar files the disclosure of which would constitute a clearly unwarranted invasion of personal privacy."
. . .

[The Court first disposed of an argument that "personnel" files were to be wholly excluded; the argument was untenable in light of the clear expectation that private and public interests would be in tension in each Exemption 6 proceeding.]

Thus, § 552(b) now provides that "[a]ny reasonably segregable portion of a record shall be provided to any person requesting such record after deletion of the portions which are exempt under this subsection." And § 552(a)(4)(B) was added explicitly to authorize in camera inspection of matter claimed to be exempt "to determine whether such records *or any part* thereof shall be withheld." The Senate Report accompanying this legislation explains, without distinguishing "personnel and medical files" from "similar files," that its effect is to require courts to look beneath the label on a file or record when the withholding of information is challenged. . . . [W]here files are involved [courts will] have to examine the records themselves and require disclosure of portions to which the purposes of the exemption under which they are withheld does not apply. S.Rep. No. 854, 93d Cong., 2d Sess., 32. . . .

The Agency argues secondly that . . . the Court of Appeals nevertheless improperly ordered the Agency to produce the case summaries in the District Court for an in camera examination to eliminate information that could result in identifying cadets involved in Honor or Ethics Code violations.

This contention has no merit. First, the argument implies that Congress barred disclosure in any case in which the conclusion could not be guaranteed that disclosure would not trigger recollection of identity in any person whatever. But this ignores Congress' limitation of the exemption to cases of "clearly unwarranted"[2] invasions of personal privacy. Second, Congress vested the courts with the responsibility ultimately to determine "de novo" any dispute as to whether the exemption was properly invoked in order to constrain agencies from withholding nonexempt matters. No court has yet seen the case histories, and the Court of Appeals was therefore correct in holding that the function of examination must be discharged in the first instance by the District Court.

In striking the balance whether to order disclosure of all or part of the case summaries, the District Court, in determining whether disclosure will entail a "clearly unwarranted" invasion of personal privacy, may properly discount its probability in light of Academy tradition to keep identities confidential within the Academy. Respondents sought only such disclosure as was consistent with this tradition. . . . As the Court of Appeals recognized, however, what constitutes identifying information regarding a subject cadet must be weighed not only from the viewpoint of the public, but also from the vantage of those who would have been familiar, as fellow cadets or Academy staff, with other aspects of his career at the Academy. . . . [T]he risk to the privacy interests of a former cadet, particularly one who has remained in the military, posed by his identification by otherwise unknowing former colleagues or instructors cannot be rejected as trivial.

To be sure, redaction cannot eliminate all risks of identifiability, as any human approximation risks some degree of imperfection, and the

---

2. The addition of this qualification was a considered and significant determination. Robles v. EPA, 484 F.2d 843, 846 (4th Cir. 1973); Getman v. NLRB, 450 F.2d 670, 674 (D.C.Cir.1971). The National Labor Relations Board and Treasury Department urged at the hearings on the Act that the "clearly" or "clearly unwarranted" qualification in Exemption 6 be deleted. The terms objected to were nevertheless retained, as a "proper balance," H.R. No. 1497, at 11, to keep the "scope of the exemption . . . within bounds," S.Rep. No. 819, at 9.

The legislative history of the 1974 amendment of Exemption 7, which applies to investigatory files compiled for law enforcement purposes, stands in marked contrast. . . . In response to a Presidential request to delete "clearly unwarranted" from the amendment in the interests of personal privacy, the Conference Committee dropped the "clearly," and the Bill was enacted as reported by the Conference.

consequences of exposure of identity can admittedly be severe. But redaction is a familiar technique in other contexts and exemptions to disclosure under the Act were intended to be practical workable concepts. Moreover, we repeat, Exemption 6 does not protect against disclosure every incidental invasion of privacy—only such disclosures as constitute "clearly unwarranted" invasions of personal privacy.

Affirmed.

MR. CHIEF JUSTICE BURGER, dissenting.

The Court correctly notes that Congress, in enacting Exemption 6, intended to strike "a proper balance between the protection of the individual's right of privacy and the preservation of the public's right to Government information by excluding those kinds of files the disclosure of which might harm the individual." H.R.Rep. No. 1497, at 11. Having acknowledged the necessity of such a balance, however, the Court, in my view, blandly ignores and thereby frustrates the congressional intent by refusing to weigh, realistically, the grave consequences implicit in release of this particular information, in any form, against the relatively inconsequential claim of "need" for the material alleged in the complaint.

The opinions of this Court have long recognized the opprobrium which both the civilian and the military segments of our society attribute to allegations of dishonor among commissioned officers of our Armed Forces. . . . The absence of the broken sword, the torn epaulets and the Rogue's March from our military ritual does not lessen the indelibility of the stigma. . . .

Admittedly, the Court requires that, before release, these documents be subject to in camera inspection with power of excising parts. But, as the Court admits, any such attempt to "sanitize" these summaries would still leave the very distinct possibility that the individual would still be identifiable and thereby injured. In light of Congress' recent manifest concern in the Privacy Act of 1974 for "governmental respect for the privacy of citizens . . . " it is indeed difficult to attribute to Congress a willingness to subject an individual citizen to the risk of possible severe damage to his reputation simply to permit law students to invade individual privacy to prepare a law journal article. Its definition of a "clearly unwarranted invasion of personal privacy" as equated with "protecting an individual's private affairs from *unnecessary* public scrutiny . . . ," S.Rep. No. 813, at 9 (emphasis applied), would otherwise be rendered meaningless.

Moreover, excision . . . would place an intolerable burden upon a district court. . . . [T]here is nothing in the legislative history of the original Act or its amendments which would require a district court to construct, in effect, a new document. Yet, the excision process mandated here could only require such a sweeping reconstruction of the material that the end product would constitute an entirely new document.

. . .

Accordingly, I would reverse the judgment of the Court of Appeals.

[BLACKMUN and REHNQUIST, JJ., also dissented. STEVENS, J., did not participate.]

NOTES

(1) ARIEFF v. UNITED STATES DEPARTMENT of the NAVY, 712 F.2d 1462 (D.C.Cir.1983): The possibility that a court will use "in camera" readings or affidavits to determine FOIA issues assumes added complexity for requesters attempting to force disclosure in the face of an exemption 6 claim, where the court must balance competing interests ("clearly unwarranted") as well as determine whether the exemption, in terms, applies ("invasion of personal privacy"). An investigative journalist sought information from the Navy about prescription drugs that had been supplied to a congressional office serving members of Congress, Supreme Court Justices and others. Although the reporter specifically denied wanting information identifying the recipients, the Navy denied the request, voicing a fear that, for some drugs, "just a single bit of information . . . would transform speculation about Members' medical conditions . . . into certain knowledge." An in camera affidavit— consequently one not revealed to the requester—identified several drugs and the disease-specific inferences that could be drawn from knowing they had been prescribed.

The D.C. Circuit concluded that a generalized fear—"a 'mere possibility' that the medical condition of a particular individual might be disclosed"—could not suffice to invoke the exemption. In examining whether the risk to privacy in a particular case might be greater, however, a court would be free to use "in camera" affidavits:

"The Freedom of Information Act specifically authorizes the courts to 'examine the contents of . . . agency records in camera to determine whether such records or any part thereof shall be withheld under any of the exemptions . . . .' 5 U.S.C. § 552(a)(4)(B). The in camera presentation in the present case consisted not of "the contents of . . . agency records" but of factual assertions and expert opinion relating to those contents—a greater distortion of normal judicial process, since it combines the element of secrecy with the element of one-sided, ex parte presentation. However, the statutory authorization for in camera examination of records was merely a confirmation of (and perhaps encouragement to the use of) a power that the courts already possessed. And like that power, the receipt of in camera affidavits is also, when necessary, 'part of a trial judge's procedural arsenal.' . . .

"Appellant suggests that, even if receipt of the in camera affidavit was proper, at least the court should have permitted his counsel and his expert, Dr. Wolfe, to examine the affidavit and respond to it under appropriate protective order restricting further disclosure. . . .

"Although dictum in one of our FOIA cases refers to the court's 'inherent discretionary power' to adopt such a procedure of selective access, the decisions of this court cited for that proposition all involved the assertion of executive privilege. That class of case is quite different from FOIA litigation. Ordinarily, it involves pretrial discovery demands, so that what is disclosed to selected agents of the demanding party is merely data that may be useful as evidence or as a lead to further investigation—not information which it is the very object of the law suit to obtain. Even in that context, the procedure (as applied to access by counsel) strains the attorney-client relationship, but at least it does not put the attorney in the position of knowing, and being unable to disclose to his principal, the very data he has been retained to acquire. . . .

"Citizens whose personal privacy or commercial data is at issue, foreign governments that may have provided secret information to our Executive Branch, and, for that matter, the officials of our Executive Branch itself, will hardly have the assurance which it is the purpose of the FOIA exemptions to provide if hostile counsel and experts can ordinarily obtain access to assertedly exempt information. . . .

"Therefore, when an affidavit disclosing information assertedly exempt from production under the FOIA is proffered, we think that the district court—at least as a general matter—is limited to the stark choice of receiving it ex parte and in camera, or receiving it not at all. We have said that the former course should be chosen only ' "where absolutely necessary." ' Salisbury v. United States, 690 F.2d 966, 973 n. 3 (D.C.Cir.1982), quoting from Allen v. CIA, 636 F.2d 1287, 1298 n. 63 (D.C.Cir.1980). That necessity exists when (1) the validity of the government's assertion of exemption cannot be evaluated without information beyond that contained in the public affidavits and in the records themselves, and (2) public disclosure of that information would compromise the secrecy asserted. There is no basis for setting aside the district court's application of that test to the facts of the present case. Evaluation of the claim that the name of the drug would disclose the disease for which it was prescribed would be impossible without further explanation; and that explanation would of necessity disclose the name of the drug itself.

"We cannot pretend to be comfortable in endorsing regular use of ex parte procedures—a practice out of accord with normal usage under our common law tradition, in which the judge functions as the impartial arbiter of a dispute fully argued by both parties before him. But FOIA cases as a class present an unusual problem that demands an unusual solution: One party knows the contents of the withheld records while the other does not; and the courts have been charged with the responsibility of deciding the dispute without altering that unequal condition, since that would involve disclosing the very material sought to be kept secret. The task can often not be performed by proceeding in the traditional fashion, so that what is a rarity among our cases generally must become a commonplace in this unique field."

(2) Elaborating on the Freedom of Information Act's recognition of privacy interests, Congress in 1974 enacted the Federal Privacy Act, 5 U.S.C. § 552a. The Act is concerned wholly with the privacy interests of individuals, not corporations and in general reflects five principles of "fair information practice" identified by an influential Report of the Secretary of Health, Education and Welfare's Advisory Committee on

Automated Personnel Data Systems, Records, Computers, and the Rights of Citizens 41 (1973):

"(1) There must be no personal data recordkeeping systems whose very existence is secret.

(2) There must be a way for an individual to find out what information about him is in a record and how it is used.

(3) There must be a way for an individual to prevent information about him that was obtained for one purpose from being used or made available for other purposes without his consent.

(4) There must be a way for an individual to correct or amend a record of identifiable information about him.

(5) Any organization creating, maintaining, using, or disseminating records of identifiable personal data must assure the reliability of the data for their intended use and must take reasonable precautions to prevent misuse of the data."

As these principles suggest, the Act is more concerned with regularity of information use than with restrictions on use.[1] Accordingly, information seekers are encouraged to obtain it from the subject of the inquiry or with her knowledge. Notice, actual or formal, is to be provided of the reasons for which information is being sought, the authority on which it is being sought, and any consequences of failure to respond. Only "relevant" information is to be sought or retained in government files. With exceptions reminiscent of the first, third and seventh exemptions of the FOIA (those having to do with restricted access materials and investigations), an individual is entitled to access to identifiable records concerning her and procedures are set out by which she may seek to have information she regards as inaccurate corrected.

For some individuals, for example federal employees concerned about the contents of their personnel files, the Act provides new rights and remedies of substantial importance. But it does not provide as significant a remedy as the FOIA. The limitations on acquisition and use of information, while responsive to privacy needs in the computer era, "explicitly recognize the legitimate needs of government departments to acquire, rely on and disseminate relevant personal information. . . . A fair reading of [the Act's provisions intended to enhance information quality] reveals that high standards of information quality are by no means inevitable. . . . In contrast to the FOIA, the right of access afforded by the Privacy Act is not designed to free up public entry to the full range of government files. Rather, access under the Privacy Act is merely a necessary adjunct to the broader objective of assuring information quality by obtaining the views of persons with the interest and ability to contribute to the accuracy of agency records."

1. Because of this differing character, Privacy Act exemptions are not to be regarded as establishing a specific exemption from disclosure for purposes of section 552(b)(3) of FOIA. 5 U.S.C. § 552a(q)(2), added by P.L. 98–477, 98 Stat. 2212. For some types of files—criminal investigation or intelligence files—Congress might well decide to direct disclosure under FOIA procedures without believing that the correction/response procedures of the Privacy Act were appropriate, H.Rep. No. 98–726, 98th Cong. 2d Sess., Pt. II, pp. 15–17 (1984).

Smiertka v. United States Dept. of Treasury, 447 F.Supp. 221, 226–227 (D.D.C.1978), remanded for consideration of possible mootness, 604 F.2d 698 (D.C.Cir.1979). See also, A. Alder & M. Hadperin, Litigation Under the Federal FOIA and Privacy Acts (9th ed. 1984); Report of the Privacy Protection Study Commission, Personal Privacy in an Information Society (1977); Project, Government Information and the Rights of Citizens, 73 Mich.L.Rev. 1323 (1975); J. Hanus and H. Relyea, A Policy Assessment of the Privacy Act of 1974, 25 Amer.U.L.Rev. 555 (1976).

(3) The federal government is not alone in opening official files to public view. Virtually all states have statutory counterparts of the Freedom of Information Act, and of the Privacy Act as well.[2] In addition, the common law right of access to information held by public bodies has been an important source for legal development in the states, albeit one which may be receding as statutory enactments come increasingly to dominate the field. Thus, in City of St. Matthews v. Voice of St. Matthews, 519 S.W.2d 811 (Ky.1974), the Court of Appeals of Kentucky recognized the right of a newspaper to inspect tax assessment records, payroll records, building permits, and a wide variety of other "public records," subject only to showing "a purpose which tends to advance or further a wholesome public interest or a legitimate private interest," and that "(1) The inspection shall be conducted at reasonable times and places and in such a manner as not to unduly interfere with the proper operation of the office of the custodian of the records. (2) The records sought to be inspected are not exempt from inspection by law. (3) The disclosure of the information would not be detrimental to the public interest or violative of confidentiality under a countervailing public policy entitled to greater weight than the policy favoring free access to public records." While ordinarily, the court remarked, it would look to the legislature to establish public policy in such matters, in the absence of legislative action "it is entirely proper and strictly in keeping with the ancient tradition of the common law for the courts to provide a policy when necessity demands it." Other courts employing the common law right, it may be remarked, have often demanded a greater showing of interest as a prerequisite to inspection, taken a more restrictive view of what constitutes a "public record," and evidenced a willingness to recognize claims of common law privilege grounded in rather diffuse considerations of public policy.[3]

2. State law is surveyed in J. O'Reilly, Federal Information Disclosure, ch. 27 and B. Braverman & Heppler, A Practical Review of State Open Records Laws, 49 Geo. Wash.L.Rev. 720 (1981). As to particular state laws, see e.g., Note, Public Access to Governmental Records and Meetings in Arizona, 16 Ariz.L.Rev. 891 (1974); Comment, The California Public Records Act: the Public's Right of Access to Governmental Information, 7 Pac.L.J. 105 (1976); Note, California Privacy Act: Controlling Government's Use of Information? 32 Stan.L.Rev. 1001 (1980); Comment, Public Access to Government Held Records, 55 N.C.L.Rev. 1187 (1977); Note, The Texas Open Records Act, 14 Hous.L.Rev. 398 (1977); Note, The Wisconsin Public Records Law, 67 Marq.L.Rev. 65 (1983).

Representative state laws include Iowa Code § 68A (1971), discussed in Note, The Iowa Freedom of Information Act, 47 Iowa L.Rev. 1163 (1972); Or.Rev.Stat. 192.410 ff.; West's Ann. Cal. Gov. Code §§ 6250–6260; and Mich.Comp.L.Ann. § 15.23 et seq.; see Op.Atty.Gen. 1972, No. 4730.

3. Note, Access to Public Documents in Kentucky, 64 Ky.L.J. 165 (1975). Project, Government Information and the Rights of Citizens, 73 Mich.L.Rev. 971, 1164, 1170, 1178–1180. In the Spring of 1973, the Northwestern University Law Review published an issue wholly devoted to Public

The Kentucky court's decision was doubtless one factor in the enactment during the next General Assembly of an Open Records law which in some, but not all, respects resembles the FOIA.[4]

While some states have looked to federal decisions or interpretive material in construing their own laws, statutory differences have played as large a part in the outcome as have the similarities. Thus, in School Bd. of Marion County v. Public Employees Relations Comm., 334 So.2d 582 (Fla.1976), the Florida Supreme Court permitted access to union authorization cards under the state open records law; it recognized that the NLRB could successfully deny access under the FOIA but concluded that Florida law gave the employer a greater stake in obtaining the information, and was not so solicitous of employee privacy. See also Industrial Foundation of the South v. Texas Industrial Accident Bd., 540 S.W.2d 668 (Tex.1976) (Department of the Air Force v. Rose balancing test will not be applied. "Although the [Texas] Open Records Act is similar in many ways to the Freedom of Information Act, our State law contains no exception comparable to exception 6 of the federal act.")

SECTION 2. GOVERNMENT IN THE SUNSHINE

COMMON CAUSE v. NUCLEAR REGULATORY COMMISSION

United States Court of Appeals, District of Columbia Circuit, 1982.
674 F.2d 921.

[The Nuclear Regulatory Commission, like other agencies, meets yearly to formulate its requests to the Office of Management for inclusion in the Presidential budget. As the materials of Chapter 2, Section 3 of this casebook suggest, the process of formulating spending priorities and limits is both a major opportunity for setting policy and a time of significant competition and horse-trading—within an agency, among agencies generally, between the agencies and the President, and, finally, with Congress. Historically, it has been a closed process, and that closure—particularly from congressional oversight—has been zealously guarded by OMB.

The Federal Government in the Sunshine Act, 5 U.S.C. § 552b enacted in 1976, required multi-member federal agencies such as the NRC to open their meetings to the public unless (and to the extent that)

Access to Information, 68 Nw.U.L.Rev. 176, and largely concerned with practice rather than legal framework. The bulk of the issue reports, in detail, what appears to have been a well-controlled experiment testing the availability of information from a variety of state and local agencies in the vicinity of Chicago, Illinois. Illinois, at the time, had no single public information law, but many documents were nonetheless regarded as public, and legally available, under existing common and statutory law. (The current provision is at Ill.Rev.Stat. ch. 116, §§ 43.4–.28 (Supp.1974)). A wide variation in response to inquiry occurred. Not

surprisingly, perhaps, relatively cordial inquiries, or inquiries that promised to show the agency in a good light, or inquiries appearing "moderate" politically, were more apt to attract response, and fuller response, than their opposites, even though more work might be required to answer these inquiries than the hostile ones. At 263–267.

4. KRS 61.870–.884, Enact. Acts 1976, Ch. 273. See E. Ziegler, Jr., The Kentucky Open Records Act: A Preliminary Analysis, 7 N.Ky.L.Rev. 7 (1980).

the subject-matter to be discussed fell within ten defined exemptions. (The Act is set out in Appendix A, within.) The Commission decided that its July 18, 1980 budget meeting fell within exemption 9(B) of the Act, which permits closing of meetings if premature disclosure of the discussion would be "likely to significantly frustrate implementation of a proposed agency action." 5 U.S.C. § 552b(c)(9)(B) (1976). A representative of the public interest group Common Cause, who wished to attend the meeting, was excluded. At that meeting the Commissioners received a preliminary briefing from the staff concerning the Commission's budgetary needs and the relationship of each office's budget requests to agency and Office of Management and Budget (OMB) guidelines and previous appropriation levels.

Common Cause brought, and won, an action in District Court challenging this closure.[1] During the summer of 1981, while its appeal from this ruling remained pending, the NRC met to consider the next year's budget requests. On the advice of its General Counsel it divided these meetings into two categories: preliminary staff briefings, designed to provide Commission members with background information and staff advice; and meetings in which the Commissioners would decide on specific funding levels for the agency's budget proposals to OMB (markup), and would also consider intra-agency appeals from initial markup decisions. While it held the preliminary staff briefings, which it thought "similar in nature" to the July 18, 1980 meeting, in public, it closed the markup/appeal meeting, relying on Exemptions 2 and 6[2] as well as Exemption 9(B).

Common Cause, notified of this decision, again sought and obtained from district court a ruling that the closure had been improper, and this ruling also was appealed. A final matter arose while both appeals remained pending, when in the fall of 1981 OMB proposed substantial reductions in the Commission's budget, but gave the agency an opportunity to appeal the cutbacks. The Commission held a two-part budget meeting to prepare its appeal to OMB. The first part, which dealt generally with the status of the Commission's budget request, was open to the public. The second part, which considered the specific budget items involved in the appeal, was held in closed session. The Commission asserted in justification of this closure that unless the discussion of its priorities, negotiation strategy, and fallback positions could be closed the agency's goal of minimizing OMB's reductions would be "significantly frustrated" within the meaning of Exemption 9(B). It also invoked Exemptions 2, 6 and 10 of the Sunshine Act.[3] Again its arguments were rejected by the district court.]

1. In the interest of simplification this statement of facts does not recount the relief ordered by the District Court, and resulting complexities during the appeal process. The remedy found appropriate by the court of appeals was release to the public of the transcripts the Act requires agencies keep of closed meetings. 5 U.S.C. § 552b(f)(1).

2. Exemption 2, for "internal personnel rules and practices," 5 U.S.C. § 552b(c)(2), and Exemption 6, for "information of a personal nature where disclosure would constitute a clearly unwarranted invasion of personal privacy," 5 U.S.C. § 552b(c)(6), essentially replicate Exemptions 2 and 6 of the FOIA.

3. Exemption 10 shields discussions that "specifically concern an agency's issuance of a subpena," or its participation in a civil proceeding or arbitration, or its con-

Before WRIGHT, WILKEY, and GINSBURG, CIRCUIT JUDGES.

WRIGHT, CIRCUIT JUDGE: . . .

A. The Purposes of the Sunshine Act

Congress enacted the Sunshine Act to open the deliberations of multi-member federal agencies to public view. It believed that increased openness would enhance citizen confidence in government, encourage higher quality work by government officials, stimulate well-informed public debate about government programs and policies, and promote cooperation between citizens and government. In short, it sought to make government more fully accountable to the people. In keeping with the premise that "government should conduct the public's business in public," the Act established a general presumption that agency meetings should be held in the open. Once a person has challenged an agency's decision to close a meeting, the agency bears the burden of proof. Even if exempt subjects are discussed in one portion of a meeting, the remainder of the meeting must be held in open session.

The Act went farther than any previous federal legislation in requiring openness in government. In general the Sunshine Act's exemptions parallel those in the Freedom of Information Act (FOIA), but there is an important difference. Unlike FOIA, which specifically exempts "predecisional" memoranda and other documents on the premise that government cannot "operate in a fishbowl," the Sunshine Act was designed to open the predecisional process in multi-member agencies to the public. During the legislative process a number of federal agencies specifically objected to the Sunshine Act's omission of an exemption for predecisional deliberations. Congress deliberately chose to forego the claimed advantages of confidential discussions among agency heads at agency meetings.

Express language in the Sunshine Act also demonstrates that Congress did not intend to follow the FOIA pattern for predecisional discussions at agency meetings.[4] The Sunshine Act applies to all "meetings," which are defined as deliberations which determine or result in "the joint conduct or disposition of official agency business[.]" 5 U.S.C. § 552b(a)(2) (1976). The legislative history demonstrates that

---

duct of formal agency proceedings. 5 U.S.C. § 552b(c)(10).

4. The Senate Report explained that the Freedom of Information Act did not provide enough information to enable the public to "understand the reasons an agency has acted in a certain way, or even what exactly it has decided to do," because "[f]ormal statements in support of agency action are frequently too brief, or too general, to fully explain the Commission's reasoning, or the compromises that were made." S.Rep. No. 94–354, supra note 1, at 5. "By requiring important decisions to

be made openly," the Senate committee added "this bill will create better public understanding of agency decisions." Id.

A leading commentary on the Sunshine Act has recognized the "unavoidable tension between FOIA exemption (5), which recognizes a legitimate governmental interest in protecting the agency deliberative process as such," and the Sunshine Act "which aims at maximum exposure of that process, at least at the collegial level." [R. Berg & S. Klitzman, An Interpretive Guide to the Government in the Sunshine Act] 98 (1978).

"official agency business" means far more than reviewable final action. The Senate report expressly stated:

> The definition of meetings includes the conduct, as well as the disposition, of official agency matters. It is not sufficient for the purposes of open government to merely have the public witness final agency votes. The meetings opened by Section 201(a) are not intended to be merely reruns staged for the public after agency members have discussed the issue in private and predetermined their views. The whole decisionmaking process, not merely its results, must be exposed to public scrutiny.

S.Rep. No. 94–354, 94th Cong., 1st Sess. 18 (1975).

Notwithstanding the omission of a deliberative process privilege from the Sunshine Act, the Commission asks us to hold that the deliberative process leading to formulation of an agency's budget request is exempt from the Sunshine Act. To resolve this question, we must examine the statutory underpinnings of the budget process and the specific exemptions from the Sunshine Act which the Commission invokes.

B. The Budget and Accounting Act of 1921

. . .

The Commission first relies on the President's authority, under the Budget and Accounting Act, to prescribe rules and regulations for preparation of the budget, 31 U.S.C. § 16 (1976), and on the "longstanding practice of confidentiality for Executive Branch discussions leading to the formulation of the President's Budget." The statute, however, makes no reference to confidentiality, nor does it authorize the President to prescribe budgetary rules and regulations without regard to the requirements of other federal statutes. The President's rulemaking authority under 31 U.S.C. § 16 is therefore subject to the specific requirements of the Sunshine Act. Indeed, the OMB directive to agencies, OMB Circular A–10, recognizes that "[c]ertain agencies headed by a collegial body may be required to hold their meetings open to public observation unless the agency properly determines that the matter to be discussed warrants the closing of those meetings for reasons enumerated in the Government in the Sunshine Act . . . ."

Second, the Commission reasons that . . . [i]f the proposals of individual agencies must be adopted in public, . . . development of the presidential budget would be "fragmented" and the President's discretion to choose among alternatives would be impaired. This contention reads too much into the 1921 Act, which simply requires that the President submit a single, unified Executive Branch budget proposal to Congress for consideration. It does not prescribe any method by which he must develop the consolidated budget figures which he submits. Nor does it require that the President's proposals be the only budgetary information available to the public.[5]

5. Common Cause asserts that 22 out of 30 federal agencies which reported on budget meetings in their annual Sunshine Act reports in 1979 held budget meetings

. . .

Therefore, the budget process is exempt from the open meeting requirement, in whole or in part, only if it fits within the terms of other specific Sunshine Act exemptions.

C. No Blanket Exemption for Budget Meetings

Exceptions to the Sunshine Act's general requirement of openness must be construed narrowly. H.R.Rep. No. 94–880 (part 1), 94th Cong., 2d Sess. 2 (1976). . . .

Exemption 9(B) permits closing of meetings to prevent "premature disclosure" of information whose disclosure would be likely to "significantly frustrate implementation of a proposed agency action." For two reasons, the precept of narrow construction applies with particular force to this exemption, upon which the Commission principally relies. First, as we have seen, Congress decided not to provide any exemption for predecisional deliberations because it wished the process of decision as well as the results to be open to public view. . . . Second, an overly broad construction of Exemption 9(B), which applies to all agencies subject to the Act, would allow agencies to "circumvent the spirit of openness which underlies this legislation."

. . . The House and Senate committee reports give four concrete examples of Exemption 9(B) situations. First, an agency might consider imposing an embargo on foreign shipment of certain goods; if this were publicly known, all of the goods might be exported before the agency had time to act, and the effectiveness of the proposed action would be destroyed. Second, an agency might discuss whether to approve a proposed merger; premature public disclosure of the proposal might make it impossible for the two sides to reach agreement. Third, disclosure of an agency's proposed strategy in collective bargaining with its employees might make it impossible to reach an agreement. Fourth, disclosure of an agency's terms and conditions for purchase of real property might make the proposed purchase impossible or drive up the price.

We construe Exemption 9(B) to cover those situations delineated by the narrow general principles which encompass all four legislative examples. In each of these cases, disclosure of the agency's proposals or negotiating position could affect private decisions by parties other than those who manage the federal government—exporters, potential corporate merger partners, government employees, or owners of real property. . . .

The budget process differs substantially from the examples given by the House and Senate reports. Disclosure of the agency's discussions would not affect private parties' decisions concerning regulated activity or dealings with the government. Rather, the Commission contends that opening budget discussions to the public might affect

in open session. Although these reports do not specify the substance and format of the budget meetings, they do suggest that a sizable number of federal agencies did not consider that their actions would be "significantly frustrated" by allowing the public to attend their budget meetings.

political decisions by the President and OMB. . . . [T]he Commission fears that disclosure of its time-honored strategies of item-shifting, exaggeration, and fall-back positions would give it less leverage in its "arm's length" dealings with OMB and the President, who make the final budget decisions within the Executive Branch. . . .

Moreover, in the budget context the public interest in disclosure differs markedly from its interest in the four situations described in the committee reports.   In those cases disclosure would permit either financial gain at government expense or circumvention of agency regulation.   In contrast, disclosure of budget deliberations would serve the affirmative purposes of the Sunshine Act: to open government deliberations to public scrutiny, to inform the public "what facts and policy considerations the agency found important in reaching its decision, and what alternatives it considered and rejected," and thereby to permit "wider and more informed public debate of the agency's policies. . . ."

. . .

If Congress had wished to exempt these deliberations from the Sunshine Act—to preserve the prior practice of budget confidentiality, to reduce the opportunities for lobbying before the President submits his budget to Congress, or for other reasons—it would have expressly so indicated.   Absent any such statement of legislative intent, we will not construe Exemption 9(B) of the Sunshine Act to allow budget deliberations to be hidden from the public view.[6]

. . .

D. Particularized Exemptions

The Sunshine Act contains no express exemption for budget deliberations as a whole, and we do not read such an exemption into Exemption 9(B).   We recognize, nevertheless, that specific items discussed at Commission budget meetings might be exempt from the open meetings requirement of the Act, and might justify closing portions of Commission meetings on an individual and particularized basis.[7]   After examining the transcripts of the Commission's closed meetings of July

---

6. The Sunshine Act does not, however, prevent agencies from making decisions by sequential, notational voting rather than by gathering at a meeting for deliberation and decision. See Communications Systems, Inc. v. FCC, 595 F.2d 797, 799–800 (D.C.Cir.1978); S.Rep. No. 94–1178, supra note 19, at 11 (conference report). Therefore, an agency might make its budget decisions by circulating staff memoranda and voting by notation; these documents might be protected under Exemption 5 of FOIA. If the agency holds a meeting, however, the Sunshine Act requires the meeting to be in open session. If there is an anomaly here, it was created by the choice of Congress.

7. Even if a portion of a budget meeting may lawfully be closed because that part of the discussion is protected by a specific

exemption, the Commission may not close the entire meeting. . . . When the Commission expects that exempt subject matter will arise at a budget meeting, it should make reasonable efforts to arrange its agenda so that these matters will not be interspersed with non-exempt portions of the discussion. If segregation of exempt and non-exempt material would make a coherent discussion impossible, then it may be reasonable to close the entire meeting. See, e.g., A.G. Becker Inc. v. Board of Governors of Federal Reserve System, 502 F.Supp. 378, 387 (D.D.C.1980). However, in this case the agency's contentions regarding the impracticality of segregating exempt and non-exempt material appear to rest on overly broad readings of Exemptions 2, 6, and 9(B).

. . .

27, 1981 and October 15, 1981, however, we conclude that none of the subject matter discussed at either meeting comes within any of the exemptions cited by the Commission. The Commission must therefore release the full transcripts of these meetings to the public.

[The court's discussion of the particularized exemptions is omitted.]

NOTES

(1) The Sunshine Act, like the Freedom of Information Act, reflects the tension between a general wish for openness in the conduct of governmental affairs, and particular needs for privacy and (what may not be the same thing) efficiency. FCC v. ITT WORLD COMMUNICATIONS, 466 U.S. 463 (1984), reversing 699 F.2d 1219, 1239–45 (D.C.Cir.1983), well illustrates the problems—and an initial Supreme Court reading of the Act more disposed to protect the latter interests than FOIA jurisprudence might suggest.

Three members of the FCC, less than a quorum but the full membership of that agency's Telecommunications Committee, regularly met with European and Canadian counterparts as part of a Consultative Process. One such meeting was to discuss expansion of overseas telecommunications services. The American position was to urge enlargement of the number of competitors; the three companies already serving the American market—understandably interested in retaining their position—sought to require these meetings to be held openly.

For the court of appeals, the presumption of openness established by the Act imposed on the Commission the burden of showing that the Act did not apply—a burden it had not met. The Committee was a "subdivision . . . authorized to act on behalf of the agency" and hence subject to the Act. The Act's application to "deliberations that determine or result in the joint conduct . . . of official agency business" must be interpreted to reach meetings at which agency interests are pursued; while legislative history supported the view that "informal background discussions" were not within the Act's reach, "the Act's presumption of openness requires that all doubts be resolved against closure.

"The thrust of the [legislative history] therefore concerns 'informal background discussions' among agency members rather than between members and outsiders. Although we believe that the Sunshine Act does not per se forbid all informal off-the-record discussions between a quorum of an agency and outside parties, we conclude that an agency's burden of persuasion must be especially great in such situations. Congress intended that 'hearings' and 'meetings with the public' be open; many such gatherings could easily be characterized as 'informal background discussions which clarify issues and expose varying views.' If we did not apply the narrowest of interpretations to this language, it would readily swallow up the requirement of open 'hearings' and 'meetings with the public.'" To the argument that a meeting of the Consultative Process group was not a meeting "of" the Committee, the court had a similar response: "An agency cannot avoid [the Act] through the facile expedient of having an outside party 'hold' the discussion, for the Sunshine Act's policy that hearings and meetings with the public be open could otherwise be ignored with impunity."

The Supreme Court unanimously and tersely rejected these conclusions. While agreeing that the Committee was within reach of the Act, the Court concluded that its "official agency business" could include only the exercise of authority formally delegated to it—in effect, the taking of "agency action" within the meaning of the APA. For the Court, the important consideration was that Congress had "recognized that the administrative process cannot be conducted entirely in the public eye." Rather than a presumption of openness, it spoke of avoiding the "impair[ment of] normal agency operations without achieving significant public benefit," of "the limited scope of the statute's requirements" and of congressional "intent . . . clearly . . . to permit preliminary discussion among agency members." To reach "any group of members who exchange views or gather information on agency business . . . would require public attendance at a host of informal conversations of the type Congress understood to be necessary for the effective conduct of agency business." Even more curtly the Court found that the Consultative Process, neither convened by the FCC nor subject to its unilateral control, could not be regarded as a meeting "of" the agency.

(2) D. WELBORN, W. LYON & L. THOMAS, IMPLEMENTATION AND EFFECTS OF THE FEDERAL GOVERNMENT IN THE SUNSHINE ACT (1984) is an empirical survey of the Act undertaken for the Administrative Conference of the United States, based on judicial opinions, agency annual reports, personal interviews and roughly 700 questionnaires received from agency officials, former agency officials, and members of public groups likely to be attentive to, and benefited by, Sunshine activities. Members, the study found, tend to behave somewhat differently in open than in closed meetings—preparing more thoroughly for the open meetings, but using them more often to appeal to special interests, refraining from asking important questions, engaging less frequently in either candid exchange, sharp debate, or efforts at reconciliation of conflict. The authors found "reasons to believe that there has been a shift in patterns of decision-making behavior, at least in a number of agencies, away from collegial processes toward segmented, individualized processes in which, in the words of one commissioner, 'members are isolated from one another.' One reason is a decline of the importance of meetings as decisional vehicles, a dynamic suggested in two major ways.

"First, an increase in notation voting is perceived by more than half (54.0%) the agency respondents. It is probably true that some of the increase is to dispose of minor items previously handled in meetings, in order to avoid the red tape involved in including them on a meeting agenda. But a part of it appears to result from an aversion to public discussion of certain topics. Second, although open meetings in which collegial interactions are quite evident do take place, meetings often have no bearing on results. The inhibitions which mark the behavior of many members and staff . . . obviously imply diminished collegiality. . . . A more direct indication is the perception of a large number (83.1%) of respondents from agencies with full-time membership that members now typically make up their minds on matters dealt with in open meetings *prior* to collective discussions. The expectation that members would prepare better for meetings held in the open appears to have been realized, but at some cost to collegial processes. . . .

"Another reason for suggesting diminished collegiality is an indication of a sense that collegial bodies are impaired in the performance of the agency leadership responsibilities placed in them by statute. . . . Of 18 agencies surveyed, only officials associated with the Federal Election Commission think that the act has strengthened the collegium. Members of attentive publics perceive increased collegiality in one instance and no impact in three others, and a decline is shown for the remainder. . . .

"The essential underlying problem appears to be that policy and strategic planning and the provision of meaningful direction to the staff commonly require the speculative exploration of sensitive matters at an early stage if there are to be productive results. This is difficult to do in public when there are uncertainties about the dimensions of problems, the options, and staff and member views, and when public reactions to speculative discussions and tentative strategic thinking might cause undesirable and unwarranted reactions. Consequently, collective discussions of important matters often do not take place, or they come so late in the process that the positive effects of free collegial interaction are substantially forfeited.

"As the incidence of meaningful collective debate and negotiation among members has declined, the focus of decision-making activity has shifted toward the offices of individual members and to the staff level and involves three key sets of interactions. The first is between staff at the operating level who are handling a particular matter and the offices of the chairman and other members. The second is between members one-on-one, except presumably in three member agencies. The third is among staff assistants to members acting as surrogates for their principals, and exercising, as one member put it, 'proxies of a sort.' [1]

1. [Ed.] An apparent example of this phenomenon can be found in Republic Airlines v. CAB, 756 F.2d 1304 (8th Cir.1985). An informal proceeding before the CAB concerned the approval of agreements among several airlines about the marketing of airline tickets. The Board referred investigation to an ALJ, who heard 57 days of testimony, and compiled 40,000 pages of exhibits, and rendered a proposed opinion. The Board then undertook to review the outcome, with staff assistance. "Petitioners allege that between August and December of 1982, nineteen meetings were held between Board members and staff concerning the case. There never were more than two members of the Board present at any of these meetings. 100 CAB at 443–44 (1983). In addition, various memoranda, including a draft of a proposed opinion by the Board were circulated among the members of the Board prior to any public hearing by the Board as a whole. Petitioners contend that through these actions the Board reached its decision in secret prior to the December 9 and 16 meetings, thus shielding the decision-making process from the full scrutiny of a public hearing. We disagree.

"The discussions between Board members and staff and the circulation of memoranda among Board members were activities common to any body of responsible

"All have distinct limitations as substitutes for collegial discussions. Processes of essentially individual interactions as a means for reaching accord in particular decision situations are cumbersome and time consuming. The chain of communications is elongated, risking the filtration and distortion of views. Members may not be exposed to the full range of staff advice and expertise, and staff may experience difficulty in ascertaining clearly the thinking of members and relating the views of one of those of others. Members may also find themselves in this situation. It is difficult for a member in the position of being a swing vote to forge accommodations under such circumstances, as one who at times had been in that position observed."

Taken as a group, respondents to the survey were equally divided whether the costs or benefits of the act were greater; as might be expected, members of the public were the most enthusiastic—finding a net benefit twice as often as a net cost—and officials who had served both before and after the Act's passage, the least so.

"One result of the act about which there is fairly general agreement is that public access to information has been enlarged. More information than before about what agencies are doing, how they go about their business, and in some respects the basic forces and rationales that underpin their action, is there for the taking. There also is substantial agreement that it is the attentive publics, the journalists and those who do business with agencies and seek to influence their actions, who take advantage of the new opportunities. The major justification for the act was not the advancement of particularistic interests, however; it was a set of diffuse, systemic benefits, the most prominent of which were broadened general public knowledge and understanding of government, increased public trust and confidence in government (which polls show to have continued to decline), and improved agency responsibility and accountability. Whether any such benefits have been realized remains problematic. Respondents are quite divided in their views, and there is no independent evidence one way or the other.

"There are reasons to believe that whatever the benefits resulting from the act, they have not come without certain costs, albeit distributed somewhat unevenly across agencies. . . . The cost that is clearest and most generally felt is impairment of collegial decision-making processes, a consequence noted even by many respondents generally favorable to the sunshine law, in addition to those less positive in their attitudes. . . . A movement toward individualized, segmented processes as the setting for evaluating information, testing views and other aspects of decision making does not mean that other features of

public officials preparing to make an important decision. A review of the transcript of the public hearings reveals that although individual Board members may have had definable public policy orientations when entering the hearings, the decision was not cast in stone at the outset of the hearings. Section 552b was not intended to prevent Board members from receiving the advice of staff or to prevent the exchange of views between two Board members off-the-record. Rather, it was meant to prevent government agencies from meeting in secret as rule making bodies to deliberate and decide issues with public impact. We are satisfied that the kind of activity forbidden by the Sunshine Act did not occur here."

collegial systems are lost, such as the representation of diverse views and interests and a measure of continuity at the agency leadership level. But the most important advantages of collegial structures are diminished, to the extent that the diverse views of members are not tested in authentic deliberations, and the specialized expertise of the staff cannot be easily conjoined with the generalist perspectives of the members as a group.

"There are variations among agencies in their willingness to treat what might be considered sensitive matters in open meetings when they do not fall under one or another of the exemptions. Yet in many settings, the evidence indicates, there is an absence of meaningful meetings on fundamental questions of policy and strategy if those meetings must be in public. The major difficulty is not when the question is, 'What shall we decide in regard to this particular matter before us?' but, when it is, 'Is there a problem, and, if so, what general approaches to dealing with it might be well to consider?'

"Unfortunately, human nature dictates that the public spotlight may often inhibit the kind of behavior called for in authentic collegial deliberations on complex problems where the uncertainties may be considerable and the views diverse and in an early stage of formulation. Deliberations in this type of situation are strengthened by such behavior as the expression of views, even if they are tentative and not fully informed; the testing of views through critical queries, even if put forth only for the purpose of debate; and raising alternatives for discussion, even though one does not necessarily favor them. People, especially public officials in positions of responsibility, generally do not wish to appear unknowledgeable, uncertain, or unprincipled, which such behavior might suggest. Furthermore, there are public and policy consequences officials might appropriately wish to avoid. These include inciting public alarm about conditions that after examination are found not to pose problems; stimulating public reactions in markets and elsewhere to an anticipated action that ultimately may not be taken; generating political pressures at an early stage of attention to a problem may preclude or distort further consideration; and providing interests subject to the authority of or otherwise affected by an agency with information which weakens it in the exercise of its responsibilities, to the general public's detriment.

". . .

"In summary, clearly the Sunshine Act has proved to be no panacea for the ills besetting the relationship between the American administrative state and the American people. . . . More will will be required to determine whether the balance it strikes between the public's right to know and, particularly, the confidentiality of administrative deliberations up to a certain point is a felicitious one, or whether over the long term, it contributes to further deterioration in the relationship between citizens and their government by impeding the sound and effective administration of governmental affairs."

(3) Now that many agency meetings are open, and many that are closed must be transcribed, may resourceful counsel make what tran-

spires part of the record against which the outcome will be judicially assessed—to support, for example, an argument that although the agency's opinion states only legitimate reasons A and B for its conclusions, unlawful reason C was actually central? One occasionally finds courts unselfconsciously using Sunshine transcripts to *defeat* arguments that irregularities have occurred. See, e.g., Republic Airlines v. CAB, p. 788 n. 1 above. To date, however, the courts appear generally to have resisted the temptation to use Sunshine Act transcripts to impeach agency results. SAN LUIS OBISPO MOTHERS for PEACE v. NRC, 751 F.2d 1287 (D.C.Cir.1984), vacated in part pending rehearing en banc, 760 F.2d 1320 (D.C.Cir.1985), affirmed 789 F.2d 26 (D.C.Cir. en banc 1986) raised the issues sharply. The NRC had approved operation of a nuclear reactor in Southern California after fifteen years of proceedings marked by determined and tenacious resistance. On review, petitioners attempted to add Sunshine Act materials to the record supplied by the agency, supported with statements by a dissenting Commissioner and a congressional subcommittee chairman who had examined the materials that they demonstrated (1) the absence of a factual basis for one part of the Commission's action; (2) the use by the Commission of extra-record material; and (3) improper motivation in licensing the plant. Two judges of the initial panel, Judges Wilkey (writing) and Bork, refused even to examine the materials in camera. Where the agency has supplied a record and articulated a basis for its decision, the majority reasoned, that is the basis on which the agency's action is to be assessed.[2]

"Precedent aside, judicial reliance on an agency's stated rationale and findings is central to a harmonious relationship between agency and court, one which recognizes that the agency and not the court is the principal decisionmaker. . . . Inclusion in the record of documents recounting deliberations of agency members is especially worrisome because of its potential for dampening candid and collegial exchange between members of multi-head agencies. While *public* disclosure stifles debate to some extent, *judicial* disclosure would suppress candor still further since off-hand remarks could turn out to have *legal* significance they would not have if barred from the record on review. . . .

"The Supreme Court has declared that 'where there are administrative findings that were made at the same time as the decision . . . there must be a *strong showing* of bad faith or improper behavior before such inquiry [into the mental processes of administrative decisionmakers] may be made.'[3] Petitioners assert that the Commission denied it a hearing not because the 'earthquake/emergency preparedness' issue is not 'material,' as required under our case law, but because it did not want to delay the start of power production at Diablo Canyon.

---

2. The court had earlier permitted access to Sunshine materials where these elements were lacking. Pan American World Airways, Inc. v. CAB, 684 F.2d 31 (D.C.Cir.1982).

3. Citizens to Preserve Overton Park v. Volpe, 401 U.S. at 420 (emphasis added); see Hercules Inc. v. Environmental Protection Agency, 598 F.2d 91, 123 (D.C.Cir. 1978).

"Petitioners' allegations, while serious, have not been documented with the requisite degree of specificity to warrant either supplementing the record or reviewing the transcripts in camera. The ease with which charges of 'bad faith' could be leveled, combined with the inordinate burden resolution of such claims would entail for courts, persuade us to decline petitioners' invitation to review the transcripts and to supplement the record.

". . . A great many parties could make similar accusations of impropriety in future litigation. On their view of the law, petitioners, and other parties to future proceedings of this sort, could successfully move for supplementation as long as one sympathetic Commissioner, Congressman, or investigative reporter was willing to attest that, based on his reading of the transcript, the agency's decision was rendered in 'bad faith.' Allegations of an 'unbalanced presentation,' 'insufficient attention to arguments of the agency's staff'—indeed, virtually any accusation of irregularity in the agency's decisionmaking process— would require discovery and supplementation of the record.

"The ease with which accusations of impropriety can be made must be compared to the difficulty judges would face investigating such charges—difficulties the dissent ignores. Courts do not have a limitless capacity to review documents in camera on the off-chance that something might turn up. 'In camera inspection of disputed documents places very burdensome demands on federal trial courts,' and even greater demands on appellate courts, which, unlike the district courts, do not have experience with discovery and factfinding on a day-to-day basis. These demands are exacerbated still further when the affected documents may be voluminous and concern technical regulatory issues such as those raised by the licensing of nuclear power plants. . . . In addition . . . over-eagerness by courts to review documents in camera and to supplement the administrative-created record fails to respect the autonomy of administrative agencies. . . ."

While Judge Wald, in dissent, agreed that "a court should not routinely grant motions to supplement the record based on discontented parties' general allegations of misconduct, the unprecedented nature of the *specific* allegations of misconduct lodged by the chairman of one of the NRC oversight committees and one of the commissioners of the NRC, viewed against the disturbing background of the plant's troubled safety history, seem to me clearly sufficient to meet the special exceptions criteria allowing further inquiry by this court. Courts have recognized that supplementation of an administrative record may be justified, in the interest of effective judicial review, where there are *credible* accusations that an agency has relied on material outside the record or has acted improperly or in bad faith. Even if the Commission's position that supplementation of the record is not warranted here were to prove ultimately correct, I see no reason not to take the middle course, i.e., an in camera examination by the court of the transcripts and related documents before making the ultimate determination to deny Petitioners' Motion to Supplement the Record. I simply believe the stakes are so high and the nature and source of the accusations sufficiently credible as to make a 'business as usual'—'see no evil, hear no evil, confront no evil'—attitude on our part untenable, if we are to provide meaningful judicial review."

When en banc consideration was ordered, petitioners were permitted to file the transcripts with the court. The en banc majority, Judge Bork now writing, reiterated the panel majority's conclusion that the transcripts alone could not be sufficient to establish "the requisite bad faith and improper conduct" to warrant an inquiry into the deliberative processes of the Commission. Judge Bork stressed "the analogy to the deliberative processes of a court . . . . Without the assurance of secrecy, the court could not fully perform its functions." Judge Mikva, who indicated that he had reviewed the transcripts, concurred only in the result on this issue. He thought supplementation of the record to include the transcripts would have been justified had petitioners made an allegation "strongly supported by the record, affidavits, and specific references to the transcripts, that the agency has acted in bad faith or with improper purpose. . . . [A]n absolute judicial refusal to inspect transcripts at the threshold of judicial inquiry sweeps too broadly . . . [and] creates incentives for concealment from the public and reviewing courts . . .." On the facts, petitioners had not met Judge Mikva's standard. Four dissenting judges did not reach this issue.

(4) Open meeting statutes had been adopted in each of the fifty states by 1976, when the federal Government in The Sunshine Act, 5 U.S.C. § 552b, came into effect. That state governments led the federal government in turning to publicity for the perceived ills of government may suggest a more immediate practical impact at the state and local levels for such measures. For the press, a major and acknowledged beneficiary of such laws, the daily routines of the Interstate Commerce Commission compete with many significant "national news" items for the attention of their necessarily limited Washington News Bureaus; aside from the trade press, whose access to the doings of bureaucratic Washington may not have required improvement, most journalists appear to be resolving this competition in favor of covering the Congress, the President, and the state of the economy. At the state or local level, the number of newspapers possibly interested may be less, but the news competition is not nearly so great; one readily imagines that Atlantic City's newspaper and broadcast reporters would find meetings of commission charged to revise the city charter worthy of serious consideration for coverage. See Polillo v. Deane, 74 N.J. 562, 379 A.2d 211 (1977). (Citizens, too, seem more likely to travel downtown for a meeting than to the nation's capital.) And the reported cases give some evidence that journalists are ready to sue to enforce access—access which in this instance can provide grist for tomorrow's news, not delivery of documents weeks after a request, when their newsworthiness may have evaporated. Missoulian v. Board of Regents of Higher Educ., ___ Mont. ___, 675 P.2d 962 (1984) (performance rating of University presidents); Mayor & Alderman v. Vicksburg Printing and Publishing, 434 So.2d 1333 (Miss.1983) (city planning commission strategy session to discuss "reasonably likely" litigation); Fiscal Court of Jefferson County v. Courier Journal and Louisville Times Co., 554

S.W.2d 72 (Ky.1977) (city officials substituted telephone calls and boat club lunches for "meetings").[4]

(5) A precursor of the Sunshine Act was the Federal Advisory Committee Act, P.L. 92–463 (1972), 5 U.S.C.App.I. The Act principally seeks to control the number, composition, and mandates of advisory committees established by agencies to assist them in their work. Such committees, typically composed of unpaid or part-time members drawn from the community to advise on policy issues, can serve a valuable "sounding board" function. A common perception however, is that they often do not represent a balanced cross section of the community. Represented interests, consulted at an early stage by an agency, have an opportunity to shape agency policy superior in time and influence to interests not represented on such panels. Section 10 of the Act required open meetings and advanced public notice, as one means of countering this perceived difficulty; closure was permitted in accordance with the Freedom of Information Act's exemptions (the Sunshine Act now governs). See Wegman, The Utilization and Management of Federal Advisory Committees (1983); M. Cardozo, The Federal Advisory Committee Act in Operation, 33 Ad.L.Rev. 1 (1981); [5] H.H. Perritt and J.A. Wilkinson, Open Advisory Committees and the Political Process: The Federal Advisory Committee Act After Two Years, 63 Geo.L.J. 725 (1975).

4. The state provisions and the techniques for the vigor of their enforcement vary so widely that generalization proves difficult. Publications of the Freedom of Information Center, School of Journalism, University of Missouri at Columbia, and of Common Cause, may provide gravitational assistance. Some of the difficulties are suggested by the following titles. Note, Sunshine or Shade? The University and Open Meetings Acts, 49 Mo.L.Rev. 867 (1984); A. Sussman, The Illinois Open Meetings Act: A Reappraisal, 1978 S.I.U.L. Rev. 193.

Comment, Invalidation as a Remedy for Open Meeting Law Violations, 55 Or.L. Rev. 519 (1976); N. Shurtz, The University in the Sunshine: Application of the Open Meeting Laws to the University Setting, 5

J. of Law & Ed. 453 (1976); Symposium, What is the Effect of a "Sunshine Law" on Public Sector Collective Bargaining, 5 J. of Law & Ed. 479 (1976); Note, The Iowa Open Meetings Act: A Lesson in Legislative Ineffectiveness, 62 Iowa L.Rev. 1108 (1977); D. Wickham, Tennessee's Sunshine Law: A Need for Limited Shade and Clearer Focus, 42 Tenn.L.Rev. 557 (1975); Comment, Pennsylvania's "Sunshine Law": Problems of Construction and Enforcement, 124 U.Pa.L.Rev. 536 (1975); Project, 73 Mich.L.Rev. 971 at 1182–1221.

5. This report generated an Administrative Conference recommendation, ACUS 80–3, 1 CFR § 305.80–3 urging that the Act be interpreted *not* to apply to one-time or occasional meetings with ad hoc, instructured, non-continuing groups.

Chapter VII

DETERMINING FACTS IN ADMINISTRATIVE DECISIONMAKING

This chapter concerns a variety of topics bearing on agency fact-finding. Such fact-finding can range from determining the details of an event involving the parties to a particular administrative proceeding (what did employer Jones say to employee Smith when she fired him?), to fixing the asserted factual basis for a policy of broad and general application. (What is the impact on union organization of making membership lists available to employers?) Fact-finding is the predicate of all characteristic forms of agency action. Understandably, then, the materials of this chapter have strong connections with other chapters—notably chapter 3, which considers the formal procedures of rulemaking and adjudication; chapter 4, which addresses the circumstances in which a particular sort of decisional process, a trial-type hearing, may be demanded; and chapter 8, which addresses the decision process within agencies once contending descriptions of the state-of-affairs and views about what ought to be done about it are in hand. Here, the emphasis is on issues of evidence, of fact-determination.

"Evidence" is, of course, another subject, and we will make no effort to be comprehensive here. But surely if we are interested in administrative process we must ask whether rules of evidence which were fashioned for judicial proceedings should apply in administrative ones. Even in formal administrative hearings, it may be, for example, that the scope of official notice, or the reach of the hearsay rule, should be different from what would apply in court, because the trier of fact is different.[1]

Approaching the matter from the other end of the spectrum, there are, one may say, no rules of "evidence" applicable to legislative hearings. It does not necessarily follow that private parties should have no procedural control over the introduction or testing of evidence in an administrative rulemaking proceeding. The agency's absence of direct political legitimacy, not to mention the need to keep it within more or less delineated statutory boundaries, may argue for recognition of evidence-testing techniques that would not be required in the halls of Congress.

---

1. In June, 1986, the Administrative Conference of the United States adopted recommendations stressing the inappropriateness of *requiring* "agencies to apply the Federal Rules of Evidence, with or without the qualification 'so far as practicable,' to limit the discretion of presiding officers to admit evidence in formal adjudications." Recommendation 86–2, 1 CFR § 305.86–2. The farthest the Conference was willing to go towards recommending use of those rules in agency proceedings was a suggestion that agencies adopt regulations that would permit presiding officers "to exclude unreliable evidence and to use the weighted balancing test of Rule 403 of the Federal Rules of Evidence. . . ." The recommendations were based upon a study by Professor Richard Pierce, "Use of the Federal Rules of Evidence in Federal Agency Adjudications," which is to appear in 39 Ad.L.Rev. (Winter 1987).

Thus, one purpose of the materials that follow is to ask the question, how much does it matter that it is an *agency* that is deciding a question of fact.

But that is not the only purpose.

As the last few paragraphs have implicitly suggested, questions of fact are handled differently in different institutional settings. An agency, we have learned, often has a choice of the type of forum it will use to decide a particular issue. Now we must ask whether the way facts are to be decided should differ depending on the procedural frame the agency decides to use. Should, for example, the availability of jobs in the national economy for persons with certain disabilities be determined in the same way regardless of whether the issue arises in an individual disability pension adjudication or in a rulemaking which will then be applicable to all such hearings? Or does the choice of adjudication or rulemaking as a starting point condition all further procedural operations?

One famous effort to deal with such questions, which has had a considerable impact on the growth of the law, is Professor Kenneth Davis' insistence on the difference between "adjudicative facts" and "legislative facts" in adjudicatory proceedings.

Davis defines "adjudicative facts" as "facts concerning immediate parties," respecting which the judicial "tradition for centuries has been that a court may not decide a disputed issue . . . without evidence and without allowing opportunity for rebuttal and cross-examination." [2] "Legislative facts" are those used "for informing . . . judgment on questions of law and policy"—judgments at least as suitably made by legislatures as by courts. "[W]hen a court is confronted with a question of law or policy on which it needs facts to guide its judgment, the judicial custom over the centuries has been that the court may go anywhere for its facts."

As Professor Davis' choice of terms suggests, his thesis is that there is a functional fit between the distinctive processes of fact-finding used in a court of law—for example, cross-examination, confrontation, and the use of focused rebuttal—and the determination of issues uniquely about "the immediate parties—who did what, where, when, how and with what motive of intent." If there is such a fit, it would seem that the same procedures should be used regardless of the forum. Correspondingly, there may be procedures best suited to developing to developing the kinds of facts needed for the framing of rules; if so, it would seem (leaving elected legislators aside) that "judges, administrative adjudicators, and rulemakers should be subject to the same law about use of facts in lawmaking."

Professor Davis' thesis, which needless to say has been simplified here, raises several large questions. First, it highlights the importance of the point already made: even if the exact same issue is in question,

---

2. 4 K. Davis, Administrative Law Treatise 135, 139 (1982); early versions of the argument appear in K. Davis, An Approach to Problems of Evidence in the Administrative Process, 55 Harv.L.Rev. 364 (1942) and K. Davis, Judicial Notice, 55 Colum.L.Rev. 945 (1955).

might not there be reasons for saying that agency personnel should operate differently from judges and juries, or from legislators?

Second, is a two-fold distinction between "legislative" and "adjudicative" facts sufficient to capture the relevant possibilities? How narrowly shall the notion of "adjudicative fact" be confined? What number appeared on Officer Green's radar-scope as Mrs. Blue drove by is clearly "adjudicative". What of questions about the general reliability of electronic speed-detection? This is a matter of no small moment to Mrs. Blue or the fact-finder at her speeding trial, but it is not a fact concerning the immediate parties—the who, what, where, when, how or why of the speeding violation with which she stands charged. The particular actors involved in the dispute are the persons most likely to know and be able to testify about Mrs. Blue's speed, an issue unique to their situation; both functional and fairness considerations argue for their full participation. Neither Officer Green nor Mrs. Blue herself will know much about the question of reliability—a general question that must arise again and again in speeding trials.[3] While the adversary trial is the paradigmatic fact-finding device of courts, it is *not* the mode chosen by other disciplines interested in testing the truth of general propositions. Statisticians apply standard measures of deviance in assessing significance.[4] Scientists test by experimentation and replication, efforts at achieving consensus. Economists and others who rely on simplifying models of enormously complex reality in their efforts to describe what will probably occur, use still other "accepted" professional tests. Such matters, if not party-specific, are with equal clarity not readily labelled as suited to determination by "feel" or political vote. We are confident that Mrs. Blue (or others sharing her interests) should have some opportunity to bring one or another appropriate regime for fact-testing to bear.

Finally, can the determination of proper process really be based on a functional match between technique and issue? Justice Rehnquist in Vermont Yankee seems to suggest that the choice of proper procedure is a political act. Certainly commentators have said that the allocation of procedural modes is meant to be, at least in part, an allocation of weapons to impede or expedite a substantive program. If that is so, can the choice of fact-finding process, especially as regards very costly processes like cross-examination, be divorced from the choice of general framework through which a program is conducted?

The following materials are meant to spur thoughts on all these issues. On the assumption that most users of this book will be most familiar with issues of "adjudicative fact" raised in judicial procedures, the materials are arranged to begin with the more familiar and move to less familiar, but by no means less important, matters. We start with the judicial context, and Rule 201 of the Federal Rules of Evidence:

3. Be careful to distinguish the general issue of reliability from facts bearing on it that may be strongly case-specific: whether the volume of traffic at the time Mrs. Blue drove by precluded a clear reading, for example. See California v. Trombetta, p. 837 within.

4. See generally D. Barnes, Statistics as Proof: Fundamentals of Quantitative Evidence (1983); A. Conard, The Quantitative Analysis of Justice, 2d J.Leg.Ed. 1 (1967); H. Zeisel, And Then There Were None: The Diminution of the Federal Jury, 38 U.Chi.L.Rev. 710 (1971).

RULE 201
Federal Rules of Evidence

(a) Scope of Rule. This rule governs only judicial notice of adjudicative facts.

(b) Kinds of facts. A judicially noticed fact must be one not subject to reasonable dispute in that it is either (1) generally known within the territorial jurisdiction of the trial court or (2) capable of accurate and ready determination by resort to sources whose accuracy cannot reasonably be questioned.

(c) When discretionary. A court may take judicial notice, whether requested or not.

(d) When mandatory. A court shall take judicial notice if requested by a party and supplied with the necessary information.

(e) Opportunity to be heard. A party is entitled upon timely request to an opportunity to be heard as to the propriety of taking judicial notice and the tenor of the matter noticed. In the absence of prior notification, the request may be made after judicial notice has been taken.

(f) Time of taking notice. Judicial notice may be taken at any stage of the proceeding.

NOTES

(1) ADVISORY COMMITTEE'S NOTE TO F.R.Ev. 201:

"Subdivision (a). This is the only evidence rule on the subject of judicial notice. It deals only with judicial notice of "adjudicative" facts. No rule deals with judicial notice of "legislative" facts. . . .

"The omission of any treatment of legislative facts results from fundamental differences between adjudicative facts and legislative facts. Adjudicative facts are simply the facts of the particular case. Legislative facts, on the other hand, are those which have relevance to legal reasoning and the lawmaking process, whether in the formulation of a legal principle or ruling by a judge or court or in the enactment of a legislative body. The terminology was coined by Professor Kenneth Davis. . . .

"The usual method of establishing adjudicative facts is through the introduction of evidence, ordinarily consisting of the testimony of witnesses. If particular facts are outside the area of reasonable controversy, this process is dispensed with as unnecessary. A high degree of indisputability is the essential prerequisite.

"Legislative facts are quite different. . . . Professor Morgan gave the following description of the methodology of determining domestic law:

In determining the content or applicability of a rule of domestic law, the judge is unrestricted in his investigation and conclusion. He may reject the propositions of either party or of both parties. He may consult the sources of pertinent data to which they refer, or he may refuse to do so. He may make an independent search for persuasive data or rest content with what he has or what the parties present. . . . [T]he parties do no more than to assist; they control no part of the process. Morgan, Judicial Notice, 57 Harv.L.Rev. 269, 270–271 (1944).

"This is the view which should govern judicial access to legislative facts. It renders inappropriate any limitation in the form of indisputability, any formal requirements of notice other than those already inherent in affording opportunity to hear and be heard and exchanging briefs, and any requirement of formal findings at any level. It should, however, leave open the possibility of introducing evidence through regular channels in appropriate situations. . . ."

(2) SECTION 7(d) of the APA, 5 U.S.C. § 556(e):

"When an agency decision [in a proceeding required to be decided on the record after a formal hearing] rests on official notice of a material fact not appearing in the evidence in the record, a party is entitled, on timely request, to an opportunity to show the contrary." [1]

(3) Now consider the following issues, all of which have arisen in licensing and rulemaking proceedings before the Nuclear Regulatory Commission:

Statistics: What are the peak and mean electricity usage rates in a large geographical region where a reactor might be located?

Science, ranging from the readily testable to the highly judgmental: What is the half-life of a particular isotype of plutonium? What is the impact on human flesh of exposure to a given, relatively substantial amount of radiation? What is the impact of prolonged human exposure to a given, very slight amount of radiation? What will be the impact on the tensile strength and other qualities of steel used in constructing reactors of forty years' exposure to the intense but varying radiation generated in running a nuclear power plant?

Probability: What is the chance that a certain kind of valve used in nuclear reactors, call it valve A, will fail in forty years' use? In the event of failure of valve A in a nuclear reactor of design B that has been operating for 20 years, what are the possible outcomes for the safety of the plant, with what probability for each? What are the environmental impacts, potential costs, and probable benefits of a decision to encourage the recycling of used reactor fuel through the development of so-called "breeder" reactors?

(4) BRUCE A. ACKERMAN, RECONSTRUCTING AMERICAN LAW 67–68 (1984): ". . . [W]e are already in the midst of a revolution in information processing that permits, for the first time in history, a disciplined empirical analysis of the structural facts of central importance to activist legal decision. Increasingly, the call for an appropriate "statement of the facts" will generate mountains of computer printout detailing a proliferating number of scenarios of obvious relevance to responsible . . . decisionmaking. Until such time as lawyers under-

---

1. The comparable provisions of the Model State Administrative Act (1981) are §§ 4–212(f) and 4–215(d) (formal adjudication), and, arguably, 3–112 (Rulemaking), pp. 1270, 1273, and 1258 within.

stand the formal economic, political, and sociological presuppositions of particular computer analyses, they can play only three roles in the fact-finding process. Most obviously, they may play the obscurantist and deny that the computer printout is worth the paper it is written on; or they may worship blindly before the shiny new shrine of the American Enlightenment and believe everything the computer tells them (so long as it is not patently absurd); or they may play the moralizer and make sure that the manipulators of the black box are not obviously corrupt or biased. . . . . The only thing they will not be able to do is to engage in a meaningful dialogue with the model builders concerning the basic assumptions that guided them in their construction of the social reality with which the law will have to deal. Yet it is only through this dialogue that lawyers can help unearth a host of controversial legal questions that are raised in every effort to state the structural facts. . . . It is, in short, past time to redeem Holmes's century-old prediction that the future of the law belongs to the master of statistics, no less than economics. . . ."

Test Professor Ackerman's assertions against the challenges facing lawyers before the agency, and on judicial review, in PUBLIC CITIZEN HEALTH RESEARCH GROUP v. TYSON, 796 F.2d 1479 (D.C.Cir. 7/25/86), noted at p. 860 below. In this case epidemiological and experimental studies, mathematical models and the databases on which they operated formed the basis for regulatory decisions concerning the industrial chemical ethylene oxide; questions about their validity, constituted the only significant "factual" disputes.

SECTION 1. INVESTIGATION AS A SUBSTITUTE FOR ADVERSARY PROCESS

With some exceptions, judges and jurors do not go out to see, or to investigate, the "facts" of a case. Instead, "evidence" is presented to them, through witnesses, in a very structured proceeding. If this process seems natural to you, it is because you are thinking like a lawyer. Lawyers need to remind themselves from time to time that investigation rather than hearing is the customary prelude to fact-finding. The chemical composition and the action of a drug compound, for example, are best ascertained by tests and experiments. Direct visual observation in many cases provides information that could be, but rarely is, obtained at second hand through the lips of witnesses; if the Coast Guard, for instance, must pass on the issue of the condition of a vessel's lifeboats, it sends a competent inspector to look at them, rather than a trial examiner to listen to someone else who has looked at them. If the Motor Vehicle Commissioner wishes to learn whether an applicant can handle a motor car, he administers a practical driving test and decides accordingly. If there is a dispute, retesting is generally deemed to be the method best fitted to resolving it.

These commonplace examples are reflections of behavior in the non-official sector of life. Everybody finds facts, but very infrequently by means of a formal hearing even when testimony provides the main basis of decision. Banks grant or withhold loans; insurance companies pass on applications and settle claims; employers hire and fire personnel—and they do so with confidence even though their decisional techniques are not the same as lawyers'. The great bulk of administrative determinations are similarly the products of "informal" methods of investigation or inquiry. They rest on evidence, to be sure; but it is not evidence adduced in the same way as at a court trial.

Surely, however, if the decision has been made (by statute or otherwise) to hold an adjudicatory hearing, the assumption must be that what we might call "every day" investigation will not substitute for evidence. A result such as that in COWAN v. BUNTING GLIDER CO., 159 Pa.Super. 573, 49 A.2d 270 (1946) is not surprising. There, the claimant was injured during working hours when his sweater caught fire while he was lighting a cigarette. He was awarded workmen's compensation, and his employer appealed. "[T]he case presents only one controverted question: Was the act of smoking such a violation of the employer's direct and positive order as to take claimant out of the course of his employment and thereby preclude him from compensation? The record shows that defendant had promulgated a general rule forbidding smoking and had placed 'No Smoking' signs at various points in the plant. However, it does not appear that such a sign was continuously displayed in the men's room during claimant's term of employment. . . . There is evidence to the effect that claimant, on numerous occasions and in the company of others, used the men's room as a smoking rendezvous, and that this practice was known to defendant's supervisory officials. On the rehearing before the referee the structural plans of the plant were introduced and explained. . . . While considering this evidence, on review, the board deemed it advisable to make a personal visit to the plant in order to further familiarize itself with the plant's physical layout. While there it observed that the floor of the men's room was littered with cigarette butts, and, partly, perhaps mainly on that ground, the board found that the company had condoned smoking, at least in the men's room. This the court below properly condemned because the personal observations of the board were not buttressed by evidence introduced into the record, and because they related to a time too remote from the date of the accident. . . . [W]e do not have a finding based exclusively upon evidence in the record, and we have concluded that . . . the case should be returned to the board, not only for findings based upon competent evidence but to take further and additional testimony in a hearing de novo." [1]

At the other extreme, one would expect a good deal of respect for the standardized, specialized tests routinely administered by an agency, and indeed Section 5(3) of the Administrative Procedure Act, 5 U.S.C. § 554(a)(3), excludes from the ordinary procedures of adjudication "pro-

---

1. Compare Matter of State Bank Charter Application of the Security Bank, Buffalo, 606 P.2d 296 (Wyo.1980). Following a hearing on an application to charter what would be Buffalo's third bank, the examiner visited town, to the knowledge of all parties, to learn informally about a variety of community matters important to the application. The reviewing court declined to regard the practice as, in itself, disabling error; if an existing bank believed the visit produced impressions that should be subject to challenge, its obligation was to seek to reopen the proceeding before the examiner.

ceedings in which decisions rest solely on inspections, tests, or elections." [2] This approach is typified by PEOPLE v. PORPORA, 154 Cal.Rptr. 400, 91 Cal.App.3d Supp. 13 (Super.L.A.Co.1979). There California's Fish and Game Code prohibited commercial fishermen from making a catch containing more than 40% Pacific mackerel. Fish and Game Department officials took fourteen thirty-pound samples of fish from the conveyor belt carrying defendant's 71½ ton catch into the cannery for processing. The sampling was done in accordance with a prescribed technique, with each sample returned to the conveyor once it had been sorted and each species weighed. It showed a catch that was 52.6% Pacific mackerel, leading to a prosecution for a violation of the Code. The sampler and others who had observed her work and knew the technique testified fully, but appellant complained that "the failure . . . . to preserve the fish, or make them available, denied him access to evidence that would have enabled him to impeach the reliability of the sampling technique and [its] results." Impressed in part by the presumed knowledge of "a sea captain of a fishing vessel," in part by the difficulty of "preserving 71½ tons of deteriorating fish or, at best, [the] 14 samples," the court readily upheld the conviction based on this testimony.

Now for a somewhat harder issue:

HUNTER v. ZENITH DREDGE CO.
Supreme Court of Minnesota, 1945.
220 Minn. 318, 19 N.W.2d 795.

GALLAGHER, JUSTICE. Certiorari to review a decision of the industrial commission holding relator ineligible for compensation and other benefits under the workmen's compensation act.

Relator's claim petition asked compensation for disability due to an accident arising out of and in the course of his employment as a slagger at the Zenith Dredge Company, employer, or for disability due to an occupational disease arising out of such employment. The answer denied these allegations.

On June 7, 1944, at the close of the hearing, the referee determined that the employee had not sustained an accidental injury and ordered that a medical board [1] be appointed in the manner provided by L.1943,

---

2. To similar effect see § 4–502(3) of the Model State Administrative Procedure Act (1981).

1. [Ed.] Section 11 provided that when occupational disease was a central issue, a medical board of three doctors should be drawn from a distinguished panel of fifteen chosen by the dean of the University of Minnesota medical school, the executive committee of the State Medical Association, and the Governor. Each of the parties would name one member of the medical board, and these two were to select the third. The medical board was then to "determine such medical questions raised by the pleadings. . . . Its findings among others shall state whether the employee is affected with an occupational disease as claimed in his petition, and whether such disease is an occupational disease as claimed in his petition, and whether such disease is an occupational disease within the provisions and definitions of occupational disease as contained in this act. . . . The medical board may examine the employee, including X-ray examinations, hear and examine witnesses on controverted medical issues, and make such other examinations as it deems necessary to a full presentation and understanding of the medical issue before them. . . . "

c. 633, § 11, to determine whether the employee had been afflicted with an occupational disease within the provisions and definitions of L.1943, c. 633, § 3(n). On August 24, 1944, the medical board, pursuant to § 11 of the 1943 act, made its report [2] determining that relator was affected with synovitis of the right knee and that such synovitis was not an occupational disease within the provisions of the 1943 act.[3]

The referee . . . adopted such report as part of his findings and disallowed relator's claim.[4] Relator thereupon appealed to the industrial commission, which duly affirmed and adopted the findings of the referee. In the memorandum attached to the commission's decision it was stated:

> . . . If the law had made this commission the arbiter of the facts in occupational disease cases we would have had no hesitancy upon the record before us in holding that the petitioner was disabled as a result of an occupational disease. We would not even have thought it necessary to appoint a neutral physician, who would have been subject to cross-examination. However, the law does not make us the judges of controverted medical questions involving occupational disease. That becomes the exclusive function of the medical board, and the medical board is not required to determine that question upon the testimony taken before the referee at a hearing prior to the appointment of the medical board.

The medical board's report filed with the commission included the following:

"1. Names and addresses of doctors other than members of the board appearing at examinations or hearings: S.S. Houkom, M.D., Duluth; F.J. Lepak, M.D., Duluth; C.A. Scherer, Duluth.

". . .

"3. Medical reports and exhibits considered by board. (Submit to Industrial Commission with this report): Transcript of the hearing before referee C.H. Schaefer, March 29, 1944, and X-ray of the knees of Mr. Hunter taken at St. Mary's Hospital, 8/19/44."

Three witnesses testified before the referee as to the nature and cause of relator's disability. These were relator, Dr. F.J. Lepak, called on his behalf, and Dr. S.S. Houkom [sic], called on behalf of the employer and its insurer. [All three testified, at length and in detail,

---

2. [Ed.] Section 11 provided that a signed report be made immediately after the board had completed its "examinations and hearings." The medical board was commanded to include in its report "the names of the doctors who appeared at such examinations and hearings and such medical reports and exhibits as were considered by it."

3. [Ed.] "Occupational disease" is defined by the statute as one "arising out of and in the course of employment peculiar to the occupation in which the employee is engaged and due to causes in excess of the ordinary hazards of employment. . . . An employer is not liable for compensation for any occupational disease which cannot be traced to the employment as a direct and proximate cause . . . or which results from a hazard to which the workman would have been equally exposed outside of the employment."

4. [Ed.] The statute directed that the medical board's "findings and conclusions" about "controverted medical questions" were to be automatically "adopted by the commission as its decision on such questions."

in ways that connected the relator's conceded synovitis with his employment. Thus, the relator testified that "he worked on steel plates in the open air, resting his right knee thereon as he applied an air gun to such plates to remove particles of slag . . . ; that he moved about on the plates by raising his knee, alternatively with his left foot and walking ahead in that manner, applying the air gun as he moved; that he first observed difficulty with his right knee about two weeks before he was forced to quit his employment on November 26, 1943." . . .

Dr. Lepak . . . "testified that working on cold steel plates or on cold surfaces and floors frequently led to bursitis, and that in the shipyards where relator was working they had similar, although not identical, difficulties with other workers." Dr. Houkom's testimony was to the effect, that trauma caused by jerking of the air gun and constant contact with the cold steel plates contributed to relator's disability. . . . He diagnosed the disability as synovitis, which he described as more generalized than simple bursitis—that in reality relator had bursitis coupled with synovitis and that his disability might be diagnosed as either bursitis or synovitis, or both. He testified that in his opinion bursitis and synovitis may be characterized as diseases, although they may also be caused by trauma; . . . that there was a true relationship between the type of work relator was doing on the cold steel plates and his disability; that a main factor in this respect was relator's constant use of his right knee, kneeling on it, getting up and down on it quite a bit, and flexing and extending the knee joint rather often; that there was more strain on relator's knee joint in the position in which he worked than in ordinary activities such as standing; that irritation caused by jarring of the air hammer might be a factor, although not as much a factor as the process of kneeling and using the knee as described. . . .

Counsel for relator, on appeal to the industrial commission, served a Notice to Produce upon respondents and upon the members of said medical board, directing them to furnish relator with a full, complete, and certified transcript of the proceedings had by the board. No response was made thereto, and relator has at no time been able to ascertain whether additional testimony or evidence was considered by the board, and, if so, what comprised the same. . . . No provision or requirement in said act makes it necessary for the medical board to file a transcript of the evidence upon which its findings or determination is based.

Due process requires that the evidence on which an agency, board, or commission bases its findings be ascertainable. This court must have the necessary data on which to determine the correctness thereof. . . . Here, the provisions of the statute creating the medical board and defining its duties require the board to determine questions of occupational disease and to hear the evidence and report findings thereon to the industrial commission. Such findings are made binding upon the commission. Therefore, the only review thereof to which a claimant is entitled is a review by this court pursuant to § 176.61 (§ 4320). Our power to review findings of the medical board and to determine whether they are supported by sufficient foundation in fact is accordingly frustrated, because such findings are binding on the commission and the board is not required, under the statute, to file with its report a transcript of the evidence, testimony, or exhibits upon which such findings are based. Thus a claimant is denied the right of review guaranteed him by the workmen's compensation law, § 176.61. . . .

It is our opinion that because the delegation of power to the medical board here in effect denied relator and other claimants under the occupational-disease provisions of the workmen's compensation law an effective right of review or appeal as prescribed by said workmen's compensation act, as well as under the due process guarantees of both the state and federal constitutions, the statute insofar as it creates said medical board and sets forth its functions constitutes an invasion of rights protected and guaranteed by said constitutions, and is therefore null and void.

2. By this, of course, it does not necessarily follow that the entire statute relating to occupational diseases must fall. . . .

3. With the elimination of those provisions creating the medical board and defining its powers, it is clear that the undisputed evidence here compels a finding that relator was disabled as a result of an occupational disease and is entitled to recover under the occupational disease sections of the workmen's compensation law. There is no evidence to support a contrary conclusion. The industrial commission, under the aforesaid invalid sections of the workmen's compensation act, was required to affirm the findings of the medical board even though in disagreement therewith. We hold that the undisputed evidence, as above set forth, requires a reversal of the findings of the commission and a determination that relator has established that his disability is due to an occupational disease within the provisions of L.1943, c. 633, § 3(n). . . .

NOTES

(1) H. Korn, LAW, FACT AND SCIENCE IN THE COURTS, 66 COLUM.L.REV. 1080, 1093–1094 (1966): "[P]erhaps the most fundamental source of difficulty in technical fact determination is that the law and the scientific knowledge to which it refers often serve different purposes. Concerned with ordering men's conduct in accordance with certain standards, values, and societal goals, the legal system is a prescriptive and normative one dealing with the 'ought to be.' Much scientific knowledge, on the other hand, is purely descriptive; its 'laws' seek not to control or judge the phenomena of the real world, but to describe and explain them in neutral terms. . . . The result of these disparities is that the law sometimes deals with the subject matter of a science in terms that are foreign to the conceptual system of the scientist. The concepts of monopoly and competition in the antitrust laws find no exact counterpart in analogous concepts used by the economist. The causal relationship between employment and heart failure that suffices for a compensable claim under workmen's compensation laws may bear

little resemblance to the etiology of heart disease known to doctors. In each of these cases the law deals with a subject within the province of one of the sciences but utilizes a concept which has been skewed from analogous scientific ones by policy and value considerations which do not concern the scientist."

(2) To what extent do the difficulties in this case derive from the requirement that the medical board not only assess the relator's medical condition and its cause, about which there was little dispute, but also whether it constituted an "occupational disease" within the meaning of the statute? What arguments could be made that the latter need not have been taken as the decision of "controverted medical questions," as to which the board's conclusions bound the commission? Why do you suppose the legislature chose to have the issue of *accidental injury* decided by a referee, but *occupational disease* by an expert board?

(3) What is the nature of the due process claim here? Does the court reject as inherently unconstitutional the idea that an expert medical board can be designated to decide diagnostic issues by inspection—i.e., despite the care taken to assure the board's objectivity/ acceptability to the participants? Is the problem the failure to provide for confrontation or cross-examination? Or was the problem simply the board's failure to give an account (notice) of what it considered and how it reasoned to its conclusion, that might have permitted understanding of its decision and an effort at response?[1] How does the case differ, in this respect, from the decision of bar examiners to flunk an individual who, in their judgment, does not adequately respond to the questions they have set to measure qualification for legal practice?

(4) J. Mashaw, Bureaucratic Justice 204–05 (1983): Reconsider Mashaw's three models of justice, described in Chapter 4, p. 607 above. Later in the book, addressing possible reforms in the disability insurance process, Professor Mashaw considers as one possibility

"that the DI program shift its decision process to a professional judgment model employing physician-deciders. One variation on such a system, for example, might use a panel of three physicians who would personally examine the claimant and decide the disability question at the reconsideration stage. The process might be organized around existing hospitals and clinics or special diagnostic centers that could provide all the basic tests that the physician panel would require. Vocational information and other data not available from the initial development, including prior medical findings, would be gathered and supplied by a development staff. If the staff's development suggested that a grant would be appropriate, it might also be authorized to remand cases to the initial stage prior to submitting the case to the medical panel. The specialist composition of the medical panel would respond to the claimant's medical condition or conditions, and the panel

---

1. To the extent the opinion is grounded specifically in assertions about the requisites of, and entitlement to, judicial review, it raises issues discussed in connection with Commodity Futures Trading Commission v. Schor, p. 107 above.

physicians would be trained in the basic policies of the DI program and in the demands of major categories of work.

"This model has a number of attractive features. It applies a more consistent level of medical expertise to cases by eliminating significant reliance on treating physician reports or the findings of a single consultative physician. The claimant would have personal contact with the decisionmaker, which would permit the evaluation of subjective factors but at the same time harness that evaluation to direct clinical observation and to the trained diagnostic intuition of medical professionals. The combined opinions of three doctors who had personally examined the claimant would also presumably have a strong symbolic effect—hopefully, strong enough to counteract both prior medical advice and the desire to get yet another opinion (appeal).

"There are, of course, problems as well: Administrative costs might be substantial. Physicians' aptitudes for assessing vocational factors or applying other program policies are unknown. The dominant medical culture might overwhelm the adjudicatory function. Floating panels might produce substantially inconsistent results. In some areas of the country the medical manpower to run the process may simply be unavailable.

"Yet, in my view, these do not seem to be determinative objections. . . . A priori, . . . I do not see solid reasons for rejecting the medical examination model. To be sure, we know much less about how it would function than we know about the current system. Obviously there are variations on the theme that would have to be carefully considered—panel composition, collegiate versus individual decisionmaking, staging of the decision process, degree of physician independence from SSA oversight, relations between the panels and treating physicians, and the like. But this seems to me to argue for careful design and subsequent testing, rather than for rejection."

SECTION 2. HEARSAY AND OTHER "INCOMPETENT" EVIDENCE

The preceding section dealt with circumstances in which the decider substituted personal observation for adversary procedure. We now turn to cases in which the observation has been done by another, but embodied in a report or in some other way presented in a manner that deprives participants of an opportunity to confront and cross-examine the observer.

The objection to such evidence, that it constitutes inadmissible hearsay, has been trenchantly criticized and sharply limited even in the context of judicial trials—a subject that can interest us here only for purposes of comparison. Consider, for example, the views of Jack B. Weinstein, Chief Judge of the United States District Court for the Eastern District of New York and a productive and influential scholar in the field of evidence:[1]

1. Alternatives to the Present Hearsay Rules, 44 F.R.D. 375 (1968).

"In a recent criminal prosecution for filing a fraudulent income tax return, there was a very close question as to whether the defendant knew what was being done in his name—someone else had concededly signed the returns. On cross-examination by the government, the firm's new certified public accountant stated that the prior accountant, who prepared the returns and was now dead, had told him that he had dealt only with the mother of the defendant and never with the defendant himself. This hearsay was never discredited and was supported by the defendant's circumstances as developed at trial. The court, in effect, held that the hearsay, considered with all the other evidence, had sufficient minimum probative force to require an acquittal. Had the defendant wished to elicit this testimony it could have been excluded as hearsay, the case would have gone to the jury and, in view of some unavoidable prejudicial factors, a conviction would have been likely.

"In a recent civil jury trial the plaintiff testified that he had never had certain neurological symptoms prior to an auto accident. All his experts' medical testimony rested on this chronology. Defendant produced a hospital medical record which predated the accident and showed a long history of similar complaints. When plaintiff's lawyer, after being given two days to check the record, failed to produce an explanation, the case was dismissed. The unimpeached hearsay business record had infinitely more probative force than the plaintiff's testimony."

Commenting on cases like these, Judge Weinstein remarks: "Since what we are trying to do at a trial is to get as close an approximation to the truth as practicable, a seeker of the facts not trained in Anglo-American law would expect all evidence with probative force to be considered by the trier. A proposal of free admissibility of hearsay thus seems sensible. It is, after all, the system used abroad and at home before administrative agencies, arbitrators and, increasingly, in bench trials. In effect, what is suggested is the same reform accomplished in this country some hundred years ago with respect to competency. Parties, spouses, felons and the like whose testimony was previously inadmissible were permitted to testify. What had been judge-decided issues of exclusion became jury-decided issues of credibility." [2]

Hearsay evidence is generally accepted even in formal administrative proceedings, although the issue of reliability, or relative weight, remains open.[3] The Federal Administrative Procedure Act provides in part, in 5 U.S.C. § 556(d): "Any oral or documentary evidence may be

---

2. See also I. Younger, Reflection on the Rule Against Hearsay, 32 S.Car.L.Rev. 281 (1980), suggesting that reliability, rather than the availability of cross-examination, is the key to understanding contemporary court uses of the hearsay rule; Note, The Theoretical Foundation of the Hearsay Rules, 93 Harv.L.Rev. 1786 (1980); T. Smith, The Hearsay Rule and the Docket Crisis, 54 A.B.A.J. 231 (1968).

3. See R. Pierce, Use of Federal Rules of Evidence in Federal Agency Adjudications, 39 Ad.L.Rev. (Winter 1987), n. 1, p. 795 above; E. Gellhorn, Rules of Evidence and Official Notice in Formal Administrative Hearings, 1971 Duke L.J. 1; R. Stern, The Substantial Evidence Rule in Administrative Proceedings: Restrictions on the Use of Hearsay Since Richardson v. Perales, 36 Ark.L.Rev. 102 (1983).

received, but the agency as a matter of policy shall provide for the exclusion of irrelevant, immaterial, or unduly repetitious evidence. A sanction may not be imposed or rule or order issued except on consideration of the whole record or those parts thereof cited by a party and supported by and in accordance with the reliable, probative, and substantial evidence. A party is entitled to present his case or defense by oral or documentary evidence, and to conduct such cross-examination as may be required for a full and true disclosure of the facts." Commenting specifically on this language, the Attorney General's Manual says that "It is clear that, as heretofore, the technical rules of evidence will not be applicable to administrative hearings." At p. 76. The Uniform Law Commissioners' Revised Model State Administrative Procedure Act (1981) similarly provides in Sec. 4–212(a) that "the presiding officer [in a formal adjudication] shall exclude evidence that is irrelevant, immaterial, unduly repetitious, or excludable on constitutional or statutory grounds or on the basis of evidentiary privilege recognized in the courts of this state. . . . Evidence may not be excluded solely because it is hearsay." Section 4–215(d) adds that "Findings [of fact] must be based upon the kind of evidence on which reasonably prudent persons are accustomed to rely in the conduct of their serious affairs and may be based upon such evidence even if it would be inadmissible in a civil trial. The presiding officer's experience, technical competence, and specialized knowledge may be utilized in evaluating evidence."

RICHARDSON v. PERALES
Supreme Court of the United States, 1971.
402 U.S. 389.

[Perales, 34 years old, was a truck driver who, while at work, injured his back by lifting an object. He was seen by neurosurgeon Munslow, who, after conservative treatment had not ended Perales' pain, undertook extensive spinal surgery in a fruitless search for disc protrusion or other definitive pathology. He concluded that Perales suffered from mild lumbar neuritis. Perales continued to complain. Neurologist Lampert was consulted. He found no neurological explanation. Munslow advised Perales to return to work. Instead Perales consulted general practitioner Morales, who put him in the hospital for two weeks and then discharged him with a diagnosis of "Back sprain, lumbo-sacral spine."

At that point Perales filed a claim for total disability insurance benefits under the federal Social Security Act, saying that his physical impairment precluded gainful employment. General practitioner Morales, in support of the claim, reaffirmed his diagnosis of back sprain, but this time added "moderately severe" and "Ruptured disk [sic] not ruled out."

The administrative agency arranged to have Perales examined at no cost by orthopedic surgeon Langston. In his subsequent report Langston blasted claimant Perales; "neurological examination [by various methods] is entirely normal"—"reflexes are very active"—"may have a very mild chronic back sprain"—"long time since I have been so impressed with the obvious attempt of a patient to exaggerate his difficulties"—"he has a tremendous psychological overlay to this illness, and I sincerely suggest that he be seen by a psychiatrist." Langston proposed that Perales, who had suffered from "inactivity and sitting around," should do a lot of walking, bicycling, and the like as a prelude to returning to work.

When Perales' claim was thereupon initially denied, Perales asked for reconsideration. Dr. Morales furnished another report, expressing his own confidence that Perales was not malingering. His conclusion, based on more than thirty visits, was that Perales had been totally and permanently disabled, though further surgery seemed inadvisable.

Next, the agency arranged to have Perales examined by psychiatrist Bailey, who had a subspecialty in neurology. Bailey concluded that Perales had a "paranoid personality" which was "conducive to anger, frustration, etc."

Then the file was again reviewed by two levels of administrators, independently of one another. The claim having been denied by them, Perales asked for a hearing. Before this occurred Perales was once more examined by orthopedist Langston and freshly by electromyographer Mattson (myography is a means of measuring the velocity and intensity of muscular contractions). Mattson, corroborating Langston's earlier impression, found indications "strongly suggestive of lack of maximal effort," with no evidence of "any active process affecting the nerves at present."

At this point the case was set for hearing. The notice to Perales, with copy to his lawyer, contained a definition of disability, told the claimant to present medical or other evidence not already proffered by him, stated that he could examine all the documentary material in the file, and informed him that he could bring his own physician and other witnesses and be represented by counsel.

The claimant appeared at the hearing with Dr. Morales and his attorney, who objected to receiving in evidence any of the medical reports other than those of Dr. Morales and Dr. Munslow (the neurosurgeon who had operated on Perales). The grounds of objection included hearsay, absence of opportunity to cross-examine, and conclusory nature of the reports. All objections were overruled.

Perales, Morales, and a former fellow employee testified for the claimant. Also heard by the hearing examiner were a vocational expert and Dr. Leavitt, chief of the Department of Physical Medicine, Baylor University. The hearing examiner called Leavitt as an independent "medical adviser." Leavitt did not himself examine Perales, but he listened to Morales' testimony, read all the medical reports, and then stated that, according to the consensus of the medical reports, Perales had a low back syndrome involving muscles and ligaments, but nothing momentous.

The hearing examiner found accordingly, almost in Dr. Leavitt's words. He also found that Perales could hold down a number of specified jobs, and was therefore not entitled to total disability benefits.

Review by the Appeals Council was sought. The Appeals Council upheld the hearing examiner. Action was begun to obtain judicial review of the final administrative decision which had been made by the Appeals Council acting in behalf of the Secretary of Health, Education, and Welfare. The district court held for Perales, indicating unwillingness to assign probative value to unsworn medical reports whose authors were not cross-examined. The Fifth Circuit said that Perales had not in timely manner requested opportunity to cross-examine,[1] and it also said that the challenged hearsay was admissible, as was Dr. Leavitt's opinion concerning it; so to that extent the court of appeals disagreed with the district court. But the two courts reached the same result because, in the Fifth Circuit's view, hearsay evidence (that is, the medical reports) fell short of being "substantial evidence" when the claimant had objected to it and had contradicted it by a live medical witness—Morales—and by his own testimony.]

MR. JUSTICE BLACKMUN delivered the opinion of the Court. . . . .

The Social Security Act has been with us since 1935. It affects nearly all of us. The system's administrative structure and procedures, with essential determinations numbering into the millions, are of a size and extent difficult to comprehend. But, as the Government's brief here accurately pronounces, "Such a system must be fair—and it must work."

> Congress has provided that the Secretary
>
> shall have full power and authority to make rules and regulations and to establish procedures . . . necessary or appropriate to carry out such provisions, and shall adopt reasonable and proper rules and regulations to regulate and provide for the nature and extent of the proofs and evidence and the method of taking and furnishing the same in order to establish the right to benefits hereunder. § 205(a), 42 U.S.C. § 405(a).

Section 205(b) directs the Secretary to make findings and decisions; on request to give reasonable notice and opportunity for a hearing; and in the course of any hearing to receive evidence. It then provides:

> Evidence may be received at any hearing before the Secretary even though inadmissible under rules of evidence applicable to court procedure.

In carrying out these statutory duties the Secretary has adopted regulations that state, among other things:

> The hearing examiner shall inquire fully into the matters at issue and shall receive in evidence the testimony of witnesses and any documents which are relevant and material to such

---

1. The Secretary of HEW has power to issue subpoenas. The Secretary's procedural regulations say that a claimant may request issuance of subpoenas to compel attendance of witnesses, production of evidence, and so on. Perales' attorney never did request that subpoenas be issued.

matters. . . . The . . . procedure at the hearing generally
. . . shall be in the discretion of the hearing examiner and of
such nature as to afford the parties a reasonable opportunity
for a fair hearing. 20 CFR § 404.927.

From this it is apparent that (a) the Congress granted the Secretary
the power by regulation to establish hearing procedures; (b) strict rules
of evidence, applicable in the courtroom, are not to operate at social
security hearings so as to bar the admission of evidence otherwise
pertinent; and (c) the conduct of the hearing rests generally in the
examiner's discretion. There emerges an emphasis upon the informal
rather than the formal. This, we think, is as it should be, for this
administrative procedure, and these hearings, should be understandable to the layman claimant, should not necessarily be stiff and comfortable only for the trained attorney, and should be liberal and not strict
in tone and operation. This is the obvious intent of Congress so long as
the procedures are fundamentally fair.

IV

With this background and this atmosphere in mind, we turn to the
statutory standard of "substantial evidence" prescribed by § 205(g).
The Court has considered this very concept in other, yet similar,
contexts. The National Labor Relations Act, § 10(e), in its original
form, provided that the NLRB's findings of fact "if supported by
evidence, shall be conclusive." 49 Stat. 454. The Court said this meant
"supported by substantial evidence" and that this was "more than a
mere scintilla. It means such relevant evidence as a reasonable mind
might accept as adequate to support a conclusion." Consolidated Edison Co. v. NLRB, 305 U.S. 197, 229 (1938).

The Court has adhered to that definition in varying statutory
situations. . . .

V

We may accept the propositions advanced by the claimant, some of
them long established, that procedural due process is applicable to the
adjudicative administrative proceeding involving "the differing rules of
fair play, which through the years, have become associated with differing types of proceedings," Hannah v. Larche, 363 U.S. 420, 442 (1960);
that "the 'right' to Social Security benefits is in one sense 'earned,'"
Flemming v. Nestor, 363 U.S. 603, 610 (1960); and that the

extent to which procedural due process must be afforded the
recipient is influenced by the extent to which he may be
"condemned to suffer grievous loss" . . . . Accordingly
. . . "consideration of what procedures due process may
require under any given set of circumstances must begin with
a determination of the precise nature of the government function involved as well as of the private interest that has been
affected by governmental action." Goldberg v. Kelly, 397 U.S.
254, 262–263 (1970).

The question, then, is as to what procedural due process requires with respect to examining physicians' reports in a social security disability claim hearing.

We conclude that a written report by a licensed physician who has examined the claimant and who sets forth in his report his medical findings in his area of competence may be received as evidence in a disability hearing and, despite its hearsay character and an absence of cross-examination, and despite the presence of opposing direct medical testimony and testimony by the claimant himself, may constitute substantial evidence supportive of a finding by the hearing examiner adverse to the claimant, when the claimant has not exercised his right to subpoena the reporting physician and thereby provide himself with the opportunity for cross-examination of the physician.

We are prompted to this conclusion by a number of factors that, we feel, assure underlying reliability and probative value:

1. The identity of the five reporting physicians is significant. Each report presented here was prepared by a practicing physician who had examined the claimant. A majority (Drs. Langston, Bailey, and Mattson) were called into the case by the state agency. Although each received a fee, that fee is recompense for his time and talent otherwise devoted to private practice or other professional assignment. We cannot, and do not, ascribe bias to the work of these independent physicians, or any interest on their part in the outcome of the administrative proceeding beyond the professional curiosity a dedicated medical man possesses.

2. The vast workings of the social security administrative system make for reliability and impartiality in the consultant reports. We bear in mind that the agency operates essentially, and is intended so to do, as an adjudicator and not as an advocate or adversary. This is the congressional plan. We do not presume on this record to say that it works unfairly.[2]

3. One familiar with medical reports and the routine of the medical examination, general or specific, will recognize their elements of detail and of value. The particular reports of the physicians who examined claimant Perales were based on personal consultation and personal examination and rested on accepted medical procedures and tests. The operating neurosurgeon, Dr. Munslow, provided his pre-operative observations and diagnosis, his findings at surgery, his post-operative diagnosis, and his post-operative observations. Dr. Lampert, the neurologist, provided the history related to him by the patient, Perales' complaints, the physical examination and neurologic tests, and his professional impressions and recommendations. Dr. Langston, the orthopedist, did the same post-operatively, and described the orthopedic tests and neurologic examination he performed, the results and his impressions and prognosis. Dr. Mattson who did the post-operative

---

2. We are advised by the Government's brief, p. 18, nn. 7 and 8, that in fiscal 1968, 515,938 disability claims were processed; that, of these, 343,628 (66.601%) were allowed prior to the hearing stage; that ap- proximately one-third of the claims that went to hearing were allowed; and that 320,164 consultant examinations were obtained.

electromyography, described the results of that test, and his impressions. And Dr. Bailey, the psychiatrist, related the history, the patient's complaints, and the psychiatric diagnosis that emerged from the typical psychiatric examination.

These are routine, standard, and unbiased medical reports by physician specialists concerning a subject whom they had seen. That the reports were adverse to Perales' claim is not in itself bias or an indication of nonprobative character.

4. The reports present the impressive range of examination to which Perales was subjected. A specialist in neurosurgery, one in neurology, one in psychiatry, one in orthopedics, and one in physical medicine and rehabilitation add up to definitive opinion in five medical specialities, all somewhat related, but different in their emphases. It is fair to say that the claimant received professional examination and opinion on a scale beyond the reach of most persons and that this case reveals a patient and careful endeavor by the state agency and the examiner to ascertain the truth.

5. So far as we can detect, there is no inconsistency whatsoever in the reports of the five specialists. Yet each result was reached by independent examination in the writer's field of specialized training.

6. Although the claimant complains of the lack of opportunity to cross-examine the reporting physicians, he did not take advantage of the opportunity afforded him under 20 C.F.R. § 404.926 to request subpoenas for the physicians. The five-day period specified by the regulation for the issuance of the subpoenas surely afforded no real obstacle to this, for he was notified that the documentary evidence on file was available for examination before the hearing and, further, a supplemental hearing could be requested. In fact, in this very case there was a supplemental hearing more than two and a half months after the initial hearings. This inaction on the claimant's part supports the Court of Appeals' view, 412 F.2d, at 50–51, that the claimant as a consequence is to be precluded from now complaining that he was denied the rights of confrontation and cross-examination.

7. Courts have recognized the reliability and probative worth of written medical reports even in formal trials and, while acknowledging their hearsay character, have admitted them as an exception to the hearsay rule. . . .

8. Past treatment by reviewing courts of written medical reports in social security disability cases is revealing. Until the decision in this case, the courts of appeals, including the Fifth Circuit, with only an occasional criticism of the medical report practice, uniformly recognized reliability and probative value in such reports. The courts have reviewed administrative determinations, and upheld many adverse ones, where the only supporting evidence has been reports of this kind, buttressed sometimes, but often not, by testimony of a medical adviser such as Dr. Leavitt. In these cases admissibility was not contested, but the decisions do demonstrate traditional and ready acceptance of the written medical report in social security disability cases.

9. There is an additional and pragmatic factor which, although not controlling, deserves mention. This is what Chief Judge Brown has described as "[t]he sheer magnitude of that administrative burden," and the resulting necessity for written reports without "elaboration through the traditional facility of oral testimony." Page v. Celebrezze, 311 F.2d 757, 760 (CA5 1963). With over 20,000 disability claim hearings annually, the cost of providing live medical testimony at those hearings, where need has not been demonstrated by a request for a subpoena, over and above the cost of the examinations requested by hearing examiners, would be a substantial drain on the trust fund and on the energy of physicians already in short supply.

VI

1. Perales relies heavily on the Court's holding and statements in Goldberg v. Kelly, supra, particularly the comment that due process requires notice "and an effective opportunity to defend by confronting any adverse witnesses. . . . " 397 U.S. at 267–268. Kelly, however, had to do with termination of AFDC benefits without prior notice. It also concerned a situation, the Court said, "where credibility and veracity are at issue, as they must be in many termination proceedings." 397 U.S., at 269.

The Perales proceeding is not the same. We are not concerned with termination of disability benefits once granted. Neither are we concerned with a change of status without notice. Notice was given to claimant Perales. The physicians' reports were on file and available for inspection by the claimant and his counsel. And the authors of those reports were known and were subject to subpoena and to the very cross-examination that the claimant asserts he has not enjoyed. Further, the specter of questionable credibility and veracity is not present; there is professional disagreement with the medical conclusions, to be sure, but there is no attack here upon the doctors' credibility or veracity. Kelly affords little comfort to the claimant.

2. Perales also, as the Court of Appeals stated 412 F.2d, at 53, 416 F.2d, at 1251, would describe the medical reports in question as "mere uncorroborated hearsay" and would relate this to Mr. Chief Justice Hughes' sentence in Consolidated Edison Co. v. NLRB, 305 U.S., at 230: "Mere uncorroborated hearsay or rumor does not constitute substantial evidence."

Although the reports are hearsay in the technical sense, because their content is not produced live before the hearing examiner, we feel that the claimant and the Court of Appeals read too much into the single sentence from Consolidated Edison. The contrast the Chief Justice was drawing, at the very page cited, was not with material that would be deemed formally inadmissible in judicial proceedings but with material "without a basis in evidence having rational probative force." This was not a blanket rejection by the Court of administrative reliance on hearsay irrespective of reliability and probative value. The opposite was the case.

3. The claimant, the District Court, and the Court of Appeals also criticize the use of Dr. Leavitt as a medical adviser. Inasmuch as

medical advisers are used in approximately 13% of disability claim hearings, comment as to this practice is indicated. We see nothing "reprehensible" in the practice, as the claimant would describe it. The trial examiner is a layman; the medical adviser is a board-certified specialist. He is used primarily in complex cases for explanation of medical problems in terms understandable to the layman-examiner. He is a neutral adviser. This particular record discloses that Dr. Leavitt explained the technique and significance of electromyography. He did offer his own opinion on the claimant's condition. That opinion, however, did not differ from the medical reports. Dr. Leavitt did not vouch for the accuracy of the facts assumed in the reports. No one understood otherwise. . . . We see nothing unconstitutional or improper in the medical adviser concept and in the presence of Dr. Leavitt in this administrative hearing.

4. Finally, the claimant complains of the system of processing disability claims. . . . [The claimant asserts that] the hearing procedure is invalid on due process grounds. He says that the hearing examiner has the responsibility for gathering the evidence and "to make the Government's case as strong as possible"; that naturally he leans toward a decision in favor of the evidence he has gathered;
. . . .

The matter comes down to the question of the procedure's integrity and fundamental fairness. We see nothing that works in derogation of that integrity and of that fairness in the admission of consultants' reports, subject as they are to being material and to the use of the subpoena and consequent cross-examination. This precisely fits the statutorily prescribed "cross-examination as may be required for a full and true disclosure of the facts." [Admin.Proc.Act § 556(d).] That is the standard. It is clear and workable and does not fall short of procedural due process.

Neither are we persuaded by the advocate-judge-multiple-hat suggestion. It assumes too much and would bring down too many procedures designed, and working well, for a governmental structure of great and growing complexity. The social security hearing examiner, furthermore, does not act as counsel. He acts as an examiner charged with developing the facts. The 44.2% reversal rate for all federal disability hearings in cases where the state agency does not grant benefits, M. Rock, An Evaluation of the SSA Appeals Process, Report No. 7, U.S. Department of HEW, p. 9 (1970), attests to the fairness of the system and refutes the implication of impropriety.

We therefore reverse and remand for further proceedings. We intimate no view as to the merits. It is for the District Court now to determine whether the Secretary's findings, in the light of all material proffered and admissible, are supported by "substantial evidence" within the command of § 205(g). . . .

MR. JUSTICE DOUGLAS, with whom MR. JUSTICE BLACK and MR. JUSTICE BRENNAN concur, dissenting.

This claimant for social security disability benefits had a serious back injury. The doctor who examined him testified that he was permanently disabled. His case is defeated, however, by hearsay evidence of doctors and their medical reports about this claimant. Only one doctor who examined him testified at the hearing. Five other doctors who had once examined the claimant did not testify and were not subject to cross-examination. But their reports were admitted in evidence. Still another doctor testified on the hearsay in the documents of the other doctors. All of this hearsay may be received, as the Administrative Procedure Act [§ 556(d)] provides that "[a]ny oral or documentary evidence may be received." But this hearsay evidence cannot by itself be the basis for an adverse ruling. The same section of the Act states that "[a] party is entitled . . . to conduct such cross-examination as may be required for a full and true disclosure of the facts." . . .

Cross-examination of doctors in these physical injury cases is, I think, essential to a full and fair disclosure of the facts. . . .

One doctor whose word cast this claimant into limbo never saw him, never examined him, never took his vital statistics or saw him try to walk or bend or lift weights.

He was a "medical adviser" to HEW. The use of circuit-riding doctors who never see or examine claimants to defeat their claims should be beneath the dignity of a great nation. Three other doctors who were not subject to cross-examination were experts retained and paid by the Government. Some, we are told, who were subject to no cross-examination were employed by the workmen's compensation insurance company to defeat respondent's claim. . . .

Review of the evidence is of no value to us. The vice is in the procedure which allows it in without testing it by cross-examination. Those defending a claim look to defense-minded experts for their salvation. Those who press for recognition of a claim look to other experts. The problem of the law is to give advantage to neither, but to let trial by ordeal of cross-examination distill the truth.

The use by HEW of its stable of defense doctors without submitting them to cross-examination is the cutting of corners—a practice in which certainly the Government should not indulge. The practice is barred by the rules which Congress has provided; and we should enforce them in the spirit in which they were written.

I would affirm this judgment.

NOTES

(1) How much of one's reaction to cases such as this depends on such characterizations as Justice Douglas' "stable of defense doctors" or Justice Blackmun's "professional curiosity a dedicated medical man possesses"? On the one hand, particular administrations may seem driven to avoid "welfare chiselers." On the other, recall Professor Mashaw's concern that the characteristic bias of procedures in which decisions are committed to responsible professionals is pro-treatment:

"The physician is committed to treatment even if the patient's complaints cannot be characterized or explained within current scientific modes"; if doctors were empowered to decide, Mashaw opined, "the dominant medical culture [of treatment] might overwhelm the adjudicatory function." Bureaucratic Justice 27, 204. Rather than characterize HEW's (now HHS's) orientation as defensive, he sees its dilemma as that of obtaining cost-effective accuracy ("bureaucratic rationality") in carrying out a program that makes it responsible for awarding benefits in those cases—and only those cases—for which Congress had provided relief. Charged *equally* with awarding benefits to those who are "disabled" and denying benefits to those who are not, the agency has a three-fold task: avoiding error entirely in cases "clearly" within or without the statute; reducing the general incidence of error so far as a reasonable level of expenditures for administration permits; and for those errors that will invariably occur, seeking a balance point between errors of under-inclusion *and* of over-inclusion.[1]

Evidently, the use of "hearsay" in the form of doctor's reports has appeal as a device for cost-containment; by avoiding the waiting time invariably associated with oral hearings as well as those hearings' sometimes emotional confrontations, it conserves the beneficial use of a valuable resource (doctors' time and engagement) as well as direct dollar costs. Nor is it hard to characterize such reports as the type of data on which reasonable persons are disposed to rely in important affairs of life; one may seek a second opinion, but does not ordinarily cross-examine one's doctor regarding his techniques or possible biases. Yet, also, the doctors one chooses, one *chooses*—and they are unambiguously committed to accurate diagnosis of one's condition and reestablishment of one's health. Are the issues the same if their mandate is assisting an agency in cost-containment? Or if they were chosen by someone else, and share a cultural background distinct from that of the person they are examining, possibly infected with racial or other stereotypes?[2]

Here, then, are two distinct possibilities of bias in the ostensibly professional reports of the examining doctors—one systemic, the hypothesis that their job has been skewed by their employer toward

1. The importance of the last policy may not be self-evident; it may seem, as well, inhumane. Yet, as Professor Mashaw remarks, a defining characteristic of systems such as the disability insurance scheme is that their administrators have programmatic responsibilities. "The administration [is] not merely a neutral decider of disability claims. It [has] a positive program . . . to administer. And, like any goal-oriented enterprise, it [is] viewed as responsible for active pursuit of information sufficient to pursue its decisional task. . . . A correct classification of the claimant as disabled or not furthers the statutory goals; an incorrect classification retards their achievement." J. Mashaw, Bureaucratic Justice 39, 49

(1981). Orientation toward error of a certain kind (over-inclusion) would have not only this formal consequence but, repeated over time through the precedential process, would tend to overwhelm the agency's budget.

2. The principal case arose in Texas. Mr. Perales and his personal physician Dr. Morales, were "opposed" by doctors Munslow, Langston, Bailey, Mattson, and Leavitt, several of whose opinions suggested malingering. Assuming that these surnames reflect an ethnic pattern, that could cut in either direction. The question is merely whether there are issues here worthy of exploration.

denial; the other, more individual, involving distorting attitudes toward this particular benefit applicant. How would one establish or refute that either had been present? Note that both opinions in Perales take firm positions on the first of these issues. How do the Justices know the things they say? Are these issues of legislative or of adjudicative fact? If Professor Mashaw's book had been published at the time, would it have been a sufficient response for a court pressed with the argument about systemic bias to have responded that it had "read Professor Mashaw's study and had been persuaded by his conclusion that, on the whole, the administrators of that program have 'succeeded remarkably well in embracing both the neutrality, expertise and efficacy that are the promise of bureaucracy and the concern for individual circumstances and well-being that is promised by systems oriented toward moral entitlements and professional treatment'?" [3] As to the possibility of individual bias (or other error) in dealing with Mr. Perales, is the opportunity for subpoena a sufficient recognition of his interests? Is it usual in our jurisprudence to require an individual to call adverse witnesses? Is the tolerance for imposing that requirement here in part a function of the nature of the proceeding and the interest at stake? Note that there is no question here of *notice* to the claimant about the evidence on which the ALJ may rely.

(2) COMMONWEALTH UNEMPLOYMENT COMPENSATION BOARD OF REVIEW v. CEJA, 493 Pa. 588, 427 A.2d 631 (1981) arose from an administrative decision that a former state employee should be denied unemployment benefits because she had been discharged for willful misconduct. All the evidence of that misconduct had been presented in the form of memoranda and letters about the claimant Ceja's employment history. Appearing pro se, she had denied the truth of what they said but had not objected to their admission. The majority concluded that the hearsay was properly admitted and could be relied upon in reaching decision; it rejected a rule previously in force that although the commission could accept any evidence offered, still in the end there must be a "residuum" of legal evidence to support the claim before an award can be made.

"We do not fault the *objective* of . . . the residuum rule, i.e. the prevention of administrative decisions based on insubstantial evidence. But this objective can be better achieved by developing simple guidelines for judging whether evidence is sufficiently reliable to support a finding, rather than by creating inflexible mechanical requirements. . . . The notion that uncorroborated hearsay may be 'legally competent' is not revolutionary. The common law recognized this fact for centuries before evidence rules were codified. Hearsay, then, is certainly legally competent and could be substantial evidence in support of an administrative finding if it falls within the statutory or common law exceptions to the traditional hearsay rule . . . [or] if it has circumstantial guarantees of reliability equivalent to those implicit in the recognized exceptions.

---

3. J. Mashaw, Bureaucratic Justice 214 (1983); see also the excellent, earlier analysis, R. Dixon, Social Security Disability and Mass Justice (1973).

"Although indicia of reliability must ultimately be evaluated on a case by case basis, several factors typically would be significant: E.g., whether the hearsay statements are contradicted by direct testimony; whether the statements are sworn or unsworn, written or oral, signed or anonymous; whether the declarant is disinterested or is potentially biased; or whether the hearsay is corroborated. The type of hearsay offered is also a factor: For example, some documents, such as reports and itemized statements of charge from licensed professionals, may be typically more trustworthy than documents of more subjective content. If hearsay is introduced by live testimony, the credibility of the witness is, of course, to be considered.

"The element of necessity for the use of hearsay is equally critical . . . . Inquiry must be made whether the declarant is available to testify or whether other, perhaps better, evidence is available if the declarant is unavailable."

The majority concluded that the administrative result could not be sustained, in light of the referee's failure to protect the interests of an uncounseled claimant, and the unreliability of the documents submitted:

"She was given virtually no meaningful opportunity to challenge the hearsay documents, upon which employer's entire case was based, much less cross-examine the declarants. Moreover, although employer made no attempt to lay a foundation for reliability of the hearsay documents, the referee failed to put employer's evidence to any test of reliability. The referee also fell short of the regulatory mandate by failing to aid claimant's efforts to articulate her challenge. When employer's representative began reading the exhibits into the record, claimant attempted to interrupt the presentation but was cut off by the referee:

QC: May I say something.

R: Let him finish please, you could make an objection.

Rather than being instructive, the referee's comment may well have prevented this and later attempts to dispute the reliability of the hearsay evidence. . . . At the end of the submissions, the referee sought to dismiss claimant without any questions or further proceedings. When claimant again asked, 'May I say something?,' the referee replied in a manner designed to abbreviate claimant's reply, rather than to elicit probative testimony. Not surprisingly, claimant launched into a confused and convoluted account of the episodes detailed in the exhibits, in a vain attempt to answer all at once the myriad accusations therein. Instead of making a sincere effort to unravel claimant's testimony and clarify her grounds for challenging employer's adverse evidence, the referee, aided by employer's counsel, in effect cross-examined her for what appears from the record to be the contrary purpose of reinforcing employer's case.

"The employer's documents lack the indicia of reliability sufficient to provide them with prima facie circumstantial guarantees of trustworthiness. They were unsworn, subjective statements prepared at the employer's request, and were directly contradicted by claimant's live testimony. Moreover, the declarants may well have been biased against claimant, and no effort was made to demonstrate the necessity for relying solely upon hearsay documents when credibility was the central issue in dispute."

Two concurrences rejected the majority's reasoning as requiring analyses too confusing and uncertain for use in routine administrative proceedings, and "repugnant to centuries of tradition" in its rejection of the "residuum" rule.

SECTION 3. THE USE OR MISUSE OF OFFICIAL NOTICE

Rule 201 of the Federal Rules of Evidence, set out at page 798, supra, provides that in trials "adjudicative facts" may be noticed if they are either "generally known" or capable of being determined from "sources whose accuracy cannot reasonably be questioned." The applicable APA provision, § 556(e), also applies only to formal proceedings, and speaks only generally of "official notice of a material fact not appearing in the evidence." The Attorney General's Manual on the Administrative Procedure Act (1947) discussed this provision as follows:

"The process of official notice should not be limited to the traditional matters of judicial notice but extends properly to all matters as to which the agency by reason of its functions is presumed to be expert, such as technical or scientific facts within its specialized knowledge.

". . .

"Agencies may take official notice of facts at any stage in a proceeding—even in the final decision—but the matters thus noticed should be specified and 'any party shall on timely request be afforded an opportunity to show the contrary.' The matters thus noticed become a part of the record and, unless successfully controverted, furnish the same basis for findings of fact as does 'evidence' in the usual sense." (Pp. 79–80). . . .

These formulations provide a jumping-off point for the topic of "official notice." Whether they are sufficient to cabin the entire subject is, naturally, another matter.

BANKS v. SCHWEIKER
United States Court of Appeals, 654 F.2d 637, Ninth Circuit, 1981.

Before ALARCON and BOOCHEVER, CIRCUIT JUDGES, and THOMPSON,* DISTRICT JUDGE.

BOOCHEVER, CIRCUIT JUDGE:

In this appeal, we consider the scope of official notice in a Social Security Administration hearing (SSA) before an administrative law judge (ALJ).

. . .

* Sitting by designation.

The evidence indicated that while on state welfare, Banks began receiving supplemental security income disability (SSID) benefits in 1976. Thereafter, he applied for social security disability insurance benefits (SSDB). He signed a statement indicating that he understood that he could receive both benefits and knew the effect of SSDB on his SSID. Moreover, he acknowledged that he might receive an SSID overpayment in the first quarter that he would receive SSDB. Banks testified that a social security representative explained this to him, but told him to call when he got the checks and the representative would inform him whether he could keep them or not.

In the second quarter of 1977, Banks received his first SSDB check for $2,604. He also got SSID checks for April and May of 1977 totaling $335. Banks testified that he called the social security office and talked to "the guy I usually talk to." Banks described the color of the checks and told him the amounts of the respective checks.[1] According to Banks, the representative said that Banks was entitled to the checks and that the green check for approximately $2,600 was a social security make-up check. Banks "figured" the make-up check was for the two years when he filed for SSDB and was turned down, and not the regular SSDB check he would eventually receive. In fact, he was entitled to the retroactive SSDB check, but not the SSID checks totaling $335. After allegedly being told that he was entitled to the money, Banks spent the entire amount within three days to pay his bills and buy some clothes.

When Banks received an overpayment notice for $335, he went to the social security office, but did not ask to speak with the person who had told him that he was entitled to keep the checks. According to Banks, he was told that a different person handled overpayment notices.

When the SSA learned that Banks had been overpaid, it sought recovery. Banks requested that the overpayment be waived, but the request was denied. Under the SSA's regulations, Banks could avoid repayment only if he showed that: (1) he was without fault and (2) recovery would defeat the purposes of the Social Security Act (Act), be against equity or impede efficient administration of the Act.

Banks sought and was granted an administrative hearing. In his written opinion prepared at the conclusion of the hearing, the ALJ found that Banks' testimony was incredible. The ALJ first stated that he had "some familiarity" with a Social Security District Office and that based on that knowledge he inferred that "no . . . representative . . . empowered to deal with claims would tell anyone that he should cash and spend SSI checks for the same quarter in which he received a large SSA check". The ALJ stated that Banks may have called the office and asked if he could spend the SSI checks, but, if so, he did not state that he received the SSA check. In addition, the ALJ disbelieved Banks because: (1) the details of his testimony were unconvincing and the testimony was glib; (2) when notified of the overpayment he did not

1. Banks' mother testified that she was present when he called the office and that she heard him describe the checks and their amount.

ask to see, and made no further attempt to locate, the representative who allegedly authorized him to spend money; and (3) he spent the money almost immediately. Accordingly, the ALJ held that Banks was not without fault, and therefore not entitled to keep the overpayment.

Banks appealed the ALJ's decision to the SSA's Appeals Council contending the ALJ took improper administrative notice. The Appeals Council affirmance of the ALJ's decision became the final decision of the Secretary. Thereafter, Banks filed an action for review of the decision in district court which affirmed the SSA's decision. This timely appeal followed.

. . .

We shall first consider whether the ALJ properly took official notice of the practices and customs of SSA district offices.[2] Banks argues that since 42 U.S.C. § 1383(c)(1) of the Act and the agency's regulations, 20 CFR 416.1457(a), require that the Secretary's decision be based on evidence adduced at the hearing, it is improper to take official notice in disability cases.

If read literally, these provisions do prohibit the use of official notice in disability cases. Congress, however, clearly did not intend a literal interpretation for it would be difficult for any agency to function without taking official notice. . . . Nor can it be said that the SSA intended that official notice should not be taken. The permissible scope of official notice depends upon whether a "rule of convenience" or a "rule of caution" is applied.

Under Rule 201(b) of the Federal Rules of Evidence, judicial notice of adjudicative facts is limited to facts that are "not subject to reasonable dispute." The Advisory Committee notes make clear that limitation upon taking judicial notice is to further the tradition that extreme caution should be used in taking notice of adjudicative facts. Fed.R. Evid. 201, subdivision (b). The reason for this tradition is the belief that the taking of evidence, subject to established safeguards, is the best way to resolve controversies involving disputes of adjudicative facts. Id. A rule of extreme caution may be unwarranted in view of the right to a hearing now provided by Rule 201(e). In any event, under SSA regulations, "[e]vidence may be received at the hearing even though inadmissible under rules of evidence applicable to court procedures." 20 C.F.R. § 416.1442. Thus Rule 201 is not applicable.

We believe that the SSA may, within the scope of its discretion, adopt a rule of convenience. Because the SSA must handle a huge volume of cases [3] and the ALJ has the affirmative duty in such cases for developing the facts fairly, the ALJ should take notice of adjudicative facts, whenever, "the ALJ at the hearing knows of information that will be useful in making the decision." Davis § 15:18 at 200. The

2. This is an adjudicative fact because it is a fact "concerning the immediate parties." For a discussion of the difference between adjudicative facts and legislative facts, see the Advisory Notes to Fed.R.Evid. 201 and 3 K. Davis, Administrative Law Treatise § 15:5 (2d ed. 1980) (hereinafter cited as "Davis").

3. See Dobrowolsky v. Califano, 606 F.2d 403, 409 n. 18 (3rd Cir. 1979) (SSA received 92,000 requests for hearings on disability insurance benefits in 1978).

Supreme Court has recognized a difference between evidence which is to be admitted at SSA administrative hearings and litigation in a court. See Richardson v. Perales, [page 809 above]. . . . [T]he ALJ acted properly in taking official notice of the district office customs and practices.[4]

When the rule of convenience is applied to allow wide latitude in taking official notice, however, it is essential that the parties be afforded an opportunity to present information "which might bear upon the propriety of noticing the fact, or upon the truth of the matter to be noticed." C. McCormick, Law of Evidence § 333, at 771 (2d ed. 1972). In fact, the administrative procedure act in 5 U.S.C. § 556(e) requires that when an agency decision rests on official notice, a party be given "on timely request, . . . an opportunity to show the contrary." The SSA's own regulations recognize the importance of the opportunity helpful to a claimant's case [sic] by providing that the claimant may request subpoenas, see 20 CFR 416.1440, or permitting continuances, see 20 CFR 416.4441.

When the facts in this case were noticed, Banks was entitled to an opportunity to introduce the contrary evidence if a timely request was made. The failure to afford such an opportunity is grounds for remanding the case to the Secretary. See McDaniel v. Celebrezze, 331 F.2d 426, 428 n. 4 (4th Cir.1964). Because Banks was never given such an opportunity, the case must be remanded if Banks made a timely request.

This in turn depends upon when the ALJ took official notice.

> When official notice is taken after the hearing rather than at the hearing, the difference between information introduced as evidence and officially noticed information may be a large one, but the difference relates only to adequacy of opportunity "to show the contrary," and not to anything else. If the claimant has a chance to show the contrary at a reopened hearing and if he is not inconvenienced by having his chance at the reopened hearing instead of at the original hearing, then his procedural interest is as fully protected as it would have been by introducing the noticed facts as a part of the evidence at the original hearing.

Davis § 15:18, at 201.[5] If the ALJ did not take official notice until his written decision, then Banks made a timely objection because he requested the SSA's Appeals Council to review the ALJ's decision on the grounds that the ALJ took improper administrative notice.

During the hearing a colloquy occurred during which the ALJ discussed the agency's procedures.[6] Although an ALJ is not generally required to give a claimant advance notice of his intent to take official

---

4. Although we believe the ALJ might properly take official notice of district office customs and practices as some indication of the probability that Banks was told to cash the checks, we do not share his belief that such practices are invariably followed or that district offices give infalli-ble advice. See, e.g., Kendrick v. Califano, 460 F.Supp. 561, 570–71 (E.D.Va.1978).

5. For a general discussion, see Davis § 15:15 (procedures for challenging facts an agency uses an adjudication).

6. The following exchange took place:

notice, the ALJ must adequately inform the claimant that he is, in fact, taking official notice and must indicate the facts noticed and their source with a degree of precision and specificity. Without such information, a party cannot be expected to offer an objection. Clearly, if the ALJ stated "I take official notice of this fact," or gave similar indication the requirement would be fulfilled. We do not believe the ALJ's passing reference at the hearing made it sufficiently clear that he was taking official notice of the agency's procedures. Thus, Banks could not have been expected to offer an objection.[7]

The ALJ's written decision stated with clarity that he was noticing the fact that it is not the customary practice for social security employees to tell claimants to cash and spend checks when there is some doubt as to whether there has been an overpayment. Banks filed formal objections to the written decision's notice of this fact and the filing was timely. He was denied the opportunity to respond. Accordingly, the judgment of the district court is reversed, and the case must be remanded to the Secretary.

OHIO BELL TELEPHONE CO. v. PUBLIC UTILITIES COMMISSION OF OHIO

Supreme Court of the United States, 1937.
301 U.S. 292.

[In a valuation proceeding for rate-making purposes, the Commission undertook to ascertain the value of the company's property as of June 30, 1925. After protracted hearings, the Commission, ten years

"MR. BANKS: . . . I told him I got these three checks in the mail and I hadn't cashed them yet. He said I had to find out—'cause I had a green one—it was social security, plus my other two SSI checks and I said I got two gold ones and a green one and I told him the amount of them and I said, 'Shall I bring them in or something?' He said, 'No, they're your checks that you're supposed to be getting every month and that your green one was social security make-up check for when I filed.' And he says, 'You're entitled to that,' so I said, 'Then that's all (inaudible)' He said, 'Yes,'—that I had to notify them.

"ALJ: How much was the social security—SSA check—the disability insurance benefit check?

"MR. BANKS: It's $2200 I think it was.

"ALJ: Are you telling me that you told him that you got a $2200 check the same time you got that and he said 'Cash it.'

"MR. BANKS: He said I was entitled to it. He said that was for my back—

"ALJ: Did he say, 'Cash it.'

"MR. BANKS: I can't remember—

"ALJ: This is exactly contrary to the training of everybody in the whole bureau. (inaudible)

"MR. BANKS: Well, I can't remember if he said 'Cash it.' He said I was entitled to it.

"ALJ: On what ground?

"MR. BANKS: For—for when I filed twice before, he said I'd be getting a make-up check.

"ALJ: For SSA, yes, but how about SSI? Did he say that you were entitled to SSI checks?

"MR. BANKS: Oh them SSI checks weren't that much. The SSI checks were only $176.

"ALJ: Well, go ahead. I might say to you that is—they make mistakes there, but that's the sort of mistake that almost nobody would make if you explained it just in those terms unless they're incompetent entirely. I don't know."

7. Banks was represented at the hearing by counsel. We need not decide now whether more safeguards would be required to be given a pro se claimant such as informing the claimant of the right to rebut, to a continuance, to request subpoenas.

having elapsed since the start of the proceedings, filed a report in which it recorded its valuation of the property not only as of 1925, but for each of the years 1926–1933, inclusive. In doing so it "took judicial notice" of price trends during those years, modifying the value which it had found as of 1925 by the percentage of decline or rise applicable to the years thereafter. "The trend of land values was ascertained," the Commission stated, "from examination of the tax value in communities where the company had its largest real estate holdings." "For building trends resort was had to price indices of the Engineering News Record, a recognized magazine in the field of engineering construction," from which source labor trends were also developed. Reference was made to the findings of a Federal court in another case to determine price levels upon sales of certain telephone equipment.

The company protested, saying that the Commission's information did not come from sources which the Commission had the right to notice judicially; that they had not been introduced in evidence; and that failure to give the company opportunity to explain or rebut them constituted a denial of due process. The company's demand for this opportunity, as well as for permission to submit evidence bearing upon the value of its property in the years in question, was denied by the Commission.]

MR. JUSTICE CARDOZO delivered the opinion of the Court. . . .

First: The fundamentals of a trial were denied to the appellant when rates previously collected were ordered to be refunded upon the strength of evidential facts not spread upon the record.

The Commission had given notice that the value of the property would be fixed as of a date certain. Evidence directed to the value at that time had been laid before triers of the facts in thousands of printed pages. To make the picture more complete, evidence had been given as to the value at cost of additions and retirements. Without warning or even the hint of warning that the case would be considered or determined upon any other basis than the evidence submitted, the Commission cut down the values for the years after the date certain upon the strength of information secretly collected and never yet disclosed. The company protested. It asked disclosure of the documents indicative of price trends, and an opportunity to examine them, to analyze them, to explain and to rebut them. The response was a curt refusal. Upon the strength of these unknown documents refunds have been ordered for sums mounting into millions, the Commission reporting its conclusion but not the underlying proofs. The putative debtor does not know the proofs today. This is not the fair hearing essential to due process. It is condemnation without trial.

An attempt was made by the Commission and again by the state court to uphold this decision without evidence as an instance of judicial notice. Indeed, decisions of this court were cited . . . as giving support to the new doctrine that the values of land and labor and buildings and equipment with all their yearly fluctuations, no longer call for evidence. Our opinions have been much misread if they have been thought to point that way. Courts take judicial notice of matters of common knowledge. 5 Wigmore, Evidence, secs. 2571, 2580, 2583; Thayer, Preliminary Treatise on Evidence, pp. 277, 302. They take judicial notice that there has been a depression, and that a decline of market values is one of its concomitants. . . . How great the decline has been for this industry or that, for one material or another, in this year or the next, can be known only to the experts, who may even differ among themselves. . . . The distinction is the more important in cases where as here the extent of the fluctuations is not collaterally involved but is the very point in issue. Moreover, notice, even when taken, has no other effect than to relieve one of the parties to a controversy of the burden of resorting to the usual forms of evidence. Wigmore, Evidence, sec. 2567; 1 Greenleaf, Evidence, 16th ed., p. 18. "It does not mean that the opponent is prevented from disputing the matter by evidence if he believes it disputable." Ibid. Cf. Shapleigh v. Mier, 299 U.S. 468. . . . Here the contention would be futile that the precise amount of the decline in values was so determinate or notorious in each and every year between 1925 and 1933 as to be beyond the range of question. . . . [T]o press the doctrine of judicial notice to the extent attempted in this case and to do that retroactively after the case had been submitted, would be to turn the doctrine into a pretext for dispensing with a trial.

What was done by the Commission is subject, however, to an objection even deeper. . . . There has been more than an expansion of the concept of notoriety beyond reasonable limits. From the standpoint of due process—the protection of the individual against arbitrary action—a deeper vice is this, that even now we do not know the particular or evidential facts of which the Commission took judicial notice and on which it rested its conclusion. Not only are the facts unknown; there is no way to find them out. When price lists or trade journals or even government reports are put in evidence upon a trial, the party against whom they are offered may see the evidence or hear it and parry its effect. Even if they are copied in the findings without preliminary proof, there is at least an opportunity in connection with a judicial review of the decision to challenge the deductions made from them. The opportunity is excluded here. The Commission, withholding from the record the evidential facts that it has gathered here and there, contents itself with saying that in gathering them it went to journals and tax lists, as if a judge were to tell us, "I looked at the statistics in the Library of Congress, and they teach me thus and so." This will never do if hearings and appeals are to be more than empty forms.

. . . To put the problem more concretely: how was it possible for the appellate court to review the law and the facts and intelligently decide that the findings of the Commission were supported by the evidence when the evidence that it approved was unknown and unknowable? In expressing that approval the court did not mean that, traveling beyond the record, it had consulted price lists for itself and had reached its own conclusion as to the percentage of decline in value from 1925 onwards. It did not even mean that it had looked at the particular lists made use of by the Commission, for no one knows what they were in any precise or certain way. Nowhere in the opinion is there even a hint of such a search. What the Supreme Court of Ohio did was to take the word of the Commission as to the outcome of a secret investigation, and let it go at that. "A hearing is not judicial, at least in any adequate sense, unless the evidence can be known." West Ohio Gas Co. v. Public Utilities Comm. (No. 1), 294 U.S. 63. Cf. Interstate Commerce Comm'n v. Louisville & N.R. Co., 227 U.S. 88, 91; United States v. Abilene & Southern Ry. Co., 265 U.S. 274, 288. . . .

NOTES

(1) PUERTO RICO MARITIME SHIPPING AUTHORITY v. FEDERAL MARITIME COMMISSION, 678 F.2d 327, 337–342 (D.C.Cir.1982): One issue in this rate-setting proceeding for intercoastal carriers serving Puerto Rico and the Virgin Islands was the likely price of fuel during the period the proposed rates would be in effect. One carrier submitted a forecast of rising prices based on a statistical analysis of recent past experience and industry projections. The Commission rejected the forecast as a deficient statistical analysis—a discussion omitted here—and, the court said, because " 'dramatic changes in world oil markets have caused [the] forecasts to change substantially since the initiation of the proceeding.' . . . Faced with the problem . . . that no reliable alternative forecast had been presented, it determined that the proper course was a 'pragmatic adjustment of the carrier's projections.' Therefore, it accepted as a base fuel cost to be applied . . . the last known price actually paid by PRMSA at the beginning of the test year:

> . . . . (1) PRMSA's last known fuel cost approximates the test year projections of the other carriers, and (2) all of the petroleum "trade intelligence" entered into the record in this proceeding support [sic] the conclusion that petroleum prices are likely to level off the remainder of 1981.

"In addition, the Commission took cognizance of the legal right under the statute of the carrier to file a cost-pass-through rate increase if it turned out that fuel prices actually were above the base cost, whereas shippers would have no adequate remedy if the allowed estimate turned out to be too high. . . . Although the newspaper articles and other materials inserted in the record dealing with potential stagnation in the oil market might not compel any particular conclusion as to the future of world oil prices, they were sufficient to arouse in the Commission a legitimate uneasiness and skepticism about a prediction based solely on the experience of the prior year that would result in an 88-percent rise, totaling over $25,000,000, in PRMSA's fuel costs over the next year.

"PRMSA urges that it was improper for the agency to take 'official notice' of any leveling off of fuel prices not contained in the submission of the parties, relying on the Supreme Court's decision in Ohio Bell Telephone Co. v. Public Util. Comm'n, 301 U.S. 292, 301 (1937). . . . We think this case is not at one with Ohio Bell, because of both the nature of the information noticed and the use made of it by the Commission.

"First, the Commission used the changes occurring in world oil markets that were documented in the record to reject PRMSA's forecast methodology, which assumes unchanging conditions. This was a judgment it was authorized to make in the course of deciding whether the carrier had carried its burden of proof. To the extent that the Commission may have looked beyond the record to the 'common knowledge' that an oil glut might be in the making which was likely to retard the increase of prices, it was making use of the kind of general and gross economic and financial information condoned in Ohio Bell. Our conclusion might be very different had the agency tried to use the existence of turbulence in the oil market to determine an exact rate.

"The base fuel cost adopted by the Commission was not the result of computations based on evidence not on the record. Instead it was a pragmatic adjustment in the absence of persuasive proof by either the carrier or shippers as to an appropriate estimate of fuel prices for the forthcoming test year. . . . [A]n agency is permitted to accept an estimate that does not comport with what actually happened later on, but the agency is not required to blindfold itself, ignoring dramatic changes in circumstances which surface during the ratemaking proceeding and are bound to affect the estimate. It may take into account evidence which contradicts the reasonableness of the estimate beforehand as well as the magnitude of the disparity between the estimate and experience afterward. PRMSA points out nonetheless that under FMC regulations it must make its case in chief well before the hearing begins and before the agency even decides a hearing is appropriate. In light of the restrictions placed on updating its submissions for cost increases, PRMSA . . . would restrict the issue before the Commission to whether any estimates were reasonable in light of information available at the time of their initial submission to the Commission.

"We have some sympathy for PRMSA's plight. It may seem at first glance unfair to a carrier operating in a fast-breaking energy market to be forced to react and adjust to events up to the moment of decision. But it would be even more unfair to saddle shippers for an entire year with unrealistically high rates based on already inflated fuel costs simply to preserve the orderliness of the ratemaking scenario. The FMC is not merely a referee, ensuring fair play with no interest in the particular outcome. It is charged with determining whether the rates proposed by the carrier are just and reasonable. This difficult responsibility requires use of the information properly before it to arrive at a conclusion consistent with the public welfare."

(2) The preceding cases arose, of course, from a matrix of formal agency hearings. How different would the problem be if the underlying procedure were informal rulemaking? Section 556, in terms, is not applicable. Yet does the idea of "a chance to prove the contrary" of "noticed" facts resonate with some of the more expansive interpretations of the "notice" provision in § 553, underlying development of "paper hearing" requirements, pp. 259 and 475 ff. above? Are Justice Cardozo's final remarks so different from some of the uses to which the requirement of a "statement of . . . basis and purpose" has been put?

Similar questions, of course, may be put respecting the use of social data by appellate courts.[1] Return to Richardson v. Perales, p. 809 above, now to assess, not what the agency "knew," but what facts influenced the Supreme Court in its own general, "expert" assessment of what procedures would be "fair," and how the Court knew *them*— whether the medical reports were "routine, standard, and unbiased" and reflected "that the claimant received professional examination and opinion on a scale beyond the reach of most persons"; what are the number of disability hearings held annually; in what proportion of cases medical advisers are used; what has been the reversal rate for state denials of benefits in disability hearings before federal ALJs; and so forth. Sometimes material of this character is presented to the Court in briefs, to which there *may* be an opportunity to reply. See, for example, note 2 at p. 813 above. But it is sometimes the product of what a Justice "just knows"[2] or of a law clerk's research. Professor Maurice Rosenberg commented on this some years ago as follows:

"I have the sense that today a judge—especially in an appellate court—who confronts a problem such as whether six-member juries function differently from twelve member juries proceeds to get information pretty much as fancy dictates. . . . Indexes in law libraries are improving, but they still leave much to be desired as gateways to materials in the social, hard, or life sciences.

"At least two serious flaws characterize the present hit-or-miss approach. One is that most judges and law clerks lack training or knowledge about how to find or evaluate empirical data in the form of reports or experiments, surveys, or systematic observational studies. The other is that litigants are not assured by definite rule that they will have an opportunity to comment on the strengths or weaknesses of the reports and materials the court may find critical to its determination on the law.

"What about creating a public agency to act as an information resource or depository for social and technological data? . . . Its mission would be to receive and catalogue social impact studies that qualify for judicial attention. The criteria for determining whether a study qualifies for approval would not be agreement or disagreement with its content or recommendations but only a finding that its design and methods fall within the range of accepted standards of scientific inquiry. These standards would be akin to 'standard accounting principles' in financial practice.

"Procedures would be developed to regulate the manner by which courts utilize the studies in the depository. A study found acceptable in its methods would be available for judicial notice if and only if timely notification is given to the parties and an opportunity afforded to submit briefs supporting, contesting, or commenting on the material

1. K. Davis, 3 Admin.L.Treatise § 15:9 (1980).

2. Justice Blackmun, for example, numbered the Mayo Clinic among his clients for many years before becoming a federal judge; surely the opinion would have been written differently by someone without that background, and resulting comfort with medical practice and documentation.

the court proposes to use. The comments could go both to the methods and the substance of the study."

M. Rosenberg, Anything Legislatures Can Do, Courts Can Do Better? 62 A.B.A.J. 587, 590 (1976).[3] The years since that proposal have seen no rush to adopt it, nor any retreat from judicial fact-finding of this character.

(3) Whether "general" information of the sort that is more easily "noticed" is sufficient with or without an opportunity to respond, depends, one must remember, in part on what is the governing substantive law. For example, the Federal Trade Commission is authorized, after an adjudicatory hearing, to proscribe "unfair or deceptive" advertising. If an advertisement is "deceptive" only if a substantial number of people are actually deceived by it into thinking something that is not true, then presumably there is no way to "notice" that crucial fact. The predominant interpretation of the statutory standard, however, is that an advertisement is "deceptive" if it has the "capacity to deceive" a substantial number of people. Using this more prophylactic interpretation of governing law, the courts have sustained the Commission when it has conducted surveys to find out what people thought an advertisement meant—and when it has accepted the "expert" testimony of those who deal with customers—and when it has by itself "inferred" what the probable interpretation of an advertisement would be.

(4) Suppose the agency wishes to notice, not general fact, but materials in its files submitted by the participants outside the pending proceedings? UNITED STATES V. ABILENE & SOUTHERN RY. CO., 265 U.S. 274 (1924), is often cited as a discouragement of free use of such files. The case involved a division between railroads of the freight charges paid by shippers whose goods were carried over the tracks of more than one carrier when moving from place of origin to destination. The ICC based its decision in part upon annual reports that the railroads had made to the Commission in past years, as required by law—tonnage carried, mileage, revenues per ton mile, operating expenses, return per $1,000 of investment, and so on, in great detail. None of this information had been formally introduced in evidence, though the trial examiner had said in the course of the hearing that "no doubt it will be necessary to refer to the annual reports of these carriers." The ICC's order was attacked because it rested upon evidence that was said not to have been legally before the Commission. The Court agreed with this contention. Justice Brandeis wrote: "Papers in the Commission's files are not always evidence in a case. Nothing can be treated as evidence which is not introduced as such. . . . The objection to the use of the data contained in the annual reports is not lack of authenticity or untrustworthiness. It is that the carriers were left without notice of the evidence with which they were, in fact, confronted, as later disclosed by the finding made. The requirement that in an adversary proceeding specific reference be made, is essential to the preservation of

---

3. Note E.I. du Pont de Nemours Co. v. Collins, 432 U.S. 46, 57 (1977) disapproving a court's use of a business school dean to help understand the record on issues concerning the valuation of shares.

the substantial rights of the parties. . . . The general notice that the Commission would rely upon the voluminous annual reports is tantamount to giving no notice whatsoever. The matter improperly treated as evidence may have been an important factor in the conclusions reached by the Commission. The order must, therefore, be held void. . . . "

(5) Do the procedures of Section 556(e) provide sufficiently for notice and the opportunity to contravene in this context? Suppose, for example, that after a hearing record had closed, an agency searched its files for indications of other dealings by the participants bearing on the outcome, then published its findings offering a reasonable period for reopening the record to dispute what had been asserted? [4] MARKET ST. RY. CO. v. RAILROAD COMM. OF CALIFORNIA, 324 U.S. 548 (1945), sheds some light on this question. The Company's rates and service were investigated by the Commission on its own motion. After hearing, the Commission ordered a reduction in the fare from seven to six cents. The order was attacked on the ground, among others, that the Commission had gone outside the record to the Company's monthly reports to the Commission, in order to ascertain the Company's operating revenues in 1943 as compared with 1942. As to this, the Court (per Jackson, J.) said: "No contention is made here that the information was erroneous or was misunderstood by the Commission, and no contention is made that the Company could have disproved it or explained away its effect for the purpose for which the Commission used it. The most that can be said is that the Commission in making its predictive findings went outside of the record to verify its judgment by reference to actual traffic figures that became available only after the hearings closed. It does not appear that the Company was in any way prejudiced thereby, and it makes no showing that, if a rehearing were held to introduce its own reports, it would gain much by cross-examination, rebuttal, or impeachment of its own auditors or the reports they had filed. Due process, of course, requires that commissions proceed upon matters in evidence and that parties have opportunity to subject evidence to the test of cross-examination and rebuttal. But due process deals with matters of substance and is not to be trivialized by formal objections that have no substantial bearing on the ultimate rights of parties. The process of keeping informed as to regulated utilities is a continuous matter with commissions. We are unwilling to say that such an incidental reference as we have here to a party's own reports, although not formally marked in evidence in the proceeding, in the absence of any showing of error or prejudice constitutes a want of due process. . . . "

(6) In AIR PRODUCTS & CHEMICALS, INC. v. FERC, 650 F.2d 687 (5th Cir.1981), on the other hand, the Commission reviewing an ALJ judg-

---

4. Dayton Power & Light, 8 S.E.C. 950 (1941): The various financings the SEC analyzed in order to infer too close a relationship between banker and borrower had been "announced in newspapers and financial and statistical services as they occurred and . . . were, moreover, reported to us as required by the Act. . . . To ignore them would not only be self-stultifying but would be closing our eyes to the very type of knowledge which we are supposed to acquire and bring to bear upon our exercise of administrative function under the Act. . . . "

ment entered in 1975 had relied upon "various reports" in its files to establish that a situation the ALJ had identified was continuing. The issue thus addressed concerned the general curtailment of natural gas supplies—a matter of continuing and general interest to the Commission; producers persuaded the court that they had evidence of a contrary trend, and the court found the Commissioner's use of unspecified information improper:

"At this time, neither this court nor any petitioner knows what information the FERC looked to in reaching this decision. Yet, the question of the curtailment situation in the interstate market was critical in the FERC's reasoning. The perceived curtailment situation was a major factor given by the FERC as to why it was terminating its producer reservation policy. It also was a major factor in its antitrust findings and its finding that producer reservation conflicted with other FERC policies. . . . Section 556(e) of the APA recognizes that agency decisions often will rest on official notice of material facts not appearing in the record evidence. However, the statute requires that a party shall have an opportunity to rebut such evidence. . . .

"We do not accept the FERC's argument that no substantial prejudice has been shown here. It maintains that the extra-record material merely upgraded and corroborated evidence of record with regard to the curtailment situation in the interstate market. Because evidence on curtailment was presented to the ALJ during the initial stages of this proceeding, the FERC argues that the issue was clearly present in the case and the producers were not deprived of the opportunity to present relevant information due to lack of notice that the issue was there. . . . First, the agency's action deprived the parties of fairness in denying them the opportunity to be heard on their views of the facts on which the agency took notice. . . . Second, . . . official notice of unspecified information in the files of an agency precludes effective judicial review. . . . [M]eaningful review of the FERC's action has been prevented by FERC's reliance upon extra-record evidence. We do not know what evidence the FERC relied upon. Also, in order to have effective judicial review, adversarial comment among the parties regarding the evidence and an opportunity to rebut is essential. . . .

"The FERC argues that reliance on the extra-record evidence was permissible because the curtailment situation in the interstate pipe line is a matter within the FERC's particular expertise. The FERC, in effect, argues that notice of the current curtailment situation is more akin to a legislative fact or legislative judgment than an adjudicative resolution of disputed fact.

"The FERC not only made a prediction concerning future curtailment situations, but grounded the decision at issue on data concerning the curtailment situation during the interim period. Such data are not forecasts of the future similar to the forecasts which the Supreme Court held were not required to be supported by testimonial and documentary evidence in FPC v. Transcontinental Gas Corp., 365 U.S. 1 (1961). Nor are such data of a judgmental or predictive nature for which complete factual support is not possible or required. . . . The curtailment situation in the interim period is a purely factual matter. Moreover, the interstate pipelines who were participants in this action below are well-equipped to offer rebuttal evidence to the FERC's file information. Accordingly, the FERC was obliged to allow the producer petitioners to present their own evidence on the curtailment situation. . . ."

(7) In FEINSON v. CONSERVATION COMMISSION OF THE TOWN OF NEWTOWN, 180 Conn. 421, 429 A.2d 910, 913–15 (1980), a property owner sought permission to install septic facilities for a one-family house he wanted to build himself. The facilities might have imperiled a local marsh; his expert witness testified that the design was adequate, and was questioned by some commissioners of the responsible state board. No other witnesses appeared. The application was denied on the basis of concerns expressed by one commissioner, not an engineer, that "there was an 'extreme possibility of septic failure, constituting a public health hazard. . . . ' " The court reversed and remanded for further hearing, remarking that "The sparsity of reliable evidence in this record is underscored by the fact that the commission, in relying on its own knowledge and experience, acted in a manner which placed its data base beyond the plaintiff's scrutiny. Nowhere in the public hearing, or at any other time and place, was the plaintiff afforded a fair opportunity to hear the commissioner's fears and to attempt to allay them. The questioning of the plaintiff's witness . . . at the public hearing did not give warning that his evidence was to be entirely discredited; on the contrary, that hearing as transcribed suggests that the proffered evidence was on the whole satisfactory to the commission. If an administrative agency chooses to rely on its own judgment, it has a responsibility to reveal publicly its special knowledge and experience, to give notice of the material facts that are critical to its decision, so that a person adversely affected thereby has an opportunity for rebuttal at an appropriate stage in the administrative proceedings. . . ." [5]

SECTION 4. DETERMINING FACTS OF A GENERAL CHARACTER

At some point the question of "official notice" becomes the yet more general issue of how facts of a general character are to be "found." We ask that question first in a case in which a question of general fact is imbedded in a formal adjudicatory proceeding.

SEACOAST ANTI–POLLUTION LEAGUE v. COSTLE
United States Court of Appeals, First Circuit, 1978.
572 F.2d 872.

[Earlier portions of the opinion are set out at pp. 241–244 above. As those pages reflect, this EPA proceeding concerned authorization to

---

5. An earlier opinion, dealing with a board more self-evidently expert, had been more accepting of agency expertise. See Jaffe v. State Department of Health, 135 Conn. 339, 64 A.2d 330 (1949) (state medical board presumed qualified to conclude without expert assistance that fee was exorbitant and use of unsterilized instruments unprofessional.)

construct a nuclear power plant, following APA formal hearing procedures. The following portions of the opinion concern one aspect of the procedures employed on review by the EPA Administrator of the initial decision reached after hearing in the field.]

2. PARTICIPATION OF THE TECHNICAL REVIEW PANEL

Petitioners object to the Administrator's use of a panel of EPA scientists to assist him in reviewing the Regional Administrator's initial decision. The objection is two-fold: first, that the Administrator should not have sought such help at all; and, second, that the panel's report (the Report) to the Administrator included information not in the administrative record.

Petitioners point out that by the EPA's own regulations "*[t]he Administrator shall decide* the matters under review on the basis of the record presented and any other consideration he deems relevant." 40 CFR § 125.36(n)(12) (emphasis added). It is true that when a decision is committed to a particular individual that individual must be the one who reviews the evidence on which the decision is to be based. See Morgan v. United States, 298 U.S. 468, 481 (1936). But it does not follow that all other individuals are shut out of the decision process. That conclusion runs counter to the purposes of the administrative agencies which exist, in part, to enable government to focus broad ranges of talent on particular multi-dimensional problems. The Administrator is charged with making highly technical decisions in fields far beyond his individual expertise. "The strength [of the administrative process] lies in staff work organized in such a way that the appropriate specialization is brought to bear upon each aspect of a single decision, the synthesis being provided by the men at the top." 2 K. Davis, Administrative Law Treatise 84 (1958) . . . The decision ultimately reached is no less the Administrator's simply because agency experts helped him to reach it.

A different question is presented, however, if the agency experts do not merely sift and analyze but also add to the evidence properly before the Administrator. The regulation quoted above cannot allow the Administrator to consider evidence barred from consideration by the APA, 5 U.S.C. § 556(e), "The transcript of testimony and exhibits, together with all papers and requests filed in the proceeding, constitutes the exclusive record for decision . . . ." To the extent the technical review panel's Report included information not in the record on which the Administrator relied,[1] § 556(e) was violated. In effect the agency's staff would have made up for PSCO's failure to carry its burden of proof.

Our review of the Report indicates that such violations did occur. The most serious instance is on page 19 of the Report where the technical panel rebuts the Regional Administrator's finding that PSCO had failed to supply enough data on species' thermal tolerances by

---

[1]. The use of the extra-record evidence must substantially prejudice petitioners in order to constitute fatal error. The Administrator's reliance on extra-record evidence for important facts, we feel, makes out such prejudice.

saying: "There is little information in the record on the thermal tolerances of marine organisms exposed to the specific temperature fluctuation associated with the Seabrook operation.[2] However, the scientific literature does contain many references to the thermal sensitivity of members of the local biota." Whether or not these references do exist and whether or not they support the conclusions the panel goes on to draw does not concern us here. What is important is that the record did not support the conclusion until supplemented by the panel. The panel's work found its way directly into the Administrator's decision at page 27 where he discusses the Regional Administrator's concerns about insufficient data but then precipitously concludes, "On the recommendation of the panel, however, I find that . . . local indigenous populations will not be significantly affected." This conclusion depends entirely on what the panel stated about the scientific literature.

Similar, though less egregious, examples occur [elsewhere] in the Report. . . .

We do not challenge the reliability of the panel, nor do we question the principle that informed opinion may be able to determine that information the Regional Administrator found lacking was either unavailable or irrelevant. On such issues the Administrator would be free to reverse the Regional Administrator. But the instances pointed to above . . . are of a different sort. The panel did not say that the information missing was unavailable or irrelevant; instead they supplied the information. They are free to do that as witnesses, but not as deciders.

The appropriate remedy under these circumstances is to remand the decision to the Administrator because he based his decision on material not part of the record. . . .

The Administrator will have the options of trying to reach a new decision not dependent on the panel's supplementation of the record; of holding a hearing at which all parties will have the opportunity to cross-examine the panel members and at which the panel will have an opportunity to amplify its position; or of taking any other action within his power and consistent with this opinion.

NOTES

(1) To understand what was at issue in this case, one must distinguish the uniquely local issues from the more general. What species teemed in Hampton Bay ("the local biota") and what were the ordinary temperatures of its waters were local issues—although one might believe the choice of adversarial hearing curious even for these. How about the question "What is the thermal sensitivity of the soft-shell clam?" Such clams are widely distributed, and could have been studied outside Hampton Bay. If, as appears, *that* was the question on which

2. [Ed.] A nuclear power plant may be the source of large volumes of warm water passed through its cooling systems. Sealife that becomes accustomed to this, if intoler- ant of changing temperatures, will be harmed when the flow stops for reactor shut-downs or is shifted by changing currents.

the technical panel consulted the books, what was the objection to their doing so? Would this have been judicial notice of "adjudicatory fact" under Fed.R.Evid. 201, p. 798 above, if it had occurred in a federal court? If so, would taking notice have been permissible under the rule, so long as its procedures were followed? Or would this have been notice of a "legislative fact," as to which the rule leaves judges free? In the agency context, could the Administrator have argued that he was entitled to take official notice of the literature, subject only to the requirement that he respond to a "timely request [for] an opportunity to show the contrary," 5 U.S.C. § 556(e)—a request which apparently had not been made? Why, in other words, does the court not continue reading Section 556(e), on the first part of which it relies, to its end?

(2) CALIFORNIA V. TROMBETTA, 467 U.S. 479 (1984): At issue was whether California was constitutionally required to preserve breath samples given by automobile drivers suspected of—and then on the strength of a breath test charged with—driving under the influence of alcohol. California officials had employed a testing device called the Intoxilyzer that did not capture samples in preservable form, as some other breath analyzers (or blood and urine tests) did, but it would have been possible to preserve a breath sample using other techniques. Now, the defendants reasoned, they had been prejudicially deprived of the opportunity to challenge the reliability of the test. Unanimously rejecting this claim, the Court noted the calibration procedures required by the state [1] and reasoned, in part:

"Although the preservation of breath samples might conceivably have contributed to respondents' defenses, a dispassionate review of the Intoxilyzer and the California testing procedures can only lead one to conclude that the chances are extremely low that preserved samples would have been exculpatory. The accuracy of the Intoxilyzer has been reviewed and certified by the California Department of Health. To protect suspects against machine malfunctions, the Department has developed test procedures that include two independent measurements (which must be closely correlated for the results to be admissible) bracketed by blank runs designed to ensure that the machine is purged of alcohol traces from previous tests. In all but a tiny fraction of cases, preserved breath samples would simply confirm the Intoxilyzer's determination that the defendant had a high level of blood-alcohol concentration at the time of the test. Once the Intoxilyzer indicated that respondents were legally drunk, breath samples were much more likely to provide inculpatory than exculpatory evidence.

1. "Prior to any test, the device is purged by pumping clean air through it until readings of 0.00 are obtained. The breath test requires a sample of 'alveolar' (deep lung) air; to assure that such a sample is obtained, the subject is required to blow air into the Intoxilyzer at a constant pressure for a period of several seconds. A breath sample is captured in the Intoxilyzer's chamber and infrared light is used to sense the alcohol level. Two samples are taken, and the result of each is indicated on a printout card. The two tests must register within 0.02 of each other in order to be admissible in court. After each test, the chamber is purged with clean air and then checked for a reading of zero alcohol. The machine is calibrated weekly, and the calibration results, as well as a portion of the calibration samples, are available to the defendant."

"Even if one were to assume that the Intoxilyzer results in this case were inaccurate and that breath samples might therefore have been exculpatory, it does not follow that respondents were without alternative means of demonstrating their innocence. Respondents and amici have identified only a limited number of ways in which an Intoxilyzer might malfunction: faulty calibration, extraneous interference with machine measurements, and operator error. Respondents were perfectly capable of raising these issues without resort to preserved breath samples. To protect against faulty calibration, California gives drunk driving defendants the opportunity to inspect the machine used to test their breath as well as that machine's weekly calibration results and the breath samples used in the calibrations. . . . As to improper measurements, the parties have identified only two sources capable of interfering with test results: radio waves and chemicals that appear in the blood of those who are dieting. For defendants whose test results might have been affected by either of these factors, it remains possible to introduce at trial evidence demonstrating that the defendant was dieting at the time of the test or that the test was conducted near a source of radio waves. Finally, as to operator error, the defendant retains the right to cross-examine the law enforcement officer who administered the Intoxilyzer test, and to attempt to raise doubts in the mind of the fact-finder whether the test was properly administered."

Note that the first paragraph of quoted material concerns the *general* reliability of the test; the second, matters bearing on the particular administrations at issue. As to the first, one may ask again how the *Court* knows the matters it asserts? How many, if any, of these propositions were developed using trial procedures? Do they differ, and if so how, from the propositions about the thermal sensitivity of soft-shell clams (e.g.) at issue in the principal case?

(3) Another option in the principal case, at least for a recurring, general issue, would be to hold an informal rulemaking proceeding, and then use the results of that rulemaking to determine authoritatively the issue in subsequent adjudication. See Vermont Yankee Nuclear Power Corp. v. NRDC, p. 248 above, and Heckler v. Campbell, p. 295. If an agency could hold an informal rulemaking to set values for the thermal sensitivities of marine organisms, does that mean the court was wrong to require adversary process in the principal case?

(4) NATIONAL TOUR BROKERS ASSOCIATION v. INTERSTATE COMMERCE COMMISSION, 671 F.2d 528, 532–33 (D.C.Cir.1982): In an ICC rulemaking, the Commission had based its conclusions supporting deregulatory change in licensing requirements applicable to four brokers on its perceptions of experience under prior arrangements. "Certainly these findings provide a rational basis for the Commission's decision to alter the existing licensing requirements. However, these findings must themselves be factually supported in the administrative record in order to assure that the ICC's decision to alter existing licensing requirements was the rational result of reasoned analysis. . . .

"Our examination of the record confirms the NTBA's contention that the ICC presented no systematic study of the tour broker industry.

However, the ICC's decision to promulgate new tour broker licensing rules . . . was based on the Commission's long experience administering the existing licensing rules and its consequential dissatisfaction with those procedures. The Commission's decision fully explained its perception that existing rules requiring individual examinations of the public interest are without substantial value and of minor importance in achieving the goals of [the statute] while contributing unnecessary expense and time to the licensing process.

"While the practice is not without problems, an agency may rely on its 'experience' to provide the necessary factual support for its decision to engage in informal rulemaking so long as that experience is made part of the record and susceptible to judicial review. A problem for the agency in relying on its experience as factual support for its decision to promulgate a rule is the necessity of adequately recording and explaining that experience on the record. In the present case, the ICC's explanation of its experience provides sufficient support under the arbitrary and capricious standard to sustain the rule change as a rational decision."

(5) Consider the following observation: "When the question was merely whether Tommy Tucker stuck in his thumb and pulled out a plum, or whether, as Tommy said, he bit into a stray stone in the pie, a jury could easily be expected to decide on its own which was right; but when the question is whether Tommy contracted bone cancer because he has been drinking milk from cows allegedly irradiated by the defendant's nuclear reactor seventy-five miles away, the answer may be too hard for a layman to reach without expert help. The more sophisticated the technology, the more subtle the invasions of personal rights, the more likely we shall need scientific experts." [2]

Note that the difficulty is not simply one of understanding, but one of a different character of "truth." There was a physical pie, a broken tooth. Tommy's bone cancer, however, has no better than a statistical relationship to those irradiated cows. There would have been *some* bone cancer even without the radiation; the cancers that occur do not come labeled as to source of origin. Beyond that, it may be no better than a hypothesis that any bone cancers at all can be attributed to the milk; laboratory experiments may have established that much higher levels of radiation produced cancer in mice, and extrapolation to humans and to lower doses is, at best, an educated guess. The following cases, and their notes, are intended to open questions about the use of statistics, econometrics, and science in administrative decision.

WIRTZ v. BALDOR ELECTRIC CO.
United States Court of Appeals, District of Columbia Circuit, 1963.
337 F.2d 518.

[The Walsh-Healey Act provides in part that a person who contracts to sell supplies to the federal government must agree to pay "not

---

2. M. Rosenberg, The Adversary Process in the Year 2000, 1 Prospectus 5, 18 (1968).

less than the minimum wages as determined by the Secretary of Labor to be the prevailing minimum wages for persons employed on similar work . . . in the locality in which the . . . supplies . . . are to be manufactured or furnished under said contract." Another section of the Act says that "all wage determinations . . . shall be made on the record after opportunity for hearing."

As a step toward determining the prevailing minimum wage in the electric motors and generators industry, the Secretary directed the Bureau of Labor Statistics (an element of the Department of Labor) to conduct a broad survey of the industry's practices. This it did by sending a questionnaire to 775 establishments, asking for information about total employment, total number of employees engaged in work related to government contracts, and hourly earnings of the latter. The suppliers of these data were promised that their responses would "be seen only by sworn employees of the Bureau of Labor Statistics and no information identified by company name will be released." The BLS compiled six tables summarizing the wage data of 216 firms determined by it to be within the scope of the survey, but the 216 were not identified.

A hearing to make a minimum wage determination was then scheduled, after notice had been duly given by publication. About five weeks before the scheduled date, the BLS wage tables were furnished to the dominant trade association, the National Electrical Manufacturers Association (NEMA). NEMA's counsel subsequently sought, unsuccessfully, the permission of BLS to see the questionnaire responses and to have a list of the respondents whose data were reflected in the tables.

Shortly before the hearing date NEMA told the BLS that it had requested and had obtained from 61 companies copies of their answers to the Bureau's questionnaire and, in addition, wage data independently of the data provided by them to the BLS; and NEMA had detected differences between the two sets of figures. The BLS examined the cited differences, found two that the Bureau thought were significant, accepted the NEMA figures instead of those the companies had originally given, and modified its estimates of prevailing wage levels accordingly.

On the day before the hearing NEMA counsel asked the hearing officer to order the Commissioner of Labor Statistics to provide, among other things, the completed questionnaire forms on the basis of which the wage tables had presumably been formulated, as well as all related correspondence. Its sampling of respondents showed, according to NEMA, that significant mistakes might have been made by respondents because they misunderstood the questionnaire. The requested material was needed, NEMA argued, in order to evaluate the BLS tabulations and test their accuracy by cross-examination.

The hearing officer denied the application for a subpoena duces tecum, however, after counsel for the Labor Department had argued that the BLS pledge of confidentiality would be broken if the desired information were to be produced; violating that pledge would, he contended, seriously impede future BLS efforts to obtain needed economic data.

When the hearing took place, the BLS survey supervisor was asked by NEMA counsel to examine the complete questionnaires in order to refresh his recollection of the information various respondents had supplied. An objection was sustained. Then NEMA tried, at first without success, to introduce affidavits by company officials that their companies had given the BLS erroneous data. Finally, NEMA unsuccessfully moved to strike the BLS supervisor's testimony because it had been "based on a perusal of records which have not been made available to us and on the further ground that we are not being allowed to impeach his testimony with respect to the wage tables. . . . " Before the hearing ended, however, the BLS agreed to accept the company officials' affidavits as evidence, and it then revised the wage tables somewhat.

At the stage of final review, Secretary of Labor Arthur Goldberg (who became Mr. Justice Goldberg) upheld the hearing officer's refusal to issue the subpoena NEMA had sought or to strike the BLS supervisor's testimony about the wage tables. The Secretary stressed that maintaining the BLS pledge of confidentiality was essential if survey work was to continue successfully. A stark choice had to be made, he said, between "the possibility that NEMA may be able to find some reporting or tabulating mistakes in this survey on the one hand, and an end to all of the useful work of the BLS." Then Secretary Goldberg asked whether the BLS's having made changes in its tables after reading company officials' affidavits warranted the assumption that as yet undetected errors existed. He thought that "these eight changes only constituted a basis for making minor improvements in a survey which was substantially accurate to begin with." The industry represented by NEMA possessed a good deal of "legal sophistication" and had had "long experience in supplying the Government with vast quantities of materials." The definitions of terms used in the questionnaire were "readily comprehensible" and the question whose clarity had been chiefly disputed had been "successfully used in recent years in wage surveys of many other industries, including several divisions of the electrical industry."

Nevertheless, Secretary Goldberg acknowledged, "some degree of reporting error is inherent in any statistical survey. The risk is, however, reduced to a minimum by the standard practice of BLS to review carefully and evaluate each response for internal consistency and subsequently to contact the company either through additional correspondence, telephone calls, or personal visits, on all doubtful matters. Furthermore, it is not clear that any alterations in the BLS survey questionnaire would have resulted in a more accurate survey of the industry than the one presented in the record. In fact, NEMA in effect admits that the responses which it obtained from the survey questionnaire which it composed were of no greater accuracy than it believed the BLS responses to be. . . . "

"Based upon a careful evaluation of all the evidence of record I find that the BLS survey constitutes a sound basis for determining the minimum wages that prevail in the industry."]

WASHINGTON, CIRCUIT JUDGE. . . . We are faced with two separate, but related, issues: whether—in the face of the receipt in evidence of the summary wage tabulations with the refusal to produce or to permit inspection of the answered questionnaires or to disclose the names of the 216 establishments tabulated—the administrative hearing afforded the appellees the opportunity "to submit rebuttal evidence, and to conduct such cross-examination as may be required for a full and true disclosure of the facts," within the meaning of . . . the Administrative Procedure Act; and whether, in light of the evidence offered by appellees in an effort to impeach the survey, the determination was "supported by and in accordance with the reliable, probative, and substantial evidence" . . . . or must be set aside . . . as "unsupported by substantial evidence." . . .

There is of course no question as to the admissibility of the summary tabulations compiled by the Bureau. But it is also the general requirement that where tables of this kind are received in evidence, the documents supporting the tables and on which they are based must also be introduced or at least be made available to the opposing party to the extent that they are necessary for purposes of rebuttal and cross-examination. We think that the statute which placed the burden on the Secretary and gave appellees a right to rebut and cross-examine with a view to a full and true disclosure of the facts clearly would require that the general rule be applied here, unless the fact that the questionnaire answers were obtained under a pledge of confidentiality compels a different rule—an issue which will be considered presently. Putting that issue to one side for the moment, we think our conclusion that at least some disclosure is required is compellingly supported by the decision in Powhatan Mining Co. v. Ickes, 118 F.2d 106 (6th Cir.1941), which reviewed an order of the Director of the Bituminous Coal Division of the Department of the Interior refusing changes in the minimum prices for coal set by him. Producing companies were required to file prices and other information relating to spot orders for coal under a statute which provided that the information be held confidential within the Division. From this data tabulations were prepared and received in evidence. Petitioners demanded that the tables be decoded so that, for purposes of cross-examination, they would know the identity of the producers who made the sales and other facts surrounding the transactions. The court held that "in all fairness the data should have been disclosed," saying:

"It is difficult to see how the accuracy, authenticity and relevancy of these tabulations could be tested in any way without the disclosure of the names of the code members who reported the data upon which the tabulations are based. The tabulations were compiled from data which was kept secret, but which was in the possession of the Division. Errors in computation could not be checked unless they appeared upon the face of the tabulation, and the real meaning of the figures could not be developed unless the character of the individual sales could be inquired into. . . . When the Division introduces the tabulations, the evidence is put in at its instance and the petitioners should be given the opportunity to cross-examine as to the weight and authenticity of the figures. . . . "

. . . Much has been argued to us about the confidential nature of the BLS survey, and the damage that disclosure of the data received would cause to the procurement of information in the future for minimum wage determinations and for important economic investigations in other areas. The Secretary rejects appellees' argument that the subpoena power could effectively achieve the results obtained by solicitation under a pledge of confidentiality, and denies that in camera disclosure would be consistent with the pledge. All of this may be quite true. We are not without sympathy for the problems faced by the Secretary, but we have found nothing in the Walsh-Healey Act or any other legislation that has been called to our attention which would empower us to release the Secretary from conforming to the procedural commands of the controlling statutes because of such considerations. Nor do we find any opinions of the Supreme Court or of this court which suggest that the difficulties advanced by the Secretary excuse him from fulfilling what appear to be his statutory obligations to appellees. . . . The Government, in situations of the present sort, has an option: it can hold back confidential material, and take the risk of not being able to prove its case, or it can produce the material and allow it to be the subject of direct and cross-examination. . . .

We must necessarily conclude that the admission of the wage tabulations compiled from undisclosed confidential data, as to which we will not compel disclosure, failed to accord to appellees the adequate opportunity for rebuttal and cross-examination that the Congress prescribed. But this does not entirely dispose of the matter.

On the record before us, we could sustain the minimum wage determination only if the wage tabulations, used as the sole basis for the determination, themselves meet the requirements of "reliable, probative and substantial evidence". . . .

In the instant case, the appellees mounted a strong attack on the reliability of the survey. As we have seen, after receiving the Bureau's tabulations, appellees made a limited survey in the short time remaining before the hearing and discovered alleged errors in the tabulations. Two of these were accepted by the Bureau and caused changes in the wage conclusions reached in the tables. During the hearing appellees submitted evidence, in the form of affidavits and testimony of company officials, which resulted in additional downward modifications of the Bureau's minimum wage estimates. The total effect of the eight reductions accepted by the Bureau was by no means de minimis.

. . . In view of the evidence casting serious doubt on the validity of the Bureau's survey results, it was certainly incumbent upon the Bureau, if it meant to rely on the survey, to offer some evidence in rebuttal of the attack. The Secretary, however, offered nothing tending to substantiate the accuracy and reliability of the underlying data.

For these reasons the Secretary's determination must be set aside for the further reason that it is not supported by "reliable, probative, and substantial evidence." . . .

NOTES

(1) Does the principal case hold that an agency may not rely on statistical compilations without exposing the underlying data to inspection and possibly adversarial challenge? Or should one stress an alternative reading, that resourceful counsel may prove able to cast a statistical analysis in such doubt as to deprive it of "substantiality" as support for the result? If the challenge is to the quality of the survey, or the model used to manipulate the data once obtained, access to the data itself may seem less central and—correspondingly—the threat to confidentiality of business data a competitor might dearly wish to see may seem a more important consideration.

At least in the absence of showings placing the accuracy of a statistical compilation in doubt, courts are not likely to be impressed by "technical" arguments about hearsay or the best evidence rule, when statistical analyses are the only practical alternative to receiving vast quantities of unanalyzed documentary material.[1] Much the same kind of remark might be made about the use of computer print-outs. Everyone knows that computers are fallible because (altogether apart from rare electronic or mechanical malfunctions) the humans who feed data into them and then retrieve the data in various combinations are fallible. Yet to disregard the materials computers can make readily available would be to close judges' and administrators' eyes to technologically produced information of a kind other decisionmakers cherish.[2]

(2) CARTER-WALLACE, INC. v. GARDNER, 417 F.2d 1086 (4th Cir.1969), grew out of a proceeding to subject meprobamate, a tranquilizer, to special controls under the Food, Drug, and Cosmetic Act. One issue was whether the drug had a "potential for abuse" because supplies were readily available outside legitimate drug channels. If this were so, individuals (on their own initiative rather than on the basis of

1. See, e.g., Chicago Board of Trade v. FCC, 223 F.2d 348 (D.C.Cir.1955): Western Union, seeking a rate increase, prepared summations of cost figures, derived from great numbers of invoices and similar original data. All the underlying material was assembled at Western Union's office. Opposing counsel were given time to examine the material and to check the accuracy of the summaries. No instance of inaccuracy having been advanced, the FCC received the summaries and based decision on them, despite opponents' objection that they were not the best evidence. The court affirmed the FCC, praising the avoidance of delay and expense.

2. For an impressive examination of the state of the law, see Note, A Reconsideration of the Admissibility of Computer-Generated Evidence, 126 U.Pa.L.Rev. 425 (1977). Compare Teubner, The Computer as Expert Witness: Toward a Unified Theory of Computer Evidence, 19 Jurimetrics J. 274 (1979); J. Sprowl, Evaluating the Credibility of Computer-Generated Evidence, 52 Chi.-Kent L.Rev. 547 (1976); M. Jenkins, Computer-Generated Evidence Especially Prepared for Use at Trial, 52 Chi.-Kent L.Rev. 600 (1976). For extensive reference material and analysis, see D. Bender, Computer Law: Evidence and Procedure (1978); R. Freed, Computers and Law (4th ed. 1974). And see also Comment, Guidelines for the Admission of Evidence Generated by Computer for Purposes of Litigation, 15 U.C.D.L.Rev. 951 (1982); Note, Admissibility of Computer-Kept Business Records, 55 Corn.L.Q. 1033 (1970); J. Roberts, A Practitioner's Primer on Computer-Generated Evidence, 41 U.Chi.L. Rev. 254 (1974).

medical advice) might consume the drug hazardously. In the end, the order subjecting the drug to controls was sustained as being supported by substantial evidence. Along the way, however, the reviewing court had this to say (at 1096–1097): "Carter-Wallace objected to government exhibit 202, which is a summary purporting to show, among other things, that an audit of 99 pharmacies disclosed a shortage of 796,000 tablets of meprobamate. The shortage represented 77% of the total amount of the drug received by the pharmacies in a one-year period. The witness through whom the summary was introduced was not familiar with all of the underlying data, and some of the underlying documents were not available for use in cross-examination. While hearsay evidence is generally admissible in an administrative hearing, we think the deficiencies concerning the underlying data made it difficult for the government to establish the reliability of its audit and precluded meaningful cross-examination by Carter-Wallace.

"However, other evidence supports the finding that there has been a significant diversion of meprobamate from legitimate channels. Furthermore, proof of the drug's potential for abuse does not rest solely upon showing its diversion. Other findings, amply supported, suffice to establish that meprobamate has a potential for abuse. Introduction of exhibit 202, therefore, is not cause for setting aside the Commissioner's order. Willapoint Oysters, Inc. v. Ewing, 174 F.2d 676, 690 (9th Cir.), cert. denied, 338 U.S. 860 (1949)."[3]

SIERRA CLUB v. COSTLE

United States Court of Appeals, District of Columbia Circuit, 1981.
657 F.2d 298.

[In June of 1979 the Environmental Protection Agency (EPA) issued revised new source performance standards (NSPS) to govern the extent to which new coal-fired power stations must control their atmospheric emissions of sulfur dioxide and particulates. The standards

---

3. [Ed.] The importance of methodology as distinct from evidentiary tradition is well developed by H. Zeisel, The Uniqueness of Survey Evidence, 45 Corn.L.Q. 322 (1960). And see Pittsburgh Press Club v. United States, 579 F.2d 751 (3d Cir.1978), rejecting as hearsay a taxpayer's "survey" of former customers, which the court characterized as "no more than a summary and distillation of 281 extrajudicial declarations offered to prove the truth of the matters asserted in those declarations." But the court by no means thought that surveys would invariably be inadmissible. As to well conducted surveys, the court said (at 758): "In the context of polls and surveys, the circumstantial guarantees of trustworthiness are for the most part satisfied if the poll is conducted in accordance with generally accepted survey principles, and if the results are used in a statistically correct way, since proper survey and statistical methods are intended to assure a poll's reliability. . . . The Judicial Conference Study Group, in its Handbook of Recommended Procedures for the Trial of Protracted Litigation, 25 F.R.D. 351, 429 (1960), discusses the several factors which must be examined when determining whether a poll meets generally accepted survey principles. A proper universe must be examined and a *representative* sample must be chosen; the persons conducting the survey must be experts; the data must be properly gathered and accurately reported. It is essential that the sample design, the questionnaires and the manner of interviewing meet the standards of objective surveying and statistical techniques. Just as important, the survey must be conducted independently of the attorneys involved in the litigation. The interviewers or sample designers should, of course, be trained, and ideally should be unaware of the purposes of the survey or the litigation. A fortiori, the *respondents* should be similarly unaware." (Emphasis in original.)

resulted from a lengthy, prominent and heated rulemaking proceeding conducted under the hybrid rulemaking procedures of the Clean Air Act, a proceeding on which considerable political pressure had been brought to bear.[1] They were promptly challenged from all sides.

Among the issues the agency had to resolve in conducting the rulemaking was how to predict the impact of various possible standards on utility planning and, consequently, on overall reduction in sulfur dioxide pollution.[2] These were standards for *new* sources; if they made construction of new plants expensive, that might encourage utilities to continue using older facilities that would have higher emission levels.[3] Further, sulfur dioxide emission standards stated in terms of the total amount that could be emitted might be met by three strategies— removing sulfur dioxide from the emissions of the plant ("scrubbing"); burning coal with a low sulfur content; or a combination of these strategies. Scrubbing could be achieved by varying technologies differing in their effectiveness, reliability, and cost. Scrubbing 70% of the sulfur dioxide out of plant emissions might permit using a technology less expensive and more reliable than would be needed to remove 90%; and removing 70% of the sulfur dioxide resulting from the burning of low-sulfur coal will produce much lower total emissions than removing 90% while burning high-sulfur coal. (Indeed, some low-sulfur coal might be burned without *any* scrubbing and still produce less sulfur dioxide than high-sulfur coal subject to 90% scrubbing.) Against these apparent advantages of joining low-sulfur coal and limited scrubbing other considerations were posed:

"Maximal scrubbing would reduce emissions yet further; much low-sulfur coal is located in the West, where preventing any degradation of air quality is highly valued by many.

"Permitting utilities to use reduced scrubbing if low-sulfur coal is used creates an economic disincentive to buy high-sulfur coal, threaten-

1. The political pressures are considered at pp. 963–969 infra. For a thorough, spirited and highly critical account of this rulemaking see B. Ackerman and W. Hassler, Clean Coal/Dirty Air (1981); a preliminary version appears as B. Ackerman and W. Hassler, Beyond the New Deal: Coal and the Clean Air Act, 89 Yale L.J. 1466 (1980).

The dimensions of the controversy are suggested by the following footnote from the Court's opinion:

"The briefs submitted to this court on the merits total over 670 pages, the Joint Appendix contains 5,620 pages in twelve volumes, and the certified index to the record lists over 2,520 submissions. By the time of the publication of the final rule (EPA's statement accompanying the final rule took up 43 triple columns of single spaced type), EPA had performed or obtained from contractors approximately 120 studies, and collected over 400 items of reference literature, received almost 1,400 comments, written 650 letters and 200 in-

teragency memos, held over 50 meetings and substantive telephone conversations with the public, and conducted four days of public hearings. The complexity of the subject matter is discussed in C. Schultze, The Public Use of Private Interest 9–10 (1977) and Del Duca, The Clean Air Act: A Realistic Assessment of Cost Effectiveness, 5 Harv.Env.L.Rev. 184 (1981)."

2. Ackerman and Hessler strongly argue that the concern of the agency should have been with *sulfates*, chemicals produced after sulfur dioxide has been airborn a significant time, rather than the sulfur dioxide itself; their analysis suggests reducing long-range sulfate pollution by permitting increased sulfur dioxide fallout locally. Clean Coal/Dirty Air 60–65. This issue, however, was not raised before the court.

3. For a general discussion of the new source-old source problem see P. Huber, The Old-New Division in Risk Regulation, 69 Va.L.Rev. 1025 (1983).

ing the economic future of parts of the country where coal deposits have high sulfur content;

"Encouraging new plants to use low-sulfur coal would lead to higher prices for that coal for all plants, including old plants that might be able to reduce emissions economically only in this way.

"It will always be cheaper to install control equipment when building a new plant than to retrofit the plant later on."

Thus, one had a "new-old" problem and a fuel choice problem to consider in predicting what would be the total sulfur dioxide emissions experienced for any given standard being considered.

To make this analysis—which ultimately resulted in adoption of a variable standard for required scrubbing [4]—EPA developed a computer program to assess the impacts of various standards on a number of complex factors, including the following: total air emissions; new plant investment; consumer costs; energy production and consumption; fuel choice (coal, oil, gas, etc.); and the regional impacts on coal production and transportation. The program and the assumptions on which it was based were reviewed within government by a working group of representatives from several agencies (EPA, Energy, Council of Economic Advisors, Council on Wage and Price Stability), subjected to public comments, and revised; the results were published and publicly discussed. Subsequently the model was used to evaluate alternative standards and indicated that the standard chosen would "result in more coal capacity in newer and 'cleaner' utility plants, have a clear cost advantage, use less oil, and have an equivalent impact on coal production."

On review the Sierra Club attacked EPA's conclusions on a number of grounds; of interest here is the assertion that "the econometric model employed by EPA was so speculative and otherwise unreliable that the modeling results are not substantial evidence." [5]]

Before ROBB, WALD and GINSBURG, CIRCUIT JUDGES.

WALD, CIRCUIT JUDGE: . . . Such models, despite their complex design and aura of scientific validity, are at best imperfect and subject to manipulation as EPA forthrightly recognizes.[6] The results ultimately are shaped by the assumptions adopted at the outset, and can change drastically for a given range of input data if key assumptions are

---

4. Plants were under no circumstances to exceed emissions of 1.2 lbs of sulfur dioxide for each defined large amount of heat produced by burning coal, and were to use 90% scrubbing if their emissions were in the upper half of the permitted range; plants with lower emission rates were required to employ 70% scrubbing.

5. See Industrial Union Dept., AFL–CIO v. Hodgson, p. 481 above.

6. EPA's Administrator stated:

"The truth of the matter is that the model that we are using is a reasonably good model, but you can alter the outcome from that model dramatically by just simply changing a few key initial assumptions that you crank into the model. I think those assumptions need to be tested, frankly, in a public debate and in a formal rulemaking proceeding, where people comment for the record, set out their alternative assumptions, saying, 'We think this is really more realistic.'"

adjusted even slightly.[7] The accuracy of the model's predictions also hinge on whether the underlying assumptions reflect reality, which is no small feat in this volatile world.[8]

Still we cannot agree with Sierra Club that it was improper for EPA to employ an econometric computer model, or hold as a matter of law that EPA erred by relying on the model to forecast the future impacts of alternative standards fifteen years hence.

Realistically, computer modeling is a useful and often essential tool for performing the Herculean labors Congress imposed on EPA in the Clean Air Act. In addition to the competing objectives that EPA must satisfy under section 111, the Act explicitly requires EPA to prepare an Economic Impact Statement before promulgating NSPS. The assessment of potential impacts in this statement must be as "extensive as practicable" and must determine the potential inflationary or recessionary effects of the standard, the effects on competition, consumer costs, and energy use.[9] Given the complexity and magnitude of the analyses EPA must perform on economic impacts alone, computer modeling, for all its flaws, is invaluable.

Even absent such statutory requirements, we would deem it reasonable to use computer modeling, and to design the model to consider not just "present day" factors, but the consequences over time of the proposed agency action. In American Public Gas Ass'n v. FPC, a challenge was raised that the results of economic modeling, similar to that used here, did not rise to the level of "substantial evidence" necessary to support the agency's findings and conclusions. This court disagreed, stating that "[r]easoned decisionmaking can use an economic

7. . . . Although the model "produces precise numbers, it is not a precise model because of the uncertainties and inaccuracies of its assumptions. Its chief value is the aid it provides to organized thinking about important policy variables and the qualitative relations between them." Del Duca, The Clean Air Act: A Realistic Assessment of Cost Effectiveness, 5 Harv.Env.L.Rev. 184, 195 (1981).

8. For example, the task of anticipating trends in oil prices is obviously fraught with difficulty. Or, as the Administrator pointed out:

"Those models are terribly sensitive to the assumptions that you make. For example, they assume that, when utility managers must manage these investments and make a decision, they choose the most economically efficient alternative. This is a modeling assumption; it may not be true in real life."

9. 42 U.S.C. § 7617 requires EPA to perform an Economic Impact Assessment for, inter alia, the promulgation or revision of NSPS. Section 7617(c) requires EPA to assess:

(1) the costs of compliance with any such standard or regulation, including extent to which the costs of compliance will vary depending on (A) the effective date of the standard or regulation, and (B) the development of less expensive, more efficient means or methods of compliance with the standard or regulation;

(2) the potential inflationary or recessionary effects of the standard or regulation;

(3) the effects on competition of the standard or regulation with respect to small business;

(4) the effects of the standard or regulation on consumer costs; and

(5) the effects of the standard or regulation on energy use.

Nothing in this section shall be construed to provide that the analysis of the factors specified in this subsection affects or alters the factors which the Administrator is required to consider in taking any action referred to in subsection (a) of this section.

42 U.S.C. § 7617(d) states that this assessment shall be "as extensive as practicable." See also Exec. Order No. 12044, 3 C.F.R. 152–56 (March 24, 1978).

model to provide useful information about economic realities. . . . "
However, the agency must sufficiently explain the assumptions and
methodology used in preparing the model; it must provide a "complete
analytic defense of its model [and] respond to each objection with a
reasoned presentation." The technical complexity of the analysis does
not relieve the agency of the burden to consider all relevant factors and
to identify the stepping stones to its final decision. There must be a
rational connection between the factual inputs, modeling assumptions,
modeling results and conclusions drawn from these results.

In this case, the utility model itself and its key assumptions were
discussed in the proposed rule and background documents. EPA invited public comments on the model and its assumptions, with the agency
recognizing the sensitivity of the model to a "few key initial assumptions." The joint interagency working group reviewed results of model
runs, revised assumptions, and required new runs of the model when it
was deemed appropriate. The principal comments received by EPA on
the model and the initial assumptions were discussed, together with the
results of the three phases of the modeling and the major post-proposal
changes to the model, in the preamble to the final NSPS. In reviewing
this record on the use of the econometric model we have carefully
examined, within the limits of our competence, EPA's explanation for
the model's premises, the results, and the conclusions drawn therefrom
to test them for internal consistency and reasonableness. Although
EPA has the benefit of the presumption of good faith and regularity in
agency action, we have attempted to ascertain whether the results have
been improperly skewed by the modeling format. We conclude that
EPA's reliance on its model did not exceed the bounds of its usefulness
and that its conduct of the modeling exercise was proper in all respects.
We are in fact reassured by EPA's own consciousness of the limits of its
model, and its invitation and response to public comment on all aspects
of the model. The safety valves in the use of such sophisticated
methodology are the requirement of public exposure of the assumptions
and data incorporated into the analysis and the acceptance and consideration of public comment, the admission of uncertainties where they
exist,[10] and the insistence that ultimate responsibility for the policy
decision remains with the agency rather than the computer. With
these precautions the tools of econometric computer analysis can intelligently broaden rather than constrain the policymaker's options and

---

10. "[T]he precise purpose of a statute
may be to grant an agency responsibility
for deciding questions characterized by a
high degree of uncertainty." DeLong, Informal Rulemaking and the Integration of
Law and Policy, 65 Va.L.Rev. 257, 289
(1978): "Rulemaking invokes an amalgam
of beliefs about the present facts; explicit
or implicit theories about the way an industry, the economy, or the society works;
predictions about the future development
with and without a rule; analyses and
guesses about costs and benefits as they
will affect different groups; identification

and assessment of risks and uncertainties;
value judgments, and political calculations
about the acceptability of regulation. The
number of facts possibly relevant to some
or all of the considerations is infinite. In
some cases factual elements will predomi-
nate. In others the major issues may require the construction of predictive models
about the effect of a rule. In still others,
the question may concern the appropriate
weighing of the risks involved."
Id. at 294.

avoid the "artificial narrowing of options that [can be] arbitrary and capricious."

Sierra Club has not only challenged the use of the model itself, but has also questioned here, as it has throughout the rulemaking, some of the specific assumptions built into the model. In some instances EPA actually adjusted the model to account for Sierra Club's objections and demonstrated that the outcome of the final rule would not have changed. . . . The most critical assumptions Sierra Club still objects to are those concerning utility behavior which incorporate what it terms a "perverse hypothesis" that less stringent controls can result in lower total emissions. EPA answered that charge by explaining why variable control could promise equivalent or better reduction of emissions than the stricter full control option:

"One finding that has been clearly demonstrated by the two years of analysis is that lower emission standards on new plants do not necessarily result in lower national SO emissions when total emissions from the entire utility system are considered. There are two reasons for this finding. First, the lowest emissions tend to result from strategies that encourage the construction of new coal capacity. This capacity, almost regardless of the alternative analyzed, will be less polluting than the existing coal- or oil-fired capacity that it replaces. Second, the higher cost of operating the new capacity (due to higher pollution costs) may cause the newer, cleaner plants to be utilized less than they would be under a less stringent alternative. These situations are demonstrated by the analyses presented here."

The crucial assumption leading to these findings is that utilities are "cost minimizers." The cost minimization assumption implies that when faced with a decision the utility will choose the low-cost option, if risks between the options are neutral. Under the cost minimization model the higher the costs of pollution controls required by the NSPS, the more utilities will delay the retirement of older plants which do not have to comply with the NSPS, and the more utilities will be discouraged from building and operating new plants which must meet the NSPS. Since uniform control is costlier than variable control, uniform control is expected to result in greater reliance on old plants and less utilization of new plants than will variable control, which in turn leads to higher emissions. We see no basis for concluding that the adoption of this assumption about utility preferences constituted a clear error of judgment; indeed we are hard pressed to conjure up an alternative assumption about utility behavior that could be put into the computer model.

[The court continued in like vein for a total of 125 pages (plus appendices). Additional excerpts, on the problem of political oversight, appear at p. 963 below. Ultimately, the court upheld the standard in all respects, concluding with the following observations:]

Since the issues in this proceeding were joined in 1973 when the Navajo Indians first complained about sulfur dioxide fumes over their Southwest homes, we have had lawsuits, almost four years of substantive and procedural maneuvering before the EPA, and now this extended court challenge. In the interim, Congress has amended the Clean Air Act once and may be ready to do so again. The standard we uphold has already been in effect for almost two years, and could be revised within another two years.

We reach our decision after interminable record searching (and considerable soul searching). We have read the record with as hard a look as mortal judges can probably give its thousands of pages. We have adopted a simple and straight-forward standard of review, probed the agency's rationale, studied its references (and those of appellants), endeavored to understand them where they were intelligible (parts were simply impenetrable), and on close questions given the agency the benefit of the doubt out of deference for the terrible complexity of its job. We are not engineers, computer modelers, economists or statisticians, although many of the documents in this record require such expertise—and more.

Cases like this highlight the enormous responsibilities Congress has entrusted to the courts in proceedings of such length, complexity and disorder. Conflicting interests play fiercely for enormous stakes, advocates are prolific and agile, obfuscation runs high, common sense correspondingly low, the public intent is often obscured.

We cannot redo the agency's job; Congress has told us, at least in proceedings under this Act, that it will not brook reversal for small procedural errors; Vermont Yankee reinforces the admonition. So in the end we can only make our best effort to understand, to see if the result makes sense, and to assure that nothing unlawful or irrational has taken place. In this case, we have taken a long while to come to a short conclusion: the rule is reasonable.

Affirmed.

NOTES

(1) BUILDING CODE ACTION v. ENERGY RESOURCES CONSERVATION AND DEVELOPMENT COMMISSION, 102 Cal.App.3d 577, 162 Cal.Rptr. 734 (1st Dist.Ct.App.1980) permitted a challenge to rulemaking by a state commission that had used computer analyses of cost-effectiveness to help it decide how broadly to impose a requirement that home builders use double glazing (a measure that decreases the amount of energy lost through glass windows and doors at the cost of increasing the amount of glass that must be used). On the one hand was the reduction in energy consumption for heating the houses—a saving that would vary with the temperateness of the climate; on the other, the energy and environmental costs of making additional glass. The computer analyses were made known on March 7 before a March 11 informal hearing, at which builders opposing the rule as too stringent were limited to presentations challenging those analyses. The builders asserted unsuccessfully that they should have had more time to study and respond to this analysis: ". . . [R]ebuttal is not an 'ineluctable right' at quasi-legislative hearings and . . . whether it is required depends on the nature of the particular evidence sought to be rebutted.

"At issue here are computer studies showing the proposed regulations to be cost-effective. The Commission relied on conclusions drawn from these studies. The conclusions were presented at a public hearing. At the hearing, and even prior to the hearing, the studies themselves were available to the public. The public, including BCA, had an opportunity to present factual statements and arguments contrary to the conclusions drawn from the studies.

"We hold that the opportunity was reasonable. All BCA had to do was to identify the assertedly wrong variables or values and state why they were wrong. It did not have to provide the right answers; concededly, that would have required a longer period of time than the time available after the studies were released. But the preparation of this 'positive' showing did not have to await the release of the studies. BCA's director was sufficiently informed of the regulations which were being formulated and acquainted with the nature of the computer studies which were under way that he could have proceeded to produce calculations showing the regulations not to be cost-effective even before the studies were complete."

(2) Thomas O. McGarity, Substantive and Procedural Discretion in Administrative Resolution of Science Policy Questions: Regulating Carcinogens in EPA and OSHA, 67 Geo.L.J. 729, 732–736, 740–45, 750 (1979)*:

"In deciding whether to reduce human exposure to potentially carcinogenic chemicals, the agencies have been forced to resolve scientific questions that the scientific community itself has been unable to resolve. Due to these factual uncertainties, agencies and reviewing courts have recognized that they must resolve these questions partially on policy grounds. . . .

Trans–Scientific Issues

"Many highly technical questions that are cast in scientific terms cannot for various practical or moral reasons be answered by science. Alvin Weinberg, a prominent scientist, has coined the term 'trans-scientific' to describe this kind of issue. A perfect example of a trans-scientific issue is the extrapolation of carcinogenic effects at high-dose levels to low-dose levels. . . . [T]o demonstrate with ninety-five percent confidence that the carcinogenic response rate is less than one in a million, an experimenter need only feed three million animals at the human exposure rate and compare the response with three million control animals that have been raised under identical conditions but with no exposure to the chemical. As a practical matter, however, . . . this 'mega-mouse' experiment . . . would require feeding and caring for six million rodents for eighteen to twenty-four months. Scientists therefore test significantly fewer animals at much higher dosage rates. . . . The agency can never be certain whether a chemical that causes cancer at high doses will cause cancer at the lower doses to which humans are typically exposed.

"Regulators cannot, however, postpone decisions involving trans-scientific issues . . . . Moreover, although most trans-scientific issues appear to be questions of fact, rather than questions of law or policy, a regulator clearly cannot reduce them to findings of fact in the traditional sense of that term. Correct answers to these questions may exist as a philosophical matter, but the 'truth' is ultimately unascertainable in either the scientific or the legal forum. Thus, a regulator who is given the responsibility for establishing a safe level for human exposure to a carcinogen has been given an impossible task if this entails establishing a threshold 'no-effect' level. The regulator cannot find as a factual matter whether a threshold 'no-effect' level exists.[1] Nor can he establish an 'acceptable' exposure to a carcinogen, because he cannot determine the shape of the dose-response curve at low-dosage rates.[2] Therefore, a regulator must make a subjective, or policy-dominated decision. Moreover, the very nature of such trans-scientific issues deprives a regulator of any legitimate excuse for delaying a decision on these issues.

DECISIONMAKING BASED ON INSUFFICIENT SCIENTIFIC DATA

"Regulators frequently must decide scientific questions when data sufficient to reach a scientifically adequate decision do not exist. This situation differs from the trans-scientific problem because theoretically the scientific community could resolve the issue with whatever accuracy the regulator desires given sufficient time and resources. Thus, a regulator may be tempted to delay deciding a question until scientists develop more data, a solution that invariably receives the enthusiastic endorsement of the scientists who are performing experiments in the field. On the other hand, a regulator's delay in deciding whether to

1. . . . . [S]cientists have thus far been unable to agree on any threshold dosage level for a particular chemical. EPA and OSHA have therefore rejected chemical manufacturers' assertions that human exposure to their chemicals is below the hypothetical thresholds. In re Velsicol Chem. Corp., Decision of the Administrator on the Suspension of Heptachlor/Chlordane, 41 Fed.Reg. 7552, 7575 (1976) (rejecting threshold limit on heptachlor/chlordane; no evidence that there is minimum dosage below which a known carcinogen has no carcinogenic effect); In re Shell Chem. Co., Opinion of the Administrator, EPA, on the Suspension of Aldrin/Dieldrin, 39 Fed.Reg. 37,246, 37,267 (1974) (rejecting threshold limit on aldrin/dieldrin; no uniform model explaining relationship between dose and cancerous response); Occupational Safety and Health Administration, Standard for Exposure to Vinyl Chloride, 39 Fed.Reg. 35,890, 35,892 (1974) (rejecting threshold limit on vinyl chloride; cannot assume no cancerous effect below

threshold level advanced by industry). In taking this position both agencies can find support in statements by eminent expert scientific bodies.

2. A dose response curve shows the relationship between different exposure levels and the risk of cancer associated with those exposure levels. For the same reason that scientists cannot determine whether thresholds exist for certain chemicals, they cannot determine the shape of the dose-response curve for a chemical at low doses: The experiment to determine that question would require millions of animals. Several extrapolation models are currently vying for regulatory attention. All of the models fit the data well in the experimental dose range, but they diverge, often by several orders of magnitude, in the unexplored range that approximates human exposure. It is therefore impossible to choose among the models based solely on the experimental data available to the regulator.

reduce human exposure to a potentially carcinogenic substance also prolongs public exposure to the chemical until a final decision is made. Therefore, as in the case of trans-scientific questions, regulators occasionally will have to decide questions on the basis of incomplete information even though these questions are, in theory, scientifically resolvable.

.   .   .

VARYING SCIENTIFIC INTERPRETATIONS

"Even though adequate information may be available concerning a particular scientific issue, scientists may differ in their interpretations of those data. For example, even when adequate bioassays for a chemical are available, pathologists often disagree in their diagnoses of the lesions they observe under their microscopes. .   .   .

"Differences in interpretation also arise over epidemiological studies. Because retrospective epidemiological data often lie on the borderline of statistical significance, how a scientist interprets particular findings often depends on subjective considerations. .   .   .

"Finally, disagreements over the adequacy of test methodologies can give rise to differences in interpretation of the results of a given experiment. .   .   .

"At stake in all of these disputes is a nebulous concept occasionally referred to as 'scientific judgment.' Scientists can objectively explain their interpretations of some kinds of data only to a point; past that point subjective considerations weigh heavily in their conclusions. These subjective considerations generally are not what lawyers label policy considerations. Although scientists are not immune from public policy preferences when they advise policymakers, scientific judgment has more to do with scientists' views, arising out of long years of study, on how things operate in the physical world with which they are familiar. As a result different scientists interpret the same data differently. The lay decisionmaker, having no scientific judgment of his own, is therefore unguided in determining which of the conflicting scientific judgments is the best. .   .   .

DISAGREEMENT OVER INFERENCES

"Scientists often agree upon a single interpretation for existing data, but disagree over the proper inferences to draw from that interpretation. Scientists, like lawyers, draw inferences about unobserved events from observed data. For example, most scientists will infer that a substance will be carcinogenic in man if it is carcinogenic in laboratory animals. .   .   . The most compelling argument in favor of this use of animal tests is the lack of any better system for risk evaluation.[3]

.   .   . Scientists still debate, however, whether a carcinogenic response

---

3. The most scientifically sound study of a chemical's carcinogenic properties would consist of feeding large quantities of the chemical to a cohort of humans over a period of 20 to 40 years and then sacrific-ing the humans to observe the presence or absence of neoplastic changes in particular organs. Obviously this experiment is morally unacceptable. .   .   .

in a single rodent species without duplication in another species is a sufficient basis to infer that a chemical poses a carcinogenic risk to man.

. . .

"[S]cience policy questions are by their very nature policy-dominated. Formal procedures such as cross-examination will seldom aid the agency in deciding these questions; indeed, adjudicatory procedures often provide an effective roadblock to agency action for parties who disagree with the agency and Congress on the policies underlying a proper resolution of science policy questions. Further, the inherent uncertainties surrounding science policy questions dictate that the agency will never be able to reduce its solution of these questions to 'findings of fact' within the traditional legal meaning of that term. Thus, judicial insistence on formal proceedings can only needlessly delay agency decisionmaking. Moreover, close judicial scrutiny of the administrative record, even if it results from formal procedures, will not reveal unequivocal support for the agency's decision. Scouring the record of an agency's resolution of science policy questions will only reveal unresolved conflicts between qualified scientists on highly technical questions, and strict judicial insistence upon formal 'findings of fact' will impose an impossible burden upon the agency. Finally, to the extent that a reviewing court is willing to defer to agency 'expertise' in choosing between the theories of equally respectable scientists, the court will simply force the agency to disguise policy decisions as factual determinations. Ultimately, this will result in less stringent judicial review of the legal and policy determinations upon which the agency in reality grounds its decisions."

(3) S. TAYLOR, MAKING BUREAUCRACIES THINK 269–70, 316–20 (1984),[*] analyzes at considerable length the special "fact-finding" procedures associated with environmental impact statements under the National Environmental Policy Act of 1969. He is concerned with interactions both within the bureaucracy (among various interested agencies) and between responsible bureaucrats and persons outside government; and with the differences between the fact-finding models of scientific and of policy inquiry.[4]

[*] Copyright © 1984 Stanford University Press and reprinted with permission.

4. "One obvious contrast is that the scientific community can afford to wait as long as necessary for the correct answer to a problem. Additional rules are . . . needed for public organizations: decision rules which specify when analysis should stop in order for action to be undertaken and how uncertainties are to be treated.

Equally striking, commitment to analytical norms is not so high in politics as it is in science. Largely because recruitment into the scientific community is voluntary, and confirmed after a long period of intense study and work, members have a mutual dedicated interest in the ideals and standards of science. . . . The typical public organization, on the other hand, must contend with the wider political community, . . . in which the motives behind a political argument are fair game in ways that scientists can safely ignore. . . . Since the uncertainties in policy disputes may not be resolvable in the short term, and decisions nevertheless may have to be made, there must be rules specifying who is to bear the burden of proof in analytical disputes with significant policy implications.

But motivation is imperiled in another way as well: the rewards to analysts for showing that their own organization has made an error are not likely to be high. . . . If a scientist finds a major anomaly in a scientific theory currently believed in

"Quite clearly, it is worthwhile for development agencies to talk with potential critics before the draft EIS [Environmental Impact Statement] becomes public, so that criticisms can be anticipated and perhaps countered. If consulted early in the planning cycle, the commenting agencies are usually willing to tell the development agency's project manager and environmental analysts if they see a problem with a proposed project. The private groups may not be so candid. They want the agency to study environmental problems and alternatives carefully, and can supply a long list of both, but they often prefer to conceal their detailed criticisms until the release of the Draft EIS initiates the expected public brawl. Much depends, of course, on the private group's prior experience with the agency, and on the legal incentives (both of which may vary), but generally the private groups do not want to be drawn into giving detailed critiques of an agency's proposed 'draft of a draft' EIS if they will only be used to make the project more politically and legally defensible, rather than more environmentally acceptable. But avoiding legally and politically perilous surprises that the commenting agencies might come up with is not the only motivation for the development agencies in the commenting process.

"The development agencies have learned that the commenting agencies may be a good deal more 'reasonable' and 'accommodating' than the private groups, to the extent of making it possible for the development agency to protect its reputation by dividing the environmental opposition. . . . The simple fact of frequent personal interaction, in many instances, and a common interest in certain problems, probably work to bring about a degree of mutual respect, or at least an accurate understanding of one another's motives; they are less likely to construct distrust-inducing explanations of each other's behavior when it is not warranted than the private groups. The two types of agencies are also more likely than the average environmental group to perceive themselves as involved in a long-term relationship. A reputation for candor, understanding, and trustworthiness is thus valuable in itself.

. . .

"In considering the role of science-like norms in politics we should look at what science can and cannot do, and the comparative advantage of science in helping us figure out what to do when knowledge is incomplete. . . . [T]he promise of an impact statement system is neither easily achieved nor free of unwanted side effects. In relying on competition among policy partisans to produce better knowledge, and through better knowledge, better decisions, impact statement systems

by his colleagues at a research institute, . . . the discoverer will be praised by all scientists, including his immediate colleagues. By contrast, an environmental analyst in a development agency who finds a major environmental defect in his agency's favored proposal cannot expect to receive great applause. . . . In addition, policy relevant research . . . often comes under intense pressure from interested parties who have special reasons for wanting to control its assumptions, methodology, resources, or dissemination.

Finally, and not least, a public organization rarely has a full consensus on goals. In the absence of such consensus, agreement on what "good analysis" consists of, and on what constitutes an "advance" in fundamental knowledge, is difficult or even impossible. . . ." At pp. 25–26.

are vulnerable to the ills associated with conflict of interest. Because the parties developing the information have policy stakes, they cannot be trusted to pursue or state the 'truth.' Because the participants cannot be trusted to value empirical objectivity more highly than political expediency, truth is pursued by an openly adversary process. In turn, for this adversary process to work effectively, analytical resources among the contending parties must not be extremely unbalanced. So 'analytical' resources are more widely distributed among the potential private and governmental critics of an agency. By having access to the development agency's data base, for example, these outsiders gain additional resources; through adjustments in burden-of-proof rules, the potency of their existing analytical resources is multiplied. But solving the problem of merely pro forma adversariness exacerbates another problem: if policy partisans are used to enforce norms of analytical quality by way of competition, they will almost unavoidably be able to convert the procedures and analytical resources into political bargaining assets whose use does not necessarily serve a larger social purpose. Indeed, the mere anticipation that the other side will act to maximize its chances of prevailing on the policy issue, rather than to ascertain the evidence, may maintain a vicious circle in which both sides play fast and loose with the evidence. The convertibility of analytical into political assets puts a heavy burden on the oversight arrangements for formulating and adjudicating the rules of analysis. Rules of analysis must be detailed and precise, requiring of the 'judges' a deep knowledge of the standard methodologies employed in many diverse settings. Since it is difficult to find an oversight body with both scientific and political authority, the excesses of competition are hard to control.

    ". . .

    "Is it possible and desirable to institutionalize expert judgment that is 'policy neutral'—to obtain an authoritative resolution or evaluation of the technical disputes without the undesirable aspects of competition among policy-interested experts whose arguments are evaluated by nonexperts?

    "It has been suggested that a 'Science Court' might resolve the technical-scientific questions most important to policy controversies. Like a regular court, a Science Court would involve adversary parties; unlike the federal courts, the judges would be eminent scientists of neutral policy disposition. The court would separate 'fact' from 'value' issues, then decide who had the soundest evidence on the former questions.

    "Attractive as such a proposal may at first sound, a Science Court has several fundamental difficulties.

    "First, it is often very difficult to separate factual and value issues. Beyond this problem is a related one: many conclusions of even the 'hard' sciences contain—if not exactly value choices—untested, not yet fully tested, hard-to-test, or even presently untestable assumptions about the way the world works; the social sciences even more. When it suits their purposes, scientists can be very skilled at highlighting these assumptions in order to save or discredit a hypothesis. Many of these are 'meta-theoretical' or 'trans-scientific' issues—issues that can be stated in apparently empirical form but as a practical matter cannot be resolved, at least not today.

. . .

"A second difficulty with a Science Court is that the 'technical' issues that scientists can be surest about are not necessarily the issues of greatest policy concern. This is especially likely when assumptions about social processes enter the calculations. . . . In this regard, Nelkin cites energy expert John Holdren's observation about the nuclear power debate: '[Holdren has] ranked the policy importance of nuclear power risks in the following (decreasing) order: proliferation, theft, sabotage, accidents, routine emissions. Technical data, he argued, are most useful in resolving the issues at the lower end of the policy-importance scale (i.e., routine emissions). The resolution of the more significant questions, proliferation and theft, has little to do with scientific "fact." ' Little to do, that is, with scientifically certifiable 'fact' based on an unforced consensus among experts—but much to do with judgments that benefit from being technically well informed.

"Finally, the losers are unlikely to accept the judgment of a Science Court as definitive. They will point to the fact-value boundary disputes and, as time goes on, 'new' evidence, as impeaching the judges' decision.

". . . The need for institutions to enforce stronger norms of analysis does not mean that we need an authoritative body to *resolve* technical disputes. When technical issues are not amenable to quick resolution, it is preferable to have forums in which the parties are forced to act according to analytic norms of fair play, showing what evidence they have, sharing their data base, responding to the questions of opponents, and airing unarticulated assumptions. When uncertainties cannot be eliminated, it is better to strive for greater clarity than for an unattainable or falsely reassuring 'scientific' consensus. Such arrangements may increase the probability of systematic learning. And greater clarity about the true range of alternatives and the probable consequences of a proposal allows the potentially affected parties to assess what risks they want to take and what alternatives they want to investigate further."

(4) R. CRANDALL and L. LAVE, EDS., THE SCIENTIFIC BASIS OF HEALTH AND SAFETY REGULATION 13–17 (1981)* presents fifteen separate papers addressing five health and safety regulatory issues—passive restraints for automobiles, cotton dust, saccharin, waterborn carcinogens and sulfur dioxide; for each issue "A Scientist's View," "An Economist's View" and "A Regulator's View" are presented.

"Several generalizations emerge from the five case studies. The first is that scientific evidence was not the determining factor in the regulatory action, and in only one instance—that of passive restraints— were scientists able to estimate risks with reasonable confidence. The underlying scientific basis for each regulation was far from complete in each case: anyone asserting that scientific evidence determined the regulation simply did not have the correct information. . . . The evidence did not replace the regulator's judgment, but it did provide facts and a structure in which a complicated decision could be made. The regulator needed to make judgments about risks, the effect of the regulation, induced changes in behavior, and the desirability of the regulation to the population generally and to involved interest groups. ". . .

"A second conclusion that emerges from all five papers is that uncertainty confounds the attempt to use scientific information. None of the regulators provides a detailed decision analysis embodying the facts and uncertainties—both scientific and economic—involved in setting a standard. . . . An administrator's judgment is required, and the decision cannot be driven by any systematic decision analysis of uncertain evidence. . . . [E]conomists can usually question the cost-effectiveness of a regulation, but they are generally unable to quantify the benefits and costs of alternative standards. Uncertainty becomes the basis for informal decisionmaking. . . .

"No matter how much . . . health evidence [about saccharin] is improved, . . . there will still be enormous uncertainty as to dose-response relationships, interactions with other carcinogens, and differences in individual tolerances. Until regulators develop a decisionmaking framework that admits uncertainty in some systematic way, reducing the variance of the estimates of the important coefficients will not necessarily improve the quality of regulatory decisions. Without a better approach to dealing with uncertainty, scientific evidence cannot be used to determine whether society might be better off with no regulatory intervention at all. . . .

"The cases concerned with exposure to toxic substances are dominated by political judgments, and the resulting regulations are inevitably challenged by those groups not favored by the regulators' judgment. Rather than ask that science play a greater part in the regulatory process, Congress seems to be looking more toward judicial and legislative review. . . . The case studies support another conclusion: regulators do not seek scientific contributions in a way that is likely to elicit the most helpful analysis and are not able to use the material they do receive. Both problems stem partly from an inability of agency heads to understand the limitations of science and to interpret inconclusive information. The problems are exacerbated by scientists' alienation from the chaotic, pressured world of the regulator, with its need for timely answers, even if such answers require making arbitrary assumptions. Regulators have learned that scientific data and analysis often cannot provide firm answers to their questions. With few scientific constraints, regulators find themselves driven by political forces, using an intuitive decisionmaking process.

"The difficulty is not that science has nothing to offer; rather it is that the science is not perceived as helpful because it is inconclusive. Since regulators do not see scientific data as helpful, they assign research a lower priority and a lesser role in policy formulation. . . .

For example, the Environmental Protection Agency must review its regulations on sulfur oxides, but it has supported little research that would help clarify the consequences of various alternative standards.

"When a regulatory decision must be made, the scientific data will always be somewhat incomplete, and important questions will be unanswered. What decisions can and should be made in light of the prevailing uncertainties? What can be gained at various periods by additional research? How should the current uncertainties in scientific knowledge be reflected in public policy? The answers to these questions require careful policy analysis. Fortunately, such analysis can be done relatively quickly and at a relatively low cost. Unfortunately, deciding to use policy analysis requires giving more emphasis to scientific evidence and less to political horse trading. The case studies show that there is substantial room for improvement in regulatory decisionmaking through better use of scientific information, but we doubt that such improvement will be realized soon."

(5) PUBLIC CITIZEN HEALTH RESEARCH GROUP v. TYSON, 796 F.2d 1479 (D.C.Cir.1986) was a proceeding for judicial review of an Occupational Safety and Health Administration rule setting standards for the exposure of workers to the industrial chemical ethylene oxide; the rulemaking had been characterized by vigorous debate over a variety of problems of "scientific fact" and judgment: "As we noted in United Steelworkers v. Marshall, 647 F.2d 1189, 1206–07 (D.C.Cir.1980), cert. denied, 453 U.S. 913 (1981):

> The peculiar problem of reviewing the rules of agencies like OSHA lies in applying the substantial evidence test to regulations which are essentially legislative and rooted in inferences from complex scientific and factual data, and which often necessarily involve highly speculative projections of technological development in areas wholly lacking in scientific and economic certainty.
>
> . . .

"[The Supreme Court's opinion in the Benzene case, p. 50 above,] established that the burden of proving that the subject of the proposed regulation presents a significant health risk remains with the agency. 448 U.S. at 653. Three of the Justices in the plurality in the Benzene case, however, were careful to preserve courts' traditional deference to agency decisionmaking. Thus, 'the requirement that a "significant" risk be identified is not a mathematical straitjacket. It is the Agency's responsibility to determine, in the first instance, what it considers to be a "significant" risk.' Id. at 655. The plurality opinion further stated that 'OSHA is not required to support its finding that a significant risk exists with anything approaching scientific certainty.' Id. at 656. Noting that the statute allows the Secretary to regulate on the basis of the 'best available evidence,' 29 U.S.C. § 655(b)(5) (1982), the opinion stated that 'a reviewing court (must) give OSHA some leeway where its findings must be made on the frontiers of scientific knowledge.' Id."

The court then proceeded to examine at some length the reasonableness of OSHA's ascription of validity to both epidemiological and experimental studies on which it had relied in determining that worker exposure to given levels of ethylene oxide presented significant risks of carcinogenicity. "OSHA . . . did not blindly rely on these studies; the agency recognized and accounted for the methodological weaknesses inherent in the studies. . . . 'Contrary to the apparent suggestion of some of the petitioners, we need not seek a single dispositive study that fully supports the Administrator's determination. Science does not work that way; nor, for that matter, does adjudicatory factfinding. Rather, the Administrator's decision may be fully supportable if it is based, as it is, on the inconclusive but suggestive results of numerous studies. By its nature, scientific evidence is cumulative: the more supporting, albeit inconclusive, evidence available, the more likely the accuracy of the conclusion. . . . Thus, after considering the inferences that can be drawn from the studies supporting the Administrator, and those opposing him, we must decide whether the cumulative effect of all this evidence, and not the effect of any single bit of it, presents a rational basis for the . . . regulations.' Ethyl Corp. v. EPA, 541 F.2d 1, 37–38 (D.C.Cir.) (en banc) (footnote omitted), cert. denied, 426 U.S. 941 (1976). . . . OSHA need only gather evidence from which it can reasonably draw the conclusion it has reached. . . . The scientific evidence in the instant case is incomplete but what evidence we have paints a striking portrait of serious danger to workers exposed to the chemical. When the evidence can be reasonably interpreted as supporting the need for regulation, we must affirm the agency's conclusion, despite the fact that the same evidence is susceptible of another interpretation. Our expertise does not lie in technical matters." A similar question was presented by the mathematical model OSHA had employed to determine the substantiality of the risk the workers faced, and the court undertook a similar examination of OSHA's database, methodology and assessment of the respective functions of agency and court.

Chapter VIII

STRUCTURES FOR DECISION

SECTION 1. THE ADMINISTRATIVE LAW JUDGE

Sections 5, 7 and 8 of the Administrative Procedure Act, 5 U.S.C. §§ 554, 556 and 557, provide in some detail for the conduct of on-the-record proceedings in federal administrative agencies. You should review them now, and may wish to compare Sections 9 through 13 of the Revised Model State Administrative Procedure Act, which serve a similar function. Many issues having to do with the actual conduct of hearing will be familiar in broad outline from courses on Civil Procedure and Evidence; others have been considered in the immediately preceding chapter.

One matter important to discuss in a casebook specifically about Administrative Law is the role of the hearing officer. As you will already have gathered from your readings, the impartiality and aloofness of the courtroom is often neither desirable nor sought in the administrative setting. To the extent agencies are problem-solvers and policy-implementers, their leadership and their staff, as a whole, can be expected to have a point of view; and they can be expected to be pursuing that point of view through a variety of means—rulemakings, public addresses, congressional appearances, private meetings—rather than solely through the retrospective, highly structured, and somewhat leisurely activity of formal hearing on the record. Yet some circumstances may seem to require, at least at an initial stage, the detachment and objectivity of an impartial hearer, an individual or panel unacquainted with a controversy except as it may be revealed in the presence of the parties. The federal administrative law judge serves this function.

a. Background and Institutional Setting for the Administrative Law Judge

NASH v. CALIFANO

United States Court of Appeals, Second Circuit, 1980.
613 F.2d 10.

Before KAUFMAN, CHIEF JUDGE, and SMITH and TIMBERS, CIRCUIT JUDGES.

IRVING R. KAUFMAN, CHIEF JUDGE: . . .

I

The appellant, Simon Nash, is an Administrative Law Judge (ALJ) of 22 years' experience in the Social Security Administration's Bureau of Hearings and Appeals. The Bureau's ALJs, under authority directly delegated by the Secretary of Health, Education and Welfare (HEW), hold hearings and decide appeals from agency denials of various claims for Social Security benefits.

The Bureau's corps of approximately 650 ALJs is divided among 145 field offices, each one headed by an Administrative Law Judge in Charge (ALJIC), who has managerial authority over all personnel assigned to his or her field office, in addition to responsibility for the same caseload as other ALJs. ALJICs receive the same salaries as other ALJs. Each ALJIC reports to one of the ten Regional Chief Administrative Law Judges who, in turn, are under the managerial authority of the Director of the Bureau of Hearings and Appeals and his chief assistant, the Chief Administrative Law Judge. While Administrative Law Judges are civil service employees, the Director of the Bureau is appointed by, and serves at the pleasure of the Commissioner of the Social Security Administration.

In December of 1967, Judge Nash became ALJIC for the Buffalo field office. During his tenure in that position, he, along with numerous other ALJICs, urged adoption of a number of administrative reforms—including the hiring of staff attorneys and the use of summary opinions in appropriate cases—to cope with the mounting backlog of cases before the Bureau of Hearings and Appeals. These pleas for reform went unheeded until 1975, when appellee Robert Trachtenberg was appointed Director of the Bureau. Facing a record backlog of 113,000 cases, Director Trachtenberg instituted many of the reforms long advocated by Nash and his colleagues.

Trachtenberg's goal of eliminating unconscionable delays in processing appeals is, of course, commendable. Appellant, however, alleges that appellees and their staff employees have interfered with the decisional independence of the administrative law judges in violation of the Administrative Procedure Act, the Social Security Act and the due process clause of the Fifth Amendment. . . . .

The first practice challenged in [Nash's] complaint is the Bureau's "Regional Office Peer Review Program." According to Nash, Trachtenberg [and other officials], as well as non-ALJ members of their staffs, known as "Development Center Analysts" and "Program Operation Officers," review the work of ALJs outside the normal appellate process. In conjunction with this ongoing review, the appellees or their staffs give plaintiff and all other ALJs detailed, purportedly mandatory instructions concerning the proper length of hearings and opinions, the amount of evidence required in specific cases, and the proper use of expert witnesses. Through the Peer Review Program, the Bureau has allegedly arrogated to itself the power to control the conduct of hearings vested in ALJs by the Administrative Procedure Act, 5 U.S.C. § 556.

Nash also avers that an arbitrary monthly production quota has been established for him and all his colleagues. Unless an ALJ renders a specified number of decisions per month, the agency, appellant claims, threatens to file incompetence charges against him with the

Civil Service Commission. In his view, the agency's production quota constitutes a performance rating forbidden by the Administrative Procedure Act, 5 U.S.C. § 4301(2)(E) and 5 C.F.R. § 930.211.

An additional threat to the ALJs statutory independence is allegedly posed by the so-called "Quality Assurance Program," which attempts to control the number of decisions denying Social Security Benefits. The agency has "let it be known" that the average 50% "reversal rate" for all ALJs is an "acceptable" one. Appellant further claims in his amended complaint that the reversal rates of all ALJs are monitored, and those who deviate from the mean are counseled and admonished to bring their rates in line with the national average. This attempt to influence the ALJs' decisionmaking process, it is urged, violates 5 U.S.C. §§ 556 & 3105 and the Fifth Amendment to the Constitution.
. . .

[The district court had dismissed the complaint on finding that ALJ Nash lacked standing to bring this action; review of this determination required the court to decide whether he had been threatened with a palpable injury, one both within judicial power to correct and arguably within the zone of interests protected by relevant law—here, the APA and the Social Security Act. See Chapter 9, Section 3, within. The court was thus required to discuss ALJ Nash's claim on the merits under the APA for the limited purpose of determining whether the APA creates interests personal to ALJ Nash that may have been violated by the SSA actions.]

As originally enacted in 1946, the Administrative Procedure Act (APA) vested hearing examiners (as ALJs were then called) with a limited independence from the agencies they served. The hearing examiners had previously been on a par with other agency employees, their compensation and promotion dependent upon agency ratings. The expanding scope of agency activity during the 1930s and early 1940s led to increasingly heavy criticism, however, because the hearing examiners came to be perceived as "mere tools of the agency concerned." Ramspeck v. Trial Examiners Conference, 345 U.S. 128, 131 (1953). In response, Congress enacted § 11 of the APA, removing control over the hearing examiners' tenure and compensation from the agencies and vesting it, to a large degree, in the Civil Service Commission.

The APA provides that ALJs "are entitled to pay prescribed by the Office of Personnel Management independently of agency recommendations or ratings." 5 U.S.C. § 5372. In addition, section 4301 and its implementing regulation (5 C.F.R. § 930.211) exempts ALJs from the performance ratings prescribed for other civil service employees. ALJ tenure, moreover, is specially safeguarded by 5 U.S.C. § 554, which provides that ALJs, unlike other civil servants, may not be removed without a formal adjudication.

These statutory provisions draw upon the more ancient wisdom grounded in history and contained in Article III, which safeguards federal judicial independence through still more stringent compensation and tenure provisions. See Kaufman, Chilling Judicial Independence, 88 Yale L.J. 681 (1979). The independent judiciary is structurally insulated from the other branches to provide a safe haven for individual liberties in times of crisis.[1] By analogy, "the process of agency adjudication is currently structured so as to assure that the hearing examiner exercises his independent judgment on the evidence before him, free from pressures by the parties or other officials within the agency." Butz v. Economou, 438 U.S. 478, 513 (1978).

It is clear that these provisions confer a qualified right of decisional independence upon ALJs. First recognized by the Supreme Court in Ramspeck v. Trial Examiners Conference, 345 U.S. 128 (1953), this special status is a creation of statute, rather than the Constitution. And as their role has expanded, the ALJs functional comparability to judges has gained recognition. . . .

The APA creates a comprehensive bulwark to protect ALJs from agency interference. The independence granted to ALJs is designed to maintain public confidence in the essential fairness of the process through which Social Security benefits are allocated by ensuring impartial decisionmaking. Since that independence is expressed in terms of such personal rights as compensation, tenure and freedom from performance evaluations and extraordinary review, we cannot say that ALJs are so disinterested as to lack even standing to safeguard their own independence.

The scrutiny and affirmative direction alleged by Nash reaches virtually every aspect of an ALJ's daily role. Under the Quality Assurance System and the Peer Review Program, the number of reversals, the number of dispositions, and the manner of trying and deciding each case are recorded and measured against prescribed standards. ALJ Nash and his colleagues allegedly receive mandatory, unlawful instructions regarding every detail of their judicial role. Nash, therefore, has "the personal stake and interest that impart the concrete adverseness required by Article III." Barlow v. Collins, 397 U.S. 159, 164 (1970). . . .

NOTES

(1) How would you have decided the merits of the questions raised in Nash? In Social Security Administration v. Goodman, 58 Pike & Fisher, Ad.L.2d 780 (MSPB 1984), the Merit Systems Protection Board denied effect to the proposed removal of an ALJ for deficient productivity—for 29 months he had decided cases at half the national average rate—but *not* because "insufficient productivity" could never constitute "good cause" for removal. The Board concluded, rather, that an unelaborated statistical showing was not enough to "prove the agency's charge that respondent had failed to achieve a minimally acceptable level of productivity." In 1980, responding to concern at the high rate with which ALJs were reversing state agency decisions to deny applica-

1. *See* E. Burke, Reflections on the Revolution in France 242 (T. Mahoney ed. 1952). The ideal of judicial independence antedates the Constitution. Indeed, one of the grievances against George III listed in the Declaration of Independence was: "He has made Judges dependent on his will alone, for the tenure of their offices, and the amount and payment of their salaries." [Ed.] Compare CFTC v. Schor, p. 107 above.

tions for disability benefits and, especially, at the wide variations in this rate among individual ALJs,[2] Congress instructed the Secretary of Health and Human Services to review ALJ decisions on her own motion.[3] The agency initially focused on ALJs with unusually high grant rates, asserting that denials were reviewed on appeal, and that the targeted decisions more frequently proved erroneous. The program gradually changed, so that an ALJ's grant rate ceased to determine whether or at what intensity her decisions were reviewed. Litigation brought by SSA ALJs to challenge the program's assault on their independence was dismissed in light of the changes. While conceding "the worthiness of defendants' stated goal of improving the quality and accuracy of decisions," the court nonetheless warned, "targeting high allowance ALJs for review, counseling and possible disciplinary action was of dubious legality," given its impact on their independence. Association of Administrative Law Judges v. Heckler, 594 F.Supp. 1132, 1141 (D.D.C.1984).[4]

(2) Judge Kaufman's brief account of the development of the APA's provisions for hearing officers,[5] now called "administrative law judges,"[6] reflects a history of tension between the need for fact-finder independence, on the one hand, and the need for policy and management control, on the other. Professor Victor Rosenblum has argued that the failures of independence from political pressure and other "undue influence" resulting from the previous institutional arrangements did much to fuel the apparent hostility of the Supreme Court to administrative fact-finding during the first four decades of the century.[7] If the objectivity of administrative fact-finding could not be assured, he suggests, it was natural for courts to develop categories of central fact requiring judicial redetermination; the notions of "constitutional" and "jurisdictional" fact you have met elsewhere in this casebook may be so

2. A 1976 survey, for example, showed 12% of ALJs awarded benefits in less than one out of three proceedings before them; 15% in more than two out of every three proceedings before them; 45% fell into the 40%–60% range. No systematic differences were discovered to explain the variation. J. Mashaw, et al., Social Security Hearings and Appeals: A Study of the Social Security Administration Hearing System 21 (1978).

3. Section 340(q), Social Security Disability Amendments of 1980, P.L. 96–265 (1980). A disappointed claimant is entitled to seek review of an ALJ's adverse decision before the agency's Appeals Council, which decides cases on the Secretary's behalf. That Council may also review any decision—either a grant or an unappealed denial—on its own motion. This authority had fallen into disuse prior to the 1980 amendment.

4. To the same effect, see Stieberger v. Heckler, 615 F.Supp. 1315 (S.D.N.Y.1985), a challenge brought by persons threatened with denial of disability benefits.

5. See F. Davis, Judicialization of Administrative Law: The Trial-Type Hearing and the Changing Status of the Hearing Officer, 1977 Duke L.J. 389 for useful discussion of the origins and later development of the office of hearing examiner.

6. Initially accomplished by regulation in 1972, the change in title was confirmed in 1978 by a statute, P.L. 95–251, 92 Stat. 183, that also designated 340 of the roughly 1,000 ALJ positions in the government (about twice the number of district court judgeships) as entitled to pay at levels generally reserved for the government's senior executives, ranging from $52,000 to $81,000 in 1985.

7. V. Rosenblum, The Administrative Law Judge in the Administrative Process, in Subcommittee on Social Security, House Committee on Ways and Means, 94th Cong., 1st Sess., Report on Recent Studies Relevant to Disability Hearings and Appeals Crisis 171–245 (Comm.Print 1975).

understood. The Supreme Court's decisions in the 30's and 40's supporting administrative fact-finding,[8] he believes, reflect a growing trust in administrative fact determination as recognition of the need for examiner independence spread.

Yet the first regulations adopted by the Civil Service Commission to carry out its responsibilities for hearing officers under the APA [9] did not unequivocally embrace the judicial model. They established various salary classifications depending upon the difficulty of the cases to be heard, and allowed agencies to consider each examiner's experience and competence in assigning cases to him. Hearing examiners, opposing this plan, argued that their independence could be safeguarded only by withholding from the employing administrative agencies any power whatsoever to determine their work assignments and, thus, their salary levels. But the Supreme Court upheld the regulations in Ramspeck v. Federal Trial Examiners Conference, 345 U.S. 128 (1953), cited for other purposes in Judge Kaufman's opinion; with Justices Black, Frankfurter, and Douglas dissenting, it concluded that "Congress did not provide for the classification of examiners by the Commission, and then provide for the Commission to ignore such classification by a mechanical rotation." The statutes and regulations remain a compromise and, in the nature of a compromise, are not fully satisfying to all concerned.[10]

Prominent among the concerns still voiced is the concern underlying the administrative actions in the principal case, whether sufficient controls over the quality and productivity of ALJ performance have been retained. Administrative law judges do not share with the government's Senior Executive Service—civil servants at comparable levels of pay and responsibility—any exposure to probationary periods, performance appraisals, productivity-governed pay decisions, or the like. In effect, they acquire the protection of tenure immediately upon their appointment. A comprehensive report to Congress by the Comptroller General of the United States, Administrative Law Process: Better Management is Needed (May 15, 1978) discussed the widespread variations of productivity among administrative law judges and the difficulties perceived by agencies in devising means to respond. For example, in fiscal 1975, the NLRB's 62 ALJ's brought about 1100 cases to conclusion after hearing; the nine most productive averaged 29 cases per year; the 23 least productive, 12.[11] But, the GAO reported, no ALJ

---

8. E.g., Crowell v. Benson, 285 U.S. 22 (1932), p. 105 above; United States v. Morgan, 313 U.S. 409 (1941), p. 455 above.

9. The former authority of the Civil Service Commission is now allocated to the Office of Personnel Management and Office of Special Counsel, both executive agencies responsible for policymaking and implementation, and to an independent adjudicator, the Merit Systems Protection Board.

10. For a most valuable over-all account, including rich Civil Service Commission documentation, see J.W. Macy, Jr.,

The APA and the Hearing Examiner: Products of a Viable Political Society, 27 Fed.B.J. 351 (1967). Mr. Macy was then the chairman of the Civil Service Commission. See also Symposium, Administrative Law Judges, 6 W.New Eng.L.Rev. 587 (1984).

11. GAO Report at 32. The GAO found similar variations elsewhere; at the Occupational Safety and Health Review Commission, 34 ALJ's averaged 62 dispositions each; but the most productive decided 95, and the least, 44. In each agency there were eight individual ALJ's who failed to

had ever been removed by the Civil Service Commission for poor performance; only the powers of persuasion—and, perhaps, the benefits of peer pressure and professional education—are available. Among the GAO's recommendations to the Congress were that it establish an initial probationary period of up to 3 years to eliminate immediate, initially guaranteed appointment and tenure; and clarify and formalize means for continuing performance review.[12]

This issue has been given particular point by a striking shift in the character of the ALJ function in the years since adoption of the APA. In 1947, 125 hearing officers, 64% of those employed by the federal government, worked for one of the independent regulatory agencies. In general, the cases they heard concerned regulatory issues of some complexity and social importance. Another 35 (18%) heard labor cases, 23 (12%) worked in the executive branch, and only 13 (7%) worked for the Social Security Administration. The principal issues presented about hearing officer function in that setting might be thought to be reconciling quasi-judicial detachment with the weaving together of many strands of expertise needed to arrive at sound policy conclusions.[13] In 1983, under the combined impact of deregulation and the due process explosion, only 89 ALJs remained in the regulatory bodies—8% of the total; 812 ALJs, 69% of a total of 1176, were at the Social Security Administration; 233, or 20%, were at labor-related agencies; and 42 were elsewhere in executive government. As Nash and other cases already encountered[14] reflect, the proceedings before these ALJs have more of the character of mass justice, in which factual issues are somewhat repetitive and individual results are unlikely to be regarded as important by agency administrators. Instead, productivity and general adherence to agency policy assume major significance. If one ALJ decides only 190 cases per year while his colleagues average 380[15] or if the ALJs of one office in a state find for applicants 90% (or 10%) of the time while another office in the same state finds for applicants at about the national average rate of 50%,[16] an administrator may believe herself confronting a problem requiring attention—and, as Nash indicates, an ALJ who gets that attention may conclude that his necessary independence has been tampered with. See V. Rosenblum, Contexts and Contents of "For Good Cause" as Criterion for Removal of Administrative Law Judges: Legal and Policy Factors, 6 W.New Eng.L.Rev. 593 (1984).

(3) Should the use of ALJs for these decisions be reconsidered? Professor Robert G. Dixon thought so; he told the Social Security Subcommittee of the House Committee on Ways and Means in 1975 that

meet the average productivity level in *any* of the four years surveyed. Ibid.

12. See also A. Scalia, The ALJ Fiasco—A Reprise, 47 U.Chi.L.Rev. 57 (1979).

13. See, e.g., R. Fuchs, The Hearing Officer Problem—Symptom and Symbol, 40 Corn.L.Q. 281 (1955); W. Pedersen, Jr., The Decline of Separation of Functions in Regulatory Agencies, 64 Va.L.Rev. 991 (1978).

14. Mathews v. Eldridge, pp. 597 above; Richardson v. Perales, p. 809 above; Heckler v. Campbell, p. 295 above.

15. SSA v. Goodman, 58 Ad.L.2d 780 (MSPB 1984).

16. Association of Administrative Law Judges v. Heckler, 594 F.Supp. 1132 (D.D.C.1984).

"There is a need for Congress to give more attention to the significant difference between the adjudication of benefit claims, where the intake numbers millions per year, and the older and more familiar type of regulatory administration exemplified by the Interstate Commerce Commission and later independent commissions. Our perceptions of the administrative process, of administrative laws, and of the proper content of the Administrative Procedure Act have been drawn almost exclusively from the leisurely, low-volume, high visibility, rich-litigant world of regulatory administration.

"We have all heard the expression: 'you get the justice you pay for.' The unspoken premise is that in a properly organized society there would be enough resources to pay for all the justice desired. Only when pushed as we are being pushed, I suggest, in the rapidly expanding field of claim adjudication, do we begrudgingly face the question: how nearly judicial should administrative claims determination be? Is it feasible to give every one of the millions of claimants annually in the programs I have mentioned an attorney, a full evidentiary hearing, an administrative appeal, and court review? Indeed, is it necessary, in order to achieve an acceptable level of accuracy and consistency in treatment of similar claimants? An even more serious question is whether such high formality does achieve the virtues of accuracy and consistency among claimants. The answer is no, according to some provocative evidence I gathered for my book, Social Security Disability and Mass Justice: A Problem in Welfare Adjudication (Praeger, 1973). . . .

"I too, have a thirst for perfection. But resources of both time and talent are not in infinite supply."

Two years later the National Center for Administrative Justice published the results of its Study of the Social Security Administration Hearing System, under the directorship of Professor Jerry Mashaw. "Our general conclusion," the group reported, "is that the more dramatic proposals for reform are inadvisable, either because they are not directed at real problems, because they would be on balance dysfunctional or because their effects are unknown." At xix. The study drew on much empirical data as well as existing literature; the changes it suggested were largely incremental and ameliatory, not dramatic. "Public trust in the SSA scheme of social insurance would be significantly undermined were the opportunity for a face-to-face encounter with a demonstrably independent decisionmaker eliminated from the system." At xxiv. Short of committing more resources, changes to speed the process would often if not inevitably risk lowering its quality; and, indeed, the problems of leading the ALJ's to "accurate" and "consistent" decisions were, in the group's view, at least as urgent and difficult as assuring "timely" decision.

If, then ALJ's are still to be used, what may be done to control their productivity and the quality of their work? "There are wide variations in the work methods and the work products of the ALJs employed by [The Bureau of Hearings and Appeals]. We have observed an ALJ who disposes of about 120 cases per month and one who averages 10, ALJs who seldom use [vocational experts] and those who use them in a majority of cases. . . . Some ALJs do extensive prehearing development; some develop almost exclusively after the hearing. Some never see many of the decisions written for them by staff attorneys; others will not use a staff attorney at all. Estimates of the administrative costs per case for the judges we have observed suggest a variance of 300 percent, and quarterly reversal rates sometimes vary by the same factor. . . . " Although "the protection of ALJ decisional independence in the APA is significant," in the authors' view, "ALJs are not policy-independent. . . . [T]he agency may control their exercise of discretion by regulation, guidelines, instructions, opinions, and the like . . . . There is no prohibition even on consultation with agency employees on questions of law or policy in a particular case." Nor can ALJs "expect a totally free hand in deciding how many cases to decide. . . . Whether a claimant is really disabled is a question that can be explored endlessly. BHA would be shirking its clear responsibility to provide timely adjudications if it did not attempt to make the process as expeditious as possible." [17]

Other aspects of the problem of mass justice have been treated in Chapter 4, above, pp. 597 ff. and 626 ff.

(4) Arguments are increasingly heard for responding to these and like problems by removing ALJs completely from the individual agencies and creating a general federal administrative law judge corps for initial decision of all administrative trials, with appeals (for policy control) to the responsible agency. Centralized systems are said to have succeeded in a number of states, although a prominent federal administrative law judge has suggested that data concerning their operation may be "too sparse, the various central panel studies too diverse and the current panels too dependent on the chief judges appointed to give effect to the legislative changes to pinpoint with accuracy what the future may hold for a central system." [18] Proponents urge that this would heighten the appearance and reality of independence, enhance the standing of the ALJ, promote more efficient use of ALJs (who could readily move among a variety of "jurisdictions" as caseload required), require clearer articulation of policy by agencies and even permit tighter discipline by removing the threat that discipline would appear tied to results. Opponents see little demonstrable need for additional protection for ALJ independence, note a substantial imbalance in the numbers and tasks of ALJs working in various federal agencies, and envision substantial risks to the unity of agency policy-making if cases of importance from a policy perspective must be tried

17. J. Mashaw, C. Goetz, F. Goodman, W. Schwartz, P. Verkuil, M. Carrow, Social Security Hearings and Appeals: A Study of the Social Security Administration Hearing System (Lexington Books, 1978).

18. N. Litt. Review of M. Rich and E. Bincar, The Central Panel System for Administrative Law Judges: A Survey of Seven States (1983), 69 A.B.A.J. 1876 (1983). See also D. Harves, The 1981 Model Administrative Procedure Act: The Impact on Central Panel States, 6 W.New Eng.L.Rev. 661 (1984); N. Abrams, Administrative Law Judge Systems: The California View, 29 Ad.L.Rev. 487 (1977); F. Davis, Judicialization of Administrative Law: The Trial-Type Hearing and The Changing Status of the Hearing Officer, 1977 Duke L.J. 389.

before persons removed from the agency, persons who may also lack relevant expertise. Observed one experienced Washington lawyer generally opposed to an ALJ corps, "Agency funding limitations often foreclose or restrict staff testimony even in impartial proceedings, and also sometimes limit the effectiveness and quality of staff briefs. The ALJ presently housed in the agency receives through his pores, as it were, in informal contacts a great deal of relevant information about agency policy developments which will not be available to the corps judges." [19] Another might find in this, of course, a major argument for a separate corps. And if—as in the case of SSA ALJs—overt policymaking is rarely a significant function, one is left with the rather more diffuse assertion that an independent corps, lacking any connection at all to fiscal responsibility, may not be as sympathetic to programmatic constraints. [20]

b. Selection, Disqualification and Replacement

GROLIER, INC. v. FEDERAL TRADE COMMISSION
United States Court of Appeals, Ninth Circuit, 1980.
615 F.2d 1215.

Before WALLACE and ANDERSON, CIRCUIT JUDGES, and SOLOMON,[1] DISTRICT JUDGE.

WALLACE, CIRCUIT JUDGE:

On March 13, 1978, the Federal Trade Commission (FTC) entered a final cease and desist order against Grolier, Incorporated and 14 of its wholly-owned subsidiaries . . . designed to correct Grolier's adjudged violations of 15 U.S.C. § 45. . . .

Grolier is engaged in the door-to-door and mail order sale of encyclopedias and related reference publications. On March 9, 1972, the FTC issued an administrative complaint charging Grolier with unfair methods of competition and unfair or deceptive acts or practices in connection with its sales activities, pricing representations, promotion techniques, recruitment practices, debt collection, and mail order operations. The case was initially assigned to an Administrative Law Judge (ALJ), who, after presiding at hearings throughout 1973 and 1974, retired from federal service before rendering a decision. A second ALJ was then assigned to complete the case, but he promptly recused himself. In February 1975, Theodore P. von Brand, the third ALJ assigned to the case, began hearings and decided to recall many of the witnesses who had previously testified in the proceedings. In January 1976, four months before completion of the hearings, ALJ von Brand informed the parties that he had served as an attorney-advisor to

19. W. Ross, Statement to the 8th Annual Symposium of the National Conference of Administrative Law Judges, Feb. 11, 1983, pp. 8–9.

20. See, for discussion of these and other issues, A. Scalia, The ALJ Fiasco—A Reprise, 47 U.Chi.L.Rev. 57 (1979); Symposium, Administrative Law Judges, 6 W.N. Eng.L.Rev. 587 (1984); J. Lubbers, A Unified Corps of Administrative Law Judges: A Proposal to Test the Idea at the Federal Level, 65 Judic. 266 (1981).

1. Honorable Gus J. Solomon, United States District Judge, District of Oregon, sitting by designation.

former FTC Commissioner A. Everett MacIntyre from 1963 through January 1971, during which period Grolier was intermittently investigated and charged by the FTC. Records available to Grolier indicated that Commissioner MacIntyre attended at least one meeting between it and representatives of the FTC.

Upon learning of ALJ von Brand's advisory responsibilities during the eight-year period, Grolier requested that the judge disqualify himself from further participation in the proceedings. The judge denied the request, stating that he did not recall working on matters involving Grolier while serving as legal advisor to the Commissioner. Grolier then filed with the FTC a formal motion for disqualification and removal of ALJ von Brand, at the same time requesting the FTC to permit discovery of specified FTC records which would have tended to show the nature and extent of the judge's contact with the Grolier case. The FTC denied both the motion for disqualification and the requested discovery.

After hearing a substantial part of the case de novo, ALJ von Brand concluded the hearings in May 1976 and issued his decision and recommended cease and desist order in October 1976. On appeal, the FTC adopted in large part the decision and order of ALJ von Brand and reaffirmed denial of the disqualification motion and request for discovery.

II

Most federal administrative agencies combine within one organization a number of responsibilities that our system of government normally seeks to separate. They formulate policy as does the legislature, administer policy as does the executive, and adjudicate controversies as does the judiciary. They investigate infractions of statutes or regulations, prosecute those against whom their investigation has established a prima facie case, and judge the case they themselves have presented. . . .

In an effort to minimize any unfairness caused by this consolidation of responsibilities, [in Section 554(d),] the APA mandates an internal separation of the investigatory-prosecutorial functions from adjudicative responsibilities. . . . To violate section 554(d), then, an agency employee must, in the same or a factually related case, (1) engage in "investigative or prosecuting functions," [2] and (2) "participate or advise in the decision." Neither Grolier nor the FTC contests the fact that ALJ von Brand's actions meet the latter of these two requirements. The point of their disagreement, and the issue which we must resolve, is whether ALJ von Brand meets the first requirement, i.e.,

---

2. . . . . Congress did not intend to limit the separation of functions to those persons contemporaneously performing both. Such a reading would permit an agency employee to become immersed in the investigation of a case, resign from the investigative position, and then be appointed judge to render the decision. Such was not the intention of Congress. See S.Rep. No. 572, 79th Cong., 1st Sess. 18 (1945), reprinted in Administrative Procedure Act—Legislative History, 79th Congress 1944–46, at 204 (1946); H.R.Rep. No. 1980, 79th Cong., 1st Sess. 27 (1946); reprinted in Administrative Procedure Act—Legislative History, 79th Congress 1944–46, at 262 (1946).

whether his employment as an attorney-advisor to Commissioner MacIntyre constituted "investigative or prosecuting functions" in this or a factually related case. . . .

[The provisions reflect a recommendation contained in the Report of the Attorney General's Committee on Administrative Procedure 50 (1941), S.Doc. No. 8, 77th Cong., 1st Sess. 50 (1941), which gave at least] two reasons . . . for this recommended separation: "the investigators, if allowed to participate [in adjudication], would be likely to interpolate facts and information discovered by them ex parte and not adduced at the hearing, where the testimony is sworn and subject to cross-examination and rebuttal"; and "[a] man who has buried himself in one side of an issue is disabled from bringing to its decision that dispassionate judgment which Anglo-American tradition demands of officials who decide questions."

. . . We conclude that by forbidding adjudication by persons "engaged in the performance of investigative or prosecuting functions," Congress intended to preclude from decisionmaking in a particular case not only individuals with the title of "investigator" or "prosecutor," but all persons who had, in that or a factually related case, been involved with ex parte information, or who had developed, by prior involvement with the case, a "will to win." An attorney-advisor may, therefore, come within the prohibition of section 554(d) if he has had such involvement. The FTC decision to the contrary was error.[3]

. . . Grolier contends that ALJ von Brand is chargeable with knowledge of all investigative and prosecutorial activities undertaken by the FTC during his tenure as an attorney-advisor. Therefore, it argues, actual possession of ex parte information in the Grolier case need not be shown; ALJ von Brand is disqualified per se by virtue of his former position. . . . On the contrary, those courts which have considered the question have focused not upon the former position of the challenged adjudicator, but upon his actual involvement, while in that former position, with the case he is now deciding.[4]

In resolving the question of ALJ von Brand's qualification to adjudicate the Grolier case, then, we must look to his activity during the time that he served as attorney-advisor to Commissioner MacIntyre. If he was sufficiently involved with the case to be apprised of ex parte information, 554(d) requires his disqualification. His current inability to recall that information is irrelevant. Once an attorney-advisor is shown to have been "engaged in the performance of investigative or prosecuting functions" through prior acquaintance with ex parte infor-

---

3. In concluding that former attorney-advisors are not within the proscription of 554(d), the FTC focused solely upon the congressional desire to prevent adjudication by those who had developed a "will to win." In re Grolier, Inc., 87 F.T.C. 179, 180 (1976). With such a narrow focus, their conclusion was not unreasonable. It was erroneous, however, because it overlooked the equally important congressional desire to prevent adjudicative interpolation of ex parte facts.

4. The position urged by Grolier would . . . produce an unnecessarily impractical approach to the problem of separation of functions. ALJ von Brand, who served as an attorney-advisor from 1963 to 1971, would be disqualified from judging any case that was investigated or prosecuted by the FTC during that eight-year period. We need not adopt such a restrictive approach in order to comply with the mandate of section 554(d).

mation, 554(d) says he "may not . . . participate or advise in the decision . . . " of the case. It does not condition this disqualification upon recollection of the ex parte facts.

Grolier has the burden of showing ALJ von Brand's prior acquaintance with ex parte information. Where, as here, the court is presented with no evidence of actual involvement in the Grolier case by then attorney-advisor von Brand, the normal course of action would be to refuse to disqualify him. In this case, however, Grolier attempted to require such evidence by requesting discovery of specified FTC documents. . . .

The FTC's denial of Grolier's request for discovery was the direct result of its erroneous conclusion that attorney-advisors did not perform "investigative or prosecuting functions" within the meaning of 554(d). . . . We conclude, therefore, that the case should be remanded to the FTC for reconsideration of the discovery denial and, in light of the results of that reconsideration, the disqualification motion. We do not say that the FTC must grant discovery; but we do say that a flat refusal to disclose anything at all about ALJ von Brand's prior involvement in the Grolier case is error. The FTC must produce sufficient information to permit it and a reviewing court, to make an accurate 554(d) determination. . . . While the FTC may grant discovery, it may, initially, respond in the form of affidavits as to the existence and extent of ALJ von Brand's involvement with the Grolier case while he served as attorney-advisor. . . . If these sworn statements adequately disclose the existence or nonexistence of ALJ von Brand's involvement in prior Grolier matters, Grolier, who has the burden of proof on the disqualification issue, may rightfully be "obliged either to offer evidence contradicting the sworn statements of the [FTC], or to point out the inadequacy and inconsistency, if any, in the sworn statements" before it will be permitted to subpoena FTC records. . . .

NOTES

(1) On remand, ALJ von Brand denied receiving any ex parte information during his service as Commissioner MacIntyre's attorney-advisor. Commissioner MacIntyre provided an affidavit indicating that he could remember no discussions with von Brand about Grolier, and knew of no contacts von Brand might himself have had with the investigation while on his staff. That sufficed, for both the FTC and the court, to warrant von Brand's continuing participation. Grolier, Inc. v. FTC, 699 F.2d 983 (9th Cir.1983), cert. denied 464 U.S. 891 (1983). Are you satisfied that both the "will to win" and prior involvement with ex parte information in some official capacity warrant disqualification? See M. Asimow, When the Curtain Falls: Separation of Functions in the Federal Administrative Agencies, 81 Colum.L.Rev. 759 (1981).

(2) JONAL CORP. v. DISTRICT OF COLUMBIA, 533 F.2d 1192 (D.C.Cir. 1975), cert. denied 429 U.S. 825 (1976), reviewed the District of Columbia's Contract Appeals Board's decision of a dispute arising out of Jonal's contract with the District to construct two buildings. Jonal

challenged the fairness of the Board's action on the ground, inter alia, that it had been appointed by the Corporation Counsel of the District, who also appeared before the Board to argue the city's case. The majority, Judge Merhige writing, easily disposed of the case on the basis of Marcello v. Bonds, 349 U.S. 302 (1955), p. 246 above, which in their view sustained similar arrangements in federal immigration cases.[1] Absent demonstrated personal bias, pecuniary interest, or prejudice apparent in the conduct of the proceedings, the majority concluded, Jonal had no complaint.

For Judge Harold Leventhal, in dissent, Marcello was not dispositive. In that case, rulings of inquiry officers were subject to "full administrative review" by a national board of immigration appeals *not* subject to INS supervision, and it was the judgment of this "insulated" review board that was found "entitled to substantial evidence deference by the courts." Here, on the other hand, the Corporation Counsel not only designated the members of the board from his staff, but also "considers itself free . . . to make such assignments, on a part-time duty basis, in such a way that on one day a lawyer may be a member of the board, . . . although the day before and the day after he may be working alongside [the attorney who argued the city's case], or even under his supervision, in another matter." For Judge Leventhal, further inquiry was required to determine, in light of these working relationships, "whether, and to what extent, [the board's] decisions are entitled to the benefit of the 'substantial evidence' rule."[2]

(3) Under the APA, ALJ's are permanent employees selected from lists provided by the Office of Personnel Management. For many years, agencies used a practice known as "selective certification," in which specific experience in the agency's work was made one of the bases for qualification. The agency had to select from among the three highest-rated candidates provided it, but the natural tendency of an experience requirement was to favor candidates from among its own legal staff, like ALJ von Brand.[3] In 1984 The Office of Personnel Management ended the practice as a general matter, leaving it open to agencies to demonstrate case by case that such experience was so important as to warrant preferring an agency attorney over persons with otherwise equal qualifications. Do you share the view of Bernard Segal, a former president of the ABA, that selective certification

---

1. "[T]he objection that the special inquiry officer was subject to the supervision and control of officials in the Immigration Service charged with investigative and prosecuting functions . . . is without substance when considered against the longstanding practice in deportation proceedings, judicially approved in numerous decisions in the federal courts, and against the special considerations applicable to deportation which the Congress may take into account in exercising its particularly broad discretion in immigration matters." 349 U.S. at 311.

2. Compare Kalaris v. Donovan, 697 F.2d 376 (D.C.Cir.1983), cert. denied 462

U.S. 1119 (1983) (sitting member of Labor Department's Benefits Review Board may constitutionally be made subject to summary removal); NLRB v. Ohio New and Rebuilt Parts, Inc., 760 F.2d 1443 (6th Cir. 1985) (performance ratings of NLRB regional directors as members of Federal Senior Executive Service did not create constitutionally unfair financial or other incentives).

3. In addition to selective certification, selection criteria most likely to have been met by government attorneys are said to have been employed for screening purposes. See Dugan v. Ramsay, 727 F.2d 192 (1st Cir.1984).

created an inbreeding which contributed significantly to the appearance of bias? "For example, of the thirteen administrative law judges assigned to the Federal Trade Commission, twelve are former employees of that commission; and of the seven new administrative law judges whose appointment was announced in May by the National Labor Relations Board, every one was either a current or a former member of the board's legal staff.

.   .   .

"A partner in our firm resigned in 1969 to become a judge of a United States court of appeals. Even after a seven-year absence from private practice, this judge still will not sit in any case in which his former law firm or any lawyer now with that firm appears as counsel, and I am certain that he never will sit in a case involving a party whom his former law firm, or any member of it, represented while he was a member of the firm. By contrast, agency attorneys who become administrative law judges, can sit as judges in an endless chain of cases in which their former employer, and in many instances client as well, is a party. How can such a system maintain the appearance of fairness?" The Administrative Law Judge, Thirty Years of Progress and the Road Ahead, 62 A.B.A.J. 1424, 1426 (1976).

Even as concerns lawyers elevated to the bench from private practice, the behavior Mr. Segal reports is more punctilious than the law or the ABA's Code of Judicial Conduct requires. Disqualification on the basis of prior representation is mandatory in such circumstances only if the judge or her associates were involved in the matter at the time she was in private practice. 28 U.S.C. § 455(b)(2); ABA Code 3(C) (1). For the government attorney, both these sources require disqualification only in the event of personal, not merely institutional, involvement in the particular case in controversy. 28 U.S.C. § 455(b)(3). While disqualification is also called for "in any proceeding in which [the judge's] impartiality might reasonably be questioned," 28 U.S.C. § 455(a), the specific situations addressed in section 455(b), the statute's legislative history, and available ABA opinions on ethical issues all suggest that judgments about the "reasonableness" of questioning impartiality may be influenced by the specific prohibitions of section 455(b).[4] In particular, these sources suggest that impartiality is not "reasonably" to be questioned merely because the trier in a case to which the government is a party has moved to that position from a concerned government agency—whether from the Department of Jus-

---

4. The Civil Procedure Code's provision on disqualification, 28 U.S.C. § 455, was amended in 1974 to conform generally with Canon 3 of the ABA's Code of Judicial Conduct, itself freshly adopted in 1972. P.L. 93–512, 88 Stat. 1609; S.Rep. 95–419, 95th Cong. 1st Sess. (1973); The development of the Code of Judicial Conduct by the ABA is discussed in J.P. Frank, Commentary on Disqualification of Judges, Canon 3C, 1972 Utah L.Rev. 377. Informal opinions published by the ABA's Professional Ethics Committee both before and after adoption of the Code suggest that "good taste and a desire to avoid any seeming impropriety"—but no firm requirement—would counsel disqualification of a judge in cases presented by his former private firm only where the case was in the firm, or the party was a private client, during his membership there. Informal Decisions No. 594 (Oct. 22, 1962), 1158 (July 10, 1970), and 1306 (Nov. 19, 1974).

tice to United States District Court, or from the office of the NLRB's General Counsel to a post as NLRB administrative law judge.

(4) While the APA does not repeat the detailed provisions of 28 U.S.C. § 455 respecting disqualification, that section and the ABA Code of Judicial Conduct are certain to be looked to for substantial guidance on what may serve to disqualify.[5] Plainly enough, the right to an *impartial* trier of fact is not to be confused with a claim to one utterly indifferent to or unshaped by events such as may be put before him. All humans have attitudes of mind that, consciously or unconsciously, influence their judgments. The late Jerome Frank declared with characteristic pungency that the world's affairs could not go on at all without preconceptions, predispositions, prejudgments; if a person were "obliged to treat every event as an unprecedented crisis presenting a wholly new problem he would go mad." In re Linahan, 138 F.2d 650, 652 (2d Cir.1943). Neither judges nor administrators approach their tasks with minds untouched by experience, reflection, and myth. Judges are shaped by "the predilections and the prejudices, the complex of instincts and emotions and habits and convictions, which make the man. . . . The great tides and currents which engulf the rest of men do not turn aside in their course, and pass the judges by." B.N. Cardozo, The Nature of the Judicial Process 167–168 (1921). If a bias is to be regarded as so incapacitating as to prevent the tribunal's acting in a specific case, it must be much more focused upon particular parties, much more distorting in its results, much less amenable to modification by fuller information, by reason, or by competing social desiderata than are such generalized attitudes of mind.

Two widely known disqualification controversies may illustrate the point. Before becoming chairman of the FTC, Paul Rand Dixon had been Counsel to a Senate Judiciary Committee subcommittee investigating drug industry pricing policies that included the antibiotic tetracycline. He could not sit on a subsequent FTC proceeding involving tetracycline, the Sixth Circuit ruled. "A 'strong conviction' or a 'crystallized point of view' on questions of law and policy are not grounds for disqualification. . . . [But the records of Mr. Dixon's service with the subcommittee] demonstrate to us that he then had formed the opinion that tetracycline prices quoted by petitioners were artificially high and collusive and that the patent interference settlement between Pfizer and Cyanamid involved improper aid by Cyanamid to Pfizer in obtaining the tetracycline patent. Any opinions so formed were conclusions as to facts, and not merely an 'underlying philosophy' or a 'crystallized point of view on questions of law or policy.' . . . " AMERICAN CYANAMID CO. V. FTC, 363 F.2d 757 (6th Cir.1966). On the other hand, Justice Rehnquist concluded (in a case that later became a focal point of debate over his qualifications to become Chief Justice) that he was not required to recuse himself from Supreme Court hearing of a case by his mention of it (at earlier stages) in testimony before a Senate committee in his former capacity as an Assistant Attorney

---

5. See generally P. Strauss, Disqualification of Decisional Officials in Rulemaking, 80 Colum.L.Rev. 990 (1980).

General of the United States, and his public statement of views on the questions of law involved. The mention of the case, he asserted, was purely formal—although as a committee witness he was required to be informed, he said that he had not participated or advised in the conduct of the case. As for his stated views on the legal issues, he remarked, "Since most Justices come to this bench no earlier than their middle years, it would be unusual if they had not by that time formulated at least some tentative notions which would influence them in their interpretation of the sweeping clauses of the Constitution and their interaction with one another. It would be not merely unusual, but extraordinary, if they had not at least given opinions as to constitutional issues in their previous legal careers. Proof that a Justice's mind at the time he joined the Court was a complete tabula rasa in the area of constitutional adjudication would be evidence of lack of qualification, not lack of bias." LAIRD V. TATUM, 409 U.S. 824 (1972).

Constitutional holdings respecting the necessary demands of the due process clause set the basic requirements. Prior involvement in a non-judicial capacity respecting the particular facts of the controversy may be constitutionally disabling in the welfare context, Goldberg v. Kelly, set out at p. 562 above, or in the setting of American Cyanamid; but it need not be so in other less freighted contexts, such as school discipline. Compare Goss v. Lopez, noted at p. 619 above. Years ago the Supreme Court held, in Tumey v. Ohio, 273 U.S. 510 (1927), that the due process clause forbids a trial before a judge who has a direct, personal, pecuniary interest in the outcome; there, an alleged violator of liquor laws had been fined and committed to jail by a township judge who received his compensation only from the fines paid by persons he had convicted. A financial interest in the outcome of a proceeding produces a distortion of judgment not readily correctable by persuasive evidence in the hearing. The bias—that is, the judge's self-interest—is unrelated to the merits of the issues. It is produced by external circumstances that cannot be modified by the present proceedings.[6]

What has just been said about the distortions of pecuniary involvement applies equally to other distractions from the quest for justice—a relationship to one of the parties, for example, or an individual and

---

6. In its most recent similar pronouncement, the Court required recusal of an Alabama Supreme Court judge who, it was revealed, was engaged in litigation whose outcome would be affected by the case in which his participation was challenged. Aetna Life Ins. Co. v. Lavoie, 106 S.Ct. 1580 (1986). See also Ward v. Monroeville, 409 U.S. 57 (1972) and Gibson v. Berryhill, 411 U.S. 564 (1973), discussed at p. 956 within.

Consider whether directness and magnitude of gain may be significant elements in any such judgment; a district judge was not obliged to recuse himself in litigation involving a local electric utility (also serving all his brethren) by a realization that one outcome might possibly have an impact on his utility bills. The odds were such, the court thought, as to lead "a reasonable man [to] prefer a $2 ticket at Churchill Downs on the first Saturday in May." In re Virginia Electric & Power Co., 539 F.2d 357 (4th Cir.1976). Greater remoteness from judicial function has also been significant. Marshall v. Jerrico, Inc., 446 U.S. 238 (1980) (not objectionable that civil penalty actions brought by enforcement officials, if successful, would enlarge agency budgetary resources). More broadly, see J.P. Frank, Disqualification of Judges, 35 L. & Contemp.Probs. 43 (1970); Comment Meeting the Challenge: Rethinking Judicial Disqualification, 69 Calif.L.Rev. 1445 (1981).

well-focused antagonism, or a corrupt conspiracy to decide one way rather than another. Extraneous circumstances like these create an unseemly atmosphere inconsistent with the values summed up by the phrase "due process." In general, however, these "personal" antagonisms, commitment, or involvements must have arisen *outside* the judicial process. Thus, United States District Judge John Sirica's lengthy involvement in judicial proceedings arising out of the Watergate scandal gave rise to no ground for his disqualification. United States v. Haldeman, 559 F.2d 31, 131–34 (D.C.Cir.1976). Judges regularly sit for a second or third time in cases factually related to others already heard, or which may have been remanded to them after reversal for "further proceedings not inconsistent with this opinion."

c. Intermediate Report by Hearing Officer

To what extent does the magnification of the hearing officer lead to a requirement that he make an initial or recommended decision disclosing his own views concerning the case just heard? In early years, as has been pointed out previously, the hearing officer was often no more than a presiding officer. When a hearing was at an end, so was his responsibility; the record then passed to others for analysis and for the final judgment. Today, both federal and state statutes have created a different level of duty.

The Administrative Procedure Act provides in part, in 5 U.S.C. § 557(b), that after a required trial-type hearing before an examiner he "shall initially decide the case unless the agency requires, either in specific cases or by general rule, the entire record to be certified to it for decision." Even in those cases (with a few exceptions), either the hearing examiner who presided over the hearing or another fully qualified hearing examiner must "first recommend a decision." Omission of an intermediate report of this character was sustained however, in an unusually protracted case that the Federal Communications Commission was pushing vigorously to conclusion. Communications Satellite Corp. v. FCC, 611 F.2d 883 (D.C.Cir.1977).

Some of the various state administrative procedure acts similarly take pains to assure that hearing officers will share in decision-making. The Ohio Administrative Procedure Act, for example, provides that whenever a case has been heard by a referee or examiner, he "shall submit to the agency a written report setting forth his findings of fact and conclusions of law and a recommendation of the action to be taken by the agency. A copy of such written report and recommendation . . . shall within five days of the date of filing thereof, be served upon the party. . . . "[1] The Wisconsin Administrative Procedure Act even more tightly requires that for most important on-the-record hearings, if a "majority of the officials of the agency who are to render the final decision are not present for the hearing, the hearing examiner presiding at the hearing shall prepare a proposed decision, including findings of fact, conclusions of law, order and opinion. . . . The proposed decision shall be a part of the record and shall be served by

---

1. Baldwin's Ohio Rev.Code § 119.09.

the agency on all parties. Each party adversely affected by the proposed decision shall be given an opportunity to file objections to the
proposed decision . . . and to argue with respect to them before the
officials who are to participate in the decision." Moreover, if the
agency's decision runs counter to the hearing officer's recommendations, "the agency's decision shall include an explanation of the basis
for each variance." [2] Sections 4–215 and 4–216 of the Model State
Administrative Procedure Act (1981), set out in Appendix B infra, are
to similar effect.

Does the Constitution require an intermediate report? It would be
generally agreed today that no such requirement exists, although
meeting related constitutional requisites—timely and adequate notice
of the matters in dispute—could be facilitated by having such a report.
NLRB v. MACKAY RADIO & TELEGRAPH CO., 304 U.S. 333 (1938) provides
the footing for this view.

The Mackay case began with a formal complaint by the Board that
the Company had discharged five men because of their union activities.
Later, after the evidence was in, some question existed as to whether
the Company had in fact discharged the five or had merely refused to
re-employ them after a strike. At the conclusion of the testimony, and
prior to oral argument before the trial examiner or the making of an
intermediate report by him, the Board transferred the case to Washington for its own decision. The respondent moved to resubmit the cause
to the trial examiner with directions to prepare and file an intermediate report, as was the usual practice. The Board's denial of that
motion was assailed by the respondent as a fatal unfairness. The
Supreme Court found no merit in this contention: "All parties to the
proceeding knew from the outset that the thing complained of was
discrimination against certain men by reason of their alleged union
activities. . . . A review of the record shows that at no time during
the hearings was there any misunderstanding as to what was the basis
of the Board's complaint. . . . What we have said sufficiently indicates the issues and contentions of the parties were clearly defined and
as no other detriment or disadvantage is claimed to have ensued from
the Board's procedure the matter is not one calling for a reversal of the
order. The Fifth Amendment guarantees no particular form of procedure; it protects substantial rights. . . . The contention that the
respondent was denied a full and adequate hearing must be rejected."

Rather different questions would be raised if, having received a
transcript of proceedings assembled by its examiner, an agency received
her report out of the presence of the parties. Or if rather than receive
an examiner's report, the agency received private communications from
its staff which had conducted the agency's case before the examiner,
suggesting how the record should be analyzed. Or even, it may be
thought, if the agency turned to staff *not* previously in the proceedings
for an analysis of the raw data generated by the hearing. (The same

2. West's Wis.Stat.Ann. 227.09, as
amended in 1977. See also Iowa Code
§§ 17A.15, 17A.16, discussed in A. Bonfield, The Definition of Formal Agency Adjudication under the Iowa Administrative
Procedure Act, 63 Iowa L.Rev. 285, 289
(1977).

questions can also arise when an intermediate report has been filed, but further views of the examiner, participating staff, or uninvolved staff are privately sought). Resolution of these questions requires preliminary analysis of decision "on the record"; of the function *in* a "record" of a hearing officer's report; and of the strains produced at the top of an agency by the conjoint responsibilities to formulate and execute policy, to supervise staff, and to decide impartially cases brought in the adjudicatory mode. These issues are among those dealt with in the sections immediately following.

SECTION 2. AGENCY DECISION IN "ON THE RECORD" PROCEEDINGS

The working assumption of this Section is that a hearing "on the record" has been concluded, and that decision on the issues presented is now to be reached at the highest levels of the agency concerned. At the hearing, it is also assumed, some individuals working for the agency have appeared as witnesses and/or as presenters of one of the points of view presented. In a proceeding to revoke a liquor license, an attorney employed by the Alcoholic Beverage Control Commission has presented the evidence and legal contentions which might support the proposed revocation. In a hearing on proposed rates, the staff of the Public Utility Commission have testified to their analysis of the proposal and the reasons for rejecting contrary views, under the guidance of a Commission attorney who has also engaged opposing witnesses in cross-examination. It is not inevitable that the government's case in on-the-record proceedings thus be presented in the traditional adversary mode; as has already been seen, rights to disability payments under the Social Security laws are determined in on-the-record proceedings in which the ALJ inquires for the government as well as decides the claim made.[1] But it is common to find the government's case presented in an adversary proceeding; the constraints which that model imposes on decision by agency heads are the primary focus of this section. Left for development in later pages are complications arising from the fact that agency heads may have responsibilities other than decision in on-the-record proceedings; or may be subject to a variety of political or other pressures as a result of their position at the apex. For the moment, our concerns may be captured in the following summary question: With whom may agency heads converse, and under what circumstances, in seeking to reduce the unruly mass of evidence and views expressed in the record of a concluded hearing to a reasoned decision?

The preceding section has discussed the trend toward personalizing the decision of the administrative law judge. She has been pushed to higher status. Her "independence" has been rendered more secure. Yet, especially in the more complex and portentous administrative hearings, the ALJ serves only as the eyes and ears of the head of the department or the members of the agency's governing body, who are themselves too busy to preside over hearings, but who (as we shall

1. See Richardson v. Perales, 402 U.S. 389 (1971), p. 809 above.

shortly see) remain fully responsible for the factual as well as the legal aspects of the final decision. Participation by these officers evidently must be less personal. To what extent, then, may such decisions be taken institutionally?

a. Institutional Decisionmaking

Lawyers, with the image of the personally responsible judge before their mind's eye, generally detest the anonymity of the "institutional decision." They believe that it encourages resort to information not embodied in the evidence of record; they fear that staff members with ideological axes to grind may exert an undetectable pressure upon the agency's announced judgment; they think that agency heads who are not themselves immersed in the facts of a case or who have not themselves weighed the arguments are especially easy prey for outside influences of various kinds.

On the other hand, institutional decisions are commonplaces of life outside the courtroom. Executives responsible for any large non-governmental organization, for example, would be surprised to learn that cutting themselves off from staff assistants would somehow make their decisions wiser or fairer. When various insights may enter into an important industrial judgment (such as whether a plant should be closed or whether a new manufacturing process should be initiated or whether funds for expansion should be raised by one device instead of another), business executives expect that economists, lawyers, engineers, public relations specialists, accountants, sales staff, and assorted underlings will cooperate in shaping the decision. The successful executive is usually more concerned about arriving at a sound decision than about his own virtuoso performance, more interested in results than in precedents. What is true of the business bureaucracy is equally true of other major non-governmental undertakings. In few universities, service clubs, trade associations, labor unions, or civic organizations, for example, do the chief officers individually form the conclusions they announce.

It will be instructive to turn first to the first two decisions in Morgan v. United States, a series of decisions the fourth and last of which has already been encountered. P. 455 above. Morgan I, set out immediately below, reviewed a judgment entered on the pleadings; Morgan II, the result of the trial which followed the Supreme Court's reversal of that judgment in Morgan I. Together, the cases set a framework for analyzing high-level consideration of hearing records which remains influential to this day.[1]

---

1. In The Morgan Cases: A Retrospective View, 30 Ad.L.Rev. 237 (1978) Professor Daniel J. Gifford compendiously discusses recent administrative law developments, particularly those concerning informal rulemaking on subjects of technical diversity, from four perspectives suggested by these decisions:

"[First,] these cases were premised upon the application of a judicial model of deci-

sion-making to the Department of Agriculture. They provided the initial stimulus for subsequent reassessments of the extent to which decisional norms drawn from that model are properly applicable to administrative proceedings. . . . Second, the Court's articulation of some of the requirements of a judicial model of decision-making in the Morgan cases have had a major influence upon the development of admin-

MORGAN v. UNITED STATES

Supreme Court of the United States, 1936.
298 U.S. 468.

[Fifty suits, consolidated for the purpose of trial, were brought to restrain the enforcement of an order of the Secretary of Agriculture fixing the maximum rates to be charged by market agencies for buying and selling livestock at the Kansas City Stockyards. In 1930, acting under the authority of the Packers and Stockyards Act, the Secretary ordered an inquiry into the reasonableness of existing rates. The ultimate order fixing the rates was made in June, 1933. The plaintiffs in these suits attacked that order on the merits and also because (so they alleged) they had not been accorded the hearing required by Section 310 of the statute. This provided that the Secretary might fix rates "Whenever after full hearing . . . the Secretary is of the opinion that any rate . . . is or will be unjust, unreasonable or discriminatory. . . . " In substance, the plaintiffs complained that they had not had a "full hearing" because their respective cases had not been heard separately; because the trial examiner had prepared no tentative report, to be subject to oral argument and exceptions; because the Secretary had unlawfully delegated to the Acting Secretary the determination of issues with respect to the reasonableness of the rates involved; and because the Secretary, so they asserted on information and belief, "had not personally heard or read any of the evidence presented at any hearing in connection with this proceeding and had not heard or considered oral arguments relating thereto submitted on behalf of this petitioner and had not read or considered any briefs submitted by petitioner in this proceeding," but had obtained all his information about the proceeding by consulting "with employees in the Department of Agriculture, out of the presence of this petitioner or any representative of this petitioner." The Government successfully moved to strike these allegations, thus denying the plaintiffs any opportunity to require an answer or to prove the facts alleged. On the merits the District Court then sustained the order.

The record disclosed that the testimony in the case had been taken before an examiner; that there had been no formulation of an intermediate report; that oral argument upon the evidence was had before the Acting Secretary of Agriculture; that subsequently a brief was filed on plaintiffs' behalf; and that thereafter the Secretary had signed an order which prescribed rates upon the basis of findings of fact and of

istrative law, especially concerning the degree to which decision makers should be isolated from other constituent functions of the total decisional process, such as investigation, fact-development, or advocacy. Third, and perhaps most important, the Morgan cases highlighted the ubiquitous task presented to regulatory agencies of synthesizing and evaluating large amounts of unstructured input so as to usefully employ it in their decisional processes.

Fourth, the second and fourth Morgan cases placed a veil of secrecy over the 'mental process' of the decision makers. In all of these areas the law has developed significantly, and much of that development has been in different directions from those indicated by the decisions. These decisions remain important, however, because they provided the initial focus upon the significance of the decision-making structure. . . ."

conclusions made, it was said, after "careful consideration of the entire record in this proceeding."]

Mr. Chief Justice Hughes delivered the opinion of the Court. . . .

All questions touching the regularity and validity of the proceeding before the Secretary are open to review. . . . When the Secretary acts within the authority conferred by the statute, his findings of fact are conclusive. . . . But, in determining whether in conducting an administrative proceeding of this sort the Secretary has complied with the statutory prerequisites, the recitals of his procedure cannot be regarded as conclusive. Otherwise the statutory conditions could be set at naught by mere assertion. If upon the facts alleged, the "full hearing" required by the statute was not given, plaintiffs were entitled to prove the facts and have the Secretary's order set aside. Nor is it necessary to go beyond the terms of the statute in order to consider the constitutional requirement of due process as to notice and hearing. For the statute itself demands a full hearing and the order is void if such a hearing was denied. . . .

Second. The outstanding allegation, which the District Court struck out, is that the Secretary made the rate order without having heard or read any of the evidence, and without having heard the oral arguments or having read or considered the briefs which the plaintiffs submitted. That the only information which the Secretary had as to the proceeding was what he derived from consultation with employees of the Department.

The other allegations of the stricken paragraph do not go to the root of the matter. Thus, it cannot be said that the failure to hear the respondents separately was an abuse of discretion. Again, while it would have been good practice to have the examiner prepare a report and submit it to the Secretary and the parties, and to permit exceptions and arguments addressed to the points thus presented—a practice found to be of great value in proceedings before the Interstate Commerce Commission—we cannot say that that particular type of procedure was essential to the validity of the hearing. The statute does not require it and what the statute does require relates to substance and not form.

Nor should the fundamental question be confused with one of mere delegation of authority. . . . If the Secretary had assigned to the [Acting] Secretary the duty of holding the hearing, and the [Acting] Secretary accordingly had received the evidence taken by the examiner, had heard argument thereon and had then found the essential facts and made the order upon his findings, we should have had simply the question of delegation. But while the [Acting] Secretary heard argument he . . . assumed no responsibility for the findings or order, and the Secretary, who had not heard, did assume that responsibility.

We may likewise put aside the contention as to the circumstances in which an Acting Secretary may take the place of his chief. . . . The Acting Secretary did not assume to make the order.

Third. What is the essential quality of the proceeding under review, and what is the nature of the hearing which the statute prescribes?

The proceeding is not one of ordinary administration, conformable to the standards governing duties of a purely executive character. It is a proceeding looking to legislative action in the fixing of rates of market agencies. And, while the order is legislative and gives to the proceeding its distinctive character (Louisville & Nashville R. Co. v. Garrett, 231 U.S. 298, 307), it is a proceeding which by virtue of the authority conferred has special attributes. The Secretary, as the agent of Congress in making the rates, must make them in accordance with the standards and under the limitations which Congress has prescribed. Congress has required the Secretary to determine, as a condition of his action, that the existing rates are or will be "unjust, unreasonable, or discriminatory." If and when he so finds, he may "determine and prescribe" what shall be the just and reasonable rate, or the maximum or minimum rate, thereafter to be charged. That duty is widely different from ordinary executive action. It is a duty which carries with it fundamental procedural requirements. There must be a full hearing. There must be evidence adequate to support pertinent and necessary findings of fact. Nothing can be treated as evidence which is not introduced as such. United States v. Abilene & Southern Ry. Co. [265 U.S. 274]. Facts and circumstances which ought to be considered must not be excluded. Facts and circumstances must not be considered which should not legally influence the conclusion. Findings based on the evidence must embrace the basic facts which are needed to sustain the order. . . .

A proceeding of this sort requiring the taking and weighing of evidence, determinations of fact based upon the consideration of the evidence, and the making of an order supported by such findings, has a quality resembling that of a judicial proceeding. Hence it is frequently described as a proceeding of a quasi-judicial character. The requirement of a "full hearing" has obvious reference to the tradition of judicial proceedings in which evidence is received and weighed by the trier of the facts. The "hearing" is designed to afford the safeguard that the one who decides shall be bound in good conscience to consider the evidence, to be guided by that alone, and to reach his conclusion uninfluenced by extraneous considerations which in other fields might have play in determining purely executive action. The "hearing" is the hearing of evidence and argument. If the one who determines the facts which underlie the order has not considered evidence or argument, it is manifest that the hearing has not been given.

There is thus no basis for the contention that the authority conferred by Section 310 of the Packers and Stockyards Act is given to the Department of Agriculture, as a department in the administrative sense, so that one official may examine evidence, and another official who has not considered the evidence may make the findings and order. In such a view, it would be possible, for example, for one official to hear the evidence and argument and arrive at certain conclusions of fact, and another official who had not heard or considered either evidence or argument to overrule those conclusions and for reasons of policy to announce entirely different ones. It is no answer to say that the question for the court is whether the evidence supports the findings and the findings support the order. For the weight ascribed by the law to the findings—their conclusiveness when made within the sphere of the authority conferred—rests upon the assumption that the officer who makes the findings has addressed himself to the evidence and upon that evidence has conscientiously reached the conclusions which he deems it to justify. That duty cannot be performed by one who has not considered evidence or argument. It is not an impersonal obligation. It is a duty akin to that of a judge. The one who decides must hear.

This necessary rule does not preclude practicable administrative procedure in obtaining the aid of assistants in the department. Assistants may prosecute inquiries. Evidence may be taken by an examiner. Evidence thus taken may be sifted and analyzed by competent subordinates. Argument may be oral or written. The requirements are not technical. But there must be a hearing in a substantial sense. And to give the substance of a hearing, which is for the purpose of making determinations upon evidence, the officer who makes the determinations must consider and appraise the evidence which justifies them. That duty undoubtedly may be an onerous one, but the performance of it in a substantial manner is inseparable from the exercise of the important authority conferred. . . .

Our conclusion is that the District Court erred in striking out the allegations of Paragraph IV of the bill of complaint with respect to the Secretary's action. The defendants should be required to answer these allegations and the question whether plaintiffs had a proper hearing should be determined.

The decree is reversed and the cause is remanded for further proceedings in conformity with this opinion.

MORGAN v. UNITED STATES
Supreme Court of the United States, 1938.
304 U.S. 1.

[The trial held on remand permitted the Court to assess the procedures that had actually been followed by the Secretary:]

MR. CHIEF JUSTICE HUGHES delivered the opinion for the Court:

. . . The original administrative proceeding was begun on April 7, 1930, when the Secretary of Agriculture issued an order of inquiry and notice of hearing with respect to the reasonableness of the charges of appellants for stockyards services at Kansas City. The taking of evidence before an examiner of the Department was begun on December 3, 1930, and continued until February 10, 1931. The Government and appellants were represented by counsel and voluminous testimony and exhibits were introduced. In March, 1931, oral argument was had before the Acting Secretary of Agriculture and appellants submitted a brief. On May 18, 1932, the Secretary issued his findings and an order prescribing maximum rates. In view of changed economic conditions, the Secretary vacated that order and granted a rehearing. That was begun on October 6, 1932, and the taking of evidence was concluded on November 16, 1932. The evidence received at the first hearing was resubmitted and this was supplemented by additional testimony and exhibits. On March 24, 1933, oral argument was had before Rexford G. Tugwell as Acting Secretary.

It appears that there were about 10,000 pages of transcript of oral evidence and over 1,000 pages of statistical exhibits. The oral argument was general and sketchy. Appellants submitted the brief which they had presented after the first administrative hearing and a supplemental brief dealing with the evidence introduced upon the rehearing. No brief was at any time supplied by the Government. Apart from what was said on its behalf in the oral argument, the Government formulated no issues and furnished appellants no statement or summary of its contentions and no proposed findings. Appellants' request that the examiner prepare a tentative report, to be submitted as a basis for exceptions and argument, was refused.

Findings were prepared in the Bureau of Animal Industry, Department of Agriculture, whose representatives had conducted the proceedings for the Government, and were submitted to the Secretary, who signed them, with a few changes in the rates, when his order was made on June 14, 1933. These findings, 180 in number, were elaborate. . . . No opportunity was afforded to appellants for the examination of the findings thus prepared in the Bureau of Animal Industry until they were served with the order. Appellants sought a rehearing by the Secretary but their application was denied on July 6, 1933, and these suits followed.

The part taken by the Secretary himself in the departmental proceedings is shown by his full and candid testimony. The evidence had been received before he took office. He did not hear the oral argument. The bulky record was placed upon his desk and he dipped into it from time to time to get its drift. He decided that probably the essence of the evidence was contained in appellants' briefs. These, together with the transcript of the oral argument, he took home with him and read. He had several conferences with the Solicitor of the Department and with the officials in the Bureau of Animal Industry and discussed the proposed findings. He testified that he considered the evidence before signing the order. The substance of his action is stated in his answer to the question whether the order represented his independent conclusion, as follows:

> My answer to the question would be that that very definitely was my independent conclusion as based on the findings of the men in the Bureau of Animal Industry. I would say, I will try to put it as accurately as possible, that it represented my own independent reactions to the findings of the men in the Bureau of Animal Industry.

Save for certain rate alterations, he "accepted the findings."

In the light of this testimony there is no occasion to discuss the extent to which the Secretary examined the evidence, and we agree with the Government's contention that it was not the function of the court to probe the mental processes of the Secretary in reaching his conclusions if he gave the hearing which the law required. The Secretary read the summary presented by appellants' briefs and he conferred with his subordinates who had sifted and analyzed the evidence. We assume that the Secretary sufficiently understood its purport. But a "full hearing"—a fair and open hearing—requires more than that. The right to a hearing embraces not only the right to present evidence but also a reasonable opportunity to know the claims of the opposing party and to meet them. The right to submit argument implies that opportunity; otherwise the right may be but a barren one. Those who are brought into contest with the Government in a quasi-judicial proceeding aimed at the control of their activities are entitled to be fairly advised of what the Government proposes and to be heard upon its proposals before it issues its final command.

No such reasonable opportunity was accorded appellants. The administrative proceeding was initiated by a notice of inquiry into the reasonableness of appellants' rates. No specific complaint was formulated. . . . In the absence of any report by the examiner or any findings proposed by the Government, and thus without any concrete statement of the Government's claims, the parties approached the oral argument.

Nor did the oral argument reveal these claims in any appropriate manner. The discussion by counsel for the Government was "very general," as he said, in order not to take up "too much time." It dealt with generalities both as to principles and procedure. . . .

Congress, in requiring a "full hearing," had regard to judicial standards—not in any technical sense but with respect to those fundamental requirements of fairness which are of the essence of due process in a proceeding of a judicial nature. If in an equity cause, a special master or the trial judge permitted the plaintiff's attorney to formulate the findings upon the evidence, conferred ex parte with the plaintiff's attorney regarding them, and then adopted his proposals without affording an opportunity to his opponent to know their contents and present objections, there would be no hesitation in setting aside the report or decree as having been made without a fair hearing. The requirements of fairness are not exhausted in the taking or consideration of evidence but extend to the concluding parts of the procedure as well as to the beginning and intermediate steps.

The answer that the proceeding before the Secretary was not of an adversary character, as it was not upon complaint but was initiated as a general inquiry, is futile. . . . In all substantial respects, the Government acting through the Bureau of Animal Industry of the Department was prosecuting the proceeding against the owners of the market agencies. The proceeding had all the essential elements of contested litigation, with the Government and its counsel on the one side and the appellants and their counsel on the other. It is idle to say that this was not a proceeding in reality against the appellants when the very existence of their agencies was put in jeopardy. Upon the rates for their services the owners depended for their livelihood, and the proceeding attacked them at a vital spot. . . .

The Government adverts to an observation in our former opinion that, while it was good practice—which we approved—to have the examiner, receiving the evidence in such a case, prepare a report as a basis for exceptions and argument, we could not say that that particular type of procedure was essential to the validity of the proceeding. That is true, for, as we said, what the statute requires "relates to substance and not form." . . . But what would not be essential to the adequacy of the hearing if the Secretary himself makes the findings is not a criterion for a case in which the Secretary accepts and makes as his own the findings which have been prepared by the active prosecutors for the Government, after an ex parte discussion with them and without according any reasonable opportunity to the respondents in the proceeding to know the claims thus presented and to contest them. That is more than an irregularity in practice; it is a vital defect.

The maintenance of proper standards on the part of administrative agencies in the performance of their quasi-judicial functions is of the highest importance and in no way cripples or embarrasses the exercise of their appropriate authority. On the contrary, it is in their manifest interest. For, as we said at the outset, if these multiplying agencies deemed to be necessary in our complex society are to serve the purposes for which they are created and endowed with vast powers, they must accredit themselves by acting in accordance with the cherished judicial tradition embodying the basic concepts of fair play.

As the hearing was fatally defective, the order of the Secretary was invalid. In this view, we express no opinion upon the merits. The decree of the District Court is

Reversed.

Mr. Justice Black dissents.

Mr. Justice Cardozo and Mr. Justice Reed took no part in the consideration and decision of this case.[1]

NOTES

(1) *Delegation of decisional responsibility.* A.H. Feller, Prospectus for the Further Study of Federal Administrative Law, 47 Yale L.J. 647, 662–663 (1938): "[Morgan I] seems so eminently reasonable on its face that some explanation is needed before its revolutionary character can be appreciated. The Secretary of Agriculture administers forty-two regulatory statutes. In addition, he administers a host of non-regulatory statutes, some of them, like the Soil Conservation and Domestic Allotment Act, of high national importance. Finally, he is a major political officer and takes part in the formulation of national policy as a member of the Cabinet. If he were to give to every order which he signs the consideration which the Morgan case requires, he would

1. A petition for rehearing, filed on May 20, 1938, was denied on May 31, 1938.

probably have to devote all his time to the conduct of matters which must be considered petty from a national viewpoint.[1]

"What is to be done about this situation? Should the function of making orders be delegated to subordinate officials? There is considerable psychological value in having the signature of the Secretary himself on the order. It would carry less weight if signed by an unknown subordinate. There is also the danger of a relaxation of responsibility in case of a complete delegation. Even if the Secretary does not give full consideration to the evidence, he at least brings his attention to bear upon the problem and does review the order, however sketchily, before signing it. . . . "

Complete delegation of decisional power is exactly what did occur in the Agriculture Department as the end result of Morgan I. Exercising power conferred on him to organize the department and to prescribe the duties of its officials, the Secretary of Agriculture in 1945 sloughed off even his nominal responsibility for decisions to be made on the record after a trial-type hearing. He vested final authority in such matters in the "Judicial Officer" of the Department of Agriculture, who issues final departmental decisions in his own name.

A survey done for the Administrative Conference of the United States in 1983 by Professor Ronald A. Cass of Boston University revealed a variety of current institutional arrangements—many the creature of statute but others formed administratively by delegation. At the Departments of Housing and Urban Development, Interior, Health and Human Resources, and Labor, review boards have been given final authority to act for the agency, replacing review by the agency head; in the case of occupational safety and health regulation, review authority is placed in a separate independent regulatory commission, the Occupational Safety and Health Review Commission. Some independent commissions—the Nuclear Regulatory Commission, Interstate Commerce Commission and Federal Communications Commission—supply intermediate review boards and make Commission review following their judgment a matter of discretion only. Even without such a board, review of ALJ judgments is often made a matter of agency discretion rather than participant right. In one way or another, and unsurprisingly, those agencies with the heaviest caseloads are the most likely to make access to the very top of the agency discretionary.[2]

1. [Ed.] For a more contemporary account to the same effect, see N. Johnson and J. Dystel, A Day in the Life: The Federal Communications Commission, 82 Yale L.J. 1575 (1973). Commissioner Johnson, then completing a seven year term as an FCC Commissioner, describes a single day's agenda of fifty-nine items presented to the Commission for action; twenty-four could be adopted without discussion, seven were passed over, and the remaining twenty-eight, covering "an incredibly broad range of communications matters," were discussed. Commissioner Johnson's solution to the difficulties thus created for

sound decision bears a notable resemblance to Congress': he believed the Commission should formulate national communications policy, and then delegate to its staff the work of policy application.

2. R. Cass, Agency Review of Administrative Law Judges' Decisions 46–48 (1983); see also J. Freedman, Review Boards in the Administrative Process, 117 U.Pa.L.Rev. 546 (1969); W. Gilliland, The Certiorari-Type Review, 26 Ad.L.Rev. 53 (1974); GAO, Administrative Law Process: Better Management is Needed (FPCD 78–79, May 15, 1978).

(2) *Delegated authority and policy control.* A 1978 GAO survey of the administrative law process concluded that "Agencies review ALJs' decisions primarily because (1) they want to maintain decision and policymaking authority and (2) in some instances, because agencies have little assurance that some ALJs' decisions are reasonable and in accordance with agency policy." The tension between seeking policy compliance while respecting fact-finding independence is familiar from the preceding section; it could be thought both more difficult and more important at the level of a review tribunal, where formulation of policy becomes more central to the body's tasks. How to secure employees' appropriate behavior is a general problem for large organizations, Professor Cass notes, even without the complications introduced by tenure protections, constraints on communication, and other familiar accoutrements of a judicialized process. "[T]here is . . . no guarantee . . . that decisions by subordinates who are in theory fully subject to the agency head's control will conform to a single policy view. . . . So long as all decisions cannot be made by a single individual, disparate perceptions of what agency policy is and should be—as well as divergent interpretations and assumptions on a host of subsidiary matters that inform policy—promote differences among the decisions. . . .

"Finding people whose views closely match yours is not easy, nor is it simple to give people incentives correctly to identify and fully to implement your views, in part simply because of difficulties ex ante in articulating (indeed, arriving at) your views on every relevant subject. . . . [A]bsent some form of review it is difficult to reward conforming behavior or punish behavior that departs from your wishes, the stuff incentives are made of. . . . Obviously, however, review is apt to be its most effective when attached to the full complement of job controls."

If it is true, as Professor Cass' study suggests, that review board officials are even more likely than ALJs to be selected from long-time agency employees, does recognition of the need for policy congruence justify such in-breeding? Does it warrant the D.C. Circuit's conclusion in Kalaris v. Donovan, 697 F.2d 376, 397 (D.C.Cir.1983), cert. denied 462 U.S. 1119 (1983) that "in the absence of a congressional statement to the contrary, inferior officers such as [the members of the Department of Labor's Benefits Review Board] serve indefinite terms at the discretion of their appointing officers"—so that they may be summarily removed from their posts?[3] Does it sufficiently explain the First Circuit's decision to prefer OSHA's administrative interpretation of the Occupational Safety and Health Act over the conflicting interpretation made by OSHRC in a judgment OSHA was challenging on review? The court said that the OSHA interpretation was entitled to deference if reasonable, as the interpretation made by the body primarily responsible for administration of the Act?[4]

---

3. The court went on to find the arrangement "clearly constitutional" despite the spectre that the dismissal power would permit the Secretary to influence claims decisions outside the review process by replacing the Board. "Congress has been creating quasi-judicial boards subject to Executive control for years, and the courts have not previously prevented them from doing so." At 401.

4. Donovan v. A. Amorello & Sons, Inc., 761 F.2d 61 (1st Cir.1985).

Photo by Robert Phillips—Courtesy of FORTUNE Magazine

"This paper mountain is only part of the testimony and documents pertaining to a single FPC gas case. The hearings to determine which new pipe line should be certified to serve midwestern markets ran for 143 days. Every one had his say *in extenso* and no doubt FPC hearing examiners like Edward B. Marsh, above, read each of the thousands of transcript pages. To the commissioners, however, they are mainly a monument to free speech. Said one: 'The industry spends so much time developing the records, they run from 10,000 to 20,000 pages, but we just haven't the time to read them'", R. A. Smith, The Unnatural Problems of Natural Gas, 60 FORTUNE 120 (Sept. 1959).

What are or ought to be the implications for the Secretary of having given up a "final say" in policy matters in this way? Enhanced use of rulemaking (which binds the adjudicators) is certainly one possibility; but recall from Chapter 3, Section 2, and our discussion of the Chenery litigation that in certain situations adjudication may be an essential or at least preferable technique for policy formulation. If the Secretary has given up participation in that process at the administrative level, does his responsibility for implementation of the statute suggest that he ought to be able to seek judicial review of decisions of his Judicial Officer of which he disapproves? Or ignore them in other, like cases subject to his administration? The Secretary of Labor has been permitted to appeal decisions of Benefits Review Boards within his Department,[5] the Secretary of Health, Education & Welfare has been rather emphatically told that, absent new rulemaking, he *must* conform his instructions to Departmental staff administering welfare programs to rulings made by the Appeals Council to which he has delegated some of *his* decisional authority.[6] Do these outcomes answer the concerns Chenery suggests? See P.L. Strauss, Rules, Adjudications, and Other Sources of Law in an Executive Department, 74 Colum.L.Rev. 1231, 1254–75 (1974).

b. The Role of Agency Staff in the Decisional Process

(1) The materials of Chapter 3, Section 3 treating substantial evidence review—notably Universal Camera Corp. v. NLRB, p. 357 above, and Penasquitos Village, Inc. v. NLRB, p. 370 above, illustrate the role that an administrative law judge's *report* plays in agency process. The weight assigned it on judicial review, of what are understood to be the *agency's* findings of fact, permit us now to see that report as one of the important instruments by which "separation of functions" objectivity is enforced in the agency setting. The agency (which almost inevitably transcends those separations) must pay a "substantial evidence" price for any disagreement it may have with its hearing officer (who does not transcend those separations) as to the facts of the matter before it.

Can the agency properly make use of the hearing officer herself to help it understand the proceedings it has under review? Suppose a proceeding with a record like that shown on the facing page—one with which the ALJ is far more familiar than the agency head can ever hope to become. Do you agree, in that context, with the following observation of H.L. Russell, a prominent Atlanta practitioner of administrative law? "The role of the hearing examiner generally ends with the issuance of his recommended or initial decision. However, I have never been convinced that, at that point, his unsurpassed knowledge of the pleadings and evidence should be thrown down the drain and that the agency members themselves should be denied the further advice of the best informed impartial person having comprehensive knowledge of the

5. Director, Office of Workers' Compensation Programs v. Eastern Coal Corp., 561 F.2d 632 (6th Cir.1977).

6. Jones v. Califano, 576 F.2d 12 (2d Cir.1978).

situation. That seems to be a waste of man hours which must cost millions of dollars in delay." The Role of the Hearing Examiner in Agency Proceedings, 12 Admin.L.Bull. 23 (1959).

(2) MAZZA V. CAVICCHIA, 15 N.J. 498, 105 A.2D 545 (1954), raises a like question in a state law context. In that case, a liquor license had been suspended after a hearing concerning the licensee's alleged improprieties. At the close of the hearing the officer who had presided as the delegate of Director Cavicchia of the Division of Alcoholic Beverage Control sent the record to the Director, along with his own findings and conclusions concerning what he had heard. Though Mazza, the licensee, had a copy of the transcript of what had occurred at the hearing, he was not given a copy of the hearer's report to the Director. He appealed from the final order of license suspension, saying that he had been denied due process as required by the state constitution.

The Director maintained that he himself had "examined and reexamined the entire record" and had decided the case "upon the basis of his own independent findings," without reliance on his subordinate's remarks. The court brushed aside this assurance, noting that the procedure in Mazza's case had been the standard practice for more than twenty years; the court deduced that the Division would not have continuously required hearing officers to file reports if the reports were then to be ignored by the ultimate decision maker.

In the court's view, the hearer's suggested findings became a part of the material upon which the Director based his conclusions. Since, however, the hearer's report had not been disclosed to Mazza by being made a part of the record, the Director should not have had access to it. "In any proceeding that is judicial in nature, whether in a court or in an administrative agency, the process of decision must be governed by the basic principle of the exclusiveness of the record," Chief Justice Vanderbilt wrote. " 'Where a hearing is prescribed by statute, nothing must be taken into account by the administrative tribunal in arriving at its determination that has not been introduced in some manner into the record of the hearing.' Benjamin, Administrative Adjudication in New York, 207 (1942). Unless this principle is observed, the right to a hearing itself becomes meaningless. Of what real worth is the right to present evidence and to argue its significance at a formal hearing, if the one who decides the case may stray at will from the record in reaching his decision? Or consult another's findings of fact, or conclusions of law, or recommendations, or even hold conferences with him? . . .

". . . The hearer's report obviously played a part in the decision in this case. For it to have played such a part without having been shown to the appellant clearly violates his right to have the decision based exclusively upon matters in the record, which are known to him and can consequently be controverted by him. The individual litigant is entitled to be apprised of the materials upon which the agency is acting. He has a right not only to refute but, what in a case like this is usually more important, to supplement, explain, and give different perspective to the hearer's view of the case. . . .

"The hearer may have drawn some erroneous conclusion in his report, or he may even have made some factual blunders. . . . But if a party has no knowledge of the secret report or access to it, how is he to protect himself? An unjust decision may very likely be the result where no opportunity is given to those affected to call attention to such mistakes. That is why it is a fundamental principle of all adjudication, judicial and administrative alike, that the mind of the decider should not be swayed by materials which are not communicated to both parties and which they are not given an opportunity to controvert. In the instant case the hearer can be characterized as a 'witness' giving his evidence to the judge behind the back of the appellant, who has no way of knowing what has been reported to the judge. . . . "

Acknowledging that cases like Mackay Radio, discussed at p. 880 above, had held that a hearing officer's report was not a constitutional requisite, the New Jersey court insisted that if one were nevertheless prepared for use by the agency head, it must be made available to all concerned so that they may have a meaningful opportunity to correct the hearing officer's mistaken impressions. This, the court said, was an "elemental due process requirement," at least in New Jersey.[1]

To Justices Jacobs and Burling, two of New Jersey's more distinguished jurists, the Director's procedure "did not materially differ from that followed by appellate judges whose law clerks prepare preliminary memoranda often embodying analyses of the testimony and their views. . . . Although the majority have dealt at length with them, we are in nowise concerned here with instances in which administrative officials have gone beyond the evidence in the strict record for their decisions. . . . We are concerned here only with an instance in which the administrative official, after exhaustive examination thereof, has determined the matter on the evidence in the strict record properly before him and now presented to us for judicial review; in this situation the pertinent authorities clearly recognize that the presence of a subordinate's factual analysis and recommendation does not impair the constitutional validity of the proceedings and determination."

(3) The Mazza dissenters' comment raises the question whether the commands of justice dictate a complete suppression of informal communication between the hearing officer and the ultimate decider. Chief Justice Vanderbilt thought that if the agency head consulted with the hearing officer, he would be hearing a "witness" secretly. The dissenters thought, on the contrary, that he would simply be using an aide, as a judge uses his law clerk. Which do you find the more accurate characterization, and why?

(4) Do you have a different reaction if the Administrator wishes to confer with members of his staff—persons unconnected with the prior stages of the litigation either as decisionmakers or as participants? Here recall Seacoast Anti-Pollution League v. Costle, set out at page 834 above. In relying on a technical panel of agency experts not previously connected with the litigation, Administrator Costle was

---

1. The majority opinion in Mazza v. Cavicchia is critically discussed in 3 Davis, Administrative Law Treatise 304–306 (2d ed. 1980).

doubtless more remarkable for his frankness than for the practice itself—as readings already encountered must have suggested. Here the dissent in Mazza, echoing remarks in Morgan I, is fully persuasive. It bears remembering that an administrator's budget may not always be so richly endowed as to permit assembly of a second staff of experts, separate from those who may have testified or assisted in preparing the agency's staff for hearing. Administrator Costle's own opinion in the case included the following thought-provoking commentary:

"[T]he [Regional Administrator] apparently felt constrained to avoid discussion of the merits of the case with his technical staff after the hearing because they were 'parties' to the case and could not be consulted in the absence of the other parties. Consequently the RA was deprived of the opportunity to consult with experts experienced in the matter of thermal discharges, and reviewed the record with only the assistance of his legal staff and a biologist hired for the purpose. This unfortunate result appears to have occurred partly because the Agency took a position in favor of its determinations (i.e., in support of PSCo) at the hearings, thus becoming 'party' as well as judge. This seems to me to have been unnecessary and of dubious propriety.

"I am requesting my staff to review this aspect of the case with a view toward assuring that in future . . . cases RAs will have available to them adequate Agency resources to assist in the review of the record. In connection with the review of the regulations mentioned above, I am asking the Office of General Counsel to review the question of whether the Agency should act as a 'party' in 316(a) proceedings."

Of course, you may say, the problem in that case *seemed* to be the introduction of extra-record "evidence," not the use of a panel as such. The First Circuit simply may not have been sufficiently astute to distinguish permissible use of agency expertise from "adding to the record." Now suppose, however, that in fact the agency only has one relevant expert in-house—the one who testified on the agency's behalf during the course of the hearings below—and the question is whether the agency head may consult with *that* person in getting to understand the record so that she can formulate her opinion. That, it may appear, brings us back to Morgan.

(5) DANIEL J. GIFFORD, THE MORGAN CASES: A RETROSPECTIVE VIEW,* 30 Ad.L.Rev. 237, 256–57, 259 (1978): "That approximately 11,000 pages of transcript and exhibits had to be evaluated suggests that the major decisional problem in the Morgan cases was one of synthesizing vast amounts of material into an understandable form. But the Court never really addressed itself to the process of synthesis and evaluation, except negatively. It objected to the synthesizing function being performed off-the-record by officials from the Bureau of Animal Industry, but it did not suggest how that function ought to be performed. The Court said that the Secretary could use assistants to 'sift' and 'analyze' evidence, but that his decision nonetheless must be a 'personal' one based upon his own weighing of the evidence. It is unclear how the

* The excerpts from Prof. Gifford's article, here and elsewhere in this chapter, are reprinted with permission of the author and publisher.

assistants may both sift and analyze on one hand, while the Secretary, on the other hand, makes a personal decision by weighing the evidence himself. The Court might have been thinking of the personal responsibility of a judge, who nevertheless receives assistance from his law clerk. Extrapolated to the functioning of a large agency, the Secretary might be said to decide 'personally' when he closely supervises his assistants and discusses their conclusions with them. Yet the line between the close supervision of assistants and a 'departmental' decision-making process which the Court condemned as impersonal is not easily drawn.

"But there is more at stake than just the condensing of data. In a rate proceeding like that involved in the Morgan cases, there is likely to be little dispute as to what physical events did or did not transpire. Rather, it is the significance of those events which tends to be disputed, and it is the methods employed to evaluate the events which are crucial to the decision. While in a typical negligence trial the issues may be simple and the processes of evaluating the evidence require only the application of ordinary experience, in technical litigation the function of synthesizing the vast quantity of data into an understandable form and the process of evaluating it require both substantial time and special skills. Yet, the busy head of a large agency cannot normally devote a large amount of time to a single case, and he may not possess the necessary skills. Thus, it is both the mass of data and the complexities of the evaluation process which magnify the decision-making burden.

" .   .   .

"When the drafters of the APA incorporated the mechanism of a preliminary decision issued prior to final argument before the agency, they had been educated by the first two Morgan decisions and the Ohio Bell decision. Those decisions dramatized the decisional problems faced by a large, centralized agency in evaluating masses of data and complex exhibits. The drafters recognized that a means needed to be found for focusing the issues which did not command a large amount of the decision maker's time. They opted for a means involving a preliminary decision plus argument. As they saw it, that mechanism not only reduced the need for behind-the-scenes participation in the decisional process by the agency's employees (who have played an adversarial role in the formal proceedings), but it also permitted the parties to participate to a greater degree in the process of evaluating the evidence."

(6) As Morgan is easily read to do, judicial opinions have often given emphatic voice to the perception that the decision-maker in an on-the-record proceeding should not hold off-the-record discussions with those elements of her staff that have assisted in presenting the agency's "case." In some circumstances, as already seen, "variable due process" has been said to exclude such approaches.[2] Yet the APA incorporates three broad exceptions to the principle: § 554(d) does not apply (1) to the "agency or a member or members of the body comprising the

---

2. See, e.g., Goldberg v. Kelly, 397 U.S. 254, 271 (1970) (welfare social worker); Morrissey v. Brewer, 408 U.S. 471, 485–486 (1972) (parole revocation).

agency," (2) "in determining applications for initial licenses," or (3) to rate-making proceedings. For agency personnel, these exceptions apparently survived the addition of § 557(d) in 1976, which explicitly prohibits only those interested persons "outside the agency" from ex parte communications in all on-the-record proceedings, whatever their character [3]—and this despite long-standing and "non-controversial" recommendations by the ABA and the Administrative Conference for their elimination.[4] Does the following case suggest sufficient justifications?

AMERICAN TELEPHONE & TELEGRAPH CO.
Federal Communications Commission, 1976.
60 FCC 1.

[The FCC had for a long time been considering revision of AT & T's rates for certain commercial services—for so long, indeed, that it had now come under judicial order to resolve the issues presented within the next few months. Nader v. FCC, 520 F.2d 182, 205 (D.C.Cir.1975). Hearings before an ALJ were complete; the Chief of its Common Carrier Bureau, acting as a "responsible employee," 5 U.S.C. § 557(b) (1), had filed a recommended decision with the Commission. The Common Carrier Bureau had represented the FCC as one party before the ALJ, and AT & T and other parties now sought an order from the Commission prohibiting members of the Bureau from further participation in the decision.]

By the COMMISSION:

2. . . . Pointing out that the Bureau staff adduced evidence through its own witnesses, cross-examined witnesses, and took positions on the highly controverted issues in the case, Bell argues that a fair and objective treatment of the evidence by the Bureau staff is precluded. As a result, Bell asserts, the Recommended Decision represents almost exclusively positions heretofore taken by the Bureau, crucial parts of the evidentiary record are disregarded, misstated or mischaracterized, and numerous statements are unsupported by the evidence. To permit the Bureau to advise the Commission ex parte as to the merits of the exceptions and briefs of the parties and to participate

3. Section 557(d) prohibits outsiders to make "an ex parte communication relevant to the merits of the proceeding" to any person "who is or may reasonably be expected to be involved in the decisional process." If licensing or ratemaking staff "may reasonably be expected to be involved," then, outsiders would be prohibited in engaging in informal discussions with that staff (as they are unquestionably prohibited from engaging in such discussions with an ALJ or Commissioner); in this way, § 557(d) might be taken as limiting if not eliminating the force of the § 554 exemptions. H. Shulman, Separation of Functions in Formal Licensing Adjudications, 56 Notre Dame Law. 351, 377–380 (1981). A contrasting view, supported in the legislative history, is that § 557(d) would apply only to prevent staff serving

as a conduit for outsider views, and that the possibilities of consultation within the agency are not meant to be addressed in § 557(d). M. Asimow, When the Curtain Falls: Separation of Functions in the Federal Administrative Agencies, 81 Colum.L. Rev. 762 n. 17 (1981).

4. See, e.g., W. Ross, ABA Legislative Proposals to Improve Administrative Procedures in Federal Departments & Agencies, 27 Ad.L.Rev. 395 (1975); K. Davis, Revising the Administrative Procedure Act, 29 Ad.L.Rev. 35, 42–43 (1977). That the recommendation was more controversial than appeared was suggested by the failure of the Administrative Conference in 1980 to adopt recommendations based on an extensive empirical survey, M. Asimow, n. 3 above.

in the drafting of the Final Decision would, Bell urges, in effect permit the Bureau to review and evaluate the criticisms of its own decision; and that the procedure authorized herein is inconsistent with the principles of fairness and due process. Only by precluding the Bureau from further participation in the decision-making process, Bell maintains, can a fair and objective review of the Recommended Decision be obtained.

. . .

4. The Commission and the courts have consistently held that a tariff proceeding, such as the one under consideration, is rulemaking and separation of the Bureau from the decision-making process is not required by the Communications Act, the Administrative Procedure Act, or the due process clause of the Constitution.[1] American Telephone and Telegraph Co. v. FCC, 449 F.2d 439 (2d Cir.1971). While the court in American Telephone and Telegraph did indicate that the participation of a staff member of the Bureau in the preparation of a recommended decision was, as Bell asserts, "ill-advised," the fact remains that the court sustained the lawfulness of the Commission's procedure. The court therein expressly held that "despite our belief as to what might be desirable in such cases, we cannot see how, under present law, the commingling of functions practiced here is proscribed either by Section 409(c) of the Communications Act or by the due process clause of the Constitution" (449 F.2d at 454).

5. The Commission recently amended its rules to provide for a separated trial staff in restricted rulemaking proceedings involving common carrier matters.[2] However, it was specifically provided therein that the Commission would not "order separation of functions retroactively in proceedings wherein we had assigned the trial staff a decisional role, owing to the disruption this would entail." . . .

6. . . . In their exceptions to the Recommended Decision and in their briefs in support thereof the parties undoubtedly will advance all of their objections to the recommended findings and conclusions and will provide in detail the evidence of record and the arguments and contentions which, in their view, require contrary findings and conclusions. All such evidence, arguments and contentions will be given careful and thorough consideration. While we shall, of course, give like consideration to the views of the Common Carrier Bureau, the fact remains that the responsibility for making the final decision is ours and

---

1. [Ed.] A similar conclusion respecting the licensing exception to 5 U.S.C. § 554(d) is reached in Marathon Oil Co. v. Environmental Protection Agency, 564 F.2d 1253 (9th Cir.1977).

2. [Ed.] See Delay in the Regulatory Process, IV Study on Federal Regulation prepared pursuant to S.Res. 71, Senate Committee on Governmental Affairs, 95th Cong., 1st Sess. 24 (Comm.Point 1977):

". . . Since the passage of the APA, . . . the distinction it makes between adjudicatory proceedings which are accusatory (in which separation of functions is required) and those which are not accusatory (in which separation of functions is not required), has largely been eroded. Instead, almost all agencies have voluntarily adopted approximately the same separation of functions rules that apply to other forms of adjudication for use in ratemaking and initial licensing as well. Similarly, agencies, for the most part, provide for decisions to be written by presiding ALJ's even where that is not legally required."

we shall discharge that responsibility in a fair and impartial manner upon the basis of what we determine will best serve the public interest after weighing and analyzing the evidence and the contentions of all parties. Moreover, as we stated in answer to a previous request by Bell in this proceeding for a separation of functions (A.T.&T., et al., 32 FCC2d at 90): "The final decision in 18128 will be made by the Commission. We will expect the participating staff to play its usual role of providing impartial expert advice and assistance to the Commission in its decisional process." We have no reason to believe that the staff of the Bureau will not continue to provide "impartial" as well as expert advice.

. . .

Separate Statement of CHAIRMAN RICHARD E. WILEY, in which COMMISSIONERS REID, WASHBURN AND QUELLO join:

. . .

If the question of separating the functions of the Bureau in this proceeding were being addressed for the first time, I believe that the better approach—from the standpoint of sound administrative procedure, but not necessarily as a matter of mandatory procedural due process—would be to grant the relief requested. And, certainly, this is my and the Commission's announced intention in future cases. Quite frankly, however, the time has passed when such an approach is feasible in the instant proceeding. The Court of Appeals has mandated that time is of the essence in this important and extremely complex docket and has established a deadline for its administrative conclusion. At this late date, the Commission realistically cannot turn to an entirely new staff which is unfamiliar with the complicated and interrelated issues raised in this rulemaking. Instead, I believe that the Commission must proceed, with appropriate caution, to consider the Bureau's Recommended Decision with the assistance of all available staff resources.

Dissenting Statement of COMMISSIONER GLEN O. ROBINSON in which COMMISSIONER BENJAMIN L. HOOKS joins:

. . .

While separation of Common Carrier Bureau staff may not be required by the Administrative Procedure Act or by the due process clause of the Fifth Amendment, American Telephone and Telegraph Co. v. FCC, 449 F.2d 439 (2d Cir.1971) (Telpak Sharing case), I think it is nevertheless injudicious to permit Bureau staff who participated in the investigation and prosecution of this case to advise us in its final disposition. More than injudicious, I consider it unfair.

The fact that the APA exempts cases such as this from the separations requirements imposed on other agency hearings (5 U.S.C. § 554(d)) does not persuade me to the contrary.[3] Whatever may be the

3. I say this mindful of the court's suggestion in Telpak Sharing that rate-making cases such as this involve, in Professor Davis' terminology, "legislative" rather than "adjudicatory" facts—a distinction which Davis developed for determining the appropriateness of evidentiary procedures in deciding "factual" questions. I have elsewhere questioned the usefulness of that distinction as a general guideline in deter-

strict legal requirements of the APA, where, as here, there is a clearly focused contest between specifically identified private interests and where the facts and arguments have been developed exclusively on the record in an evidentiary hearing, we should insulate ourselves from the investigative/prosecutorial staff of the Bureau as a matter of administrative discretion. The Commission does not dispute this in principle; in fact, it formally adopted new separation procedures in 1974 to deal with this very problem. Restricted Rulemaking Proceedings, 47 FCC 2d 1183 (1974). The only reason given by the majority for refusing to apply this concededly important element of fair procedure to this case is that to do so would cause disruption and delay while new, non-separated staff made itself familiar with the case. But this explanation seems to me more an excuse than a reason. We are not required—we have not even been requested—to separate the entire Bureau or even all persons having familiarity with the general issues. All that is required is to separate those who have actively participated in the prosecution of the case through the time of the preparation of the recommended decision of the Bureau Chief. . . .

The fact that the majority is unwilling to separate itself from even part of the Bureau staff seems to me to underscore the very concern that AT&T and other parties have expressed: that the Commission will depend more on their advice than the arguments and facts on the official record which has been so elaborately and exhaustively constructed. Certainly one could forgive the parties, and the public, from so viewing it—and this appearance in itself should be a matter of concern to us.

NOTES

(1) DANIEL J. GIFFORD, THE MORGAN CASES: A RETROSPECTIVE VIEW, 30 Ad.L.Rev. 237, 241–243 (1978): "When the [Morgan] Court seemingly equated a 'judicial model' of decision-making with a 'full hearing' and perhaps with the fair procedure demanded by the due process clause, it made no distinction about the types of proceedings to which its strictures would apply. In the aftermath of those decisions, however, several widely-shared assessments of those opinions gradually emerged: First, the Morgan cases focused attention upon the contribution of the institutional structure of an agency to its ultimate decision. They raised questions about the roles which could properly be assigned to the

mining what form of agency proceeding is appropriate. See Robinson, The Making of Administrative Policy: Another Look at Rulemaking and Adjudication and Administrative Procedure Reform, 118 Pa.L.Rev. 485, 503–504 (1970). And I question its utility in this particular case in deciding what kinds of hearing procedures are fair. For one thing, I cannot say that all the issues here are "legislative" as opposed to "adjudicatory." Certainly the mere fact they involve "matters of statistics, economics and expert interpretation," American Tel. and Tel. Co., supra, at 455, does not make them such to my mind. Moreover,

labels aside, I doubt that the court in Telpak Sharing intended to suggest that all "matters of statistics, economics and expert interpretation" are properly determinable outside the accepted processes of hearing procedures—particularly when the case is one for which an evidentiary hearing has been prescribed. [I]t is noteworthy that Professor Davis himself would not apply his legislative/adjudicative fact test in the manner suggested by the court in Telpak Sharing since he criticizes the FCC severely for its refusal to separate the Bureau staff in such cases. See Davis, supra, 1970 Supp. at pp. 445–57.

same individual. They also raised questions about the extent to which administrators assigned to decide cases might properly engage in ex parte consultation concerning those cases. Second, the Court had correctly articulated some of the characteristics of a judicial model of decision-making, and this model did accord with fair procedure in a wide area of administrative decision-making. Indeed, for a broad class of administrative decision-making, the drafters of the Administrative Procedure Act accepted the basic position of the Morgan cases that a judicial model provides appropriate procedural norms. Third, it also became apparent in the aftermath of the Morgan decisions that the pristine judicial model by which the Court seemed to be guided was inappropriate for ratemaking cases like the Morgan cases themselves, and perhaps was also inappropriate for other kinds of highly technical and complex cases. The studies and investigations of the Attorney General's Committee, which took place in 1940, had indicated that ex parte consultation, at least as to background matters, was common in rate proceedings, and that without such consultation the decisional process would be unduly hampered.

"These assessments profoundly affected the design of the Administrative Procedure Act. . . . These exemptions from the section 5(c) provisions were justified on two grounds; first, that the hearing officer would be likely to need expert assistance in the decision of complex and technical issues and, second, that the isolation of the decision maker which a strict judicial decision-making model would impose would not be as necessary in non-accusatory proceedings where no stigma attached to an adverse determination."

(2) HARVEY J. SHULMAN, SEPARATION OF FUNCTIONS IN FORMAL LICENSING ADJUDICATIONS, 56 Notre Dame Law. 351 (1981): "In its report, the President's Commission on the Accident at Three Mile Island found that the NRC commissioners 'have adopted unnecessarily stringent ex parte rules to preserve their adjudicative impartiality. . . . '[1] Although the President's Commission declined to make any recommendations regarding these rules, the report of the Chief Counsel of the President's Commission blamed the ex parte rules, in part, for the 'strained communication system within NRC' which interferes with the agency's ability to protect public health and safety.[2] The Chief Counsel's Report noted that, although not required by the APA, the NRC's ex parte rules apply to initial licensing cases and to all NRC staff. Thus, the report suggests that if the NRC were willing to relax its ex parte rules, many of the agency's problems could be better resolved. Similarly, [an NRC-commissioned report known as] the 'Rogovin Report' concluded that NRC members are isolated 'from detailed consideration of case-related safety issues by the so-called "ex parte rule." '[3]

1. U.S. President's Commission on the Accident at Three Mile Island, Report of the President's Commission on the Three Mile Island Accident 51 (1979).

[Ed.] Note that "ex parte" is being used here, as it often is, to denote internal separation-of-function barriers as well as constraints on communications with outsiders.

That is, the rules treated the Commission's staff as if they were outsiders.

2. Report of the Office of Chief Counsel on the Nuclear Regulatory Commission 31 (1979).

3. NRC Special Inquiry Group, Three Mile Island: A Report to the Commissioners and to the Public 141 (1980).

The report stated that the NRC rule goes far beyond APA requirements in separating commissioners from 'those within their own agency who have the most knowledge and expertise about these questions.' The Rogovin Report called for the NRC ex parte rule to be 'very significantly limited and applied more rationally.' "

(3) WILLIAM F. PEDERSON, JR., THE DECLINE OF SEPARATION OF FUNCTIONS IN REGULATORY AGENCIES, 64 Va.L.Rev. 991 (1978): * "The current debate over when and to what extent administrative agencies should use trial-type hearings to make decisions has focused primarily on the costs and the benefits of the hearings themselves. 'Separation-of-functions' requirements, however, are a more important but largely unperceived defect of these hearings. These provisions forbid agency employees who worked on a matter in its early stages from advising or consulting with those who handle succeeding stages. These barriers can hinder efficient agency operation and lower the quality of final administrative decisions.

"Admittedly, a separation-of-functions rule has its place in an 'accusatory' proceeding, in which one group of agency employees prosecutes a private party for a violation of the law and another group must sit in judgment. Most significant decisions by government agencies, however, simply do not fit this model. Instead, they involve the formulation or the application of policy, without any connotation of wrongdoing, regarding persons who are being regulated. Agencies and their staffs exist to make policy decisions, and there is no reason to suspect that staff members who work on the early stages of a nonaccusatory proceeding view the choices confronting them in a manner any less valid than do those who handle succeeding stages. . . .

"Five independent characteristics of formal adjudication may contribute to a fair disposition of a particular case: (1) a decision based on a publicly defined and publicly accessible record, (2) a mechanism for confrontation between opposing points of view, (3) a mechanism for probing and, where possible, resolving differences on factual and other matters, (4) separation-of-functions requirements, and (5) an independent, judge-like hearing officer. The framers of the APA concluded that all five of these elements must be present in accusatory cases but only the first three in policy decisions. They undermined their own work, however, by requiring the factual probing to take the form of a trial-type hearing even in policy-dominated cases.

"Whether a decision requires separation of functions depends not only upon its basic nature but also upon the procedures used to make it. Trial-type hearings cast the agency's trial staff in an adversarial role, which almost inevitably calls forth a partisan attitude, but the APA also expressly sanctions informal reliance on the advice of these same staff members in reaching a final decision. Naturally enough, private lawyers who have confronted this staff in the hearing object fiercely to its taking any part in the subsequent deliberations within the agency.

* Reprinted with permission of the author, the Virginia Law Review, and Fred B. Rothman & Co.

Accordingly, in the years since passage of the APA, agencies gradually have adopted rules to bar those who take part in the hearing from playing any role in the preparation of the resulting decision, even when the APA would permit their involvement. . . .

"Clothing non-accusatory administrative hearings with more of the trappings of adjudicatory proceedings may make better theater, but it probably reduces their substantive importance. Agency trial staffs, because of the separation-of-functions rules, and hearing examiners, because of their misconceptions of their proper role, do not participate in the informal discussions that often generate the agency's governing policies. Unawareness of these policies or simple separation from their development may prevent the outcome of the initial hearing from reflecting what the agency as an institution would consider to be the proper result."

(4) JAMES O. FREEDMAN, "EXPERTISE AND THE ADMINISTRATIVE PROCESS," 28 Ad.L.Rev. 363 (1976) *: "To the extent that skepticism of administrative expertise is based on the premise that agency members have often lacked expertise in the substantive areas that they have been appointed to regulate, it misses the mark in a crucial respect. The continuing expertness of an administrative agency as to matters of technical substance can be more properly understood as deriving primarily from its staff, and not from the shifting membership of those who temporarily serve as commissioners.[4] It is, indeed, the experience and specialization of a large and dedicated staff that has permitted agencies to channel the diverse expertise of many individuals into the process of institutional decisionmaking—one of the unique contributions of the modern administrative process. . . .

". . . Because so many agency members are themselves generalists rather than experts in any professional sense, they may be particularly well qualified to perform the necessary function of moderating the staff's assertions of expertise.

* Reprinted with the permission of the author and publisher.

4. [Ed.] At the beginning of 1973, just before President Nixon made a significantly large number of new appointments to the independent regulatory agencies, the average length of service of all then members of boards and commissions was slightly over 5½ years. The most recently appointed members who would constitute a majority (that is, "the least experienced majority") had an average length of service, however, of only 2⅔ years, which suggests a high rate of turnover, with a few "old hands" whose long stay in office brings up the overall average. Comparable figures for agencies at the beginning of 1973: ICC, 3⅓ years and 10 months; SEC, 3¾ years and 1⅔ years; FPC—3¾ years and 1⅓ years; FTC—8 years and 5 years; CAB—10½ years and 6⅔ years; FCC—5⅔ years and 3 years: NLRB—7 years and 3 years. In point of fact, a congressional study has recently concluded, "regulatory commissioners spend significantly longer periods in office than other political executives"—on the average, about four years. The Regulatory Appointments Process, I Study on Federal Regulation pursuant to S.Res. 71, Senate Committee on Government Operations, 95th Cong. 1st Sess. 89 (Comm.Print 1977); see also V. Kramer & J. Graham, Appointments to the Regulatory Agencies, printed for the use of the Senate Committee on Commerce, 94th Cong.2d Sess. (1976).

"The great turnover of top men, particularly in certain agencies, is much deplored, but it is questionable whether long tenures are preferable. Can it be said with any assurance that the members of the FTC and the ICC have been better than those of the FCC or the SEC, that they have displayed more courage, more ingenuity, more flexibility?" L. Jaffe, The Effective Limits of the Administrative Process: A Re-evaluation, 67 Harv.L.Rev. 1105, 1132 (1954).

"This function requires agency members to use the staff's expertise wisely but not uncritically: to measure the staff's expertise against the counsels of common sense, to place the staff's expertise within the context of a wider experience with the world of affairs, to coordinate the staff's various kinds of expertise into a coherent program, and to estimate the extent to which the staff's technical expertise must share the direction of agency policy with values drawn from the world of political and social experience.

". . . [T]hose who point to the absence of a technical expertise in agency members may actually be directing attention to an expertise of a different kind—an expertise in the art of skepticism about expertise, a competence in the worldly art of the politically acceptable and socially wise.

". . . [T]he agency member who is not a technical expert becomes an essential guarantor of the common sense and political acceptability of proposals that originate from experts, whether they be agency staff members or private retainers. As Laski so well understood:

> In convincing the non-specialist Minister that a policy propounded is either right or wrong, the expert is already halfway to convincing the public of his plans; and if he fails in that effort to convince, the chances are that his plans are, for the environment he seeks to control, inadequate or mistaken.

"The agency member who is not an expert thus performs one of the defining acts of the statesman: he serves, in Laski's words, as 'the broker of ideas without whom no bridges can be built between the expert and the multitude.'[5] "

c. "Off-the-Record" Communications From Others

PROFESSIONAL AIR TRAFFIC CONTROLLERS ORGANIZATION v. FEDERAL LABOR RELATIONS AUTHORITY

United States Court of Appeals, District of Columbia Circuit, 1982.
685 F.2d 547.

[The Professional Air Traffic Controllers Organization called its members out on strike August 3, 1981, in violation of a statutory

---

5. [Ed.] Report of Committee on Independent Regulatory Commissions 22–24 (Hoover Commission, 1949): "There can be no doubt that the main source of expertness in a commission must lie in its staff. The work of most of these agencies requires the collaboration of many technical skills, such as engineering, accounting, and law. At most, a commissioner can be expected to be proficient in only one of these disciplines and many do not have such training at all. As a whole, the commission must rely for expert help and advice on its staff technicians. . . .

". . . Taken as a whole . . . the staffs of most agencies do appear to be familiar with the problems of the industry and qualified to handle them.

"The situation with respect to members of the commissions is different. There is probably no need for the members to be true experts in the area of regulation. They should have sufficient familiarity with it to understand the problems and the policy issues and to make full use of the technical experts on the staff. Their main contribution should be wise and intelligent judgment which does not necessarily require expertness beyond the intelligent familiarity just described."

prohibition of federal employees from striking their employer. Among the several proceedings resulting was an unfair labor practice hearing before the Federal Labor Relations Authority, threatening the revocation of PATCO's certification as the recognized union for the nation's air traffic controllers. That hearing was held before an FLRA ALJ August 10–11 and on August 14, after briefing, a recommended decision was announced stripping PATCO of its certification. Oral argument on review was held before the three members of the FLRA September 16, and the ALJ's decision was affirmed October 22. Members Frazier and Applewhaite voted unconditionally to revoke PATCO's certification; Chairman Haughton would have permitted PATCO a brief period to end the strike before that revocation, but joined the other two when that period elapsed without an appropriate PATCO response. The case was then brought to the D.C. Circuit on judicial review, where expedited argument was heard December 3, 1981.]

Before ROBINSON, CHIEF JUDGE, MacKINNON and EDWARDS, CIRCUIT JUDGES.

HARRY T. EDWARDS, CIRCUIT JUDGE:

. . .

II. EX PARTE COMMUNICATIONS DURING THE FLRA PROCEEDINGS

Unfortunately, allegations of improprieties during the FLRA's consideration of this case forced us to delay our review on the merits. Only a day before oral argument, the Department of Justice, which represents the FAA in this review, informed the court that the Department of Justice Criminal Division and the FBI had investigated allegations of an improper contact between a "well-known labor leader" and FLRA Member Applewhaite during the pendency of the PATCO case. . . . [W]e invoked a procedure that this court has occasionally employed in like situations in the past.[1] Without assuming that anything improper had in fact occurred or had affected the FLRA Decision in this case, we ordered the FLRA "to hold, with the aid of a specially-appointed administrative law judge, an evidentiary hearing to determine the nature, extent, source and effect of any and all ex parte communications and other approaches that may have been made to any member or members of the FLRA while the PATCO case was pending before it."

Following our remand on the ex parte communications issue, John M. Vittone, an Administrative Law Judge with the Civil Aeronautics Board, was appointed to preside over an evidentiary proceeding. . . . A.L.J. Vittone's inquiry led to the disclosure of a number of communications with FLRA Members that were at least arguably related to the Authority's consideration of the PATCO case. We find the vast majority of these communications unobjectionable. Three occurrences, however, are somewhat more troubling and require our careful review and

---

1. See, e.g., Home Box Office, Inc. v. FCC, 567 F.2d 9, 58–59 (D.C.Cir.), cert. denied 434 U.S. 829 (1977); United Air Lines v. CAB, 281 F.2d 53, 58 (D.C.Cir.1960); Sangamon Valley Television Corp. v. United States, 269 F.2d 221, 225 (D.C.Cir.1959); WKAT, Inc. v. FCC, 258 F.2d 418, 419–420 (D.C.Cir.1958) (per curiam).

discussion. We first summarize A.L.J. Vittone's findings regarding them.

1. The Meeting Between Member Applewhaite and FLRA General Counsel Gordon

On August 10, 1981 (one week after the unfair labor practice complaint against PATCO was filed), H. Stephan Gordon, the FLRA General Counsel, was in Member Applewhaite's office discussing administrative matters unrelated to the PATCO case. During Gordon's discussion with Member Applewhaite, Ms. Ellen Stern, an attorney with the FLRA Solicitor's office, entered Member Applewhaite's office to deliver a copy of a memorandum . . . Ms. Stern had prepared at the request of Member Frazier.[2] With General Counsel Gordon present, Ms. Stern proceeded to discuss her memorandum, which dealt with whether the Civil Service Reform Act makes revocation of a striking union's exclusive recognition status mandatory or discretionary and, assuming it is discretionary, what other disciplinary actions might be taken.

During Ms. Stern's discussion, both Member Applewhaite and General Counsel Gordon asked her general questions (e.g., regarding the availability of other remedies and whether she had researched the relevant legislative history). . . . While the conversation at least implicitly focused on the PATCO case, the facts of the case and the appropriate disposition were not discussed. The discussion ended after ten or fifteen minutes.

A.L.J. Vittone concluded that "[t]he conversation had no effect or impact on Member Applewhaite's ultimate decision in the PATCO case."

2. Secretary Lewis' Telephone Calls to Members Frazier and Applewhaite

During the morning of August 13, 1981, Secretary of Transportation Andrew L. Lewis, Jr. telephoned Member Frazier. Secretary Lewis stated that he was not calling about the substance of the PATCO case, but wanted Member Frazier to know that, contrary to some news reports, no meaningful efforts to settle the strike were underway. Secretary Lewis also stated that the Department of Transportation would appreciate expeditious handling of the case. Not wanting to discuss the PATCO case with Secretary Lewis, Member Frazier replied, "I understand your position perfectly, Mr. Secretary." . . .

Member Frazier also advised Member Applewhaite of Secretary Lewis' telephone call. In anticipation of a call, Member Applewhaite located the FLRA Rules regarding the time limits for processing an appeal from an A.L.J. decision in an unfair labor practice case. When Secretary Lewis telephoned and stated his concern that the case not be delayed, Member Applewhaite interrupted the Secretary to inform him

---

2. The Solicitor is the general legal advisor of the FLRA, including the Members. The Solicitor also represents the FLRA on appeals from FLRA orders and in other legal proceedings.

that if he wished to obtain expedited handling of the case, he would have to comply with the FLRA Rules and file a written motion. Secretary Lewis stated that he was unaware that papers had to be filed and that he would contact his General Counsel immediately. The conversation ended without further discussion.

During the afternoon of August 13, the FAA filed a Motion to Modify Time Limits for Filing Exceptions, requesting that the time limit be reduced from the usual twenty-five days to seven days. On August 14, the FLRA General Counsel filed a similar motion. On August 17, PATCO filed an opposition to these motions and a motion to extend the time for filing exceptions to sixty days. On August 18, 1981, the FLRA Members considered the three pending motions, denied all three, and decided instead to reduce the usual twenty-five day period for filing exceptions to nineteen days.

Upon considering this evidence, Judge Vittone concluded that: (1) the FAA's filing of a motion to expedite may have been in response to Secretary Lewis' conversation with Member Applewhaite; (2) Chairman Haughton was unaware of Secretary Lewis' telephone calls when he considered the motions on August 18; (3) "Secretary Lewis' call had an undetermined effect on Member Applewhaite's and Member Frazier's decision to reduce the time period for filing exceptions,"; and (4) the telephone calls "had no effect on Member Applewhaite's or Member Frazier's ultimate decision on the merits of the PATCO case."

3. Member Applewhaite's Dinner with Albert Shanker

Since 1974 Albert Shanker has been President of the American Federation of Teachers, a large public-sector labor union, and a member of the Executive Council of the AFL–CIO.[3] Since 1964 Mr. Shanker has been President of the AFT's New York City Local, the United Federation of Teachers. Before joining the FLRA, Member Applewhaite had been associated with the New York Public Employment Relations Board. Through their contacts in New York, Mr. Shanker and Member Applewhaite had become professional and social friends.

During the week of September 20, 1981, Mr. Shanker was in Washington, D.C. on business. On September 21, Mr. Shanker made arrangements to have dinner with Member Applewhaite that evening. Although he did not inform Member Applewhaite of his intentions when he made the arrangements, Mr. Shanker candidly admitted that he wanted to have dinner with Member Applewhaite because he felt strongly about the PATCO case and wanted to communicate directly to Member Applewhaite his sentiments, previously expressed in public statements, that PATCO should not be severely punished for its strike. . . . After accepting the invitation, Member Applewhaite informed Member Frazier and Chairman Haughton that he was having dinner with Mr. Shanker.

3. The AFL–CIO presented oral argument to the FLRA in the PATCO case as amicus curiae. Mr. Shanker, however, was unaware of the amicus status of the AFL–CIO at all times relevant to our consideration.

Member Applewhaite and Mr. Shanker talked for about an hour and a half during their dinner on September 21. Most of the discussion concerned the preceding Saturday's Solidarity Day Rally, an upcoming tuition tax credit referendum in the District of Columbia, and mutual friends from New York. Near the end of the dinner, however, the conversation turned to labor law matters relevant to the PATCO case. The two men discussed various approaches to public employee strikes in New York, Pennsylvania and the federal government. Mr. Shanker expressed his view that the punishment of a striking union should fit the crime and that revocation of certification as a punishment for an illegal strike was tantamount to "killing a union." The record is clear that Mr. Shanker made no threats or promises to Member Applewhaite; likewise, the evidence also indicates that Member Applewhaite never revealed his position regarding the PATCO case.

Near the end of their conversation, Member Applewhaite commented that because the PATCO case was hotly contested, he would be viewed with disfavor by whichever side he voted against. Member Applewhaite also observed that he was concerned about his prospects for reappointment to the FLRA in July 1982. Mr. Shanker, in turn, responded that Member Applewhaite had no commitments from anyone and urged him to vote without regard to personal considerations. The dinner concluded and the two men departed.

The FLRA Decisional Process. On the afternoon of September 21, before the Applewhaite/Shanker dinner, the FLRA Members had had their first formal conference on the PATCO case, which had been argued to them five days earlier. Members Frazier and Applewhaite both favored revocation of PATCO's exclusive recognition status and took the position that PATCO would no longer be a labor organization within the meaning of the Civil Service Reform Act. Member Frazier favored an indefinite revocation; Member Applewhaite favored a revocation for a fixed period of one to three years. Chairman Haughton agreed that an illegal strike had occurred, but favored suspension, not revocation, of PATCO's collective bargaining status.

After September 21, Member Applewhaite considered other remedies, short of revocation, to deal with the PATCO strike. For over two weeks Member Applewhaite sought to find common ground with Chairman Haughton. Those efforts to agree on an alternative solution failed and, on October 9, Member Applewhaite finally decided to vote with Member Frazier for revocation. (Member Applewhaite apparently was concerned that the FLRA have a majority favoring one remedy, rather than render three opinions favoring three different dispositions.) . . . While these negotiations within the Authority were going on, Member Frazier became concerned that Mr. Shanker might have influenced Member Applewhaite's position in the case. On September 22, Member Frazier visited Member Applewhaite to inquire about his dinner with Mr. Shanker. Member Frazier understood Member Applewhaite to say that Shanker had said that if Member Applewhaite voted against PATCO, then Applewhaite would be unable to get work as an arbitrator when he left the FLRA. Member Frazier also understood Member Applewhaite to say that he was then leaning against voting for revocation. (A.L.J. Vittone found that Shanker had made no such threats during the dinner, and concluded that Member Frazier reached this conclusion based on some miscommunication or misunderstanding.)

On September 22 and again on September 28, Member Frazier advised Member Applewhaite to talk to Solicitor Freehling about his dinner with Mr. Shanker. . . . Member Frazier later asked Solicitor Freehling if Member Applewhaite had discussed his dinner with Mr. Shanker. Solicitor Freehling told Member Frazier that they had talked and that Member Applewhaite had concluded that there were no problems involved. Despite these assurances, Member Frazier contacted his personal attorney. Sometime in early October, Member Frazier's attorney contacted the FBI. The FBI interviewed Member Frazier on October 17 and then other FLRA Members and staff. FBI agents interviewed Member Applewhaite on October 22, the day the FLRA Decision issued. (Member Applewhaite was thus unaware of the FBI investigation until after he reached his final decision in the PATCO case.)

. . .

C. Applicable Legal Standards

1. The Statutory Prohibition of Ex Parte Contacts and the FLRA Rules

The Civil Service Reform Act requires that FLRA unfair labor practice hearings, to the extent practicable, be conducted in accordance with the provisions of the Administrative Procedure Act. 5 U.S.C. § 7118(a)(6) (Supp. IV 1980). Since FLRA unfair labor practice hearings are formal adjudications within the meaning of the APA, see 5 U.S.C. § 551(7) (1976), section 557(d) governs ex parte communications. Id. § 557(d). . . .

Three features of the prohibition on ex parte communications in agency adjudications are particularly relevant to the contacts here at issue. First, by its terms, section 557(d) applies only to ex parte communications to or from an "interested person." . . . Second, the Government in the Sunshine Act defines an "ex parte communication" as "an oral or written communication not on the public record to which reasonable prior notice to all parties is not given, but . . . not includ[ing] requests for status reports on any matter or proceeding. . . ." 5 U.S.C. § 551(14) (1976). Requests for status reports are thus allowed under the statute, even when directed to an agency decisionmaker rather than to another agency employee. . . . Third, and in direct contrast to status reports, section 557(d) explicitly prohibits communications "relevant to the merits of the proceeding." The congressional reports state that the phrase should "be construed broadly and . . . include more than the phrase 'fact in issue' currently used in [section 554(d)(1) of] the Administrative Procedure Act."

. . .

The disclosure of ex parte communications serves two distinct interests. Disclosure is important in its own right to prevent the appearance of impropriety from secret communications in a proceeding that is required to be decided on the record. Disclosure is also important as an instrument of fair decisionmaking; only if a party knows the arguments presented to a decisionmaker can the party respond effectively and ensure that its position is fairly considered. When these interests of openness and opportunity for response are threatened by an ex parte communication, the communication must be disclosed. . . .

2. Remedies for Ex Parte Communications

Section 557(d) contains two possible administrative remedies for improper ex parte communications. The first is disclosure of the communication and its content. 5 U.S.C. § 557(d)(1)(C) (1976). The second requires the violating party to "show cause why his claim or interest in the proceeding should not be dismissed, denied, disregarded, or otherwise adversely affected on account of [the] violation." Id. § 557(d)(1)(D); see also id. § 556(d). . . . [T]he statutory language clearly states that a party's interest in the proceeding may be adversely affected only "to the extent consistent with the interests of justice and the policy of the underlying statutes." 5 U.S.C. § 557(d)(1)(D) (1976).

The Government in the Sunshine Act contains no specific provisions for judicial remedy of improper ex parte communications.

Under the case law in this Circuit, improper ex parte communications, even when undisclosed during agency proceedings, do not necessarily void an agency decision. . . . [A] court must consider whether, as a result of improper ex parte communications, the agency's decisionmaking process was irrevocably tainted so as to make the ultimate judgment of the agency unfair, either to an innocent party or to the public interest that the agency was obliged to protect.[4] In making this determination, a number of considerations may be relevant: the gravity of the ex parte communications;[5] whether the contacts may have influenced the agency's ultimate decision; whether the party making the improper contacts benefited from the agency's ultimate decision; whether the contents of the communications were unknown to opposing parties, who therefore had no opportunity to respond; and whether vacation of the agency's decision and remand for new proceedings

---

4. We have also considered the effect of ex parte communications on the availability of meaningful judicial review. Where facts and arguments "vital to the agency decision" are only communicated to the agency off the record, the court may at worst be kept in the dark about the agency's actual reasons for its decision. At best, the basis for the agency's action may be disclosed for the first time on review. If the off-the-record communications regard critical facts, the court will be particularly ill-equipped to resolve in the first instance any controversy between the parties. . . .

5. Compare, e.g., WKAT, Inc. v. FCC, 296 F.2d 375, 383 (D.C.Cir.) ("corrupt tampering with the adjudicatory process"), cert. denied, 368 U.S. 841, 82 S.Ct. 63, 7 L.Ed.2d 40 (1961), with United Air Lines v. CAB, 309 F.2d 238, 241 (D.C.Cir.1962) (nothing "savoring of corruption or attempt to corrupt"). If the ex parte contacts are of such severity that an agency decision-maker should have disqualified himself, vacation of the agency decision and remand to an impartial tribunal is mandatory. Cf. Cinderella Career & Finishing Schools v. FTC, 425 F.2d 583, 591–92 (D.C.Cir.1970) (failure of single member of agency to disqualify himself for bias requires vacation of agency decision).

would serve a useful purpose. . . . [A]ny such decision must of necessity be an exercise of equitable discretion.

D. Analysis of the Alleged Ex Parte Communications with FLRA Members

. . .

1. The Meeting Between Member Applewhaite and FLRA General Counsel Gordon

When General Counsel Gordon met with Member Applewhaite on August 10, the General Counsel's office was prosecuting the unfair labor practice complaint against PATCO before Chief A.L.J. Fenton. General Counsel Gordon was therefore a "person outside the agency" within the meaning of section 557(d) and the FLRA Rules. 5 C.F.R. § 2414.3(a) (1981). Still, the undisputed purpose of the meeting was to discuss budgetary and administrative matters. It was therefore entirely appropriate. The shared concerns of the Authority are not put on hold whenever the General Counsel prosecutes an unfair labor practice complaint.

The discussion relevant to the PATCO case arose only when Ms. Stern delivered a copy of her memorandum regarding decertification of striking unions to Member Applewhaite. . . . Some occasional and inadvertent contacts between the prosecuting and adjudicating arms of a small agency like the FLRA may be inevitable. . . . In hindsight, it may have been preferable if Member Applewhaite had postponed even this general conversation with Ms. Stern or if General Counsel Gordon had temporarily excused himself from Member Applewhaite's office. Nonetheless, we do not believe that this contact tainted the proceeding or unfairly advantaged the General Counsel in the prosecution of the case. Thus, we conclude that the conversation at issue here, even though possibly indiscreet and undesirable, does not void the FLRA Decision in this case.

2. Secretary Lewis' Telephone Calls to Members Frazier and Applewhaite

Transportation Secretary Lewis was undoubtedly an "interested person" within the meaning of section 557(d) and the FLRA Rules when he called Members Frazier and Applewhaite on August 13. Secretary Lewis' call clearly would have been an improper ex parte communication if he had sought to discuss the merits of the PATCO case. . . . Although Secretary Lewis did not in fact discuss the merits of the case, even a procedural inquiry may be a subtle effort to influence an agency decision. . . . We need not decide, however, whether Secretary Lewis' contacts were in fact improper. . . . Member Applewhaite explicitly told Secretary Lewis that if he wanted the case handled more quickly than the normal course of FLRA business, then the FAA would have to file a written request. If, as A.L.J. Vittone found likely, Member Applewhaite's comments led to the FAA's Motion to Modify Time Limits, *that was exactly the desired result.* Once the FAA filed a motion, PATCO filed its own responsive motions, and the FLRA was able to decide the timing issue based on the pleadings before it. . . .

In the end, the FLRA denied all of the motions and only reduced the time for filing exceptions from twenty-five days to nineteen days. In these circumstances, and given A.L.J. Vittone's inability to find any effect of the calls on the Members' decision, we cannot find that the disposition of the motions was improperly influenced. . . .

3. Member Applewhaite's Dinner with Albert Shanker

. . . At the outset, we are faced with the question whether Mr. Shanker was an "interested person" to the proceeding under section 557(d) and the FLRA Rules. . . . The House and Senate Reports agreed that the term covers "any individual or other person with an interest in the agency proceeding that is greater than the general interest the public as a whole may have. The interest need not be monetary, nor need a person be a party to, or intervenor in, the agency proceeding . . . ."

. . . Mr. Shanker was (and is) the President of a major public-sector labor union. As such, he has a special and well-known interest in the union movement and the developing law of labor relations in the public sector. . . . From August 3, 1981 to September 21, 1981, Mr. Shanker and his union made a series of widely publicized statements in support of PATCO.

. . . Thus, Mr. Shanker's actions, as well as his union office, belie his implicit claim that he had no greater interest in the case than a member of the general public. . . .

Even if we were to adopt Mr. Shanker's position that he was not an interested person, we are astonished at his claim that he did nothing wrong.[6] Mr. Shanker frankly concedes that he "desired to have dinner with Member Applewhaite because he felt strongly about the PATCO case and he wished to communicate directly to Member Applewhaite sentiments he had previously expressed in public." While we appreciate Mr. Shanker's forthright admission, we must wonder whether it is a product of candor or a failure to comprehend that his conduct was improper. . . .

It is simply unacceptable behavior for any person directly to attempt to influence the decision of a judicial officer in a pending case outside of the formal, public proceedings. This is true for the general public, for "interested persons," and for the formal parties to the case. This rule

---

6. Mr. Shanker suggests that "[s]ince there is no sanction available against amici, it is reasonable to assume that the ex parte rules are not intended to apply in these circumstances." Shanker's Brief at 14. This argument is simply a non sequitur. The principal purpose of the ex parte rules is not to punish violators, but to preserve the integrity of the administrative process. Even when a nonparty is the source of an ex parte communication, a proceeding may be voided if the decision is irrevocably tainted. In such a case, the principal purpose of the statute would be served, even though a direct sanction against the violator might be unavailable. Cf. S.Rep. No. 354, 94th Cong., 1st Sess. 39 (1975), Sunshine Act Sourcebook at 234 (inadvertent ex parte contact not a basis for sanction against a party, but nonetheless voids an irrevocably tainted proceeding).

applies to administrative adjudications as well as to cases in Article III courts. . . .

We do not hold, however, that Member Applewhaite committed an impropriety when he accepted Mr. Shanker's dinner invitation. Member Applewhaite and Mr. Shanker were professional and social friends. We recognize, of course, that a judge "must have neighbors, friends and acquaintances, business and social relations, and be a part of his day and generation." . . . When Mr. Shanker called Member Applewhaite on September 21, Member Applewhaite was unaware of Mr. Shanker's purpose in arranging the dinner. He therefore had no reason to reject the invitation.

The majority of the dinner conversation was unrelated to the PATCO case. Only in the last fifteen minutes of the dinner did the discussion become relevant to the PATCO dispute, apparently when Mr. Shanker raised the topic of local approaches to public employee strikes in New York and Pennsylvania. At this point, and as the conversation turned to the discipline appropriate for a striking union like PATCO, Member Applewhaite should have promptly terminated the discussion. . . .

This indiscretion, this failure to steer the conversation away from the PATCO case, eventually led to the special evidentiary hearing in this case.

. . . We now know that Mr. Shanker did *not* in any way threaten Member Applewhaite during their dinner. Mr. Shanker did *not* tell Member Applewhaite that if he voted to decertify PATCO he would be unable to get cases as an arbitrator if and when he left the FLRA. Mr. Shanker did *not* say that he was speaking "for top AFL-CIO officials" or that Member Applewhaite would need labor support to secure reappointment. Moreover, Mr. Shanker did *not* make any promises of any kind to Member Applewhaite, and Member Applewhaite did *not* reveal how he intended to vote in the PATCO case.

In these circumstances, we do not believe that it is necessary to vacate the FLRA Decision and remand the case. . . .

Though plainly inappropriate, the ex parte communication was limited to a ten or fifteen minute discussion, often couched in general terms, of the appropriate discipline for a striking public employee union. This behavior falls short of the "corrupt tampering with the adjudicatory process" found by this court in WKAT, Inc. v. FCC, 296 F.2d 375, 383 (D.C.Cir.), cert. denied, 368 U.S. 841 (1961).

Second, A.L.J. Vittone found that the Applewhaite/Shanker dinner had no effect on the ultimate decision of Member Applewhaite or of the FLRA as a whole in the PATCO case. None of the parties have disputed this finding. Indeed, even Member Frazier, who initiated the FBI investigation of the dinner, testified that "in his opinion the Shanker-Applewhaite dinner did not have an effect on Member Applewhaite's ultimate decision in the PATCO case."

Third, no party benefited from the improper contact. . . .

Finally, we cannot say that the parties were unfairly deprived of an opportunity to refute the arguments propounded in the ex parte communication. . . .

E. Member Applewhaite's Alleged "Personal Interest" in the PATCO Case

. . .

A.L.J. Vittone found that near the end of their conversation Member Applewhaite observed [to Mr. Shanker] that "he was concerned about his prospects for reappointment in July 1982." He also commented that, "because the PATCO case was hotly contested, he would be viewed with disfavor by whichever side he voted against." In response, "Mr. Shanker urged Applewhaite to vote without regard to personal considerations."

Based essentially on this brief conversation, Member Frazier now proposes that Member Applewhaite had a personal interest in the outcome of the PATCO case. . . . [and] argues that Member Applewhaite was disqualified from hearing the PATCO case.

We do not read as much into this conversation as does Member Frazier. It is not surprising that an agency member appointed by the President might be concerned about his prospects for reappointment. We are not so naive as to believe that such thoughts do not cross a member's mind. Nor would we assume that an Authority Member would believe that his decisions are irrelevant to the President's determination whether to reappoint him. Similarly, it is hardly surprising for Member Applewhaite to recognize that his decision in a hotly contested case would not receive universal approbation. The appropriate question here is not whether Member Applewhaite recognized that his decision might not be universally approved; rather, the correct inquiry is whether Member Applewhaite's concerns rendered him incapable of reaching a fair decision on the merits of the case before him.

The cited brief conversation between Member Applewhaite and Mr. Shanker does not demonstrate an inability to fairly decide the case. Courts have long recognized "a presumption of honesty and integrity in those serving as adjudicators." Absent a strong showing to the contrary, an agency adjudicator is presumed to act in good faith and to be capable of ignoring considerations not on the record. . . . Member Applewhaite explained that this was no different from any arbitration case in which he had ruled—one party wins and the other loses. He testified: "I have always faced that problem[,] so I just have to call it like it is and . . . take my chances." Tr. 744. We have no reason to doubt this testimony. A remand on the basis of personal interest is therefore unnecessary.

. . .

[On the merits, the court upheld the FLRA order.]

SPOTTSWOOD W. ROBINSON, III, CHIEF JUDGE, concurring in part, and concurring in the judgment.

. . .

From the special hearing emerges an appalling chronicle of attorneys, high government officials, and interested outsiders apparently without compunction about intervening in the course of FLRA's decisionmaking by means of private communications with those charged with resolving the case on the merits. We have an even more distressing picture of agency decisionmakers—whose role in this formal adjudication concededly approximated that of judges—seemingly ignorant of the substance of the ex parte rules, insensitive to the compromising potentialities of certain official and social contacts, and unwilling to silence peremptorily and firmly improper discussions that did transpire. Although the special hearing disclosed no such taint on the agency's ultimate decision as would require additional corrective proceedings, ... the court's opinion administers a mild chiding where a ringing condemnation is in order.

I. THE APPLEWHAITE–GORDON INCIDENT

. . .

It is one of the facts of administrative life that agencies such as FLRA fulfill, often simultaneously, the several roles of investigator, prosecutor, adjudicator, and policy formulator. Undoubtedly, this commingling of functions makes it more difficult to maintain a strict separation between those personnel who, on any given case, are cast in the role of advocate from those who occupy the position of judge in the matter. Once the agency is engaged in formal adjudication, however, such a separation is mandated by the APA, and is essential to the integrity of the administrative process. The perils of laxness on this point are well illustrated by the Applewhaite-Gordon incident. The prosecutor in an important and controversial case is permitted access to the substance of an internal legal memorandum on a pivotal issue. He hears and participates in discussion of the analysis being formulated on the question. At one point, the decisionmaker, apparently without any conception of the seriousness of what he is about to do, turns to the prosecutor and asks for the latter's opinion on the problem. . . . The conversation was not merely indiscreet or undesirable; it was, purely and simply, a prohibited ex parte contact that should never have occurred. Gordon had no business remaining in the room once he realized that PATCO was the object of discussion. Applewhaite had no business permitting him to remain, and certainly was grossly at fault in soliciting Gordon's opinion on the issue.

. . .

II. SECRETARY LEWIS' CALLS TO MEMBERS FRAZIER
AND APPLEWHAITE

. . .

The testimony of Frazier and Applewhaite confirms that Secretary Lewis' calls were highly unusual. Both stated that they had never before been contacted by a Cabinet member on a pending case. Applewhaite also explained that persons seeking status information normally contact the staff in lieu of discussing such matters directly with the members. . . .

Agencies, like courts, promulgate rules of practice to assist outsiders in communicating in proper fashion with decisionmakers. These channels are quite adequate to accommodate any information that legitimately could be sought from or provided to those who will judge the case. For a high government officer to bypass established procedures and approach, directly and privately, members of an independent decisionmaking body about a case in which he has an official interest and on which they will be called to rule suggests, at the minimum, a deplorable indifference toward safeguarding the purity of the formal adjudicatory process. Regardless of the officer's actual intent, such a call could be felt by the recipient as political pressure; regardless of its actual effect, such a call could be perceived by the public as political pressure. Either way, the integrity of the process is dealt a sore blow.

. . .

IV. THE APPLEWHAITE–SHANKER DINNER

. . .

I cannot accede to the assertion that, by itself, a private dinner engagement between Applewhaite and Shanker was not improper. . . . Can the public really be expected to believe in the fairness and neutrality of the agency's formal adjudicatory processes when one of its decisionmakers permits an outspoken, highly visible official of a participating union to wine and dine him during deliberations on the case? . . . [T]hose who take on this judicial role may no longer participate in the daily intercourse of life as freely as do others. They have a duty to the judicial system in which they have accepted membership fastidiously to safeguard their integrity—at the expense, if need be, of "neighbors, friends and acquaintances, business and social relations." This *is* their "part" in their "day and generation," and one who is unwilling to make the sacrifice is unsuited to the office.

. . .

While it might be possible to attribute Applewhaite's actions in placing himself in a compromising position to thoughtless imprudence, his unprotesting submission to blatant ex parte advocacy on the merits of a case then pending before the members defies explanation. . . . Such remissness on the part of a powerful and highly-placed administrator deserves, by my estimate, a harsher verdict from this court than "unfortunate."

. . .

MacKINNON, CIRCUIT JUDGE (concurring).

Subject to the fact that I might differ in the characterization of some of the ex parte contacts, I concur in Judge Edwards' opinion but wish to record some additional comments. . . .

The number of ex parte contacts that were disclosed at the remand hearing is appalling, as are the statements by counsel that such contacts were nothing more than what is normal and usual in administrative agencies and even in courts of law. That statement is categorically denied insofar as our courts are concerned. If that ever turns out to be true some very severe penalties are going to be meted out. . . .

In this connection 18 U.S.C. § 1505 should be noted. This section of the Criminal Code provides that it is an offense if one "corruptly . . . *endeavors to influence,* obstruct or impede the due and proper administration of the law under which [a] proceeding is being had before [an] . . . agency of the United States . . . ." (emphasis added). Private contacts with agency officials, with respect to pending adjudicatory matters, by interested parties or their agents, that endeavor to affect the decisional process, however subtle such contract may be, are *corrupt* endeavors to influence the "due and proper administration of the law" and those who so attempt may be indicted. The authorized punishment is imprisonment for not more than five years, or a $5,000 fine, or both. 18 U.S.C. § 1505.

NOTE

The PATCO court was able to conclude that no remedy was required for the indiscretions that had occurred. What might an effective remedy have been? In some cases, disqualification has been administered, and plainly the threat that the agency will withhold whatever the communicator is seeking to gain can serve as a significant control. See WKAT, Inc. v. FCC, 296 F.2d 375 (D.C.Cir.1961), cert. denied 368 U.S. 841 (1961), in which the court disqualified a successful applicant for a television license worth millions, because of its improper ex parte efforts to influence the role of an FCC commissioner. This sanction cannot be applied invariably, however, without risking a hurt instead of an advantage to the public interest. The Reopened Kansas-Oklahoma Local Service Case, 38 C.A.B. 163, 13 Ad.L.2d 694 (1963), provides an example. Two small airlines, Central and Ozark, were seeking permission to provide transportation service between St. Louis and Tulsa, with a number of intermediate stops. The trial examiner found that both of the contestants had violated the Board's principles of practice. Central had sought to communicate ex parte with a Board member and had encouraged others to "pressure" him. Ozark's officers had stirred up a campaign in the press and in Congress to influence the Board in favor of Ozark. What should be done? The innocent public would benefit from having the service the guilty applicants were desirous of supplying. The trial examiner ruled, and the Board agreed, that the violations should not be regarded as absolutely disqualifying, but should be considered when appraising the comparative fitness of the violators. Taking all the pertinent facts into account, the Board granted the Ozark application.

The Board added that the actions of both lines "fall short of the standards of conduct which the public and this Board are entitled to expect from public service companies that have been granted valuable rights and have assumed important responsibilities in the over-all public interest. It is to be fervently hoped that the conduct of the applicants herein is not representative of the ethical standards of the aviation business community. Nothing less than misfortune can follow such actions if pursued." Apart from fervently hoping, the Board could do little more unless it were ready to disregard the convenience of those who needed air transportation.

SECTION 3.   AGENCY DECISIONS IN PROCEEDINGS NOT REQUIRED TO BE DECIDED "ON THE RECORD"

It would be appropriate to begin the materials of this section by reviewing William Pedersen's description of the course of a typical EPA rulemaking, p. 34 above, and Chapter 3, Section 4's treatment of judicial review of informal proceedings, from p. 436 (Overton Park) through the materials on "hard look," p. 475. The emphasis there was on the judicial view; here, it is on agency functioning, and the possible impact of judicial procedural norms in shaping that functioning. For example, it would be worth considering to what extent proposed § 553(f) of S. 1080, p. 451 above, or any effort at definition of the record in informal rulemaking or adjudication, risks engrafting judicial values on the underlying procedures—as by impairing the possibilities for institutional decision, or establishing as a norm that the opportunity to comment (provide information) is also an opportunity to respond (rebut). Under current section 553, if an agency announces that the public has until 5:00 p.m. on Wednesday, July 10 to comment on a proposal, is a 4:55 p.m. filing on that date timely? Does the statute, then, appear to contemplate a right to respond to the filings of other commenters? Does the statute treat differently material in the agency's possession? Should it? And, if so, why? Or should the chance to respond be provided for *all* submitted filings?

a.   "Ex Parte Contacts" in Proceedings not "On the Record"?

Before Overton Park and like developments started lawyers thinking about what might constitute the "full administrative record," informal (off-record) contacts between an agency and persons interested in the outcome of agency proceedings were not a matter for legal concern outside the narrow constraints of adjudicatory, "on the record" hearings. The whiff of possible corruption, of course, might be a different matter, and this could explain why much was made of contacts which occurred in a proposed FCC rulemaking, the effect of which would have been to award to a St. Louis, Mo. television station a VHF license in lieu of the UHF channel the station was currently assigned.[1]

1. Section 307(b) of the Communications Act directs the Federal Communications Commission so to distribute frequencies and power "among the several States and communities as to provide a fair, efficient, and equitable distribution of radio service to the same." For some years the FCC had considered "de-intermixing" various areas of the country where television service had been provided by both UHF (ultra high frequency) and VHF (very high frequency channels). Many engineers had expressed belief that coverage would increase and conflicts would decrease if available channels were reassigned so that all television dissemination in one area would be in the UHF band (which has seventy channels) and all dissemination in

The commercially less desirable UHF channel would have been reassigned to Springfield, Illinois. Congressional testimony disclosed that the St. Louis station's president had personally called on and had written and telephoned to Commissioners to advocate shifting Channel 2 to St. Louis, had taken them to lunch, and had sent them turkeys as Christmas presents, while the matter was still under consideration. Its attention called to the matter, the Court of Appeals concluded that "whatever the proceeding may be called it involved not only allocation of TV channels among communities but also resolution of conflicting private claims to a valuable privilege, and that basic fairness requires such a proceeding to be carried on in the open. . . . Accordingly the private approaches to the members of the Commission vitiated its action and the proceeding must be reopened." The court directed the Commission to hold a hearing before a special examiner "to determine the nature and source of all ex parte and other approaches that were made to Commissioners while the former proceeding was pending, and any other factors that might be thought to require either disqualification of some Commissioners from participating in the reopened proceeding or disqualification of some parties from receiving any award that may ultimately result." SANGAMON VALLEY TELEVISION CORP. V. UNITED STATES, 269 F.2d 221, 225 (D.C.Cir.1959).[2]

Cornelius J. Peck wrote of the ensuing administrative proceedings in Regulation and Control of Ex Parte Communications with Administrative Agencies, 76 Harv.L.Rev. 233, 273–274 (1962): "In the Sangamon case, the proceedings before the special hearing examiner revealed only that limited ex parte communications were made in a rulemaking proceeding and at a time when commissioners, senators, congressmen and the chief of the Broadcaster's Bureau shared the view of the petitioner that there was nothing improper about such communications.[3] The Commission decided that these did not constitute grounds

another area would be in the VHF band (which has twelve channels).

In 1956 the FCC gave notice of a proposed rulemaking, to amend the existing Table of Television Channel Assignment. The proposed change involved shifting VHF Channel 2 from Springfield, Illinois, to St. Louis, Missouri, and Terre Haute, Indiana, while UHF Channels 26 and 36 would shift from St. Louis and Terre Haute to Springfield. Before the Commission was to reach its final decision about the Springfield-St. Louis-Terre Haute imbroglio, it would substantially have given up its deintermixture campaign. In another effort to encourage development of UHF telecasting, the Commission successfully sponsored a bill to require manufacturers to include a UHF band on all television receivers. Once all-channel receivers became commonplace, intermixture (utilizing both UHF and VHF channels) would be the way to achieve a comprehensive national television system.

2. When that hearing resulted, not in fresh consideration of the assignment of the VHF channel, but merely in a reconsideration (and reaffirmation) of the original action, the Court of Appeals again reversed, directing the Commission to conduct "an entirely new proceeding." 294 F.2d 742 (D.C.Cir.1961). It was again concluded that St. Louis should keep the VHF Channel, and on this occasion the court was satisfied. Fort Harrison Telecasting Corp. v. FCC, 324 F.2d 379 (D.C.Cir. 1963), cert. denied 376 U.S. 915 (1964). For comment on the case, see Note, Are Ex Parte Representations Permissible in Administrative Agency Rule-Making Functions? 28 U.Cin.L.Rev. 338 (1959). And see also Note, Ex Parte Contacts with the Federal Communications Commission, 73 Harv.L.Rev. 1178 (1960).

3. [Ed.] The hearing officer had found that "apart from letters to the Commissioners and personal interviews with them, Tenenbaum [the St. Louis Station's presi-

for disqualification, though it might be considered in a future licensing proceeding as indicative of the applicant's character. . . .

"Most of the cases involving ex parte communications which have come to light involve not cases of injustice actually done, but only cases in which it was possible that justice had not been done. To a certain extent, then, the attention devoted to the problem has been the attention of perfectionists searching for an ideal. . . .

"However, the trapping and punishment of violators is not the reason for enactment of a statute regulating ex parte communications. Nor is the concern that many cases have resulted in decisions different from what they would have been without any such law. The major objective of such legislation would be that of setting a standard of behavior to be followed; its importance would be more in the ethical guide it offered than in the coercive power it made available for enforcement."

As we have seen, Congress subsequently did enact a statute concerning ex parte contacts—but one limited to "on-the-record" proceedings. 5 U.S.C. § 557(d). Informal rulemaking, "conflicting private claims to a valuable privilege," Overton Park review, and "the appearance of justice" coalesced in the following decision:

HOME BOX OFFICE, INC. v. FEDERAL COMMUNICATIONS COMMISSION

United States Court of Appeals, District of Columbia Circuit, 1977.
567 F.2d 9, cert. denied 434 U.S. 829 (1977).

[In March, 1975 the FCC had adopted four amendments to its rules governing the programs which could be shown by paid television services—both subscription broadcasting, and subscription cable television. If contemporary films and sports could be shown over these services, the commercial or advertising television services feared, they

dent], during the years here in review, had a few more or less casual social contacts with some of them—not, however, of such frequency or importance as to warrant more than a passing reference. On visits to Washington, especially during the time of the Congressional committee hearings, he may have had an occasional offhand lunch with one or more of them as his guests. When Commissioner Lee visited St. Louis in August, 1955, to survey the condition of UHF operation there, Tenenbaum had him to dinner at his house, and when Commissioner Webster and his wife were there the following May the Tenenbaums drove them around and invited them to their home for tea. On one occasion in the fall of 1956 Commissioner Bartley went to the theatre with the Tenenbaums as Tenenbaum's guest. These incidents, infrequent as they were, amounted to nothing more than what was normal and not improper under the circumstances, especially in view of the per-

sonal relations that had gradually developed to some extent between them. The same, however, can scarcely be said for Tenenbaum's sending a turkey to the home of each of the Commissioners for Christmas of 1955 and again on Thanksgiving Day of 1956, . . . attentions which were manifestly in bad taste because rendered while proceedings in which he was vitally interested were pending before the Commission and the motive for which could readily have been misconstrued. However, these modest holiday gifts can hardly be said to have risen to the dignity—or descended to the indignity—of bribes or bids for favor."

The St. Louis station had not been alone in interviewing the Commissioners in their offices and "there undoubtedly prevailed a general impression at the time that ex parte presentations were not improper in rulemaking proceedings." 19 Pike & Fischer Radio Reg. 1055 (1960).

would be at a pronounced competitive disadvantage and the quality of conventional television would inevitably be reduced; not all viewers could be reached by, or afford to pay for, subscription television, and these viewers would be injured by this change. Other participants in the rulemaking—metropolitan viewers and subscription service owners—both doubted the asserted competitive effect, and believed that restrictions on the material subscription services could show would inhibit their commercial growth and deprive viewers of diversity. The amendments adopted by the FCC were the product of informal rulemaking initiated during the summer of 1972, including in this instance an oral argument to the Commission, held in October, 1974. While reducing somewhat the rigor of prior restraints, the amendments satisfied neither the commercial nor the subscription broadcast interests (including associated viewer groups) and all promptly sought review in the D.C. Circuit.]

Before WRIGHT, MACKINNON, CIRCUIT JUDGES, and WEIGEL *, DISTRICT JUDGE:

Per Curiam.[1]

. . .

IV. EX PARTE CONTACTS

During the pendency of this proceeding Mr. Henry Geller,[2] a participant before the Commission and an amicus here, filed with the Commission a "Petition for Revision of Procedures or for Issuance of Notice of Inquiry or Proposed Rule Making." In this petition amicus Geller sought to call the Commission's attention to what were alleged to be violations in these proceedings of the ex parte communications doctrine set out by this court in Sangamon Valley Television Corp. v. United States. The Commission took no action in response to the petition, and amicus now presses us to set aside the orders under review here because of procedural infirmity in their promulgation.

. . . In an attempt to clarify the facts this court sua sponte ordered the Commission to provide "a list of all of the ex parte presentations, together with the details of each, made to it, or to any of its members or representatives, during the rulemaking proceedings." In response to this order the Commission filed a document over 60 pages long which revealed, albeit imprecisely, widespread ex parte communications involving virtually every party before this court, including amicus Geller.[3]

---

* Of the United States District Court for the Northern District of California, sitting by designation pursuant to 28 U.S.C. § 292(d) (1970).

1. The opinion in this case is issued as a per curiam, not because it has received less than full consideration by the court, but because the complexity of the issues raised on appeal made it useful to share the effort required to draft this opinion among the members of the panel.

2. [Ed.] Mr. Geller was General Counsel of the FCC until the middle of 1973; he later became Chairperson of the Citizens Communication Center, a public interest group concentrating on broadcast matters.

3. . . . There can be no waiver or estoppel raised here against our consideration of an issue vital to the public as a whole. Therefore, Mr. Geller's "dirty hands," if such they be, present no bar.

. . .

. . . To give a flavor of the effect of these contacts, . . . we think it useful to quote . . . from the brief of amicus Geller: "[Ex parte] presentations have in fact been made at crucial stages of the proceeding. Thus, in early 1974, then-Chairman Burch sought to complete action in this proceeding. Because the Commission was 'leaning' in its deliberations towards relaxing the existing rules . . . American Broadcasting Company's representatives contacted 'key members of Congress,' who in turn successfully pressured the Commission not to take such action.[4] . . . " [I]n the crucial period between the close of oral argument on October 25, 1974 and the adoption of the First Report and Order on March 20, 1975, when the rulemaking record should have been closed while the Commission was deciding what rules to promulgate, . . . broadcast interests met some 18 times with Commission personnel, cable interests some nine times, motion picture and sports interests five times each, and "public interest" intervenors not at all.

Although it is impossible to draw any firm conclusions about the effect of ex parte presentations upon the ultimate shape of the pay cable rules, the evidence is certainly consistent with often-voiced claims of undue industry influence over Commission proceedings, and we are particularly concerned that the final shaping of the rules we are reviewing here may have been by compromise among the contending industry forces, rather than by exercise of the independent discretion in the public interest the Communications Act vests in individual commissioners. Our concern is heightened by the submission of the Commission's Broadcast Bureau to this court which states that in December 1974 broadcast representatives "described the kind of pay cable regulation that, in their view, broadcasters 'could live with.'" If actual positions were not revealed in public comments, . . . the elaborate public discussion in these dockets has been reduced to a sham.

Even the possibility that there is here one administrative record for the public and this court and another for the Commission and those "in the know" is intolerable. Whatever the law may have been in the past, there can now be no doubt that implicit in the decision to treat the promulgation of rules as a "final" event in an ongoing process of administration is an assumption that an act of reasoned judgment has occurred, an assumption which further contemplates the existence of a body of material—documents, comments, transcripts, and statements in various forms declaring agency expertise or policy—with reference to which such judgment was exercised. Against this material, "the full administrative record that was before [an agency official] at the time he

---

4. [S]ee remarks by Everett H. Erlich, Senior Vice President and General Counsel, ABC, before the ABC Television Network Affiliates, Los Angeles, May 10, 1974, at 1: "As most of you know, the FCC just prior to Chairman Burch's sudden departure was on the verge of modifying Pay-TV rules applicable to movies by loosening the 2 and 10–years limitations. They were also considering a so-called 'wild card' exception for 12 to 18 pictures a year which would have exempted entirely the most popular features from the application of any rule. We took the leadership in opposing these proposals with the result that key members of Congress made it known in no uncertain terms that they did not expect the Commission to act on such a far-reaching policy matter without guidance. The Commission got the message and has postponed for several months reconsideration of this particular issue . . . ."

made his decision," Citizens to Preserve Overton Park v. Volpe, supra,
. . . it is the obligation of this court to test the actions of the
Commission for arbitrariness or inconsistency with delegated authority.
Yet here agency secrecy stands between us and fulfillment of our
obligation. As a practical matter, Overton Park's mandate means that
the public record must reflect what representations were made to an
agency so that relevant information supporting or refuting those representations may be brought to the attention of the reviewing courts by
persons participating in agency proceedings. This course is obviously
foreclosed if communications are made to the agency in secret and the
agency itself does not disclose the information presented. Moreover,
where, as here, an agency justifies its actions by reference only to
information in the public file while failing to disclose the substance of
other relevant information that has been presented to it, a reviewing
court cannot presume that the agency has acted properly, but must
treat the agency's justifications as a fictional account of the actual
decisionmaking process and must perforce find its actions arbitrary.

The failure of the public record in this proceeding to disclose all the
information made available to the Commission is not the only inadequacy we find here. Even if the Commission had disclosed to this court
the substance of what was said to it ex parte, it would still be difficult
to judge the truth of what the Commission asserted it knew about the
television industry because we would not have the benefit of an adversarial discussion among the parties. The importance of such discussion
to the proper functioning of the agency decisionmaking and judicial
review processes is evident in our cases. We have insisted, for example,
that information in agency files or consultants' reports which the
agency has identified as relevant to the proceeding be disclosed to the
parties for adversarial comment. Similarly, we have required agencies
to set out their thinking in notices of proposed rulemaking. This
requirement not only allows adversarial critique of the agency but is
perhaps one of the few ways that the public may be apprised of what
the agency thinks it knows in its capacity as a repository of expert
opinion. From a functional standpoint, we see no difference between
assertions of fact and expert opinion tendered by the public, as here,
and that generated internally in an agency: each may be biased,
inaccurate, or incomplete—failings which adversary comment may illuminate. Indeed, the potential for bias in private presentations in
rulemakings which resolve "conflicting private claims to a valuable
privilege," seems to us greater than in cases where we have reversed
agencies for failure to disclose internal studies. . . .

Equally important is the inconsistency of secrecy with fundamental
notions of fairness implicit in due process and with the ideal of
reasoned decisionmaking on the merits which undergirds all of our
administrative law. This inconsistency was recognized in Sangamon,
and we would have thought that the principles announced there so
clearly governed the instant proceeding that there could be no question
of the impropriety of ex parte contacts here. Certainly any ambiguity
in how Sangamon should be interpreted has been removed by recent

congressional and presidential actions.[5] In the Government in the Sunshine Act, for example, Congress has declared it to be "the policy of the United States that the public is entitled to the fullest practicable information regarding the decisionmaking processes of the Federal Government," and has taken steps to guard against ex parte contacts in formal agency proceedings.[6] Perhaps more closely on point is Executive Order 11920, 12 Weekly Comp. of Presidential Documents 1040 (1976), which prohibits ex parte contacts with members of the White House staff by those seeking to influence allocation of international air routes during the time route certifications are before the President for his approval. . . . Thus this is a time when all branches of government have taken steps "designed to better assure fairness and to avoid suspicions of impropriety," White House Fact Sheet on Executive Order 11920 (June 10, 1976), and consequently we have no hesitation in concluding with Sangamon that due process requires us to set aside the Commission's rules here.

From what has been said above, it should be clear that information gathered ex parte from the public which becomes relevant to a rulemaking will have to be disclosed at some time. On the other hand, we recognize that informal contacts between agencies and the public are the "bread and butter" of the process of administration and are completely appropriate so long as they do not frustrate judicial review or raise serious questions of fairness. Reconciliation of these considerations in a manner which will reduce procedural uncertainty leads us to conclude that communications which are received prior to issuance of a formal notice of rulemaking do not, in general, have to be put in a public file. Of course, if the information contained in such a communication forms the basis for agency action, then, under well established principles, that information must be disclosed to the public in some form. Once a notice of proposed rulemaking has been issued, however, any agency official or employee who is or may reasonably be expected to be involved in the decisional process of the rulemaking proceeding, should "refus[e] to discuss matters relating to the disposition of a [rulemaking proceeding] with any interested private party, or an attorney or agent for any such party, prior to the [agency's] decision

---

5. For this reason, we do not think our opinion in Courtaulds (Alabama) Inc. v. Dixon, 294 F.2d 899 (1961), should be interpreted to narrow Sangamon. In Courtaulds it was stipulated that the Federal Trade Commission had considered ex parte communications in formulating its final rules defining rayon. Nonetheless, in upholding the procedures used this court said, "We find no evidence that the Commission improperly did anything in secret or gave to any interested party advantages not shared by all." This finding alone distinguishes Courtaulds from Sangamon and the instant case, in both of which the substance of the contacts was kept secret. Indeed, the Courtaulds court specifically noted that ex parte submissions were "canvassed with the appellant, Government spokesmen and others . . . ." Courtaulds also contained a footnote distinguishing Sangamon on the ground that the rulemaking in Courtaulds did not decide competing private claims to a valuable privilege.

To the extent this same footnote also suggests that Sangamon did not involve rulemaking, it is plainly in error. . . .

6. Of course, the Sunshine Act by its terms does not apply here. Its ex parte contact provisions are couched as an amendment to 5 U.S.C. § 557, and as such the rules do not apply to rulemaking under § 4 of the Administrative Procedure Act, 5 U.S.C. § 553. Moreover, the Act was not in effect at the time of the events in question here.

. . . ," Executive Order 11920, § 4, supra, at 1041. If ex parte contacts nonetheless occur, we think that any written document or a summary of any oral communication must be placed in the public file established for each rulemaking docket immediately after the communication is received so that interested parties may comment thereon. Compare Executive Order 11920, § 5.[7]

. . . [W]e today remand the record to the Commission for supplementation with instructions "to hold, with the aid of a specially appointed hearing examiner, an evidential hearing to determine the nature and source of all ex parte pleas and other approaches that were made to" the Commission or its employees after the issuance of the first notice of proposed rulemaking in these dockets. "All parties to the former proceeding and to the present review may on request participate fully in the evidential hearing," and may further participate in any proceedings before the Commission which it may hold for the purpose of evaluating the report of the hearing examiner.

. . .

[WEIGEL, DISTRICT JUDGE, concurred on other grounds.]

MACKINNON, CIRCUIT JUDGE, concurring specially:

Belatedly, I file the following special concurrence.

. . .

To the extent that our Per Curiam opinion relies upon Overton Park to support its decision as to ex parte communications in this case, it is my view that it is exceeding the authority it cites because here there is no statutory requirement for specific findings nor are the regulations limited to the full administrative record. And our opinion follows up this excessive reliance on Overton Park by an overly broad statement of the rule. . . .

---

7. We do not think these reporting requirements will be unduly burdensome. The overall effect of our opinion will be to require procedures similar to those already in effect in the Consumer Product Safety Commission which the head of that Commission has stated are not burdensome. . . . The scheme we require here is also no more burdensome than that required by the Sunshine Act for formal rulemaking, see 5 U.S.C. § 557(d)(1)(C) or by Executive Order 11920. In addition, agency compliance with this opinion would be in accordance with Recommendations 74–4 of the Administrative Conference of the United States which provides: "1. In the absence of a specific statutory requirement to the contrary, the following are the administrative materials that should be before a court for its use in evaluating, on preenforcement judicial review, the factual basis for rules adopted pursuant to informal procedures prescribed in 5 U.S.C. § 553: (1) the notice of proposed rulemaking and any documents referred to therein; (2) comments and other documents submitted by interested persons; (3) any transcripts of oral presentations made in the course of the rulemaking; (4) *factual information not included in the foregoing that was considered by the authority responsible for promulgation of the rule or that is proffered by the agency as pertinent to the rule;* (5) reports of any advisory committees; and (6) the agency's concise general statement or final order and any documents referred therein. References to the 'record' or 'whole record' in statutes pertaining to judicial review of rules adopted under Section 553 should be construed as references to the foregoing in the absence of a legislative intent to the contrary. The Conference does not assume that the reviewing court should invariably be confined to the foregoing materials in evaluating the factual basis for the rule." 3 Recommendations & Reports of the Administrative Conference of the United States 49 (1974) (emphasis added; footnote omitted). . . .

. . . . [I]n this case . . . the rulemaking undeniably involved competitive interests of great monetary value and conferred preferential advantages on vast segments of the broadcast industry to the detriment of other competing business interests. The rule as issued was in effect an adjudication of the respective rights of the parties vis-a-vis each other. And since that is the nature of the case and controversy that we are deciding and to which our opinion is limited, I would make it clear that that is all we are deciding. I would not make an excessively broad statement to include dictum that could be interpreted to cover the entire universe of informal rulemaking. . . .

NOTES

(1) In ACTION FOR CHILDREN'S TELEVISION [ACT] v. FCC, 564 F.2d 458 (D.C.Cir.1977), a different panel of the D.C.Circuit (Tamm, MacKinnon and Wilkey) refused to apply Home Box Office to another FCC rulemaking proceeding, this time involving television programming and advertising practices for children. In response to a notice of rulemaking based on ACT proposals, over 100,000 comments had been filed; six days of panel discussions and arguments had been held. Early in this proceeding, the broadcast industry had undertaken "limited self-regulation"; after a private meeting with the FCC's Chairman following the Commission hearings, it adopted further measures to control advertising practice. The Commission suspended its rulemaking, pending promised monitoring of these self-regulatory measures. ACT then sought to compel promulgation of specific rules like those the Commission had been considering.

The court declined to apply Home Box Office, holding only that its "broad prescription is not to be applied retroactively . . . inasmuch as it constitutes a clear departure from established law when applied to informal rulemaking proceedings [which do not involve conflicting private claims to a valuable privilege]. . . . " The panel's lengthy opinion, however, left little doubt that it would generally prefer not to apply Home Box Office to such proceedings, whenever they might occur. "We do not propose to argue . . . that ex parte contacts always are permissible in informal rulemaking proceedings—they are of course not—but we do think . . . that ex parte contacts do not per se vitiate agency informal rulemaking action, but only do so if it appears from the administrative record under review that they may have materially influenced the action ultimately taken." Overton Park, this panel felt, was "a somewhat Delphic opinion . . . which . . . should not be read as mandating that the public record upon which our review is based reflect every informational input that may have entered into the decisionmaker's deliberative process.

"If we go as far as Home Box Office does in its ex parte ruling in ensuring a 'whole record' for our review, why not go further to require the decisionmaker to summarize and make available for public comment every status inquiry from a Congressman or any germane material—say a newspaper editorial—that he or she reads or their evening-hour ruminations? In the end, why not administer a lie-detector test to ascertain whether the required summary is an accurate and complete one? The problem is obviously a matter of degree, and the appropriate line must be drawn somewhere. In light of what must be presumed to be Congress' intent not to prohibit or require disclosure of all ex parte contacts during or after the public comment stage, we would draw that line at the point where the rulemaking proceedings involve 'competing claims to a valuable privilege.' It is at that point where the potential for unfair advantage outweighs the practical burdens, which we imagine would not be insubstantial, that such a judicially conceived rule would place upon administrators."

On the merits, the court found the Commission's action "a reasoned exercise of its discretion" and affirmed.

(2) In the wake of the Home Box Office and ACT decisions, the Administrative Conference of the United States, drawing on a report by Professor Nathaniel L. Nathanson,[1] stated that it opposed a general prohibition on ex parte contacts in informal rulemakings, given the flexibility necessary for effective rulemaking. Nonetheless the Conference believed "certain restraints upon such communications may be desirable. Ex parte communications during the rulemaking process can give rise to three principal types of problems. First, decision makers may be influenced by communications made privately, thus creating a situation seemingly at odds with the widespread demand for open government; second, significant information may be unavailable to reviewing courts; and third, interested persons may be unable to reply effectively to information, proposals or arguments presented in an ex parte communication. In the context of Section 553 rulemaking, the first two problems can be alleviated by placing written communications addressed to a rule proposal in a public file, and by disclosure of significant oral communications by means of summaries or other appropriate techniques. The very nature of such rulemaking, however, precludes any simple solution to the third difficulty. The opportunity of interested persons to reply could be fully secured only by converting rulemaking proceedings into a species of adjudication in which such persons were identified as parties, and entitled to be, at least constructively, present when all information and arguments are assembled in a record. In general rulemaking, where there may be thousands of interested persons and where the issues tend to be broad questions of policy with respect to which illumination may come from a vast variety

---

1. Professor Nathanson's report, published at 30 Ad.L.Rev. 377 (1978), concluded with an expression of "concern that [an absolute ban upon ex parte communications] might well prove self-defeating. It is obviously impracticable to apply such a ban to communications occurring before the formal notice of proposed rulemaking is issued. Consequently, the effect of the ban might well be to encourage the agency and the more active or influential members of the industry involved to carry on their most significant discussions before the notice of proposed rulemaking is issued, thus reducing the statutory part of the proceeding to a relatively insignificant formality. If that should happen it would not be the first time that the complications of formal proceedings may have induced administrative agencies to accomplish their most important business by less formal means."

Compare the discussion of the Government in the Sunshine Act, at p. 787 above.

of sources not specifically identifiable, the constraints appropriate for adjudication are neither practicable nor desirable." 1 CFR 305.77–3.

The restraints suggested by the Conference have been widely heeded. Nearly every agency with a substantial rulemaking docket has reported that it follows the Conference's recommendation that all written communications received from the public promptly be made public. The Department of Agriculture, for example, requires "all written submissions made after publication of a notice of proposed rulemaking to be made available for public inspection, unless the submitter has requested confidentially and a determination is made that the records can be withheld under the Freedom of Information Act. . . . Agency practice on handling oral ex parte communications is more varied. The independent regulatory agencies have the most restrictive policies regarding such contacts in rulemaking. . . . The Federal Communications Commission prohibits ex parte communications in the deliberative stage of rulemaking, and it imposes strict disclosure requirements on earlier stages. The Federal Trade Commission is required by the 1980 amendments to the FTC Act to place a verbatim record or summary of ex parte contacts in the rulemaking record. . . . The independent regulatory agencies' policies probably reflect experience with the open-meeting requirements of the Government in the Sunshine Act, . . . Executive agencies which have formal policies governing ex parte communications include the Department of Transportation, the Environmental Protection Agency, and the Federal Emergency Management Agency." Office of the Chairman of the Administrative Conference of the United States, A Guide to Federal Agency Rulemaking 166–68 (1983).

(3) UNITED STATES LINES, INC. v. FEDERAL MARITIME COMMISSION, 584 F.2d 519 (D.C.Cir.1978) gave the D.C. Circuit an opportunity to reconsider Home Box Office in the context of an informal adjudication (see p. 244 above) and in the wake of the Supreme Court's decision in Vermont Yankee. The proceeding concerned possible amendment to a joint operating agreement between two European-based shipping lines, to add a third such line; the amendment was opposed by United States Lines. The ex parte contacts in question were official representations by the French and German governments that they strongly supported the proposed amendments; these were made to the Commission staff after the Commission had tentatively decided to investigate and hear further before permitting the amendment to take effect even provisionally. When the representations were communicated to the Commission, it permitted the amendment to take effect without further proceedings. Judge Wright, the author of the ex parte portions of Home Box Office, wrote the opinion for the court:

"Although the notices from the French and German governments were in no way classified it appears that they were never mentioned or made available to the parties or to the public. . . . The public right to participate in a hearing . . . is effectively nullified when the agency decision is based not on the submissions and information known and available to all, but rather on the private conversations and secret points and arguments to which the public and the participating parties have no access. In such cases the exercise of permitting public comment and response by interested parties—the 'hearing'—is nothing more than a sham.

"The inconsistency of secret ex parte contacts with the notion of a fair hearing and with the principles of fairness implicit in due process has long been recognized. . . . Ex parte contacts . . . also foreclose effective judicial review of the agency's final decision according to the arbitrary and capricious standard of the Administrative Procedure Act. Under this standard the reviewing court must test the actions of the FMC for arbitrariness or inconsistency with delegated authority against 'the full administrative record that was before the [agency official] at the time he made his decision.' Overton Park, supra, 401 U.S. at 420. . . .

"To be sure, while we do not know the precise content of the agency communications or what was revealed of them to the Commission by its staff, we have some idea of the substance of the communications from the memorandum excerpted in the joint appendix. This memorandum, however, hardly provides a substitute sufficient to allow for the 'searching and careful' judicial inquiry required by Overton Park. Moreover, even if the detailed contents of the ex parte contacts were revealed by the agency on judicial review, we would still be deprived of the benefit of an adversarial discussion among the parties. . . . Such comment serves not only to clarify the issues and positions being considered at the agency level, but also to ensure that factual questions underlying the agency's decision are not raised, by necessity, for the first time on judicial review. And adversarial comment is particularly critical where, as here, ex parte communications are made by a party interested in securing the Commission approval necessary for the legality of its contracts; clearly, the potential for bias in Euro-Pacific's presentation is as great as that posed in rulemaking proceedings which resolve 'conflicting private claims to a valuable privilege,' and is indeed greater than in those cases where we have reversed agencies for failure to disclose internal studies.

"The statutory requirement of a hearing in Section 15 proceedings as well as the governing standards for judicial review make clear that ex parte contacts should not have been allowed in these proceedings.[2]

2. . . .

The freedom of administrative agencies to fashion their procedures recognized in Vermont Yankee . . . does not encompass freedom to ignore statutory requirements. The Vermont Yankee Court was careful to point out that "[o]f course, the court must determine whether the agency complied with the procedures mandated by the relevant statutes." Nor does Vermont Yankee provide a basis for agency procedures or practices which effectively foreclose judicial review where, as here, such review is provided for by statute. Nothing in that decision calls into question the well established principle, found in the Administrative Procedure Act and in the decisions of the Supreme Court, that the court is required to conduct a "searching and careful" inquiry to determine whether agency action is arbitrary or capricious, or, in appropriate cases, supported by substantial evidence. Indeed, the Vermont Yankee decision remanded the case to the Court of Appeals for just such an inquiry.

In our decision today we have consistently recognized the freedom of the FMC to structure its hearings as it finds appropriate. We have rejected petitioner's arguments that a full evidentiary hearing with opportunities for oral presentations and cross-examination must of necessity be provided. Our prohibition of ex parte contacts is not based on our choice as to

It is the obligation of the agency, consistent with its duty to afford a hearing and its responsibility to provide a record for judicial review, to guard against such contacts. And where they do unforeseeably occur, the agency must . . . at least disclose the substance of these comments publicly and afford an opportunity for public response. Fairness requires no less." [3]

ERNEST GELLHORN [*] and GLEN O. ROBINSON,[**] RULEMAKING "DUE PROCESS": AN INCONCLUSIVE DIALOGUE [†]

48 University of Chicago Law Review 201, 237–246 (1981).

III.　THE EX PARTE PROBLEM

Publius

. . . [I]n Vermont Yankee the Supreme Court emphatically instructed the court of appeals that "[a]bsent constitutional constraints or extremely compelling circumstances," agencies could not be required to follow procedures beyond those set forth by Congress in the APA (or, presumably, in an agency's authorizing statute). Inasmuch as a rule against ex parte contacts, unlike a rule requiring impartiality, necessarily results in procedural requirements, this language threatens the continued vitality of Home Box Office. The Vermont Yankee Court went on to note that additional procedures could not be justified on the grounds that "a more adequate record . . . will give interested parties more of an opportunity to participate and contribute to the proceedings." This statement undercuts the principal policy justification for the ban on ex parte contacts.

Brutus

Although I would accept your implied conclusion that neither constitutional constraints nor compelling circumstances bar outside contact with agency rulemakers, I do not think Vermont Yankee will carry all the freight you want to load on it. The Court there recognized that rules are still subject to review under the APA's arbitrariness standard to determine whether they are "sustainable on the administrative record made"; this review, which the APA states may be of the "whole record," can examine everything before the agency decision maker, including all ex parte contacts. An effort to control ex parte contacts in rulemaking is therefore well within the traditional role of judicial oversight mandated by Congress. The Home Box Office rule can be explained, consistently with Vermont Yankee, as expressing the

"which procedures are 'best' or most likely to further some vague, undefined public good."

3. [Ed.] Consider again Independent U.S. Tanker Owners Committee v. Lewis, p. 467 above.

* Mr. Gellhorn, a Washington, D.C. practitioner, was Dean of the Case Western Reserve Law School.

** Professor Robinson, of the University of Virginia Law School, was for a time Commissioner of the Federal Communications Commission.

† Reprinted with permission of the authors and the publisher.

determination that the existence of ex parte contacts means that a rule could never be sustained on the record. . . . Home Box Office . . . attempts to ensure the integrity of the rulemaking process as far as practicable by confining basic evidence to that produced "on the record". . . .

Publius

Saying that Home Box Office is necessary to ensure the integrity of the rulemaking process begs the question. Ex parte contacts during notice-and-comment rulemaking were commonplace at the FCC and other agencies before Home Box Office, and no one asserted that such contacts impeached the integrity of rulemaking. . . . [T]he fact that the agencies constantly engaged in ex parte consultations on issues of policy confronting them in rulemaking proceedings without evoking any complaints is clearly relevant to the question of whether such contacts compromise the integrity of the process.

Brutus

You exaggerate the unanimity of acceptance for this practice. The Sangamon Valley case would never have been brought nor decided as it was if ex parte contacts were regarded as wholly innocuous. That the issue of a general ban on ex parte contacts is only now squarely before the courts is probably the result of the same several factors that explain the recent emergence of the bias issue for the first time: the relative newness of agency use of rulemaking to develop important policy issues; an increased concern with open government; and a more active judicial role in reviewing agency action in general and rulemaking in particular. Thus I would not put much reliance on the old test-of-time criterion. It may seem surprising that such basic issues of due process are emerging as questions of first impression this late in the game. But most of the jurisprudence of administrative due process is the creation of the last thirty years.

Publius

Obviously courts can and do change the law not only to accommodate changing social needs but also to reflect changing social and ethical norms. I only meant to suggest that this new ethic created by Home Box Office is indeed new. . . . If the proceeding in Home Box Office is an appropriate occasion for invoking the Sangamon Valley principle, it is difficult to imagine what rulemaking proceedings would not qualify. . . .

I would be more satisfied to see Home Box Office recognized for what it purports to be: a flat ban on ex parte contacts in *all* rulemaking. Only then can the full ramifications of the case be understood, and I hope, corrected.

Brutus

When you say corrected, I assume you mean the case should be overturned.

Publius

I confess to ambivalence on that score. The absence of any constraint on how and where agency officials obtain their information bothers me. I have some sympathy for the argument made to the court in Home Box Office that the ex parte contacts had circumvented the formalities prescribed to ensure reliability in oral argument before the agency. Similar consequences follow, I suppose, whether or not there is oral argument. Whenever interested persons are able to present their facts and arguments to individual agency members and staff without notifying other parties, the rulemaking process imposes no check on the reliability of information presented to the decision makers. This raises obvious concerns of fairness, as well as substantial problems of effectiveness and efficiency, given the problems inherent in evaluating such information. Allowing unfettered ex parte communications also undermines the incentive for interested persons to submit reliable, carefully prepared documents because their work is so easily lost in the shuffle of off-the-record encounters. Many regulatory policy makers are forced to place great reliance on oral briefing and discussion because of the massive quantities of paper confronting them. Because of this reliance, even the most carefully produced commentary of one party can be negated by the offhand, ex parte comments of another.

On the other hand, ex parte contacts also operate as an important check on the reliability of staff information and interpretation. Given the potential unreliability of staff-provided information, ex parte contacts with persons outside the agency are an important means of avoiding "staff capture." To be sure, one does not want an agency to rely entirely on outside informants, but neither does one want it to be the prisoner of agency staff. Indeed, depending on the rigor of the ex parte prohibition, the staff itself may have difficulty obtaining information.

Brutus

I do not understand this concern about possibly inadequate access to information. Surely the agency can ask that any information it feels is necessary to or influential in its decision be submitted on the record, where it is subject to public scrutiny and rebuttal as appropriate.

Publius

Your incomprehension results from your initial mischaracterization of my concern. Obtaining information is not the problem. Agencies seldom want for information or argument in a quantitative sense. If anything, they suffer from the opposite, what Alvin Toffler has described as "information overload." If you examine the docket in any major rulemaking, such as the proceeding at issue in Home Box Office, you will see what I mean. What the agency rulemaker needs is both a means to get to the heart of the case, and an exchange of views with the advocates of competing positions in which he can test his, and their, understanding of the issues. It is somewhat ironic that one of the principal proponents of a ban on ex parte contacts, Judge Wright, should also interpret the APA as requiring rulemaking to provide "a genuine dialogue between agency experts and concerned members of the public." The formal submission of documents to an agency, in response to a formal public notice, seems unlikely to constitute a "genuine" dialogue—but this would be the only permissible communication between the agency and the parties if the ban on ex parte contacts stands. . . . In the absence of a market for the sale of public choice decisions of the kind made in rulemaking, we have no accurate way to evaluate the true demand for different outcomes. Yet this is a vital component of rulemaking, just as it is of legislative lawmaking. . . . An agency is not simply an issuer of edicts; it is also an arbitrator of interests. Again Home Box Office is illustrative. Some of the ex parte contacts involved in that case apparently took place partly for the purpose of exploring possible compromises among the competing groups. It is difficult to envision how such compromise efforts, which are clearly desirable, could be made without some informal contacts.

Brutus

. . . [T]he rulemaker-as-arbitrator is not an appropriate model for agencies. No doubt rules often reflect compromises among competing interest groups. I do not deplore that. Even where rulemaking is a zero-sum game among different interests, agencies are properly sensitive to minimizing the losses to any particular group as a consequence of the rule being adopted. Bargaining is not objectionable except where it is done without rules, which would allow the decision to be unfairly skewed by irrelevant factors such as who was able to contact whom, when, and so forth. On the other hand, why do we have a structured rulemaking process with notice and comment and, in the Home Box Office case, even oral argument? Is this just a warmup for negotiations? I think not. It would seem to be an attempt to require rulemakers to do more than rubberstamp agreements by the affected parties. Instead, they must independently assure themselves, from the evidence produced by these procedures, that the rule is in fact in the public interest. That determination could be rendered illusory by unregulated ex parte contacts creating a predisposition in the rulemaker's mind.

Moreover, I think it is somewhat naive to suppose that it is necessary for an agency rulemaker to have informal discussions with particular parties in order to gain an adequate understanding of their "bottom line." For example, I think your FCC commissioner in Home Box Office would, from the outset, have a pretty good sense of what was soft and what was firm in the positions of the parties as a result of his familiarity with the industry. If he did not, I doubt he would obtain it from ex parte discussions. The parties would be just as likely to seize such an opportunity to impress him with the fervor of their opinions and the rational basis thereof in hopes of securing a completely favorable decision, as they would be to reveal which of their claims they would be willing to concede without any quid pro quo.

Regarding your point about agencies being overloaded with information, your cure is puzzling: ex parte contacts will only add to the overload.[1]

1. [Ed.] See also G. Carberry, Ex Parte Communications in Off-The-Record Administrative Proceedings: A Proposed Limitation on Judicial Innovation, 1980 Duke L.J.

b. Constraints on *Internal* Communications?

As already seen, "ex parte contacts" involving outsiders are carefully distinguished under the Administrative Procedure Act from constraints on communication among co-workers within a government agency. The former, dealt with under 5 U.S.C. § 557(d), are prohibited in all "on the record" proceedings, and an elaborate remedial scheme for exposure of comments not deterred (and possible sanction of the participant) is created. The latter are the concern of 5 U.S.C. §§ 554(d) and 557(b); the prohibition does *not* reach rulemaking, ratemaking, or initial licensing even when these occur "on the record"; and no remedies are directly provided for. These on-the-record settings not reached by Section 554(d) are typically activities of a general policy-making character involving choice of one out of a multitude of possible solutions, rather or more than resolution of an adversary confrontation between two contending forces. "The formation of government policy is not an event but a process. It takes place over a period of time and involves legions of participants, who may never see or know each other. From a distance, government action may appear to be the work of a handful of influential members of Congress or perhaps the head of a federal agency. On close look that image fractures into a thousand pieces." John Quarles, Cleaning Up America 166 (1976).

"Where regulation is enacted there is conflict. Large forces find themselves in opposition, each seeking solutions which threaten social unity. In our society there is a broad basis of consent to the proposition that just at these points administration has a legitimate role in creating solutions. The agencies, specialized and experienced each in its way, are in a position to offer solutions that do not depart so far from the given technical base as to be unacceptable or unworkable. The permanent staff in particular is the repository of this experience. It is the matrix of thinking which can transcend the positions of the parties. Because it is anonymous it is more autonomous. It is politically less vulnerable, its opportunity for 'passing over' to the 'other side' is more restricted. For these reasons it has at times become the target for private interests who fear and resent its influence over the commissioners. To my mind this has much to do with the persistent efforts to devise procedures which isolate the commissions from their staffs." Louis L. Jaffe, The Effective Limits of the Administrative Process: A Re-evaluation, 67 Harv.L.Rev. 1105, 1132–1133 (1954). How, then, ought the concerns with "the record" and communications outside it reflected in the materials just considered be treated where the communications in question originate within the agency?

65 (would limit judicial prohibition on ex parte contacts to informal adjudications where statutory context nonetheless indicates strong public participatory claims, or due process requires on-the-record characteristics); N. Preston, A Right of Rebuttal in Informal Rulemaking, 32 Ad.L.Rev. 621 (1980) (similar argument; "if the 'meaningful public participation' doctrine survives at all, it does so only with respect to agency-generated material, and even that is doubtful").

UNITED STEELWORKERS OF AMERICA, AFL–CIO–CLC
v. MARSHALL

United States Court of Appeals, District of Columbia Circuit, 1980.
647 F.2d 1189, cert. denied 453 U.S. 913 (1981).

Before WRIGHT, CHIEF JUDGE, and ROBINSON and MacKINNON, JUDGES.

J. SKELLY WRIGHT, CHIEF JUDGE:

In November 1978 the Occupational Safety and Health Administration (OSHA), exercising its authority and responsibility under Section 6 of the Occupational Safety and Health Act, 29 U.S.C. § 655 (1976), issued new rules designed to protect American workers from exposure to airborne lead in the workplace. In these consolidated appeals petitioners representing both labor union and industry interests challenge virtually every aspect of the new lead standard and the massive rulemaking from which it emerged. The unions claim that OSHA has failed to carry out its statutory duty to ensure that "no employee will suffer material impairment of health." Id. § 655(b)(5). The industry parties charge OSHA with almost every procedural sin of which an agency can be guilty in informal rulemaking, attack some of the most important substantive provisions of the standard as exceeding OSHA's statutory authority, and assert that the agency has failed to present substantial evidence to support the factual bases of the standard.

. . .

III. PROCEDURAL CLAIMS

OSHA was occasionally careless or inefficient in its procedures throughout this rulemaking, and we readily concede that procedural purists will never place the lead standard in the Pantheon of administrative proceedings. Moreover, we concede that most of the Lead Industry Association [LIA]'s procedural claims raise difficult legal issues, and indeed force us to consider a number of important questions of informal rulemaking procedure that have not been fully resolved by this circuit in recent years. Nevertheless, we enter this area under two important restraints. First, as a legal matter, we generally have no power to impose extra-statutory procedural requirements on the agency unless it has violated the Constitution or flagrantly disregarded minimal principles of procedural fairness. Vermont Yankee Nuclear Power Corp. v. Natural Resources Defense Council, Inc., 435 U.S. 519 (1978). Second, as both a legal and a practical matter, we must recognize the procedural flexibility inherent in informal rulemaking, as well as the difficulty an agency faces in managing hundreds of comments and witnesses and developing a coherent standard out of tens of thousands of pages of record evidence.

The OSH Act requires the agency to follow procedures more stringent than the minimal ones established in the Administrative Procedure Act. Thus the agency must give interested parties the opportunity to request a public hearing on objections to a proposed rule, and must publish notice of the time and place for such hearing in the

Federal Register. Moreover, the agency has added to these statutory procedures by rule. Thus OSHA itself requires a hearing examiner at oral hearings, who must provide an opportunity for cross-examination on important issues and offer interested persons verbatim transcripts of the hearing.

Nevertheless, Congress' decision to impose the substantial evidence test on OSHA does not alter the essentially informal character of OSHA rulemaking. Industrial Union Dep't, AFL–CIO v. Hodgson, 499 F.2d 467, 472–473 (D.C.Cir.1974). . . . Thus, as we examine the procedural claims in the lead proceeding, we must avoid imposing procedural constraints beyond those in APA Section 553, the OSH Act, and the Due Process Clause, and we remain bound by judicial construction of the demands of APA Section 553 as our source for the general principles of informal rulemaking. . . .

B. Improper Staff Role and Separation of Functions

LIA aims its . . . procedural attack at OSHA staff attorneys who, LIA argues, acted essentially as advocates for a stringent lead standard by consulting with and persuading the Assistant Secretary as she drew her conclusions from the record. LIA would have us conclude that the agency decisionmaker engaged in ex parte, off-the-record contacts with one of the adverse sides in the rulemaking, thereby rendering the proceedings unfair. Grounding its contention somewhat equivocally on due process, the procedural principles inherent in hybrid rulemaking, and OSHA's own regulations providing for cross-examination, LIA asks us to invalidate the entire proceeding.

The key agency employee in question was Richard Gross, a lawyer in the Office of the Solicitor at OSHA, who served as a so-called "standard's attorney" throughout the rulemaking. . . . The standard's attorney was at the center of activity throughout the rulemaking. He worked with the regular OSHA staff in reviewing preliminary research and drafting the proposed standard, all the while offering informal legal advice. He helped organize the public hearings and, having immersed himself in the scientific literature and in the submitted public comments, he communicated regularly with the prospective expert witnesses. In these communications he briefed the witnesses on the issues they were to address in their testimony, explained the positions of the agency, the industry, and the unions on key questions, discussed the likely criticism of the experts' testimony, and asked the experts for any new information that supported or contradicted the OSHA proposal.[1] During the hearing itself he conducted all initial

---

1. The letters of Gross' colleague, Donald Kuchenbecker, to two of the expert medical witnesses best reveal the work of the standard's attorney. ALD 66–82. The letters are exhaustively detailed and generally quite neutral in briefing the witnesses on the important medical issues and urging them to supply all new relevant evidence, including any at odds with a stringent lead standard. Nevertheless, Kuchenbecker did make some imprudent remarks. He told Dr. Piomelli that it "would not be helpful to OSHA" if the latter were to state that there was no correlation between air-lead and blood-lead measurements, and told both Dr. Piomelli and Dr. Seppalainen that OSHA wanted to avoid the "ticklish issue" of how to accommodate female workers of child-bearing age if feasibility limits required OSHA to set a standard that threatened such women but not other workers.

questioning of OSHA witnesses and cross-examined all other witnesses. After the hearings he assisted the Assistant Secretary by reviewing the evidence in the record, preparing summaries, analyses, and recommendations, and helping draft the Preamble to the final standard.

In a proceeding to create a general rule it makes little sense to speak of an agency employee advocating for one "side" over another. However contentious the proceeding, the concept of advocacy does not apply easily where the agency is not determining the specific rights of a specific party, and where the proposed rule undergoes detailed change in its journey toward a final rule. Indeed, as OSHA notes, the true adversaries here may well have been the industry and the unions, since the final standard, while in no sense a mathematical compromise, did fall between the old standard, to which the industry had resigned itself, and the extremely stringent one the unions urged. Thus, the standard's attorney may have been an advocate for *some* new lead standard, and probably even a stringent one, but not necessarily for one specific standard supported by one specific party.

Nevertheless, the adversary tone and format of the proceedings are obvious. . . . The Assistant Secretary might well have been able to assess the record more objectively—if less efficiently—had the standard's attorney not been constantly at her side. Therefore, although we have some doubt about calling the standard's attorney an "advocate" in the context of such rulemaking,[2] we will *assume* he played that role so we can measure his conduct against the legal constraints on the agency.[3]

We note at the outset that nothing in the Administrative Procedure Act bars a staff advocate from advising the decisionmaker in setting a final rule. . . . Moreover, in establishing the special hybrid procedures in the OSH Act, Congress never intended to impose the separation-of-functions requirement it imposes in adjudications.

In context, these remarks do not overcome the generally objective import of the letters; moreover, Kuchenbecker himself did not advise the Assistant Secretary on the final standard, and we are loath to project his attitude onto Gross.

2. We also have some doubt as to the wisdom of singling out a staff *lawyer* in this case, when other, nonlegal, staff people probably participated with great vigor both in developing the agency position during the hearings and in advising the Assistant Secretary in drafting the final standard. . . .

3. We assume, however, only that the standard's attorney may have influenced the Assistant Secretary by reinforcing, according to his bias, certain information and arguments that they were put in the record of the public proceedings. Thus this is not a case where agency employees supplied the decisionmaker with actual new evidence which the agency has identified as part of the basis of its decision, but which it has refused to disclose except through a "blind reference." The distinction is important, since we were referring only to the latter situation when we stated, in the course of restricting ex parte contacts, in Home Box Office, Inc. "From a functional standpoint, we see no difference between assertions of fact and expert opinion tendered by the public . . . and that generated internally in an agency . . . ."

In the absence of proof by LIA that the staff did supply the decisionmaker with new hard data off the record, our assumption that the staff lawyer was an advocate does not mean that he was anything other than a *staff* advocate. That is, even if he were predisposed on the lead standard, the standard's attorney's conduct remained within the general boundaries of the *deliberative* process and, however biased, his communications with the Assistant Secretary remained within the boundaries of *deliberative* material. . . .

The legislative history shows that Congress consistently turned back efforts to impose such formal procedures on OSHA standard-setting. . . . [U]nder the Supreme Court's decision in Vermont Yankee that is virtually the end of the inquiry. Unless we find that the standard's attorney here violated the due process rights of the petitioners, or that this is one of those "extremely compelling circumstances" in which courts remain free to impose nonconstitutional extra-statutory procedures on agencies, id., we must reject LIA's challenge here.

In Home Box Office, of course, we expressed our general concern that whenever the record fails to disclose important communications that may have influenced the agency decisionmaker, the court cannot fully exercise its power of review. But we spoke there in the context of massive evidence that industry parties financially interested in the rulemaking secretly lobbied with FCC staff and commissioners. . . . Influence from within an agency poses no such threat. . . . Moreover, an OSHA rulemaking proceeding is of a character wholly distinct from that of a proceeding which resolves "conflicting private claims to a valuable privilege," Sangamon Valley Television Corp. v. United States, 269 F.2d 221, 224 (D.C.Cir.1959), and from a "quasi-adjudicatory" proceeding in which we found the potential for bias as great as that in a case of competing claims, United States Lines, Inc. v. FMC, supra.

In only one recent case have we actually addressed the propriety of ex parte contacts between agency decisionmakers and agency staff, but even there our discussion of the issue was only dictum, and indeed essentially supports OSHA here. In Hercules, Inc. v. EPA, 598 F.2d 91 (D.C.Cir.1978) we dealt with a claim that the chief judicial officer of the Environmental Protection Agency, who assisted the Administrator in setting final regulations on two toxic substances, consulted after the record was closed with staff experts, including two staff lawyers who had represented the staff position at the administrative hearing. We noted that the problem was one "of great sensitivity," which caused us some "uneasiness," and on which we suggested we might rule when a more concrete case than the one there presented itself.

To be sure, most of the special factors we cited in avoiding ruling on the issue in Hercules, Inc. are absent here.[4] Nevertheless, LIA's reading of Hercules, Inc. ignores the almost unmistakable conclusion we drew there: that the issue was one for Congress or the agencies to resolve. . . .

---

4. The judicial officer in Hercules, Inc. v. EPA, supra note 19, only consulted the staff attorneys on the location of documents in the record; she did not discuss facts and policy with them. 598 F.2d at 121–122. The proceeding in that case was complete before we handed down Home Box Office, so we followed Action for Children's Television, Inc. v. FCC, 564 F.2d 458, 474 (D.C.Cir.1977), in refusing to apply Home Box Office retroactively. Hercules, Inc. v. EPA, supra, 598 F.2d at 126. These two factors obviously distinguish Hercules, Inc. from the present case. Of a third factor, however, we are less sure. We noted in Hercules, Inc. that Congress had created, and the courts had reinforced, severe and rigid timetables for rulemaking on toxic substances, so the agency needed all the help it could get in the face of the massive record there to comply with the law. Id. Although OSHA is not under the same specific restraints, its proceedings, like EPA's, involve records of "extraordinary bulk and complexity," id., and its mandate, like EPA's, invokes "the rule of ancient origin that expedition in protecting the public health justifies less elaborate procedure than may be required in other contexts." Id. (citing cases).

Rulemaking is essentially an institutional, not an individual, process, and it is not vulnerable to communication within an agency in the same sense as it is to communication from without. In an enormously complex proceeding like an OSHA standard setting, it may simply be unrealistic to expect an official facing a massive, almost inchoate, record to isolate herself from the people with whom she worked in generating the record. In any event, we rest our decision not on our own theory of agency management, but on the state of the law.

C. Improper Use of Consultants

LIA makes two attacks on OSHA's reliance on out-of-house consultants in developing the lead standard.

The first attack goes to the *general use* of consultants and the effect thereof on the Assistant Secretary's exercise of her duty to determine the final standard. LIA contends that the Assistant Secretary hired so many consultants and relied on them so heavily for so many tasks that she essentially abdicated her responsibility for setting the lead standard to outsiders. . . .

The record shows that OSHA did make rather broad requests for help from the consultants. As we discuss below, OSHA relied heavily on David Burton Associates (DBA) and Nicholas Ashford and his Center for Policy Alternatives (CPA) in examining the data on feasibility and developing a "technology-forcing" rationale for the standard. The agency hired a number of other expert consultants, giving them fairly broad mandates to summarize and evaluate data in the record, prepare record data for computer processing, and help draft portions of the Preamble and the final standard. LIA argues that such reliance on outsiders invites abuse, even if one assumes the honesty of the ones in this case, since hired hands have a financial incentive to tell the agency what it wants to hear, and have no civil service protection against retaliation for telling uncomfortable truths.

. . .

LIA's position . . . comes down to the challenge that OSHA has violated the principle of Morgan I: "The one who decides must hear," and an agency denies the parties a true hearing if the official who acts for the agency has not personally confronted the evidence and the arguments. Though Morgan I expressly allowed agency officials to rely on their subordinates in reviewing the record, it did not, of course, address the question of outside consultants. Nevertheless, applying the general principle of Morgan I, we see that LIA cannot buttress its general allegation of excessive reliance with any specific proof that the Assistant Secretary failed to confront personally the essential evidence and arguments in setting the final standard. Without at this point addressing the substantive validity of the lead standard, we note that in the lengthy Preamble and Attachments to the final standard the decisionmaker reviewed the evidence and explained the evidentiary bases for each part of the standard. Moreover, the Assistant Secretary demonstrated her independence from the consultants by strongly criticizing some of their conclusions on the key issue of feasibility.

To inquire further would be to probe impermissibly into the mental processes by which the Assistant Secretary made her decision. The unsupported allegation that hired consultants might have an incentive to act dishonestly cannot overcome the presumption that agency officials and those who assist them have acted properly. Thus we generally see no reason to force agencies to hire enormous regular staffs versed in all conceivable technological issues, rather than use their appropriations to hire specific consultants for specific problems.

LIA's second attack goes to *specific* uses of consultants, and alleges damage to the state of the rulemaking record, rather than to the Assistant Secretary's fulfillment of her personal responsibility. After closing the record, OSHA sought help from outside consultants in reviewing the record and preparing the Preamble. Two consultants were primary. The agency asked David Burton and DBA to help review the record to determine the feasibility of a permissible air-lead standard of 50 ug/m^3, as opposed to the 100 ug/m^3 standard the agency had proposed in the original notice of rulemaking, and on which most of the public commentary had focused. And OSHA asked Nicholas Ashford and CPA to analyze, in light of the record, the possibility of marking a correlation between air-lead levels and blood-lead levels. Both these consultants had previously aided OSHA by supplying on-the-record reports and testifying as expert witnesses at the public hearings. Both fulfilled the new requests by submitting written reports, of 117 and 192 pages respectively, neither of which the agency has released or placed in the rulemaking record. LIA contends that the reports are illegal ex parte communications which, like the communications with the staff advocates described earlier, constitute "secret briefs" and off-the-record evidence which LIA was deprived of a chance to rebut and the court a chance to review.

We note first that, as in the case of the staff-influence charge discussed earlier, LIA has not identified any hard data or new legal arguments which are contained only in the allegedly improper *ex parte* communications and on which OSHA demonstrably relied in setting the standard. Thus LIA has not shown that OSHA has materially prejudiced parties who were not privy to the communications. Rather, LIA asks us to infer that there must have been such *ex parte* evidence or legal argument, its request essentially relying on three factors: (1) The consultants were not agency employees; (2) they had previously testified as expert witnesses and prepared on-the-record reports; and (3) the documents we have before us, which describe the agreements and expectations between OSHA and the consultants and the content of the undisclosed reports, imply that actual new evidence was requested and supplied. We find the first two factors legally irrelevant, or at least insufficient to prove impropriety. As for the third, as we demonstrate below, we simply reject LIA's construction of the documents.

The documents show that the communications between the agency and the consultants were simply part of the deliberative process of drawing conclusions from the public record. The consultants acted after the record was closed as the functional equivalent of agency staff, so the question of the legal propriety of OSHA's reliance on DBA and CPA is foreclosed by our earlier conclusion that neither the APA nor the Home Box Office doctrine imposes a separation-of-functions requirement on the agencies. Thus, even though we readily assume that OSHA used the consultants' reports—and even incorporated parts of them verbatim in the Preamble—LIA has suffered no legal prejudice from such use.

. . .

When performed by agency *staff,* [the] sort of sophisticated review of evidence [the consultants performed in this case] has always been recognized as legitimate participation in the deliberative process. And the circuit courts, in applying the intra-agency exemption to the Freedom of Information Act, 5 U.S.C. § 552(b)(5) (1976), have recognized that where outside consultants so engage in the deliberative process there is no *functional* difference between staff and consultants, and so there should be no *legal* difference. . . .

In Lead Industries Ass'n, Inc. v. OSHA, 610 F.2d 70 (2d Cir. 1979), Judge Friendly examined the same affidavits, agreements, and indices that we have examined, and concluded that both the DBA report and the CPA report contributed to the process by which the Assistant Secretary made her final decision. He conceded that the reports might contain some factual matter, but asserted that in a vast rulemaking like this one such information was necessarily incident to and not severable from the process of summary and analysis. He suggested, moreover, that to the extent the reports drew inferences from and weighed the evidence they were more truly "deliberative" and thus better candidates for [Freedom of Information Act] exemption than mere summaries of the record. . . .

MacKINNON, CIRCUIT JUDGE (dissenting): . . .

Subsequent to the close of the record in this rulemaking, and prior to the promulgation of the final standard, OSHA contracted with outside consultants to perform an evaluation, presumably only of record evidence,[5] on two topics. First, the agency asked David Burton and David Burton Associates (DBA) to review the voluminous record and evaluate the feasibility of a permissible air-lead exposure standard of 50 ug/m^3. The rule as proposed in the notice, and virtually all of the record evidence, referred only to the feasibility of a permissible expo-

---

5. Without a review of the actual reports submitted by the consultants, which are not available, it cannot be determined whether or not they contain new, extra-record evidence. The majority reads vague statements from the contracts which designate the evaluating responsibilities of DBA and CPA, and concludes that only record evidence was to have been reviewed to formulate their analyses. However, far too little weight is given to the statement in the CPA contract to the effect that the consultant was permitted "to conduct additional research and prepare material supplementary to the above testimony. . . . " This concern only magnifies the insuperable handicap with which the Court is afflicted by being forced to rule on the propriety of these reports, without ever seeing them. *This is a fatal defect in the record.*

sure limit of 100 ug/m³. Burton and DBA had previously prepared reports for OSHA which had been introduced into the record, and *had testified as expert witnesses during the public hearings in support of the economic and technological feasibility of the 100 ug/m³ proposed level.* After the record was closed the agency also contracted with the Center for Policy Analysis and Nicholas Ashford to analyze the scientific and medical correlation between air-lead and blood-lead levels. Ashford had submitted a preliminary report on this correlation during the record period as an expert witness for OSHA. The lengthy analyses prepared by the consultants in fulfillment of their contractual responsibilities have *never* been released to the parties or the public, despite the fact that as far as the report on the economic and technological feasibility of 50 ug/m³ is concerned, it is the only in depth evidence on the topic in existence. The delegation of this task to these biased witnesses, and the failure to introduce the reports into evidence, constitute prejudicial error which requires the remand of the case to the agency on this point. As Chief Justice Hughes remarked in Morgan I, "[n]othing can be treated as evidence which is not introduced as such." In the absence of this report there is insufficient evidence to support the finding.

The majority is correct in the first part of its section addressing the use of outside consultants, in concluding that they may be hired to aid the agency perform many of its tasks. See 29 U.S.C. § 656(c) (1976). However, fundamental requirements of fairness and due process in administrative law compel that these outside consultants to whom the agency delegates its obligation to evaluate the evidence must be unbiased and neutral in their evaluation of the record. Just as the actual decision-maker is to be unbiased, so must those to whom such duty is delegated. No court should condone allowing paid consultants to legally change their hats from expert witnesses subject to cross-examination during the hearings, to "agency staff" hired after the close of hearings to evaluate the credibility of *their own testimony* and others. . . . Subjecting these consultants to cross-examination initially, and then giving them free reign to evaluate and weigh all contrary testimony, is in effect giving them free and unbridled rebuttal without the benefits that might flow from cross-examination. And OSHA cannot contend that the substance of these secret reports does not relate to "crucial issues" because they go to the very core of the standard. . . .

NOTES

(1) LEAD INDUSTRIES ASS'N v. EPA, 647 F.2d 1130 (D.C.Cir.1980), cert. denied 449 U.S. 1042 (1981) was a companion case challenging EPA's regulation of air-borne emissions of lead into public spaces. One branch of the argument here was that the lead standards were rendered invalid by the participation of David Hawkins, head of EPA's Office of Air, Noise and Radiation. Hawkins had previously been a staff attorney for the Natural Resources Defense Council, a participant in the rulemaking, and while there had appeared for it before a Senate hearing and an executive advisory committee to present testimony on

air-borne lead as a pollutant; he appeared as a spokesman, and within NRDC had apparently not been involved in the particular issues raised in the lead standards rulemaking. He had resigned from NRDC before joining EPA. LIA's effort to disqualify Hawkins was clouded by questions about its timeliness in raising the issue; if it had raised the issue in timely fashion, ought it to have succeeded? Or are there important distinctions to be made between judicial figures previously involved in adjudication, and policy-makers previously involved in presenting an organization's position on an issue in other forums? Between involvement with particular factual issues and association with general (albeit fact-driven) policy concerns? See P. Strauss, Disqualifications of Decisional Officials in Rulemaking, 80 Colum.L.Rev. 990 (1980).

(2) Do you agree with the argument that, for informal proceedings, the appropriate claims of outsiders to know about staff/agency communications are limited to significant new factual data [1] or the use of staff as a conduit to convey the views of outsiders,[2] as distinct from policy analyses privileged from disclosure under Exemption 5 of the Freedom of Information Act, pp. 735–748 above?

NATIONAL SMALL SHIPMENTS TRAFFIC CONFERENCE, INC. v. ICC, 725 F.2d 1442 (D.C.Cir.1984) concerns a recent outcome of informal rulemaking begun in 1969 to reexamine the way in which handling costs at freight truck terminals were allocated among shippers of high and low bulk commodities. One complaint about the outcome, which found a higher proportion of the costs should be borne by smaller-size shippers, was that the bureaucratic decision process within the ICC had prevented staff analyses favorable to the smaller-size shippers from reaching the Commission:

"Under existing law, an agency decisionmaking body such as the Commission may delegate detailed consideration of the administrative record to its subordinates while retaining the final power of decision for itself. Rather than wade through the entire record personally, then, members of the body are free to rely on summaries prepared by agency staff. Because of the strong presumption of regularity in administrative proceedings, reviewing courts will not normally entertain procedural challenges that members of the body inadequately considered the issues before reaching a final decision, or that staff reports on which the body relied imperfectly summarized the record under review, cf. Montrose Chemical Corp. v. Train, 491 F.2d 63, 71 (D.C.Cir.1974).

"At some point, however, staff-prepared synopses may so distort the record that an agency decisionmaking body can no longer rely on them in meeting its obligations under the law. . . . Certainly, if subordinates systematically eliminated from their reports all mention of record comments adverse to the agency's final action, the consideration requirement would not be satisfied unless the decisionmakers took

---

1. Portland Cement Ass'n v. Ruckleshaus, p. 480 above; National Wildlife Federation v. Marsh, 568 F.Supp. 985 (D.D.C.1983) ("new data introduced by the [100 page, post-hearing] Staff Evaluation was not simply 'a bit of background information'. . . . ")

2. Cf. United States Lines v. FMC, p. 929 above.

independent steps to familiarize themselves with withheld portions of the record.

"This analysis suggests that petitioners do have a legal right that their comments reach Commission members in at least summary form, and that those comments be considered before final action is taken.[3] Neither the APA nor the due process clause, however, accords similar treatment to staff evaluations that move beyond a mere summary of record comments to express the independent judgments of subordinate agency personnel. An agency is free to structure its internal policy debate in any manner it deems appropriate. Mid-level managers may therefore filter out the evaluations of lower-level personnel if they so choose, so long as relevant record comments are not eliminated in the process as well. . . . [W]hat appears to have occurred is a lively debate in which other ICC offices seriously questioned the soundness of various aspects of the study methodolgy, and in which the Bureau responded with refined statistical analyses to support its conclusions. The Bureau of Accounts ultimately prevailed, not because it unfairly suppressed legitimate internal dissent, but because it convinced other division heads that its weight-only formula was not materially flawed by admitted shortcomings in the study's design and execution."

(3) COMMODITY EXCHANGE v. COMMODITY FUTURES TRADING COMMISSION, 543 F.Supp. 1340 (S.D.N.Y.1982), affirmed per curiam 703 F.2d 682 (2d Cir.1983), concerned a proceeding in which the CFTC disapproved a rule that had been adopted for self-governance by Comex, a commodity exchange subject to its supervision; by statute such disapprovals were to follow "notice and an opportunity for hearing." The CFTC followed notice and comment rulemaking procedures in considering the disapproval; after Comex and others had filed detailed written comments, and Comex met to discuss its position with CFTC staff, the CFTC met with its staff for a final discussion that—pursuant to the Government in the Sunshine Act, p. 788ff. above—was open to the public. The court rejected any claim that the Exchange was entitled to adjudicatory or on-the-record proceedings; "[e]xamination of the record shows that the Commission's action was rulemaking in nature. Its inquiry into the operation of the Straddle Rules involved consideration of general economic and policy matters upon which it based its judgment. Its ultimate determination was not only of particular applicability to Comex, but also established a policy which applied to all contract markets in the same manner. . . . [E]ven when only one entity is the immediate subject of an agency's action, this alone does not change its rulemaking nature for other entities may nevertheless be affected. As the Commission pointed out, disapproval of a contract market rule often affects the interests of other exchanges and market participants, particularly traders. In order to allow the participation of all concerned, only rulemaking not adjudication, provides the appropriate procedural format." Nonetheless, the court concluded that the statutory hearing provision required the CFTC to afford Comex an opportunity

---

3. This right remains subject, however, to the long-standing rule that courts will not probe the mental processes of administrative decisionmakers absent strong evidence of bad faith or other misconduct. *Overton Park*, 401 U.S. at 420.

to make an oral presentation. "Since the Commission permitted its own staff to make oral statements in support of its recommendation for disapproval, to respond to questions by the Commission, and to negate Comex's prior written submission, there is no reason why Comex should not be afforded a similar opportunity.[4]" Do you agree?

SECTION 4. SOME COMPLICATIONS AT THE TOP

Thus far, we have looked at the process of decision largely as it concerns an individual proceeding—as if that were the sole relevant matter before the decision-maker, without particular regard for the activities of yesterday or tomorrow. This is an easy perspective for those accustomed to thinking in judicial terms. Though a court may have many cases pending at any given moment, all require similar intellectual functions, and analyses of the judicial function tend *not* to focus on the interrelatedness of pending matters in either fact or policy terms. We expect that the particular facts a judge learns in proceeding A will not be used in deciding proceeding B; and to the extent we notice a flow of related legal (or policy) issues passing before a judicial tribunal, the observation that these might be seized upon to accomplish a consciously formed objective of legal development is as likely to provoke criticism as admiration. Similarly, the common use of life tenure or at least lengthy terms of office, frees our thinking about judicial behavior from concern for the impact of the judge's future career.

If such a perspective is apt for judicial activities, the cases of the last two sections—PATCO and Home Box Office in particular—must suggest that it is seriously flawed in administrative settings. The interrelatedness of issues arising before an administrator very likely sparked the creation of her agency; she may virtually be commanded to detect and to domesticate the patterns which emerge from the flow of facts passing before her. Often, moreover, that effort is one not limited to one type of activity: investigation, enforcement, and general policy-making are as much part of the daily apparatus of operation as quasi-judicial decision. The administrator must answer to the world of politics—to the legislature, the executive, the press, the trade association, the consumer group—as well as to the judiciary, and this supposes meetings, pressures, and demands few judges encounter. "[P]ublic administrators at every level are enveloped by a matrix of contending policy initiators . . . —the legislature, the administrative network, and the nongovernmental environment. Public administration is marked by multiple points of access, which reproduce a bewildering array of problems in the never-ending process of policy administration." W. Boyer, Bureaucracy on Trial 67 (1964). Finally, the impermanence of administrative position may be considered—administrators at the highest rank are *neither* permanent nor even particularly long-term

---

4. Providing Comex an opportunity for oral presentation of its views resolves its claim that providing only the staff with such an opportunity was an ex parte communication in violation of 5 U.S.C. § 554(d) (1977).

employees. They come from another economic life and move on to other activity after an average four or five years, often much less. Even if they have ambitions in government for the longer term, like Commissioner Applewhaite in PATCO, they must pursue them within a designedly political process for appointment. Each of these factors should suggest complications, additional strains on the fabric of decision possibly requiring correction in individual cases in which they appear or institutional reform to avoid their effects generally.

a. Multiplicity of Function

Early in this chapter, in considering the role of the administrative law judge, we discussed preliminarily the problem of disqualifying bias. The rules there developed are not tuned to the possibly special circumstances of administration, but are equally applied to—indeed largely arise from—judicial decisions. In general, we saw, the concern of those cases was for preserving circumstances conducive to objective and impartial decision of factual issues, free from the influence of extrajudicial knowledge about the particular circumstances of the controversy and from the warping influences of financial gain, friendship and other externalities. We saw, inter alia, that prior service as a judge in such a context is *not* disqualifying; the judge whose verdict has once been reversed is ordinarily regarded as fully capable to preside over a second trial despite what he "knows" from the first. We now turn to knowledge that comes to an administrator, not from prior "judicial" involvement, but from his prior activities in *other* functions, as investigator, rulemaker, congressional witness, or featured luncheon speaker.

In this discussion, we will continue to be concerned with predisposition as to particular fact, not policy, outcomes. See Comment, Prejudice and the Administrative Process, 59 Nw.U.L.Rev. 216 (1966). Although the wisdom or even the permissibility of a given policy or rule may be open to heated debate, persistent support of particular policies is what the public expects (and does not always receive) from its administrators, not an ill to be guarded against. Judges are not expected to "be neutral toward the purposes of the law" they enforce. L.L. Jaffe, The Reform of Administrative Procedure, 2 Pub.Admin.Rev. 141, 149 (1942). No more are administrators supposed to lack enthusiasm for the policies they believe to be embodied in the statutes they administer. If the FTC is poorly disposed toward anti-competitive activity, or a workmen's compensation board tends to resolve doubtful points in favor of allegedly disabled claimants, each can be charged with no more than effectuating the policy it was established to administer.

ASH GROVE CEMENT CO. v. FTC
United States Court of Appeals, Ninth Circuit, 1978.
577 F.2d 1368.

Before CARTER and HUG, CIRCUIT JUDGES and HAUK, DISTRICT JUDGE.

JAMES M. CARTER, CIRCUIT JUDGE:

Ash Grove is a major supplier and manufacturer of portland cement (hereafter "portland") which is the major and most expensive ingredient of ready-mix cement (hereafter "ready-mix"). Between 1961 and 1966 Ash Grove sold an average of about 400,000 barrels of portland annually in the Kansas City Metropolitan Area (KCMA). This amounted to between 13% and 18% of the total annual sales of portland in the KCMA. Most portland was sold to manufacturers of ready-mix.

On June 1, 1964, Ash Grove purchased 50% of the stock of Fordyce Concrete, a ready-mix manufacturer engaged in business in the KCMA since 1961. About two and one-half years later, on November 8, 1966, Ash Grove purchased the outstanding 50% of Fordyce stock, thereby obtaining 100% ownership. . . .

In the early 1960's Ash Grove also acquired . . . the stock of Lee's Summit, another ready-mix manufacturer in the KCMA. . . . In effect Ash Grove, through these two acquisitions, had acquired customer firms which, combined, represented nearly one-fifth of the KCMA ready-mix industry. . . . In April, 1964, the FTC announced that due to the "growing importance and urgency" of the industry-wide trend toward integration of the cement industry, it would institute a trade regulation rule proceeding to organize and appraise "the general economic facts involving [the cement] industry and market structure. . . . " Permanente Cement Co., 65 F.T.C. 410, 494 (1964). . . .

After nearly two years of study [by its Division of Industry Analysis,] the Bureau of Economics on April 4, 1966, transmitted to the Commissioners the staff report entitled Economic Report on Mergers and Vertical Integration in the Cement Industry (hereafter "Economic Report"). The Economic Report analyzed twenty-two target metropolitan areas, including the KCMA, to determine the extent and anticompetitive effects of vertical integration in the cement industry. No trade regulation rule was ever issued.

The Economic Report was the subject of public hearings in June 1966.[1] On January 3, 1967, the FTC, based on the report and the public hearings, issued its Enforcement Policy with Respect to Vertical Mergers in the Cement Industry (hereafter "Enforcement Policy"). The Enforcement Policy concluded that vertical mergers in the cement industry, particularly those involving ready-mix companies, "can have substantial adverse effects on competition in the particular market areas where they occur." Guidelines were promulgated to indicate which mergers the FTC would be likely to challenge. However, it was expressly stated that any enforcement proceedings would be judged on the basis of the facts presented in the individual adjudicative proceedings instituted.

On July 8, 1969, the FTC issued a complaint charging Ash Grove with violation of § 7 of the Clayton Act, as amended, 15 U.S.C.A. § 18, by its acquisitions of Fordyce and Lee's Summit. . . . [After exten-

---

1. [Ed.] The Federal Register notice of the hearing, in which Ash Grove participated, described the Report as a staff document the Commission "has not approved, disapproved, or passed upon." 31 Fed.Reg. 6285 (1986).

sive hearing, an administrative law judge sustained the complaint; he was upheld in most respects by the Commission, which] decreed that Ash Grove divest itself of all stock, assets and properties acquired as a result of the acquisitions of the stock of Fordyce and Lee's. . . .

II. DUE PROCESS OF LAW

Ash Grove contends its constitutional right to due process of law was violated because the FTC's investigation of the cement industry and subsequent promulgation of the Economic Report and the Enforcement Policy, . . . even if legally permissible, . . . caused it to unlawfully prejudge the adjudicative proceeding below. Claims that an administrative agency is impermissibly biased because of its combination of investigative and adjudicative functions must overcome a presumption of honesty and integrity on the part of the decisionmaker. . . .

. . . That facts revealed by the staff investigation subsequently formed a part of the foundation for an enforcement proceeding is to be expected. Indeed, one of the purposes of industry investigations is to provide the agency with increased expertise in administering the law by exposing it to the factual background of relevant industries against which to judge individual mergers and acquisitions.

Likewise, the fact that some of the Commissioners' conclusions expressed in the Enforcement Policy were mirrored in the complaint does not prove prejudgment.[1] The Enforcement Policy was openly cautious to phrase its conclusions tentatively. . . .

Ash Grove maintains that the Commission cannot avoid the implication that it has unfairly prejudged all the material issues by self-serving statements that it will judge each case on its individual merits. However, we reiterate that the presumption favors the Commission and it is incumbent on Ash Grove to make a showing that undue prejudice did occur. The facts suggest otherwise. In its proceeding against Ash Grove the FTC did not rely solely or even primarily on the Economic Report or the Enforcement Policy to prove its case. Extensive independent evidence was introduced before the administrative law judge and was available upon review by the Commission.[2] . . .

The issue here is not dissimilar to that in F.T.C. v. Cement Institute et al., 333 U.S. 683 (1948). There the Commissioner charged and after hearing determined that the respondents' use of a multiple basing-point delivered-price system in the cement industry violated Section 5 of the F.T.C. Act and Section 2 of the Clayton Act. On judicial review one of the respondents contended it did not receive a

---

1. Note that four of the five members of the Commission who decided the Ash Grove case (including three of the four member majority) were not members of the Commission when the Enforcement Policy was developed.

2. [Ed.] Pangburn v. CAB, 311 F.2d 349 (1st Cir.1962) is to like effect; here, wearing its "safety investigator" hat, the CAB released a report ascribing fault to the pilot in an accident, at the same time as one of its ALJs was considering suspending the pilot's license as a disciplinary matter. The report was not part of the record in the disciplinary proceeding, and the court found the conjunction of the two matters before the CAB unobjectionable.

fair hearing before the Commission since the Commission was biased against the portland cement industry generally. Respondent noted that the Commission had, prior to the filing of its complaint, conducted an investigation resulting in the conclusion that "the multiple basing point system as they had studied it was the equivalent of a price fixing restraint of trade in violation of the Sherman Act," and that the Commission had reported this conclusion to Congress and the President. The Supreme Court "decide[d] this contention [of prejudgment] . . . on the assumption that such an opinion [of the illegality of multiple basing-point delivered-price systems] had been formed by the entire membership of the Commission as a result of its prior official investigations." The Court concluded, however, that the Commission had not so prejudged the issues as to impermissibly taint their action in the adjudicative proceeding. It was held not to be a denial of due process for the Commission to express an opinion on the legality of a particular trade practice and thereafter pass upon the lawfulness of the practice while sitting as judges during an adjudicatory proceeding: ". . . [no] decision of this Court would require us to hold that it would be a violation of procedural due process for a judge to sit in a case after he had expressed an opinion as to whether certain types of conduct were prohibited by law. In fact, judges frequently try the same case more than once and decide identical issues each time, although these issues involve questions both of law and fact. Certainly, the Federal Trade Commission cannot possibly be under stronger constitutional compulsions in this respect than a court."

Ash Grove has not overcome the presumption of fairness by the FTC in its adjudicative enforcement procedures. [The court then considered the sufficiency of the evidence, and the appropriateness of the remedy ordered, and upheld the Commission in all respects.]

In the case just seen, the court was dealing with a large, busy agency—one structured below the very top to keep the work of investigating, prosecuting and judging in separate, if not watertight, compartments. It is wholly unrealistic to regard most federal agencies as though all of their parts were moved by a single brain, instead of as an aggregation whose moves are responsive to many minds, often without awareness of movements dictated by yet other minds. On the whole, federal courts have been scantily impressed by lawyers' outcries against the combination of responsibilities to be found in large administrative bodies. Might a difference be perceived between a small agency (in which by hypothesis, the right hand may in fact know what the left hand is doing) and a larger, more bureaucratized agency?

WITHROW v. LARKIN

Supreme Court of the United States, 1975.
421 U.S. 35.

[Appellee Larkin, a resident of Michigan, obtained a license to practice medicine in Wisconsin, and began performing abortions at a Milwaukee office. In June of 1973, he was informed that appellants, members of the state medical examining board, intended to conduct an investigation into certain aspects of his practice at a closed hearing which he and his attorney could attend. After unsuccessfully seeking to restrain the investigatory hearing, Larkin (through counsel) was present at the hearing; he was told that he could, if he wished, explain any of the evidence that had been presented, but was not otherwise invited to participate. In September, the board formally charged Larkin with practicing under an assumed name and other professional violations, and set a contested hearing for October. The possible outcomes of this hearing included temporary license suspension. Before the hearing could be held, Larkin persuaded a federal district court to restrain it pending trial of his claim that the statute was unconstitutional in its assignment of investigating and adjudicating roles to the same tribunal. Under distinct statutory authority, the Board then held a further investigatory hearing which resulted in a finding of "probable cause" to believe that Larkin had committed criminal violations of state law and a reference of the matter to the Milwaukee district attorney for prosecution in state court; possible outcomes in this proceeding included license revocation. A three-judge district court later found (after procedural complications not important to understanding here) that Larkin had shown a high likelihood of success in his constitutional claim not to be subjected to a contested hearing before the Board; accordingly, it enjoined preliminarily the conduct of the October hearing. The board then appealed to the Supreme Court.]

MR. JUSTICE WHITE delivered the opinion of the Court.

.   .   .

Concededly, a "fair trial in a fair tribunal is a basic requirement of due process." In re Murchison, 349 U.S. 133, 136 (1955). This applies to administrative agencies which adjudicate as well as to courts. Not only is a biased decisionmaker constitutionally unacceptable but "our system of law has always endeavored to prevent even the probability of unfairness." In pursuit of this end, various situations have been identified in which experience teaches that the probability of actual bias on the part of the judge or decisionmaker is too high to be constitutionally tolerable. Among these cases are those in which the adjudicator has a pecuniary interest in the outcome and in which he has been the target of personal abuse or criticism from the party before him.

The contention that the combination of investigative and adjudicative functions necessarily creates an unconstitutional risk of bias in administrative adjudication has a much more difficult burden of persuasion to carry. It must overcome a presumption of honesty and integrity in those serving as adjudicators; and it must convince that, under a realistic appraisal of psychological tendencies and human weakness, conferring investigative and adjudicative powers on the same individuals poses such a risk of actual bias or prejudgment that the practice must be forbidden if the guarantee of due process is to be adequately implemented.   .   .   .

That is not to say that there is nothing to the argument that those who have investigated should not then adjudicate. The issue is substantial, it is not new, and legislators and others concerned with the operations of administrative agencies have given much attention to whether and to what extent distinctive administrative functions should be performed by the same persons. . . . Within the Federal Government itself, Congress has addressed the issue in several different ways, providing for varying degrees of separation from complete separation of functions to virtually none at all. For the generality of agencies, Congress has been content with § 5 of the Administrative Procedure Act, 5 U.S.C. § 554(d), which provides that no employee engaged in investigating or prosecuting may also participate or advise in the adjudicating function, but which also expressly exempts from this prohibition "the agency or a member or members of the body comprising the agency."

It is not surprising, therefore, to find that "[t]he case law, both federal and state, generally rejects the idea that the combination [of] judging [and] investigating functions is a denial of due process. . . ." 2 K. Davis, Administrative Law Treatise, § 13.02 (1958), at 175. Similarly, our cases, although they reflect the substance of the problem, offer no support for the bald proposition applied in this case by the District Court that agency members who participate in an investigation are disqualified from adjudicating. The incredible variety of administrative mechanisms in this country will not yield to any single organizing principle.

Appellee relies heavily on In re Murchison, supra, in which a state judge, empowered under state law to sit as a "one-man grand jury" and to compel witnesses to testify before him in secret about possible crimes, charged two such witnesses with criminal contempt, one for perjury and the other for refusing to answer certain questions, and then himself tried and convicted them. This Court found the procedure to be a denial of due process of law not only because the judge in effect became part of the prosecution and assumed an adversary position, but also because as a judge, passing on guilt or innocence, he very likely relied on "his own personal knowledge and impression of what had occurred in the grand jury room," an impression that "could not be tested by adequate cross-examination."

Plainly enough, Murchison has not been understood to stand for the broad rule that the members of an administrative agency may not investigate the facts, institute proceedings, and then make the necessary adjudications. The court did not . . . lay down any general principle that a judge before whom an alleged contempt is committed may not bring and preside over the ensuing contempt proceedings. The accepted rule is to the contrary.

Nor is there anything in this case that comes within the strictures of Murchison. When the Board instituted its investigative procedures, it stated only that it would investigate whether proscribed conduct had occurred. Later in noticing the adversary hearing, it asserted only that it would determine if violations had been committed which would warrant suspension of appellee's license. Without doubt, the Board then anticipated that the proceeding would eventuate in an adjudication of the issue; but there was no more evidence of bias or the risk of bias or prejudgment than inhered in the very fact that the Board had investigated and would now adjudicate.[1] Of course, we should be alert to the possibilities of bias that may lurk in the way particular procedures actually work in practice. The processes utilized by the Board, however, do not in themselves contain an unacceptable risk of bias. The investigative proceeding had been closed to the public, but appellee and his counsel were permitted to be present throughout; counsel actually attended the hearings and knew the facts presented to the Board. No specific foundation has been presented for suspecting that the Board had been prejudiced by its investigation or would be disabled from hearing and deciding on the basis of the evidence to be presented at the contested hearing. . . . Without a showing to the contrary, state administrators "are assumed to be men of conscience and intellectual discipline, capable of judging a particular controversy fairly on the basis of its own circumstances." United States v. Morgan, 313 U.S. 409, 421 (1941).

. . .

Nor do we think the situation substantially different because the Board, when it was prevented from going forward with the contested hearing, proceeded to make and issue formal findings of fact and conclusions of law asserting that there was probable cause to believe that appellee had engaged in various acts prohibited by the Wisconsin statutes [, and transmitted them to the district attorney for his initiation of proceedings.] . . .

Judges repeatedly issue arrest warrants on the basis that there is probable cause to believe that a crime has been committed and that the person named in the warrant has committed it. Judges also preside at preliminary hearings where they must decide whether the evidence is sufficient to hold a defendant for trial. Neither of these pretrial involvements has been thought to raise any constitutional barrier against the judge presiding over the criminal trial and, if the trial is without a jury, against making the necessary determination of guilt or innocence. Nor has it been thought that a judge is disqualified from presiding over injunction proceedings because he has initially assessed the facts in issuing or denying a temporary restraining order or a preliminary injunction. It is also very typical for the members of administrative agencies to receive the results of investigations, to approve the filing of charges or formal complaints instituting enforcement proceedings, and then to participate in the ensuing hearings. This mode of procedure does not violate the Administrative Procedure Act, and it does not violate due process of law. We should also remember that it is not contrary to due process to allow judges and administrators . . . reversed on appeal to confront the same questions a second time around. . . .

1. Appellee does claim that state officials harassed him . . . because he performed abortions. . . . [T]he record does not provide a basis for finding . . . actual bias or prejudgment . . . .

The risk of bias or prejudgment in this sequence of functions has not been considered to be intolerably high or to raise a sufficiently great possibility that the adjudicators would be so psychologically wedded to their complaints that they would consciously or unconsciously avoid the appearance of having erred or changed position. Indeed, just as there is no logical inconsistency between a finding of probable cause and an acquittal in a criminal proceeding, there is no incompatibility between the agency filing a complaint based on probable cause and a subsequent decision, when all the evidence is in, that there has been no violation of the statute. Here, if the Board now proceeded after an adversary hearing to determine that appellee's license to practice should not be temporarily suspended, it would not implicitly be admitting error in its prior finding of probable cause. Its position most probably would merely reflect the benefit of a more complete view of the evidence afforded by an adversary hearing.

. . .

That the combination of investigative and adjudicatory functions does not, without more, constitute a due process violation, does not, of course, preclude a court from determining from the special facts and circumstances present in the case before it that the risk of unfairness is intolerably high. Findings of that kind made by judges with special insights into local realities are entitled to respect, but injunctions resting on such factors should be accompanied by at least the minimum findings required by Rules 52(a) and 65(d).

The judgment of the District Court is reversed and the case is remanded to that court for further proceedings consistent with this opinion.

So ordered.

Judgment reversed and case remanded.

NOTE ON THE DOCTRINE OF NECESSITY

Suppose circumstances in which there is no doubt that the bearer is personally—not just officially—interested. Is it permissible for the bearer nonetheless to sit, if no alternative hearing body is authorized or available?

Analysis of this issue conventionally begins with judges asked to pass on matters affecting their pay, which under the Constitution may not be reduced during their terms of office. UNITED STATES V. WILL, 449 U.S. 200 (1980), arose when Congress in several consecutive years passed legislation suspending cost-of-living increases that would otherwise have taken effect for all federal employees, including judges. Two of these suspensions became law before the beginning of the fiscal year to which they related, but two did not take effect until just after the fiscal year had begun. The Supreme Court concluded that the first two statutes did not, but the second two did, constitute forbidden reductions in judicial compensation. En route, it paused to consider the obvious and direct interest each of its members (and all other federal judges) had in the outcome:

"The Rule of Necessity had its genesis at least five and a half centuries ago and has been consistently applied in this country in both state and federal courts. In State ex rel. Mitchell v. Sage Stores Co., 157 Kan. 622, 143 P.2d 652 (1943), the Supreme Court of Kansas observed:

> [I]t is well established that actual disqualification of a member of a court of last resort will not excuse such member from performing his official duty if failure to do so would result in a denial of a litigant's constitutional right to have a question, properly presented to such court, adjudicated.

Similarly, the Supreme Court of Pennsylvania held:

> The true rule unquestionably is that wherever it becomes necessary for a judge to sit even where he has an interest— where no provision is made for calling another in, or where no one else can take his place—it is his duty to hear and decide, however disagreeable it may be. Philadelphia v. Fox, 64 Pa. 169, 185 (1870)."

At 213–14. The Court went on to find that Section 455 of the Judicial Code, discussed briefly above at page 876, was not intended to alter this "time-honored" rule. The legislative reports "reflect a constant assumption that upon disqualification of a particular judge, another would be assigned to the case. And we would not casually infer that the Legislative and Executive Branches sought by the enactment of Para. 455 to foreclose federal courts from exercising 'the province and duty of the judicial department to say what the law is.' Marbury v. Madison, 5 U.S. (1 Cranch) 137, 177 (1803)." At 216–17.

Is the problem somewhat more difficult when the designated hearer is not a life-tenured judge but the part-time members of a professional board; and the issue is not the validity of a general statute, but the facts of a particular case the members may have encountered in their private, professional lives and in whose outcome they may have a personal financial interest?

Place yourself in the position of a dentist who is a part-time member of the State Dental Board, with responsibilities which include acting in disciplinary cases. In the course of his professional work he repeatedly encounters first-hand the prior efforts of his professional colleagues, and over time he has involuntarily acquired in this way a knowledge of their respective skills and practices. Wearing his office whites, he knows whether the cracked crown under his gaze is another sad example of Jones' general incompetence or, rather, an aberrational departure from Brown's customary skill. Does this necessary but wholly private acquisition of extra-record information about the skills of fellow professionals who may one day be subjected to disciplinary proceedings argue for, or against, a State's choice to ask him for similar judgments in particular cases while wearing quasi-judicial black? If he is chosen, should he be expected to put that information wholly out of mind? Are public protection and/or individual fairness, on the whole, advanced or retarded by designating as judge of particular circumstances one who may find it easy to set those circumstances in a context of general performance?   See Leonard v. Board of Directors, Prowers County Hospital Dist., 673 P.2d 1019 (Colo.App.1983); Klinge v. Lutheran Charities Ass'n of St. Louis, 523 F.2d 56 (8th Cir.1975); Robbins v. Ong, 452 F.Supp. 110 (S.D.Ga.1978).

Introduce now the element of possible financial self-interest that may be endemic for such tribunals.   We saw in Section 1 of this chapter, p. 878 above, that a financial interest in the outcome of an adjudicatory proceeding will ordinarily require disqualification.   In GIBSON v. BERRYHILL, 411 U.S. 564 (1973), the Supreme Court found that members of the Alabama State Board of Optometry, all *independent* optometrists, could not consistently with due process adjudicate charges of "unprofessional conduct" brought against *employed* optometrists. "Independent" and "employed" optometrists enjoyed roughly equal shares of the Alabama market for eyeglasses, but the independents controlled the regulatory board and its policies.   The protection they could thus provide for their trade gave them, the Court concluded, too substantial a pecuniary interest in the license revocation proceedings. The "doctrine of necessity" had been argued by the state in support of its board's competence; the Court did not mention the argument.   Did it follow that state legislation might no longer create licensing boards composed in whole or in substantial part of professional members empowering them to define "unauthorized practice" by rule or adjudication in ways tending to enrich existing members of the profession, board members included?   That proposition was emphatically rejected in Friedman v. Rogers, 440 U.S. 1 (1979), holding that impartiality was a matter to be assessed in the particular circumstances of individual disciplinary proceedings.   In the view of a perceptive student analyst, ". . . If members of a profession are to be utilized, the possibility of bias based on personal economic interest will always be present.   Given the advantages of professional expertise, courts are more likely to focus on the substantiality of the possible bias in each case, drawing the line only when the image of unfairness is quite distinct.   Under this view, pecuniary interest based only on membership in the same profession seems unlikely to be considered disqualifying in many future cases. Yet Berryhill can be important if for no other reason than to indicate that courts should analyze the realities of the occupational licensing situation. If it is unworkable in this area to demand that all possibilities of bias be eliminated, then courts should recognize that bias might exist and adjust the procedural requirements and intensity of judicial review accordingly."   Note, Due Process Limitations on Occupational Licensing, 59 U.Va.L.Rev. 1097, 1119 (1973).

Finally, note that the complaints emerging from the caselaw about professional self-regulation are most likely to come from fellow professionals.   The loudest of these may be he whom the current profession regards as a charlatan—an accolade, it should be remembered, once bestowed on Louis Pasteur.   The complaints emerging from public policy debates may be quite different, and have a strikingly different source.   From the public's perspective, it is more likely to be argued that assignment of fellow professionals to regulate professional conduct tends to produce too *much* understanding, a latitudinarianism that results for attorneys in disciplinary proceedings being brought only against the ambulance chaser, the misappropriator of funds, or the convicted felon and not against the more subtly unethical or inept practitioner. The decisions of some authorities to confer disciplinary functions on a civil service "professional disciplinary board" with responsibility for all professions, or to include non-professionals in the tribunals, are in part the result of such suggestions. Putting aside their possible contribution to greater discipline, ought boards so constituted also to be favored as enhancing fairness? Or do you find persuasive the argument that their verdicts, whether destroying a career or failing to give the public full protection, are more likely to be irrational in relating the particular cases before them to general levels of professional skill and bearing than the conclusions of a panel of fellow professionals, some of whom may have had exposure to the individual's work ex cathedra?

b. "Political Influence" and "Pressure"

The atomistic approach to decision taken earlier in this chapter has another major weakness. Not only may agencies perform multiple functions in their own decision-making—the FTC conducting economic surveys *and* bringing anti-trust proceedings, Wisconsin state officials initiating disciplinary charges *and* deciding their merit. As important, and again unlike courts, agencies frequently act in the context of policies or issues whose administration or resolution is *shared* with other official actors or spread over a variety of activities and they act in the unruly world of politics, subject to a range of official and unofficial controls courts simply do not encounter.[1] To what extent shall courts seek to control these external influences? We have already seen that judicial attitudes toward alleged bias may turn substantially on consideration whether the challenged distorting influence arose "extrajudicially," outside the hearing. Courts also are prone to distinguish impermissible "ex parte contacts" by interested outside participants in agency proceedings from permissible advice and support, as to policy issues, from the agency's own staff. The matters treated in this part of the materials might be thought to fall on middle ground, and resolution of the questions to which they give rise is correspondingly uncertain.

Suppose, for example, that the President, in pursuit of his constitutional obligation to "take care that the laws be faithfully executed," Art. II, Sec. 3, wishes to be sure that the Administrator of EPA is kept up to date on developing national economic policy, and that he gives appropriate consideration to possible inflationary aspects of rules he has under consideration. In such a case, the President is neither a "party" nor acting for one. Are distinctions to be drawn between the covert telephone call seeking to influence the outcome of particular, pending "on-the-record" adjudication as a political favor, on the one hand, and confidential presentations respecting developing, not yet

---

1. These controls are discussed in Ch. II, Sec. 3 above, which could profitably be reviewed at this point.

public national policy, on the other? Or are administrators meant to be untouchable by the President and his personal staff under any circumstances?

Alternatively, suppose that a recent course of decision by a particular agency suggests to its oversight committee—responsible under the Legislative Reorganization Act of 1946, Sec. 136, 60 Stat. 832, to "exercise continuous watchfulness of the execution by the administrative agencies" of the laws within the committee's jurisdiction—that the agency is straying from the correct policy path. May oversight hearings be convened while aspects of the policy issues remain unresolved before the agency? Senatorial whispering in the ears of commissioners who are considering a television license, done on behalf of particular constituents, seems offensive. Indeed, direct, paid Congressional representation of clients in governmental proceedings is absolutely forbidden by law, though evasion is not unknown.[2] But how about legislators' expressions of opinion concerning the merits of an as yet unresolved and highly important policy question that may be brought to the fore by a pending application—such as, for example, whether a license should be granted for nuclear energy power plants or whether the effective date of a pollution control order should be postponed? Should legislators scrupulously abstain from indicating their judgment about a public policy until the administrators have finally announced their own conclusion? Certainly Americans are accustomed to talking to their elected representatives about grievances against officials.[3] A major change in contemporary mores would be effected if Congressmen were to be rigorously precluded from asking questions about or making remarks concerning current administrative cases. Where is the line to be drawn between legislative vigilance and legislative intermeddling?

Finally, consider the importance to effective regulation of continuing contact with a regulated industry, the public, and the press. Informal contacts, press interviews, convention addresses and the like serve valuable functions. The agency may be able to win needed support, reduce future enforcement requirements (by helping industry anticipate and plan for compliance), float a trial balloon, spur the provision of needed information, or otherwise achieve wholly understandable and worthy ends, if it can discuss its program informally as it unfolds. For such reasons, speech-writing staffs burgeon, and Commissioner Jones devotes fully as much attention to the emerging draft of his upcoming luncheon talk to the Environmental Alliance as to his draft opinion in the Gesellschaft case. Businessmen need to know how they might be planning for future requirements; the public, a basis on which to assess the agency's program and effectiveness. Courts, having no direct policy responsibilities, are not faced with the need to defend

---

2. 18 U.S.C. § 203(a) prohibits direct or indirect compensation to a Member of Congress in any proceeding in which the United States is a party or has a "substantial interest" before any department or agency. Other statutes explicitly prohibit Congressmen's practicing before named tribunals. For discussion of continuing problems, see J.C. Kirby, Congress and the Public Trust 91–117 (1970).

3. See W. Gellhorn, When Americans Complain ch. II (1966); P.H. Douglas, Ethics in Government 85–88 (1952); M.G. Paulsen ed., Legal Institutions Today and Tomorrow 97 (1959).

their policies or budget before a concerned legislature, or to enlist the understanding or reluctant support of industry at a convocation. How sharply should courts respond when administrators, performing in those settings, let slip some hint of their views on matters not yet finally decided?

The materials of this section take up another side, then, of the issues addressed previously in the third part of Chapter II. There, we looked at the political controls over agency action from a structural perspective, the issue being what makes for a "good government." Here the same controls reappear, from the perspective of individual participants in particular administrative proceedings, the issues being the more familiar ones of procedural fairness and legality.

PILLSBURY CO. v. FEDERAL TRADE COMMISSION
United States Court of Appeals, Fifth Circuit, 1966.
354 F.2d 952.

[In 1952 the FTC filed a complaint against Pillsbury, challenging its then-recent acquisition of competing flour millers as having had a substantial anti-competitive effect. In 1953 its trial examiner dismissed the complaint; the FTC reinstated it on appeal and remanded for what proved to be a lengthy hearing. The complaint might have been reinstated on either of two bases—(1) as FTC complaint counsel urged, a "per se" rule was possible to preclude a merger in which one company already having a substantial share of the business absorbed an active competitor; or (2) even if proof was required that competition had actually been diminished, the Commission's staff might be said to have met that burden, now requiring Pillsbury to come forward. In its 1953 order, the Commissioner adopted the latter, less dramatic approach. This was, of course, a conclusion of "law," which could be expected to govern many cases then pending or likely to come before the Commission, and to increase the difficulty it would encounter in blocking or discouraging corporate mergers.

The remanded hearings before the trial examiner were still in progress when, in 1955, the antitrust subcommittee of the Senate Judiciary Committee under Senator Kefauver's chairmanship summoned then FTC Chairman Howrey and members of his staff to appear. Chairman Howrey came before the Kefauver committee with the FTC's General Counsel Kintner, Commissioner Secrest, and Director of Litigation Sheehy (whose assistant Kern later became a commissioner). The Kefauver committee was volubly dissatisfied with the Commission's failure to adopt a "per se" rule. Especially critical were the questions and observations of Senator Kefauver, who commented at length on what he believed to be imperfections in the Commission's approach to the Pillsbury case. At one stage Chairman Howrey protested bitterly about the Senator's having "delved too deeply into the quasi-judicial mind in the Pillsbury matter"; he announced that he would have to disqualify himself from further participation in the Pillsbury case.[1]

1. At the time of this inquest, Chairman Howrey is said already to have in- formed the White House of his intention to resign; he had been a very forceful chair-

This case or the Pillsbury name was referred to more than 100 times during three hearings before this and other Congressional committees.

Five years later, in 1960, the FTC ordered Pillsbury to divest itself of the companies it had acquired, restoring them as effective competitors. By this time, Howrey was no longer on the FTC. Kintner, who wrote the opinion, had become Chairman; Secrest was still a member; Kern, who had been Sheehy's assistant but was not personally at the hearings, had become a Commissioner; Commissioner Anderson, the fourth and last sitting member in the 1960 opinion, had had no contact with the hearings. Pillsbury sought review of the divestiture order on the grounds that the Commission had misapplied the statute, had acted on improper evidence, and had not accorded Pillsbury due process because Congressional committees had interfered with the decisional process while the case was under consideration. The court focused on the last point alone. The alleged interference, as the reviewing court later remarked, was not an impropriety concealed from public view, but consisted, rather, of "questions and statements made by members of two Senate and House subcommittees having responsibility for legislation dealing with antitrust matters all clearly spread upon the record."]

Before TUTTLE, CHIEF JUDGE, and JONES and ANDERSON, CIRCUIT JUDGES.

TUTTLE, CHIEF JUDGE, [after reviewing the facts, including six pages devoted to reproducing questions and answers taken from Hearings Before the Subcommittee on Antitrust and Monopoly of the Committee on the Judiciary, United States Senate, Eighty-Fourth Congress (First Session) Part I]:

. . . We conclude that the proceedings just outlined constituted an improper intrusion into the adjudicatory processes of the Commission and were of such a damaging character as to have required at least some of the members in addition to the chairman to disqualify themselves. We think it illuminating to quote Chairman Howrey's statement relative to his decision to disqualify himself, which he read into the record at the House subcommittee hearing. He said:

". . . I wrote the opinion [in the Pillsbury case]. It is still a pending adjudication; and because of some of the penetrating questions over on the Senate side, I felt compelled to withdraw from the case because I did not think I could be judicial any more when I had been such an advocate of its views in answering questions."

In view of the inordinate lapse of time in this proceeding, brought to undo what was done by mergers completed in 1951, we are naturally loathe to frustrate the proceedings at this late date. However, common justice to a litigant requires that we invalidate the order entered by a quasi-judicial tribunal that was importuned by members of the United

---

man for the FTC who had repeatedly "been summoned before committees in both houses to defend his sweeping staff reorganization and his FTC policies which—it was said—'were partial to big business.'" V. Kramer and J. Graham, Appointment to the Regulatory Agencies, 77, Senate Committee on Commerce, 94th Cong., 2d Sess. (Comm. Print 1976). In this context, his "withdrawal" from the case may have the guise of tactics more than injured judicial mien.

States Senate, however innocent they intended their conduct to be, to arrive at the ultimate conclusion which they did reach. . . .

We are sensible of the fact that, pursuant to its quasi-legislative function, it frequently becomes necessary for a commission to set forth policy statements or interpretative rules (to be distinguished from strict "legislative" rules, see generally 1 Davis, Administrative Law §§ 5.03–04 (1958)) in order to inform interested parties of its official position on various matters. This is as it should be.

At times similar statements of official position are elicited in Congressional hearings. In this context, the agencies are sometimes called to task for failing to adhere to the "intent of Congress" in supplying meaning to the often broad statutory standards from which the agencies derive their authority, e.g., "substantially to lessen competition" or "to tend to create a monopoly." There are those who "take a rather dim view of [such] committee pronouncements as to what agency policy should be, save when this is incident to proposals for amendatory legislation." Friendly, The Federal Administrative Agencies 169 (Harvard University Press 1962). Although such investigatory methods raise serious policy questions as to the de facto "independence" of the federal regulatory agencies, it seems doubtful that they raise any constitutional issues. However, when such an investigation focuses directly and substantially upon the mental decisional processes of a Commission in a case which is pending before it, Congress is no longer intervening in the agency's legislative function, but rather, in its *judicial* function. . . .

To subject an administrator to a searching examination as to how and why he reached his decision in a case still pending before him, and to criticize him for reaching the "wrong" decision, as the Senate subcommittee did in this case, sacrifices the appearance of impartiality—the sine qua non of American judicial justice—in favor of some short-run notions regarding the Congressional intent underlying an amendment to a statute, unfettered administration of which was committed by Congress to the Federal Trade Commission (see 15 U.S.C. § 21).

It may be argued that such officials as members of the Federal Trade Commission are sufficiently aware of the realities of governmental, not to say "political," life as to be able to withstand such questioning as we have outlined here. However, this court is not so "sophisticated" that it can shrug off such a procedural due process claim merely because the officials involved should be able to discount what is said and to disregard the force of the intrusion into the adjudicatory process. We conclude that we can preserve the rights of the litigants in a case such as this without having any adverse effect upon the legitimate exercise of the investigative power of Congress. What we do is to preserve the integrity of the judicial aspect of the administrative process. See United States v. Morgan, 313 U.S. 409, 422 (1941).

We are fully aware of the reluctance expressed by the Supreme Court to disqualify the members of the Federal Trade Commission for bias or prejudice (a somewhat different basis than that urged here) in

Federal Trade Commission v. Cement Institute, 333 U.S. 683. There the Court seems to have placed its decision largely on the grounds of necessity [which do not apply here]. . . .

Although we conclude that the course of the questioning before the Senate subcommittee in June 1955 deprived the petitioner of [a fair and impartial hearing], we are convinced that the Commission is not permanently disqualified to decide this case. We are convinced that the passage of time, coupled with the changes in personnel on the Commission, sufficiently insulate the present members from any untoward effect from what occurred in 1955.

It is extremely unfortunate that this complaint, seeking divestiture by Pillsbury of two other companies acquired by it, has taken this long to reach the present stage of the litigation. It commenced as a pioneer case under the new amendment to the law. However, in the meantime much law has been written as to the quantity and quality of proof needed under a Section 7 complaint while it has been pending. . . .

We conclude that the order appealed from must be vacated and the case remanded to the Commission. The Commission as now constituted can then determine what steps should then appropriately be taken in view of both the lapse of time and the present state of the case law applying Section 7.[3]

NOTE

UNITED STATES EX REL. PARCO v. MORRIS, 426 F.Supp. 976 (E.D.Pa. 1977), concerned married aliens' effort to secure permission from the Immigration & Naturalization Service to remain in the United States. Under a prior Operating Instruction, such permission would have been routinely granted. In July, 1972, before the Parcos' unsuccessful application, that instruction was rescinded by a memorandum stating, in part: "[U]nlawful employment of nonresident aliens in the United States has been having an increasingly unfavorable effect on the domestic job market. . . . Subcommittee No. 1 of the House of Representatives Committee on the Judiciary . . . has . . . recommended to the Service that the practice be terminated of routinely

---

3. [Ed.] On remand in 1966 the Commission (now with a membership wholly different from that of 1960) dismissed the complaint, noting sadly that the case was then fourteen years old, had elicited some 40,000 pages of testimony which pertained to market conditions more than a decade ago, and presented grave difficulties in fashioning effective relief after so long a passage of time. Bearing in mind that its funds and personnel resources were limited, the Commission concluded that the public interest would not be served by further proceedings. But the order which dismissed the complaint ended with a small growl: "Any future acquisitions by respondent will receive careful attention, and the Commission will take such action thereon as may be required in the public interest." Matter of Pillsbury Mills, Inc., 69 F.T.C. 482 (1966).

The Pillsbury case was distinguished by the Third Circuit in Gulf Oil Corp. v. FPC, 563 F.2d 588, cert. denied 434 U.S. 1062 (1977), on the ground that the challenged congressional questioning in Gulf Oil was not directed to the FPC's particular factual judgments in the case; the congressmen were concerned by the FPC's decision to conduct lengthy show cause hearings rather than seek immediate injunctive relief in court, in Gulf Oil and other cases. This concern with the efficient operation of a regulatory agency was, the court thought, wholly legitimate.

permitting alien professionals . . . to remain in the United States pending the availability of immigrant visas.

"The Service has accepted the Subcommittee's recommendations. Accordingly OI 242.10(a)(6) is terminated effective July 31, 1972, except for the following: . . . ."

The Parcos contended, inter alia, that the rescission was invalidated by the congressional "pressure" thus noted. Acknowledging that congressional pressure did force the change, the court found it unobjectionable: "[W]e see no Constitutional violation in a Congressional attempt to influence the regulatory interpretation of statutes. Interrogation of agency officials at Congressional hearings often serves such a purpose and is part of the give and take of democratic government. We think that the contention the Parcos seek to raise is really one of administrative law, i.e., that an agency decision may be invalid if induced by secret or otherwise improper influence. . . . [Proper] analysis of this principle distinguishes sharply between agency action which is 'judicial' or 'quasi-judicial' and agency action which is 'legislative.' The former concept relates to agency adjudication of a particular, individual case, or when it renders a decision on the record compiled in formal hearings; in such instance the consideration of extraneous pressuring influences undermines the fairness of the hearing accorded the adverse parties. On the other hand, when the agency action is purely 'legislative,' as in the informal rulemaking involved here, the decision 'cannot be invalidated merely because the . . . action was motivated by impermissible considerations' any more than can that of a legislature. Cf. Fletcher v. Peck, 10 U.S. (6 Cranch) 87, 129–31 (1810). The Parcos do not contend that Congressman Rodino or anyone else improperly interfered with the 'quasi-judicial' decision to deny *them* extended voluntary departure. Rather, they seek to challenge the motivation of the Administrator in taking the purely 'legislative' action of rescinding OI 242.10(a)(6). This they cannot successfully do."

The court went on to hold that the new policy could not be applied to the Parcos' detriment, in view of the government's failure to publish it.

SIERRA CLUB v. COSTLE
United States Court of Appeals, District of Columbia Circuit, 1981.
657 F.2d 298.

[Other portions of the opinion are set out at p. 845 above, including a description of the general background of this complex dispute over emissions standards set by the Environmental Protection Agency under the Clean Air Act to govern release of air-borne sulfur dioxide and particulates from new coal-fired electric power plants. Here we are concerned with a procedural challenge to one standard EPA adopted, setting a ceiling of 1.2 lbs of sulfur dioxide emissions for each million British thermal units (MBtu) of heat energy produced. A lower ceiling would have been possible, and (it appears) fully sustainable on the record, but could have been adopted only at the cost of impairing the

market for coal produced in the Eastern Midwest and Northern Appalachian coal regions. The Environmental Defense Fund (EDF) asserted
that in fact EPA initially decided to adopt a ceiling of 0.55 lb./MBtu,
and backed away from this under an "ex parte blitz" from the coal
industry, the President, and Senator Robert Byrd of West Virginia—at
the time, majority leader in the Senate and obviously interested in the
economic health of the Northern Appalachian coal region. The "blitz"
occurred partly through the submission of late comments, partly
through high-level meetings with Executive branch officials (including
one meeting with the President himself) and with congressional officials, including two with Senator Byrd. In discussion omitted here, the
court found that the written submissions had been docketed in sufficient time to permit response and satisfy the requirements of the
"procedural record" established by Section 307 of the Clean Air Act.
See p. 450 above. It then turned to the meetings that had been held.]

WALD, CIRCUIT JUDGE:

The Clean Air Act does not explicitly treat the issue of post-
comment period meetings with individuals outside EPA. Oral face-to-
face discussions are not prohibited anywhere, anytime, in the Act. The
absence of such prohibition may have arisen from the nature of the
informal rulemaking procedures Congress had in mind. Where agency
action resembles judicial action, where it involves formal rulemaking,
adjudication, or quasi-adjudication among "conflicting private claims to
a valuable privilege," the insulation of the decisionmaker from ex parte
contracts is justified by basic notions of due process to the parties
involved. But where agency action involves informal rulemaking of a
policymaking sort, the concept of ex parte contacts is of more questionable utility.

Under our system of government, the very legitimacy of general
policymaking performed by unelected administrators depends in no
small part upon the openness, accessibility, and amenability of these
officials to the needs and ideas of the public from whom their ultimate
authority derives, and upon whom their commands must fall. As
judges we are insulated from these pressures because of the nature of
the judicial process in which we participate; but we must refrain from
the easy temptation to look askance at all face-to-face lobbying efforts,
regardless of the forum in which they occur, merely because we see
them as inappropriate in the judicial context. Furthermore, the importance to effective regulation of continuing contact with a regulated
industry, other affected groups, and the public cannot be underestimated. Informal contacts may enable the agency to win needed support for
its program, reduce future enforcement requirements by helping those
regulated to anticipate and shape their plans for the future, and spur
the provision of information which the agency needs. The possibility of
course exists that in permitting ex parte communications with
rulemakers we create the danger of "one administrative record for the
public and this court and another for the Commission."[2] Under the

2. Home Box Office, Inc. v. FCC, 567
F.2d 9, 54 (D.C.Cir.1977), cert. denied 434
U.S. 829 (1977).

Clean Air Act procedures, however, "[t]he promulgated rule may not be based (in part or whole) on any information or data which has not been placed in the docket . . . ." Thus EPA must justify its rulemaking solely on the basis of the record it compiles and makes public. . . .

It still can be argued, however, that if oral communications are to be freely permitted after the close of the comment period, then at least some adequate summary of them must be made in order to preserve the integrity of the rulemaking docket, which under the statute must be the sole repository of material upon which EPA intends to rely. . . . [U]nless oral communications of central relevance to the rulemaking are also docketed in some fashion or other, information central to the justification of the rule could be obtained without ever appearing on the docket, simply by communicating it by voice rather than by pen, thereby frustrating the command of section 307 that the final rule not be "based (in part or whole) on any information or data which has not been placed in the docket . . . ."

EDF is understandably wary of a rule which permits the agency to decide for itself when oral communications are of such central relevance that a docket entry for them is required. Yet the statute itself vests EPA with discretion to decide whether "documents" are of central relevance and therefore must be placed in the docket; surely EPA can be given no less discretion in docketing oral communications, concerning which the statute has no explicit requirements whatsoever.

. . .

Turning to the particular oral communications in this case, we find that only two of the nine contested meetings were undocketed by EPA.[3] The agency has maintained that, as to the May 1 meeting where Senate staff people were briefed on EPA's analysis concerning the impact of alternative emissions ceilings upon coal reserves, its failure to place a summary of the briefing in the docket was an oversight. We find no evidence that this oversight was anything but an honest inadvertence; furthermore, a briefing of this sort by EPA which simply provides background information about an upcoming rule is not the type of oral communication which would require a docket entry under the statute.

---

3. [Ed.] The meetings were as follows:

March 14, 1979—one and one-half hours White House briefing for high level executive branch officials.

April 5, 1979—Meeting of principal participants in the rulemaking called by EPA, with discussion among all of new data presented in connection with the meeting by EPA staff and the National Coal Association (NCA).

April 23, 1979—30–45 minute meeting in Senator Byrd's office with high level executive branch officials and NCA officials attending.

April 27, 1979—Briefing on technological issues for executive branch officials.

April 30, 1979—One hour briefing for the President and other executive branch officials.

April 30, 1979—Briefing on technological issues for White House staff.

May 1, 1979—Additional White House briefing on technological issues.

May 1, 1979—One hour briefing for Senate Committee staff members.

May 2, 1979—Meeting with Senator Byrd, executive branch and NCA officials.

The rule was promulgated in final form June 11, 1979.

The other undocketed meeting occurred at the White House and involved the President and his White House staff. . . .

(a) Intra-Executive Branch Meetings

We have already held that a blanket prohibition against meetings during the post-comment period with individuals outside EPA is unwarranted, and this perforce applies to meetings with White House officials. We have not yet addressed, however, the issue whether such oral communications with White House staff, or the President himself, must be docketed on the rulemaking record, and we now turn to that issue.

. . .

We note initially that section 307 makes specific provision for including in the rulemaking docket the "written comments" of other executive agencies along with accompanying documents on any proposed draft rules circulated in advance of the rulemaking proceeding. Drafts of the final rule submitted to an executive review process prior to promulgation, as well as all "written comments," "documents," and "written responses" resulting from such interagency review process, are also to be put in the docket prior to promulgation.[4] This specific requirement does not mention informal meetings or conversations concerning the rule which are not part of the initial or final review processes, nor does it refer to oral comments of any sort. Yet it is hard to believe Congress was unaware that intra-executive meetings and oral comments would occur throughout the rulemaking process. We assume, therefore, that unless expressly forbidden by Congress, such intra-executive contacts[5] may take place, both during and after the public comment period; the only real issue is whether they must be noted and summarized in the docket.

The court recognizes the basic need of the President and his White House staff to monitor the consistency of executive agency regulations with Administration policy. He and his White House advisers surely must be briefed fully and frequently about rules in the making, and

---

4. These materials, although docketed, are excluded from the "record for judicial review." 42 U.S.C. § 7607(d)(7)(A). The logic of this exclusion of final draft comments from the agency's "record for judicial review" is not completely clear, but we believe it evinces a Congressional intent for the reviewing court to judge the rule solely upon the data, information, and comments provided in the public docket, as well as the explanations EPA provides when it promulgates the rule, and not to concern itself with who in the Executive Branch advised whom about which policies to pursue. . . .

5. In this case we need not decide the effect upon rulemaking proceedings of a failure to disclose so-called "conduit" communications, in which administration or inter-agency contacts serve as mere conduits for private parties in order to get the latter's off-the-record views into the pro-

ceeding. EDF alleges that many of the executive comments here fell into that category. We note that the Department of Justice Office of Legal Counsel has taken the position that it may be improper for White House advisers to act as conduits for outsiders. It has therefore recommended that Council of Economic Advisers officials summarize and place in rulemaking records a compilation of all written or oral comments they receive relevant to particular proceedings. EDF has given us no reason to believe that a policy similar to this was not followed here, or that unrecorded conduit communications exist in this case; we therefore decline to authorize further discovery simply on the unsubstantiated hypothesis that some such communications may be unearthed thereby. Cf. Citizens to Preserve Overton Park, Inc. v. Volpe, 401 U.S. 402, 420 (1971).

their contributions to policymaking considered. The executive power under our Constitution, after all, is not shared—it rests exclusively with the President. The idea of a "plural executive," or a President with a council of state, was considered and rejected by the Constitutional Convention. Instead the Founders chose to risk the potential for tyranny inherent in placing power in one person, in order to gain the advantages of accountability fixed on a single source. . . .

The authority of the President to control and supervise executive policymaking is derived from the Constitution; the desirability of such control is demonstrable from the practical realities of administrative rulemaking. Regulations such as those involved here demand a careful weighing of cost, environmental, and energy considerations. They also have broad implications for national economic policy. Our form of government simply could not function effectively or rationally if key executive policymakers were isolated from each other and from the Chief Executive. Single mission agencies do not always have the answers to complex regulatory problems. An overworked administrator exposed on a 24-hour basis to a dedicated but zealous staff needs to know the arguments and ideas of policymakers in other agencies as well as in the White House.

We recognize, however, that there may be instances where the docketing of conversations between the President or his staff and other Executive Branch officers or rulemakers may be necessary to ensure due process. This may be true, for example, where such conversations directly concern the outcome of adjudications or quasi-adjudicatory proceedings; there is no inherent executive power to control the rights of individuals in such settings.[6] Docketing may also be necessary in some circumstances where a statute like this one *specifically requires* that essential "information or data" upon which a rule is based be docketed. But in the absence of any further Congressional requirements, we hold that it was not unlawful in this case for EPA not to docket a face-to-face policy session involving the President and EPA officials during the post-comment period, since EPA makes no effort to base the rule on any "data or information" arising from that meeting.
. . . .

The purposes of full-record review which underlie the need for disclosing ex parte conversations in some settings do not require that courts know the details of every White House contact, including a Presidential one, in this informal rulemaking setting. After all, any rule issued here with or without White House assistance must have the requisite *factual support* in the rulemaking record, and under this particular statute the Administrator may not base the rule in whole or in part on any *"information or data "* which is not in the record, no matter what the source. The courts will monitor all this, but they need not be omniscient to perform their role effectively. Of course, it is always possible that undisclosed Presidential prodding may direct an

---

6. Myers v. United States, 272 U.S. 52, 135 (1926) ("there may be duties of a quasi-judicial character imposed on executive tribunals whose decisions after hearings affect the interest of individuals, the discharge of which the President cannot in a particular case properly influence or control").

outcome that *is* factually based on the record, but different from the outcome that would have obtained in the absence of Presidential involvement. In such a case, it would be true that the political process did affect the outcome in a way the courts could not police. But we do not believe that Congress intended that the courts convert informal rulemaking into a rarified technocratic process, unaffected by political considerations or the presence of Presidential power. In sum, we find that the existence of intra-Executive Branch meetings during the post-comment period, and the failure to docket one such meeting involving the President, violated neither the procedures mandated by the Clean Air Act nor due process.

(b) Meetings Involving Alleged Congressional Pressure

Finally, EDF challenges the rulemaking on the basis of alleged Congressional pressure, citing principally two meetings with Senator Byrd. EDF asserts that under the controlling case law the political interference demonstrated in this case represents a separate and independent ground for invalidating this rulemaking. But among the cases EDF cites in support of its position, only D.C. Federation of Civic Associations v. Volpe, [459 F.2d 1231 (D.C.Cir.1971), cert. denied 405 U.S. 1030 (1972).] seems relevant to the facts here.

In D.C. Federation the Secretary of Transportation, pursuant to applicable federal statutes, made certain safety and environmental findings in designating a proposed bridge as part of the interstate highway system. Civic associations sought to have these determinations set aside for their failure to meet certain statutory standards, and because of possible tainting by reason of improper Congressional influence. Such influence chiefly included public statements by the Chairman of the House Subcommittee on the District of Columbia, Representative Natcher, indicating in no uncertain terms that money earmarked for the construction of the District of Columbia's subway system would be withheld unless the Secretary approved the bridge. While a majority of this court could not decide whether Representative Natcher's extraneous pressure had in fact influenced the Secretary's decision, a majority did agree on the controlling principle of law: "that the decision [of the Secretary] would be invalid if based in whole or in part on the pressures emanating from Representative Natcher." In remanding to the Secretary for new determinations concerning the bridge, however, the court went out of its way to "emphasize that we have not found—nor, for that matter, have we sought—any suggestion of impropriety or illegality in the actions of Representative Natcher and others who strongly advocate the bridge." The court remanded simply so that the Secretary could make this decision strictly and solely on the basis of considerations made relevant by Congress in the applicable statute.

D.C. Federation thus requires that two conditions be met before an administrative rulemaking may be overturned simply on the grounds of Congressional pressure. First, the content of the pressure upon the Secretary is designed to force him to decide upon factors not made relevant by Congress in the applicable statute. Representative Natcher's threats were of precisely that character, since deciding to approve the bridge in order to free the "hostage" mass transit appropriation was not among the decisionmaking factors Congress had in mind when it enacted the highway approval provisions of Title 23 of the United States Code. Second, the Secretary's determination must be affected by those extraneous considerations.

In the case before us, there is no persuasive evidence that either criterion is satisfied. Senator Byrd requested a meeting in order to express "strongly" his already well-known views that the SO_2 standards' impact on coal reserves was a matter of concern to him. EPA initiated a second responsive meeting to report its reaction to the reserve data submitted by the NCA.[7] In neither meeting is there any allegation that EPA made any commitments to Senator Byrd. The meetings did underscore Senator Byrd's deep concerns for EPA, but there is no evidence he attempted actively to use "extraneous" pressures to further his position. Americans rightly expect their elected representatives to voice their grievances and preferences concerning the administration of our laws. We believe it entirely proper for Congressional representatives vigorously to represent the interests of their constituents before administrative agencies engaged in informal, general policy rulemaking, so long as individual Congressmen do not frustrate the intent of Congress as a whole as expressed in statute, nor undermine applicable rules of procedure. Where Congressmen keep their comments focused on the substance of the proposed rule—and we have no substantial evidence to cause us to believe Senator Byrd did not do so here[8]—administrative agencies are expected to balance Congressional pressure with the pressures emanating from all other sources. To hold otherwise would deprive the agencies of legitimate sources of information and call into question the validity of nearly every controversial rulemaking.

In sum, we conclude that EPA's adoption of the 1.2 lbs./MBtu emissions ceiling was free from procedural error. The post-comment period contacts here violated neither the statute nor the integrity of the proceeding.

NOTES

(1) Prior to the decision in Sierra Club, the Administrative Conference of the United States had adopted the following general policy for intra-executive branch communications:

7. [Ed.] See note 3 above.

8. The only hint we are provided that extraneous "threats" were made comes from a newspaper article which states, in part,

"The ceiling decision came after two weeks of what one Senate source called 'hard-ball arm-twisting' by Byrd and other coal state Senators. Byrd summoned Costle and White House adviser Stuart Eizenstat *strongly hinting* that the Administration needs his support on strategic arms limitation treaty (SALT) and the windfall profits tax, according to Senate and Administration sources."

The Washington Post, May 5, 1979, at A–1 (emphasis supplied). We do not believe that a single newspaper account of strong "hint[s]" represents substantial evidence of extraneous pressure significant enough to warrant a finding of unlawful congressional interference.

"1. Any Executive department or agency engaged in informal rulemaking in accordance with the procedural requirements of section 553 of the Administrative Procedure Act should be free to receive written or oral policy advice and recommendations at any time from the President, advisers to the President, the Executive Office of the President, and other administrative bodies, without having a duty to place these intragovernmental communications in the public file of the rulemaking proceeding except to the extent called for in paragraph 2.

"2. When the rulemaking agency receives communications from the President, advisers to the President, the Executive Office of the President, or other administrative bodies which contain material factual information (as distinct from indications of governmental policy) pertaining to or affecting a proposed rule, the agency should promptly place copies of the documents, or summaries of any oral communications, in the public file of the rulemaking proceeding. All communications from these sources containing or reflecting comments by persons outside the government should be so identified and placed in the public file, regardless of their content. A rulemaking agency should consider the importance of giving public participants adequate opportunity to respond if the material presents new and important issues or creates serious conflicts of data.

"3. The Administrative Conference takes no position in the present recommendation concerning rulemaking by other than Executive departments and agencies."

1 CFR § 305.80–6. See P. Verkuil, Jawboning Administrative Agencies: Ex Parte Contacts by the White House, 80 Colum L.Rev. 943 (1980).

Recall that OMB administration of Executive Orders 12291 and 12498, pp. 147–163 above, has made involvement in agency rulemaking by presidential staff increasingly routine. In light of that experience, is the Conference recommendation sufficient? See Symposium on Presidential Control of Rulemaking, 56 Tul.L.Rev. 811 (1982). Or, on the other hand, ought Sierra Club be regarded as a case putting unusual demands for openness on the President and agency, in light of the special character of the Clean Air Act—so that under the APA alone, not even the ACUS constraints need be observed? See Center for Science in the Public Interest v. Department of the Treasury, 573 F.Supp. 1168, 1178 (D.D.C.1983).

(2) SEC v. WHEELING-PITTSBURGH STEEL CORP., 648 F.2d 118 (3d Cir. 1981) (en banc) was a subpoena enforcement proceeding in the course of an investigation said to have resulted from political pressure; a prominent Senator, friendly to a competitor firm, was said to have put the SEC under great pressure to initiate an inquiry likely to jeopardize the subject corporation. Was the investigation, therefore, illicit?

"At bottom, this case raises the question whether based on objective factors, the SEC's decision to investigate reflected its independent determination, or whether that decision was the product of external influences. The reality of prosecutorial experience, that most investigations originate on the basis of tips, suggestions, or importunings of third parties, including commercial competitors, need hardly be noted. That the SEC commenced these proceedings as a result of the importunings of Senator Weicker or Wheeling's competitor, even with malice on their part, is not a sufficient basis to deny enforcement of the subpoena. But beginning an informal investigation by collecting facts at the request of a third party, even one harboring ulterior motives, is much different from entering an order directing a private formal investigation . . . without an objective determination by the Commission and only because of political pressure. . . . The SEC order must be supported by an independent agency determination, not one dictated or pressured by external forces. If an allegation of improper influence and abdication of the agency's objective responsibilities is made, and supported by sufficient evidence to make it facially credible, respondents are entitled to examine the circumstances surrounding the SEC's . . . investigation order."

Four dissenters thought this paid too much attention to the contributions of the Senator and his friends:

"If the target of an agency investigation may resist enforcement of a subpoena whenever there is cause to believe that the agency received information from a competitor or from a Congressman acting on behalf of a constituent, resistance to investigations may well become the order of the day. . . . I recognize, of course, the potential danger presented when members of Congress or the Executive Branch suggest that an enforcement agency undertake an investigation. If, for example, the head of an agency wishes to harass a former political or personal opponent by conducting an investigation, such conduct should not be approved. See United States v. Fensterwald, 553 F.2d 231 (D.C.Cir. 1977) (per curiam). But not every investigative referral by a Congressman or other official should be considered suspect or condemned per se. The Supreme Court recognized in Gravel v. United States, 408 U.S. 606, 625 (1972), that members of Congress 'are constantly in touch with the Executive Branch of Government—they may cajole, and exhort with respect to the administration of a federal statute.'"

See Note, The Abuse of Process Defense, 82 Colum.L.Rev. 811 (1982).

(3) The incidence of decisions like those preceding is trivial when compared with the extent of Congressional and executive oversight activity. "Congressional Oversight of Regulatory Agencies," II Study on Federal Regulation pursuant to S.Res. 71, Senate Committee on Government Operations, 95th Cong., 1st Sess. (1977) gives a full and not surprisingly complimentary picture of legislative activity, with suggestions for future development. Over four recent congresses, it found, oversight hearings had increased more than three-fold; EPA alone appeared more than 200 times in the 93d and 94th Congresses. Success is reported in provoking bank regulators into enforcement of anti-discrimination regulations, the CAB into deregulation. Problems are described—assuring better coordination, higher priority for oversight, more information, and the like. Neither the possibility that Congressional pressure could override or distort administrative judgment, nor

the risk of judicial disapproval of the result, are among the problems listed.

A NOTE ON THE PERILS OF CANDOR

Now let us turn our attention briefly to other interactions—with the press, the public, regulated industry, or other agencies of government. An agency in the course of developing policy approaches to the problems placed in its charge may often find it expedient to let slip the probable direction of development. Reasons have already been suggested. With the Freedom of Information Act and Sunshine Act in place, such expressions are increasingly accessible in convenient form. If, with a proceeding not yet complete, already formulated views are evident in these expressions, may the speaker be thereby disqualified? Does it matter whether the expressions concern fact or policy, rules or adjudicatory outcomes, formal or informal proceedings? Consider the following:

(1) TEXACO INC. v. FTC, 336 F.2d 754 (D.C.Cir.1964), vac. and remanded on other issues, 381 U.S. 739 (1965).

As did many large producers of petroleum products, Texaco strongly encouraged its franchised dealers to procure tires, batteries, and accessories (TBA) exclusively from a particular supplier, which then gave Texaco a commission on each sale made by Texaco dealers. The FTC had for years been seeking to establish that this sort of link between a TBA supplier and a gasoline producer was illegal because it tended to restrict competition in TBA products. While proceedings against Texaco were still in progress, Chairman Dixon was invited to make a speech before the National Congress of Petroleum Retailers, Inc., meeting in Denver in 1961. In the course of his speech, Mr. Dixon said: "Your problems are many, and many of them are the problems of the Federal Trade Commission, too; for the Commission is concerned with promoting fair competition . . . We at the Commission are well aware of the practices which plague you and we have challenged their legality in many important cases. You know the practices—price fixing, price discrimination, and overriding commissions on TBA. You know the companies—Atlantic, Texas, Pure, Shell, Sun, Standard of Indiana, American, Goodyear, Goodrich, and Firestone. . . . Some of these cases are still pending before the Commission; some have been decided and are in the courts on appeal. You may be sure that the Commission will continue and, to the extent that increased funds and efficiency permit, will increase its efforts to promote fair competition in your industry."

In proceedings to review a final order directing Texaco to cease the promotion of Goodrich products, the Court of Appeals was confident that "a disinterested reader of Chairman Dixon's speech could hardly fail to conclude that he had in some measure decided that Texaco had violated the Act. . . . We conclude that Chairman Dixon's participation in the hearing amounted in the circumstances to a denial of due process which invalidated the order under review. . . . His Denver speech, made before the matter was submitted to the Commission, but while it was before the examiner, plainly reveals that he had already concluded that Texaco and Goodrich were violating the Act, and that he would protect the petroleum retailers from such abuses." [1]

Do you agree? What would you have done in the circumstances of this case if you had been the FTC's General Counsel? a fellow commissioner? a member of a reviewing court?

(2) KENNECOTT COPPER CORP. v. FTC, 467 F.2d 67 (10th Cir.1972). Kennecott was the subject of divestiture proceedings as the result of its acquisition of a coal company. The Commission had relied on a new theory in finding the merger unlawful; Kennecott was not a competitor in the coal industry, but the Commission concluded that *it would have become one* had it not purchased Peabody, a large coal company, outright. The Tenth Circuit sustained this theory, and turned to a news interview given during the pendency of the case by Commissioner Mary Jones:

" 'Comm. Jones. When we look at the structure of a market, we must look at the barriers to entry. We have to determine whether the acquired company could have gone into the market on its own or whether its new presence might keep others out. Perhaps it's easier to see in a case like the Kennecott Copper-Peabody Coal *complaint.* We have here an instance of a copper company that was actually moving into the coal industry on its own. Kennecott was experimenting with a small, previously acquired coal property. The *complaint says* that Kennecott, in effect, eliminated itself as a probable new entrant into the coal industry when it went out and bought a major coal company. (Emphasis added.)'

"We have examined the cases and in each instance in which the courts considering the facts have ruled that the Commissioner had to be disqualified, action was entirely justified based on comments showing what appeared to be a prejudice or a viewpoint. No such commenting or editorializing is present here. From a reading of the statement in its entirety, it is clear that Commissioner Jones was discussing the *complaint* and was doing so in an effort to illustrate a point. . . . In other words, she is not shown to have prejudged the central issue of the case, namely, whether 'the effect of such acquisition may be substantially to lessen competition or to tend to create a monopoly.' See Skelly Oil Company v. Federal Power Commission, 375 F.2d 6 at 17–18 (10th Cir.1967).

"Effort was there being made to show that one of the Commissioners was disqualified based upon a public address. It was there said: '. . . In our opinion no basis for disqualification arises from the fact or assumption that a member of an administrative agency enters a

---

1. Instead of remanding for reconsideration by the FTC without Chairman Dixon's participation, the court reviewed the FTC order on the merits, found it to be unsupported by substantial evidence, and directed that the complaint against Texaco and Goodrich be dismissed. It was on this issue that the Government petitioned for certiorari and obtained a remand. After fresh FTC action (without Chairman Dixon), an order against Texaco and Goodrich was finally sustained in FTC v. Texaco, Inc., 393 U.S. 223 (1968), rev'g 383 F.2d 942 (D.C.Cir.1967).

proceeding with advance views on important economic matters in issue.
. . . ' 375 F.2d at 18.

"Public expressions with regard to pending cases cannot, of course,
be approved because regardless of what is said such expressions tend
not only to mar the image but to create embarrassment and to subject
the proceedings to question. We do not, however, perceive any evidence of prejudging or the appearance of it."

(3) ASSOCIATION OF NATIONAL ADVERTISERS v. FTC, 627 F.2d 1151
(D.C.Cir.1979), cert. denied 447 U.S. 921 (1980): The FTC had been
concerned for some time with the special hazards of advertising to
children; and those who do such advertising had as long been vigilant
to see that Commissioners acquired (or at least expressed) outside the
somewhat controllable milieu of a proceeding no views respecting the
impressionability of children. See, e.g., Re ITT Continental Baking Co.,
82 FTC 1183 (1973) (memorandum of Commissioner Jones refusing to
disqualify herself). In April, 1978, the Commission initiated a rulemaking proceeding governed by special hybrid procedures under the
Magnuson-Moss Federal Trade Commission Improvement Act, 15 U.S.C.
§ 57a: A record was to be compiled; using informal procedures, parties
were to have the opportunity to show particular disputes of fact,
material to the outcome, requiring on-the-record oral proceedings replete with cross-examination and the like, with review in accordance
with the substantial evidence test. As soon as the proposed rule had
been published, industry representatives moved to disqualify the Chairman, Michael Pertschuk; FOIA requests had disclosed, inter alia, a
November 17, 1977 memo from Pertschuk to the head of the Food and
Drug Administration, seeking to enlist his interest:

> Setting legal theory aside, the truth is that we've been drawn
> into this issue because of the conviction which I know you
> share, that one of the evils flowing from the unfairness of
> children's advertising is the resulting distortion of children's
> perception of nutritional values. I see, at this point, our
> logical process as follows—Children's advertising is inherently
> unfair . . . .

When the Chairman and the Commission denied the motion to disqualify, a district court action brought the desired result. Judge Gerhard
Gesell wrote:

"Upon examination of the Chairman's public statements and correspondence of record, a very substantial showing has been made that the
Chairman has conclusively prejudged factual issues which will be
disputed in the rule making proceeding and whose resolution will be
necessary for a fair determination of the rule making as a whole.
Going far beyond general observations of policy and tentative statements of attitude, the Chairman has by his use of conclusory statements of fact, his emotional use of derogatory terms and characterizations, and his affirmative efforts to propagate his settled views made his
further participation improper."

The D.C. Circuit reversed. While disqualification of agency adjudicators is required when their public statements about pending cases are

such that "a disinterested observer may conclude that the [agency] has in some measure adjudged the facts as well as the law of a particular case in advance of hearing it," Cinderella Career & Finishing Schools, Inc. v. FTC, 425 F.2d 583, 591 (D.C.Cir.1970), the court concluded, the more open character of rulemaking and the special nature of rulemaking facts suggested a more permissive test: an agency official must be disqualified from rulemaking "only when there has been a clear and convincing showing that he has an unalterably closed mind on matters critical to the disposition of the proceeding." At 1195. The impossibility of separating fact from policy in rulemaking, and the administrator's corresponding need to form and express his views at an early stage—to "test his own views on different audiences"—required a test that left ample room for the political process. See also United Steelworkers of America v. Marshall, 647 F.2d 1189 (D.C.Cir.1980) [3]; P. Strauss, Disqualification of Decisional Officials in Rulemaking, 80 Colum.L.Rev. 990 (1980); E. Gellhorn and G. Robinson, Rulemaking "Due Process": In Inconclusive Dialogue, 48 U.Chi.L.Rev. 213 (1981).

Chairman Pertschuk's survival of the motion for disqualification was a Pyrrhic victory. He promptly withdrew from the rulemaking in the face of legislative proposals to restrict FTC rulemaking severely and terminate this one, saying that his "own prior statements, however appropriate the court has judged them, have given those urging Congress to terminate the rulemaking a diversionary issue. I am concerned that continuing controversy regarding my participation could become a focus of the debate, instead of the far more important issue—whether the proceeding itself should be allowed to continue." Legal Times of Washington, Jan. 14, 1980, p. 14. It was too late. The following year saw the adoption of legislation significantly curbing FTC rulemaking in general and putting an end, in particular, to the Chil-

---

3. Assistant Secretary of Labor Eula Bingham, the official responsible for OSHA rulemaking, spoke at a labor union conference on exposure to lead in the workplace shortly before OSHA's adoption of a standard to govern that subject. On three controverted issues—whether exposed workers should be given alternative work at the same rate of pay; whether harmful effects were being experienced; and what would be the economic impact of the proposed standards—she told her "Brothers and Sisters" the following: "As to the medical removal protection provision (MRP): I think that there may be some apprehension because Assistant Secretaries in the past have not always understood, or have not known how to spell the words medical removal protection, or rate retention . . . . Well, I learned to spell those words a long time ago on the Coke Oven Advisory Committee, and if you want to know how I feel about it, you need only to look up my comments during those Committee hearings. As far as I'm concerned, it is possible to have a Lead Standard without it. . . .

"As to the dangers of lead: . . . I can tell you about a plant within 300 miles of the city where workers are told to go to the hospital from work and receive therapy that would drag out poison and precious metals. And then they're sent back to be poisoned again. And then I could go down to the hospitals of this city and find a worker that is undergoing kidney dialysis, and I'll bet you a dinner that some of those workers have been in lead plants.

"As to economic feasibility: I have told some people that I have never aspired to be an economist, but I tell you I can smell phony issue when I see one. And to say that safety and health regulations are inflationary is phony.

". . . I don't understand a society such as ours who is not willing to pay a dollar more for a battery to insure that workers do not have to pay for that battery with their lives."

647 F.2d at 1208. The court found the comments politically unwise, but not disqualifying.

dren's Advertising proceeding. Federal Trade Commission Improvements Act of 1980, P.L. 96–252, 94 Stat. 374, Sec. 11. See B. Weingast and M. Moran, Bureaucratic Discretion or Congressional Control? Regulatory Policymaking by the Federal Trade Commission, p. 131 above; M. Pertschuk, Revolt Against Regulation, The Rise and Pause of the Consumer Movement (1982).

(4) *The sound of one hand clapping.* Despite the impressions that might arise from the incidents giving rise to the preceding cases, the more common public complaint is that Commissioners' informal chatter predominantly occurs with those whom they are supposed to be regulating, and conveys softness rather than firmness of purpose. Industry, of course, seeks understanding as urgently and as validly as the agency does. Absent a specific proceeding sought to be influenced outside a required record, its captains are hardly to be criticized for wishing to convey their views personally to bodies capable of inflicting substantial inconvenience and cost, through misapprehension as well as through right-thinking attention to duty.[4] Any realist knows that error is more readily corrected in its early stages of development than after man-months of staff effort have been spent in building action plans upon it.

A survey of logs some federal regulatory commissioners keep of their personal appointments made in 1977 by Common Cause, a citizen-supported organization, took no issue with the consultations as such: "Industry has a constitutional right . . . to lobby government for favorable action. Consultation between regulatory officials and industry representatives is an essential part of effective policy making in regulatory agencies."[5] Still, Common Cause concluded, its survey showed an imbalance: almost half the recorded contacts were with "industry representatives"; less than 5%, with consumer or "public interest" representatives.[6] Required logging of all contacts, and mea-

---

4. The line between a general, policy-oriented approach and an ex parte contact can be as delicate as that between congressional oversight and congressional interference. In Constraints on the Regulatory Process: A Case Study of Regulation of Cable Television § 22–24 (1976), Richard O. Berner describes meetings sought by the Association for Maximum Service Telecasters with individual commissioners in the spring of 1967 to discuss what AMST regarded as accelerating erosion of rules restricting cable TV systems' use of distant television signals. AMST's memo discusses no particular case; the issue was a timely one and its position, unsurprising. As it happened, however, the AMST memo was presented the day before the Commission was to take up a particular request for waiver of the "eroding" rules, and three of the five members of the AMST "team" had executive positions with TV stations which, the AMST position would suggest, would be negatively affected by granting of that request. Forbidden ex parte contacts?

5. With Only One Ear i (1977).

6. Id. at 22. Press (13%), foreign visitors (11%), Congress (6%), Consultants (4%) and others (16%) supplied the balance. The "industry" group could not be broken down to reflect possibly competing interests. At 9. Professor, formerly FCC Commissioner, Glen O. Robinson, remarks, "[I]ndustry capture is at best an awkward explanation for regulatory behavior in dealing with competing industry interests. For example, it is easy to find evidence of FCC bias towards the broadcast industry, but that very bias undermines any particular solicitude towards the cable industry. It also would be difficult for the FCC to be captured simultaneously by AT & T and interconnect equipment suppliers, nor could the agency at once be cozy with Motorola *and* radio common carriers. Because most important controversies involve conflicting industry constituents, the 'capture' explanation would appear to have limited value as a guide to agency behavior. . . .

"Because economic security is a characteristic of many, if not most, regulatory

sures to increase the level of public participation, were among the reforms suggested. Contemporaneous congressional studies found that the level of public participation in discrete agency proceedings was similarly slight [7]—a phenomenon taken by many, including Common Cause, as an important indication of the need for government subvention of such participation.

c. "Conflict of Interests" and "The Revolving Door"

LASALLE NATIONAL BANK v. COUNTY OF LAKE
United States Court of Appeals, Seventh Circuit, 1983.
703 F.2d 252.

Before PELL and CUDAHY, CIRCUIT JUDGES, and BONSAL,[*] SENIOR DISTRICT JUDGE.

CUDAHY, CIRCUIT JUDGE.

This case confronts us with some of the ethical problems involved when a former government attorney takes up the practice of law with a large law firm. Lake County, Illinois, one of the parties to this appeal, is the former employer of an attorney now practicing law with the firm representing the plaintiffs-appellants. Lake County moved to disqualify the plaintiff's law firm because of the County's former relationship with one of the firm's associates. The district court granted the motion, finding that the past association gave rise to an appearance of impropriety and holding that both the attorney and the entire law firm must be disqualified. Plaintiffs are here appealing the disqualification as a collateral order appealable under the doctrine set forth in Cohen v. Beneficial Loan Corp., 337 U.S. 541 (1949). We affirm the order of the district court.

I

Marc Seidler, the attorney upon whose career our attention must focus in this case, served as an Assistant State's Attorney in Lake County from 1976 until January 31, 1981. On December 1, 1976, Mr. Seidler was appointed Chief of the Civil Division of the Lake County State's Attorney's office, and in September 1979, he was appointed First Assistant State's Attorney. As such, he had general supervisory re-

schemes, business interests tend to prefer regulation to the unsettling vicissitudes of competition. Herein lies the larger problem: not that *regulators* have been captured by industry but rather that *regulation* has been captured by industry. As I discovered during my term as a Commissioner, the FCC is entreated to promote many 'public interests,' but few are advanced with such heartfelt eloquence as the pleas of businessmen—most notably broadcasters and telephone company representatives—to protect their 'services' from the corrosive, unstabilizing effects of competition by imposing some new layer of anticompetitive regulations." The Federal Communications Commission: An Essay on Regulatory Watchdogs, 64 Va.L.Rev. 169, 191–192 (1978).

7. "Public Participation in Regulatory Agency Proceedings," III Study on Federal Regulation pursuant to S.Res. 71, Senate Committee on Governmental Affairs, 95th Cong. 1st Sess. (1977); "Federal Regulation and Regulatory Reform," Subcommittee on Oversight and Investigations, House Committee on Interstate and Foreign Commerce, 94th Cong. 2d Sess. 539 (1976).

* The Honorable Dudley B. Bonsal, Senior District Judge of the United States District Court for the Southern District of New York, is sitting by designation.

sponsibility with respect to all civil cases handled by the State's Attorney's office. On February 2, 1981, Mr. Seidler joined the Chicago law firm of Rudnick & Wolfe as an associate, working in the firm's Northbrook, Illinois office.

On June 5, 1981, Rudnick & Wolfe filed suit against the County of Lake and the Village of Grayslake, on behalf of its clients, the LaSalle National Bank as Trustee ("LaSalle National") and Lake Properties Venture ("Lake Properties"). [The lawsuit challenged Grayslake's denial of sewer access to developments on a tract of land in which plaintiffs had an interest. The issues would turn, in part, on construction of a sewage disposal agreement between Grayslake and Lake County; while that agreement had been signed before Mr. Seidler joined the State Attorney's office, he was privy to discussions with the county about the validity of similar agreements with other entities, and at one point had begun work on a requested opinion letter on the matter.]

Mr. Seidler has submitted a sworn affidavit stating that he has not disclosed to his law firm or any of its personnel any information about the Agreement, about the County's legal strategy or about any other matter relevant to the present litigation. In addition, Theodore J. Novak, a partner at Rudnick & Wolfe involved in the representation of Lake Properties, has filed an affidavit swearing that Mr. Seidler had been screened from all involvement in the litigation since the motion to disqualify was filed.

[The court first considered whether the disqualification of Attorney Seidler himself was proper. Because, in its view, "information relating to any of the similar sewage agreements or to the attitude or policies of Lake County toward provision of sewer service in general to new developments is relevant to the issues in the present litigation," the court had no difficulty upholding that disqualification.]

IV

Having found that Mr. Seidler was properly disqualified from representation of the plaintiffs in this case, we must now address whether this disqualification should be extended to the entire law firm of Rudnick & Wolfe. Although the knowledge possessed by one attorney in a law firm is presumed to be shared with the other attorneys in the firm, . . . this presumption may be rebutted. The question arises here whether this presumption may be effectively rebutted by establishing that the "infected" attorney was "screened," or insulated, from all participation in and information about a case, thus avoiding disqualification of an entire law firm based on the prior employment of one member.

. . . .

If past employment in government results in the disqualification of future employers from representing some of their long-term clients, it seems clearly possible that government attorneys will be regarded as "Typhoid Marys." Many talented lawyers, in turn, may be unwilling to spend a period in government service, if that service makes them unattractive or risky for large law firms to hire. In recognition of this problem, several other circuits have begun either explicitly or implicitly to approve the use of screening as a means to avoid disqualification of an entire law firm by "infection." The Second Circuit has expressed its approval of the use of screening in a situation where the law firm's continued representation of a client results in no threat of a taint to the trial process. Armstrong v. McAlpin, 625 F.2d 433, 445 (2d Cir.1980) (en banc), vacated on other grounds, 449 U.S. 1106 (1981). The Fourth Circuit, similarly, has approved an arrangement under which a former Justice Department attorney's new employer was not disqualified, on the basis that the disqualified individual was denied access to all the relevant files and did not participate in fees from the barred litigation. Greitzer & Locks v. Johns-Manville Corp., No. 81–1379, slip op. at 7 (4th Cir. Mar. 5, 1982). Similarly, the Court of Claims has held that a former government attorney's entire firm need not be disqualified where screening procedures insure that he did not consult with the other attorneys about the case or share in fees derived from it. Kesselhaut v. United States, 555 F.2d 791 (Ct.Cl.1977).

In 1975 the Committee on Ethics and Professional Responsibility of the American Bar Association turned its attention to the acceptability of screening in its Formal Opinion No. 342. The specific question under consideration was whether Disciplinary Rule 5–105(D) ("If a lawyer is required to decline employment or to withdraw from employment under a disciplinary rule, no partner, or associate, or any other lawyer affiliated with him or his firm, may accept or continue such employment") applied in the case of the many former government attorneys now in private practice. The Committee stated that it did not interpret DR 5–105(D) to require disqualification of an entire law firm if the former government attorney had been screened from any direct or indirect participation in the matter. ABA, Comm. on Ethics and Professional Responsibility, Formal Op. 342 (1975) at 11. . . . Scholarly commentary has also generally approved screening as a device to avoid the wholesale disqualification of law firms with which former government attorneys are associated.

The screening arrangements which courts and commentators have approved, however, contain certain common characteristics. The attorney involved in the Armstrong v. McAlpin case, for example, was denied access to relevant files and did not share in the profits or fees derived from the representation in question; discussion of the suit was prohibited in his presence and no members of the firm were permitted to show him any documents relating to the case; and both the disqualified attorney and others in his firm affirmed these facts under oath. 625 F.2d at 442–43. The screening approved in the Kesselhaut case was similarly specific: all other attorneys in the firm were forbidden to discuss the case with the disqualified attorney and instructed to prevent any documents from reaching him; the files were kept in a locked file cabinet, with the keys controlled by two partners and issued to others only on a "need to know" basis. 555 F.2d at 793. In both cases, moreover, as well as in Greitzer & Locks, the screening arrangement was set up at the time when the potentially disqualifying event occured, either when the attorney first joined the firm or when the firm accepted a case presenting an ethical problem.

In the case at hand, by contrast, Mr. Seidler joined the firm of Rudnick & Wolfe on February 2, 1981; yet screening arrangements were not established until the disqualification motion was filed in August 1981. Although Mr. Seidler states in his affidavit that he did not disclose to any person associated with the firm any information about the validity of the Agreement or the County's strategy on any matter relevant to this litigation, no specific institutional mechanisms were in place to insure that that information was not shared, even inadvertently, between the months of February and August.[1] Recognizing that this is an area in which the relevant information is singularly within the ken of the party defending against the motion to disqualify and in which the reputation of the bar as a whole is implicated, we hold that the district court did not abuse its discretion in extending the disqualification of Marc Seidler to the entire firm of Rudnick & Wolfe. The district court order is therefore affirmed.

NOTES

(1) ABA, MODEL RULES OF PROFESSIONAL CONDUCT (1983), RULE 1.11, "SUCCESSIVE GOVERNMENT AND PRIVATE EMPLOYMENT":

"(a) Except as law may otherwise expressly permit, a lawyer shall not represent a private client in connection with a matter in which the lawyer participated personally and substantially as a public officer or employee, unless the appropriate government agency consents after consultation. No lawyer in a firm with which that lawyer is associated may knowingly undertake or continue representation in such a matter unless:

"(1) the disqualified lawyer is screened from any participation in the matter and is apportioned no part of the fee therefrom; and

"(2) written notice is promptly given to the appropriate government agency to enable it to ascertain compliance with the provisions of this rule.

"(b) Except as law may otherwise expressly permit, a lawyer having information that the lawyer knows is confidential government information about a person acquired when the lawyer was a public officer or employee, may not represent a private client whose interests are adverse to that person in a matter in which the information could be used to the material disadvantage of that person. A firm with which that lawyer is associated may undertake or continue representation in the matter only if the disqualified lawyer is screened from any participation in the matter and is apportioned no part of the fee therefrom.

"(c) Except as law may otherwise expressly permit, a lawyer serving as a public officer or employee shall not:

---

1. We, of course, recognize that our analysis frequently requires identification of problems at the time attorneys are hired. In some cases, this may be difficult or even impossible. Nevertheless, we believe that timely screening arrangements are essential to the avoidance of firm disqualification.

"(1) participate in a matter in which the lawyer participated personally and substantially while in private practice or nongovernmental employment, unless under applicable law no one is, or by lawful delegation may be, authorized to act in the lawyer's stead in the matter; or

"(2) negotiate for private employment with any person who is involved as a party or as attorney for a party in a matter in which the lawyer is participating personally and substantially.

"(d) As used in this Rule, the term 'matter' includes:

"(1) any judicial or other proceeding, application, request for a ruling or other determination, contract, claim, controversy, investigation, charge, accusation, arrest or other particular matter involving a specific party or parties, and

"(2) any other matter covered by the conflict of interest rules of the appropriate government agency.

"(e) As used in this Rule, the term 'confidential government information' means information which has been obtained under governmental authority and which, at the time this rule is applied, the government is prohibited by law from disclosing to the public or has a legal privilege not to disclose, and which is not otherwise available to the public."

(2) Early drafts of Rule 1.11 contained no provision for screening; disqualification was to be absolute. Should the "revolving door" be locked . . . or oiled? It has its beneficial aspects: without it, we might be forced to adopt a permanent civil service, even at policy levels of government [1]; the possibility of leaving government service for connected private sector employment makes government service more desirable and reduces the pressure to conform while one is in it; while informed evasion or excessive influence is the fear, having persons in the private sector who have the experience of public service may in fact promote understanding, voluntary compliance, and constructive compromise. On the other hand lie concerns about agency capture, personal trading on a government connection for private advantage,[2] and the

---

1. In Armstrong v. McAlpin, 625 F.2d 433, 443 (2d Cir.1980) (en banc), vacated on other grounds 449 U.S. 1106 (1981), cited in the principal case, amicus briefs were filed by the United States, FTC, CAB, FERC, Federal Legal Council, SEC, ICC, FMC, CFTC and a number of distinguished former government lawyers, "all attesting to the importance of the issues raised on appeal. Thus, the United States asserts that a 'decision to reject screening procedures is certain to have a serious, adverse effect on the ability of Government legal offices to recruit and retain well-qualified attorneys'; this view is seconded by the other government amici. And the former government lawyers, including two former Attorneys General of the United States and two former Solicitors General of the United States, state that they are all 'affected at

least indirectly, by the panel opinion's underlying assumption that government lawyers cannot be trusted to discharge their public responsibilities faithfully while in office, or to abide fully by screening procedures afterwards.' While the tone of these assertions may be overly apocalyptic, it is true that a decision rejecting the efficacy of screening procedures in this context may have significant adverse consequences."

2. "There is a deep public uneasiness with officials who switch sides—who become advocates for and advisors to the outside interests they previously supervised as government employees. After all, there are reasons why private clients so frequently hire former officials, and the attraction explains why some of them do so

unworkability of measures like the "Chinese Wall" built in the principal case, that depend so strongly on self-regulation.[3] One study, drawing on publicly available data for commissioners at three major federal independent regulatory commissions through 1977,[4] found that private use of government experience was the prevailing pattern. Although about half of the 174 persons *appointed* commissioners to the agencies came from related *public* sector jobs, and only one fifth from the regulated industry, the proportions were reversed on exit: fifty percent took jobs in or serving the regulated industries; only eleven percent, jobs in the related public sector. In addition to works already cited, recent thoughtful discussion may be found in R. Mundheim, Conflict of Interest and the Former Government Employee: Rethinking the Revolving Door, 14 Creighton L.Rev. 707 (1981); T. Morgan, Appropriate Limits on Participation by Former Agency Official in Matters Before an Agency, 1980 Duke L.J. 1; Developments: Conflicts of Interest, 94 Harv.L.Rev. 1244 (1981); and Comment, The Chinese Wall Defense to Law Firm Disqualification, 128 U.Pa.L.Rev. 677 (1980).

(3) Within the federal government, conflicts of interest during and after public service are regulated under the Ethics in Government Act of 1978, 5 U.S.C. App., and implementing regulations of the Office of Personnel Management, 5 C.F.R. Part 737. Conflicts of interest during federal service are guarded against, in part, by requiring civil servants and political appointees alike to file detailed reports about financial matters and institutional responsibilities. Agency officials or the Director of the Office of Government Ethics review the reports to determine whether conflicts of interest exist and recommend corrective action, such as divestiture, or limitation of duties to eliminate the conflict.[5] The innovation of this aspect of the statute lies in the detail of reporting required and the provision that the reports be public. What actually constitutes a conflict remains as defined since 1962 by 18 U.S.C. §§ 203, 205, 208, and by agency regulation. The statute is well discussed by Bayless Manning, formerly dean of Stanford Law School and one of the chief movers of the matter, in Federal Conflict of Interest Law (1964); and see also R.B. Perkins, The New Federal Conflict-of-Interest Law, 76 Harv.L.Rev. 1113 (1963); United States v. Mississippi Valley Generating Co., 364 U.S. 520 (1961); Comment, Fighting Conflicts of Interest in Officialdom: Constitutional and Practi-

---

well in subsequent careers in the private sector. Private clients know well that they are hiring persons with special skill and knowledge of particular departments and agencies. That is also the major reason for public concern. It is feared that officials may use information, influence, and access acquired during government service at public expense, for improper and unfair advantage in subsequent dealings with that department or agency." S.Rep. 95–170, 95th Cong. 1st Sess. 32–33 (1977).

3. See, e.g., G. Hazard, Ethics in the Practice of Law 113 (1978), comparing screening to "the alleged New England practice of bundling, having neither the credibility of real prophylaxis nor the dignity of real self-control."

4. R. Eckert, The Life Cycle of Regulatory Commissioners, 24 J. Law & Ec. 113 (1981).

5. Lest these officials be lax, each report (save for officials of the intelligence community) must be held available for public inspection; would-be thieves, insurance salesmen, and college presidents are warned, however, that their use of information contained therein for unlawful, commercial, or solicitation purposes would be unlawful. Sec. 205.

cal Guidelines for State Financial Disclosure Laws, 73 Mich.L.Rev. 758 (1975). The continuing problem has been to limit opportunities for using official positions to gain private advantage without at the same time precluding public agencies from recruiting and retaining as employees or consultants especially qualified persons drawn from the private sector.[6]

The 1978 Act also deals with the difficulties arising after government service, the problem of "the revolving door." Federal criminal law had long provided that a former official may not appear for a private client after leaving government in a distinct matter (adjudication, grant, contract—but *not* rule) in which he had been "personally and substantially" involved while in government; and that he may not appear for a year respecting any like matter for which he had official "responsibility" during the year before he left government. A moment's reflection will show that these prohibitions are limited—there is no bar to advising a client so long as one does not appear; one's partner may appear; appearance is acceptable so long as it is not in connection with a "matter" within reach of one or the other rule; and, finally, waivers could on occasion be obtained. The Ethics in Government Act tightened post-employment constraints in some respects. As amended, 18 U.S.C. § 207 now extends the lifetime ban on participation in particular matters in which the former employee was "personally and substantially" involved to informal as well as formal appearances. In addition, for two years she is forbidden to counsel, aid, consult, advise, or assist others so appearing; the same extended two year ban applies to all matters formally under her official responsibility. For one year, high-level former employees are completely forbidden to make any approach to the agency, formal or informal, oral or written, seeking to influence outcomes—in this case, including rulemaking and whether or not the matter was pending during their tenure or within their responsibility.[2] And these prohibitions are no longer to be enforced only by

---

6. In general, the regulation of bribery and petty corruption does not seem worthy of attention in these pages. Though popular opinion is sometimes otherwise, dishonesty is not characteristic of Washington—or, it is believed, other well-controlled civil service systems. Prohibitions on the acceptance of business lunches and weekend hunting trips abound in statutes and agency regulations, and the periodic emergence of some new scandal—much more often associated with the awarding of defense contracts than the decision of unfair labor practice charges—keeps such behavior at a satisfyingly low level. More alarming to some is the observation that measures adopted to detect or prevent the exchange of favors can stultify administration: "The Civil Service Commission's regulations . . . extend to all agencies the same prohibition which originated with the Department of Defense against the acceptance of entertainment, including meals, by any agency employee from a contractor in fact or aspiration. We see that meals pose a danger to morality, and that unfairness in the treatment of Citizen A versus Citizen B may spread alarmingly because of the allure which a good salad or a delicious piece of beef or a titillating highball may have for a servant of the public or his clerk. Rather than being a shield of good behavior, the enunciation of such rules seems to be an admission that the civil service is filled with weak characters whose will can be reduced to putty by a gift of spaghetti Bolognese. This is truly a libel upon the civil service." B. Boles, Correctives for Dishonest and Unfair Public Administrators, 363 The Annals 23 (1966).

Of course, civil service regulations deal with more substantial matters than spaghetti Bolognese. They discuss also such undoubted improprieties as use of government property, misuse of officially acquired information, and coercion.

2. Provision is made for the agency to seek its former employee's advice where the agency wants that advice, and the

the draconian (and consequently cumbersome and often reluctant) processes of criminal law; the agency concerned may impose a sanction as large as five years' disqualification to appear before it.

Is the former employee, then, wholly out in the cold? No, she may appear in whatever does not concern a "particular matter"—and, unless she is subject to the one year ban on *all* business appearances before her former agency, that includes all rulemakings and general policy questions. And, so far as this statute is concerned, the disqualification is wholly personal. If she joins a law firm, her partners and associates can continue *their* appearances before her former agency; and once two years have expired, they can have her aid and counsel even in those matters respecting which she could not appear.

(4) Note that conflict of interest rules generally concern interests on which a monetary value can be placed, and interests arising in particular (adjudicatory or investigative) rather than general policy (rulemaking) settings. In an era that recognizes aesthetic and environmental interests as sufficient to create standing to sue, should like interests be considered sufficient for application of conflict of interest rules? Where the increasing use of rulemaking often signals that use of that procedure will have an enormous financial or other impact on participants, should concern about changing loyalties (the revolving door) extend as well to it? Recommendation 80–4 of the Administrative Conference of the United States: 1 CFR § 305.80–4, urged agencies to adopt standards extending conflict of interest controls to these matters, but in a cautious manner. For an exploration of some of the difficulties see P. Strauss, Disqualification of Decisional Officials in Rulemaking, 80 Colum.L.Rev. 990 (1980).

agency only is paying any compensation
that may be received for it.

Chapter IX

JUDICIAL CONTROL OF ADMINISTRA-
TIVE ACTION: METHODS, AVAILABILITY,
STANDING, TIMING, SOVEREIGN
IMMUNITY AND TORT ACTION

Having explored the scope of judicial review in chapter III, this chapter considers (1) the ways in which judicial review is secured (methods), (2) whether the action is reviewable (availability), (3) who may secure judicial review (standing), (4) when the agency's action is reviewable (timing), (5) the obstacles to review presented by the doctrine of sovereign immunity and (6) special problems involved when the review action takes the form of an action in tort for money damages against an administrative official or against the government.

SECTION 1. METHODS OF OBTAINING
JUDICIAL REVIEW

Authority for judicial review of allegedly erroneous administrative action may be found in (a) a statute which specifically states that orders or other actions of the named agency may be reviewed ("specific statutory review") or (b) a statute which contains a general provision for judicial review of administrative action ("general statutory review") or (c) a grant of general jurisdiction—either by statute, such as a code of procedure, or under the common law or by the constitution—which does not in terms refer to judicial review of administrative action ("nonstatutory review") or (d) the prerogative writs.

a. Specific Statutory Review

Most federal regulatory acts and many state statutes contain provisions which specifically authorize review of actions of the agency administering the statute. Most often, in the federal area at least, the review is appellate-type, in that the reviewing court is an appellate court, a United States court of appeals, the review is based upon the record of the proceeding before the agency, and the agency's findings of fact are conclusive if supported by substantial evidence. The review is initiated by filing a petition, within a specified period—usually sixty days—after entry of the administrative order of which the petitioner complains, in an appropriate court of appeals—typically within any circuit in which the petitioner resides or has his principal place of business or in the United States Court of Appeals for the District of Columbia. This type of specific statutory review was first enacted in

985

the Federal Trade Commission Act of 1914. Since that time it has been widely adopted.[1]

Similar appellate-type review is sometimes available in an action brought by the agency to enforce its order. See Section 10(e) of the National Labor Relations Act, 29 U.S.C. § 160(e). An NLRB order to cease and desist from an unfair labor practice is not self-operative. But the statute authorizes the Board to petition a court of appeals for a decree enforcing the order. In the enforcement proceeding, the court of appeals acts on the basis of the administrative record and reviews the administrative action as it would had an aggrieved person filed a petition to review.

Another group of federal statutes provides for enforcement in an original—as distinguished from an appellate—action in a United States district court. Reparation orders (i.e., orders for the payment of money) of the Interstate Commerce Commission and of the Secretary of Agriculture under the Packers and Stockyards Act and the Perishable Commodities Act are enforced by civil suits for damages in the district courts; in the judicial proceedings the administrative findings and orders are "prima facie evidence of the facts therein stated." 49 U.S.C. § 11705(d), 7 U.S.C. §§ 210(f), 499g(b).

Occasionally Congress provides for review in a United States district court rather than in a court of appeals. A notable example is section 205(g) of the Social Security Act which provides that the final administrative decision may be reviewed, "irrespective of the amount in controversy . . . [in] a civil action . . . brought in the district court of the United States for the judicial district in which the plaintiff resides or has his principal place of business. . . ." 42 U.S.C. § 405(g).

In some instances administrative actions are reviewable in specialized courts such as the United States Court of Appeals for the Federal Circuit, United States Claims Court, United States Court of International Trade, Temporary Emergency Court of Appeals and the United States Tax Court. For discussion of the advantages and disadvantages of specialized courts, see D. Currie and F. Goodman, supra note 1 at 63–85.

b. General Statutory Review

Instead of, or in some cases in addition to, a statute which authorizes review of orders of named agencies, the legislature may enact a

1. See H. Friendly, Federal Jurisdiction: A General View 34–35 n. 108 (1973), summarizing "a representative sample" of a "host of recent but as yet relatively little known statutes providing for direct review by the courts of appeals of determinations of administrators under specialized administrative schemes."

For an illuminating discussion of "the considerations that determine which federal administrative actions are best reviewed by the district courts, which by the courts of appeals, and which by separate courts of administrative review," see D. Currie and F. Goodman, Judicial Review of Federal Administrative Action: Quest for the Optimum Forum, 75 Colum.L.Rev. 1 (1975). This study underlay ACUS Recommendation 75–3, The Choice of Forum for Judicial Review of Administrative Action, 1 CFR 305.75–3.

general provision for review. See section 5–102 of the Model Administrative Procedure Act (1981), infra Appendix B; 2 Cooper, State Administrative Law 608 (1965). Compare sections 701–706 of the Federal Administrative Procedure Act, infra Appendix A. Such general provisions may themselves define judicial jurisdiction or, as in the case of the federal act, may simply define a cause of action on the basis of which jurisdiction created by other statutes may be invoked. Califano v. Sanders, 430 U.S. 99 (1977).

c. Nonstatutory Review: Tort Action, Injunction and Declaratory Judgment

The existence of a specific or general statutory provision for judicial review does not, as we shall see, eliminate all difficulties. Indeed, many problems are common to both statutory and nonstatutory methods of review; and considerations which influence judges in deciding whether a particular statutory review provision is applicable to the case at bar may be operative also when the issue is whether review should be allowed in absence of a statute, but there are important differences between the two types of judicial review.

The theory of statutory review is that the legislature has expressed its will. The problem in each instance is to ascertain the legislative objective. That this will not be easy in many cases is apparent. But the court's responsibility is to utilize all legitimate aids to determine the legislative purpose, and once it has been ascertained, to give it effect unless doing so would infringe constitutional principles.

Absent a statutory provision for review, the complainant obviously cannot proceed on the theory that the legislature has directed the court to consider his alleged grievance. In such a case he must advance some other reason for judicial intervention. An important basis of nonstatutory review is the proposition that if an official invades a person's "legal rights"—or in other words, commits a "legal wrong"—the ordinary courts of the land should be open to his plea for suitable relief, just as they would be if controversy arose between two private persons.

The litigant who seeks federal judicial review under this theory will institute a "civil action" in a federal district court against the individual whose action or inaction as a government official allegedly invades his legal rights.[2] In the words of the Attorney General's Committee on Administrative Procedure:[3] "[T]he basic judicial remedy for the protection of the individual against illegal official action is a private action for damages against the official in which the court

2. Although the theory of nonstatutory review is that the defendant official has, as an individual, infringed the plaintiff's legal rights, a 1961 amendment to the Federal Rules of Civil Procedure provides that "[w]hen a public officer sues or is sued in his official capacity, he may be described as a party by his official title rather than by name. . . . " Fed.R.Civ.P. 25(d)(2). The Advisory Committee's Note makes it clear that the words "official capacity" include nonstatutory review actions. See Judicial Conf. of the United States, Report of Proposed Amendments to Certain Rules of Civil Procedure for the United States District Courts 3–5 (1961).

3. Report of the Attorney General's Committee on Administrative Procedure, S.Doc. No. 8, 77th Cong., 1st Sess. 81 (1941).

determines, in the usual common-law manner and with the aid of a jury, whether or not the officer was legally authorized to do what he did in the particular case. The plaintiff cannot sue to redress merely any unauthorized action by an officer. To maintain the suit the plaintiff must allege conduct by the officer which, if not justified by his official authority, is a private wrong to the plaintiff, entitling the latter to recover damages."[4]

Increasingly in recent years 42 U.S.C. § 1983 has been utilized as the basis for a damage action against state or local officials. That statute provides: "Every person who, under color of any statute, ordinance, regulation, custom, or usage, of any State or Territory, subjects, or causes to be subjected, any citizen of the United States or other person within the jurisdiction thereof to the deprivation of any rights, privileges, or immunities secured by the Constitution and laws, shall be liable to the party injured in an action at law, suit in equity, or other proper proceeding for redress." [5] Although there is no similar statute applicable to federal officials, comparable actions for "constitutional torts" may be maintained against federal officers. Bivens v. Six Unknown Named Agents of the Federal Bureau of Narcotics, 403 U.S. 388 (1971), infra p. 1170. Actions for common-law torts such as libel or slander may, of course, be brought against federal as well as state and local officials.

"While the private action for damages is the basic remedy, . . . the equity injunction has become in the United States the common remedy. It rests on the same theory, namely, the answerability of a Government officer as a private individual for conduct injurious to another, and depends upon the assumption that unless enjoined the officer will commit acts which will entitle the plaintiff to maintain an action for damages." [6]

The prayer for an injunction usually is accompanied by a request for relief under the Declaratory Judgment Act.[7] Since federal district

---

4. Similarly, a defendant prosecuted for violating an agency rule or order ordinarily can defend on the ground that the rule or order is not valid and thus secure judicial review of the agency's action in the criminal proceeding.

5. The statute's jurisdictional counterpart is 28 U.S.C. § 1343(3) which states in relevant part: "The district courts shall have original jurisdiction of any civil action authorized by law to be commenced by any person:

". . .

"(3) To redress the deprivation, under color of any State law, statute, ordinance, regulation, custom or usage, of any right, privilege or immunity secured by the Constitution of the United States or by any Act of Congress providing for equal rights of citizens or of all persons within the jurisdiction of the United States. . . . "

6. Report of the Attorney General's Committee on Administrative Procedure, supra note 3.

7. 28 U.S.C. §§ 2201, 2202:

"§ 2201. . . . In a case of actual controversy within its jurisdiction, except with respect to Federal taxes, any court of the United States, upon the filing of an appropriate pleading, may declare the rights and other legal relations of any interested party seeking such declaration, whether or not further relief is or could be sought. Any such declaration shall have the force and effect of a final judgment or decree and shall be reviewable as such.

"§ 2202. . . . Further necessary or proper relief based on a declaratory judgment or decree may be granted, after reasonable notice and hearing, against any adverse party whose rights have been determined by such judgment."

For discussion of declaratory judgment review in the states, see D. Gifford, Declar-

courts exercise only that jurisdiction conferred upon them by act of Congress, the plaintiff must base her action upon an appropriate section of the United States Code. Sometimes it will be possible to utilize a specific jurisdictional provision enacted as a part of a substantive statute, such as section 279 of the Immigration and Nationality Act of 1952, which states that district courts shall have jurisdiction of "all causes, civil and criminal, arising under any of the provisions of this subchapter." 8 U.S.C. § 1329. Or the nonstatutory review action may be grounded upon a jurisdictional provision of title 28 of the United States Code such as sections 1337 or 1339 which state that the district courts shall have "original jurisdiction of any civil action arising under" any act of Congress "regulating commerce" or "relating to the postal service." [8] Most often the nonstatutory action will be based on section 1331 of title 28—the general "federal question" jurisdictional grant which gives district courts jurisdiction of a civil action "arising under the Constitution, laws, or treaties of the United States."

d. The Prerogative Writs as a Method of Review

These writs (mandamus, certiorari, habeas corpus, prohibition, and quo warranto), often called the "extraordinary legal remedies," were issued by the judges of the King's Bench in England to control or review the actions of inferior officials. American courts, particularly in the states, regarding themselves as the inheritors of the judicial power exercised by the King's Bench, have used the writs—especially mandamus and certiorari—to review administrative determinations.

(i) Mandamus

The conventional formulation of the central idea of the law of mandamus is that the writ will issue to compel an official to perform a "ministerial" duty but not to control the officer's exercise of "discretion", although "arbitrary" or "capricious" action or an "abuse of discretion" may be remedied by the writ. As a mode of analysis, the ministerial-discretionary dichotomy is largely illusory because few administrative determinations do not involve an element of discretion and few are wholly discretionary. Examples of the latter might be the President's selection of members of his Cabinet and his conduct of foreign affairs; but except for this very limited class of completely discretionary functions, administrative officials typically have discretion concerning some elements of their decisions and lack discretion concerning other elements. For example, issuance of passports is a discretionary act, but that discretion does not include withholding a passport because of the applicant's beliefs or associations.[1] The fact

---

atory Judgments under the Model State Administrative Procedure Acts, 13 Hous.L. Rev. 825 (1976).

8. 28 U.S.C. §§ 1337, 1339:

"§ 1337. . . . The district courts shall have original jurisdiction of any civil action or proceeding arising under any Act of Congress regulating commerce or protect-

ing trade and commerce against restraints and monopolies."

"§ 1339. . . . The district courts shall have original jurisdiction of any civil action arising under any Act of Congress relating to the postal service."

1. Kent v. Dulles, 357 U.S. 116 (1958).

that the officer has discretion is not conclusive; the determinative issue is the scope of the discretion. Only after that issue has been resolved can it be decided whether the act in question is subject to judicial control.

Perhaps the most effective step in the development of a rational law of mandamus would be judicial rejection or abandonment of the ministerial-discretionary distinction. Short of that reform, it should be possible to administer the ministerial-discretionary distinction so as to achieve reasoned judicial review. Chief Justice Taft long ago pointed the way:

> Mandamus issues to compel an officer to perform a purely ministerial duty. It cannot be used to compel or control a duty in the discharge of which by law he is given discretion. The duty may be discretionary within limits. He cannot transgress those limits, and if he does so, he may be controlled by injunction or mandamus to keep within them. The power of the court to intervene, if at all, thus depends upon what statutory discretion he has. . . . [The] extent [of the officer's discretion] and the scope of judicial action in limiting it depend upon a proper interpretation of the particular statute and the congressional purpose.[2]

Adherence to this analysis would lead court and counsel to focus upon the basic issue of the scope of the delegated authority. All that is needed is that in mandamus cases federal courts recognize that the

---

2. Work v. Rives, 267 U.S. 175 (1925). In the Work case the Secretary of Interior rejected plaintiff's application for an award of $9,600, an amount he had expended to obtain a release from a contract to buy land containing manganese, after the land had lost much of its value because of the termination of World War I. The Dent Act, 40 Stat. 1272 (1919), was passed by Congress in an effort to do justice and equity to the many persons who could not obtain from the Government compensation for supplies or services furnished or losses incurred in helping the Government during the war, because of a lack of enforceable contracts or equities. Section 5 of the Act directed the Secretary of Interior to make such payments as he should determine would be just and equitable to persons who had made expenditures or incurred obligations "in good faith for or upon property which contained manganese. . . ." The Secretary's decision was to be "conclusive and final." From the beginning, the Interior Department interpreted expenditures "for and upon property" to be confined to expenditures for construction equipment and machinery in the development of property and *not* to include expenditures for real estate or mining rights, because the latter would be too speculative.

The Supreme Court held the plaintiff was not entitled to a writ of mandamus. Chief Justice Taft's opinion pointed out: (1) The Department's construction of the statute was "based in part at least upon the legislative history of the" statute; (2) Congress had no legal obligation to provide for the payments but instead had authorized "a gratuity based on equitable and moral considerations;" (3) the Secretary's decision was to be conclusive and final against the claimant. The Chief Justice concluded: "Congress intended the Secretary to act for it and to construe the [statute] and to give effect to his interpretation without the intervention of the courts. . . . There is nothing in the case at bar which would characterize it as arbitrary or capricious or fraudulent or an abuse of discretion."

Judged by today's standards, the result reached by the Chief Justice may be criticized, for the question was strictly legal and the "gratuity" justification is less weighty today than in 1925. But whether the result is right or wrong, the Chief Justice's mode of analysis is exemplary, for his opinion demonstrates that he focused on what should be the central issue in every mandamus case, that is, "a proper interpretation of the particular statute and the congressional purpose."

terms "ministerial," "discretionary," and "clear duty to act" [3] more often obscure than facilitate analysis. As they would in injunction or statutory review proceedings, the courts should utilize all relevant aids to determine the scope of the delegated power.

Before 1962 federal district courts other than those in the District of Columbia did not have power to issue original writs of mandamus. This lack of mandamus jurisdiction was remedied by the Mandamus and Venue Act of 1962, which created a new section 1361 of title 28 of the United States Code:

"§ 1361. Action to compel an officer of the United States to perform his duty

"The district courts shall have original jurisdiction of any action in the nature of mandamus to compel an officer or employee of the United States or any agency thereof to perform a duty owed to the plaintiff."

After enactment of this statute making mandamus available throughout the nation, federal district and courts of appeal judges other than those in the District of Columbia were required to cope with the intricacies of the ministerial-discretionary distinction.[4] A survey of the manner in which the federal courts responded to this challenge concludes that they "have adopted two approaches. . . . Under the first approach, the court makes the traditional determination of whether the alleged duty is ministerial or discretionary. If the duty is determined to be ministerial in nature, mandamus will issue. However, if the administrative action sought to be compelled is found to be discretionary, the court will find itself lacking in jurisdiction under section 1361. This first approach seems to have been approved by many courts which have dealt with the problem in recent years. In some of these decisions, courts have specifically indicated that the ministerial duty requirement precludes judicial review under section 1361 *even if* an administrator *abuses* his discretion.

"Under the second approach adopted by courts when construing the duty element for mandamus, the court first determines whether the duty alleged to be owed is ministerial or discretionary. If the duty is found to be ministerial in nature, mandamus will lie as in the first approach. However, even if the duty is found to be discretionary, the court will further determine whether, by failing to perform the duty, the administrator exceeded the *permissible scope* of his discretion. The court will typically examine the statute granting the authority to the administrator, the congressional purpose, and other data such as the

---

3. The rule that a court will compel performance of a duty only when there is a "clear duty to act" is essentially an alternative formulation of the ministerial-discretionary distinction and is equally objectionable. Fortunately it is subject to the same refinement and rational administration that Chief Justice Taft employed in the Work case and that we advocate here.

4. For discussion of the development and application of section 1361, see C.

Byse, Proposed Reforms in Federal "Nonstatutory" Judicial Review: Sovereign Immunity, Indispensable Parties, Mandamus, 75 Harv.L.Rev. 1479, 1499–1502 (1962); C. Byse and J.V. Fiocca, Section 1361 of the Mandamus and Venue Act of 1962 and "Nonstatutory" Judicial Review of Federal Administrative Action, 81 Harv.L.Rev. 308, 333–335 (1967).

pertinent administrative regulations, in order to delineate the boundaries within which the officer may permissibly exercise his discretion; if those bounds are exceeded, mandamus will lie." Note, Mandamus in Administrative Actions: Current Approaches, 1973 Duke L.J. 207, 209–211.[5]

Two conclusions concerning mandamus expressed by Professor Davis deserve mention here:

1. "A court has jurisdiction under either § 1331 or § 1361 to require an agency to perform such duties as the law imposes on it and the scope of review is governed by 5 U.S.C. § 706." 4 K. Davis, Admin. L. Treatise § 23:10 (1983).

2. "The best way to compel agency action unlawfully withheld is by injunction or declaratory judgment or both, but without the word 'mandatory' before 'injunction.' Jurisdiction under § 1331 always suffices; mention of § 1361 unnecessarily risks judicial advertence to mandamus technicalities." Id. § 23:11.[6]

(ii) Certiorari

Certiorari's roots extend into the thirteenth century, when the King's Bench had come to be recognized as England's highest court, with superintendence over all others. The writ of certiorari did not issue to litigants as a matter of right. It was not, in short, one of the writs ex debito justitiae. Rather, it was a "prerogative writ" in the sense that the King (acting, of course, through his judges) decided in each instance that certiorari should issue so that an allegedly gross injustice could be investigated. It was used, on a case by case basis, to remove a cause from one tribunal to another before final judgment, if for some reason an impartial trial would be difficult to obtain in the original forum; or as an auxiliary remedy to cause additional material to be sent up to the reviewing court, where the clerk of the lower court had omitted something one of the litigants regarded as important (this was called "certiorari for diminution of the record"); or, finally as a pure instrument of review, after a judgment had been entered by lower judges such as justices of the peace. This last use seems, however, to have been infrequent because the existence of other appellate procedures made recourse to this "prerogative writ" unnecessary.

This very abbreviated historical statement has not been inserted for ornamental reasons. It provides the basis for understanding how certiorari became important in American administrative law.

---

5. An example of the "second approach" is Murray v. Vaughn, 300 F.Supp. 688 (D.R.I.1969) ("Unquestionably, mandamus will not compel an officer to do a 'discretionary' act. Yet, the pivotal inquiry must be directed at the permissible scope of the officer's discretion, for that discretion is circumscribed by constitutional, statutory, and regulatory strictures."). Compare Jarrett v. Resor, 426 F.2d 213 (9th Cir.1970) (mandamus may not issue unless the claim is "clear and certain and the duty of the officer . . . [is] free from doubt.").

6. Note, however, that if § 1331 jurisdiction is precluded by statute, mandamus may be an appropriate method of review. See American Association of Councils of Medical Staffs of Private Hospitals v. Califano, infra p. 1016, at 1018 n. 3.

In the nineteenth century, when the growth of public administration in this country had already become very noticeable but there had not as yet been a corresponding growth of statutory procedures, judges turned to certiorari as a means of reviewing administrative judgments. The judges, like their counterparts on the King's Bench of ancient times, thought of themselves as overseers of their inferiors. And in a country where judicial supremacy had prevailed at least since Marbury v. Madison was decided in 1803, administrators were not surprisingly regarded as subordinate to judges rather than, as in civil law countries, somewhat on a parity with them.

Typically, certiorari has been used only when the administrative action sought to be reviewed has been of a "judicial" character. However, what is judicial and what is, on the other hand, merely "administrative" or "legislative" has never been effectively defined. To learn where the line is drawn in any particular jurisdiction would require a search of that jurisdiction's decisions. But even a detailed state-by-state review would, in the words of the leading commentator on state administrative law, leave "many questions unanswered; for uncertainties as to the availability and scope of review by certiorari present a never-ending source of baffling difficulties for the bench and bar of each state." 2 F. Cooper, State Administrative Law 644 (1965).

The situation in the federal courts can be described more confidently. In sum, certiorari simply is not used at all as a means of reviewing administrative agencies' decisions. Degge v. Hitchcock, 229 U.S. 162 (1913).

(iii) Habeas Corpus, Prohibition, and Quo Warranto

Habeas corpus. The writ is available to a person whose bodily liberty has been unlawfully restrained by an administrative official. Thus the writ would be suitable to test the legality of administrative action involving enforced military service, commitment to mental institutions, and health quarantine.

Proceedings can be brought by an aggrieved individual or in his behalf by his "next best friend." The relief ultimately granted is an order to release the party affected. Meanwhile, the detained person gains access to a court for an inquiry into the propriety of his detention.

Ordinarily habeas corpus will not lie where a different method of review has been provided. It is itself a means of judicial review by indirection, for in order to pass on the question of the legality of detaining the relator, the court must inquire into questions of jurisdiction, deviation from statutory authority, fairness of the hearing, and other issues such as challenges to the constitutionality of the underlying statute. Occasionally a court will say that habeas corpus proceedings do not enable a judge to "review the evidence." If this means that the court will not itself weigh the evidence, the statement is undoubtedly correct. But upon suitable presentation of the issue courts have normally scrutinized the evidence to the extent of deciding whether it reasonably supports the challenged detention—and they have done so even where speaking otherwise.

The fact that a statute makes the administrative decision "final" does not bar examination of the legality of detention. Habeas corpus, as Justice Holmes said in one of his famous opinions, "comes in from the outside" quite independently of the prior proceedings, "and although every form may have been preserved, opens the inquiry whether they have been more than an empty shell." [1]

Prohibition. The writ is used to prevent the performance of action "judicial" in nature—by an administrative body as well as by a court. It is supposedly inapposite if the administrative activity is purely "administrative" or "ministerial" or some such adjective. It has to do with restraining a *tribunal.* The action to be restrained is an attempted assumption of jurisdiction when it clearly does not exist. The writ will not be granted if there is another available remedy and issuance of the writ is said to be discretionary. [2]

Since prohibition is aimed at halting action on the threshold it is not a means of reviewing errors that have already occurred nor of inquiring into irregularities (such as deficient notice and the like) that do not go to the issue of fundamental power.

Like all such generalized statements, the above will be found to have numerous exceptions, chiefly because many state court judges seemingly do not understand what the writ's functions really are.

In determining whether an administrative proceeding is "judicial" in nature, the easy and sensible test for present purposes is simply whether the matter involves a court-type procedure. The purpose of prohibition is to shut off the necessity of going through a hearing, a trial, before a tribunal that has no power to deal with the subject matter at all. Prohibition is not appropriately used to forestall a merely erroneous exercise of jurisdiction. On the other hand, it exactly fills the bill if the tribunal can in no circumstances whatsoever act validly as to the subject matter involved in the hearings it proposes to conduct.

Quo warranto. Quo warranto sounds like judicial review, but it rarely is. It dates from at least as early as the twelfth century, when it was used by the King against the barons and other competitors for power as a demand that they show by what right—quo warranto—they were exercising the prerogatives of some office or enjoying the perquisites of some franchise that was allegedly the crown's to dispose of as it wished. The writ came down through the centuries—at one time, indeed, becoming a criminal proceeding to fine the usurper as well as to oust him from the office or franchise he had usurped. [3] In most states today it is an entirely civil proceeding to test the respondent's right to hold office—as, for example when an elected official seeks to continue

---

1. Frank v. Mangum, 237 U.S. 309, 346 (dissenting opinion) (1915).

For discussion of habeas corpus, see H. Hart and H. Wechsler, The Federal Courts and the Federal System c. 10 (P. Bator, P. Mishkin, D. Shapiro and H. Wechsler, 2d ed. 1973); C. Wright, The Law of Federal Courts § 53 (4th ed. 1983).

2. 2 F. Cooper, State Administrative Law 661 (1965).

3. See 3 Blackstone's Commentaries 263; Ames v. Kansas, 111 U.S. 449, 460–461 (1884).

beyond his term, or when a de facto officeholder takes over public functions, or when an aspirant to a post asserts that someone else has been unlawfully appointed. Some states require that such a proceeding be instituted by the public prosecutor or a similar official, usually upon the relation of a private individual having a special interest in the matter (such as a claim to the office in question); other states permit individuals to initiate the proceedings directly, but only if they have an interest that sets them apart from the generality of citizens and taxpayers.[4]

The orthodox view is that quo warranto affords no relief against official misconduct, nor can it be used to test the legality of any particular action that an officeholder has taken or proposes to take. The only issue to be considered is whether the asserted official really is an official at all. But numerous local variations diminish the generality of this "general rule." Thus, for instance, cases may be found in which quo warranto has been successfully used to challenge allegedly ultra vires acts by concededly lawful officeholders.[5]

SECTION 2. AVAILABILITY OF JUDICIAL REVIEW: STATUTORY PRECLUSION AND "COMMITTED TO DISCRETION"

Section 701(a) of the APA provides that the sections of the APA governing judicial review (i.e., 5 U.S.C. §§ 702–706) shall apply "except to the extent that—(1) statutes preclude judicial review or (2) agency action is committed to agency discretion by law." Two aspects of this section should be noted at the outset.

First, § 701 qualifies or modifies everything that appears in §§ 702–706. Thus, despite the first sentence of § 702, a litigant "suffering legal wrong" would not be entitled to judicial review if a statute completely precluded review to the class of which the litigant was a member; in this way § 701 would operate to limit the *availability* of review. Similarly, "to the extent that" a statute committed the interpretation of a statute to the agency's discretion, the agency's—not the reviewing court's—interpretation would prevail despite the provision in the first sentence of § 706 that the "reviewing court shall . . . interpret . . . statutory provisions"; in this instance § 701 would operate to limit the *scope* of review.[1]

4. See R. Madigan, Quo Warranto to Enforce a Corporate Duty not to Pollute the Environment, 1 Ecology L.Q. 653, 662–666 (1971); Quo Warranto—Persons Entitled to Relief, 57 W.Va.L.Rev. 120 (1955).

5. See, e.g., State ex inf. McKittrick v. Murphy, 347 Mo. 484, 148 S.W.2d 527 (1941). Members of the Unemployment Compensation Commission of Missouri were about to move their headquarters from the state capital to another city; held, the "respondents should be and are hereby ousted from locating . . . the cen-

tral office of the Commission outside the City of Jefferson."

In jurisdictions where quo warranto would be held inapplicable, the misfeasant commissioners would of course be subject to political controls such as proceedings to remove them from office, legislative investigation, restrictions in the appropriations act, and the like. In some states, a taxpayer's suit could be maintained to prevent expenditures for an unlawful purpose.

1. At this point the interested student might profitably refer to the 1925 opinion

The second introductory caveat is that § 701 does not have all or nothing consequences. The section does not state that §§ 702–706 apply according to their terms *"unless"* (1) another statute precludes review or (2) agency action is committed to agency discretion by law. Instead it provides that the various provisions of §§ 702–706 apply *"except to the extent that* (1) . . . . or (2) . . . ."* Accordingly, if a statute completely precludes review, or if a matter is wholly committed to agency discretion §§ 702–706 would be totally inapplicable. But if the preclusion or commitment to discretion is partial, the provisions of §§ 702–706 would be partly applicable and partly inapplicable.[2] In this light, § 701 is an aspect of that pervasive topic of administrative law: the *scope* of judicial review. For unless there is complete preclusion or complete commitment—neither of which is a common occurrence in American law—the questions in every § 701 case will be the same as those identified above at p. 352 in connection with our consideration of the scope of judicial review of administrative action, namely, "[P]recisely what error [does] the complaining party claim the agency [has] committed"? and "[J]ust what is the extent of the power delegated to the agency for the function under review?" Thus do scope, preclusion and commitment to discretion overlap and become if not the proverbial seamless web, a reasonable facsimile.

a. Statutory Preclusion of Judicial Review

The problem of statutory preclusion of judicial review arises in two contexts: (1) where no express statutory provision relates to the issue— *implied preclusion,* and (2) where an express provision purports to bar or restrict review—*express preclusion.* We consider each in turn.

(i) Implied Preclusion

The Supreme Court decision most often cited in support of the conclusion that judicial review has not been precluded by statute is Abbott Laboratories v. Gardner, 387 U.S. 136 (1967), infra p. 1105. There Justice Harlan emphasized that the APA "embodies the basic presumption of review" and that "only upon a showing of 'clear and convincing evidence' of a contrary legislative intent should the courts restrict access to judicial review." The language of that case and its

in Work v. Rives, supra note 2, p. 990, and consider whether, if sections 701 and 706 had been in effect at that time, the scope of review would have been the same or different than that exercised by the Court in that case.

2. Attorney General's Manual on the Administrative Procedure Act 95 (1947): "[T]he clear result [is] that some other statute, while not precluding review altogether, will have the effect of preventing the application of some of the provisions of section[s 702–706]. The net effect, clearly intended by the Congress, is to provide for a dovetailing of the general provisions of the Administrative Procedure Act with the particular statutory provisions which the Congress has moulded for special situations. Thus, a civil service employee of the Federal Government who alleges unlawful removal from office, can obtain judicial review only of the question of whether the procedures of the Civil Service Act were followed. Levine v. Farley, 107 F.2d 186 (D.C.Cir.1939), cert. denied 308 U.S. 622. In such a case, the provisions of section [706], for example, relating to substantial evidence and to review of abuses of discretion, will not apply."

repetition in numerous other Supreme Court opinions [3] indicate that the Court will not readily find a Congressional intention to foreclose access to the courts. The problem, of course, is how to determine whether there is "clear and convincing evidence" of a legislative intent to bar judicial review.

Dunlop v. Bachowski, 421 U.S. 560 (1975), discussed above at pp. 317, 472, is an example of the usual refusal to imply a preclusion of review from statutory materials. The Secretary of Labor contended that judicial review of his refusal to sue to set aside an allegedly invalid labor union election was precluded by statute. He argued that "the structure of the statutory scheme, its objectives, its legislative history, the nature of the administrative action involved, and the conditions spelled out with respect thereto, combine to evince a congressional meaning to prohibit judicial review of his decision." The Court replied:

"We have examined the materials the Secretary relies upon. They do not reveal to us any congressional purpose to prohibit judicial review. Indeed, there is not even the slightest intimation that Congress gave thought to the matter of the preclusion of judicial review. The only reasonable inference is that the possibility did not occur to the Congress. Wirtz v. Local 153, Glass Bottle Blowers Ass'n, 389 U.S. 463 (1968).

"We therefore reject the Secretary's argument as without merit. He has failed to make a showing of 'clear and convincing evidence' that Congress meant to prohibit all judicial review of his decision. . . . Our examination of the relevant materials persuades us, however, that although no purpose to prohibit all judicial review is shown, a congressional purpose narrowly to limit the scope of judicial review of the Secretary's decision can, and should, be inferred in order to carry out congressional objectives in enacting LMRDA."

Occasionally, however, despite the failure of Congress to address the issue, the Court will divine the necessary "clear and convincing evidence" of a Congressional intention to preclude review. For a recent instance of such a divination, consider:

BLOCK v. COMMUNITY NUTRITION INSTITUTE
Supreme Court of the United States, 1984.
467 U.S. 340.

[To bring destabilizing competition among dairy farmers under control, the Agricultural Marketing Agreement Act of 1937 authorizes the Secretary of Agriculture, after "due notice of and opportunity for a hearing" to issue milk market orders establishing minimum prices that processers of dairy products (handlers) must pay to producers (dairy farmers) for their milk. Pursuant to this authority, the Secretary issued some 45 milk market orders covering different regions of the country. The orders designated raw milk that is processed and bottled for fluid consumption as "Class I" milk. Raw milk that is used to produce milk products such as butter, cheese, or dry milk powder is

3. See, e.g., Citizens to Preserve Overton Park v. Volpe, supra p. 436; Association of Data Processing Service Organizations v. Camp, infra p. 1046.

termed "Class II" milk. The orders require handlers to pay a higher price for Class I products than for Class II products; all payments are made to a regional pool from which distributions are made to dairy farmers based on how much milk they have produced, regardless of its class. While Class I and Class II milk are physically indistinguishable, this mechanism permits accommodating the cyclical nature of a cow's milk production. Class I products have a short shelf life and constant yearly demand; cows produce much more milk in the spring than in other seasons.

The orders require handlers to pay the lower minimum Class II price for "reconstituted milk," which is milk manufactured by mixing milk powder with water. The orders assume that handlers will use the reconstituted milk to manufacture Class II milk products, but for any portion of reconstituted milk not so used handlers must make a "compensatory payment" to the regional pool equal to the difference between Class I and Class II milk product prices. Three individual consumers of fluid dairy products, a handler regulated by the market orders, and a nonprofit organization brought suit in federal district court, contending that by raising handlers' costs the compensatory payment requirement makes reconstituted fluid milk uneconomical for handlers to process. The district court held that the consumers and the nonprofit organization did not have standing and, in addition, that the Act precluded such persons from obtaining judicial review; the milk handler's action was dismissed because of failure to exhaust administrative remedies. The circuit court of appeals agreed that the handler and the nonprofit organization had been properly dismissed but held that the consumers had standing. The court also rejected the contention that the statute impliedly precluded consumers from challenging milk market orders because the statutory structure and purposes of the Act did not reveal "the type of clear and convincing evidence of congressional intent needed to overcome the presumption in favor of judicial review," citing Abbott Laboratories. 698 F.2d 1252 n.75. The Supreme Court granted certiorari.]

JUSTICE O'CONNOR delivered the opinion of the Court. . . .

II

Respondents filed this suit under the Administrative Procedure Act (APA), 5 U.S.C. § 701 et seq. The APA confers a general cause of action upon persons "adversely affected or aggrieved by agency action within the meaning of a relevant statute," but withdraws that cause of action to the extent the relevant statute "preclude[s] judicial review,". Whether and to what extent a particular statute precludes judicial review is determined not only from its express language, but also from the structure of the statutory scheme, its objectives, its legislative history, and the nature of the administrative action involved. See . . . generally Note, Statutory Preclusion of Judicial Review Under the Administrative Procedure Act, 1976 Duke L.J. 431, 442–449. Therefore, we must examine this statutory scheme "to determine whether Congress precluded all judicial review, and, if not, whether

Congress nevertheless foreclosed review to the class to which the [respondents] belon[g]." Barlow v. Collins, 397 U.S. 159, 173 (1970) (Opinion of Brennan, J.,); see also Data Processing Service v. Camp, 397 U.S. 150, 156 (1970).

It is clear that Congress did not intend to strip the judiciary of all authority to review the Secretary's milk market orders. The Act's predecessor, the Agricultural Adjustment Act of 1933, 48 Stat. 31, contained no provision relating to administrative or judicial review. In 1935, however, Congress added a mechanism by which dairy handlers could obtain review of the Secretary's market orders. That mechanism was retained in the 1937 legislation and remains in the Act as § 608c(15) today. Section 608c(15) requires handlers first to exhaust the administrative remedies made available by the Secretary. After these formal administrative remedies have been exhausted, handlers may obtain judicial review of the Secretary's ruling in any federal district court "in which [they are] inhabitant[s], or ha[ve their] principal place[s] of business." These provisions for handler-initiated review make evident Congress' desire that *some* persons be able to obtain judicial review of the Secretary's market orders.

The remainder of the statutory scheme, however, makes equally clear Congress' intention to limit the classes entitled to participate in the development of market orders. The Act contemplates a cooperative venture among the Secretary, handlers, and producers the principal purposes of which are to raise the price of agricultural products and to establish an orderly system for marketing them. Handlers and producers—but not consumers—are entitled to participate in the adoption and retention of market orders. The Act provides for agreements among the Secretary, producers, and handlers, for hearings among them, and for votes by producers and handlers. Nowhere in the Act, however, is there an express provision for participation by consumers in any proceeding. In a complex scheme of this type, the omission of such a provision is sufficient reason to believe that Congress intended to foreclose consumer participation in the regulatory process. See Switchmen v. National Mediation Board, 320 U.S. 297 (1943).

To be sure, the general purpose sections of the Act allude to general consumer interests. See 7 U.S.C. §§ 602(2), (4).[1] But the

---

1. [Ed.] Sections 602(2) and (4) provide as follows:

§ 602. "It is declared to be the policy of Congress—. . .

"(2) To protect the interest of the consumer by (a) approaching the level of [parity] prices which it is declared to be the policy of Congress to establish in subsection (1) of this section by gradual correction of the current level at as rapid a rate as the Secretary of Agriculture deems to be in the public interest and feasible in view of the current consumptive demand in domestic and foreign markets, and (b) authorizing no action under this chapter which has for its purpose the maintenance of

prices to farmers above the [parity] level which it is declared to be the policy of Congress to establish in subsection (1) of this section. . . .

"(4) Through the exercise of the powers conferred upon the Secretary of Agriculture under this chapter, to establish and maintain such orderly marketing conditions for any agricultural commodity enumerated in section 608c(2) of this title as will provide, in the interests of producers and consumers, an orderly flow of the supply thereof to market throughout its normal marketing season to avoid unreasonable fluctuations in supplies and prices."

preclusion issue does not only turn on whether the interests of a particular class like consumers are implicated. Rather, the preclusion issue turns ultimately on whether Congress intended for that class to be relied upon to challenge agency disregard of the law. See Barlow v. Collins, 397 U.S., at 167. The structure of this Act indicates that Congress intended only producers and handlers, and not consumers, to ensure that the statutory objectives would be realized.

Respondents would have us believe that, while Congress unequivocally directed handlers first to complain to the Secretary that the prices set by milk market orders are too high, it was nevertheless the legislative judgment that the same challenge, if advanced by consumers, does not require initial administrative scrutiny. There is no basis for attributing to Congress the intent to draw such a distinction. The regulation of agricultural products is a complex, technical undertaking. Congress channelled disputes concerning marketing orders to the Secretary in the first instance because it believed that only he has the expertise necessary to illuminate and resolve questions about them. Had Congress intended to allow consumers to attack provisions of marketing orders, it surely would have required them to pursue the administrative remedies provided in § 608c(15)(A) as well. The restriction of the administrative remedy to handlers strongly suggests that Congress intended a similar restriction of judicial review of market orders.

Allowing consumers to sue the Secretary would severely disrupt this complex and delicate administrative scheme. It would provide handlers with a convenient device for evading the statutory requirement that they first exhaust their administrative remedies. A handler may also be a consumer and, as such, could sue in that capacity. Alternatively, a handler would need only to find a consumer who is willing to join in or initiate an action in the district court. The consumer or consumer-handler could then raise precisely the same exceptions that the handler must raise administratively. . . . For these reasons, we think it clear that Congress intended that judicial review of market orders issued under the Act ordinarily be confined to suits brought by handlers in accordance with 7 U.S.C. § 608c(15).

III

. . .

The presumption favoring judicial review of administrative action is just that—a presumption. This presumption, like all presumptions used in interpreting statutes, may be overcome by specific language or specific legislative history that is a reliable indicator of congressional intent. The congressional intent necessary to overcome the presumption may also be inferred from contemporaneous judicial construction barring review and the congressional acquiescence in it or from the collective import of legislative and judicial history behind a particular statute. More important for purposes of this case, the presumption favoring judicial review of administrative action may be overcome by inferences of intent drawn from the statutory scheme as a whole. See, e.g., Switchmen v. National Mediation Board, 320 U.S. 297 (1943). In particular, at least when a statute provides a detailed mechanism for judicial consideration of particular issues at the behest of particular persons, judicial review of those issues at the behest of other persons may be found to be impliedly precluded.

. . .

In this case, the Court of Appeals did not take [a] balanced approach to statutory construction. . . . Rather, it recited this Court's oft-quoted statement that "only upon a showing of 'clear and convincing evidence' of a contrary legislative intent should the courts restrict access to judicial review." Abbott Laboratories v. Gardner, 387 U.S. 136, 141 (1967). See also . . . Dunlop v. Bachowski, 421 U.S. 560, 568 (1975). According to the Court of Appeals, the "clear and convincing evidence" standard required it to find unambiguous proof, in the traditional evidentiary sense, of a congressional intent to preclude judicial review at the consumers' behest. Since direct statutory language or legislative history on this issue could not be found, the Court of Appeals found the presumption favoring judicial review to be controlling.

This Court has, however, never applied the "clear and convincing evidence" standard in the strict evidentiary sense the Court of Appeals thought necessary in this case. Rather, the Court has found the standard met, and the presumption favoring judicial review overcome, whenever the congressional intent to preclude judicial review is "fairly discernible in the statutory scheme." Data Processing Service v. Camp, 397 U.S., at 157. In the context of preclusion analysis, the "clear and convincing evidence" standard is not a rigid evidentiary test but a useful reminder to courts that, where substantial doubt about the congressional intent exists, the general presumption favoring judicial review of administrative action is controlling. That presumption does not control in cases such as this one, however, since the congressional intent to preclude judicial review is "fairly discernible" in the detail of the legislative scheme. Congress simply did not intend for consumers to be relied upon to challenge agency disregard of the law.

. . .

[P]reclusion of consumer suits will not threaten realization of the fundamental objectives of the statute. Handlers have interests similar to those of consumers. . . . Handlers can therefore be expected to challenge unlawful agency action and to ensure that the statute's objectives will not be frustrated.[2] Indeed, as noted above, consumer suits might themselves frustrate achievement of the statutory purposes. The Act contemplates a cooperative venture among the Secretary, producers, and handlers; consumer participation is not provided for or desired under the complex scheme enacted by Congress. Consumer suits would undermine the congressional preference for administrative

---

2. Whether handlers would pass on to consumers any savings they might secure through a successful challenge to the market order provisions is irrelevant. Consumers' interest in market orders is limited to lowering the prices charged to handlers in the hope that consumers will then reap some benefit at the retail level.

remedies and provide a mechanism for disrupting administration of the congressional scheme. . . .

. . . .

JUSTICE STEVENS did not participate in the decision of this case.

NOTES

(1) SWITCHMEN'S UNION v. NATIONAL MEDIATION BOARD, 320 U.S. 297 (1943), cited by Justice O'Connor in the Block opinion, involved a dispute between the Brotherhood of Railroad Trainmen and the Switchmen's Union over representation of railroad employees for collective bargaining purposes. The Brotherhood sought to represent all yardmen of the New York Central system. The Union contended that yardmen of certain designated parts of the system should be permitted to vote for separate representatives instead of being compelled to take part in a system-wide election. The National Mediation Board, authorized by § 2, Ninth of the Railway Labor Act to resolve such disputes, decided that the statute did not give it power to permit representation of a unit of less than all of the employees of a given craft. Accordingly, it directed a system-wide election. With all yardmen voting as a unit, the Brotherhood won the election and the Board certified it as the collective bargaining representative of all the yardmen in the system. The Switchmen's Union then sought injunctive relief in the district court to cancel the Board's decision on the ground that the Board had incorrectly interpreted § 2, Ninth.

The lower federal courts upheld the Board. The Supreme Court affirmed on the ground that the district court did not have power to review the decision of the Board. Justice Douglas wrote for four of the seven justices who participated:

". . . Congress for reasons of its own decided upon the method for the protection of the 'right' which it created. It selected the precise machinery and fashioned the tool which it deemed suited to that end. . . .

"[T]he history of § 2, Ninth is highly relevant. It was introduced into the Act in 1934 as a device to strengthen and make more effective the processes of collective bargaining. It was aimed not only at company unions which had long plagued labor relations but also at numerous jurisdictional disputes between unions. Commissioner Eastman, draftsman of the 1934 amendments, explained the bill at the Congressional hearings. He stated that whether one organization or another was the proper representative of a particular group of employees was one of the most controversial questions in connection with labor organization matters. He stated that it was very important 'to provide a neutral tribunal which can make the decision and get the matter settled.' But the problem was deemed to be so 'highly controversial' that it was thought that the prestige of the Mediation Board might be adversely affected by the rulings which it would have to make in these jurisdictional disputes. Accordingly § 2, Ninth was drafted so as to give to the Mediation Board the power to 'appoint a committee of three neutral persons who after hearing shall within ten days designate the employees who may participate in the election.' That was added so that the Board's 'own usefulness of settling disputes that might arise thereafter might not be impaired.' Where Congress took such great pains to protect the Mediation Board in its handling of an explosive problem, we cannot help but believe that if Congress had desired to implicate the federal judiciary and to place on the federal courts the burden of having the final say on any aspect of the problem, it would have made its desire plain.

. . .

"In the present case the authority of the Mediation Board in election disputes to interpret the meaning of 'craft' as used in the statute is . . . clear and . . . essential to the performance of its duty. The statutory command that the decision of the Board shall be obeyed is . . . explicit. Under this Act Congress did not give the Board discretion to take or withhold action, to grant or deny relief. It gave it no enforcement functions. It was to find the fact and then cease. . . .

"[T]he intent seems plain—the dispute was to reach its last terminal point when the administrative finding was made. There was to be no dragging out of the controversy into other tribunals of law.[1] . . .

"What is open when a court of equity is asked for its affirmative help by granting a decree for the enforcement of a certificate of the Mediation Board under § 2, Ninth raises questions not now before us."

(2) To be compared with Switchmen's Union is LEEDOM v. KYNE, 358 U.S. 184 (1958). The National Labor Relations Board included both professional and nonprofessional employees in a bargaining unit. The professional employees brought an action in the district court against the members of the Board to vacate the Board's determination. The plaintiffs pointed to a provision in the Act which stated that in determining the unit appropriate for collective bargaining purposes, "The Board shall not decide that any unit is appropriate for such purposes if such unit includes both professional employees and [nonprofessional employees] unless a majority of such professional employees vote for inclusion in such unit." The district court found that the Board had refused to take a vote among the professional employees. On appeal, the Board did not contest the district court's conclusion that it had violated the statute but instead contended only that the district court lacked jurisdiction. The Board relied upon American Federation of Labor v. National Labor Relations Board, 308 U.S. 401 (1940). In the AFL case a labor union, whose contentions concerning the appropriate bargaining unit had been rejected by the Board, filed a petition for review in a court of appeals pursuant to section 10(f) of the Act; the Court held that a Board order in certification proceedings under section

---

1. Switchmen's Union has often been cited but, as Professor Jaffe has noted, the case "has borne little fruit." L. Jaffe, Judicial Control of Administrative Action 345 (1965). He also observes: "This decision is in some measure, I believe, an expression of the mood of judicial self-deprecation and abdication into which the Court of that period had fallen. Haunted by a past of judicial arrogance, beguiled by the promise of administrative action, a majority of the judges who participated were easily persuaded of the irrelevance of the judicial role." Id. at 344.

9 of the Act was not a "final order" within the meaning of section 10. The proper occasion for contesting the validity of the certification would be when and if an appropriate party sought review or enforcement of an unfair labor practice order that was based on the certification; therefore, the certification determination was not subject to review at that time. The Supreme Court rejected the Board's argument based on the AFL case and held that the Leedom action could be maintained in the district court:

"... This case, in its posture before us involves unlawful action of the Board [which] has inflicted an injury on the [respondent]. Does the law, apart from the review provisions of the ... Act, afford a remedy? We think the answer surely must be yes. This suit is not one to 'review,' in the sense of that term as used in the Act, a decision of the Board made within its jurisdiction. Rather, it is one to strike down an order of the Board made in excess of its delegated powers and contrary to a specific prohibition in the Act. Section 9(b)(1) is clear and mandatory. ...

"Where, as here, Congress has given a 'right' to the professional employees it must be held that it intended that right to be enforced, and 'the courts ... encounter no difficulty in fulfilling its purpose.' " [2]

(3) BOWEN v. MICHIGAN ACADEMY OF FAMILY PHYSICIANS, 106 S.Ct. 2133 (1986). The Michigan Academy, an association of family physicians, and several individual family physicians brought an action against the Secretary of Health and Human Services challenging the validity of a regulation promulgated by the Secretary pursuant to Part B of Title XVIII of the Social Security Act, commonly known as the Medicare Act (Act).[3] Under the regulation, services performed by family physicians who were board certified were reimbursed at a higher rate than identical services performed by family physicians who were not board certified. Plaintiffs contended that the regulation violated the Medicare Act and the equal protection and due process components

---

2. [Ed.] See Boire v. Greyhound Corp., 376 U.S. 473 (1964) (contending it was not an employer, Greyhound sued in the district court to enjoin a representation election; held, the district court does not have jurisdiction; the Leedom v. Kyne exception "is a narrow one, not to be extended to permit plenary district court review of Board orders in certification proceedings whenever it can be said that an erroneous assessment of the particular facts before the Board has led it to a conclusion which does not comport with the law"); McCulloch v. Sociedad Nacional De Marineros de Honduras, 372 U.S. 10 (1963) (the NLRB ordered a representation election to be conducted among seamen working on vessels legally owned by a foreign subsidiary of an American corporation; the foreign owner and a foreign labor union representing the seamen sued in the district court to enjoin the election; held, the district court has

jurisdiction; although here, unlike the situation in Leedom v. Kyne, "the Board has violated no specific prohibition of the Act ..., the presence of public questions particularly high in the scale of our national interest because of their international complexion is a uniquely compelling justification for prompt judicial resolution of the controversy over the Board's power").

For general discussion, see II The Developing Labor Law 1716 (C. Morris, ed., 2d ed. 1983); R. Gorman, Basic Text in Labor Law 64 (1976).

3. Part A of the Act provides insurance for the cost of hospital and related posthospital services. Part B supplements Part A's coverage by insuring against a portion of some medical expenses, such as certain physician services and x-rays that are excluded from the Part A program.

of the Fifth Amendment. The lower courts held that the regulation violated the Act. The Secretary did not challenge this holding but sought certiorari on the ground that the Act precluded judicial review.

The Secretary argued, first, that § 1395ff(b)[4] of the Act which authorizes "appeal by individuals" impliedly precludes judicial review "of any action taken under Part B . . . by failing to authorize such review while simultaneously authorizing . . . review of 'any determination . . . as to . . . the amount of benefit under part A.' § 1395ff(b)(1)(C)." In a unanimous opinion by Justice Stevens, Rehnquist, J., not participating, the Supreme Court rejected the Secretary's argument:

"In the Medicare program, however, the situation is somewhat more complex. Under Part B of [the Medicare] program, which is at issue here, the Secretary contracts with private health insurance carriers to provide benefits for which individuals voluntarily remit premiums. This optional coverage, which is federally subsidized, supplements the mandatory institutional health benefits (such as coverage for hospital expenses) provided by Part A. . . . [I]ndividuals aggrieved by delayed or insufficient payment with respect to benefits payable under Part B are afforded an 'opportunity for a fair hearing by the *carrier*,' 42 U.S.C. § 1395u(b)(3)(C) (emphasis added); in comparison . . . a similarly aggrieved individual under Part A is entitled 'to a hearing thereon by the *Secretary* . . . and to judicial review,' 42 U.S.C. § 1395ff(b)(1)(C), (b)(2). 'In the context of the statute's precisely drawn provisions,' we held in United States v. Erika, Inc., 456 U.S. 201, 208 (1982), that the failure 'to authorize further review for determinations of the amount of Part B awards . . . provides persuasive evidence that Congress deliberately intended to foreclose further review of such claims.' . . . Respondents' federal-court challenge to the validity of the Secretary's regulation is not foreclosed by § 1395ff as we construed that provision in Erika. The reticulated statutory scheme, which carefully details the forum and limits of review of 'any determination . . . of . . . the amount of benefits under part A,' 42 U.S.C. § 1395ff(b)(1)(C), and of the 'amount of . . . payment' of benefits under Part B, 42 U.S.C. § 1395u(b)(3)(C), simply does not speak to

---

4. Section 1395ff provides in pertinent part:

"(a) Entitlement to and amount of benefits

"The determination of whether an individual is entitled to benefits under part A or part B, and the determination of the amount of benefits under part A, shall be made by the Secretary in accordance with regulations prescribed by him.

"(b) Appeal by individuals

"(1) Any individual dissatisfied with any determination under subsection (a) of this section as to—

"(A) whether he meets the conditions of section 426 or section 426a of this title [which set forth eligibility requirements to

be satisfied before an individual is permitted to participate in Part A of the Medicare program], or

"(B) whether he is eligible to enroll and has enrolled pursuant to the provisions of part B of [the Medicare program] . . . , or,

"(C) the amount of the benefits under part A (including a determination where such amount is determined to be zero)

shall be entitled to a hearing thereon by the Secretary to the same extent as is provided in section 405(b) of this title and to judicial review of the Secretary's final decision after such hearing as is provided in section 405(g) of this title."

challenges mounted against the *method* by which such amounts are to be determined rather than the *determinations* themselves. As the Secretary has made clear, 'the legality, constitutional or otherwise, of any provision of the Act or regulations relevant to the Medicare Program' is not considered in a 'fair hearing' held by a carrier to resolve a grievance related to a determination of the amount of a Part B award.[5] As a result, an attack on the validity of a regulation is not the kind of administrative action that we described in Erika as an 'amount determination' which decides 'the amount of the Medicare payment to be made on a particular claim' and with respect to which the Act impliedly denies judicial review. . . .

". . . As we found in Erika, Congress has precluded judicial review only 'of adverse hearing officer determinations of the amount of Part B payments.'

"Careful analysis of the governing statutory provisions and their legislative history thus reveals that Congress intended to bar judicial review only of determinations of the amount of benefits to be awarded under Part B. Congress delegated this task to carriers who would finally determine such matters in conformity with the regulations and instructions of the Secretary. We conclude, therefore, that those matters which Congress did *not* leave to be determined in a 'fair hearing' conducted by the carrier—including challenges to the validity of the Secretary's instructions and regulations—are not impliedly insulated from judicial review by 42 U.S.C. § 1395ff."

The Secretary also argued that review was expressly precluded by the third sentence of § 405(h) of Title II of the Social Security Act which § 1395ii of the Medicare Act stated "shall also apply" to the Medicare program. Section 405(h) provides:

"The findings and decision of the Secretary after a hearing shall be binding upon all individuals who were parties to such hearing. No findings of fact or decision of the Secretary shall be reviewed by any person, tribunal, or governmental agency except as herein provided. No action against the United States, the Secretary, or any officer or employee thereof shall be brought under section 1331 or 1346 of title 28 to recover on any claim arising under this subchapter."

The court again rejected the Secretary's contention:

"The legislative history of both the statute establishing the Medicare program and the 1972 amendments thereto provides specific evidence of Congress' intent to foreclose review only of 'amount determinations'—i.e., those 'quite minor matters,' 118 Cong.Rec. 33992 (1972)

---

5. Medicare Carrier's Manual § 12016 (1985). In a "fair hearing" conducted pursuant to § 1395u(b)(3)(C); see 42 CFR § 405.820 (1985), the carrier designates a hearing officer, § 405.823, whose jurisdiction is circumscribed by regulation as follows: . . .

"Authority—the HO [Hearing Officer] occupies a significant position in the administration appeals process. Authority of the HO is limited to the extent that he

must comply with all provisions of title XVIII of the Act and regulations issued thereunder, as well as with HCFA. The HO may not overrule the provisions of the law or interpret them in a way different than HCFA does when he disagrees with their intent; nor may he use hearing decisions as a vehicle for commenting upon the legality, constitutional or otherwise, of any provision of the Act or regulations relevant to the Medicare Program."

(remarks of Sen. Bennett), remitted finally and exclusively to adjudication by private insurance carriers in a 'fair hearing.' By the same token, matters which Congress did *not* delegate to private carriers, such as challenges to the validity of the Secretary's instructions and regulations, are cognizable in courts of law. In the face of this persuasive evidence of legislative intent, we will not indulge the Government's assumption that Congress contemplated review by carriers of 'trivial' monetary claims, ibid., but intended no review at all of substantial statutory and consitutional challenges to the Secretary's administration of Part B of the Medicare program. This is an extreme position, and one we would be most reluctant to adopt without 'a showing of "clear and convincing evidence," ' Abbott Laboratories v. Gardner, 387 U.S., at 141, to overcome the 'strong presumption that Congress did not mean to prohibit all judicial review' of executive action, Dunlop v. Bachowski, 421 U.S., at 567. We ordinarily presume that Congress intends the executive to obey its statutory commands and, accordingly, that it expects the courts to grant relief when an executive agency violates such a command. That presumption has not been surmounted here." [6]

(4) For those who may have thought that the Community Nutrition Institute case represented a weakening of the presumption of judicial review, a portion of the Michigan Academy opinion not reproduced above suggests that such a conclusion may be premature. For although he does quote from Community Nutrition Institute [7]—thus suggesting that no sharp break with that case is intended—part I of Justice Stevens' opinion in Michigan Academy is an essay in support of the presumption. He commences with the statement, "We begin with the strong presumption that Congress intends judicial review of administrative action" and continues with discussion of and quotations from (1) judicial precedent—inter alia, Rusk v. Cort, Abbott Laboratories, Mar-

---

6. "Our disposition avoids the 'serious constitutional question' that would arise if we construed § 1395ii to deny a judicial forum for constitutional claims arising under Part B of the Medicare program. Weinberger v. Salfi, 422 U.S., at 762 (citing Johnson v. Robison, 415 U.S. 361, 366–367 (1974). See Yakus v. United States, 321 U.S. 414, 433–444 (1944); St. Joseph Stock Yards Co. v. United States, 298 U.S. 38, 84 (1936) (Brandeis, J., concurring); Gunther, Congressional Power to Curtail Federal Court Jurisdiction: An Opinionated Guide to the Ongoing Debate, 36 Stanford L.Rev. 895, 921, n. 113 (1984) ('[A]ll agree that Congress cannot bar all remedies for enforcing federal constitutional rights'). Cf. Hart, The Power of Congress to Limit the Jurisdiction of Federal Courts: An Exercise in Dialectic, 66 Harv.L.Rev. 1362, 1378–1379 (1953). . . . [W]e cannot, as the Government would have us, dismiss respondents' constitutional attack as insubstantial—that is to say, 'essentially fictitious,' 'obviously frivolous,' and 'obviously without merit'—under Hagans v. Lavine, 415 U.S. 528, 537 (1974) (internal quota-

tions omitted), as would be necessary to decline jurisdiction over the case. Both courts below found the classification embodied in the regulation to be 'irrational,' and although this finding was made with respect to respondents' statutory claims, it surely casts sufficient doubt on the constitutionality of the classification under the Due Process and Equal Protection Clauses to merit resolution of the constitutional challenge."

7. "Subject to constitutional constraints, Congress can, of course, make exceptions to the historic practice whereby courts review agency action. The presumption of judicial review is, after all, a presumption, and 'like all presumptions used in interpreting statutes, may be overcome by,' inter alia, 'specific language or specific legislative history that is a reliable indicator of congressional intent,' or a specific congressional intent to preclude judicial review that is ' "fairly discernible" in the detail of the legislative scheme.' Block v. Community Nutrition Institute, 467 U.S. 340, 349, 351 (1984)."

bury v. Madison ("[t]he very essence of civil liberty certainly invests in the right of every individual to claim the protection of the laws"), Dunlop v. Bachowski; (2) reports of the 1945 House and Senate Judiciary Committees recommending enactment of the APA ("Very rarely do statutes withhold judicial review. . . . To preclude review a . . . statute . . . must upon its face give clear and convincing evidence of an itent to withhold it"); and (3) scholarly literature—K. Davis (praising "the case law since 1974" for being "strongly on the side of reviewability"); L. Jaffe ("[J]udicial review is the rule. . . . It is a basic right; it is a traditional power and the intention to exclude it must be made specifically manifest"); B. Schwartz ("The responsibility of enforcing the limits of statutory authority is a judicial function; . . . [w]ithout judicial review, statutory limits would be naught but empty words"); M. Shapiro (since the passage of the APA, the sustained effort of administrative law has been to "continuously narro[w] the category of actions considered to be so discretionary as to be exempted from review").

Note that Justice Stevens did not participate in Community Nutrition Institute. Note also that there were no dissenting or concurring opinions in either case.

(ii) Express Preclusion

Although explicit statutory provisions purporting to bar judicial review are not common, Congress sometimes has provided that designated administrative action shall be "final." When vital personal interests are at stake, finality clauses customarily are given a restrictive interpretation. Examples are Lloyd Sabaudo Societa v. Elting, 287 U.S. 329 (1932), and Shaughnessy v. Pedreiro, 349 U.S. 48 (1955), interpreting the 1917 and 1952 Immigration Acts. The Lloyd case held that although the statute made the deportation decision of the Secretary of Labor "final," it was "nevertheless subject to some review" in habeas corpus proceedings; Shaughnessy held that notwithstanding the finality clause the deportee could seek injunctive and declaratory relief under the APA: "It is more in harmony with the generous review provisions of the Administrative Procedure Act to construe the ambiguous word 'final' in the 1952 Immigration Act as referring to finality in administrative procedure rather than as cutting off the right of judicial review in whole or in part."

Another instance of restrictive interpretation of a finality clause in a case involving a personal liberty is Estep v. United States, 327 U.S. 114 (1946). The Selective Training and Service Act of 1940 granted local selective service boards "power within their respective jurisdictions to hear and determine . . . all questions or claims with respect to . . . exemption or deferment" and provided that the boards' decisions "shall be final." There was no provision for judicial review. Section 11 of the Act made criminal a failure to submit to induction and conferred jurisdiction on district courts to try one charged with such offense; but § 11 was silent as to the defenses, if any, which could be interposed in the criminal proceeding. The Court, per Justice

Douglas, said that in this case where "we are dealing . . . with a question of personal liberty . . . , we are loath to believe" that Congress intended a registrant should "go to jail for not obeying an unlawful order of an administrative agency." The provision making the decision of local boards "final" is interpreted to mean "that Congress chose not to give administrative action under this Act the customary scope of judicial review which obtains under other statutes." Accordingly, the board's decision concerning the registrant's application for an exemption as an ordained minister is "final" only if it is within its "jurisdiction"; and if there is "no basis in fact" for the board's refusal to classify the registrant as an ordained minister, the board's decision would be beyond its jurisdiction. Therefore, in a criminal prosecution for refusing to submit to induction, the registrant-defendant may defend on the ground that there was "no basis in fact" for his classification. Three justices disagreed with this interpretation.[1]

That the technique of restrictive interpretation of finality clauses is not limited to cases involving vital personal interests is illustrated by the opinion of then-Judge Warren E. Burger in Gonzalez v. Freeman, 334 F.2d 570 (D.C.Cir.1964), involving debarment from participation in government-financed programs of the Commodity Credit Corporation for a period of five years: "The language . . . relating to 'final and conclusive' determinations of the Secretary has as its primary thrust the removal from judicial scrutiny of the operational policy decisions and programs of the agency, not standards of procedure for debarment. . . . Appellants here do not challenge broad policy decisions . . . , but narrowly attack as beyond agency authority a debarment or 'blacklisting' which the complaint alleges inflicted a special injury on appellants and was accomplished in a procedurally unfair and unauthorized manner. Nothing in the statute confers unreviewable finality on determinations of the Secretary as to questions of the scope of his congressional authority or of the requisite procedural safeguards." [2]

Probably because finality clauses often are interpreted restrictively, Congress occasionally adds to a finality provision an explicit jurisdictional prohibition. Before being amended in 1970, § 211(a) of 38 U.S.C. stated: "[T]he decisions of the Administrator [of Veterans' Affairs] on any question of law or fact concerning a claim for benefits or payments

1. See also Harmon v. Brucker, 355 U.S. 579 (1958) (per curiam: although the applicable statute provided that the findings of the Army Discharge Review Board shall be "final subject only to review by the Secretary of the Army," the validity of a less-than-honorable discharge from the Army is reviewable; "[g]enerally, judicial relief is available to one who has been injured by an act of a government official which is in excess of his express or implied powers").

2. Compare Work v. Rives, 267 U.S. 175 (1925), summarized above, p. 990 n. 2, involving what the Court described as "a gratuity based on equitable and moral considerations," in which a finality clause was accorded, if not a literal, at least a sympathetic interpretation.

See Note, Judicial Review of Federal Administrative Decisions Concerning Gratuities, 49 Va.L.Rev. 313 (1963); Rubin v. Weinberger, 524 F.2d 497 (7th Cir.1975) (judicial review of denial of claim for $722 of Medicare benefits is precluded by statute which provides: "[N]or shall judicial review be available to an individual . . . if the amount in controversy is less than $1,000").

For discussion of state courts' treatment of finality clauses, see 2 F. Cooper, State Administrative Law 677–679 (1965).

under any law administered by the Veterans' Administration shall be final and conclusive and no other official or any court of the United States shall have power or jurisdiction to review any such decision." This preclusion of judicial review usually was respected by the courts. But in Wellman v. Whittier, 259 F.2d 163 (D.C.Cir.1958), Thompson v. Gleason, 317 F.2d 901 (D.C.Cir.1962), and Tracy v. Gleason, 379 F.2d 469 (D.C.Cir.1967), the court held that since by its terms section 211(a) applied to a *"claim* for benefits," it was not applicable to administrative action *terminating* benefits. Soon after the latter decision, an increasing number of suits seeking resumption of terminated benefits were instituted; as of March 8, 1970, 353 actions of this type had been filed in the District of Columbia Circuit. The Veterans' Administration and Congress were unhappy with this state of affairs and Congress responded by amending § 211(a) in 1970 "to make it perfectly clear that the Congress intends to exclude from judicial review all determinations with respect to noncontractual benefits provided for veterans and their dependents and survivors." H.Rep. No. 91–1166, 91st Cong. 1st Sess. 8, 11 (1970). Four years later the Supreme Court interpreted the amended statute in:

JOHNSON v. ROBISON
Supreme Court of the United States, 1974.
415 U.S. 361.

[Under the relevant statutes, a draftee who had been accorded conscientious objector status and had completed alternate civilian service—in this case two years at the Peter Bent Brigham Hospital in Boston—was ineligible for educational benefits available to veterans "who served on active duty . . . in the Armed Forces." After the Veterans' Administration had denied conscientious objector Robison's application for educational benefits, he instituted a class action against the Administrator of Veterans' Affairs seeking a declaratory judgment that the statutes violated the First Amendment's guarantee of religious freedom and the Fifth Amendment's guarantee of equal protection of the laws. The Administrator moved to dismiss the action on the ground, among others, that the district court lacked jurisdiction because of amended § 211(a). The district court denied the motion to dismiss and, on the merits, rejected the First Amendment claim but held that the statutes did deny plaintiff and his class equal protection of the laws. The Administrator appealed to the Supreme Court.]

Mr. Justice Brennan delivered the opinion of the Court. . . .

We consider first appellants' contention that § 211(a) bars federal courts from deciding the constitutionality of veterans' benefits legislation. Such a construction would, of course, raise serious questions concerning the constitutionality of § 211(a), and in such case "it is a cardinal principle that this Court will first ascertain whether a construction of the statute is fairly possible by which the [constitutional] question[s] may be avoided."

Plainly, no explicit provision of § 211(a) bars judicial consideration of appellee's constitutional claims. That section provides that "the *decisions* of the Administrator on any question of law or fact *under* any law administered by the Veterans' Administration providing benefits for veterans . . . shall be final and conclusive and no . . . court of the United States shall have power or jurisdiction to review any such decision . . . ." (Emphasis added.) The prohibitions would appear to be aimed at review only of those decisions of law or fact that arise in the *administration* by the Veterans' Administration of a *statute* providing benefits for veterans. A decision of law or fact "under" a statute is made by the Administrator in the interpretation or application of a particular provision of the statute to a particular set of facts. Appellee's constitutional challenge is not to any such decision of the *Administrator,* but rather to a decision of *Congress* to create a statutory class entitled to benefits that does not include I–O conscientious objectors who performed alternate civilian service. Thus, as the District Court stated, "the questions of law presented in these proceedings arise under the Constitution, not under the statute whose validity is challenged."

This construction is also supported by the administrative practice of the Veterans' Administration. . . . The Board of Veterans' Appeals expressly disclaimed authority to decide constitutional questions in Appeal of Peter W. Sly, C 27 593 725 (May 10, 1972). There the Board, denying a claim for educational assistance by a I–O conscientious objector, held that "this decision does not reach the issue of constitutionality of the pertinent laws as this matter is not within the jurisdiction of this Board." Sly thus accepts and follows the principle that "[a]djudication of the constitutionality of congressional enactments has generally been thought beyond the jurisdiction of administrative agencies."

Nor does the legislative history accompanying the 1970 amendment of § 211(a) demonstrate a congressional intention to bar judicial review even of constitutional questions. No-review clauses similar to § 211(a) have been a part of veterans' benefits legislation since 1933. While the legislative history accompanying these precursor no-review clauses is almost nonexistent, the Administrator, in a letter written in 1952 in connection with a revision of the clause under consideration by the Subcommittee of the House Committee on Veterans' Affairs, comprehensively explained the policies necessitating the no-review clause and identified two primary purposes: (1) to insure that veterans' benefits claims will not burden the courts and the Veterans' Administration with expensive and time-consuming litigation, and (2) to insure that the technical and complex determinations and applications of Veterans' Administration policy connected with veterans' benefits decisions will be adequately and uniformly made.

The legislative history of the 1970 amendment indicates nothing more than a congressional intent to preserve these two primary purposes. . . .

[T]he 1970 amendment was enacted to overrule the interpretation of the Court of Appeals for the District of Columbia [in the Wellman, Thompson and Tracy cases], and thereby restore vitality to the two primary purposes to be served by the no-review clause. Nothing whatever in the legislative history of the 1970 amendment, or predecessor no-review clauses, suggests any congressional intent to preclude judicial cognizance of constitutional challenges to veterans' benefits legislation. Such challenges obviously do not contravene the purposes of the no-review clause, for they cannot be expected to burden the courts by their volume, nor do they involve technical considerations of Veterans' Administration policy. We therefore conclude, in agreement with the District Court, that a construction of § 211(a) that does not extend the prohibitions of that section to actions challenging the constitutionality of laws providing benefits for veterans is not only "fairly possible" but is the most reasonable construction, for neither the text nor the scant legislative history of § 211(a) provide the "clear and convincing" evidence of congressional intent required by this Court before a statute will be construed to restrict access to judicial review. See Abbott Laboratories v. Gardner, 387 U.S. 136, 141 (1967).

[On the merits, the Court agreed with the district court's rejection of the First Amendment claim but held that the statutes did not deny equal protection of the laws. Justice Douglas dissented on the ground that the statutes violated the First Amendment.]

NOTES

(1) Johnson v. Robison shows how the Supreme court uses the technique of statutory construction to enable the affected citizen to secure judicial evaluation of the claim that denying him an alleged entitlement would violate the constitution. A certain consequence of a decision like Johnson v. Robison in our adversary system is that counsel will seek to extend its holding and reasoning to new situations; almost as certain, opposing (in this case, government) counsel will argue against such extensions. How should the lower federal courts respond to such thrusts and counter thrusts in the Johnson v. Robison context?

The answer of the majority of federal courts is that § 211(a) "should not be interpreted to bar judicial scrutiny of a variety of VA 'decisions' relating to veterans' benefits law. See, e.g., American Fed'n of Gov't Employees v. Nimmo, 711 F.2d 28, 31 (4th Cir.1983) ('[C]ourts are not precluded from considering the VA's statutory authority for promulgating regulations and the constitutionality of its actions.'); Evergreen State College v. Cleland, 621 F.2d 1002, 1007–08 (9th Cir. 1980) (§ 211(a) does not bar review to determine whether VA regulations exceed its statutory authority); University of Maryland v. Cleland, 621 F.2d 98, 100–01 (4th Cir.1980) (same); Merged Area X (Education) v. Cleland, 604 F.2d 1075, 1078 (8th Cir.1979) (same); Wayne State Univ. v. Cleland, 590 F.2d 627, 631–32 (6th Cir.1978) (same); Arnolds v. Veterans' Admin., 507 F.Supp. 128, 130–31 (N.D.Ill.1981) (§ 211(a) does not bar review where VA procedures allegedly violate the due process clause); Plato v. Roudebush, 397 F.Supp. 1295, 1301–04 (D.Md.1975) (same)." [3]

3. Judge Wald dissenting in the Gott v. Walters case about to be considered.

(2) The construction of § 211(a) reflected by these decisions was sharply challenged in GOTT v. WALTERS, 756 F.2d 902 (D.C.Cir.1985), opinion and judgment vacated, rehearing granted, and action dismissed on joint motion of the parties 791 F.2d 172 (D.C.Cir.1985). The Veterans' Administration (VA) issued three documents concerning the standards and procedures for determining when veterans exposed to radiation are entitled to VA disability benefits. Plaintiffs—veterans, veterans' wives and veterans' organizations—brought suit in the district court under the APA seeking a ruling that the documents were "rules" subject to the notice and comment provisions of the APA. The district court, noting that the plaintiffs did not seek review of actual benefit determinations, held that the documents were rules and invalidated them because of the VA's failure to comply with the APA's notice and comment provisions. On appeal, the court of appeals held that § 211(a) precluded judicial review of the validity of the "rules." Judge Scalia, for himself and Judge Bork, reasoned as follows.[1]

Plaintiffs contend that § 211(a) by its terms is inapplicable because the legal question at issue—the necessity of rulemaking procedures—"arises under the APA and not 'under the statute' concerning veterans' benefits." Central to this contention is the statement in the Johnson opinion that the constitutional challenges in that case "arise under the constitution, not under the statute whose validity is challenged." This, said Judge Scalia, reflects a misunderstanding of Johnson:

"[T]he consequence of the fact that the case presented a question (concerning the validity of the statute) 'under the Constitution' was *not* that therefore it did not present a 'question of law . . . under any law administered by the Veterans' Administration' within the meaning of § 211(a); but rather, that therefore there had been no 'decision of the Administrator' within the meaning of § 211(a), since the Administrator does not consider the constitutionality of the statutes he is directed to administer (as he does consider the compliance of his regulations with the APA). It was, the Court concluded, a decision of the Congress rather than of the Administrator that was under review. . . . All that is necessary for § 211(a) to apply is that the question of law or fact have been decided by the Administrator, and that the decision have been made in the course of applying the veterans' benefit statutes. . . ."

Plaintiffs also argued that the word "decisions" refers only to adjudications of individual claims and not to the promulgation of regulations. The court replied that "in light of the language, the legislative history and the purposes of § 211(a), we reject the . . . argument." Concerning the purposes of the section, the court stated:

"Coverage of regulations is . . . supported by the basic purposes of § 211(a), which the Supreme Court has said are twofold: first, to prevent the courts from becoming 'involve[d] . . . in day-to-day determination and interpretation of Veterans' Administration policy,' with

---

1. Judge Scalia noted at the outset that the court was "confronted with a jurisdictional problem, raised and argued in the district court but not asserted in this ap-   peal. . . . Since we consider it substantial, and since it pertains to our power to decide this case, we feel compelled to address it on our own."

the accompanying prospect of ' "judicial review of millions of decisions terminating or reducing many types of benefits" '; and second, 'to insure that the technical and complex determinations and applications of Veterans' Administration policy connected with veterans' benefits will be adequately and uniformly made,' Johnson v. Robison, 415 US at 370, 372. . . .

"Review of the *substance* of regulations obviously would frustrate the second of these purposes. Regulations are at least as likely as adjudications to involve 'technical and complex' policy determinations regarding benefits. In fact the appellees' principal complaint about the documents at issue here is that they are for all practical purposes final decisions of issues which would otherwise be resolved by adjudication: the health effects of exposure to low levels of radiation, the kinds of diseases radiation may cause, and the best method for calculating the dosages of radiation to which appellees were exposed. It is hard to see why these determinations are too technical and complex to be 'adequately' reviewed in the context of individual adjudications, but less so when reviewed in the context of rule making; or why the destruction of 'uniformity' in these determinations—presumably attributable to the differing views of the various federal circuits as opposed to the unitary view of the Administrator—is any more tolerable when achieved through review of rules than through review of the same policies adopted in adjudication.

"Moreover, both review of the *substance* of regulations and review of the *procedures* by which they are adopted conflict with the first purpose the Supreme Court found Congress was pursuing in enacting § 211(a)—avoiding the courts' embroilment in numerous individual claims decisions. That is evident from considering what would happen in this case if we were to proceed with review of the appellees' complaint that the documents and methodologies at issue are substantive regulations and therefore should have been adopted in accordance with informal rule making procedures. All parties to this litigation agree that whether they are substantive regulations turns on whether they are given a dispositive effect in the adjudication of individual claims. The VA asserts they are not determinative, the appellees the contrary. It is quite impossible to resolve this issue without looking at the actual use of the documents and methodologies in individual proceedings. But even if we were to resolve it on some philosophical basis, and were to conclude that the documents and methodologies *are* dispositive, *are* substantive rules and therefore *are* improperly adopted, it is difficult to imagine any effective order we could issue. In prohibiting the VA from giving them binding legal effect, we would be telling the VA not to do what it believes it is not doing anyway. It would presumably continue to act as it says (though we disagree) it has been acting—and how would we ever stop that behavior? Our order is a vain act, in other words, *unless we can review subsequent adjudications for compliance.* And that will always be so, with regard to any regulation that governs the adjudication of claims. Review of such regulations, therefore, either frustrates the first purpose of § 211(a) described by the Supreme Court, or else requires the courts to issue embarrassingly impotent mandates. The former consequence is not, given the Supreme Court's pronouncement, a permissible assumption of legislative intent; and the latter is not a plausible one."

Finally, the court considered the plaintiffs' argument that "even if some types of judicial review of regulations, such as review to ensure that they are not arbitrary or capricious, or review to ensure that they have adequate evidentiary support, *are* barred by § 211(a), the type of review they seek here, merely to assure that the APA's procedural requirements have been observed, is not barred" by § 211(a):

"They rely for that proposition upon decisions in other circuits holding that § 211(a) does not preclude judicial review of regulations to ensure that they do not exceed the VA's statutory authority, citing Wayne State University v. Cleland, 590 F.2d 627 (6th Cir.1978), and cases that accept the reasoning of that opinion without additional analysis. . . .

"Wayne State rested upon the assumption that 'clear and convincing evidence of congressional intent [is] required by the Supreme Court before a statute will be construed to restrict access to judicial review,' citing, inter alia, Citizens to Preserve Overton Park, Inc. v. Volpe, 401 U.S. 402, 410 (1971). . . . Subsequent Supreme Court authority makes clear, however, that a 'clear and convincing evidence' test, in the normal sense in which we and other courts had interpreted that phrase, does not apply . . . [citing and quoting from] Community Nutrition Institute v. Block, 104 S.Ct. at 2457."

Judge Wald dissented in an opinion of approximately twelve pages—about the same length as Judge Scalia's. She concluded as follows:

"Judicial review to ensure that VA rule makings comply with the notice and comment provisions of the APA would not frustrate any 'fairly discernible' congressional intent to preclude court scrutiny of certain VA actions. The specific language of Section 211(a), as interpreted in Robison, is not sufficiently unambiguous to carry the burden of demonstrating a specific intent to preclude review of a VA rule making to ensure compliance with the APA. The purpose, legislative history and overall structure of the provision, in turn, indicate that Congress did not seek to bar review of a VA rule making that admittedly violates the notice and comment provisions of the APA. Moreover, the VA has told Congress that it does not interpret the no-review clause to insulate VA rule makings from court scrutiny. Given all of this, the case for the majority's all-preclusive reading of Section 211(a) must fail. That interpretation, even if *plausible* standing by itself, is by no means mandatory and, against the backdrop of legislative history, it falls far short of overcoming the presumption favoring judicial review of administrative action. At bottom, today's decision not only ignores the relevant indicators of congressional intent but also constitutes rank judicial interference with a reasonable statutory interpretation agreed upon by both political branches of government." [2]

2. See 43 Cong.Quar.Weekly Report 1555 (Aug. 3, 1985):   "A bill allowing veterans to appeal to federal courts decisions by the Veterans

(3) AMERICAN ASSOCIATION OF COUNCILS OF MEDICAL STAFFS OF PRIVATE HOSPITALS, INC. v. CALIFANO, 575 F.2d 1367 (5th Cir.1978), cert. denied 439 U.S. 1114 (1979). The Social Security Act provided that institutional health care providers should be reimbursed for services to Medicare patients. To be eligible, however, a hospital must have a "utilization review plan" that would minimize the danger of needlessly prolonged hospitalization or other unnecessary services. The reviewing group, the statute added, should be made up of a committee containing at least two physicians on the institution's staff or a similarly constituted group outside the institution or a group established jointly by the local medical society and all or some of the local health care institutions. The Secretary of HEW, pursuant to his authority to issue regulations, adopted a Manual (known as HIM–7) indicating a preference for an in-house utilization review committee "when a hospital has a sufficiently large staff;" the other statutory approaches were rarely to be approved, the Manual said.

Many staff physicians and the professional association that represented them objected on the grounds that it needlessly consumed physicians' time and exposed staff members to unpleasant conflicts with colleagues and, indeed, perhaps with their own interests. They filed suit to enjoin the HEW Secretary from enforcing HIM–7 and for declaratory relief. They contended that he had no statutory authority to establish an essentially mandatory choice among the methods the Social Security Act allowed; they argued, too, that the Manual had not been adopted in accord with rulemaking procedures required by the APA; and, finally, they said that HIM–7 violated their due process rights. They lost on all counts in the district court. On review of that decision, the court of appeals held for the Secretary, but on the embracive ground that the merits of the physicians' objections should never have been considered.

Judge Wisdom, writing for himself and Judges Gewin and Ainsworth, first considered whether the Medicare Act or the Social Security Act in general contained any pertinent authorizations of judicial review. After examining past decisions, the court concluded that the statutes precluded review. Section 405(h) of the Social Security Act provides in part: "No findings of fact or decision of the Secretary shall be reviewed by any person, tribunal, or governmental agency except as herein provided. No action against the United States, the Secretary, or any officer or employee thereof shall be brought under section [1331] of

Administration (VA) denying claims for benefits was approved by the Senate July 30 by voice vote.

"The measure (S 367—S Rept 99–100) also eliminates the present limit of $10 on fees for attorneys representing veterans before the VA and allows the VA to set 'reasonable fees' of up to $500.

"Similar bills passed in 1979, 1982 and 1983 were blocked in the House Veterans' Affairs Committee because its chairman, G.V. 'Sonny' Montgomery, D-Miss., opposes judicial review."

See also F. Davis, Report to ACUS, Judicial Review of Benefits Decisions of the Veterans Administration, Nov. 20, 1978; K. Morris, Judicial Review of Non-Reviewable Administrative Action: Veterans Administration Benefits Claims, 29 Admin.L. Rev. 65 (1977); R. Rabin, Preclusion of Judicial Review in the Processing of Claims for Veterans' Benefits: A Preliminary Analysis, 27 Stan.L.Rev. 905 (1975); F. Davis, Veterans' Benefits, Judicial Review and the Constitutional Problems of "Positive" Government, 39 Ind.L.J. 183 (1964).

title 28 to recover on any claim arising under this subchapter." Neither "statutory nor constitutional claims," the court asserted, were excepted from this sweeping ouster of the court's jurisdiction. The barrier was against "any *action*" of whatever nature.

Did so broad a preclusion itself violate the requirements of due process? Doubt had been expressed in earlier cases about foreclosing all review of constitutional issues (a doubt, one may add, that remains as yet unresolved).[1] Judge Wisdom was able to avoid that difficult issue by finding that the objectors to HIM–7 might have access to another forum in an original action against the United States, rather than, as they had here attempted, in a suit against the Secretary to review the provisions of his Manual. "The question of Congressional power over jurisdiction is both ancient and difficult", Judge Wisdom acknowledged. "It involves the most sensitive relationships between coequal branches of the federal government. Courts and commentators have long discussed the issue. While many commentators may have decided it, it is fair to say that the Supreme Court has not. Under MacDonald [Foundation v. Califano, 554 F.2d 714 (5th Cir.1977)], this Court can only say: 'Happily, we need resolve neither Congress' intent to preclude review of constitutional claims nor the constitutionality of a statute so construed. We would face these issues only if *all* avenues of review were precluded . . . .'

"This particular suit cannot be brought in the Court of Claims. . . . It has jurisdiction over claims against the United States, without limitation as to jurisdictional amount. That Court cannot provide the equitable or declaratory relief sought in this suit. United States v. King, 1969, 395 U.S. 1. Nevertheless, the issue raised by the plaintiff could be heard by that Court if [plaintiff group] can state a claim for damages or at least for nominal damages.[2] Only the relief granted would be different, and Congress has power over the relief granted suitors against the United States and its officers.

"The resolution we have reached is not pleasant. [Plaintiff group] has waited nearly three years for the resolution of its suit. The parties

1. The Court has recently expressed doubts about the constitutionality of foreclosing all review of constitutional issues.

"There is another reason why Johnson v. Robison is inapposite. It was expressly based, at least in part, on the fact that if § 211(a) reached constitutional challenges to statutory limitations, then absolutely no judicial consideration of the issue would be available. Not only would such a restriction have been extraordinary, such that 'clear and convincing' evidence would be required before we would ascribe such intent to Congress, [citations omitted] but it would have raised a serious constitutional question of the validity of the statute as so construed." Weinberger v. Salfi, 422 U.S. at 749, 762 (1975).

A thorough discussion of this whole area is found in P. Bator, P. Mishkin, D. Shapi-ro, and H. Wechsler, The Federal Courts and the Federal System, Note on the Power of Congress to Limit the Jurisdiction of Federal Courts, 313–375 (2d ed. 1973). See also Caulfield v. U.S. Dept. of Agriculture, 5 Cir.1961, 293 F.2d 217 (en banc); K. Davis, Administrative Law in the Seventies, § 28.09 (1976); L. Jaffe, Judicial Control of Administrative Action, 376–94 (1965). [Footnote by Judge Wisdom]

2. For example, violation of due process rights, standing alone, has been held to found a claim for nominal damages. Carey v. Piphus, 1978, 435 U.S. 247. This plaintiff also alleges that its members' time is being wasted in violation of their constitutional rights. Therefore, a successful action would also involve actual damages. We note the plaintiff alleged that more than $10,000 was in controversy.

have briefed and argued their cases. . . . Now, we must deny both parties a decision on the merits where at least one argument is substantial. But the alternative is to find that Congress cannot cut off our jurisdiction over these issues while providing another court, the Court of Claims, to hear the issues. That is a decision we cannot make. Moreover, we respect the ingenuity of lawyers. We do not exclude the possibility of plaintiff's counsel casting an action in terms of mandamus that might resolve what is obviously an important issue to the private hospitals in this country." [3]

(4) ADAMO WRECKING CO. v. UNITED STATES, 434 U.S. 275 (1978). The Clean Air Act of 1970 authorized the Administrator of the EPA to promulgate "emission standards" for hazardous air pollutants. Knowing violators were subject to fine and imprisonment. Paragraph (1) of § 307(b) of the statute provided that a petition for review of the promulgation of any emission standard could be filed only in the Court of Appeals for the District of Columbia Circuit and "shall be filed within 30 days from the date of promulgation of the standard or after such date if such petition is based solely on grounds arising after such 30th date." Paragraph (2) of § 307(b) provided that "[a]ction of the Administrator with respect to which review could have been obtained under paragraph (1) shall not be subject to judicial review in civil or criminal proceedings for enforcement."

Adamo was indicted for violating a standard promulgated by the Administrator that had not been subjected to § 307(b) review. Adamo argued and the district court agreed that while § 307(b) prevented its obtaining judicial review of an emission standard in this criminal proceeding, it was nonetheless entitled to show that the EPA regulation cited in the indictment—although titled an "emission standard"—actually was not an emission standard at all. The court of appeals, relying on Yakus v. United States, 321 U.S. 414 (1944), reversed. The Supreme Court, per Rehnquist, J., distinguished the Yakus case, emphasized that "when there is ambiguity in a criminal statute, doubts are resolved in favor of the defendant", and held that § 307(b)(2) did "not relieve the Government of the duty of proving . . . that the regulation allegedly violated is an emission standard."

---

3. [Ed.] See Ellis v. Blum, 643 F.2d 68 (2d Cir.1981) in which the court, in an opinion by Judge Friendly, held that § 405(h) does not foreclose mandamus jurisdiction.

Compare Heckler v. Ringer, 466 U.S. 602 (1984):

"We have on numerous occasions declined to decide whether the third sentence of § 405(h) bars mandamus jurisdiction over claims arising under the Social Security Act, either because we have determined that jurisdiction was otherwise available under § 405(g) or because we have determined that the merits of the mandamus claim were clearly insubstantial. We need

not decide the effect of the third sentence of § 405(h) on the availability of mandamus jurisdiction in Social Security cases here either [because plaintiff has not exhausted his remedies under § 405(g) and mandamus provides a] remedy for a plaintiff only if he has exhausted all other avenues of relief and only if the defendant owes him a clear nondiscretionary duty."

The proper interpretation of § 405(h) has been widely litigated with results that are not always harmonious. For a helpful analysis and survey, see Colonial Penn Insurance Co. v. Heckler, 721 F.2d 431 (3d Cir.1983).

Justices Stewart, Brennan, Blackmun and Stevens dissented. Justice Powell entered the following concurring opinion:

"If the constitutional validity of § 307(b) of the Clean Air Act had been raised by petitioner, I think it would have merited serious consideration. This section limits judicial review to the filing of a petition in the United States Court of Appeals for the District of Columbia Circuit within 30 days from the date of the promulgation by the Administrator of an emission standard. No notice is afforded a party who may be subject to criminal prosecution other than publication of the Administrator's action in the Federal Register.[1] The Act in this respect is similar to the preclusion provisions of the Emergency Price Control Act before the Court in Yakus v. United States, 321 U.S. 414 (1944), and petitioner may have thought the decision in that case effectively foreclosed a due process challenge in the present case.[2]

"Although I express no considered judgment, I think Yakus is at least arguably distinguishable. The statute there came before the Court during World War II, and it can be viewed as a valid exercise of the war powers of Congress under Art. I, § 8, of the Constitution. Although the opinion of Mr. Chief Justice Stone is not free from ambiguity, there is language emphasizing that the price controls imposed by the Congress were a 'war emergency measure.' Indeed, the Government argued that the statute should be upheld under the war powers authority of Congress. Brief for United States in Yakus v. United States, O.T. 1943, No. 374, p. 35. As important as environmental concerns are to the country, they are not comparable—in terms of an emergency justifying the shortcutting of normal due process rights— to the need for national mobilization in wartime of economic as well as military activity.

"The 30–day limitation on judicial review imposed by the Clean Air Act would afford precariously little time for many affected persons even if some adequate method of notice were afforded. It also is totally unrealistic to assume that more than a fraction of the persons and entities affected by a regulation—especially small contractors scattered across the country—would have knowledge of its promulgation or

1. Section 112(b)(1)(B) of the Act requires the Administrator to publish proposed emission standards and to hold a public hearing before standards are promulgated. But there is no more assurance that notice of proposed standards will come to the attention of the thousands of persons and entities affected than that notice of their actual promulgation will. Neither is it realistic to assume that more than a fraction of these persons and entities could afford to follow or participate in the Administrator's hearing. [Footnote by Justice Powell.]

2. [Ed.] "Yakus v. United States involved an attempt to challenge the validity of price control regulations in a criminal proceeding initiated to enforce those regulations against Yakus. A majority of the Court held that Yakus was precluded from challenging the regulations in the enforcement proceeding because: (1) Congress had provided a prior opportunity to challenge the validity of the regulations in the preenforcement context; (2) Yakus had not availed himself of that opportunity; (3) the 60 day time period provided by Congress for preenforcement judicial review of the regulations had expired; and, (4) Congress had explicitly limited review of the validity of the regulations to the period 60 days after their promulgation. The Court reasoned that, since Congress had provided an adequate alternative method of judicial review, it could prohibit review of the regulations in a later enforcement action." R. Pierce, S. Shapiro and P. Verkuil, Administrative Law and Process 130–131 (1985).

familiarity with or access to the Federal Register. Indeed, following Yakus, and apparently concerned by Mr. Justice Rutledge's eloquent dissent,[3] Congress amended the most onerous features of the Emergency Price Control Act.

"I join the Court's opinion with the understanding that it implies no view as to the constitutional validity of the preclusion provisions of § 307(b) in the context of a criminal prosecution." [4]

For enlightening discussion of the extent of Congressional power to limit judicial review of administrative rules to pre-enforcement review actions, see P. Verkuil, Congressional Limitations on Judicial Review of Rules, 57 Tulane L.Rev. 733 (1983); F. Davis, Judicial Review of Rulemaking: New Patterns and New Problems, 1981 Duke L.J. 279; W. Allen, Thoughts on the Jeopardy of Rules of Long Standing to Procedural Challenge, 33 Admin.L.Rev. 203 (1981); See also ACUS, Recommendation 82–7: Judicial Review of Rules in Enforcement Proceedings, 1 CFR § 305.82–7:

. . . .

"2. When Congress decides to limit the availability of judicial review of rules at the enforcement stage, it should ordinarily preclude review only of issues relating to procedures employed in the rulemaking or the adequacy of factual support for the rule in the administrative record. Judicial review of issues relating to the constitutional basis for the rule or the application of the rule to a particular respondent or defendant should be permitted when these issues are raised in subsequent suits or as defenses to subsequent enforcement actions (subject to the principles of collateral estoppel and stare decisis). Judicial review of issues relating to the statutory authority for the rule should be precluded at the enforcement stage only where Congress has concluded that there is a compelling need to achieve prompt compliance with the rule on a national or industry-wide basis.

"3. When Congress limits the availability of judicial review of rules at the enforcement stage as described in paragraph 2, it should provide that, in an exceptional case when foreclosure of issues will work a severe hardship or otherwise produce a manifestly unjust

---

3. [Ed.] In his dissent, Justice Rutledge argued that although Congress might withhold jurisdiction, it could not invoke the judicial power and at the same time prevent the court from complying with the constitution in the enforcement action: "[W]henever the judicial power is called into play, it is responsible directly to the fundamental law and no other authority can intervene to force or authorize the judicial body to disregard it. The problem . . . is not solely one . . . of due process of law. It is equally one of . . . separation of . . . powers . . . and the constitutional integrity of the judicial process, more especially in criminal trials.
. . . .

"[C]learly Congress could not require judicial enforcement of an unconstitutional

statute. The same is true of an unconstitutional regulation."

4. [Ed.] In Harrison v. PPG Industries, Inc., 446 U.S. 578 (1980) Justice Powell, again concurring, noted that Congress had extended to 60 days the period within which a petition for review could be filed under Section 307(b). Nevertheless, "I continue to have reservations about the constitutionality of the notice and review preclusion provisions of Section 307(b). . . . [P]ublication in the Federal Register still is unlikely to provide constitutionally adequate notice that a failure to seek immediate review will bar affected parties from challenging the noticed action in a subsequent criminal prosecution."

outcome, a court may either dismiss or stay the proceedings and refer the rule to the affected agency for its reconsideration."

b. Committed to Agency Discretion

CITIZENS TO PRESERVE OVERTON PARK, INC. v. VOLPE
Supreme Court of the United States, 1971.
401 U.S. 402.

The opinion is set out at p. 436 supra.

HECKLER v. CHANEY
Supreme Court of the United States, 1985.
105 S.Ct. 1649.

[Several prisoners sentenced to death by lethal injection of drugs under the laws of the States of Oklahoma and Texas petitioned the Food and Drug Administration (FDA), alleging that the use of the drugs for capital punishment violated the Federal Food, Drug, and Cosmetic Act (FDCA). They contended that the drugs used, although approved by the FDA for the medical purposes stated on their labels, were not approved for use in human executions and thus were misbranded in violation of 21 U.S.C. § 352(f) which provides, "A drug or device shall be misbranded . . . [u]nless its label bears (1) adequate directions for use . . . ." They also suggested that the FDCA's requirements for approval of "new drugs" applied since these drugs were now being used for a new purpose. Accordingly, they urged that the FDA was required to approve the drugs as "safe and effective" for human executions before they could be distributed in interstate commerce. The prisoners therefore requested the FDA to take the following enforcement actions to prevent these perceived violations of the Act: (1) affix warnings to the labels of all the drugs stating that they were unapproved and unsafe for human execution; (2) send statements to the drug manufacturers and prison administrators stating that the drugs should not be so used; (3) adopt procedures for seizing the drugs from state prisons; and (4) recommend the prosecution of all those in the chain of distribution who knowingly distribute or purchase the drugs with intent to use them for human execution.

The FDA Commissioner responded, refusing to take the requested actions. He first asserted that the FDA's jurisdiction did not extend to the regulation of state-sanctioned use of lethal injections. He also stated: "Were FDA clearly to have jurisdiction in the area, moreover, we believe we would be authorized to decline to exercise it under our inherent discretion to decline to pursue certain enforcement matters. The unapproved use of approved drugs is an area in which the case law is far from uniform. Generally, enforcement proceedings in this area are initiated only when there is a serious danger to the public health or a blatant scheme to defraud. We cannot conclude that those dangers are present under State lethal injection laws, which are duly authorized statutory enactments in furtherance of proper State functions. . . . [W]e decline, as a matter of enforcement discretion, to pursue supplies of drugs under State control that will be used for execution by lethal injection."

The prisoners then filed suit in the United States District Court for the District of Columbia which granted summary judgment for the defendant. A divided panel of the D.C. Circuit reversed. The Supreme Court granted certiorari.]

JUSTICE REHNQUIST delivered the opinion of the Court. . . . .

II

. . . For us, this case turns on the important question of the extent to which determinations by the FDA *not to exercise* its enforcement authority over the use of drugs in interstate commerce may be judicially reviewed. That decision in turn involves the construction of two separate but necessarily interrelated statutes, the APA and the FDCA.

The APA's comprehensive provisions for judicial review of "agency actions" are contained in 5 U.S.C. §§ 701–706. Any person "adversely affected or aggrieved" by agency action, see § 702, including a "failure to act," is entitled to "judicial review thereof," as long as the action is a "final agency action for which there is no other adequate remedy in a court," see § 704. The standards to be applied on review are governed by the provisions of § 706. But before any review at all may be had, a party must first clear the hurdle of § 701(a). That section provides that the chapter on judicial review "applies, according to the provisions thereof, except to the extent that—(1) statutes preclude judicial review; or (2) agency action is committed to agency discretion by law." Petitioner urges that the decision of the FDA to refuse enforcement is an action "committed to agency discretion by law" under § 701(a)(2).

This Court has not had occasion to interpret this second exception in § 701(a) in any great detail. On its face, the section does not obviously lend itself to any particular construction; indeed, one might wonder what difference exists between § (a)(1) and § (a)(2). The former section seems easy in application; it requires construction of the substantive statute involved to determine whether Congress intended to preclude judicial review of certain decisions. That is the approach taken with respect to § (a)(1) in cases such as . . . Dunlop v. Bachowski, 421 U.S., at 567. But one could read the language "committed to agency discretion *by law*" in § (a)(2) to require a similar inquiry. In addition, commentators have pointed out that construction of § (a)(2) is further complicated by the tension between a literal reading of § (a)(2), which exempts from judicial review those decisions committed to agency "discretion," and the primary scope of review prescribed by § 706(2)(A)—whether the agency's action was "arbitrary, capricious, or an *abuse of discretion*." How is it, they ask, that an action committed to agency discretion can be unreviewable and yet courts still can review agency actions for abuse of that discretion? See 5 K. Davis, Administrative Law § 28.6 (1984); Berger, Administrative Arbitrariness and Judicial Review, 65 Colum.L.Rev. 55, 58 (1965). The APA's legislative history provides little help on this score. Mindful, however, of the commonsense principle of statutory construction that sections of a statute generally should be read "to give effect, if possible, to every clause . . . ," we think there is a proper construction of § (a)(2) which satisfies each of these concerns.

This Court first discussed § (a)(2) in Citizens to Preserve Overton Park v. Volpe. That case dealt with the Secretary of Transportation's approval of the building of an interstate highway through a park in Memphis, Tennessee. The relevant federal statute provided that the Secretary "shall not approve" any program or project using public parkland unless the Secretary first determined that no feasible alternatives were available. Overton Park, 401 U.S., at 411. Interested citizens challenged the Secretary's approval under the APA, arguing that he had not satisfied the substantive statute's requirements. This Court first addressed the "threshold question" of whether the agency's action was at all reviewable. After setting out the language of § 701(a), the Court stated:

"In this case, there is no indication that Congress sought to prohibit judicial review and there is most certainly no 'showing of "clear and convincing evidence" of a . . . legislative intent' to restrict access to judicial review. Abbott Laboratories v. Gardner, 387 U.S. 136, 141 (1967). . . .

"Similarly, the Secretary's decision here does not fall within the exception for action 'committed to agency discretion.' This is a very narrow exception. . . . The legislative history of the Administrative Procedure Act indicates that it is applicable in those rare instances where statutes are drawn in such broad terms that in a given case there is no law to apply. S.Rep. No. 752, 79th Cong., 1st Sess., 26 (1945)."[1]

The above quote answers several of the questions raised by the language of § 701(a), although it raises others. First, it clearly separates the exception provided by § (a)(1) from the § (a)(2) exception. The former applies when Congress has expressed an intent to preclude judicial review. The latter applies in different circumstances; even where Congress has not affirmatively precluded review, review is not to be had if the statute is drawn so that a court would have no meaningful standard against which to judge the agency's exercise of discretion. In such a case, the statute ("law") can be taken to have "committed" the decisionmaking to the agency's judgment absolutely. This construction avoids conflict with the "abuse of discretion" standard of review in § 706—if no judicially manageable standards are available for judging

---

1. [Ed.] The relevant paragraph of S.Rep. No. 752, 79th Cong., 1st Sess., 26 (1945), reads as follows:

"The basic exception of matters committed to agency discretion would apply even if not stated at the outset. If, for example, statutes are drawn in such broad terms that in a given case there is no law to apply, courts of course have no statutory question to review. That situation cannot be remedied by an administrative proce-dure act but must be treated by the revision of statutes conferring administrative powers. However, where statutory standards, definitions, or other grants of power deny or require action in given situations or confine an agency within limits as required by the Constitution, then the determination of the facts does not lie in agency discretion but must be supported by either the administrative or judicial record."

how and when an agency should exercise its discretion then it is impossible to evaluate agency action for "abuse of discretion." In addition, this construction satisfies the principle of statutory construction mentioned earlier, by identifying a separate class of cases to which § 701(a)(2) applies.

To this point our analysis does not differ significantly from that of the Court of Appeals. That court purported to apply the "no law to apply" standard of Overton Park. We disagree, however, with that court's insistence that the "narrow construction" of § (a)(2) required application of a presumption of reviewability even to an agency's decision not to undertake certain enforcement actions. Here we think the Court of Appeals broke with tradition, case law, and sound reasoning.

Overton Park did not involve an agency's refusal to take requested enforcement action. It involved an affirmative act of approval under a statute that set clear guidelines for determining when such approval should be given. Refusals to take enforcement steps generally involve precisely the opposite situation, and in that situation we think the presumption is that judicial review is not available. This Court has recognized on several occasions over many years that an agency's decision not to prosecute or enforce, whether through civil or criminal process, is a decision generally committed to an agency's absolute discretion. . . . This recognition of the existence of discretion is attributable in no small part to the general unsuitability for judicial review of agency decisions to refuse enforcement.

The reasons for this general unsuitability are many. First, an agency decision not to enforce often involves a complicated balancing of a number of factors which are peculiarly within its expertise. Thus, the agency must not only assess whether a violation has occurred, but whether agency resources are best spent on this violation or another, whether the agency is likely to succeed if it acts, whether the particular enforcement action requested best fits the agency's overall policies, and indeed, whether the agency has enough resources to undertake the action at all. An agency generally cannot act against each technical violation of the statute it is charged with enforcing. The agency is far better equipped than the courts to deal with the many variables involved in the proper ordering of its priorities. Similar concerns animate the principles of administrative law that courts generally will defer to an agency's construction of the statute it is charged with implementing, and to the procedures it adopts for implementing that statute.

In addition to these administrative concerns, we note that when an agency refuses to act it generally does not exercise its *coercive* power over an individual's liberty or property rights, and thus does not infringe upon areas that courts often are called upon to protect. Similarly, when an agency *does* act to enforce, that action itself provides a focus for judicial review, inasmuch as the agency must have exercised its power in some manner. The action at least can be reviewed to determine whether the agency exceeded its statutory powers. Finally, we recognize that an agency's refusal to institute proceedings shares to some extent the characteristics of the decision of a prosecutor in the Executive Branch not to indict—a decision which has long been regarded as the special province of the Executive Branch, inasmuch as it is the executive who is charged by the Constitution to "take Care that the Laws be faithfully executed." U.S. Const., Art. II, § 3.

We of course only list the above concerns to facilitate understanding of our conclusion that an agency's decision not to take enforcement action should be presumed immune from judicial review under § 701(a)(2). For good reasons, such a decision has traditionally been "committed to agency discretion," and we believe that the Congress enacting the APA did not intend to alter that tradition. Cf. Davis, § 28.5 (APA did not significantly alter the "common law" of judicial review of agency action). In so stating, we emphasize that the decision is only presumptively unreviewable; the presumption may be rebutted where the substantive statute has provided guidelines for the agency to follow in exercising its enforcement powers.[2] Thus, in establishing this presumption in the APA, Congress did not set agencies free to disregard legislative direction in the statutory scheme that the agency administers. Congress may limit an agency's exercise of enforcement power if it wishes, either by setting substantive priorities, or by otherwise circumscribing an agency's power to discriminate among issues or cases it will pursue. How to determine when Congress has done so is the question left open by Overton Park.

Dunlop v. Bachowski, 421 U.S. 560, (1975), relied upon heavily by respondents and the majority in the Court of Appeals, presents an example of statutory language which supplied sufficient standards to rebut the presumption of unreviewability. . . . This Court . . . rejected the Secretary's argument that the statute precluded judicial review, and in a footnote it stated its agreement with the conclusion of the Court of Appeals that the decision was not "an unreviewable exercise of prosecutorial discretion." 421 U.S., at 567, n. 7. Our textual references to the "strong presumption" of reviewability in Dunlop were addressed only to the § (a)(1) exception; we were content to rely on the Court of Appeals' opinion to hold that the § (a)(2) exception did not apply. The Court of Appeals, in turn, had found the "principle of absolute prosecutorial discretion" inapplicable, because the language of the LMRDA indicated that the Secretary was required to file suit if certain "clearly defined" factors were present. The decision therefore was not " 'beyond the judicial capacity to super-

---

2. We do not have in this case a refusal by the agency to institute proceedings based solely on the belief that it lacks jurisdiction. Nor do we have a situation where it could justifiably be found that the agency has "consciously and expressly adopted a general policy" that is so extreme as to amount to an abdication of its statutory responsibilities. See, e.g., Adams v. Richardson, 156 U.S.App.D.C. 267, 480 F.2d 1159 (1973) (en banc). Although we express no opinion on whether such decisions would be unreviewable under § 701(a)(2), we note that in those situations the statute conferring authority on the agency might indicate that such decisions were not "committed to agency discretion."

vise.' " Bachowski v. Brennan, 502 F.2d 79, 87–88 (CA3 1974) (quoting K. Davis, Administrative Law § 28.16, p. 984 (1970 Supp.)).

Dunlop is thus consistent with a general presumption of unreviewability of decisions not to enforce. The statute being administered quite clearly withdrew discretion from the agency and provided guidelines for exercise of its enforcement power. Our decision that review was available was not based on "pragmatic considerations," such as those cited by the Court of Appeals, see 718 F.2d, at 1185, that amount to an assessment of whether the interests at stake are important enough to justify intervention in the agencies' decisionmaking. The danger that agencies may not carry out their delegated powers with sufficient vigor does not necessarily lead to the conclusion that courts are the most appropriate body to police this aspect of their performance. That decision is in the first instance for Congress, and we therefore turn to the FDCA to determine whether in this case Congress has provided us with "law to apply." If it has indicated an intent to circumscribe agency enforcement discretion, and has provided meaningful standards for defining the limits of that discretion, there is "law to apply" under § 701(a)(2), and courts may require that the agency follow that law; if it has not, then an agency refusal to institute proceedings is a decision "committed to agency discretion by law" within the meaning of that section.

III

[In this section of the opinion, the Court rejected plaintiffs' arguments that there was law to apply. The Court first found that the "Act's enforcement provisions commit complete discretion to the Secretary to decide how and when they should be exercised." It then considered the "three separate authorities that [plaintiffs] claim provide the courts with sufficient indicia of an intent to circumscribe enforcement discretion." One of these the Court characterized as "simply irrelevant"; a second was "singularly unhelpful." The] third argument, based upon § 306 of the FDCA, merits only slightly more consideration. That section provides:

> Nothing in this chapter shall be construed as requiring the Secretary to report for prosecution, or for the institution of libel or injunction proceedings, minor violations of this chapter whenever he believes that the public interest will be adequately served by a suitable written notice or ruling. 21 U.S.C. § 336.

Respondents seek to draw from this section the negative implication that the Secretary is *required* to report for prosecution all "major" violations of the Act, however those might be defined, and that it therefore supplies the needed indication of an intent to limit agency enforcement discretion. We think that this section simply does not give rise to the negative implication which respondents seek to draw from it. The section is not addressed to agency proceedings designed to discover the existence of violations, but applies only to a situation where a violation has already been established to the satisfaction of the agency. We do not believe the section speaks to the criteria which shall be used by the agency for investigating *possible* violations of the Act.

IV

We therefore conclude that the presumption that agency decisions not to institute proceedings are unreviewable under § 701(a)(2) of the APA is not overcome by the enforcement provisions of the FDCA. The FDA's decision not to take the enforcement actions requested by respondents is therefore not subject to judicial review under the APA. The general exception to reviewability provided by § 701(a)(2) for action "committed to agency discretion" remains a narrow one, see Overton Park, but within that exception are included agency refusals to institute investigative or enforcement proceedings, unless Congress has indicated otherwise. In so holding, we essentially leave to Congress, and not to the courts, the decision as to whether an agency's refusal to institute proceedings should be judicially reviewable. No colorable claim is made in this case that the agency's refusal to institute proceedings violated any constitutional rights of respondents, and we do not address the issue that would be raised in such a case. Cf. Johnson v. Robison. The fact that the drugs involved in this case are ultimately to be used in imposing the death penalty must not lead this Court or other courts to import profound differences of opinion over the meaning of the Eighth Amendment to the United States Constitution into the domain of administrative law.

JUSTICE BRENNAN, concurring.

Today the Court holds that individual decisions of the Food and Drug Administration not to take enforcement action in response to citizen requests are presumptively not reviewable under the Administrative Procedure Act, 5 U.S.C. §§ 701–706. I concur in this decision. This general presumption is based on the view that, in the normal course of events, Congress intends to allow broad discretion for its administrative agencies to make particular enforcement decisions, and there often may not exist readily discernible "law to apply" for courts to conduct judicial review of nonenforcement decisions. See Citizens to Preserve Overton Park v. Volpe, 401 U.S. 402, 410 (1971).

I also agree that, despite this general presumption, "Congress did not set agencies free to disregard legislative direction in the statutory scheme that the agency administers." Ante, at 1025. Thus the Court properly does not decide today that nonenforcement decisions are unreviewable in cases where (1) an agency flatly claims that it has no statutory jurisdiction to reach certain conduct; (2) an agency engages in a pattern of nonenforcement of clear statutory language, as in Adams v. Richardson, 480 F.2d 1159 (1973) (en banc); (3) an agency has refused to enforce a regulation lawfully promulgated and still in effect;[3] (4) a nonenforcement decision violates constitutional rights. It is possible to

---

3. Compare Motor Vehicle Manufacturers Assn. v. State Farm Mutual Ins. Co., 463 U.S. 29 (1983) (failure to revoke lawfully a previously promulgated rule is reviewable under the APA).

imagine other nonenforcement decisions made for entirely illegitimate reasons, for example, nonenforcement in return for a bribe, judicial review of which would not be foreclosed by the nonreviewability presumption. It may be presumed that Congress does not intend administrative agencies, agents of Congress' own creation, to ignore clear jurisdictional, regulatory, statutory, or constitutional commands, and in some circumstances including those listed above the statutes or regulations at issue may well provide "law to apply" under 5 U.S.C. § 701(a)(2). Individual, isolated nonenforcement decisions, however, must be made by hundreds of agencies each day. It is entirely permissible to presume that Congress has not intended courts to review such mundane matters, absent either some indication of congressional intent to the contrary or proof of circumstances such as those set out above.

On this understanding of the scope of today's decision, I join the Court's opinion.

JUSTICE MARSHALL, concurring in the judgment.

Easy cases at times produce bad law, for in the rush to reach a clearly ordained result, courts may offer up principles, doctrines, and statements that calmer reflection, and a fuller understanding of their implications in concrete settings, would eschew. In my view, the "presumption of unreviewability" announced today is a product of that lack of discipline that easy cases make all too easy. . . .

I write separately to argue for a different basis of decision: that refusals to enforce, like other agency actions, are reviewable in the absence of a "clear and convincing" congressional intent to the contrary, but that such refusals warrant deference when, as in this case, there is nothing to suggest that an agency with enforcement discretion has abused that discretion.

I

[The FDA's statement explaining] its decision not to take the action [plaintiff's] requested . . . provide[s] a sufficient basis for holding, *on the merits,* that the FDA's refusal to grant the relief requested was within its discretion.

. . .

[A]rguments about prosecutorial discretion do not necessarily translate into the context of agency refusals to act. . . . Criminal prosecutorial decisions vindicate only intangible interests, common to society as a whole, in the enforcement of the criminal law. The conduct at issue has already occurred; all that remains is society's general interest in assuring that the guilty are punished. See Linda R.S. v. Richard D., 410 U.S. 614, 619 (1973) ("a private citizen lacks a judicially cognizable interest in the prosecution or nonprosecution of another"). In contrast, requests for administrative enforcement typically seek to prevent concrete and future injuries that Congress has made cognizable—injuries that result, for example, from misbranded drugs, such as alleged in this case, or unsafe nuclear power plants, see, e.g., Florida Power & Light Co. v. Lorion, 105 S.Ct. 1598 (1985)—or to obtain palpable benefits that Congress has intended to bestow—such as labor union elections free of corruption, see Dunlop v. Bachowski, 421 U.S. 560 (1975). Entitlements to receive these benefits or to be free of these injuries often run to specific classes of individuals whom Congress has singled out as statutory beneficiaries. The interests at stake in review of administrative enforcement decisions are thus more focused and in many circumstances more pressing than those at stake in criminal prosecutorial decisions. A request that a nuclear plant be operated safely or that protection be provided against unsafe drugs is quite different from a request that an individual be put in jail or his property confiscated as punishment for past violations of the criminal law. Unlike traditional exercises of prosecutorial discretion, "the decision to enforce—or not to enforce—may itself result in significant burdens on a . . . statutory beneficiary." . . .

Perhaps most important, the sine qua non of the APA was to alter inherited judicial reluctance to constrain the exercise of discretionary administrative power—to rationalize and make fairer the exercise of such discretion. Since passage of the APA, the sustained effort of administrative law has been to "continuously narro[w] the category of actions considered to be so discretionary as to be exempted from review." Shapiro, Administrative Discretion: The Next Stage, 92 Yale L.J. 1487, 1489, n. 11 (1983). Discretion may well be necessary to carry out a variety of important administrative functions, but discretion can be a veil for laziness, corruption, incompetency, lack of will, or other motives, and for that reason *the presence of discretion should not bar a court from considering a claim of illegal or arbitrary use of discretion.* L. Jaffe, Judicial Control of Administrative Action 375 (1965). Judicial review is available under the APA in the absence of a clear and convincing demonstration that Congress intended to preclude it precisely so that agencies, whether in rulemaking, adjudicating, acting or failing to act, do not become stagnant backwaters of caprice and lawlessness. . . .

For these and other reasons, reliance on prosecutorial discretion, itself a fading talisman, to justify the unreviewability of agency inaction is inappropriate. See generally Stewart & Sunstein, Public Programs and Private Rights, 95 Harv.L.Rev. 1195, 1285–1286, n. 386 (1982) (discussing differences between agency inaction and prosecutorial discretion); Note, Judicial Review of Administrative Inaction, 83 Colum.L.Rev. 627, 658–661 (1983) (same). To the extent arguments about traditional notions of prosecutorial discretion have any force at all in this context, they ought to apply only to an agency's decision to decline to seek penalties against an individual for past conduct, not to a decision to refuse to investigate or take action on a public health, safety, or welfare problem.

II

The "tradition" of unreviewability upon which the majority relies is refuted most powerfully by a firmly entrenched body of lower court case law that holds reviewable various agency refusals to act.[4] This case law recognizes that attempting to draw a line for purposes of judicial review between affirmative exercises of coercive agency power and negative agency refusals to act, is simply untenable. . . . The lower courts, facing the problem of agency inaction and its concrete effects more regularly than do we, have responded with a variety of solutions to assure administrative fidelity to congressional objectives: a demand that an agency explain its refusal to act, a demand that explanations given be further elaborated, and injunctions that action "unlawfully withheld or unreasonably delayed," 5 U.S.C. § 706, be taken. See generally Stewart & Sunstein, 95 Harv.L.Rev., at 1279. Whatever the merits of any particular solution, one would have hoped the Court would have acted with greater respect for these efforts by responding with a scalpel rather than a blunderbuss.

. . .

Perhaps the Court's reference to guidance from the "substantive statute" is meant to . . . allow the "common law" of judicial review of agency action to provide standards by which inaction can be reviewed. But in that case I cannot fathom what content the Court's "presumption of unreviewability" might have. If inaction can be reviewed to assure that it does not result from improper abnegation of jurisdiction, from complete abdication of statutory responsibilities, from violation of constitutional rights, or from factors that offend principles of rational and fair administrative process, it would seem that a court must always inquire into the reasons for the agency's action before deciding whether the presumption applies. . . . In that event, we would not be finding enforcement decisions unreviewable, but rather would be reviewing them on the merits, albeit with due deference, to assure that such decisions did not result from an abuse of discretion.

III

The problem of agency refusal to act is one of the pressing problems of the modern administrative state, given the enormous powers,

---

4. [Ed.] Justice Marshall's footnote of supporting authority is omitted. The footnote cited twenty four federal district and circuit court of appeals cases decided between 1970 and 1983.

See also R. Stewart, The Reformation of American Administrative Law, 88 Harv. L.Rev. 1669, 1754–56 (1975):

"Courts have, in a variety of . . . contexts . . . scrutinize[d] hitherto informal agency choices on regulation and enforcement priorities. By affording all affected interests with a recognized stake in agency policy the right to demand and participate in such procedures . . ., [these] cases . . . facilitate effective judicial review of asserted agency laxity or bias. When the agency has clearly failed to protect the beneficiaries of the administration scheme, courts have gone so far as to mandate appropriate enforcement measures. For

example, judges have required HEW to enforce Title VI of the 1964 Civil Rights Act; HUD to ensure removal of lead paint from the interior of federally subsidized housing; the Interior Department to protect Indians from exploitation by trading posts; the FHA to ensure that federally insured housing meets local code requirements; and the Secretary of the Treasury to protect domestic milk producers from assertedly unlawful competition. Where the agency has already initiated enforcement proceedings, courts have, in selected cases, scrutinized settlements of these proceedings. The judges have thus begun to assume the ultimate protection of the collective social interests which administrative schemes were designed to secure."

And see C. Sunstein, Reviewing Agency Inaction after Heckler v. Chaney, 52 U.Chi. L.Rev. 653 (1985).

for both good and ill, that agency inaction, like agency action, holds over citizens. . . . Over time, I believe the approach announced today will come to be understood, not as mandating that courts cover their eyes and their reasoning power when asked to review an agency's failure to act, but as recognizing that courts must approach the substantive task of reviewing such failures with appropriate deference to an agency's legitimate need to set policy through the allocation of scarce budgetary and enforcement resources. Because the Court's approach, if taken literally, would take the courts out of the role of reviewing agency inaction in far too many cases, I join only the judgment today.

NOTES

(1) LITTELL v. MORTON, 445 F.2d 1207 (4th Cir.1971). 25 U.S.C. § 82 provides that no money shall be paid to an attorney under a contract or agreement for services to Indians unless "the Secretary of the Interior and the Commissioner of Indian Affairs shall determine . . . whether, in their judgment, such contract or agreement has been complied with or fulfilled. . . . " Littell filed a claim for compensation.[1] The Secretary denied the claim and Littell "sought judicial review by mandamus." The district court dismissed the action. The court of appeals reversed and remanded in an opinion by Judge Winter:

". . . While nothing in § 82, or in any other statute relating to Indian affairs, explicitly precludes judicial review of a decision denying compensation under § 82, the argument of the Secretary is that since he and the Commissioner of Indian Affairs shall determine whether, '*in their judgment*,' Littell is entitled to compensation for professional services, their determination is not subject to judicial review under the APA.

"Although § 10(a) renders the APA inapplicable to 'agency action . . . committed to agency discretion by law,' § 10(e), defining the scope of judicial review, directs a reviewing court to hold unlawful and set aside agency action found to be 'arbitrary, capricious *an abuse of discretion* or otherwise not in accordance with law' (emphasis supplied), as well as that which is unconstitutional, in excess of statutory jurisdiction and, in certain instances, not supported by substantial evidence. 5 U.S.C. § 706. How to reconcile the withdrawal from judicial scrutiny

---

1. Littell sought payment of (1) a fixed annual retainer for acting as general counsel for the Navaho Tribe of Indians and (2) contingent fees with respect to five land claim cases brought by the Tribe against the United States. "The Secretary denied [Littell's] claim for payment for services as general counsel, ruling that notwithstanding that termination of the contract by the Secretary had been enjoined for a substantial period of time, the effective date of termination was December 1, 1963, so that Littell was not entitled to payment for services rendered thereafter. Littell's claims for compensation for claims cases were also rejected for a variety of reasons. First, the Secretary determined that three of the cases were not claims cases, so that Littell was not entitled to be paid a contingent fee for his services in regard to them but, rather, was obligated to handle them in consideration of his fixed annual retainer. The fourth case was deemed a claims case but payment was denied on the ground that Littell had breached his fiduciary duty to the Tribe and, hence, had forfeited his right to a fee. The same position was taken with respect to the fifth case. . . . " 445 F.2d 1209–1210.

of discretionary agency action in § 10(a) with the mandatory judicial review for abuse of discretion in § 10(e) has been the subject of sharp dispute.

"Professor Davis has argued that these two sections are reconciled by saying that whenever a decision is committed to agency discretion by law, then a reviewing court can afford no review, not even for abuse of discretion. 4 K. Davis, Administrative Law Treatise, § 28.16 at 80 (1958). This view has also been adopted by other commentators. See, e.g. Saferstein Nonreviewability: A Functional Analysis of "Committed to Discretion," 82 Harv.L.Rev. 367 (1968).[2] On the other hand, Professor Jaffe has argued that § 10(e) permits a limited review to determine whether the agency has exercised its discretion within permissible bounds. L. Jaffe, Judicial Control of Administrative Action 359 (1965). This view in turn has its other supporters. See, e.g., Berger, Administrative Arbitrariness: A Synthesis, 78 Yale L.J. 965 (1969). While the controversy is far from settled, we prefer the latter rationale. . . .

"Thus, we conclude that, while § 82 commits the decision to deny compensation to an Indian attorney to the discretion of the Secretary, the APA provides limited judicial review to determine if there was an abuse of that discretion. In defining the scope of this limited review, we would adopt the formulation of Judge Friendly in Wong Wing Hang v. Immigration & Naturalization Service, 360 F.2d 715, 718 (2d Cir. 1966). Thus, the Secretary's decision here would be an abuse of discretion 'if it were made without a rational explanation, inexplicably departed from established policies, or rested . . . on other "considerations that Congress could not have intended to make relevant." ' "

Judge Winter concluded his opinion with the following paragraph: "Finally, we are constrained to add that this would appear to be a most appropriate case for judicial review. The essential issues in this case are ones of contract interpretation and appropriate remedies if breach of contract is established. There is certainly no compelling agency expertise in this area of the law. These are questions always considered to have been within the special competence of the courts. The

---

2. [Ed.] In this widely cited article, Mr. Saferstein lists nine "factors which most often shape decisions that review be denied." He states that only rarely "is any of these factors, standing alone, controlling; rather, their cumulative effect on the interests of the individual, the agency, and the courts determines whether review should be denied." p. 379. The factors are: (1) broad agency discretion; (2) expertise and experience required to understand subject matter of agency action; (3) managerial nature of agency; (4) impropriety of judicial intervention; (5) necessity of informal agency decision making; (6) inability of reviewing court to ensure correct result; (7) need for expeditious operation of Congressional programs; (8) quantity of potentially appealable agency actions; (9) existence of other methods of preventing abuses of discretion.

Compare G. Leedes, Understanding Judicial Review of Federal Agency Action: Kafkaesque and Langdellian, 12 U. of Rich. L.Rev. 469, 475 (1978), advocating the utility of the following factors "in the analysis of reviewability questions as well as other" issues of judicial review: "1. The nature and degree of the injury. 2. The nature of the question presented (legal, factual, mixed, discretionary, narrow or broad). 3. The obviousness of the agency error as it relates to the challenger (as shown by the record before the court.) 4. The opportunity of the rightholder to obtain relief without court intervention, and the ability of the court to provide the challenger with meaningful relief. 5. The impact of judicial intervention on the orderly conduct of governmental business (including the court's business)."

notion that the government can administratively give a unilateral and final interpretation to a contract under which it may be obligated to pay, and thereby avoid payment, is one that should not be encouraged." [3]

(2) LANGEVIN v. CHENANGO COURT, INC., 447 F.2d 296 (2d Cir.1971), held unreviewable the decision of the Federal Housing Administration (FHA) to approve a rent increase proposed by a federally subsidized landlord which had agreed not to increase rents unless the FHA approved. Judge Friendly said in part:

"Assuming as we do that the FHA's approval constitutes 'agency action' within the broad definition of 5 U.S.C. § 551(13), it would be most unusual for Congress to subject to judicial review discretionary action by an agency in administering a contract which Congress authorized it to make. Other factors tending in the direction of nonreviewability are the managerial nature of the responsibilities confided to the FHA, the need for expedition to achieve the Congressional objective . . . and the quantity of appeals that would result if FHA authorizations to increase rents were held reviewable, see Saferstein, supra, 82 Harv.L.Rev. at 384–86, 390–93.[4] . . . Like the First Circuit [in Hahn v. Gottlieb, 430 F.2d 1243 (1st Cir.1970), which held similar FHA action unreviewable], 'we do not reach the question whether courts may intervene in those rare cases where the FHA has ignored a

---

3. [Ed.] Schonbrun v. Commanding Officer, 403 F.2d 371 (2d Cir.1968), cert. denied 394 U.S. 929 (1969), held that granting or denying a request for exemption from active duty because of "extreme personal and community hardship" is committed to agency discretion. In response to the argument that the Army had violated its own regulations by failing to give notice and reasons for denial of applicant's initial request, Judge Friendly said that while this might be grounds for review in many instances, in this case applicant "was not prejudiced thereby."

Compare Feliciano v. Laird, 426 F.2d 424 (2d Cir.1970). An enlisted man's application for hardship discharge or compassionate reassignment was denied by the Army. The court held that the Army's failure to follow its own regulation "is the kind of error" that warrants reversal and an order to the Army to reconsider the application de novo. The regulation in question provided in part: "If the application does not contain conclusive evidence upon which to base a clear-cut decision that release is or is not warranted, the application and supporting evidence will be forwarded by letter to the Director of Selective Service of the State in which the individual's local board of jurisdiction is located. The letter will request a statement as to whether the circumstances presented in the application would result in deferment on the basis of undue and genuine hardship to the individual's dependents if he were being consid-

ered for induction. . . . It is not mandatory in any way that the officer having discharge authority follow the recommendation of the State Director of Selective Service, but when such statement is received it will be considered in relation to the other supporting evidence."

4. Judge Coffin's opinion in Hahn v. Gottlieb also relies on these factors, 430 F.2d at 1250. We suppose there would rarely be a rent increase which some tenant would not challenge in court if he could.

[Ed.] In the Hahn case Judge Coffin stated:

"In approaching this question [of whether 'agency action is committed to agency discretion by law'] we recognize a strong presumption in favor of review, which is overcome only by "clear and convincing evidence" that Congress intended to cut off review above the agency level. Such evidence may, however, be drawn not only from explicit language, but also from a statute's purpose and design [citing Switchmen's Union]. In the absence of a clear declaration of Congressional intent, three factors seem to us determinative: first, the appropriateness of the issues raised for review by the courts; second, the need for judicial supervision to safeguard the interests of the plaintiffs; and third, the impact of review on the effectiveness of the agency in carrying out its assigned role."

plain statutory duty, exceeded its jurisdiction, or committed constitutional error,' including cases where it is alleged that the agency decision clearly 'rested on an impermissible basis such as an invidious discrimination against a particular race or group.' Wong Wing Hang v. I.N.S., 360 F.2d 715, 719 (2 Cir.1966). We hold only that a mere claim of error, even of gross error, is not enough to escape the second exception in 5 U.S.C. § 701(a). And, whatever bounds the due process clause may set upon nonreviewability of agency action, no case goes to the extent of holding that due process mandates judicial review of an order approving—on the basis of an ex parte submission of facts—a rent increase to a landlord who has benefited from a federal aid program. As already indicated, our decision leaves room for court review of questions as to agency jurisdiction and compliance with constitutional and statutory demands."

(3) CURRAN v. LAIRD, 420 F.2d 122 (D.C.Cir.1969). The Cargo Preference Act provides that if United States vessels are available, "only [such] vessels . . . may be used in the transportation by sea" of military supplies. Another statute provides that United States "vessels placed in [national defense] reserve should be preserved . . . for the purpose of national defense . . . except that any such vessel may be used for account of any agency or department of the United States. . . ."

Plaintiff, president of the National Maritime Union, brought an action against the Secretary of Defense and other officials to enforce the Cargo Preference Act. Defendants admitted that foreign vessels had been used to transport military cargo to Vietnam but contended that United States vessels were not available. Plaintiff replied that Government owned vessels in the national defense reserve were available United States vessels that must be used to transport military cargo pursuant to the Cargo Preference Act before resort could be had to foreign vessels.

The court en banc, in an opinion by Judge Leventhal, held that the legislation providing for the reserve fleet "authorizes a span of executive actions—pertaining to the fleet's establishment, expansion, curtailment, maintenance and use—that are committed to agency discretion within the meaning of § 10(a)(2) of the Administrative Procedure Act, and are not subject to judicial surveillance and correction for error in the exercise of discretion."

The court stated that it recognized the "general rule" that official action is judicially reviewable "when a person claims injury from an act taken by a government official in excess of his powers." But the rule is subject to exceptions and the "exceptions do not violate, rather they define, the rule of reviewability."

"That the matter before us for consideration lies in the special zones of the exceptions, rather than the ordinary area of judicial reviewability is established by several cardinal aspects of the issues. The case involves decisions relating to the conduct of national defense; the President has a key role; the national interest contemplates and requires flexibility in management of defense resources; and the particular issues call for determinations that lie outside sound judicial domain in terms of aptitude, facilities, and responsibility."

"Our decision does not involve personal rights and liberties, does not involve constitutional rights and does not involve a right expressly granted by statute that qualifies what would otherwise be non-reviewable discretion.

"Furthermore, our decision does not contradict the principle that even where an official action is of a type which generally involves the exercise of discretion the court has power to inquire into a claim of abuse of discretion, or use of procedurally unfair and unauthorized techniques, inflicting injury on private citizens. The point of our decision is that there is a narrow band of matters that are wholly committed to official discretion, and that the inappropriateness or even mischief involved in appraising a claim of error or of abuse of discretion, and testing it in an evidentiary hearing, leads to the conclusion that there has been withdrawn from the judicial ambit any consideration of whether the official is arbitrary or constitutes an abuse of discretion. . . .

"We do not deal with officials who are operating under discernible statutory standards, or a mandate to develop standards to assure evenhanded justice. They are rather likely to be called on to make and revise judgments freely, perhaps to draw heavily on information from sources abroad or in the domain of the military in making global guesstimates. Not all operations of government are subject to judicial review, even though they may have a profound effect on our lives."

Judge Wright, with whom Bazelon, C.J. and Robinson, J., concurred, dissented: "I would hold that the policy of the [Cargo Preference] Act .   .   .—that American seamen be favored in the shipment of American military cargo—must be taken into account in the exercise of the power to break out the reserve fleet" and that the administrative decision should be "subject to review only for abuse of discretion."

(4) INTERNATIONAL UNION, UNITED AUTOMOBILE AEROSPACE & AGRICULTURAL IMPLEMENT WORKERS OF AMERICA v. BROCK, 783 F.2d 237 (D.C.Cir. 1986). The Labor-Management Reporting and Disclosure Act required employers to file annual reports with the Secretary of Labor on a variety of activities including their relationships with unions. The Union petitioned the Secretary to enforce the Act by requiring a named employer to file reports concerning specified labor activities. The Secretary of Labor refused to take enforcement action on the grounds, inter alia, that doing so would not be the best expenditure of the agency's resources and that as the Secretary now interpreted the statute, it did not require reporting the activities in question. Held: the "ultimate decision not to enforce" is nonreviewable under Chaney, but the statutory interpretation is reviewable. "Even if a statutory interpretation is announced in the course of a nonenforcement decision, that does not mean that it escapes review altogether. . . . Were we to accept the Department's contention, we would be handling agencies carte blanche to avoid review by

announcing new interpretations of statutes only in the context of decisions not to take enforcement action."

SECTION 3. STANDING TO SECURE JUDICIAL REVIEW

Justice Douglas observed in the Data Processing case, infra p. 1046, "Generalizations about standing to sue are largely worthless. . . . " He might well have added that comprehending the subject of standing is a difficult, complex and frustrating task. In Standing in the Supreme Court—A Functional Analysis, 86 Harv.L.Rev. 645 (1973), Professor Kenneth E. Scott discusses one important reason for the confused state of standing doctrine: the judiciary's failure to distinguish between two very different functions performed by the law of standing. In Professor Scott's terminology the first function involves *access standing,* i.e., who should be able to invoke the subsidized machinery of the federal courts to secure a determination of the validity of the challenged government action.[1] The second function involves *decision standing*—i.e., whether the unrepresentative judiciary should decide the question tendered by the plaintiff. Professor Scott notes that although "standing narrowly and properly refers to access standing," sometimes a "particular case may raise issues of both access standing and justiciability [i.e., decision standing]" and the court will blend together discussion of access and decision doctrines.

Notwithstanding its intricacies and indeterminacies, the law of standing usually must be confronted by law students, not once but twice or thrice or more—in courses in Administrative Law, Constitutional Law, Federal Courts and sometimes also in Civil Procedure. Although very likely there is something to be said in favor of studying the same cases and the same problems in several law school courses, such a repetitious process does raise problems of cost effectiveness.

A possible answer to this lack of coordination would be rigid curriculum planning. But the typical American law school curriculum is more likely to be shaped by laissez faire considerations than by strict decanal or curriculum committee planning and control. Our resolution of the problem is not a unilateral abdication to the other courses but a partial cession. Accordingly, after an appropriate bit of background, this section focuses in the main on the problem of standing in the context of the APA and other statutes purportedly authorizing a described class of persons to seek the aid of the judiciary. This does not mean that we completely eschew constitutional issues. It does mean that we do not purport to provide rounded coverage of standing doctrines in this volume but instead refer the Administrative Law student to courses in Constitutional Law and Federal Courts for more comprehensive treatment.

1. "Access standing . . . means a judicial determination of whether the nature and extent of the alleged harm to a plaintiff are such as to warrant deciding his case." 86 Harv.L.Rev. at 670.

ASSOCIATED INDUSTRIES OF NEW YORK STATE, INC. v. ICKES

United States Court of Appeals, Second Circuit, 1943.
134 F.2d 694.

[Associated Industries of New York, an organization of industrial and commercial firms, many of which were substantial consumers of coal, participated as a party in proceedings conducted by the Bituminous Coal Division (sometimes referred to by the court as "the Commission") and Secretary Ickes to fix minimum prices for coal. Section 6(b) of the Bituminous Coal Act of 1937 authorized "any person aggrieved by an order issued by the Commission in a proceeding to which such person is a party" to seek review by a petition in an appropriate Court of Appeals. Associated Industries petitioned for court review and respondents Ickes and the Director of the Division moved to dismiss.]

FRANK, CIRCUIT JUDGE. . . . The motion to dismiss is not based on any contention as to the general non-reviewability of the orders or their validity, but solely on the contention that, assuming them to be invalid and reviewable, petitioner is not the kind of person entitled to seek court review. Respondents' basic position is frankly that consumers of coal can never appear in court to complain of such price-fixing orders, even if invalid, no matter how great the financial burdens imposed on those consumers by the increase in the cost of coal which will result from those orders. . . .

Respondents . . . insist that petitioner is not a "person aggrieved" by the orders. They assert that those words mean merely to describe the kind of person who, in the absence of § 6(b), would have had a "standing" to maintain a suit in a district court seeking to enjoin respondents from enforcing its order or a declaratory judgment with respect to the validity of those orders. In considering that contention, it is necessary to have in mind that an action in a Court of Appeals to review administrative orders under such a provision as that contained in § 6(b) is a suit begun in an appellate court, i.e., that such provision has the effect of conferring original jurisdiction upon an appellate court; such a proceeding is sometimes called an "appeal" but it is, of course, not the equivalent of an appeal from a lower court, since the proceedings under review were not judicial. In the absence, then, of an appropriate statutory provision, such as § 6(b) of the act here, a suit of this kind, assailing administrative orders, could be brought only in a district court. In other words, the review proceeding is, in effect, a substitute for a district court injunction or declaratory judgment suit. It follows that the doctrine of so-called "standing to sue," as worked out in district court injunction or declaratory judgment suits against government officers, is applicable to the present review proceedings.

That doctrine, as ordinarily applied, may be summarized as follows: In a suit in a federal court by a citizen against a government officer, complaining of alleged past or threatened future unlawful conduct by the defendant, there is no justiciable "controversy," without which, under Article III, § 2 of the Constitution, the court has no jurisdiction, unless the citizen shows that such conduct or threatened conduct invades or will invade a private substantive legally protected interest of the plaintiff citizen; such invaded interest must be either of a "recognized" character at "common law"[2] or a substantive private legally protected interest created by statute.[3] In other words, unless the citizen first shows that, if the defendant were a private person having no official status, the particular defendant's conduct or threatened conduct would give rise to a cause of action against him by that particular citizen, the court cannot consider whether the defendant officer's conduct is or is not authorized by statute;[4] for the statute comes into the case, if at all, only by way of a defense or of justification for acts of the defendant which would be unlawful as against the plaintiff unless the defendant had official authority, conferred upon him by the statute, to do those acts. Unless, then, the citizen first shows that some substantive private legally protected interest possessed by him has been invaded or is threatened with invasion by the defendant officer thus regarded as a private person, the suit must fail for want of a justiciable controversy, it being then merely a request for a forbidden advisory opinion. That the plaintiff shows financial loss on his part resulting from unlawful official conduct is not alone sufficient, for such a loss, absent any such invasion of the plaintiff's private substantive legally protected interest, is damnum absque injuria. Thus, for instance, financial loss resulting from increased lawful competition with a plaintiff, made possible solely by the defendant official's unlawful action, is insufficient to create a justiciable controversy.

2. [Ed.] Joint Anti-Fascist Refugee Committee v. McGrath, 341 U.S. 123 (1951), is an example of standing based upon an interest protected by the common law. The Attorney General published a list of "communist" organizations. Three of the organizations so listed sued the Attorney General for injunctive and declaratory relief. "[T]he standing of the petitioners to bring these suits is clear. The touchstone to justiciability is injury to a legally protected right and the right of a bona fide charitable organization to carry on its work, free from defamatory statements of the kind discussed, is such a right."

3. [Ed.] Hardin v. Kentucky Utilities Co., 390 U.S. 1 (1968), is an example of standing based on an interest created by statute. In 1959 Congress amended the Tennessee Valley Authority Act to provide that the "Corporation [TVA] shall make no contracts for the sale or delivery of power which would have the effect of making the Corporation or its distributors, directly or indirectly, a source of power supply outside the area for which the Corporation or its distributors were the primary source of power supply on July 1, 1957. . . . " Held: "[I]t is clear and undisputed that protection of private utilities from TVA competition was . . . the primary objective of the limitation. Since [Kentucky Utilities] is thus in the class which [the statute] is designed to protect, it has standing under familiar judicial principles to bring this suit [to enjoin the TVA from violating the statute] and no explicit statutory provision is necessary to confer standing. . . . [Defendants'] reliance on Kansas City Power & Light Co. v. McKay, 225 F.2d 924, cert. denied 350 U.S. 884 (1955), is thus misplaced. The Court in McKay ruled that an explicit statutory provision was necessary to confer standing because of the 'long established rule' that an injured competitor cannot sue to enforce statutory requirements not designed to protect competitors. In the case of statutes concerned with protecting competitive interests, the 'long established rule' is of course precisely the opposite."

Justice Frankfurter, concurring in the Joint Anti-Fascist Refugee Committee Case, supra note 2, noted that "standing [also] may be based on an interest created by the Constitution."

4. Of course, the discussion here is not applicable to a suit by a citizen to compel an officer affirmatively to perform a plain ministerial duty owed to that citizen. See, e.g., Board of Liquidation v. McComb, 92 U.S. (2 Otto) 531, 541.

More is required "than a common concern for obedience to law." There is the related rule that Congress cannot constitutionally enact a statute authorizing a suit to be brought to test out the abstract question of the constitutionality of the statute where there is no actual justiciable controversy.

Insisting that the doctrine, substantially as above outlined, is fully applicable here, respondents cite as directly in point the memorandum opinion in City of Atlanta v. Ickes, 308 U.S. 517. There a city, as a substantial coal consumer, brought a suit in a federal district court, to enjoin the Coal Commission from establishing minimum prices by orders, alleged to be invalid, purporting to have been issued pursuant to the Act now before us, and for a declaratory judgment that the Act was unconstitutional. The trial court, holding that it had jurisdiction, dismissed the suit on the merits. On appeal, the Supreme Court affirmed, but not on the merits, holding that the trial court was without jurisdiction. The opinion in its entirety reads as follows: "The judgment is affirmed on the ground that the appellant has no standing to maintain the suit. . . . [citing cases]."

There can be little doubt, then, that if this Act made no provisions for review in a Court of Appeals and if (without any statutory provision covering the mode of bringing such actions) petitioner had brought a suit in a district court, setting forth the allegations now contained in its petition, and seeking an injunction or declaratory judgment, the City of Atlanta decision would have been in point, and dismissal of the suit would have been necessary. But the City of Atlanta case was not an action brought in a Court of Appeals under § 6(b) and consequently did not raise the question whether a "person aggrieved" in that section means merely the sort of person who would have "standing to sue" in the absence of a statutory provision thus worded. For light on the effect of such a provision, we must turn to two cases subsequently decided.

In those cases, Federal Communications Commission v. Sanders Radio Station, 309 U.S. 470, 642 (1940), and Scripps-Howard Radio, Inc. v. Federal Communications Commission, 316 U.S. 4 (1942), it has been held that a "person aggrieved," seeking review under such a statutory provision need not show that he has such a "standing" as is ordinarily required either in injunction suits to restrain action by officials alleged to be unlawful or in declaratory judgment suits brought to determine the validity of such action. . . .

[In the Sanders case, the Telegraph-Herald, published in Dubuque, Iowa, filed an application for a construction permit to erect a broadcasting station in that city. Sanders, who operated station WKBB at East Dubuque, Illinois, directly across the Mississippi River from Dubuque, Iowa, intervened in the Commission proceedings in opposition to issuance of the permit. The Commission granted the application, and on] Sanders' petition for review in the Court of Appeals, it was held that the Commission's order granting a license to the Telegraph-Herald was invalid because the Commission had failed to make any findings as to whether Sanders would suffer "economic injury" from the resulting competition. On certiorari, the Supreme Court held that the "economic injury" to a rival station is not, in and of itself and apart from consideration of public convenience, interest or necessity, an element which the Commission was obliged to weigh or as to which it must make findings in passing on applications for a broadcasting license. The court said that the Act recognizes that the field of broadcasting is one of free competition, that Congress had not in the Act "abandoned the principle of free competition," that "the broadcasting field is open to anyone," and that the policy of the Act was clearly that "no person is to have anything in the nature of a property right as a result of the granting of a license. . . . " It said that while the Commission should take into account the question of competition in its bearing upon the ability of the applicant adequately to serve the public, such matters "are distinct from the consideration that, if a license be granted, competition between the licensee and any other existing station may cause economic loss to the latter. If such economic loss were a valid reason for refusing a license this would mean that the Commission's function is to grant a monopoly in the field of broadcasting, a result which the Act itself expressly negatives. . . . " Nevertheless, the court went on to say: "It does not follow that, because the licensee of the station cannot resist the grant of a license to another, on the ground that the resulting competition may work economic injury to him, he has no standing to appeal from an order of the Commission granting the application. Section 402(b) of the Act provides for an appeal to the Court of Appeals of the District of Columbia (1) by an applicant for a license or permit, or (2) 'by any other person aggrieved or whose interests are adversely affected by any decision of the Commission granting or refusing any such application.' The petitioner insists that as economic injury to the respondent was not a proper issue before the Commission it is impossible that § 402(b) was intended to give the respondent standing to appeal, since *absence of right implies absence of remedy. This view would deprive subsection (2) of any substantial effect.* Congress had some purpose in enacting section 402(b)(2). It may have been of opinion that one likely to be financially injured by the issue of a license would be the only person having a sufficient interest to bring to the attention of the appellate court errors of law in the action of the Commission in granting the license. *It is within the power of Congress to confer such standing to prosecute an appeal.* We hold, therefore, that the respondent had the requisite standing to appeal and to raise, in the court below, any relevant question of law in respect of the order of the Commission. . . . "

In the Scripps-Howard case, supra, the same doctrine as to "standing" was reiterated. There the . . . [Court] said: "The Communications Act of 1934 did not create new private rights. The purpose of the Act was to protect the public interest in communications. By § 402(b) (2), Congress gave the right of appeal to persons 'aggrieved or whose interests are adversely affected' by Commission action. . . . But *these private litigants have standing only as representatives of the public interest.*"

[W]e believe that the usual "standing to sue" cases [such as City of Atlanta v. Ickes] can be reconciled with the Sanders and Scripps-Howard cases, as follows: While Congress can constitutionally authorize no one, in the absence of an actual justiciable controversy, to bring a suit for the judicial determination either of the constitutionality of a statute or the scope of powers conferred by a statute upon government officers, it can constitutionally authorize one of its own officials, such as the Attorney General, to bring a proceeding to prevent another official from acting in violation of his statutory powers; for then an actual controversy exists, and the Attorney General can properly be vested with authority, in such a controversy, to vindicate the interest of the public or the government. Instead of designating the Attorney General, or some other public officer, to bring such proceedings, Congress can constitutionally enact a statute conferring on any non-official person, or on a designated group of non-official persons, authority to bring a suit to prevent action by an officer in violation of his statutory powers; for then, in like manner, there is an actual controversy, and there is nothing constitutionally prohibiting Congress from empowering any person, official or not, to institute a proceeding involving such a controversy, even if the sole purpose is to vindicate the public interest. Such persons, so authorized, are, so to speak, private Attorney Generals. . . .

The court, in the Sanders and Scripps-Howard cases, as we understand them, construed the "person aggrieved" review provision as a constitutionally valid statute authorizing a class of "persons aggrieved" to bring suit in a Court of Appeals to prevent alleged unlawful official action in order to vindicate the public interest, although no personal substantive interest of such persons had been or would be invaded. Although one threatened with financial loss through increased competition resulting from unlawful action of an official cannot, solely on that account, make the proper showing to maintain a suit against the official, absent such a statute, yet the "person aggrieved" statute gives the needed authority to do so to one who comes within that description. True, in the Sanders and Scripps-Howard cases, the review provisions of the statute referred not only, as here, to a "person aggrieved" but also to a "person adversely affected" by the administrative order; we think, however, that the omission of the latter clause in § 6(b) of the Act before us makes no significant difference. If, then, one is a "person aggrieved," he has authority by review proceedings under § 6(b), to vindicate the public interest involved in a violation of the Act by respondents, even if he can show no past or threatened invasion of any private legally protected substantive interest of his own.

Of course, not every person is a "person aggrieved." But the Supreme Court has explicitly told us that one threatened with financial loss through increased competition resulting from a Commission's order is "aggrieved," and entitled as such to a review notwithstanding that the very statute pursuant to which he obtains review is designed to keep competition alive and confers upon him no property right which gives him any kind of immunity from competition. It would seem clear, then, that a consumer threatened with financial loss by a

Commission's order, which fixes prices and prevents competition among those from whom the consumer purchases, is also a "person aggrieved." Indeed there is more reason why Congress should be deemed to have intended to confer such a power on consumers than to authorize a holder of a radio station license to obtain review of an administrative order, issued under the Communication Act, subjecting him to increased competition. For the common law has always zealously regarded competition as inherently desirable.

Respondents contend that Congress could not have intended to construe § 6(b) to include consumers, because such an interpretation will open up the "possibilities of separate law suits by hundreds of thousands of individual consumers" attacking Commission orders, with the result of impairing the effective administration of a statute designed for the stabilization of the coal industry. But there are no such horrendous possibilities. A review proceeding under § 6(b) must be brought within sixty days after the entry of the Commission's order and only in one of the eleven Circuit Courts of Appeals; a decision in one such action in any one of those courts would ordinarily be, at least, stare decisis in that same court. Moreover, § 6(b) contains a provision to the effect that upon the filing in a Court of Appeals of a petition for review and of the transcript of the administrative proceeding, "such court shall have exclusive jurisdiction to affirm, modify, and enforce or set aside such order, in whole or in part." . . .

The motion is denied.

NOTES

(1) OFFICE OF COMMUNICATION OF THE UNITED CHURCH OF CHRIST V. FCC, 359 F.2d 994 (D.C.Cir.1966), supra p. 333.

(2) In the United Church of Christ case, the court stated that "such community organizations as civic associations, professional societies, unions, churches, and educational institutions or associations might well be helpful to the Commission," and therefore have standing. An illustration of this type of "associational" standing may be found in SCENIC HUDSON PRESERVATION CONFERENCE v. FPC, 354 F.2d 608 (2d Cir. 1965), cert. denied 384 U.S. 941 (1966). The conference was an unincorporated association consisting of a number of non-profit conservationist organizations. The Court of Appeals for the Second Circuit, in an opinion by Judge Hays, held that the conference and several towns in the affected area were "aggrieved" within the meaning of the Federal Power Act provision that "any party to a proceeding . . . aggrieved by an order issued by the Commission in such proceeding may obtain a review" in an appropriate court of appeals. The Commission's orders in question granted a license to the Consolidated Edison Company to construct a pumped storage hydroelectric project consisting of a storage reservoir, a powerhouse, and transmission lines near the Hudson River at Storm King Mountain in Cornwall, New York. The court rejected the Commission's contention that "petitioners do not have standing to obtain review" because they "make no claim of any personal economic injury resulting from the Commission's action." The Commission itself,

the court remarked, had stated that the area involved is one "of great scenic beauty" and that it must decide "whether the project's effect on the scenic, historical and recreational values of the area are such that we should deny the application." [1] The court thought that the present parties had a suitable degree of interest in the "values" the Commission had said it should weigh. Judge Hays wrote: "In order to insure that the Federal Power Commission will adequately protect the public interest in the aesthetic, conservational, and recreational aspects of power development, those who by their activities and conduct have exhibited a special interest in such areas, must be held to be included in the class of 'aggrieved' parties under § 313(b). We hold that the Federal Power Act gives petitioners a legal right to protect their special interests. . . .

"Moreover, petitioners have sufficient economic interest to establish their standing. The New York-New Jersey Trail Conference, one of the two conservation groups that organized Scenic Hudson, has some seventeen miles of trailways in the area of Storm King Mountain. Portions of these trails would be inundated by the construction of the project's reservoir. . . .

"We see no justification for the Commission's fear that our determination will encourage 'literally thousands' to intervene and seek review in future proceedings. We rejected a similar contention in Associated Industries, Inc. v. Ickes, 134 F.2d 694, 707 (2d Cir.), vacated as moot, 320 U.S. 707 (1943), noting that 'no such horrendous possibilities' exist. Our experience with public actions confirms the view that the expense and vexation of legal proceedings is not lightly undertaken."

Finally, the Federal Power Act creates no absolute right to intervene in the administrative proceedings themselves. The Act, Sec. 308(a), says, simply, that the Commission "may admit as a party any . . . person whose participation may be in the public interest." "Since the right to seek review under § 313(a) and (b) is limited to a 'party' to the Commission proceeding, the Commission has ample authority reasonably to limit those eligible to intervene or to seek review. . . . Representation of common interests by an organization such as Scenic Hudson serves to limit the number of those who might otherwise apply for intervention and serves to expedite the administrative process." [2]

---

1. [Ed.] Section 10(a) of the Federal Power Act, 16 U.S.C. § 803(a) provides in part as follows:

"All licenses issued . . . shall be on the following conditions:

"(a) That the project adopted . . . shall be such as in the judgment of the Commission will be best adapted to a comprehensive plan for improving or developing a waterway or waterways for the use or benefit of interstate or foreign commerce, for the improvement and utilization of waterpower development, and for other beneficial public uses, including recreational purposes; and if necessary in order to se-

cure such plan the Commission shall have authority to require the modification of any project and of the plans and specifications of the project works before approval."

2. [Ed.] "The Scenic Hudson case showed that private groups may do much to represent the public interest. But they too have their limitations. The typical conservation organization operates on an annual budget of about $350,000, and with perhaps 25 staff members. Often the office and travel expenses, combined with modest salaries, more than exhaust the treasury. By the time of the rehearing in Scenic Hudson, the conservationists had

The court remanded the case to the Federal Power Commission, directing the Commission in its renewed proceedings to "include as a basic concern the preservation of natural beauty and of national historic shrines, keeping in mind that, in our affluent society, the cost of the project is only one of several factors to be considered." Extensive and lengthy litigation ensued and finally Consolidated Edison terminated the project.[3]

(3) Louis L. Jaffe, Judicial Control of Administrative Action 528–530 (1965): "[In Kansas City Power and Light Co. v. McKay, 225 F.2d 924 (D.C.Cir.1955), cert. denied 350 U.S. 884, utility companies] attacked the statutory validity of certain federally supported power programs. The Supreme Court in Tennessee Electric Power Co. v. TVA, [306 U.S. 118 (1939)], had dismissed precisely such a suit on the ground that a person had no legal claim to protection against competition whether illegal or not. The court in McKay was asked to hold that the petitioners were within Section 10 of the APA giving a 'right of review' to 'any person suffering legal wrong . . . or adversely affected or aggrieved within the meaning of any relevant statute.' Judge Washington, writing for the court, regarded the provision of the APA, correctly in my opinion, as no more than declaratory of existing law.[4]

already spent almost $250,000—an astounding sum for such an organization to amass. . . ." Note, Of Birds, Bees and the FPC, 77 Yale L.J. 117, 120 (1967).

And see N.Y. Times, Oct. 31, 1976, sec. 1, p. 55, cols, 1–6 ("the Scenic Hudson Preservation Conference . . . has fought the Storm King project for the last 13 years and has spent more than $1 million in litigation to stave it off"); id., Feb. 25, 1979, Sec. 4, p. 16, col. 2 ("capital costs [of Storm King] have jumped from an estimated $300 million in 1970 to $1.3 billion"); id., Jan. 6, 1974, Sec. 1, pg. 53, col. 2 ("had the plant been built when originally proposed, the cost would have been $165 million").

3. See N.Y. Times, Dec. 20, 1980, p. 1, cols. 1–2:

"Consolidated Edison agreed yesterday to halt construction on a pumped-storage power plant at Storm King Mountain and to donate the 500-acre site in Cornwall, N.Y., for park use. The settlement ended a 17-year dispute between the utility and environmentalists and Government agencies over the preservation of river life.

"In exchange for a host of concessions from Con Edison and four other utilities, opponents of the plant agreed that the utilities would not be required to install closed-cycle cooling systems at three [other] electric generating plants on the Hudson River.

"The utilities, in turn, must spend nearly $18 million on projects to reduce fish kills by about 35 percent, stock the river

and study the impact on fish by power plants.

"The agreement, which could serve as a model for settlements of at least 20 similar disputes around the country, was hailed by environmentalists. The utility companies were less ebullient."

See also A. Talbot, Power Along the Hudson: The Storm King Case and the Birth of Environmentalism (1972); W. Tucker, Environmentalism and the Leisure Class, 255 Harper's Mag. 49 (Dec. 1977).

4. [Ed.] In the Kansas City Power case Judge Washington stated in part: "Section 10(a) is for the benefit of 'any person suffering legal wrong', that is, one whose legal rights have been violated. As we have seen, these plaintiffs cannot effectively make such a claim. Nor are we confronted with any relevant statute within the meaning of which the plaintiffs are 'adversely affected or aggrieved.' Plaintiffs-appellants cite and rely on the view expressed in American President Lines v. Federal Maritime Board, D.C.D.C.1953, 112 F.Supp. 346, at page 349, which would in effect delete from Section 10(a) the phrase 'within the meaning of any relevant statute'. That view cannot, of course, be accepted."

In the American President Lines case the Federal Maritime Board had granted a subsidy to two steamship lines. A competing shipping line brought an action to set aside the subsidies. The court held plaintiff had standing because the APA provided for review by any person "adversely affected or aggrieved" and in the Sanders

Professor Davis says of the APA that 'although the legislative history is not entirely free from conflicting views, the part of the legislative history that is both clear and authoritative is the statement made by the committees of both the Senate and the House. . . . "This subsection confers a right of review upon any person adversely affected *in fact* by agency action or aggrieved within the meaning of any statute." ' (Emphasis added.) The words 'in fact' are not, however, in the statute. The statute as enacted conforms to the draft which came out of conferences between the Government and the American Bar Association and of which the Attorney General stated to Congress: 'This reflects existing law.' To be sure the understanding of the Attorney General is not so authoritative as that of the committees but it does throw into high relief the omission of the words 'in fact.' And if we put aside this 'conflicting' legislative history, the case for Professor Davis' view is logically very difficult to support. It appears to be argued that if any statute would class the petitioner as 'aggrieved' in the context of that statute, a person similarly situated, in so far as such similarity can be thought to exist logically, is aggrieved with respect to action under any other statute. Thus since under Sanders illegally certified competition gives rise to standing the same is true of any illegally certified or assisted competition. This to my mind gives no weight to the word 'relevant,' which would seem to limit standing clauses in particular statutes to actions under those or perhaps under closely related statutes. If the APA had meant to make the test grievance in fact, most of the provision becomes unnecessary. It would have sufficed to provide simply, 'any person aggrieved' shall be entitled to judicial review." [5]

(4) SCANWELL LABORATORIES, INC. v. SHAFFER, 424 F.2d 859 (D.C.Cir. 1970). Scanwell, the second lowest bidder on a government contract, sued the Administrator of the Federal Aviation Administration (FAA), contending that in awarding the contract to the lowest bidder, the FAA had violated its own procurement regulations. The district court dismissed the plaintiff's action on the ground it lacked standing to sue.

The court of appeals reversed. After noting the "incredible complexity" of the law of standing "as developed by the Supreme Court, Judge Tamm's opinion, joined by Judge Bazelon, concluded: "[I]n spite of the fact that the Supreme Court has not yet chosen to hold that the Administrative Procedure Act applies to all situations in which a party who is in fact aggrieved seeks review, regardless of a lack of legal right or specific statutory language, it is clearly the intent of that Act that this should be the case. . . .

"Of course it is true that the grant of standing must be carefully controlled by the exercise of judicial discretion in order that completely

case the court had held that the competitor was adversely affected or aggrieved. "If a competitor who fears adverse economic effects, has a right to challenge the legality of official action under one of the Acts [i.e., the FCC Act], the conclusion is inescapable that he may do so under the other Act [i.e., the APA]." Nowhere in its opinion did the court deal with the clause "within the meaning of any relevant statute."

5. [Ed.] Professor Davis' "reply" to Professor Jaffe's argument appears in K. Davis, "Judicial Control of Administrative Action": A Review, 66 Colum.L.Rev. 635, 668–669 (1966).

frivolous lawsuits will be averted. There must be a practical separation of the meritorious sheep from the capricious goats . . . . However, responsible federal judges will be able to discern a case in which there is injury in fact, a sufficient adversary interest to constitute a case or controversy under Article III, and an otherwise reviewable subject matter to prevent the dockets from becoming overcrowded. The court should have discretion to grant standing, provided the other criteria listed above are properly met. . . . " [6]

ASSOCIATION OF DATA PROCESSING SERVICE ORGANIZATIONS v. CAMP

Supreme Court of the United States, 1970.
397 U.S. 150.

MR. JUSTICE DOUGLAS delivered the opinion of the Court.

Petitioners sell data processing services to business generally. In this suit they seek to challenge a [1966] ruling by respondent, Comptroller of the Currency, that, as an incident to their banking services, national banks, including respondent American National Bank & Trust Company, may make data processing services available to other banks and to bank customers. The District Court dismissed the complaint for lack of standing of petitioners to bring the suit.

Generalizations about standing to sue are largely worthless as such. One generalization is, however, necessary and that is that the question of standing in the federal courts is to be considered in the framework of Article III which restricts judicial power to "cases" and "controversies." As we recently stated in Flast v. Cohen, 392 U.S. 83, 101, ". . . [I]n terms of Article III limitations on federal court jurisdiction, the question of standing is related only to whether the dispute sought to be adjudicated will be presented in an adversary

---

6. Having subjected federal procurement decisions to judicial review by its holding in Scanwell, the court in later decisions limited the judicial role in the procurement process by emphasizing the broad discretion delegated to procurement officials. See M. Steinthal & Co. v. Seamans, 455 F.2d 1289 (D.C.Cir.1971) ("the court must refrain from judicial intervention unless the actions of the executive officials are without any rational basis"); Wheelabrator Corp. v. Chafee, 455 F.2d 1306 (D.C.Cir.1971) (in this case "we have an action, or more truly a failure to take action, that is 'committed to agency discretion by law' within the meaning of the Administrative Procedure Act").

See also Gull Airborne Instruments, Inc. v. Weinberger, 694 F.2d 838, 846 n. 9 (D.C. Cir.1982):

"Post-Scanwell courts have considered several factors in exercising their discretion to issue or refuse to issue an injunction [in behalf of a disappointed bidder]. . . . They have looked carefully at the interests to be affected by injunctive relief, recognizing that substantial harm may accrue to the government and the public when agencies are unable to make necessary procurements without undue delay. Although finding merit in the claims of disappointed bidders, they have struck the balance of equities in favor of the government's interests in the smooth and efficient functioning of the procurement process at the expense of the interests of the unsuccessful bidder in the integrity of the bidding process and equal access to the procurement dollar (and of the public in fairness and competitive bidding).

"[C]ourts have also taken into account the availability of a damage remedy in the Court of Claims for bid preparation losses resulting from illegal agency action. See M. Steinthal & Co. v. Seamans, 455 F.2d at 1302–03. And partial performance of a contract has been considered to be a substantial factor in the denial of injunctions to unsuccessful bidders. Keco Indus. v. Laird, 318 F.Supp. 1361, 1364 (D.D.C.1970)."

context and in a form historically viewed as capable of judicial resolution." Flast was a *taxpayer's* suit. [Ed. See note 2, p. 1051 below, for fuller reference to this case.] The present is a *competitor's* suit. And while the two have the same Article III starting point, they do not necessarily track one another.

The first question is whether the plaintiff alleges that the challenged action has caused him injury in fact, economic or otherwise. There can be no doubt but that petitioners have satisfied this test. The petitioners not only allege that competition by national banks in the business of providing data processing services might entail some future loss of profits for the petitioners, they also allege that respondent American National Bank & Trust Company was performing or preparing to perform such services for two customers for whom petitioner Data Systems, Inc., had previously agreed or negotiated to perform such services. The petitioners' suit was brought not only against the American National Bank & Trust Company, but also against the Comptroller of the Currency. The Comptroller was alleged to have caused petitioners injury in fact by his 1966 ruling . . . .

[P]rior decisions of this Court, such as Tennessee Power Co. v. TVA, 306 U.S. 118, where private power companies sought to enjoin TVA from operating, claiming that the statutory plan under which it was created was unconstitutional, . . . [have] denied . . . competitors standing, holding that they did not have that status "unless the right invaded is a legal right—one of property, one arising out of contract, one protected against tortious invasion, or one founded on a statute which confers a privilege."

The "legal interest" test goes to the merits. The question of standing is different. It concerns, apart from the "case" or "controversy" test, the question whether the interest sought to be protected by the complainant is arguably within the zone of interests to be protected or regulated by the statute or constitutional guarantee in question. Thus the Administrative Procedure Act grants standing to a person "aggrieved by agency action within the meaning of a relevant statute." 80 Stat. 392, 5 U.S.C. § 702. That interest, at times, may reflect "aesthetic, conservational, and recreational" as well as economic values. Scenic Hudson Preservation Conf. v. Federal Power Commission, 354 F.2d 608, 616; United Church of Christ v. FCC, 359 F.2d 994, 1000–1006. A person or a family may have a spiritual stake in First Amendment values sufficient to give him standing to raise issues concerning the Establishment Clause and the Free Exercise Clause. Abington School District v. Schempp, 374 U.S. 203. We mention these noneconomic values to emphasize that standing may stem from them as well as from the economic injury on which petitioner relies here. Certainly he who is "likely to be financially" injured, Commission v. Sanders Radio Station, 309 U.S., at 477, may be a reliable private attorney general to litigate the issues of the public interest in the present case.

Apart from Article III jurisdictional questions, problems of standing, as resolved by this Court, have involved a "rule of self-restraint for its own governance." Barrows v. Jackson, 346 U.S. 249, 255. Congress can, of course, resolve the question one way or another, save as the requirements of Article III dictate otherwise. Muskrat v. United States, 219 U.S. 346.

Where statutes are concerned, the trend is toward enlargement of the class of people who may protest administrative action. The whole drive for enlarging the category of aggrieved "persons" is symptomatic of that trend. . . . In that tradition was Hardin v. Kentucky Utilities Co., 390 U.S. 1, which involved a section of the TVA Act designed primarily to protect, through area limitations, private utilities against TVA competition. We held that no explicit statutory provision was necessary to confer standing, since the private utility bringing suit was within the class of persons which the statutory provision was designed to protect.

It is argued that . . . the Hardin case [is] relevant here because of § 4 of the Bank Service Corporation Act of 1962, 76 Stat. 1132, 12 U.S.C. § 1864, which provides: "No bank service corporation may engage in any activity other than the performance of bank services for banks."

The Court of Appeals for the First Circuit held in Arnold Tours Inc. v. Camp, 408 F.2d 1147, 1152–1153, that by reason of § 4 a data processing company has standing to contest the legality of a national bank performing data processing services for other banks and bank customers: "Section 4 had a broader purpose than regulating only the service corporations. It was also a response to the fears expressed by a few senators, that without such a prohibition, the bill would have enabled 'banks to engage in a nonbanking activity,' S.Rep. No. 2105, [87th Cong., 2d Sess., pp. 7–12] (Supplemental views of Senators Proxmire, Douglas, and Neuberger), and thus constitute 'a serious exception to the accepted public policy which strictly limits banks to banking.' (Supplemental views of Senators Muskie and Clark.) We think Congress has provided the sufficient statutory aid to standing even though the competition may not be the precise kind Congress legislated against."

We do not put the issue in those words, for they implicate the merits. We do think, however, that § 4 arguably brings a competitor within the zone of interests protected by it.

That leaves the remaining question, whether judicial review of the Comptroller's action has been precluded. We do not think it has been.

. . .

The Administrative Procedure Act provides that the provisions of the Act authorizing judicial review apply "except to the extent that—(1) statutes preclude judicial review; or (2) agency action is committed to agency discretion by law." . . .

We read § 701(a) as sympathetic to the issue presented in this case. As stated in the House Report: "The statutes of Congress are not merely advisory when they relate to administrative agencies, any more than in other cases. To preclude judicial review under this bill a statute, if not specific in withholding such review, must upon its face give clear and convincing evidence of an intent to withhold it. The mere failure to provide specially by statute for judicial review is certainly no evidence of intent to withhold review." H.R.Rep. No. 1980, 79th Cong., 2d Sess., 41.

There is no presumption against judicial review and in favor of administrative absolutism . . . unless that purpose is fairly discernible in the statutory scheme. Cf. Switchmen's Union v. National Mediation Board, 320 U.S. 297.

We find no evidence that Congress in either the Bank Service Corporation Act or the National Bank Act sought to preclude judicial review of administrative rulings by the Comptroller as to the legitimate scope of activities available to national banks under those statutes. Both Acts are clearly "relevant" statutes within the meaning of § 702. The Acts do not in terms protect a specified group. But their general policy is apparent; and those whose interests are directly affected by a broad or narrow interpretation of the Act are easily identifiable. It is clear that petitioners, as competitors of national banks which are engaging in data processing services, are within that class of "aggrieved" persons who, under § 702, are entitled to judicial review of "agency action."

Whether anything in the Bank Service Corporation Act or the National Bank Act gives petitioners a "legal interest" which protects them against violations of those Acts, and whether the actions of respondents did in fact violate either of those Acts, are questions which go to the merits and remain to be decided below.

We hold that petitioners have standing to sue and that the case should be remanded for a hearing on the merits.

Reversed.[1]

[The concurring and dissenting opinion of Justice Brennan is printed at p. 1051 below.]

BARLOW v. COLLINS
Supreme Court of the United States, 1970.
397 U.S. 159.

[Tenant farmers were eligible to receive cash subsidy payments under the Upland Cotton Program; the payments could not be assigned by a participant in the program except as security to enable him to obtain "cash or advances to finance making a crop." Until 1966 the Secretary of Agriculture's regulations made clear that financing "making a crop" did not include whatever cash rent a tenant might have to pay. Then the Secretary changed the regulations by expressly defining "making a crop" to include assignments to secure the tenant's "payment of cash rent for land" used in cotton farming. The petitioners in

---

1. [Ed.] See K. Scott, Standing in the Supreme Court—A Functional Analysis, 86 Harv.L.Rev. 645, 688 n. 167 (1973): "On remand, the Association of Data Processing Service Organizations dropped the case, the actions of Congress and the Federal Reserve Board in permitting provision of data processing services via the holding company device having rendered pointless any attempt to impose a direct limitation on banks. . . . "

the present case were cash rent tenant farmers, suing as a class. They attacked the new regulation because, they said, it enabled their landlords to demand that tenants assign the Upland Cotton Program's benefits as a precondition of getting leases to work the land. They said that the landlords, newly armed with the amended regulation, gouged them economically, so that they suffered irreparable injury traceable to the Secretary's action. They sought a declaration that the regulation was itself unauthorized by statute and they asked for an injunction prohibiting federal officials from permitting the benefit assignments the regulation contemplated. In short, they alleged that the regulation injured them in fact, though it neither commanded nor forbade them to do anything.

The district court held that the tenants lacked standing because the officials whom they sought to enjoin had not "taken any action which invades any legally protected interest of the plaintiffs." The Fifth Circuit affirmed.]

MR. JUSTICE DOUGLAS delivered the opinion of the Court. . . .

Our decision in Data Processing Service v. Camp . . . leads us to reverse here.

First, there is no doubt that in the context of this litigation the tenant farmers, petitioners here, have the personal stake and interest that impart the concrete adverseness required by Article III.

Second, the tenant farmers are clearly within the zone of interests protected by the Act.

Implicit in the statutory provisions and their legislative history is a congressional intent that the Secretary protect the interests of tenant farmers. Both of the relevant statutes expressly enjoin the Secretary to do so. The Food and Agriculture Act of 1965 states that "[t]he Secretary shall provide adequate safeguards to protect the interests of tenants. . . . " . . . The legislative history of the "making a crop" provision, though sparse, similarly indicates a congressional intent to benefit the tenants. They are persons "aggrieved by agency action within the meaning of a relevant statute" as those words are used in 5 U.S.C. § 702.

Third, judicial review of the Secretary's action is not precluded. The Court of Appeals rested its holding on the view that no provision of the Food and Agriculture Act of 1965 "expressly or impliedly . . . gives the Courts authority to review such administrative action."

. . . The amended regulation here under challenge was promulgated under 16 U.S.C. § 590(d)(3) which authorizes the Secretary to "prescribe such regulations, as he may deem proper to carry out the provisions of this chapter." Plainly this provision does not expressly preclude judicial review, nor does any other provision in either the 1938 or 1965 Acts. Nor does the authority to promulgate such regulations "as he may deem proper" in § 590(d)(3) constitute a commitment of the task of defining "making a crop" entirely to the discretionary judgment of the Executive Branch without the intervention of the courts. On the contrary, since the only or principal dispute relates to the meaning of the statutory term, the controversy must ultimately be resolved, not on the basis of matters within the special competence of the Secretary, but by judicial application of canons of statutory construction. . . . Therefore the permissive term "as he may deem proper," by itself, is not to be read as a congressional command which precludes a judicial determination of the correct application of the governing canons.

The question then becomes whether nonreviewability can fairly be inferred. . . . It is, however, "only upon a showing of 'clear and convincing evidence' of a contrary legislative intent" that the courts should restrict access to judicial review. Abbott Laboratories v. Gardner, 387 U.S. 136, 141 . . . . .

We hold that the statutory scheme at issue here is to be read as evincing a congressional intent that petitioners may have judicial review of the Secretary's action.

The judgments of the Court of Appeals and of the District Court are vacated and the case is remanded to the District Court for a hearing on the merits.

Mr. Justice Brennan, with whom Mr. Justice White joins, concurring and dissenting.

I concur in the result in both [the Data Processing and Barlow] cases but dissent from the Court's treatment of the question of standing to challenge agency action.

The Court's approach to standing, set out in Data Processing, has two steps: (1) since "the framework of Article III . . . restricts judicial power to 'cases' and 'controversies,'" the first step is to determine "whether the plaintiff alleges that the challenged action has caused him injury in fact"; (2) if injury in fact is alleged the relevant statute or constitutional provision is then examined to determine "whether the interest sought to be protected by the complainant is arguably within the zone of interests to be protected or regulated by the statute or constitutional guarantee in question."

My view is that the inquiry in the Court's first step is the only one which need be made to determine standing. I had thought we discarded the notion of any additional requirement when we discussed standing solely in terms of its constitutional content in Flast v. Cohen, 392 U.S. 83 (1968).[2] . . .

---

2. [Ed.] In the Flast case, federal taxpayers, alleging a violation of the establishment and free exercise clauses of the first amendment, sued to enjoin federal officials from expending federal funds to finance instruction and materials in religious schools. Distinguishing Frothingham v. Mellon, 262 U.S. 447 (1923), the Court held that plaintiffs had standing as taxpayers.

". . . Whether such individuals have standing . . . turns on whether they can demonstrate the necessary stake as taxpayers in the outcome of the litigation to satisfy Article III requirements.

"The nexus demanded of federal taxpayers has two aspects to it. First, the taxpayer must establish a logical link between that status and the type of legislative enactment attacked. Thus, a taxpayer will be a proper party to allege the unconstitutionality only of exercises of congressional power under the taxing and spending clause of Art. I, § 8, of the Constitution. It will not be sufficient to allege an incidental expenditure of tax funds in the administration of an essentially regulatory statute. . . . Secondly the taxpayer must establish a nexus between that status and the precise nature of the constitutional in-

I submit that . . . [w]hen agency action is challenged, standing, reviewability, and the merits pose discrete, and often complicated, issues which can best be resolved by recognizing and treating them as such.

STANDING

Although Flast v. Cohen was not a case challenging agency action, its determination of the basis for standing should resolve that question for all cases. We there confirmed what we said in Baker v. Carr, 369 U.S. 186, 204 (1962), that the "gist of the question of standing" is whether the party seeking relief has "alleged such a personal stake in the outcome of the controversy as to assure that concrete adverseness which sharpens the presentation of issues upon which the court so largely depends for illumination of difficult . . . questions." "In other words," we said in Flast, "when standing is placed in issue in a case, the question is whether the person whose standing is challenged is a proper party to request an adjudication of a particular issue" and not whether the controversy is otherwise justiciable, or whether, on the merits, the plaintiff has a legally protected interest which the defendant's action invaded. 392 U.S., at 99–100. The objectives of the Article III standing requirement are simple: the avoidance of any use of a "federal court as a forum [for the airing of] generalized grievances about the conduct of the government," and the creation of a judicial context in which "the questions will be framed with the necessary specificity. . . . the issues . . . contested with the necessary adverseness and . . . the litigation . . . pursued with the necessary vigor to assure that the . . . challenge will be made in a form traditionally thought to be capable of judicial resolution. Id. at 106. . . . ."

In light of Flast, standing exists when the plaintiff alleges, as the plaintiffs in each of these cases alleged, that the challenged action has caused him injury in fact economic or otherwise. He thus shows that he has the requisite "personal stake in the outcome" of his suit. Baker

fringement alleged. Under this requirement, the taxpayer must show that the challenged enactment exceeds specific constitutional limitations imposed upon the exercise of the congressional taxing and spending power and not simply that the enactment is generally beyond the powers delegated to Congress by Art. I, § 8. When both nexuses are established, the litigant will have shown a taxpayer's stake in the outcome of the controversy and will be a proper and appropriate party to invoke a federal court's jurisdiction.

"The taxpayer-appellants in this case have satisfied both nexuses to support their claim of standing under the test we announce today. Their constitutional challenge is made to an exercise by Congress of its power under Art. I, § 8, to spend for the general welfare, and the challenged program involves a substantial expenditure of federal tax funds. In addition, appellants have alleged that the challenged expenditures violate the Establishment and Free Exercise Clauses of the First Amendment."

See also Boryszewski v. Brydges, 37 N.Y.2d 361, 372 N.Y.S.2d 623, 334 N.E.2d 579 (1975), in which taxpayers challenged the constitutionality of "lulus"—lump sum payments to legislators in lieu of expenses—and a retirement plan for members of the legislative and executive branches. The court, overruling prior cases, upheld plaintiffs' standing: "We are satisfied that the time has now come when the judicially formulated restriction on standing (which we recognize has had a venerable existence . . . .) should be modified to bring our State's practice into conformity . . . with the practice in the majority of other States. . . . "

v. Carr, supra, at 204. We may reasonably expect that a person so harmed will, as best he can, frame the relevant questions with specificity, contest the issues with the necessary adverseness, and pursue the litigation vigorously. Recognition of his standing to litigate is then consistent with the Constitution, and no further inquiry is pertinent to its existence.

REVIEWABILITY

When the legality of administrative action is at issue standing alone will not entitle the plaintiff to a decision on the merits. Pertinent statutory language, legislative history and public policy considerations must be examined to determine whether Congress precluded all judicial review, and, if not, whether Congress nevertheless foreclosed review to the class to which the plaintiff belongs. Under the Administrative Procedure Act (APA), "statutes [may] preclude judicial review" or "agency action [may be] committed to agency discretion by law." 5 U.S.C. § 701(a). In either case, the plaintiff is out of court, not because he had no standing to enter, but because Congress has stripped the judiciary of authority to review agency action. . . .

. . . Where, as in the instant cases, there is no express grant of review, reviewability has ordinarily been inferred from evidence that Congress intended the plaintiff's class to be a beneficiary of the statute under which the plaintiff raises his claim. See, for example, Hardin v. Kentucky Utilities Co., 390 U.S. 1 (1968). In light of Abbott Laboratories, slight indicia that the plaintiff's class is a beneficiary will suffice to support the inference.[3]

THE MERITS

If it is determined that a plaintiff who alleged injury in fact is entitled to judicial review, inquiry proceeds to the merits—to whether the specific legal interest claimed by the plaintiff is protected by the statute and to whether the protested agency action invaded that interest. It is true, of course, that matters relevant to the merits will already have been touched tangentially in the determination of standing and, in some cases, in the determination of reviewability. The aspect of the merits touched in establishing standing is the identification of injury in fact, the existence of which the plaintiff must prove. The merits are also touched in establishing reviewability in cases where the plaintiff's right to review must be inferred from evidence that his class is a statutory beneficiary. The same statutory indicia that afford the plaintiff a right to review also bear on the merits because they provide evidence that the statute protects his class, and thus that he is entitled to relief if he can show that the challenged agency action violated the statute. Evidence that the plaintiff's class is a statutory beneficiary, however, need not be as strong for the purpose of obtaining review as for the purpose of establishing the plaintiff's claim on the

3. This is particularly the case when the plaintiff is the only party likely to challenge the action. Refusal to allow him review would, in effect, commit the action wholly to agency discretion, thus risking frustration of the statutory objectives.

merits. Under Abbott Laboratories, slight beneficiary indicia will suffice to establish his right to have review and thus to reach the merits. . . .[4]

NOTE

ARNOLD TOURS, INC. v. CAMP, 400 U.S. 45 (1970). The Comptroller of the Currency issued a ruling that "national banks may provide travel services for their customers and receive compensation therefor." Arnold Tours and some forty other travel agencies in Massachusetts instituted an action against the Comptroller seeking a declaration that the ruling was illegal and an injunction to restrain him from permitting any national bank to engage in the travel agency business. The district court dismissed the action on the ground plaintiffs lacked standing. The court of appeals affirmed. Chief Judge Aldrich, writing before the Supreme Court decisions in Data Processing and Barlow, found no "statutory aid to standing" and rejected petitioners' arguments that either section 10(a) of the Administrative Procedure Act or Flast v. Cohen, 392 U.S. 83 (1968) had so changed the law as to grant standing.

The travel agents petitioned for certiorari. The Supreme Court, per curiam, granted the petition, vacated the judgment, and remanded the case "for further consideration in light of" Data Processing and Barlow. 397 U.S. 315 (1970). On remand, Chief Judge Aldrich again wrote for the court and again held that the travel agents lacked standing: "Under any standard, plaintiffs have no standing. They have produced no scintilla of evidence tending to show that Congress was specifically concerned with the competitive interests of travel agencies; nor have they shown enough evidence of concern for general business competitors to create a 'zone' within which they are arguably included. . . . Clearly the Court did not feel that the mere fact that [the travel agents] were in competition with the defendant bank gave them standing. Had it intended so substantial a change in the law it would not only have written quite a different opinion in Data Processing; it would have reversed us out of hand." 428 F.2d 359 (1st Cir. 1970).

The Supreme Court, per curiam, granted certiorari and reversed and remanded: "Here, as in Data Processing, we are concerned with § 4 of the Bank Service Corporation Act, 76 Stat. 1132, 12 U.S.C. § 1864.[1] In Data Processing we did not rely on any legislative history showing that Congress desired to protect data processors alone from competition.[2] Moreover, we noted a growing trend 'toward enlargement of the class of people who may protest administrative action.'

---

4. [Ed.] For general discussion of standing, see J. Vining. Legal Identity: The Coming of Age of Public Law (1978).

1. "No bank service corporation may engage in any activity other than the performance of bank services for banks."

2. [Ed.] This sentence apparently was prompted by the following statement in the circuit court's opinion: "The [Supreme Court's] decision in Data Processing was not based on the wording of the statute, but on a showing that Congress, in connection with authorizing entities to engage in data processing for banks, had protection of data processing competitors specifically in mind." 428 F.2d at 361.

397 U.S. at 154. We held that § 4 'arguably brings a competitor within the zone of interests protected by it.' Id., at 156. Nothing in the opinion limited § 4 to protecting only competitors in the data-processing field. When national banks begin to provide travel services for their customers, they compete with travel agents no less than they compete with data processors when they provide data-processing services to their customers."[3]

CONTROL DATA CORPORATION v. BALDRIDGE

United States Court of Appeals, District of Columbia Circuit, 1981.
655 F.2d 283, cert. denied 454 U.S. 881 (1981).

[The Secretary of Commerce promulgated standards establishing specifications to which automatic data processing (ADP) equipment had to conform in order to be eligible for government purchase. Manufacturers and suppliers of ADP systems and equipment brought suit in the district court seeking a judgment declaring the specifications to be invalid and enjoining the Secretary from enforcing the specifications. Plaintiffs argued that because the specifications were similar to those of IBM to which plaintiffs' equipment did not presently conform, plaintiffs would be required to expend large amounts of time and money in order to compete for government ADP contracts, that IBM would thus occupy a highly favored position vis-a-vis plaintiffs, and that because plaintiffs' equipment provided the only major alternative to IBM's equipment, enforcement of the specifications would hinder competition. Plaintiffs also urged that Congress desired to promote competition in order to achieve economic and efficient government procurement.[1] The district court held that plaintiffs lacked standing to challenge the specifications and dismissed the action. Plaintiffs appealed.]

Before TAMM and EDWARDS, CIRCUIT JUDGES, and LLOYD F. MACMAHON, U.S. DISTRICT JUDGE for the Southern District of New York.

TAMM, CIRCUIT JUDGE: . . .

We begin our standing inquiry with a statement of the standard against which we must evaluate appellants' right to sue in the present instance. This standard establishes three requirements: 1) appellants

---

3. [Ed.] On remand, the travel agents prevailed on the merits. Arnold Tours, Inc. v. Camp, 472 F.2d 427 (1st Cir.1972) ("it is illegal for a national bank to operate a full-scale travel agency since such an operation is not an exercise of the incidental powers referred to in 12 U.S.C. § 24, Seventh," which provides that banks may exercise "such incidental powers as shall be necessary to carry on the business of banking. . . . ")

See also Investment Co. Institute v. Camp, 401 U.S. 617 (1971), following Data Processing and Arnold Tours in holding that a trade association of open-end investment companies has standing to challenge a ruling of the Comptroller of the Currency which permitted national banks to operate collective investment funds.

1. See 40 U.S.C. § 759(a) ("Administrator is authorized and directed to coordinate and provide for the economic and efficient purchase, lease, and maintenance of automatic data processing equipment by Federal agencies"); 40 U.S.C. § 471 ("It is the intent of Congress in enacting this legislation to provide for the Government an economical and efficient system for . . . the procurement and supply of personal property and nonpersonal services. . . . "); 41 U.S.C. § 253 ("[S]pecifications and invitations for bids shall permit such full and free competition as is consistent with the procurement of the type of property and services necessary to meet the requirements of the agency concerned").

must allege injury in fact;[2] 2) appellants must assert that arbitrary or capricious agency action injured an interest arguably within the zone of interests to be protected or regulated by the statute or constitutional guarantee in question; 3) there must be no "clear and convincing" indication of a legislative intent to withhold judicial review.[3] The first requirement need not detain us long. Appellants have alleged here that the implementation of the . . . standards will cause them substantial economic injury. They claim that if they choose to comply with the standards, they must expend considerable time and effort to ensure the equipment's conformance to the mandated specifications. If they choose not to comply, they will be effectively precluded from offering their products in the government ADP market. Such allegations sufficiently describe the specific injury appellants will sustain as a result of the Secretary's action. Like the district court, then, we believe that appellants have demonstrated the requisite "personal stake" in the litigation and meet, thereby, their constitutional burden.

Appellants' attempts to fulfill the prudential requirement, on the other hand, require extended consideration. . . .

A careful evaluation of the parties' contentions demands, in the first instance, a viable standard against which they can be measured. In this case the acknowledged standard is the zone of interests test. The test's amorphous nature, however, makes application difficult and careful evaluation impossible absent some refinement. To apply the zone of interests standard in a principled fashion, then, we must attempt to give it content and form, definition and scope. For this purpose we proceed to an examination of the origins of the test and of its present status.

The zone of interests test made its initial appearances in four cases decided by the Supreme Court in 1970 and 1971. . . .

[At this point the court summarized the holdings in Data Processing, Barlow, Arnold Tours and Investment Co. Institute, supra.]

In these four cases the Supreme Court discarded the outdated legal interest criterion and interposed a new zone of interest test more compatible with the perceived trend toward the enlargement of the class of persons entitled to protest administrative action. Data Processing, 397 U.S. at 154. This new test was starkly stated, however, without accompanying expression of the methods to be utilized in its application. Moreover, the Court's own applications of the fledgling

---

2. The Supreme Court has expounded upon the nature of this constitutional aspect of the standing inquiry. . . . In Simon v. Eastern Kentucky Welfare Rights Organization, 426 U.S. 26 (1976), for example, the Court emphasized that a plaintiff must show "an injury to himself that is likely to be redressed by a favorable decision." As the Court explained, this constitutional requirement mandates "that a federal court act only to redress injury that fairly can be traced to the challenged action of the defendant, and not injury that results from the independent action of some third party not before the court." As we point out, appellants here have alleged a specific economic injury caused by the Government. This constitutional requirement has therefore been met.

3. In light of our disposition of this case, we find it unnecessary to reach this third criterion.

standard were generally conclusory in nature, and consequently failed to provide the desired clarification.

Despite the difficulties engendered by this lack of guidance, the Court has not attempted to develop, in the years since Data Processing and its immediate progeny, a more mature zone of interests standard. In that time the Court has specified no guidelines for the test's application nor has it even undertaken to apply the zone test in a standing inquiry. At least one commentator has suggested that this neglect indicates the Court's implicit abandonment of the zone standard.[4] The Court's express reaffirmation of the test's existence, albeit in summary fashion,[5] requires us to assume, however, the test's continued role as a prudential limitation.[6] We must, therefore, apply the test despite the Court's failure to provide more specific guidance. . . .

A survey of [the law of the federal courts reveals] more variety than uniformity among the approaches to the zone test. Some courts, reacting strongly to the Supreme Court's vague formulation of the test, have expressed disagreement with the standard,[7] clearly misapplied it,[8] or virtually ignored it.[9] Other courts, taking a more active approach, have attempted to refine the test into a workable standard. As a result of these efforts, it is generally recognized that in applying the zone test a court must discern whether the interest asserted by a party in the particular instance is one intended by Congress to be protected or regulated by the statute under which suit is brought. Most courts also acknowledge that the sources pertinent to this examination are the language of the relevant statutory provisions and their legislative history. An application of the test under even this approach, however, still affords a court great latitude in defining the scope of the relevant

---

4. K. Davis, Administrative Law Treatise § 22–02–11, at 509 (Supp.1976) ("a second reason for doubting that the 'zone' test is the law is that the Supreme Court itself has not followed it.")

5. See, e.g., Sierra Club v. Morton, 405 U.S. 727, 733 & n. 5 (1972); United States v. SCRAP, 412 U.S. 669, 686 & n. 13 (1973); Simon v. Eastern Kentucky Welfare Rights Organization, 426 U.S. 26, 39 n. 19 (1976). . . .

6. Congress has the power to eliminate this prudential limitation, and apparently attempted to do so in 1976. At that time the subcommittee on Administrative Practice and Procedure of the Senate Judiciary Committee examined several bills "to expand and improve the Administrative Procedure Act." Included among the proposed "Administrative Procedure Act Amendments of 1976" was S. 3296. . . . The explicit intent of the provision was . . . . to "eliminate nonessential, 'prudential limitations' on standing . . . ." Administrative Procedure Act Amendments of 1976: Hearings Before the Subcomm. on Administrative Practice and Procedure of the Senate Comm. on the Judiciary, 94th Cong., 2d Sess. 40 (1976).

7. See, e.g., Park View Heights Corp. v. City of Black Jack, 467 F.2d 1208 (8th Cir. 1972). In this case the court recorded its "preference for simplifying the 'law on standing.' We think that all that is required for a plaintiff to have standing to sue for a constitutional or statutory violation is a showing of 'injury in fact.'" Id. at 1212 n. 4.

8. See Upper Pecos Ass'n v. Stans, 452 F.2d 1233, 1235 (10th Cir.1971), vacated on other grounds, 409 U.S. 1021, (1972), and Izaak Walton League of America v. St. Clair, 313 F.Supp. 1312, 1316–17 (D.Minn. 1970). . . .

9. See, e.g., Florida v. Weinberger, 492 F.2d 488, 494 (5th Cir.1974) (grant of standing to the state plaintiff solely on the basis of its "clear interest . . . in the manner in which the Medicaid program is administered vis-a-vis its citizens and in being spared the reconstitution of its statutory program. . . . "); William F. Wilke, Inc. v. Department of Army of United States, 485 F.2d 180 (4th Cir.1973) (grant of standing to a disappointed bidder for a government contract without mentioning the zone standard).

zone; the conclusions it derives from these legislative sources will vary according to the nature and quantity of the "beneficial indicia" it requires.

This court has stated that "slight" beneficial indicia will be sufficient to sustain a party's assertion of standing. Although this standard would seem to invite a liberal interpretation of congressional intent, our review of the relevant statutory provisions and legislative history reveals *no* evidence of an intent to protect or benefit these appellants. [The relevant statute in this case is the Brooks Act [10] passed in 1965] as an amendment to the Federal Property and Administrative Services Act of 1949. Both statutes express congressional interest in economic and efficient procurement of property, 40 U.S.C. § 759(a) (1976) and 40 U.S.C. § 471 (1976); in both Congress recognized the maximization of competition as an important means to its objective. 41 U.S.C. § 253(a) (1976) and H.R.Rep. No. 802, 89th Cong., 1st Sess. 25 (1965). This interest in competition is not, however, congruent with that interest in competition asserted by appellants. Appellants, as major suppliers, wish to challenge the . . . standards promulgated by the Secretary of Commerce because these standards will require appellants to make considerable expenditures of time and money to produce equipment suitable for the government ADP market. Appellants believe that these resulting costs will destroy not only their individual competitive positions but also their collective position as the sole realistic alternative to IBM. Thus appellants' interest in competition is rooted in economic self-preservation.

The congressional interest in competition, when viewed in its proper context, is grounded upon a quite different premise. The Brooks Act resulted from a growing perception that certain trends in ADP acquisition and use were leading to "costly inefficiencies." H.R.Rep. No. 802, 89th Cong., 1st Sess. 18 (1965). To avoid these inefficiencies, Congress established in the Act a coordinated management program directed particularly toward the economic acquisition of ADP equipment. Such acquisition, in turn, depended upon the successful implementation of several proposals, including the improvement of the government's bargaining position vis-a-vis ADP suppliers through volume acquisition, the selection of equipment offering the largest purchase advantage on a government-wide basis, the creation of adequate standards, and the increase of competition among suppliers, id. at [22–34]. Despite this variety of approaches, however, only one end was sought—lower government ADP costs. Competition was not, therefore, valued for itself, but for the benefits it could bring the government.

---

10. The Brooks Act provides in pertinent part:

The Secretary of Commerce is authorized (1) to provide agencies, and the Administrator of General Services in the exercise of the authority delegated in this section, with scientific and technological advisory services relating to automatic data processing and related systems, and (2) to make appropriate recommendations to the President relating to the establishment of uniform Federal automatic data processing standards. The Secretary of Commerce is authorized to undertake the necessary research in the sciences and technologies of automatic data processing computer and related systems, as may be required under provisions of this subsection. 40 U.S.C. § 759(f) (1976). [Footnote by the court. See also note 1, supra p. 1055.]

Since the passage of the Brooks Act, Congress has maintained its interest in competition.[11] The standards challenged here were intended to foster competition among systems manufacturers and between such manufacturers and peripheral suppliers. Consistent with the indications of congressional intent just discussed, however, this increased competition was expected to inure to the benefit of the government, rather than ADP suppliers. We note, moreover, that to enjoy these advantages Congress was determined to obtain an effective . . . interface standard, despite its recognition of the possible adverse effects on ADP suppliers such as appellants. In light of these consistent congressional indicators, therefore, we cannot find that appellants' interest lies within that zone of interests intended to be protected by the Brooks Act.[12]

In sustaining the district court's denial of standing, we do not feel that we have insulated the Secretary's action from critical review. The Secretary has stated that the standards will be reviewed within three years of their effective date and are subject at that time to revision or withdrawal if technological trends or other factors so require. 44 Fed. Reg. 10,100 (1979). More importantly, however, if these standards do seriously discourage the competition they were intended to promote, it is very likely that Congress will interject itself into the process and insist upon the necessary corrective measures. Certainly, Congress has been quite zealous in its previous oversight of the Brooks Act. It has held numerous hearings and made voluminous criticisms of the agencies' implementations of the Act's provisions and policies in the years since that Act's passage. We find no reason to assume that these congressional efforts will decrease either in vigor or number.

While we realize that these observations offer small comfort in the face of the economic injury appellants may suffer, we feel our decision is compelled by the present law of standing. Although confusing and perhaps inconsistent,[13] that law dictates the continued role of the zone of interests tests as a prudential limitation. We must therefore apply

---

11. See, e.g., H.R.Rep. No. 96–694, 96th Cong., 1st Sess. 62 (1979):

"The Brooks Act is grounded upon two basic objectives: (1) ADP resources should be procured as economically and efficiently as possible; and (2) only those resources should be procured which are needed and which can assist (rather than retard) the management of Government programs.

"To accomplish the first objective, *it is essential that Federal agencies be required to procure their ADP requirements on a fully competitive basis unless exceptional circumstances intervene.*

(Emphasis added).

We realize, of course, that post-enactment congressional discussion of legislation is to be given limited weight in statutory construction. We include such discussion here, however, for its value as a persuasive manifestation of the consistent congressional approach to the Brooks Act.

12. Appellants also argue that their interest lies within that zone protected by the Federal Property and Administrative Services Act of 1949 (FPASA). Ch. 288, 63 Stat. 377 (codified in scattered sections of 40 & 41 U.S.C.). The Brooks Act and the FPASA share the purpose of economical and efficient procurement and an interest in maximizing competition. As with the Brooks Act, however, there is no indication that the competition sought by Congress was intended to inure to the benefit of those in appellants' position. . . .

13. We are not unmindful of the quality of fantasy or play in the search for beneficiaries. "Litigants search for a personality that will fit the demands of the court, tailor their attributes, paint their faces, manipulate their identities, and attend a masked ball where they hope to receive a prize for the imagination and ingenuity they display." J. Vining, Legal Identity 123 (1978). We do not believe that

the test in appropriate circumstances and in a manner calculated to serve its intended purpose of "allowing courts to define those instances when it believes the exercise of its power at the instigation of a particular party is not congruent with the mandate of the legislative branch in a particular subject area." Tax Analysts, 566 F.2d at 140.

We have found no justification for avoiding the application of the zone test to the present circumstances. We believe, moreover, that because these circumstances involve the government's prerogative to dictate the specifications of those products it will purchase, our application must fully reflect our awareness of the test's importance as a limitation on the role of the courts in resolving public disputes. In light of this obligation we have scrutinized carefully the legislative history and defined accordingly the scope of the zone of interests protected by the Brooks Act. As drawn, this zone of interests must exclude appellants. . . .

NOTES

(1) COPPER & BRASS FABRICATORS COUNCIL, INC. v. DEPARTMENT OF THE TREASURY, 679 F.2d 951 (D.C.Cir.1982). Responding to rising copper prices and the withdrawal from circulation of substantial quantities of pennies as a result of the public hoarding which followed, Congress enacted the following statute in 1974: "Whenever in the judgment of the Secretary of the Treasury such action is necessary in order to assure an adequate supply of coins to meet national needs, he may prescribe such composition of the copper and zinc in the alloy of the one-cent piece as he may deem appropriate. Such one-cent pieces shall have such weight as may be prescribed by the Secretary." 31 U.S.C. § 317(b).

Sometime in 1980, the Department of the Treasury announced that it planned to alter the composition of the penny from 95% copper and 5% zinc to a copper-plated zinc blank containing 2.4% copper and 97.6% zinc. Plaintiff, a nonprofit "membership association" representing 23 domestic fabricators of copper and copper alloy products, brought an action against the Treasury Department and the Secretary of the Treasury seeking a declaratory judgment that the proposed change was not authorized by Section 317(b) and an injunction barring the defendants from taking any steps to further the proposed change. The district court dismissed the action on the ground that plaintiffs lacked standing.

A panel of the D.C. Circuit (Tamm and Ginsburg, JJ., and Palmieri, J., sitting by designation) affirmed in an opinion by District Judge Palmieri. In a relatively brief discussion the court said that the case was governed by the "zone of interests standard [which], as Control Data explains, requires some indicia—however slight—that the litigant before the court was intended to be protected, benefited or regulated by the statute under which suit is brought. . . . The clear intent [of Congress] to permit discretionary reduction in copper content, in favor

it is our place, however, to call a halt to
this "masked ball."

of zinc, can in no respect be viewed as an intent to benefit or protect the copper industry. . . . It follows that appellant does not fall within the zone of interests sought to be protected, benefited, or regulated by Section 317(b)."

Judge Ginsburg filed a separate opinion stating that since Control Data "prescribes the manner in which the 'zone of interests' test is to be applied in this Circuit[,] I therefore concur in the result reached today." She continued:

"However, I write separately (1) to emphasize the need for 'further enlightenment from Higher Authority' [1] as to the vitality and proper application of the 'zone' test, and (2) because I am uncertain whether the Control Data standard, which constitutes the law of this Circuit, is fully consistent with the leading Supreme Court decisions announcing and applying the 'zone' test. . . .

"It is less than apparent that the standard adopted in Control Data, and applied today, is altogether consistent with the terse instruction provided by the Supreme Court concerning the 'zone' test's proper application. As the opinion of the court points out, the Control Data standard 'requires some indicia . . . that the litigant before the court *was intended* to be protected, benefitted or regulated by the statute under which suit is brought.' (Emphasis added). However, the 'zone' test announced by the Supreme Court requires only that the litigant be '*arguably* within the zone of interests to be protected or regulated by the statute or constitutional guarantee in question.' Data Processing, 397 U.S. at 153, (emphasis added). Further, Control Data identifies the statute's legislative history as pertinent to the standing inquiry. But the Supreme Court's Arnold Tours decision raises significant doubt whether examination of legislative history is proper when applying the 'arguably within the zone of interests' test. . . .

"[I]n view of the Control Data 'indicia of intent' requirement, I cannot dissent from the court's judgment. Were redressable 'injury in fact' the sole test for standing, the copper fabricators would clear the first threshold to adjudication of their claim. How much more the 'zone' test demands and even the situations in which the test applies present questions left murky by the Supreme Court. Clarification from the Court would facilitate the expeditious, even-handed disposition of standing controversies by lower courts."

(2) SIERRA CLUB v. MORTON, 405 U.S. 727 (1972). Sierra Club, "a large and long-established organization, with a historic commitment to the cause of protecting our Nation's natural heritage from man's depredations," sought a declaratory judgment and an injunction to restrain federal officials from approving the creation of an extensive ski-resort development in the scenic Mineral King Valley of the Sequoia National Forest. The Sierra Club claimed standing to maintain its "public interest" lawsuit because it had "a special interest in the conservation and [the] sound maintenance of the national parks, game

1. See United States v. Martino, 664 F.2d 860, 881 (2d Cir.1981) (Oakes, J., concurring).

refuges and forests of the country. . . . " The Court held those allegations insufficient.

Justice Stewart—writing for the majority which consisted of himself, Chief Justice Burger and Justices White and Marshall [2]—stated in part: "The [Sierra] Club apparently regarded any allegations of individualized injury as superfluous, on the theory that this was a 'public' action involving questions as to the use of natural resources, and that the Club's longstanding concern with and expertise in such matters were sufficient to give it standing as a 'representative of the public.'

. . .

"Some courts have indicated a willingness to . . . [c]onfer standing upon organizations that have demonstrated 'an organizational interest in the problem' of environmental or consumer protection. Environmental Defense Fund v. Hardin, 138 U.S.App.D.C. 391, 395, 428 F.2d 1093, 1097. It is clear that an organization whose members are injured may represent those members in a proceeding for judicial review." See, e.g., NAACP v. Button, 371 U.S. 415, 428. "But a mere 'interest in a problem,' no matter how longstanding the interest and no matter how qualified the organization is in evaluating the problem, is not sufficient by itself to render the organization 'adversely affected' or 'aggrieved' within the meaning of the APA. [I]f a 'special interest' in this subject were enough to entitle the Sierra Club to commence this litigation, there would appear to be no objective basis upon which to disallow a suit by any other bona fide 'special interest' organization however small or short-lived. And if any group with a bona fide 'special interest' could initiate such litigation, it is difficult to perceive why any individual citizen with the same bona fide special interest would not also be entitled to do so.

"The requirement that a party seeking review must allege facts showing that he is himself adversely affected does not insulate executive action from judicial review, nor does it prevent any public interests from being protected through the judicial process. It does serve as at least a rough attempt to put the decision as to whether review will be sought in the hands of those who have a direct stake in the outcome. That goal would be undermined were we to construe the APA to authorize judicial review at the behest of organizations or individuals who seek to do no more than vindicate their own value preferences through the judicial process. The principle that the Sierra Club would have us establish in this case would do just that." [3]

---

2. Justices Powell and Rehnquist did not participate.

3. [Ed.] The majority opinion explicitly stated that its "decision does not, of course, bar the Sierra Club from seeking in the District Court to amend its complaint by a motion under Rule 15, Federal Rules of Civil Procedure." 405 U.S. 735–736 n. 8.

Acting in apparent response to this suggestion, Sierra Club did amend its complaint in the district court, alleging that its chapters and members regularly conduct outings in Mineral King, and that over the years it had conducted conservation campaigns to have Mineral King included in Sequoia National Park. The amended complaint also added a new cause of action that the defendants had failed to prepare an environmental impact statement required by the National Environmental Policy Act of 1969, which was not law when the original complaint was filed in 1969. The defendants' motion to dismiss the amended complaint was denied. 57 Sierra Club Bulletin 24–25, 16–17, (July-Aug., Oct.-Nov., 1972).

Justices Douglas, Brennan and Blackmun dissented. In his opinion, Justice Douglas expressed the view that the "critical question of 'standing' would be simplified and also put neatly in focus if we fashioned a federal rule that allowed environmental issues to be litigated before federal agencies or federal courts in the name of the inanimate object about to be despoiled, defaced, or invaded by roads and bulldozers and where injury is the subject of public outrage. Contemporary public concern for protecting nature's ecological equilibrium should lead to the conferral of standing upon environmental objects to sue for their own preservation. See Stone, Should Trees Have Standing? Toward Legal Rights for Natural Objects, 45 S.Cal.L.Rev. 450 (1972). This suit would therefore be more properly labeled as Mineral King v. Morton." [4]

UNITED STATES v. STUDENTS CHALLENGING REGULATORY AGENCY PROCEDURES (SCRAP)

Supreme Court of the United States, 1973.
412 U.S. 669.

[A railroad seeking an increase in rates must provide at least 30 days notice to the Interstate Commerce Commission and the public before putting the new rate into effect. During that period, the Commission may suspend the operation of the proposed rate for a maximum of seven months pending an investigation and decision on the lawfulness of the new rate. At the end of the seven-month period, the carrier may put the suspended rate into effect unless the Commission has earlier completed its investigation and found the rate unlawful.

Pursuant to this procedure substantially all the nation's railroads sought a 2.5% surcharge on nearly all freight rates as an interim emergency measure pending adoption of selective rate increases on a permanent basis. Shippers, competing carriers and various environmental groups requested the Commission to suspend the surcharge for the statutory seven-month period. Students Challenging Regulatory Agency Procedures (SCRAP), an unincorporated association formed by five law students in September 1971 to enhance the quality of the environment, brought an action to restrain enforcement of the Commission's orders which allowed the carriers to collect the surcharge.[1]

Additional litigation ensued and finally in 1978 Congress transferred Mineral King Valley to the contiguous Sequoia National Park, thereby preventing commercial development of the area. See N.Y. Times, Nov. 27, 1978, p. A17, col. 1.

4. A Michigan statute provides: "[A]ny person . . . may maintain an action in the circuit court having jurisdiction where the alleged violation occurred or is likely to occur for declaratory and equitable relief . . . for the protection of the air, water and other natural resources and the public trust therein from pollution, impairment or destruction." 35 Mich.Comp.L. § 691.1202. Similar statutes have been adopted in Connecticut, Florida, Indiana, Massachusetts and Minnesota. For discussion, see J. Sax and J. DiMento, Environmental Citizen Suits: Three Years' Experience Under the Michigan Environmental Protection Act, 4 Ecology L.Q. 1 (1974); N.Y. Times, Mar. 24, 1973, p. 15, col. 4.

1. Three other environmental groups (Environmental Defense Fund, National Parks and Conservation Association, and Izaak Walton League of America) intervened as plaintiffs.

The theory of SCRAP's action was that the across-the-board increase in freight rates would increase the cost of shipping recyclable materials and discourage the environmentally desirable use of recyclable goods; therefore, the Commission's orders allowing the carriers to collect the surcharge were "major federal actions significantly affecting the quality of the human environment," which, under the terms of the National Environmental Policy Act of 1969 (NEPA), cannot take effect before a "detailed statement . . . on . . . the environmental impact of the proposed action" is prepared.[2] Plaintiffs alleged that their members used the forests, streams, mountains and other resources in the Washington Metropolitan Area for camping, hiking, fishing, and sightseeing, and that these uses were adversely affected because the rate increase would discourage the reuse of recyclable commodities, such as bottles and cans, and encourage the depletion of natural resources. Defendants argued, inter alia, that SCRAP did not have standing, that the Commission's orders were not "major Federal actions significantly affecting the quality of the human environment" within the meaning of NEPA, and that, in any event, issuance of an injunction was barred by the Supreme Court's decision in Arrow Transportation Co. v. Southern R. Co., 372 U.S. 658 (1963). The district court rejected these arguments and issued an injunction forbidding the Commission from permitting, and the railroads from collecting, the surcharge on goods being transported for the purpose of recycling. Appeals to the Supreme Court were filed by the United States, the Commission and the railroads.]

MR. JUSTICE STEWART delivered the opinion of the Court. . . .

The appellants challenge the appellees' standing to sue, arguing that the allegations in the pleadings as to standing were vague, unsubstantiated and insufficient under our recent decision in Sierra Club v. Morton, [405 U.S. 727 (1972)]. The appellees respond that unlike the petitioner in Sierra Club, their pleadings sufficiently alleged that they

---

2. Section 102 of NEPA, 42 U.S.C. § 4334, provides:

"The Congress authorizes and directs that, to the fullest extent possible: (1) the policies, regulations, and public laws of the United States shall be interpreted and administered in accordance with the policies set forth in this chapter, and (2) all agencies of the Federal Government shall—

" . . .

"(C) include in every recommendation or report on proposals for legislation and other major Federal actions significantly affecting the quality of the human environment, a detailed statement by the responsible official on—

"(i) the environmental impact of the proposed action,

"(ii) any adverse environmental effects which cannot be avoided should the proposal be implemented,

"(iii) alternatives to the proposed action,

"(iv) the relationship between local short-term uses of man's environment and the maintenance and enhancement of long-term productivity, and

"(v) any irreversible and irretrievable commitments of resources which would be involved in the proposed action should it be implemented.

"Prior to making any detailed statement, the responsible Federal official shall consult with and obtain the comments of any Federal agency which has jurisdiction by law or special expertise with respect to any environmental impact involved. Copies of such statement and the comments and views of the appropriate Federal, State, and local agencies, which are authorized to develop and enforce environmental standards, shall be made available to the President, the Council on Environmental Quality and to the public . . . and shall accompany the proposal through the existing agency review processes. . . . "

were "adversely affected" or "aggrieved" within the meaning of § 10 of the Administrative Procedure Act (APA), 5 U.S.C. § 702,[3] and they point specifically to the allegations that their members used the forests, streams, mountains and other resources in the Washington Metropolitan Area for camping, hiking, fishing, and sightseeing, and that this use was disturbed by the adverse environmental impact caused by the nonuse of recyclable goods brought about by a rate increase on those commodities. The District Court found these allegations sufficient to withstand a motion to dismiss. We agree. . . .

Relying upon our prior decisions in Association of Data Processing Services v. Camp, 397 U.S. 150, and Barlow v. Collins, 397 U.S. 159, we held [in Sierra Club] that § 10 of the APA conferred standing to obtain judicial review of agency action only upon those who could show "that the challenged action had caused them 'injury in fact,' and where the alleged injury was to an interest 'arguably within the zone of interests to be protected or regulated' by the statutes that the agencies were claimed to have violated." 405 U.S., at 733.[4]

In interpreting "injury in fact" we made it clear that standing was not confined to those who could show "economic harm" although both Data Processing and Barlow had involved that kind of injury. Nor, we said, could the fact that many persons shared the same injury be sufficient reason to disqualify from seeking review of an agency's action any person who had in fact suffered injury. Rather, we explained: "Aesthetic and environmental well-being, like economic well-being, are important ingredients of the quality of life in our society, and the fact that particular environmental interests are shared by the many rather than the few does not make them less deserving of legal protection through the judicial process." Id., at 734. Consequently, neither the fact that the appellees here claimed only a harm to their use and enjoyment of the natural resources of the Washington area, nor the fact that all those who use those resources suffered the same harm, deprives them of standing.

In Sierra Club, though, we went on to stress the importance of demonstrating that the party seeking review be himself among the injured, for it is this requirement that gives a litigant a direct stake in the controversy and prevents the judicial process from becoming no more than a vehicle for the vindication of the value interests of concerned bystanders. No such specific injury was alleged in Sierra Club. In that case the asserted harm "will be felt directly only by those who use Mineral King and Sequoia National Park, and for whom the

---

3. Like the petitioner in Sierra Club, the appellees here base their standing to sue upon § 10 of the Administrative Procedure Act (APA), 5 U.S.C. § 702, which provides:

"A person suffering legal wrong because of agency action, or adversely affected or aggrieved by agency action within the meaning of a relevant statute, is entitled to judicial review thereof."

4. As in Sierra Club, it is unnecessary to reach any question concerning the scope of the "zone of interests" test or its application to this case. It is undisputed that the "environmental interest" that the appellees seek to protect is within the interests to be protected by NEPA, and it is unnecessary to consider the various allegations of economic harm on which the appellees also relied in their pleadings and which the Government contends are outside the intended purposes of NEPA.

aesthetic and recreational values of the area will be lessened by the highway and ski resort," id., at 735, yet "[t]he Sierra Club failed to allege that it or its members would be affected in any of their activities or pastimes by the . . . development." Ibid. Here, by contrast, the appellees claimed that the specific and allegedly illegal action of the Commission would directly harm them in their use of the natural resources of the Washington Metropolitan Area.

Unlike the specific and geographically limited federal action of which the petitioner complained in Sierra Club, the challenged agency action in this case is applicable to substantially all of the Nation's railroads, and thus allegedly has an adverse environmental impact on all the natural resources of the country. Rather than a limited group of persons who used a picturesque valley in California all persons who utilize the scenic resources of the country, and indeed all who breathe its air, could claim harm similar to that alleged by the environmental groups here. But we have already made it clear that standing is not to be denied simply because many people suffer the same injury. See, e.g., . . . Reade v. Ewing, 2 Cir., 205 F.2d 630, 631–632 (interests of consumers of oleomargarine in fair labeling of product regulated by Federal Security Administration). To deny standing to persons who are in fact injured simply because many others are also injured, would mean that the most injurious and widespread Government actions could be questioned by nobody. We cannot accept that conclusion.

But the injury alleged here is also very different from that at issue in Sierra Club because here the alleged injury to the environment is far less direct and perceptible. The petitioner there complained about the construction of a specific project that would directly affect the Mineral King Valley. Here, the Court was asked to follow a far more attenuated line of causation to the eventual injury of which the appellees complained—a general rate increase would allegedly cause increased use of nonrecyclable commodities as compared to recyclable goods, thus resulting in the need to use more natural resources to produce such goods, some of which resources might be taken from the Washington area, and resulting in more refuse that might be discarded in national parks in the Washington area. The railroads protest that the appellees could never prove that a general increase in rates would have this effect, and they contend that these allegations were a ploy to avoid the need to show some injury in fact.

Of course, pleadings must be something more than an ingenious academic exercise in the conceivable. A plaintiff must allege that he has been or will in fact be perceptibly harmed by the challenged agency action, not that he can imagine circumstances in which he could be affected by the agency's action. And it is equally clear that the allegations must be true and capable of proof at trial. But we deal here simply with the pleadings in which the appellees alleged a specific and perceptible harm that distinguished them from other citizens who had not used the natural resources that were claimed to be affected.[5] If, as

---

5. The Government urges us to limit standing to those who have been "significantly" affected by agency action. But, even if we could begin to define what such a test would mean, we think it fundamentally misconceived. "Injury in fact" re-

the railroads now assert, these allegations were in fact untrue, then the appellants should have moved for summary judgment on the standing issue and demonstrated to the District Court that the allegations were sham and raised no genuine issue of fact. . . . [6]

[On the merits, reaffirming Arrow Transportation Co. v. Southern R. Co., 372 U.S. 658 (1963), the Court held that the district court lacked power to grant the injunction, because the Interstate Commerce Act vested exclusive power in the Commission to suspend rates pending its final decision on their lawfulness. The Court specifically rejected the district court's conclusion that NEPA, enacted in 1969, had amended the Interstate Commerce Act sub silentio, thus creating an implicit exception to the Arrow holding and authorizing injunctive relief in an environmental case.]

[R]eversed and . . . remanded. . . .

MR. JUSTICE POWELL took no part in the consideration or decision of these cases.

[Justice Blackmun, with whom Justice Brennan joined, concurred in a separate opinion. Justice Douglas dissented on the merits but agreed that the plaintiffs had standing for the reasons stated in his dissenting opinion in Sierra Club. Justice Marshall dissented on the merits. Justice White, with whom the Chief Justice and Justice Rehnquist joined, dissented on the standing issue, stating in part: "To me, the alleged injuries are so remote, speculative and insubstantial in fact that they fail to confer standing. They become no more concrete, real or substantial when it is added that materials will cost more at the marketplace and that somehow the freight rate increase would increase air pollution. Allegations such as these are no more substantial and direct and no more qualify these plaintiffs to litigate than allegations of a taxpayer that governmental expenditures will increase his taxes and

flects the statutory requirement that a person be "adversely affected" or "aggrieved," and it serves to distinguish a person with a direct stake in the outcome of a litigation—even though small—from a person with a mere interest in the problem. We have allowed important interests to be vindicated by plaintiffs with no more at stake in the outcome of an action that a fraction of a vote, see Baker v. Carr, 369 U.S. 186; a five dollar fine and costs, see McGowan v. Maryland, 366 U.S. 420; and a $1.50 poll tax, Harper v. Virginia Bd. of Elections, 383 U.S. 663. While these cases were not dealing specifically with § 10 of the APA, we see no reason to adopt a more restrictive interpretation of "adversely affected" or "aggrieved." As Professor Davis has put it: "The basic idea that comes out in numerous cases is that an identifiable trifle is enough for standing to fight out a question of principle; the trifle is the basis for standing and the principle supplies the motivation." Davis, Standing: Taxpayers and Others, 35 U.Chi.L.Rev. 601, 613. See also K. Davis, Administrative Law Trea-

tise, §§ 22.09–5 to 22.09–6 (1970 Supplement).

6. The railroads object to the fact that the allegations were not more precise— that no specific "forest" was named, that there was no assertion of the existence of any lumbering camp or other extractive facility in the area. They claim that they have no way to answer such allegations which were wholly barren of specifics. But, if that were really a problem, the railroads could have moved for a more definite statement, see Rule 12(e), Fed.Rule Civ.Proc., and certainly normal civil discovery devices were available to the railroads.

Similarly, the District Court cannot be faulted for failing to take evidence on the issue of standing. This case came before the Court on motions to dismiss and for a preliminary injunction. If the railroads thought that it was necessary to take evidence, or if they believed summary judgment was appropriate, they could have moved for such relief.

have an impact on his pocketbook, Massachusetts v. Mellon, 262 U.S. 447, 486–489 (1923). . . . As I see the allegations in this case, they are in reality little different from the general interest allegations found insufficient and too remote in Sierra Club. If they are sufficient here, we are well on our way to permitting citizens at large to litigate any decisions of the Government which fall in an area of interest to them and with which they disagree."]

SIMON v. EASTERN KENTUCKY WELFARE RIGHTS ORGANIZATION

Supreme Court of the United States, 1976.
426 U.S. 26.

[Indigent persons and organizations composed of indigents sued the Secretary of the Treasury and the Commissioner of Internal Revenue, alleging that the Internal Revenue Service (IRS) had violated the Internal Revenue Code and the APA by issuing a Revenue Ruling which changed the standards under which a hospital could qualify for tax-exempt status as a corporation operated for "charitable purposes." [1] The prior ruling had required that the hospital "be operated to the extent of its financial ability for those not able to pay for the service rendered . . . ." The later ruling relaxed this requirement by providing that a hospital would be tax exempt as a "charitable" corporation if it "operates a full time emergency room and no one requiring emergency care is denied treatment," although it "otherwise ordinarily limits admissions to those who can pay the cost of their hospitalization . . . ."

The individual plaintiffs alleged that they subsisted below the poverty income levels established by the Federal Government and that they were suffering from medical conditions requiring hospital services. Each of the individuals described incidents in which they had applied to tax-exempt hospitals but had been refused admission because of their inability to pay a deposit or advance fee. Both lower courts upheld the plaintiffs' standing.]

MR. JUSTICE POWELL delivered the opinion of the Court. . . .

[W]hen a plaintiff's standing is brought into issue the relevant inquiry is whether, assuming justiciability of the claim, the plaintiff has shown an injury to himself that is likely to be redressed by a favorable decision. Absent such a showing, exercise of its power by a federal court would be gratuitous and thus inconsistent with the Art. III limitation. . . .

A federal court cannot ignore this requirement without overstepping its assigned role in our system of adjudicating only actual cases and controversies.[2] It is according to this settled principle that the

---

1. Hospitals operated for "charitable purposes" are exempt from income taxation and donors may deduct from their income contributions to such hospitals.

2. The Data Processing decision established a second, nonconstitutional standing requirement that the interest of the plaintiff, regardless of its nature in the absolute, at least be "arguably within the zone of interests to be protected or regulated" by the statutory framework within which his claim arises. As noted earlier, respondents in this case claim that they, and of course their particular interests involved

allegations of both the individual respondents and the respondent organizations must be tested for sufficiency. . . .

The complaint alleges specific occasions on which each of the individual respondents sought but was denied hospital services solely due to his indigency. . . . We thus assume, for purpose of analysis, that some members have been denied service. But injury at the hands of a hospital is insufficient by itself to establish a case or controversy in the context of this suit, for no hospital is a defendant. The only defendants are officials of the Department of the Treasury, and the only claims of illegal action respondents desire the courts to adjudicate are charged to those officials. . . . [T]he "case or controversy" limitation of Art. III still requires that a federal court act only to redress injury that fairly can be traced to the challenged action of the defendant, and not injury that results from the independent action of some third party not before the court.

The complaint here alleged only that petitioners, by the adoption of Revenue Ruling 69–545, had "encouraged" hospitals to deny services to indigents. The implicit corollary of this allegation is that a grant of respondents' requested relief, resulting in a requirement that all hospitals serve indigents as a condition to favorable tax treatment, would "discourage" hospitals from denying their services to respondents. But it does not follow from the allegation and its corollary that the denial of access to hospital services in fact results from petitioners' new Ruling, or that a court-ordered return by petitioners to their previous policy would result in these respondents' receiving the hospital services they desire. It is purely speculative whether the denials of service specified in the complaint fairly can be traced to petitioners' "encouragement" or instead result from decisions made by the hospitals without regard to the tax implications.

It is equally speculative whether the desired exercise of the court's remedial powers in this suit would result in the availability to respondents of such services. So far as the complaint sheds light, it is just as plausible that the hospitals to which respondents may apply for service would elect to forgo favorable tax treatment to avoid the undetermined financial drain of an increase in the level of uncompensated services. . . .

The principle of . . . Warth [infra p. 1070] controls this case. As stated in Warth . . . , indirectness of injury, while not necessarily fatal to standing, "may make it substantially more difficult to meet the minimum requirement of Art. III: to establish that, in fact, the asserted injury was the consequence of the defendants' actions, or that prospective relief will remove the harm." Respondents have failed to carry this burden. Speculative inferences are necessary to connect their injury to the challenged actions of petitioners.[3] Moreover, the complaint suggests no substantial likelihood that victory in this suit

in this suit, are the intended beneficiaries of the charitable organization provisions of the Code. In view of our disposition of this case, we need not consider this "zone of interests" test.

3. The courts below erroneously believed that United States v. SCRAP, supported respondents' standing. In SCRAP, although the injury was indirect and "the Court was asked to follow [an] attenuated

would result in respondents' receiving the hospital treatment they desire. A federal court, properly cognizant of the Art. III limitation upon its jurisdiction, must require more than respondents have shown before proceeding to the merits.[4]

[Justice Stevens did not participate. Justice Stewart concurring stated in part, "I cannot now imagine a case, at least outside the First Amendment area, where a person whose own tax liability was not affected ever could have standing to litigate the federal tax liability of someone else." Justices Brennan and Marshall concurred in the result on grounds of lack of ripeness but dissented from the Court's standing analysis, stating in part:

"Of course, the most disturbing aspect of today's opinion is the Court's insistence on resting its decision regarding standing squarely on the irreducible Art. III minimum of injury in fact, thereby effectively placing its holding beyond congressional power to rectify. Thus, any time Congress chooses to legislate in favor of certain interests by setting up a scheme of incentives for third parties, judicial review of administrative action that allegedly frustrates the congressionally intended objective will be denied, because any complainant will be required to make an almost impossible showing. Clearly the Legislative Branch of the Government cannot supply injured individuals with the means to make the factual showing in a specific context that the Court today requires. More specific indications of a congressional desire to confer standing upon such individuals would be germane, not to the Art. III injury-in-fact requirement, but only to the Court's 'zone of interest' test for standing, that branch of standing lore which the Court assiduously avoids reaching."][5]

NOTES

(1) In WARTH v. SELDIN, 422 U.S. 490 (1975), cited in Simon v. EKWRO, members of low-income and minority groups, and others, brought an action against the Town of Penfield and its officers, alleging a violation of constitutional rights because Penfield's restrictive zoning

line of causation," the complaint nevertheless "alleged a specific and perceptible harm" flowing from the agency action. Such a complaint withstood a motion to dismiss, although it might not have survived challenge on a motion for summary judgment. But in this case the complaint is insufficient even to survive a motion to dismiss, for it fails to allege an injury that fairly can be traced to petitioners' challenged action.

4. [Ed.] For discussion of Justice Powell's opinions on standing in Warth v. Seldin and Simon v. EKWRO, see G. Leedes, Mr. Justice Powell's Standing, 11 U.Rich.L. Rev. 269 (1977).

5. [Ed.] See N. Lewin, Avoiding the Supreme Court, N.Y. Times Mag. Sec., Oct. 1, 1976, p. 31, 98: "The public-interest lawyers are still holding their heads over East-

ern Kentucky, which aggravates limitations imposed by earlier 'standing' decisions. [One public interest lawyer] says the most damaging effect of these rulings is that they 'unleashed hostile district judges' who are able to stop a public-interest case in its early stages by dismissing it on the ground that the plaintiffs have no legal right to sue. 'We eat up our energies submitting memoranda and presenting legal argument on these preliminary questions, and if a trial judge decides against us—even if we have *his* decision quickly overruled—we have been stalled for months or years.' The public-interest groups are now wondering what possessed them to bring so unpromising a case as Eastern Kentucky up to the Supreme Court and give it the opportunity to administer such a crushing blow."

practices had made "practically and economically impossible the construction of sufficient numbers of low and moderate income . . . housing . . . to satisfy the minimum housing requirements" of Penfield and the Metropolitan Rochester, N.Y. area. The Court held, per Justice Powell, that plaintiffs lacked standing:

". . . In essence the question of standing is whether the litigant is entitled to have the court decide the merits of the dispute or of particular issues. This inquiry involves both constitutional limitations on federal-court jurisdiction and prudential limitations on its exercise. In both dimensions it is founded in concern about the proper—and properly limited—role of the courts in a democratic society.

"In its constitutional dimension, standing imports justiciability: whether the plaintiff has made out a 'case or controversy' between himself and the defendant within the meaning of Art. III . . . on his behalf. The Art. III judicial power exists only to redress or otherwise to protect against injury to the complaining party, even though the court's judgment may benefit others collaterally. A federal court's jurisdiction therefore can be invoked only when the plaintiff himself has suffered 'some threatened or actual injury resulting from the putatively illegal action . . . .'

"Apart from this minimum constitutional mandate, this Court has recognized other [prudential] limits on the class of persons who may invoke the courts' decisional and remedial powers. First, the Court has held that when the asserted harm is a 'generalized grievance' shared in substantially equal measure by all or a large class of citizens, that harm alone normally does not warrant exercise of jurisdiction. Second, even when the plaintiff has alleged injury sufficient to meet the 'case or controversy' requirement, this Court has held that the plaintiff generally must assert his own legal rights and interests, and cannot rest his claim to relief on the legal rights or interests of third parties. Without such limitations—closely related to Art. III concerns but essentially matters of judicial self-governance—the courts would be called upon to decide abstract questions of wide public significance even though other governmental institutions may be more competent to address the questions and even though judicial intervention may be unnecessary to protect individual rights.

. . .

"With these general considerations in mind, we turn . . . to the claims of petitioners . . ., each of whom asserts standing as a person of low or moderate income and, coincidentally, as a member of a minority racial or ethnic group. We must assume, taking the allegations of the complaint as true, that Penfield's zoning ordinance and the pattern of enforcement by respondent officials have had the purpose and effect of excluding persons of low and moderate income, many of whom are members of racial or ethnic minority groups. We also assume, for purposes here, that such intentional exclusionary practices, if proved in a proper case, would be adjudged violative of the constitutional and statutory rights of the persons excluded. . . .

"In their complaint, petitioners . . . alleged in conclusory terms that they are among the persons excluded by respondents' actions. None of them has ever resided in Penfield; each claims at least implicitly that he desires, or has desired, to do so. Each asserts, moreover, that he made some effort, at some time, to locate housing in Penfield that was at once within his means and adequate for his family's needs. Each claims that his efforts proved fruitless. We may assume, as petitioners allege, that respondents' actions have contributed, perhaps substantially, to the cost of housing in Penfield. But there remains the question whether petitioners' inability to locate suitable housing in Penfield reasonably can be said to have resulted, in any concretely demonstrable way, from respondents' alleged constitutional and statutory infractions. Petitioners must allege facts from which it reasonably could be inferred that, absent the respondents' restrictive zoning practices, there is a substantial probability that they would have been able to purchase or lease in Penfield and that, if the court affords the relief requested, the asserted inability of petitioners will be removed.

"We find the record devoid of the necessary allegations. As the Court of Appeals noted, none of these petitioners has a present interest in any Penfield property; none is himself subject to the ordinance's strictures; and none has ever been denied a variance or permit by respondent officials. Instead, petitioners claim that respondents' enforcement of the ordinance against third parties—developers, builders, and the like—has had the consequence of precluding the construction of housing suitable to their needs at prices they might be able to afford. . . .

"Here, by their own admission, realization of petitioners' desire to live in Penfield always has depended on the efforts and willingness of third parties to build low- and moderate-cost housing. The record specifically refers to only two such efforts . . . . But the record is devoid of any indication that these projects, or other like projects, would have satisfied petitioners' needs at prices they could afford, or that, were the court to remove the obstructions attributable to respondents, such relief would benefit petitioners. Indeed, petitioners' descriptions of their individual financial situations and housing needs suggest precisely the contrary—that their inability to reside in Penfield is the consequence of the economics of the area housing market, rather than of respondents' assertedly illegal acts. In short, the facts alleged fail to support an actionable causal relationship between Penfield's zoning practices and petitioners' asserted injury. . . .

"We hold only that a plaintiff who seeks to challenge exclusionary zoning practices must allege specific, concrete facts demonstrating that the challenged practices harm *him,* and that he personally would benefit in a tangible way from the court's intervention.[1] . . ."

---

1. This is not to say that the plaintiff who challenges a zoning ordinance or zoning practices must have a present contractual interest in a particular project. A particularized personal interest may be shown in various ways, which we need not undertake to identify in the abstract. But usually the initial focus should be on a particular project. We also note that zoning laws and their provisions, long consid-

Justices Douglas, Brennan, White and Marshall dissented.

(2) VILLAGE OF ARLINGTON HEIGHTS V. METROPOLITAN HOUSING DEVEL-
OPMENT CORP., 429 U.S. 252 (1977). Metropolitan Housing Development
Corp. (MHDC) contracted to buy land in the Village of Arlington
Heights in order to build racially integrated low- and moderate-income
housing. The contract was contingent upon MHDC's securing a rezoning of the land from single-family to multiple-family classification. The
Village denied the rezoning request; MHDC and three black individuals sued the Village in federal district court alleging a violation of the
Fourteenth Amendment and the Fair Housing Act. The Court, in an
opinion by Justice Powell, held that MHDC and one of the three
individuals had standing:

"[T]here can be little doubt that MHDC meets the constitutional
standing requirements. The challenged action of the petitioners stands
as an absolute barrier to constructing the housing MHDC had contracted to place on the Viatorian site. If MHDC secures the injunctive relief
it seeks, that barrier will be removed. An injunction would not, of
course, guarantee that Lincoln Green will be built. MHDC would still
have to secure financing, qualify for federal subsidies, and carry
through with construction. But all housing developments are subject
to some extent to similar uncertainties. When a project is as detailed
and specific as Lincoln Green, a court is not required to engage in
undue speculation as a predicate for finding that the plaintiff has the
requisite personal stake in the controversy. MHDC has shown an
injury to itself that is 'likely to be redressed by a favorable decision.'
Simon v. Eastern Ky. Welfare Rights Org., 426 U.S., at 38.

"Clearly MHDC has met the constitutional requirements and it
therefore has standing to assert its own rights. Foremost among them
is MHDC's right to be free of arbitrary or irrational zoning actions.
But the heart of this litigation has never been the claim that the
Village's decision [violates our zoning decisions]. Instead it has been
the claim that the Village's refusal to rezone discriminates against
racial minorities in violation of the Fourteenth Amendment. As a
corporation, MHDC has no racial identity and cannot be the direct
target of the petitioners' alleged discrimination. In the ordinary case, a
party is denied standing to assert the rights of third persons. Warth v.
Seldin, 422 U.S., at 499. But we need not decide whether the circumstances of this case would justify departure from that prudential
limitation and permit MHDC to assert the constitutional rights of its
prospective minority tenants. For we have at least one individual
plaintiff who has demonstrated standing to assert these rights as his
own.

"Respondent Ransom, a Negro, works at the Honeywell factory in
Arlington Heights and lives approximately 20 miles away in Evanston
in a 5-room house with his mother and his son. The complaint alleged
that he seeks and would qualify for the housing MHDC wants to build

ered essential to effective urban planning,
are peculiarly within the province of state
and local legislative authorities. They are,
of course, subject to judicial review in a
proper case. But citizens dissatisfied with
provisions of such laws need not overlook
the availability of the normal democratic
process.

in Arlington Heights. Ransom testified at trial that if Lincoln Green were built he would probably move there, since it is closer to his job.

"The injury Ransom asserts is that his quest for housing nearer his employment has been thwarted by official action that is racially discriminatory. If a court grants the relief he seeks, there is at least a 'substantial probability,' Warth v. Seldin, at 504, that the Lincoln Green project will materialize, affording Ransom the housing opportunity he desires in Arlington Heights. His is not a generalized grievance. Instead, as we suggested in Warth, it focuses on a particular project and is not dependent on speculation about the possible actions of third parties not before the court. Unlike the individual plaintiffs in Warth, Ransom has adequately averred an 'actionable causal relationship' between Arlington Heights' zoning practices and his asserted injury."

Justice Stevens did not participate. Justices Brennan, White and Marshall dissented on other grounds.

(3) The causation and redressability requirement emphasized in Simon and Warth continues to play its frustrating role in standing law. See, e.g., ALLEN v. WRIGHT, 468 U.S. 737 (1984). The case is summarized as follows in The Supreme Court, 1983 Term, 98 Harv.L.Rev. 1, 237 (1984):[2]

"Until 1971, the IRS generally accepted all private schools as charitable organizations; the schools' income was therefore tax-exempt and their donors' contributions deductible. In 1971, however, the District Court for the District of Columbia enjoined the IRS from granting such tax benefits to private schools in Mississippi that discriminated on the basis of race. The IRS soon thereafter implemented a nationwide policy similar to that embodied in the court order and adopted corresponding guidelines to identify the discriminatory private schools that would be subject to the new policy.

"In 1976, parents of black children who attended public schools in districts in the process of desegregation challenged the adequacy of the IRS's guidelines in a nationwide class action in the District Court for the District of Columbia. While the suit was pending, the IRS prepared new guidelines that would have identified more private schools as discriminatory. Extremely hostile public and congressional reaction to the new guidelines prompted the House of Representatives quickly to pass two amendments to its Treasury Department appropriations bill— measures designed to deny the IRS the funds to enforce the new guidelines or to promulgate any other guidelines that would alter the tax-exempt status of any private school. Soon after this congressional action, the district court dismissed the parents' class action suit, partly on the basis that the plaintiffs lacked standing because they could not show injury in fact. The United States Court of Appeals for the District of Columbia Circuit reversed. It found that the plaintiffs had standing to maintain the lawsuit because the injury they alleged was one that had traditionally been shown special solicitude by the federal courts.

---

2. The editors' extensive footnote documentation has been omitted.

"The Supreme Court reversed, holding that the plaintiffs lacked standing. Writing for a 5–3 majority, Justice O'Connor began the Court's analysis with the generalization that the 'law of Art. III standing is built on a single basic idea—the idea of separation of powers.' The Court then examined the two injuries alleged by the plaintiffs. The plaintiffs claimed, first, that the tax exemptions injured them directly because the exemptions constituted 'tangible federal financial aid . . . for racially segregated institutions.' The Court, noting that the mere fact of government noncompliance with the law could not itself constitute injury in fact, characterized the allegation of injury as a claim that tax exemptions for racially segregated private schools injured plaintiffs by stigmatizing them. The Court rejected this argument on the ground that the plaintiffs, by failing to allege that their children had ever applied or planned to apply to such schools, had not claimed to have been personally denied equal treatment. Without alleging the personal denial of equal treatment, the Court asserted, the plaintiffs could not claim as an article III injury their having been stigmatized by government conduct.

"Plaintiffs also claimed that the preferential tax treatment helped to provide segregated private school alternatives for white children and thus diminished the ability of plaintiffs' children to obtain a public education in integrated schools. The Court acknowledged that such injury is 'one of the most serious injuries recognized in our legal system,' but nonetheless found that the plaintiffs lacked standing because they failed to meet either prong of the causality requirement. The injury was not 'fairly traceable' to the challenged conduct, and the prospect that the relief requested would remedy the harm was 'entirely speculative.' The majority stated that the injury would be fairly traceable to the challenged conduct 'only if there were enough racially discriminatory private schools receiving tax exemptions . . . for withdrawal of those exemptions to make an appreciable difference in public school integration.' The majority also maintained that there was insufficient likelihood of redressability because there was no showing that a change in the IRS guidelines would affect the behavior of even admittedly discriminatory schools or the students attending them."

Justices Brennan and Stevens each filed a dissenting opinion. Justice Blackmun joined Justice Stevens and Justice Marshall did not participate.

DUKE POWER CO. v. NORTH CAROLINA ENVIRONMENTAL GROUP, INC.

Supreme Court of the United States, 1978.
438 U.S. 59.

[In order to protect the public and encourage the development of the atomic energy industry, the Price-Anderson Act limits the aggregate liability for a single nuclear accident to a fixed amount, now $560 million. Duke Power Co., an investor-owned public utility was licensed by the Atomic Energy Commission to construct a nuclear power plant in North Carolina and another in South Carolina. Two organizations and 40 individuals who live within close proximity to the proposed plants instituted an action against Duke and the Atomic Energy Commission (later replaced by the Nuclear Regulatory Commission (NRC) as the licensing and regulatory authority) which in part sought a declaration that the Price-Anderson Act is unconstitutional. Defendants moved to dismiss on grounds that the plaintiffs lacked standing and that the claims were not ripe for decision. The district court, after conducting four days of hearings on these issues, held that plaintiffs had standing, the matter was ripe, and the Act was unconstitutional in that it violated (1) the due process clause of the Fifth Amendment because it allowed injuries to occur without assuring adequate compensation to the victims and (2) the equal protection component of the Fifth Amendment by forcing the victims of nuclear incidents to bear the burden of injury, whereas society as a whole benefits from the existence and development of nuclear power. The Supreme Court affirmed the standing and ripeness holdings but reversed on the merits.]

MR. CHIEF JUSTICE BURGER delivered the opinion of the Court.
. . .

The essence of the standing inquiry is whether the parties seeking to invoke the court's jurisdiction have "alleged such a personal stake in the outcome of the controversy as to assure that concrete adverseness which sharpens the presentation of issues upon which the court so largely depends for illumination of difficult constitutional questions." Baker v. Carr, 369 U.S. 186, 204 (1962). As refined by subsequent reformulation, this requirement of a "personal stake" has come to be understood to require not only a "distinct and palpable injury," to the plaintiff, Warth v. Seldin, 422 U.S. 490, 501, but also a "fairly traceable" causal connection between the claimed injury and the challenged conduct. Arlington Heights v. Metropolitan Housing Corp., 429 U.S. 252, 261 (1977). Application of these constitutional standards to the factual findings of the District Court persuades us that the Art. III requisites for standing are satisfied by appellees.

We turn first to consider the kinds of injuries the District Court found the appellees suffered. It discerned two categories of effects which resulted from the operation of nuclear power plants in potentially dangerous proximity to appellees' living and working environment. The immediate effects included: (a) the production of small quantities of non-natural radiation which would invade the air and water; (b) a "sharp increase" in the temperature of two lakes presently used for recreational purposes resulting from the use of the lake waters to produce steam and to cool the reactor; (c) interference with the normal use of the waters of the Catawba River; (d) threatened reduction in property values of land neighboring the power plants; (e) "objectively reasonable" present fear and apprehension regarding the "effect of the increased radioactivity in the air, land and water upon [appellees] and their property, and the genetic effects upon their descendants"; and (f) the continual threat of "an accident resulting in uncontrolled release of large or even small quantities of radioactive material" with no assurance of adequate compensation for the resultant damage. Into a second category of potential effects were placed the damages "which may result from a core melt or other major accident in the operation of a reactor. . . . "

For purposes of the present inquiry, we need not determine whether all the putative injuries identified by the District Court, particularly those based on the possibility of a nuclear accident and the present apprehension generated by this future uncertainty, are sufficiently concrete to satisfy constitutional requirements. It is enough that several of the "immediate" adverse effects were found to harm appellees. Certainly the environmental and aesthetic consequences of the thermal pollution of the two lakes in the vicinity of the disputed power plants is the type of harmful effect which has been deemed adequate in prior cases to satisfy the "injury in fact" standard. See United States v. SCRAP. And the emission of non-natural radiation into appellees' environment would also seem a direct and present injury given our generalized concern about exposure to radiation and the apprehension flowing from the uncertainty about the health and genetic consequences of even small emissions like those concededly emitted by nuclear power plants.

The more difficult step in the standing inquiry is establishing that these injuries "fairly can be traced to the challenged action of the defendant," Simon v. Eastern Kentucky Welfare Rights Org., 426 U.S. 26, 41, or put otherwise, that the exercise of the Court's remedial powers would redress the claimed injuries. The District Court discerned a "but for" causal connection between the Price-Anderson Act, which appellees challenged as unconstitutional, "and the construction of the nuclear plants which the [appellees] view as a threat to them." 431 F.Supp. 219. Particularizing that causal link to the facts of the instant case, the District Court concluded that "there is a substantial likelihood that Duke would not be able to complete the construction and maintain the operation of the McGuire and Catawba Nuclear Plants but for the protection provided by the Price-Anderson Act."

These findings, which, if accepted, would likely satisfy the second prong of the constitutional test for standing as elaborated in Simon,[1] are challenged on two grounds. First, it is argued that the evidence presented at the hearing, contrary to the conclusion reached by the District Court, indicated that the McGuire and Catawba nuclear plants would be completed and operated without the Price-Anderson Act's limitation on liability. And second, it is contended that the Price-Anderson Act is not, in some essential sense, the "but for" cause of the disputed nuclear power plants and resultant adverse effects since if the Act had not been passed Congress may well have chosen to pursue the nuclear program as a government monopoly as it had from 1946 until 1954. We reject both of these arguments. . . .

1. Our recent cases have required no more than a showing that there is a "substantial likelihood" that the relief requested will redress the injury claimed to satisfy the second prong of the constitutional standing requirement. See Arlington Heights v. MHDC, 429 U.S. 252, 262, quoting Simon v. Eastern Kentucky Welfare Rights Organization, 426 U.S. 26, 38 ("MHDC has shown an injury to itself that is 'likely to be redressed by a favorable decision' "). See also Warth v. Seldin, 422 U.S. 490, 504, 506–507.

[As to the first, the district court's finding was not clearly erroneous and therefore the Court is required to accept it. As to the second:]

[I]t is not responsive to the simple proposition that private power companies now do in fact operate the nuclear powered generating plants injuring appellees and that their participation would not have occurred but for the enactment and implementation of the Price-Anderson Act. Nothing in our prior cases requires a party seeking to invoke federal jurisdiction to negate the kind of speculative and hypothetical possibilities suggested in order to demonstrate the likely effectiveness of judicial relief.

It is further contended that in addition to proof of injury and of a causal link between such injury and the challenged conduct, appellees must demonstrate a connection between the injuries they claim and the constitutional rights being asserted. This nexus requirement is said to find its origin in Flast v. Cohen, 392 U.S. 83 (1968), where the general question of taxpayer standing was considered. "The nexus demanded of federal taxpayers has two aspects to it. First, the taxpayers must establish a logical link between that status and the type of legislative enactment attacked. . . . Secondly, the taxpayer must establish a nexus between that status and the precise nature of the constitutional infringement alleged." Since the environmental and health injuries claimed by appellees are not directly related to the constitutional attack on the Price-Anderson Act, such injuries, the argument continues, cannot supply a predicate for standing.[2] We decline to accept this argument.

The major difficulty with the argument is that it implicitly assumes that the nexus requirement formulated in the context of taxpayer suits has general applicability in suits of all other types brought in the federal courts. No cases have been cited outside the context of taxpayer suits where we have demanded this type of subject matter nexus between the right asserted and the injury alleged and we are aware of none. We . . . cannot accept the contention that, outside the context of taxpayers' suits, a litigant must demonstrate anything more than injury in fact and a substantial likelihood that the judicial relief requested will prevent or redress the claimed injury to satisfy the "case and controversy" requirement of Art. III.

Our prior cases have, however, . . . narrowly limited the circumstances in which one party will be given standing to assert the legal rights of another. "[E]ven when the plaintiff has alleged injury sufficient to meet the 'case or controversy' requirement, this Court has held that the plaintiff generally must assert his own legal rights and interests, and cannot rest his claim to relief in the legal rights or interests of third parties." Warth v. Seldin, supra.

This limitation on third party standing arguably suggests a connection between the claimed injury and the right asserted bearing some resemblance to the nexus requirement now urged upon us.

---

2. The only injury that would possess the required subject matter nexus to the due process challenge is the injury that would result from a nuclear accident causing damages in excess of the liability limitation provisions of the Price-Anderson Act.

There are good and sufficient reasons for this prudential limitation on standing when rights of third parties are implicated—the avoidance of the adjudication of rights which those not before the Court may not wish to assert, and the assurance that the most effective advocate of the rights at issue is present to champion them. We do not, however, find these reasons a satisfactory predicate for applying this limitation or a similar nexus requirement to all cases as a matter of course. Where a party champions his own rights, and where the injury alleged is a concrete and particularized one which will be prevented or redressed by the relief requested, the basic practical and prudential concerns underlying the standing doctrine are generally satisfied when the constitutional requisites are met.

We conclude that appellees have standing to challenge the constitutionality of the Price-Anderson Act.[3] . . .

MR. JUSTICE STEWART, concurring in the result. . . .

On the issue of standing, the Court relies on the "present" injuries of increased water temperatures and low-level radiation emissions. Even assuming that but for the Act the plant would not exist and therefore neither would its effects on the environment, I cannot believe that it follows that the appellees have standing to attack the constitutionality of the Act. Apart from a but-for connection in the loosest sense of that concept, there is no relationship at all between the injury alleged for standing purposes and the injury alleged for federal subject matter jurisdiction.

Surely a plaintiff does not have standing simply because his challenge, if successful, will remove the injury relied on for standing purposes *only* because it will put the defendant out of existence. Surely there must be *some* direct relationship between the plaintiff's federal claim and the injury relied on for standing. . . . An interest in the local water temperature does not, in short, give these appellees standing to bring a suit under 28 U.S.C. § 1331 to challenge the constitutionality of a law limiting liability in an unrelated and as-yet-to-occur major nuclear accident.

For these reasons, I would remand this case to the District Court with instructions to dismiss the complaint.

MR. JUSTICE REHNQUIST, with whom MR. JUSTICE STEVENS joins, concurring in the judgment.

3. Mr. Justice Rehnquist undertakes to sever the action of the NRC in executing indemnity agreements under the Act from the Act's alleged constitutional infirmities—particularly the liability limitation provisions. Careful examination of the statutory mechanism indicates that such a separation simply cannot be sustained. The execution of the indemnification agreements by the NRC triggers the statutory ceiling on liability which in terms, applies only to "persons indemnified." See 42 U.S.C. § 2210(e). Thus, absent the exe- cution of such agreements between the NRC and the licensees, the liability limitation provisions of the Act, to which appellees object, would simply not come into play. This fact coupled with the District Court's finding that "but for" the liability limitation provisions there is a substantial likelihood that the contemplated plants would not be built or operated, is sufficient to establish the justiciability of appellees' claim against the Commission. See Simon v. Eastern Ky. Welfare Rights Org., 426 U.S., at 44–46.

I can understand the Court's willingness to reach the merits of this case and thereby remove the doubt which has been cast over this important federal statute. In so doing, however, it ignores established limitations on District Court jurisdiction as carefully defined in our statutes and cases. Because I believe the preservation of these limitations is in the long run more important to this Court's jurisprudence than the resolution of any particular case or controversy, however important, I too would reverse the judgment of the District Court, but would do so with instructions to dismiss the complaint for want of jurisdiction. . . .

. . . [T]here is no allegation in this complaint that the Nuclear Regulatory Commission has taken or will take any unconstitutional action at all. The complaint alleges only that the Commission granted construction permits to Duke, and that it will enter into an agreement "to indemnify Duke for any nuclear incident exceeding the amount of $125,000,000, subject to a maximum liability of $560,000,000." Neither of these actions is alleged to be unconstitutional. The gist of the complaint is the asserted unconstitutionality of 42 U.S.C. § 2210(e) which limits Duke's liability. But this limitation of liability is separate and apart from the indemnity agreement which the Commission is authorized to execute under 42 U.S.C. § 2210(d). The Commission has nothing whatever to do with the administration of the limitation of liability; whatever administration of that statute there is to be is left in the hands of the District Court. 42 U.S.C. § 2210(o). The District Court, of course, is not a party to this suit.

It simply cannot be said that these allegations make out an actual controversy against the Commission. While the Commission may be quite interested in the constitutionality of the statute, that is hardly sufficient to establish a justiciable controversy. Muskrat v. United States, 219 U.S. 346, 361–362 (1911). While appellees may have been damaged by Duke's decision to construct these plants, there is no "challenged action of the defendant" Commission to which their damage "fairly can be traced." Simon v. Eastern Kentucky Welfare Rights Org., 426 U.S. 26, 41 (1976). If Duke decided to proceed with construction despite a declaration of the statute's unconstitutionality, there would be nothing that the Commission could do to aid appellees. Where the prospect of effective relief against a defendant depends on the actions of a third party, no justiciable controversy exists against that defendant. Warth v. Seldin, 422 U.S. 490, 505 (1975). In short, appellees' only conceivable controversy is with Duke, over whom the District Court had no jurisdiction. . . .

MR. JUSTICE STEVENS, concurring in the judgment.

The string of contingencies that supposedly holds this case together is too delicate for me. We are told that but for the Price-Anderson Act there would be no financing of nuclear power plants, no development of those plants by private parties; and hence no present injury to persons such as appellees; we are then asked to remedy an alleged due process violation that may possibly occur at some uncertain time in the future, and may possibly injure the appellees in a way that has no significant connection with any present injury. It is remarkable that such a series of speculations is considered sufficient either to make this case ripe for decision or to establish appellees' standing;[4] it is even more remarkable that this occurs in a case in which, as Mr. Justice Rehnquist demonstrates, there is no federal jurisdiction in the first place.

The Court's opinion will serve the national interest in removing doubts concerning the constitutionality of the Price-Anderson Act. I cannot, therefore, criticize the statesmanship of the Court's decision to provide the country with an advisory opinion on an important subject. Nevertheless, my view of the proper function of this Court, or of any other federal court, in the structure of our government is more limited. We are not statesmen; we are judges. When it is necessary to resolve a constitutional issue in the adjudication of an actual case or controversy, it is our duty to do so. But whenever we are persuaded by reasons of expediency to engage in the business of giving legal advice, we chip away a part of the foundation of our independence and our strength.[5]

SECTION 4. TIMING OF JUDICIAL REVIEW

The problem considered here is whether a petitioner seeking judicial assistance has prematurely resorted to the courts. Assuming that petitioner has selected the proper method of review, that review is not precluded by statute, that the agency's action is not committed to agency discretion and that petitioner has standing, will the administrative action in question be reviewed at this stage of the proceedings, or will it only be reviewed at a later time if and when further administrative action has been taken? The law's answer to this problem of timing is contained in the overlapping doctrines of: (1) exhaustion—petitioner must exhaust available administrative remedies before seeking judicial assistance; (2) finality—in order for agency action to be reviewed, it must be "final agency action" within the meaning of section 704 of the APA;[1] and (3) ripeness—the agency's action must be "ripe" for review. Primary jurisdiction presents a different but related problem—whether a plaintiff who institutes a traditional lawsuit against a private party will be required to postpone that lawsuit until an administrative agency has expressed its judgment concerning some or all of the issues involved in the lawsuit.

In considering these doctrines, note that considerations relevant to solving problems of availability of review and standing often are appli-

---

4. With respect to whether appellees' claim of present injury is sufficient to establish standing, it should be noted that some sort of financing is essential to almost all projects, public or private. Statutes that facilitate and may be essential to the financing abound—from tax statutes to statutes prohibiting fraudulent securities transactions. One would not assume, however, that mere neighbors have standing to litigate the legality of a utility's financing.

5. [Ed.] For critical discussion of Duke Power, see W. Rudolph and J. Rudolph,

Standing: A Legal Process Approach, 36 S.W.L.J. 857, 891–894 (1982).

1. Or otherwise made reviewable by statute. The first two sentences of section 704 provide as follows:

"Agency action made reviewable by statute and final agency action for which there is no other adequate remedy in a court are subject to judicial review. A preliminary, procedural, or intermediate agency action or ruling not directly reviewable is subject to review on the review of the final agency action."

cable also to issues of exhaustion, finality and ripeness. As Professor Davis has observed, "In many cases . . . problems of standing and ripeness are merged; a party may lack standing because what has happened to him is not far enough developed, but the lack of development may be the essence of unripeness. . . . Similarly, an unripe question can be called an unreviewable question. . . . Both ripeness and exhaustion deal with timing of judicial review; the ripeness focus is on the types of functions that courts should perform, and the exhaustion focus is on the narrow question of how far a party must pursue an administrative remedy before going to court; the two often overlap." 4 K. Davis, Admin.Law Treatise 350 (1983).[2]

a. Exhaustion of Administrative Remedies

MYERS v. BETHLEHEM SHIPBUILDING CORP.

Supreme Court of the United States, 1938.
303 U.S. 41.

[Bethlehem brought a bill in equity against officials of the National Labor Relations Board to enjoin them from holding a hearing on a complaint issued by the Board against Bethlehem. The injunction issued and the court of appeals affirmed. The Supreme Court granted certiorari.]

MR. JUSTICE BRANDEIS delivered the opinion of the Court. . . .

First. There is no claim by the Corporation that the statutory provisions and the rules of procedure prescribed for such hearings are illegal; or that the Corporation was not accorded ample opportunity to answer the complaint of the Board; or that opportunity to introduce evidence on the allegations made will be denied. The claim is that the provisions of the Act are not applicable to the Corporation's business at the Fore River Plant, because the operations conducted there are not carried on, and the products manufactured are not sold, in interstate or foreign commerce; that, therefore, the Corporation's relations with its employees at the plant cannot burden or interfere with such commerce; that hearings would, at best, be futile; and that the holding of them would result in irreparable damage to the Corporation, not only by reason of their direct cost and the loss of time of its officials and employees, but also because the hearings would cause serious impairment of the good will and harmonious relations existing between the Corporation and its employees, and thus seriously impair the efficiency of its operations.[3]

Second. The District Court is without jurisdiction to enjoin hearings because the power "to prevent any person from engaging in any unfair practice affecting commerce" has been vested by Congress in the Board and the Circuit Court of Appeals, and Congress has declared:

---

2. See also Leedes, supra note 2, p. 1032.

3. It is alleged that in 1934 and 1935 the predecessor of the present National Labor Relations Board instituted somewhat similar action against the Corpora-

tion. Although the proceedings were eventually dismissed, the hearings consumed a total of some 2500 hours of working time of officials and employees and cost the Corporation more than $15,000, none of which could be recovered.

"This power shall be exclusive, and shall not be affected by any other means of adjustment or prevention that has been or may be established by agreement, code, law, or otherwise." The grant of that exclusive power is constitutional, because the act provided for appropriate procedure before the Board and in the review by the Circuit Court of Appeals an adequate opportunity to secure judicial protection against possible illegal action on the part of the Board. No power to enforce an order is conferred upon the Board. To secure enforcement, the Board must apply to a Circuit Court of Appeals for its affirmance. And, until the Board's order has been affirmed by the appropriate Circuit Court of Appeals, no penalty accrues for disobeying it. The independent right to apply to a Circuit Court of Appeals to have an order set aside is conferred upon any party aggrieved by the proceeding before the Board. The Board is even without power to enforce obedience to its subpoena to testify or to produce written evidence. To enforce obedience it must apply to a District Court; and to such an application appropriate defense may be made. . . .

It is true that the Board has jurisdiction only if the complaint concerns interstate or foreign commerce. Unless the Board finds that it does, the complaint must be dismissed. And if it finds that interstate or foreign commerce is involved, but the Circuit Court of Appeals concludes that such finding was without adequate evidence to support it, or otherwise contrary to law, the Board's petition to enforce it will be dismissed, or the employer's petition to have it set aside will be granted. Since the procedure before the Board is appropriate and the judicial review so provided as adequate, Congress had power to vest exclusive jurisdiction in the Board and the Circuit Court of Appeals. . . .

Third. The Corporation contends that, since it denies that interstate or foreign commerce is involved and claims that a hearing would subject it to irreparable damage, rights guaranteed by the Federal Constitution will be denied unless it be held that the District Court has jurisdiction to enjoin the holding of a hearing by the Board. So to hold would, as the government insists, in effect substitute the District Court for the Board as the tribunal to hear and determine what Congress declared the Board exclusively should hear and determine in the first instance. The contention is at war with the long-settled rule of judicial administration that no one is entitled to judicial relief for a supposed or threatened injury until the prescribed administrative remedy has been exhausted.[4] That rule has been repeatedly acted on in cases where, as here, the contention is made that the administrative body lacked power over the subject matter.

Obviously, the rule requiring exhaustion of the administrative remedy cannot be circumvented by asserting that the charge on which the complaint rests is groundless and that the mere holding of the prescribed administrative hearing would result in irreparable damage. Lawsuits also often prove to have been groundless; but no way has

---

4. The rule has been most frequently applied in equity where relief by injunction was sought. . . . But because the rule is one of judicial administration—not merely a rule governing the exercise of discretion—it is applicable to proceedings at law as well as suits in equity. . . .

been discovered of relieving a defendant from the necessity of a trial to establish the fact. . . .

Decrees for preliminary injunction reversed, with direction to dismiss the bills.

MR. JUSTICE CARDOZO took no part in the consideration or decision of this case.[5]

NOTES

(1) The Myers decision is a leading case in the law of exhaustion of remedies and later courts often have repeated Justice Brandeis' statement concerning "the long-settled rule of judicial administration that no one is entitled to judicial relief for a supposed or threatened injury until the prescribed administrative remedy has been exhausted." As you study the materials in this section you should appraise the validity of this well known dictum.[1]

(2) TOUCHE ROSS & CO. v. SECURITIES AND EXCHANGE COMMISSION, 609 F.2d 570 (2d Cir.1979). Pursuant to Rule 2(e) of its Rules of Practice [2], the SEC instituted an administrative proceeding to determine whether Touche Ross & Co., a nationwide accounting firm, and three of its former partners (hereafter referred to collectively as "Touche Ross") should be censured or suspended from appearing or practicing before the Commission. Six weeks later Touche Ross brought an action against the SEC and four of its members to enjoin the administrative proceeding and for a declaratory judgment that Rule 2(e) had been promulgated "without any authority;" that the proceeding had been instituted against them "without authority of law;" and that since the SEC does not constitute an impartial forum, the administrative proceedings would deny Touche Ross due process of law. The district court

---

5. [Ed.] See also Leedom v. Kyne, 358 U.S. 184 (1958) and Boire v. Greyhound Corp., 376 U.S. 473 (1964), supra pp. 1003–1004.

Compare Grutka v. Barbour, 549 F.2d 5 (7th Cir.), cert. denied 431 U.S. 908 (1977), in which the Bishop of the Roman Catholic Diocese of Gary, Indiana, sued the NLRB's regional director seeking a declaration that the National Labor Relations Act was unconstitutional as applied to lay teachers in parochial schools and an injunction prohibiting the NLRB from holding a representation election in the schools operated by the Diocese. The court distinguished Leedom and held that "[s]ince the dimension of state-church entanglement can only be intelligently assessed against a developed factual background and since developing a factual record in labor disputes is a task peculiarly within the competence of the Board, we recognize the importance here of permitting the exhaustion doctrine to run its normal course. Because the Bishop does not seek review of agency action bottomed on the plain wording of a statute which is alleged to be facially unconstitu-

tional, the Boire teachings on the rare availability of district court review are freely transferrable to the constitutional realm."

1. See also M. Gelpe, Exhaustion of Administrative Remedies: Lessons from Environmental Cases, 53 Geo.Wash.L.Rev. 1 (1985).

2. Rule 2(e) of the SEC's Rules of Practice in relevant part provides:

"(e) Suspension and disbarment. (1) The Commission may deny, temporarily or permanently, the privilege of appearing or practicing before it in any way to any person who is found by the Commission after notice of and opportunity for hearing in the matter (i) not to possess the requisite qualifications to represent others, or (ii) to be lacking in character or integrity or to have engaged in unethical or improper professional conduct, or (iii) to have willfully violated, or willfully aided and abetted the violation of, any provision of the Federal securities laws (15 U.S.C. §§ 77a to 80b–20), or the rules and regulations thereunder."

dismissed the action on the ground that Touche Ross had not exhausted its administrative remedies. Touche Ross appealed.

Judge Timbers, writing for himself and Chief Judge Kaufman and Judge Gurfein, said that in the context of the case there were "three possible situations in [which] . . . the exhaustion issue arises: (1) when a litigant, such as Touche Ross, seeks to challenge a final Commission decision and order pursuant to Rule 2(e) which imposes sanctions or disciplines professionals for improper or unprofessional conduct; (2) when a litigant, such as Touche Ross, seeks judicial review of claims of agency bias; and (3) when, as in the particular circumstances of this case, Touche Ross requests this Court to adjudicate the question whether the Commission has the *authority* to promulgate Rule 2(e) and to proceed thereunder."

As to issue (1): "The rationale behind the exhaustion doctrine is that a court's refusal to intervene prematurely in the administrative process gives the agency an opportunity to develop factual findings, to apply its expertise to new issues and to exercise its discretionary powers. See McKart v. United States, 395 U.S. 185, 193–94 (1969). Moreover, '[n]otions of administrative autonomy require that the agency be given a chance to discover and correct its own errors'—a practice that will protect the integrity of the administrative process and prevent litigants from flouting the agency's procedures. We emphasize at the outset that normally we will not tolerate the interruption of the administrative process to hear piecemeal appeals of a litigant's claims on the merits. This is exactly what the exhaustion doctrine was designed to prevent. Accordingly, we wish to make it clear that Touche Ross must exhaust their administrative remedies by submitting to the Rule 2(e) proceedings before we will consider any challenges which they may assert with respect to any disciplinary action that the Commission may determine is appropriate under the circumstances."

As to issue (2) involving the contention that the Commission is "biased" as indicated by the institution of public rather than non-public proceedings, exhaustion also is required. The Court of Appeals for the District of Columbia Circuit has held that "allegations of agency bias or prejudgment based on ex parte communications are insufficient for injunctive relief and cannot be reviewed until the agency has made an adverse determination and an appeal has been taken raising these claims on the record as a whole. We agree. Until the Commission has acted and actual bias has been demonstrated, the orderly administrative procedures of the agency should not be interrupted by judicial intervention."

As to issue (3)—that in promulgating Rule 2(e) the SEC acted in excess of its statutory authority and now is proceeding against them without jurisdiction—the problem is more difficult. Touche Ross relies on Leedom v. Kyne [p. 1003 above.] as an exception to the exhaustion requirement. But Leedom v. Kyne is a narrow exception applicable only when "an agency refuses to dismiss a proceeding that is *plainly* beyond its jurisdiction as a matter of law or is being conducted in a manner that cannot result in a valid order." Unlike the Board's action in Leedom, "the action of the Commission in promulgating Rule 2(e) is not specifically *prohibited* by statute." The most that might be said is that the Commission's authority to promulgate Rule 2(e) is not specifically *provided* by statute.

However, said the court, in the McKart case, the Supreme Court weighed the hardships of a jail sentence, the fact that the issue there required only statutory interpretation and that there was no need for agency expertise or the exercise of agency discretion. The Court also emphasized that had the case involved the exercise of discretion or the application of expertise, exhaustion should be required and distinguished McKart in McGee v. United States, 402 U.S. 479 (1971) on that ground:

"Similar considerations are present in the instant case. Appellants challenge the legal authorization of the Commission to proceed against them pursuant to Rule 2(e). While the Commission's administrative proceeding is not 'plainly beyond its jurisdiction', nevertheless to require appellants to exhaust their administrative remedies would be to require them to submit to the very procedures which they are attacking.

"Moreover, the issue is one of purely statutory interpretation. Further agency action is unnecessary to enable us to determine the validity of Rule 2(e). There is no need for the exercise of discretion on the part of the agency nor for the application of agency expertise. While the Commission has the power to declare its own rule invalid, it is unlikely that further proceedings would produce such a result. Accordingly, we now turn to the merits of that question."

The court then pointed to the Commission's statutory authority to "make such rules as may be necessary or appropriate to implement the provision of this title" and concluded that Rule 2(e) was a valid exercise of the Commission's rulemaking power.

(3) LEEDOM v. KYNE, 358 U.S. 184 (1958), p. 1003, supra.

(4) ALLEN v. GRAND CENTRAL AIRCRAFT CO., 347 U.S. 535 (1954). If a violation of wage ceilings was found by the National Enforcement Commission, it could notify the Internal Revenue Service that all or part of the violator's unlawful wage payments should be disallowed for income tax purposes. Grand Central Aircraft was charged with violating the ceilings. The potential disallowance, if the charges were sustained, amounted to $5,500,000. The Commission notified Grand Central that a hearing would be held. Grand Central sued to enjoin the hearing, contending that holding the hearing would inflict irreparable damage on it and that neither the Constitution nor any statute authorized the administrative procedure proposed to be followed by the Commission. The trial court granted the requested injunction. The Supreme Court reversed in an opinion by Justice Burton:

". . . Appellee argues that such proceedings carry the possibility of the disallowance as a business expense, for income-tax purposes, of $750,000, more or less, up to the total wages paid, exceeding $5,500,000. Appellee contends also that the mere threat of such action would jeopardize the bank credit upon which it depends for essential working capital. There is grave doubt of the right of appellee thus to test the validity of administrative procedure before exhausting it or bringing the issues closer to a focus than it has done. However, it is clear that once the right of the Government to hold administrative hearings is established, a litigant cannot enjoin them merely because they might jeopardize his bank credit or otherwise be inconvenient or embarrassing. Aircraft & Diesel Equipment Corp. v. Hirsch, 331 U.S. 752, 777–779. [T]he expense and annoyance of litigation is 'part of the social burden of living under government.'

"It is appellee's principal claim that there is no properly authorized administrative procedure for it to exhaust and that the administrative authorities who seek to determine its case have no lawful right to do so. We, therefore, go directly to the heart of this controversy, which is the question whether the administrative enforcement of the 1950 wage stabilization program has been validly authorized."

The Court discussed section 405(b) of the Defense Production Act and the various Executive and administrative orders establishing the Office of Economic Stabilization, the Wage Stabilization Board and the National Enforcement Commission and authorizing the administrative procedures here complained of. Relying principally upon the fact that similar procedures had been authorized under a prior statute, the Stabilization Act of 1942, whose language had been closely followed in drafting section 405(b), the Court held that the procedure was authorized by the statute. This portion of the opinion ended with the following sentence: "We have noted the other arguments submitted by appellee concerning the interpretation and constitutionality of the statute but it would be premature action on our part to rule upon these until after the required administrative procedures have been exhausted."

The Court here appended the following footnote: "The constitutional objections suggested are that the Act and proceedings which have been taken and are proposed under it violate (1) the Fifth Amendment by depriving appellee of property without due process of law; (2) the Sixth or Seventh Amendment by depriving appellee of the right to a jury trial; (3) the Eighth Amendment in authorizing excessive fines; (4) Article I, § 9, by authorizing an unapportioned direct tax; (5) Article I, § 1, by improper delegation of legislative power to the Executive; and (6) the Tenth Amendment by attempting to legislate on matters reserved to the States."

(5) ROSENTHAL & CO. v. BAGLEY, 581 F.2d 1258 (7th Cir.1978). Section 14 of the Commodities Futures Trading Commission Act of 1974 confers on the Commission authority to adjudicate reparation claims brought by members of the public against registered commodities brokers and certain other registered persons. Upon finding a statutory violation, the Commission may make an award of damages. The Commission's order awarding reparations is enforceable in a federal district court. "Subject to the right of appeal" to a court of appeals, the Commission's reparation order "shall be final and conclusive." Any

party aggrieved by a reparation order may secure review in an appropriate court of appeals.

Plaintiff, a registered commodities brokerage firm defending approximately 25 reparations proceedings before the Commission, brought an action in the district court against the Commission and its members to enjoin the administrative proceedings on the ground that the statutory scheme violates the Seventh Amendment by abridging the right to jury trial in civil cases. Plaintiff argued that the reparations claims are "suits at common law" within the meaning of the Seventh Amendment and are therefore subject to the guarantee of trial by jury. The district court, dismissed the action, holding that, because the plaintiff could present its claim of unconstitutionality to the court of appeals in a direct review of the administrative proceeding, declaratory or injunctive relief interrupting the administrative proceedings was unavailable. The court affirmed in an opinion by Judge Tone:

"The exhaustion doctrine retains its vitality even when the collateral judicial action challenges the constitutionality of the basic statute under which the agency functions, even though one frequently asserted reason for requiring exhaustion, viz., to give the agency an opportunity to avoid or correct error, is inapplicable because an agency will not ordinarily pass on the constitutionality of the statute under which it operates.[3]

"An exception has been recognized in our cases, whether the asserted right is based on the Constitution, statute, or regulation: When the agency would violate a clear right of the plaintiff if allowed to proceed, the court will intervene.

"We do not view this case as falling within the clear-right exception. To reach that conclusion we need go no further than Atlas Roofing Co. v. Occupational Safety and Health Review Commission, 430 U.S. 442 (1977) [p. 117 supra.]. That the Seventh Amendment prevents the relegation of reparations claims to the Commodity Futures Trading Commission is arguable but far from clear. At least when only 'public rights' are involved, Congress may provide for administrative fact finding with which a jury trial would be incompatible. And the fact that new statutory 'public rights' are enforceable in favor of a private party does not mean they cannot be committed to an administrative agency for determination. . . . Moreover, 'the right to a jury trial turns not solely on the nature of the issue to be resolved but also on the forum in which it is to be resolved.'

. . .

3. [Ed.] But see Southern Pacific Transportation Co. v. Public Utilities Comm., 18 Cal.3d 308, 134 Cal.Rptr. 189, 556 P.2d 289 (1976), holding that an administrative agency has power to determine the constitutionality of statutes. For discussion, see Note, The Authority of Administrative Agencies to Consider the Constitutionality of Statutes, 90 Harv.L.Rev. 1682, 1684 (1977), urging that "[w]hile the Southern Pacific Transportation Co. rationale may reach too far and prove too much, the insight that the sweeping rule against agency determinations of the validity of statutes is unwarranted appears well-founded." The Note suggests "criteria that should define a new, more flexible approach to agency power." The Southern Pacific Transportation Co. case is also discussed in The Supreme Court of California 1976–1977, 66 Cal.L.Rev. 178, 180–201 (1978).

". . . [T]he number of reparations claims asserted against plaintiff before the agency does not require a different result. Twenty-five claims may present fewer litigation difficulties than a single complex claim. 'Mere litigation expense, even substantial and unrecoupable cost, does not constitute irreparable injury.' " Renegotiation Board v. Bannercraft Clothing Co., 415 U.S. 1, 24 (1974).[4]

(6) In ASSOCIATION OF NATIONAL ADVERTISERS V. FEDERAL TRADE COMMISSION, 627 F.2d 1151 (D.C.Cir.1979), cert. denied 447 U.S. 921 (1980), involving ANA's attempt to disqualify Chairman Pertschuk, see supra p. 974, the D.C. Circuit did not require exhaustion. Judge Tamm concluded that "immediate review of the prejudgment claim will not thwart the purposes of [the exhaustion doctrine because the] challenge to Chairman Pertschuk's further participation involves no disputed factual issues that demand the creation of a better administrative record. The agency has had an adequate opportunity to explain why Chairman Pertschuk need not be recused. Second, the issue involved in this case—the prejudgment standard required by due process for section 18 rulemaking—is a pure question of law. The Commission can bring no particular expertise to bear on its determination. Consideration of this question of first impression will not necessarily permit future piecemeal attacks on administrative processes.[5] Under the particular circumstances of this case, we therefore conclude that the appellees' claim may be heard."

Judge Leventhal disagreed with this analysis:

"To the extent that there is any judicial jurisdiction to halt an ongoing agency proceeding—or what is the equivalent, to enter a declaratory judgment that it cannot result in a valid final action—that jurisdiction, . . . is available only in a limited class of cases, not including the case at bar. There is always some problem of analysis when a court's determination of whether it has jurisdiction requires it

---

4. [Ed.] Compare Wolff v. Selective Service Local Bd. No. 16, 372 F.2d 817 (2d Cir.1967). Plaintiffs who had been classified II–S—student deferred—were reclassified I–A—available for immediate induction. Alleging that they had been reclassified because of their participation in a demonstration against the Viet Nam war, plaintiffs sued to have their II–S classification reinstated. Defendants contended that plaintiffs had not exhausted their administrative remedies. Judge Medina rejected the argument: "[W]hen as here a serious threat to the exercise of First Amendment rights exists, the policy favoring preservation of these rights must prevail" over the policies supporting the exhaustion doctrine.

5. In this sense, review of the Commission's decision not to recuse Chairman Pertschuk is analogous to the interlocutory review of a district court order permitted under 28 U.S.C. § 1292(b) (1976) when the "order involves a controlling question of law as to which there is substantial ground

for difference of opinion and . . . an immediate appeal from the order may materially advance the ultimate termination of the litigation." See also Kennedy, The Federal Courts Improvement Act: a first step for Congress to take, 63 Judicature 8, 12 (1979) (proposed S. 678 balances need for finality against desirability of hearing interlocutory appeals by allowing "immediate appeals in cases of 'extraordinary importance,' with the Court of Appeals deciding—even in the absence of district court certification—whether or not to entertain an appeal").

Similarly, appellate courts reviewing claims that a district court judge improperly refused to recuse himself, see 28 U.S.C. §§ 144, 455 (1976), have demonstrated sensitivity to the expeditious hearing of prejudgment cases. Although a refusal to recuse is not appealable as a final order, commentators have detected a liberal trend toward use of mandamus to consider disqualification claims.

to take a 'peek at the merits.' But I think the doctrine can be etched fairly clearly. . . .

"If a federal court . . . is to take jurisdiction before final agency action, it can only be in a case of 'clear right' such as outright violation of a clear statutory provision (Leedom) or violation of basic rights established by a *structural* flaw, and not requiring *in any way* a consideration of interrelated aspects of the merits—which can only be done appropriately on review of a final order. . . .

"The case at bar is one where the very inquiry posed by plaintiff obviously requires some analysis of the views expressed by Chairman Pertschuk, and comparison with the issues as they will actually be focused in the ongoing proceeding. The Government puts forward substantial considerations in justification of Chairman Pertschuk's remarks—the proper purpose of calling the public's attention to possible abuses and to factors enhancing public understanding, the propriety of a hortatory role on a wide range of issues, the breadth of the underlying policy issues, as contrasted with the quality of rulings on specific, adjudicative effects (with the corollary likelihood of specific condemnation and stigma). But even if one pretermits all such considerations, the actual conduct of the proceeding may bear significantly on the relationship of the remarks to ultimate issues, let alone dispositions, which are necessary aspects of any claim of prejudicial bias."

Also, the case does not involve a structural flaw and thus is distinguishable from the cases relied on by ANA: Amos Treat & Co. v. SEC, 306 F.2d 260 (D.C.Cir.1962) ("the court enjoined an adjudicatory proceeding because one of the commissioners who had participated in certain rulings had previously, as a member of the staff, participated in the investigation. That decision was a ruling of a *structural* incapacity, which was necessary for a 'fair trial'"); Fitzgerald v. Hampton, 467 F.2d 755 (D.C.Cir.1972) ("that, too, was a structural violation—the denial of a public hearing").[6]

Judge MacKinnon dissented from the holding on the merits that Pertschuk could be disqualified only upon a showing by clear and convincing evidence that he had an unalterably closed mind on matters critical to the disposition of the rulemaking. But he summarily concurred in the ruling that the Association of National Advertisers was not required to exhaust the rulemaking process before instituting a court action to disqualify Pertschuk.

(7) MCKART v. UNITED STATES, 395 U.S. 185 (1969), an often cited case relied on in Touche Ross, supra NOTE (2), presents a different kind of exhaustion problem from that involved in Myers. Whereas in Myers plaintiff could secure judicial consideration of its claim on review of the

---

6. Emphasizing that if a similar case should arise in the future—i.e., a case that did not involve "defiance of an explicit statute, or a structural flow denying basic rights"—exhaustion would be required, Judge Leventhal nevertheless concurred in the ruling that exhaustion would not be required in this case. He explained: "This is partly due to the area of doubt left in the wake of our previous rulings" and partly because the district court's ruling on the merits has "for more than a year constituted a stain on the FTC proceeding" and that "stain would persist if the appellate court confined itself to a jurisdictional ruling, to the detriment of sound governmental process."

final unfair labor practice order, in McKart that expedient was fore-closed because it was too late to go back to the agency. The question thus becomes not one of timing but of "excuse" or "waiver" or perhaps one of preclusion of judicial review. Whatever the terminology, the underlying considerations are essentially the same, although the hard-ship element typically will be greater in the McKart-type case.

In the McKart case, McKart had been deferred pursuant to a statute stating that the sole surviving son of [a] family whose father had been killed in action should not be inducted into the army. After McKart's mother died, he was reclassified and ordered to report for induction; the reasoning of the Selective Service System was that since both parents were dead, there no longer was a family. McKart did not report for induction and he did not utilize available Selective Service procedures to challenge his reclassification. He was then convicted for wilful failure to report for induction and sentenced to three years imprisonment. His only defense at the criminal trial was that he was exempt because he was the sole surviving son of his family. The lower courts held that he could not raise that defense because he had failed to exhaust the Selective Service procedures.

The Supreme Court reversed in an opinion by Justice Marshall. The Court first held for McKart on the merits. It then turned to the ex-haustion issue and reasoned as follows:

1. "[U]se of the exhaustion doctrine in criminal cases can be exceedingly harsh."

2. "The question of whether petitioner is entitled to exemption as a sole surviving son is . . . solely one of statutory interpretation."

3. We are unimpressed with the "Government's argument that failure to require exhaustion in the present case will induce registrants to bypass available administrative remedies."

"[W]e doubt whether many registrants will be foolhardy enough to deny the Selective Service System the opportunity to correct its own errors by taking their chances with a criminal prosecution and a possibility of five years in jail. The very presence of the criminal sanction is sufficient to ensure that the great majority of registrants will exhaust all administrative remedies before deciding whether or not to continue the challenge to their classifications. And, today's holding does not apply to every registrant who fails to take advantage of the administrative remedies provided by the Selective Service System. For, as we have said, many classifications require exercise of discretion or application of expertise; in these cases, it may be proper to require a registrant to carry his case through the administrative process before he comes into court. Moreover, we are not convinced that many in this rather small class of registrants will bypass the Selective Service System with the thought that their ultimate chances of success in the courts are enhanced thereby. In short, we simply do not think that the exhaustion doctrine contributes significantly to the fairly low number of registrants who decide to subject themselves to criminal prosecution for failure to submit to induction. Accordingly, in the present case, where there appears no significant interest to be served in having the

System decide the issue before it reaches the courts, we do not believe that petitioner's failure to appeal his classification should foreclose all judicial review."

Justices Douglas and White wrote separate concurring opinions.

Compare McGee v. United States, 402 U.S. 479 (1971). McGee, who also was reclassified, refused to avail himself of the appeal procedures provided by the Selective Service System and was convicted for refusing to report for induction. The Supreme Court affirmed his conviction. Justice Marshall wrote:

". . . Unlike the dispute about statutory interpretation involved in McKart, McGee's claims to exempt status—as a ministerial student or a conscientious objector—depended on the application of expertise by administrative bodies in resolving underlying issues of fact. Factfinding for purposes of Selective Service classification is committed primarily to the administrative process, with very limited judicial review to ascertain whether there is a 'basis in fact' for the administrative determination. . . . McKart expressly noted that as to classification claims turning on the resolution of particularistic fact questions, 'the Selective Service System and the courts may have a stronger interest in having the question decided in the first instance by the local board and then by the appeal board, which considers the question anew.' . . . This 'stronger interest,' in the circumstances of the present case, has become compelling and fully sufficient to justify invocation of the exhaustion doctrine. . . .

"That petitioner's failure to exhaust should cut off judicial review of his conscientious objector claim may seem too hard a result, assuming, as the Government admits, that the written information available to the board provided no basis in fact for denial of the exemption, and, as the Court of Appeals ruled, that neither did petitioner's conduct in relation to the conscription system or other acts that came into view. . . . But even assuming the above, petitioner's dual failure to exhaust—his failure either to secure a personal appearance or to take an administrative appeal—implicates decisively the policies served by the exhaustion requirement, especially the purpose of ensuring that the Selective Service System have full opportunity to 'make a factual record' and apply its expertise in relation to a registrant's claims. When a claim to exemption depends ultimately on the careful gathering and analysis of relevant facts, the interest in full airing of the facts within the administrative system is prominent, and as the Court of Appeals noted, the exhaustion requirement 'cannot properly be limited to those persons whose claims would fail in court anyway.' " Justice Douglas dissented.[7]

(8) Telecommunications Research and Action Center v. FCC, 750 F.2d 70 (D.C.Cir.1984). Plaintiff (TRAC) and other public interest groups petitioned the court for a writ of mandamus to compel the FCC

---

7. Compare Patsy v. Florida Board of Regents, 457 U.S. 496 (1982) (exhaustion of state administrative remedies is not a condition precedent to filing a section 1983 action). For discussion, see S. Nahmod, Civil Rights Litigation, A Guide to Section 1983, § 5.10 [2d ed. 1986].

to decide certain unresolved matters then pending before the agency. Judge Edwards wrote for the panel, consisting of himself and Judges Tamm and Wilkey, that the case "raises two significant and recurring jurisdictional questions. First, where a statute commits final agency action to review by the court of appeals, does that court have jurisdiction to hear suits seeking relief that would affect its future statutory power of review? Second, if the court of appeals does have jurisdiction, is that jurisdiction exclusive . . . ?"

The Court answered both questions in the affirmative. With respect to the first, it is well established that although the All Writs Act [8] does not expand the jurisdiction of a court, the Act does empower a federal court "to issue writs of mandamus to protect its prospective jurisdiction. Because the statutory obligation of a court of appeals to review on the merits may be defeated by an agency that fails to resolve disputes, a circuit court may resolve claims of unreasonable delay in order to protect its future jurisdiction."

As to the second question, the court held that where a statute commits review of agency action to the court of appeals, any suit seeking relief that might affect the circuit court's future jurisdiction is subject to the *exclusive* review of the court of appeals. The court reasoned that a statute which vests jurisdiction in .a particular court impliedly deprives all other courts of jurisdiction in all cases covered by the statute. Accordingly, since the court of appeals has jurisdiction by virtue of a statutory provision for review and the All Writs Act, the district court is deprived of jurisdiction in all cases in which the court of appeals has jurisdiction. [9]

The Court concluded its discussion of the jurisdictional problem with the following paragraph:

"There may be a small category of cases in which the underlying claim is not subject to the jurisdiction of the court of appeals (and thus adjudication of the claim in the district court will not affect any future statutory review authority of the circuit court). In such cases, where a denial of review in the district court will truly foreclose all judicial review, district court review might be predicated on the general federal question jurisdiction statute, 28 U.S.C. § 1331. For example, in Leedom v. Kyne, 358 US 184 (1958), the Supreme Court held that, even though there is a statutory prohibition against review of representation orders of the National Labor Relations Board, a district court has jurisdiction under Section 1331 in the *very limited circumstance* where

---

8. [Ed.] The All Writs Act, 28 U.S.C. § 1651, provides as follows:

"(a) The Supreme Court and all courts established by Act of Congress may issue all writs necessary or appropriate in aid of their respective jurisdictions and agreeable to the usages and principles of law.

"(b) An alternative writ or rule nisi may be issued by a justice or judge of a court which has jurisdiction."

9. The Court stated in a footnote: "Because this holding resolves inconsistencies among our prior decisions, this part of our decision has been considered separately and approved by the whole court, and thus constitutes the law of the circuit."

In a companion case, Air Line Pilots Association v. CAB, 750 F.2d 81 (D.C.Cir. 1984), the Court held that the TRAC principle of exclusive jurisdiction applied as well to a claim of bias as to one of unreasonable delay.

the Board has clearly violated an express mandate of the statute and the plaintiff has no alternative means of review. However, we need not tarry over this narrow exception because it is in no way implicated in the case before us. The principal point of this decision is to make clear that where a statute commits review of agency action to the court of appeals, any suit seeking relief that might affect the circuit court's future jurisdiction is subject to the exclusive review of the court of appeals." [10]

Judicial Stays Pending Administrative Action or Judicial Review.

The so-called All Writs statute, 28 U.S.C. § 1651, states, "The Supreme Court and all courts established by Act of Congress may issue all writs necessary or appropriate in aid of their respective jurisdictions and agreeable to the usages and principles of law." Section 10(d) of the Administrative Procedure Act, 5 U.S.C. § 705, provides, "On such conditions as may be required and to the extent necessary to prevent irreparable injury, the reviewing court, including the court to which a case may be taken on appeal from or on application for certiorari or other writ to a reviewing court, may issue all necessary and appropriate process to postpone the effective date of an agency action or to preserve status or rights pending conclusion of the review proceedings." Other statutes, such as the Review Act of 1950, 28 U.S.C. § 2349, or the Federal Aviation Act of 1958, 49 U.S.C. § 1486(a), specifically authorize a stay. Finally, in Scripps-Howard Radio, Inc. v. FCC, 316 U.S. 4 (1942), the Supreme Court, in an opinion by Justice Frankfurter, implied that the power of a federal reviewing court to issue a stay did not depend upon specific statutory authorization but was "part of its traditional equipment for the administration of justice," citing in support the All Writs statute. 316 U.S. 10 n. 4.[1]

The practical question concerning stays thus relates not to power but to the propriety of issuance or denial. In a case which has been widely cited by other lower federal courts and occasionally by the Supreme Court, the Court of Appeals for the District of Columbia Circuit outlined the factors which govern issuance or denial of a stay order, as follows:

---

10. [Ed.] See 28 U.S.C. § 1631:

Whenever a civil action is filed in a [federal] court . . . or an appeal, including a petition for review of administrative action, is noticed for or filed with such a court and that court finds that there is a want of jurisdiction, the court shall, if it is in the interest of justice, transfer such action or appeal to any other such court in which the action or appeal could have been brought at the time it was filed or noticed, and the action or appeal shall proceed as if it had been filed in or noticed for the court to which it is transferred on the date upon which it was actually filed in or noticed for the court from which it is transferred.

This statute was adopted in 1982, P.L. 97–164, 96 Stat. 55, and is discussed in P. Caron, Confronting Unforeseen Problems Under 28 U.S.C. § 1631: The Tenth Circuit Struggles to Properly Dispose of Tucker Act Claims Within the Exclusive Jurisdiction of the Claims Court, 1985 Brig.Y.L. Rev. 505.

1. Section 5–111 of the Model State Administrative Procedure Act (1981) provides that unless precluded by law, an agency may grant a stay pending judicial review; the section also authorizes interlocutory judicial review of the agency's action on an application for a stay.

"(1) Has the petitioner made a strong showing that it is likely to prevail on the merits of its appeal? Without such a substantial indication of probable success, there would be no justification for the court's intrusion into the ordinary processes of administration and judicial review.[2]

"(2) Has the petitioner shown that without such relief, it will be irreparably injured? The key word in this consideration is *irreparable.* Mere injuries, however substantial, in terms of money, time and energy necessarily expended in the absence of a stay, are not enough. The possibility that adequate compensatory or other corrective relief will be available at a later date, in the ordinary course of litigation, weighs heavily against a claim of irreparable harm. But injury held insufficient to justify a stay in one case may well be sufficient to justify it in another, where the applicant has demonstrated a higher probability of success on the merits.

"(3) Would the issuance of a stay substantially harm other parties interested in the proceedings? On this side of the coin, we must determine whether, despite showings of probable success and irreparable injury on the part of petitioner, the issuance of a stay would have a serious adverse effect on other interested persons. Relief saving one claimant from irreparable injury, at the expense of similar harm caused another, might not qualify as the equitable judgment that a stay represents.

"(4) Where lies the public interest? In litigation involving the administration of regulatory statutes designed to promote the public interest, this factor necessarily becomes crucial. The interests of private litigants must give way to the realization of public purposes. The public interest may, of course, have many facets—favoring at once both the rapid expansion of utilities and the prevention of wasteful and repetitive proceedings at the taxpayers' or consumers' expense; both fostering competition and preserving the economic viability of existing public services; both expediting administrative or judicial action and preserving orderly procedure." Virginia Petroleum Jobbers Ass'n v. FPC, 259 F.2d 921 (D.C.Cir.1958).[3]

The case involved an application by the Blue Ridge Gas Company to the Federal Power Commission for a certificate authorizing it to

---

2. [Ed.] But see M. Wilkey, Judicial Review 245, 284–285, in Federal Administrative Law Practice and Procedure (C. Christensen and R. Middlekauf eds. 1977): "A number of circuits, notably the Second and the Ninth, have adopted an alternative approach to the merits. To quote fully from the Second Circuit, Charlie's Girls, Inc. v. Revlon, Inc., 483 F.2d 953, 954 (1973): 'One moving for a preliminary injunction assumes the burden of demonstrating *either* a combination of probable success and the possibility of irreparable injury *or* that serious questions are raised and the balance of hardships tips sharply in his favor.' (emphasis supplied). Under this approach the questions of comparative injury are necessarily balanced, in order to set the standard for review of the merits. . . . This approach departs from the more traditional analysis, which may dispose of the petition solely on the merits. Compare Siff v. State Democratic Executive Committee, 500 F.2d 1307 (5th Cir. 1974) (no likelihood of success; no injunction)."

3. [Ed.] See also A. Wolf, Preliminary Injunctions: The Varying Standards, 7 Western N.Eng.L.Rev. 173, 236 (1984): "[T]his article shows that the Supreme Court and the courts of appeal have not articulated or applied consistent criteria for preliminary injunctive relief."

distribute natural gas in three Virginia cities. Virginia Petroleum Jobbers Association (Jobbers), which marketed petroleum products in Virginia, sought to intervene in the FPC hearing. The Commission denied intervention and proceeded with the hearing. Jobbers then filed a petition for judicial review of the Commission's order denying intervention. Jobbers also requested the court to stay the administrative proceedings pending review. The court denied the motion for a stay. In applying the four factors the court reasoned as follows:

[1] Under the applicable precedents petitioner, i.e., Jobbers, had a right to intervene in the Blue Ridge proceedings and denial of that right is an immediately appealable order. Accordingly, "petitioner has shown a probability of success on the merits of its appeal. . . .

"[2] [P]etitioner has not indicated any way in which we can consider it irreparably harmed in the absence of a stay. Its bare claims that if the court were ultimately to reverse and remand the case to the Commission, the latter would not provide Jobbers with an adequate hearing, or permit it to develop the record successfully, can be given no credence. . . .

"[3] The question of harm to others if a stay were granted is not really before us. Except insofar as it may reflect on the public interest in saving taxpayers and consumers needless expense, we do not think petitioner has standing to complain of potential losses or inconvenience to the other parties in this case, should the proceedings before the Commission have to be repeated on court order. The gas companies must be aware that they are now proceeding at their own risk, and without a claim for relief from them, it is neither the petitioner's nor the court's place to protect them from hypothetical, self-inflicting losses.

"[4] We come then to the public interest considerations, which we have indicated are crucial in this type of case. We note that Congress has charged the Commission with administering the Natural Gas Act in the public interest. In so doing, the Commission may find that a grant of the Blue Ridge application would not be in the public interest, thus mooting the case from petitioner's point of view. On the other hand, the Commission may well conclude that prompt expansion of natural gas distribution to the area Blue Ridge proposes to serve would be in the public interest. We must hesitate before we say what the Commission may find necessary and convenient, and we must be, and are, reluctant to interfere with administrative proceedings. Lastly, we note that the Commission has now completed the hearing, participation in which was at the heart of petitioner's claim for relief. A stay at this juncture would not, therefore, expedite resolution of the issues on which this appeal turns. It would not further the public interest in orderly procedure or the petitioner's cause. It is within petitioner's power to accelerate court consideration of its petition for review. In the circumstances of this case we consider this an adequate remedy, and conclude that the stay petitioner requests must be denied." [4]

4. Utilizing the Virginia Petroleum Jobbers factors, the Court held in Sampson v. Murray, 415 U.S. 61 (1974), that a probationary employee, who had been dis-

Consider also the converse of the Jobbers situation, that is when the agency requests a court to grant temporary relief pending the outcome of agency proceedings. Here again specific statutes sometimes confer the necessary authority. See, for example, § 13(a) of the Federal Trade Commission Act, 15 U.S.C. § 53(a), which provides that whenever the Commission has reason to believe that a person is violating or is about to violate any provision of law enforced by the Commission and that temporarily enjoining the violation during the pendency of an FTC hearing concerning the alleged violation would be in the interest of the public, the Commission may request, and a district court may issue, a temporary restraining order or a preliminary injunction. The NLRB has been given similar authority to secure appropriate temporary injunctive relief pending the final adjudication of the board concerning alleged unfair labor practices or boycotts on illegal strikes. 29 U.S.C. §§ 160(j), 160(*l*).

But suppose there is no specific statutory authorization for interim judicial relief. See FTC v. Dean Foods Co., 384 U.S. 597 (1966), a 5–4 decision in which the Supreme Court held that the All Writs Act empowered the court of appeals (to which a final order could be appealed) to enjoin two corporations from merging until the FTC could conduct a hearing to determine the legality of the merger. The Court said that the All Writs Act enabled the court of appeals to protect its *potential* jurisdiction to decide an appeal from the Commission's order in the merger hearing.

b. Final Agency Action

FEDERAL TRADE COMMISSION v. STANDARD OIL COMPANY OF CALIFORNIA

Supreme Court of the United States, 1980.
449 U.S. 232.

[In July 1973 the Federal Trade Commission issued and served on Standard Oil Company of Southern California (Socal) and seven other major oil companies a complaint stating that the Commission "had reason to believe" that the companies were violating Section 5 of the Federal Trade Commission Act.[1] An adjudication of the complaint's

charged for failure to follow directions and who would be entitled to back pay if she were successful in her administrative appeal, was not entitled to a stay pending her appeal to the Civil Service Commission. Compare Schwartz v. Covington, 341 F.2d 537 (9th Cir.1965), also applying the Virginia Petroleum Jobbers tests and staying the discharge of an Army sergeant who, after sixteen years of service, had been accused of engaging in homosexual activities: it is likely that plaintiff will prevail on the merits; the "injury and the stigma attached to an undesirable discharge are clear;" and "there is no showing that irreparable harm to the government or harm to the public would occur [if the discharge were stayed since the] record dis-

closes that his service [as an orderly] has been excellent and subject to no complaints."

1. Section 5 provides in pertinent part:

"(a)(1). Unfair methods of competition in commerce, and unfair or deceptive acts or practices in commerce, are declared unlawful. . . .

"(b) Whenever the Commission shall have reason to believe that any . . . corporation has been or is using any unfair method of competition or unfair or deceptive act or practice in commerce . . . it shall issue and serve upon such . . . corporation a complaint stating its charges in that respect and containing a notice of a hearing. . . ."

charges began soon thereafter before an administrative law judge. Socal moved to dismiss the complaint on the ground that when the Commission issued the complaint it lacked sufficient evidence to warrant a belief that Socal was violating the Act. The Commission denied the motion, stating in part, "Once the Commission has . . . issued a complaint, the issue to be litigated is not the adequacy of the Commission's pre-complaint information . . . but whether the alleged violation has in fact occurred." Socal then brought an action against the Commission in a federal district court in California seeking an order declaring that issuance of the complaint was unlawful and requiring the complaint to be withdrawn. The district court dismissed Socal's complaint on the ground that "a review of preliminary decisions made by administrative agencies, except under most unusual circumstances, would be productive of nothing more than chaos." The Ninth Circuit reversed. It held the Commission's determination whether evidence before it provided the requisite reason to believe is "committed to agency discretion" and therefore is unreviewable. The court of appeals held, however, that the district court could inquire whether the Commission *in fact* had made the determination that it had reason to believe that Socal was violating the Act. If the district court were to find upon remand that the Commission had issued the complaint "solely because of outside pressure or with complete absence of a 'reason to believe' determination," then it was to order the Commission to dismiss the complaint. The court of appeals also held that the issuance of the complaint was "final agency action" under § 704 of the APA. [The Supreme Court granted certiorari.]

JUSTICE POWELL delivered the opinion of the Court. . . .

The Commission averred in its complaint that it had reason to believe that Socal was violating the Act. That averment is subject to judicial review before the conclusion of administrative adjudication only if the issuance of the complaint was "final agency action" or otherwise was "directly reviewable" under § [704] of the APA. We conclude that the issuance of the complaint was neither.[2]

The Commission's issuance of its complaint was not "final agency action." . . . By its terms, the Commission's averment of "reason to believe" that Socal was violating the Act is not a definitive statement of position. It represents a threshold determination that further inquiry is warranted and that a complaint should initiate proceedings. To be sure, the issuance of the complaint is definitive on the question whether the Commission avers reason to believe that the respondent to the complaint is violating the Act. But the extent to which the respondent may challenge the complaint and its charges proves that the averment

2. In addition to contending that the issuance of the complaint is not "final" agency action, the Commission argues that the issuance is not "agency action" under § [551(13)] of the APA, and that, if agency action, it is "committed to agency discretion by law" under § [701(a)(2).]

We agree with Socal and with the Court of Appeals that the issuance of the com-

plaint is "agency action." The language of the APA and its legislative history support this conclusion. . . .

In view of our conclusion that the issuance of the complaint was not "*final* agency action," we do not address the question whether the issuance of a complaint is "committed to agency discretion by law." 5 U.S.C. § 701(a)(2).

of reason to believe is not "definitive" in a comparable manner to the regulation in Abbott Laboratories [infra p. 1105].   .   .   .

.   .   .   [T]he averment of reason to believe is a prerequisite to a definitive agency position on the question whether Socal violated the Act, but itself is a determination only that adjudicatory proceedings will commence.

Serving only to initiate the proceedings, the issuance of the complaint averring reason to believe has no legal force comparable to that of the regulation at issue in Abbott Laboratories, nor any comparable effect upon Socal's daily business. The regulations in Abbott Laboratories forced manufacturers to "risk serious criminal and civil penalties" for noncompliance, or "change all their labels, advertisements, and promotional materials;   .   .   .   destroy stocks of printed matter; and .   .   .   invest heavily in new printing type and new supplies." Socal does not contend that the issuance of the complaint had any such legal or practical effect, except to impose upon Socal the burden of responding to the charges made against it. Although this burden certainly is substantial, it is different in kind and legal effect from the burdens attending what heretofore has been considered to be final agency. action.

In contrast to the complaint's lack of legal or practical effect upon Socal, the effect of the judicial review sought by Socal is likely to be interference with the proper functioning of the agency and a burden for the courts. Judicial intervention into the agency process denies the agency an opportunity to correct its own mistakes and to apply its expertise. Weinberger v. Salfi, 422 U.S. 749, 765 (1975). Intervention also leads to piecemeal review which at the least is inefficient and upon completion of the agency process might prove to have been unnecessary. Furthermore, unlike the review in Abbott Laboratories, judicial review to determine whether the Commission decided that it had the requisite reason to believe would delay resolution of the ultimate question whether the Act was violated. Finally, every respondent to a Commission complaint could make the claim that Socal had made. Judicial review of the averments in the Commission's complaints should not be a means of turning prosecutor into defendant before adjudication concludes.

In sum, the Commission's issuance of a complaint averring reason to believe that Socal was violating the Act is not a definitive ruling or regulation.   .   .   .

Socal relies, however, upon different considerations than these in contending that the issuance of the complaint is "final agency action."

Socal first contends that it exhausted its administrative remedies by moving in the adjudicatory proceedings for dismissal of the complaint. By thus affording the Commission an opportunity to decide upon the matter, Socal contends that it has satisfied the interests underlying the doctrine of administrative exhaustion. The Court of Appeals agreed. We think, however, that Socal and the Court of Appeals have mistaken exhaustion for finality. By requesting the Commission to withdraw its complaint and by awaiting the Commission's refusal to do so, Socal may well have exhausted its administrative remedy as to the averment of reason to believe. But the Commission's refusal to reconsider its issuance of the complaint does not render the complaint a "definitive" action. The Commission's refusal does not augment the complaint's legal force or practical effect upon Socal. Nor does the refusal diminish the concerns for efficiency and enforcement of the Act.

Socal also contends that it will be irreparably harmed unless the issuance of the complaint is judicially reviewed immediately. Socal argues that the expense and disruption of defending itself in protracted adjudicatory proceedings constitutes irreparable harm. As indicated above, we do not doubt that the burden of defending this proceeding will be substantial. But "the expense and annoyance of litigation is 'part of the social burden of living under government.'" As we recently reiterated: "Mere litigation expense, even substantial and unrecoupable cost, does not constitute irreparable injury."

Socal further contends that its challenge to the Commission's averment of reason to believe can never be reviewed unless it is reviewed before the Commission's adjudication concludes. . . .

We are not persuaded. . . . [T]he APA specifically provides that a "preliminary, procedural, or intermediate agency action or ruling not directly reviewable is subject to review on the review of the final agency action," 5 U.S.C. § 704, and . . . the APA also empowers a court of appeals to "hold unlawful and set aside agency action . . . found to be . . . without observance of procedure required by law." 5 U.S.C. § 706. Thus, assuming that the issuance of the complaint is not "committed to agency discretion by law," a court of appeals reviewing a cease-and-desist order has the power to review alleged unlawfulness in the issuance of a complaint. We need not decide what action a court of appeals should take if it finds a cease-and-desist order to be supported by substantial evidence but the complaint to have been issued without the requisite reason to believe. It suffices to hold that the possibility does not affect the application of the finality rule.

There remains only Socal's contention that the claim of illegality in the issuance of the complaint is a "collateral" order subject to review under the doctrine of Cohen v. Beneficial Loan Corp., 337 U.S. 541 (1949). It argues that the Commission's issuance of the complaint averring reason to believe "fall[s] in that small class [of decisions] which finally determine claims of right separable from, and collateral to, rights asserted in the action, too important to be denied review and too independent of the cause itself to require that appellate consideration be deferred until the whole case is adjudicated." Id., at 546. In that diversity case, a District Court refused to apply a state statute requiring shareholders bringing a derivative suit to post a security bond for the defendant's litigation expenses. This Court held that the District Court's order was subject to immediate appellate review under 28 U.S.C. § 1291. Giving that section a "practical rather than a technical construction," the Court concluded that this order "did not make any step toward final disposition of the merits of the case and will not be merged in final judgment."

Cohen does not avail Socal. What we have said above makes clear that the issuance of the complaint averring reason to believe is a step toward, and will merge in, the Commission's decision on the merits. Therefore, review of this preliminary step should abide review of the final order.

Because the Commission's issuance of a complaint averring reason to believe that Socal has violated the Act is not "final agency action" under § [704] of the APA, it is not judicially reviewable before administrative adjudication concludes. We therefore reverse the Court of Appeals and remand for the dismissal of the complaint.

[Justice Stewart did not participate. Justice Stevens concurred in the judgment on the ground that "the Commission's decision to initiate a complaint is not 'agency action' within the meaning" of the APA.]

NOTES

(1) PEPSICO, INC. v. FEDERAL TRADE COMMISSION, 472 F.2d 179 (2d Cir. 1972), cert. denied 414 U.S. 876 (1973). The FTC issued a complaint against PepsiCo alleging that PepsiCo had hindered competition by restricting bottlers of its products from selling outside a designated geographical area. PepsiCo moved to dismiss the complaint on the ground that the 513 bottlers of Pepsi products were indispensable parties who had not been joined. The FTC denied the motion. PepsiCo thereupon sued in the district court to enjoin the FTC from proceeding unless it joined all the bottlers. The district court granted the defendants' motion to dismiss and the court of appeals affirmed in an opinion by Judge Friendly:

"Although the Federal Trade Commission Act limits review by a court of appeals to 'any person, partnership, or corporation required by an order of the Commission to cease and desist,' 15 U.S.C. § 45(c), we agree with appellants that the fact that the order here assailed is not one requiring PepsiCo to cease and desist from anything does not lead inexorably to the conclusion that it is not reviewable, but only that it is not reviewable by petition to a court of appeals. Whether it was reviewable by suit in a district court depends on the construction given to the first two sentences of § 10(c) of the APA, now 5 U.S.C. § 704. . . . Since the order was not one 'made reviewable by statute,' its reviewability hinges on whether it constitutes 'final agency action for which there is no other adequate remedy in a court . . . .'

"If the APA uses the term 'final agency action' in the same sense that the Judicial Code speaks of a 'final decision' of a lower court, 28 U.S.C. § 1291, there could be little doubt about the answer. It is clear that "[d]enial of a motion to dismiss is not a final order and is therefore not appealable,' 2A Moore, Federal Practice ¶ 12.14, at 2338 & n. 16 (2d ed. 1968), and this principle has been applied to a refusal to dismiss for failure to join indispensable parties. . . . Many of the considerations supporting the final judgment rule with respect to appeals from decisions of lower courts are equally present in the case of agency action:

The agency may find in favor of the respondent; the case may be settled; the reviewing court, in any event, will be in a better position to assess the matter when all the cards have been played.

"The legislative history of the APA sheds little light on what the framers meant by 'final agency action for which there is no other adequate remedy in a court.' S.Rep. No. 752, 79th Cong., 1st Sess. 27 (1945), says that the phrase 'includes any effective agency action for which there is no other adequate remedy in any court.' H.R.Rep. No. 1980, 79th Cong., 2d Sess. 43 (1946), . . . , speaks of any effective or operative agency action. The adjectives tend against a construction that would include denial of a motion to dismiss a complaint. A quick reading of the second sentence of § 10(c) might suggest that interlocutory rulings were never to be reviewed until there had been final agency action in the usual sense. However, the phrase '[a] preliminary, procedural, or intermediate agency action or ruling *not directly reviewable*' (emphasis supplied) suggests that some action may be directly reviewed, although it does not explain by what authority unless the reference is to special statutory review procedures. Perhaps the second sentence could best be read as designed to insure that, like similar orders in civil actions . . . , preliminary orders in administrative proceedings which are not immediately reviewable do not remain beyond review forever. . . . It is arguable also that the framers must have been familiar with the well-known decision in Myers v. Bethlehem Shipbuilding Corp., 303 U.S. 41 (1938), and that, if they intended to overrule it, they would have spoken more clearly. The decisions on the subject, both by the Supreme Court and by lower courts, are conflicting, as Professor Davis has pointed out, 3 Administrative Law Treatise §§ 20.01–.05 (1958). Moreover, most of them do not address themselves to what one would suppose to be the crucial issue, i.e., the proper interpretation of § 10(c).[3]

"We find no need to proffer a definitive solution to the question of the reviewability of agency orders which are not 'final' in the ordinary sense—something which, in any event, is beyond the capability of an inferior court. Rather we shall accept for the sake of argument . . . that we can extrapolate from cases such as Leedom v. Kyne, 358 U.S. 184 (1958) and McCulloch v. Sociedad Nacional de Marineros, 372 U.S. 10 (1963), a principle that one can find 'final agency action for which there is no other adequate remedy in a court' if an agency refuses to dismiss a proceeding that is plainly beyond its jurisdiction as a matter of law or is being conducted in a manner that cannot result in a valid

---

3. The courts instead speak of "exhaustion." This case shows how little help that term offers in the context here relevant. If the rule is simply that plaintiff must have "exhausted" administrative remedies with respect to the issue for which judicial review is sought, as he clearly must, PepsiCo has done that. The real question is under what circumstances a court should review an order which, in Mr. Justice Brandeis' famous phrase, does not command the carrier to do, or to refrain from doing, any thing; which does not grant or withhold any authority, privilege, or license; which does not extend or abridge any power or facility; which does not subject the carrier to any liability, civil or criminal; which does not change the carrier's existing or future status or condition; which does not determine any right or obligation." United States v. Los Angeles & S.L.R.R., 273 U.S. 299, 309–310 (1927). . . .

order.[4] The injury against which a court would protect is not merely the expense to the plaintiff of defending in the administrative proceeding, which Myers held not to be enough, but, in a case like this, the enormous waste of governmental resources and the continuing threat of a complete restructuring of an industry. While PepsiCo and its bottlers cannot be heard to complain of the Commission's attempt to accomplish this restructuring, arguably they should not be placed under that threat in a proceeding that must prove to be a nullity."

The court then held that the "decision whether to accede to PepsiCo's request for joinder was within the Commission's discretion."

Judge Medina dissented. He would have remanded the case to the district court with instructions to enjoin the FTC until it made the PepsiCo bottlers parties.

At the time the FTC issued its complaint against PepsiCo, it issued similar complaints against six other manufacturers of soft drink syrups: Dr. Pepper, Seven-Up, Royal Crown Cola, Coca-Cola, Cott, and Crush. At least two of these, Coca-Cola and Seven-Up, also brought actions to enjoin the FTC. The Fifth Circuit affirmed the district court's dismissal of Coca-Cola's action: "The court below did not reach the merits of the controversy about the indispensability of the contract bottlers . . . nor do we. We agree that judicial resolution of that question at this juncture would be premature. . . . The extraordinary remedy of judicial intervention in agency proceedings still in progress is unavailable unless necessary to vindicate an unambiguous statutory or constitutional right. . . .

"In part plaintiffs' argument is grounded not on a right unequivocally vested in them by statute but on asserted constitutional rights of third parties, namely the non-joined bottlers' respective rights to due process. It is always refreshing when giant corporations evince solicitous regard for others' rights—and we have learned to expect refreshment from the Coca-Cola Company—but it is no occasion for judicial review of interlocutory agency decisions." Coca-Cola Co. v. Federal Trade Commission, 475 F.2d 299 (5th Cir.), cert. denied 414 U.S. 877 (1973).

The Eighth Circuit disposed of Seven-Up's contention in a relatively brief opinion in which Judge Stephenson stated in part, "We particularly agree with the reasoning of the Fifth Circuit. . . . Seven-Up must await a cease and desist order by the FTC, if such is ever to be issued, before jurisdiction will lie for a review of the interlocutory ruling it challenges." Seven-Up Co. v. Federal Trade Commission, 478 F.2d 755 (8th Cir.), cert. denied 414 U.S. 1013 (1973).

4. PepsiCo argues this to be the real thrust of Interstate Broadcasting Co. v. United States, 109 U.S.App.D.C. 255, 286 F.2d 539 (1960), and American Communications Ass'n v. United States, 298 F.2d 648 (2 Cir.1962), holding orders denying intervention in administrative proceedings to be immediately appealable in circumstances where erroneous denial might invalidate any future order, although the decisions are technically distinguishable since the precise issue was whether the orders fell within the statute permitting review of "final" FCC orders, now 28 U.S.C. § 2342. . . .

(2) GULF OIL CORP. v. UNITED STATES DEPARTMENT OF ENERGY, 663 F.2d 296 (D.C.Cir.1981). The Department of Energy (DOE) initiated an administrative proceeding by issuing a Proposed Remedial Order (PRO) which alleged that seven major producers of oil had charged prices 1.7 billion dollars in excess of what the applicable regulations permitted. A crucial issue in the case was whether the producers had misclassified "properties" from which crude oil was produced. The producers argued that the agency's regulations, particularly the definition of "property," were ambiguous on their face and had a history of inconsistent interpretation and application. The producers contended that they should not be penalized for failing to adhere to regulations whose meaning had neither been intelligently defined nor agreed upon by agency personnel themselves. Accordingly, they sought extensive discovery before the Office of Hearings and Appeals (OHA) of the agency's contemporaneous construction of its regulations and of agency documents relating to the issuance of PROs.

During the discovery process two incidents of alleged document destruction came to the producers' attention. They also learned that various agency personnel had engaged in numerous ex parte communications and in violation of an agency rule had not promptly made the communications available to the public and the participants in the proceeding. Producers filed over twenty discovery requests seeking extensive deposition and document discovery into both the document destruction and ex parte incidents. OHA held several hearings on these requests but did not rule on them for several months. Producers filed suit in the district court seeking declaratory and injunctive relief. The district court, although expressing its reluctance to interfere with the ongoing administrative proceeding, ordered the Secretary of Energy to appoint an independent ALJ "for the sole purpose of supervising such further document and deposition discovery as the [ALJ] determines is appropriate and reasonable to develop fully all facts concerning ex parte contacts with the hearing officer and any destruction of relevant documents by agency personnel." Defendants appealed, arguing that the district court had no jurisdiction "because the agency proceeding was still ongoing, and judicial intervention in an ongoing proceeding is barred by the twin doctrines of exhaustion and ripeness."

The court, per Judge Wald, rejected the arguments, concluding that "we have here a combination of (1) serious allegations originating in the agency itself of document destruction and prohibited ex parte communications between adjudicator and enforcement counsel, (2) backed by admissions of agency personnel that some such actions had already taken place, (3) along with a history of extremely restrictive discovery permitted to the parties to explore the extent of alleged document destruction or their cover-up and (4) the unavailability for an estimated five years under the agency's procedures of any judicial review of proceedings of massive scope and complexity. The totality of these circumstances in our view permitted the district court to make an exception to the normal exhaustion, finality, and ripeness rules and justified its limited order requiring that an agency-appointed ALJ conduct discovery into the allegations and report back to the court."

The court distinguished the FTC v. Standard Oil case as follows: "[T]he crucial difference between Standard Oil and this case is the nature of the judicial review sought. In Standard Oil, the plaintiffs sought an order requiring the FTC complaint to be withdrawn because it was issued as a result of political pressures and on the basis of insufficient evidence. Here, appellees are not in court challenging [DOE's] proposed remedial order or asking for its withdrawal. They want help in getting the proceeding tried fairly."

(3) Consider whether legislation similar to the following statute governing civil litigation should be made applicable to administrative agencies:

"When a district judge, in making in a civil action an order not otherwise appelable . . . , shall be of the opinion that such order involves a controlling question of law as to which there is substantial ground for difference of opinion and that an immediate appeal from the order may materially advance the ultimate termination of the litigation, he shall so state in writing in such order. The Court of Appeals may thereupon, in its discretion, permit an appeal to be taken from such order, if application is made to it within ten days after the entry of the order: Provided, however, That application for an appeal hereunder shall not stay proceedings in the district court unless the district judge or the Court of Appeals or a judge thereof shall so order." 28 U.S.C. § 1292(b).

c. Ripeness for Review

ABBOTT LABORATORIES v. GARDNER
Supreme Court of the United States, 1967.
387 U.S. 136.

MR. JUSTICE HARLAN delivered the opinion of the Court.

In 1962 Congress amended the Federal Food, Drug, and Cosmetic Act . . . to require manufacturers of prescription drugs to print the "established name" of the drug "prominently and in type at least half as large as that used thereon for any proprietary name or designation for such drug," on labels and other printed material . . . . The "established name" is one designated by the Secretary of Health, Education, and Welfare pursuant to § 502(e)(2) of the Act, 21 U.S.C. § 352(e)(2); the "proprietary name" is usually a trade name under which a particular drug is marketed. The underlying purpose of the 1962 amendment was to bring to the attention of doctors and patients the fact that many of the drugs sold under familiar trade names are actually identical to drugs sold under their "established" or less familiar trade names at significantly lower prices. The Commissioner of Food and Drugs, exercising authority delegated to him by the Secretary, published proposed regulations designed to implement the statute. After inviting and considering comments submitted by interested parties the Commissioner promulgated the following regulation for the "efficient enforcement" of the Act, § 701(a):

"If the label or labeling of a prescription drug bears a proprietary name or designation for the drug or any ingredient thereof, the established name, if such there be, corresponding to such proprietary name or designation, shall accompany each appearance of such proprietary name or designation." 21 CFR § 1.104(g)(1).

A similar rule was made applicable to advertisements for prescription drugs, 21 CFR § 1.105(b)(1).

The present action was brought by a group of 37 individual drug manufacturers and by the Pharmaceutical Manufacturers Association, of which all the petitioner companies are members, and which includes manufacturers of more than 90% of the Nation's supply of prescription drugs. They challenged the regulations on the ground that the Commissioner exceeded his authority under the statute by promulgating an order requiring labels, advertisements, and other printed matter relating to prescription drugs to designate the established name of the particular drug involved every time its trade name is used anywhere in such material.

The District Court, on cross motions for summary judgment, granted the declaratory and injunctive relief sought, finding that the statute did not sweep so broadly as to permit the Commissioner's "every time" interpretation. 228 F.Supp. 855. The Court of Appeals for the Third Circuit reversed without reaching the merits of the case. 352 F.2d 286. It held first that under the statutory scheme provided by the Federal Food, Drug, and Cosmetic Act pre-enforcement [1] review of these regulations was unauthorized and therefore beyond the jurisdiction of the District Court. Second, the Court of Appeals held that no "actual case or controversy" existed and, for that reason, that no relief under the Administrative Procedure Act or under the Declaratory Judgment Act was in any event available. Because of the general importance of the question, and the apparent conflict with the decision of the Court of Appeals for the Second Circuit in Toilet Goods Assn. v. Gardner, 360 F.2d 677, which we also review today, we granted certiorari.

I

The first question we consider is whether Congress by the Federal Food, Drug, and Cosmetic Act intended to forbid pre-enforcement review of this sort of regulation promulgated by the Commissioner. The question is phrased in terms of "prohibition" rather than "authorization" because a survey of our cases shows that judicial review of a final agency action by an aggrieved person will not be cut off unless there is persuasive reason to believe that such was the purpose of Congress. Early cases in which this type of judicial review was entertained have been reinforced by the enactment of the Administrative Procedure Act, which embodies the basic presumption of judicial review to one "suffering legal wrong because of agency action, or adversely

1. That is, a suit brought by one before any attempted enforcement of the statute or regulation against him.

affected or aggrieved by agency action within the meaning of a relevant statute," 5 U.S.C. § 702, so long as no statute precludes such relief or the action is not one committed by law to agency discretion, 5 U.S.C. § 701(a). The Administrative Procedure Act provides specifically not only for review of "[a]gency action made reviewable by statute" but also for review of "final agency action for which there is no other adequate remedy in a court," 5 U.S.C. § 704. The legislative material elucidating that seminal act manifests a congressional intention that it cover a broad spectrum of administrative actions,[2] and this Court has echoed that theme by noting that the Administrative Procedure Act's "generous review provision" must be given a "hospitable" interpretation . . . [and] that only upon a showing of "clear and convincing evidence" of a contrary legislative intent should the courts restrict access to judicial review. See also Jaffe, Judicial Control of Administrative Action 336–359 (1965).

Given this standard, we are wholly unpersuaded that the statutory scheme in the food and drug area excludes this type of action. The Government relies on no explicit statutory authority for its argument that pre-enforcement review is unavailable, but insists instead that because the statute includes a specific procedure for such review of certain enumerated kinds of regulations, not encompassing those of the kind involved here, other types were necessarily meant to be excluded from any pre-enforcement review. The issue, however, is not so readily resolved; we must go further and inquire whether in the context of the entire legislative scheme the existence of that circumscribed remedy evinces a congressional purpose to bar agency action not within its purview from judicial review. As a leading authority in this field has noted, "The mere fact that some acts are made reviewable should not suffice to support an implication of exclusion as to others. The right to review is too important to be excluded on such slender and indeterminate evidence of legislative intent." Jaffe, supra, at 357. . . .

[Justice Harlan's opinion here considers the specific review provisions of § 701(f) of the Act, their legislative history, the savings clause of § 701(f)(6) ("The remedies provided for in this subsection shall be in addition to and not in substitution for any other remedies provided by law"), and concludes that "nothing in the Food, Drug, and Cosmetic Act itself precludes this action."]

II

A further inquiry must, however, be made. The injunctive and declaratory judgment remedies are discretionary, and courts traditionally have been reluctant to apply them to administrative determinations unless these arise in the context of a controversy "ripe" for judicial resolution. Without undertaking to survey the intricacies of the ripeness doctrine it is fair to say that its basic rationale is to

---

2. See H.R.Rep. No. 1980, 79th Cong., 2d Sess., 41 (1946), U.S.Code Cong.Serv. 1946, p. 1195: "To preclude judicial review under this bill a statute, if not specific in withholding such review, must upon its face give clear and convincing evidence of an intent to withhold it. The mere failure to provide specially by statute for judicial review is certainly no evidence of intent to withhold review." . . .

prevent the courts, through avoidance of premature adjudication, from entangling themselves in abstract disagreements over administrative policies, and also to protect the agencies from judicial interference until an administrative decision has been formalized and its effects felt in a concrete way by the challenging parties. The problem is best seen in a twofold aspect, requiring us to evaluate both the fitness of the issues for judicial decision and the hardship to the parties of withholding court consideration.

As to the former factor, we believe the issues presented are appropriate for judicial resolution at this time. First, all parties agree that the issue tendered is a purely legal one: whether the statute was properly construed by the Commissioner to require the established name of the drug to be used *every time* the proprietary name is employed. Both sides moved for summary judgment in the District Court, and no claim is made here that further administrative proceedings are contemplated. It is suggested that the justification for this rule might vary with different circumstances, and that the expertise of the Commissioner is relevant to passing upon the validity of the regulation. This of course is true, but the suggestion overlooks the fact that both sides have approached this case as one purely of congressional intent, and that the Government made no effort to justify the regulation in factual terms.

Second, the regulations in issue we find to be "final agency action" within the meaning of § 10 of the Administrative Procedure Act, 5 U.S.C. § 704, as construed in judicial decisions. An "agency action" includes any "rule," defined by the Act as "an agency statement of general or particular applicability and future effect designed to implement, interpret, or prescribe law or policy," §§ 2(c), 2(g), 5 U.S.C. §§ 551(4), 551(13). The cases dealing with judicial review of administrative actions have interpreted the "finality" element in a pragmatic way. Thus in Columbia Broadcasting System v. United States, 316 U.S. 407, a suit under the Urgent Deficiencies Act, 38 Stat. 219, this Court held reviewable a regulation of the Federal Communications Commission setting forth certain proscribed contractual arrangements between chain broadcasters and local stations. The FCC did not have direct authority to regulate these contracts, and its rule asserted only that it would not license stations which maintained such contracts with the networks. Although no license had in fact been denied or revoked, and the FCC regulation could properly be characterized as a statement only of its intentions, the Court held that "Such regulations have the force of law before their sanctions are invoked as well as after. When as here they are promulgated by order of the Commission and the expected conformity to them causes injury cognizable by a court of equity, they are appropriately the subject of attack . . . ."

Two more recent cases have taken a similarly flexible view of finality. In Frozen Food Express v. United States, 351 U.S. 40, at issue was an Interstate Commerce Commission order specifying commodities that were deemed to fall within the statutory class of "agricultural commodities." Vehicles carrying such commodities were exempt from

ICC supervision. An action was brought by a carrier that claimed to be transporting exempt commodities, but which the ICC order had not included in its terms. Although the dissenting opinion noted that this ICC order had no authority except to give notice of how the Commission interpreted the Act and would have effect only if and when a particular action was brought against a particular carrier, and argued that "judicial intervention [should] be withheld until administrative action has reached its complete development," the Court held the order reviewable.

Again, in the United States v. Storer Broadcasting Co., 351 U.S. 192, the Court held to be a final agency action within the meaning of the Administrative Procedure Act an FCC regulation announcing a Commission policy that it would not issue a television license to an applicant already owning five such licenses, even though no specific application was before the Commission. The Court stated: "The process of rulemaking was complete. It was final agency action . . . by which Storer claimed to be 'aggrieved.' "

We find decision in the present case following a fortiori from these precedents. The regulation challenged here, promulgated in a formal manner after announcement in the Federal Register and consideration of comments by interested parties [3] is quite clearly definitive. There is no hint that this regulation is informal, see Helco Products Co. v. McNutt, 78 U.S.App.D.C. 71, 137 F.2d 681, 149 A.L.R. 345, or only the ruling of a subordinate official, or tentative. It was made effective upon publication, and the Assistant General Counsel for Food and Drugs stated in the District Court that compliance was expected.

The Government argues, however, that the present case can be distinguished from cases like Frozen Food Express on the ground that in those instances the agency involved could implement its policy directly, while here the Attorney General must authorize criminal and seizure actions for violations of the statute. In the context of this case, we do not find this argument persuasive. These regulations are not meant to advise the Attorney General, but purport to be directly authorized by the statute. Thus, if within the Commissioner's authority, they have the status of law and violations of them carry heavy criminal and civil sanctions. Also, there is no representation that the Attorney General and the Commissioner disagree in this area; the Justice Department is defending this very suit. It would be adherence to a mere technicality to give any credence to this contention. Moreover, the agency does have direct authority to enforce this regulation in the context of passing upon applications for clearance of new drugs or certification of certain antibiotics.

This is also a case in which the impact of the regulations upon the petitioners is sufficiently direct and immediate as to render the issue appropriate for judicial review at this stage. These regulations purport to give an authoritative interpretation of a statutory provision that has

---

3. Compare similar procedures followed in Frozen Food Express, supra, 351 U.S. at 41–42, and Storer, supra, 351 U.S. at 193– 194. The procedure conformed with that prescribed in § 4 of the Administrative Procedure Act, 5 U.S.C. § 1003.

a direct effect on the day-to-day business of all prescription drug companies; its promulgation puts petitioners in a dilemma that it was the very purpose of the Declaratory Judgment Act to ameliorate. As the District Court found on the basis of uncontested allegations, "Either they must comply with the every time requirement and incur the costs of changing over their promotional material and labeling or they must follow their present course and risk prosecution." The regulations are clear-cut, and were made effective immediately upon publication; as noted earlier the agency's counsel represented to the District Court that immediate compliance with their terms was expected. If petitioners wish to comply they must change all their labels, advertisements, and promotional materials; they must destroy stocks of printed matter; and they must invest heavily in new printing type and new supplies. The alternative to compliance—continued use of material which they believe in good faith meets the statutory requirements, but which clearly does not meet the regulation of the Commissioner—may be even more costly. That course would risk serious criminal and civil penalties for the unlawful distribution of "misbranded" drugs.[4]

It is relevant at this juncture to recognize that petitioners deal in a sensitive industry, in which public confidence in their drug products is especially important. To require them to challenge these regulations only as a defense to an action brought by the Government might harm them severely and unnecessarily. Where the legal issue presented is fit for judicial resolution, and where a regulation requires an immediate and significant change in the plaintiffs' conduct of their affairs with serious penalties attached to noncompliance, access to the courts under the Administrative Procedure Act and the Declaratory Judgment Act must be permitted, absent a statutory bar or some other unusual circumstance, neither of which appears here.

The Government does not dispute the very real dilemma in which petitioners are placed by the regulation, but contends that "mere financial expense" is not a justification for pre-enforcement judicial review. It is of course true that cases in this Court dealing with the standing of particular parties to bring an action have held that a possible financial loss is not by itself a sufficient interest to sustain a judicial challenge to governmental action. Frothingham v. Mellon, 262 U.S. 447; Perkins v. Lukens Steel Co., 310 U.S. 113. But there is no question in the present case that petitioners have sufficient standing as plaintiffs: the regulation is directed at them in particular; it requires them to make significant changes in their everyday business practices; if they fail to observe the Commissioner's rule they are quite clearly exposed to the imposition of strong sanctions. Compare Columbia Broadcasting System v. United States, 316 U.S. 407; 3 Davis, Administrative Law Treatise, c. 21 (1958). This case is, therefore, remote from the Mellon and Perkins cases.

4. Section 502(e)(1)(B) declares a drug not complying with this labeling requirement to be "misbranded." Section 301, 21 U.S.C. § 331, designates as "prohibited acts" the misbranding of drugs in interstate commerce. Such prohibited acts are subject to injunction, § 302, 21 U.S.C. § 332, criminal penalties, § 303, 21 U.S.C. § 333, and seizure, § 304(a), 21 U.S.C. § 334(a).

The Government further contends that the threat of criminal sanctions for noncompliance with a judicially untested regulation is unrealistic; the Solicitor General has represented that if court enforcement becomes necessary, "the Department of Justice will proceed only civilly for an injunction . . . or by condemnation." We cannot accept this argument as a sufficient answer to petitioners' petition. This action at its inception was properly brought and this subsequent representation of the Department of Justice should not suffice to defeat it.

Finally, the Government urges that to permit resort to the courts in this type of case may delay or impede effective enforcement of the Act. We fully recognize the important public interest served by assuring prompt and unimpeded administration of the Pure Food, Drug, and Cosmetic Act, but we do not find the Government's argument convincing. First, in this particular case, a pre-enforcement challenge by nearly all prescription drug manufacturers is calculated to speed enforcement. If the Government prevails, a large part of the industry is bound by the decree; if the Government loses, it can more quickly revise its regulation.

The Government contends, however, that if the Court allows this consolidated suit, then nothing will prevent a multiplicity of suits in various jurisdictions challenging other regulations. The short answer to this contention is that the courts are well equipped to deal with such eventualities. The venue transfer provision, 28 U.S.C. § 1404(a), may be invoked by the Government to consolidate separate actions. Or, actions in all but one jurisdiction might be stayed pending the conclusion of one proceeding. A court may even in its discretion dismiss a declaratory judgment or injunctive suit if the same issue is pending in litigation elsewhere. In at least one suit for a declaratory judgment, relief was denied with the suggestion that the plaintiff intervene in a pending action elsewhere. . . .

Further, the declaratory judgment and injunctive remedies are equitable in nature, and other equitable defenses may be interposed. If a multiplicity of suits are undertaken in order to harass the Government or to delay enforcement, relief can be denied on this ground alone. The defense of laches could be asserted if the Government is prejudiced by a delay. And courts may even refuse declaratory relief for the nonjoinder of interested parties who are not, technically speaking, indispensable.

In addition to all these safeguards against what the Government fears, it is important to note that the institution of this type of action does not by itself stay the effectiveness of the challenged regulation. There is nothing in the record to indicate that petitioners have sought to stay enforcement of the "every time" regulation pending judicial review. See 5 U.S.C. § 705. If the agency believes that a suit of this type will significantly impede enforcement or will harm the public interest, it need not postpone enforcement of the regulation and may oppose any motion for a judicial stay on the part of those challenging the regulation. Ibid. It is scarcely to be doubted that a court would refuse to postpone the effective date of an agency action if the Government could show, as it made no effort to do here, that delay would be detrimental to the public health or safety. See Associated Securities Corp. v. SEC, 10 Cir., 283 F.2d 773, 775, where a stay was denied because "the petitioners . . . [had] not sustained the burden of establishing that the requested stays will not be harmful to the public interest . . . ".

Lastly, although the Government presses us to reach the merits of the challenge to the regulation in the event we find the District Court properly entertained this action, we believe the better practice is to remand the case to the Court of Appeals for the Third Circuit to review the District Court's decision that the regulation was beyond the power of the Commissioner.

Reversed and remanded.

[In a companion case, Gardner v. Toilet Goods Association, 387 U.S. 167 (1967), the Court also upheld pre-enforcement review of regulations prescribing the use of color additives in foods, drugs and cosmetics. However, in the immediately following decision, which also was a companion case to Abbott Laboratories, the Court reached a different result.]

TOILET GOODS ASSOCIATION v. GARDNER
Supreme Court of the United States, 1967.
387 U.S. 158.

[The Commissioner of Food and Drugs promulgated the following regulation:

"(a) When it appears to the Commissioner that a person has:

. . .

"(4) Refused to permit duly authorized employees of the Food and Drug Administration free access to all manufacturing facilities, processes, and formulae involved in the manufacture of color additives and intermediates from which such color additives are derived; he may immediately suspend certification service to such person and may continue such suspension until adequate corrective action has been taken."

The Toilet Goods Association, an organization of cosmetic manufacturers and 39 individual manufacturers and distributors, sought declaratory and injunctive relief on the ground that the regulation was not authorized by the statute. The district court held that the issue was justiciable but the court of appeals reversed. The Supreme Court granted certiorari.]

MR. JUSTICE HARLAN delivered the opinion of the Court. . . .

As to the first of these [Abbott Laboratories] factors, we agree with the Court of Appeals that the legal issue as presently framed is not appropriate for judicial resolution. This is not because the regulation is not the agency's considered and formalized determination, for we are in agreement with petitioners that under this Court's decisions in Frozen Food Express v. United States, 351 U.S. 40, and United States v. Storer Broadcasting Co., 351 U.S. 192, there can be no question that this regulation—promulgated in a formal manner after notice and evaluation of submitted comments—is a "final agency action" under § 10 of the Administrative Procedure Act, 5 U.S.C. § 704. Also, we recognize the force of petitioners' contention that the issue as they have framed it presents a purely legal question: whether the regulation is totally beyond the agency's power under the statute, the type of legal issue that courts have occasionally dealt with without requiring a specific attempt at enforcement, Columbia Broadcasting System v. United States, 316 U.S. 407, or exhaustion of administrative remedies, Allen v. Grand Central Aircraft Co.

These points which support the appropriateness of judicial resolution are, however, outweighed by other considerations. The regulation serves notice only that the Commissioner *may* under certain circumstances order inspection of certain facilities and data, and that further certification of additives *may* be refused to those who decline to permit a duly authorized inspection until they have complied in that regard. At this juncture we have no idea whether or when such an inspection will be ordered and what reasons the Commissioner will give to justify his order. The statutory authority asserted for the regulation is the power to promulgate regulations "for the efficient enforcement" of the Act, § 701(a). Whether the regulation is justified thus depends not only, as petitioners appear to suggest, on whether Congress refused to include a specific section of the Act authorizing such inspections, although this factor is to be sure a highly relevant one, but also on whether the statutory scheme as a whole justified promulgation of the regulation. This will depend not merely on an inquiry into statutory purpose, but concurrently on an understanding of what types of enforcement problems are encountered by the FDA, the need for various sorts of supervision in order to effectuate the goals of the Act, and the safeguards devised to protect legitimate trade secrets (see 21 CFR § 130.14(c)). We believe that judicial appraisal of these factors is likely to stand on a much surer footing in the context of a specific application of this regulation than could be the case in the framework of the generalized challenge made here.

We are also led to this result by considerations of the effect on the petitioners of the regulation, for the test of ripeness, as we have noted, depends not only on how adequately a court can deal with the legal issue presented, but also on the degree and nature of the regulation's present effect on those seeking relief. The regulation challenged here is not analogous to those that were involved in Columbia Broadcasting System, supra, where the impact of the administrative action could be said to be felt immediately by those subject to it in conducting their day-to-day affairs.

This is not a situation in which primary conduct is affected—when contracts must be negotiated, ingredients tested or substituted, or special records compiled. This regulation merely states that the Commissioner may authorize inspectors to examine certain processes or formulae; no advance action is required of cosmetics manufacturers, who since the enactment of the 1938 Act have been under a statutory

duty to permit reasonable inspection of a "factory, warehouse, establishment, or vehicle and all pertinent equipment, finished and unfin-
ished materials; containers, and labeling therein." Moreover, no irremediable adverse consequences flow from requiring a later challenge to
this regulation by a manufacturer who refuses to allow this type of
inspection. Unlike the other regulations challenged in this action, in
which seizure of goods, heavy fines, adverse publicity for distributing
"adulterated" goods, and possible criminal liability might penalize
failure to comply, a refusal to admit an inspector here would at most
lead only to a suspension of certification services to the particular
party, a determination that can then be promptly challenged through
an administrative procedure, which in turn is reviewable by a court.
Such review will provide an adequate forum for testing the regulation
in a concrete situation.

It is true that the administrative hearing will deal with the
"factual basis" of the suspension, from which petitioners infer that the
Commissioner will not entertain and consider a challenge to his statutory authority to promulgate the regulation. Whether or not this assumption is correct, given the fact that only minimal, if any, adverse
consequences will face petitioners if they challenge the regulation in
this manner, we think it wiser to require them to exhaust this administrative process through which the factual basis of the inspection order
will certainly be aired and where more light may be thrown on the
Commissioner's statutory and practical justifications for the regulation.
Judicial review will then be available, and a court at that juncture will
be in a better position to deal with the question of statutory authority.
. . .

[Justice Brennan did not take part in any of the three cases.
Justice Douglas dissented in Toilet Goods Association v. Gardner.
Justice Fortas wrote the following concurring and dissenting opinion.]

MR. JUSTICE FORTAS, with whom THE CHIEF JUSTICE and MR. JUSTICE
CLARK join, concurring in No. 336, and dissenting in Nos. 39 and 438.

I am in agreement with the Court in No. 336, Toilet Goods
Association v. Gardner, that we should affirm the decision of the Court
of Appeals for the Second Circuit. . . .

I am, however, compelled to dissent from the decisions of the Court
in No. 39, Abbott Laboratories v. Gardner, and No. 438, Gardner v.
Toilet Goods Association. . . .

The Court, by today's decisions, has opened Pandora's box. Federal
injunctions will now threaten programs of vast importance to the public
welfare. The Court's holding here strikes at programs for the public
health. The dangerous precedent goes even further. It is cold comfort—it
is little more than delusion—to read in the Court's opinion that "It is
scarcely to be doubted that a court would refuse to postpone the effective
date of an agency action if the Government could show . . . that delay
would be detrimental to the public health or safety." Experience dictates,
on the contrary, that it can hardly be hoped that some federal judge
somewhere will not be moved as the Court is here, by the regulated's cries
of anguish and distress, to grant a disruptive injunction.

The difference between the majority and me in these cases is not with respect to the existence of jurisdiction to enjoin, but to the definition of occasions on which such jurisdiction may be invoked. I do not doubt that there is residual judicial power in some extreme and limited situations to enjoin administrative actions even in the absence of specific statutory provision where the agency has acted unconstitutionally or without jurisdiction—as distinguished from an allegedly erroneous action. But the Court's opinions in No. 39 and No. 438 appear to proceed on the principle that, even where no constitutional issues or questions of administrative jurisdiction or of arbitrary procedure are involved, exercise of judicial power to enjoin allegedly erroneous regulatory action is permissible unless Congress has explicitly prohibited it, provided only that the controversy is "ripe" for judicial determination. This is a rule that is novel in its breadth and destructive in its implications as illustrated by the present application. . . . I believe that this approach improperly and unwisely gives individual federal district judges a roving commission to halt the regulatory process, and to do so on the basis of abstractions and generalities instead of concrete fact situations, and that it impermissibly broadens the license of the courts to intervene in administrative action by means of threshold suit for injunction rather than by the method provided by statute. . . .

Now, with all respect, I submit that this controversy is clearly, transparently and obviously unsuited to adjudication by the courts in limine or divorced from a particular controversy. Every reason advanced in No. 336 (the access regulation) is applicable here with equal or greater force to repel this effort to secure judicial review at this stage. . . .

The regulation in No. 39 relates to a 1962 amendment to the Act requiring manufacturers of prescription drugs to print on the labels or other printed material, the "established name" of the drug "prominently and in type at least half as large as that used thereon for any proprietary name or designation for such drug." Obviously, this requires some elucidation, either case-by-case or by general regulation or pronouncement, because the statute does not say that this must be done "every time," or only once on each label or in each pamphlet, or once per panel, etc., or that it must be done differently on labels than on circulars, or doctor's literature than on directions to the patients, etc. This is exactly the traditional purpose and function of an administrative agency. The Commissioner acting by delegation from the Secretary, took steps to provide for the specification. He invited and considered comments and then issued a regulation requiring that the "established name" appear every time the proprietary name is used. A manufacturer—or other person who violates this regulation—has mislabeled his product. The product may be seized; or injunction may be sought; or the mislabeler may be criminally prosecuted. In any of these actions he may challenge the regulation and obtain a judicial determination.

The Court, however, moved by petitioners' claims as to the expense and inconvenience of compliance and the risks of deferring challenge by noncompliance, decrees that the manufacturers may have their suit for injunction at this time and reverses the Third Circuit. The Court says that this confronts the manufacturer with a "real dilemma." But the fact of the matter is that the dilemma is no more than citizens face in connection with countless statutes and with the rules of the SEC, FTC, FCC, ICC, and other regulatory agencies. This has not heretofore been regarded as a basis for injunctive relief unless Congress has so provided. The overriding fact here is—or should be—that the public interest in avoiding the delay in implementing Congress' program far outweighs the private interest; and that the private interest which has so impressed the Court is no more than that which exists in respect of most regulatory statutes or agency rules. Somehow, the Court has concluded that the damage to petitioners if they have to engage in the required redesign and reprint of their labels and printed materials without threshold review outweighs the damage to the public of deferring during the tedious months and years of litigation a cure for the possible danger and asserted deceit of peddling plain medicine under fancy trademarks and for fancy prices which, rightly or wrongly, impelled the Congress to enact this legislation. I submit that a much stronger showing is necessary than the expense and trouble of compliance and the risk of defiance. Actually, if the Court refused to permit this blunderbuss assault, experience and reasonably sophisticated common-sense show that there would be orderly compliance without the disaster so dramatically predicted by the industry, reasonable adjustments by the agency in real hardship cases, and where extreme intransigence involving substantial violations occurred, enforcement actions in which legality of the regulation would be tested in specific, concrete situations. I respectfully submit that this would be the correct and appropriate result. Our refusal to respond to the vastly overdrawn cries of distress would reflect not only healthy skepticism, but our regard for a proper relationship between the courts on the one hand and Congress and the administrative agencies on the other. It would represent a reasonable solicitude for the purposes and programs of the Congress. And it would reflect appropriate modesty as to the competence of the courts. The courts cannot properly—and should not—attempt to judge in the abstract and generally whether this regulation is within the statutory scheme. Judgment as to the "every time" regulation should be made only in light of specific situations, and it may differ depending upon whether the FDA seeks to enforce it as to doctors' circulars, pamphlets for patients, labels, etc.

I submit, therefore, that this invitation to the courts to rule upon the legality of these regulations in these actions for injunction and declaratory relief should be firmly rejected. . . .

NOTES

(1) Abbott Laboratories is the leading case on ripeness for review of administrative action. In Judge McGowan's words, it "dominates the field." Continental Airlines, Inc. v. CAB, 522 F.2d 107, 124 (D.C.Cir.

1975). Professor Davis believes that the ripeness law of Abbott and its progeny "is stable and satisfactory [and] is largely the opposite of what it was under the Supreme Court's decisions of the 1940s and 1950s, when the Court was rendering extreme decisions closing the judicial doors, even when plaintiffs were seriously hurt by onerous legal uncertainties." K. Davis, Admin.L. Treatise Supp. 158 (1978).[1] As you study the following materials, consider whether the judicial work product supports the view that the ripeness doctrine is now both "stable and satisfactory." Consider also whether the standards of Abbott Laboratories should continue to "dominate the field" or whether reformulation or modification would be desirable.

(2) BETTER GOVERNMENT ASSOCIATION v. DEPARTMENT OF STATE, 780 F.2d 86 (D.C.Cir.1986). The Freedom of Information Act (FOIA) authorizes agencies to impose "reasonable standard charges for document research and duplication" to recover the direct costs of such services. The statute also provides that documents "shall be furnished without charge or at a reduced charge where the agency determines that waiver or reduction of the fee is in the public interest because furnishing the information can be considered as primarily benefiting the general public." In 1980 a congressional subcommittee concluded that most agencies had been too restrictive in granting fee waivers for the indigent, news media, scholars and recommended that the Department of Justice (DOJ) develop guidelines to deal with those problems. In December 1980 DOJ promulgated interim guidelines and in January 1983 issued a new memorandum that superseded the interim guidelines. The 1983 memorandum stated DOJ's twofold commitment to "encourage waiver of fees where disclosures of the requested information will primarily benefit the general public" and to "the preservation of public funds where there will be insufficient public benefit derived from disclosure." The memorandum then listed five general factors that agencies should consider in determining whether to grant a fee waiver.[2]

1. But cf., Note, Pre-Enforcement Review of Administrative Agency Action: Developments in the Ripeness Doctrine, 53 Notre Dame Lawy. 346, 356–357 (1977): "Although the general standards for pre-enforcement review have been clearly defined since the Supreme Court's decision in Abbott Laboratories . . . , [t]here are many uncertainties with regard to the availability of pre-enforcement review . . . [which] have, at times, closed the doors of review to plaintiffs who were genuinely injured by an agency action."

2. Those factors are:

"(1) whether there is a genuine public interest in the subject matter of the documents . . . There is no universal formula by which the existence and extent of legitimate public interest in the subject matter of FOIA requests can be evaluated, so each agency must draw on its unique expertise in making these judgments about the subject matter of its own records. The 'public' to be benefited need not be so broad as to encompass all citizens, but it must be distinct from the requester alone;

"(2) the value to the public of the records themselves . . . [T]he public is benefited only if the information released meaningfully contributes to the public development or understanding of the subject;

"(3) whether the requested information is already available in the public domain;

"(4) a requester's identity and qualifications; and

"(5) any personal interest of the requester reasonably expected to be benefited by disclosure . . . . It is necessary to assess the magnitude of any such personal interest, and then to compare it with that of any discernible public benefit. . . . . "

Better Government Association (BGA) is a nonprofit organization that conducts investigations designed to expose waste, fraud and abuse in the functioning of government programs. National Wildlife Federation (NWF) is a nonprofit organization dedicated to the promotion of conservation principles. BGA made an FOIA request to the Department of State (State) for audits, inspections or reports regarding the five American embassies receiving the largest number of official visitors, and petitioned for a fee waiver. NWF submitted an FOIA request to the Department of Interior (Interior) for documents relating to the impact of proposed coal exchanges and lease sales on fish and wildlife, and petitioned for a fee waiver. Although both State and Interior had promulgated regulations pertaining to fee waivers, in these two cases the departments relied on the DOJ guidelines in denying the petitions for fee waivers; also the two departments stated their intention to employ the DOJ guidelines in processing FOIA fee waiver requests in the future. Both BGA and NWF sought relief in the district court. Thereafter State and Interior announced that the petitions for fee waivers would be granted and moved for summary judgment on the ground that granting the fee waivers rendered the cases moot as to the plaintiffs' specific requests and unripe as to their challenges to the DOJ guidelines. The district court granted the motions for summary judgments, and plaintiffs appealed.

The case was heard by D.C. Circuit Judges Wright and Edwards and Federal Circuit Judge Davis. Judge Edwards, who wrote the opinion, and Judge Davis held that the plaintiffs' "challenge to the guidelines as applied to their specific fee waiver requests is, in fact, moot."[3] But the facial challenges to the DOJ guidelines are ripe for review:

"Initially, we find that the questions presented by the instant case are fit for judicial resolution. Both appellants contend that, on their face, the DOJ guidelines violate FOIA. This question will be resolved by an analysis of FOIA, its legislative history, and its construction by relevant case law. Likewise, BGA's procedural challenge to the guidelines raises the purely legal question of whether State violated section 553(c) of the Administrative Procedure Act (APA) by its failure to give public notice of, and an opportunity to comment on the guidelines. Finally, NWF alleges that the failure of Interior to promulgate regulations establishing specific criteria to govern FOIA fee waiver requests violates a purported FOIA requirement that all agencies do so. Each claim presents purely legal questions, the understanding of which neither requires nor is facilitated by further factual development. Our appraisal of the legitimacy of the DOJ guidelines in light of the statutory requirements of FOIA and the APA would not be enhanced by the existence of a particular FOIA fee waiver request.[4]

3. Judge Wright, concurring in the result, said that he would apply "the well-established rule that when a defendant voluntarily ceases an allegedly unlawful activity, the challenge to this activity is not rendered moot unless there is no reasona-ble expectation that the wrong will not be repeated."

4. Although the meaning of the guidelines and regulation might be illustrated by their application to particular fee waiver requests, such illustrations are not nec-

"Second, we find that the agency action in question has taken its final form. The DOJ guidelines at issue have been in effect well over two years. Both appellee departments assert that they will continue to rely upon the DOJ guidelines in their evaluation of FOIA fee waiver requests. Neither appellee has indicated that it intends to subject the guidelines to public notice and comment; nor has Interior suggested that it intends to take steps to adopt revised or different regulations. In other words, on the present record, it seems clear that Interior and State have utilized and will continue to utilize the standards at issue in their present form. From what appellees have said, no further procedural or substantive evolution is expected.

"The appellees' description of the guidelines as 'informal' is not definitive in our ripeness determination.[5] Courts have taken a 'flexible' and 'pragmatic' view of the finality of agency action. Where, as here, the agency has stated that the action in question *governs and will continue to govern* its decisions, such action must be viewed as final in our analysis of ripeness.[6] [W]hat is decisive is the substance of what [the agency] has done;' here State and Interior have made final, not tentative, decisions to utilize the challenged fee waiver standards.

"Finally, we hold that the continued use of the DOJ guidelines and the Interior regulation has a 'direct and immediate' impact on the appellants that rises to the level of hardship. These guidelines 'purport to give an authoritative interpretation of a statutory provision that has a direct effect on the day-to-day business of [the appellants.]' As noted above, both BGA and NWF rely heavily and frequently on FOIA and its fee waiver provision to conduct the investigations that are essential to the performance of certain of their primary institutional activities— publicizing governmental choices and highlighting possible abuses that otherwise might go undisputed and thus unchallenged. These investigations are the necessary prerequisites to the fundamental publicizing and mobilizing functions of these organizations. Access to information through FOIA is vital to their organizational missions.

"Thus, the 'primary conduct' of the appellants is affected by the standards at issue. Moreover, this impact is 'felt immediately.' The appellants are nonprofit public interest groups that routinely make FOIA requests that potentially would not be made absent a fee waiver provision. While under normal circumstances an appellant's budgetary constraints would not weigh decisively in our hardship evaluation, here

essary to appellants' challenges. They contend that, *even without application,* the standards are facially inconsistent with FOIA and violate the APA, and are therefore illegal. It is these claims that we hereby hold ripe for review.

5. See Continental Airlines, Inc. v. CAB, 522 F.2d 107, 124 (D.C.Cir.1974) ("The label an agency attaches to its action is not determinative."). Although it is not clear whether State and Interior were *required* to adopt the DOJ guidelines, they apparently have constructively done so.

6. Although certain of the questions that are pertinent to ripeness may also go to the merits, we do not mean to prejudge the merits of these cases. The ripeness issue—concerning whether these cases are now fit for review—is separate from the questions concerning the nature of the guidelines and regulation, their alleged inconsistency with the legal mandate of FOIA, and the alleged applicability of notice and comment rulemaking under the APA. It is these latter questions that will be resolved by the District Court on remand.

we have the additional authority of a Congressional determination that such constraints should not impede the access to information for appellants *such as these.*

"Congress explicitly recognized the importance and the difficulty of access to governmental documents for such typically under-funded organizations and individuals when it enacted the 'public benefit' test for FOIA fee waivers. This waiver provision was added to FOIA 'in an attempt to prevent government agencies from using high fees to discourage certain types of requesters and requests' in a clear reference to requests from journalists, scholars and, most importantly for our purposes, nonprofit public interest groups. Congress made clear its intent that fees should not be utilized to discourage requests or to place obstacles in the way of such disclosure, forbidding the use of fees as ' "toll gate[s]" ' on the public access road to information.' Payment in advance, followed by litigation to recover costs, may often be impossible if costs are prohibitive. Thus, insofar as these appellants are correct that the DOJ guidelines and standards in question act to discourage FOIA requests and to impede access to information for precisely those groups Congress intended to aid by the fee waiver provision, they inflict a continuing hardship on the nonprofit public interest groups who depend on FOIA to supply their lifeblood—information. The appellants allege that the DOJ guidelines act to 'chill' the ability and willingness of their organizations to engage in activity that is not only voluntary, but that Congress explicitly wished to encourage.

"We recognize that this hardship analysis relies in part upon an acceptance of the appellants' view of the merits. However, when, as here, '[t]he issue of harm and the issue on the merits are intertwined,' we properly adopt such a perspective from which to address the threshold consideration of ripeness. See note 6 supra.

.   .   .

"[T]he appellants allege that, on their face, the guidelines deny them certain, purported statutory entitlements, such as, for example, a presumption that they, as nonprofit, public interest groups, must receive FOIA fee waivers. [T]he allegedly impermissible standards have been and are now employed by the appellee departments, creating a current 'impairment of rights' under FOIA.[7] .   .   .

"In sum, the prudential considerations implicated by the ripeness doctrine all militate for judicial review in the instant case. The issues are purely legal, the agency actions final, and the hardship to the parties created by withholding review are concrete and present. These facial challenges to the guidelines and to Interior's failure to promulgate specific criteria governing fee waiver determinations are now ripe for judicial resolution."

---

7. Our conclusion that appellants will suffer hardship if review is withheld also holds true for BGA's claim that State's failure to expose the guidelines to notice and comment violates the APA. BGA is an interested party and arguably suffers continuing injury to its procedural rights if State has altered its practice without following APA requirements.

(3) DIAMOND SHAMROCK CORP. v. COSTLE, 580 F.2d 670 (D.C.Cir.1978). The Federal Water Pollution Control Act provides that the discharge of pollutants into navigable rivers shall be in compliance with permits issued by the Environmental Protection Agency (EPA). A permit specifies the effluent limitations to which a permittee must adhere when discharging wastewater. Complying with the provisions of section 553 of the APA, the EPA promulgated regulations which provided that permits issued by the regional administrators of the EPA should express effluent limitations in gross terms. Thus, a permittee is given no credits for pollutants already present in its intake water. Several chemical manufacturers sought review of the regulations. The court, in an opinion by Judge Robb, joined by Judges Robinson and Wilkey, affirmed the district court's decision that the matter would not be ripe until the regulations were applied in a permit proceeding.

The appellants alleged that the regulations "now operate to control [their] business affairs" and to place them in an "acute dilemma" because of the stringent deadlines the Act imposes for achieving compliance with permits and the leadtimes needed to design and construct conforming treatment facilities. But, said the court, "appellants have failed to substantiate this bare assertion either in their briefs or at oral argument. They have not, for example alleged that design or construction must commence before a permit issues or that they could not meet the deadlines." In addition, once the regulations are applied in a permit proceeding, the statute provides for judicial review. Thus, the case is unlike Abbott Laboratories and CBS v. United States in that in those cases the affected parties were confronted with the "painful choice between immediate compliance with an agency's policy, at great expense, and the risk of serious penalties should their challenge in a later proceeding be unsuccessful" whereas in this case the "appellants have failed to point to any present damaging effect from the EPA's regulations."

Although appellants' challenges to the regulations present issues which "are for the most part 'legal', that characterization does not end the inquiry. See Toilet Goods Ass'n v. Gardner, 387 U.S. 158, 162 (1967). In this case we believe that the administrative process will benefit from our withholding review. Although the regulations were promulgated after informal rulemaking and thus the order adopting them may be considered sufficiently final to permit review, the Administrator is not barred from changing his policy as experience in applying the regulations is gained. Moreover, the regulations appear merely to be an interpretation of how the earlier promulgated effluent limitations are to be applied. The impact of the regulations will depend in part upon their interpretation by the EPA's regional administrators . . . . Accordingly, we are unwilling to disrupt this administrative process when 'no irremediable adverse consequences flow from requiring a later challenge to this regulation.' Toilet Goods, supra, 337 U.S. at 164.

"The interest of the courts will also be furthered by withholding review. Judicial review is generally facilitated by waiting until administrative policy is implemented for then a court can be freed, at least in part, from theorizing about how a rule will be applied and what its effect will be. This principle seems especially apt in this case where the effect of the regulations is derivative; unlike many regulations which prescribe the conduct required of a party, these regulations—requiring that effluent limitations be expressed in gross terms—specify no standards until applied to particular effluent limitations. Therefore, rather than speculate about the consequences the regulations will have, we believe it more appropriate in the absence of hardship to the appellants to wait until the regulations are applied and their consequences realized.   . . .

"Determination of ripeness is, as we have said, a commonsense judgment. Continental Air Lines [v. CAB], 522 F.2d 107, 124 (D.C.Cir. 1975). Here, we believe, practicalities demand that judicial review be withheld; postponing review will impose no hardship on appellants and it will enhance the administrative process and assist judicial review. Accordingly, we affirm the District Court's dismissal. Once the regulations have been applied, administrative review will then be available."

(4) Suppose that in a case similar to Diamond Shamrock, counsel for the chemical manufacturers, anticipating an adverse decision on the ripeness issue, considers whether it would be prudent to postpone seeking review until later developments made the matter ripe. Suppose also that the relevant statute provides:

> Review of any regulation promulgated under the Act may be had upon application by any interested person only in the Circuit Court of Appeals of the United States for the District of Columbia. Any such application shall be made within ninety days from the date of promulgation of such regulations. Any matter with respect to which review could have been obtained under this subsection shall not be subject to judicial review in any civil or criminal proceeding for enforcement or to obtain damages or recovery of response costs.

Should counsel seek review within 90 days of promulgation of the regulation or should she await occurrence of ripening events?

The answer of the D.C. Circuit may be found in EAGLE-PICHER INDUSTRIES v. UNITED STATES ENVIRONMENTAL PROTECTION AGENCY, 759 F.2d 905 (D.C.Cir.1985). Judge Edwards wrote for himself. Chief Judge Robinson and Judge Starr:

"Ripeness . . . is largely a prudential doctrine, 'whose basic rationale is to prevent the courts, through avoidance of premature adjudication, from entangling themselves in abstract disagreements over administrative policies, and also to protect the agencies from judicial interference until an administrative decision has been formalized and its effects felt in a concrete way by the challenging parties.' Timeliness requirements, on the other hand, are designed to protect a different set of interests. They are intended to prevent courts from 'entangling themselves' in disputes which Congress has determined have been raised too late and to protect agencies from endless judicial interference with formalized administrative policy.

"Because the principal function of the ripeness doctrine is to aid a court in ascertaining whether it should stay its hand until agency policy has crystallized, most of the case law explicating the doctrine is forward-looking, that is, looking into the future to determine the effects of deferring review.[1] Only rarely does case law depict the ripeness doctrine in the service of a tardy petitioner—looking backward to divine whether the court would have considered the request for review ripe had it been brought in a timely fashion. Indeed, we know of only one case from this circuit, Geller v. FCC, [610 F.2d 973 (D.C.Cir.1979)], where we explicitly evaluated the retrospective ripeness of an untimely challenge. There the petitioner solicited review of an FCC regulation nearly five years after the statutory review period had expired. We dismissed all of Geller's claims for lack of timeliness, except one which had clearly just become ripe with the passage of new legislation.

"We think Geller may suggest one of two kinds of cases where the court should perform a retrospective ripeness analysis for a petitioner who has failed to file a timely request for review. The Geller type can be characterized as a case in which events occur or information becomes available after the statutory review period expires that essentially create a challenge that did not previously exist.[2] The other type involves claims that, under our precedents, are without any doubt not ripe for review during the statutory period. For example, Diamond Shamrock held that certain effluent limitation regulations promulgated under the Federal Water Pollution Control Act were not ripe for review until applied in discharge permit proceedings. Obviously, other would-be petitioners in the same position as those in Diamond Shamrock—applicants for discharge permits under the same statute—can rely on the holding in that case.

"As a general proposition, however, if there is *any* doubt about the ripeness of a claim, petitioners must bring their challenge in a timely fashion or risk being barred. Courts simply are not well-suited to answering hypothetical questions which involve guessing what the court might have done in the past. Furthermore, if we were routinely to conduct retrospective ripeness analyses where a late petitioner offers no compelling justification for not having filed his claim in a timely manner, we would wreak havoc with the congressional intention that repose be brought to final agency action. Consequently, except where events occur or information becomes available after the statutory

---

1. The orientation of the ripeness doctrine toward the future is apparent in Abbott Laboratories where the Supreme Court explained that, in addition to ascertaining the fitness of the issues for judicial decision, the court must consider "the hardship to the parties of *withholding* court consideration." 387 U.S. at 149 (emphasis added).

2. In Investment Co. Inst. [v. Board of Governors, 551 F.2d 1270 (D.C.Cir.1977),] we noted the two methods by which petitioners may request review of agency regulations after the statutory period has ex-

pired. The preferred method is for the petitioners first to ask the agency to reconsider the regulation and then to request review of the agency's decision in this court. But, where not precluded by statute, the petitioners generally may challenge the rule also when it is applied to them in an agency adjudication. We emphasized there, as we do here, that absent a convincing justification for failure to request review during the statutory period, the court will refuse to hear an untimely challenge.

review period expires that essentially create a challenge that did not previously exist, or where a petitioner's claim is, under our precedents, *indisputably* not ripe until the agency takes further action, we will be very reluctant, in order to save a late petitioner from the strictures of a timeliness requirement, to engage in a retrospective determination of whether we would have held the claim ripe had it been brought on time."

NATIONAL AUTOMATIC LAUNDRY AND CLEANING COUNCIL v. SHULTZ

United States Court of Appeals, District of Columbia Circuit, 1971.
443 F.2d 689.

[Prior to 1966, section 13(a)(3) of the Fair Labor Standards Act specifically exempted "any employee employed by any establishment engaged in laundering, cleaning, or repairing clothing or fabrics." In 1963, the Administrator of the Wage and Hour Division of the Department of Labor ruled that coin-operated launderettes were "engaged in renting the service of the laundry machines rather than engaged in laundering or cleaning" and hence were not entitled to the 13(a)(3) exemption; however, they were entitled to a 13(a)(2) exemption as a retail or service establishment. In 1966, Congress amended the Act to repeal the 13(a)(3) exemption and added a provision that establishments "engaged in laundering, cleaning or repairing clothing or fabrics" could no longer qualify for the 13(a)(2) retail exemption.

Plaintiff is a national trade association of 72 manufacturers, 119 distributors, and 1260 operators or owners of coin-operated laundry and dry-cleaning enterprises. On January 17, 1967, plaintiff's attorneys wrote to the Administrator inquiring about the 1966 amendments, which were to be effective February 1, 1967. Plaintiff reasoned that since the Administrator had ruled in 1963 that its members were renting the service of laundry machines and not "engaged in laundering, cleaning or repair of clothing or fabrics," the 1966 amendments did not affect the 1963 ruling that its members were entitled to the 13(a)(2) retail exemption. The letter therefore stated, "We wish to confirm that [the 1963 ruling] still applies to our client's business." The letter concluded by setting forth three typical fact situations prevailing in the coin-operated laundry business and requested the opinion of the Administrator as to the Act's applicability to each example. The Administrator replied by letter dated April 6, 1967, which stated in part: "The legislative history of the 1966 amendments to the Fair Labor Standards Act makes it clear that a coin-operated launderette or dry cleaning service is engaged in laundering or cleaning clothing or fabrics within the meaning of the act. The amendments extend the coverage of the act to employees in enterprises engaged in laundering, cleaning or repairing clothing or fabrics."

Plaintiff then brought an action for a declaratory judgment that the Administrator's ruling was invalid. The district court dismissed the action, stating, "[T]he Court is of the opinion that there exists no case or controversy between the parties." Plaintiff appealed.]

Before WRIGHT, LEVENTHAL and ROBINSON, CIRCUIT JUDGES.

LEVENTHAL, CIRCUIT JUDGE: . . . .

The Government raises the basic question whether the courts may appropriately provide the judicial review sought by plaintiff of the interpretation by the Administrator. In past decisions refraining from judicial review courts have summoned, and often confused, a variety of concepts, finding a lack in one or another of the elements a suitor must provide to obtain judicial review: case or controversy; standing; finality (or formality); ripeness; suitability of case for relief in equity or declaratory judgment. These concepts are separable, and for clarity of analysis we discuss them separately, but with awareness that they are intermeshed in the overall determination of the appropriate occasion for judicial review. . . .

[The court first held that plaintiff had standing and then turned to " 'ripeness' and to the opinions in Abbott Laboratories . . . and the sister cases:" Toilet Goods and Gardner.]

B. RIPENESS . . . .

Fitness of Issues for Judicial Resolution

In Abbott Laboratories, the Supreme Court found the issues fit for judicial resolution because "all parties agree that the issue tendered is a purely legal one: whether the statute was properly construed by the Commissioner . . . ." This is, of course, the precise substantive issue in the instant case—the effect of the 1966 amendments to the Act on its application to coin-operated laundries. . . . There is no "record" to be studied or made, for the only record involved on this issue is that established by such materials as the law and its legislative history. . . .

Hardship to Parties of Deferring Court Consideration

. . .

Plaintiff association (NALCC) says its members are confronted with adverse financial consequences if they comply with the Administrator's view and with consequences of serious litigation if they do not. The Government brief says the coin-operated laundries are not faced with a "Hobson's choice" and continues (p. 6): "They can safely do nothing. If it later develops that the Administrator was correct, and they should have raised their wages to meet the statutory minimum, they have only to pay back the additional wages they should have been paying all along."

If the Administrator is correct in his interpretation of the 1966 law, the owners of coin-operated laundries who are paying their employees at rates which are in violation of the Act are subject not only to injunctive enforcement proceedings under § 17 of the Act; and in extreme cases to criminal liability under § 16(a); but also to actions for double damages, denominated "liquidated damages," brought by affected employees under § 16(b). The provision inserted by Congress as a meaningful penalty and deterrent cannot be passed off by Government lawyers as a prospect of no substantial legal consequence. . . .

C. FINALITY AND INFORMALITY OF RULINGS

The courts will not interfere with the executive function, whether exercised by executive officials or administrative agencies, by entertaining a lawsuit that challenges an action that is not final. The APA provides in § 10 for judicial review of "final agency action." 5 U.S.C. § 704. But the term "agency action" includes "rule," and that in turn is defined in § 2 as "an agency statement of general or particular applicability and future effect designed to implement, interpret, or prescribe law or policy." 5 U.S.C. § 551(4) (Supp. V, 1970). The term "agency action" thus embraces an agency's interpretation of its law, and it is the finality of that action that we must consider.

The issue of finality is, as the Court noted in Abbott Laboratories determined not by the name assigned by the agency to its action but "in a pragmatic way." The Court has found final action in a wide array of pronouncements and communications having the contemplation and likely consequence of "expected conformity." . . .

General Consideration of "Informal" Actions

The Government insists that the present order lacks finality because it is "informal." In Abbott Laboratories the Court took note that the interpretative regulation was issued "in a formal manner after announcement in the Federal Register and consideration of comments by interested parties," and was "quite clearly definitive." And the Court noted there was "no hint that this regulation is informal, see Helco Products Co. v. McNutt, 137 F.2d 681 . . . ."

This court's 1943 Helco opinion involved acts not yet done by the person subject to the challenged regulatory activity. Helco had written a letter to the Food and Drug Administration explaining why it did not consider its proposed shipment of white poppy seeds dyed blue at variance with the Food, Drug and Cosmetic Act and requested an FDA opinion. The FDA Commissioner wrote back a letter saying that it was "our considered opinion" that the proposed shipment would be unlawful. In affirming a dismissal of Helco's declaratory judgment suit this court said: "Obviously, the declaration of the Commissioner is several steps removed from a threat of prosecution. Neither he nor his superior, the Federal Security Administrator, has power to prosecute or to require prosecution. Moreover, . . . his advisory opinion, in answer to a hypothetical question, does not foreclose a contrary conclusion, by him, upon an actual state of facts. . . . To permit suits for declaratory judgments upon mere informal, advisory, administrative opinions might well discourage the practice of giving such opinions, with a net loss of far greater proportions to the average citizen than any possible gain which could accrue." . . .

There is no question . . . concerning the reasoning in Helco which disclaims judicial review of executive determinations on hypothetical inquiries. But that doctrine simply has no application to the instant case. The plaintiff Association did not present to the Administrator a hypothetical set of facts, rather it set out the actual and present operations of its members. . . .

Lack of Finality in Advisory Opinions Subject to Authoritative Reconsideration

In Helco the court pointed out that a ruling on a hypothetical question might be subject to reconsideration when an actual problem materialized. This aspect of nonfinality, that the ruling involved does not represent the final, that is to say, ultimate, authoritative decision of the executive official or agency may be applicable even when the inquiry is not hypothetical.

A businessman unable to obtain a final, authoritative ruling on the matter at hand is nevertheless interested in an "advisory" indication, perhaps from a subordinate official, which can serve the purpose of providing an informed though not binding prediction. There are sound reasons why such advisory letters and opinions should not be subject to judicial review. This technique of apprising persons informally as to their rights and liabilities has been termed an "excellent practice in administrative procedure." [1] There is surely a need for such informality in the administration of the Fair Labor Standards Act, a law deemed "full of baffling questions of application." Indeed, we are told that the "Wage and Hour Division of the Department of Labor answers some 750,000 inquiries from the public each year; of this number, 10,000 are signed by the Administrator." (Brief of Appellees, at 8). Advisory opinions should, to the greatest extent possible, be available to the public as a matter of routine; it would be unfortunate if the prospect of judicial review were to make an agency reluctant to give them. . . .

In view of the hundreds of thousands of inquiries the Wage and Hour Division answers each year, a lack of formality is understandable, and, of course, the overwhelming majority of these will not be appropriate for review by a court by way of declaratory judgment. But it does not follow that a letter intended as a deliberative determination of the agency's position at the highest available level on a question of importance is to be lumped together with the mass of interpretative correspondence as a mere "informal" expression. As appears from the data already cited, only 1.25% of the Division's answers to inquiries are signed by the Administrator himself.

Presumptiveness of Finality in Interpretation or Ruling by Head of an Agency

Even the head of an agency, it may be contended, operates on more than one level of deliberativeness. And it may be urged that a ruling made without that kind of assurance of deliberativeness that is presented by a hearing, or a structured controversy, may be the kind of ruling that is more truly subject to reconsideration. Certainly we know that the head of an agency may make tentative rulings and may reconsider

---

1. Commission on Organization of the Executive Branch of the Government, Task   Force Report on Legal Services and Procedure 189 (1955).

rulings previously made. This much is recognized by § 10 of the Portal-to-Portal Act of 1947, which permits employers to rely in good faith on the Administrator's rulings and interpretations at least until issuance of a subsequent ruling changing the rule previously announced.

We think the sound course is to accept the ruling of a board or commission, or the head of an agency, as presumptively final. If it does not indicate on its face that it is only tentative, it would be likely to be accepted as authoritative . . . . [E]ven in the absence of such [an indication], a court might decline to entertain a litigation if it was presented not with legal defenses interposed by counsel, but with an affidavit of the agency head advising the court that the ruling in question was tentative, and outlining the method of seeking reconsideration. . . .

The Requisite Finality of Interpretation by the Head of an Agency not Designated for Reconsideration

When a published interpretation represents the initial views of an agency, approved by the Commission or person who heads the agency, when it is the product of the process provided by the agency for taking into account the position of agency staff as well as the outside presentation, when the interpretation is not labeled as tentative or otherwise qualified by arrangement for reconsideration, it has the feature of "expected conformity" stressed in Abbott Laboratories. This embraces conformity not only by the businessman affected but by the agency personnel. And we see no basis for saying that this interpretative "agency action" is not "final" for purposes of the APA and judicial review.

. . .

D. SURVEY OF OVERALL CONSIDERATIONS INVOLVED IN PRE-ENFORCEMENT JUDICIAL REVIEW

. . .

There is the possibility that judicial review at too early a stage removes the process of agency refinement, including give-and-take with the regulated interests, that is an important part of the life of the agency process. The considerations developed in the dissent of Justice Fortas in Abbott Laboratories describe realities of the administrative process that must be taken into account.

They can be taken into account under our decision. As we have indicated, an affidavit by the agency head—not a mere argument by its court counsel—that a matter is still under meaningful refinement and development, will likely provide the element of tentativeness and reconsideration that should negative finality, or in any event ripeness.

Even if the interpretation is not being reconsidered, the agency may invoke the sound discretion of the court on the ground that an enforce[ment] action was in preparation or imminent. If filing of such an action close in time permits an equally convenient determination, the court's sound discretion permits the deferral, in effect the restraint, of the action for declaratory relief. . . .

The overruling of threshold objections does not necessarily portend the propriety of a court ruling on the merits. A declaratory judgment, like other forms of equitable relief, is granted only as a matter of judicial discretion, exercised in the public interest. . . .

The case brought by an organization plaintiff raises the problem of the binding effect on the members of the plaintiff. Typically the courts entertain such actions only when it appears that the organization suing as the representative of its members is their "authorized spokesman" and will effectively represent their interests.

Pre-enforcement review, on the other hand, may well present a situation where the defendant officials have a compelling interest in having the organization's suit for declaratory relief maintained as a class action. Before an action may be maintained as a class action, under Rule 23(a), the court must find that "the representative parties will fairly and adequately protect the interests of the class." Thus the maintenance of an action under Rule 23 provides a basis for a litigation which will settle the controversy in which the members of the class have an interest and avoid unnecessary re-litigation. . . .

It is reasonable that the Government should be able to offset the diversion of enforcement resources required to defend a pre-enforcement review action by the assurance that the determination in such a litigation will have a reasonably broad res judicata effect. . . .

An organization that is a sufficiently effective spokesman for the interests of its members to assure an adversarial presentation of the issues has standing to present their views even though the action is not brought under Rule 23. Moreover, it may well be that responsible Government officials are of the view that the public interest lies in confining rather than expanding the scope of the litigation. Or they may have confidence that their enforcement interests are adequately protected without insisting on maintenance as a class action. But the court that holds itself open to an organization that seeks access to pre-enforcement review on behalf of its members has discretion to determine that the Government's request for protection of its interests warrants an insistence that this representative suit be maintained as a class action.

In the course of time other problems of administration or litigation may emerge. We anticipate that they can be managed by reference to doctrines that govern the conduct of litigation, or the scope of relief granted. We find no threshold obstacle that requires dismissal of the action before us merely because it seeks judicial review of the "agency action" of interpretation prior to the institution of an agency action for enforcement.

[The court then turned to the merits and concluded in slightly more than two pages (as compared to the twelve devoted to the availability of review) that the Administrator had correctly interpreted the 1966 amendments.]

NOTES

(1) KIXMILLER v. SEC, 492 F.2d 641 (D.C.Cir.1974). The staff of the SEC informally advised a stockholder that the staff would not recommend action by the Commission respecting the contemplated exclusion from the management's proxy materials of the stockholder's proposals for action at a stockholders' meeting. The stockholder requested the Commission to examine the staff's ruling. The Commission informed the stockholder that it "declined to review the staff's position or hold an oral hearing . . . [or] to issue an informal statement on the matter." The stockholders petitioned for review. Said the court, per curiam: "We think members of the Commission's staff, like staff personnel of other agencies, 'have no authority individually or collectively to make "orders," ' and that, on the contrary, '[o]nly the Commission makes orders.' [1] Here the Commission made no order on the merits of petitioner's claim; rather, it emphatically 'declined to review the staff's position.' It follows that what petitioner seeks to have reviewed in this court is not an 'order issued by the Commission.' "

The court also stated that it recognized "that administrative inaction may become judicially cognizable, and that yet another question here is whether the Commission erred in flatly refusing to deal with petitioner's claim. But assuming, without deciding, that the refusal is otherwise encompassed by Section 25(a), we are not at liberty to override it. [Section 25(a) provides that any "person aggrieved by an order issued by the Commission in a proceeding . . . to which such person is a party may obtain review of such order" in a designated circuit court of appeals.]

"The Securities Exchange Act of 1934 provides that 'the Commission may, in its discretion, make such investigations as it deems necessary,' and that 'it may in its discretion bring an action' in court. An agency's decision to refrain from an investigation or an enforcement action is generally unreviewable and, as to the agency before us, the specifications of the Act leave no doubt on that score.

"The Commission, by regulation, has served notice that its informal procedures are ordinarily to be matters of staff activity, and will involve the Commission only when special circumstances so warrant.[2]
. . .

"The Commission offers informal advice by its staff on a vast number of proxy solicitations.[3] Sheer volume of this wholesome activi-

---

1. See . . . National Automatic Laundry & Cleaning Council v. Shultz, wherein we drew a clear line between opinions reflecting the definitive views of an agency head and the considerably less authoritative rulings by subordinate officials.

2. "The informal procedures of the Commission are largely concerned with the rendering of advice and assistance by the Commission's staff to members of the public dealing with the Commission. . . . In certain instances an informal statement of

the views of the Commission may be obtained. The staff, upon request, or on its motion will generally present questions to the Commission which involve matters of substantial importance and where the issues are novel or highly complex, although the granting of a request for an informal statement by the Commission is entirely within its discretion." 17 C.F.R. § 202.1(d) (1973).

3. We are informed by the Commission that during fiscal year 1973, the staff

ty belies Commission review in every such instance. It must be remembered that a dissatisfied stockholder is free to litigate proxy-solicitation questions judicially, with or without prior administrative resort to the staff or the Commission. It is for the Commission to initially draw the line on administrative review of staff decisions in this area, and we cannot say that its regulation has done so unreasonably. And finding no legal fault in the Commission's discretionary exercise here, we are powerless to upset it."

(2) NEW YORK STOCK EXCHANGE, INC. v. BLOOM, 562 F.2d 736 (D.C. Cir.1977). The Glass-Steagall Act limits national banks' purchase and sale of securities "solely" to those which are ordered by, "and for the account of, customers." Security Pacific National Bank (Security Pacific) wrote to the Comptroller of the Currency requesting an opinion whether the "Automatic Investment Service" (AIS) which the bank was proposing to establish would be consistent with the Glass-Steagall Act.[4] The Comptroller replied in a brief letter which stated that in the Comptroller's opinion AIS, as set forth in Security Pacific's letter, involves only purchases for the account of customers and not for the bank's own account; that the bank in creating and managing the Service is not engaged in the business of issuing, underwriting, selling or distributing securities; and that the operation of the Service by the bank is consistent with the Glass-Steagall Act.

The New York Stock Exchange (NYSE) and the Investment Company Institute (ICI)—a national association of mutual funds and their investment advisers and principal underwriters—wrote to the Comptroller requesting him to reconsider the position he had taken in his letter to Security Pacific. After Security Pacific, ICI and NYSE had submitted comments on the issue, the Comptroller reaffirmed the view expressed in his earlier letter to Security Pacific. But in contrast to the summary character of that letter, his reaffirmation statement contained a more extensive analysis of the underlying issues. He said in part, "We are not unmindful of the potential for abuse, but until such time as abuse develops, we should not strain the meaning of the [Glass-Steagall Act] to stifle banks' competition in the free market for the patronage of American investors." NYSE and ICI sought declaratory and injunctive relief. The Comptroller moved to dismiss on grounds that NYSE lacked standing, indispensable parties had not been joined and the informal opinions were not ripe for review. Rejecting these contentions, the district court granted summary judgment for the Comptroller on the merits. The court of appeals reversed.

Applying the "two fold aspect" approach of Abbott Laboratories, Judge McGowan first noted that unlike the opinion letter in National

---

processed 7,023 proxy statements and 141 information statements to be submitted to stockholders in lieu of proxy soliciting materials, and with respect to substantially all of these statements furnished a staff letter commenting on its apparent adequacy under the proxy rules.

4. The bank's proposed plan would permit the bank's regular checking account customers to invest, through automatic monthly deductions from their accounts, in stocks individually chosen by them from a list of 25 selected corporations. All deductions for a particular stock would be pooled and the proceeds used by the bank at least once a month to purchase the stock promptly after a specified cut-off date.

Automatic Laundry and Cleaning Council, the Comptroller's letter in this case "expressly reserved the possibility that [the Comptroller's] opinion, which extended only to the permissibility of the particular service proposed by Security Pacific, might change if and when [the Comptroller] was presented with concrete evidence that AIS involves the hazards which the Glass-Steagall Act was intended to prevent." In addition, the question decided by the Comptroller was not, as the district court concluded, "purely legal." It is true that "determining the general intent of Congress from the language and history of the Act is a matter of law, but an assessment of the factual consequences of AIS to determine whether it falls within the scope of the congressional concerns requires resolution of factual issues, and an application of law to fact. While appellants contest, at the outset, the Comptroller's reading of the legislative history, a substantial part of their argument at all stages of this case has revolved around their disagreement with the Comptroller's estimate of the factual implications of AIS. To this extent, judicial review of appellant's claims would be aided by further factual development."

As to the "hardship" element of the Abbott Laboratories test, "appellants' conduct is not directly regulated by the agency action at issue and consequently they are not facing a 'Hobson's choice' between burdensome compliance and risky noncompliance." The district court's assumption that denial of review now would mean that appellants' claim never would come under judicial scrutiny is erroneous. "Although we have been unable to find any case law squarely on point, and in any event, are without power to make an authoritative ruling on the issue since it is not currently before us, we have no reason to believe that appellant would not have a private right of action for injunctive relief under the Glass-Steagall Act. The express language of the statute neither authorizes nor precludes such an action, but under the standards set forth in recent Supreme Court decisions we would suppose first, that an implied right of action for injunctive relief would exist for appropriate parties and, second, that appellants would qualify as proper plaintiffs.[5]

"[W]hat appellants would have the courts do in this case is to determine the correctness of an informal statement by the Comptroller to the effect that he would not now take any action if Security Pacific goes forward with its proposed AIS, although he might take a different

---

5. Both of these questions apparently would be governed by the general criteria set forth in Cort v. Ash, 422 U.S. 66 (1975), and reaffirmed in Piper v. Chris-Craft Indus., Inc., 430 U.S. 1, 37–41 (1977): "First, is the plaintiff 'one of the class for whose *especial* benefit the statute was enacted,'" . . .—that is, does the statute create a federal right in favor of the plaintiff? Second, is there any indication of legislative intent, explicit or implicit, either to create a remedy or to deny one? Third, is it consistent with the underlying purposes of the legislative scheme to imply such a remedy for the plaintiff? And finally, is the cause of action one traditionally relegated to state law, in an area basically the concern of the States, so that it would be inappropriate to infer a cause of action based solely on federal law? 422 U.S. at 78 (citations omitted) (emphasis in original).

The Supreme Court's holding in ICI v. Camp, 401 U.S. 617 at 620–21 "that Congress did legislate against the competition" which ICI challenged in that case, while not dispositive of the first issue, strongly suggests that appellants are part of the class for whose "*especial* benefit" the Glass-Steagall Act was passed.

view of its compatibility with the Glass-Steagall Act at some point in the future after there has been some experience with its actual operation. This is sought to be done at the instance of parties who, although very possibly possessed of standing to litigate the question in some circumstances, are not themselves subject to regulation by the Comptroller and who will be under no compulsion to do, or to refrain from doing, anything by reason of the advisory opinion in question. Neither is there now before the court any bank currently providing AIS or proposing to do so.

"The record made in such a lawsuit would be barren indeed with respect to information highly relevant to, and informative of, the applicability of the statutory provisions in question. As indicated above, appellants have other avenues open to them for more meaningful and authoritative judicial resolution of the validity of AIS. . . . [T]he agency action challenged here is not ripe for review. . . . "

Judge Wright concurred because appellants have a private right of action and should be required to explore that avenue first. But "if it is ultimately held that appellants lack a private right of action, prudential concerns inhering in the 'hardship to the parties of withholding court consideration' would, in my judgment, remove any doubt as to the ripeness of a subsequent suit by appellants against the Comptroller. There should be some means to obtain review of the Comptroller's interpretation of the statute." [6]

d. Primary Jurisdiction

When a court refuses to engage in judicial review until administrative remedies have been exhausted or until an order has become final, it says in effect that review would be premature because the allegedly objectionable administrative action is not yet complete. The court's power to review comes into play, in such a case, only if and when a completed act can be identified. The power to *begin* the act is plainly and exclusively lodged in administrative hands—as, for example, the power to consider whether a license should be revoked or whether an unfair labor practice has occurred or whether trading on the stock market should be suspended.

In some situations, however, both a court and an administrative agency have the legal capacity to deal with the same subject matter. Thus, for instance, the courts have power and responsibility to pass on complaints against combinations in restraint of trade such as conspiracies to fix prices; at the same time, the Federal Trade Commission has authority to decide whether respondents have used unfair methods of competition such as conspiratorial price-fixing. Similarly, a court can decide a lawsuit arising out of a contract between a public utility company and a user of the company's services; at the same time, a regulatory body may have authority to decide, in a suitable proceeding, the meaning and proper application of the contract which gave rise to the lawsuit. Or a court may have power to decide whether a claimant

6. [Ed.] NYSE v. Bloom is criticized in Recent Case, 30 Vand.L.Rev. 1249 (1977).

to a decedent's estate was, in law and in fact, the spouse of the decedent; at the same time, the federal agency that administers the old age and survivors' insurance program may have power to determine precisely that issue.

When this duality of power exists, which arm of government should be regarded as having *primary* jurisdiction? Should jurisdiction simply be determined by the speedier litigant's choice, on the basis of first come, first served? If not, what principles or practicalities should induce Tribunal A to defer to Tribunal B?

TEXAS & PACIFIC R. CO. v. ABILENE COTTON OIL CO., 204 U.S. 426 (1907), a landmark case, suggested an answer to these questions. The Oil Company sued the Railroad in an ordinary common law action to recover the difference between the freight charges exacted pursuant to the carrier's published rate schedule and the amount the shipper regarded as reasonable. The applicable statute said that any person damaged by a carrier could "either make complaint" to the Interstate Commerce Commission "or may bring suit" in federal court. Moreover, the statute said that its provisions were to be regarded as additions to rather than abridgements or alterations of "remedies now existing at common law or by statute." The shipper chose to rely on the existing remedy of a law suit. The Supreme Court held, despite the statutory language, that "a shipper seeking reparation predicated upon the unreasonableness of the established rate . . . must *primarily* invoke redress through the Interstate Commerce Commission" (italics added).

The Court explained this seemingly drastic rewriting of the statutory text on a purely practical ground. Uniform rates, which were plainly an objective of the Act to Regulate Commerce, could not possibly be achieved if divers judges and juries scattered across the country were to determine the reasonableness of a carrier's established rate schedule. Further, the Court said, if courts could act independently of the ICC, their decisions might "lead to favoritism, to the enforcement of one rate in one jurisdiction and a different one in another, would destroy the prohibitions against preferences and discrimination, and afford, moreover a ready means by which, through collusive proceedings, the wrongs which the statute was intended to remedy could be successfully inflicted." [1]

The pioneer case just summarized had emphasized the desirability of uniformity as against diversity, but had not suggested that the administrative agency possessed special insights into the subject matter. Later cases added explicit recognition that the generalist should defer to the specialist. GREAT NORTHERN RY. CO. v. MERCHANTS ELEVATOR CO., 259 U.S. 285 (1922), is an often cited illustration. There, a shipper and a carrier disagreed about the propriety of the freight charges paid for shipping grain. The outcome of the dispute hinged on the meaning of two seemingly conflicting portions of the carrier's rate

---

1. [Ed.] For further discussion of the beginnings of the primary jurisdiction doctrine and acute analysis of its later development, see L. Jaffe, Judicial Control of Administrative Action ch. 4 (1965). And for critical discussion of the Abilene Oil case, see I. Convisser, Primary Jurisdiction: The Rule and Its Rationalizations, 65 Yale L.J. 315, 320–328 (1956).

schedule. The shipper sued to recover $80 which had been collected by the carrier. Should the court hear the case, or should the parties be told to take their quarrel to the Interstate Commerce Commission? In this instance the Court held that judges could decide the controverted issues because, though the case did unavoidably necessitate reading the fine print of the applicable railroad tariff, the question in the end was simply one of interpreting language and was thus "solely of law," suitable for the courts. But, Justice Brandeis quickly added, if the tariff had used words in a technical or peculiar sense which could not have been understood without considering extrinsic evidence about their meaning, the Court would have regarded the question as one "essentially of fact, and of discretion in technical matters." That kind of problem, Justice Brandeis said, must go to the ICC, not to the judges, for initial decision. Why? Because a determination about the technicalities of railroading and railroad freight charges "is reached ordinarily upon voluminous and conflicting evidence, for the adequate appreciation of which acquaintance with many intricate facts of transportation is indispensable *and such acquaintance is commonly to be found only in a body of experts*" (italics added).

The landmark cases just summarized have, then, stated two considerations that should persuade the judges to stand aside even when they apparently have statutory power to proceed. The judges are admonished to recognize the *primary jurisdiction* of another body either when this will conduce toward a desirable uniformity of decisions or when this will make possible the utilization of pertinent expertise.

The fuzziness of these criteria makes them far easier to state than to apply.

UNITED STATES v. WESTERN PACIFIC RAILROAD CO.
Supreme Court of the United States, 1956.
352 U.S. 59.

[The Army made many shipments of aerial bomb cases filled with napalm gel. Napalm is inflammable, but not self-igniting. It is a jelly-like mixture of gasoline, thickened by an aluminum powder. A functioning incendiary bomb requires, in addition, a burster charge and a fuse. These shipments were simply of the steel casings, containing the napalm but without the igniting mechanisms. What freight charges were proper?—the high rate for "incendiary bombs" or the much lower for "gasoline in steel drums"? These questions were submitted to the Court of Claims in the shape of lawsuits by the railroads to recover what the Government allegedly owed them.

The Government insisted that the lower rate applied because of the absence of bursters and fuses. If, however, the shipments were to be regarded as involving "incendiary bombs," then the Government wanted a chance to argue that the freight charges were unreasonably high in the present circumstances. As to that issue, the Government contended that the court proceedings should be suspended while this one phase of the controversy was referred to the ICC.

The Court of Claims ruled that the shipments in question were "incendiary bombs" and that the issue of reasonableness of the railroad's rates had been raised too tardily to justify asking the ICC to enter the picture now.]

MR. JUSTICE HARLAN delivered the opinion of the Court. . . .

We are met at the outset with the question of whether the Court of Claims properly applied the doctrine of primary jurisdiction in this case; that is, whether it correctly allocated the issues in the suit between the jurisdiction of the Interstate Commerce Commission and that of the court. . . . We have concluded that in the circumstances here presented the question of tariff construction, as well as that of the reasonableness of the tariff as applied, was within the exclusive primary jurisdiction of the Interstate Commerce Commission.

The doctrine of primary jurisdiction, like the rule requiring exhaustion of administrative remedies, is concerned with promoting proper relationships between the courts and administrative agencies charged with particular regulatory duties. "Exhaustion" applied where a claim is cognizable in the first instance by an administrative agency alone; judicial interference is withheld until the administrative process has run its course. "Primary jurisdiction," on the other hand, applies where a claim is originally cognizable in the courts, and comes into play whenever enforcement of the claim requires the resolution of issues which, under a regulatory scheme, have been placed within the special competence of an administrative body; in such a case the judicial process is suspended pending referral of such issues to the administrative body for its views. General American Tank Car Corp. v. El Dorado Terminal Co., 308 U.S. 422, 433.

No fixed formula exists for applying the doctrine of primary jurisdiction. In every case the question is whether the reasons for the existence of the doctrine are present and whether the purposes it serves will be aided by its application in the particular litigation. These reasons and purposes have often been given expression by this Court. In the earlier cases emphasis was laid on the desirable uniformity which would obtain if initially a specialized agency passed on certain types of administrative questions. . . .

More recently the expert and specialized knowledge of the agencies involved has been particularly stressed. . . .

Thus the first question presented is whether effectuation of the statutory purposes of the Interstate Commerce Act requires that the Interstate Commerce Commission should first pass on the construction of the tariff in dispute here; this, in turn, depends on whether the question raises issues of transportation policy which ought to be considered by the Commission in the interests of a uniform and expert administration of the regulatory scheme laid down by the Act. . . .

A tariff is not an abstraction. It embodies an analysis of the costs incurred in the transportation of a certain article and a decision as to how much should, therefore, be charged for the carriage of that article in order to produce a fair and reasonable return. Complex and technical cost-allocation and accounting problems must be solved in setting the tariff initially. In the case of "incendiary bombs," since it is expensive to take the elaborate safety precautions necessary to carry such items in safety, evidently there must have been calculation of the costs of handling, supervising and insuring an inherently dangerous cargo. In other words, there were obviously commercial *reasons* why a higher tariff was set for incendiary bombs than for, say, lumber. It therefore follows that the decision whether a certain item was intended to be covered by the tariff for incendiary bombs involves an intimate knowledge of these very reasons themselves. Whether steel casings filled with napalm gel are incendiary bombs is, in this context, more than simply a question of reading the tariff language or applying abstract "rules" of construction. For the basic issue is how far the reasons justifying a high rate for the carriage of extra-hazardous objects were applicable to the instant shipment. Do the factors which make for high costs and therefore high rates on incendiary bombs also call for a high rate on steel casings filled with napalm gel? To answer that question there must be close familiarity with these factors. Such familiarity is possessed not by the courts but by the agency which had the exclusive power to pass on the rate in the first instance. And, on the other hand, to decide the question of the scope of this tariff without consideration of the factors and purposes underlying the terminology employed would make the process of adjudication little more than an exercise in semantics.

The main thrust of the Government's argument on the construction question went to the fact that the shipments here involved were not as hazardous as contemplated by the term "incendiary bomb" as used in the tariff, and that therefore the tariff should not be construed to cover them. Similarly, the dissenting judges below emphasized the absence from the shipments of the commercial factors which call for a high rate on incendiary bombs: "If the reason for the high freight rate is the incendiary quality of the freight, and if the freight does not have the incendiary quality, the reason for the high rate vanishes and the rate should vanish with it." 131 F.Supp. at page 921, 132 Ct.Cl. at page 118. The difficulty with this line of argument is that we do not know whether the "incendiary quality of the freight" was in fact the reason for the high rate, still less whether that was the only reason and how much weight should be assigned to it. Courts which do not make rates cannot know with exactitude the factors which go into the rate-making process. And for the court here to undertake to fix the limits of the tariff's application without knowledge of such factors, and the extent to which they are present or absent in the particular case, is tantamount to engaging in judicial guesswork. It was the Commission and not the court which originally determined why incendiaries should be transported at a high rate. It is thus the Commission which should determine whether shipments of napalm gel bombs, minus bursters and fuses, meet those requirements; that is, whether the factors making for certain costs and thus a certain rate on incendiaries are present in the carriage of such incompleted bombs.

This conclusion is fortified by the artificiality of the distinction between the issues of tariff construction and of the reasonableness of the tariff as applied, the latter being recognized by all to be one for the Interstate Commerce Commission. For the Government's thesis on the issue of reasonableness is not that the rate on incendiary bombs is, in general, too high. It argues only that the rate "as applied" to these particular shipments is too high—i.e., that since the expenses which have to be met in shipping incendiaries have not been incurred in this case, the carriers will be making an unreasonable profit on these shipments. This seems to us to be but another way of saying that the wrong tariff was applied. In both instances the issue is whether the factors which call for a high rate on incendiary bomb shipments are present in a shipment of bomb casings full of napalm gel but lacking bursters and fuses. And the mere fact that the issue is phrased in one instance as a matter of tariff construction and in the other as a matter of reasonableness should not be determinative on the jurisdictional issue. To hold otherwise would make the doctrine of primary jurisdiction an abstraction to be called into operation at the whim of the pleader.

By no means do we imply that matters of tariff construction are never cognizable in the courts. We adhere to the distinctions laid down in Great Northern R. Co. v. Merchants Elevator Co. [p. 1134, above], which call for decision based on the particular facts of each case. Certainly there would be no need to refer the matter of construction to the Commission if that body, in prior releases or opinions, has already construed the particular tariff at issue or has clarified the factors underlying it. See Crancer v. Lowden, 315 U.S. 631. And in many instances construing the tariff does not call for examination of the underlying cost-allocation which went into the making of the tariff in the first instance. We say merely that where, as here, the problem of cost-allocation is relevant, and where therefore the questions of construction and reasonableness are so intertwined that the same factors are determinative on both issues, then it is the Commission which must first pass on them.

We hold, therefore, that both the issues of tariff construction and the reasonableness of the tariff as applied were initially matters for the Commission's determination. . . .

Reversed and remanded.[1]

NOTES

(1) Cases like the one just considered may be and often are retained on the court's docket, rather than dismissed for want of jurisdiction. That is to say, the court when it recognizes that primary jurisdiction

---

1. [Ed.] Justice Douglas dissented on the ground that "the principles of Great Northern R. Co. v. Merchants Elevator Co., 259 U.S. 285," made it inappropriate to refer the issues to the ICC. Justices Reed and Brennan did not participate.

lies with an administrative agency, stays its own further consideration and tells the parties to knock on another door.[2]

When the administrative decision will dispose of the entire controversy (as seems likely to have been true in the Western Pacific "incendiary bomb" case), then the referral by the court to the agency saves the judges' time; the courts serve only as reviewers rather than as initial deciders. But when the issue to be passed upon by the administrative agency is only partially dispositive of the controversy, then complaints begin to be heard about added expense and delay. The primary jurisdiction doctrine is by no means universally adored by lawyers.[3]

Nor, indeed, does the doctrine arouse enthusiasm among all judges. A five-to-four decision in 1973 suggests the clash of considerations involved in determining whether or not to recognize another tribunal's primary jurisdiction. RICCI v. CHICAGO MERCANTILE EXCHANGE, 409 U.S. 289 (1973). Ricci sued under the antitrust laws for damages caused by an allegedly unlawful transfer of his membership in the Chicago Mercantile Exchange to a third person, thereby excluding him from trading on the Exchange with resulting loss of business. The transfer, he alleged, was unlawful because it violated the rules of the Mercantile Exchange and also the provisions of the Commodity Exchange Act. That statute is administered by the Secretary of Agriculture and the Commodity Exchange Commission. The latter has power to conduct hearings and to issue orders to cease engaging in acts which violate the law; the Commission may receive requests to initiate proceedings or it may begin a case on its own motion, and provision is made for allowing private parties to intervene. Should Ricci's complaint, though couched in terms which bring it within the reach of the antitrust laws and thus within the federal trial court's jurisdiction, be referred by the court to the Commodity Exchange Commission because the allegedly unlawful conduct is assertedly prohibited by the Commodity Exchange Act and the rules of the Exchange?

The majority of the Court answered that question affirmatively, saying that the antitrust action should be stayed until the administrative officials had had opportunity to act. If the Commission were to agree with Ricci's assertion that he had been victimized by an illegal disregard of Exchange rules, then the antitrust action could go forward without having to inquire into that aspect of the matter; if, on the other hand, the Commission were to conclude that the Exchange had acted in accord with a valid membership rule, then the court would be able to focus on whether or not the antitrust laws reach conduct which does not in itself violate the Commodity Exchange Act. For the majority, Justice White wrote that the Court simply recognizes that "Congress has established a specialized agency that would determine either that a membership rule of the Exchange has been violated or

2. The practice in this regard is well described in L. Jaffe, Judicial Control of Administrative Action 132–141 (1965).

3. See K. Hoffman, The Doctrine of Primary Jurisdiction Misconceived: End to

Common Law Environmental Protection? 2 Fla.S.U.L.Rev. 491 (1974).

that it has been followed. Either judgment would require determination of facts and the interpretation and application of the Act and exchange rules. And either determination will be of great help to the antitrust court in arriving at the essential accommodation between the antitrust and the regulatory regime . . . ". Accordingly, the district court should stay further judicial proceedings pending an administrative determination that the rule of the Exchange had or had not been violated.

Justice Douglas protested against requiring a seeker of justice to travel a road which is "long and expensive and available only to those with long purses. . . . " He joined, too, with Justices Stewart and Powell in supporting Justice Marshall's dissenting opinion. Justice Marshall acknowledged that the Commodity Exchange Commission might possibly "make findings of fact or statements as to the law within the area of its expertise which the court might find helpful." He added, however:

"But I had not thought that petitioner need meet the burden of showing that resort to administrative remedies would be totally useless before securing adjudication from a court. Indeed, in virtually every suit involving a regulated industry, there is something of value which an administrative agency might contribute if given the opportunity. But we have never suggested that such suits must therefore invariably be postponed while the agency is consulted. . . . [I]n these days of crowded dockets and long court delays, the [primary jurisdiction] doctrine frequently prolongs and complicates litigation. More fundamentally, invocation of the doctrine derogates from the principle that except in extraordinary situations, every citizen is entitled to call upon the judiciary for expeditious vindication of his legal claims of right.
. . . .

". . . Wise use of the doctrine necessitates a careful balance of the benefits to be derived from utilization of agency processes as against the costs in complication and delay. Where the plaintiff has no means of invoking agency jurisdiction, where the agency rules do not guarantee the plaintiff a means of participation in the administrative proceedings, and where the likelihood of a meaningful agency input into the judicial process is remote, I would strike a balance in favor of immediate court action. Since the majority's scale is apparently differently calibrated, I must respectfully dissent."

(2) In commenting on the Ricci case, Professors Areeda and Turner suggest that "[w]here agency input is sought to determine only whether a rule has been followed, it might be preferable to proceed with an antitrust adjudication and seek an amicus brief from the regulators to resolve unfamiliar questions and gain insights into factual problems." 1 P. Areeda and D. Turner, Antitrust Law 178 (1978). This expedient was utilized in DISTRIGAS OF MASSACHUSETTS CORP. v. BOSTON GAS CO., 693 F.2d 1113 (1st Cir.1982), involving litigation in which two gas companies each sued the other for money that each believed the other owed it under tariffs filed with the Federal Energy Regulatory Commission (FERC). Judge Breyer wrote for the court:

"We intend to invoke the doctrine of 'primary jurisdiction' to obtain the view of FERC before proceeding to interpret the tariffs. We do so despite the fact that neither party has directly pressed the primary jurisdiction issue before this court, although Boston Gas did raise the issue without success below. It is now well established that the doctrine is not waived by the failure of the parties to present it in the trial court or on appeal, since the doctrine exists for the proper distribution of power between judicial and administrative bodies and not for the convenience of the parties. . . .

"The conventional practice in primary jurisdiction cases is to stay judicial proceedings and require the parties to initiate proceedings before the relevant administrative body. In the present case, however, we believe that a more efficient and expeditious alternative exists— that of requesting the agency to develop its views and then to present them through an amicus brief. Cf. Jaffe, Primary Jurisdiction, 77 Harv.L.Rev. 1037, 1047 (1964). Parties are ordinarily required to enter into full-blown administrative proceedings because only then can the agency adequately resolve the complex issues of fact and policy that underlie the usual primary jurisdiction case. In this case, however, the agency's task is only secondarily to make traditional factual findings and policy judgments; the primary question before it is simply what it meant to do when it approved the Long Term Program in December 1978. We think that this question can be answered fully and quickly through amicus participation. If more elaborate agency proceedings are required, the agency can so inform us.

"We therefore shall hold this case on the docket, while instructing the clerk to send a copy of this opinion to the Solicitor General along with this court's request that FERC file an amicus brief. The parties may file responses to FERC's brief. This court will then take such further action as is apropriate."[4]

(3) Note that the examples thus far discussed have had to do with a broad, continuing administrative relationship to the subject matter. Hence, quite apart from considerations of uniformity and expertness, a judge who has been asked to pass upon a novel point might reasonably hesitate to render piecemeal judicial decisions that might collaterally and unforeseeably affect some aspect of administration not immediately involved. Consider, for example, SPENCE v. BALTIMORE & OHIO R. Co., 360 F.2d 887 (7th Cir.), cert. denied 385 U.S. 946 (1966). There, a seed and grain company complained to a court that a railroad was refusing to provide freight cars which were immediately needed if the complainant's business was to be saved from ruin. The railroad, the complainant contended, was under a duty to render transportation service; it was failing to discharge this duty; and the complainant was suffering irreparable injury as a consequence. Did the district court have jurisdiction, then? The trial judge thought he did have power to order the railroad to provide box cars to move the complainant's shipments. But the appellate court thought otherwise. The problem arose apparently

4. [Ed.] Pursuant to the court's request, FERC filed a brief and the parties then settled the case.

because the railroad (through its own neglect) possessed at that time an insufficient number of box cars to satisfy all shippers' demands; a court order to furnish cars to meet a particular shipper's need might inadvertently create a discrimination against other shippers; the Interstate Commerce Commission is responsible for trying to avoid discriminatory allocation of available transportation facilities; so the district court erred in not leaving in the Commission's hands the problem at the heart of this controversy, namely, "the reasonableness of the defendant's method of car distribution for seasonal loading during a car shortage"—a description of the issue that makes it sound very different from "irreparable injury, no adequate remedy at law."

(4) NADER v. ALLEGHENY AIRLINES, INC., 426 U.S. 290 (1976). Nader's confirmed reservation was not honored because the airline had overbooked. He brought a common-law tort action based on fraudulent misrepresentation arising from the airline's alleged failure to inform him in advance of its deliberate overbooking practices. The court of appeals reversed a judgment for Nader on the ground that the CAB must be allowed to determine in the first instance whether the defendant's failure to disclose the practice of overbooking violated section 411 of the Federal Aviation Act which provides in part that if it considers such action to be in the public interest, the CAB may order an air carrier to cease and desist from engaging in an "unfair or deceptive" practice.

The Supreme Court reversed in an opinion by Justice Powell. In this case, unlike Abilene Cotton Oil Co., there is no conflict between the regulatory scheme and the existence of common-law remedies because the CAB had not required the carriers to engage in overbooking or to fail to disclose that they do so. Nor is there any need to secure the Board's expert judgment on the question. "The standards to be applied in an action for fraudulent misrepresentation are within the conventional competence of the courts and the judgment of a technically expert body is not likely to be helpful in the application of these standards to the facts of this case." Also a determination by the CAB that the carrier had not violated section 411 would not immunize the carrier from common-law tort liability for fraudulent misrepresentation because the statutory and the common-law issues are not co-extensive; the one relates to the public interest, the other to private rights.

(5) Judicial disinclination to acknowledge an administrative body's primary jurisdiction mounts, too, when the litigant before the court is incapable of initiating the administrative process. ROSADO v. WYMAN, 397 U.S. 397 (1970), makes this point rather dramatically. Rosado and other welfare recipients sued to prevent expenditure of federal monies in support of New York's amended program of Aid to Families with Dependent Children; they asserted that the New York welfare plan was incompatible with federal law whose requirements needed to be met before the expenditure could be made lawfully. The federal law indubitably gave the Department of Health, Education, and Welfare power to cut off federal funds if a state's plan did not conform with federal statutory requirements. The cut off power could be exercised

by HEW only after suitable notice to the state and an opportunity for hearing. HEW had in fact initiated an investigation of New York's plan before the Rosado suit came to court, but the investigation had not yet reached the point of formal administrative proceedings to halt federal payments to New York. In this posture of the case, should the court defer to the administrative agency especially charged with responsibility for analyzing the validity of state welfare programs, or should a district court judge exercise his own power to pass upon a question of compliance with federal law?

The Supreme Court majority, speaking through Justice Harlan, decided that the judge need not defer to the administrator. Special note was taken that the complainants before the court—that is, the welfare recipients who thought New York's plan was invalid under federal law—could not "have obtained an administrative ruling since HEW has no procedures whereby welfare recipients may trigger and participate in the Department's review of state welfare programs." In concluding that HEW's power to cut off funds did not limit a federal court's power to review state welfare provisions, the Court said that it was "most reluctant to assume Congress has closed the avenue of effective judicial review to those individuals most directly affected by the administration of its program."

The other side of the coin is shown in the dissenting opinion of Justice Black, joined by Chief Justice Burger. The dissenters criticized the majority's disregard of "the unmistakable intent of the Social Security Act to give HEW primary jurisdiction over these highly technical and difficult welfare questions;" not recognizing the administrative agency's role "plunges this Court and other federal courts into an ever-increasing and unnecessary involvement in the administration of the Nation's categorical assistance programs administered by the States." The Congressionally created "unified, coherent scheme for reviewing state welfare rules and practices" would if the courts would only allow it to function as intended, "render unnecessary countless lawsuits by welfare recipients." Permitting cases like Rosado's to lead to judicial decrees "can only lead to the collapse of the enforcement scheme envisioned by Congress . . . ."[5]

(6) In any event, however, propositions about primary jurisdiction cannot be stated as flat rules or, even, as altogether confident predictions. Rosado v. Wyman in 1970 said that the federal district court should proceed to decide the case before it because the complainants did not themselves have access to an administrative forum in which their contentions could be considered. But in 1973 Ricci v. Chicago Mercantile Exchange, p. 1139 supra, said equally firmly that 'taint necessarily so. There, the Court held that Ricci could not ask a court to decide for itself an issue which the Commodity Exchange Commission was capable

---

5. [Ed.] Rosado v. Wyman is discussed in Note, Federal Administrative Law Developments—1970, 1971 Duke L.J. 149, 152–159. A later case, National Welfare Rights Organization v. Finch, 429 F.2d 725 (D.C.Cir.1970), discussed above at page 336, held that welfare recipients should be allowed to intervene in HEW conformity hearings which had been scheduled for the purpose of passing upon certain states' plans. Thus persons in Rosado's position were in that instance given opportunity to participate directly in the administrative proceedings.

of determining, *even though Ricci could not himself force the Commission to institute proceedings and no provision had been made to allow intervention as of right in proceedings when and if the Commission chose to launch them.* All that Ricci was capable of doing was to report to the Commission his belief that a violation of law had occurred. Then, if the Commission decided to go further, Ricci could request permission to participate. The Court dealt with the point in a footnote, as follows: "The dissent complains . . . that the Commission need not institute proceedings, that the complainant must intervene to become a party and that agency remedies are discretionary. But proceeding by complaint and intervention is not an unusual system for invoking administrative action. And surely if administrative proceedings are sought in vain, there would be no further problem for the antitrust court. In any event it should be pointed out that the regulations require investigation of complaints and provide that 'the Commission *will institute* an appropriate proceeding' if investigation reveals reason to believe that the Act is being violated."

(7) PORT OF BOSTON MARINE TERMINAL ASS'N v. REDERI. TRANSATLANTIC, 400 U.S. 62 (1970). The Terminal Association sued an association which represented ship owners to recover charges it said were owed by the shipping companies. The Federal Maritime Commission, the agency with primary jurisdiction over ocean freight rates, was asked to pass upon the propriety of the charges while the court stayed the proceedings. The Commission decided that the charges were permissible, without the need of the Commission's approval. The time for seeking review of that administrative decision expired. Then Transatlantic, a shipping company which was dissatisfied with representation by the ship owners' association, intervened in the district court proceedings and sought to challenge the validity of the Commission's order. The Court held that this kind of collateral attack on the administrative judgment was impossible. Since the time for review had elapsed before the case returned for district court action on the Terminal Association's lawsuit, "neither the District Court nor any Court of Appeals nor this Court had or has any authority to review the merits of that [Commission] decision." [6]

FAR EAST CONFERENCE v. UNITED STATES
Supreme Court of the United States, 1952.
342 U.S. 570.

[The Far East Conference was an association of steamship companies, organized in 1922, which had agreed to maintain two sets of freight rates—one for shippers who contracted to use exclusively the ships of Conference members and a higher rate for those who would not bind themselves by such an exclusive patronage contract. The Govern-

---

6. [Ed.] For discussion of the effect of an administrative ruling upon a matter referred by a court, see Note, Federal Administrative Law Developments—1970, 1971 Duke L.J. 149, 159–164. See also E. Crew, Antitrust Policy, Primary Jurisdic-tion and the Equitable Doctrine of Tolling, 11 U.SanFran.L.Rev. 429 (1977), proposing that the statute of limitations be tolled while the antitrust plaintiff is before the agency.

ment, alleging that this practice violated the antitrust provisions of the Sherman Act sought an injunction in a federal district court; the Act gave district courts "jurisdiction to prevent and restrain violations. . . . ." The Conference admitted engaging in the practices complained of, defended them on the merits, and added that, in any event, the Government's complaint should be dismissed because "the nature of the issues required that resort must first be had to the Federal Maritime Board before a district court could adjudicate the Government's complaint." The district court denied the motion to dismiss.]

MR. JUSTICE FRANKFURTER delivered the opinion of the Court.

. . . We see no reason to depart from United States Navigation Co. v. Cunard Steamship Co., 284 U.S. 474. That case answers our problem. There a competing carrier invoked the Antitrust Acts for an injunction against a combination of carriers in the North Atlantic trade which were alleged to operate a dual-rate system similar to that here involved. The plaintiff had not previously challenged the offending practice before the United States Shipping Board, the predecessor in authority of the present Maritime Board. This Court sustained the two lower courts, dismissing the bill because initial consideration by the Shipping Board of the circumstances in controversy had not been sought. After a detailed analysis of the provisions of the Shipping Act and their relation to the construction theretofore given to the Interstate Commerce Act, this was the conclusion:

"The [Shipping] act is restrictive in its operation upon some of the activities of common carriers by water, and permissive in respect of others. Their business involves questions of an exceptional character, the solution of which may call for the exercise of a high degree of expert and technical knowledge. Whether a given agreement among such carriers should be held to contravene the act may depend upon a consideration of economic relations, of facts peculiar to the business or its history, of competitive conditions in respect of the shipping of foreign countries, and of other relevant circumstances, generally unfamiliar to a judicial tribunal, but well understood by an administrative body especially trained and experienced in the intricate and technical facts and usages of the shipping trade, and with which that body, consequently, is better able to deal. . . .

"A comparison of the enumeration of wrongs charged in the bill with the provisions of the sections of the Shipping Act above outlined conclusively shows, without going into detail, that the allegations either constitute direct and basic charges of violations of these provisions, or are so interrelated with such charges as to be in effect, a component part of them; and the remedy is that afforded by the Shipping Act, which to that extent supersedes the anti-trust laws. . . .

"The matter therefore is within the exclusive preliminary jurisdiction of the Shipping Board. The scope and evident purpose of the Shipping Act, as in the case of the Interstate Commerce Act, are demonstrative of this conclusion." 284 U.S. 474, 485.

The Court thus applied a principle, now firmly established that in cases raising issues of fact not within the conventional experience of judges or cases requiring the exercise of administrative discretion, agencies created by Congress for regulating the subject matter should not be passed over. This is so even though the facts after they have been appraised by specialized competence serve as a premise for legal consequences to be judicially defined. Uniformity and consistency in the regulation of business entrusted to a particular agency are secured, and the limited functions of review by the judiciary are more rationally exercised, by preliminary resort for ascertaining and interpreting the circumstances underlying legal issues to agencies that are better equipped than courts by specialization, by insight gained through experience, and by more flexible procedure. . . .

The sole distinction between the Cunard case and this is that there a private shipper invoked the Anti-Trust Acts and here it is the Government. This difference does not touch the factors that determined the Cunard case. The same considerations of administrative expertise apply, whoever initiates the action. The same Anti-Trust Laws and the same Shipping Act apply to the same dual-rate system. To the same extent they define the appropriate orbits of action as between court and Maritime Board. . . .

Having concluded that initial submission to the Federal Maritime Board is required, we may either order the case retained on the District Court docket pending the Board's action . . . or order dismissal of the proceeding brought in the District Court. As distinguished from the situation presented by [General American Tank Car Corp. v. El Dorado Terminal Co., 308 U.S. 422], which was a contract action raising only incidentally a question proper for initial administrative decision, the present case involves questions within the general scope of the Maritime Board's jurisdiction. An order of the Board will be subject to review by a United States Court of Appeals, with opportunity for further review in this Court on writ of certiorari. If the Board's order is favorable to the United States, it can be enforced by process of the District Court on the Attorney General's application. We believe that no purpose will here be served to hold the present action in abeyance in the District Court while the proceeding before the Board and subsequent judicial review or enforcement of its order are being pursued. A similar suit is easily initiated later, if appropriate. Business-like procedure counsels that the Government's complaint should now be dismissed. . . .

The judgment of the District Court must be reversed.

MR. JUSTICE CLARK took no part in the consideration or decision of this case.

MR. JUSTICE DOUGLAS, with whom MR. JUSTICE BLACK concurs, dissenting.

The Shipping Act would have to be amended for me to reach the result of the majority. The Conference agreement, approved by the Board in 1922, provides for the adoption by the Conference of a tariff of rates and charges. It states that there shall be no unjust discrimination against shippers and no rebates paid to them. There is no provision in the agreement for dual rates—no arrangement for allowing one rate to shippers who give all their business to the members and for retaliations against nonsubscribing shippers by exacting from them a higher rate. Nevertheless petitioners have prescribed this dual rate system for the purpose of barring from the outbound Far East trade steamship lines that are not members of the combination. At least these are the facts if we are to believe the allegations of the complaint, as we must on the motion to dismiss.

If the Board had expressly approved the dual rate system, and the dual rate system did not violate the Shipping Act, then there would be immunity from the Sherman Act, since § 15 of the Shipping Act, 39 Stat. 733, as amended, 46 U.S.C. § 814, gives the Board authority to approve agreements fixing or regulating rates, in effect makes "lawful" the rates so approved, and exempts from the Sherman Act every "lawful" agreement concerning them. But that exemption from the Sherman Act can be acquired only in the manner prescribed by § 15.[1] Here no effort was made to obtain it. Hence the petitioners are at large, subject to all of the restraints of the Sherman Act.

Why should the Department of Justice be remitted to the Board for its remedy? The Board has no authority to enforce the Sherman Act. If the rates were filed, of course the Board would have exclusive jurisdiction to pass on them. . . .

The jurisdiction of the Department of Justice must commence at this point, unless we are to amend the Act by granting an anti-trust exemption to rate fixing not only when the rates are filed by the companies and approved by the Board but also when they are not filed at all. . . . I would read the Act as written and require the steamship companies to obtain the anti-trust exemption in the precise way Congress has provided.

NOTES

(1) Observe that the Government's suit in this instance was dismissed altogether, rather than retained on the court's docket pending action by the Board. Presumably it would have been retained if the suit had involved matters beyond the administrative agency's reach. Suppose, for example, that this case had come before the court in the form of a lawsuit for treble damages under the Sherman Act. If the Federal Maritime Board were now to disapprove the dual rate plan, it

1. [Ed.] Section 15 of the Shipping Act, 46 U.S.C. § 814 (1952), provides in part: "Every common carrier by water . . . shall file immediately with the Federal Maritime Board a true copy, or, if oral, a true and complete memorandum, of every agreement, with another such carrier . . . fixing or regulating transportation rates or fares; giving or receiving special rates, accommodations, or other special privileges or advantages; controlling, regulating, preventing, or destroying competition; . . . or in any manner providing for an exclusive, preferential, or cooperative working arrangement. The term 'agreement' in this section includes understandings, conferences, and other arrangements."

The Board is then empowered to disapprove or modify any agreement it finds to be "unjustly discriminatory or unfair." An agreement "shall be lawful only when and as long as approved by the Board. . . . " An approved agreement, however, "shall be excepted from the provisions of the [Sherman Antitrust Act]." A violation of any portion of this section subjects the violator to a civil penalty of $1,000 for each day the violation continues.

still could in no way satisfy the plaintiff's claim to treble damages. So in such a situation, presumably, the court would retain jurisdiction over the lawsuit, would refer the issue of the rate plan's approvability to the Board, and would simply withhold further judicial consideration until the administrative phase of the matter had been concluded. See CARNATION CO. v. PACIFIC WESTBOUND CONFERENCE, 383 U.S. 213 (1966), distinguishing Far East and holding that the lower court should not have dismissed an antitrust treble damage action by a shipper against associations of shipping companies. In Far East, said Chief Justice Warren, the Court dismissed the action rather than staying the proceeding pending Commission action "because it found that dismissal would not prejudice the plaintiffs' right to obtain antitrust relief at the appropriate time. That plaintiff was seeking injunctive relief from continuing conduct. Such a suit could easily be reinstituted if and when the Commission determined that the activities in question violated the Shipping Act. But a treble-damage action for past conduct cannot be easily reinstituted at a later time. Such claims are subject to the Statute of Limitations and are likely to be barred by the time the Commission acts. Therefore, we believe that the Court of Appeals should have stayed the action instead of dismissing it."

(2) The agreement involved in the Far East Conference case was patently illegal because, whether or not it could legally be approved, the fact is that it had never been submitted for approval. Professor Jaffe pertinently inquires: "What is the function of expertness if the agreement is illegal per se? It may still be argued that it is futile to enjoin what may be immunized. The injunction, however, would put pressure on the association to file, though as the Court held, the Government itself could bring the matter before the Board for approval." [2]

(3) The aftermath of the Far East case was somewhat bizarre. The Federal Maritime Board did give approval to the dual rate structure, and the Government went no farther with the Far East injunction matter. But an independent steamship company (a party aggrieved by the agency's final order) then sought judicial review of the Board's order of approval, arguing that the approval ran counter to an express provision of the Shipping Act forbidding retaliation by common carriers against a shipper for patronizing a competitor. The Court agreed that the statute precluded approval of dual rate systems "where they are employed as predatory devices." And so the upshot of shuffling the case to and fro was, in the end, a judicial decision on an issue of

---

2. L. Jaffe, Judicial Control of Administrative Action 146 (1965).

And see L. Jaffe, Primary Jurisdiction Reconsidered: The Antitrust Laws, 102 U.Pa.L.Rev. 577, 598 (1954): "I am to some extent troubled that the sole organ for resolving the issues of consumer and competitor protection involved in the antitrust laws becomes an agency so powerfully moved to support industry price regulation."

Compare R. von Mehren, The Antitrust Laws and Regulated Industries: The Doctrine of Primary Jurisdiction, 67 Harv.L. Rev. 929, 965 (1954): "The doctrine of primary jurisdiction is essential. . . . Without it, members of regulated industries would be subject to two masters—the regulatory statute as administered by the agency and the antitrust laws as administered by the courts."

statutory interpretation.   Federal Maritime Board v. Isbrandtsen Co., 356 U.S. 481 (1958).[3]

(4) The complicated subject of the relationship of antitrust law and regulation—facets of which are involved in Ricci, Far East, and Carnation, supra,—is explored by Professors Areeda and Turner in their treatise, Antitrust Law, vol. 1, pp. 134–178 (1978).   They state at the outset that a court "confronted with an antitrust claim concerning conduct by a regulated firm must face one or more of the following questions:

"(1) Does the very existence of the regulatory regime administered by the agency immunize the challenged conduct, or does the agency have the express or implied power by affirmative action to confer such an immunity?

"(2) Has the agency already immunized it?

"(3) If not, should the agency now have the opportunity to do so?

"(4) Even if there is no immunity for future or past conduct, should the court require the parties to seek the agency's judgment on either the 'reasonableness' of the challenged conduct or on any relevant fact?

"Note that the courts do not always address these questions in the sequence stated.   For example, a court may ask the second question first, with a possible hope (i) that the agency will completely dispose of the problem somehow, or (ii) that the hard first question can sometimes be evaded if the agency finds that it had not approved the challenged conduct, or (iii) that the antitrust court will in any event be aided by the agency's exploration of fact or judgment of reasonableness."

Students interested in the interaction between regulation and antitrust would do well to consult this reference.[4]

SECTION 5. RELIEF AGAINST "THE SOVEREIGN"

The origins of the rule that the United States cannot be sued without its consent are unclear.[1]   No provision of the Constitution so dictates.   The doctrine was not applied as the ground of a decision of the Supreme Court until 1846.   United States v. McLemore, 45 U.S. (4 How.) 286 (1846).   As late as 1882, Justice Miller observed that "while the exemption of the United States and of the several States from being subjected as defendants to ordinary actions in the courts . . . has been repeatedly asserted here, the principle has never been discussed or the reasons for it given, but it has always been treated as an established doctrine."   United States v. Lee, 106 U.S. 196, 207 (1882).   The reasons

---

3. The problems raised by the Isbrandtsen case in relation to primary jurisdiction questions are trenchantly considered by C. Auerbach, The Isbrandtsen Case and Its Aftermath II, 1959 Wis.L.Rev. 369, 370–386.

4. For general discussion of primary jurisdiction problems including an interesting report concerning a "quasi-empirical

study" of the manner in which agencies handle their primary jurisdiction responsibilities, see M. Botein, Primary Jurisdiction: The Need for Better Court/Agency Interaction, 29 Rutg.L.Rev. 867 (1976).

1. For discussion, see D. Engdahl, Immunity and Accountability for Positive Governmental Wrongs, 44 U.Colo.L.Rev. 1, 2–21 (1972).

that have been advanced include the argument that "the King can do no wrong" and the similarly conceptual contention that the sovereign's immunity rests on the "logical and practical ground that there can be no legal right as against the authority that makes the law on which the right depends." Holmes, J., in Kawananakoa v. Polyblank, 205 U.S. 349, 353 (1907). The practical or policy justification of the immunity is avoidance of undue judicial interference in the affairs of government.

In light of the failure of Congress to provide a statutory method of review during the formative era of administrative law, a literal application of the sovereign immunity doctrine often would have left the citizen remediless against harsh and illegal acts of his government. Such a result could not be tolerated. The courts were equal to the challenge. They reasoned that although the sovereign principal might be immune from suit the privilege of the principal could not be claimed by the agent, who therefore could be restrained from committing the wrongful act. In the words of a leading case, a public official who acts under an unconstitutional statute or outside his statutory authority is "stripped of his official or representative character and is subjected in his person to the consequences of his individual conduct." Ex parte Young, 209 U.S. 123, 160 (1908). Thus a controversy that was in fact between a private person and the government was transmuted into a controversy between two private persons. By means of this fiction the courts were able to exert a significant measure of control over the bureaucracy. But because the control rested on a fiction, because the rule of the sovereign's immunity was in terms so clear and undisputed, and because the practical ground for the fiction was to protect the citizen from illegal administrative actions whereas the practical ground for the immunity was to prevent improper judicial intervention in the affairs of government, confusions and difficulties developed and the decisions moved in variant directions. As the Supreme Court said in 1883, it is not "an easy matter to reconcile all the decisions of the court in this class of cases." Cunningham v. Macon & Brunswick R. Co., 109 U.S. 446, 451 (1883). The task of reconciliation, difficult in 1883, had become no less complex when, in 1949, the Supreme Court was called upon to decide:

LARSON v. DOMESTIC & FOREIGN COMMERCE CORP.
Supreme Court of the United States, 1949.
337 U.S. 682.

[The following statement is taken from the dissenting opinion of MR. JUSTICE FRANKFURTER:

"The Government had some surplus coal at an Army camp in Texas. On March 11, 1947, the War Assets Administration, through the Regional Office in Dallas, Texas, invited a bid from the plaintiff, respondent here, for purchase of the coal. The Dallas office expressed thus its approval of the bid submitted by the plaintiff: '. . . your terms of placing $17,500 with the First National Bank, Dallas, Texas, for payment upon presentation of our invoices to said bank are accepted.' Thereupon the plaintiff arranged for resale of the coal and its shipment abroad. On April 1, 1947, the Dallas office wired the plaintiff that unless the sum of $17,500 was deposited in the First National Bank in Dallas by noon April 4, 'the sale will be cancelled and other disposition made.' Though claiming that this demand was in the teeth of the contract, the plaintiff arranged for an irrevocable letter of credit payable through the First National Bank of Dallas to the War Assets Administration. The Dallas office now insisted that unless cash was deposited 'the sale of 10,000 tons of coal . . . will be cancelled ten days from this date.' That office disregarded further endeavors by the plaintiff to adjust the matter, and on April 16 it informed the plaintiff that the contract was cancelled. Having learned that the coal was to be sold to another concern, the plaintiff, asserting ownership in the coal and the threat of irreparable damage, brought this suit in the District Court of the United States for the District of Columbia to restrain the War Assets Administrator and those under his control from transferring the coal to any other person than the plaintiff.

"After issuing a temporary restraining order the District Court on May 6, 1947, dismissed the suit with this oral observation: 'I am satisfied that this suit is in effect a suit for specific performance and the United States is a necessary party, and this Court is without jurisdiction.' The Court of Appeals took a different view: 'Appellant, . . . did not seek the court's aid to interfere in the use of official discretion by the appellee. Such discretion was exercised at the time the contract with appellant was entered into. If that contract served to vest title immediately in appellant then it follows that the ruling in Philadelphia Co. v. Stimson, 223 U.S. 605, is controlling here. . . . Clearly, then, it was incumbent upon the lower court in determining its jurisdictional capacity to decide the ultimate question of whether or not a contract of sale had been consummated between appellant and appellee.' " Certiorari was granted.]

MR. CHIEF JUSTICE VINSON delivered the opinion of the Court. . . .

[C]ontroversy there has been, in this field above all others, because it has long been established that the crucial question is whether the relief sought in a suit nominally addressed to the officer is relief against the sovereign. In a suit against the officer to recover damages for the agent's personal actions that question is easily answered. The judgment sought will not require action by the sovereign or disturb the sovereign's property. There is, therefore, no jurisdictional difficulty. The question becomes difficult and the area of controversy is entered when the suit is not one for damages but for specific relief: i.e., the recovery of specific property or monies, ejectment from land, or injunction either directing or restraining the defendant officer's actions. In each such case the question is directly posed as to whether, by obtaining relief against the officer, relief will not, in effect, be obtained against the sovereign. For the sovereign can act only through agents and, when the agents' actions are restrained, the sovereign itself may, through him, be restrained. As indicated, this question does not arise because of any distinction between law and equity. It arises whenever suit is brought against an officer of the sovereign in which the relief sought from him is not compensation for an alleged wrong but, rather, the prevention or discontinuance, in rem, of the wrong. In each such case the compulsion, which the court is asked to impose, may be compulsion against the sovereign, although nominally directed against the individual officer. If it is, then the suit is barred, not because it is a suit against an officer of the Government, but because it is, in substance, a suit against the Government over which the court, in the absence of consent, has no jurisdiction.

The relief sought in this case was not the payment of damages by the individual defendant. To the contrary, it was asked that the court order the War Assets Administrator, his agents, assistants, deputies and employees and all persons acting under their direction, not to sell the coal involved and not to deliver it to anyone other than the respondent. . . .

There may be, of course, suits for specific relief against officers of the sovereign which are not suits against the sovereign. If the officer purports to act as an individual and not as an official, a suit directed against that action is not a suit against the sovereign. If the War Assets Administrator had completed a sale of his personal home, he presumably could be enjoined from later conveying it to a third person. On a similar theory, where the officer's powers are limited by statute, his actions beyond those limitations are considered individual and not sovereign actions. The officer is not doing the business which the sovereign has empowered him to do or he is doing it in a way which the sovereign has forbidden. His actions are ultra vires his authority and therefore may be made the object of specific relief. It is important to note that in such cases the relief can be granted, without impleading the sovereign, only because of the officer's lack of delegated power. A claim of error in the exercise of that power is therefore not sufficient. And, since the jurisdiction of the court to hear the case may depend, as we have recently recognized, upon the decision which it ultimately reaches on the merits, it is necessary that the plaintiff set out in his complaint the statutory limitation on which he relies.

A second type of case is that in which the statute or order conferring power upon the officer to take action in the sovereign's name is claimed to be unconstitutional. Actions for habeas corpus against a warden and injunctions against the threatened enforcement of unconstitutional statutes are familiar examples of this type. Here, too, the conduct against which specific relief is sought is beyond the officer's powers and is, therefore, not the conduct of the sovereign. The only difference is that in this case the power has been conferred in form but the grant is lacking in substance because of its constitutional invalidity.

These two types have frequently been recognized by this Court as the only ones in which a restraint may be obtained against the conduct of Government officials. The rule was stated by Mr. Justice Hughes in Philadelphia Co. v. Stimson, 1912, 223 U.S. 605, 620, where he said: ". . . in case of an injury threatened by his illegal action, the officer cannot claim immunity from injunction process. The principle has frequently been applied with respect to state officers seeking to enforce unconstitutional enactments. [Citing cases.] And it is equally applicable to a Federal officer acting in excess of his authority or under an authority not validly conferred." [2]

It is not contended by the respondent that the present case falls within either of these categories. There was no claim made that the Administrator and his agents, etc., were acting unconstitutionally or pursuant to an unconstitutional grant of power. Nor was there any allegation of a limitation on the Administrator's delegated power to refuse shipment in cases in which he believed the United States was not obliged to deliver. There was, it is true, an allegation that the Administrator was acting "illegally," and that the refusal to deliver was "unauthorized." But these allegations were not based and did not purport to be based upon any lack of delegated power. Nor could they be, since the Administrator was empowered by the sovereign to administer a general sales program encompassing the negotiation of contracts, the shipment of goods and the receipt of payment. A normal concomitant of such powers, as a matter of general agency law, is the power to refuse delivery when, in the agent's view, delivery is not called for under a contract and the power to sell goods which the agent believes are still his principal's to sell.

The respondent's contention, which the Court of Appeals sustained, was that there exists a third category of cases in which the action of a Government official may be restrained or directed. If, says the respondent, an officer of the Government wrongly takes or holds specific property to which the plaintiff has title then his taking or holding is a tort, and "illegal" as a matter of general law, whether or not it be within his delegated powers. He may therefore be sued individually to prevent the "illegal" taking or to recover the property "illegally" held.

If this is an adequate theory on which to rest the conclusion that the relief asked is not relief against the sovereign, then the respondent's complaint made out a sufficient basis for jurisdiction. The complaint alleged that the respondent's contract with the United States

---

2. Of course, a suit may fail, as one against the sovereign, even if it is claimed that the officer being sued has acted unconstitutionally or beyond his statutory powers, if the relief requested cannot be granted by merely ordering the cessation of the conduct complained of but will require affirmative action by the sovereign or the disposition of unquestionably sovereign property. North Carolina v. Temple, 1890, 134 U.S. 22.

[Ed.] Professor Jaffe refers to this footnote as "troublesome" and comments as follows: "If [Chief Justice] Vinson's *may* is read as *may* and not as *must*, it is unobjectionable. North Carolina v. Temple was a suit to require the state to levy taxes to fund bonds and no type of suit, as we know, is more centrally within the prohibi-

tion of the eleventh amendment. But if a decree which requires 'affirmative action by the sovereign,' e.g., grant of a license, of a civil service post or any other of the actions traditionally enforced by mandamus, if such a decree could no longer be made, then Larson would have worked a sharp and startling change. And, similarly, if it excludes an order to dispose 'of unquestionably sovereign property,' it would overrule a long line of Supreme Court decisions. There is nothing whatever in the opinion to indicate an intention to override such well-established doctrines, let alone any reason to do so. The only possible explanation would be a desire for some abstract doctrinal purity." L.L. Jaffe, Judicial Control of Administrative Action 226–227 (1965).

was an immediate contract of sale under which title to the coal had passed. The coal was thus alleged to be the respondent's coal, not the United States' coal. Retention of it by the Administrator after demand was claimed to be a conversion; sale to a third party would aggravate the conversion. Since these actions were tortious they were "illegal" in the respondent's sense and hence were contended to be individual actions, not properly taken on behalf of the United States, which could be enjoined without making the United States a party.

We believe the theory to be erroneous. It confuses the doctrine of sovereign immunity with the requirement that a plaintiff state a cause of action. It is a prerequisite to the maintenance of any action for specific relief that the plaintiff claim an invasion of his legal rights, either past or threatened. He must, therefore, allege conduct which is "illegal" in the sense that the respondent suggests. If he does not, he has not stated a cause of action. This is true whether the conduct complained of is sovereign or individual. In a suit against an agency of the sovereign, as in any other suit, it is therefore necessary that the plaintiff claim an invasion of his recognized legal rights. If he does not do so, the suit must fail even if he alleges that the agent acted beyond statutory authority or unconstitutionally. But, in a suit against an agency of the sovereign, it is not sufficient that he make such a claim. Since the sovereign may not be sued, it must also appear that the action to be restrained or directed is not action of the sovereign. The mere allegation that the officer, acting officially, wrongfully holds property to which the plaintiff has title does not meet that requirement. True, it establishes a wrong to the plaintiff. But it does not establish that the officer, in committing that wrong, is not exercising the powers delegated to him by the sovereign. If he is exercising such powers the action is the sovereign's and a suit to enjoin it may not be brought unless the sovereign has consented.

It is argued, however, that the commission of a tort cannot be authorized by the sovereign. Therefore, the argument goes, the allegation that a Government officer has acted or is threatening to act tortiously toward the plaintiff is sufficient to support the claim that he has acted beyond his delegated powers. It is on this contention that the respondent's position fundamentally rests, since it is admitted that, if the action to be prevented or compelled is authorized by the sovereign, the demand for it must fail as a demand against the sovereign. It has been said, in a very special sense, that, as a matter of agency law, a principal may never lawfully authorize the commission of a tort by his agent. But that statement, in its usual context, is only a way of saying that an agent's liability for torts committed by him cannot be avoided by pleading the direction or authorization of his principal. The agent is himself liable whether or not he has been authorized or even directed to commit the tort. This, of course, does not mean that the principal is not liable nor that the tortious action may not be regarded as the action of the principal. It does not mean, therefore, that the agent's action, because tortious, is, for that reason alone, ultra vires his authority. . . .

There is, therefore, nothing in the law of agency which lends support to the contention that an officer's tortious action is ipso facto beyond his delegated powers. Nor, do we think, is there anything in the doctrine of sovereign immunity which requires us to adopt such a view as regards Government agencies. If, of course, it is assumed that the basis of the doctrine of sovereign immunity is the thesis that the king can do no wrong then it may be also assumed that if the king's agent does wrong that action cannot be the action of the king. It is on some such argument that the position of the respondent rests. It is argued that an officer given the power to make decisions is only given the power to make correct decisions. If his decisions are not correct, then his action based on those decisions is beyond his authority and not the action of the sovereign. There is no warrant for such a contention in cases in which the decision made by the officer does not relate to the terms of his statutory authority. . . . We hold that if the actions of an officer do not conflict with the terms of his valid statutory authority, then they are the actions of the sovereign, whether or not they are tortious under general law, if they would be regarded as the actions of a private principal under the normal rules of agency. A Government officer is not thereby necessarily immunized from liability, if his action is such that a liability would be imposed by the general law of torts. But the action itself cannot be enjoined or directed, since it is also the action of the sovereign.

United States v. Lee, 1882, 106 U.S. 196, is said to have established the rule for which the respondent contends. It did not. It represents, rather, a specific application of the constitutional exception to the doctrine of sovereign immunity. The suit there was against federal officers to recover land held by them, within the scope of their authority, as a United States military station and cemetery. The question at issue was the validity of a tax sale under which the United States, at least in the view of the officers, had obtained title to the property. The plaintiff alleged that the sale was invalid and that title to the land was in him. The Court held that if he was right the defendants' possession of the land was illegal and a suit against them was not a suit against the sovereign. Prima facie, this holding would appear to support the contention of the plaintiff. Examination of the Lee case, however, indicates that the basis of the decision was the assumed lack of the defendants' constitutional authority to hold the land against the plaintiff. The Court said (106 U.S. at page 219):

"It is not pretended, as the case now stands, that the president had any lawful authority to [take the land], or that the legislative body could give him any such authority except upon payment of just compensation. The defense stands here solely upon the absolute immunity from judicial inquiry of every one who *asserts* authority from the executive branch of the government, however clear it may be made that the executive possessed no such power. Not only that no such power is given, but that it is absolutely prohibited, both to the executive and the legislative, to deprive any one of life, liberty, or property without due process of law, or to take private property without just compensation. . . .

"Shall it be said . . . that the courts cannot give a remedy when the citizen has been deprived of his property by force, his estate seized and converted to the use of the government without any lawful authority, without any process of law, and without any compensation, because the president has ordered it and his officers are in possession?"

The Court thus assumed that if title had been in the plaintiff the taking of the property by the defendants would be a taking without just compensation and, therefore, an unconstitutional action.[3] On that assumption, and only on that assumption, the defendants' possession of the property was an unconstitutional use of their power and was, therefore, not validly authorized by the sovereign. For that reason, a suit for specific relief, to obtain the property, was not a suit against the sovereign and could be maintained against the defendants as individuals.

The Lee case, therefore, offers no support to the contention that a claim of title to property held by an officer of the sovereign is, of itself, sufficient to demonstrate that the officer holding the property is not validly empowered by the sovereign to do so. Only where there is a claim that the holding constitutes an unconstitutional taking of property without just compensation does the Lee case require that conclusion.[4] . . . [T]he action of an officer of the sovereign (be it holding, taking or otherwise legally affecting the plaintiff's property) can be regarded as so "illegal" as to permit a suit for specific relief against the officer as an individual only if it is not within the officer's statutory powers or, if within those powers, only if the powers, or their exercise in the particular case, are constitutionally void.

The application of this principle to the present case is clear. The very basis of the respondent's action is that the Administrator was an officer of the Government, validly appointed to administer its sales program and therefore authorized to enter, through his subordinates, into a binding contract concerning the sale of the Government's coal. There is no allegation of any statutory limitation on his powers as a sales agent. In the absence of such a limitation he, like any other sales agent, had the power and the duty to construe such contracts and to refuse delivery in cases in which he believed that the contract terms had not been complied with. His action in so doing in this case was, therefore, within his authority even if, for purposes of decision here, we assume that his construction was wrong and that title to the coal had, in fact, passed to the respondent under the contract. There is no claim that his action constituted an unconstitutional taking. It was, there-

3. The Lee case was decided in 1882. At that time there clearly was no remedy available by which he could have obtained compensation for the taking of his land. Whether compensation could be obtained today in such a case is, of course, not the issue here.

4. For this reason the availability of a remedy in the Court of Claims may, in some cases, be relevant to the question of sovereign immunity. Where the action against which specific relief is sought is a taking, or holding, of the plaintiffs' property, the availability of a suit for compensation against the sovereign will defeat a contention that the action is unconstitutional as a violation of the Fifth Amendment. Compare Hurley v. Kincaid, 1932, 285 U.S. 95.

fore, inescapably the action of the United States and the effort to enjoin it must fail as an effort to enjoin the United States.

It is argued that the principle of sovereign immunity is an archaic hangover not consonant with modern morality and that it should therefore be limited wherever possible. There may be substance in such a viewpoint as applied to suits for damages. The Congress has increasingly permitted such suits to be maintained against the sovereign and we should give hospitable scope to that trend. But the reasoning is not applicable to suits for specific relief. For, it is one thing to provide a method by which a citizen may be compensated for a wrong done to him by the Government. It is a far different matter to permit a court to exercise its compulsive powers to restrain the Government from acting, or to compel it to act. There are the strongest reasons of public policy for the rule that such relief cannot be had against the sovereign. The Government as representative of the community as a whole, cannot be stopped in its tracks by any plaintiff who presents a disputed question of property or contract right. . . .

There are limits, of course. Under our constitutional system, certain rights are protected against governmental action and, if such rights are infringed by the actions of officers of the Government, it is proper that the courts have the power to grant relief against those actions. But in the absence of a claim of constitutional limitation, the necessity of permitting the Government to carry out its functions unhampered by direct judicial intervention outweighs the possible disadvantage to the citizen in being relegated to the recovery of money damages after the event.

It is argued that a sales agency, such as the War Assets Administration, is not the type of agency which requires the protection from direct judicial interference which the doctrine of sovereign immunity confers. We do not doubt that there may be some activities of the Government which do not require such protection. There are others in which the necessity of immunity is apparent. But it is not for this Court to examine the necessity in each case. That is a function of the Congress. The Congress has, in many cases, entrusted the business of the Government to agencies which may contract in their own names and which are subject to suit in their own names. In other cases it has permitted suits for damages, but significantly not for specific relief, in the Court of Claims. The differentiations as to remedy which the Congress has erected would be rendered nugatory if the basis on which they rest—the assumed immunity of the sovereign from suit in the absence of consent—were undermined by an unwarranted extension of the Lee doctrine.

The cause is reversed with directions that the complaint be dismissed.

It is so ordered.

Reversed with directions.

MR. JUSTICE DOUGLAS.

I think that the principles announced by the Court are the ones which should govern the selling of government property. Less strict applications of those principles would cause intolerable interference with public administration. To make the right to sue the officer turn on whether by the law of sales title had passed to the buyer would clog this governmental function with intolerable burdens. So I have joined the Court's opinion.

Mr. Justice Rutledge concurs in the result.

Mr. Justice Jackson dissents.

[The dissenting opinion of Justice Frankfurter, Justice Burton concurring, is omitted.]

NOTE

Vishnevsky v. United States, 581 F.2d 1249 (7th Cir.1978). Taxpayers sought a writ of mandamus to compel Internal Revenue officials to credit them with an overpayment of taxes. The defendants argued that the action should be dismissed because the "effect of mandamus relief . . . will expend itself on the public treasury, and the action is thus effectively one against the United States without its consent, in violation of the principles of sovereign immunity." The court, per Pell, J., rejected the contention:

"It is true enough that in ordinary suits, a plaintiff may not avoid the bar of sovereign immunity merely by casting his action against individual Government officials. The result of the judgment or decree sought, not the identity of the parties, is dispositive. If relief would operate against the sovereign, the suit is barred unless consented to. See Minnesota v. Hitchcock, 185 U.S. 373, 386 (1902). And it is clearly the law that an ordinary action which will result in depletion of the public treasury operates against the sovereign. See Dugan v. Rank, 372 U.S. 609, 620–21 (1963), and the cases discussed therein.

"The problem with this theory is that it simply does not apply to actions for mandamus. After stating that courts must inquire into the effects of judgments or decrees sought and may not rely on the identity of the parties, the Supreme Court in Minnesota v. Hitchcock, supra, said that 'this statement has no reference to and does not include those cases in which officers of the United States are sued, in appropriate form, to compel them to perform some ministerial duty imposed upon them by law, and which they wrongfully neglect or refuse to perform. Such suits would not be deemed suits against the United States within the rule that the government cannot be sued except by its consent. . . . ' The precise conceptual basis for this distinction was not made clear. It may be that Congress, by giving federal courts jurisdiction of mandamus actions has waived any immunity, or that to command the performance of a clear and ministerial legal duty does not impinge on the discretionary functions which comprise the essence of sovereignty. In any event, so far as we are aware, the Supreme Court has yet to deem it necessary to invoke sovereign immunity problems as being includable in the issues in a mandamus action, and none of the cases articulating the rules of sovereign immunity were themselves, or purported to deal with, mandamus actions."[5]

The court then cited the "long line of cases" in which the Supreme Court "specifically affirmed the appropriateness of mandamus relief to compel federal officers to pay monies out of the public treasury, where the duty to do so was clear and ministerial," and directed entry of summary judgment for the plaintiffs. Judge Tone dissented on the ground that the taxpayers had not exhausted their administrative remedies.

SENATE COMMITTEE ON THE JUDICIARY, JUDICIAL REVIEW OF AGENCY ACTION

Sen.Rep.No. 94–996 on S. 800, 94th Cong., 2d Sess. 3–8 (1976).

Congress has made great strides toward establishing monetary liability on the part of the Government for wrongs committed against its citizens by passing the Tucker Act of 1875, 28 U.S.C. sections 1346, 1491, and the Federal Tort Claims Act of 1946, 28 U.S.C. section 1346(b)[1] S. 800 would strengthen this accountability by withdrawing the defense of sovereign immunity in actions seeking relief other than money damages, such as an injunction, declaratory judgment, or writ of mandamus. Since S. 800 would be limited only to actions of this type for specific relief, the recovery of money damages contained in the Federal Tort Claims Act and the Tucker Act governing contract actions would be unaffected.

It is now generally accepted that courts can make a useful contribution to the administration of Government by reviewing the legality of official conduct which adversely affects private persons. This acceptance of judicial review is reflected not only in court decisions but in the many statutes in which Congress has provided a special procedure for reviewing particular administrative activity. For years almost every regulatory statute enacted by Congress has contained provisions authorizing Federal courts to review the legality of administrative action that has adversely affected private citizens.

Unfortunately, these special statutes do not cover many of the functions performed by the older executive departments, such as the

---

5. [Ed.] Note, however, Judge Wisdom's caveat in Jarecki v. United States, 590 F.2d 670 (7th Cir.1979): "Other courts have observed that the mandamus statute, 28 U.S.C. § 1361, is not a consent to suit by the sovereign and, therefore, sovereign immunity can be a bar to mandamus jurisdiction."

1. At the state level, the trend has also been toward the reduction or elimination of the sovereign immunity defense. For example, 21 states and the District of Columbia have by judicial decision overturned, in varying degrees, the sovereign immunity defense to tort actions. (Alaska, Arizona, Arkansas, California, Colorado, Florida, Idaho, Illinois, Indiana, Kansas, Kentucky, Louisiana, Michigan, Minnesota, Nebraska, Nevada, New Jersey, Pennsylvania, Rhode Island, West Virginia, and Wisconsin.) Approximately ten other states (Connecticut, Delaware, North Dakota, Ohio, Oregon, Pennsylvania, South Carolina, South Dakota, Washington and Wyoming) have constitutional provisions which enable the legislature to prescribe the manner and venue in which a suit against the sovereign may be brought. The jurisdictions of Iowa, New York, Oregon, and Utah have ended by statute the sovereign immunity defense to tort actions. Furthermore, the state of Montana has completely abrogated the doctrine by constitutional amendment. . . .

Departments of State, Defense, Treasury, Justice, Interior, and Agriculture. In addition, there are omissions and gaps in the application of
special review statutes. In these instances, judicial review is available,
if at all, through so-called "nonstatutory review" actions in United
States district courts.

These actions usually take the form of a suit for injunctive,
declaratory or mandamus relief against a named Federal officer on the
theory he is exceeding his legal authority. That such actions are
against the officer and not against the Government for whom he is
acting is a legal fiction developed by the courts to mitigate the injustice
caused by strict application of the sovereign immunity doctrine. As
Richard K. Berg, executive secretary of the Administration Conference
of the United States noted: ". . . if this fiction were logical, easy to
apply and did substantial justice, perhaps there would be no problem.
But it does not. On the contrary, it has set lawyers and courts to
chasing conceptual will-o'-the-wisps." . . .

Dean Roger Cramton of Cornell Law School . . . has described
the effect of these wispy fictions on the judicial process: "The basic
problem with the sovereign immunity doctrine is that it has developed
by fits and starts through a series of fictions. The resulting patchwork
is an intricate, complex and not altogether logical body of law. The
basic issue—balancing the public interest in preventing undue judicial
interference with ongoing governmental programs against the desire to
provide judicial review to individuals claiming that Government has
harmed or threatens to harm them—is obscured rather than assisted by
the doctrine of sovereign immunity in its present form." . . .

Perhaps the only situation under recent case law, other than suits
for damages where it was fairly predictable—and intended by Congress—that a court would uphold a claim of sovereign immunity,
involved disputed title to real property.[2] The results in these cases
were so obviously unjust that in 1972 Congress enacted legislation to
permit actions to quiet title to be brought against the United States, 28
U.S.C. sections 1346(f), 1402(d), 2409(a).

Just as there is little reason why the United States as a landowner
should be treated any differently from other landowners in an action to
quiet title, so too has the time now come to eliminate the sovereign
immunity defense in all equitable actions for specific relief against a
Federal agency or officer acting in an official capacity.

The importance of ameliorating the effect of the sovereign immunity doctrine in other areas besides quiet title actions is emphasized by
the number and variety of cases in which the defense is still raised.
The doctrine has been invoked in hundreds of cases each year concern-

---

2. [Ed.] For discussion of the land
cases, see J. Steadman, "Forgive U.S. Its
Trespasses?": Land Title Disputes with the
Sovereign—Present Remedies and Prospective Reform, 1972 Duke L.J. 15; A. Scalia,
Sovereign Immunity and Nonstatutory Review of Federal Administrative Action:
Some Conclusions from the Public-Lands
Cases, 68 Mich.L.Rev. 867, 920–924 (1970);
See also One Third of the Nation's Land:
A Report to the President and to the Congress by the Public Land Law Review Commission (1970); C. McFarland, Administrative Procedures and the Public Lands
(1969).

ing agricultural regulations, governmental employment, tax investigations, postal-rate matters, administration of labor legislation, control of subversive activities, food and drug regulation, and administration of Federal grant-in-aid programs.

In each instance, the sovereign immunity doctrine distracts the court's attention from the basic issue concerning the availability or scope of judicial review and diverts it toward sophistry and semantics. Sovereign immunity beclouds the real issue whether a particular governmental activity should be subject to judicial review, and, if so, what form of relief is appropriate. Its elimination as proposed in S. 800, in the words of Richard K. Berg, . . . "would be a major step in rationalizing the law of judicial review of agency action. It might not change many outcomes, but it would force the courts to ask and to answer the right questions."

PUBLIC LAW 94–574, 90 STAT. 2721
94th Cong. 2d Sess. (1976).

Be it enacted by the Senate and House of Representatives of the United States of America in Congress assembled, That sections 702 and 703 of title 5, United States Code, are amended to read as follows:

"§ 702. Right of review

"A person suffering legal wrong because of agency action, or adversely affected or aggrieved by agency action within the meaning of a relevant statute, is entitled to judicial review thereof. An action in a court of the United States seeking relief other than money damages and stating a claim that an agency or an officer or employee thereof acted or failed to act in an official capacity or under color of legal authority shall not be dismissed nor relief therein be denied on the ground that it is against the United States or that the United States is an indispensable party. The United States may be named as a defendant in any such action, and a judgment or decree may be entered against the United States: Provided, That any mandatory or injunctive decree shall specify the Federal officer or officers (by name or by title), and their successors in office, personally responsible for compliance. Nothing herein (1) affects other limitations on judicial review or the power or duty of the court to dismiss any action or deny relief on any other appropriate legal or equitable ground; or (2) confers authority to grant relief if any other statute that grants consent to suit expressly or impliedly forbids the relief which is sought.

"§ 703. Form and venue of proceeding

"The form of proceeding for judicial review is the special statutory review proceeding relevant to the subject matter in a court specified by statute or, in the absence or inadequacy thereof, any applicable form of legal action, including actions for declaratory judgments or writs of prohibitory or mandatory injunction or habeas corpus, in a court of competent jurisdiction. If no special statutory review proceeding is applicable, the action for judicial review may be brought against the

United States, the agency by its official title, or the appropriate officer. Except to the extent that prior, adequate, and exclusive opportunity for judicial review is provided by law, agency action is subject to judicial review in civil or criminal proceedings for judicial enforcement.".

. . .

Sec. 3. The first paragraph of section 1391(e) of title 28, United States Code, is amended to read as follows:

"(e) A civil action in which a defendant is an officer or employee of the United States or any agency thereof acting in his official capacity or under color of legal authority, or an agency of the United States, or the United States, may, except as otherwise provided by law, be brought in any judicial district in which (1) a defendant in the action resides, or (2) the cause of action arose, or (3) any real property involved in the action is situated, or (4) the plaintiff resides if no real property is involved in the action. Additional persons may be joined as parties to any such action in accordance with the Federal Rules of Civil Procedure and with such other venue requirements as would be applicable if the United States or one of its officers, employees, or agencies were not a party.".[3]

SENATE COMMITTEE ON THE JUDICIARY, JUDICIAL REVIEW OF AGENCY ACTION
Sen.Rep. No. 94–996 on S. 800, 94th Cong., 2d Sess. 11–12 (1976).

S. 800 is not intended to affect or change defenses other than sovereign immunity. All other than the law of sovereign immunity remain unchanged. This intent is made clear by clause (1) of the third new sentence added to § 702: "Nothing herein (1) affects other limitations on judicial review or the power or duty of the court to dismiss any action or deny relief on any other appropriate legal or equitable ground."

These grounds include, but are not limited to, the following: (1) extraordinary relief should not be granted because of the hardship to the defendant or to the public ("balancing the equities") or because the plaintiff has an adequate remedy at law; (2) action committed to agency discretion; (3) express or implied preclusion of judicial review; (4) standing; (5) ripeness; (6) failure to exhaust administrative remedies; and (7) an exclusive alternative remedy.

Special doctrines favoring the United States as a litigant, such as the inapplicability of statutes of limitations to claims asserted by the United States, are unaffected. Statutory or rule provisions denying authority for injunctive relief (e.g., the Anti-Injunction Act, 26 U.S.C. § 7421, and 28 U.S.C. § 2201, prohibiting injunctive and declaratory relief against collection of federal taxes) and other matters (e.g., Rule 13(d), dealing with counterclaims against the United States) also remain unchanged. It should be noted in particular that 5 U.S.C. § 701(a) is unchanged and remains applicable.

3. [Ed.] The statute is discussed in S. Jacoby, Roads to the Demise of the Doc- trine of Sovereign Immunity, 29 Admin.L. Rev. 265 (1977).

Likewise, the amendment to 5 U.S.C. § 702 is not intended to permit suit in circumstances where statutes forbid or limit the relief sought. Clause (2) of the third new sentence added to § 702 contains a second proviso concerned with situations in which Congress has consented to suit and the remedy provided is intended to be the exclusive remedy. For example, in the Court of Claims Act, Congress created a damage remedy for contract claims with jurisdiction limited to the Court of Claims except in suits for less than $10,000. The measure is intended to foreclose specific performance of government contracts. In the terms of the proviso, a statute granting consent to suit, i.e., the Tucker Act, "impliedly forbids" relief other than the remedy provided by the Act. Thus, the partial abolition of sovereign immunity brought about by this bill does not change existing limitations on specific relief, if any, derived from statutes dealing with such matters as government contracts, as well as patent infringement, tort claims, and tax claims.[4]

The language of clause (2) of the proviso directs attention to particular statutes and the decisions interpreting them. If a statute "grants consent to suit" with respect to a particular subject matter, specific relief may be obtained only if Congress has not intended that provision for relief to be exclusive.

Clause (2) of the proviso does not withdraw specific relief in any situation in which it is now available. It merely provides that new authority to grant specific relief is not conferred when Congress has dealt in particularity with a claim and intended a specified remedy to be the exclusive remedy.

Clause (2) of the proviso, at the request of the Department of Justice, has been amended to read as follows: "Nothing herein . . . (2) confers authority to grant relief if any other statute that grants consent to suit [for money damages] *expressly or impliedly* forbids the relief which is sought. (Emphasis added.)"

This language makes clear that the committee's intent to preclude other remedies will be followed with respect to all statutes which grant consent to suit and prescribe particular remedies. The proviso as amended also emphasizes that the requisite intent can be implied as well as expressed.

Question

Would application of amended § 702 to the facts of the Larson case change the result in that case?

NOTE

SPECTRUM LEASING CORP. v. UNITED STATES, 764 F.2d 891 (D.C.Cir. 1985). Spectrum contracted with the General Services Administration (GSA) to develop and install a communications network to be used by

---

4. See, e.g., The Anti-Injunction Act, 26 U.S.C. § 7421 prohibiting suit "for the purpose of restricting the assessment or collection of any tax. . . . " Cf. Bob Jones University v. Simon, et al., 416 U.S. 725 (1974) (action to enjoin revocation of letter ruling declaring qualification for tax-exempt status held to be within and barred by the Act).

the Veterans' Administration. After Spectrum commenced delivery and GSA began to make specified lease payments, difficulties developed and GSA eventually invoked the contract's liquidated damage clause and collected the assessed liquidated damages by returning Spectrum's invoices unpaid. The amount so withheld amounted to approximately $1,800,000. Spectrum sued in the district court seeking a declaration that GSA had violated the procedures set forth in the Debt Collection Act (DCA)[5] and an injunction compelling GSA to cease withholding payments due under the contract. The district court dismissed the action. Spectrum's appeal was heard by Judges Tamm, Bork and McGowan who affirmed the district court in an opinion by Judge Tamm.

The issue, said the court, is "whether Spectrum's claim is a contract dispute subject to the jurisdiction of the Claims Court under the Tucker Act or a request for review of agency action under the APA and § 1331." A claim "founded upon" a contract for purposes of the Tucker Act "depends both upon [1] the source of the rights upon which the plaintiff bases its claims and upon [2] the type of relief sought (or appropriate)." A court will not find that a particular claim is one contractually based merely because resolution of that claim requires *some* reference to a contract.

In this case Spectrum seeks an injunction requiring the government to pay monies owed for computer hardware. "The right to these monies is created by the contract not by the DCA. The DCA . . . confers no such right in the absence of the contract itself. Although the DCA might impose procedural requirements on the government having some impact on the contract, the Act in no way creates the substantive right to the remedy Spectrum seeks."

Also, the type of relief sought by Spectrum is a typical contract remedy. "Spectrum seeks an order compelling the government to pay money owed in exchange for goods procured under an executory contract. In other words, Spectrum seeks the classic contractual remedy of specific performance."

Since Spectrum's claim is founded upon a contract and since it "is clear from the APA's legislative history that § 702's waiver of sovereign immunity may not be used to circumvent the jurisdictional and remedial limitations of the Tucker Act,"[6] the district court properly dismissed the suit.

5. The Debt Collection Act provides a set of procedures and safeguards designed to assure due process protections to delinquent government debtors and to enhance the ability of the federal government to collect its debts.

6. The legislative history reveals that Congress intended the remedies available under the Tucker Act to be exclusive in cases against the United States based on contracts. The House Report states that in 28 U.S.C. § 1491: "Congress created a damage remedy for contract claims with jurisdiction limited to the Court of Claims except in suits for less than $10,000. The measure is intended to foreclose specific performance of government contracts. In terms of the proviso, a statute granting consent to suit, i.e., the Tucker Act, 'impliedly forbids' relief other than the remedy provided by the Act." H.R.Rep. No. 1656, 94th Cong., 2d Sess. 12–13 (1976). [Footnote by the court.]

SECTION 6.   TORT ACTION AS A FORM OF REVIEW

a.   Tort Action Against Administrative Official

As the materials in this book demonstrate, the litigant who seeks judicial review typically requests the court to grant *specific* relief: a determination that the agency has acted unlawfully and a judicial order or declaration that the agency should remedy the illegality by acting or ceasing to act in a particular way—set aside the rule, refrain from adjudicating, provide procedural safeguards, restore the license, grant the welfare funds, and so on.   Sometimes, however, the relief sought is not a declaration or order—specific relief—but instead a judgment for money damages.   When this is the desired remedy, the plaintiff must be prepared to overcome the defense of sovereign immunity.   This can be done if the sovereign has consented to be sued as the United States has done in the Tucker Act and the Tort Claims Act. But if there is no consent to be sued, plaintiff's suit for money damages must be based upon a different theory—a theory that we considered, supra p. 987, where attention was invited to the statement of the Attorney General's Committee on Administrative Procedure that "the basic judicial remedy for the protection of the individual against illegal official action is a private action for damages against the official in which the court determines, in the usual common-law manner and with the aid of a jury, whether or not the officer was legally authorized to do what he did in the particular case.   The plaintiff cannot sue to redress merely any unauthorized action by an officer.   To maintain the suit the plaintiff must allege conduct by the officer which, if not justified by his official authority, is a private wrong to the plaintiff, entitling the latter to recover damages."   North American Cold Storage Co. v. Chicago, p. 546 above, discusses this theory of liability.

The plaintiff who sues an officer for damages thus must allege, and be prepared to prove, a cause of action—that the defendant officer has violated a right conferred on plaintiff by the common law, the Constitution or a statute.   If plaintiff surmounts this obstacle, the likely next hurdle will be the defendant's assertion of an official immunity—that is, that even if defendant did commit an act that violated plaintiff's legal rights, the law confers upon its officials an immunity from liability for acts arising out of their official conduct.   Depending on the office and act involved, the defendant officer might be entitled to no immunity whatever, to a "qualified" immunity, or to an "absolute" immunity.

Early opinions made no distinction between public officers and the ordinary citizen when considering answerability for tortious conduct.[1]

---

1. In 1703, Chief Justice Holt put the matter even more strongly: "[I]f public officers will infringe men's rights, they ought to pay greater damages than other men, to deter and hinder other officers from the like offences."   Ashby v. White, 2 Ld. Raym. 938, 956.

Courts at times imposed personal liability for official acts that were not even shown to be negligent, let alone willfully despotic. In effect, judges and jurors reviewed what had been done by a governmental functionary, to determine whether he had done his duty as it was supposed to be done. A famous case of this type was Miller v. Horton, 152 Mass. 540, 26 N.E. 100 (1891). A Massachusetts statute directed health officers to examine horses believed to be infected with glanders, and summarily to destroy and bury diseased animals in order to prevent spread of the infection. A farmer sued an officer who had ordered destruction of the farmer's horse. The court, in an opinion by Holmes, J., held damages to be recoverable if the jury found that the beast had not actually been diseased. The officer, said the court, could not successfully defend by showing that action had been undertaken reasonably and in a good faith effort to execute the statutory duty. The officer was authorized to destroy *infected* horses only, and not horses he *believed* (contrary to a jury's later belief) were infected. The result thus was that the defendant's official status did not confer any immunity at all.[2]

At the other extreme, the classic example of an absolute immunity from liability for allegedly tortious misconduct in office was that which common-law judges awarded themselves. Even when a judge was accused of having caused loss to a private individual by reason of having "exceeded his jurisdiction" and even when he was charged with having made a malicious or corrupt decision, no redress could be had in a tort action. Easily imagining their own responses to such threats, judges thought that to allow defeated suitors to sue a judge would destroy the administration of justice; for judges might then proceed in constant fear that their judgments would expose them to liability, and in any case judges would find themselves incapable of sitting on the bench to dispense justice if their time and energies had to be devoted to private litigation in which they were defendants. Moreover, as Justice Field noted in his classic statement of the reasons for immunity in BRADLEY v. FISHER, 13 Wall. 335 (1871): "Against the consequences of [judges'] erroneous or irregular action, from whatever motives proceeding, the law has provided for private parties numerous [alternative] remedies, and to those remedies they must, in such cases, resort."

Justice Field characterized the principle of absolute judicial immunity as of "the highest importance," for a judicial officer in discharging his functions must be "free to act upon his own convictions, without apprehension of personal consequences to himself." A dramatic confirmation of this assertion was given in STUMP v. SPARKMAN, 435 U.S. 349 (1978). Without affording notice or hearing, or appointing a guardian

---

2. Miller v. Horton was overruled in Gildea v. Ellershaw, 363 Mass. 800, 298 N.E.2d 847 (1973): "[W]e hold that the law of the Commonwealth should be, and therefore is, that if a public officer, other than a judicial officer, is either authorized or required, in the exercise of his judgment and discretion, to make a decision and to perform acts in the making of that deci-sion, and the decision and acts are within the scope of his duty, authority and juris-diction, he is not liable for negligence or other error in the making of that decision, at the suit of a private individual claiming to have been damaged thereby. This rule is presently limited to public officers acting in good faith, without malice and without corruption."

ad litem, and without any express statutory authority to do so, defendant, an Indiana circuit judge, approved a mother's petition for authority to have her "somewhat retarded" 15-year-old daughter sterilized. The daughter had kept pace with her public school class, but had begun to have sexual encounters with older youth; she was told she was to have her appendix removed, and learned the truth only after her marriage, two years later, proved barren. The Court, per White J., found no "clear absence of all jurisdiction" and held that the defendant was "immune from damages liability even if his approval of the petition was in error." Justices Stewart, Marshall and Powell dissented on the ground that the judge's approval of the petition was not a "judicial act." Justice Brennan did not participate.

The question of immunity for government employees acting in executive capacity has proved much more variable over the years. In the strongest terms, Lord Mansfield early rebuffed an English colonial governor (of the island of Minorca) who claimed absolute immunity: "Therefore to lay down in an English court of Justice such a monstrous proposition, as that a governor acting by virtue of letters patent under the great seal, is accountable only to God and his own conscience; that he is absolutely despotic, and can spoil, plunder, and affect his Majesty's subjects, both in their liberty and property, with impunity, is a doctrine that cannot be maintained." [3] While the judicial immunity recognized in Bradley v. Fisher was extended to a cabinet officer in SPALDING v. VILAS, 161 U.S. 483 (1896),[4] its spread was slow. Ultimately, what appears to have emerged from the tension between protecting the vigor of administration by honest officials from inhibition by lawsuit, and redressing the harm that can be done citizens by unchecked discretion, is a form of qualified privilege—one whose reach may vary somewhat with the importance of the office held by the defendant. Understanding the principal case responsible for this development, Butz v. Economou, p. 1175 within, requires some knowledge of earlier cases, beginning with:

3. Mostyn v. Fabrigas, 1 Cowp. 161, 175 (1744).

For a brief survey of immunity in English common law and American common law before 1871, see W. Theis, Official Immunity and the Civil Rights Act, 38 La.L. Rev. 281 (1978).

4. In that case the plaintiff alleged that the defendant Postmaster General had maliciously circulated information which he knew to be false, thereby "placing the plaintiff before the country as a common swindler." Justice Harlan wrote for the Court that "the same general considerations of public policy and convenience which demand for judges of courts of superior jurisdiction immunity from civil suits for damages arising from acts done by them in the course of the performance of their judicial functions apply to a large extent to official communications made by heads of Executive Departments when engaged in the discharge of duties imposed upon them by law. The interests of the people require that due protection be accorded to them in respect of their official acts. . . . In exercising the functions of his office, the head of an Executive Department, keeping within the limits of his authority, should not be under an apprehension that the motives that control his official conduct may, at any time, become the subject of inquiry in a civil suit for damages. It would seriously cripple the proper and effective administration of public affairs as entrusted to the executive branch of the government, if he were subjected to any such restraint." Accordingly, so long as the defendant "did not exceed his authority, nor pass the line of his duty, as Postmaster General, [the] motive that impelled him to do that of which the plaintiff complains is . . . wholly immaterial."

(1) BARR v. MATTEO, 360 U.S. 564 (1959), a libel case that grew out of bureaucratic struggles at the Office of Housing Expediter. In 1950 Matteo and Madigan, personnel officials, had devised a plan which Barr had opposed, but had not been in a position to block. When the plan later came under congressional fire, Madigan prepared a defensive letter over Barr's signature, which was signed by Barr's secretary in his absence and sent to an enraged Congress. When he learned of this, Barr *was* in a position to act, as reflected in the following press release:

"William G. Barr, Acting Director of Rent Stabilization, today served notice of suspension on the two officials of the agency who in June 1950 were responsible for the plan which allowed 53 of the agency's 2,681 employees to take their accumulated annual leave in cash.

"Mr. Barr's appointment as Acting Director becomes effective Monday, February 9, 1953, and the suspension of these employees will be his first act of duty. The employees are John J. Madigan, Deputy Director for Administration, and Linda Matteo, Director of Personnel.

" 'In June 1950,' Mr. Barr stated, 'my position in the agency was not one of authority which would have permitted me to stop the action. Furthermore, I did not know about it until it was almost completed. . . .'

"While I was advised that the action was legal, I took the position that it violated the spirit of the Thomas Amendment and I violently opposed it. Monday, February 9th, when my appointment as Acting Director becomes effective, will be the first time my position in the agency has permitted me to take any action on this matter, and the suspension of these employees will be the first official act I shall take. . . ."

Madigan and Matteo subsequently sued Barr, contending that the press release, coupled with contemporaneous news accounts of Senatorial ire, had defamed and injured them. They alleged that Barr had been actuated by malice in composing and issuing the press release. Barr defended on the ground, among others, of immunity, but the trial court sent the case to the jury, and the jury found that the plaintiffs had indeed been damaged by Barr.

Justice Harlan wrote the principal opinion, and was able to command only a plurality: Justices Frankfurter, Clark and Whittaker. He resolved the tension between protection of the citizen from "oppressive or malicious" official action and protection of responsible governmental officials from "harassment" and "vindictive or ill-founded suits" in favor of the officials:

"The reasons for the recognition of the privilege have been often stated. It has been thought important that officials of government should be free to exercise their duties unembarrassed by the fear of damage suits in respect of acts done in the course of those duties—suits which would consume time and energies which would otherwise be devoted to governmental service and the threat of which might appreciably inhibit the fearless, vigorous, and effective administration of policies of government. . . . We do not think that the principle announced in [Spalding v.] Vilas can properly be restricted to executive officers of cabinet rank, and in fact it never has been so restricted by the lower federal courts. The privilege is not a badge or emolument of exalted office, but an expression of a policy designed to aid in the effective functioning of government. The complexities and magnitude of governmental activity have become so great that there must of necessity be a delegation and redelegation of authority as to many functions, and we cannot say that these functions become less important simply because they are exercised by officers of lower rank in the executive hierarchy. . . . "

While conceding the closeness of the issue, the plurality found Barr's issuance of the press release to have been an appropriate "exercise of the discretion with which an executive officer of petitioner's rank is necessarily clothed" and "within the outer perimeter of petitioner's line of duty."

". . . The integrity of the internal operations of the agency which he headed, and thus his own integrity in his public capacity, had been directly and severely challenged in charges made on the floor of the Senate and given wide publicity; and without his knowledge correspondence which could reasonably be read as impliedly defending a position very different from that which he had from the beginning taken in the matter had been sent to a Senator over his signature and incorporated in the Congressional Record. The issuance of press releases was standard agency practice, as it has become with many governmental agencies in these times. . . .

"We are told that we should forbear from sanctioning any such rule of absolute privilege lest it open the door to wholesale oppression and abuses on the part of unscrupulous government officials. It is perhaps enough to say that fears of this sort have not been realized within the wide area of government where a judicially formulated absolute privilege of broad scope has long existed. . . . To be sure, as with any rule of law which attempts to reconcile fundamentally antagonistic social policies, there may be occasional instances of actual injustice which will go unredressed, but we think that price a necessary one to pay for the greater good. And there are of course other sanctions than civil tort suits available to deter the executive official who may be prone to exercise his functions in an unworthy and irresponsible manner. We think that we should not be deterred from establishing the rule which we announce today by any such remote forebodings."

Justice Black made the fifth vote for the "absolute privilege" position, and emphasized his view that the result was compelled by the need for "informed public opinion. This calls for the widest possible understanding of the quality of government service rendered by all elective or appointed public officials or employees. Such an informed understanding depends, of course, on the freedom people have to applaud or to criticize the way public employees do their jobs, from the least to the most important. . . .

"Subjecting [Mr. Barr] to libel suits for criticizing the way the Agency or its employees perform their duties would certainly act as a restraint upon him. So far as I am concerned, . . . the restraint will have to be imposed expressly by Congress and not by the general libel laws of the States or of the District of Columbia. . . . "

Three dissenting opinions were filed. Chief Justice Warren, with Justice Douglas, would have limited Spalding v. Vilas to cabinet officials; "[g]iving officials below cabinet or equivalent rank qualified privilege for statements to the public would in no way hamper the internal operation of the Executive Department of government, nor would it unduly subordinate the interest of the individual in obtaining redress for the public defamation uttered against him. . . . "

Justice Brennan, also, thought only a qualified privilege was appropriate. He characterized the majority's "findings" about the impact of exposure to liability on the robustness of officials' performance of duty as "a gossamer web self-spun without a scintilla of support to which one can point," one which "demands the resolution of large imponderables which one might have thought would be better the business of the Legislative Branch. To what extent is it in the public interest that the Executive Branch carry on publicity campaigns in relation to its activities? . . . To what extent does fear of litigation actually inhibit the conduct of officers in carrying out the public business? To what extent should it? Where does healthy administrative frankness and boldness shade into bureaucratic tyranny? To what extent is supervision by an administrator's superiors effective in assuring that there will be little abuse of a freedom from suit? To what extent can the referral of constituent complaints by Congressmen to the executive agencies (already myriad in number and quite routinized in processing) take the place of actions in the courts of law in securing the injured citizen redress? Can it be assumed, as the opinion appears to assume, that an absolute privilege so broadly enjoyed will not be subject to severe abuse? . . . "

"If the fears expressed materialized and great inconvenience to the workings of the Government arose out of allowing defamation actions subject to a showing of malice, Congress might well be disposed to intervene. And its intervention might take a less drastic form than the solution today."

Justice Stewart, finally, agreed with the Harlan analysis but would not have applied it to this case. "By publicizing the action which he intended to take when he became permanent Acting Director, and his past attitude as a lesser functionary, the petitioner was seeking only to defend his own individual reputation. This was not within, but beyond 'the outer perimeter of petitioner's line of duty.' "

(2) BIVENS v. SIX UNKNOWN NAMED AGENTS OF THE FEDERAL BUREAU OF NARCOTICS, 403 U.S. 388 (1971), grew out of an early morning raid upon a private apartment. The agents had no warrant when they burst in. They handcuffed Bivens in front of his wife and children, ransacked his home in a fruitless search for contraband, arrested him without a warrant, forced him to accompany them to their quarters,

interrogated him, subjected him to a strip search, filed charges against him, and brought him before a United States Commissioner—who found no basis at all for detaining Bivens. If in fact the agents had discovered the evidence for which they were apparently searching, it could not have been used in a proceeding against Bivens had he moved to suppress it as having been illegally obtained. But, as we say, no evidence whatsoever was found. Was Bivens remediless? Being an ignorant as well as an indignant man, he believed the law must be on his side. This was perhaps remarkable since, at that time, Bivens was free on bail, awaiting trial upon a felony charge which later led to conviction and the penitentiary. While serving his sentence Bivens, representing himself, initiated a rather inartistic law suit in federal court against the agents whose names he did not know, asking $15,000 damages from each. His complaint was dismissed in the district court. The court of appeals affirmed, reasoning that "with rare exceptions . . . , the choice of ways and means to enforce a constitutional right should be left with Congress. It is when a clearly declared right is left so wanting of remedies as to render it a mere 'form of words' that an appropriate occasion for judicial initiative has been reached. . . . [T]he primary thrust of the Bill of Rights is to shield citizens from certain actions by the government. The implication of judicial remedies [such as injunctive relief or the exclusionary rule] to provide this shield follows naturally from the declaration of a right; far less natural is the conversion of this shield into a sword directed against individual officers."

The Supreme Court, when the case finally came before it, decided for the first time that violation of the Fourth Amendment could give rise to an implied cause of action for damages. Justice Brennan's majority opinion said that the "present case involves no special factors counselling hesitation in the absence of affirmative action by Congress. . . . [W]e have here no explicit congressional declaration that persons injured by a federal officer's violation of the Fourth Amendment may not recover money damages from the agents, but must instead be remitted to another remedy, equally effective in the view of Congress. The question is merely whether petitioner, if he can demonstrate an injury consequent upon the violation by federal agents of his Fourth Amendment rights, is entitled to redress his injury through a particular remedial mechanism normally available in the federal courts. Cf. J.I. Case Co. v. Borak, 377 U.S. 426, 433 (1964). 'The very essence of civil liberty certainly consists in the right of every individual to claim the protection of the laws, whenever he receives an injury.' Marbury v. Madison, 1 Cranch 137, 163 (1803). Having concluded that petitioner's complaint states a cause of action under the Fourth Amendment, we hold that petitioner is entitled to recover money damages for any injuries he has suffered as a result of the agents' violation of the Amendment."

Justice Harlan, concurring, pointed to the fact that "in suits for damages based on violations of federal statutes lacking any express authorization of a damage remedy, this Court has authorized such relief where, in its view, damages are necessary to effectuate the congression-

al policy underpinning the substantive provisions of the statute. J.I.
Case v. Borak, 377 U.S. 426 (1964).⁵ " In Justice Harlan's view:

"[I]t would be anomalous to conclude that the federal judiciary—
while competent to choose among the range of traditional judicial
remedies to implement statutory and common-law policies . . . —is
powerless to accord a damages remedy to vindicate social policies
which, by virtue of their inclusion in the Constitution, are aimed
predominantly at restraining the Government as an instrument of the
popular will.

"And I think it is clear that Bivens advances a claim of the sort
that, if proved, would be properly compensable in damages. The
personal interests protected by the Fourth Amendment are those we
attempt to capture by the notion of 'privacy'; while the Court today
properly points out that the type of harm which officials can inflict
when they invade protected zones of an individual's life are different
from the types of harm private citizens inflict on one another, the
experience of judges in dealing with private trespass and false imprisonment claims supports the conclusion that courts of law are capable of
making the types of judgment concerning causation and magnitude of
injury necessary to accord meaningful compensation for invasion of
Fourth Amendment rights. . . .⁶

"Putting aside the desirability of leaving the problem of federal
official liability to the vagaries of common-law actions, it is apparent
that some form of damages is the only possible remedy for someone in
Bivens' alleged position. It will be a rare case indeed in which an
individual in Bivens' position will be able to obviate the harm by
securing injunctive relief from any court. However desirable a direct
remedy against the Government might be as a substitute for individual
official liability, the sovereign still remains immune to suit. Finally,
assuming Bivens' innocence of the crime charged, the "exclusionary
rule" is simply irrelevant. For people in Bivens' shoes, it is damages or
nothing."

Chief Justice Burger and Justices Black and Blackmun dissented.

Since the court of appeals had not considered the question whether
the defendants were immune from liability by virtue of their official
position, the Bivens case was remanded for further proceedings. Upon

---

5. The Borak case is an especially clear
example of the exercise of federal judicial
power to accord damages as an appropriate
remedy in the absence of any express statutory authorization of a federal cause of
action. There we "implied"—from what
can only be characterized as an "exclusively procedural provision" affording access to
a federal forum, a private cause of action
for damages for violation of Section 14(a) of
the Securities Exchange Act of 1934. We
did so in an area where federal regulation
has been singularly comprehensive and
elaborate administrative enforcement machinery had been provided. The exercise
of judicial power involved in Borak simply
cannot be justified in terms of statutory

construction; nor did the Borak Court purport to do so. The notion of "implying" a
remedy, therefore, as applied to cases like
Borak, can only refer to a process whereby
the federal judiciary exercises a choice
among *traditionally available* judicial remedies according to reasons related to the
substantive social policy embodied in an
act of positive law.

6. The same, of course, may not be true
with respect to other types of constitutionally protected interests, and therefore the
appropriateness of money damages may
well vary with the nature of the personal
interest asserted. . . .

remand, the Second Circuit concluded in 1972 (456 F.2d 1339) that unlike the officials in Barr, these defendant narcotic agents should not be accorded an absolute immunity from damage liability because, although the defendants were acting within "the outer perimeter of [their] line of duty," they were not performing "discretionary" functions. The court stated that in determining whether the defendants' duties were discretionary, it recognized that "words such as 'discretion' are not particularly helpful" because the "real question" is: "[I]s the act complained of the result of a judgment or decision which it is necessary that the Government official be free to make without fear or threat of vexatious or fictitious suits and alleged personal liability? "

The court then balanced law enforcement needs against the "right of citizens to be free from unlawful arrests and searches" and concluded that a police officer who allegedly has violated the Fourth Amendment may be held answerable in damages unless he can "allege and prove not only [1] that he believed, in good faith, that his conduct was lawful, but also [2] that his belief was reasonable"—the first condition being subjective and the second objective. The court also noted that in its opinion in this case, "the Supreme Court recognized a right of action against federal officers that is roughly analogous to the right of action against state officers that was provided when Congress enacted the Civil Rights Act" and expressed the view that it would be "incongruous and confusing" for it to hold that the damage liability of federal officers should be different from the damage liability imposed by the Civil Rights Act on state officers for similar constitutional violations.[7]

Thus, in Bivens the Supreme Court provided a federal money damage remedy for a "constitutional tort"—in that instance, a violation of the Fourth Amendment prohibition against unreasonable search and seizure; the Second Circuit held that the officers' immunity should be qualified, not absolute, and intimated that the scope of the immunity accorded federal officers sued for constitutional torts should be the same as the immunity accorded state officials sued for violating the Civil Rights Act.[8]

---

7. "Webster Bivens' claims were never determined at trial after remand, since an out-of-court settlement was reached which provided for a payment of $100.00 from each defendant narcotics agent." 454 F.Supp. at 767 n. 2.

8. The Civil Rights Act of 1871, 42 U.S.C. § 1983, provides in part as follows: "Every person who, under color of any statute, ordinance, regulation, custom or usage, of any State . . . subjects, or causes to be subjected, any . . . person . . . to the deprivation of any rights, privileges or immunities secured by the Constitution and laws, shall be liable to the party injured in an action at law, suit in equity, or other proper proceeding for redress." Actions under this statute may be brought directly in the federal courts.

In Patsy v. Board of Regents, 457 U.S. 496 (1982), the Supreme Court reaffirmed

that exhaustion of state administrative remedies is not required in § 1983 actions.

The Civil Rights of Institutionalized Persons Act, P.L. No. 96–247, 94 Stat. 349 (1980), requires exhaustion in certain circumstances in § 1983 prisoner cases. "[T]he Act . . . provides that an inmate who sues under 1983 shall, if appropriate and the interests of justice warrant, have his or her case continued by the court for 90 days so that the inmate may exhaust 'such plain, speedy, and effective administrative remedies as are available.' Exhaustion may only be ordered, however, where the applicable administrative procedures are either certified by the Attorney General or are determined by the court to comply substantially with certain minimum acceptable standards. These standards, promulgated by the Attorney General . . . include: (1) An advisory role for

(3) MONROE v. PAPE, 365 U.S. 167 (1961). Local police officers smashed their way into living quarters at an early hour, abused the resident family both verbally and physically, violently searched the premises though without a warrant, and then detained and questioned the family head without preferring charges against him or taking him before a magistrate. Suit was brought under § 1983 to recover damages for this deprivation of constitutional "rights, privileges, or immunities." The defense argued that the policemen had not acted "under color" of state authority, because no statute or ordinance conceivably empowered them to break into the plaintiff's home and to mistreat its occupants as they had done; if suit were to be brought, the defense contended, let it be brought in a state court for unlawful entry, assault, or what not. As to this, the Supreme Court in an opinion by Justice Douglas (Justice Frankfurter dissenting and Justices Harlan and Stewart concurring rather hesitantly) confirmed an earlier decision that "Misuse of power, possessed by virtue of state law and made possible only because the wrongdoer is clothed with the authority of state law, is action taken 'under color of' state law." United States v. Classic, 313 U.S. 299, 326 (1941). And the Court added that litigation growing out of this kind of misuse of power need not be brought in state courts; the federal remedy given by the Civil Rights Act "is supplementary to the State remedy, and the latter need not be first sought and refused before the federal one is invoked. Hence the fact that Illinois by its constitution and laws outlaws unreasonable searches and seizures is no barrier to the present suit in the federal court."

After Monroe v. Pape, lawsuits in mounting number were brought against public officials under § 1983.[9] While this is not the place to

the inmates. (2) Time limits for written replies to inmate grievances. (3) Priority processing of emergency grievances. (4) Safeguards to avoid reprisals. (5) Independent review of the disposition of grievances." S. Nahmod, Civil Rights and Civil Liberties Litigation (1979) 1985 Supp. § 5.10

9. See P. Schuck, Suing Government 199 (1983):

"Only nineteen decisions were rendered under § 1983 in the first sixty-five years after its adoption in 1871. Today, however, § 1983 is the second most heavily litigated section of the United States Code; only federal habeas corpus claims are more numerous. [Since] § 1983 cases are not identified separately in the statistics published by the Administrative Office of the United States Courts, the . . . statistics do not permit one to isolate § 1983 suits from other cases . . . in the 'civil rights' categories in the data base. Hence, the data on 'civil rights' litigation must be the statistical proxy for the volume of § 1983 cases.

"In the period 1960–81, the volume of civil litigation in federal courts increased steadily, from just under 60,000 cases commenced in 1960 to 175,694 cases commenced in the statistical year ending March 31, 1981—an increase of some 193 percent. During the same period, however, the 'civil rights statute' subcategory grew even more dramatically, from 280 filings in 1960 to just over 27,000 in 1980—an increase of 9,578 percent. In the decade 1970–80 alone, 'federal question' civil rights cases (including prisoner civil rights petitions) rose by 350 percent."

Compare T. Eisenberg and S. Schwab, The Realities of Constitutional Tort Litigation, 13 Corn.L.Forum 7 (1986), reporting concerning an "empirical study of . . . 965 cases classified by the Administrative Office of the U.S. Courts as civil rights or habeas corpus cases and filed in fiscal 1980 in the Central District of California (Los Angeles)": "The popular wisdom suggests a large and growing number of constitutional tort cases. We have discovered, however, that that common wisdom seriously overstates the facts. Our study suggests that less than a third of the 965 filings . . . are [§ 1983 and Bivens-type] constitutional tort cases."

attempt to discuss this burgeoning development,[10] two matters of significance to the current theme of official privilege may be noted: although
the Civil Rights Act speaks to "every person" whose acts cause another
to be deprived of rights under the Constitution and laws, state legislators retain their traditional absolute immunity for legislative conduct;[11] and absolute judicial immunity also survives.[12] The cases
establishing these propositions, like their federal analogs, were developed solely on the basis of judicial reasoning. As one commentator
expressed it, "[T]he question of immunity under § 1983 [was to] be
resolved by: common law rules; neither the language of the statute nor
its legislative history spoke directly to questions of official immunity,
and absent direct evidence to the contrary, Congress must be presumed
to have intended to preserve common law rules. However, these
principles did not necessarily define the scope of immunity, if any, to be
afforded executive officers other than policemen. While absolute immunity of legislators and judges, and perhaps the protective defense of
good faith and probable cause for police officers, were established at
common law, the rules as to immunity of executive officials other than
policemen were not so clear. The federal courts applied a rather broad
common law rule of absolute immunity to federal executive officials,
while state courts more typically rejected absolute immunity. How
these executive officials would be treated in suits under the Civil Rights
Act remained unresolved after Tenney and Pierson. The lower federal
courts were divided on this issue, some applying the federal officer rule
of absolute immunity, others extending a qualified immunity."[13] The
Supreme Court's answer came in a series of cases beginning with
Scheuer v. Woods in 1974. Those cases, together with a considerable
change in applicable federal law, are discussed in Justice White's
opinion in:

BUTZ v. ECONOMOU

Supreme Court of the United States, 1978.
438 U.S. 478.

[The Department of Agriculture (DOA) instituted a proceeding
under the Commodity Exchange Act to revoke or suspend the registration of Arthur N. Economou and Co., a corporation controlled by
Arthur N. Economou. DOA charged that while a registered futures
merchant the company had willfully failed to maintain the minimum
financial requirements prescribed by DOA. The proceeding was insti-

10. For discussion, see S. Nahmod, Civil
Rights and Civil Liberties Litigation (2d ed.
1986); 4 K. Davis, Admin.L. Treatise
§§ 27.30–27.40 (1984); P. Schuck, Suing
Government (1983); T. Eisenberg, Civil
Rights Legislation c. 2 (1981 and Supp.
1986); Civil Actions Against State Governments (Shepard's McGraw-Hill, 1982); P.
Bator, P. Mishkin, D. Shapiro and H.
Wechsler, Hart and Wechsler's The Federal Courts and the Federal System c. 7; § 3
(2d ed. 1973 and Supp.1981); Developments
in the Law—Section 1983 and Federalism,
90 Harv.L.Rev. 1133 (1977).

See also the useful compilation of law
review literature in T. Madden and N.
Allard, Advice on Official Liability and Immunity, Appendix C, 2 ACUS Recommendations and Reports 201, 327–442 (1982).

11. Tenney v. Brandhove, 341 U.S. 367
(1951).

12. Pierson v. Ray, 386 U.S. 547 (1967).

13. M. Freed, Executive Official Immunity for Constitutional Violations: An
Analysis and A Critique, 72 Nw.U.L.Rev.
526, 536–7 (1977).

tuted without issuing a warning letter to the company. The hearing examiner's decision upholding the charge was affirmed by the Judicial Officer of DOA, but was reversed by the Second Circuit on the ground that "the essential finding of willfulness . . . was made in a proceeding instituted without the customary warning letter." While the administrative proceeding was pending on appeal, the company, Economou and another corporation headed by Economou brought an action for $32,000,000 against DOA, the Commodity Exchange Authority (CEA), the Secretary, and Assistant Secretary of Agriculture, the Judicial Officer and Chief Hearing Examiner, the DOA attorney who had prosecuted the enforcement proceeding, auditors who had investigated or testified against the company, and several CEA officials.[1] Plaintiffs alleged constitutional violations such as deprivations of the first amendment right to free expression and the fifth amendment right to notice; common-law torts of abuse of process, malicious prosecution, invasion of privacy, negligence and trespass were also alleged.[2]

The district court dismissed the actions against DOA and CEA on grounds of sovereign immunity. Apparently relying on the plurality opinion in Barr v. Matteo, the court also dismissed the actions against the individual defendants "since [they] have shown that their alleged unconstitutional acts were both within the scope of their authority and discretionary." The Second Circuit affirmed as to DOA and CEA[3] but reversed as to the individual defendants, holding that they were not entitled to an absolute Barr v. Matteo type of immunity but, instead, to a qualified immunity of good faith and reasonable grounds similar to that accorded state officers sued for constitutional violations under the Civil Rights Act. Certiorari was granted.]

MR. JUSTICE WHITE delivered the opinion of the Court. . . .

The single submission by the United States on behalf of petitioners is that all of the federal officials sued in this case are absolutely immune from any liability for damages even if in the course of enforcing the relevant statutes they infringed respondent's constitutional rights and even if the violation was knowing and deliberate. Although the position is earnestly and ably presented by the United States, we are quite sure that it is unsound and consequently reject it. . . .

Bivens established that compensable injury to a constitutionally protected interest could be vindicated by a suit for damages invoking the general federal question jurisdiction of the federal courts,[4] but we

---

1. The Administrator of CEA, the Director of the Compliance Division, the Deputy Director of the Registration and Audit Division and the New York Regional Administrator.

2. One of the charges was that the defendants had issued a "deceptive" press release that "falsely indicated to the public that [plaintiff's] financial resources had deteriorated when Defendants knew that their statement was untrue and so acknowledge[d] previously that said assertion was untrue."

3. The court also said it would not "accept appellant's suggestion that the complaint now be amended to name the United States of America as a defendant, since the 'intentional tort' exclusion of the Federal Tort Claims Act, would deny us jurisdiction over such claims against the United States, even though appellant's claims of malicious prosecution, abuse of process, and libel be cast in constitutional terms."

4. The Court's opinion in Bivens concerned only a Fourth Amendment claim and therefore did not discuss what other

reserved the question whether the agents involved were "immune from liability by virtue of their official position," and remanded the case for that determination. On remand, the Court of Appeals for the Second Circuit, as has every other court of appeals that has faced the question, held that the agents were not absolutely immune and that the public interest would be sufficiently protected by according the agents and their superiors a qualified immunity.

In our view, the courts of appeals have reached sound results. We cannot agree with the United States that our prior cases are to the contrary and support the rule it now urges us to embrace. . . .

[The Court then discussed and distinguished to its satisfaction the cases relied on by the Government. Two of these cases were Barr v. Matteo, supra p. 1168, and Spalding v. Vilas, supra p. 1167, note 4. As to them:]

The liability of officials who have exceeded constitutional limits was not confronted in either Barr or Spalding.[5] Neither of those cases supports the Government's position. Beyond that, however, neither case purported to abolish the liability of federal officers for actions manifestly beyond their line of duty; and if they are accountable when they stray beyond the plain limits of their statutory authority, it would be incongruous to hold that they may nevertheless willfully or knowingly violate constitutional rights without fear of liability.

Although it is true that the Court has not dealt with this issue with respect to federal officers, we have several times addressed the immunity of state officers when sued under 42 U.S.C. § 1983 for alleged violations of constitutional rights. These decisions are instructive for present purposes. . . .

In Scheuer v. Rhodes, [416 U.S. 232 (1974)], the issue was whether "higher officers of the executive branch" of state governments were immune from liability under § 1983 for violations of constitutionally protected rights. There, the governor of a State, the senior and subordinate officers of the state national guard, and a state university president had been sued on the allegation that they had suppressed a civil disturbance in an unconstitutional manner. We explained that the doctrine of official immunity from § 1983 liability, although not constitutionally grounded and essentially a matter of statutory construction, was based on two mutually dependent rationales: "(1) the injustice, particularly in the absence of bad faith, of subjecting to liability an officer who is required, by the legal obligation of his

personal interests were similarly protected by provisions of the Constitution. We do not consider that issue here. Cf. Doe v. McMillan, 412 U.S. 306, 325 (1973).

5. [Ed.] In a portion of its opinion not reproduced here, the Court stated in a footnote: "We view this case, in its present posture, as concerned only with constitutional issues. The District Court Memorandum focused exclusively on respondent's constitutional claims. It appears from the language and reasoning of its opinion that the Court of Appeals was also essentially concerned with respondent's constitutional claims. See, e.g., 535 F.2d, at 695 n. 7. The Second Circuit has subsequently read Economou as limited to that context. See Huntington Towers, Ltd. v. Franklin Nat. Bank, 559 F.2d 863, 870, and n. 2 (1977), cert. denied 434 U.S. 1012 (1978). The argument before us as well has focused on respondent's constitutional claims, and our holding is so limited."

position, to exercise discretion; (2) the danger that the threat of such liability would deter his willingness to execute his office with the decisiveness and the judgment required by the public good." The opinion also recognized that executive branch officers must often act swiftly and on the basis of factual information supplied by others, constraints which become even more acute in the "atmosphere of confusion, ambiguity and swiftly moving events" created by a civil disturbance. Although quoting at length from Barr v. Matteo, we did not believe that there was a need for absolute immunity from § 1983 liability for these high-ranking state officials. Rather the considerations discussed above indicated that: "in varying scope, a qualified immunity is available to officers of the executive branch of government, the variation being dependent upon the scope of discretion and responsibilities of the office and all the circumstances as they reasonably appeared at the time of the action on which liability is sought to be based. It is the existence of reasonable grounds for the belief formed at the time and in light of all the circumstances, coupled with good-faith belief, that affords a basis for qualified immunity of executive officers for acts performed in the course of official conduct."

Subsequent decisions have applied the Scheuer standard in other contexts. In Wood v. Strickland, 420 U.S. 308 (1975), school administrators were held entitled to claim a similar qualified immunity. A school board member would lose his immunity from a § 1983 suit only if "he knew or reasonably should have known that the action he took within his sphere of official responsibility would violate the constitutional rights of the student affected, or if he took the action with the malicious intention to cause a deprivation of constitutional rights or other injury to the student." In O'Connor v. Donaldson, 422 U.S. 563 (1975), we applied the same standard to the superintendent of a state hospital. In Procunier v. Navarette, 434 U.S. 555, we held that prison administrators would be adequately protected by the qualified immunity outlined in Scheuer and Wood. We emphasized, however, that, at least in the absence of some showing of malice, an official would not be held liable in damages under § 1983 unless the constitutional right he was alleged to have violated was "clearly established" at the time of the violation.

None of these decisions with respect to state officials furnishes any support for the submission of the United States that federal officials are absolutely immune from liability for their constitutional transgressions. On the contrary, with impressive unanimity, the federal courts of appeals have concluded that federal officials should receive no greater degree of protection from *constitutional* claims than their counterparts in state government. . . .

We agree with the perception of these courts that, in the absence of congressional direction to the contrary, there is no basis for according to federal officials a higher degree of immunity from liability when sued for a constitutional infringement as authorized by Bivens, than is accorded state officials when sued for the identical violation under § 1983. The constitutional injuries made actionable by § 1983 are of no greater magnitude than those for which federal officials may be responsible. The pressures and uncertainties facing decisionmakers in state government are little if at all different from those affecting federal officials. . . . Surely, *federal* officials should enjoy no greater zone of protection when they violate *federal* constitutional rules than do *state* officers.

. . .

Our opinion in Bivens put aside the immunity question; but we could not have contemplated that immunity would be absolute. If, as the Government argues, all officials exercising discretion were exempt from personal liability, a suit under the Constitution could provide no redress to the injured citizen, nor would it in any degree deter federal officials from committing constitutional wrongs. Moreover, no compensation would be available from the Government, for the Tort Claims Act prohibits recovery for injuries stemming from discretionary acts, even when that discretion has been abused.[6]

The extension of absolute immunity from damages liability to all federal executive officials would seriously erode the protection provided by basic constitutional guarantees. . . . It makes little sense to hold that a Government agent is liable for warrantless and forcible entry into a citizen's house in pursuit of evidence, but that an official of higher rank who actually orders such a burglary is immune simply because of his greater authority. . . .

This is not to say that considerations of public policy fail to support a limited immunity for federal executive officials. We consider here, as we did in Scheuer, the need to protect officials who are required to exercise their discretion and the related public interest in encouraging the vigorous exercise of official authority. Yet Scheuer and other cases have recognized that it is not unfair to hold liable the official who knows or should know he is acting outside the law, and that insisting on an awareness of clearly established constitutional limits will not unduly interfere with the exercise of official judgment. We therefore hold that, in a suit for damages arising from unconstitutional action, federal executive officials exercising discretion are entitled only to the qualified immunity specified in Scheuer, subject to those exceptional situations where it is demonstrated that absolute immunity is essential for the conduct of the public business. . . .

[W]e see no substantial basis for holding, as the United States would have us do, that executive officers generally may with impunity discharge their duties in a way that is known to them to violate the United States Constitution or in a manner that they should know transgresses a clearly established constitutional rule. The principle should prove as workable in suits against federal officials as it has in the context of suits against state officials. Insubstantial lawsuits can be quickly terminated by federal courts alert to the possibilities of

---

6. Pursuant to 28 U.S.C. § 2680, the Government is immune from "(a) any claim . . . based upon the exercise or performance or the failure to exercise or perform a discretionary function or duty on the part of a federal agency or an employee of the Government, whether or not the discretion involved be abused." See generally Dalehite v. United States, 346 U.S. 15 (1953).

artful pleading. Unless the complaint states a compensable claim for relief under the Federal Constitution, it should not survive a motion to dismiss. Moreover, the Court recognized in Scheuer that damage suits concerning constitutional violations need not proceed to trial, but can be terminated on a properly supported motion for summary judgment based on the defense of immunity.[7] In responding to such a motion, plaintiffs may not play dog in the manger; and firm application of the Federal Rules of Civil Procedure will ensure that federal officials are not harassed by frivolous lawsuits.

Although a qualified immunity from damages liability should be the general rule for executive officials charged with constitutional violations, our decisions recognize that there are some officials whose special functions require a full exemption from liability. . . .

[The Court then discussed Bradley v. Fisher, supra p. 1166, which held that judges should be accorded an absolute immunity, and Imbler v. Pachtman, 424 U.S. 409 (1976), which held that a state prosecutor was entitled to absolute immunity with respect to his activities as an advocate, "activities [which] were intimately associated with the judicial phase of the criminal process, and thus were functions to which the reasons for absolute immunity apply with full force."[8]]

Despite these precedents, the Court of Appeals concluded that all of the defendants in this case—including the hearing examiner, Judicial Officer, and prosecuting attorney—were entitled to only a qualified immunity. The Court of Appeals reasoned that officials within the Executive Branch generally have more circumscribed discretion . . . . .

We think that the Court of Appeals placed undue emphasis on the fact that the officials sued here are—from an administrative perspective—employees of the Executive Branch. Judges have absolute immunity not because of their particular location within the Government, but because of the special nature of their responsibilities. This point is underlined by the fact that prosecutors—themselves members of the Executive Branch—are also absolutely immune. "It is the functional comparability of their judgments to those of the judge that has resulted in both grand jurors and prosecutors being referred to as 'quasi-judicial' officers, and their immunities being termed 'quasi-judicial' as well." Imbler v. Pachtman, 424 U.S., at 423 n. 20.

The cluster of immunities protecting the various participants in judge-supervised trials stems from the characteristics of the judicial

---

7. The defendant official may also be able to assert on summary judgment some other common law or constitutional privilege. For example, in this case the defendant officials may be able to argue that their issuance of the press release was privileged as an accurate report on a matter of public record in an administrative proceeding. See Handler & Klein, The Defense of Privilege in Defamation Suits Against Government Executive Officials, 74 Harv.L.Rev. 44, 61–62, 75–76 (1960). Of course, we do not decide this issue at this time.

8. [Ed.] In a portion of the opinion not reproduced here, the Court stated in a footnote: "The Imbler Court specifically reserved the question 'whether like or similar reasons require immunity for those aspects of the prosecutor's responsibility that cast him in the role of an administrator or investigative officer rather than that of advocate.'"

process rather than its location. . . . The loser in one forum will frequently seek another, charging the participants in the first with unconstitutional animus. Absolute immunity is thus necessary to assure that judges, advocates, and witnesses can perform their respective functions without harassment or intimidation.

At the same time, the safeguards built into the judicial process tend to reduce the need for private damage actions as a means of controlling unconstitutional conduct. The insulation of the judge from political influence, the importance of precedent in resolving controversies, the adversary nature of the process, and the correctability of error on appeal are just a few of the many checks on malicious action by judges. Advocates are restrained not only by their professional obligations, but by the knowledge that their assertions will be contested by their adversaries in open court. Jurors are carefully screened to remove all possibility of bias. Witnesses are, of course subject to the rigors of cross-examination and the penalty of perjury. Because these features of the judicial process tend to enhance the reliability of information and the impartiality of the decisionmaking process, there is a less pressing need for individual suits to correct constitutional error.

We think that adjudication within a federal administrative agency shares enough of the characteristics of the judicial process that those who participate in such adjudication should also be immune from suits for damages. . . .

[W]e think that the risk of an unconstitutional act by one presiding at an agency hearing is clearly outweighed by the importance of preserving the independent judgment of these men and women. We therefore hold that persons subject to these restraints and performing adjudicatory functions within a federal agency are entitled to absolute immunity from damages liability for their judicial acts. . . .

We also believe that agency officials performing certain functions analogous to those of a prosecutor should be able to claim absolute immunity with respect to such acts.[9] . . .

---

9. [Ed.] A particularly powerful opinion supporting such immunity, written by Learned Hand, one of the country's most distinguished jurists, is Gregoire v. Biddle, 177 F.2d 579 (2d Cir.1949):

"It does indeed go without saying that an official, who is in fact guilty of using his powers to vent his spleen upon others, or for any other personal motive not connected with the public good, should not escape liability for the injuries he may so cause; and, if it were possible in practice to confine such complaints to the guilty, it would be monstrous to deny recovery. The justification for doing so is that it is impossible to know whether the claim is well founded until the case has been tried, and that to submit all officials, the innocent as well as the guilty, to the burden of a trial and to the inevitable danger of its outcome, would dampen the ardor of all but the most resolute, or the most irresponsible, in the un-flinching discharge of their duties. Again and again the public interest calls for action which may turn out to be founded on a mistake, in the face of which an official may later find himself hard put to it to satisfy a jury of his good faith. There must indeed be means of punishing public officers who have been truant to their duties; but that is quite another matter from exposing such as have been honestly mistaken to suit by anyone who has suffered from their errors. As is so often the case, the answer must be found in a balance between the evils inevitable in either alternative. In this instance it has been thought in the end better to leave unredressed the wrongs done by dishonest officers than to subject those who try to do their duty to the constant dread of retaliation. Judged as res nova, we should not hesitate to follow the path laid down in the books."

The discretion which executive officials exercise with respect to the initiation of administrative proceedings might be distorted if their immunity from damages arising from that decision was less than complete. Cf. Imbler v. Pachtman, supra. While there is not likely to be anyone willing and legally able to seek damages from the officials if they do *not* authorize the administrative proceeding . . . , there is a serious danger that the decision to authorize proceedings will provoke a retaliatory response. An individual targeted by an administrative proceeding will react angrily and may seek vengeance in the courts. . . .

The defendant in an enforcement proceeding has ample opportunity to challenge the legality of the proceeding. . . . Indeed, respondent in this case was able to quash the administrative order entered against him by means of judicial review.

We believe that agency officials must make the decision to move forward with an administrative proceeding free from intimidation or harassment. Because the legal remedies already available to the defendant in such a proceeding provide sufficient checks on agency zeal, we hold that those officials who are responsible for the decision to initiate or continue a proceeding subject to agency adjudication are entitled to absolute immunity from damages liability for their parts in that decision.

We turn finally to the role of an agency attorney in conducting a trial and presenting evidence on the record to the trier of fact. We can see no substantial difference between the function of the agency attorney in presenting evidence in an agency hearing and the function of the prosecutor who brings evidence before a court. . . . We therefore hold that an agency attorney who arranges for the presentation of evidence on the record in the course of an adjudication is absolutely immune from suits based on the introduction of such evidence.

There remains the task of applying the foregoing principles to the claims against the particular petitioner-defendants involved in this case. Rather than attempt this here in the first instance, we vacate the judgment of the Court of Appeals and remand the case to that Court with instructions to remand the case to the District Court for further proceedings consistent with this opinion.

MR. JUSTICE REHNQUIST, with whom THE CHIEF JUSTICE, MR. JUSTICE STEWART, and MR. JUSTICE STEVENS join, concurring in part and dissenting in part.

. . . I cannot agree . . . with the Court's conclusion that in a suit for damages arising from allegedly unconstitutional action federal executive officials, regardless of their rank or the scope of their responsibilities, are entitled to only qualified immunity even when acting within the outer limits of their authority. . . .

[I]f we allow a mere allegation of unconstitutionality, obviously unproven at the time made, to require a Cabinet-level official, charged

---

For criticism of Gregoire v. Biddle, see D. Engdahl, Immunity and Accountability for Positive Governmental Wrongs, 44 U.Colo. L.Rev. 1, 53–56 (1972).

with the enforcement of the responsibilities to which the complaint pertains, to lay aside his duties and defend such an action on the merits, the defense of official immunity will have been abolished in fact if not in form. The ease with which a constitutional claim may be pleaded in a case such as this, where a violation of statutory or judicial limits on agency action may be readily converted by any legal neophyte into a claim of denial of procedural due process under the Fifth Amendment, will assure that. The fact that the claim fails when put to trial will not prevent the consumption of time, effort, and money on the part of the defendant official in defending his actions on the merits. . . .

It likewise cannot seriously be argued that an official will be less deterred by the threat of liability for unconstitutional conduct than for activities which might constitute a common-law tort. The fear that inhibits is that of a long, involved lawsuit and a significant money judgment, not the fear of liability for a certain type of claim. Thus, even viewing the question functionally—indeed, *especially* viewing the question functionally—the basis for a distinction between constitutional and common-law torts in this context is open to serious question. Even the logical justification for raising such a novel distinction is far from clear. That the Framers thought some rights sufficiently susceptible of legislative derogation that they should be enshrined in the Constitution does not necessarily indicate that the Framers likewise intended to establish an immutable hierarchy of rights in terms of their importance to individuals. The most heinous common-law tort surely cannot be less important to, or have less of an impact on, the aggrieved individual than a mere technical violation of a constitutional proscription. . . .

The Court . . . looks to the question of immunity of state officials for causes arising under § 1983 and . . . finds no reason why those principles should not likewise apply when federal officers are the target. . . . [E]ven a moment's reflection on the nature of the Bivens-type action and the purposes of § 1983 . . . supplies a compelling reason for distinguishing between the two different situations. In the first place . . . , a grant of absolute immunity to high-ranking executive officials on the federal side would not eviscerate the cause of action recognized in Bivens. The officials who are the most likely defendants in a Bivens-type action have generally been accorded only a qualified immunity. But more importantly, Congress has expressly waived sovereign immunity for this type of suit. This allows a direct action against the government, while at the same time limiting those risks which might "dampen the ardor of all but the most resolute, or the most irresponsible, in the unflinching discharge of their duties." And the Federal Government can internally supervise and check its own officers. The Federal Government is not situated such that it can control state officials or strike this same balance, however. Hence the necessity of § 1983 and the differing standards of immunity. . . . [10]

---

10. [Ed.] See District of Columbia v. Carter, 409 U.S. 418, 429–430 (1973): "[The basic] rationale underlying Congress' decision not to enact legislation similar to § 1983 with respect to federal officials [was] the assumption that the Federal Government could keep its own officers under control. . . . "

My biggest concern, however, is not with the illogic or impracticality of today's decision, but rather with the potential for disruption of government that it invites. The steady increase in litigation, much of it directed against governmental officials and virtually all of which could be framed in constitutional terms, cannot escape the notice of even the most casual observer. From 1961 to 1977, the number of cases brought in the federal courts under civil rights statutes increased from 296 to 13,113. . . . It simply defies logic and common experience to suggest that officials will not have this in the back of their minds when considering what official course to pursue. . . .

The Court, of course, recognizes this problem and suggests two solutions. First, judges, ever alert to the artful pleader, supposedly will weed out insubstantial claims. . . . [T]his very case, unquestionably frivolous in the extreme, belies any hope in that direction. And summary judgment on affidavits and the like is even more inappropriate when the central, and perhaps only, inquiry is the official's state of mind. . . .

The second solution offered by the Court is even less satisfactory. The Court holds that in those special circumstances "where it is demonstrated that absolute immunity is essential for the conduct of the public business," absolute immunity will be extended. But this is a form of "absolute immunity" which in truth exists in name only. If, for example, the Secretary of Agriculture may never know until inquiry by a trial court whether there is a possibility that vexatious constitutional litigation will interfere with his decisionmaking process, the Secretary will obviously think not only twice but thrice about whether to prosecute a litigious commodities merchant who has played fast and loose with the regulations for his own profit. Careful consideration of the rights of every individual subject to his jurisdiction is one thing; a timorous reluctance to prosecute any of such individuals who have a reputation for using litigation as a defense weapon is quite another. Since Cabinet officials are mortal, it is not likely that we shall get the precise judgmental balance desired in each of them, and it is because of these very human failings that the principles of Spalding, dictate that absolute immunity be accorded once it be concluded by a court that a high level executive official was "engaged in the discharge of duties imposed upon [him] by law." . . .

. . . [W]hile I believe that history will look approvingly on the motives of the Court in reaching the result it does today, I do not believe that history will be charitable in its judgment of the all but inevitable result of the doctrine espoused by the Court in this case. That doctrine seeks to gain and hold a middle ground which, with all deference, I believe the teachings of those who were at least our equals suggest cannot long be held. That part of the Court's present opinion from which I dissent will, I fear, result in one of two evils, either one of which is markedly worse than the effect of according absolute immunity to the Secretary and the Assistant Secretary in this case. The first of these evils would be a significant impairment of the ability of responsible public officials to carry out the duties imposed upon them by law. If that evil is to be avoided after today, it can be avoided only by a necessarily unprincipled and erratic judicial "screening" of claims such as those made in this case, an adherence to the form of the law while departing from its substance. Either one of these evils is far worse than the occasional failure to award damages caused by official wrongdoing, frankly and openly justified by the rule of Spalding v. Vilas, Barr v. Matteo, and Gregoire v. Biddle.[11]

NOTES

(1) *Does Barr v. Matteo still live?* The Supreme Court has not answered this question, see footnote 5, supra p. 1177. The lower federal courts usually view Barr as controlling in cases involving common-law torts. See 5 Davis, Admin.L. Treatise 120–121 (1984) for citation of authority. Professor Davis believes that the Court should "declare a single rule about absolute or qualified immunity . . . that will be the same for constitutional and nonconstitutional torts unless some reason can be found for distinguishing between the two classes of torts for purpose of immunity." Id. at 120. What do you think?

(2) *Implication of Bivens-type actions based on constitutional provisions other than the Fourth Amendment.* The Supreme Court has recognized Bivens-type actions for violation of the First, Bush v. Lucas, 462 U.S. 367 (1983), Fifth, Davis v. Passman, 442 U.S. 228 (1979), and Eighth Amendments, Carlson v. Green, 446 U.S. 14 (1980); lower federal courts have extended Bivens to actions based on the Sixth and Fourteenth Amendments. See Note, Rethinking Sovereign Immunity After Bivens, 57 N.Y.U.L.Rev. 597, 598 n.7 (1982).

(3) *Limitations on implying a Bivens-type action.* In the Bivens case, Justice Brennan's majority opinion stated that "the case involves no special factors counselling hesitation in the absence of affirmative action by Congress." Justice Harlan, concurring, said that "[f]or people in Bivens' shoes, it is damages or nothing." And in Davis v. Passman, Justice Brennan, again writing for the Court, concluded that in the circumstances of that case—a congressman's dismissal of plaintiff because of her sex—"there are available no other alternative forms of judicial relief. For Davis, as for Bivens, 'it is damages or nothing.' " 442 U.S. at 245. Suppose, however, that the law does provide another remedy for the plaintiff whose constitutional rights have been violated by a federal officer. Does existence of such a remedy mean that plaintiff has no Bivens-type action but instead is limited to the alternative remedy? Compare the answers of:

11. [Ed.] On remand, the district court held that all the defendants except two auditors were entitled to absolute immunity because (1) as to common-law tort claims, they were performing discretionary acts within the outer perimeter of their duties and (2) as to constitutional tort claims, they were performing discretionary functions similar to those of prosecutors. As to the two auditors, plaintiff alleges they deliberately falsified the results of their audits in an effort to cause the commencement of the CEA proceeding in retaliation for plaintiff's criticism of the agency; this states a cause of action for a constitutional tort for violation of the First Amendment. Economou v. Butz, 466 F.Supp. 1351 (S.D.N.Y.1979), affirmed 633 F.2d 203 (2d Cir.1980).

(a) CARLSON v. GREEN, 446 U.S. 14 (1980). Plaintiff sued federal prison officials on behalf of her deceased son's estate, seeking compensatory and punitive damages and alleging that her son had died because defendants had violated, inter alia, son's Eighth Amendment right to be free from cruel and unusual punishment because of their failure to give him proper medical attention.

Justice Brennan, writing for the majority, said that Bivens had "established that victims of a constitutional violation by a federal agent have a right to recover against the official in federal court despite the absence of any statute conferring such a right." However, such a cause of action may be defeated when (1) "defendants demonstrate 'special factors counselling hesitation in the absence of affirmative action by Congress'" or (2) "defendants show that Congress has provided an alternative remedy which it explicitly declared to be a *substitute* for recovery directly under the constitution and viewed as equally effective."

In a brief, somewhat conclusory paragraph, the Court found that there were no "special factors counselling hesitation." As to the alternative remedy problem, it is true that the Federal Tort Claims Act (FTCA) authorizes recovery against the United States for intentional torts committed by federal law enforcement officers. But there is "nothing in the FTCA or its legislative history to show that Congress meant to pre-empt a Bivens remedy or to create an equally effective remedy for constitutional violations.[1]" Also, there are four "additional factors, each suggesting that the Bivens remedy is a more effective remedy, [that] support our conclusion that Congress did not intend to limit [plaintiff] to an FTCA action": (1) because the Bivens remedy is recoverable against individuals it is a more effective deterrent than the FTCA remedy against the United States; (2) punitive damages are recoverable in a Bivens action but not under the FTCA; (3) plaintiff cannot opt for a jury in an FTCA action as she may in a Bivens suit; and (4) whereas a Bivens action exists nationwide, FTCA liability must be "in accordance with the law of the place where the act or omission occurred," 28 U.S.C. § 1346(b). Justice Brennan concluded, "Plainly FTCA is not a sufficient protection of the citizens' constitutional rights, and without a clear congressional mandate we cannot hold that Congress relegated responsibility exclusively to the FTCA remedy."

The Chief Justice and Justice Rehnquist dissented. Justice Powell, for himself and Justice Stewart, concurring, agreed that in this case the FTCA remedy would not be adequate. But he criticized the majority's statement that in order to preclude the Bivens-type action, the defendant must show that Congress "explicitly declared [its remedy] to be a *substitute* for recovery directly under the Constitution and viewed [it] as equally effective. . . . The Court cites no authority and advances no policy reason—indeed no reason at all—for imposing this threshold burden upon the defendant in an implied remedy case. . . .

1. To satisfy this test, petitioners need not show that Congress recited any specific "magic words." Instead, our inquiry at this step in the analysis is whether Congress has indicated that it intends the statutory remedy to replace, rather than to complement, the Bivens remedy. . . .

"One is left to wonder whether judicial discretion in this area will hereafter be confined to the question of alternative remedies, which is in turn reduced to the single determination that congressional action does or does not comport with the specifications prescribed by this Court. Such a drastic curtailment of discretion would be inconsistent with the Court's long-standing recognition that Congress is ultimately the appropriate body to create federal remedies. A plaintiff who seeks his remedy directly under the Constitution asks the federal courts to perform an essentially legislative task. In this situation, as Mr. Justice Harlan [said in Bivens, a] court should 'take into account [a range of policy considerations] at least as broad as the range of those a legislature would consider with respect to an express statutory authorization of a traditional remedy.' The Court does not explain why this discretion should be limited in the manner announced today."

(b) BUSH v. LUCAS, 462 U.S. 367 (1983). Plaintiff, an engineer employed at the NASA George C. Marshall Space Flight Center, publicly criticized the Center. Subsequently, defendant, the Director of the Center, asserting that plaintiff's statements were false and misleading, demoted plaintiff for making the statements. The Federal Employee Appeals Authority upheld the demotion, but the Civil Service Commission's Appeals Review Board found that the demotion had violated plaintiff's First Amendment rights. NASA accepted the Board's recommendation that plaintiff be restored to his former position retroactively and that he receive backpay. While his administrative appeal from the demotion was pending, plaintiff sued defendant in an Alabama state court, seeking to recover damages for violation of his First Amendment rights. The defendant removed the action to a federal district court, which granted summary judgment for defendant. The court of appeals affirmed, holding that "plaintiff had no cause of action for damages under the First Amendment for retaliatory demotion in view of the available remedies under the Civil Service Commission regulations."

The Supreme Court affirmed in an opinion by Justice Stevens. The introductory paragraphs of the Court's opinion framed the issue as follows:

"We assume for purposes of decision that petitioner's First Amendment rights were violated by the adverse personnel action. We also assume that, as petitioner asserts, civil service remedies were not as effective as an individual damages remedy and did not fully compensate him for the harm he suffered.[2] Two further propositions are undisputed. Congress has not expressly authorized the damages remedy that petitioner asks us to provide. On the other hand, Congress has not expressly precluded the creation of such a remedy by declaring that existing statutes provide the exclusive mode of redress.

"Thus, we assume, a federal right has been violated and Congress has provided a less than complete remedy for the wrong. If we were writing on a clean slate, we might answer the question whether to supplement the statutory scheme in either of two quite simple ways.

2. His attorney's fees were not paid by the Government, and he claims to have suffered uncompensated emotional and dignitary harms. . . .

We might adopt the common-law approach to the judicial recognition of new causes of action and hold that it is the province of the judiciary to fashion an adequate remedy for every wrong that can be proved in a case over which a court has jurisdiction.[3] Or we might start from the premise that federal courts are courts of limited jurisdiction whose remedial powers do not extend beyond the granting of relief expressly authorized by Congress.[4] Under the former approach, petitioner would obviously prevail; under the latter, it would be equally clear that he would lose.

"Our prior cases, although sometimes emphasizing one approach and sometimes the other, have unequivocally rejected both extremes. They establish our power to grant relief that is not expressly authorized by statute, but they also remind us that such power is to be exercised in the light of relevant policy determinations made by the Congress."

The Court then reviewed the prior cases, Bivens, Davis v. Passman and Carlson v. Green, concluding:

"This much is established by our prior cases. The federal courts' statutory jurisdiction to decide federal questions confers adequate power to award damages to the victim of a constitutional violation. When Congress provides an alternative remedy, it may, of course, indicate its intent, by statutory language, by clear legislative history, or perhaps even by the statutory remedy itself, that the Court's power should not be exercised. In the absence of such a congressional directive, the federal courts must make the kind of remedial determination that is appropriate for a common-law tribunal, paying particular heed, however, to any special factors counselling hesitation before authorizing a new kind of federal litigation.

"Congress has not resolved the question presented by this case by expressly denying petitioner the judicial remedy he seeks or by providing him with an equally effective substitute. There is, however, a good deal of history that is relevant to the question whether a federal employee's attempt to recover damages from his superior for violation of his First Amendment rights involves any 'special factors counselling hesitation.' "

After reviewing the "elaborate, comprehensive scheme" established by statute, executive orders and administrative regulations to protect federal civil servants from retaliatory demotion or discharge because of the exercise of First Amendment rights, the Court concluded:

"Given the history of the development of civil service remedies and the comprehensive nature of the remedies currently available, it is clear that the question we confront today is quite different from the

3. In Marbury v. Madison, 1 Cranch 137, 163 (1803), Chief Justice Marshall invoked the authority of Blackstone's Commentaries in support of this proposition. Blackstone had written, "it is a general and indisuptable rule, that where there is a legal right, there is also a legal remedy by suit, or action at law, whenever that right is invaded. . . . [I]t is a settled and invariable principle in the laws of England, that every right, when withheld, must have a remedy, and every injury its proper redress." 3 Commentaries 23, 109.

4. See Bivens v. Six Unknown Fed. Narcotics Agents, 403 U.S. 388, 428 (1971) (Black, J., dissenting).

typical remedial issue confronted by a common-law court. The question is not what remedy the court should provide for a wrong that would otherwise go unredressed. It is whether an elaborate remedial system that has been constructed step by step, with careful attention to conflicting policy considerations, should be augmented by the creation of a new judicial remedy for the constitutional violation at issue. That question obviously cannot be answered simply by noting that existing remedies do not provide complete relief for the plaintiff. The policy judgment should be informed by a thorough understanding of the existing regulatory structure and the respective costs and benefits that would result from the addition of another remedy for violations of employees' First Amendment rights.

"The costs associated with the review of disciplinary decisions are already significant—not only in monetary terms, but also in the time and energy of managerial personnel who must defend their decisions. The Government argues that supervisory personnel are already more hesitant than they should be in administering discipline, because the review that ensues inevitably makes the performance of their regular duties more difficult. Whether or not this assessment is accurate, it is quite probable that if management personnel face the added risk of personal liability for decisions that they believe to be a correct response to improper criticism of the agency, they would be deterred from imposing discipline in future cases. In all events, Congress is in a far better position than a court to evaluate the impact of a new species of litigation between federal employees on the efficiency of the civil service. Not only has Congress developed considerable familiarity with balancing governmental efficiency and the rights of employees, but it also may inform itself through factfinding procedures such as hearings that are not available to the courts. . . .

"Thus, we do not decide whether or not it would be good policy to permit a federal employee to recover damages from a supervisor who has improperly disciplined him for exercising his First Amendment rights. . . . [W]e decline 'to create a new substantive legal liability without legislative aid and as at the common law,' because we are convinced that Congress is in a better position to decide whether or not the public interest would be served by creating it."

Justice Marshall, with whom Justice Blackmun joined, concurred, stating in part, "I join the Court's opinion because I agree that 'there are special factors counselling hesitation in the absence of affirmative action by Congress.' " [5]

(4) *Refinement of the qualified immunity.* In HARLOW v. FITZGERALD, 457 U.S. 800 (1982), the Court held that unlike the President, who was entitled to absolute immunity, Nixon v. Fitzgerald, 457 U.S. 731

5. See also Chappell v. Wallace, 462 U.S. 296 (1983), decided the same day as Bush v. Lucas. Chief Justice Burger wrote for a unanimous Court that enlisted military personnel may not maintain a suit to recover damages from a superior officer for alleged racial discrimination in violation of the Fifth Amendment. "Taken together, the unique disciplinary structure of the military establishment and Congress' activity in the field constitute 'special factors' which dictate that it would be inappropriate to provide enlisted military personnel a Bivens-type remedy against their superior officers. See Bush v. Lucas."

(1982), presidential aides Bryce Harlow and Alexander Butterfield, like cabinet officer Butz in Butz v. Economou, were entitled only to a qualified immunity. The Court then said that in Butz it had identified the qualified immunity defense "as the best attainable accommodation of competing values" and had assumed that "this standard would permit '[i]nsubstantial lawsuits [to] be quickly terminated.'" Petitioners in Harlow challenged that assumption; the Court, per Justice Powell, responded:

"Qualified or 'good faith' immunity is an affirmative defense that must be pleaded by a defendant official. Decisions of this Court have established that the 'good faith' defense has both an 'objective' and a 'subjective' aspect. The objective element involves a presumptive knowledge of and respect for 'basic, unquestioned constitutional rights.' The subjective component refers to 'permissible intentions.' Characteristically the Court has defined these elements by identifying the circumstances in which qualified immunity would *not* be available. Referring both to the objective and subjective elements, we have held that qualified immunity would be defeated if an official '*knew or reasonably should have known* that the action he took within his sphere of official responsibility would violate the constitutional rights of the [plaintiff], or if he took the action *with malicious intention* to cause a deprivation of constitutional rights or other injury. . . .' (emphasis added).

"The subjective element of the good faith defense frequently has proved incompatible with our admonition in Butz that insubstantial claims should not proceed to trial. Rule 56 of the Federal Rules of Civil Procedure provides that disputed questions of fact ordinarily may not be decided on motions for summary judgment. And an official's subjective good faith has been considered to be a question of fact that some courts have regarded as inherently requiring resolution by a jury.

"In the context of Butz's attempted balancing of competing values, it now is clear that substantial costs attend the litigation of the subjective good faith of government officials. Not only are there the general costs of subjecting officials to the risks of trial—distraction of officials from their governmental duties, inhibition of discretionary action, and deterrence of able people from public service. There are special costs to 'subjective' inquiries of this kind. Immunity generally is available only to officials performing discretionary functions. In contrast with the thought processes accompanying 'ministerial' tasks, the judgments surrounding discretionary action almost inevitably are influenced by the decisionmaker's experiences, values, and emotions. These variables explain in part why questions of subjective intent so rarely can be decided by summary judgment. Yet they also frame a background in which there often is no clear end to the relevant evidence. Judicial inquiry into subjective motivation therefore may entail broad-ranging discovery and the deposing of numerous persons, including an official's professional colleagues. Inquiries of this kind can be peculiarly disruptive of effective government.

"Consistently with the balance at which we aimed in Butz, we conclude today that bare allegations of malice should not suffice to subject government officials either to the costs of trial or to the burdens of broad-reaching discovery. We therefore hold that government officials performing discretionary functions generally are shielded from liability for civil damages insofar as their conduct does not violate clearly established statutory or constitutional rights of which a reasonable person would have known.

"Reliance on the objective reasonableness of an official's conduct, as measured by reference to clearly established law, should avoid excessive disruption of government and permit the resolution of many insubstantial claims on summary judgment. On summary judgment, the judge appropriately may determine, not only the currently applicable law, but whether that law was clearly established at the time an action occurred. If the law at that time was not clearly established, an official could not reasonably be expected to anticipate subsequent legal developments, nor could he fairly be said to 'know' that the law forbade conduct not previously identified as unlawful. Until this threshold immunity question is resolved, discovery should not be allowed. If the law was clearly established, the immunity defense ordinarily should fail, since a reasonably competent public official should know the law governing his conduct. Nevertheless, if the official pleading the defense claims extraordinary circumstances and can prove that he neither knew nor should have known of the relevant legal standard, the defense should be sustained. But again, the defense would turn primarily on objective factors."

Justice Brennan, joined by Justices Marshall and Blackmun, filed a brief concurring opinion which stated in part: "I agree with the substantive standard announced by the Court today, imposing liability when a public-official defendant 'knew or should have known' of the constitutionally violative effect of his actions. . . . I write separately only to note that given this standard, it seems inescapable to me that some measure of discovery may sometimes be required to determine exactly what a public-official defendant did 'know' at the time of his actions."

(5) *Implication of private rights of action and § 1983.* In the Bivens case, the Supreme Court held that a plaintiff injured by defendants' violation of the Fourth Amendment had a cause of action notwithstanding that neither the constitution nor a statute expressly authorized such a remedy. In popular parlance, plaintiff was accorded an "implied" private right of action for violation of the constitution. Similarly, the Court has accorded plaintiffs implied private rights of action for violation of a statute in circumstances where, again, there was no statutory authorization of a private remedy. In Cort v. Ash, 422 U.S. 66, 78 (1975), the Court held that in determining whether a private remedy is implicit in a statute not expressly providing one, the following factors would be relevant: "First, is the plaintiff 'one of the class for whose *especial* benefit the statute was enacted,'—that is, does the statute create a federal right in favor of the plaintiff? Second, is there any indication of legislative intent, explicit or implicit, either to create a remedy or to deny one? Third, is it consistent with the underlying

purposes of the legislative scheme to imply such a remedy for the plaintiff? And finally, is the cause of action one traditionally relegated to state law, in an area basically the concern of the States, so that it would be inappropriate to infer a cause of action based solely on federal law?"

Decisions and opinions since Cort v. Ash indicate that the Court has been following a restrictive approach when confronted with an implied right of action question. The Court now appears to regard the question of existence of a private right of action as basically one of statutory construction and to be disinclined to find a private right of action in the absence of rather specific statutory authorization. See, e.g., Touche Ross & Co. v. Redington, 442 U.S. 560 (1979): "To the extent our analysis in today's decision differs from that of the Court in [prior cases], it suffices to say that in a series of cases since [those decisions] we have adhered to a stricter standard for the implication of private causes of action, and we follow that stricter standard today. The ultimate question is one of congressional intent, not one of whether this court thinks that it can improve upon the statutory scheme that Congress enacted into law." [1]

Compare this restrictive point of view in statutory private right cases with the Court's far more generous approach in constitutional cases. Consider also the effect of § 1983 in statutory cases. The section, it will be recalled, imposes liability on every person who under color of any state statute, ordinance, regulation, custom or usage deprives a citizen or person of "any rights, privileges or immunities secured by the Constitution *and laws . . . .*" Does this mean that notwithstanding the Court's restrictive statutory implied rights approach, every person who is accorded a right under a federal statute may bring a § 1983 action to require state officials to comply with the federal statute even though the statute contains no provision for private enforcement? [2] The answer of MAINE v. THIBOUTOT, 448 U.S. 1 (1980), is that beneficiaries of the federal AFDC program are entitled to sue state officials to require them to comply with the federal Social Security Act. Justice Brennan wrote for the majority that the plain language of § 1983 means what it says and that the legislative history does not demonstrate the contrary. Justice Powell, joined by the Chief Justice and Justice Rehnquist, dissented, contending that properly construed the term "laws" in § 1983 should be limited to equal rights laws. Justice Powell emphasized that there were "literally hundreds of [federal] regulatory and social welfare" programs in whose administration the states participate.[3] As a result of the majority's holding, he

1. See, for a stimulating discussion of the problems involved, M. Field, Sources of Law: The Scope of Federal Common Law, 99 Harv.L.Rev. 881, 930 ff. (1986).

2. Note that a condition of maintaining a § 1983 action is that the "law" in question creates a right, privilege or immunity within the meaning of § 1983. See Pennhurst State School and Hospital v. Halderman, 451 U.S. 1 (1981) in which the Court remanded for a determination whether the statute at issue there was the kind that created enforceable rights under § 1983.

3. "The States now participate in the enforcement of federal laws governing migrant labor, noxious weeds, historic preservation, wildlife conservation, anadromous fisheries, scenic trails, and strip mining. Various statutes authorize federal-state cooperative agreements in most aspects of federal land management. In addition,

argued, all who benefit from these programs will be potential § 1983 plaintiffs. "No one can predict the extent to which litigation arising from today's decision will harass state and local officials; nor can one foresee the number of new filings in our already overburdened courts."

Whatever the merits of the Thiboutot holding, the implications of the decision were far-reaching; § 1983's indiscriminate authorization of private persons to sue to enforce federal laws could seriously disrupt federal enforcement endeavors and thus undermine agency expertise and discretion to determine policy, allocate resources and coordinate regulatory programs. A possible corrective soon appeared. In MIDDLE-SEX COUNTY SEWERAGE AUTHORITY v. NATIONAL SEA CLAMMERS ASSOCIA-TION, 453 U.S. 1 (1981), the Court, per Powell, J., held that the enforcement provisions of the statutes in question—the Federal Water Pollution Control Act and the Marine Protection, Research and Sanctuaries Act—"demonstrate[ ] not only that Congress intended to foreclose implied private actions but also that it intended to supplant any remedy that otherwise would be available under § 1983." Federal statutes authorizing federal-state cooperative programs typically contain enforcement provisions of some kind but rarely do they explicitly exclude other remedies.[4] The difficult problem thus presented is how shall it be determined whether Congress implicitly "intended" that the federal statute in question involved preempts the operation of § 1983.

Professor Cass R. Sunstein trenchantly discusses this topic in Section 1983 and the Private Enforcement of Federal Law, 49 U.Chi.L. Rev. 394 (1982). He concludes that the Congress which enacted § 1983 intended to accord "private persons a federal judicial remedy against state officials who have violated federal law. That intent, embodied as it is in law, must be respected unless a subsequent Congress had at least in some sense faced the issue and decided otherwise." Thus, in his opinion, there is a "presumption in favor of the continued availability of the § 1983 remedy." But that presumption will be rebutted if there is a "necessary" or "manifest" inconsistency between the statutory enforcement scheme and a private cause of action. He then identifies the "contexts in which the § 1983 remedy and a particular regulatory scheme might be found incompatible." In "declining order of significance," these contexts are:

1. Statutes that create independent private causes of action.[5]

2. Statutes involving open-ended substantive standards.[6]

federal grants administered by state and local governments now are available in virtually every area of public administration. Unemployment, Medicaid, school lunch subsidies, food stamps, and other welfare benefits may provide particularly inviting subjects of litigation. Federal assistance also includes a variety of subsidies for education, housing, health care, transportation, public works, and law enforcement." Statement by Justice Powell.

4. For such a rarity, see Adickes v. Kress & Co., 398 U.S. 144, 150–151 n. 5 (1970) (Public Accommodations Act pro-

vides that the injunction remedy is "the exclusive means of enforcing the rights based on this title").

5. Sea Clammers is such a case. The Court said, "It is hard to believe that Congress intended to preserve the § 1983 right of action when it created so many specific statutory remedies including the two citizen-suit provisions."

6. When the statute establishes a "vague or ambiguous 'reasonableness' standard . . . . the agency, and not the court

3. Statutes that demand consistency and coordination in enforcement.[7]

4. Statutes in which there is evidence of legislative calibration of sanction to the expected enforcement level.[8]

5. Statutes in which remedies have been created against the federal government to compel state conformity with federal law.[9]

6. Statutes in which informal methods of enforcement were intended as the exclusive route.[10]

7. Statutes protecting collective interests.[11]

(6) *Municipal liability under § 1983.* In Monroe v. Pape, 365 U.S. 167 (1961), the Supreme Court held that "Congress did not undertake to bring municipal corporations within the ambit of [§ 1983]." MONELL v. DEPARTMENT OF SOCIAL SERVICES, 436 U.S. 658 (1978), overruling Monroe v. Pape in this respect, held that municipal corporations—cities, towns, counties—are "persons" within the meaning of that term as used in § 1983. Accordingly, wrote Justice Brennan for the Court, local governments may be "sued directly under § 1983 for monetary, declaratory or injunctive relief where . . . the action that is alleged to be unconstitutional implements or executes a policy, statement, ordinance, regulation or decision officially adopted and promulgated by that body's officers . . . [and] local governments like every other § 1983 'person,' by the very terms of the statute, may be sued for constitutional deprivations even though such a custom has not received formal approval through the body's official decisionmaking channels. . . . On the other hand . . . , Congress did not intend municipalities to be held liable unless action pursuant to official policy of some nature caused a constitutional tort. In particular, we conclude that a munici-

has the primary responsibility to determine the statute's proper reach."

7. "[P]rivate actions should be found precluded if it appears that a rational enforcement scheme requires the exercise of prosecutorial discretion."

8. Although such a legislative calibration is unlikely, if the "legislative history or administrative practice shows an intention to adjust sanctions to enforcement ends, and if it appears that § 1983 was not 'counted' in setting those levels, the argument for preemption is complete. Cf. Holloway v. Bristol-Myers Corp., 485 F.2d 986, 997–1001 (D.C.Cir.1973) (private right of action under the Federal Trade Commission Act denied because FTC achieved the level of enforcement intended by Congress)."

9. Although "[t]he existence of such a remedy provides evidence that Congress intended the executive, and not the courts, to be the primary guarantor of state compliance with federal law," it may be that the federal official fails to act against the state not because of a belief that there is state compliance with federal law but be-

cause of insufficient resources. In this latter event, a § 1983 action would be appropriate.

10. "Under such laws [as the Developmentally Disabled Assistance and Bill of Rights Act] enforcement is supposed to take the form of a continuous process of dialogue and accommodation on the part of the regulatory agency and the regulated states; the rigid and formal route of litigation is intended to be used, if at all, as a last resort." Again, however, in the absence of legislative history to the contrary, "the fact that informal means of enforcement were contemplated is generally not, without more, sufficient reason to overcome the presumption against implicit repeal."

11. "The fact that a statute protects collective interests [as for example the collective interest in clean air] is not . . . in itself sufficient to justify a conclusion that the § 1983 remedy is extinguished, but may strengthen an inference that Congress intended the public enforcement scheme to be exclusive."

pality cannot be held liable under § 1983 on a respondeat superior theory. . . . [T]he language of § 1983 . . . cannot be easily read to impose liability vicariously on governing bodies solely on the basis . . . of an employer-employee relationship with a tortfeasor":

"We conclude . . . that a local government may not be sued for an injury inflicted solely by its employees or agents. Instead, it is when execution of a government's policy or custom, whether made by its lawmakers or by those whose edicts or acts may fairly be said to represent official policy, inflicts the injury that the government as an entity is responsible under § 1983. Since this case unquestionably involves official policy as the moving force of the constitutional violation found by the District Court, we must reverse the judgment below. In so doing, we have no occasion to address, and do not address, what the full contours of municipal liability under § 1983 may be. We have attempted only to sketch so much of the § 1983 cause of action against a local government as is apparent from the history of the 1871 Act and our prior cases and we expressly leave further development of this action to another day.

". . .

"Since the question whether local government bodies should be afforded some form of official immunity was not presented as a question to be decided on this petition and was not briefed by the parties nor addressed by the courts below, we express no views on the scope of any municipal immunity beyond holding that municipal bodies sued under § 1983 cannot be entitled to an absolute immunity. . . ."

Justice Powell ended his concurring opinion with the following comment:

"Difficult questions nevertheless remain for another day. There are substantial line-drawing problems in determining 'when execution of a government's policy or custom' can be said to inflict constitutional injury such that 'government as an entity is responsible under § 1983.' Opinion for the Court, ante. This case, however, involves formal, written policies of a municipal department and school board; it is the clear case. The Court also reserves decision on the availability of a qualified municipal immunity. Initial resolution of the question whether the protection available at common law for municipal corporations . . . or other principles support a qualified municipal immunity in the context of the § 1983 damages action, is left to the lower federal courts.

Justice Rehnquist, joined by the Chief Justice, dissented:

"The decision in Monroe v. Pape, was the fountainhead of the torrent of civil rights litigation of the last 17 years. Using § 1983 as a vehicle, the courts have articulated new and previously unforeseeable interpretations of the Fourteenth Amendment. At the same time, the doctrine of municipal immunity enunciated in Monroe has protected municipalities and their limited treasuries from the consequences of their officials' failure to predict the course of this Court's constitutional jurisprudence. None of the Members of this Court can foresee the practical consequences of today's removal of that protection. Only the Congress, which has the benefit of the advice of every segment of this diverse Nation, is equipped to consider the results of such a drastic change in the law. It seems all but inevitable that it will find it necessary to do so after today's decision."

Since Monell, the Court has partially delineated the "contours of municipal liability under § 1983." See, e.g., Owen v. Independence, 445 U.S. 622 (1980) (individual officer's good faith qualified immunity is not available to city); Newport v. Fact Concerts, Inc., 435 U.S. 247 (1981) (municipalities are immune from punitive damages in a § 1983 action).

Clarifying what is meant by the Monell requirement that an officer's unconstitutional action must have been taken "pursuant to official municipal policy of some nature," has proved more difficult. See, e.g., CITY OF OKLAHOMA CITY v. TUTTLE, 105 S.Ct. 2427 (1985), involving a single incident in which a police officer shot and killed plaintiff's husband outside a bar in which a robbery had been reported in progress. In plaintiff's § 1983 action against the city, she contended that a municipal "custom or policy" had caused the constitutional violations. Plaintiff's theory of liability was that the "policy" in question was the city's policy of training and supervising police officers, and that this "policy" resulted in inadequate training and in the constitutional violations alleged. The trial judge instructed the jury that a municipal "policy such as to impose liability [under § 1983] cannot ordinarily be inferred from a single incident of illegality such as a first excessive use of force to stop a suspect; *but a single unusually excessive use of force may be sufficiently out of the ordinary to warrant an inference that it was attributable to inadequate training or supervision amounting to 'deliberate indifference' or 'gross negligence' on the part of the officials in charge."* The jury returned a verdict for $1,500,000.

The Supreme Court reversed. Justice Rehnquist and three other Justices held:

"Proof of a single incident of unconstitutional activity is not sufficient to impose liability under Monell, unless proof of the incident includes proof that it was caused by an existing, unconstitutional municipal policy, which policy can be attributed to a municipal policymaker. Otherwise the existence of the unconstitutional policy, and its origin, must be separately proved. But where the policy relied upon is not itself unconstitutional, considerably more proof than the single incident will be necessary in every case to establish both the requisite fault on the part of the municipality, and the causal connection between the 'policy' and the constitutional deprivation. Under the [trial judge's charge] the jury could properly have imposed liability on the city based solely upon proof that it employed a non-policymaking officer who violated the Constitution."

Justice Brennan and two other Justices concurred in the result, Justice Stevens dissented and Justice Powell did not participate.

Compare PEMBAUR v. CINCINNATI, 106 S.Ct. 1292 (1986). When two Hamilton county deputy sheriffs attempted to arrest and detain two of plaintiff's employees who had been subpoenaed as witnesses, plaintiff barred the door to his clinic and refused to let the deputies enter the room where the witnesses presumably were located. The deputies telephoned the Assistant Prosecutor assigned to the case and informed him of the situation. The Assistant then conferred with the County Prosecutor who told him to instruct the deputies to "go in and get" the witnesses. Pursuant to this instruction, city police officers obtained an axe and chopped down the door. Plaintiff brought a § 1983 action against the officers, the city of Cincinnati and the county of Hamilton for $10 million in actual and $10 million in punitive damages plus costs and attorneys' fees. The Sixth Circuit held that plaintiffs' claim against the county had been properly dismissed:

"We believe that Pembaur failed to prove the existence of a county policy in this case. [Plaintiff] claims that the deputy sheriffs acted pursuant to the policies of the Sheriff and Prosecutor by forcing entry into the medical center. [Plaintiff] has failed to establish, however, anything more than that, on this *one occasion,* the Prosecutor and the Sheriff decided to force entry into his office. . . . That single, discrete decision is insufficient, by itself, to establish that the Prosecutor, the Sheriff, or both were implementing a governmental policy."

The Supreme Court reversed in an opinion by Justice Brennan:

"[M]unicipal liability may be imposed for a single decision by municipal policymakers. . . . We hold that municipal liability under § 1983 attaches where—and only where—a deliberate choice to follow a course of action is made from among various alternatives by the official or officials responsible for establishing final policy with respect to the subject matter in question. . . . [An Ohio statute] provides that county officers may 'require . . . instructions from [the County Prosecutor] in matters connected with their official duties.' Pursuant to standard office procedure, the Sheriff's office referred this matter to the Prosecutor and then followed his instructions. The Sheriff testified that his Department followed this practice under appropriate circumstances and that it was 'the proper thing to do' in this case. We decline to accept respondent's invitation to overlook this delegation of authority by disingenuously labeling the Prosecutor's clear command mere 'legal advice.' In ordering the Deputy Sheriffs to enter petitioner's clinic the County Prosecutor was acting as the final decisionmaker for the county, and the county may therefore be held liable under Section 1983."

Justices White, Stevens, and O'Connor wrote concurring opinions. Justice Powell, joined by the Chief Justice and Justice Rehnquist, dissented. As was stated in Monell, local government units are liable under § 1983 when the action that is alleged to be unconstitutional "implements or executes a policy statement, ordinance, regulation or decision officially adopted and promulgated by that body's officers." Here there was no rule of general applicability but a mere ad hoc decision. "Nothing about the Prosecutor's response to the inquiry over the phone, nor the circumstances surrounding the response indicates that . . . . a rule of general applicability was formed." Also relevant in determining whether official policy has been formed is the process by which the decision was reached. Here the Prosecutor, "without time for thoughtful consideration or consultation, simply gave an off-the-cuff answer to a single question. There was no *process* at all. The Court's holding undercuts the basic rationale of Monell, and unfairly increases the risk of liability on the level of government least able to bear it."

(7) *Section 1983 and the Eleventh Amendment.* The Eleventh Amendment provides that "The judicial power of the United States shall not be construed to extend to any suit in law or equity, commenced or prosecuted against one of the United States by citizens of another State, or by citizens or subjects of any foreign State." By construction, "citizens of another State" has come to mean, also, citizens of the same state. Hans v. Louisiana, 134 U.S. 1 (1890).

In recent years, the Supreme Court has sustained § 1983 liability of state officers in many situations, e.g. Scheuer v. Rhodes, 416 U.S. 232 (1974). The Court also has held that Congress' authority under section 5 of the Fourteenth Amendment includes the power to make states liable for civil rights breaches, if Congress finds that useful for enforcement of the Amendment.[12]   Fitzpatrick v. Bitzer, 427 U.S. 445 (1976). But in Edelman v. Jordan, 415 U.S. 651 (1974), a majority of the Court concluded that in an action under § 1983 "a federal court's remedial power, consistent with the Eleventh Amendment, is necessarily limited to prospective injunctive relief . . . and may not include a retroactive award which requires the payment of funds from the state treasury." The suit there was for retroactive benefits alleged to be owing on account of Illinois officials' violation of the Fourteenth Amendment and federal regulations under the federal-state program of Aid to the Aged, Blind and Disabled.

After the Court's decision in Monell, Justice Brennan argued that "[g]iven our holding in Monell . . . , it is surely at least an open question whether § 1983 properly construed does not make the States liable for relief of all kinds, notwithstanding the Eleventh Amendment." Hutto v. Finney, 437 U.S. 678 (1978) (concurring opinion). The Court soon answered the question in Quern v. Jordan, 440 U.S. 332 (1979), in which it reaffirmed the Edelman holding that § 1983 does not authorize retroactive relief against states and rejected Justice Brennan's contention that Monell had cast doubt on its rationale: "[U]nlike our Brother Brennan, we simply are unwilling to believe, on the basis of such slender 'evidence' [as that advanced by Justice Brennan], that Congress intended by the general language of § 1983 to override traditional sovereign immunity of the States. . . . [Section] 1983 does not explicitly and by clear language indicate on its face an intent to sweep away the immunity of the States; nor does it have a history which focuses directly on the question of state liability and which shows that Congress considered and firmly decided to abrogate the Eleventh

12. Section 5 provides: "The Congress shall have power to enforce, by appropriate legislation, the provisions of this article."

Amendment immunity of the States." Finally, in Pennhurst State School & Hospital v. Holderman, 465 U.S. 89 (1984), by a 5–4 vote, the Court held that the Eleventh Amendment bars a federal court from issuing an injunction ordering state officials to comply with state law either prospectively or retroactively.[13]

b. Governmental Tort Liability

The preceding discussion has shown how individual administrators frequently were relieved of the threat of personal liability, lest they be deterred from vigorous action in the public interest. In these instances, as a New Jersey opinion said, "We think it not unreasonable to require [the citizen] to depend for redress upon the sense of justice of the public, rather than upon the right of action against public officers who have acted, as they thought, for the public weal in a matter of public duty." [1]

Unfortunately "the sense of justice of the public" remained largely unaroused for many years. A careful study of state statutes and practices showed that in 1954 exactly half of the then forty-eight states "seldom" or "almost never" undertook responsibility, while only New York had assumed liability for "substantially all state torts" and in only twelve others was responsibility borne "in most cases." [2] The reasons for this sluggishness were not admirable, being compounded of entangling verbiage about sovereignty, "legislative and judicial inertia, which is probably the most potent single explanation that anyone can give as to why the American Law is what it is," and fear that acceptance of liability would drain the public treasury.[3] More recently, the pace of change has quickened; acknowledgment of liability has become more characteristic of the legal landscape.[4] The materials following consider the federal experience in this regard, suggesting a question which seems equally applicable to the states: whether the changes in *individual* liability just reviewed may not prove a tonic in the field of governmental liability as well.

The United States did not broadly consent to be sued until 1946, when Congress enacted the Federal Tort Claims Act, that permitted suit to be brought against the United States, generally, "for injury or

---

13. For a thoughtful and critical discussion of the decision, consult D. Shapiro, Wrong Turns: The Eleventh Amendment and the Pennhurst Case, 98 Harv.L.Rev. 61 (1984).

1. Valentine v. Englewood, 76 N.J.L. 509, 71 A. 344 (1908).

2. R. Leflar and B. Kantrowitz, Tort Liability of the States, 29 N.Y.U.L.Rev. 1363 (1954).

3. Leflar and Kantrowitz, note 2 above, at 1364. Compare W. Gellhorn and C. Schenck, Tort Actions against the Federal Government, 47 Colum.L.Rev. 722 (1947): The survival of the immunity rule in this country after the Revolutionary War "is attributable, in all likelihood, to the financial instability of the infant American

states rather than to the stability of the doctrine's theoretical foundations."

4. See W. Prosser and P. Keeton, Prosser and Keeton on the Law of Torts 1044–1045 (1984): "Although one or two states seem to have retained something like a total sovereign immunity, the great majority have now consented to at least some liability for torts, retaining the immunity at least to the extent of basic policy or discretionary decisions. . . . [A]bout six or seven states . . . have established administrative agencies to hear and determine claims against the state. . . . [N]ine states have waived the tort immunity in [a] limited class of cases . . . [and about] thirty states have abrogated the immunity in a substantial or general way."

loss of property, or personal injury or death caused by the negligent or wrongful act or omission of any employee of the Government while acting within the scope of his office or employment, under circumstances where the United States, if a private person, would be liable to the claimant in accordance with the law of the place where the act or omission occurred." [5] The statute contained significant exceptions, however, excluding (for example) claims "arising out of assault, battery, false imprisonment, false arrest, malicious prosecution, abuse of process, libel, slander, misrepresentation, deceit, or interference with contract rights." 28 U.S.C. § 2680(h). This exclusion no doubt would have barred suit against the Government on the claim set forth in Barr v. Matteo, because the complaint arose out of an allegedly defamatory utterance.[6] In 1974, following on the heels of some especially shocking violence by narcotics law enforcement officers,[7] Congress adopted the Intentional Tort Amendment Act, P.L. 93–253, 88 Stat. 50, amending this section to acknowledge tort liability for assault, battery, false imprisonment, false arrest, abuse of process, or malicious prosecution attributable to federal investigative or law enforcement officers. But defamation, misrepresentation, deceit, and interference with contract rights continue to be nonactionable.

5. The FTCA first appeared in 60 Stat. 842 (1946). Then it was reenacted without substantive changes in the revision of the Judicial Code, 62 Stat. 869 (1948). Now its provisions are scattered widely in the Code—28 U.S.C. §§ 1346, 1402, 1504, 2110, 2401, 2402, 2411, 2412, and 2671–2680. Most of the substantive provisions appear in §§ 2671–2680. The portion quoted in the text appears, however, in § 1346(b).

6. The Act is also inapplicable to such matters as claims arising in a foreign country or arising out of the loss, miscarriage or negligent transmission of mail, assessment or collection of taxes and customs duties, fiscal operation of the Treasury, imposition of a quarantine, combatant activities of the military and naval forces in time of war, and activities of the Panama Canal Company, the Tennessee Valley Authority and Federal land banks. 28 U.S.C. § 2680.

7. The story is well told in J. Boger, M. Gitenstein and P. Verkuil, The Federal Tort Claims Act Intentional Torts Amendment: An Interpretative Analysis, 54 N.C.L.Rev. 497 (1976). They describe one incident as follows at 500–501:

"Herbert and Evelyn Giglotto awoke in their Collinsville, Illinois, townhouse at about 9:30 p.m. on April 23, 1973, to the sound of someone smashing down their door and bursting into their home. Mr. Giglotto leapt from bed; as he entered the hallway outside his bedroom, he found himself confronted by perhaps five shabbily dressed men. Brandishing pistols, they forced Giglotto back into his bedroom. They threw him face down on his bed, tied his hands behind his back, and put a pistol to his head. Said one, 'You move, you're dead. I'm going to shoot you.'

"Evelyn Giglotto, clad only in a negligee, stood horrified as one of the intruders screamed abuses at her incapacitated husband. Then several turned on her, forcing her into a similar position, while others searched the upstairs room. About fifteen men had come into the bedroom by this time, some entering and then leaving. Cursorily, the men identified themselves as federal officers, flashing a badge at Mr. Giglotto and telling him the house had been under surveillance for three weeks. The couple, unsure what to think, could hear other men beginning to ransack the downstairs. Throughout the ordeal Giglotto, a pistol held to his head, tried to identify himself, but the intruders refused to respond. Some ten to fifteen minutes after the invasion began, one of the men came into the room holding the Giglottos' bankbook and insurance papers. 'Well, we have the wrong people,' he said. The men, without apology, untied the couple and permitted them to sit up on their bed. Even at this point, when Herbert Giglotto tried to put on his pants, they were ripped from his hand. 'I told you not to move.' The agents departed without explanation, leaving behind a smashed television, a broken camera, scattered books, scratched furniture, and a shattered antique vase."

Despite the inadequacies of present tort statutes the reader should be reminded that meritorious claims are often recognized outside the statutory framework. Since 1966, federal administrators have had authority to settle tort claims without limitation as to amount, though only with the Attorney General's concurrence if the settlement exceeds $25,000.[8] A defendant, even when the defendant is the United States, may not choose to fight when it can compromise a claim without creating a major precedent by doing so.

Great masses of cases are handled by administrators who have been empowered either to make payments directly or to report to Congress that a claim is just though not compensable under the existing law.[9] Moreover, every session of Congress witnesses the adoption of numerous "private laws," each one published in the United States at Large as "An Act for the relief of . . . ."[10] These enactments are too varied for simple classification; but collectively they serve to show that many aggrieved persons who could not proceed successfully under the Federal Tort Claims Act may nevertheless receive payments out of the national treasury.

Perhaps the most important of the FTCA's exceptions preserves the Government's immunity from suits relating to its agents' discretionary acts. The courts are given no jurisdiction to consider "Any claim based upon an act or omission of an employee of the Government, exercising due care in the execution of a statute or regulation, whether or not such statute or regulation be valid, or based upon the exercise or performance or the failure to exercise or perform a discretionary function or duty on the part of a Federal agency or an employee of the Government, whether or not the discretion involved be abused" (28 U.S.C. § 2680(a)). Any suit against the government for the conduct underlying Economou v. Butz surely would have foundered on this rock.

The significance of this exception is still not easily gauged, despite the passage of many years since the statute's enactment. DALEHITE v. UNITED STATES, 346 U.S. 15 (1953), held that the United States could not be sued for an explosion in Texas City that killed hundreds of people, wounded thousands, and caused millions of dollars of property damages. The explosion occurred during the loading of a ship that was to carry a

8. 80 Stat. 306, 308 (1966), 28 U.S.C. §§ 2672, 2675. Court suits must be withheld until the possibility of an agreed settlement has been explored. See S. Jacoby, The 89th Congress and Government Litigation, 67 Colum.L.Rev. 1212, 1213–1222 (1967); J. Laughlin, A New Charter for Injured Citizens, 2 Trial 18 (1966).

9. For general discussion, see G. Berman, Federal Tort Claims at the Agency Level: The FTCA Administrative Process, 35 Case West.Res.L.Rev. 509 (1985). This article is based on the author's report as consultant to the Administrative Conference of the United States on "Administrative Handling of Monetary Claims: Tort Claims at the Agency Level," Administrative Conference of the United States, Rec-

ommendations and Reports, 1984, p. 639, which in turn provides the background for ACUS Recommendation 84–7 Administrative Settlement of Tort and Other Monetary Claims Against the Government, 1 CFR § 305.84–7.

10. The legislative procedures involved in private relief acts are examined in M. Jones and F. Davis, Profile of a Congressional Reference Case, 28 Mo.B.J. 69 (1972); and see also J. Glosser, Congressional Reference Cases in the United States Court of Claims: A Historical and Current Perspective, 25 Amer.U.L.Rev. 595 (1976); W. Gellhorn and L. Lauer, Settlement of Tort Claims Against the United States, 55 Colum.L.Rev. 1 (1955).

cargo of ammonium nitrate to France as part of the foreign aid program. The nitrate, originally produced as an explosive element, was valuable as fertilizer. In the immediate postwar period a high level decision was made to reactivate ordnance plants to supply the substance for shipment abroad, to help restore the productivity of ravaged farmlands. The trial court found that negligence had occurred in bagging the volatile material at too high a temperature, in using paper bags that prevented access of air or water, and in sending coated granules that were resistant to water. But the Supreme Court, by a four-to-three decision, concluded that a policy decision had been made to ship the ammonium nitrate, despite attendant risks, because of the felt need for expediting the fertilizer program. Congress never meant, said Justice Reed for the majority to expose the United States to claims for damages "however negligently caused, that affected the governmental functions." This caused Justice Jackson to exclaim bitterly in dissent: "The Government's negligence here was not in policy decisions of a regulatory or governmental nature, but involved actions akin to those of a private manufacturer, contractor, or shipper. . . . Surely a statute so long debated was meant to embrace more than traffic accidents. If not, the ancient and discredited doctrine that 'The King can do no wrong' has not been uprooted; it has merely been amended to read, 'The King can do only little wrongs.'"

Two years later, in a five-to-four decision, the Court appeared to veer away from the Dalehite case. INDIAN TOWING CO. v. UNITED STATES, 350 U.S. 61 (1955), involved a suit for cargo damage. The damage occurred when a vessel ran aground because the Coast Guard had negligently failed to maintain a beacon light. The Government did not contend here that the Coast Guard had been engaged in a "discretionary function" when one of its petty officers had carelessly tested the light. It did insist, however, that maintaining lighthouses and beacons was a peculiarly governmental activity, without private counterparts; and it asked the Court to rule that no recovery could be had for negligent performance of the so-called "end-objective" of the governmental activity in question. Thus, for illustration, the Government conceded that it could be held liable if its agent had carelessly operated a government launch on his way to perform his assigned duty of inspecting the light; but the negligence in inspecting the light itself, which was the "end-objective," could give rise to no justifiable claim.

The Court rejected the distinction. True, nobody but the Government maintains navigation guides. But a private individual could have been held liable in circumstances similar to those of the present case, for "one who undertakes to warn the public of danger and thereby induces reliance must perform his 'good Samaritan' task in a careful manner." (We may note, incidentally, that the plaintiff failed to prove governmental negligence when the case was finally tried on the merits. See Indian Towing Co. v. United States, 276 F.2d 300 (5th Cir.1960).)

RAYONIER, INC. v. UNITED STATES, 352 U.S. 315 (1957), is another indication of apparent unwillingness to follow the Dalehite lead in the direction of minimizing governmental liability. One of the claims in

Dalehite had been that after a fire had broken out on the laden vessel, greater care in fighting the blaze would have minimized the consequences. The majority bluntly rejected liability on this ground because, Justice Reed said, the Federal Tort Claims Act "did not change the normal rule that an alleged failure or carelessness of public firemen does not create private actionable rights." The opposite view was taken in Rayonier. There, the Forest Service had been negligent in its attempts to extinguish a forest fire that ultimately spread far from its beginnings and destroyed the claimant's property. In the state of Washington, where the disaster had occurred, private persons or corporations could have been held liable in somewhat comparable circumstances. The Court held that the assertedly "governmental" nature of firefighting conferred no immunity, and said that "to the extent there was anything to the contrary in the Dalehite case it was necessarily rejected by Indian Towing."

In its most recent encounter with the discretionary function exemption (in the Varig Airlines case, below), the Court unanimously rejected the argument that "the view of § 2680(a) expressed in Dalehite has been eroded, if not overruled, by subsequent cases . . . , particularly Indian Towing. . . . While the Court's reading of the act admittedly has not followed a straight line, we do not accept the supposition that Dalehite no longer represents a valid interpretation of the discretionary function exception."

UNITED STATES v. S.A. EMPRESA DE VIACAO AEREA RIO GRANDENSE (VARIG AIRLINES), ET AL.
Supreme Court of the United States, 1984.
467 U.S. 797.

[Aircraft, that had been certificated as airworthy by the Civil Aeronautics Agency (CAA) and its successor, the Federal Aviation Administration (FAA), caught fire, resulting in deaths of passengers and damage to the airplanes. Representatives of the passengers and owners of the planes sued the United States under the FTCA claiming that the CAA and FAA had been negligent in inspecting the planes and issuing certificates of compliance with safety requirements.]

CHIEF JUSTICE BURGER delivered the opinion of the Court. . . .

As in Dalehite, it is unnecessary—and indeed impossible—to define with precision every contour of the discretionary function exception. From the legislative and judicial materials, however, it is possible to isolate several factors useful in determining when the acts of a Government employee are protected from liability by Section 2680(a). First, it is the nature of the conduct, rather than the status of the actor, that governs whether the discretionary function exception applies in a given case. . . . Thus, the basic inquiry concerning the application of the discretionary function exception is whether the challenged acts of a Government employee—whatever his or her rank—are of the nature and quality that Congress intended to shield from tort liability.

Second, whatever else the discretionary function exception may include, it plainly was intended to encompass the discretionary acts of the Government acting in its role as a regulator of the conduct of private individuals. Time and again the legislative history refers to the acts of regulatory agencies as examples of those covered by the exception, and it is significant that the early tort claims bills considered by Congress specifically exempted two major regulatory agencies by name. This emphasis upon protection for regulatory activities suggests an underlying basis for the inclusion of an exception for discretionary functions in the Act: Congress wished to prevent judicial "second-guessing" of legislative and administrative decisions grounded in social, economic, and political policy through the medium of an action in tort. By fashioning an exception for discretionary governmental functions, including regulatory activities, Congress took "steps to protect the Government from liability that would seriously handicap efficient government operations."

We now consider whether the discretionary function exception immunizes from tort liability the FAA certification process involved in this case. . . .

[T]he Secretary of Transportation has the duty to promote safety in air transportation by promulgating reasonable rules and regulations governing the inspection, servicing, and overhaul of civil aircraft. In her discretion, the Secretary may also prescribe "the periods for, and *the manner in, which such inspection, servicing, and overhaul shall be made,* including provision for examinations and reports by properly qualified private persons whose examinations or reports the Secretary of Transportation may accept in lieu of those made by its officers and employees." § 1421(a)(3)(C) (emphasis added). Thus, Congress specifically empowered the Secretary to establish and implement a mechanism for enforcing compliance with minimum safety standards according to their "judgment of the best course." Dalehite v. United States.

In the exercise of this discretion, the FAA, as the Secretary's designee, has devised a system of compliance review that involves certification of aircraft design and manufacture at several stages of production. The FAA certification process is founded upon a relatively simple notion: the duty to ensure that an aircraft conforms to FAA safety regulations lies with the manufacturer and operator, while the FAA retains the responsibility for policing compliance. Thus, the manufacturer is required to develop the plans and specifications and perform the inspections and tests necessary to establish that an aircraft design comports with the applicable regulations; the FAA then reviews the data for conformity purposes by conducting a "spot-check" of the manufacturer's work.

The operation of this "spot-check" system is outlined in detail in the handbooks and manuals developed by the CAA and FAA for the use of their employees. . . .[1]

---

1. In a recent report, the National Academy of Sciences recognized that because "FAA engineers cannot review each of the thousands of drawings, calculations, reports and tests involved in the type certification process," the agency must place great reliance on the manufacturer. Improving Aircraft Safety 6, 29, 31. The report also noted that "in most cases the FAA staff performs only a cursory review of the substance of th[e] overwhelming vol-

Respondents' contention that the FAA was negligent in failing to inspect certain elements of aircraft design before certificating the Boeing 707 and DeHavilland Dove necessarily challenges two aspects of the certification procedure: the FAA's decision to implement the "spot-check" system of compliance review, and the application of that "spot-check" system to the particular aircraft involved in these cases. In our view, both components of respondents' claim are barred by the discretionary function exception to the Act.

The FAA's implementation of a mechanism for compliance review is plainly discretionary activity of the "nature and quality" protected by § 2680(a). When an agency determines the extent to which it will supervise the safety procedures of private individuals, it is exercising discretionary regulatory authority of the most basic kind. Decisions as to the manner of enforcing regulations directly affect the feasibility and practicality of the Government's regulatory program; such decisions require the agency to establish priorities for the accomplishment of its policy objectives by balancing the objectives sought to be obtained against such practical considerations as staffing and funding. Here, the FAA has determined that a program of "spot-checking" manufacturers' compliance with minimum safety standards best accommodates the goal of air transportation safety and the reality of finite agency resources. Judicial intervention in such decisionmaking through private tort suits would require the courts to "second-guess" the political, social, and economic judgments of an agency exercising its regulatory function. It was precisely this sort of judicial intervention in policymaking that the discretionary function exception was designed to prevent.

It follows that the acts of FAA employees in executing the "spot-check" program in accordance with agency directives are protected by the discretionary function exception as well. See Dalehite v. United States. The FAA employees who conducted compliance reviews of the aircraft involved in this case were specifically empowered to make policy judgments regarding the degree of confidence that might reasonably be placed in a given manufacturer, the need to maximize compliance with FAA regulations, and the efficient allocation of agency resources. In administering the "spot-check" program, these FAA engineers and inspectors necessarily took certain calculated risks, but those risks were encountered for the advancement of a governmental purpose and pursuant to the specific grant of authority in the regulations and operating manuals. Under such circumstances, the FAA's alleged negligence in failing to check certain specific items in the course of certificating a particular aircraft falls squarely within the discretionary function exception of Section 2680(a).

In rendering the United States amenable to some suits in tort, Congress could not have intended to impose liability for the regulatory enforcement activities of the FAA challenged in this case. The FAA has a statutory duty to *promote* safety in air transportation, not to

ume of documents" submitted for its approval.

insure it. We hold that these actions against the FAA for its alleged negligence in certificating aircraft for use in commercial aviation are barred by the discretionary function exception of the Federal Tort Claims Act.

[The Court distinguished Indian Towing and Rayonier as follows:]

Indian Towing involved a claim under the Act for damages to cargo aboard a vessel that ran aground, allegedly owing to the failure of the light in a lighthouse operated by the Coast Guard. The plaintiffs contended that the Coast Guard had been negligent in inspecting, maintaining, and repairing the light. Significantly, the Government *conceded* that the discretionary function exception was not implicated in Indian Towing, arguing instead that the Act contained an implied exception from liability for "uniquely governmental functions." The Court rejected the Government's assertion, reasoning that it would "push the courts into the 'non-governmental'-'governmental' quagmire that has long plagued the ·law of municipal corporations. . . .[2]"

FEDERAL OFFICIALS' LIABILITY FOR CONSTITUTIONAL VIOLATIONS

Recommendation 82–6, adopted by the Administrative Conference of the United States, Dec. 16, 1982, 1 C.F.R. § 305.82–6

This recommendation focuses on the increasing risk to federal executive branch officials of civil liability for monetary damages for alleged violations of federal constitutional rights. This vulnerability has expanded dramatically in recent years, as a result of judicially-discovered rights enunciated in Bivens v. Six Unknown Named Agents, 403 U.S. 388 (1971), and subsequent court cases involving allegations of official misconduct. Under the present system of officials' liability, as developed piecemeal by the courts, an individual federal employee (except certain categories of officials, including the President, who have been ruled to have absolute immunity) may be held personally liable for acts that, though committed while the employee was acting within the scope of office or employment, may subsequently be found to violate a constitutional provision. Juries may hold officials liable for actual damages where they cannot show that their actions were taken in good faith—that is, in the belief that their conduct was lawful—and for punitive damages where they are shown to have acted maliciously or with reckless disregard of the plaintiff's constitutional rights. At present, damages may not be recovered against the United States for

---

2. Respondents' reliance upon Rayonier is equally misplaced. In Rayonier the Court revisited an issue considered briefly in Dalehite: whether the United States may be held liable for the alleged negligence of its employees in fighting a fire. In Dalehite, the Court held that alleged negligence in firefighting was not actionable under the Act, basing its decision upon "the normal rule that an alleged failure or carelessness of public firemen does not create private actionable rights." In so holding, the Dalehite Court did not discuss or rely upon the discretionary function exception. The Rayonier Court rejected the reasoning of Dalehite on the ground that the liability of the United States under the Act is not restricted to that of a municipal corporation or other public body. . . . While the holding of Rayonier obviously overrules one element of the judgment in Dalehite, the more fundamental aspects of Dalehite, including its construction of Section 2680(a), remain undisturbed. [Footnote by the Court.]

violations of constitutional rights as such, although claims arising out of the same conduct may or may not be stated against the Government under the Federal Tort Claims Act.

The existing system of civil sanctions for constitutional violations by federal officials does not provide adequate assurance of compensation for victims of such violations and discourages proper conduct by government officials. In addition, the federal government often has interests at stake in constitutional tort litigation involving its officials which may not be represented adequately when individual officials themselves are the defendants on trial.

In Carlson v. Green, 446 U.S. 14 (1980), the Supreme Court suggested that the courts may properly refuse to entertain monetary damage actions against federal officials if Congress has expressly substituted a different remedy or made available an alternative to the Bivens remedy. In the Conference's view, such an alternative system is likely to improve the effectiveness with which federal programs and laws are administered.

To serve the primary goals of compensation, deterrence, and fairness in dealing with constitutional violations assertedly committed by federal officials, and to afford a solution to the problems perceived to flow from the current system of individual liability, Congress should replace the existing system by accepting public liability for wrongs done in the public's name and by strengthening the means of dealing with the wrongdoers. When defending against constitutional tort claims, the Government should be able to assert any immunity or good faith defense available to the officials. . . .

RECOMMENDATION

1. Congress should enact legislation providing that the United States shall be substituted as the exclusive party defendant in all actions for damages for violations of rights secured by the Constitution of the United States committed by federal executive branch officers and employees while acting within the scope of their office or employment. The legislation should provide adequate procedures to ensure that, where a damage action for violation of such rights is brought against an executive branch officer or employee, such action should be deemed to have been brought against the United States upon certification by the Attorney General that the defendant officer or employee was acting within the scope of his office or employment at the time of the incident out of which the suit arose. The Attorney General's failure to make such certification should be judicially reviewable.

2. Such legislation should provide that, in actions alleging constitutional violations, the United States may assert as a defense any qualified immunity or good faith defense available to the executive branch officer or employee whose conduct gave rise to the claim, or his reasonable good faith belief in the lawfulness of his conduct. The United States should also be free to assert such other defenses as may be available, including the absolute immunity of those officers entitled to such immunity.

3. The agency that employed the offending official should be responsible for investigation and, where appropriate, for disciplining the official and implementing any other appropriate corrective measures. The Office of Personnel Management should assure, via guidance promulgated through the Federal Personnel Manual and other devices, that agencies are authorized to employ existing mechanisms to impose sanctions on officers and employees who have violated the constitutional rights of any person. Employees should be permitted to assert as a defense in any disciplinary proceeding their good faith in taking the action in question, as well as such other defenses as may be available.

4. Congressional legislation should preserve the opportunity for jury trial only with respect to claims that arose prior to the effective date of the legislation implementing this recommendation.[3]

3. [Ed.] See also K. Davis, 4 Admin. L. Treatise § 27:45 (1984) (recommending that Congress enact eight "major changes" in the law of government tort liability); T. Madden, N. Allard and D. Remes, Bedtime for Bivens: Substituting the United States as Defendant in Constitutional Torts, 20 Harv.J.Legis. 469 (1983) (analyzing proposed legislation to modify the immunity available to the federal government for constitutional torts committed by its officials); P. Schuck, Suing Government 111 (1983) (proposing that "government be obliged to compensate for every harmful act or omission committed by its agents within the scope of their employment that is tortious under applicable law"); G. Bermann, Integrating Governmental and Officer Tort Liability, 77 Colum.L.Rev. 1175 (1977) (discussing alternative models of integration: officer liability, with or without indemnification by the government versus government liability, with or without indemnification by the officer); T. Madden and N. Allard, Advice on Official Liability and Immunity, 2 Administrative Conference of the United States, Recommendations and Reports, 1982, pp. 201–442 (the background report for Recommendation 82–6).

APPENDIX A

ADMINISTRATIVE PROCEDURE ACT

[Public Law 404—79th Congress, approved June 11, 1946, 60 Stat. 237–244; as codified by An Act to enact title 5, United States Code, September 6, 1966, Public Law 89–554, 80 Stat. 378; and as amended through the conclusion of the 95th Congress, Second Session.]

TITLE 5. GOVERNMENT ORGANIZATION AND EMPLOYEES

CHAPTER 5. ADMINISTRATIVE PROCEDURE

. . .

Subchapter II—Administrative Procedure

§ 551. Definitions

Parallel sections of 1946 Act

For the purpose of this subchapter—

(1) "agency" means each authority of the Government of the United States, whether or not it is within or subject to review by another agency, but does not include—   SEC. 2(a).

(A) the Congress;

(B) the courts of the United States;

(C) the governments of the territories or possessions of the United States;

(D) the government of the District of Columbia;

or except as to the requirements of section 552 of this title—

(E) agencies composed of representatives of the parties or of representatives of organizations of the parties to the disputes determined by them;

(F) courts martial and military commissions;

(G) military authority exercised in the field in time of war or in occupied territory; or

1209

(H) functions conferred by sections 1738, 1739, 1743, and 1744 of title 12; chapter 2 of title 41; or sections 1622, 1884, 1891–1902, and former section 1641(b)(2), of title 50, appendix;

(2) "person" includes an individual, partnership, corporation, association, or public or private organization other than an agency;   SEC. 2(b).

(3) "party" includes a person or agency named or admitted as a party, or properly seeking and entitled as of right to be admitted as a party, in an agency proceeding, and a person or agency admitted by an agency as a party for limited purposes;

(4) "rule" means the whole or a part of an agency statement of general or particular applicability and future effect designed to implement, interpret, or prescribe law or policy or describing the organization, procedure, or practice requirements of an agency and includes the approval or prescription for the future of rates, wages, corporate or financial structures or reorganization thereof, prices, facilities, appliances, services or allowances therefor or of valuations, costs, or accounting, or practices bearing on any of the foregoing;   SEC. 2(c).

(5) "rule making" means agency process for formulating, amending, or repealing a rule;

(6) "order" means the whole or a part of a final disposition, whether affirmative, negative, injunctive, or declaratory in form, of an agency in a matter other than rule making but including licensing;   SEC. 2(d).

(7) "adjudication" means agency process for the formulation of an order;

(8) "license" includes the whole or a part of an agency permit, certificate, approval, registration, charter, membership, statutory exemption or other form of permission;   SEC. 2(e).

(9) "licensing" includes agency process respecting the grant, renewal, denial, revocation, suspension, annulment, withdrawal, limitation, amendment, modification, or conditioning of a license;

(10) "sanction" includes the whole or a part of an agency—   SEC. 2(f).

(A) prohibition, requirement, limitation, or other condition affecting the freedom of a person;

(B) withholding of relief;

(C) imposition of penalty or fine;

(D) destruction, taking, seizure, or withholding of property;

(E) assessment of damages, reimbursement, restitution, compensation, costs, charges, or fees;

(F) requirement, revocation, or suspension of a license; or

(G) taking other compulsory or restrictive action;

(11) "relief" includes the whole or a part of an agency—

(A) grant of money, assistance, license, authority, exemption, exception, privilege, or remedy;

(B) recognition of a claim, right, immunity, privilege, exemption, or exception; or

(C) taking of other action on the application or petition of, and beneficial to, a person;

(12) "agency proceeding" means an agency process   SEC. 2(g).
as defined by paragraphs (5), (7), and (9) of this section; and

(13) "agency action" includes the whole or a part of an agency rule, order, license, sanction, relief, or the equivalent or denial thereof, or failure to act.

(14)[1] "Ex parte communication" means an oral or written communication not on the public record with respect to which reasonable prior notice to all parties is not given, but it shall not include requests for status reports on any matter or proceeding covered by this subchapter.

[2] § 552. Public information; agency rules, opinions, orders, records, and proceedings

SEC.   3.   (as amended)

(a) Each agency shall make available to the public information as follows:

(1) Each agency shall separately state and currently publish in the Federal Register for the guidance of the public—

(A) descriptions of its central and field organization and the established places at which, the employees (and in the case of a uniformed service, the members) from whom, and the methods whereby, the public may obtain information, make submittals or requests, or obtain decisions;

(B) statements of the general course and method by which its functions are channeled and determined, including the nature and requirements of all formal and informal procedures available;

1. Added by P.L. 94–409, 90 Stat. 1247.   409, 90 Stat. 1247; P.L. 95–454, 92 Stat.
2. As amended by P.L. 90–23, 81 Stat.   1225; and P.L. 98–620, 98 Stat. 2428.
54; P.L. 93–502, 88 Stat. 1561; P.L. 94–

(C) rules of procedure, descriptions of forms available or the places at which forms may be obtained, and instructions as to the scope and contents of all papers, reports, or examinations;

(D) substantive rules of general applicability adopted as authorized by law, and statements of general policy or interpretations of general applicability formulated and adopted by the agency; and

(E) each amendment, revision, or repeal of the foregoing.

Except to the extent that a person has actual and timely notice of the terms thereof, a person may not in any manner be required to resort to, or be adversely affected by, a matter required to be published in the Federal Register and not so published. For the purpose of this paragraph, matter reasonably available to the class of persons affected thereby is deemed published in the Federal Register when incorporated by reference therein with the approval of the Director of the Federal Register.

(2) Each agency, in accordance with published rules, shall make available for public inspection and copying—

(A) final opinions, including concurring and dissenting opinions, as well as orders, made in the adjudication of cases;

(B) those statements of policy and interpretations which have been adopted by the agency and are not published in the Federal Register; and

(C) administrative staff manuals and instructions to staff that affect a member of the public;

unless the materials are promptly published and copies offered for sale. To the extent required to prevent a clearly unwarranted invasion of personal privacy, an agency may delete identifying details when it makes available or publishes an opinion, statement of policy, interpretation, or staff manual or instruction. However, in each case the justification for the deletion shall be explained fully in writing. Each agency also shall maintain and make available for public inspection and copying a current index providing identifying information for the public as to any matter issued, adopted, or promulgated after July 4, 1967, and required by this paragraph to be made available or published. Each agency shall promptly publish, quarterly or more frequently, and distribute (by sale or otherwise) copies of each index or supplements thereto unless it determines by order published in the Federal Register that the publication would be unnecessary and impracticable, in which case the agency shall nonetheless provide copies of such index on request at a cost not to exceed the direct cost of duplication. A final order, opinion, statement of policy, interpretation, or staff manual or instruction that affects a member of the public may be relied on, used, or cited as precedent by an agency against a party other than an agency only if—

(i) it has been indexed and either made available or published as provided by this paragraph; or

(ii) the party has actual and timely notice of the terms thereof.

(3) Except with respect to the records made available under paragraphs (1) and (2) of this subsection, each agency upon any request for records which (A) reasonably describes such records and (B) is made in accordance with published rules stating the time, place, fees (if any), and procedures to be followed, shall make the records promptly available to any person.

(4)(A)(i) In order to carry out the provisions of this section, each agency shall promulgate regulations, pursuant to notice and receipt of public comment, specifying the schedule of fees applicable to the processing of requests under this section and establishing procedures and guidelines for determining when such fees should be waived or reduced. Such schedule shall conform to the guidelines which shall be promulgated, pursuant to notice and receipt of public comment, by the Director of the Office of Management and Budget and which shall provide for a uniform schedule of fees for all agencies.

(ii) Such agency regulations shall provide that—

(I) fees shall be limited to reasonable standard charges for document search, duplication, and review, when records are requested for commercial use;

(II) fees shall be limited to reasonable standard charges for document duplication when records are not sought for commercial use and the request is made by an educational or noncommercial scientific institution, whose purpose is scholarly or scientific research; or a representative of the news media; and

(III) for any request not described in (I) or (II), fees shall be limited to reasonable standard charges for document search and duplication.

(iii) Documents shall be furnished without any charge or at a charge reduced below the fees established under clause (ii) if disclosure of the information is in the public interest because it is likely to contribute significantly to public understanding of the operations or activities of the government and is not primarily in the commercial interest of the requester.

(iv) Fee schedules shall provide for the recovery of only the direct costs of search, duplication, or review. Review costs shall include only the direct costs incurred during the initial examination of a document for the purposes of determining whether the documents must be disclosed under this section and for the purposes of withholding any portions exempt from disclosure under this section. Review costs may not include any costs incurred in resolving issues of law or policy that may be raised in the course of processing a request under this section. No fee may be charged by any agency under this section—

(I) if the costs of routine collection and processing of the fee are likely to equal or exceed the amount of the fee; or

(II) for any request described in clause (ii)(II) or (III) of this subparagraph for the first two hours of search time or for the first one hundred pages of duplication.

(v) No agency may require advance payment of any fee unless the requester has previously failed to pay fees in a timely fashion, or the agency has determined that the fee will exceed $250.

(vi) Nothing in this subparagraph shall supersede fees chargeable under a statute specifically providing for setting the level of fees for particular types of records.

(vii) In any action by a requester regarding the waiver of fees under this section, the court shall determine the matter de novo: Provided, That the court's review of the matter shall be limited to the record before the agency.*

(B) On complaint, the district court of the United States in the district in which the complainant resides, or has his principal place of business, or in which the agency records are situated, or in the

* As amended by the Anti-Drug Abuse
Act of 1986, P.L. 99–570, 100 Stat. 3207.

District of Columbia, has jurisdiction to enjoin the agency from withholding agency records and to order the production of any agency records improperly withheld from the complainant. In such a case the court shall determine the matter de novo, and may examine the contents of such agency records in camera to determine whether such records or any part thereof shall be withheld under any of the exemptions set forth in subsection (b) of this section, and the burden is on the agency to sustain its action.

(C) Notwithstanding any other provision of law, the defendant shall serve an answer or otherwise plead to any complaint made under this subsection within thirty days after service upon the defendant of the pleading in which such complaint is made, unless the court otherwise directs for good cause shown.

(D) [Repealed, P.L. 98–620, 98 Stat. 2428.]

(E) The court may assess against the United States reasonable attorney fees and other litigation costs reasonably incurred in any case under this section in which the complainant has substantially prevailed.

(F) Whenever the court orders the production of any agency records improperly withheld from the complainant and assesses against the United States reasonable attorney fees and other litigation costs, and the court additionally issues a written finding that the circumstances surrounding the withholding raise questions whether agency personnel acted arbitrarily or capriciously with respect to the withholding, the Special Counsel [3] shall promptly initiate a proceeding to determine whether disciplinary action is warranted against the officer or employee who was primarily responsible for the withholding. The Special Counsel, after investigation and consideration of the evidence submitted, shall submit his findings and recommendations to the administrative authority of the agency concerned and shall send copies of the findings and recommendations to the officer or employee or his representative. The administrative authority shall take the corrective action that the Special Counsel recommends.

(G) In the event of noncompliance with the order of the court, the district court may punish for contempt the responsible employee, and in the case of a uniformed service, the responsible member.

---

3. [Ed.] The Special Counsel of the Merit Systems Protection Board was assigned, in this respect, the responsibilities formerly held by the Civil Service Commission. See the "Civil Service Reform Act of 1978," P.L. 95–251, 92 Stat. 183.

(5) Each agency having more than one member shall maintain and make available for public inspection a record of the final votes of each member in every agency proceeding.

(6)(A) Each agency, upon any request for records made under paragraph (1), (2), or (3) of this subsection, shall—

(i) determine within ten days (excepting Saturdays, Sundays, and legal public holidays) after the receipt of any such request whether to comply with such request and shall immediately notify the person making such request of such determination and the reasons therefor, and of the right of such person to appeal to the head of the agency any adverse determination; and

(ii) make a determination with respect to any appeal within twenty days (excepting Saturdays, Sundays, and legal public holidays) after the receipt of such appeal. If on appeal the denial of the request for records is in whole or in part upheld, the agency shall notify the person making such request of the provisions for judicial review of that determination under paragraph (4) of this subsection.

(B) In unusual circumstances as specified in this subparagraph, the time limits prescribed in either clause (i) or clause (ii) of subparagraph (A) may be extended by written notice to the person making such request setting forth the reasons for such extension and the date on which a determination is expected to be dispatched. No such notice shall specify a date that would result in an extension for more than ten working days. As used in this subparagraph, "unusual circumstances" means, but only to the extent reasonably necessary to the proper processing of the particular request—

(i) the need to search for and collect the requested records from field facilities or other establishments that are separate from the office processing the request;

(ii) the need to search for, collect, and appropriately examine a voluminous amount of separate and distinct records which are demanded in a single request; or

(iii) the need for consultation, which shall be conducted with all practicable speed, with another agency having a substantial interest in the determination of the request or among two or more components of the agency having substantial subject-matter interest therein.

(C) Any person making a request to any agency for records under paragraph (1), (2), or (3) of this subsection shall be deemed to have exhausted his administrative remedies with respect to such request if the agency fails to comply with the applicable time limit provisions of this paragraph. If the Government can show exceptional circumstances exist and that the agency is exercising due diligence in responding to the request, the court may retain jurisdiction and allow the agency additional time to complete its review of the records. Upon any determination by an agency to comply with a request for records, the records shall be made promptly available to such person making such request. Any notification of denial of any request for records under this subsection shall set forth the names and titles or positions of each person responsible for the denial of such request.

(b) This section does not apply to matters that are—

(1)(A) specifically authorized under criteria established by an Executive order to be kept secret in the interest of national defense or foreign policy and (B) are in fact properly classified pursuant to such Executive order;

(2) related solely to the internal personnel rules and practices of an agency;

(3) specifically exempted from disclosure by statute (other than section 552b of this title), provided that such statute (A) requires that the matters be withheld from the public in such a manner as to leave no discretion on the issue, or (B) establishes particular criteria for withholding or refers to particular types of matters to be withheld;

(4) trade secrets and commercial or financial information obtained from a person and privileged or confidential;

(5) inter-agency or intra-agency memorandums or letters which would not be available by law to a party other than an agency in litigation with the agency;

(6) personnel and medical files and similar files the disclosure of which would constitute a clearly unwarranted invasion of personal privacy;

(7) records or information compiled for law enforcement purposes, but only to the extent that the production of such law enforcement records or information (A) could reasonably be expected to interfere with enforcement proceedings, (B) would deprive a person of a right to a fair trial or an

impartial adjudication, (C) could reasonably be expected to constitute an unwarranted invasion of personal privacy, (D) could reasonably be expected to disclose the identity of a confidential source, including a State, local, or foreign agency or authority or any private institution which furnished information on a confidential basis, and, in the case of a record or information compiled by criminal law enforcement authority in the course of a criminal investigation or by an agency conducting a lawful national security intelligence investigation, information furnished by a confidential source, (E) would disclose techniques and procedures for law enforcement investigations or prosecutions, or would disclose guidelines for law enforcement investigations or prosecutions if such disclosure could reasonably be expected to risk circumvention of the law, or (F) could reasonably be expected to endanger the life or physical safety of any individual; *

(8) contained in or related to examination, operating, or condition reports prepared by, on behalf of, or for the use of an agency responsible for the regulation or supervision of financial institutions; or

(9) geological and geophysical information and data, including maps, concerning wells.

Any reasonably segregable portion of a record shall be provided to any person requesting such record after deletion of the portions which are exempt under this subsection.

(c)(1) Whenever a request is made which involves access to records described in subsection (b)(7)(A) and—

(A) the investigation or proceeding involves a possible violation of criminal law; and

(B) there is reason to believe that (i) the subject of the investigation or proceeding is not aware of its pendency, and (ii) disclosure of the existence of the records could reasonably be expected to interfere with enforcement proceedings,

the agency may, during only such time as that circumstance continues, treat the records as not subject to the requirements of this section.

---

* As amended by the Anti-Drug Abuse
Act of 1986, P.L. 99–570, 100 Stat. 3207.

(2) Whenever informant records maintained by a criminal law enforcement agency under an informant's name or personal identifier are requested by a third party according to the informant's name or personal identifier, the agency may treat the records as not subject to the requirements of this section unless the informant's status as an informant has been officially confirmed.

(3) Whenever a request is made which involves access to records maintained by the Federal Bureau of Investigation pertaining to foreign intelligence or counterintelligence, or international terrorism, and the existence of the records is classified information as provided in subsection (b)(1), the Bureau may, as long as the existence of the records remains classified information, treat the records as not subject to the requirements of this section.*

(d) This section does not authorize withholding of information or limit the availability of records to the public, except as specifically stated in this section. This section is not authority to withhold information from Congress.

(e) On or before March 1 of each calendar year, each agency shall submit a report covering the preceding calendar year to the Speaker of the House of Representatives and President of the Senate for referral to the appropriate committees of the Congress. The report shall include—

(1) the number of determinations made by such agency not to comply with requests for records made to such agency under subsection (a) and the reasons for each such determination;

(2) the number of appeals made by persons under subsection (a)(6), the result of such appeals, and the reason for the action upon each appeal that results in a denial of information;

(3) the names and titles or positions of each person responsible for the denial of records requested under this section, and the number of instances of participation for each;

(4) the results of each proceeding conducted pursuant to subsection (a)(4)(F), including a report of the disciplinary action taken against the officer or employee who was primarily responsible for improperly withholding records or an explanation of why disciplinary action was not taken;

* Added by the Anti-Drug Abuse Act of 1986, P.L. 99–570, 100 Stat. 3207.

(5) a copy of every rule made by such agency regarding this section;

(6) a copy of the fee schedule and the total amount of fees collected by the agency for making records available under this section; and

(7) such other information as indicates efforts to administer fully this section.

The Attorney General shall submit an annual report on or before March 1 of each calendar year which shall include for the prior calendar year a listing of the number of cases arising under this section, the exemption involved in each case, the disposition of such case, and the cost, fees, and penalties assessed under subsections (a)(4)(E), (F), and (G). Such report shall also include a description of the efforts undertaken by the Department of Justice to encourage agency compliance with this section.

(f) For purposes of this section, the term "agency" as defined in section 551(1) of this title includes any executive department, military department, Government corporation, Government controlled corporation, or other establishment in the executive branch of the Government (including the Executive Office of the President), or any independent regulatory agency.

§ 552a. Records maintained on individuals

[This section, also known as the Privacy Act, is omitted.]

§ 552b. Open meetings

[See p. 1233 within].

§ 553. Rule making

SEC. 4.

(a) This section applies, accordingly to the provisions thereof, except to the extent that there is involved—

(1) a military or foreign affairs function of the United States; or

(2) a matter relating to agency management or personnel or to public property, loans, grants, benefits, or contracts.

(b) General notice of proposed rule making shall be   SEC. 4(a).
published in the Federal Register, unless persons subject thereto are named and either personally served or otherwise have actual notice thereof in accordance with law. The notice shall include—

(1) a statement of the time, place, and nature of public rule making proceedings;

(2) reference to the legal authority under which the rule is proposed; and

(3) either the terms or substance of the proposed rule or a description of the subjects and issues involved.

Except when notice or hearing is required by statute, this subsection does not apply—

(A) to interpretative rules, general statements of policy, or rules of agency organization, procedure, or practice; or

(B) when the agency for good cause finds (and incorporates the finding and a brief statement of reasons therefor in the rules issued) that notice and public procedure thereon are impracticable, unnecessary, or contrary to the public interest.

(c) After notice required by this section, the agency shall give interested persons an opportunity to participate in the rule making through submission of written data, views, or arguments with or without opportunity for oral presentation. After consideration of the relevant matter presented, the agency shall incorporate in the rules adopted a concise general statement of their basis and purpose. When rules are required by statute to be made on the record after opportunity for an agency hearing, sections 556 and 557 of this title apply instead of this subsection.

(d) The required publication or service of a substantive rule shall be made not less than 30 days before its effective date, except—

(1) a substantive rule which grants or recognizes an exemption or relieves a restriction;

(2) interpretative rules and statements of policy; or

(3) as otherwise provided by the agency for good cause found and published with the rule.

(e) Each agency shall give an interested person the right to petition for the issuance, amendment, or repeal of a rule.

§ 554. Adjudications

(a) This section applies, according to the provisions thereof, in every case of adjudication required by statute to be determined on the record after opportunity for an agency hearing, except to the extent that there is involved—

(1) a matter subject to a subsequent trial of the law and the facts de novo in a court;

(2) the selection or tenure of an employee, except an administrative law judge appointed under section 3105 of this title;

(3) proceedings in which decisions rest solely on inspections, tests, or elections;

(4) the conduct of military or foreign affairs functions;

(5) cases in which an agency is acting as an agent for a court; or

(6) the certification of worker representatives.

(b) Persons entitled to notice of an agency hearing shall be timely informed of—   SEC. 5(a).

(1) the time, place, and nature of the hearing;

(2) the legal authority and jurisdiction under which the hearing is to be held; and

(3) the matters of fact and law asserted.

When private persons are the moving parties, other parties to the proceeding shall give prompt notice of issues controverted in fact or law; and in other instances agencies may by rule require responsive pleading. In fixing the time and place for hearings, due regard shall be had for the convenience and necessity of the parties or their representatives.

(c) The agency shall give all interested parties opportunity for—   SEC. 5(b).

(1) the submission and consideration of facts, arguments, offers of settlement, or proposals of adjustment when time, the nature of the proceeding, and the public interest permit; and

(2) to the extent that the parties are unable so to determine a controversy by consent, hearing and decision on notice and in accordance with sections 556 and 557 of this title.

(d) The employee who presides at the reception of evidence pursuant to section 556 of this title shall make the recommended decision or initial decision required by section 557 of this title, unless he becomes unavailable to the agency. Except to the extent required for the disposition of ex parte matters as authorized by law, such an employee may not—   SEC. 5(c).

(1) consult a person or party on a fact in issue, unless on notice and opportunity for all parties to participate; or

(2) be responsible to or subject to the supervision or direction of an employee or agent engaged

in the performance of investigative or prosecuting functions for an agency.

An employee or agent engaged in the performance of investigative or prosecuting functions for an agency in a case may not, in that or a factually related case, participate or advise in the decision, recommended decision or agency review pursuant to section 557 of this title, except as witness or counsel in public proceedings. This subsection does not apply—

(A) in determining applications for initial licenses;

(B) to proceedings involving the validity or application of rates, facilities, or practices of public utilities or carriers; or

(C) to the agency or a member or members of the body comprising the agency.

(e) The agency, with like effect as in the case of other orders, and in its sound discretion, may issue a declaratory order to terminate a controversy or remove uncertainty.   SEC. 5(d).

§ 555. Ancillary matters   SEC. 6.

(a) This section applies, according to the provisions thereof, except as otherwise provided by this subchapter.

(b) A person compelled to appear in person before an agency or representative thereof is entitled to be accompanied, represented, and advised by counsel or, if permitted by the agency, by other qualified representative. A party is entitled to appear in person or by or with counsel or other duly qualified representative in an agency proceeding. So far as the orderly conduct of public business permits, an interested person may appear before an agency or its responsible employees for the presentation, adjustment, or determination of an issue, request, or controversy in a proceeding, whether interlocutory, summary, or otherwise, or in connection with an agency function. With due regard for the convenience and necessity of the parties or their representatives and within a reasonable time, each agency shall proceed to conclude a matter presented to it. This subsection does not grant or deny a person who is not a lawyer the right to appear for or represent others before an agency or in an agency proceeding.   SEC. 6(a).

(c) Process, requirement of a report, inspection, or other investigative act or demand may not be issued, made, or enforced except as authorized by law. A person compelled to submit data or evidence is entitled   SEC. 6(b).

to retain or, on payment of lawfully prescribed costs, procure a copy or transcript thereof, except that in a nonpublic investigatory proceeding the witness may for good cause be limited to inspection of the official transcript of his testimony.

(d) Agency subpenas authorized by law shall be issued to a party on request and, when required by rules of procedure, on a statement or showing of general relevance and reasonable scope of the evidence sought. On contest, the court shall sustain the subpena or similar process or demand to the extent that it is found to be in accordance with law. In a proceeding for enforcement, the court shall issue an order requiring the appearance of the witness or the production of the evidence or data within a reasonable time under penalty of punishment for contempt in case of contumacious failure to comply. SEC. 6(c).

(e) Prompt notice shall be given of the denial in whole or in part of a written application, petition, or other request of an interested person made in connection with any agency proceeding. Except in affirming a prior denial or when the denial is self-explanatory, the notice shall be accompanied by a brief statement of the grounds for denial. SEC. 6(d).

§ 556. Hearings; presiding employees; powers and duties; burden of proof; evidence; record as basis of decision

SEC. 7.

(a) This section applies, according to the provisions thereof, to hearings required by section 553 or 554 of this title to be conducted in accordance with this section.

(b) There shall preside at the taking of evidence— SEC. 7(a).

    (1) the agency;

    (2) one or more members of the body which comprises the agency; or

    (3) one or more administrative law judges appointed under section 3105 of this title.

This subchapter does not supersede the conduct of specified classes of proceedings, in whole or in part, by or before boards or other employees specially provided for by or designated under statute. The functions of presiding employees and of employees participating in decisions in accordance with section 557 of this title shall be conducted in an impartial manner. A presiding or participating employee may at any time disqualify himself. On the filing in good faith of a timely and sufficient affidavit of personal bias or other disqualification of a presiding or participating employee, the agency shall determine the matter as a part of the record and decision in the case.

(c) Subject to published rules of the agency and within its powers, employees presiding at hearings may— SEC. 7(b).

    (1) administer oaths and affirmations;

    (2) issue subpenas authorized by law;

    (3) rule on offers of proof and receive relevant evidence;

    (4) take depositions or have depositions taken when the ends of justice would be served;

    (5) regulate the course of the hearing;

    (6) hold conferences for the settlement or simplification of the issues by consent of the parties;

    (7) dispose of procedural requests or similar matters;

    (8) make or recommend decisions in accordance with section 557 of this title; and

    (9) take other action authorized by agency rule consistent with this subchapter.

(d) Except as otherwise provided by statute, the proponent of a rule or order has the burden of proof. Any oral or documentary evidence may be received, but the agency as a matter of policy shall provide for the exclusion of irrelevant, immaterial, or unduly repetitious evidence. A sanction may not be imposed or rule or order issued except on consideration of the whole record or those parts thereof cited by a party and supported by and in accordance with the reliable, probative, and substantial evidence. The agency may, to the extent consistent with the interests of justice and the policy of the underlying statutes administered by the agency, consider a violation of section 557(d) of this title sufficient grounds for a decision adverse to a party who has knowingly committed such violation or knowingly caused such violation to occur.[4] A party is entitled to present his case or defense by oral or documentary evidence, to submit rebuttal evidence, and to conduct such cross-examination as may be required for a full and true disclosure of the facts. In rule making or determining claims for money or benefits or applications for initial licenses an agency may, when a party will not be prejudiced thereby, adopt procedures for the SEC. 7(c).

4. This sentence added by P.L. 94–409, 90 Stat. 1247.

submission of all or part of the evidence in written form.

(e) The transcript of testimony and exhibits, together with all papers and requests filed in the proceeding, constitutes the exclusive record for decision in accordance with section 557 of this title and, on payment of lawfully prescribed costs, shall be made available to the parties. When an agency decision rests on official notice of a material fact not appearing in the evidence in the record, a party is entitled, on timely request, to an opportunity to show the contrary.

SEC. 7(d).

§ 557. Initial decisions; conclusiveness; review by agency; submissions by parties; contents of decisions; record

SEC. 8.

(a) This section applies, according to the provisions thereof, when a hearing is required to be conducted in accordance with section 556 of this title.

(b) When the agency did not preside at the reception of the evidence, the presiding employee or, in cases not subject to section 554(d) of this title, an employee qualified to preside at hearings pursuant to section 556 of this title, shall initially decide the case unless the agency requires, either in specific cases or by general rule, the entire record to be certified to it for decision. When the presiding employee makes an initial decision, that decision then becomes the decision of the agency without further proceedings unless there is an appeal to, or review on motion of, the agency within time provided by rule. On appeal from or review of the initial decision, the agency has all the powers which it would have in making the initial decision except as it may limit the issues on notice or by rule. When the agency makes the decision without having presided at the reception of the evidence, the presiding employee or an employee qualified to preside at hearings pursuant to section 556 of this title shall first recommend a decision, except that in rule making or determining application for initial licenses—

SEC. 8(a).

    (1) instead thereof the agency may issue a tentative decision or one of its responsible employees may recommend a decision; or

    (2) this procedure may be omitted in a case in which the agency finds on the record that due and timely execution of its functions imperatively and unavoidably so requires.

(c) Before a recommended, initial, or tentative decision, or a decision on agency review of the decision of

SEC. 8(b).

subordinate employees, the parties are entitled to a reasonable opportunity to submit for the consideration of the employees participating in the decisions—

(1) proposed findings and conclusions; or

(2) exceptions to the decisions or recommended decisions of subordinate employees or to tentative agency decisions; and

(3) supporting reasons for the exceptions or proposed findings or conclusions.

The record shall show the ruling on each finding, conclusion, or exception presented. All decisions, including initial, recommended, and tentative decisions, are a part of the record and shall include a statement of—

(A) findings and conclusions, and the reasons or basis therefor, on all the material issues of fact, law, or discretion presented on the record; and

(B) the appropriate rule, order, sanction, relief, or denial thereof.

(d)(1) [5] In any agency proceeding which is subject to subsection (a) of this section, except to the extent required for the disposition of ex parte matters as authorized by law—

(A) no interested person outside the agency shall make or knowingly cause to be made to any member of the body comprising the agency, administrative law judge, or other employee who is or may reasonably be expected to be involved in the decisional process of the proceeding, an ex parte communication relevant to the merits of the proceeding;

(B) no member of the body comprising the agency, administrative law judge, or other employee who is or may reasonably be expected to be involved in the decisional process of the proceeding, shall make or knowingly cause to be made to any interested person outside the agency an ex parte communication relevant to the merits of the proceeding;

(C) a member of the body comprising the agency, administrative law judge, or other employee who is or may reasonably be expected to be involved in the decisional process of such proceeding who receives, or who makes or knowingly

5. Subsection (d) was added by P.L. 94–409, 90 Stat. 1247.

causes to be made, a communication prohibited by this subsection shall place on the public record of the proceeding:

    (i) all such written communications;

    (ii) memoranda stating the substance of all such oral communications; and

    (iii) all written responses, and memoranda stating the substance of all oral responses, to the materials described in clauses (i) and (ii) of this subparagraph;

(D) upon receipt of a communication knowingly made or knowingly caused to be made by a party in violation of this subsection, the agency, administrative law judge, or other employee presiding at the hearing may, to the extent consistent with the interests of justice and the policy of the underlying statutes, require the party to show cause why his claim or interest in the proceeding should not be dismissed, denied, disregarded, or otherwise adversely affected on account of such violation; and

(E) the prohibitions of this subsection shall apply beginning at such time as the agency may designate, but in no case shall they begin to apply later than the time at which a proceeding is noticed for hearing unless the person responsible for the communication has knowledge that it will be noticed, in which case the prohibitions shall apply beginning at the time of his acquisition of such knowledge.

(2) This subsection does not constitute authority to withhold information from Congress.

§ 558. Imposition of sanctions; determination of applications for licenses; suspension, revocation, and expiration of licenses   Sec. 9.

(a) This section applies, according to the provisions thereof, to the exercise of a power or authority.

(b) A sanction may not be imposed or a substantive rule or order issued except within jurisdiction delegated to the agency and as authorized by law.   Sec. 9(a).

(c) When application is made for a license required by law, the agency, with due regard for the rights and privileges of all the interested parties or adversely affected persons and within a reasonable time, shall set and complete proceedings required to be conducted in accordance with sections 556 and 557 of this title or other proceedings required by law and shall make its decision. Except in cases of willfulness or those in   Sec. 9(b).

which public health, interest, or safety requires otherwise, the withdrawal, suspension, revocation, or annulment of a license is lawful only if, before the institution of agency proceedings therefor, the licensee has been given—

    (1) notice by the agency in writing of the facts or conduct which may warrant the action; and

    (2) opportunity to demonstrate or achieve compliance with all lawful requirements.

When the licensee has made timely and sufficient application for a renewal or a new license in accordance with agency rules, a license with reference to an activity of a continuing nature does not expire until the application has been finally determined by the agency.

§ 559. Effect on other laws; effect of subsequent statute   SEC. 12.

This subchapter, chapter 7, and sections 1305, 3105, 3344, 4301(2)(E), 5372, and 7521, and the provisions of section 5335(a)(B) of this title that relate to administrative law judges, do not limit or repeal additional requirements imposed by statute or otherwise recognized by law. Except as otherwise required by law, requirements or privileges relating to evidence or procedure apply equally to agencies and persons. Each agency is granted the authority necessary to comply with the requirements of this subchapter through the issuance of rules or otherwise. Subsequent statute may not be held to supersede or modify this subchapter, chapter 7, sections 1305, 3105, 3344, 4301(2)(E), 5372, or 7521, or the provisions of section 5335(a)(B) of this title that relate to administrative law judges, except to the extent that it does so expressly.

. . .

CHAPTER 7.   JUDICIAL REVIEW

§ 701. Application; definitions

    (a) This chapter applies, according to the provisions   SEC. 10.
thereof, except to the extent that—

    (1) statutes preclude judicial review; or

(2) agency action is committed to agency discretion by law.

(b)(1) ["agency" is defined precisely as in § 551(1) (A) through (H), above];

(2) "person", "rule", "order", "license", "sanction", "relief", and "agency action" have the meanings given them by section 551 of this title.

§ 702. Right of review

A person suffering legal wrong because of agency action, or adversely affected or aggrieved by agency action within the meaning of a relevant statute, is entitled to judicial review thereof.[6] An action in a court of the United States seeking relief other than money damages and stating a claim that an agency or an officer or employee thereof acted or failed to act in an official capacity or under color of legal authority shall not be dismissed nor relief therein be denied on the ground that it is against the United States or that the United States is an indispensable party. The United States may be named as a defendant in any such action, and a judgment or decree may be entered against the United States: Provided, That any mandatory or injunctive decree shall specify the Federal officer or officers (by name or by title), and their successors in office, personally responsible for compliance. Nothing herein (1) affects other limitations on judicial review or the power or duty of the court to dismiss any action or deny relief on any other appropriate legal or equitable ground; or (2) confers authority to grant relief if any other statute that grants consent to suit expressly or impliedly forbids the relief which is sought.

SEC. 10(a).

§ 703. Form and venue of proceeding

The form of proceeding for judicial review is the special statutory review proceeding relevant to the subject matter in a court specified by statute or, in the absence or inadequacy thereof, any applicable form of legal action, including actions for declaratory judgments or writs of prohibitory or mandatory injunction or habeas corpus, in a court of competent jurisdiction. If no special statutory review proceeding is applicable, the action for judicial review may be brought against the United States, the agency by its official title, or the appropriate officer.[7] Except to the extent that prior, adequate, and exclusive opportunity for judicial review is provided by law, agency action is subject to judicial

SEC. 10(b).

---

6. Material after first sentence added by P.L. 94–574, 90 Stat. 2721.

7. Preceding sentence added by P.L. 94–574, 90 Stat. 2721.

review in civil or criminal proceedings for judicial enforcement.

§ 704. Actions reviewable

Agency action made reviewable by statute and final   SEC. 10(c).
agency action for which there is no other adequate
remedy in a court are subject to judicial review. A
preliminary, procedural, or intermediate agency action or
ruling not directly reviewable is subject to review on the
review of the final agency action. Except as otherwise
expressly required by statute, agency action otherwise
final is final for the purposes of this section whether or not
there has been presented or determined an application for
a declaratory order, for any form of reconsideration, or,
unless the agency otherwise requires by rule and provides
that the action meanwhile is inoperative, for an appeal to
superior agency authority.

§ 705. Relief pending review

When an agency finds that justice so requires, it may   SEC. 10(d).
postpone the effective date of action taken by it, pending
judicial review. On such conditions as may be required
and to the extent necessary to prevent irreparable injury,
the reviewing court, including the court to which a case
may be taken on appeal from or on application for
certiorari or other writ to a reviewing court, may issue all
necessary and appropriate process to postpone the effective date of an agency action or to preserve status or rights
pending conclusion of the review proceedings.

§ 706. Scope of review

To the extent necessary to decision and when pre-   SEC. 10(e).
sented, the reviewing court shall decide all relevant
questions of law, interpret constitutional and statutory
provisions, and determine the meaning or applicability
of the terms of an agency action. The reviewing court
shall—

   (1) compel agency action unlawfully withheld
or unreasonably delayed; and

   (2) hold unlawful and set aside agency action,
findings, and conclusions found to be—

      (A) arbitrary, capricious, an abuse of discretion, or otherwise not in accordance with law;

      (B) contrary to constitutional right, power,
privilege, or immunity;

      (C) in excess of statutory jurisdiction, authority, or limitations, or short of statutory
right;

(D) without observance of procedure required by law;

(E) unsupported by substantial evidence in a case subject to sections 556 and 557 of this title or otherwise reviewed on the record of an agency hearing provided by statute; or

(F) unwarranted by the facts to the extent that the facts are subject to trial de novo by the reviewing court.

In making the foregoing determinations, the court shall review the whole record or those parts of it cited by a party, and due account shall be taken of the rule of prejudicial error.

. . .

§ 3105. Appointment of administrative law judges [8]

Each agency shall appoint as many administrative law judges as are necessary for proceedings required to be conducted in accordance with sections 556 and 557 of this title. Administrative law judges shall be assigned to cases in rotation so far as practicable, and may not perform duties inconsistent with their duties and responsibilities as administrative law judges.

SEC. 11 (1st sentence).

§ 7521. Actions against administrative law judges [9]

(a) An action may be taken against an administrative law judge appointed under section 3105 of this title by the agency in which the administrative law judge is employed only for good cause established and determined by the Merit Systems Protection Board on the record after opportunity for hearing before the Board.

SEC. 11 (2d sentence).

(b) The actions covered by this section are—

(1) a removal;

(2) a suspension;

(3) a reduction in grade;

(4) a reduction in pay; and

(5) a furlough of 30 days or less;

but do not include—

(A) a suspension or removal [in the interest of national security];

(B) a reduction-in-force action . . . ; or

8. Substitution of "administrative law judge" for "hearing examiner," here and elsewhere in the APA, was effected by P.L. 95–251, 92 Stat. 183.

9. As amended by the Civil Service Reform Act of 1978, P.L. 95–454, 92 Stat. 1137. The following sections were also amended in minor respects.

(C) any action initiated [by the Special Counsel of the Board].

§ 5372. Administrative law judges

Administrative law judges appointed under section 3105 of this title are entitled to pay prescribed by the Office of Personnel Management independently of agency recommendations or ratings and in accordance with subchapter III of this chapter and chapter 51 of this title.

SEC. 11 (3d sentence).

§ 3344. Details; administrative law judges

An agency as defined by section 551 of this title which occasionally or temporarily is insufficiently staffed with administrative law judges appointed under section 3105 of this title may use administrative law judges selected by the Office of Personnel Management from and with the consent of other agencies.

SEC. 11 (4th sentence).

§ 1305. Administrative law judges

For the purpose of sections 3105, 3344, 4301(2)(D), and 5372 of this title 7521 and the provisions of section 5335(a)(B) of this title that relate to administrative law judges, the Office of Personnel Management may, and for the purpose of section 7521 of this title, the Merit Systems Protection Board may investigate, require reports by agencies, issue reports, including an annual report to Congress, prescribe regulations, appoint advisory committees as necessary, recommend legislation, subpena witnesses and records, and pay witness fees as established for the courts of the United States.

SEC. 11 (5th sentence).

§ 552b. Open meetings [10]

(a) For purposes of this section—

(1) the term "agency" means any agency, as defined in section 552(e) of this title, headed by a collegial body composed of two or more individual members, a majority of whom are appointed to such position by the President with the advice and consent of the Senate, and any subdivision thereof authorized to act on behalf of the agency;

(2) the term "meeting" means the deliberations of at least the number of individual agency members required to take action on behalf of the agency where such deliberations determine or result in the joint conduct or disposition of official agency business, but does not include deliberations required or permitted by subsection (d) or (e); and

(3) the term "member" means an individual who belongs to a collegial body heading an agency.

10. Added by P.L. 94–409, 90 Stat. 1241 (1976).

(b) Members shall not jointly conduct or dispose of agency business other than in accordance with this section. Except as provided in subsection (c), every portion of every meeting of an agency shall be open to public observation.

(c) Except in a case where the agency finds that the public interest requires otherwise, the second sentence of subsection (b) shall not apply to any portion of an agency meeting, and the requirements of subsections (d) and (e) shall not apply to any information pertaining to such meeting otherwise required by this section to be disclosed to the public, where the agency properly determines that such portion or portions of its meeting or the disclosure of such information is likely to—

(1) disclose matters that are (A) specifically authorized under criteria established by an Executive order to be kept secret in the interests of national defense or foreign policy and (B) in fact properly classified pursuant to such Executive order;

(2) relate solely to the internal personnel rules and practices of an agency;

(3) disclose matters specifically exempted from disclosure by statute (other than section 552 of this title), provided that such statute (A) requires that the matters be withheld from the public in such a manner as to leave no discretion on the issue, or (B) establishes particular criteria for withholding or refers to particular types of matters to be withheld;

(4) disclose trade secrets and commercial or financial information obtained from a person and privileged or confidential;

(5) involve accusing any person of a crime, or formally censuring any person;

(6) disclose information of a personal nature where disclosure would constitute a clearly unwarranted invasion of personal privacy;

(7) disclose investigatory records compiled for law enforcement purposes, or information which if written would be contained in such records, but only to the extent that the production of such records or information would (A) interfere with enforcement proceedings, (B) deprive a person of a right to a fair trial or an impartial adjudication, (C) constitute an unwarranted invasion of personal privacy, (D) disclose the identity of a confidential source and, in the case of a record compiled by a criminal law enforcement authority in the course of a criminal investigation, or by an agency conducting a lawful national security intelligence investigation, confidential information furnished only by the confidential source, (E) disclose investigative techniques and procedures, or (F) endanger the life or physical safety of law enforcement personnel;

(8) disclose information contained in or related to examination, operating, or condition reports prepared by, on behalf of, or for the use of an agency responsible for the regulation or supervision of financial institutions;

(9) disclose information the premature disclosure of which would—

(A) in the case of an agency which regulates currencies, securities, commodities, or financial institutions, be likely to (i) lead to significant financial speculation in currencies, securities, or commodities, or (ii) significantly endanger the stability of any financial institution; or

(B) in the case of any agency, be likely to significantly frustrate implementation of a proposed agency action,

except that subparagraph (B) shall not apply in any instance where the agency has already disclosed to the public the content or nature of its proposed action, or where the agency is required by law to make such disclosure on its own initiative prior to taking final agency action on such proposal; or

(10) specifically concern the agency's issuance of a subpena, or the agency's participation in a civil action or proceeding, an action in a foreign court or international tribunal, or an arbitration, or the initiation, conduct, or disposition by the agency of a particular case of formal agency adjudication pursuant to the procedures in section 554 of this title or otherwise involving a determination on the record after opportunity for a hearing.

(d)(1) Action under subsection (c) shall be taken only when a majority of the entire membership of the agency (as defined in subsection (a)(1)) votes to take such action. A separate vote of the agency members shall be taken with respect to each agency meeting a portion or portions of which are proposed to be closed to the public pursuant to subsection (c), or with respect to any information which is proposed to be withheld under subsection (c). A single vote may be taken with respect to a series of meetings, a portion or portions of which are proposed to be closed to the public, or with respect to any information concerning such series of meetings, so long as each meeting in such series involves the same particular matters and is scheduled to be held no more than thirty days after the initial meeting in such series. The vote of each agency member participating in such vote shall be recorded and no proxies shall be allowed.

(2) Whenever any person whose interests may be directly affected by a portion of a meeting requests that the agency close such portion to the public for any of the reasons referred to in paragraph (5), (6), or (7) of subsection (c), the agency, upon request of any one of its members, shall vote by recorded vote whether to close such meeting.

(3) Within one day of any vote taken pursuant to paragraph (1) or (2), the agency shall make publicly available a written copy of such vote reflecting the vote of each member on the question. If a portion of a meeting is to be closed to the public, the agency shall, within one day of the vote taken pursuant to paragraph (1) or (2) of this subsection, make publicly available a full written explanation of its action closing the portion together with a list of all persons expected to attend the meeting and their affiliation.

. . .

(e)(1) In the case of each meeting, the agency shall make public announcement, at least one week before the meeting, of the time, place, and subject matter of the meeting, whether it is to be open or closed to the public, and the name and phone number of the official designated by the agency to respond to requests for information about the meeting. Such announcement shall be made unless a majority of the members of the agency determines by a recorded vote that agency business requires that such meeting be called at an earlier date, in which case the agency shall make public announcement of the time, place, and subject matter of such meeting, and whether open or closed to the public, at the earliest practicable time.

(2) The time or place of a meeting may be changed following the public announcement required by paragraph (1) only if the agency publicly announces such change at the earliest practicable time. The subject matter of a meeting, or the determination of the agency to open or close a meeting, or portion of a meeting, to the public, may be changed following the public announcement required by this subsection only if (A) a majority of the entire membership of the agency determines by a recorded vote that agency business so requires and that no earlier announcement of the change was possible, and (B) the agency publicly announces such change and the vote of each member upon such change at the earliest practicable time.

. . .

(f)(1) For every meeting closed pursuant to paragraphs (1) through (10) of subsection (c), the General Counsel or chief legal officer of the agency shall publicly certify that, in his or her opinion, the meeting may be closed to the public and shall state each relevant exemptive provision. A copy of such certification, together with a statement from the presiding officer of the meeting setting forth the time and place of the meeting, and the persons present, shall be retained by the agency. The agency shall maintain a complete transcript or electronic recording adequate to record fully the proceedings of each meeting, or portion of a meeting, closed to the public, except that in the case of a meeting, or portion of a meeting, closed to the public pursuant to paragraph (8), (9)(A), or (10) of subsection (c), the agency shall maintain either such a transcript or recording, or a set of minutes. Such minutes shall fully and clearly describe all matters discussed and shall provide a full and accurate summary of any actions taken, and the reasons therefor, including a description of each of the views expressed on any item and the record of any rollcall vote (reflecting the vote of each member on the question). All documents considered in connection with any action shall be identified in such minutes.

(2) The agency shall make promptly available to the public, in a place easily accessible to the public, the transcript, electronic recording, or minutes (as required by paragraph (1)) of the discussion of any item on the agenda, or of any item of the testimony of any witness received at the meeting, except for such item or items of such discussion or testimony as the agency determines to contain information which may be withheld under subsection (c). . . .

(h)(1) The district courts of the United States shall have jurisdiction to enforce the requirements of subsections (b) through (f) of this section by declaratory judgment, injunctive relief, or other relief as may be appropriate. Such actions may be brought by any person against an agency prior to, or within sixty days after, the meeting out of which the violation of this section arises, except that if public announcement of such meeting is not initially provided by the agency in accordance with the requirements of this section, such action may be instituted pursuant to this section at any time prior to sixty days after any public announcement of such meeting. Such actions may be brought in the district court of the United States for the district in which the agency meeting is held or in which the agency in question has its headquarters, or in the District Court for the District of Columbia. In such actions a defendant shall serve his answer within thirty days after the service of the complaint. The burden is on the defendant to sustain his action. In deciding such cases the court may examine in camera any portion of the transcript, electronic recording, or minutes of a meeting closed to the public, and may take such additional evidence as it deems necessary. The court, having due regard for orderly administration and the public interest, as well as the interests of the parties, may grant such equitable relief as it deems appropriate, including granting an injunction against future violations of this section or ordering the agency to make available to the public such portion of the transcript, recording, or minutes of a meeting as is not authorized to be withheld under subsection (c) of this section.

(2) Any Federal court otherwise authorized by law to review agency action may, at the application of any person properly participating in the proceeding pursuant to other applicable law, inquire into violations by the agency of the requirements of this section and afford such relief as it deems appropriate. Nothing in this section authorizes any Federal court having jurisdiction solely on the basis of paragraph (1) to set aside, enjoin, or invalidate any agency action (other than an action to close a meeting or to withhold information under this section) taken or discussed at any agency meeting out of which the violation of this section arose.

(i) The court may assess against any party reasonable attorney fees and other litigation costs reasonably incurred by any other party who substantially prevails in any action brought in accordance with the provisions of subsection (g) or (h) of this section, except that costs may be assessed against the plaintiff only where the court finds that the suit was initiated by the plaintiff primarily for frivolous or dilatory purposes. In the case of assessment of costs against an agency, the costs may be assessed by the court against the United States.

(j) Each agency subject to the requirements of this section shall annually report to Congress regarding its compliance with such requirements . . . .

(*l*) This section does not constitute authority to withhold any information from Congress, and does not authorize the closing of any agency meeting or portion thereof required by any other provision of law to be open.

. . .

APPENDIX B

UNIFORM LAW COMMISSIONERS' REVISED MODEL STATE ADMINISTRATIVE PROCEDURE ACT (1981)

Introductory Note. In the late 1930's, the American Bar Association and the National Conference of Commissioners on Uniform State Laws initiated efforts to draft legislation relating to state administrative rule making, adjudication and judicial review. The Model State Administrative Procedure Act was first approved by the two organizations in 1946, revised in 1961, and again in 1981. The Model Act is reproduced below. With a prefatory note and comments it is published in Uniform Laws Annotated (West), vol. 14, 1985 Pamphlet, p. 69.

Acceptance of the Model Act came slowly at first. By 1959 it was in force in only five states, but publication of the 1961 revision marked a turning point. Today, more than half of the states have APAs based wholly or partly on the Model Act.[1] In 1977, the House of Delegates of the ABA adopted a proposal urging every state without an administrative procedure act to adopt one. 63 A.B.A.J. 1234 (1977). See Arthur Bonfield, The Federal APA and State Administrative Law, 72 Va.L.Rev. 297 (1986).

1. See generally, Model State Administrative Procedure Act, 13 Uniform State Laws Ann. 347 (Pamphlet 1978). The states that have adopted the Model Act are designated by an asterisk (*) or (†) for adoption of the 1981 revision.

* **Alabama:** Ala.Code §§ 41-22-1 to 41-22-27 (1982 and Supp.1984). See McCurley, Alabama Administrative Procedure Act, 42 Ala.L.Rev. 409 (1981); Prentwood, Implementing the Administrative Procedure Act in Alabama—A Report from the Administrative Law Section, 43 Ala.L.Rev. 680 (1982).

Alaska: Alaska Stat. 24.20.400 to 24.20.460 (1978 & Supp.1984) (legislative oversight) and 44.62.010 to 44.62.650 (1984 & Supp.1984).

Arizona: Ariz.Rev.Stat. §§ 12-901 to 12-932 (1982 & Supp.1984-85) (judicial review) and 41-1001 to 41-1015 (1974 & Supp.1975-1984). Special Project on State Regulatory Reform, 1985 Ariz.St. L.J. 249; Comment, Judicial Review of Administrative Action in Arizona, 1975 Ariz.St.L.J. 741.

* **Arkansas:** Ark.Stats. §§ 5-701 to 5-715.3, 6-608 to 6-612 (1976 & Supp.1983) (legislative oversight). See Wilson and Carnes, Judicial Review of Administrative Agencies in Arkansas, 25 Ark.L.Rev. 397 (1972); Derden, Survey of Arkansas

Law: Administrative Law, 2 U.Ark.Little Rock L.J. 157 (1979).

California: West's Ann.Cal.Gov't Code §§ 11340 to 11370.5, 11500 to 11528 (1980 & Supp.1985). See Clarkson, History of the California Administrative Procedure Act, 15 Hastings L.J. 237 (1964), and Bobby, Introduction to Practice and Procedure Under the California Administrative Procedure Act, id. at 258; California and Federal Administrative Due Process: Development, Interrelation and Direction, 5 U.C.D.L.Rev. 1 (1972); Comment, Administrative Decisions Review: Proposed Single Uniform Substantial Evidence Rule, 12 Pacific L.J. 41 (1980).

Colorado: Colo.Rev.Stat. 24-4-101 to 24-4-108 (1982 & Supp.1984). See Henry, The Colorado Administrative Procedure Act: Exclusions Demanding Reform, 44 Den.L.J. 42 (1967); Comment, Administrative Law—The Colorado Administrative Procedure Act—Colo.Rev.Stat.Ann. § 3-16-6. 51 Den.L.J. 275 (1974).

* **Connecticut:** Conn.Gen.Stat.Ann. §§ 4-166 to 4-189 (Supp.1985). See Feigen, Uniform Administrative Procedure Act—An Overview, 54 Conn.B.J. 537 (1980).

Delaware: Del.Code tit. 29., §§ 10101 to 10161 (1983).

* **District of Columbia:** D.C.Code 1981, §§ 1–1501 to 1–1542 (Supp.1985). See Frana, Current Problems Concerning the District of Columbia Administrative Procedure Act, 23 Ad.L.Rev. 3 (1970); Comment, Administrative Procedure in the District of Columbia—The APA and Beyond, 20 Am.U.L.Rev. 457 (1970–1971).

Florida: West's Fla.Stat.Ann. §§ 120.50 to 120.73 (1985). See Alford, Administrative Procedure Act, 48 Fla.B.J. 683 (1974); Levinson, The Florida Administrative Procedure Act: 1974 Revision and Amendments, 29 U.Miami L.Rev. 617 (1975); Oertal, Hearings Under the New Administrative Procedure Act, 49 Fla.B.J. 356 (1975); Note, Rulemaking and Adjudication Under the Florida Administrative Procedure Act, 27 U.Fla.L. Rev. 755 (1975); Symposium on the New Florida Administrative Procedure Act. 3 Fla.St.U.L.Rev. 64 (1976); Note, Can the Administrative Procedures Commission Solve Administrative Conflict? 4 Fla.St.U.L.Rev. 350 (1976); England and Levinson, Administrative Law, 31 U.Miami L.Rev. 749 (1977); Fox and Carson, A Comparison of the Federal and Florida Systems of Administrative Procedure 55 Fla.B.J. 699 (1980); Karl and Lehrman, Trends in Administrative Law, 54 Fla.B.J. 24 (1980); Dore, Access to Florida Administrative Proceedings, 13 Fla.St.U.L.Rev. 967 (1986).

* **Georgia:** Official Code Ga.Ann. §§ 50–13–1 to 50–13–22 (1982 & Supp.1985). See Feild, The Georgia Uniform Administrative Procedure Act, 1 Ga.St.B.J. 269 (1965); Hinchey, Administrative Law, 29 Mercer L.Rev. 1 (1977).

* **Hawaii:** Hawaii Rev.Stat. §§ 91–1 to 91–18 (1976 & Supp.1984). See Brown and Blankley, Standing to Challenge Administrative Action in the Federal and Hawaiian Courts, 8 Hawaii B.J. 37 (1971).

* **Idaho:** Idaho Code §§ 67–5201 to 67–5218 (1980 & Supp.1985). See Haman and Tunnicliff, Idaho Administrative Agencies and the New Administrative Procedure Act, 3 Idaho L.Rev. 61 (1966).

* **Illinois:** Ill.—S.H.A. ch. 110, §§ 3–101—3–112 (Smith-Hurd 1983 & Supp.1985) (judicial review), ch. 127, §§ 1001 to 1021 (Smith-Hurd 1981 & Supp.1985). See Freehling, Administrative Procedure Legislation in Illinois, 57 Ill.B.J. 364 (1969); Doering, Illinois Administrative Law, 23 De Paul L.Rev. 1 (1973); Note, The Illinois Administrative Procedure Act, 1976 U.Ill.L.F. 803; Gray, Administrative Law in Illinois, 8 Loy.U.Chi.L.J. 511 (1977); Note, Legislative Review of Administrative Actions, 50 Ill.L.J. 579 (1978); Burns, Judicial Enforcement of Illinois Administrative Procedure Act's

Rulemaking Provisions, 55 Chi.-Kent L.Rev. 383 (1979).

Indiana: Ind.Code Ann. 4–22–1–1 to 4–22–1–12 (Burns 1982 & Supp.1984). See Fuchs, Judicial Control of Administrative Agencies in Indiana, 28 Ind.L.J. 1 (1952), id. at 293 (1953); Dionisopoulos, Procedural Safeguards in Administrative Rulemaking in Indiana, 37 Ind.L.J. 423 (1962); Utken, Recent Developments in Indiana Law II: Administrative Law, 11 Ind.L.Rev. 20 (1978); Greenberg, Survey of Recent Developments in Indiana Law II: Administrative Law, 13 Ind.L.Rev. 39 (1980).

* **Iowa:** Iowa Code Ann. §§ 17A.1 to 17A.33 (West 1978 & Supp.1985). See Bezanson, Judicial Review of Administrative Action in Iowa, 21 Drake L.Rev. 1 (1971); Bonfield, The Iowa Administrative Procedure Act: Background, Construction, Applicability, Public Access to Agency Law, the Rulemaking Process, 60 Iowa L.Rev. 731 (1975), and The Definition of Formal Agency Adjudication Under the Iowa Administrative Procedure Act, 63 Iowa L.Rev. 285 (1977).

Kansas: Kan.Stat.Ann. 60–2101(d) (Supp. 1984) (judicial review) and 77–415 to 77–436 (1984). See Note, Kansas Administrative Regulations: A Tentative Step, 7 Washburn L.J. 61 (1967); Ainsworth and Shapiro, Rethinking Kansas Administrative Procedure, 28 Kansas L.Rev. 419 (1980); Ryan, Judicial Review of Administrative Action—Kansas Perspectives, 19 Washburn L.J. 423 (1980); Kansas Comment, Administrative Law, Findings of Fact, A Review of the Federal Administrative Procedure Act and Kansas Law, 22 Washburn L.J. 58 (1982).

Kentucky: Ky.Rev.Stat. 13A.010 to 13A.350 (Supp.1984). See Ziegler, Jr., A Primer on Administrative Rules and Rulemaking in Kentucky, 64 Ky.L.J. 103 (1978).

* **Louisiana:** LSA—Rev.Stat. 49:950 to 49:970 (West Supp.1985). See Baier, Administrative Regulation: Law and Procedure, 35 La.L.Rev. 349 (1975); Louisiana's "New" Administrative Procedure Act, 35 La.L.Rev. 629 (1975); R. Force and L. Griffith, The Louisiana Administrative Procedure Act, 42 La.L.Rev. 1227 (1982).

* **Maine:** Me.Rev.Stat.Ann. tit. 5, §§ 8001 to 10051, 11001 to 11116 (Supp.1985–1986). See Sawyer, The Quest for Justice in Maine Administrative Procedure: The Administrative Code in Application and Theory, 18 Me.L.Rev. 218 (1966).

* **Maryland:** Md.Code SG 10–101 to SG 10–405 (1984). See Sybert, Maryland Administrative Procedure—The Law and

the Lawyer, 61 Md.St.B.A. 175 (1956); Cohen, Some Aspects of Maryland Administrative Law, 24 Md.L.Rev. 1 (1964).

Massachusetts: Mass.Gen.Laws Ann. c. 30A, §§ 1 to 17 (Michie/Law.Co-op.1983 & Supp.1985). See Segal, The New Administrative Procedure Law of Massachusetts, 39 Mass.L.Q. (Oct.1954) at 31; Curran and Sacks, Massachusetts Administrative Procedure Act, 37 B.U.L. Rev. 70 (1957); Crowther, Jr. and F. Davis, The Massachusetts and Federal Efforts to Establish Uniform Procedural Rules for Administrative Agencies, 24 Ad.L.Rev. 213 (1972); Gahan, The Headless Fourth Branch of Government, 64 Mass.L.Rev. 21 (1979).

* Michigan: Mich.Comp.Laws Ann. §§ 24.201 to 24.315 (West 1981 and Supp. 1985). B.D. Figot, Annual Survey: Administrative Law, 30 Wayne L.Rev. 201 (1984); See Cramton and Holmes, The New Administrative Procedure Course Handbook (1970); Michigan—Comment, Legislative Veto: A Survey Constitutional Analysis and Empirical Study of its Effect in Michigan, 29 Wayne L.Rev. 91 (1982).

Minnesota: Minn.Stat.Ann. §§ 3.965 (West Supp.1982) (legislative oversight), 14.01 to 14.70 (West 1977 & Supp.1985). See Baird, Remedies by Judicial Review of Agency Action, 4 Wm.Mitchell L.Rev. 277 (1978); Auerbach, Administrative Rulemaking in Minnesota, 63 Minn.L. Rev. 151 (1979); Note, Definition of "Rule" under the Minnesota Administrative Procedure Act, 7 Wm.Mitchell L.Rev. 665 (1981).

* Mississippi: Miss.Code §§ 25–43–1 to 25–43–19 (Supp.1984).

* Missouri: Vernons Ann.Mo.Stat. §§ 536.010 to 536.215 (1949 & Supp. 1985). See Note, Federal and Missouri Administrative Procedure Acts: A Comparison, 17 Mo.L.Rev. 286 (1952); Shewmaker, Procedure Before, and Review of Decisions of, Missouri Administrative Agencies, 37 Mo.Ann.Stat. 145 (Vernon 1957); Spradley and Daugherty, A Present Look at Administrative Law Practice in Missouri, 27 Mo.B.J. 257 (1971); Lynch, Judicial Determination of the Validity of Administrative Agency Rules: A Forum Without Substance? 37 Mo.B.J. 81 (1981).

* Montana: Mont.Code Ann. 2–4–101 to 2–4–711 (1983). See McCrory, Administrative Procedures in Montana: A View After Four Years With the Montana Administrative Procedure Act, 38 Mont.L. Rev. 1 (1977).

* Nebraska: Neb.Rev.St. §§ 84–901 to 84–919 (Supp.1983). See Willborn, Time for

Change: A Critical Analysis of the Nebraska Administrative Procedure Act, 60 Neb.L.Rev. 1, (1981).

* Nevada: Nev.Rev.Stat. 233B.010 to 233B.150 (1983).

†New Hampshire: N.H.Rev.Stat.Ann. 541.1 to 541.22 (adjudication and judicial review), 541–A.1 to 541–A.21 (rulemaking) (Supp.1983).

New Jersey: N.J.Stat.Ann. 52:14B–1 to 52:14B–15 (West 1970 & Supp.1985). See Note, A Comparative Study of Administrative Procedure in New Jersey and the Model State Administrative Procedure Act, 7 Rutgers L.Rev. 465 (1953); Thomas, New Jersey Administrative Law: The Nature and Scope of Judicial Review, 8 Vill.L.Rev. 1 (1962); Note, The Department of Public Advocate—Public Interest Representation and Administrative Oversight, 30 Rutgers L.Rev. 386 (1977).

New Mexico: N.M.Stat.Ann. §§ 12–8–1 to 12–8–25 (Supp.1984). See Glidden and Utton, An Administrative Procedure Act for New Mexico, 8 Nat.Resources J. 114 (1968); Utton, How to Stand Still Without Really Trying: A Critique of the New Mexico Administrative Procedure Act, 10 Nat.Resources J. 840 (1970); Note, Administrative Law, 6 N.M.L.Rev. 401 (1976); Utton, The Use of the Substantial Evidence Rule to Review Administrative Findings of Fact in New Mexico, 10 N.M.L.Rev. 103 (1980).

* New York: N.Y.Ad.Proc.Act §§ 101 to 501 (Consol.1976 & Supp.1984), (N.Y.Civ. Prac.Law §§ 7801 to 7806 (Consol.1978 & Supp.1983) (judicial review). See Schwartz, Administrative Law, 26 Syracuse L.Rev. 1 (1975); Gifford, The New York State Administrative Procedure Act, 26 Buffalo L.Rev. 589 (1977); R.A. Herman, The New York Rulemaking Process: Rulemaking Procedures in New York, 47 Alb.L.Rev. 1051 (1983).

* North Carolina: N.C.Gen.Stat. §§ 150A–1 to 150A–64 (1983). See Daye, North Carolina's New Administrative Procedure Act: An Interpretive Analysis, 53 N.C.L.Rev. 833 (1975); Note, The Problems of Procedural Delay in Contested Case Hearings Under the North Carolina Administrative Procedure Act, 7 N.C.Cent.L.J. 347 (1976); Survey of Developments in North Carolina Law, 1980—Administrative Law, 59 N.C.L. Rev. 1017 (1981).

North Dakota: N.D.Cent.Code 28–32–1 to 28–32–21 (1974 & Supp.1983).

Ohio: Ohio Rev.Code §§ 119.01 to 119.12 (Baldwin 1982 & Supp.1984). See Pollack and Leach, Re-appraisal of Ohio

State Administrative Procedure Act, 11 Ohio St.L.J. (1950); Symposium on Administrative Law in Ohio, 13 Ohio St.L.J. 427 (1952); Anderson, A Comparative Analysis of the Federal and Ohio Administrative Procedure Acts, 24 U.Cin.L.Rev. 365 (1955); Melville, Legislative Control Over Administrative Rule Making, 32 U.Cin.L.Rev. 33 (1963); Note, A Survey of the Ohio Administrative Procedure Act, 22 Clev.St.L.Rev. 320 (1973); Note, Judicial Review of Administrative Decisions in Ohio, 34 Ohio St.L.J. 853 (1973); Warner, Remarks on the Attorney General's Proposed New Administrative Procedure Act for Ohio, 2 Ohio N.U.L.Rev. 462 (1975).

* **Oklahoma:** Okl.St.Ann. tit. 75, §§ 301 to 326 (West 1976 & Supp.1984–1985). See Merrill, Oklahoma's New Administrative Procedures Act, 17 Okla.L.Rev. 1 (1964); Cox, The Oklahoma Administrative Procedures Act: Fifteen Years of Interpretation, 31 Okla.L.Rev. 886 (1978). Oklahoma—M.P. Cox, The Oklahoma Administrative Procedures Act: an aid or a hindrance? 37 Okla.L.Rev. 1 (1984).

* **Oregon:** Or.Rev.Stat. 183.025 to 183.725 (1983). See Comment, The Oregon Administrative Procedure Act, 1 Willamette L.J. 233 (1960); Comment, Judicial Review Under the Oregon Apa: The Present Act and S.B. 300 Compared, 49 Or.L.Rev. 394 (1970); Comment, Validity of Agency Action Under the Oregon Apa: The Acid Test, 51 Or.L.Rev. 696 (1972); Frohnmayer, Oregon Administrative Procedure Act: An Essay on State Administrative Rulemaking Procedure Reform, 58 Or.L.Rev. 411 (1980); Frohnmayer, Oregon Attorney General's Administrative Law Manual (1986).

Pennsylvania: Pa.Stat. tit. 2 appendix §§ 101 to 754 (Purdon Supp.1964–1985); tit. 45, §§ 1102 to 1208 (Purdon Supp. 1965–1984) (rulemaking), Regulatory Review Act, 1982 Pa.Legis.Serv. 181 (Purdon). See Byse, Administrative Procedure Reform in Pennsylvania, 97 U.Pa.L. Rev. 22 (1948); Administrative Agency Practice and Procedure in Pennsylvania: A Symposium, 36 Temp.L.Q. 385 (1963), including Ruben, The Administrative Agency Law: Reform of Adjudicative Procedure and the Revised Model Act, at 388; Zieder, Pennsylvania General Rules of Practice and Procedure—A Surprising By-Product of a State Register System, 24 Ad.L.Rev. 275 (1972); Nalmod, Thoughts on Pennsylvania Administrative Law, 15 Duq.L.Rev. 573 (1977).

* **Rhode Island:** R.I.Gen.Laws §§ 42–35–1 to 42–35–18 (1984 & Supp.1984). See Note, Administrative Law in Rhode Island: The Judiciary's Search for a Path Toward Efficient Democratic Government, 13 Suffolk U.L.Rev. 553 (1979).

South Carolina: S.C.Code §§ 1–23–10 to 1–23–400 (Law, Co-op. Supp.1984). See Steer, Administrative Procedure Act, 30 S.C.L.Rev. 1 (1979); Comment, Legislative Oversight and the South Carolina Experience, 34 S.C.L.Rev. 595 (1982).

* **South Dakota:** S.D.Codified Laws 1–26–1 to 1–26–41, 1–26A–1 to 1–26A–10 (publication of rules), 1–26B–1 to 1–26B–12 (legislative oversight) (Supp.1984).

* **Tennessee:** Tenn.Code Ann. §§ 4–5–101 to 4–5–323 (Supp.1984). See Symposium, Tennessee Administrative Law, 13 Memphis St.L.Rev. 461 (1983); Symposium, The Tennessee Uniform Administrative Procedure Act, 6 Mem.St.U.L.Rev. 143 (1976); Bates, State Rulemaking Under the Administrative Procedure Act: Legal Remedies, 16 Tenn.B.J., May 1980 at 21.

Texas: Tex.Civ.Stat.Ann. art. 6252–13(a) (Vernon Supp.1985). See Guinn, Administrative Law, 24 SW.L.J. 216 (1970); Guinn, Administrative Law, 25 SW.L.J. 201 (1971); Hamilton and Jewett, The Administrative Procedure and Texas Register Act: Contested Cases and Judicial Review, 54 Tex.L.Rev. 285 (1976); McCalla, The Administrative Procedure and Texas Evidence in Texas Register Act, 28 Baylor L.Rev. 445 (1976); Kuhl, Evidence in Texas Administrative Adjudication), 15 Hous.L.Rev. 682 (1978); Note, The Future of Judicial Review Under the Administrative Procedure and Texas Register Act, 57 Tex.L.Rev. 253 (1979); Hill and Kent, Annual Survey of Texas Law: Administrative Law, 34 SW.L.J. 471 (1980); Shannon and Ewbank II, Texas Administrative Procedure and Texas Register Act Since 1976—Selected Problems, 33 Baylor L.Rev. 393 (1981); Watkins and Beck, Judicial Review of Rulemaking Under the Texas Administrative Procedure and Texas Register Act, 34 Baylor L.Rev. 1 (1982); Comment, Emergency Rulemaking in Texas: What's the Rush?, 35 Baylor L.Rev. 323 (1983).

Utah: Utah Code Ann. 63–46–1 to 63–46–13 (Supp.1983) (rulemaking), Utah R.Civ. P. 81(a). See Note, Recent Developments in Utah Law, 1980 Utah L.Rev. 649.

* **Vermont:** Vt.Stat.Ann. tit. 3, §§ 801 to 849 (Supp.1984).

Virginia: Va.Code §§ 9–6.14:1 to 9–6.14:25, 9–6.15 to 9–6.22 (1978 & Supp. 1985). See Comment, Administrative Law, 61 Va.L.Rev. 1632 (1975).

* **Washington:** West's Rev.Code Wash. Ann. 34.04.010 to 34.04.940 (1965 & Supp.1985); 34.08.010 to 34.08.910 (Supp.

UNIFORM LAW COMMISSIONERS' MODEL STATE ADMINISTRATIVE PROCEDURE ACT (1981)

ARTICLE I

GENERAL PROVISIONS

ARTICLE II

PUBLIC ACCESS TO AGENCY LAW AND POLICY

1985) (publication of rules). See Comment, Administrative Law—Combination of Functions: May an Administrative Tribunal be Both Prosecutor and Judge? 45 Wash.L.Rev. 411 (1971); Andersen, Judicial Review of Agency Fact-Finding in Washington 13 Willamette L.J. 397 (1977); Abrahams, Scope of Review of Administrative Action in Washington, 14 Gonz.L.Rev. 75 (1978).

* **West Virginia:** W.Va.Code, 29A-1-1 to 29A-7-4 (1980 & Supp.1984). See Harrison, The West Virginia Administrative Procedure Act, 66 W.Va.L.Rev. 159 (1964); Note, Administrative Procedure—Judicial Review—Abolition of Extraordinary Writs, 77 W.Va.L.Rev. 548 (1975); Neely, Rights and Responsibilities in Administrative Rule Making in West Virginia, 79 W.Va.L.Rev. 513 (1977); Note, Survey of Developments in West Virginia Law: 1977—Administrative Law, 80 W.Va.L.Rev. 113 (1978).

* **Wisconsin:** Wis.Stat.Ann. 227.01 to 227.26 (West 1982 & Supp.1984-85). See Simon, Administrative Procedure, 43 Wis.B.Bull., Feb. 1970 at 42; Van Susteren, Administrative Procedure: "Something is Being Done", 43 Wis.B.Bull., April 1970 at 42; Mayer, Methods of Judicial Review of Administrative Agency Decisions in Wisconsin, 53 Wis.B. Bull., Jan. 1980 at 27; Leonhardt, Administrative Rules, 53 Wis.B.Bull., Dec. 1980 at 28; Comment, Standard of Review of Administrative Rules in Wisconsin, 1982 Wis.L.Rev. 691.

* **Wyoming:** Wyo.Stat. §§ 16-3-101 to 16-3-115 (1982). See Bloomenthal, Administrative Law in Wyoming—An Introduction and Preliminary Report. 16 Wyo. L.J. 191 (1962); Legislative Comment, The Wyoming Administrative Procedure Act, 1 Land & Water L.Rev. 497 (1966); Comment, Wyoming's Administrative Regulation Review Act, 14 Land & Water L.Rev. 189 (1979); Singer, Administrative Regulation Review Act II, 15 Land & Water L.Rev. 207 (1980); Battle, Jackson B., Administrative Law, Wyoming Style, 18 Land & Water L.Rev. 223 (1983).

ARTICLE III

RULE MAKING

Chapter I

Adoption and Effectiveness of Rules

Chapter II

Review of Agency Rules

ARTICLE IV

ADJUDICATIVE PROCEEDINGS

Chapter I

Availability of Adjudicative Proceedings; Applications; Licenses

Chapter II

Formal Adjudicative Hearing

Chapter III

Office of Administrative Hearings

Chapter IV

Conference Adjudicative Hearing

Chapter V

Emergency and Summary Adjudicative Proceedings

ARTICLE V

JUDICIAL REVIEW AND CIVIL ENFORCEMENT

Chapter I

Judicial Review

Chapter II

Civil Enforcement

ARTICLE I

GENERAL PROVISIONS

§ 1–101. [Short Title]

This Act may be cited as the [state] Administrative Procedure Act.

§ 1–102. [Definitions]

As used in this Act:

(1) "Agency" means a board, commission, department, officer, or other administrative unit of this State, including the agency head, and one or more members of the agency head or agency employees or other persons directly or indirectly purporting to act on behalf or under the authority of the agency head. The term does not include the [legislature] or the courts [, or the governor] [, or the governor in the exercise of powers derived directly and exclusively from the constitution of this State]. The term does not include a political subdivision of the state or any of the administrative units of a political subdivision, but it does include a board, commission, department, officer, or other administrative unit created or appointed by joint or concerted action of an agency and one or more political subdivisions of the state or any of their units. To the extent it purports to exercise authority subject to any provision of this Act, an administrative unit otherwise qualifying as an "agency" must be treated as a separate agency even if the unit is located within or subordinate to another agency.

(2) "Agency action" means:

(i) the whole or a part of a rule or an order;

(ii) the failure to issue a rule or an order; or

(iii) an agency's performance of, or failure to perform, any other duty, function, or activity, discretionary or otherwise.

(3) "Agency head" means an individual or body of individuals in whom the ultimate legal authority of the agency is vested by any provision of law.

(4) "License" means a franchise, permit, certification, approval, registration, charter, or similar form of authorization required by law.

(5) "Order" means an agency action of particular applicability that determines the legal rights, duties, privileges, immunities, or other legal interests of one or more specific persons. [The term does not include an "executive order" issued by the governor pursuant to Section 1–104 or 3–202.]

(6) "Party to agency proceedings," or "party" in context so indicating, means:

(i) a person to whom the agency action is specifically directed; or

(ii) a person named as a party to an agency proceeding or allowed to intervene or participate as a party in the proceeding.

(7) "Party to judicial review or civil enforcement proceedings," or "party" in context so indicating, means:

(i) a person who files a petition for judicial review or civil enforcement or

(ii) a person named as a party in a proceeding for judicial review or civil enforcement or allowed to participate as a party in the proceeding.

(8) "Person" means an individual, partnership, corporation, association, governmental subdivision or unit thereof, or public or private organization or entity of any character, and includes another agency.

(9) "Provision of law" means the whole or a part of the federal or state constitution, or of any federal or state (i) statute, (ii) rule of court, (iii) executive order, or (iv) rule of an administrative agency.

(10) "Rule" means the whole or a part of an agency statement of general applicability that implements, interprets, or prescribes (i) law or policy, or (ii) the organization, procedure, or practice requirements of an agency. The term includes the amendment, repeal, or suspension of an existing rule.

(11) "Rule making" means the process for formulation and adoption of a rule.

§ 1–103. [Applicability and Relation to Other Law]

(a) This Act applies to all agencies and all proceedings not expressly exempted.

(b) This Act creates only procedural rights and imposes only procedural duties. They are in addition to those created and imposed by other statutes. To the extent that any other statute would diminish a right created or duty imposed by this Act, the other statute is superseded by this Act, unless the other statute expressly provides otherwise.

(c) An agency may grant procedural rights to persons in addition to those conferred by this Act so long as rights conferred upon other persons by any provision of law are not substantially prejudiced.

§ 1–104. [Suspension of Act's Provisions When Necessary to Avoid Loss of Federal Funds or Services]

(a) To the extent necessary to avoid a denial of funds or services from the United States which would otherwise be available to the state, the [governor by executive order] [attorney general by rule] [may] [shall] suspend, in whole or in part, one or more provisions of this Act. The [governor by executive order] [attorney general by rule] shall declare the termination of a suspension as soon as it is no longer necessary to prevent the loss of funds or services from the United States.

[(b) An executive order issued under subsection (a) is subject to the requirements applicable to the adoption and effectiveness of a rule.]

(c) If any provision of this Act is suspended pursuant to this section, the [governor] [attorney general] shall promptly report the suspension to the [legislature]. The report must include recommendations concerning any desirable legislation that may be necessary to conform this Act to federal law.]

§ 1–105. [Waiver]

Except to the extent precluded by another provision of law, a person may waive any right conferred upon that person by this Act.

§ 1–106. [Informal Settlements]

Except to the extent precluded by another provision of law, informal settlement of matters that may make unnecessary more elaborate proceedings under this Act is encouraged. Agencies shall establish by rule specific procedures to facilitate informal settlement of matters. This section does not require any party or other person to settle a matter pursuant to informal procedures.

§ 1–107. [Conversion of Proceedings]

(a) At any point in an agency proceeding the presiding officer or other agency official responsible for the proceeding:

(1) may convert the proceeding to another type of agency proceeding provided for by this Act if the conversion is appropriate, is in the public interest, and does not substantially prejudice the rights of any party; and

(2) if required by any provision of law, shall convert the proceeding to another type of agency proceeding provided for by this Act.

(b) A conversion of a proceeding of one type to a proceeding of another type may be effected only upon notice to all parties to the original proceeding.

(c) If the presiding officer or other agency official responsible for the original proceeding would not have authority over the new proceeding to which it is to be converted, that officer or official, in accordance with agency rules, shall secure the appointment of a successor to preside over or be responsible for the new proceeding.

(d) To the extent feasible and consistent with the rights of parties and the requirements of this Act pertaining to the new proceeding, the record of the original agency proceeding must be used in the new agency proceeding.

(e) After a proceeding is converted from one type to another, the presiding officer or other agency official responsible for the new proceeding shall:

(1) give such additional notice to parties or other persons as is necessary to satisfy the requirements of this Act pertaining to those proceedings;

(2) dispose of the matters involved without further proceedings if sufficient proceedings have already been held to satisfy the requirements of this Act pertaining to the new proceedings; and

(3) conduct or cause to be conducted any additional proceedings necessary to satisfy the requirements of this Act pertaining to those proceedings.

(f) Each agency shall adopt rules to govern the conversion of one type of proceeding to another. Those rules must include an enumeration of the factors to be considered in determining whether and under what circumstances one type of proceeding will be converted to another.

§ 1–108. [Effective Date]

This Act takes effect on [date] and does not govern proceedings pending on that date. This Act governs all agency proceedings, and all proceedings for judicial review or civil enforcement of agency action, commenced after that date. This Act also governs agency proceedings conducted on a remand from a court or another agency after the effective date of this Act.

§ 1–109. [Severability]

If any provision of this Act or the application thereof to any person or circumstance is held invalid, the invalidity does not affect other provisions or applications of the Act which can be given effect without the invalid provision or application, and for this purpose the provisions of this Act are severable.

ARTICLE II

PUBLIC ACCESS TO AGENCY LAW AND POLICY

§ 2–101. [Administrative Rules Editor; Publication, Compilation, Indexing, and Public Inspection of Rules]

(a) There is created, within the executive branch, an [administrative rules editor]. The governor shall appoint the [administrative rules editor] who shall serve at the pleasure of the governor.

(b) Subject to the provisions of this Act, the [administrative rules editor] shall prescribe a uniform numbering system, form, and style for all proposed and adopted rules caused to be published by that office [, and shall have the same editing authority with respect to the publication of rules as the [reviser of statutes] has with respect to the publication of statutes].

(c) The [administrative rules editor] shall cause the [administrative bulletin] to be published in pamphlet form [once each week]. For purposes of calculating adherence to time requirements imposed by this Act, an issue of the [administrative bulletin] is deemed published on the later of the date indicated in that issue or the date of its mailing. The [administrative bulletin] must contain:

(1) notices of proposed rule adoption prepared so that the text of the proposed rule shows the text of any existing rule proposed to be changed and the change proposed;

(2) newly filed adopted rules prepared so that the text of the newly filed adopted rule shows the text of any existing rule being changed and the change being made;

(3) any other notices and materials designated by [law] [the administrative rules editor] for publication therein; and

(4) an index to its contents by subject.

(d) The [administrative rules editor] shall cause the [administrative code] to be compiled, indexed by subject, and published [in loose-leaf form]. All of the effective rules of each agency must be published and indexed in that publication. The [administrative rules editor] shall also cause [loose-leaf] supplements to the [administrative code] to be published at least every [3 months]. [The loose-leaf supplements must be in a form suitable for insertion in the appropriate places in the permanent [administrative code] compilation.]

(e) The [administrative rules editor] may omit from the [administrative bulletin or code] any proposed or filed adopted rule the publication of which would be unduly cumbersome, expensive, or otherwise inexpedient, if:

(1) knowledge of the rule is likely to be important to only a small class of persons;

(2) on application to the issuing agency, the proposed or adopted rule in printed or processed form is made available at no more than its cost of reproduction; and

(3) the [administrative bulletin or code] contains a notice stating in detail the specific subject matter of the omitted proposed or adopted rule and how a copy of the omitted material may be obtained.

(f) The [administrative bulletin and administrative code] must be furnished to [designated officials] without charge and to all subscribers at a cost to be determined by the [administrative rules editor]. Each agency shall also make available for public inspection and copying those portions of the [administrative bulletin and administrative code] containing all rules adopted or used by the agency in the discharge of its functions, and the index to those rules.

(g) Except as otherwise required by a provision of law, subsections (c) through (f) do not apply to rules governed by Section 3–116, and the following provisions apply instead:

(1) Each agency shall maintain an official, current, and dated compilation that is indexed by subject, containing all of its rules within the scope of Section 3–116. Each addition to, change in, or deletion from the official compilation must also be dated, indexed, and a record thereof kept. Except for those portions containing rules governed by Section 3–116(2), the compilation must be made available for public inspection and copying. Certified copies of the full compilation must also be furnished to the [secretary of state, the administrative rules counsel, and members of the administrative rules review committee], and be kept current by the agency at least every [30] days.

(2) A rule subject to the requirements of this subsection may not be relied on by an agency to the detriment of any person who does not have actual, timely knowledge of the contents of the rule until the requirements of paragraph (1) are satisfied. The burden of proving that knowledge is on the agency. This provision is also inapplicable to the extent necessary to avoid imminent peril to the public health, safety, or welfare.

§ 2–102. [Public Inspection and Indexing of Agency Orders]

(a) In addition to other requirements imposed by any provision of law, each agency shall make all written final orders available for public inspection and copying and index them by name and subject. An agency shall delete from those orders identifying details to the extent required by any provision of law [or necessary to prevent a clearly unwarranted invasion of privacy or release of trade secrets]. In each case the justification for the deletion must be explained in writing and attached to the order.

(b) A written final order may not be relied on as precedent by an agency to the detriment of any person until it has been made available for public inspection and indexed in the manner described in subsection (a). This provision is inapplicable to any person who has actual timely knowledge of the order. The burden of proving that knowledge is on the agency.

§ 2–103. [Declaratory Orders]

(a) Any person may petition an agency for a declaratory order as to the applicability to specified circumstances of a statute, rule, or order within the primary jurisdiction of the agency. An agency shall issue a declaratory order in response to a petition for that order unless the agency determines that issuance of the order under the circumstances would be contrary to a rule adopted in accordance with subsection (b). However, an agency may not issue a declaratory order that would substantially prejudice the rights of a person who would be a necessary party and who does not consent in writing to the determination of the matter by a declaratory order proceeding.

(b) Each agency shall issue rules that provide for: (i) the form, contents, and filing of petitions for declaratory orders; (ii) the procedural rights of persons in relation to the petitions and (iii) the disposition of the petitions. Those rules must describe the classes of circumstances in which the agency will not issue a declaratory order and must be consistent with the public interest and with the general policy of this Act to facilitate and encourage agency issuance of reliable advice.

(c) Within [15] days after receipt of a petition for a declaratory order, an agency shall give notice of the petition to all persons to whom notice is required by any provision of law and may give notice to any other persons.

(d) Persons who qualify under Section 4–209(a)(2) and (3) and file timely petitions for intervention according to agency rules may intervene in proceedings for declaratory orders. Other provisions of Article IV apply to agency proceedings for declaratory orders only to the extent an agency so provides by rule or order.

(e) Within [30] days after receipt of a petition for a declaratory order an agency, in writing, shall:

(1) issue an order declaring the applicability of the statute, rule, or order in question to the specified circumstances;

(2) set the matter for specified proceedings;

(3) agree to issue a declaratory order by a specified time; or

(4) decline to issue a declaratory order, stating the reasons for its action.

(f) A copy of all orders issued in response to a petition for a declaratory order must be mailed promptly to petitioner and any other parties.

(g) A declaratory order has the same status and binding effect as any other order issued in an agency adjudicative proceeding. A declaratory order must contain the names of all parties to the proceeding on which it is based, the particular facts on which it is based, and the reasons for its conclusion.

(h) If an agency has not issued a declaratory order within [60] days after receipt of a petition therefor, the petition is deemed to have been denied.

§ 2–104. [Required Rule Making]

In addition to other rule-making requirements imposed by law, each agency shall:

(1) adopt as a rule a description of the organization of the agency which states the general course and method of its operations and where and how the public may obtain information or make submissions or requests;

(2) adopt rules of practice setting forth the nature and requirements of all formal and informal procedures available to the public,

including a description of all forms and instructions that are to be used by the public in dealing with the agency; [and]

(3) as soon as feasible and to the extent practicable, adopt rules, in addition to those otherwise required by this Act, embodying appropriate standards, principles, and procedural safeguards that the agency will apply to the law it administers[; and][.]

[(4) as soon as feasible and to the extent practicable, adopt rules to supersede principles of law or policy lawfully declared by the agency as the basis for its decisions in particular cases.]

§ 2–105. [Model Rules of Procedure]

In accordance with the rule-making requirements of this Act, the [attorney general] shall adopt model rules of procedure appropriate for use by as many agencies as possible. The model rules must deal with all general functions and duties performed in common by several agencies. Each agency shall adopt as much of the model rules as is practicable under its circumstances. To the extent an agency adopts the model rules, it shall do so in accordance with the rule-making requirements of this Act. Any agency adopting a rule of procedure that differs from the model rules shall include in the rule a finding stating the reasons why the relevant portions of the model rules were impracticable under the circumstances.

ARTICLE III

RULE MAKING

CHAPTER I

ADOPTION AND EFFECTIVENESS OF RULES

§ 3–101. [Advise on Possible Rules Before Notice of Proposed Rule Adoption]

(a) In addition to seeking information by other methods, an agency, before publication of a notice of proposed rule adoption under Section 3–103, may solicit comments from the public on a subject matter of possible rule making under active consideration within the agency by causing notice to be published in the [administrative bulletin] of the subject matter and indicating where, when, and how persons may comment.

(b) Each agency may also appoint committees to comment, before publication of a notice of proposed rule adoption under Section 3–103, on the subject matter of a possible rule making under active consideration within the agency. The membership of those committees must be published at least [annually] in the [administrative bulletin].

§ 3–102. [Public Rule-Making Docket]

(a) Each agency shall maintain a current, public rule-making docket.

(b) The rule-making docket [must] [may] contain a listing of the precise subject matter of each possible rule currently under active consideration within the agency for proposal under Section 3–103, the name and address of agency personnel with whom persons may communicate with respect to the matter, and an indication of the present status within the agency of that possible rule.

(c) The rule-making docket must list each pending rule-making proceeding. A rule-making proceeding is pending from the time it is commenced, by publication of a notice of proposed rule adoption, to the time it is terminated, by publication of a notice of termination or the rule becoming effective. For each rule-making proceeding, the docket must indicate:

(1) the subject matter of the proposed rule;

(2) a citation to all published notices relating to the proceeding;

(3) where written submissions on the proposed rule may be inspected;

(4) the time during which written submissions may be made;

(5) the names of persons who have made written requests for an opportunity to make oral presentations on the proposed rule, where those requests may be inspected, and where and when oral presentations may be made;

(6) whether a written request for the issuance of a regulatory analysis of the proposed rule has been filed, whether that analysis has been issued, and where the written request and analysis may be inspected;

(7) the current status of the proposed rule and any agency determinations with respect thereto;

(8) any known timetable for agency decisions or other action in the proceeding;

(9) the date of the rule's adoption;

(10) the date of the rule's filing, indexing, and publication; and

(11) when the rule will become effective.

§ 3-103. [Notice of Proposed Rule Adoption]

(a) At least [30] days before the adoption of a rule an agency shall cause notice of its contemplated action to be published in the [administrative bulletin]. The notice of proposed rule adoption must include:

(1) a short explanation of the purpose of the proposed rule;

(2) the specific legal authority authorizing the proposed rule;

(3) subject to Section 2–101(e), the text of the proposed rule;

(4) where, when, and how persons may present their views on the proposed rule; and

(5) where, when, and how persons may demand an oral proceeding on the proposed rule if the notice does not already provide for one.

(b) Within [3] days after its publication in the [administrative bulletin], the agency shall cause a copy of the notice of proposed rule adoption to be mailed to each person who has made a timely request to the agency for a mailed copy of the notice. An agency may charge persons for the actual cost of providing them with mailed copies.

§ 3–104. [Public Participation]

(a) For at least [30] days after publication of the notice of proposed rule adoption, an agency shall afford persons the opportunity to submit in writing, argument, data, and views on the proposed rule.

(b)(1) An agency shall schedule an oral proceeding on a proposed rule if, within [20] days after the published notice of proposed rule adoption, a written request for an oral proceeding is submitted by [the administrative rules review committee,] [the administrative rules counsel,] a political subdivision, an agency, or [25] persons. At that proceeding, persons may present oral argument, data, and views on the proposed rule.

(2) An oral proceeding on a proposed rule, if required, may not be held earlier than [20] days after notice of its location and time is published in the [administrative bulletin].

(3) The agency, a member of the agency, or another presiding officer designated by the agency, shall preside at a required oral proceeding on a proposed rule. If the agency does not preside, the presiding official shall prepare a memorandum for consideration by the agency summarizing the contents of the presentations made at the oral proceeding. Oral proceedings must be open to the public and be recorded by stenographic or other means.

(4) Each agency shall issue rules for the conduct of oral rule-making proceedings. Those rules may include provisions calculated to prevent undue repetition in the oral proceedings.

§ 3–105. [Regulatory Analysis]

(a) An agency shall issue a regulatory analysis of a proposed rule if, within [20] days after the published notice of proposed rule adoption, a written request for the analysis is filed in the office of the [secretary of state] by [the administrative rules review committee, the governor, a political subdivision, an agency, or [300] persons signing the request]. The [secretary of state] shall immediately forward to the agency a certified copy of the filed request.

(b) Except to the extent that the written request expressly waives one or more of the following, the regulatory analysis must contain:

(1) a description of the classes of persons who probably will be affected by the proposed rule, including classes that will bear the costs of the proposed rule and classes that will benefit from the proposed rule;

(2) a description of the probable quantitative and qualitative impact of the proposed rule, economic or otherwise, upon affected classes of persons;

(3) the probable costs to the agency and to any other agency of the implementation and enforcement of the proposed rule and any anticipated effect on state revenues;

(4) a comparison of the probable costs and benefits of the proposed rule to the probable costs and benefits of inaction;

(5) a determination of whether there are less costly methods or less intrusive methods for achieving the purpose of the proposed rule; and

(6) a description of any alternative methods for achieving the purpose of the proposed rule that were seriously considered by the agency and the reasons why they were rejected in favor of the proposed rule.

(c) Each regulatory analysis must include quantification of the data to the extent practicable and must take account of both short-term and long-term consequences.

(d) A concise summary of the regulatory analysis must be published in the [administrative bulletin] at least [10] days before the earliest of:

(1) the end of the period during which persons may make written submissions on the proposed rule;

(2) the end of the period during which an oral proceeding may be requested; or

(3) the date of any required oral proceeding on the proposed rule.

(e) The published summary of the regulatory analysis must also indicate where persons may obtain copies of the full text of the regulatory analysis and where, when, and how persons may present their views on the proposed rule and demand an oral proceeding thereon if one is not already provided.

(f) If the agency has made a good faith effort to comply with the requirements of subsections (a) through (c), the rule may not be invalidated on the ground that the contents of the regulatory analysis are insufficient or inaccurate.

§ 3–106. [Time and Manner of Rule Adoption]

(a) An agency may not adopt a rule until the period for making written submissions and oral presentations has expired.

(b) Within [180] days after the later of (i) the publication of the notice of proposed rule adoption, or (ii) the end of oral proceedings thereon, an agency shall adopt a rule pursuant to the rule-making proceeding or terminate the proceeding by publication of a notice to that effect in the [administrative bulletin].

(c) Before the adoption of a rule, an agency shall consider the written submissions, oral submissions or any memorandum summarizing oral submissions, and any regulatory analysis, provided for by this Chapter.

(d) Within the scope of its delegated authority, an agency may use its own experience, technical competence, specialized knowledge, and judgment in the adoption of a rule.

§ 3–107. [Variance Between Adopted Rule and Published Notice of Proposed Rule Adoption]

(a) An agency may not adopt a rule that is substantially different from the proposed rule contained in the published notice of proposed rule adoption. However, an agency may terminate a rule-making proceeding and commence a new rule-making proceeding for the purpose of adopting a substantially different rule.

(b) In determining whether an adopted rule is substantially different from the published proposed rule upon which it is required to be based, the following must be considered:

(1) the extent to which all persons affected by the adopted rule should have understood that the published proposed rule would affect their interests;

(2) the extent to which the subject matter of the adopted rule or the issues determined by that rule are different from the subject matter or issues involved in the published proposed rule; and

(3) the extent to which the effects of the adopted rule differ from the effects of the published proposed rule had it been adopted instead.

§ 3–108. [General Exemption From Public Rule-Making Procedures]

(a) To the extent an agency for good cause finds that any requirements of Sections 3–103 through 3–107 are unnecessary, impracticable, or contrary to the public interest in the process of adopting a particular rule, those requirements do not apply. The agency shall incorporate the required finding and a brief statement of its supporting reasons in each rule adopted in reliance upon this subsection.

(b) In an action contesting a rule adopted under subsection (a), the burden is upon the agency to demonstrate that any omitted requirements of Sections 3–103 through 3–107 were impracticable, unnecessary, or contrary to the public interest in the particular circumstances involved.

(c) Within [2] years after the effective date of a rule adopted under subsection (a), the [administrative rules review committee or the governor] may request the agency to hold a rule-making proceeding thereon according to the requirements of Sections 3–103 through 3–107. The request must be in writing and filed in the office of the [secretary of state]. The [secretary of state] shall immediately forward to the agency and to the [administrative rules editor] a certified copy of the request. Notice of the filing of the request must be published in the next issue of the [administrative bulletin]. The rule in question ceases to be effective [180] days after the request is filed. However, an agency, after the filing of the request, may subsequently adopt an identical rule in a rulemaking proceeding conducted pursuant to the requirements of Sections 3–103 through 3–107.

§ 3–109. [Exemption for Certain Rules]

(a) An agency need not follow the provisions of Sections 3–103 through 3–108 in the adoption of a rule that only defines the meaning of a statute or other provision of law or precedent if the agency does not possess delegated authority to bind the courts to any extent with its definition. A rule adopted under this subsection must include a statement that it was adopted under this subsection when it is published in the [administrative bulletin], and there must be an indication to that effect adjacent to the rule when it is published in the [administrative code].

(b) A reviewing court shall determine wholly de novo the validity of a rule within the scope of subsection (a) that is adopted without complying with the provisions of Sections 3–103 through 3–108.

§ 3–110. [Concise Explanatory Statement]

(a) At the time it adopts a rule, an agency shall issue a concise explanatory statement containing:

(1) its reasons for adopting the rule; and

(2) an indication of any change between the text of the proposed rule contained in the published notice of proposed rule adoption and the text of the rule as finally adopted, with the reasons for any change.

(b) Only the reasons contained in the concise explanatory statement may be used by any party as justifications for the adoption of the rule in any proceeding in which its validity is at issue.

§ 3–111. [Contents, Style, and Form of Rule]

(a) Each rule adopted by an agency must contain the text of the rule and:

(1) the date the agency adopted the rule;

(2) a concise statement of the purpose of the rule;

(3) a reference to all rules repealed, amended, or suspended by the rule;

(4) a reference to the specific statutory or other authority authorizing adoption of the rule;

(5) any findings required by any provision of law as a prerequisite to adoption or effectiveness of the rule; and

(6) the effective date of the rule if other than that specified in Section 3–115(a).

[(b) To the extent feasible, each rule should be written in clear and concise language understandable to persons who may be affected by it.]

(c) An agency may incorporate, by reference in its rules and without publishing the incorporated matter in full, all or any part of a code, standard, rule, or regulation that has been adopted by an agency of the United States or of this state, another state, or by a nationally recognized organization or association, if incorporation of its text in agency rules would be unduly cumbersome, expensive, or otherwise inexpedient. The reference in the agency rules must fully identify the incorporated matter by location, date, and otherwise, [and must state that the rule does not include any later amendments or editions of the incorporated matter]. An agency may incorporate by reference such matter in its rules only if the agency, organization, or association originally issuing that matter makes copies of it readily available to the public. The rules must state where copies of the incorporated matter are available at cost from the agency issuing the rule, and where copies are available from the agency of the United States, this State, another state, or the organization or association originally issuing that matter.

(d) In preparing its rules pursuant to this Chapter, each agency shall follow the uniform numbering system, form, and style prescribed by the [administrative rules editor].

§ 3–112. [Agency Rule-Making Record]

(a) An agency shall maintain an official rule-making record for each rule it (i) proposes by publication in the [administrative bulletin] of a notice of proposed rule adoption, or (ii) adopts. The record and materials incorporated by reference must be available for public inspection.

(b) The agency rule-making record must contain:

(1) copies of all publications in the [administrative bulletin] with respect to the rule or the proceeding upon which the rule is based;

(2) copies of any portions of the agency's public rule-making docket containing entries relating to the rule or the proceeding upon which the rule is based;

(3) all written petitions, requests, submissions, and comments received by the agency and all other written materials considered by the agency in connection with the formulation, proposal, or adoption of the rule or the proceeding upon which the rule is based;

(4) any official transcript of oral presentations made in the proceeding upon which the rule is based or, if not transcribed, any tape recording or stenographic record of those presentations, and any memorandum prepared by a presiding official summarizing the contents of those presentations;

(5) a copy of any regulatory analysis prepared for the proceeding upon which the rule is based;

(6) a copy of the rule and explanatory statement filed in the office of the [secretary of state];

(7) all petitions for exceptions to, amendments of, or repeal or suspension of, the rule;

(8) a copy of any request filed pursuant to Section 3–108(c);

[(9) a copy of any objection to the rule filed by the [administrative rules review committee] pursuant to Section 3–204(d) and the agency's response;] and

(10) a copy of any filed executive order with respect to the rule.

(c) Upon judicial review, the record required by this section constitutes the official agency rule-making record with respect to a rule. Except as provided in Section 3–110(b) or otherwise required by a provision of law, the agency rule-making record need not constitute the exclusive basis for agency action on that rule or for judicial review thereof.

§ 3–113. [Invalidity of Rules Not Adopted According to Chapter; Time Limitation]

(a) A rule adopted after [date] is invalid unless adopted in substantial compliance with the provisions of Sections 3–102 through 3–108 and Sections 3–110 through 3–112. However, inadvertent failure to mail a notice of proposed rule adoption to any person as required by Section 3–103(b) does not invalidate a rule.

(b) An action to contest the validity of a rule on the grounds of its noncompliance with any provision of Sections 3–102 through 3–108 or Sections 3–110 through 3–112 must be commenced within [2] years after the effective date of the rule.

§ 3–114. [Filing of Rules]

(a) An agency shall file in the office of the [secretary of state] each rule it adopts and all rules existing on the effective date of this Act that have not previously been filed. The filing must be done as soon after adoption of the rule as is practicable. At the time of filing, each rule adopted after the effective date of this Act must have attached to it the explanatory statement required by Section 3–110. The [secretary of state] shall affix to each rule and statement a certification of the time and date of filing and keep a permanent register open to public inspection of all filed rules and attached explanatory statements. In filing a rule, each agency shall use a standard form prescribed by the [secretary of state].

(b) The [secretary of state] shall transmit to the [administrative rules editor], [administrative rules counsel], and to the members of the [administrative rules review committee] a certified copy of each filed rule as soon after its filing as is practicable.

§ 3–115. [Effective Date of Rules]

(a) Except to the extent subsection (b) or (c) provides otherwise, each rule adopted after the effective date of this Act becomes effective [30] days after the later of (i) its filing in the office of the [secretary of state] or (ii) its publication and indexing in the [administrative bulletin].

(b)(1) A rule becomes effective on a date later than that established by subsection (a) if a later date is required by another statute or specified in the rule.

(2) A rule may become effective immediately upon its filing or on any subsequent date earlier than that established by subsection (a) if the agency establishes such an effective date and finds that:

(i) it is required by constitution, statute, or court order;

(ii) the rule only confers a benefit or removes a restriction on the public or some segment thereof;

(iii) the rule only delays the effective date of another rule that is not yet effective; or

(iv) the earlier effective date is necessary because of imminent peril to the public health, safety, or welfare.

(3) The finding and a brief statement of the reasons therefor required by paragraph (2) must be made a part of the rule. In any action contesting the effective date of a rule made effective under paragraph (2), the burden is on the agency to justify its finding.

(4) Each agency shall make a reasonable effort to make known to persons who may be affected by it a rule made effective before publication and indexing under this subsection.

(c) This section does not relieve an agency from compliance with any provision of law requiring that some or all of its rules be approved by other designated officials or bodies before they become effective.

§ 3–116. [Special Provision for Certain Classes of Rules]

Except to the extent otherwise provided by any provision of law, Sections 3–102 through 3–115 are inapplicable to:

(1) a rule concerning only the internal management of an agency which does not directly and substantially affect the procedural or substantive rights or duties of any segment of the public;

(2) a rule that establishes criteria or guidelines to be used by the staff of an agency in performing audits, investigations, or inspections, settling commercial disputes, negotiating commercial arrangements, or in the defense, prosecution, or settlement of cases, if disclosure of the criteria or guidelines would:

(i) enable law violators to avoid detection;

(ii) facilitate disregard of requirements imposed by law; or

(iii) give a clearly improper advantage to persons who are in an adverse position to the state;

(3) a rule that only establishes specific prices to be charged for particular goods or services sold by an agency;

(4) a rule concerning only the physical servicing, maintenance, or care of agency owned or operated facilities or property;

(5) a rule relating only to the use of a particular facility or property owned, operated, or maintained by the state or any of its subdivisions, if the substance of the rule is adequately indicated by means of signs or signals to persons who use the facility or property;

(6) a rule concerning only inmates of a correctional or detention facility, students enrolled in an educational institution, or patients admitted to a hospital, if adopted by that facility, institution, or hospital;

(7) a form whose contents or substantive requirements are prescribed by rule or statute, and instructions for the execution or use of the form;

(8) an agency budget; [or]

(9) an opinion of the attorney general [; or] [.]

(10) [the terms of a collective bargaining agreement.]

§ 3–117. [Petition for Adoption of Rule]

Any person may petition an agency requesting the adoption of a rule. Each agency shall prescribe by rule the form of the petition and the procedure for its submission, consideration, and disposition. Within [60] days after submission of a petition, the agency shall either (i) deny the petition in writing, stating its reasons therefor, (ii) initiate rule-making proceedings in accordance with this Chapter, or (iii) if otherwise lawful, adopt a rule.

CHAPTER II

REVIEW OF AGENCY RULES

§ 3–201. [Review by Agency]

At least [annually], each agency shall review all of its rules to determine whether any new rule should be adopted. In conducting that review, each agency shall prepare a written report summarizing its findings, its supporting reasons, and any proposed course of action. For each rule, the [annual] report must include, at least once every [7] years, a concise statement of:

(1) the rule's effectiveness in achieving its objectives, including a summary of any available data supporting the conclusions reached;

(2) criticisms of the rule received during the previous [7] years, including a summary of any petitions for waiver of the rule tendered to the agency or granted by it; and

(3) alternative solutions to the criticisms and the reasons they were rejected or the changes made in the rule in response to those criticisms and the reasons for the changes. A copy of the [annual] report must be sent to the [administrative rules review committee and the administrative rules counsel] and be available for public inspection.

[§ 3–202. [Review by Governor; Administrative Rules Counsel]

(a) To the extent the agency itself would have authority, the governor may rescind or suspend all or a severable portion of a rule of an agency. In exercising this authority, the governor shall act by an executive order that is subject to the provisions of this Act applicable to the adoption and effectiveness of a rule.

(b) The governor may summarily terminate any pending rule-making proceeding by an executive order to that effect, stating therein the reasons for the action. The executive order must be filed in the office of the [secretary of state], which shall promptly forward a certified copy to the agency and the [administrative rules editor]. An executive order terminating a rule-making proceeding becomes effective on [the date it is filed] and must be published in the next issue of the [administrative bulletin].

(c) There is created, within the office of the governor, an [administrative rules counsel] to advise the governor in the execution of the authority vested under this Article. The governor shall appoint the [administrative rules counsel] who shall serve at the pleasure of the governor.]

[§ 3–203. [Administrative Rules Review Committee]

There is created the ["administrative rules review committee"] of the [legislature]. The committee must be [bipartisan] and composed of [3] senators appointed by the [president of the senate] and [3] representatives appointed by the [speaker of the house]. Committee members must be appointed within [30] days after the convening of a regular legislative session. The term of office is [2] years while a member of the [legislature] and begins on the date of appointment to the committee. While a member of the [legislature], a member of the committee whose term has expired shall serve until a successor is appointed. A vacancy on the committee may be filled at any time by the original appointing authority for the remainder of the term. The committee shall choose a chairman from its membership for a [2]-year term and may employ staff it considers advisable.]

§ 3–204. [Review by Administrative Rules Review Committee]

(a) The [administrative rules review committee] shall selectively review possible, proposed, or adopted rules and prescribe appropriate committee procedures for that purpose.

ARTICLE IV

ADJUDICATIVE PROCEEDINGS

CHAPTER I

AVAILABILITY OF ADJUDICATIVE PROCEEDINGS; APPLICATIONS; LICENSES

§ 4–101. [Adjudicative Proceedings; When Required; Exceptions]

(a) An agency shall conduct an adjudicative proceeding as the process for formulating and issuing an order, unless the order is a decision:

(1) to issue or not to issue a complaint, summons, or similar accusation;

(2) to initiate or not to initiate an investigation, prosecution, or other proceeding before the agency, another agency, or a court; or

(3) under Section 4–103, not to conduct an adjudicative proceeding.

(b) This Article applies to rule-making proceedings only to the extent that another statute expressly so requires.

§ 4–102. [Adjudicative Proceedings; Commencement]

(a) An agency may commence an adjudicative proceeding at any time with respect to a matter within the agency's jurisdiction.

(b) An agency shall commence an adjudicative proceeding upon the application of any person, unless:

(1) the agency lacks jurisdiction of the subject matter;

(2) resolution of the matter requires the agency to exercise discretion within the scope of Section 4–101(a);

(3) a statute vests the agency with discretion to conduct or not to conduct an adjudicative proceeding before issuing an order to resolve the matter and, in the exercise of that discretion, the agency has determined not to conduct an adjudicative proceeding; to resolve the matter and, in the exercise of that discretion, the agency has determined not to conduct an adjudicative proceeding;

(4) resolution of the matter does not require the agency to issue an order that determines the applicant's legal rights, duties, privileges, immunities, or other legal interests;

(5) the matter was not timely submitted to the agency; or

(6) the matter was not submitted in a form substantially complying with any applicable provision of law.

(c) An application for an agency to issue an order includes an application for the agency to conduct appropriate adjudicative proceedings, whether or not the applicant expressly requests those proceedings.

(d) An adjudicative proceeding commences when the agency or a presiding officer:

(1) notifies a party that a pre-hearing conference, hearing, or other stage of an adjudicative proceeding will be conducted; or

(2) begins to take action on a matter that appropriately may be determined by an adjudicative proceeding, unless this action is:

(i) an investigation for the purpose of determining whether an adjudicative proceeding should be conducted; or

(ii) a decision which, under Section 4–101(a), the agency may make without conducting an adjudicative proceeding.

§ 4–103. [Decision Not to Conduct Adjudicative Proceeding]

If an agency decides not to conduct an adjudicative proceeding in response to an application, the agency shall furnish the applicant a copy of its decision in writing, with a brief statement of the agency's reasons and of any administrative review available to the applicant.

§ 4–104. [Agency Action on Applications]

(a) Except to the extent that the time limits in this subsection are inconsistent with limits established by another statute for any stage of the proceedings, an agency shall process an application for an order, other than a declaratory order, as follows:

(1) Within [30] days after receipt of the application, the agency shall examine the application, notify the applicant of any apparent errors or omissions, request any additional information the agency wishes to obtain and is permitted by law to require, and notify the applicant of the name, official title, mailing address and telephone number of an agency member or employee who may be contacted regarding the application.

(2) Except in situations governed by paragraph (3), within [90] days after receipt of the application or of the response to a timely request made by the agency pursuant to paragraph (1), the agency shall:

(i) approve or deny the application, in whole or in part, on the basis of emergency or summary adjudicative proceedings, if those proceedings are available under this Act for disposition of the matter;

(ii) commence a formal adjudicative hearing or a conference adjudicative hearing in accordance with this Act; or

(iii) dispose of the application in accordance with Section 4–103.

(3) If the application pertains to subject matter that is not available when the application is filed but may be available in the future, including an application for housing or employment at a time no vacancy exists, the agency may proceed to make a determination of eligibility within the time provided in paragraph (2). If the agency determines that the applicant is eligible, the agency shall maintain the application on the agency's list of eligible applicants as provided by law and, upon request, shall notify the applicant of the status of the application.

(b) If a timely and sufficient application has been made for renewal of a license with reference to any activity of a continuing nature, the existing license does not expire until the agency has taken final action upon the application for renewal or, if the agency's action is unfavorable, until the last day for seeking judicial review of the agency's action or a later date fixed by the reviewing court.

§ 4–105. [Agency Action Against Licensees]

An agency may not revoke, suspend, modify, annul, withdraw, or amend a license unless the agency first gives notice and an opportunity for an appropriate adjudicative proceeding in accordance with this Act or other statute. This section does not preclude an agency from (i) taking immediate action to protect the public interest in accordance with Section 4–501 or (ii) adopting rules, otherwise within the scope of its authority, pertaining to a class of licensees, including rules affecting the existing licenses of a class of licensees.

CHAPTER II

FORMAL ADJUDICATIVE HEARING

§ 4–201. [Applicability]

An adjudicative proceeding is governed by this chapter, except as otherwise provided by:

(1) a statute other than this Act;

(2) a rule that adopts the procedures for the conference adjudicative hearing or summary adjudicative proceeding in accordance with the standards provided in this Act for those proceedings;

(3) Section 4–501 pertaining to emergency adjudicative proceedings; or

(4) Section 2–103 pertaining to declaratory proceedings.

§ 4–202. [Presiding Officer, Disqualification, Substitution]

(a) The agency head, one or more members of the agency head, one or more administrative law judges assigned by the office of administrative hearings in accordance with Section 4–301 [, or, unless prohibited by law, one or more other persons designated by the agency head], in the discretion of the agency head, may be the presiding officer.

(b) Any person serving or designated to serve alone or with others as presiding officer is subject to disqualification for bias, prejudice, interest, or any other cause provided in this Act or for which a judge is or may be disqualified.

(c) Any party may petition for the disqualification of a person promptly after receipt of notice indicating that the person will preside or promptly upon discovering facts establishing grounds for disqualification, whichever is later.

(d) A person whose disqualification is requested shall determine whether to grant the petition, stating facts and reasons for the determination.

(e) If a substitute is required for a person who is disqualified or becomes unavailable for any other reason, the substitute must be appointed by:

(1) the governor, if the disqualified or unavailable person is an elected official; or

(2) the appointing authority, if the disqualified or unavailable person is an appointed official.

(f) Any action taken by a duly-appointed substitute for a disqualified or unavailable person is as effective as if taken by the latter.

§ 4–203. [Representation]

(a) Any party may participate in the hearing in person or, if the party is a corporation or other artificial person, by a duly authorized representative.

(b) Whether or not participating in person, any party may be advised and represented at the party's own expense by counsel or, if permitted by law, other representative.

§ 4–204. [Pre-hearing Conference—Availability, Notice]

The presiding officer designated to conduct the hearing may determine, subject to the agency's rules, whether a pre-hearing conference will be conducted. If the conference is conducted:

(1) The presiding officer shall promptly notify the agency of the determination that a pre-hearing conference will be conducted. The agency shall assign or request the office of administrative hearings to assign a presiding officer for the pre-hearing conference, exercising the same discretion as is provided by Section 4–202 concerning the selection of a presiding officer for a hearing.

(2) The presiding officer for the pre-hearing conference shall set the time and place of the conference and give reasonable written notice to all parties and to all persons who have filed written petitions to intervene in the matter. The agency shall give notice to other persons entitled to notice under any provision of law.

(3) The notice must include:

(i) the names and mailing addresses of all parties and other persons to whom notice is being given by the presiding officer;

(ii) the name, official title, mailing address, and telephone number of any counsel or employee who has been designated to appear for the agency;

(iii) the official file or other reference number, the name of the proceeding, and a general description of the subject matter;

(iv) a statement of the time, place, and nature of the pre-hearing conference;

(v) a statement of the legal authority and jurisdiction under which the pre-hearing conference and the hearing are to be held;

(vi) the name, official title, mailing address and telephone number of the presiding officer for the pre-hearing conference;

(vii) a statement that at the pre-hearing conference the proceeding, without further notice, may be converted into a conference adjudicative hearing or a summary adjudicative proceeding for disposition of the matter as provided by this Act; and

(viii) a statement that a party who fails to attend or participate in a pre-hearing conference, hearing, or other state of an adjudicative proceeding may be held in default under this Act.

(4) The notice may include any other matter that the presiding officer considers desirable to expedite the proceedings.

§ 4–205. [Pre-hearing Conference—Procedure and Pre-hearing Order]

(a) The presiding officer may conduct all or part of the pre-hearing conference by telephone, television, or other electronic means if each participant in the conference has an opportunity to participate in, to hear, and, if technically feasible, to see the entire proceeding while it is taking place.

(b) The presiding officer shall conduct the pre-hearing conference, as may be appropriate, to deal with such matters as conversion of the proceeding to another type, exploration of settlement possibilities, preparation of stipulations, clarification of issues, rulings on identity and limitation of the number of witnesses, objections to proffers of evidence, determination of the extent to which direct evidence, rebuttal evidence, or cross-examination will be presented in written form, and the extent to which telephone, television, or other electronic means will be used as a substitute for proceedings in person, order of presentation of evidence and cross-examination, rulings regarding issuance of subpoenas, discovery orders and protective orders, and such other matters as will promote the orderly and prompt conduct of the hearing. The presiding officer shall issue a pre-hearing order incorporating the matters determined at the pre-hearing conference.

(c) If a pre-hearing conference is not held, the presiding officer for the hearing may issue a pre-hearing order, based on the pleadings, to regulate the conduct of the proceedings.

§ 4–206. [Notice of Hearing]

(a) The presiding officer for the hearing shall set the time and place of the hearing and give reasonable written notice to all parties and to all persons who have filed written petitions to intervene in the matter.

(b) The notice must include a copy of any pre-hearing order rendered in the matter.

(c) To the extent not included in a pre-hearing order accompanying it, the notice must include:

(1) the names and mailing addresses of all parties and other persons to whom notice is being given by the presiding officer;

(2) the name, official title, mailing address and telephone number of any counsel or employee who has been designated to appear for the agency;

(3) the official file or other reference number, the name of the proceeding, and a general description of the subject matter;

(4) a statement of the time, place, and nature of the hearing;

(5) a statement of the legal authority and jurisdiction under which the hearing is to be held;

(6) the name, official title, mailing address, and telephone number of the presiding officer;

(7) a statement of the issues involved and, to the extent known to the presiding officer, of the matters asserted by the parties; and

(8) a statement that a party who fails to attend or participate in a pre-hearing conference, hearing, or other stage of an adjudicative proceeding may be held in default under this Act.

(d) The notice may include any other matters the presiding officer considers desirable to expedite the proceedings.

(e) The agency shall give notice to persons entitled to notice under any provision of law who have not been given notice by the presiding officer. Notice under this subsection may include all types of information provided in subsections (a) through (d) or may consist of a brief statement indicating the subject matter, parties, time, place, and nature of the hearing, manner in which copies of the notice to the parties may be inspected and copied, and name and telephone number of the presiding officer.

§ 4–207. [Pleadings, Briefs, Motions, Service]

(a) The presiding officer, at appropriate stages of the proceedings, shall give all parties full opportunity to file pleadings, motions, objections and offers of settlement.

(b) The presiding officer, at appropriate stages of the proceedings, may give all parties full opportunity to file briefs, proposed findings of fact and conclusions of law, and proposed initial or final orders.

(c) A party shall serve copies of any filed item on all parties, by mail or any other means prescribed by agency rule.

§ 4–208. [Default]

(a) If a party fails to attend or participate in a pre-hearing conference, hearing, or other stage of an adjudicative proceeding, the presiding officer may serve upon all parties written notice of a proposed default order, including a statement of the grounds.

(b) Within [7] days after service of a proposed default order, the party against whom it was issued may file a written motion requesting that the proposed default order be vacated and stating the grounds relied upon. During the time within which a party may file a written motion under this subsection, the presiding officer may adjourn the proceedings or conduct them without the participation of the party against whom a proposed default order was issued, having due regard for the interests of justice and the orderly and prompt conduct of the proceedings.

(c) The presiding officer shall either issue or vacate the default order promptly after expiration of the time within which the party may file a written motion under subsection (b).

§ 4–209. [Intervention]

(a) The presiding officer shall grant a petition for intervention if:

(1) the petition is submitted in writing to the presiding officer, with copies mailed to all parties named in the presiding officer's notice of the hearing, at least [3] days before the hearing;

(2) the petition states facts demonstrating that the petitioner's legal rights, duties, privileges, immunities, or other legal interests may be substantially affected by the proceeding or that the petitioner qualifies as an intervener under any provision of law; and

(3) the presiding officer determines that the interests of justice and the orderly and prompt conduct of the proceedings will not be impaired by allowing the intervention.

(b) The presiding officer may grant a petition for intervention at any time, upon determining that the intervention sought is in the interests of justice and will not impair the orderly and prompt conduct of the proceedings.

(c) If a petitioner qualifies for intervention, the presiding officer may impose conditions upon the intervener's participation in the proceedings, either at the time that intervention is granted or at any subsequent time. Conditions may include:

(1) limiting the intervener's participation to designated issues in which the intervener has a particular interest demonstrated by the petition;

(2) limiting the intervener's use of discovery, cross-examination, and other procedures so as to promote the orderly and prompt conduct of the proceedings; and

(3) requiring 2 or more interveners to combine their presentations of evidence and argument, cross-examination, discovery, and other participation in the proceedings.

(d) The presiding officer, at least [24 hours] before the hearing, shall issue an order granting or denying each pending petition for intervention, specifying any conditions, and briefly stating the reasons for the order. The presiding officer may modify the order at any time, stating the reasons for the modification. The presiding officer shall promptly give notice of an order granting, denying, or modifying intervention to the petitioner for intervention and to all parties.

§ 4–210. [Subpoenas, Discovery and Protective Orders]

(a) The presiding officer [at the request of any party shall, and upon the presiding officer's own motion,] may issue subpoenas, discovery orders and protective orders, in accordance with the rules of civil procedure.

(b) Subpoenas and orders issued under this section may be enforced pursuant to the provisions of this Act on civil enforcement of agency action.

§ 4–211. [Procedure at Hearing]

At a hearing:

(1) The presiding officer shall regulate the course of the proceedings in conformity with any pre-hearing order.

(2) To the extent necessary for full disclosure of all relevant facts and issues, the presiding officer shall afford to all parties the opportunity to respond, present evidence and argument, conduct cross-examination, and submit rebuttal evidence, except as restricted by a limited grant of intervention or by the pre-hearing order.

(3) The presiding officer may give nonparties an opportunity to present oral or written statements. If the presiding officer proposes to consider a statement by a nonparty, the presiding officer shall give all parties an opportunity to challenge or rebut it and, on motion of any party, the presiding officer shall require the statement to be given under oath or affirmation.

(4) The presiding officer may conduct all or part of the hearing by telephone, television, or other electronic means, if each participant in the hearing has an opportunity to participate in, to hear, and, if technically feasible, to see the entire proceeding while it is taking place.

(5) The presiding officer shall cause the hearing to be recorded at the agency's expense. The agency is not required, at its expense, to prepare a transcript, unless required to do so by a provision of law. Any party, at the party's expense, may cause a reporter approved by the agency to prepare a transcript from the agency's record, or cause additional recordings to be made during the hearing if the making of the additional recordings does not cause distraction or disruption.

(6) The hearing is open to public observation, except for the parts that the presiding officer states to be closed pursuant to a provision of law expressly authorizing closure. To the extent that a hearing is conducted by telephone, television, or other electronic means, and is not closed, the availability of public observation is satisfied by giving members of the public an opportunity, at reasonable times, to hear or inspect the agency's record, and to inspect any transcript obtained by the agency.

§ 4–212. [Evidence, Official Notice]

(a) Upon proper objection, the presiding officer shall exclude evidence that is irrelevant, immaterial, unduly repetitious, or excludable on constitutional or statutory grounds or on the basis of evidentiary privilege recognized in the courts of this state. In the absence of proper objection, the presiding officer may exclude objectionable evidence. Evidence may not be excluded solely because it is hearsay.

(b) All testimony of parties and witnesses must be made under oath or affirmation.

(c) Statements presented by nonparties in accordance with Section 4–211(3) may be received as evidence.

(d) Any part of the evidence may be received in written form if doing so will expedite the hearing without substantial prejudice to the interests of any party.

(e) Documentary evidence may be received in the form of a copy or excerpt. Upon request, parties must be given an opportunity to compare the copy with the original if available.

(f) Official notice may be taken of (i) any fact that could be judicially noticed in the courts of this State, (ii) the record of other proceedings before the agency, (iii) technical or scientific matters within the agency's specialized knowledge, and (iv) codes or standards that have been adopted by an agency of the United States, of this State or of another state, or by a nationally recognized organization or association. Parties must be notified before or during the hearing, or before the issuance of any initial or final order that is based in whole or in part on facts or material noticed, of the specific facts or material noticed and the source thereof, including any staff memoranda and data, and be afforded an opportunity to contest and rebut the facts or material so noticed.

§ 4–213. [Ex parte Communications]

(a) Except as provided in subsection (b) or unless required for the disposition of ex parte matters specifically authorized by statute, a presiding officer serving in an adjudicative proceeding may not communicate, directly or indirectly, regarding any issue in the proceeding, while the proceeding is pending, with any party, with any person who has a direct or indirect interest in the outcome of the proceeding, or with any person who presided at a previous stage of the proceeding, without notice and opportunity for all parties to participate in the communication.

(b) A member of a multi-member panel of presiding officers may communicate with other members of the panel regarding a matter pending before the panel, and any presiding officer may receive aid from staff assistants if the assistants do not (i) receive ex parte communications of a type that the presiding officer would be prohibited from receiving or (ii) furnish, augment, diminish, or modify the evidence in the record.

(c) Unless required for the disposition of ex parte matters specifically authorized by statute, no party to an adjudicative proceeding, and no person who has a direct or indirect interest in the outcome of the proceeding or who presided at a previous stage of the proceeding, may communicate, directly or indirectly, in connection with any issue in that proceeding, while the proceeding is pending, with any person serving as presiding officer, without notice and opportunity for all parties to participate in the communication.

(d) If, before serving as presiding officer in an adjudicative proceeding, a person receives an ex parte communication of a type that could not properly be received while serving, the person, promptly after starting to serve, shall disclose the communication in the manner prescribed in subsection (e).

(e) A presiding officer who receives an ex parte communication in violation of this section shall place on the record of the pending matter all written communications received, all written responses to the communications, and a memorandum stating the substance of all oral communications received, all responses made, and the identity of each person from whom the presiding officer received an ex parte communication, and shall advise all parties that these matters have been placed on the record. Any party desiring to rebut the ex parte communication must be allowed to do so, upon requesting the opportunity for rebuttal within [10] days after notice of the communication.

(f) If necessary to eliminate the effect of an ex parte communication received in violation of this section, a presiding officer who receives the communication may be disqualified and the portions of the record pertaining to the communication may be sealed by protective order.

(g) The agency shall, and any party may, report any willful violation of this section to appropriate authorities for any disciplinary proceedings provided by law. In addition, each agency by rule may provide for appropriate sanctions, including default, for any violations of this section.

§ 4–214. [Separation of Functions]

(a) A person who has served as investigator, prosecutor or advocate in an adjudicative proceeding or in its pre-adjudicative stage may not serve as presiding officer or assist or advise a presiding officer in the same proceeding.

(b) A person who is subject to the authority, direction, or discretion of one who has served as investigator, prosecutor, or advocate in an adjudicative proceeding or in its pre-adjudicative stage may not serve as presiding officer or assist or advise a presiding officer in the same proceeding.

(c) A person who has participated in a determination of probable cause or other equivalent preliminary determination in an adjudicative proceeding may serve as presiding officer or assist or advise a presiding officer in the same proceeding, unless a party demonstrates grounds for disqualification in accordance with Section 4–202.

(d) A person may serve as presiding officer at successive stages of the same adjudicative proceeding, unless a party demonstrates grounds for disqualification in accordance with Section 4–202.

§ 4–215. [Final Order, Initial Order]

(a) If the presiding officer is the agency head, the presiding officer shall render a final order.

(b) If the presiding officer is not the agency head, the presiding officer shall render an initial order, which becomes a final order unless reviewed in accordance with Section 4–216.

(c) A final order or initial order must include, separately stated, findings of fact, conclusions of law, and policy reasons for the decision if it is an exercise of the agency's discretion, for all aspects of the order, including the remedy prescribed and, if applicable, the action taken on a petition for stay of effectiveness. Findings of fact, if set forth in language that is no more than mere repetition or paraphrase of the relevant provision of law, must be accompanied by a concise and explicit statement of the underlying facts of record to support the findings. If a party has submitted proposed findings of fact, the order must include a ruling on the proposed findings. The order must also include a statement of the available procedures and time limits for seeking reconsideration or other administrative relief. An initial order must include a statement of any circumstances under which the initial order, without further notice, may become a final order.

(d) Findings of fact must be based exclusively upon the evidence of record in the adjudicative proceeding and on matters officially noticed in that proceeding. Findings must be based upon the kind of evidence on which reasonably prudent persons are accustomed to rely in the conduct of their serious affairs and may be based upon such evidence even if it would be inadmissible in a civil trial. The presiding officer's experience, technical competence, and specialized knowledge may be utilized in evaluating evidence.

(e) If a person serving or designated to serve as presiding officer becomes unavailable, for any reason, before rendition of the final order or initial order, a substitute presiding officer must be appointed as provided in Section 4–202. The substitute presiding officer shall use any existing record and may conduct any further proceedings appropriate in the interests of justice.

(f) The presiding officer may allow the parties a designated amount of time after conclusion of the hearing for the submission of proposed findings.

(g) A final order or initial order pursuant to this section must be rendered in writing within [90] days after conclusion of the hearing or after submission of proposed findings in accordance with subsection (f) unless this period is waived or extended with the written consent of all parties or for good cause shown.

(h) The presiding officer shall cause copies of the final order or initial order to be delivered to each party and to the agency head.

§ 4–216. [Review of Initial Order; Exceptions to Reviewability]

(a) The agency head, upon its own motion may, and upon appeal by any party shall, review an initial order, except to the extent that:

    (1) a provision of law precludes or limits agency review of the initial order; or

(2) the agency head, in the exercise of discretion conferred by a provision of law,

(i) determines to review some but not all issues, or not to exercise any review,

(ii) delegates its authority to review the initial order to one or more persons, or

(iii) authorizes one or more persons to review the initial order, subject to further review by the agency head.

(b) A petition for appeal from an initial order must be filed with the agency head, or with any person designated for this purpose by rule of the agency, within [10] days after rendition of the initial order. If the agency head on its own motion decides to review an initial order, the agency head shall give written notice of its intention to review the initial order within [10] days after its rendition. The [10]-day period for a party to file a petition for appeal or for the agency head to give notice of its intention to review an initial order on the agency head's own motion is tolled by the submission of a timely petition for reconsideration of the initial order pursuant to Section 4–218, and a new [10]-day period starts to run upon disposition of the petition for reconsideration. If an initial order is subject both to a timely petition for reconsideration and to a petition for appeal or to review by the agency head on its own motion, the petition for reconsideration must be disposed of first, unless the agency head determines that action on the petition for reconsideration has been unreasonably delayed.

(c) The petition for appeal must state its basis. If the agency head on its own motion gives notice of its intent to review an initial order, the agency head shall identify the issues that it intends to review.

(d) The presiding officer for the review of an initial order shall exercise all the decision-making power that the presiding officer would have had to render a final order had the presiding officer presided over the hearing, except to the extent that the issues subject to review are limited by a provision of law or by the presiding officer upon notice to all parties.

(e) The presiding officer shall afford each party an opportunity to present briefs and may afford each party an opportunity to present oral argument.

(f) Before rendering a final order, the presiding officer may cause a transcript to be prepared, at the agency's expense, of such portions of the proceeding under review as the presiding officer considers necessary.

(g) The presiding officer may render a final order disposing of the proceeding or may remand the matter for further proceedings with instructions to the person who rendered the initial order. Upon remanding a matter, the presiding officer may order such temporary relief as is authorized and appropriate.

(h) A final order or an order remanding the matter for further proceedings must be rendered in writing within [60] days after receipt of briefs and oral argument unless that period is waived or extended with the written consent of all parties or for good cause shown.

(i) A final order or an order remanding the matter for further proceedings under this section must identify any difference between this order and the initial order and must include, or incorporate by express reference to the initial order, all the matters required by Section 4–215(c).

(j) The presiding officer shall cause copies of the final order or order remanding the matter for further proceedings to be delivered to each party and to the agency head.

§ 4–217. [Stay]

A party may submit to the presiding officer a petition for stay of effectiveness of an initial or final order within [7] days after its rendition unless otherwise provided by statute or stated in the initial or final order. The presiding officer may take action on the petition for stay, either before or after the effective date of the initial or final order.

§ 4–218. [Reconsideration]

Unless otherwise provided by statute or rule:

(1) Any party, within [10] days after rendition of an initial or final order, may file a petition for reconsideration, stating the specific grounds upon which relief is requested. The filing of the petition is not a prerequisite for seeking administrative or judicial review.

(2) The petition must be disposed of by the same person or persons who rendered the initial or final order, if available.

(3) The presiding officer shall render a written order denying the petition, granting the petition and dissolving or modifying the initial or final order, or granting the petition and setting the matter for further proceedings. The petition may be granted, in whole or in part, only if the presiding officer states, in the written order, findings of fact, conclusions of law, and policy reasons for the decision if it is an exercise of the agency's discretion, to justify the order. The petition is deemed to have been denied if the presiding officer does not dispose of it within [20] days after the filing of the petition.

§ 4–219. [Review by Superior Agency]

If, pursuant to statute, an agency may review the final order of another agency, the review is deemed to be a continuous proceeding as if before a single agency. The final order of the first agency is treated as an initial order and the second agency functions as though it were reviewing an initial order in accordance with Section 4–216.

§ 4–220. [Effectiveness of Orders]

(a) Unless a later date is stated in a final order or a stay is granted, a final order is effective [10] days after rendition, but:

(1) a party may not be required to comply with a final order unless the party has been served with or has actual knowledge of the final order;

(2) a nonparty may not be required to comply with a final order unless the agency has made the final order available for public inspection and copying or the nonparty has actual knowledge of the final order.

(b) Unless a later date is stated in an initial order or a stay is granted, the time when an initial order becomes a final order in accordance with Section 4–215 is determined as follows:

(1) when the initial order is rendered, if administrative review is unavailable;

(2) when the agency head renders an order stating, after a petition for appeal has been filed, that review will not be exercised, if discretion is available to make a determination to this effect; or

(3) [10] days after rendition of the initial order, if no party has filed a petition for appeal and the agency head has not given written notice of its intention to exercise review.

(c) Unless a later date is stated in an initial order or a stay is granted, an initial order that becomes a final order in accordance with subsection (b) and Section 4–215 is effective [10] days after becoming a final order, but:

(1) a party may not be required to comply with the final order unless the party has been served with or has actual knowledge of the initial order or of an order stating that review will not be exercised; and

(2) a nonparty may not be required to comply with the final order unless the agency has made the initial order available for public inspection and copying or the nonparty has actual knowledge of the initial order or of an order stating that review will not be exercised.

(d) This section does not preclude an agency from taking immediate action to protect the public interest in accordance with Section 4–501.

§ 4–221. [Agency Record]

(a) An agency shall maintain an official record of each adjudicative proceeding under this Chapter.

(b) The agency record consists only of:

(1) notices of all proceedings;

(2) any pre-hearing order;

(3) any motions, pleadings, briefs, petitions, requests, and intermediate rulings;

(4) evidence received or considered;

(5) a statement of matters officially noticed;

(6) proffers of proof and objections and rulings thereon;

(7) proposed findings, requested orders, and exceptions;

(8) the record prepared for the presiding officer at the hearing, together with any transcript of all or part of the hearing considered before final disposition of the proceeding;

(9) any final order, initial order, or order on reconsideration;

(10) staff memoranda or data submitted to the presiding officer, unless prepared and submitted by personal assistants and not inconsistent with Section 4–213(b); and

(11) matters placed on the record after an ex parte communication.

(c) Except to the extent that this Act or another statute provides otherwise, the agency record constitutes the exclusive basis for agency action in adjudicative proceedings under this Chapter and for judicial review thereof.

CHAPTER III

OFFICE OF ADMINISTRATIVE HEARINGS

§ 4–301. [Office of Administrative Hearings—Creation, Powers, Duties]

(a) There is created the office of administrative hearings within the [Department of _____], to be headed by a director appointed by the governor [and confirmed by the senate].

(b) The office shall employ administrative law judges as necessary to conduct proceedings required by this Act or other provision of law. [Only a person admitted to practice law in [this State] [a jurisdiction in the United States] may be employed as an administrative law judge.]

(c) If the office cannot furnish one of its administrative law judges in response to an agency request, the director shall designate in writing a full-time employee of an agency other than the requesting agency to serve as administrative law judge for the proceeding, but only with the consent of the employing agency. The designee must possess the same qualifications required of administrative law judges employed by the office.

(d) The director may furnish administrative law judges on a contract basis to any governmental entity to conduct any proceeding not subject to this Act.

(e) The office may adopt rules:

(1) to establish further qualifications for administrative law judges, procedures by which candidates will be considered for employment, and the manner in which public notice of vacancies in the staff of the office will be given;

(2) to establish procedures for agencies to request and for the director to assign administrative law judges; however, an agency may neither select nor reject any individual administrative law judge for any proceeding except in accordance with this Act;

(3) to establish procedures and adopt forms, consistent with this Act, the model rules of procedure, and other provisions of law, to govern administrative law judges;

(4) to establish standards and procedures for the evaluation, training, promotion, and discipline of administrative law judges; and

(5) to facilitate the performance of the responsibilities conferred upon the office by this Act.

(f) The director may:

(1) maintain a staff of reporters and other personnel; and

(2) implement the provisions of this section and rules adopted under its authority.

CHAPTER IV

CONFERENCE ADJUDICATIVE HEARING

§ 4-401. [Conference Adjudicative Hearing—Applicability]

A conference adjudicative hearing may be used if its use in the circumstances does not violate any provision of law and the matter is entirely within one or more categories for which the agency by rule had adopted this chapter [; however, those categories may include only the following:

(1) a matter in which there is no disputed issue of material fact; or

(2) a matter in which there is a disputed issue of material fact, if the matter involves only:

(i) a monetary amount of not more than [$1,000];

(ii) a disciplinary sanction against a prisoner;

(iii) a disciplinary sanction against a student which does not involve expulsion from an academic institution or suspension for more than [10] days;

(iv) a disciplinary sanction against a public employee which does not involve discharge from employment or suspension for more than [10] days;

(v) a disciplinary sanction against a licensee which does not involve revocation, suspension, annulment, withdrawal, or amendment of a license; or

(vi) . . . .]

§ 4-402. [Conference Adjudicative Hearing—Procedures]

The procedures of this Act pertaining to formal adjudicative hearings apply to a conference adjudicative hearing, except to the following extent:

(1) If a matter is initiated as a conference adjudicative hearing, no pre-hearing conference may be held.

(2) The provisions of Section 4–210 do not apply to conference adjudicative hearings insofar as those provisions authorize the issuance and enforcement of subpoenas and discovery orders, but do apply to conference adjudicative hearings insofar as those provisions authorize the presiding officer to issue protective orders at the request of any party or upon the presiding officer's motion.

(3) Paragraphs (1), (2) and (3) of Section 4–211 do not apply; but,

(i) the presiding officer shall regulate the course of the proceedings,

(ii) only the parties may testify and present written exhibits, and

(iii) the parties may offer comments on the issues.

§ 4–403. [Conference Adjudicative Hearing—Proposed Proof]

(a) If the presiding officer has reason to believe that material facts are in dispute, the presiding officer may require any party to state the identity of the witnesses or other sources through whom the party would propose to present proof if the proceeding were converted to a formal adjudicative hearing, but if disclosure of any fact, allegation, or source is privileged or expressly prohibited by any provision of law, the presiding officer may require the party to indicate that confidential facts, allegations, or sources are involved, but not to disclose the confidential facts, allegations, or sources.

(b) If a party has reason to believe that essential facts must be obtained in order to permit an adequate presentation of the case, the party may inform the presiding officer regarding the general nature of the facts and the sources from whom the party would propose to obtain those facts if the proceeding were converted to a formal adjudicative hearing.

CHAPTER V

EMERGENCY AND SUMMARY ADJUDICATIVE PROCEEDINGS

§ 4–501. [Emergency Adjudicative Proceedings]

(a) An agency may use emergency adjudicative proceedings in a situation involving an immediate danger to the public health, safety, or welfare requiring immediate agency action.

(b) The agency may take only such action as is necessary to prevent or avoid the immediate danger to the public health, safety, or welfare that justifies use of emergency adjudication.

(c) The agency shall render an order, including a brief statement of findings of fact, conclusions of law, and policy reasons for the decision if it is an exercise of the agency's discretion, to justify the determination of an immediate danger and the agency's decision to take the specific action.

(d) The agency shall give such notice as is practicable to persons who are required to comply with the order. The order is effective when rendered.

(e) After issuing an order pursuant to this section, the agency shall proceed as quickly as feasible to complete any proceedings that would be required if the matter did not involve an immediate danger.

(f) The agency record consists of any documents regarding the matter that were considered or prepared by the agency. The agency shall maintain these documents as its official record.

(g) Unless otherwise required by a provision of law, the agency record need not constitute the exclusive basis for agency action in emergency adjudicative proceedings or for judicial review thereof.

§ 4-502. [Summary Adjudicative Proceedings—Applicability]

An agency may use summary adjudicative proceedings if:

(1) the use of those proceedings in the circumstances does not violate any provision of law;

(2) the protection of the public interest does not require the agency to give notice and an opportunity to participate to persons other than the parties; and

(3) the matter is entirely within one or more categories for which the agency by rule has adopted this section and Sections 4-503 to 4-506 [; however, those categories may include only the following:

(i) a monetary amount of not more than [$100];

(ii) a reprimand, warning, disciplinary report, or other purely verbal sanction without continuing impact against a prisoner, student, public employee, or licensee;

(iii) the denial of an application after the applicant has abandoned the application;

(iv) the denial of an application for admission to an educational institution or for employment by an agency;

(v) the denial, in whole or in part, of an application if the applicant has an opportunity for administrative review in accordance with Section 4-504;

(vi) a matter that is resolved on the sole basis of inspections, examinations, or tests;

(vii) the acquisition, leasing, or disposal of property or the procurement of goods or services by contract;

(viii) any matter having only trivial potential impact upon the affected parties; and

(ix) . . . .]

§ 4-503. [Summary Adjudicative Proceedings—Procedures]

(a) The agency head, one or more members of the agency head, one or more administrative law judges assigned by the office of administrative hearings in accordance with Section 4–301 [, or, unless prohibited by law, one or more other persons designated by the agency head], in the discretion of the agency head, may be the presiding officer. Unless prohibited by law, a person exercising authority over the matter is the presiding officer.

(b) If the proceeding involves a monetary matter or a reprimand, warning, disciplinary report, or other sanction:

(1) the presiding officer, before taking action, shall give each party an opportunity to be informed of the agency's view of the matter and to explain the party's view of the matter; and

(2) the presiding officer, at the time any unfavorable action is taken, shall give each party a brief statement of findings of fact, conclusions of law, and policy reasons for the decision if it is an exercise of the agency's discretion, to justify the action, and a notice of any available administrative review.

(c) An order rendered in a proceeding that involves a monetary matter must be in writing. An order in any other summary adjudicative proceeding may be oral or written.

(d) The agency, by reasonable means, shall furnish to each party notification of the order in a summary adjudicative proceeding. Notification must include at least a statement of the agency's action and a notice of any available administrative review.

§ 4–504. [Administrative Review of Summary Adjudicative Proceedings—Applicability]

Unless prohibited by any provision of law, an agency, on its own motion, may conduct administrative review of an order resulting from summary adjudicative proceedings, and shall conduct this review upon the written or oral request of a party if the agency receives the request within [10] days after furnishing notification under Section 4–503(d).

§ 4–505. [Administrative Review of Summary Adjudicative Proceedings—Procedures]

Unless otherwise provided by statute [or rule]:

(1) An agency need not furnish notification of the pendency of administrative review to any person who did not request the review, but the agency may not take any action on review less favorable to any party than the original order without giving that party notice and an opportunity to explain that party's view of the matter.

(2) The reviewing officer, in the discretion of the agency head, may be any person who could have presided at the summary adjudicative proceeding, but the reviewing officer must be one who is authorized to grant appropriate relief upon review.

(3) The reviewing officer shall give each party an opportunity to explain the party's view of the matter unless the party's view is apparent from the written materials in the file submitted to the reviewing officer. The reviewing officer shall make any inquiries

necessary to ascertain whether the proceeding must be converted to a conference adjudicative hearing or a formal adjudicative hearing.

(4) The reviewing officer may render an order disposing of the proceeding in any manner that was available to the presiding officer at the summary adjudicative proceeding or the reviewing officer may remand the matter for further proceedings, with or without conversion to a conference adjudicative hearing or a formal adjudicative hearing.

(5) If the order under review is or should have been in writing, the order on review must be in writing, including a brief statement of findings of fact, conclusions of law, and policy reasons for the decision if it is an exercise of the agency's discretion, to justify the order, and a notice of any further available administrative review.

(6) A request for administrative review is deemed to have been denied if the reviewing officer does not dispose of the matter or remand it for further proceedings within [20] days after the request is submitted.

§ 4–506. [Agency Record of Summary Adjudicative Proceedings and Administrative Review]

(a) The agency record consists of any documents regarding the matter that were considered or prepared by the presiding officer for the summary adjudicative proceeding or by the reviewing officer for any review. The agency shall maintain these documents as its official record.

(b) Unless otherwise required by a provision of law, the agency record need not constitute the exclusive basis for agency action in summary adjudicative proceedings or for judicial review thereof.

ARTICLE V

JUDICIAL REVIEW AND CIVIL ENFORCEMENT

CHAPTER I

JUDICIAL REVIEW

§ 5–101. [Relationship Between This Act and Other Law on Judicial Review and Other Judicial Remedies]

This Act establishes the exclusive means of judicial review of agency action, but:

(1) The provisions of this Act for judicial review do not apply to litigation in which the sole issue is a claim for money damages or compensation and the agency whose action is at issue does not have statutory authority to determine the claim.

(2) Ancillary procedural matters, including intervention, class actions, consolidation, joinder, severance, transfer, protective orders, and other relief from disclosure of privileged or confidential material, are governed, to the extent not inconsistent with this Act, by other applicable law.

(3) If the relief available under other sections of this Act is not equal or substantially equivalent to the relief otherwise available under law, the relief otherwise available and the related procedures supersede and supplement this Act to the extent necessary for their effectuation. The applicable provisions of this Act and other law must be combined to govern a single proceeding or, if the court orders, 2 or more separate proceedings, with or without transfer to other courts, but no type of relief may be sought in a combined proceeding after expiration of the time limit for doing so.

§ 5–102. [Final Agency Action Reviewable]

(a) A person who qualifies under this Act regarding (i) standing (Section 5–106), (ii) exhaustion of administrative remedies (Section 5–107), and (iii) time for filing the petition for review (Section 5–108), and other applicable provisions of law regarding bond, compliance, and other pre-conditions is entitled to judicial review of final agency action, whether or not the person has sought judicial review of any related non-final agency action.

(b) For purposes of this section and Section 5–103:

(1) "Final agency action" means the whole or a part of any agency action other than non-final agency action;

(2) "Non-final agency action" means the whole or a part of an agency determination, investigation, proceeding, hearing, conference, or other process that the agency intends or is reasonably believed to intend to be preliminary, preparatory, procedural, or intermediate with regard to subsequent agency action of that agency or another agency.

§ 5–103. [Non-final Agency Action Reviewable]

A person is entitled to judicial review of non-final agency action only if:

(1) it appears likely that the person will qualify under Section 5–102 for judicial review of the related final agency action; and

(2) postponement of judicial review would result in an inadequate remedy or irreparable harm disproportionate to the public benefit derived from postponement.

[Alternative A.]

§ 5–104. [Jurisdiction, Venue]

(a) The [trial court of general jurisdiction] shall conduct judicial review.

(b) Venue is in the [district] [that includes the state capital] [where the petitioner resides or maintains a principal place of business] unless otherwise provided by law.

[Alternative B.]

§ 5–104. [Jurisdiction, Venue]

(a) The [appellate court] shall conduct judicial review.

(b) Venue is in the [district] [that includes the state capital] [where the petitioner resides or maintains a principal place of business] unless otherwise provided by law.

(c) If evidence is to be adduced in the reviewing court in accordance with Section 5–114(a), the court shall appoint a [referee, master, trial court judge] for this purpose, having due regard for the convenience of the parties.

§ 5–105. [Form of Action]

Judicial review is initiated by filing a petition for review in [the appropriate] court. A petition may seek any type of relief available under Sections 5–101(3) and 5–117.

§ 5–106. [Standing]

(a) The following persons have standing to obtain judicial review of final or non-final agency action:

(1) a person to whom the agency action is specifically directed;

(2) a person who was a party to the agency proceedings that led to the agency action;

(3) if the challenged agency action is a rule, a person subject to that rule;

(4) a person eligible for standing under another provision of law; or

(5) a person otherwise aggrieved or adversely affected by the agency action. For purposes of this paragraph, no person has standing as one otherwise aggrieved or adversely affected unless:

(i) the agency action has prejudiced or is likely to prejudice that person;

(ii) that person's asserted interests are among those that the agency was required to consider when it engaged in the agency action challenged; and

(iii) a judgment in favor of that person would substantially eliminate or redress the prejudice to that person caused or likely to be caused by the agency action.

[(b) A standing committee of the legislature which is required to exercise general and continuing oversight over administrative agencies and procedures may petition for judicial review of any rule or intervene in any litigation arising from agency action.]

§ 5–107. [Exhaustion of Administrative Remedies]

A person may file a petition for judicial review under this Act only after exhausting all administrative remedies available within the agency whose action is being challenged and within any other agency authorized to exercise administrative review, but:

(1) a petitioner for judicial review of a rule need not have participated in the rule-making proceeding upon which that rule is based, or have petitioned for its amendment or repeal;

(2) a petitioner for judicial review need not exhaust administrative remedies to the extent that this Act or any other statute states that exhaustion is not required; or

(3) the court may relieve a petitioner of the requirement to exhaust any or all administrative remedies, to the extent that the administrative remedies are inadequate, or requiring their exhaustion would result in irreparable harm disproportionate to the public benefit derived from requiring exhaustion.

§ 5–108. [Time for Filing Petition for Review]

Subject to other requirements of this Act or of another statute:

(1) A petition for judicial review of a rule may be filed at any time, except as limited by Section 3–113(b).

(2) A petition for judicial review of an order is not timely unless filed within [30] days after rendition of the order, but the time is extended during the pendency of the petitioner's timely attempts to exhaust administrative remedies, if the attempts are not clearly frivolous or repetitious.

(3) A petition for judicial review of agency action other than a rule or order is not timely unless filed within [30] days after the agency action, but the time is extended:

(i) during the pendency of the petitioner's timely attempts to exhaust administrative remedies, if the attempts are not clearly frivolous or repetitious; and

(ii) during any period that the petitioner did not know and was under no duty to discover, or did not know and was under a duty to discover but could not reasonably have discovered, that the agency had taken the action or that the agency action had a sufficient effect to confer standing upon the petitioner to obtain judicial review under this Act.

§ 5–109. [Petition for Review—Filing and Contents]

(a) A petition for review must be filed with the clerk of the court.

(b) A petition for review must set forth:

(1) the name and mailing address of the petitioner;

(2) the name and mailing address of the agency whose action is at issue;

(3) identification of the agency action at issue, together with a duplicate copy, summary, or brief description of the agency action;

(4) identification of persons who were parties in any adjudicative proceedings that led to the agency action;

(5) facts to demonstrate that the petitioner is entitled to obtain judicial review;

(6) the petitioner's reasons for believing that relief should be granted; and

(7) a request for relief, specifying the type and extent of relief requested.

§ 5–110. [Petition for Review—Service and Notification]

(a) A petitioner for judicial review shall serve a copy of the petition upon the agency in the manner provided by [statute] [the rules of civil procedure].

(b) The petitioner shall use means provided by [statute] [the rules of civil procedure] to give notice of the petition for review to all other parties in any adjudicative proceedings that led to the agency action.

§ 5–111. [Stay and Other Temporary Remedies Pending Final Disposition]

(a) Unless precluded by law, the agency may grant a stay on appropriate terms or other temporary remedies during the pendency of judicial review.

(b) A party may file a motion in the reviewing court, during the pendency of judicial review, seeking interlocutory review of the agency's action on an application for stay or other temporary remedies.

(c) If the agency has found that its action on an application for stay or other temporary remedies is justified to protect against a substantial threat to the public health, safety, or welfare, the court may not grant relief unless it finds that:

(1) the applicant is likely to prevail when the court finally disposes of the matter;

(2) without relief the applicant will suffer irreparable injury;

(3) the grant of relief to the applicant will not substantially harm other parties to the proceedings; and

(4) the threat to the public health, safety, or welfare relied on by the agency is not sufficiently serious to justify the agency's action in the circumstances.

(d) If subsection (c) does not apply, the court shall grant relief if it finds, in its independent judgment, that the agency's action on the application for stay or other temporary remedies was unreasonable in the circumstances.

(e) If the court determines that relief should be granted from the agency's action on an application for stay or other temporary remedies, the court may remand the matter to the agency with directions to deny a stay, to grant a stay on appropriate terms, or to grant other temporary remedies, or the court may issue an order denying a stay, granting a stay on appropriate terms, or granting other temporary remedies.

§ 5–112. [Limitation on New Issues]

A person may obtain judicial review of an issue that was not raised before the agency, only to the extent that:

(1) the agency did not have jurisdiction to grant an adequate remedy based on a determination of the issue;

(2) the person did not know and was under no duty to discover, or did not know and was under a duty to discover but could not reasonably have discovered, facts giving rise to the issue;

(3) the agency action subject to judicial review is a rule and the person has not been a party in adjudicative proceedings which provided an adequate opportunity to raise the issue;

(4) the agency action subject to judicial review is an order and the person was not notified of the adjudicative proceeding in substantial compliance with this Act; or

(5) the interests of justice would be served by judicial resolution of an issue arising from:

(i) a change in controlling law occurring after the agency action; or

(ii) agency action occurring after the person exhausted the last feasible opportunity for seeking relief from the agency.

§ 5–113. [Judicial Review of Facts Confined to Record for Judicial Review and Additional Evidence Taken Pursuant to Act]

Judicial review of disputed issues of fact must be confined to the agency record for judicial review as defined in this Act, supplemented by additional evidence taken pursuant to this Act.

§ 5–114. [New Evidence Taken by Court or Agency Before Final Disposition]

(a) The court [(if Alternative B of Section 5–104 is adopted), assisted by a referee, master, trial court judge as provided in Section 5–104(c),] may receive evidence, in addition to that contained in the agency record for judicial review, only if it relates to the validity of the agency action at the time it was taken and is needed to decide disputed issues regarding:

(1) improper constitution as a decision-making body, or improper motive or grounds for disqualification, of those taking the agency action;

(2) unlawfulness of procedure or of decision-making process; or

(3) any material fact that was not required by any provision of law to be determined exclusively on an agency record of a type reasonably suitable for judicial review.

(b) The court may remand a matter to the agency, before final disposition of a petition for review, with directions that the agency conduct fact-finding and other proceedings the court considers necessary and that the agency take such further action on the basis thereof as the court directs, if:

(1) the agency was required by this Act or any other provision of law to base its action exclusively on a record of a type reasonably

suitable for judicial review, but the agency failed to prepare or preserve an adequate record;

(2) the court finds that (i) new evidence has become available that relates to the validity of the agency action at the time it was taken, that one or more of the parties did not know and was under no duty to discover, or did not know and was under a duty to discover but could not reasonably have discovered, until after the agency action, and (ii) the interests of justice would be served by remand to the agency;

(3) the agency improperly excluded or omitted evidence from the record; or

(4) a relevant provision of law changed after the agency action and the court determines that the new provision may control the outcome.

§ 5–115. [Agency Record for Judicial Review—Contents, Preparation, Transmittal, Cost]

(a) Within [_____] days after service of the petition, or within further time allowed by the court or by other provision of law, the agency shall transmit to the court the original or a certified copy of the agency record for judicial review of the agency action, consisting of any agency documents expressing the agency action, other documents identified by the agency as having been considered by it before its action and used as a basis for its action, and any other material described in this Act as the agency record for the type of agency action at issue, subject to the provisions of this section.

(b) If part of the record has been preserved without a transcript, the agency shall prepare a transcript for inclusion in the record transmitted to the court, except for portions that the parties stipulate to omit in accordance with subsection (d).

(c) The agency shall charge the petitioner with the reasonable cost of preparing any necessary copies and transcripts for transmittal to the court. [A failure by the petitioner to pay any of this cost to the agency does not relieve the agency from the responsibility for timely preparation of the record and transmittal to the court.]

(d) By stipulation of all parties to the review proceedings, the record may be shortened, summarized, or organized.

(e) The court may tax the cost of preparing transcripts and copies for the record:

(1) against a party who unreasonably refuses to stipulate to shorten, summarize, or organize the record;

(2) as provided by Section 5–117; or

(3) in accordance with any other provision of law.

(f) Additions to the record pursuant to Section 5–114 must be made as ordered by the court.

(g) The court may require or permit subsequent corrections or additions to the record.

§ 5–116. [Scope of Review; Grounds for Invalidity]

(a) Except to the extent that this Act or another statute provides otherwise:

(1) The burden of demonstrating the invalidity of agency action is on the party asserting invalidity; and

(2) The validity of agency action must be determined in accordance with the standards of review provided in this section, as applied to the agency action at the time it was taken.

(b) The court shall make a separate and distinct ruling on each material issue on which the court's decision is based.

(c) The court shall grant relief only if it determines that a person seeking judicial relief has been substantially prejudiced by any one or more of the following:

(1) The agency action, or the statute or rule on which the agency action is based, is unconstitutional on its face or as applied.

(2) The agency has acted beyond the jurisdiction conferred by any provision of law.

(3) The agency has not decided all issues requiring resolution.

(4) The agency has erroneously interpreted or applied the law.

(5) The agency has engaged in an unlawful procedure or decision-making process, or has failed to follow prescribed procedure.

(6) The persons taking the agency action were improperly constituted as a decision-making body, motivated by an improper purpose, or subject to disqualification.

(7) The agency action is based on a determination of fact, made or implied by the agency, that is not supported by evidence that is substantial when viewed in light of the whole record before the court, which includes the agency record for judicial review, supplemented by any additional evidence received by the court under this Act.

(8) The agency action is:

(i) outside the range of discretion delegated to the agency by any provision of law;

(ii) agency action, other than a rule, that is inconsistent with a rule of the agency; [or]

(iii) agency action, other than a rule, that is inconsistent with the agency's prior practice unless the agency justifies the inconsistency by stating facts and reasons to demonstrate a fair and rational basis for the inconsistency. [; or] [.]

(iv) [otherwise unreasonable, arbitrary or capricious.]

§ 5–117. [Type of Relief]

(a) The court may award damages or compensation only to the extent expressly authorized by another provision of law.

(b) The court may grant other appropriate relief, whether mandatory, injunctive, or declaratory; preliminary or final; temporary or permanent; equitable or legal. In granting relief, the court may order agency action required by law, order agency exercise of discretion required by law, set aside or modify agency action, enjoin or stay the effectiveness of agency action, remand the matter for further proceedings, render a declaratory judgment, or take any other action that is authorized and appropriate.

(c) The court may also grant necessary ancillary relief to redress the effects of official action wrongfully taken or withheld, but the court may award attorney's fees or witness fees only to the extent expressly authorized by other law.

(d) If the court sets aside or modifies agency action or remands the matter to the agency for further proceedings, the court may make any interlocutory order it finds necessary to preserve the interests of the parties and the public pending further proceedings or agency action.

[§ 5–118. [Review by Higher Court]

Decisions on petitions for review of agency action are reviewable by the [appellate court] as in other civil cases.]

CHAPTER II
CIVIL ENFORCEMENT

§ 5–201. [Petition by Agency for Civil Enforcement of Rule or Order]

(a) In addition to other remedies provided by law, an agency may seek enforcement of its rule or order by filing a petition for civil enforcement in the [trial court of general jurisdiction.]

(b) The petition must name, as defendants, each alleged violator against whom the agency seeks to obtain civil enforcement.

(c) Venue is determined as in other civil cases.

(d) A petition for civil enforcement filed by an agency may request, and the court may grant, declaratory relief, temporary or permanent injunctive relief, any other civil remedy provided by law, or any combination of the foregoing.

§ 5–202. [Petition by Qualified Person for Civil Enforcement of Agency's Order]

(a) Any person who would qualify under this Act as having standing to obtain judicial review of an agency's failure to enforce its order may file a petition for civil enforcement of that order, but the action may not be commenced:

(1) until at least [60] days after the petitioner has given notice of the alleged violation and of the petitioner's intent to seek civil enforcement to the head of the agency concerned, to the attorney general, and to each alleged violator against whom the petitioner seeks civil enforcement;

(2) if the agency has filed and is diligently prosecuting a petition for civil enforcement of the same order against the same defendant; or

(3) if a petition for review of the same order has been filed and is pending in court.

(b) The petition must name, as defendants, the agency whose order is sought to be enforced and each alleged violator against whom the petitioner seeks civil enforcement.

(c) The agency whose order is sought to be enforced may move to dismiss on the grounds that the petition fails to qualify under this section or that enforcement would be contrary to the policy of the agency. The court shall grant the motion to dismiss unless the petitioner demonstrates that (i) the petition qualifies under this section and (ii) the agency's failure to enforce its order is based on an exercise of discretion that is improper on one or more of the grounds provided in Section 5–116(c)(8).

(d) Except to the extent expressly authorized by law, a petition for civil enforcement filed under this section may not request, and the court may not grant any monetary payment apart from taxable costs.

§ 5–203. [Defenses; Limitation on New Issues and New Evidence]

A defendant may assert, in a proceeding for civil enforcement:

(1) that the rule or order sought to be enforced is invalid on any of the grounds stated in Section 5–116. If that defense is raised, the court may consider issues and receive evidence only within the limitations provided by Sections 5–112, 5–113, and 5–114; and

(2) any of the following defenses on which the court, to the extent necessary for the determination of the matter, may consider new issues or take new evidence:

(i) the rule or order does not apply to the party;

(ii) the party has not violated the rule or order;

(iii) the party has violated the rule or order but has subsequently complied, but a party who establishes this defense is not necessarily relieved from any sanction provided by law for past violations; or

(iv) any other defense allowed by law.

§ 5–204. [Incorporation of Certain Provisions on Judicial Review]

Proceedings for civil enforcement are governed by the following provisions of this Act on judicial review, as modified where necessary to adapt them to those proceedings:

(1) Section 5–101(2) (ancillary procedural matters); and

(2) Section 5–115 (agency record for judicial review—contents, preparation, transmittal, cost.)

§ 5–205. [Review by Higher Court]

Decisions on petitions for civil enforcement are reviewable by the [appellate court] as in other civil cases.

*

INDEX

1293

†